Webster's New World
Companion to
English and American
Literature

Webster's New World Companion to English and American Literature

Edited by Arthur Pollard

Associate Editor for American Literature
Ralph Willett

Compton Russell

Published by Compton Russell Ltd.
Published simultaneously in Canada
by Nelson, Foster & Scott Ltd.,
and in USA by The World Publishing Company
First printing—1973
© London International Press Ltd 1973
Printed in Great Britain by
Alden & Mowbray Ltd
at the Alden Press, Oxford
ISBN 0 85955 000 1

Foreword

This *Companion* is designed for all who have an interest in literature written in the English language. Any attempt of this kind must be less than complete, but the aim has been to produce a work as comprehensive as possible both as to range of reference and content of individual entries, whilst at the same time providing a volume that is attractive and easy to read. It was therefore decided to include both English and American literature in a single volume and to add a number of composite articles on the several areas of the Commonwealth. The select bibliography of an author's own works follows immediately upon the biographical information and critical assessment which constitute each text entry. Any selection of books about him will be found in the appendix of secondary bibliography.

ARTHUR POLLARD

Hull, 1972

Acknowledgments

The contributors have a special interest in the subjects on which they have written, and I should like first to express my thanks to them. Even within the limits of the necessarily comparatively brief entries of a volume like this they have provided something of that variety of approach which makes literary studies such a refreshing and vigorous discipline. Next, I must thank Mr. Ralph Willett, my associate editor for the American entries, for the knowledge and diligence that he has brought to his task. I also owe a very great debt of gratitude to Mr. Michael Russell, of London International Press Ltd., and Dr. G. G. Urwin for the extremely detailed and careful revision that they have supplied. They have freed the work of many errors, though, of course, I must remain responsible for those which remain. For reference to films I am grateful to Mr. A. G. S. Enser, the Borough Librarian of Eastbourne, who not only permitted me to use his *Filmed Books and Plays* (London: André Deutsch) but also supplied some references which were subsequent to the revised edition of his book in 1969. Finally, Miss Ruth Green knows in what a variety of states literary scholars can submit their drafts. With inestimable patience and unruffled calm she has reduced this variety to an impeccable uniformity of typescript. I thank her once again.

A.P.

List of Contributors

(*with initials used in text*)

A.D.M.	Dr. A. D. Mills	D.P.M.	D. P. Morse
A.E.	A. W. Easson	D.V.W.	D. V. Ward
A.G.	Dr. A. M. Goldman	D.W.	Professor D. S. R. Welland
A.J.C.	A. J. V. Cheetham	D.W.C.	D. W. Crompton
A.J.S.	A. J. Shelston	E.A.	E. A. Abramson
A.M.O.	Mrs. A. M. Oliver	E.H.R.	E. H. Robinson
A.M.R.	Dr. A. M. Ross	E.M.	E. N. W. Mottram
A.N.M.	A. N. Marlow	E.M.J.	Miss E. M. Jacka
A.P.	Professor A. Pollard	E.T.W.	E. T. Webb
A.P.H.	Dr. A. P. Hinchliffe	F.F.B.	Professor F. F. Bruce
A.S.	Dr. A. J. Stead	G.A.K.	G. A. Kearns
A.W.B.	Dr. A. W. Bower	G.B.	Mrs. G. K. P. Beer
A.Y.	A. Young	G.G.U.	Dr. G. G. Urwin
B.L.	B. C. Lee	G.P.	G. A. E. Parfitt
C.B.	Dr. C. W. E. Bigsby	G.S.	Dr. G. F. Smith
C.H.	C. Hanson	H.N.D.	H. N. Davies
C.P.	C. Partridge	I.M.W.	Miss I. M. Westcott
D.B.H.	D. B. Howard	I.W.	Dr. I. M. Walker
D.C.	D. T. Corker	J.B.	Miss J. Bazire
D.E.P.	Dr. D. E. Painting	J.B.B.	Dr. J. B. Beer
D.G.	D. Grant	J.C.	Professor J. A. V. Chapple
D.G.S.	Dr. D. G. Scragg	J.D.J.	Professor J. D. Jump
D.H.	Miss D. Hirst	J.L.M.	J. L. Mowat
D.H.R.	D. H. Roy	J.M.	J. R. D. Milroy
D.J.P.	D. J. Palmer	J.M.P.	Miss J. M. Proctor
D.L.	D. B. Locke	J.M.W.	J. M. Walton
D.M.	D. Murray	J.O'M.	J. O'Malley
D.N.C.	D. N. Clough	J.P.	Dr. Joan H. Pittock
D.P.	D. R. Parry	J.P.W.	Dr. J. P. Wainwright

J.S.	Professor A. J. Smith	R.B.	Dr. W. R. J. Barron
J.W.	J. White	R.E.	Miss R. G. Eland
K.T.	R. K. R. Thornton	R.G.C.	Dr. R. G. Cox
L.E.P.	L. E. Pearsall	R.H.B.	Professor R. H. Barback
L.S.	Mrs. L. Scragg	R.L.B.	Professor R. L. Brett
M.B.	Professor M. S. Bradbury	R.S.	Dr. R. C. Simmons
M.G.	M. Gidley	R.V.O.	R. V. Osbourn
M.L.	M. Leaf	R.W.	R. W. Willett
M.P.	Dr. M. J. W. Pittock	S.A.F.	Dr. S. A. Fender
M.S.	Mrs. M. Shaw	S.C.	Dr. Susan M. Cockroft
M.T.	Mrs. M. Taylor	S.M.S.	Miss S. M. Smith
O.E.	O. D. Edwards	T.W.	T. Wright
O.K.	O. Knowles	W.A.S.	Dr. W. A. Speck
P.B.	Mrs. P. Bawcutt	W.R.	W. Ruddick
P.G.M.	P. G. Mudford	W.S.	Dr. W. D. Sherman
P.R.	P. E. Roberts		

Explanatory Note

Dates accompanying titles denote year of first publication in book form.

f. Film version. Accompanying date signifies year of first release.

p. First stage performance (where known and when taking place in a year preceding publication in book form).

s. Serialization, including publication by parts (where known and when taking place in a year preceding publication in book form).

No specific convention attaches to the use of ? or c. preceding dates, though c. implies a greater degree of conjecture.

In certain instances the original titles of works have been modernized for ease of understanding.

A

ABERCROMBIE, Lascelles (1881–1938), born at Ashton-on-Mersey (Cheshire), was educated at Malvern and Manchester University before starting a career in journalism. After the First World War, during which he served as munitions inspector in Liverpool, he entered upon what was to be a distinguished academic career, later becoming professor of English at Leeds and London. His poems and plays in verse show occasional signs of vigor and intensity that are untypical in Georgian poetry; some of them have a taut intellectuality that is more reminiscent of Donne than of Abercrombie's own contemporaries. But his preference for the long reflective poem, which he was trying to revive, too frequently encourages an overstrained rhetoric and obtrusive erudition. Later he turned exclusively to criticism and in *The Theory of Poetry* (1924) and *The Idea of Great Poetry* (1925) argued that great poetry consists of a confluence of different energies and impulses into a single unity. (See also **Georgians, The.**)

Collected Poems, London: Oxford Univ. Press, 1930.   O.K.

ABRAHAMS, Peter. See **African Literature.**

ACHEBE, Chinua. See **African Literature.**

ADAMS, Henry (1838–1918) was born in Boston of a distinguished family. His grandfather, John Quincy Adams, had been the sixth president of the United States, and his great-grandfather, John Adams, the second. Adams acted as private secretary to his father (a congressman and minister to Great Britain between 1861 and 1868) before and during the Civil War and worked as a correspondent and free-lance political journalist for various papers, including *The New York Times*, *The Nation* and *The North American Review*. Afterwards he taught medieval history at Harvard (1870–77) and edited *The North American Review* (1870–76). He then started writing in earnest, publishing *The Life of Albert Gallatin* in 1879 and *Democracy* in 1880. The latter was a novel about Gilded Age politics, attacking American democracy from a Puritanical position which refused to countenance expediency or self-interest. Adams took up the same stance in his vast *History of the United States of America*, in which he saw the

I

Revolutionary purity and fervor dying away into partisanship and haggling—principles suborned by power.

Such a view not only alienated him from current political events but also drove him to an untenable transcendentalist Brahminism, antagonistic to all worldly power and its attendant compromises. His later writings sought a way out of this stalemate, a situation worsened in 1885 by the suicide of his wife, Marion, shortly after the publication of his second novel, *Esther*. The connection between the dilemmas of the heroines in his novels and the death of his wife has never been satisfactorily explained. *Esther* deals with a religious crisis in a young woman, torn intellectually between an Episcopalian minister and a skeptical humanist, and emotionally between marriage to the minister on the one hand, and independence and spiritual isolation on the other. She chooses independence, but the future seems to hold little hope or purpose for her.

Adams received the Loubat Prize for his *History* from Columbia University in 1894 and was elected, in absentia, president of the American Historical Association for the same year. He spent much time abroad. *Mont-Saint-Michel and Chartres* is one of the fruits of his travels. It is a survey of late medieval France focused on her architecture, literature and philosophy, and hinges upon the changes from a masculine orientated world view (Norman) to a feminine one (Gothic), and then to the bourgeoisie's disillusionment with ritualistic religion, culminating in the Reformation. Using this schema as a mirror of the nineteenth century, Adams saw in both periods an attempt to reach directly from God to man without intermediaries. In the thirteenth century the consequent strain had called the Virgin into existence as a go-between for sinful man. The only nineteenth-century parallel to this that Adams could see was the Dynamo, an expression of the forces of nature which bound man to the world around him. This idea was developed at length in *The Education of Henry Adams*, in which the author traced his century's development in a semiautobiographical work, taking the events of his life as general indicators of movement and change. In the contemporary picture and in the future he saw mankind being carried away by the materialized forces of electricity and even newer sources of power, all of which possessed their own accelerating momentum.

Adams's work, then, spans an immensely important period of American cultural development. He himself, coming from one of the most influential families in the early years of the Republic, found he was outpaced and alienated from much that was going on around him. He strove to reorientate himself in terms of the approaching twentieth century, with its mechanization, industrialization and scientific relativism—"physics stark mad in metaphysics." He believed the challenge of its enormous power would be a challenge to man himself.

The Life of Albert Gallatin, 1879.
Democracy: An American Novel (anonymously), 1880.
John Randolph, 1882.
Esther (pseud. Frances Snow Compton), 1884.
A History of the United States of America during the Administrations of Thomas Jefferson and James Madison, 9 vols., 1889–91.
Memoirs of Marau Taaroa, Last Queen of Tahiti, privately printed, 1893; revised and enlarged, as *Memoirs of Arii Taimai E. . . . .* , 1901.
Mont-Saint-Michel and Chartres, privately printed, 1904; 1913.
The Education of Henry Adams, privately printed, 1906; 1918.
A Letter to American Teachers of History, privately printed, 1910.
The Life of George Cabot Lodge, 1911.
The Degradation of the Democratic Dogma, 1919.

Letters, ed. W. C. Ford, 2 vols., Boston: Houghton Mifflin, *1858–1891*, 1930; *1892–1918*, 1938.   D.C.

ADDISON, Joseph (1672–1719), son of a dean of Lichfield, was at school in London at the Charterhouse (with Steele) before going on first to Queen's College and then to Magdalen College, Oxford. In 1697 he was elected to a fellowship of Magdalen, which he held until 1711. From 1699 to 1703 he traveled in Europe on a pension from the crown, and soon after his return was commissioned to write a poem celebrating the victory at Blenheim. This poem, *The Campaign*, was published in 1705. Addison was appointed undersecretary of state in 1706, was a member of Parliament from 1708 until his death and was twice chief secretary for Ireland. He collaborated with Steele in *The Tatler* (1709–11) before they became joint authors of *The Spectator* (1711–12 and 1714), and for a time he also enjoyed the friendship of Swift. He wrote Latin and English poetry and a tragedy, *Cato* (1713), constructed on classical lines, as well as editing a number of periodicals himself and undertaking political journalism for the Whigs. In 1716 he married the countess of Warwick. Shortly before his death he was estranged from Steele.

In recent times Addison's character and style of writing have been criticized for priggishness and superficial affectations. He was indeed didactic and genteel. He could be cloyingly sentimental. He patronizes his female readers and shows up shakily in some of his critical papers. Yet he has important claims to the literary historian's attention and still offers a good deal that interests the general reader. He grasped at once the significance of Steele's attempt to write on moral and philosophical questions in a style so firmly grounded in recognizable reality that it would entice the reader's interest and coax him into understanding the ideas being debated. Addison was a born popularizer and he showed great resourcefulness in finding new methods of presenting in an engaging form what was, in effect, moral exhortation. But his skill was always at the service of a genuine vision of an ideal modern society, gentlemanly in behavior and of cultivated intelligence. There may be too many bland assumptions in his equating of good sense and virtue (though Addison's apparent blandness is often due to stylistic factors, not to the subject matter), but his stress on cultivation and social considerateness did much good all through the eighteenth century (when *The Spectator* was a standard work) and may be clearly felt as late as Jane Austen. A great deal of eighteenth-century prose shows Addison's stylistic influence and his observant but civilized tone and dignified presence affected prose writers up to the time of his professed admirer, Macaulay.

Addison discovered important areas of fresh debate which proved popular with his contemporaries. He inherited enough of Dryden's historical sense to see that poetry of other ages needs to be judged by different standards from our own, and in *The Spectator* there are pioneer essays on wit and Metaphysical style, on *Chevy Chase* and, in particular, *Paradise Lost*, which are still of interest. They prefigure later eighteenth-century aesthetic developments in the praise they give to natural genius and sublime effects. Addison also developed the idea of Sir Roger de Coverley and his circle into a series of genre pieces which anticipate many of the characteristics of the novel.

(See also **Essays.**)

Works, ed. R. Hurd, 6 vols., 1811; London: Bohn (Bohn's British Classics), 1854–56.
The Tatler, ed. G. A. Aitken, 4 vols., London: Duckworth, 1898–99.
The Spectator, ed. D. F. Bond, 5 vols., Oxford: Clarendon Press, 1965.
Letters, ed. W. Graham, Oxford: Clarendon Press, 1941.   w.r.

"Æ." See **Russell, George William.**

AELFRIC, Abbot. See **Old English Prose.**

AFRICAN LITERATURE (including South African). English writing in Africa is found first, as might be expected, in the oldest settlements, namely, South Africa. Apart from the poems of Thomas Pringle (1789–1834), the abolitionist, who spent some years in the province, the first work to note is *The Story of an African Farm* (1883) by Olive Schreiner (1855–1920), which gives a realistic picture of Boer life and its confining conventions, especially on women. Rider Haggard (1856–1925), with his popular stories like *King Solomon's Mines* (1885) and *Allan Quatermain* (1887), was also a South African.

In the twentieth century much South African fiction has been dominated, not to say obsessed, by racial conflict. An early novel concerned with this subject is *Turbott Wolfe* (1925) by William Plomer (1903–), who with Roy Campbell (1901–57) is one of the few South Africans of any importance as a poet. The outstanding novelist of the interwar period and one who combined humane feeling with a grasp of practical realities was Sarah Gertrude Millin (1889–1968), remembered for *God's Stepchildren* (1924) and *Mary Glenn* (1925). A more widely known successor is Alan Paton (1903–) with *Cry, the Beloved Country* (1948) and *Too Late the Phalarope* (1953), the former attracting more attention but the latter the better book. Dan Jacobson (1929–) also deals with interracial relationships in *The Trap* (1955), *A Dance in the Sun* (1956) and *The Evidence of Love* (1960). In *The Beginners* (1966) he examines the problems of a Jewish family growing up in South Africa. Peter Abrahams (1919–), who is the most important colored writer of South Africa but now lives in Jamaica, gives a sensitive account of the urbanized African countryman in *Mine Boy* (1946), while other novels such as *Wild Conquest* (1950) and *A Wreath for Udomo* (1956) reveal his broad and understanding grasp of the South African predicament. Doris Lessing (1919–), who comes from Rhodesia, is also occupied with the racial problem in her *Children of Violence* sequence, the novels *Martha Quest* (1952), *A Proper Marriage* (1954), *A Ripple from the Storm* (1958), *Landlocked* (1965) and *The Four Gated City* (1969); but her concerns extend beyond this to a compassionate and at times angry study of human relationships, especially of the position of women.

Much the most active area of mid-twentieth-century writing in Africa has been West Africa. There the idea of negritude has been sedulously promoted by writers in French, of whom Leopold Senghor is best known, though we must remember that this idea takes its origins from the Antilles in the work of Fanon and Aimé Césaire. Writing in English has never had this specific direction, but the general political and cultural ferment has thrown up a host of figures, exploring imaginatively (usually in fiction) the rapid changes which have turned tribal societies into modern urbanized communities. Nigeria has produced some of the best novelists, and none better than Chinua Achebe (1930–). In his first novel, *Things Fall Apart* (1958), he analyzed the breakdown of tribal life with the invasion of white missionary and government and went on thereafter in *No Longer at Ease* (1960) and *Arrow of God* (1964) to examine the process of disintegration, until in *A Man of the People* (1966) he showed the corruption that power brings with independence. Similarly, T. M. Aluko (1918–) deals first with the clash of Christianity and African polygamous culture in *One Man, One Wife* (1959), follows it, in *One Man, One Matchet* (1964), with the theme of unrest during the decline of British control, and then proceeds to corruption, bloodshed and tragedy in an independent African state, in *Chief the Honourable Minister* (1970). East Africa's single novelist of note, the Kenyan James Ngugi (1938–), has a group of three novels not unlike in theme to those of Achebe and Aluko— *The River Between* (1965), *Weep Not, Child* (1964) and *A Grain of Wheat* (1967). All these novelists possess an intense awareness of environment, a sense of the terrible dilemmas in which their characters often find themselves and, when necessary, a penetrating capacity for satirical comment. Cyprian Ekwensi (1921–), evoking two quite different environments, concerns himself with the rural nomadic Fulani in *Burning Grass* (1962) and the urban scene in *People of the City* (1963). The pullulating life of an African city is probably most vividly caught by Wole Soyinka (1934–) in *The Interpreters* (1965), but behind the bohemianism of the group of main characters lies a quasi-symbolic exploration of purpose in life and of death and sacrifice. Amos Tutuola (1920–) is another quite different, indeed unique, novelist who is known mainly for his visionary *The Palm-Wine Drinkard* (1952), a kind of African *Pilgrim's Progress*. His is a poetical view of life which reminds us of Christopher Okigbo (1924–67), whose poems also draw upon African mythology and are fundamentally concerned with an exploration of the meaning of life's years—*Heavensgate* (1962); *Limits* (1964); *Distances* (1964).

By contrast with the white dominions, Africa has also developed a drama, of which the two principal proponents are Soyinka, whose comedy and at times acute satire includes *The Lion and the Jewel* (1963), *The Road* (1965) and *Kongi's Harvest* (1967), and John Pepper Clark (1935–), whose work, however, is not so versatile as that of Soyinka.   A.P.

AGEE, James (1909–55), a Harvard graduate, collaborated with Walker Evans, the photographer, on *Let Us Now Praise Famous Men* (1941), an ambitious, sensitive study of Alabama sharecroppers suffering in the Depression. During the 1940s he wrote regular film articles, distinguished for their descriptive exactness and eclectic sympathies. His work for the cinema included the script for *The African Queen* (*f.* 1951) and he wrote a life of Lincoln for television. *The Morning Watch* (1951) and *A Death in the Family* (1957; dramatized as *All the Way Home* and *f.* under that title, 1963) are poetic novels based partly on Agee's own Tennessee childhood. His anguished private life is partially revealed in the *Letters to Father Flye* (1962). His volume of *Collected Poems*, edited by Robert Fitzgerald, was published in 1968.   M.G.

AIKEN, Conrad (1889–) was born in Georgia but, after the violent deaths of both parents, was brought up by relatives in New Bedford (Massachusetts) and educated—in the same class as T. S. Eliot—at Harvard.

Except for a long sojourn as an informal creative arts teacher in England at Rye (Sussex), he chose to live in New England, where he could feel part of a continuing cultural tradition.

Aiken first attracted attention as the prolific author of such works as *Earth Triumphant*... (1914), *Turns and Movies* (1916), *The Jig of Forslin: A Symphony* (1916), *The Charnel Rose; Senlin: A Biography, and Other Poems* (1918) and *Priapus and the Pool* (1922), collections of mellifluous lyrics and of Eliot-like investigations into the modern psyche. His criticism, starting with *Scepticisms* (1919), is lively and individualistic; his essay of 1924 successfully promoted interest in Emily Dickinson.

The poetry of the later periods, such as *Selected Poems* (1929), *Preludes for Memnon* (1931), *Time in the Rock* (1936), *Collected Poems* (1953) and *A Letter from Li Po* (1955), still notably musical, is frequently concerned with metaphysical matters. Similarly, his fiction, especially *Blue Voyage* (1927), *Great Circle* (1933) and *King Coffin* (1935), examines the configurations of consciousness and time, often employing the resources of psychoanalysis, stream of consciousness and rhetorical prose. *Ushant* (1952) is an idiosyncratic autobiography which obscures chronology and the true identities of characters.

Collected Poems, New York: Oxford Univ. Press, 1953; 2nd edition, 1970.
Collected Short Stories, ed. M. Schorer, Cleveland: World Publishing, 1960.   M.G.

AINSWORTH, William Harrison (1805–82) was born in Manchester and began his career as a publisher before turning to fiction and magazine editing. His novel *Rookwood* (1834), based on the Dick Turpin legend, won wide acclaim, and it was followed by a long succession of historical romances including *The Tower of London* (1840), *Old St. Paul's* (1841) and *The Lancashire Witches* (1849; *s.* 1848). Ainsworth's novels owe much to Scott and the vogue for Gothic romances, and while they were widely popular as late as 1865, they lack both intelligent characterization and literary craftsmanship.   I.W.

AKENSIDE, Mark (1721–70) was born in Newcastle-upon-Tyne, the son of a Dissenter, from whom, according to Dr. Johnson, he inherited "an unnecessary and outrageous zeal for what he called and thought liberty." After training in theology, Akenside studied medicine at Edinburgh and Leyden. There in 1744 he completed his main work, *The Pleasures of Imagination*. In the following year he published a collection of odes. His life was spent in the practice of medicine, mainly at St. Thomas's Hospital, London. He may have been the prototype of the physician with leanings to the classics in Smollett's *Peregrine Pickle*.

His odes illustrate his patriotism and his zeal for liberty; one of them, "To the Evening Star," is faintly a precursor of Keats's Nightingale ode. In his long poem he is influenced by Addison's essays on the imagination (*The Spectator*, nos. 411–21) and more extensively by Shaftesbury's *Characteristics*, from which he derives many of his ideas of natural religion and his use of ridicule (see especially *The Pleasures of Imagination*, book 3). This poem, written in blank verse, owes much to Milton, but it is weighed down by conventional eighteenth-century poetic diction and by its lifeless imagery. One passage in the fragmentary and later book 4, however, presents a remarkable anticipation of Wordsworth's manner in *The Prelude*. This book was part of the enlarged and revised version of the poem published in J. Dyson's edition of *Poems* (1772).

The Pleasures of Imagination, 1744 (and see above).
Odes on Several Subjects, 1745; revised, 1760.

Poems, ed. A. Dyce, London: Pickering (Aldine edition of the British Poets), 1835.   A.P.

ALABASTER, William (1567–1640) was born at Hadleigh (Suffolk) and educated at Westminster School and Trinity College, Cambridge. After serving as a chaplain on Essex's Cadiz expedition in 1596, he became a Roman Catholic and spent some years in Spain and the Netherlands. He returned to England and the Church of England in 1610. Besides theological works and a tragedy in Latin, *Roxana*, he was the author of some sixty sonnets, in which he unites an older medieval devotional tradition with an incipient Metaphysical treatment. The result is that the meditative matter is embodied in a framework in which traditional Christian symbolic references gain striking and sometimes paradoxical expression.

Sonnets, ed. G. M. Story and H. Gardner, London: Oxford Univ. Press, 1959.   A.P.

ALBEE, Edward (1928–) was adopted at the age of two weeks by Reed Albee, the millionaire owner of a chain of theaters. His first play, *Aliqueen*, was written at the age of twelve but the first to appear in print was *Schism*, a short drama of the conflict of love and religion, which appeared in the Choate literary magazine in 1946. Albee regarded himself as a poet until well into his twenties, until, in fact, at the age of twenty-nine, he wrote *The Zoo Story*. This was produced first at the Schiller Theater Werkstatt in Berlin before its première at the Provincetown Playhouse. Together with his expressionistic satire of American life and values, *The American Dream*, this parable of the need for human contact in an age obsessed with material values and afraid of the vulnerability which is a product of genuine communication established Albee as a playwright of considerable theatrical power. His reputation was secured by his first full-length play, *Who's Afraid of Virginia Woolf?*, directed, like most other Albee plays, by Alan Schneider and produced at the Billy Rose Theater. This play presents the agonized exorcism of illusions on the part of a university professor and his wife who have created a fantasy child to compensate for their own sterility. Set in the town of New Carthage, the play constitutes a warning to American society, as it is to the individual, content to accept illusion in preference to the harsh realities of private and public life. After an unsatisfactory adaptation of Carson McCullers's *The Ballad of the Sad Café*, Albee's next play took his concern with the nature of reality a stage further. *Tiny Alice* attempts to examine the nature of religious conviction. After a brilliant first scene, the play, which seems to owe something to Eliot's drama, plunges into a highly symbolic metaphysical debate.

Following a disastrous adaptation of James Purdy's *Malcolm*, Albee's next work, *A Delicate Balance*, was awarded a Pulitzer Prize. Though inferior to *Who's Afraid of Virginia Woolf?*, this play is an effective, if somewhat mechanical examination of the private fears and public insecurity which seem to form the fabric of modern society as Albee sees it. His characters, although constructed with too overtly a metaphysical intent, test out the assumptions which have been the unspoken foundations of their existence and find them terrifyingly wanting.

After an adaptation of Giles Cooper's *Everything in the Garden*, which opened late in 1967, Albee broke new ground with two related plays, *Box* and *Quotations from Chairman Mao Tse-Tung*, which stood as a comment both on the nature of personal and political reality and the role of art in an era in which humane and liberal values no longer seem to form the basis of human intercourse. *Box* has no characters and consists of an off-stage monologue, the stage itself being dominated by the highlit outlines of a huge cube. In *Quotations from Chairman Mao Tse-Tung* lines drawn from the work of the nineteenth-century poet, Will Carleton, and from Chairman Mao are intercalated with a confessional monologue in such a way that chance assonances in the text create meanings which at times transcend the banality of the words themselves. Albee's next work, *All Over*, is a study of the nature of death: the entourage of a "great man" gather to witness his dying and to discuss their lives.

Albee's gift to the theater does not lie in his ability to produce an American version of absurdist drama; Albee is not an absurdist. It lies in his supreme mastery of language in a theater not renowned for its articulateness, a language controlled and shaped by an almost musical sense of form and rhythm. It lies also, perhaps, in his consistent commitment to humane values in an age tempted by apocalypse and despair.

The Zoo Story; The Death of Bessie Smith; The Sandbox, 1960 (*The Zoo Story* p. 1959).
The American Dream, 1961 (*p.* 1960).
Who's Afraid of Virginia Woolf?, 1962 (*f.* 1965).
Fam and Yam (edition with *The Sandbox, The Death of Bessie Smith*), 1963 (*p.* 1960).
The Ballad of the Sad Café, 1963.
Tiny Alice, 1965 (*p.* 1964).
Malcolm, 1966 (*p.* 1965).
A Delicate Balance, 1966.
Box and *Quotations from Chairman Mao Tse-Tung*, 1969 (*p.* 1968).
All Over, 1971.   C.B.

ALDINGTON, Richard (1892–1962) was born in Hampshire and educated at London University. He married the American imagist poet Hilda Doolittle ("H.D.") (see **Imagism**). He achieved some fame with his novel *Death of a Hero* (1929), which traces the life of George Winterbourne first in a satirical exposure of pre-1914 London intelligentsia circles and then in his war experiences. *All Men Are Enemies* (1933) explores the personal relations of its hero, Antony Clarendon, but also devotes much space to the political and social problems of the 1920s. Aldington also wrote a biography of D. H. Lawrence, *Portrait of a Genius, But...* (1950), and of T. E. Lawrence, *Lawrence of Arabia* (1955). His volume of *Collected Poems* was published in 1929 and his autobiography, *Life for Life's Sake*, in 1940.   A.P.

ALFRED, King. See **Middle English Literature.**

ALGER, Horatio, Jr. (1834–99), born in Massachusetts, graduated from Harvard in 1852. Puritan ethics instilled during his youth were later revealed in many of the more than 100 books he wrote for boys. After two years as a Unitarian minister, he started his literary career in New York in 1866. His most popular work was the *Ragged Dick* series (from 1867); almost equally successful were the *Luck and Pluck* series (from 1869) and the *Tattered Tom* series (from 1871). These stories were often about a boy who overcomes poverty and is rewarded by a rich benefactor, as befits his piety and virtue—a naïve but undoubtedly popular ideal.   R.W.

ALGREN, Nelson (1909–) was born in Detroit (Michigan) and educated at the University of Illinois. He has written a large number of novels that depict, with thorough detail, the lives of the lowest strata of society. His early novels, such as *Somebody in Boots* (1935), show the influence of Marxist thought. His finest work is probably *The Man with the Golden Arm* (1949; *f.* 1955), a taut and compelling story of the degradations of drug addiction. At his best Algren achieves an impressionistic control of mood and a powerful awareness of physical degradation but in later work, such as *A Walk on the Wild Side* (1956; *f.* 1962), the naturalism declines into a pervasive sentimentality.   D.V.W.

ALLINGHAM, William (1824–89), born in Ireland, became a customs official, moving in 1847 to London where he became friendly with Leigh Hunt, Carlyle and the Pre-Raphaelites. He began publishing poetry in 1850 and edited various anthologies of verse. In 1870 he left the customs to join *Fraser's Magazine* as deputy editor under Froude, and as editor from 1874 to 1879. His poetry, which is primarily lyrical, reflects his interest in Irish folk songs and mythology, music and the arts, anticipating and influencing in some respects W. B. Yeats, who edited a selection of his poems.

Diary, ed. G. Grigson, Fontwell, Sussex: Centaur Press; Carbondale: Southern Illinois Univ. Press, 1967.   D.W.

ALUKO, T. M. (Timothy Mofolorunso). See **African Literature.**

AMIS, Kingsley (1922–), born in London, of lower-middle-class origins, studied English at St. John's College, Oxford. He served in the army from 1942 to 1945 and later taught at University College, Swansea (1949–61) and Peterhouse, Cambridge (1961–63). His first novel, *Lucky Jim*, was immensely successful. Jim Dixon, its hero, sometimes considered as a prototype of the angry young men who appear in the work of such writers as Wain and Osborne, is a restive lower-middle-class radical, who tilts, not always availingly, at the establishment values of the university to which he is appointed and especially those of his professor, Welch. Amis's gift for ridicule and broad comedy served him well in his next two novels, *That Uncertain Feeling* and *I Like It Here*, both of whose heroes are cast in similar mold to that of Jim Dixon. In these as well as in later novels Amis is critical of assumed and artificial cultural allegiances. His subsequent novels still manifest his comic gift, but there is sometimes a more bitter note. Corresponding with his move away from a radical political position, there is, for instance, the anti-left-wing criticism of *Take a Girl Like You*. In *The Anti-Death League* he mounts an attack on the forces that create human suffering and especially on the God who blights human happiness. Here, however, we have another manifestation of Amis's essential love of life and belief in humanity. His best work is in the novel, but he has also published poetry and science fiction. *The Green Man* employs some of the techniques of the latter in the exploration of the supernatural.

Lucky Jim, 1954 (*f.* 1957).
That Uncertain Feeling, 1955 (*f.* as *Only Two Can Play*, 1961).
I Like It Here, 1958.
Take a Girl Like You, 1960 (*f.* 1970).
One Fat Englishman, 1963.
The Egyptologists (with Robert Conquest), 1965.
The Anti-Death League, 1966.
I Want It Now, 1968.
The Green Man, 1969.
Girl, 20, 1971.   A.P.

ANAND, Mulk Raj. See **Indian Literature.**

ANDERSON, Maxwell (1888–1959) was born in Pennsylvania and graduated from the University of North Dakota in 1911. He later met Laurence Stallings with whom he wrote his first successful play, *What Price Glory?* (1924; *f.* 1926; 1952). Commended for its realism, the play is noisy and farcical, suggesting that war is fun. Anderson's attitude in his Depression era plays deepened into romantic pessimism. In his historical plays, such as *Mary of Scotland* (1933), and his contemporary plays, notably *Winterset* (1935; *f.* 1936), hopeful idealists are defeated by those in power: rebellion is both necessary and doomed.

Eleven Verse Plays, 1929–1939, New York: Harcourt, Brace, 1940.   R.W.

ANDERSON, Sherwood (1876–1941), born in Ohio, wrote largely of the Midwest and the South. His best-known work is *Winesburg, Ohio* (1919), a collection of stories dealing with the restricted eccentric life of a small Midwest community. Anderson describes his characters as "grotesques," and the preface, "The Book of the Grotesque," is a fable which lies behind the description. To attempt to possess truth renders a character grotesque and the stories are concerned with characters who manifest this peculiarity in one way or another. In *Poor White* (1920) the impact on a rural community of a series of labor-saving inventions is seen to be corrupting, as it leads to prosperity for the few and social fragmentation. Although Anderson seems superficially folksy, his writing often plucks disconcertingly at the nerves of American life.

Windy McPherson's Son, 1916.
Winesburg, Ohio, 1919 (stories).
Poor White, 1920.
Horses and Men, 1923 (stories).
Dark Laughter, 1925.

The Sherwood Anderson Reader, ed. P. A. Rosenfeld, Boston: Houghton Mifflin, 1947.
Letters, ed. H. M. Jones and W. P. Rideout, Boston: Little, Brown, 1953.
M.L.

ANDREWES, Lancelot (1555–1626) was successively dean of Westminster (1601) and bishop of Chichester (1605), Ely (1609) and Winchester (1618). These latter promotions he owed to James I, who also made him dean of the Chapel Royal and a privy councillor. He took a prominent part in preparing the Authorized Version of the Bible and was said to know some fifteen languages. Fuller remarked of him that "the world wanted learning to know how learned this man was." His erudition characterized his sermons, especially in his knowledge of the Fathers and in his delight in analysis. The outcome often seems quaint and sometimes pedantic, but the effect is that of a powerful mind allied to deep spirituality.

Works, 11 vols., Oxford: Parker, 1841–54.
Sermons, ed. G. M. Story, Oxford: Clarendon Press, 1967.
A.P.

ANSTEY, Christopher (1724–1805), a clergyman's son, went to Eton and King's College, Cambridge, becoming a fellow in 1745. In 1754 he inherited the family estates and in 1770, after earlier visits, settled in Bath on account of ill health. Anstey is remembered as the originator of a tradition of jocular verse. In 1766 he published *The New Bath Guide*, a comic account in letters of the joys and mishaps of a stay in Bath by the various members of a family (including servants). Smollett found basic ideas for *Humphry Clinker* in the poem and Moore copies its form closely in *The Fudge Family in Paris*.

Poetical Works (with memoir), ed. J. Anstey (son), London: T. Cadell & Davies, 1808.
W.R.

ANTHONY, Michael. See Caribbean Literature.

ARBUTHNOT, John (1667–1735), expatriate Scot, member of the Scriblerus Club and Queen Anne's physician, collaborated with Swift, Pope and Gay, and led his age in medicine and mathematics. Brilliantly fertile and versatile, he is ironical, logical—and modest. "He has more wit than we all have, and more humanity than wit," wrote Swift, and Pope cheered his deathbed with the *Epistle* addressed to him. His main works are *A Sermon . . . on . . . the Union* (1706), *The History of John Bull* (1727; first published as pamphlets, 1712), *Know Thyself* (1734) and the greater part of *Memoirs of Martinus Scriblerus* (with Pope's *Works*, 1741). (See also **Political Pamphlets.**)   A.M.O.

ARCHER, William (1856–1924) was born and educated in Edinburgh, obtaining his M.A. degree from the university there in 1876. Immediately after graduation he traveled round the world. In 1878 he went to London as a dramatic critic, but to conform with the demands of his father he read law and was admitted to the bar, but never practiced. Theater was to become the center of his activity; he was friendly with Pinero, Wilde and Shaw, collaborating with the last-named in the first version of *Widowers' Houses*. Books on contemporary theater and theatrical history, *Henry Irving* (1883), *Masks or Faces?* (1888), *A National Theatre* (with H. Granville-Barker) (1907) and *Play-making* (1912), added to his reputation. His journalistic publications included *America Today* (1900) and, one of his most interesting works, *Through Afro-America* (1910).

Although much of Archer's criticism has faded with time and his one full-length play, *The Green Goddess* (1921), is forgotten, his fame as translator of Ibsen remains. His version of *Pillars of Society* was produced in December 1880, and English audiences first became aware of the Norwegian's work. Over the following thirty years Archer became responsible for translating the majority of Ibsen's plays, remarking towards the end of his task: "Though it has involved not a little sheer drudgery, it has, on the whole, been of absorbing interest." He worked in cooperation with others and thus assisted in that general discovery of Scandinavian literature at the end of the nineteenth century in which Edmund Gosse also played a notable role. Although Archer's versions of Ibsen's dialogue appear a little stiff to the modern reader, these pioneering efforts remain his most enduring achievement.   C.P.

ARDEN, John (1930–   ) trained and practiced briefly as an architect before his first professional stage play, *The Waters of Babylon*, was accepted by the English Stage Company for a Sunday-night production-without-décor in October 1957 at London's Royal Court Theatre. His next three plays were also performed there with little success at the box office. He was invited to spend the session 1960–61 as fellow in playwriting at the University of Bristol and for some years lived a comparatively withdrawn provincial life, first in Somerset and then in rural Yorkshire. Returning to London, he has had plays produced at the Mermaid, the Round House and the Arts Laboratory, Drury Lane.

Arden's output is difficult to classify. Apart from his work for radio (*The Life of Man*) and television (*Soldier, Soldier* and *Wet Fish*) and the experimental pieces for schoolchildren and amateurs, written in collaboration with his wife, Margaretta D'Arcy, he has proved possibly the most adventurous and unpredictable of young English playwrights, in terms of form and substance alike. His early "social" plays, like *The Waters of Babylon* and *Live Like Pigs*, transcend purely contemporary issues and are characterized by an interesting marriage of verse and prose dialogue and by an interpolation of song and ballad which implies a thorough absorption of Brechtian influence. These features reappear in *The Happy Haven*, an expressionistic farce set in an old people's home and conceived for masked performance on an open stage, in *The Business of Good Government*, a modern morality play for church performance centering on the figure of Herod, and in *The Workhouse Donkey*, a labyrinthine romp through party-political intrigue in a north-country town and subtitled "a vulgar melo-drama." They are used to most powerful effect, however, in his series of "historical" plays: *Serjeant Musgrave's Dance*, Arden's best-known work and a mature examination of the relationship between pacifism and violence; *Ironhand* (adapted from Goethe's *Goetz von Berlichingen*); *Armstrong's Last Goodnight*; *Left-Handed Liberty* (commissioned by the City of London to commemorate the 750th anniversary of Magna Carta); and his "romantic melodrama" on the life of Nelson, *The Hero Rises Up*.

Arden shows a consistent preoccupation with large, serious themes and an ability to pose crucial political and social questions. He avoids facile solutions by adroitly dispersing our sympathies over a range of complex, even self-contradictory characters, none of them recognizable as a mouthpiece for the author's private views or readily assimilable to any "message" in the play. This results in an ambivalence of theme, occasionally verging on obscurity, which has disconcerted audiences and so far prevented his plays from gaining widespread popular favor, but it is a quality which, coupled with Arden's pungent vitality of language and formidable irreverence towards sacred cows, may yet produce the modern masterpiece which he so nearly achieved in *Serjeant Musgrave's Dance*.

Serjeant Musgrave's Dance, 1960 (*p.* 1959).
Live Like Pigs, 1961 (*p.* 1958).

The Happy Haven (with M. D'Arcy), 1962 (*p.* 1960).
The Business of Good Government (with M. D'Arcy), 1963 (*p.* 1960).
The Workhouse Donkey, 1964 (*p.* 1963).
Armstrong's Last Goodnight, 1965 (*p.* 1964).
Ironhand, 1965.
Left-Handed Liberty, 1965.
The Royal Pardon (with M. D'Arcy), 1967 (*p.* 1966).
Soldier, Soldier and Other Plays, 1967 (*Soldier, Soldier p.* 1960).
The Hero Rises Up (with M. D'Arcy), 1969 (*p.* 1968).   D.H.R.

ARNOLD, Matthew (1822–88) was educated at Rugby, where his father was headmaster, and at Oxford. He spent most vacations at the family home in the Lake District, but he also traveled extensively in western Europe, especially in France. As a young Oxford man, and from 1847 as private secretary to Lord Lansdowne, the influential Whig statesman, he concealed behind the pose of a dandy the melancholy which found expression only in his poetry.

Visiting Thun in Switzerland in 1848, he met and fell in love with a young Frenchwoman whose name is unknown but whom he calls "Marguerite" in his poems. They met again in the same place in 1849 and then parted for ever. In 1850 he began his courtship of Frances Lucy Wightman, whom he married in 1851. To enable himself to support a wife and family, Arnold gave up his secretaryship and became an inspector of schools. His original inspectorial district was vast; so much so that his life was very unsettled. Not until 1858 did he and his wife have a permanent home away from her parents.

By this date Arnold had published most of the verse that he was ever to write. His appointment in 1857 as professor of poetry at Oxford, an appointment tenable concurrently with his inspectorship, committed him to regular literary criticism. When he relinquished this post in 1867, his career as a poet was virtually complete; but his career as a critic still lay mostly ahead.

During his middle and later years Arnold was a cheerful, sociable and well-adjusted man. His dandyism had mellowed into urbanity, and, though he could still be supercilious, his kindliness, geniality and courtesy won general recognition. He continued to travel abroad, both on educational business and for recreation. Twice during the 1880s he visited the United States. His elder daughter married an American, and it was his eagerness to greet her and his grandchild on a visit to England that placed too great a strain on a weak heart and caused his sudden death.

Arnold's poetry is dominated by a sense of limitation. Its author evidently feels a spontaneous sympathy with the high aspirations of the

Romantic poets, but he recognizes an inevitable conflict between these aspirations and the rigorous, impartial and inescapable tyranny of circumstance and natural law. In "Resignation" he speaks of the wisdom of submitting to "time" and "change," of learning "to bear rather than rejoice." Similarly, the protagonist of "Empedocles on Etna" advises his friend to "nurse no extravagant hope" and to "moderate desire" in the face of a universe which is utterly indifferent to him, which will in any case proceed in accordance with its own laws, and to which he will obviously be well advised to adjust himself. As a contemporary reviewer put it: "Mr. Arnold's *sentiment*, his aspiration for life, is almost always in conflict with his critical perception of what life really is; . . . and hence he hits exactly many of the moods of an age which finds its desires for faith in strong contrast with what it deems the inadequate justification for those desires."

"Dover Beach" embodies this conflict. In this poem the decline of religious faith leaves the poet desolate in a neutral universe. His only hope is that in a successful love relationship he may realize some of the values for which there is no longer a place in "the world." The rendering of its meaning in terms of a symbolic landscape is something that "Dover Beach" shares with others of Arnold's most successful poems—for example, "A Summer Night," "The Scholar Gipsy" and "Thyrsis."

As a literary critic Arnold stands above all for "disinterestedness." A disinterested critic resolutely rejects "ulterior, political, practical considerations" and is motivated only by "*curiosity*" in the finest sense of that word. He seeks to acquaint himself as far as he can with the best thought and the finest creative practice of his time. Having done so, he wishes to communicate his knowledge and insights to others.

This activity serves both the creative writer and society generally. It serves the creative writer by helping to educate a reading public capable of offering him the understanding and the challenge which will elicit his best work; it serves society by bringing fresh knowledge and insights to bear upon its creeds, customs, laws and institutions, and so preventing it from settling into a self-satisfaction that would retard its growth. Arnold's principal work as a social critic is *Culture and Anarchy* (1869). In this he describes his own age as energetic, complacent and blundering, and tries to inculcate in his contemporaries a more general appreciation of the value of knowledge, understanding and intelligence. One way, in particular, by which he sought to extend their intellectual horizons was by introducing them to Continental writers and forms of education, as in *Essays in Criticism*, first series, and his government reports published as *The Popular Education of France* (1861) and *Schools and Universities on the Continent* (1868).

In addition to literary and social criticism, Arnold's prose includes a number of works on religion. In these he assumes that belief in the supernatural has already become impossible for many people and will soon become impossible for many more. He does not wish to accelerate the process, but he is anxious that those affected by it should perceive that religion does not need the support of a belief in the supernatural. He maintains that the dogmatic elements in Christianity are less enduring than the poetic elements and that men must learn to rely on these poetic elements if religion is to continue to make its essential contribution to their lives.

In general, Arnold's prose has a hopefulness and an assurance which are rare in his verse. Much of it is polemical. Cool, serious, bantering and ironical, it makes him one of the most pleasing and civilized of our controversialists.

(See also **Essays.**)

The Strayed Reveller, and Other Poems, 1849.
Empedocles on Etna, and Other Poems, 1852.
Poems, 1853.
Poems: Second Series, 1855.
Merope: A Tragedy, 1858.
On Translating Homer, 1861.
Essays in Criticism, 1865.
New Poems, 1867.
On the Study of Celtic Literature, 1867.
Culture and Anarchy, 1869.
Literature and Dogma, 1873.
God and the Bible, 1875.
Essays in Criticism: Second Series, 1888.

Complete Prose Works (excludes correspondence), ed. R. H. Super, 11 vols.,
    Ann Arbor: Univ. of Michigan Press, 1960– .
Poems, ed. K. Allott, London: Longmans; New York: Barnes & Noble,
    1965.
Letters . . . to Arthur Hugh Clough, ed. H. F. Lowry, London and
    New York: Oxford Univ. Press, 1932.   J.D.J.

ASCHAM, Roger (1515–68), son of Lord Scrope's steward, was educated at Cambridge and became a fellow and teacher of Greek there. Subsequently he was tutor to Princess Elizabeth and Latin secretary to Edward VI, Mary and Elizabeth. He upholds the humanist ideal of versatility and *The Schoolmaster* proposes a humane approach to education. A fine writer of letters in English and Latin, Ascham is an early master of graceful English prose. His main English works are *Toxophilus* (1545) and *The Schoolmaster* (1570). (See also **Renaissance Humanism.**)

Whole Works, ed. J. A. Giles, 3 vols., London: J. R. Smith, 1864–65.
English Works, ed. W. A. Wright, Cambridge: Cambridge Univ. Press, 1904.   G.P.

ASHBERY, John (1927–) was born in Rochester (New York), graduated from Harvard in 1949 and Columbia in 1951. He has worked in publishing, lived in France (1955–57), where he was art critic of the Paris *Herald Tribune*, and has also worked for *Art News* and, latterly, the Museum of Modern Art in New York. His first book of poems, *Turandot and Other Poems*, appeared in 1953. In 1956 he won the Yale Series of Younger Poets contest with *Some Trees*, and has since published *The Poems* (1960), *The Tennis Court Oath* (1962), *Rivers and Mountains* (1966), *Fragment: Poem* (1969) and *The Double Dream of Spring* (1970). In prose, *A Nest of Ninnies* (1969) was a novel with James Schuyler. His plays include *The Compromise* (1960; *p.* 1955) and *The Heroes* (1960). Ashbery has described the influence on his work of Wallace Stevens, the French surrealists and the New York "action painters." His method of discontinuity is disturbing, but his themes—innocence, change, love, communion—emerge notwithstanding.   J.P.W.

ASIMOV, Isaac. See **Science Fiction.**

AUBREY, John (1626–97), antiquary, was one of the original ninety-eight fellows of the Royal Society. He combined an insatiable curiosity with an inability to organize its products into complete works of scholarship. His *Brief Lives Chiefly of Contemporaries*, about notable persons of the sixteenth and seventeenth centuries, is a fascinating product of restless inquiry and inveterate love of gossip. He allowed his fellow antiquary, Anthony à Wood, to draw on it, but the work itself was not published until the nineteenth century. Only *Miscellanies: A Collection of Hermetic Philosophy* (1696) appeared in his lifetime.

Selected Lives, ed. O. L. Dick, London: Secker & Warburg, 1949.
                                                                    J.D.J.

AUCHINCLOSS, Louis (1917–) was born in Lawrence (New York), educated at Yale and the University of Virginia, and admitted to the bar in 1941. His novels of life in New York's high society—for example, *The Great World and Timothy Colt* (1956)—reflect at times his experiences as a lawyer, and the best of his short stories, in the collections *Powers of Attorney* (1963) and *Tales of Manhattan* (1967), are set in a New York "law factory." A novelist of manners and morals in the tradition of Edith Wharton, Auchincloss fails to question sufficiently the values of the society he describes, but at his best—as in *Portrait in Brownstone* (1962)—he writes with a dry subtlety.   R.W.

AUDEN, W. H. (Wystan Hugh) (1907–   ) was born in York, where his father was a medical officer of health, but spent much of his early life in the industrial Midlands. Educated at Gresham's School, Holt, and then Oxford, he began to write verse at school, showing a talent for assimilating various styles. At Oxford he devoted most of his time to the writing of poetry, and his forceful personality attracted around him several young writers who became known as the "Auden group." He was a schoolmaster for some time, but writing and traveling were his main occupations during the 1930s. In January 1939 he went to live in the U.S.A., becoming a United States citizen in 1946, but returned in 1972 to make his home in Oxford, where he had been professor of poetry from 1956 to 1961.

Auden's reputation as a poet was firmly established before he was thirty. His air of authority in interpreting modern man and contemporary society, and his daring and technically brilliant handling of language and verse forms made him the dominant poet of the 1930s. The near-Marxist poet of the 1930s changed, after his emigration to America, into the later Christian poet of such works as *Nones* (1951). The transformation is first noticeable in *New Year Letter* (1941). In addition to regular volumes of poems Auden has produced an astonishing variety of work, including plays, opera libretti and translations. His prose essays contain perceptive and deeply felt speculations about the relationship between art and life (always a central question in Auden's writing), and some interestingly original interpretation of Shakespeare. He has also edited several anthologies, all of which reveal an alert, sympathetic and wide-ranging mind.

Like Byron, a poet he greatly admires, Auden has an extraordinary capacity for expressing directly in verse the whole "feel" of his age. His interest in discovering explanatory schemata has led him sometimes into oversimple generalizations, and his serious poetry has undoubtedly suffered from his facility in pastiche and light colloquial verse. But Auden's work cannot be pigeonholed as "detached sociological commentary." He has written some beautiful lyrics, and the playful anti-Romantic or the analytic observer are merely two of many facets of a complex, fundamentally serious and compassionate artist.

Poems, 1930.
The Orators, 1932.
The Dance of Death, 1933.
The Dog beneath the Skin (with Christopher Isherwood), 1935 (play).
The Ascent of F6 (with Isherwood), 1936 (play).
Look, Stranger!, 1936.
Letters from Iceland (with Louis MacNeice), 1937.
On the Frontier (with Isherwood), 1938 (play).
Another Time, 1940.
New Year Letter, 1941 (U.S. title: *The Double Man*).
For the Time Being, 1944.
The Age of Anxiety, 1948.
Nones, 1951.
The Shield of Achilles, 1955.
Homage to Clio, 1960.
About the House, 1966.
Secondary Worlds, 1968 (prose).
City without Walls, and Other Poems, 1969.
Epistle to a Godson, and Other Poems, 1972.

Collected Shorter Poems, 1927–1957, London: Faber & Faber, 1966; New
    York: Random House, 1967.
Collected Longer Poems, London: Faber & Faber, 1968; New York:
    Random House, 1969.   A.Y.

AUGUSTANS, The. "Augustan" is an abused definition. Historians
use it to denote various permutations of dates between 1660 and 1789.
Literary critics who stress the political and social aspects of eighteenth-
century literature use it with similar variation in meaning. Some even use
it as a synonym for "the eighteenth century," but the more perceptive
limit its scope to the beliefs, themes, styles and forms of authors such as
Dryden, Swift and Pope between the 1680s and the 1740s (see J. W.
Johnson, "The Meaning of Augustan," *Journal of the History of Ideas*, 19,
1958).
    The title was first coined by the age itself which, weaned on the Latin
classics, almost instinctively drew analogies between Roman and contemporary life, and in the early years of the eighteenth century began to
see itself as the English counterpart of the Roman state under the Emperor
Augustus. The "Augustans" pointed to the political parallel between
Augustus's establishment of civil peace after civil war and the autocratic
stability of England emanating from the Revolution Settlement of 1688.
There was also a very conscious effort to imitate the urbane and polished
literary models of the Latin Augustan Age, particularly Horace and Ovid.

They were aware of the dangers in this, as Pope's "The Art of Sinking in Poetry" wittily demonstrates, but "true" imitation meant the process of selective evaluation of the forms and styles of the literary classics, prior to their "translation" into a native English tradition. Thus Tickell, in his 1721 edition of Addison's works, could isolate "correctness," "propriety of thought" and "chastity of style" as the distinctive qualities of a deliberate English "Augustanism."

The twin foundations of politics and literature were strengthened by the influence of philosophical rationalism, particularly that of Hobbes and Locke. Stability was a hard won and still precarious balance which any irrational "enthusiasm" could threaten, be it that of the extreme Whigs, who were willing to abandon any religious, political or social principle as long as this would advance the cause of trade, or that of the extreme Tories, who still looked with furtive optimism toward the restoration of the Catholic Pretender and the feudal aristocracy. The 1688 Revolution had not usurped the law, but overthrown a king who broke the law. It was a rational compromise between Whig and Tory, city and country, Dissent and Anglicanism, which all the Augustan writers sought to defend in their several ways.

Indeed, "reason" and its applied form in "common sense" provided the basic subject and dictated the style of many Augustan masterpieces such as Pope's *The Rape of the Lock*, Addison and Steele's *The Spectator* papers and Swift's *Gulliver's Travels*. It is no coincidence that satire, particularly ironic satire, should link these works. Defensive satire, which is based on a cohesive infrastructure of related concepts such as those held by the Augustans and to which the bulk of the reading public paid at least lip service, is always a more potent force than isolated offensive satire. Irony underlined this. It proclaimed the virtues of perspicacious reason and urbane refinement in its very form, which automatically drew the reader into a flattering collaboration with the author, the one applying reason to untangle the ironic complexity which the other had rationally created.

Reason also dictated the pattern of poetic development during the age, for the Augustans accepted Hobbes's judgment that literature was only of value when it illustrated or elucidated a rational approach to life. This informed the idea of poetic diction, which was designed to reflect general truths underlying superficial differences among all phenomena (including man) through common concepts expressed by refined and polished common language. Thus diction was not divorced from life and the "proper study" was reflected not only through the subject of poetry but its expression, a reasonable refinement of life's raw materials.

Yet the Augustans knew only too well how far life fell short of the rational ideal. They believed in reason but were concurrently aware of its limitations in a proud, fallen and paradoxical compound of angel and beast such as man, and this ambivalence is eloquently expressed in Pope's *An Essay on Man* and Swift's *Gulliver's Travels*. They were equally aware of the forces in society antipathetic to their principles, and attacked them vigorously through their deep and increasingly pessimistic involvement in the violent and dangerous arena of political pamphleteering. But the rise of Whiggery, mercantilism, enthusiasm and toleration was irresistible. Defoe with his plain earthbound style, industry, inventiveness, exuberance and ecstatic reverence for trade was in many ways more typical of "the Augustan Age" than the Augustans. Ned Ward's picture of low life in *The London Spy* and Lord Hervey's virile portrait of the crude and corrupt court express the raw gusto of all Augustan society. Pope satirized Hervey as Sporus in *An Epistle to Dr. Arbuthnot* and the popular "scriblers" in *The Dunciad*, but he knew that his satire could not turn the social tide. The new reading public created by Dissenting academies and swelled by the increasingly leisured class had been brought up on practical English and mathematics, not the classical past. They responded to Defoe's journalism and the economic realism of his novels rather than to Pope's allusive urbanity.

The Augustans abhorred but accepted the situation. Indeed the cyclical pattern of Roman Augustan history, elucidated by later Roman historians, convinced them that English Augustanism must follow the inevitable pattern of flowering and decay visible in its classical model. Thus the last lines of *The Dunciad* are an almost tragic affirmation of standards in the face of encroaching darkness. Those standards lived on in a changing world to be reincarnated by writers such as Johnson and his friends, but one of them, Goldsmith, although one of the best critics and fervent admirers of Augustanism, realized that "the Augustan Age" itself had long gone.　　　　　　　　　　　　　　　　　　　　　　　　　　　　**A.W.B.**

AUROBINDO, Sri. See **Indian Literature.**

AUSTEN, **Jane** (1775–1817), the younger of two daughters in a family of eight, was born at Steventon (Hampshire), where she lived in her father's rectory for the first twenty-five years of her life. Five years were then spent at Bath, three at Southampton, and virtually the whole of the rest of her life at Chawton (Hampshire). Her education, as was then usual, was mainly at home, where she acquired a wide knowledge of English literature (particularly of the novel), considerable French and a little Italian. Her life was uneventful and normal: her days were filled with the duties and diversions proper to a lady of her class in society—a share of the housekeeping, needlework, reading, music, visiting, occasional balls, and fairly frequent holiday trips to London and Kent. It was clearly a happy and high-spirited household. The great friendship of her life was that with her sister Cassandra; they were deeply devoted to each other. It seems that at some time, probably about 1801, she fell in love with a young man who loved her in return, but he died suddenly. No details are known with any certainty.

Her novels, about family groups similar to her own, were actually written in the middle of her own, in the general parlor, with Jane hastily covering her manuscript if anyone not of the family entered the room. There were two creative periods in her life, 1796–1803 and 1811–16. The first period is particularly confused. "Elinor and Marianne" (a forerunner of *Sense and Sensibility*) was written in 1795; "First Impressions" (an early *Pride and Prejudice*) in 1796–97; "Susan" (an early *Northanger Abbey*) in 1797–98. In 1798 "First Impressions" was refused by a publisher. In 1803 another bought *Northanger Abbey* for £10, but merely put it in a drawer. In 1816, with four novels published, it was bought back from him for the same sum. Only when the transaction was completed was the news broken to him that it was by the author of *Pride and Prejudice*. The three novels of the later period offer no such difficulties, each novel appearing shortly after it was written. Her works made no great stir at the time (and she certainly made no great fortune from them—about £750 for the four published in her lifetime), but they were greatly admired by Southey, Coleridge, Sir Walter Scott and, incongruously, the Prince Regent. Jane Austen died after an unidentified illness of some eighteen months' duration on 18 July 1817 and is buried in Winchester Cathedral.

In the following years Jane Austen's novels rapidly established themselves as favorites with a wide range of readers. Her wit, her humor and her comic characters were justly admired, but unfortunately there was a rather sentimental stress on the "gentleness" of her "playful satire." In fact, although all the novels are comedies in that they end happily, and although there is often a tone of sustained and lively gaiety, the latent somberness of *Mansfield Park* and *Persuasion* is salutary in directing us towards the fundamental seriousness of them all. With all their vivacity, they are nevertheless soberly concerned with the study of the moral values of contemporary society and the nature of the good life. It is a fact often found unpalatable by readers in an egalitarian culture that she accepts the principles of social hierarchy common to her age; she, and her first readers, would see nothing ridiculous in the jingle

> God bless the squire and his relations
> And keep us in our proper stations.

But she sees the hierarchical society as an ideal, and much of her irony is directed against betrayals of that ideal; often charged with snobbery, she is the great "antisnob" of our literature. For examples, General Tilney in *Northanger Abbey*, Lady Catherine de Bourgh in *Pride and Prejudice*, Mrs. Elton (and Emma) in *Emma* and Sir Walter Elliot in *Persuasion* are all subjected in various degrees to ironic and condemnatory ridicule as people who presume on their social status, who are only too aware of the rights of their rank but forgetful of the obligations it imposes upon them. Allied to this is Jane Austen's awareness of the just demands of society: Marianne is censured openly for her failure to observe elementary social decorum; Emma's rudeness to Miss Bates is seen as doubly bad—a failure of *noblesse oblige* and a personal offense; the whole of *Persuasion* is, amongst other things, an investigation into what society is entitled to demand of its members.

But Jane Austen is very conscious of individual feeling. It is not sensibility that is seen as bad, only the unmannerly display of it. In presenting feeling, her habitual reticence can mislead us; Elinor feels as deeply as Marianne, and Emma's emotion as she realizes the enormity of her offense is painful and sincere. Although Jane Austen never deals with the inflated grandeurs of romantic passion, she shows us in her heroines qualities of strong emotion, deep feeling and lasting affection. Always she insists on self-discipline and right conduct, animated by "active principle" (her own phrase), but she makes us aware of the feelings and impulses that necessitate this control. The weak, the trivial, the foolish and the vicious she ultimately dismisses in a manner that is far from gentle. All this is achieved by an apparently straightforward style that is capable of subtle nuances and wide variation. It creates a range of characters each with a distinctive utterance; it can be simple and direct, or charged with a revealing irony; it can be boisterously comic, or incisively analytical. The characters are set beside each other in revealing ironic juxtaposition, so that we see General Tilney and John Thorpe as equals in mercenary vulgarity, and Emma and Mrs. Elton equally arrogant, presumptuous and overweening. The novels are skillfully constructed, and the plot is in continuous development: before one climax is reached, another is being quietly prepared for. The whole presents us with a complex view of individuals in society, even though, on the surface, the main interest seems to be the progression towards happy marriage of a handful of middle-class young ladies at the turn of the eighteenth century.

Sense and Sensibility, 1811.
Pride and Prejudice, 1813 (*f.* 1940).
Mansfield Park, 1814.
Emma, 1816.
Northanger Abbey, 1818.
Persuasion, 1818.

Novels, ed. R. W. Chapman, 5 vols., Oxford: Clarendon Press, 1923;
  edition 6 vols., vol. 6 *Minor Works*, London: Oxford Univ. Press,
  1954.
Letters, ed. R. W. Chapman, 2 vols., Oxford: Clarendon Press, 1932.

C.H.

AUSTRALIAN LITERATURE. The earliest fiction, like *Robinson Crusoe*, masquerades as reminiscence. Both *Tales of the Colonies* by Charles Rowcroft (c. 1781–1850) and *Settlers and Convicts* by Alexander Harris (1805–74) are such. Two other early novels worth mention are *Ralph Rashleigh* by James Tucker (1808–66), written c. 1844 and published in original form 1952, with its description of the horrors of convict life, and *Clara Morison* (1854) by Catherine Spence (1825–1910), about domestic life in the Victorian gold rush period. Henry Kingsley (1830–76) provided a romanticized version of pastoral life in *The Recollections of Geoffry Hamlyn* (1859), but the first really powerful major Australian novel is *For the Term of His Natural Life* (1874; s. 1870) by Marcus Clarke (1846–81), who traces the harrowing psychological effects of the convict system on jailer and prisoner alike.

A distinguishably intrinsic Australian flavor is first found in "Rolf Boldrewood," the pseudonym of Thomas Alexander Browne (1826–1915). He wrote in the preface to *Robbery under Arms* (1888; s. 1882; f. 1957, about the Victorian gold rush and the activities of bushrangers): "Much of the narrative is literally true, as can be verified by official records." Assertive nationalism finds expression in *Such Is Life*, written in 1896 by "Tom Collins" (Joseph Furphy, 1843–1912) and published in 1903. This novel, though formless and rambling, resembles the short stories of Henry Lawson (1867–1922) in providing an authentic feeling of Australian farming life. *The Bulletin*, the periodical founded in 1880 and edited for a long period by A. G. Stephens (1865–1933), did much to foster creative activity, especially in the short story.

These writers are, however, essentially tellers of tales. There is little study of character in their work. The best psychological study in the Australian novel before 1930 is to be found in the work of "Henry Handel Richardson" (Mrs. Ethel F. Robertson, 1870–1946) and, in particular, *Australia Felix* (1917), *The Way Home* (1925) and *Ultima Thule* (1929), the trilogy comprising *The Fortunes of Richard Mahony*. It has been called the life story of a misfit, but behind Mahony's own inadequacies is also the restless movement back and forth between England and Australia.

In general the Australian novel remained extrovert, "saga, picaresque and documentary," sometimes avowedly political, as in *The Go-Getter* (1942) by Leonard Mann (1895–   ) and *Power without Glory* (1950) by

Frank Hardy (1917–). Social indignation is also found in *Capricornia* (1938) by Xavier Herbert (1911–), the long, formless but rumbustious survey of forty years in the Northern Territory. Herbert's later *Soldiers' Women* (1961) is a much more controlled and complex work. But the greatest name by far in the Australian novel is that of Patrick White (1912–). His has been a deliberate attempt "to prove that the Australian novel is not necessarily the dreary, dun-coloured off-spring of journalistic realism"—preface to *Voss* (1957). In this novel and in others such as *The Aunt's Story* (1948), *The Tree of Man* (1955), *Riders in the Chariot* (1961) and *The Vivisector* (1970), with his more profound concept of character, his handling of language and his sense of symbolic significances, he has triumphantly succeeded. Among younger writers mention must be made of the poet-novelist Randolph Stow (1935–), author of, in particular, *To the Islands* (1958) and *Tourmaline* (1963).

In poetry the first names to be noted are those of Charles Harpur (1813–68), Henry Kendall (1839–82) and Adam Lindsay Gordon (1833–70), but all three represent little more than diluted versions of various types of English Romanticism. Christopher Brennan (1870–1932) is something of a "sport" in Australian poetry. He, too, is derivative, but he is a symbolist looking back to a European tradition, and particularly to Mallarmé. A more typically Australian voice was that of A. B. ("Banjo") Paterson (1864–1941), who, with Lawson (see earlier), turned the oral tradition of the bush ballad into literary channels, especially in *The Bulletin*.

The most notable names of the interwar period were Kenneth Slessor (1901–) and R. D. FitzGerald (1902–), Douglas Stewart (1913–) and Kenneth Mackenzie (1913–54), but the years since 1945 have produced greater talent in the work of A. D. Hope (1907–), James McAuley (1917–) and Judith Wright (1915–). Hope, with his *Collected Poems* (1966), is preoccupied with an Arnoldian sense of human loneliness. He explores attempts at communication through the act of love and through art. At times there is a sardonic note about his work. McAuley, by contrast, is more confidently affirmative. A Roman Catholic since 1952, he records in *Captain Quiros* (1964) a spiritual journey in which, though man is seen to fail, the search is proclaimed as the all-important fact—as Arnold saw his father, "On, to the City of God!" ("Rugby Chapel"). Judith Wright has a sensitive awareness of the ageless Australian landscape, where the life of trees, flowers and birds appears at times to take on a Blakean significance for her. Besides Stow, already mentioned, more recent poets of some note include Bruce Dawe (1930–) and Chris Wallace-Crabbe (1934–).

A.P.

AYTOUN, William Edmonstoune. See **Spasmodics, The.**

B

BABBITT, Irving (1865–1933) was born in Dayton (Ohio). He was educated at Harvard and returned there in 1894, to remain as a professor of Romance languages until his death. He was the leading exponent of what came to be called the New Humanism, though his version of the doctrine was different in some basic respects from that propounded by other adherents of the movement. Babbitt's philosophy insisted on the primacy of human reason and he offered models of human conduct from his wide knowledge of Greek, Chinese and European civilization. His humanism was developed more specifically in opposition to the prevailing ideas of the Naturalists, based, as he believed, on a false scientism and emotionalism. Among his works (their titles reveal his preoccupations) are *Literature and the American College: Essays in Defense of the Humanities* (1908), *The New Laokoön: An Essay on the Confusion of the Arts* (1910), *Rousseau and Romanticism* (1919) and *Democracy and Leadership* (1924).

B.L.

BACON, Francis, 1st Baron Verulam and Viscount St. Albans (1561–1626) was the youngest son of Sir Nicholas Bacon, lord keeper of the Great Seal, who died in 1579, leaving him poor, but ambitious to follow the career of lawyer and statesman. Educated at Trinity College, Cambridge, he served in the embassy of Sir Amyas Paulet in France, and then attended Gray's Inn. He was called to the bar in 1582 and made a queen's counsel in 1596. From 1584 he was a member of Parliament. Burghley's opposition and Bacon's friendship with Essex hindered his political advancement. Essex had proved a generous but rash patron, so that Bacon's involvement in the treason trial was regrettable, but legally inevitable. Under James I he was successively a commissioner for the Union with Scotland, solicitor general, attorney general, lord keeper of the Great Seal and lord chancellor. In 1621 he was created a viscount. The expenses of his offices and rank with the small emoluments received made him, according to contemporary custom, incautiously accept gifts from parties in lawsuits before him, thus giving to legal and political enemies the means of his fall in 1621. The loss of place gave him time for his studies. He had already addressed *The Advancement of Learning* to the scholar king, published *Instauratio Magna* and written *The New Atlantis*. Before his death he published the third edition of *Essays* and the *History of Henry VII*. He wrote a number of his works in Latin. He married a London merchant's daughter, but had no children.

Bacon holds a controversial place in the history of Renaissance ideas. He did not advance scientific experiment in any field, but he sought a method of acquiring and systematizing knowledge, different from that of Aristotle as pursued in the universities. There metaphysical reasons were given for the behavior of matter, so that the fall of a stone illustrated inferiority of matter to spirit rather than led to the discovery of physical laws of motion. Bacon examined with psychological insight the "idols" of the mind, shown in uncritical reverence for tradition, undiscriminating acceptance of new ideas, majority views and ill-matured judgments. He saw that knowledge must grow by concerted effort, unfettered by the unscientific dogmatism of current theology, and by methods of inquiry suited to each branch of learning, as, for example, in medicine the collection of data on causes, effects and cures of diseases. Judged by modern standards or in relation to the discoveries of Gilbert and Harvey, Bacon's own knowledge was deficient, but his historical importance remains as a promoter of the method of induction. He advocated in *The New Atlantis* a scientific research institution freed from professional interests. He stimulated the thinkers who founded the Royal Society in 1666. His *History of Henry VII* contains much realistic detail, but it is a guide to a prince's education more than a modern study. His works now most significant are *The Advancement of Learning*, *The New Atlantis* and the *Essays*.

While using Montaigne's title "essay," Bacon established an English form in the genre of "advice" literature, written from experience, with classical and contemporary usage of maxims, pithy illustrations and table-book wit. He was a master of the sententious style enriched with imagery and eloquence. His essays grew in size and number and there were numerous changes in the editions. At first "dispersed jottings," they became full, often graceful, without loss of his legal judgment or his worldly wisdom. The subjects covered interested the educated gentleman or professional man and reflected on his business and his pleasures, his public and personal life. On the surface of the essays all is reserve and detachment, but the penetrating reader can admire the idealist and the shrewd, sometimes disillusioned man of affairs who retired to Gray's Inn as treasurer and planned the gardens there. His complexities as man and writer have made him friends and enemies, but he has been discussed and weighed as a European Renaissance figure for four centuries. No man was more representative of his age. (See also **Essays; Renaissance Humanism.**)

Essays; Religious Meditations; Places of Persuasion and Dissuasion, 1597; expanded, 1612; 1625.

The Two Books . . . of the Proficience and Advancement of Learning, Divine and Human, 1605.
Instauratio Magna, 1620 (includes unfinished *Novum Organum*).
History of the Reign of King Henry the Seventh, 1622.
Sylva Sylvarum; or, A Natural History, 1627 (includes *The New Atlantis*).

Works, ed. J. Spedding, R. L. Ellis, and D. D. Heath, 14 vols., London: Longman & Co., 1857–74.   I.M.W.

BAGEHOT, Walter (1826–77), born at Langport (Somerset) and educated at Bristol College and University College, London, was the son of a prosperous Unitarian banker who sent him to London because he objected to the religious tests then applied at Oxford and Cambridge. The result was that Bagehot received a thorough but entirely non-sectarian training in an atmosphere free from the doctrinal controversies that dissipated so much intellectual energy in the older universities. After a brilliant academic career, followed by a brief visit to Paris in 1851 when he witnessed and ironically condoned Louis Napoleon's seizure of power, he abandoned his legal studies and joined his father's bank in Somerset, where he could combine his professional commitments with his activities as a journalist and reviewer. In 1855 his financial affluence enabled him to establish and edit (with his close friend R. H. Hutton) *The National Review* and in 1861 he crowned his journalistic achievement by becoming editor of *The Economist* (Hutton had been joint editor from 1855). The publication of *The English Constitution* in 1867 made him a national figure, and when he died at fifty-one, he had come to be regarded as an unofficial chancellor of the Exchequer.

In *The English Constitution*, first published in *The Fortnightly Review*, Bagehot's own aim was to examine the basic structure of British politics with the realism of a successful banker and man of affairs rather than to produce what has since become a theoretical treatise on constitutional government. He attempted to cut through the confusing expediencies and baffling compromises of a political system that had developed over several centuries. Sooner than accept the clichés of party warfare, he chose to look most carefully at what actually happened, not at what was meant to happen, and although his analysis applied more relevantly to the pre-1867 political situation than to the Parliaments which met after Disraeli's Reform Act of that year, much of what he wrote continues to excite controversy. He then broadened his evolutionary interpretation of political development in his *Physics and Politics*, where he stressed the importance of organic change in any society that was not to become fossilized by custom and tradition. His other major work, *Lombard Street*, descended from the abstract heights of anthropological speculation to the practical level of financial speculation in the City of London and can be read with profit by anyone concerned with the City's role as a monetary center of the world.

While *The English Constitution* remains Bagehot's principal achievement in literature, his claim to the title of "the greatest Victorian" (awarded him by G. M. Young) rests not only on his published work as an economist and reviewer but on his whole personality as a man who reflected all the best aspects of what, for convenience's sake, we call the Victorian period. Above all, there is his sanity, his refusal to be cajoled into approving what was acceptable and fashionable. Writing of Queen Victoria and her son he refers not to a remote monarch and a mighty prince but to "a retired widow and an unemployed youth," yet he disdains the conventional Radical prejudices. The widow and the youth perform, however inadequately, a useful symbolic function. This urbane detachment, so refreshing in the prosaic fields of politics and economics, becomes a weakness when Bagehot turns to literature and art, blinding him to the merits of a highly emotive writer like Dickens whose novels he could not understand. But even in his literary criticism his sound common sense, expressed with a conversational ease and glancing wit, places him among the most rewarding writers of his time.

The English Constitution, 1867.
Physics and Politics, 1872.
Lombard Street, 1873.
Literary Studies, 2 vols., 1879.
Biographical Studies, 1880.

Works and Life, ed. E. I. Barrington, 10 vols., London: Longmans, 1915.
Works, ed. N. St. John-Stevas, 9 vols., London: *The Economist*; Cambridge, Mass.: Harvard Univ. Press, 1965– .   D.E.P.

BAILEY, P. J. (Philip James). See **Spasmodics, The.**

BALDWIN, James (1924–) was born in Harlem (New York City). To avoid the immediate realities of the racial situation, he sought refuge in physical exile and in writing—"the only way to another world." With the help of Richard Wright, whom he was later to attack in a famous essay, "Everybody's Protest Novel," he left for France in 1948, convinced that "I would die if I stayed in America." His first book, *Go Tell It on the Mountain*, was published in 1953. Set in Harlem, it is concerned with the initiation of a young boy into a whole complex of religious, social and racial realities. Baldwin followed this with an impressive volume of essays, *Notes of a Native Son* (1955), and a novel about the relationship between two white homosexuals, *Giovanni's Room* (1956). In 1957 he returned to the United States, and a first visit to the South, combined with the increasing bitterness of the racial situation, gave a new acerbity to his next novel, *Another Country* (1962), and to a short polemical work, *The Fire Next Time* (1963). A second volume of essays, *Nobody Knows My Name*, was published in 1961. His plays are *The Amen Corner* (1968; *p.* 1964), about the personal lives of black Christians, and *Blues for Mister Charlie* (1964), a protest play set in a Southern town. The central theme running through Baldwin's work, including his volume of short stories, *Going to Meet the Man* (1965), and a further novel, *Tell Me How Long the Train's Been Gone* (1968), is the need for love, even an imperfect love, in the face of a social and racial situation which seems to erode identity and destroy the substance of human love.   C.B.

BALLADS evolved from popular social activities. The word is from Old French *ballade*, Provençal *balada*, meaning "dance, song or poem to dance to"; its root is that of *ballare*, "to dance," which is seen in *ball*, and its Italian form gives modern *ballet*. Etymologically, the word indicates a set of words for a dance tune, a social literary form, and it is in this sense that it first appears in Middle English. By the end of the fifteenth century, however, it had acquired the sense "any light and simple song" which it still retains today. During the sixteenth century there was a tendency to use the word to refer to a story told in song, and at the end of that century the traditional or popular ballads for social occasions had been joined by another type of ballad with contemporary social reference, put about by printers and often journalistic rather than poetic in manner—the broadside ballad.

The ballads were thus either a form of folk culture or a form of occasional entertainment much commercialized. During the seventeenth century the collecting of ballads began. Men such as John Selden (1584–1654), Anthony à Wood (1632–95) and Samuel Pepys collected broadside ballads (and inevitably also some traditional examples) and in 1765 Bishop Thomas Percy published his *Reliques of Ancient English Poetry* which gave a new impetus to ballad collection by such men as Joseph Ritson and Sir Walter Scott. These collections in turn influenced the poets of the eighteenth and nineteenth centuries and the literary ballad was born. In origin a poem sharing the literary characteristics of the older ballad form, the literary ballad tends to involve a greater degree of stylistic elaboration and to develop away from the popular form. As a result of this evolutionary process, the word "ballad" has a wide range of reference.

The ballad began as an oral form, a poem to be sung, and our written records of ballads are late. A long period of unrecorded oral development may well precede the earliest extant written example of an English ballad, the thirteenth-century *Judas*. The popular oral nature of the ballad causes certain difficulties, for both the stories and the tunes to which they were sung were known over a wide area, not only of Britain but of Europe. The traditional ballads were taken by settlers to British colonies and there underwent independent development. Hence a story may appear in a variety of forms, all obviously related because they have words, phrases and details in common, but none obviously the earliest or superior version; and the same is true of the tunes. Probably no two performances of a ballad were exactly the same and it is impossible to establish the descent of the modern versions.

The origins of the ballad would seem to be similar to those of the Anglo-Saxon lay and heroic poem. The heroic poem was in origin an oral composition, narrative and sung to the harp. The ballad, however, differs from the heroic poem in its stanzaic form, its essential brevity and its avoidance of any accepted standard of conduct. Ballads are also recorded much later than heroic poems and any connection between the two is obscure. There is a closer parallel between ballads and some medieval romances. Formally, some romances (e.g., *King Horn*) show the same kind of simplifying technique and concentration upon situation as the ballads do, and romances and ballads may even have the same subjects. But the ballad is not an extended narrative, does not present events in terms of a code of conduct, and lacks the detailed descriptions and extended dialogue of the romance. Despite the interaction of the two genres, the ballad, unlike the romance, takes a detached view of love, warfare and the supernatural.

More remote connections may be suggested between the ballad and the lyric. Like the ballad, the lyric is associated with music, but the stanza forms are more complex and the stress is upon mood rather than upon situation. The longer political poems of the later Middle Ages are part of the same contemporary concern that is to be found in the "public" ballads.

In part, the literary characteristics of the ballad may be the result of putting words to an already existing tune. The subjects would have an immediate appeal for an audience. Some are "personal"—tales of love (happy or tragic), of relationships between kinsmen or within marriage, accounts of death and homicide. Others were "public," celebrating local heroes or events—the ballads of Robin Hood, for example, or the Border ballads of feuds between Scots and English. Some concentrate upon the supernatural—dialogues with the Devil or tales of returning ghosts, as *The Wife of Usher's Well*. Yet it is the method of narration rather than the nature of the story that characterizes the ballad.

Ballads concentrate upon a single situation with little regard for its importance in a wider sequence of events. The situation is recounted briefly, in episodic manner, in a series of short speeches or isolated details which are connected through being in sequence and through their individual relationship to the central situation. There is no attempt to provide a close connection between the details, or to develop background or dialogue; the emotional potential of the situation is not exploited and no attitude or set of values is projected. Yet although the treatment is objective and unemotional, this detached attitude to sex, violence, love, death and the supernatural often intensifies rather than reduces the emotional impact of the situation. Selection of situation and detail, speed in narration and objectivity in presentation are the ballad's main characteristics.

The disjunctive style is offset in several ways. In the popular form, the repetition of the tune serves as a linking device, and some ballads have refrains which further link the stanzas. Repetition of words, phrases and whole lines characterizes the form in general. And although ballads show a variety of metrical forms, there is no variation in the regular sequence of primary and secondary stresses or in the use of endstopped lines, so that the metrical form is an important unifying element.

The English and Scottish Popular Ballads, ed. F. J. Child, 5 vols., London: Stevens, Son & Stiles; Boston: Houghton, Mifflin, 1882–98.

The Literary Ballad, ed. A. H. Ehrenpreis, London: Arnold, 1966.

The Oxford Book of Ballads, newly selected and ed. J. Kinsley, Oxford: Clarendon Press, 1969.   A.D.M.

BANCROFT, George (1800–91), American historian and diplomat, was born in Massachusetts, graduated from Harvard (1817) and Gottingen (1820), and studied at the University of Berlin. After a brief spell at Harvard he founded the experimental Round Hill School at Northampton where he taught for eight years, introducing European methods of progressive education. An ardent Democrat and advocate of "Manifest Destiny," Bancroft supported the movement to acquire California and to expel Mexico from the disputed territory north of the Rio Grande. As a delegate to the National Democratic Convention (1844) he helped to secure the nomination of James K. Polk for the presidency, and was appointed customs collector for the Port of Boston. His major historical work, *A History of the United States* [to 1872], very popular for the rest of the nineteenth century, is characterized by a nationalistic rhetorical approach, reflecting a romantic and Hegelian interpretation of history. An admirer of Jacksonian Democracy, Bancroft asserted that out of ancient Teutonic practices or "germs" there had evolved the superiority of Anglo-Saxon and American peoples with distinctive institutions and the triumph of Protestant individualism and civil liberty over Roman Catholic authoritarianism. Bancroft, like Hegel, viewed historical events as part of a teleological "universal history," with principles and ideas rather than materialistic factors as the keys to historical development. In 1876 he produced a "thoroughly revised" edition of his *History* in six volumes, correcting earlier errors and modifying the more chauvinistic passages. He is remembered as the "Father of American History."

A History of the United States, 10 vols., Boston: Little & Brown, 1837–74.

J.W.

BANTLEMAN, Lawrence. See **Indian Literature.**

BARAKA, Amiri Imamu. See **Jones, Leroi.**

BARBOUR, John (?1316–95) was probably born near Aberdeen and studied at Oxford and Paris. He became archdeacon of Aberdeen and journeyed abroad. He is remembered for *The Bruce* (written 1375–78), a poem of 14,000 octosyllabic lines celebrating the exploits of Robert the Bruce and James Douglas. It is composed in a simple, even bald, manner and is chiefly valuable as a historical chronicle of the time. Nevertheless, Robert is always kept in the center of the poem as a heroic figure and the embodiment of freedom, "a noble thing." The Battle of Bannockburn is the most important incident in the poem. A version within Lydgate's *Troy Book* and a translation of *Legends of the Saints* have also been ascribed to Barbour.

A.P.

BARING, Maurice (1874–1945) was born in London and educated at Eton and Cambridge. He served in the diplomatic service and as a foreign correspondent for *The Times*. In this capacity he came to know and love czarist Russia in its Indian summer of the early twentieth century. Baring was a sensitive interpreter of Russian life and literature. He was also a writer of exquisitely realized *nouvelles* and short stories, which, together with his autobiography, *The Puppet Show of Memory* (1922), display cultured aristocratic values at their best—liberal, humane, refined and subtly humorous in their view of life.

The Russian People, 1911.
An Outline of Russian Literature, 1914.
Cat's Cradle, 1925.
Daphne Adeane, 1926.

The Lonely Lady of Dulwich, 1934.

Collected Poems, London: Heinemann, 1925.
Maurice Baring Restored, ed. P. Horgan, London: Heinemann; New York:
Farrar, Straus, 1970.   A.P.

BARING-GOULD, Sabine. See **Hymns.**

BARKER, George (1913–) was born in Essex of an English father and
Irish mother. He taught for a period in a Japanese university and resided
in America during the Second World War. He returned to England in
1943, though he has lived in America and Italy since that time. His
poetry is concerned with guilt, suffering and social decay, with which
the poet identifies himself. In manner his early verse is apocalyptic and
tragic, though often hysterical; in later volumes, such as *News of the
World* (1950), his feelings are more orderly and conveyed in simpler
language.

Collected Poems, 1930–55, 1957.
The Golden Chains, 1968.
Essays, 1970.   O.K.

BARLOW, Joel (1754–1812) graduated from Yale in 1778, where he
was class poet. After serving as a chaplain to the Revolutionary troops, he
became an editor and publisher in Hartford in 1784, was admitted to the
bar in 1786, and collaborated with John Trumbull and others of the
Connecticut Wits on *The Anarchiad* (1786–87) to argue the Federalist (i.e.,
centralist) case during the Constitutional Convention. In 1787 Barlow
published *The Vision of Columbus*, an epic celebration of the history and
future of America in nine books of decasyllabic couplets. A trip to France
as a land agent (1788) developed into a long residence in Europe, during
which he met Paine, came to accept and then to argue brilliantly the
Democratic Republican (anti-Federalist) position and was involved in
French politics. In 1795 he was appointed American consul to Algiers.
He returned in 1805 to live near Washington (D.C.), where he interested himself in various public projects, such as a national institution for education and research in Washington, and in the elaboration of his old epic
poem into *The Columbiad* (1807). Appointed minister to France in 1811, he
died near Cracow, on his way to arrange a treaty with Napoleon.
    Barlow is best known for his much anthologized poem *The Hasty
Pudding*, a short, mock-heroic appreciation of cornmeal mush written in
a fit of nostalgia when he was unexpectedly served a dish of it in France.

He wanted to be remembered most by *The Columbiad*, and, although dependent on the much earlier poetic conventions of Goldsmith and Cowper, both of his "epics," if only for their energy and the optimistic scale of their conception, invite rereading. It is on his radical political prose, however, that his reputation should depend. *A Letter to the National Convention of France* and *Advice to the Privileged Orders* are clear, vigorous and rational defenses of democracy, deserving to be read alongside *The Rights of Man* and *Common Sense*. *Advice to the Privileged Orders* was suppressed in England by Pitt's government.

The Vision of Columbus, 1787.
A Letter to the National Convention of France . . ., 1792.
Advice to the Privileged Orders, 2 vols., 1792–93.
The Hasty Pudding, 1796.
Prospectus of a National Institution to Be Established in the United States, 1806.
The Columbiad, 1807.

Works, ed. W. K. Bottorff and A. L. Ford, 2 vols., Gainesville, Fla.: Scholars' Facsimiles and Reprints, 1970.   S.A.F.

BARNES, William (1801–86) shows in his poetry a loving knowledge of the life and ways of his native county, Dorset. It is his faithfulness in natural description, his realistic portrayal of character and his use of Dorset dialect that give a lasting fragrance to poems whose subject matter is often comparatively trivial in itself. Much of his philological work was concerned with the development, from Old English, of the native Dorset medium that Barnes, despite Hardy's exhortations that he write more often in "common" (Received Standard) English, considered to be most suitable for recording a dying way of life.

Poems of Rural Life in the Dorset Dialect, 3 collections [1844–62], London: Kegan Paul, 1879.
Poems, ed. B. Jones, 2 vols., London: Centaur Press; Carbondale: Southern Illinois Univ. Press, 1962.   D.P.

BARNFIELD, Richard (1574–1627) was born at Norbury (Staffordshire) and educated at Brasenose College, Oxford. Probably the author of a pamphlet defending Robert Greene, Barnfield is otherwise known for only three slim volumes, *The Affectionate Shepherd* (1594), *Cynthia, with Certain Sonnets* (1595) and *The Encomion of Lady Pecunia* (1598). His verse is chiefly remarkable for its debt to Spenser, the variety of the forms attempted, and the poignancy of some poems in the first two volumes celebrating homosexual love. Two of his best lyrics have been attributed to Shakespeare.

Poems, ed. M. Summers, London: Fortune Press, 1936.   J.M.P.

BARRIE, J. M. (Sir James Matthew) (1860–1937), the son of a weaver, was born at Kirriemuir (Forfarshire) and educated at Edinburgh University. He began his career as a journalist and then moved to London. There he wrote several novels and, after 1901, devoted his time to the theater. In many stories describing peasant life in Scotland, he employs the dialect, whimsies and sentiment of what has since become known as the "kailyard" tradition, while much of his other fiction exploits the popular themes of Edwardian literature. In plays such as *The Admirable Crichton* (1914; *p.* 1902; *f.* 1957) he combines a slight social comment with fantasy, while *Peter Pan* (*p.* 1904; *f.* 1953) has become a regular feature of London's winter theater season.

Plays, ed. A. E. Wilson, London: Hodder & Stoughton, 1942.
Letters, ed. V. Meynell, London: P. Davies, 1942.   O.K.

BARRY, Philip (1896–1949) was born in Rochester (New York) and educated at Yale and Harvard. A product of George Pierce Baker's 47 Workshop, his career effectively demonstrated the short-term advantages and ultimate liability of the techniques of playmaking inculcated there. A successful writer for Broadway with some intellectual pretensions, Barry, like his predecessors in the art of the well-made play, mastered the art of flirting with unorthodox ideas while paying every deference to convention and subordinating all to the contriving of an effective curtain. Thus the sanctity of the marriage bond was, as in *Paris Bound* (1929; *p.* 1927; *f.* 1929), the subject of many a Barry theatrical sermon. Yet this play at least carried a modicum of conviction, which *Hotel Universe* (1930) and *Here Come the Clowns* (1939; *p.* 1938), his confused stabs at profundity, utterly lack. He will probably be best remembered for the social comedy of *The Philadelphia Story* (1939; *f.* 1940; as *High Society*, 1956).   D.P.M.

BARTH, John (1930–) was born in Cambridge (Maryland). He attended the Juilliard School of Music and Johns Hopkins University where he met the Spanish poet Pedro Salinas, worked (like Borges, a writer Barth admires greatly) in the Classics Library, and received an A.B. (1951) and an M.A. (1952). From 1953 to 1965 he taught at Pennsylvania State University before taking up appointment as professor of English at the State University of New York at Buffalo.

Barth's first novel, *The Floating Opera* (1956), was reissued in 1967 with considerable textual change, including the restoration of its originally unpublished ending. His second novel, *The End of the Road* (1958), a nasty nihilistic comedy, was later made into a "sexploitation" film. Barth's third novel, *The Sot-Weed Factor*, was a radical departure from his earlier work. A big historical novel in which the medicinal properties of the aubergine figure largely, *The Sot-Weed Factor* toasts the achievements of Ebenezer Cook, poet laureate of Maryland, and drives another nail into the Pocahontas myth. *Giles Goat-Boy* (1966) carries Barth's particular brand of prose experiment to its apex.

The Floating Opera, 1956; revised, 1967.
The End of the Road, 1958; revised, 1967 (*f.* 1969).
The Sot-Weed Factor, 1960.
Giles Goat-Boy, 1966.
Lost in the Funhouse, 1968.   w.d.s.

BAXTER, J. K. See **New Zealand Literature.**

BAXTER, Richard (1615–91) was a pioneer Nonconformist, who worked mainly in the Kidderminster (Worcestershire) area. He served as a chaplain with the Parliamentarians in the Civil War, but condemned the usurpation of Cromwell. He was finally driven out of the Church of England by the Act of Uniformity (1662) and was later imprisoned, first for illegal preaching and then for publishing his *Paraphrase of the New Testament* (1685). Baxter was renowned for his piety, which is amply demonstrated in the only one of his vast output of writings to be at all remembered nowadays, his devotional *The Saints' Everlasting Rest* (1650). *Reliquiae Baxterianae* (1696) is his autobiography.

BEARD, Charles Austin (1874–1948), historian and political scientist, was born in Indiana, graduated from DePauw University, studied at Oxford, where he founded Ruskin College (1899), and received his M.A. and Ph.D. from Columbia. Professor of political science at Columbia (1907–17), he resigned in protest against the dismissal of pacifist colleagues and helped to found the New School for Social Research. Beard's seminal study, *An Economic Interpretation of the Constitution of the United States* (1913), reflected his belief in economic determinism, as did *The Economic Origins of Jeffersonian Democracy* (1915). With his wife, Mary, Beard also wrote *The Rise of American Civilization* (2 vols., 1927) and *America in Midpassage* (1939). In later years he held conservative and isolationist views, expressed in *The Old Deal and the New* (1940) and *President Roosevelt and the Coming of the War, 1941* (1948).   J.W.

BEARDSLEY, Aubrey (1872–98), mainly influenced in youth by his mother and sister, left Brighton Grammar School for jobs in the office first of a surveyor and then an insurance company. His early passion for the theater never left him and appears in his love of fantastic costume and theatrical effect. He might well have gone on the stage, as his sister did, had it not been for tuberculosis, diagnosed in 1879 and from which he died. He rose to fame with his illustrations of *Morte d'Arthur* (1893), Oscar Wilde's *Salomé* (1894) and his sensational designs in *The Yellow Book* (1894–95), of which he was art editor. Hostility from the public and fellow contributors forced him from that position, unjustly associating him with the Wilde scandal of 1895, but he became art editor of *The Savoy* (1896), a finer but more notorious magazine where he published not only drawings but also parts of his erotic novel *Under the Hill*. His last years were divided between England and France, work and illness, erotica and religion. He died, converted to Roman Catholicism, at Menton.

His art, which decorated the books of many of his contemporaries, is seen as the graphic expression of decadence, with its grotesques, its perversities, its disregard of traditional rules of art and its juxtaposition of strange images. A more detached view is that he is "the Master of the Line Block," a technical achievement which reveals his originality, the subtlety of his line, and his skill in black and white arrangement.

Early Work, London and New York: J. Lane, 1899.
Later Work, London: J. Lane, 1901.
Letters . . . to Leonard Smithers, ed. R. A. Walker, London: First Edition Club, 1937.
Letters, ed. H. Maas and others, Rutherford, N.J.: Fairleigh Dickinson Univ. Press, 1970; London: Cassell, 1971.
Collected Drawings, ed. B. S. Harris, New York: Crown Publishers, 1967.

                                                                                                K.T.

BEATTIE, James (1735–1803) studied at Marischal College, Aberdeen, and after a period of schoolmastering returned there in 1760 as professor of moral philosophy. *The Minstrel* (book 1, 1771; book 2, 1774), a long-popular poem, interestingly reveals the literary tendencies of its time. Beattie "traces the progress of genius" in a Highland shepherd boy "in Gothic days" and shows anticipation of Wordsworth with his belief that the voice of nature speaks directly to the sensitive soul and educates it.

In Beattie's poem the revived Spenserian stanza is used with full seriousness and not, as with some eighteenth-century poets, as a deliberate antiquarian move. It provided Byron with a model when he wrote *Childe Harold's Pilgrimage.*   W.R.

BEAUMONT, Francis (?1584–1616), son of Francis Beaumont, a justice of common pleas, entered Oxford (Broadgates Hall) in 1597 but left without taking a degree. Subsequently he was a student of law at the Inner Temple. His first literary endeavor was a poem in the Ovidian erotic vein, *Salmacis and Hermaphroditus* (1602), but his first play, *The Woman Hater*, a "humors" comedy redolent of Jonson's influence, was not published until 1607 (p. ?1606). *The Knight of the Burning Pestle*, the only other play generally thought to be solely by Beaumont, is a brilliantly turned dramatic burlesque of the high-flying romantic tendencies of Heywood, Dekker and other dramatists of the "popular" breed. His commendatory verses to Fletcher's *The Faithful Shepherdess* suggest that the period of collaboration between the two men began about 1608. Though the precise ratio of Beaumont's contribution to the "Fletcher" canon is still shrouded in conjecture, seven plays at least would seem to owe something to this partnership—*Philaster*, *A King and No King*, *The Maid's Tragedy*, *Four Plays in One*, *Cupid's Revenge*, *The Coxcomb* and *The Scornful Lady*. Beaumont's dramatic career would appear to have ended in 1613 when he married an heiress. During his last three years he seems to have enjoyed the life of a country gentleman.

Because of difficulties in defining individual shares in the canon, it is convenient to link the names of Beaumont (Fletcher's most important collaborator) and Fletcher in any literary assessment. Fletcher's most assured achievements, *The Maid's Tragedy*, *Philaster* and *A King and No King*, clearly owe much to the discipline and restraint imposed on his agile imagination by the more sober dramatic instincts of "judicious" Beaumont, and it was while collaborating with Beaumont that Fletcher perfected the sophisticated tragicomic form (having the distinguished persons and the dangers of tragedy, yet lacking deaths "which is enough to make it no tragedy, yet brings some near it, which is enough to make it no comedy") that was to become his hallmark. Except in the brief partnership with Shakespeare, Fletcher was never so fortunate again in his collaborating. The plays written with Massinger are generally sorry affairs, but it is clear that Fletcher was weakest when working solo; he needed the particular restraints and supports which collaboration provided.

Exploiting as well as defining the taste of the refined upper-class audiences of the Jacobean private theaters, Beaumont and Fletcher enjoyed a popularity and a high esteem in their own day (and again in the

Restoration period) which now seem rather out of proportion to their artistic merits. The word "decadence" has frequently been employed to explain the dichotomy. Beaumont and Fletcher are easy and fluent dramatists of the surface with no pretensions to intellectual depth or powerful moral discrimination. The fifty-four or so plays in the canon suffer, speaking in general terms, from a remorseless sameness; the range both of actions and characters is restricted, and situations recur tediously; the scale of emotion is similarly limited, and the plays are only marginally and very tenuously relevant to the most important social and intellectual currents of the day. The staple ingredients of these plays are complicated plotting with accent on surprise and suspense; frequent dependence on disguise, mistaken identity, misunderstood motive and "discovery" tableaux; idealized pasteboard characters torn by conflicting, though decorative, absolutes (love, friendship, loyalty, etc.); elevated emotions and exaggerated postures. Skillfully contrived though most of these plays are, in the final assessment they provide only escapist entertainment.

The Woman Hater, 1607 (*p.* ?1606).
The Knight of the Burning Pestle, 1613 (*p.* ?1607).

(See also **Fletcher, John.**)

L.E.P.

BECKETT, Samuel (1906–   ), Irish dramatist and novelist, was born in Dublin of Protestant parents. He graduated from Trinity College, Dublin with such distinction that he was sent in 1928 on an exchange program as *lecteur d'anglais* to the École Normale Supérieure in Paris. It was at this time that he first met James Joyce. In 1931 he abandoned a promising academic career to wander about Europe until he finally settled once more in Paris in 1937. It is no accident that most of his characters are tramps, wanderers and lonely men.

After the publication of his first novel, *Murphy* (1938), and the completion of *Watt* (1953) in ?1944, he began to write mainly in French, believing this would discipline his thought and style. *Molloy* and *Malone Meurt* appeared in 1951, the first two novels of a trilogy, concluded by *L'Innommable* (1953), dealing with man's search for ultimate identity.

Beckett's first play, "Eleutheria," dating from 1947, is as yet unpublished and unperformed; it was *En Attendant Godot*, first published in 1952, which made him famous. This elusive tragic farce about two tramps to whom nothing happens was followed by others, all of which more completely lack plot than other plays in the genre which Esslin has called "theater of the absurd."

Absurd drama reflects a contemporary feeling of wonder, incomprehension and frequently despair at the lack of meaning in the world, and the uselessness of reason and language to dispel this feeling. The futility and despair seem to increase as Beckett moves from play to play. Thus, although *Waiting for Godot* explores a dismal and static situation, it does contain hints which are absent from the ominously titled second play, *Endgame* (in French as *Fin de Partie*). Critics have remarked on the suggestivity of *Godot* and on the similarity in title to Simone Weil's *Attente de Dieu*, whilst Eric Bentley has pointed to a possible literary connection with Balzac's comedy *Mercadet*. Beckett's mind seems to work in such a way that none of these hints can safely be ignored. The play appears to be about salvation, hinging in one sense on the story of the two thieves at the Crucifixion and the moral dilemma of the Christian that they demonstrate—that he may not despair, but he must not presume. Thus a theme of the play could be the fortuitous grace that divides the saved from the damned. But the action of the play concerns waiting, a process of inaction that is difficult to portray. Vladimir and Estragon pass the time in various, often amusing, ways, their boredom only broken by the arrival of a master, Pozzo, and his slave, Lucky, and a small boy who tells them that Godot will not come that day. The hope that he may come tomorrow may, of course, only be a delusion shared with the audience who desire to wring some meaning out of the play.

The bare unsettling spaces of *Waiting for Godot* give way in the second (one-act) play, *Endgame*, to a claustrophobic room where things are running down. The interdependence of Vladimir and Estragon (and also of Lucky and Pozzo) is carried on in the relationship between Hamm, imprisoned in his wheelchair, and Clov, over whom he tyrannizes (a relationship which some critics have thought may be a personal emblem of Beckett's own relationship with Joyce). The futility of life represented by the dying parents in the dustbins in this play is increasingly reflected in the structure and language of *Happy Days* (1961) and *Play* (1964). Although these plays seem to defy all the rules of good theater, ignoring the apparently crucial requirements of character, plot and meaningful dialogue, they work very well in the theater, producing a powerful and in some cases poetic impression. The use, too, of music hall techniques makes them comic so that an audience is often tricked into laughter at situations which are themselves far from humorous.

Murphy, 1938.
Watt, 1953.
Waiting for Godot, 1954 (trans. Beckett from *En Attendant Godot*, 1952).
Molloy, 1955 (trans. Beckett and P. Bowles from *Molloy*, 1951).
Malone Dies, 1956 (trans. Beckett from *Malone Meurt*, 1951).
All That Fall, 1957 (radio play).
The Unnamable, 1958 (trans. Beckett from *L'Innommable*, 1953).

Endgame (trans. Beckett from *Fin de Partie*, 1957); *Act without Words*, 1958.
Knapp's Last Tape; Embers, 1959.
Happy Days, 1961.
Poems in English, 1961.
Play; and *Two Short Pieces for Radio* [*Words and Music; Cascando*], 1964.
How It Is, 1964 (novel; trans. Beckett from *Comment C'Est*, 1961).
Eh Joe, and Other Writings, 1967.
No's Knife: Collected Shorter Prose, 1945–1966, 1967.
Come and Go, 1967 ("dramaticule").
Lessness, 1970 (trans. Beckett from *Sans*, 1969).   A.P.H.

BECKFORD, William (?1760–1844) was born at Fonthill Gifford (Wiltshire) and educated privately. Inheriting vast wealth early, he traveled widely. He wrote his powerfully imaginative oriental romance *Vathek: An Arabian Tale* in French, intending to publish it simultaneously with the English translation he commissioned from Samuel Henley; but Henley published the English version in 1786 as being from an anonymous manuscript. The French version appeared in 1787. The influence of its eroticism can be sensed in Byron's tales and in the oriental imagery of Charlotte Brontë. From 1797 Beckford created the fantastic Gothic mansion at Fonthill which, till it collapsed, showed Romantic medievalism at its most dynamic. Money troubles necessitated his retirement to Bath in 1822. He was a prose stylist of distinction and his letters are excellent.

                                                                     W.R.

BEDDOES, Thomas Lovell (1803–49), the son of a well-known physician, was educated at Bath Grammar School, the Charterhouse and Oxford. He showed a precocious talent for writing and published while an undergraduate *The Improvisatore* (1821) and *The Bride's Tragedy* (1822). Three years later he left England for Germany and the remainder of his life was spent wandering between different university towns. He obtained the degree of M.D. at Würzburg in 1831, but over the following years showed increasing signs of personal eccentricity and mental derangement. In 1849 he committed suicide, leaving a note which contained the statement: "I ought to have been among other things a good poet."

Beddoes had an original vision to convey and technical skill, but the fragmentary nature of his achievement results from failure to find a literary mode appropriate to his expression. His most significant play, *Death's Jest Book* (1850), written between 1825 and 1828 but, at the instigation of his friends, revised continually through his lifetime, shows a conflict between his essentially lyrical genius and the formal dramatic structure he has chosen. Although he may have wished to describe a drama of the spirit, he had little sense of dramatic action or individual character. His control of an Elizabethan-style blank verse is adequate and some of his lyrical interludes superb, but too vast a fascination with death and cosmic chaos prevented the satisfactory integration of his thought and technique.

Works, ed. H. W. Donner, London: Oxford Univ. Press, 1935.
Plays and Poems, ed. H. W. Donner, London: Routledge; Cambridge, Mass.: Harvard Univ. Press, 1950. C.P.

BEERBOHM, Max (Sir Henry Maximilian) (1872–1956), of mixed German, Dutch and Lithuanian origin, and half brother of the celebrated actor Beerbohm Tree, was educated at Charterhouse School and Merton College, Oxford. Having already cultivated an aesthetic reputation as an undergraduate, he coolly introduced himself to the London literary world of the 1890s by publishing his juvenile essays at the age of twenty-four as *The Works of Max Beerbohm*. Surviving the eclipse of *Yellow Book* aestheticism which followed Oscar Wilde's downfall, he succeeded Shaw as dramatic critic of *The Saturday Review* and for ten years played a leading role in both literary and artistic life. In 1910 he married the American actress Florence Kahn and retired to Italy where he lived until his death at Rapallo in 1956. He was knighted in 1939.

Equally admired as essayist and caricaturist, Beerbohm worked in a narrow field and knew precisely the limitations of his talent. The elegantly mannered prose, gentle yet obliquely scathing, balances the stylized humor of his drawings. He was a cultured satirist whose dandyish pose concealed a keen eye for the fraudulent and ostentatious. A contemporary but never a rival of greater writers like Shaw, Wilde and Kipling, he appraised their artistic and personal failings with a connoisseur's discrimination. His one full-length novel, *Zuleika Dobson*, shows Max at his incomparable best and some of his finest essays appear in *And Even Now* and *Seven Men*. A Catalogue of the Caricatures of Max Beerbohm [2,052 of them] appeared in 1972.

(See also **Parody and Nonsense.**)

The Works of Max Beerbohm, 1896.
Zuleika Dobson; or, An Oxford Love Story, 1911.
A Christmas Garland, 1912.
Seven Men, 1919 (enlarged version, *Seven Men, and Two Others*, 1950).
And Even Now, 1920.
Around Theatres, 1924. D.E.P.

BEHAN, Brendan (1923–64), after a Catholic education in Dublin, joined the Irish Republican Army in 1937 and was sent to Borstal in 1939.

In 1942 he was sentenced for political offenses and served nearly six years. He then became a professional journalist. His first and best play was *The Quare Fellow* (1956; *p.* 1954; *f.* 1962), followed by *The Hostage* (1958; revised, 1962). He died before completing his third major work, *Richard's Cork Leg*. Behan's I.R.A. experience and imprisonment are his main concerns, as appears from his autobiographical *Borstal Boy* (1958). He approaches these with a bitter and futile comedy in *The Quare Fellow*, but the comedy comes too easily in *The Hostage*. The attitude to Irish problems in his plays suggests the last line of his brother Dominic's play: "Mother Ireland, get off my back."

G.A.K.

BEHN, Aphra (?1640–89) refers in her novel *Oroonoko* (1688) to a period spent in Surinam, though her early life is obscure. After the death of her Dutch husband she worked as a British secret agent (code name "Astrea") in Antwerp (1666–67), the setting for another story, *The Fair Jilt* (1688). As the first professional authoress she was highly successful, writing lively but inconsequential stories, plays, verses, including some delightful lyrics, and making translations.

Complete Works, ed. M. Summers, 6 vols., London: Heinemann, 1915.

H.N.D.

BEHRMAN, S. N. (Samuel Nathaniel) (1893–   ) was born in Worcester (Massachusetts) and educated at Harvard and Columbia. He reviewed books for *The New Republic* and *The New York Times* before scoring a success with his first and most convincing play, *The Second Man* (1927). The hero, Clerk Storey, is a writer manqué, a man whose intelligence makes him only too aware of his own limitations. Offered the Shavian choice between a beautiful young girl and a wealthy widow who will support him, he sensibly opts for the latter. Behrman established a brittle, edgy, sophisticated comedy style, which in such later works as *Brief Moment* (1931), *Biography* (1933; *p.* 1932), *Rain from Heaven* (1934) and *No Time for Comedy* (1939) lost in freshness and integrity what it gained in poise. He fell victim to his own deprecating manner, since it became difficult to take his characters any more seriously than he did. Apart from his prolific work for the theater, Behrman has also published *Portrait of Max* (U.K. title: *Conversation with Max*) [Beerbohm] (1960), a biography of Duveen (1952), *The Worcester Account* (early reminiscences, 1954), *The Burning Glass* (novel, 1968) and *People in a Diary* (memoirs, 1972; U.K. title: *Tribulations and Laughter*).

D.P.M.

BELLAMY, Edward (1850–98) was born in Chicopee Falls (Massachusetts) where his father was a Baptist minister. He spent nearly the whole of his life in his home state, at first studying law and working on the editorial staff of newspapers, including the New York *Evening Post* His first novels, *Dr Heidenhoff's Process* (1880) and *Miss Ludington's Sister* (1884), were fables and romances, but he is now remembered only for his famous *Looking Backward, 2000–1887* (1888), in which he postulated a utopia where a bureaucratic state capitalism ensured the welfare of all citizens and where, with equal wages, culture was the main item of consumption. Under the title of "Nationalism" this vision of a socialistic future was the source of numerous clubs and societies, while his writings were used by such organizations as the Labour party in London, and influenced Veblen, Dewey and Eugene V. Debs, among others. He attempted to recapitulate his success with *Equality* (1897), but failed to do so.

Selected Writings on Religion and Society, ed. J. Schiffman, New York: Liberal Arts Press, 1956.
D.C.

BELLOC, Hilaire (1870–1953) was born at La Celle St. Cloud near Paris, of a French father and an English mother, on the eve of the Franco-Prussian War. Belloc's upbringing and outlook were the more English in that his father died when he himself was two. He very early showed a precocious talent for verse, and was an outstanding pupil at the Oratory School, Edgbaston, then under the direction of Cardinal Newman. After a year of wandering, some journalism and a period as a conscript in the French army, he entered Balliol College, Oxford in 1893 and was a brilliant scholar, but his applications for fellowships at Oxford were refused and he turned to writing for a living. From 1906 to 1910 he was Liberal member of Parliament for South Salford, but from then on his influence on affairs was through his voluminous writings and his work as editor of various journals. After the First World War his increasing purpose was to proclaim the truth of Catholicism.

As a writer he has been called not one man, but a procession: historian, essayist, topographer, novelist, biographer and poet. In his historical writings he shows a preoccupation with Revolutionary and Republican France, with lives of Danton, Robespierre and Marie Antoinette. He has an unrivaled flair for topography and his historical work contains excellent reconstructions of times and places. Minor monographs such as *The Old Road* and *The Stone Street* are an individual blend of history and reminiscence, and two books, *The Path to Rome* and *The Four Men*, deserve particular mention, one as the record of a pilgrimage and the other as a Rabelaisian merrymaking punctuated by splendid lyrics.

As a poet Belloc is underrated. Apart from his nonsense verse for children, which is unsurpassed, his sonnets are among the finest of his time; his carols and sacred poems have an enchanting medieval simplicity; and not even Kipling has written more delightfully of Sussex.

(See also **Political Pamphlets**.)

The Bad Child's Book of Beasts, 1896 (light verse).
Danton, 1899.
The Path to Rome, 1902.
The Old Road, 1904.
Hills and the Sea, 1906 (essays).
Marie Antoinette, 1909.
The Four Men, 1912.
The Cruise of the "Nona," 1925.
Wolsey, 1930.
The County of Sussex, 1936.
The Great Heresies, 1938.

Complete Verse, London: Duckworth, 1971.
Letters, ed. R. Speaight, London: Hollis & Carter; New York: Macmillan Co., 1958.
A.N.M.

BELLOW, Saul (1915–) was born in Lachine (Quebec), the son of Russian-Jewish immigrants. He received an orthodox religious education and graduated from Northwestern University in 1937. His career has been largely spent in academic institutions, on visiting fellowships and lectureships. He has been three times married.

His novels deal with an individual man's relationship to family, society and belief. They vary between short, tightly constructed works of great intensity such as *Dangling Man* (1944), *The Victim* (1947), and *Seize the Day* (1956) and epic, occasionally sprawling books of much wider range like *The Adventures of Augie March* (1953) and *Herzog* (1964). Bellow's central concern is the means whereby a man may preserve his humanity within the pressures of a modern urban society. His hero is frequently in a peculiarly isolated circumstance, "dangling" like Joseph awaiting his draft papers, writing letters in solitude like Herzog, or deliberately choosing the isolation of a separate continent as does Henderson, in *Henderson the Rain King* (1959). In this solitude the hero examines his concerns: his inability to maintain belief, his disintegrating relations with his family, his sexual failures. All Bellow's heroes are alone and afraid but avoid the self-pity of exclusive concentration on one introspective consciousness by a resort to ironic self appraisal and a comic inability to function adequately in the everyday world. This concentration on a single personality has led to the charge of an absence of real dialogue between characters in the novels and particularly to the charge of stereotyped portraits of women.

Bellow has written a large body of short stories, some of which are collected in *Mosby's Memoirs* (1968). He has also had some success with stage plays, such as *The Last Analysis* (1965; *p.* 1964).

Bellow's early fiction is most successful when he examines a particular situation exhaustively. In *The Victim* he handles the subject of racial and religious prejudice with complexity and understanding by showing the ambivalent relationship between persecutor and persecuted. In *Seize the Day* he shows the paradox of failure and triumph in its hero's awareness of the world's destructiveness. Both of these works achieve a much greater artistic cohesion than that shown in the formless wanderings of the near-passive hero Augie in *The Adventures of Augie March* or the random jottings of Joseph in *Dangling Man*.

Bellow's later fiction has united the two types. *Herzog* employs a large canvas but, with system and technical versatility, the material is organized to bear on the central concern, the hero's attempts to make sense of his confused past. *Mr. Sammler's Planet* (1970) has an octogenarian hero and a multiplicity of experience, but it is used to emphasize a view of the range and limitation of man's nature and achievements. In this book the aim is no less than a survey of man's very existence on the planet at the time of his attempts on the moon.

Considerable difficulty has been found in coming to terms with the apparent ambiguity of the endings of Bellow's novels. In them the hero frequently makes a positive gesture towards the humanity which much of the book has called in question. Joseph voluntarily embraces regimentation, Leventhal in *The Victim* comes to terms with his opponent Allbee, Tommy Wilhelm in *Seize the Day* weeps for mankind, Henderson dances in the Newfoundland snow. In each case the hero seems to move away from the self-concern which is the heart of the book. Like so much of Bellow's comic art, it is difficult to tell the author's intended direction.

Dangling Man, 1944.
The Victim, 1947.
The Adventures of Augie March, 1953.
Seize the Day, 1956.
Henderson the Rain King, 1959.
Herzog, 1964.
Mosby's Memoirs and Other Stories, 1968.
Mr. Sammler's Planet, 1970.   D.V.W.

BENÉT, Stephen Vincent (1898–1943) was born in Bethlehem (Pennsylvania). Following a few semiautobiographical works, he published a pre-Revolution novel, *Spanish Bayonet* (1926), which initiated the continuing theme of America in subsequent books. *James Shore's*

Daughter (1934) finally spanned the frontier period, its ultimate wealth and freedom being coupled with future responsibility. Benét's epic poem *John Brown's Body* (1928; *f*. 1968) brought him long-lasting fame, and dramatized versions are still being presented. "The Devil and Daniel Webster" was the best known of his short stories and was adapted by him as a folk opera (1939; *f*. as *All That Money Can Buy*, 1941). He was awarded a Pulitzer Prize for poetry in 1944 for *Western Star* (1943).   R.W.

BENLOWES, Edward (1602–76), inheriting the extensive estates of a staunch Catholic family, studied at St. John's College, Cambridge and then Lincoln's Inn before traveling widely on the Continent and becoming a Protestant. The generous patron of Quarles and Phineas Fletcher, he devoted many years to the writing and elaborate printing of *Theophila* (1652), an ecstatic devotional poem. Punitive taxation, occasioned by his Royalist sympathies in the Civil War, and constant litigation reduced him to extreme poverty. He died in Oxford.   H.N.D.

BENNETT, Arnold (1867–1931) was born at Hanley in the Potteries area of Staffordshire. His father was a solicitor, and on leaving Newcastle-under-Lyme Middle School Bennett became a clerk in his father's office. He had little love for the law and left for London, where he took up journalism, becoming assistant editor of *Woman* in 1893 and editor from 1896 to 1900. His first novel, *A Man from the North*, was published in 1898. It was the beginning of a prolific career as a writer, in which he mingled serious and popular novels. This novel and a number of its successors are set in the "Five Towns," Bennett's evocation of the area from which he came. These successors include *Anna of the Five Towns* (1902), the Clayhanger trilogy, *Clayhanger* (1910), *Hilda Lessways* (1911) and *These Twain* (1916), and the greatest of his works, *The Old Wives' Tale* (1908). This last firmly established Bennett as a considerable writer. During this period Bennett collaborated in a number of plays, of which only *Milestones* (1912) is now remembered. The years that followed were marked by the acquisition of wealth and influence, both of which Bennett obviously and immensely enjoyed. During the First World War he served at the Ministry of Information, becoming head at the end of the war. At this time his marriage to the French-born Marguerite Soulié began to break up, and following a separation in 1921 Bennett lived with Dorothy Cheston, who assumed his name by deed poll and bore him a daughter. *Riceyman Steps* (1923) is the best novel of his final period. He died from typhoid fever in 1931.

Because of his success in portraying his "Five Towns," Bennett is often thought of as a regional novelist. In fact, he hated the locality of his upbringing and rarely visited it in later years. Nevertheless, his obvious subconscious attachment to his early environment is avowed by the fidelity with which he evokes it in his novels. Fidelity of detail and representation without expression of feeling were techniques which Bennett learned from the naturalistic school of French novelists. (He lived in France for much of the period 1903–12.) Like many of these French novelists, Bennett was attracted to the apparently humdrum lives of ordinary people, but he found in them the eternal significance of the passage of time, of birth and marriage and death, of youth and old age. Nowhere is this better seen than in the parallel lives of the sisters Constance and Sophia in *The Old Wives' Tale*. The harshness of life is one of Bennett's recurring themes—what it does to us, with Sophia, or what disastrously we make of it, as with her husband, Gerald Scales, or the miser Earlforward in *Riceyman Steps*. Yet there was another side to Bennett's view of life, not, significantly, the celebration of happiness but of success. With his own background of success in life and the philistinism of his father's values, he admired men like Darius Clayhanger and, even more, flashy Denry Machin of *The Card*. As he himself gained wealth and success, he turned to higher social strata in *Lord Raingo* and *Imperial Palace*. Bennett never established any compatible relationship with his father. The clash of father and son in *Clayhanger* no doubt derives from the author's own experience, and also from this relationship comes Bennett's abiding distaste for the cant of Methodism, as he believed it to be. He is not in the front rank of English novelists, but his best work is, as E. M. Forster described it, "strong, sad, sincere."

Bennett published some forty-one novels and volumes of short stories, of which the principal ones are:

A Man from the North, 1898.
Anna of the Five Towns, 1902.
Tales of the Five Towns, 1905.
The Grim Smile of the Five Towns, 1907.
The Old Wives' Tale, 1908.
Buried Alive, 1908.
Clayhanger, 1910.
The Card, 1911 (*f*. 1951).
Hilda Lessways, 1911.
The Regent, 1913.
These Twain, 1916.
Riceyman Steps, 1923.
Lord Raingo, 1926.
Imperial Palace, 1930.

Journals, ed. N. Flower, 3 vols., London: Cassell; New York: Viking Press, 1932–33.
Letters, ed. J. B. Hepburn, 3 vols., London and New York: Oxford Univ. Press, 1966–70.   A.P.

BENTHAM, Jeremy (1748–1832), utilitarian philosopher, is perhaps most famous for his proposition that the general good is best served by the individual's concentration on his own happiness. He also argued that all human experience could be measured in scientific terms and that such measurement would provide the data on which the future happiness of mankind could be based. The influence of his philosophy on Victorian social attitudes is perhaps of more interest today than his own work, which he himself rarely published. Dickens criticizes utilitarianism in *Hard Times*.

Works, ed. J. Bowring, 11 vols., Edinburgh: Tait, 1838–43.
Correspondence [1753–80], ed. T. Sprigge, 2 vols., London: Athlone Press, 1968.   A.J.S.

BERGER, Thomas (1924–) was born in Cincinnati (Ohio) and made his home in New York after his war service. His reputation as a satirical social novelist, with a streak of salutary black humor, began with *Crazy in Berlin* (1958), set amongst the American occupying forces after the Second World War. The hero, Carlos Reinhart, reappears in *Reinhart in Love* (1962), focusing Berger's comments on postwar life, and in *Vital Parts* (1970), a shrewd satire on contemporary America. *Little Big Man* (1964; *f*. 1969) is both an accurate version of the Old West and a humanist comedy. Perhaps his best novel is *Killing Time* (1967), a major dramatization of modern problems—justice and law, the frontiers of madness and criminality, the overorganized urban society.   E.M.

BERKELEY, George (1685–1753), Irish philosopher, was student and senior fellow at Trinity College, Dublin, and later bishop of Cloyne. He published *Principles of Human Knowledge* (1710) and *Three Dialogues . . .* (1713), which together form the classic statement of the idealist theory of perception: that the objects we perceive are nothing but ideas in our minds, existing only in our perception of them ("*esse* is *percipi*"). Berkeley rejects the accepted theory that these ideas are caused by the action of external objects on the grounds that such objects, lying beyond our perception, must be totally unknowable. For this reason he regards his own theory as the more commonsensical, although such contemporaries as Swift and Johnson found it totally paradoxical, taking Berkeley to deny the existence of sticks and stones.

Collected Works, ed. A. A. Luce and T. E. Jessop, 9 vols., London: Nelson, 1948–57.   D.L.

BERRYMAN, John (1914–72) was born, a Roman Catholic, in McAlester (Oklahoma). A graduate of Columbia and Cambridge, he taught at several American universities and was professor at the University of Minnesota at the time of his death. The long-unpublished *Sonnets* come closest to revealing the Berryman of the 1940s: hard-drinking, adulterous, but preeminently a professor of literature, imitating Donne's modish fusion of formal prosody, bawdry and scholarly conceit, and quoting Wallace Stevens *in coitu*.

Berryman's best work is directed towards the creation of a style and a persona adequate to express intense feeling without resorting to "confessional" verse. The short poems in *The Dispossessed* render the emotions of the war years in verse whose distorted syntax and choking consonantal agglomerates are reminiscent of Hopkins. In *Homage to Mistress Bradstreet* he found his persona in the first, and perhaps the worst, American poet. His awesomely powerful poem both re-creates his predecessor's world and probes the nature of the poet's vocation. *77 Dream Songs* and *His Toy, His Dream, His Rest* are a continuous sequence of 385 eighteen-line poems, dreamlike in their tortured syntax, dissolving into "nigger-minstrel" crosstalk and naming horrors with cool irony. Berryman's scared and comic protagonist, the white negro Henry, can be a jazz version of Eliot's wounded surgeon ("Song 67"); he is also Mr. Bones and so, perhaps, death; increasingly he is recognized as Berryman's consciousness shaping itself into an image flexible enough to contain any human experience.

Poems, 1942.
The Dispossessed, 1948.
Stephen Crane, 1950.
Homage to Mistress Bradstreet, 1956.
His Thought Made Pockets and the Plane Buckt, 1958.
77 Dream Songs, 1964.
Berryman's Sonnets, 1967.
His Toy, His Dream, His Rest, 1968.

Short Poems, New York: Farrar, Straus, 1967.   M. T

BESANT, Sir Walter (1836–1901) was born at Portsmouth (Hampshire) and educated at King's College, London and Christ's College, Cambridge. He worked as a schoolmaster in Mauritius but, after returning home for health reasons, turned to journalism and fiction (up to 1882 in collaboration with James Rice, who died in that year). *Ready-Money Mortiboy* (1872) achieved considerable popularity, but his own favorite, *Dorothy Forster* (1884), was one of his historical novels. A more important contribution, however, is to be found in his novels on social conditions in the East End of London, *All Sorts and Conditions of Men* (1882) and *Children of Gibeon* (1886). He took a practical interest in these conditions and was instrumental in founding The People's Palace (for recreation and amusement) in 1887.

Autobiography, 1902.   A.P.

BETHELL, Mary Ursula. See **New Zealand Literature.**

BETJEMAN, Sir John (1906–), son of a merchant, was educated at Marlborough and Oxford. For a time he was a schoolmaster and during the Second World War United Kingdom press attaché in Dublin. Betjeman's first volume of poems, *Mount Zion*, was published in 1933, but until the success of *Continual Dew* (1937) he was known only as a writer on architecture, especially Victorian. Several further volumes of poetry were published and then his *Collected Poems* (1958) brought wide acclaim. He continues to interest himself in British architecture and has done much to popularize the subject in numerous television programs.

As a prose writer Betjeman was a pioneer in the revival of the serious study of Victorian architecture. His poetry is reflective, always closely linked with his own interests and beliefs and often displaying his nostalgia for childhood. Throughout there runs a strong topographical element, and his interest in the atmosphere and associations of places generally leads him to personal reflections or devotional statement. His love of eighteenth-century hymnology and the English devotional tradition is obvious. He has earned a considerable reputation as a writer of light verse and as a social satirist. *Summoned by Bells*, a verse autobiography, was published in 1960. He was appointed poet laureate in 1972.

Collected Poems, London: Murray, 1958; enlarged, 1962; 1970.   W.R.

BHATTACHARYA, Bhabani. See **Indian Literature.**

BIBLE, The consists of the collected sacred books of the Christian Church, of which the earlier and major part (the Old Testament) constitutes the Jewish Bible.

The earliest Bible versions in English belong to the Old English period; extant are parts of the Bible story in verse, versions of the Psalter by Aldhelm (c. 700) and others, the Wessex Gospels (ninth to tenth centuries), interlinear glosses in the Lindisfarne and Rushworth (Latin) Gospels, and Aelfric's version of part of the Old Testament narrative (late tenth century).

To the Middle English period belong some renderings of various parts of the Bible, especially those which figured in the liturgy, and pre-eminently the two versions of the whole Bible associated with the name of John Wyclif (?1320–84). The earlier of these two (c. 1382), partly the work of Nicholas of Hereford, was a very literal translation of the Latin, perhaps intended as a law book to replace the medieval corpus of canon law. The later one (c. 1390), the work of Wyclif's secretary John Purvey, was a much more idiomatic rendering, which enjoyed a considerable circulation in manuscript for over a century. A Scots edition of it was produced by Murdoch Nisbet (c. 1520).

A new chapter in the history of the English Bible begins with William Tyndale (?1494–1536), whose translations were based on the Hebrew and Greek texts and circulated in print. Tyndale published three editions of the New Testament (1525–26; 1534; 1535), the Pentateuch (1530), with a revision of Genesis in 1534, and Jonah (1531). His translation of the Old Testament historical books remained in manuscript until it was published as part of "Matthew's" Bible in 1537. Tyndale's version, so far as it went, has formed the basis of a succession of English versions down to the Revised Standard Version (1952).

The first complete printed Bible in English was Miles Coverdale's (1535). A later edition of his Bible, together with "Matthew's" Bible ("Matthew" was a pen name used by John Rogers), received the royal license in 1537. Coverdale was also editor of the Great Bible (1539), designed for church use, which soon replaced earlier versions, only to be replaced in turn by two Elizabethan versions, the Geneva Bible (1560) and the Bishops' Bible (1568). Of these the Bishops' Bible was the more official church edition, but the Geneva Bible was both more accurate and more popular. It was, for example, the Bible of Shakespeare, and in Scotland it was the only Bible used from its publication until its displacement by the Authorized Version.

The Authorized (King James) Version, published in 1611, superseded both the Elizabethan versions and for over 300 years retained its position as *the* Bible of the English-speaking world. Its idioms, cadences and prose rhythms have become part of the literary heritage of the English language; it has proved itself superbly suitable for reading aloud. By comparison with it, more recent versions, whatever they gain in accuracy as translations of the original, inevitably suffer in point of style. No English version of the Bible approaches the Authorized Version in literary influence. Contemporaneously and at different levels, it provided the matter for an epic such as *Paradise Lost* and a popular allegory such as *The Pilgrim's Progress*. At a later date it inspired Blake's prophetic books and the prosaic *Proverbial Philosophy* of Martin Tupper. In a wider sense, it influenced modes of thinking and understanding, chief of which perhaps was the attitude towards the Creation, as it emerged during the controversy over the theory of evolution (see **Darwin, Charles**). New scientific views of this kind together with textual criticism of the Scriptures and the concomitant waning of religious belief have led to a corresponding decline in the literary influence of the Bible in the twentieth century.

Shortly before the appearance of the Authorized Version, an English version for Roman Catholics was produced by Gregory Martin of the English College in Flanders—the New Testament being published at Rheims in 1582 and the Old Testament at Douai in 1609–10. This version, based for the most part on the Latin Vulgate, was excessively latinate in vocabulary and syntax, but was given a much more idiomatic English form in the thorough revision it received from Richard Challoner in 1749 and the following years.

As the language of the Authorized Version was increasingly felt to be archaic, and the underlying text (especially in the New Testament) increasingly recognized to be based on inferior manuscripts, the necessity for a revision imposed itself. But when the Revised Version appeared (New Testament in 1881, complete Bible in 1885—except for the Apocrypha, which appeared in 1895), it was a disappointment to many. For all the pedantic precision of its renderings, it was a work for students, not for the worshiping community, and it failed to gain general acceptance. Its American counterpart, the American Standard Version of 1901, was more fortunate, but hardly replaced the Authorized Version.

It has been far different with the Revised Standard Version (1952) which, produced by American scholars, has proved increasingly acceptable in Britain and indeed throughout the English-speaking world. The publication of a Catholic edition in 1966 means that for the first time English-speaking Protestants and Catholics share substantially the same Bible.

The principal non-Roman churches of Great Britain and Ireland sponsored the New English Bible, on which panels of translators began work in 1948. This is not a revision of previous versions but a completely new translation from the Hebrew and Greek. The New Testament appeared in 1961 and the Old Testament and Apocrypha in 1970. Its idiom, described by the translators as "timeless English," has received some severe criticism, but its modernity helps to penetrate the communication barrier and speaks to those to whom older "Bible English" is a foreign tongue.

Another recent English version of the whole Bible is the Jerusalem Bible (1966), an annotated rendering into vigorous English, based on the French work of scholars of the Dominican École Biblique in Jerusalem. There has also, especially during the twentieth century, been a continuous stream of private Bible translations: well known among them are R. F. Weymouth, *The New Testament in Modern Speech* (1903), J. Moffatt, *A New Translation of the Bible* (revised and final edition, 1935), E. J. Goodspeed and others, *The Complete Bible: An American Translation* (1923–38), and J. B. Phillips, *The New Testament in Modern English* (1958). For literary effect none of these is more distinguished than R. A. Knox's version (1945–49), although already many regard it as a period piece.

F.F.B.

BIERCE, Ambrose (1842–?1914) was born in Ohio of a poor family. During the Civil War he served as a drummer boy and then as a lieuten-ant on the Union side, before turning to journalism in San Francisco. In 1914 he visited Mexico to observe the revolution led by Pancho Villa and was never heard of again.

Bierce is a surrealist whose vision penetrates beyond all beliefs and dogmas to the central meaninglessness of existence. One technique he uses in his short stories is to divorce an incident from its customary significance in order that its absurdity should be apprehended first. In "Chickamauga" the survivors of war appear as grotesque scarecrows, and nothing more, to the deaf mute who is the story's central character. Alternatively, a heightened significance is given to something as ephemeral as a daydream in "An Occurrence at Owl Creek Bridge" (*f.* as *Au Coeur de la Vie*, 1962). The substance of the story is a captive's escape but by the end of the story we realize this was only his imagination at the moment of execution. A third technique is to treat the extraordinary as commonplace. "Oil of Dog" has the Dickensian opening of "I was born of honest parents in one of the humbler walks of life . . .," but the paragraph ends with the dis-concerting information that the father manufactures dog oil and the mother is an abortionist. Bierce's stories appear in *In the Midst of Life* and *Can Such Things Be?* Also typical is *The Devil's Dictionary*.

The Fiend's Delight, 1872 (sketches).
Nuggets and Dust, 1872 (sketches).
Cobwebs from an Empty Skull, 1874 (fables and tales from *Fun*).
Tales of Soldiers and Civilians, 1891; as *In the Midst of Life*, 1892.
The Monk and the Hangman's Daughter, 1892.
Black Beetles in Amber, 1892 (poems).
Can Such Things Be?, 1893 (stories).
Fantastic Fables, 1899.

Shapes of Clay, 1903 (poems).
The Cynic's Word Book, 1906; reissued as *The Devil's Dictionary*, 1911.
The Shadow on the Dial, 1909 (essays).

Collected Writings, ed. C. Fadiman, New York: Citadel Press, 1946.
Letters, ed. B. C. Pope, San Francisco: Book Club of California, 1922.

J.L.M.

BIGG, John Stanyan. See **Spasmodics, The.**

BINYON, Laurence (1869–1943) was for forty years an official at the British Museum and most of his writings are devoted to the study of oriental art, upon which he was an authority. He published several volumes of verse, historical plays and a translation of Dante. A prolific but academic poet throughout his long life, he never wrote so well as when recording his experiences in the First World War. His poem "For the Fallen" is associated with the commemoration of the dead in war. His poetry, to be found in *Collected Poems* (2 vols., 1931), has vision, austerity and gracefulness.   O.K.

BIRNEY, Earle. See **Canadian Literature.**

BISHOP, Elizabeth (1911–), born in Massachusetts, was a student at Vassar. Her poetry, which distinctively enjoins humanism and a sense of nature, works through brilliant surfaces and the accumulation of intense moments. She won the Houghton Mifflin Poetry Prize Fellowship for her first volume of poetry, *North and South* (1946), which was later extended into *Poems: North and South—A Cold Spring* and published in 1955 (Pulitzer Prize, 1956). She settled in Brazil in 1951 and in 1957 translated the Brazilian classic *Minha Vida de Menina* (*The Diary of "Helena Morley"*). *Questions of Travel*, her third book of poems, appeared in 1965.

Complete Poems, New York: Farrar, Straus, 1969; London: Chatto & Windus, 1970.   R.W.

BLACKMORE, R. D. (Richard Doddridge) (1825–1900), after leaving Oxford, became a lawyer but, for health reasons, turned to market gardening. He published poetry, but soon realized that fiction was his real métier. He wrote fifteen novels, of which only *Lorna Doone* (1869) is now remembered. Others, however, such as *The Maid of Sker* (1872) and *Springhaven* (1887), also reveal Blackmore's essential qualities—

his affinity with the life of the countryside, his power to depict provincial manners, his love of the past and his ability to achieve striking effects.

A.P.

BLACKMUR, R. P. (Richard Palmer) (1904–65) was born in Springfield (Massachusetts). The first part of his career was passed as a free-lance poet and critic, during which time, however, he also edited *Hound and Horn* and spent two years (1936–38) as a Guggenheim Fellow. In 1951 he became professor of English at Princeton, where he continued to publish criticism of English and American literature—*Language As Gesture* (1952), *The Lion and the Honeycomb* (1955), *Form and Value in Modern Poetry* (1957). Blackmur's criticism is characterized not so much by an adherence to any particular theory (though he was obviously influenced by the New Critics) as by a penetrating attention to the subtleties of meaning and significance in the texts he chose to write about. This led to the development of his notoriously complex and often overinvolved prose style.

B.L.

BLAIR, Eric Arthur. See **"Orwell, George."**

BLAIR, Hugh (1718–1800) was born in Edinburgh and attended the university there. He was ordained in 1742 and became a leading moderate divine. He was appointed professor of rhetoric at Edinburgh in 1760. He encouraged Macpherson to publish the Ossian *Fragments* and wrote a commentary, despite the skepticism of Johnson, who had a "warm esteem" for Blair. He was a member of the famous Poker Club, and a special friend of Hume, although they differed on matters of theology. His *Lectures on Rhetoric* (1783), published on his retirement, are mostly orthodox, but a new, primitivist theory ("the poetry of the heart") is evident in the one entitled "What Is Poetry?". Blair's *Sermons* (5 vols., 1777–1801) were very popular and earned him a pension of £200 from 1780.

D.G.

BLAIR, Robert (1699–1746), son of a clergyman, was born in Edinburgh, and educated there and in Holland. He himself became a clergyman and in 1731 was appointed to the living of Athelstaneford (East Lothian). The manuscript of his poem, *The Grave*, was enthusiastically commended by Isaac Watts, who tried to get it published, and afterwards by Doddridge, who found a publisher for it in 1743. It is the first and best "mortuary" poem, a blank verse work with seventeenth-century devotional affinities, tinged with Romantic feeling. It is contemporary with Young's *Night Thoughts*, but the two poems were written independently. Apart from *The Grave*, Blair's output was negligible.   w.r.

BLAKE, William (1757–1827), born in London, son of a hosier, displayed marked visionary power even as a child, incurring his father's wrath when he spoke of seeing a tree starred with angels on Peckham Rye. He had no formal education, but at ten was sent to Parr's drawing school in the Strand and later apprenticed to the engraver Basire. A spell in Westminster Abbey making drawings of the monuments gave him an enthusiasm for Gothic art as a true and living form from which later art had declined. In August 1782 he married Catherine Boucher, daughter of a Battersea market gardener, and apart from a period at Felpham (Sussex) under the patronage of William Hayley, lived in London for the rest of his life, maintaining his household by engraving when necessary and devoting himself to creative work as much as possible. While at Felpham he expelled a soldier from his garden and as a result was brought to Chichester Assizes on a charge of sedition. Although acquitted, he was much disturbed by the experience. His later life was quiet and uneventful, though some visitors found him embittered by the failure of the British public to appreciate an art that aimed at the sublime. After engraving his long poem *Jerusalem* he devoted himself largely to art, illustrating well-known works such as the Book of Job or *The Pilgrim's Progress*, but infusing them with his own vision. He was still working on a long set of illustrations to Dante's *Divina Commedia* when he died.

From an early age Blake interested himself in imaginative metaphysics and out-of-the-way learning, drawn not by antiquarianism but by his own visionary experiences, which convinced him of the reality of another order behind the world of immediate experience. He differs from most contemplative mystics by his belief in physical energy; instead of rejecting the material world like many ascetics, he worships it wherever it displays energy and rejects it wherever it remains dull and vegetative. His view of the world is therefore ambivalent and at first sight puzzling.

Blake's urge to express his vision of the world led him to ignore many of the formal aspects of art and to use any means which offered themselves, devoting himself to poetry and the visual arts with equal intensity. His promise both as a poet and a painter were commented on from an early age. The drawings which he exhibited at the Royal Academy in 1780 and 1784 were thought by Romney to rank with those of Michelangelo, and several of his friends helped with the publishing of his first book of poems, *Poetical Sketches*, in 1783. His early work often attempts to weld a visionary style on to eighteenth-century forms: some of his most successful writing echoes the Elizabethans, especially Spenser and Shakespeare. Blake also at this period satirized fashionable intellectual trends of the time in the prose fragment, "An Island in the Moon."

The powerful contemporary political movements excited in him an interest in the nature and possibilities of human energy. The revolutions in America and France prompted him to write first a dramatic historical poem (the unfinished *The French Revolution*) and the more mythological poems *America, Europe* and *The Song of Los*, which set recent history in an interpretative context, referring it back to the eternal human principles which he saw at work beneath all events. His insistence on the importance of humanizing energy instead of exiling it (a conception remarkably prophetic of twentieth-century attitudes) comes to a climax in *The Marriage of Heaven and Hell*, where he affirms the superiority of energy over reason and overturns traditional conceptions of holiness by his affirmation that "everything that lives is holy."

Blake's growing conviction that political and social problems were all due to a central failure of humanity itself led him to create a new myth-ology of his own, allegorical of human energies. In *The First Book of Urizen, The Book of Ahania* and *The Four Zoas* (his first attempt at the epic) he countered the orthodox Christian picture of a world that had fallen away from an original holiness and purity by creating a poetic universe in which the demands for purity and holiness, and the creation of a law based on them, were in fact the real corruption, resulting from a con-traction away from an original harmony of vision and desire into estab-lishment of the isolated self as the center of the world.

Despite passages of splendid poetry and some sharp insights into human nature, the chief problem of creating an epic plot proved intractable and *The Four Zoas* was left in manuscript. During the period after 1800 Blake was also realigning his own sense of man, placing less emphasis on energy, more on vision. Further thought about society seems to have led to the recognition that in a visionless society complete liberty of desire was not available to the individual. He might, however, attain to the state of vision which would lead to forgiveness of his fellows through recognition of their individual genius, a state which, extended through society, might eventually lead to universal human freedom. The two final long prophetic books are based on these twin beliefs, the theme of *Milton* being inspiration and its ability to destroy the selfhood created by blind worship of law, while *Jerusalem* is concerned with the opposition between a jealousy based on the law and forgiveness based on vision in society at large. In these poems Blake used his previous mythology in a loose form but no longer aimed at a tight epic plot.

As a writer Blake holds an unusual position. Like D. H. Lawrence, he is an expressionist poet in a literary culture which has no expressionist tradition. In art, however, his relation to contemporaries such as Fuseli and Samuel Palmer is more easily traced. His painting cannot be separated from his literary work, since the same themes are at work in both: his most characteristic mode of expression is through the "illuminated book," where text is surrounded by a visual design which either expands or counterpoints its meaning.

Blake's longer works are by no means as obscure as they appear at first sight. They are rather related to large obsessive patterns of ideas which, once grasped, give shape to the meaning. Nevertheless, his own insistence on the importance of the "minute particulars" and of individual identities points to an important fact about his own achievement—that individual lines or stanzas may have a self-contained meaning and resonance which is independent of their context. This is especially true of *Songs of Innocence and of Experience*, where in simple measures common objects of everyday familiarity are used as images to suggest rich symbolic associations. Blake's strength as creator of short poems lies particularly in this ability to bring images into a suggestive pattern. Even in his best short lyrics, however, some awareness of his larger visionary ideas helps to give precision to what might otherwise seem vague, while acquaintance with his visual art adds further dimensions of color and vividness.

(See also **Romantic Movement, The.**)

Poetical Sketches, 1783.
Songs of Innocence, 1789.
The Book of Thel, 1789.
The French Revolution (book 1), 1791.
The Marriage of Heaven and Hell, c. 1793.
Visions of the Daughters of Albion, 1793.
America: A Prophecy, 1793.
Songs of Innocence and of Experience, 1794.
Europe: A Prophecy, 1794.
The First Book of Urizen, 1794.
The Book of Ahania, 1795.
The Song of Los, 1795.
The Book of Los, 1795.
Milton, 1804 – c. 08.
Jerusalem, 1804 – c. 20.

Vala; or, The Four Zoas (MS. 1795–1807), ed. G. E. Bentley, Jr., with facsimile, Oxford: Clarendon Press, 1963.
Tiriel (MS. c. 1789), ed. G. E. Bentley, Jr., with facsimile, Oxford: Clarendon Press, 1967.

Complete Writings, ed. G. L. Keynes, London: Nonesuch Press; New

York: Random House, 1957; revised, London: Oxford Univ. Press, 1966.

Poems, ed. W. H. Stevenson, London: Longmans; New York: Barnes & Noble, 1971.

Letters, ed. G. L. Keynes, 2nd edition, revised, London: Hart-Davis, 1968.   J.B.B.

BLOOMFIELD, Robert (1766–1823), peasant poet, was born at Honington (Suffolk). He learnt shoemaking in London after four years' farm service. Attracted to literature, he composed *The Farmer's Boy* (1800), which was an immense success. Other works followed, including *Rural Tales* (1802), *Wild Flowers* (1806) and *The Banks of Wye* (1811). Bankrupted after trying the book trade, he died leaving his family in great poverty. A competent versifier, his tales offer little except to the folklore student (as in "The Horkey"); but *The Farmer's Boy*, influenced by Thomson's *The Seasons*, though too consciously poetic in diction, describes the farming year with some sense of individuality and challenges comparison with Clare.

Remains, ed. J. Weston, 2 vols., London: Baldwin, Cradock & Joy, 1824.
Selections from Correspondence, ed. W. H. Hart, London: Spottiswoode, 1870.   A.E.

BLUESTOCKINGS was the name given to a group of women of literary tastes meeting in London around 1750 at the houses of Mrs. Vesey, Mrs. Montagu and Mrs. Ord. Their drawing rooms, and particularly that of Mrs. Elizabeth Montagu (1720–1800), became the English equivalent of the French *salon*. Boswell gives an account of the "Blue-stocking Clubs" in *The Life of Samuel Johnson* under the year 1781. Mrs. Montagu was also a patroness of authors in need, and herself the author of Lyttelton's last three *Dialogues of the Dead* (1760) and an *Essay on the Writings and Genius of Shakespeare* (1769). The most formidably intellectual member of the group, however, was the polyglot Miss Elizabeth Carter (1717–1806), who translated Epictetus (1758) and contributed two essays to Johnson's *The Rambler* (nos. 44 and 100), whilst the most renowned was the philanthropic Hannah More (1745–1833), who wrote a poem, "Bas Bleu," about the circle (printed 1786, but written some years before) and several plays. After the death of Garrick in 1779 she turned to religion and thereafter wrote edifying works. Other names connected with the Bluestockings are those of Mrs. Hester Chapone (1727–1801), friend of Richardson and another contributor to *The Rambler*, Mrs. Hester Thrale (later Piozzi) (1741–1821), another of Johnson's friends, and Fanny Burney.   A.P.

BLUNDEN, Edmund (1896–) was at Christ's Hospital and Oxford before going to France as an infantry subaltern in the First World War. His subsequent career has alternated between literary journalism (*The Athenaeum* in the 1920s and *The Times Literary Supplement* in the 1940s) and university appointments in Tokyo, Oxford and later Hong Kong, where he was professor and head of the department of English. In 1966 he was elected to the chair of poetry at Oxford.

Modest and self-effacing, he has never achieved the reputation his work deserves. In 1922 he won the Hawthornden Prize for a volume of poems called *The Shepherd*, and came to be thought of in conjunction with the Georgian poets; but his interest in rural life was deeper than their "week-end" acquaintance with it and his affinities are more with Hardy, Barnes and Clare. (The earlier volume, *The Waggoner*, had introduced a glossary of dialect words.) His poetry has a gently reflective gravity and a form-ality that is at times slightly old-fashioned but in its context very effective. His love of the countryside informs his prose as well as his poetry in books such as *Cricket Country* (1944). As a critic he has written with perceptive originality and authority on several Romantic writers and on Thomas Hardy, while his edition of Wilfred Owen (1931) established a text of those poems with the unobtrusive scholarship, patience and sensibility that characterize all Blunden's work. He may, however, be best remem-bered ultimately for *Undertones of War* (1928), his sensitive account of his experiences in the First World War.

The Waggoner, 1920.
The Shepherd, 1922.
Undertones of War, 1928.
Poems 1914–1930, 1930.
Charles Lamb and His Contemporaries, 1932.
Poems 1930–40, 1940.
Thomas Hardy, 1941.
Cricket Country, 1944.
Shells by a Stream, 1944.
Shelley: A Life Story, 1946.
Poems of Many Years, ed. R. Hart-Davis, 1957.
A Hong Kong House, 1962.   D.W·

BLUNT, Wilfrid Scawen (1840–1922), poet, pamphleteer, traveler and adventurer, came of a Sussex Roman Catholic aristocratic family. He spent some years abroad in the diplomatic service, and it was in Paris that he met Catherine Walters ("Skittles"), the famous Victorian courtesan, who inspired some of the poems that were first collected in *Sonnets and Songs*:

by Proteus (1875). Later work included more sonnets, *Esther* . . . (1892), and a novel in verse, *Griselda* (1893). His travels produced anti-imperialist propaganda—*Ideas about India* (1885); *The Secret History of the English Occupation of Egypt* (1907)—of which a rare successful example in verse is *The Wind and the Whirlwind* (1883), about Egypt. *Satan Absolved* (1899) is a vigorous epic dialogue on the ugliness of late Victorian industrialized England. Blunt's best work is undoubtedly in the sonnets with their expression of "the healthy paganism of the English Victorian aristocrat."

Poetical Works, 2 vols., London: Macmillan, 1914.   A.P.

BLY, Robert (1926–   ) was born in Madison (Minnesota). He served in the U.S. Navy from 1944 to 1946, after which he went to Harvard and the State University of Iowa. In 1958 he founded the Sixties Press and the magazine called *The Sixties* (now *The Seventies*), devoted to the publication, criticism, and especially the translation from foreign languages, of contemporary poetry. In his own first collection, *Silence in the Snowy Fields* (1962), Bly was seen as a poet of western space and silence. An admirer of Lorca and Neruda, he has favored the "deep image" which operates in the context of the poet's unconscious. In 1966 he gathered with David Ray *A Poetry Reading against the Vietnam War*, and in 1967 publicly gave his National Book Award check (for *The Light around the Body*) to the antiwar movement. *The Teeth-Mother Naked at Last* appeared in 1971.   J.P.W.

"BOLDREWOOD, Rolf." See **Australian Literature.**

BOLINGBROKE, Henry St. John, 1st Viscount (1678–1751) rose to political prominence in the Tory ministry of 1710–13. His greatest service to literature was encouragement of Pope and Swift. His works include *A Dissertation upon Parties* (1735), *Letters on the Spirit of Patriotism; On the Idea of a Patriot King;* . . . (1749) and *Letters on the Study and Use of History* (1752). Bolingbroke's brilliant but unstable mind is reflected both in his unsystematic philosophy, which influenced Pope's *An Essay on Man*, and in his diffuse and careless style.

Works, ed. D. Mallet [5 vols., 1754] and G. Parke, 7 vols., London, 1754–98.   A.W.B.

BOLT, Robert (1924–   ), son of a shopkeeper, was educated at the grammar school and university in Manchester, where he was born. He first wrote radio plays while following his profession as a teacher, then, after the stage success of *Flowering Cherry* (1958), took up writing full time. His plays are mainly traditional and realistic, though in his best play, *A Man for All Seasons* (1961; *p.* 1960; *f.* 1966), he modified certain techniques of Brecht. The plays are characterized by an obvious serious-ness of intention, as in the study of Sir Thomas More's integrity in *A Man for All Seasons*, and by an efficient use of symbol and imagery to achieve this intention. *Vivat! Vivat Regina!* (1971; *p.* 1970), a play based on the parallel fortunes of Elizabeth I and Mary, Queen of Scots, is a study of power and power politics.   O.K.

BOND, Edward (1935–   ) is a Londoner, most of whose work has been associated with the English Stage Company at the Royal Court Theatre. His first play, *The Pope's Wedding*, was staged there in 1962, to be followed in 1965 by *Saved* (1966). Performed without the cuts demanded by the censor, including a scene where a baby is stoned to death, *Saved* became a center of controversy and the subject of a notable court case. *Early Morning* (1969; *p.* 1968) was originally banned completely, its scenes of lesbianism (Queen Victoria and Florence Nightingale), fetishism and cannibalism having been considered only at their improbable literal level. Two one-act plays, *Black Mass* (written for the Sharpeville Massacre Tenth Anni-versary Commemoration, 1970) and *Passion* (written for the CND Festival of Life, Easter 1971), several film scripts, including *Blow-Up*, and two more major plays, *Narrow Road to the Deep North* (1968) and *Lear* (1972; *p.* 1971—the Shakespearean theme), have confirmed Bond as a deeply sincere writer whose vision may prove as important as that of any con-temporary playwright.   J.M.W.

BONTEMPS, Arna (1902–   ) was educated at Pacific Union College and the University of Chicago. He was professor of English and chief librarian at Fisk University from 1943 to 1966. The first of his numerous publications was *God Sends Sunday* in 1931. A novelist of some distinction, a poet, a dramatist and a biographer, Bontemps played a leading role in the development of Negro writing in the United States, reclaiming the heroes of a dubious past for the benefit of a more self-consciously militant present and establishing within his work the range and potential of the Negro writer in America. His novel *Black Thunder* (1936) remains one of the more impressive works of Negro writing.   C.B.

BORROW, George (1803–81) was born at East Dereham (Norfolk), son of a militia captain, whose wanderings he accompanied before the family settled in Norwich, where he was articled to a solicitor in

1819. Borrow had already begun to acquire languages, eventually claiming more than a dozen (though his knowledge was often superficial), and in 1824 he went to London to live by literature. He worked as a literary hack, compiling material for *The Newgate Calendar* and *Celebrated Trials*, and reviewing. From 1825 he wandered in England and on the Continent, until he obtained a post with the British and Foreign Bible Society, first in Russia and then (1835–40) in Spain. The publication of *The Bible in Spain* (1843), an account of his adventures, made him famous, and *Lavengro* (1851) and *The Romany Rye* (1857), both fictionalized autobiography, cover the earlier period of his life, emphasizing his interests in Gypsies and philology ("lavengro" is Romany for word-master). Borrow married in 1840 and settled permanently in England.

His works are a strange mixture of folklore, anecdote and prejudice, while the structure of *Lavengro* and *The Romany Rye* is reminiscent of Smollett in the constant interconnection of characters apparently casually introduced. He is deficient in powers of imagination, but manipulates the facts of his experience into a convincing narrative and contrives to praise himself through the mouths of others. Though his anti-Catholic prejudices are not to all tastes, Borrow emerges as an enterprising and determined character, fascinating in his depiction of Gypsies, whether his friend Petulengro or the villainous Mrs. Herne.

The Zincali; or, An Account of the Gypsies in Spain, 1841.
The Bible in Spain, 1843.
Lavengro, 1851.
The Romany Rye, 1857.
Wild Wales, 1862.
Romano Lavo-Lil, Word-Book of the Romany, 1874.

Works, ed. C. K. Shorter, 16 vols., London: Constable; New York: Wells, 1923–24.   A.E.

BOSWELL, James (1740–95) was born in Edinburgh, son of a Scottish judge, Lord Auchinleck, and educated at Edinburgh High School. He then reluctantly studied law at Edinburgh and Glasgow Universities. Initiated into the social, literary and sexual pleasures of London on an escapade in 1760, he returned in 1762–63 (when he first met Johnson), intending to join the Guards. He had in view endless paid leave in the capital, but he fell back on the law, studying at Utrecht before traveling adventurously on the Continent, where he sought out Rousseau, Voltaire and General Paoli. On his return he published *An Account of Corsica*, which won acclaim. In 1769 he married his cousin and settled to a legal practice in Edinburgh, reserving a month each year for London, Johnson, and release from domestic ties. He had already decided to write Johnson's life, and in 1773 persuaded him to visit Scotland. *The Journal of a Tour to the Hebrides* appeared soon after Johnson's death, in 1785. Boswell at last moved to London in 1786, but his "towering hopes" (which included a seat in Parliament) were generally disappointed. Malone encouraged him in his work on *The Life of Samuel Johnson* (1791). Boswell died, saddened by his "strange kind of life," four years later.

The discovery this century of the Boswell papers at Malahide Castle and Fettercairn House makes Boswell the man available to us in an uniquely intimate and total way, and provides at the same time a new dimension to his literary importance. Here we may see Boswell, "chilled" by his father, compulsively seeking out "great men" for their understanding and advice, confessing to his ambition, which "has ever raged in my veins like a fever," and rationalizing his "veering amorous affections." Here we learn of the melancholy, the disordered longings of the Romantic before his time.

Here also we learn the secret of his genius—his almost pathological need to write up his experience ("I should live no more than I can record, as one should not have more corn growing than one can get in"), coupled with an ability to subject chaos to orderly presentation. Boswell prescribed for Johnson what he prepared for himself, a curious literary embalming which should contradict the process of oblivion ("Had his other friends been as diligent and ardent as I was, he might have been almost entirely preserved"). So from a complicated "interweaving" of journals, notes, memoranda and letters collected since 1763 the *Life* emerged, enabling us to "see him live" as extensively as Boswell claimed, and creating a new standard, even a new ethic, for biographical writing.

The new ethic was contested and the new standard long disparaged as a mere process of mindless accretion (Macaulay thought the *Life* a great book by a great fool), but Boswell's unique talent is now more fairly acknowledged, and the two works on Johnson, supplemented as they now are by the "Life of Boswell" on an even larger scale, insist that we admit Boswell's typically spirited claim: "Surely I am a man of genius. I deserve to be taken notice of."

An Account of Corsica . . . and Memoirs of Pascal Paoli, 1768.

The Journal of a Tour to the Hebrides with Samuel Johnson, LL.D., 1785.

The Life of Samuel Johnson, LL.D., 1791 (ed. G. B. Hill, 6 vols., 1887; revised L. F. Powell, Oxford: Clarendon Press, 1934–50).

Boswell's London Journal 1762–3, ed. F. A. Pottle, London: Heinemann; New Haven: Yale Univ. Press, 1950.

Boswell in Holland 1763–4, ed. F. A. Pottle, London: Heinemann; New Haven: Yale Univ. Press, 1952.

Boswell on the Grand Tour 1764, ed. F. A. Pottle, London: Heinemann; New Haven: Yale Univ. Press, 1953.

Boswell on the Grand Tour 1765–6, ed. F. Brady and F. A. Pottle, London: Heinemann; New Haven: Yale Univ. Press, 1955.

The Private Papers of James Boswell from Malahide Castle, ed. G. Scott and F. A. Pottle, 18 vols., private edition, 1928–34; ed. F. A. Pottle and others, London: Heinemann; New Haven: Yale Univ. Press, as above and in progress.

The Correspondence and Other Papers of James Boswell Relating to the Making of the Life of Johnson, ed. M. Waingrow, London: Heinemann, 1969; New York: McGraw-Hill, 1970.   D.G.

BOTTOMLEY, Gordon (1874–1948) was born in Yorkshire. Ill health compelled him to cut short a career in banking. He wrote a considerable amount of latter-day Romantic verse, but his best work is to be found in his poetic dramas, notably *King Lear's Wife* (1916), where Celtic influences can be seen at work. As with Yeats, the supernatural element in some of his other plays seems to reflect the influence of Japanese No plays. He was at one time particularly popular with amateur and experimental drama groups. (See also **Georgians, The.**)

Poems and Plays, London: Bodley Head, 1953.   A.P.

"BOURNE, George" was the pen name of George Sturt (1863–1927), a craftsman who was befriended by Arnold Bennett. His writings reflect his work and his interest in his fellow men. In particular, they recall the world before mass production, and especially the life of rural England. Sturt was a teacher before joining his family's wheelwright business. His writings show him as a craftsman with his roots in the soil of the place in which he lived. His *Journals* cover the period from 1890 to 1927 and span a world that recalls the machine breakers of the 1830s and ends with radio and the General Strike. His best-known works are *Change in the Village* (1912) and *The Wheelwright's Shop* (1923), but *The Bettesworth Book* (1901), *Memoirs of a Surrey Labourer* (1907) and *A Small Boy in the Sixties* (1927) are also very readable.

Journals, ed. E. D. Mackerness, Cambridge: Cambridge Univ. Press, 1967.
                          A.P.

BOURNE, Randolph (1886–1918) was born in New Jersey and graduated from Columbia (1913), where he was taught and influenced by John Dewey and Charles Beard. A brilliant student, Bourne became a radical critic of American social and literary values and a spokesman of his generation. He joined the editorial staff of *The New Republic* in 1914 and his pacifist articles, collected as *Untimely Papers* (1919) and *War and the Intellectuals* (1964), have as their common theme Bourne's refusal to invest the war with any spiritual or moral purpose. An admirer called him "the intellectual hero" of the First World War. His other writings, reflecting the influence of Dewey's pragmatism, include *Youth and Life* (1913), *The Gary Schools* (1916) and *Education and Living* (1917). J.W.

BOWEN, Sir Charles Christopher. See **New Zealand Literature.**

BOWEN, Elizabeth (1899–   ) was born in Dublin and educated in Kent. After leaving home at nineteen she lived alone in London and abroad until her marriage in 1923, the year in which her first work was published. This was *Encounters*, a collection of short stories written when she was twenty. Since then she has published four collections of short stories, some autobiography, a book of essays and an account of her family —*Bowen's Court* (1942). But she is best known for her novels, the first of which was *The Hotel* (1927).

As a writer Elizabeth Bowen has two predominant characteristics— the ability to convey nuances of feeling, atmosphere and personality with great subtlety and a talent for biting social satire. These are attributes respectively of the two writers most often associated with her, Henry James and Jane Austen, though she lacks the largeness of vision of either. Knowing her limitations, however, she usually confines herself to a middle-class setting and a fairly narrow range of emotions, often the feelings involved in a love affair. When she tries to suggest a life outside these bounds, as with the spy element in *The Heat of the Day*, she is generally less successful.

Perhaps her two best novels are *The House in Paris* and *The Death of the Heart*. In the latter particularly, the story of innocence confronted and betrayed by unsympathetic sophistication provided her with a situation which was not beyond her artistic capabilities but which embodied a large and moving theme.

The Hotel, 1927.
The Last September, 1929.
Friends and Relations, 1931.
To the North, 1932.
The House in Paris, 1935.
The Death of the Heart, 1938.
Seven Winters, 1942.
The Heat of the Day, 1949.

A World of Love, 1955.
The Little Girls, 1964.
A Day in the Dark, 1965.
Eva Trout, 1968.   T.W.

BOWLES, W. L. (William Lisle) (1762–1850) was educated at
Winchester (under Joseph Warton) and Trinity College, Oxford. He became vicar of Bremhill (Wiltshire) in 1804, prebendary and then canon of
Salisbury (1804, 1828) and chaplain to the Prince Regent (1818). Bowles's
Fourteen Sonnets Written Chiefly on Picturesque Spots during a Journey
(1789) exactly hit contemporary taste for sentimental nature poetry. He
furthered Warton's revival of the sonnet form, and such poets as Coleridge
and Lamb were inspired by him. His edition of Pope's *Works* (1806) led to
a vigorous controversy with Byron.

Poetical Works, ed. G. Gilfillan, 2 vols., Edinburgh: Nichol, 1855.   W.R.

BRACKENRIDGE, Hugh Henry (1748–1816) was born in Scotland. His family emigrated to Pennsylvania in 1753 to farm on the
frontier. Educated at Princeton (1768–71), where he met Philip Freneau
and collaborated in the epic poem *The Rising Glory of America* (1772),
he made a versatile career as a teacher, preacher, journalist, lawyer, judge,
politician, poet, patriotic playwright—*The Battle of Bunker's Hill* (1776);
The Death of General Montgomery (1777)—and novelist. His major work
was the picaresque *Modern Chivalry*, published in installments (1792–1815).
The continuing adventures of Captain John Farrago and his Irish servant
Teague O'Regan, it portrays and gently satirizes frontier democracy.
Important as a pioneer American work of fiction, *Modern Chivalry*
remains readable and amusing; the prose is often admirable.   D.B.H.

BRADFORD, William (1590–1657) was born in Austerfield (Yorkshire). Joining the separatists at Scrooby (Nottinghamshire), he went with
them to Holland and later, on the *Mayflower*, to North America. In
1621 he became governor of the Plymouth Colony and was regularly
reelected. His major work, *Of Plymouth Plantation*, written between 1630
and 1651, was both an authoritative historical document and a personal
accounting to be judged by God. The emphasis is on loneliness and
struggle; nature is malignant and the pilgrims' human adversaries formidable. Bradford's tone combines nostalgic sadness with the love he felt for
the heroic community he controlled. His literary contrivances, however,
do not prevent his ugly self-righteousness showing through.   R.W.

BRADSTREET, Anne (?1612–72) emigrated to New England in 1630 with her husband and father, a cultivated Elizabethan man of affairs, later to be governor of Massachusetts. She wrote long, encyclopedic poems reminiscent of the versified treatises of Ralegh, John Davies and Sylvester's Du Bartas, to whom she gladly acknowledged her debt. Friends and relatives, probably without her knowledge, arranged for these to be published in London as *The Tenth Muse Lately Sprung Up in America* (1650). Later she prepared a second edition, but died before it was completed. When published posthumously, *Several Poems* (1678) contained thirteen extra poems found among her papers and possibly not intended for a wide public—short lyrics on family occasions such as the temporary absence of her husband, the death of a relative, the birth of one of her eight children. More of these poems, together with letters and verse and prose meditations, were later found and included in the first complete (1867) edition.

"I found a new world and new manners, at which my heart rose," she wrote in one of her letters. "But after I was convinced it was the way of God, I submitted . . . ." Most of her public poetry (e.g., "The Four Elements" and "The Four Monarchies" in *The Tenth Muse*) was a fence against this world, a traditional assertion of the cosmological, physiological and historical structures which seemed to underpin her culture. She is valued now almost exclusively for the shorter, more personal poems. But she was not limited to the "homely" tone, nor was this apparent simplicity anything less than a conscious, sophisticated achievement of another style. Her long poems, by which she was known to a wide audience in seventeenth-century England, are a display of technical skill, wide knowledge and wit enough to play off the new against the old "philosophy" (with her line "Since first the Sun did run his ne'er run race," compare Donne's "At the round earth's imagin'd corners"). Hers was the first volume of poetry to be published by a woman in English.

The Tenth Muse Lately Sprung Up in America, 1650.
Several Poems . . . . by a Gentlewoman in New-England, 1678.

Works, ed. J. Hensley, Cambridge, Mass.: Harvard Univ. Press, 1967.

S.A.F.

BRAINE, John (1922–) was born in Bradford (Yorkshire) and after war service worked for some years as a librarian. He made his name with *Room at the Top* (1957; *f.* 1958), the hero of which, the opportunist and not overscrupulous Joe Lampton, achieves success not least by marrying the boss's daughter. The story of the somewhat disillusioned Joe Lampton continues in *Life at the Top* (1962; *f.* 1965). Both these novels derive strength from their solidly realized Yorkshire setting, a quality that one finds again in the work of Stan Barstow (*A Kind of Loving*) and David Storey (*This Sporting Life*). In *The Jealous God* (1964) Braine turned to spiritual problems associated with his own Catholicism and in *The Crying Game* (1968) he gives expression to his vehement anti-left-wing views. *Stay with Me Till Morning* (1970) embodies some of Braine's dislike of some "advanced" contemporary literature, with its emphasis on perversion, mainly sexual.   A.P.

BRASCH, Charles. See **New Zealand Literature.**

BRATHWAITE, Edward. See **Caribbean Literature.**

BRENNAN, Christopher. See **Australian Literature.**

BRETON, Nicholas (?1545–?1626), descended from an ancient but poor family, probably received no university education. He was introduced into the literary world by his stepfather, George Gascoigne, and became a prolific but undistinguished poet, a few of his poems appearing in *England's Helicon* (1600). Breton also wrote a number of moderately successful prose works. In the genre of character he extended the conventional tripartite syntactic structure into a fourfold unit, resulting in obsession with pattern for its own sake. (See also **Elizabethan Miscellanies.**)

Works in Verse and Prose, ed. A. B. Grosart, 2 vols., Edinburgh: for private circulation, Chertsey Worthies Library, 1879.
A Mad World, My Masters and Other Prose Works, ed. U. Kentish-Wright, London: Cresset Press, 1929.
Poems (Not Hitherto Reprinted), ed. J. Robertson, Liverpool: Liverpool Univ. Press; New York: Grove Press, 1952.   A.W.B.

BRIDGES, Robert (1844–1930) was ten when his father died, leaving him well provided for. His Eton and Oxford career was happy and successful in both intellectual and physical fields. Free to choose his life's work, he decided to be a poet and equip himself by practicing medicine until he was forty. He took his M.B. in 1874 and held posts in London as physician until a serious illness forced him to retire in 1881. He was made poet laureate in 1913 and given the Order of Merit in 1929.

By date Victorian and a contemporary of Gerard Manley Hopkins, whose poems he edited and with whom he had an important correspondence (though only Hopkins's letters survive), he is not, however, markedly influenced by that period, being concerned for the perfection and purity of his own work. His concern for the philosophical and technical problems of poetry and language involved him in 1913 in the formation of the Society for Pure English, whose pamphlets he edited. He wrote frequently on linguistic topics, pronunciation and spelling.

He was more successful in his chastely simple lyrics than in his eight verse dramas. Towards the end of his life he devoted much time to *The Testament of Beauty* (1929), a poem in four books which embodies both experimental ideas and mature reflections on art and life.

Poetical Works, 6 vols., London: Smith, Elder, 1898–1905; revised, London: Oxford Univ. Press, 1936.
Collected Essays, 30 parts, 10 vols., London: Oxford Univ. Press, 1927–36.
Correspondence of Bridges and Henry Bradley, 1900–23, Oxford: Clarendon Press, 1940.   K.T.

"BRIDIE, James" was the pseudonym of Osborne Henry Mavor (1888–1951), who was born and educated in Glasgow, qualified as a doctor and practiced medicine most of his life. As playwright and founder of the Glasgow Citizens' Theatre, he was responsible for a minor revival of Scottish theater. He is a witty and inventive dramatist, whose intellectual liveliness is reminiscent of Shaw and whose whimsy is like that of Barrie. He delights in the miraculous and quaint, as in *Tobias and the Angel* (1931; *p.* 1930). His unusual methods are not always successful; his extraneous prologues and soliloquies have much to do with the fact that his plays seldom leave a unified impression.

Jonah and the Whale, 1932.
A Sleeping Clergyman, 1933 (*f.* as *Flesh and Blood*, 1951).
Mr. Bolfry, 1943.
Dr. Angelus, 1947.   O.K.

BRIGGS, G. W. (George Wallace). See **Hymns.**

BRIGHOUSE, Harold (1882–1958), born in Eccles (Lancashire) and educated at Manchester Grammar School, began his career as a dramatist by writing plays for the Gaiety Theatre, Manchester, then under the control of Miss Horniman. He continued as a playwright until late in life, though he also wrote novels and worked as dramatic critic for *The Manchester Guardian*. His first popular success was *Hobson's Choice* (1916; *f.* 1931; 1953), in which old Hobson's daughter insists on marrying her father's timid employee. Many of his plays reach a creditable, and some of them a high, standard of merit. Using local middle-class life and suburban settings, he renders the spirit of both by means of sharp characterization and racy dialogue.   O.K.

BROME, Richard (?1590–1653) was Ben Jonson's servant in 1614 and later wrote a number of plays, fifteen of which have survived. *A Jovial Crew* (1652; *p.* 1641), a romantic comedy, is often considered his masterpiece, but *The Antipodes* (1640; *p.* 1638) and *The City Wit* (1653; *p.* 1629), comedies in the Jonsonian manner, have also considerable merits. The former, in particular, is a lively "humors" play. Its antipodean scenes, exhibiting an exact reversal of customary situations and relationships, provide lively entertainment by their patent absurdity but at the same time reflect satirically on a familiar reality.

Dramatic Works, 3 vols., London: Pearson, 1873.   J.D.J.

BRONTË, Anne (1820–49), the youngest of the Brontës, shared with her sisters a Celtic heredity and Yorkshire upbringing, but it was the Calvinistic teaching of her mother's family which doubtless gave her writings their distinctive somber and religious tone. After intermittent schooling and an unhappy period as a governess, she was compelled to return to Haworth with her sisters and care for their brother, a chronic dipsomaniac. This period of enforced isolation initiated a fruitful period of writing, for bitter, shared experience had matured the vision portrayed in the Angrian fantasies of the Brontës' childhood. Anne's poems were published under the pseudonym of Acton Bell in 1846. Two novels appeared shortly afterwards, bringing some recognition, but the happiness was short-lived. Early in 1849 she developed consumption and died at Scarborough in May of that year.

Anne's novels, comparable to her sisters', vividly portray a closed-in world with the heroine as captive or in frantic flight. The emotional driving force of *Agnes Grey* is simple and single—homesickness. It is a linear narrative without depth or conflict, but its line defines a genuine, self-sustaining world, at times suggestive of the stormier terrors of *The Tenant of Wildfell Hall*, where the effect of dipsomania on married life is made painfully clear. This obligation "to speak an unpalatable truth" stems from a deep sense of religion manifest in the poems. Though lacking breadth of ideas and verbal coloring, Anne Brontë's poetry nevertheless expresses a real intensity of feeling and spiritual integrity, which, together with a clear, gray style and calm truthfulness, make her a minor classic in her own right.

Poems by Currer, Ellis, and Acton Bell, 1846.
Agnes Grey (pseud. Acton Bell), 1847.
The Tenant of Wildfell Hall (pseud. Acton Bell), 1848.

The Shakespeare Head Brontë, ed. T. J. Wise and J. A. Symington, 19 vols.,
   Oxford: Blackwell, 1931–38.
Poems, ed. C. K. Shorter and C. W. Hatfield, London: Hodder &
   Stoughton, 1923; New York: Doran, 1924.   J.O'M.

BRONTË, Charlotte (1816–55), the daughter of a somewhat eccentric
Anglican clergyman of Irish origin, spent most of her life at Haworth on
the Yorkshire moors, where her father was incumbent. The history of
the Brontë family is a sad one. The mother died when Charlotte was only
five and the children came under the care of their aunt. Some of them,
including Charlotte, went to the Clergy Daughters' School at Cowan
Bridge and were there subjected to such rigors that as a result the two eldest
sisters became ill and died. In later years Charlotte and her two remaining
sisters, Emily and Anne, had to bear the burden of their dipsomaniac
brother Branwell. Charlotte herself married her father's curate, the Rev.
A. B. Nicholls, in 1854, the year before her death.

   The harshness of their circumstances undoubtedly drove the Brontë
children in upon themselves and led to the development of their intense, if
rather narrow, imaginative life. They created their own fantasy world.
As a result they have left us a considerable quantity of juvenile and
adolescent writings, of which the *Legends of Angria* is the most interesting.
The claustrophobic atmosphere of Haworth parsonage stimulated the
desire to leave it, and Charlotte in turn taught at Roe Head where she had
been a pupil, acted as a governess and went with Emily to Brussels as a
pupil-teacher in M. Héger's school in 1842. But the sisters were soon
back at Haworth. The *Poems* of Currer, Ellis and Acton Bell (their
pseudonyms) appeared in 1846, but made little impact. It was a different
story with *Jane Eyre* in the following year, and the success established by
this novel was consolidated by its successors, *Shirley* and *Villette*. Charlotte's
first novel, *The Professor*, which had met with several rejections, was
published in 1857 after her death. Literary fame brought her literary
friendships and thereby gave occasion to one of the great biographies of the
nineteenth century, Mrs. Gaskell's *Life of Charlotte Brontë*.

   There is a strong autobiographical strain in the novels. *Jane Eyre* has
Lowood School and Mr. Brocklehurst, closely based on Cowan Bridge
and its founder Carus Wilson. *Villette* and *The Professor* are set in Brussels;
Lucy Snowe's relationship with Paul Emanuel and the role of Madame
Beck in the former may reflect something of Charlotte Brontë's relation-
ship with M. and Mme. Héger. Moreover, both Jane and Lucy tell their

stories in first-person narrative, giving us an intense realization from the central woman character's point of view. One cannot help feeling also the strong femininity in the delineation of dominant men characters like Rochester (*Jane Eyre*) and Robert Moore (*Shirley*) together with more than a hint of wish fulfillment in the union of the heroines with these men. Charlotte Brontë often heightens, occasionally exaggerates. Her situations remind one of the Gothic novel at times, verging on the melodramatic, encompassing the sensational. Fire, storm, madness, apparitions, persecution, desertion, destitution are among the elements of her narrative. But she never indulges in the sensational for its own sake and, above all, her novels retain their hold on our credibility by their firm moral basis. Her heroines are dominated by a sense of their duty, of what is right and of their need to do what they know to be right, come what may. Charlotte Brontë saw life as a tense and sublime battle in which there was much suffering and not always a commensurate reward. Whatever one may say of her delineation, her vision remains always true to life.

Poems by Currer, Ellis, and Acton Bell, 1846.
Jane Eyre: An Autobiography, 1847 (*f.* 1934; 1944; 1971).
Shirley, 1849.
Villette, 1853.
The Professor, 1857.   (All pseud. Currer Bell.)

Legends of Angria, ed. F. E. Ratchford and W. C. De Vane, New Haven: Yale Univ. Press, 1933.
Five Novelettes, ed. W. Gérin, Oxford: Clarendon Press, 1971.
The Shakespeare Head Brontë, ed. T. J. Wise and J. A. Symington, 19 vols., Oxford: Blackwell, 1931–38.
Poems, ed. C. K. Shorter and C. W. Hatfield, London: Hodder & Stoughton, 1923; New York: Doran, 1924.   A.P.

BRONTË, Emily (1818–48) was the fifth of the six Brontë children, the most reserved in temperament and in literary terms the most distinguished of them. Apart from a brief spell at Roe Head School in Yorkshire, at which her sister Charlotte was successively pupil and teacher, a few months as a teacher near Halifax in 1837 and rather less than a year spent with Charlotte learning French in Brussels in 1842, Emily spent her entire life at her father's parsonage at Haworth. There, apart from her writing, she was occupied only with domestic duties, spending her leisure roaming the Yorkshire moors that surrounded her home. She died in December 1848, having refused all medical attention. Her decline had set in after the death of her brother Branwell, of alcoholism and opium addiction, in the September of that year. It was due to the galloping consumption that wracked the Brontë family and was largely responsible for the deaths of Anne Brontë, only six months after that of Emily, and of Charlotte in 1855.

While it now surpasses that of her sisters, Emily Brontë's literary reputation was completely posthumous and depends almost entirely on her one novel, *Wuthering Heights*. This was originally published under the pseudonym of Ellis Bell in 1847 and was censured by contemporary critics for its violence of expression. For some time it was overshadowed by Charlotte's *Jane Eyre*, but critical opinion is now unanimous in reversing this valuation. Set amongst the Yorkshire moors of the Brontës' home, *Wuthering Heights* concerns the interrelationships of its central character, the foundling Heathcliff, and the members of two families, the Earnshaws and the Lintons. Brought up on the Earnshaws' farm—"Wuthering Heights"—Heathcliff sets out to destroy the more cultivated Lintons after the marriage to Edgar Linton of Catherine Earnshaw, whom he loves absolutely and who, in moments of supreme self-knowledge, declares her unqualified love for him. The story is thus a romantic account of emotional potency confronted by sophistication and repression, that is, nevertheless, firmly controlled by an extremely complex narrative method involving the use of several narrators within the story itself. The consistency of its imagery, drawn largely from nature and affirming themes of destruction and recovery, restriction and freedom, is a further controlling factor, and a novel that might well have failed through romantic excess is, in fact, a masterpiece of psychological insight and statement. Its uniqueness of expression has made it impossible for critics to place it satisfactorily within any of the accepted traditions of the English novel.

Emily Brontë's poetry, some of which was published, again pseudony-mously, along with that of Charlotte and Anne in 1846, can help us best perhaps in our understanding of *Wuthering Heights*, expressing as it does her isolation of temperament, which approaches that of the mystic, and her vivid awareness of the symbolic potential of the forces of nature. Her output apart from *Wuthering Heights* and the poems consists of little more than juvenilia. Though the quality of the poems is varied, they have recently received increasing critical attention.

Poems by Currer, Ellis, and Acton Bell, 1846.
Wuthering Heights (pseud. Ellis Bell), 1847 (*f.* 1939; 1971).

Gondal's Queen: A Novel in Verse, ed. F. E. Ratchford, Austin: Univ. of Texas Press, 1955.

The Shakespeare Head Brontë, ed. T. J. Wise and J. A. Symington, 19 vols., Oxford: Blackwell, 1931–38.
Complete Poems, ed. C. W. Hatfield, New York: Columbia Univ. Press, 1941.

A.J.S.

BROOKE, Lord. See **Greville, Fulke.**

BROOKE, Rupert (1887–1915) was born at Rugby (Warwickshire), where his father was housemaster at the school. At Cambridge, Brooke was popular and socially active; he became president of the Fabian Society and a founder member of the Marlowe Society. In 1911 he moved to the Old Vicarage, Grantchester, and here and in London he met many influential literary figures. He returned from extensive travels just before the outbreak of war and enlisted in September 1914, obtaining a commission in the Royal Naval Division. He died of septicemia on 23 April 1915 on his way to Gallipoli and became a symbol of young English sacrifice. Dean Inge read his sonnet "The Soldier" in St. Paul's Cathedral at Easter 1915.

His early verse, sometimes self-consciously "shocking" and cynical, is generally conventional, accomplished and pleasant; it has a strong nostalgic appeal achieved through simple sensual images. The war sonnets are regarded by most recent critics as his weakest poems, vague, facile, hollow, sentimentally self-dramatizing and even life-weary, though they clearly harmonized with the public mood in the early part of the First World War.

(See also **Georgians, The; War Poets.**)

Poems, 1911.
1914 and Other Poems, 1915.
John Webster and the Elizabethan Drama, 1916.

Poetical Works, ed. G. L. Keynes, London: Faber & Faber; as *Collected Poems*, New York: Dodd, Mead, 1946.
Prose, ed. C. Hassall, London: Sidgwick & Jackson, 1956.
Letters, ed. G. L. Keynes, London: Faber & Faber; New York: Harcourt, Brace, 1968.   A.Y.

BROOKS, Van Wyck (1886–1963) was born in New Jersey and educated at Harvard. His long and prolific career as critic and biographer began with *The Wine of the Puritans* (1908), in which he expounded his theory that the effect of Puritanism on American culture had produced a sterile literary climate. *America's Coming-of-Age* (1915) continued this thesis, which was amplified further in critical biographies of Mark Twain, Henry James and Emerson, among others. His later works, notably the Pulitzer Prize winning *The Flowering of New England, 1815–1865* (1936), dealt more sympathetically with the history of American life and displayed greater confidence in future creativity.   R.W.

BROWN, Charles Brockden (1771–1810) was born in Philadelphia, the son of a well-to-do Quaker, and educated as a lawyer, but soon gave up this profession, moving in 1796 to New York as a professional writer. He had already published essays in *The Columbia Magazine*, and his income was made throughout his life by his journalism. His bookish youth, which laid the foundation of his lifelong ill health, had made him familiar with the common ideas of his time. He was a patriot and, also in the spirit of the Enlightenment, ranged widely over many fields of intellectual investigation, becoming one of the founders of the American Society for the Attainment of Useful Knowledge. He had ambitious nationalist aspirations of bringing into being a body of truly American writing, comparable in every way with the literary culture of Europe. From 1799 to 1802 he edited *The Monthly Magazine and American Review*, a New York periodical that became a quarterly in 1801; and from 1803 to 1807 he edited a Philadelphia periodical, *The Literary Magazine and American Register*. Brown's particular union of literary interests with general scientific knowledge was a fragile one, though characteristic of the age, as may be seen in such a writer as Shelley, who admired Brown's fiction. One of the principal influences on Brown's thinking was William Godwin, and Brown's first book, *Alcuin* (1798), was a discussion of the rights of women, one of Godwin's preoccupations and the special interest of his wife, Mary Wollstonecraft. It was a theme that recurred in Brown's own works.

The most important of these are the six novels he published in the three years from 1798 to 1801, the best of which is *Wieland* (1798). This book has all the marks of Brown's achievement, its remarkable insights and equally remarkable failures. It is a Gothic story of horror and sensation, a melodrama in which the good characters are saintly and the evil, not unadmired by Brown, have a very perceptible whiff of other world brimstone. It also introduces what, with hindsight, we call pseudo-science, the kind of promising psychosomatic theory which fascinated him, in this case the domination of one mind by another through the skill of ventriloquism. The theories of Mesmer provide a contemporary parallel. The events of the novel take place in a country house outside Philadelphia, a foretaste of Brown's innovation of getting rid of the castles and Italian bric-a-brac of the Gothic tale in favor of a real American wilderness setting. In this Brown took a step paralleled in England by Godwin in his novel *Caleb Williams* (1794) and in Scotland by Hogg in his *Confessions of a Justified Sinner* (1824); only in American fiction, though, did it have such permanent and far-reaching consequences, to be felt in the works of Poe, Faulkner, Capote and many others.

Ormond (1798), unfolding a typically rambling plot, introduces two skills of Brown's: the first is a somewhat surprising knack for creating scenes of realism in the streets of Philadelphia, the second, in the character of Constantia Dudley, a successful exploration of the psychology of woman. The novel also deals with a yellow fever epidemic, another instance of Brown's scientific and psychosomatic bent. Brown is very much influenced by Richardson, the eighteenth-century master of "sentiment," not only in technique, as in the letter form of *Wieland*, but most significantly in the emphasis given to the exploration of immediate sensation and abnormal psychological states. It is in this that, despite his often incompetent rhetoric and poor skill at writing, Brown succeeds admirably. *Edgar Huntly* (1799) is his second best novel. In it sleepwalking and some kind of thought transference produce the psychosomatic problem. The native scenes introduce Indians for the first time in indigenous American fiction. The melodrama allows Brown to develop the transcendental, symbolic soul-searching that is so typical of American fiction.

Brown's novels influenced Hawthorne and Cooper, but never became popular. In them may be discerned the simplified moral structure, overstrained rhetoric, conscious use of pathological mental states, unflinching attempts to grapple with profound questions, and an importation of occasionally undigested information and theoretical structures that have characterized American fiction from Melville to Mailer.

Alcuin: A Dialogue, 1798.
Wieland; or, The Transformation, 1798.
Ormond; or, The Secret Witness, 1799.
Arthur Mervyn; or, Memoirs of the Year 1793, 1799.
Edgar Huntly; or, Memoirs of a Sleep-Walker, 1799.
Clara Howard; or, The Enthusiasm of Love, 1801.
Jane Talbot, 1801.

Novels, 7 vols. in 6, Boston: Goodrich, 1827.   A.M.R.

BROWNE, Charles Farrar. See **"Ward, Artemus."**

BROWNE, Sir Thomas (1605–82), educated at Winchester and Oxford, studied medicine and received the degree of M.D. from the University of Leyden. He returned to England and set up practice in Norwich in 1637. Although asserting that "the whole world was made for man, but the twelfth part of man for woman," he married in 1641 Dorothy Mileham, a Norfolk lady who, according to a contemporary, was "of such symmetrical proportion to her worthy husband . . . that they seemed to come together by a kind of natural magnetism."

A version of *Religio Medici*, originally written as "a private exercise directed to myself," was published without his knowledge in 1642. Browne carefully prepared a corrected version for publication the following year. This work emphasizes his intellectual position as an Anglican, belonging to a Christian group which has "reformed from, not against" the Church of Rome. Browne stresses individual reason as a guide where no guidance is offered by Scripture or church teaching; at the same time he recognizes the limits of reason and accepts the necessity of revelation. He thus fashions an area of intellectual freedom where his "solitary and retired imagination" may wander in speculation.

In 1646 he published *Pseudodoxia Epidemica*, usually known as *Vulgar Errors*. It is a work interesting in portions but tedious as a whole and was of greater fascination in the seventeenth century than it is today. *Hydriotaphia*, or *Urn Burial*, appeared in 1658. Browne's speculations were probably made two years previously when, in a field at Old Walsingham (Norfolk), forty or fifty urns containing burnt remains of human bones were unearthed. The discovery prompted Browne's scholarly mind to range over the burial customs of various nations and ages, while simultaneously commenting on human vanity and rhapsodizing on the splendors of unchanging eternity. *The Garden of Cyrus* was published in the same volume as *Urn Burial*. It is an inadequately integrated series of speculations on a quincunx—the figure of five as formed by a domino. To this unlikely subject Browne brings his characteristic erudition, but the full power of his harmonious arrangement of material is not as evident as in *Religio Medici* and *Urn Burial*.

When Charles II visited Norwich in 1671, Thomas Browne was knighted. Father of twelve children, a physician of local repute and a widely known author who had displayed in his writings an encyclopedic knowledge, he continued his comfortable existence in that city. He published nothing between 1658 and his death in 1682. *Christian Morals* appeared posthumously in 1716.

For a modern reader Browne's intellectual curiosity, rather than his his encyclopedic knowledge, is an abiding fascination. In *Religio Medici* he asserts that revelation is offered as profoundly in nature as in the Bible. His own studies have taught him that "there are no grotesques in Nature," and that always a general beauty exists in the works created by God. It was in eulogy of this natural harmony that Browne's published works were composed. Although it has been frequently stated that he relished the task of committing his speculations to paper, perhaps equally important to him was the deliberate organization of his material so that no "grotesque" or "deformity" might clash in the harmony of his rhetoric. The unpolished style and spontaneous recording of ideas in his domestic correspondence are very different from the conscious use of language and careful organization of material in his published works. Consequently, the strength of his rhetoric is a reflection of his comfortable belief in the God-given natural harmony of the universe. He is read today for his magnificent demonstrations of the resources of the English language, perhaps most clearly evident in the final chapter of *Urn Burial*. He is a Protestant Bossuet whose panegyrics and unsubstantiated assertions, backed by a wealth of erudite references, are conveyed in the private rhetoric of a continually speculative mind.

Religio Medici, 1642.
Pseudodoxia Epidemica, 1646.
Hydriotaphia, Urn Burial . . . *Together with The Garden of Cyrus*, 1658.
Certain Miscellany Tracts, 1683.
A Letter to a Friend, 1690.
Christian Morals, 1716.

Works, ed. G. L. Keynes, 6 vols., London: Faber & Gwyer, 1928–31; Chicago: Univ. of Chicago Press, 1964.   G.P.

BROWNE, William (?1591–?1643) was born at Tavistock (Devonshire) and educated at Exeter College, Oxford. In 1611 he was enrolled at the Inner Temple and returned to Oxford in 1624, graduating B.A. in the same year. Complimentary poems and incidental remarks make it clear that Browne was well known in London literary circles and was particularly friendly with Michael Drayton.

Apart from the *Inner Temple Masque* (completed by 1615), Browne's main works are the poems *Britannia's Pastorals* and *The Shepherd's Pipe*. The former (book 1, 1613; book 2, 1616; book 3, 1852) is mainly in couplets and clearly, especially in the use of allegory, influenced by Spenser. *The Shepherd's Pipe* (1614) consists of seven pastoral eclogues in various forms, with Spenserian archaisms. Browne's other verse includes songs, epistles, elegies and epitaphs; particular mention may be made of "On the Countess Dowager of Pembroke," a fine epitaph, often ascribed to Jonson, but a good indication of Browne at his best. His work is not remarkable for wit, imagination or narrative skill, but shows fluency, a certain delicacy of rhythm, pleasant simplicity of imagery, and an occasional fresh responsiveness to natural phenomena. He influenced Milton, especially in "L'Allegro," and Keats in his early poems.

Works, ed. W. C. Hazlitt, 2 vols., London: Roxburghe Library, 1868–69.
Poems, ed. G. Goodwin, 2 vols., London: Lawrence & Bullen, 1894; reissued, London: Routledge; New York: Dutton, 1905.   G.P.

BROWNING, Elizabeth Barrett (1806–61) was born at Coxhoe Hall, near Durham, the eldest child of Edward and Mary Moulton Barrett. A precocious child, she wrote poetry and read widely, including Greek and Latin. She greatly admired Byron. She spent her childhood and youth with her family at Hope End, a country house in Herefordshire. Then, after a move to Devonshire, the Barretts settled in London in 1836. Because of a serious illness in adolescence she led the life of an invalid, but intellectually was very active. She published poems and essays, and corresponded with many artists and intellectuals including Carlyle, Wordsworth, Mary Russell Mitford, R. H. Horne and Benjamin Robert Haydon. Robert Browning wrote to her in 1845. They met that summer, were married secretly on 12 September 1846 and made their home in Italy, with occasional visits to England. They had one child, Robert Wiedemann Barrett. Elizabeth's father, whose love for her was jealous and overprotective, never forgave her marrying. During the later years of her life Elizabeth became interested in spiritualism, which was then fashionable. She also had great sympathy with the Italian revolutionary movement.

Her first collection of poems, *The Seraphim and Other Poems*, appeared in 1838 and was favorably reviewed. But her *Poems* (1844) made her famous, and included "The Cry of the Children," inspired by evidence collected by R. H. Horne for the 1842 royal commission on child labor. The second edition in 1850 contained "Sonnets from the Portuguese," not in fact translations but original sonnets describing the growth of her love for Robert Browning. She was a contributor to R. H. Horne's collection of essays on contemporaries, *A New Spirit of the Age* (1844). *Casa Guidi Windows*, a poem about the Tuscan struggle for freedom, was published in 1851. *Aurora Leigh*, her most ambitious work—nine books in blank verse—appeared in 1857. Elizabeth described the poem as "the one into which my highest convictions upon Life and Art have entered." The improbable plot concerns the love story of Aurora Leigh and her cousin, Robert, and is told by Aurora, who digresses freely on subjects such as the nature of poetry, the value of art, and women's place in society. Both Aurora's attempt to be an independent artist and Robert's schemes for regenerating society fail, and finally they discover happiness together. Technically, the poem is an interesting attempt to create a modern form which shall be poetry yet have the social consciousness and analytic power of the contemporary novel. The poet courageously rejects escapist romance and tackles urgent modern problems. Unfortunately, "good aims not always make good books" (*Aurora Leigh*, book 1). The blank verse is often diffuse and flat, and the poem is disappointingly escapist after all. It ends in a retreat from social action to undefined hard work, blessed by a vague God, and a renunciation of woman's claim to be anything more than a creature made to love a man.

Elizabeth Browning is a minor poet whose romantic biography has obscured her poetry. She was a serious professional poet, experimenting tirelessly with form, rhyme, assonance and rhythm. Her best poetry has an urgent, arresting tone and a startling use of metaphor. Her worst luxuriates in imprecise and abundant emotion; in several of the "Sonnets from the Portuguese," for instance, the feelings remain so private as to be embarrassing. She writes best when she re-creates mood in a precisely imagined setting, as in "The Deserted Garden" or "Bianca among the Nightingales," in which situation and mood are gradually revealed by the narrator, a technique probably learnt from Robert Browning. Sometimes she achieves images of nightmare intensity, as in the abortive wedding in *Aurora Leigh*, book 4.

(See also **Spasmodics, The.**)

The Seraphim and Other Poems, 1838.
Poems, 1844.
Casa Guidi Windows, 1851.
Aurora Leigh, 1857.
Poems before Congress, 1860.
Last Poems, 1862.

Complete Poetical Works, ed. L. Whiting, New York: Nelson, 1919.
Letters of Elizabeth Barrett Browning, ed. F. G. Kenyon, 2 vols., London: Smith, Elder; New York: Macmillan Co., 1897.
Letters of Robert Browning and Elizabeth Barrett Browning, 1845–1846, ed. E. Kintner, 2 vols., London: Oxford Univ. Press; Cambridge, Mass.: Harvard Univ. Press, 1969.
Elizabeth Barrett to Miss Mitford, ed. B. Miller, London: Murray; New Haven: Yale Univ. Press, 1954.
Letters of the Brownings to George Barrett, ed. P. Landis, Urbana: Univ. of Illinois Press, 1958.
Unpublished Diary of Elizabeth Barrett Barrett, 1831–1832, ed. P. Kelley and R. Hudson, Athens: Ohio Univ. Press, 1969.   s.m.s.

BROWNING, Robert (1812–89) was born in Camberwell in South London on 7 May 1812, the son of a clerk in the Bank of England, whose central interest lay in the pleasures of books and scholarship. His mother, a strict Congregationalist of Scottish origin, dominated the household where Browning's early and formative education took place in his father's extensive library. In 1828 Browning enrolled in the new University of London, but he found the courses unpalatable and resigned with the intention of becoming a poet. In the early years of his practicing life Browning was influenced by Shelley; it was he who played some part in Browning's rejection of his mother's faith, the conflict over which is recorded in *Sordello* (1840). Although Browning ceased to be an orthodox Christian, much of his poetry reflected in various ways his belief that the soul is above and behind the intellect.

Under the influence of the actor-manager William Macready, Browning attempted from 1835 to 1842 to write for the theater. His plays did not succeed, but they helped to develop that aspect of his poetic personality which expressed itself with complete mastery in the dramatic monologue. In 1842 he had already begun to demonstrate his talent in this form with the publication of *Dramatic Lyrics*, expanded in 1845 into *Dramatic Romances and Lyrics*. It was in that year also that he first met Elizabeth Barrett who was to become his wife in 1846. During the greater part of their marriage they lived in Italy, where Browning completed *Poems* (2 vols., 1849) and *Men and Women* (2 vols., 1855). Neither of these achieved success, at the time, comparable to that of his wife's work. After her death in 1861 Browning produced two further major works, *Dramatis Personae* (1864) and *The Ring and the Book* (1868–69). Between then and his own death twenty years later he published fourteen more volumes of verse which show technical skill but do not represent any further development.

During the later years of his life Browning spent most of his time in England where he had belatedly become a public figure. He also made frequent visits to Italy to visit his son, "Pen," and it was whilst staying with him that Browning died in Venice. His body was brought back to England and buried in Westminster Abbey.

The range of Browning's interests has found its reflection in those of his critics, many of whom have been attracted by his philosophical and theological views that are often amplified in his poems of least artistic merit such as *Christmas-Eve and Easter-Day* (1850). In the second half of the nineteenth century, when skepticism was making incursions upon traditional belief, Browning's faith bore witness to the existence of the Infinite and the Good outside the bounds of orthodox religious practice. In this way he gave expression to a sense of crisis that has continued to exercise its influence on culture, in various forms, to the present time. But Browning's poetic effects were least interesting where he merely stated his beliefs. In "Caliban upon Setebos" (1864), on the other hand, he achieves a concrete exploration of the speaker's religious mind through the poem's idiom and imagery. Here, as in many other of his monologues (a form that has been discussed by R. Langbaum in *The Poetry of Experience*), we have the combination of terseness with deep and original feeling so typical of Browning's mature style. But this very compression can also conceal inadequately gestated personal emotions, as in "In a Balcony," and can involve the reader in the obscurity of an idiom not justified by newness of feeling. On any estimate, the quality of Browning's verse varies considerably, even within individual poems where the weight of particular lines and the quality of rhymes can be coarse and ineffective. At his best, though, the individuality of his mind and his understanding of the effects which could be attained in verse—particularly through the use of a persona or *alter ego*—constituted a major originality which, apart from its intrinsic interest, has proved a creative influence in twentieth-century verse.

Browning's achievement can most easily be considered in two types of poem. In the first, of which "Andrea del Sarto" and "A Heretic's Tragedy" are good examples, he uses a richly stored historical imagination to express, with subtle penetration, the emotions of his central characters. These talents are again broadly exercised in *The Ring and the Book* where Browning examines, from twelve different points of view, the murder by Count Guido Franceschini of his wife, Pompilia. In spite of periods of narrative prolixity, Browning's handling of the themes of truth and evil in this work is formidably effective. It falls short, however, of the artistic perfection he achieves in many of the shorter poems.

His second major success lies in more personal poetry. In "Childe Roland to the Dark Tower Came" he projects the terrors and depressions of psychic life with a power unequalled by any other nineteenth-century poet except Wordsworth. In love poems like "Two in the Campagna," "By the Fire-side," and "A Woman's Last Word" he combines lyric strength and rhythmic control to produce a fusion of thought and feeling that is only less perfect than that of seventeenth-century love poetry because he too frequently moves from the concrete experience to abstract affirmation.

Pauline: A Fragment of a Confession, 1833.
Paracelsus, 1835.
Strafford, 1837.
Sordello, 1840.
Dramatic Lyrics, 1842.
Dramatic Romances and Lyrics, 1845.
Poems, 2 vols., 1849.
Christmas-Eve and Easter-Day, 1850.
Men and Women, 1855.
Dramatis Personae, 1864.
The Ring and the Book, 1868–69.
Balaustion's Adventure, 1871.
Fifine at the Fair, 1872.

Pacchiarotto and How He Worked in Distemper; with Other Poems, 1876.
La Saisiaz, 1878.
Jocoseria, 1883.
Ferishtah's Fancies, 1884.
Parleying with Certain People of Importance in Their Day, 1887.
Asolando: Fancies and Facts, 1889.

Complete Works, ed. R. A. King, Jr., and others, 13 vols., Athens: Ohio
Univ. Press, 1969– .
Letters of Robert Browning and Elizabeth Barrett Browning, 1845–1846, ed.
E. Kintner, 2 vols., London: Oxford Univ. Press; Cambridge, Mass.:
Harvard Univ. Press, 1969.   P.G.M.

BROWNSON, Orestes (1803–76), born in Vermont, was successively
a Universalist, an Independent, a Unitarian minister and a Roman Catholic
(1844). Influenced by Robert Owen, Brownson was an advocate of various
liberal and socialistic programs, supporting the Workingmen's party (1828)
and the Utopian socialism of Brook Farm. He expressed his ideas in the
journals he edited, *The Boston Quarterly Review* (1838–42) and *Brownson's
Quarterly Review* (1844–64; 1873–75), a journal reflecting his religious
beliefs. His other writings include *New Views of Christianity, Society and
the Church* (1836), *Charles Elwood; or, The Infidel Converted* (1840), a semiautobiographical novel, *The Convert* (1857), an account of his conversion
to Catholicism, and *The Spirit-Rapper* (1854), concerned with spiritualism.

Works, ed. H. F. Brownson, 20 vols., Detroit: T. Nourse, 1882–87.   J.W.

BRYANT, W. C. (William Cullen) (1794–1878) was born at
Cummington (Massachusetts). His father was a successful physician and
active public figure with developed literary tastes which included English
Romantic poetry of the time. From childhood Bryant had an affinity with
the countryside, but his first publication, *The Embargo* (1808), a lampooning
attack on Jefferson, written when he was thirteen, reflected the Federalist
views of his family and local school together with his own neoclassicist
reading. After studying at Cummington School, and being tutored at
home, he spent less than a year at Williams College (1810–11), then studied
law at Worthington and Bridgewater and was admitted to the bar in 1815.
"Thanatopsis" (first version, 1811) and "To a Waterfowl" belong to this
period, but he published nothing until "Thanatopsis" appeared in *The
North American Review* in 1817. In *Poems* (1821) he revised the "view of
death" expressed in this work, so that, whereas in the first version the
author's "better genius" offers at best a stoical consolation that all men face
death with their own particular faith and that they can all be equally
efficacious, in the final version nature replaces the "better genius" and

speaks of death as within her dispensation. Death, then, is made less final and less threatening. This faith in nature is also found in "To a Waterfowl" where the sight of the bird on the skyline reaffirms the poet's faith that nature "will lead my steps aright." This belief in the moral agency of nature was confirmed by Bryant's reading of Wordsworth and the Lake Poets and represented a break from Calvinist thought, but it moderated as he grew older into a fairly orthodox Unitarianism, into which faith he was eventually baptized in 1858. His later revisions to his *Hymns* (1864) reveal a growing willingness to regard Christ as God as well as man.

In 1821 he married Frances Fairchild, continuing to practice law in Massachusetts until 1825, when his published work, particularly poems in *The United States Literary Gazette* during 1824–25, led to the offer of the joint editorship of *The New York Review and Athenaeum Magazine* and then of the New York *Evening Post*. He became full editor and part owner in 1829 and remained so for fifty years, during the early part of which he was one of the leading Democratic editors, supporting free trade, free speech and Abolition. His support for the Abolitionist cause, however, eventually brought him into the new Republican party. As he grew older, his attitudes to literature and politics, originally radical and progressive, hardened. He took seriously, both as editor and poet, his public responsibilities, which meant that as representative poet and public figure he increasingly confirmed and tastefully articulated the orthodox view.

His real strength as a poet lies in the expression of his feeling for "analogies and correspondences . . . between the things of the moral and of the natural world," but the expression is always economical and restrained. His verse experiments were among the first in America to break from the heroic couplet, and he perfected the unrhymed pentameter and the quatrain. He makes no large intellectual or emotional claims and his faith in nature does not preclude the existence of God. Bryant's experience of nature is, in fact, one of delight but not of mystical fusion; he is observing nature as manifestation of God, rather than experiencing unity with it. Almost all Bryant's best poetry was completed by the time of *Poems* (1832) and although he continued to write, his output of poetry slowed down. After his third visit to Europe he produced the prose *Letters of a Traveller* (1850), a second series in 1859, and *Letters from the East* in 1869, and in old age he translated into relatively unadorned blank verse *The Iliad* (1870) and *The Odyssey* (1871–72).

(See also **Hymns**.)

The Embargo; or, Sketches of the Times: A Satire, 1808.
Poems, 1821.
Poems, 1832.
The Fountain and Other Poems, 1842.

The White-Footed Deer and Other Poems, 1844.
Letters of a Traveller, 1850; second series, 1859.
Thirty Poems, 1864.
Hymns, 1864.
Letters from the East, 1869.
The Iliad of Homer, Translated into English Blank Verse, 1870.
The Odyssey of Homer, 1871–72.
Poems, 1875.
The Flood of Years, 1878.

Life and Works, ed. P. Godwin, 6 vols., New York: Appleton, 1883–84.

D.M.

BUCHAN, John (1st Baron Tweedsmuir) (1875–1940) was born in Perth, the son of a minister, educated at Glasgow and Oxford Universities and called to the bar at the Middle Temple in 1901. He had a distinguished career as politician and administrator both at home and abroad. In 1935 he was made governor general of Canada, a post which he held until his death. One of the most successful writers of his day, he wrote a number of popular histories, showing in *The Marquis of Montrose* (1913; *Montrose,* 1928) and *Sir Walter Scott* (1932) a particular interest in Scottish character and history. He is chiefly remembered now for his stories about Richard Hannay, a gentleman-adventurer who foreshadows Ian Fleming's James Bond. These stories, the best known of which are *The Thirty-Nine Steps* (1915) and *Greenmantle* (1916), exploit the adventure of secret service and intelligence work, and illustrate Buchan's art of transforming melodrama into credible narratives. His autobiography was published under the title of *Memory, Hold-the-Door* (1940). O.K.

BUNYAN, John (1628–88) is best known for his allegory, *The Pilgrim's Progress,* written in the "dream convention," using the pattern of the soul's pilgrimage from earth to heaven with the simplicity of perfection. He was born in November 1628 at Elstow near Bedford, of Thomas Bunyan, "brasier" (or mender of pots and pans), and Mary Bentley, his second wife. His books are all records of his own heart-searching. They are written by a man with a sharp ear for the idioms of popular speech and a shrewd knowledge of the life around him. Fits of remorse began to strike him early, leading him to renounce pastimes like country dancing and bell ringing, for which he had a passion; he was convinced that he had been ringleader in vice to the youth of Elstow. After overhearing some poor women "sitting at a door in the sun and talking about the things of God," he eventually joined the sect to which they belonged, John Gifford's Baptist congregation at Bedford. Made a deacon in 1655, he preached at meetings and started publishing polemical works. His first book, *Some Gospel Truths Opened*, an attack on Quaker doctrine, appeared in 1656 after he had become involved in controversy on the reality of Christ's earthly life.

Bunyan had served with the local Newport Pagnell garrison of the Parliamentary army from November 1644 until his return to Elstow in 1648 to follow his father's trade as a tinker and to marry. His qualms about his wild youth were roused by two books his wife brought with her, Lewis Bailey's *The Practice of Piety* (1601) and Arthur Dent's *The Plain Man's Pathway to Heaven* (1612). Many of his own books were written in Bedford county jail where he spent about twelve years after his arrest in November 1660, when measures against Dissenting preachers were enforced after the Restoration. *The Holy City; or, The New Jerusalem* was published in 1665, and Bunyan's revealing autobiographical work, *Grace Abounding to the Chief of Sinners*, followed in 1666. As became his custom, Bunyan included touches in later editions stressing his sorrow at separation from his family, especially from his blind daughter.

During a second imprisonment of six months in the Bedford town lockup in 1675 Bunyan began *The Pilgrim's Progress*, the story of Christian's journey to the New Jerusalem, with all the elements in it that have made the great myths and fairy tales endure. It is less easy for the reader to identify with Christiana in the sequel, since she and her companions are defended on their way by Mr. Greatheart and no one can fight another's spiritual battles. Notable portraits in it can be appreciated, however, in the same way as the vivid picture of the contemporary world in *The Life and Death of Mr. Badman* and Bunyan's reflections on politics and on his Civil War experiences in *The Holy War*. Emblem literature and romances such as his early favorite, *Bevis of Southampton*, clearly influenced Bunyan, and he may have known works like Symon Patrick's *A Parable of the Pilgrim*, (1663) and Richard Bernard's *The Isle of Man* (1627).

After years of fame as author and preacher to widespread Baptist congregations Bunyan died on 31 August 1688 at his friend John Strudwick's house in London and is buried in Bunhill Fields.

The Holy City; or, The New Jerusalem, 1665.
Grace Abounding to the Chief of Sinners, 1666.
The Pilgrim's Progress from This World, to That Which Is to Come; Delivered under the Similitude of a Dream, 1678.
The Life and Death of Mr. Badman, Presented to the World in a Familiar Dialogue, 1680.
The Holy War, Made by Shaddai upon Diabolus, for the Regaining of the Metropolis of the World, 1682.
The Pilgrim's Progress ... The Second Part, 1684.   D.H.

"BURGESS, Anthony" is the pen name of John Burgess Wilson (1917–   ), who was born and educated in Manchester. His life as an instructor in the army and as an education officer in Malaya provides most of the material for his early novels, in particular his *Malayan Trilogy* (1956–59). Since 1960, when he became a full-time writer, he has been prolific as critic and novelist. While continuing to derive inspiration from exotic and colonial settings, Burgess has become increasingly interested in the values of contemporary and future England. Two of his best novels, *A Clockwork Orange* (1962; *f.* 1971) and *The Wanting Seed* (1962), combine verbal and satirical humor with darkly pessimistic observation. His works as a critic include a study of Joyce, *Re Joyce* (1965; U.K. title: *Here Comes Everybody*), and *The Novel Now* (1967).   o.k.

BURKE, Edmund (1729–97), the son of an Irish attorney, was educated first by a Quaker schoolmaster, then studied at Trinity College, Dublin, and later at the Middle Temple. He married the daughter of an Irish Catholic in 1756. Burke began his career as a writer, editing *The Reformer* in Dublin after graduating in 1748. In 1756 he published *A Vindication of Natural Society*, and in 1757 *A Philosophical Enquiry into the Origin of Our Ideas of the Sublime and the Beautiful*. From 1759 to 1789 he was chief editor of *The Annual Register*, though he was assisted in his editorial duties after he entered Parliament in 1766.

Burke's political career was distinguished by his opposition to repression at home and abroad. He attacked ministerial attempts to control Parliament in *Thoughts on the Cause of the Present Discontents* (1770). When his patron, Lord Rockingham, became prime minister in 1782, Burke carried a measure aimed at reducing the crown's influence in the Commons by curtailing its powers of patronage. He championed the causes of Irish Catholics, American colonists and Indian natives against the British government and its agents. His letters and speeches on these issues did not prepare his colleagues for his denunciation of the French Revolution in *Reflections on the Revolution in France* . . . (1790).

Yet, as he argued in *An Appeal from the New to the Old Whigs* . . . (1791), he had remained consistent to the principles of the Glorious Revolution (1688). After that date the Whigs became a conservative force, intent on preserving the benefits of the Revolution Settlement. Politically, this involved maintaining the balance of power struck between crown, peers and people; socially, it meant upholding the privileges of the Whig oligarchy. Thus, while opposing any increase in the power of the crown, Burke had consistently resisted encroachments by the electorate. He refused to receive instructions from his consistituents when elected at Bristol in 1774 and had little time for the advocates of electoral reform.

His great reputation as a political philospher rests mainly on his defense of Whig conservatism. He accepted the view of Locke that civil society originated in a social contract, but where other disciples of Locke stressed the natural rights which men enjoyed before the signing of the contract, Burke regarded these as irrelevant and emphasized the way in which civil society had developed as an organism since its formation. His stress on history rather than on origins led him to oppose theories of politics based on deductive reasoning a priori and to advocate the inductive method in political philosophy.

Burke's political philosophy found literary expression not only in his own writings but in those of the Lake Poets, who were sympathetic to his views, and in the novels of Disraeli. But even more than his politics his aesthetics have played a prominent role in English literature. In the *Enquiry* Burke tried to provide an objective basis for aesthetic criticism, arguing that ideas of the sublime and the beautiful could all be accounted for on the pleasure/pain principle. His attempt found favor among his own wide circle of literary friends, being praised by Dr. Johnson as "an example of pure criticism." On the other hand, it was dismissed by Blake for its narrowness of vision and held little attraction for Romantic writers, though Wordsworth made use of it in his *Guide to the English Lakes*. In the second half of the nineteenth century, however, Burke was held in high esteem in literary circles. His *Enquiry* directly influenced the work of Thomas Hardy, while the Victorian admiration for Burke received its fullest expression in Matthew Arnold's claim that he was "our greatest English prose writer."

(See also **Political Pamphlets.**)

A Vindication of Natural Society, 1756.
A Philosophical Enquiry into the . . . Sublime and the Beautiful, 1757.
Thoughts on the Cause of the Present Discontents, 1770.
Speech on American Taxation, April 19, 1774, 1775.
Speech on Conciliation with the Colonies, 1775.
Reflections on the Revolution in France, 1790.
An Appeal from the New to the Old Whigs . . ., 1791.
A Letter to a Noble Lord, 1796.

Works, 12 vols., Boston: Little, Brown, 1865–67; ed. W. Willis, F. W. Raffety, and F. H. Willis, 6 vols., London: Oxford Univ. Press, 1906–07.
Correspondence, ed. T. W. Copeland and others, 10 vols., Cambridge: Cambridge Univ. Press; Chicago: Univ. of Chicago Press, 1958– .

W.A.S.

BURKE, Kenneth (1897–) born in Pittsburgh and educated in Ohio, has pursued a number of different professions. He was music critic for *The Dial* (1927–29) and *The Nation* (1934–36) during part of which time he also worked for the Bureau of Social Hygiene. He has also taught at the University of Chicago and Bennington College (Vermont). He won the *Dial* Award for service to American letters in 1928, and was awarded a Guggenheim Fellowship in 1935.

The variety of pursuits and preoccupations in Burke's career is reflected in his published criticism. He has insisted that "the main ideal of criticism, as I conceive it, is to use all that there is to use." His own work manifests a profound knowledge of psychology, sociology, theology and linguistics, all of which are brought together "to show an integral relationship existing among a great variety of cultured manifestations which are often considered in isolation." More specifically he has attempted a synthesis of economics and psychology in the work of Freud and Marx, seeing in the content of both philosophies a basic concern with the symbols of authority. Burke's literary criticism has been largely based on the idea of language as a form of symbolic action. A symbolic act is that act "which a man does because he is interested in doing it exactly as he does do it." They revolve around rituals of initiation, change of identity, rebirth, purification, etc., and determine not only the content, but also the form and language of literary works. The task for literary criticism is therefore that of analyzing and interpreting the symbolic structures embodied in novels, poems and plays. Burke's own erudition and the complexity of his thought have prevented his criticism from reaching a wide audience, but he has influenced many contemporary professional critics.

The White Oxen, and Other Stories, 1924.
Counter-Statement, 1931; revised, 1953.
Permanence and Change, 1935.
Attitudes toward History, 2 vols., 1937.
The Philosophy of Literary Form, 1941; revised, 1957.
A Grammar of Motives, 1945.
A Rhetoric of Motives, 1950.
Collected Poems 1915–1967, 1968.   B.L.

BURNET, Gilbert (1643–1715) was an uncompromising supporter of religious toleration from his early years in Scotland to his death as bishop of Salisbury. A key figure in the 1688 Revolution, he was the target of satiric Tory attacks, notably by Swift and Arbuthnot. *Bishop Burnet's History of His Own Time* (vol. 1, 1724; vol. 2, 1734) must be valued for integrity rather than brilliance of mind or style.

Bishop Burnet's History of His Own Time, ed. O. Airy, Oxford: Clarendon Press, 1897–1900.
A Supplement to Burnet's History, ed. H. C. Foxcroft, Oxford: Clarendon Press, 1902. A.W.B.

BURNEY, Frances ("Fanny"), Madame d'Arblay (1752–1840), daughter of Charles Burney, the celebrated music historian, began to write at an early age, starting in 1768 the diary which she kept for most of her life. In 1778 she published her first novel, *Evelina*. It was immediately successful and led to personal friendship with Mrs. Thrale and Johnson. Her other novels, *Cecilia* (1782), *Camilla* (1796) and *The Wanderer* (begun before 1800, published 1814) are much less interesting. Fanny Burney also wrote several plays and the *Memoirs of Dr. Burney* (1832). Between 1786 and 1791 she was a keeper of the robes to Queen Charlotte and in 1793 married Alexandre d'Arblay, with whom she spent several years on the Continent.

Until she misguidedly allowed her admiration for Dr. Johnson to lead her into "Johnsonese" and stiffness of approach, Fanny Burney wrote graphically, often humorously, and well; this her early journals show. As a novelist she was, even at her best, very conscious of serious aims and didactic intentions, but *Evelina* at least shows a lively, if snobbish, gift for middle-class comedy, a great enjoyment of the surface of life and admirably firm characterization. She combines this with an interest in social behavior and the formation of female personality through social experiences which owed much to Richardson, *The Spectator* and the Courtesy Books, yet was still new. Refined and improved upon, Fanny Burney's example persists in the work of Jane Austen, Maria Edgeworth and Susan Ferrier.

(See also **Bluestockings.**)

Evelina; or, The History of a Young Lady's Entrance into the World, 1778.
Cecilia; or, Memoirs of an Heiress, 1782.
Camilla; or, A Picture of Youth, 1796.
The Wanderer; or, Female Difficulties, 1814.

The Early Diary of Frances Burney, 1768–78, ed. A. R. Ellis, 2 vols., London: Bell (Bohn's Standard Library), 1907.
Diary and Letters of Madame d'Arblay, ed. C. F. Barrett and A. Dobson, 6 vols., London: Macmillan, 1904–05.
Journals and Letters, vol. 1, ed. J. Hemlow and C. D. Cecil; vol. 2, ed. J. Hemlow and A. Douglas, Oxford: Clarendon Press, 1972. W.R.

BURNS, John Horne (1916–53) was born in Andover (Massachusetts) and educated at Harvard. As a result of war service in Italy, he wrote his best-known book, *The Gallery* (1947), a brutal but compassionate account of the lives of people who happened to be in the Galleria Umberto in Naples in 1944. Never quite unified, the book transfers the Jamesian theme of the American experience of Europe into the context of wartime and produces a rich tapestry of character, vital and sympathetic. Burns's subsequent books were badly received. *Lucifer with a Book* (1949), set in a school, is a well-written and well-constructed novel, but without the powerful motivating experience of the first book. *A Cry of Children* (1952) is a weak work. Burns died of sunstroke at Leghorn, Italy.   D.V.W.

BURNS, Robert (1759–96) was born of a peasant family in a clay cottage at Alloway (Ayrshire) which his father, William, had built with his own hands. Despite extreme poverty, Burns's family background embodied many fine aspects of Scottish rural life. His father clung desperately to the precarious independence of farm tenancy, personally taught his children an austere but not fanatical religious morality, and, when Burns was six, joined some neighbors in engaging John Murdoch as a tutor for Robert and his brother Gilbert. Burns was educated by his father when Murdoch had to give up his appointment, but he was able to study with Murdoch again for three weeks in 1773 and managed to master some French in that period. Thereafter Burns was mainly self-educated through such books as he was able to obtain. His poems contain clear evidence of his knowledge of such writers as Shakespeare, Milton, Pope and Gray; and a collection of eighteenth-century letters which he possessed were of some importance to him, especially in forming his prose style. His father died in 1784, exhausted by a lifetime of labor, and Robert and Gilbert began farming at Mossgiel, near Mauchline. Burns engaged in much social activity, founding the Tarbolton Bachelors' Club in 1780 and joining the Freemasons in 1781, and his involvement in church controversy also stimulated his poetic output.

Jean Armour, whom Burns eventually married in 1788, became pregnant by him in 1786. In the same year he published the Kilmarnock edition of his poems, which contains some of his greatest work. The volume's success led to his being lionized in Edinburgh, where between late 1786 and early 1788 he received the adulation of the city's social and literary aristocracy with dignified independence. At this time Burns began collecting and rewriting old poems and songs for *The Scots Musical Museum* edited by James Johnson, work that continued throughout his life and for which he would never accept payment. For a time he attempted to combine farming with work as an excise officer, but concentrated on the latter from 1791 when he moved to Dumfries. He died there in 1796, worn out by hard work, illness and the dissipation that had continued throughout his life.

Burns poses many problems to the academic critic who seeks to place him within a tradition, for he contains elements which seem to stem from English neoclassicism (the epistles and satires), the pre-Romantic movement (sentimentalism) and the native Scottish tradition (fierce humor and the supernatural). But for a worldwide audience Burns's simplicity, gaiety and his compassionate understanding of the joys and sorrows of the ordinary man have made him a genuine people's poet. He may lack a quality of imagination necessary to place him in the very highest rank of poets, but his range and variety is staggering, and with John Donne he is the greatest love poet in English literature. At the opposite pole from Donne's tortuous analysis, his love songs have a piercing directness that celebrates unforgettably the briefly snatched joy which the common man finds in the experience of love. The savage satire of "Holy Willie's Prayer," the joyous fun of "Tam o' Shanter" and the noble humanitarianism of "Auld Lang Syne" are all presented with matchless technical skill in the robustness of the Scots language in which Burn's best work was composed.

Poems Chiefly in the Scottish Dialect, 1786; enlarged, 2 vols., 1793.
The Scots Musical Museum, ed. J. Johnson, 6 vols., 1787–1803.
The Cotter's Saturday Night, in Roach's *Beauties of the Poets*, no. 21, 1795.

Poems and Songs, ed. J. Kinsley, 3 vols., London and New York: Oxford Univ. Press, 1968.
Letters, ed. J. De Lancey Ferguson, 2 vols., Oxford: Clarendon Press, 1931.
The Merry Muses of Caledonia, London: Macdonald, 1959.   G.S.

BURROUGHS, William (1914–   ) was born in St Louis (Missouri), graduated from Harvard University, worked in Europe and America, and finally became a professional writer living in Tangiers, Paris and London. His work extends the inventions of Joyce, Gertrude Stein and the avant-garde of the 1920s into a new prose based on experiences derived from drugs and other consciousness-expanding devices. The resultant styles and forms have exerted a major influence on prose and verse in the 1960s and beyond, and his radicalism in social and political opinion has helped to shape the "underground" of the period. *Junkie* (1953) documents the experiences of drug addiction and the world of narcotic agents and pushers. Burroughs's most important work is his fiction tetralogy—*The Naked Lunch* (1959), *The Soft Machine* (1961; rewritten,

1968), *The Ticket That Exploded* (1962) and *Nova Express* (1964). *The Yage Letters* (1963, with Allen Ginsberg) reports on South American drug experience, and *The Exterminator* (1960, with Brion Gysin) and *Minutes to Go* (1960, with Brion Gysin, Sinclair Beiles and Gregory Corso) present compositional experiments in cut-up methods. *The Job* (1970, with Daniel Odier) further extends discussion of methods of consciousness and of political and literary revolution. *The Last Words of Dutch Schultz* (1970) is a film script based on the life of the famous gangster.   E.M.

BURTON, (Sir) Richard (1821–90), though he received no formal education, mastered more than twenty languages and wrote over forty books, which reveal his specialized knowledge of Indian, Arabic and African customs and culture. Like Havelock Ellis, he was a crusader against sexual ignorance, as well as a fierce critic of Victorian indifference to the traditions of countries within the British Empire. In 1853 he became the first European to penetrate Mecca, and later explored the sources of the Nile with Speke. Officially disapproved of, he spent the later part of his life as British consul in various parts of the world. His most important work, after his anthropological studies, is the [*Arabian Nights*] sixteen-volume translation, *The Thousand Nights and a Night* (1885–88).

Works, ed. I. Burton, 7 vols., London: Tylston & Edwards, 1893–94.
                                                            P.G.M.

BURTON, Robert (1577–1640) was born in Lindley (Leicestershire) and entered Brasenose College, Oxford in 1593. The remainder of his life was passed at Oxford, the life of a scholar with an insatiable curiosity, an extraordinary memory and the ability to make all knowledge his province. His only important work, *The Anatomy of Melancholy*, appearing in 1621, was revised continually during his lifetime. Beginning as an analysis of melancholia, "an inbred malady in every one of us," the scope of the investigation is extended to discuss social and political anti-dotes to man's melancholic disposition. Although Burton's prose lacks the harmonic richness of that of Sir Thomas Browne, his encyclopedic knowledge is displayed with wit, irony, satire and colloquial directness. *The Anatomy of Melancholy* is tedious as a whole, but sections such as the "Satirical Preface," the discussion on suicide (part 1) and on the nature of love (part 3) reveal the quaint dignity of a scholarly mind surveying and commenting on a world which appears "giddy, vertiginous and lunatic."

The Anatomy of Melancholy (pseud. Democritus Junior), ed. A. R. Shilleto, 3 vols., London: Bell, 1893.   C.P.

BUTLER, Joseph (1692–1752), son of a Presbyterian draper, became bishop of Durham after being preacher at the Rolls Chapel and bishop of Bristol. His *Fifteen Sermons Preached at the Chapel of the Rolls Court* (1726) places Butler in the highest rank of moral theologians. In these sermons he sought to overthrow the egoistic system of Hobbes by the assertion of a moral principle, or conscience, in man acting as a guide to his behavior. Butler's *The Analogy of Religion* (1736), based on the argument from probability and asserting the analogy between natural and revealed religion, is an important statement of the orthodox case in the Deist controversy of the early eighteenth century.

Works, ed. W. E. Gladstone, 2 vols., Oxford: Clarendon Press, 1896.

A.P.

BUTLER, Samuel (1612–80), born in Strensham (Worcestershire), the son of a prosperous farmer, was educated at King's School, Worcester. At different times he was in the service of the countess of Kent and the earl of Carbery, but the story that he was once employed by Sir Samuel Luke, a rigid Presbyterian, is improbable. He sprang to fame with the publication of the first part of *Hudibras* in 1663. This poem satirizing Puritans was highly popular and found favor with Charles II, though Butler was not granted a pension until 1677. He is also said to have helped the duke of Buckingham, whose secretary he was for a few years, with the composition of a satirical play, *The Rehearsal* (1672; *p.* 1671). In addition, Butler wrote a number of miscellaneous poems and prose "characters," not published till well after his death.

Hudibras is in rhymed octosyllabics, a form Butler used with vigor and point. It is far from simple as satire, being directed at a number of targets, religious and political, literary and intellectual, and written in an exceptionally varied style. Butler's own outlook was "unsettled, sceptical and pessimistic," yet his irresistible inventiveness and wit raise *Hudibras* far above mere scurrility and lampoon.

Hudibras, 1, 1663; 2, 1664; 3, 1678; ed. J. Wilders, Oxford: Clarendon Press, 1967.

Collected Works, ed. A. R. Waller and R. Lamar, 3 vols., Cambridge: Cambridge Univ. Press, 1905–28.

J.C.

BUTLER, Samuel (1835–1902) was born in Nottinghamshire, the son of Dr. Thomas Butler. After leaving St. John's College, Cambridge, he went to work in a poor London parish with a view to following his father's plan for ordination, but quickly decided against it. In 1859 he emigrated to New Zealand where he became a successful sheep farmer. He abandoned orthodox belief under the influence of Charles Darwin's theories and collected material for his first book, *A First Year in Canterbury Settlement* (1863). He returned in 1864 to London where he spent the rest of his life, except for an eighteen-month visit to Montreal and several sojourns in Italy, to which he was greatly attached—see *Alps and Sanctuaries of Piedmont and the Canton Ticino* (1882).

Admired, in both *Erewhon* and the posthumously published *The Way of All Flesh*, for his clearheaded appraisal of Victorian attitudes to family, wealth and religion, Butler still occupies an unsettled position in English literature. A master of pleasantry and of a style that subtly mixes fact with fantasy, he has been justly attacked for his complacency and for his failure to take himself or his writing with sufficient seriousness. Nevertheless, his ideas on evolution in his four books against Darwin (1880–87) were an important influence on Shaw; and E. M. Forster acknowledges a particular debt to Butler's style. *The Way of All Flesh* remains, for the period and the social group it reviews, a classic account of the struggle between father and son. (See also **New Zealand Literature.**)

Erewhon; or, Over the Range, 1872; revised, 1872; 1901.
Erewhon Revisited . . ., 1901.
The Way of All Flesh, 1903.

Complete Works, Shrewsbury edition, ed. H. F. Jones and A. T. Bartholomew, 20 vols., London: Dent; New York: Dutton, 1923–26.
Notebooks, ed. G. L. Keynes and B. Hill, London: Cape; New York: Dutton, 1951.
Family Letters 1841–86, ed. A. Silver, London: Cape; Stanford: Stanford Univ. Press, 1962.   P.G.M.

BYRD, William (1674–1744) was born in Westover (Virginia) and lived the life of a wealthy planter, lawyer and public official. He wrote only as a hobby and his work remained in manuscript until 1841. In works such as *The History of the Dividing Line* and *A Journey to the Land of Eden,* Byrd writes of Virginia with lively style and effective satire. He also kept a *Secret Diary* which remained unprinted until 1941. Invaluable as a work of social history, the diary is full of lively incident, often lewd, and presents a revealing portrait of its author as an engaging mixture of cynicism and innocence.   D.V.W.

BYRON, George Gordon, Lord (6th Baron) (1788–1824) spent most of his early childhood in Aberdeen with his widowed mother. When he succeeded to the barony at the age of ten, they moved to England. Mrs.

Byron was emotionally unbalanced and, though fond of her son, could indulge in the most violent and scurrilous abuse of him. As he lost sympathy with her, he drew closer to his half sister, Augusta.

In 1809 he set out on a Mediterranean tour with J. C. Hobhouse, who had become his friend at Cambridge. They visited Portugal, Spain, Malta, and those parts of the Ottoman Empire now known as Albania, Greece and Turkey. Returning in 1811, Byron published a long poem based on these travels, *Childe Harold's Pilgrimage*, cantos 1 and 2 (1812). This was tremendously successful.

After a stormy love affair with the sensitive, impulsive and unstable Lady Caroline Lamb and a calmer one with the mature and worldly Lady Oxford, Byron may possibly have become Augusta's lover. Then, in January 1815, he married the high-minded and intellectual Annabella Milbanke. In January 1816, one month after the birth of their daughter, she left him. A public scandal resulted, and hostility towards the husband was widespread. In April 1816 Byron sailed from England for the second and last time.

He journeyed up the Rhine to Switzerland, where he saw much of the Shelleys, and then moved on to Italy. These regions provided him with materials for *Childe Harold's Pilgrimage*, cantos 3 (1816) and 4 (1818). A period of dissipation in Venice preceded the formation of his last and firmest sexual attachment, that to Teresa Guiccioli. To be near her, he lived in Ravenna and later in Pisa. Italy remained his home until he left for Greece in 1823. In Italy he had supported the Italian national movement; in Greece, too, he worked to free a subject people from foreign rule. He was at Missolonghi organizing an artillery force—with which, despite his lameness, he was ready to go into action—when he contracted a fever and died.

In *Hours of Idleness* (1807) Byron is sentimental and affected; in the succeeding volume, *English Bards and Scotch Reviewers* (1809), he is satirical and realistic. His years of fame in England (1812–16) saw the sentimental and affected poet prevail in *The Giaour*, *The Bride of Abydos*, *The Corsair*, *Lara* and *The Siege of Corinth*. These immensely popular poems projected upon the public mind the romantic image of the Byronic hero, or fatal man: "a man proud, moody, cynical, with defiance on his brow, and misery in his heart, scorner of his kind, implacable in revenge, yet capable of deep and strong affection" (T. B. Macaulay). Childe Harold, in the earlier cantos of his *Pilgrimage*, and Manfred, in the dramatic poem which bears his name, are also examples of this type. Like *Manfred*, the later cantos of *Childe Harold's Pilgrimage* are products of the months of mortification and despondency through which Byron passed after his separation from Lady Byron. Childe Harold himself fades out by the middle of canto 3, and the work

becomes undisguisedly Byron's own poetic travel journal. The scenes
through which he passes provide occasions for him to express not only
his gloomy personal resentments but also his passion for freedom,
his admiration for energy in all its forms, and his melancholy sense of the
transience of human power and glory. These two cantos contain the
finest work produced by Byron before 1818.

Nevertheless, he had not yet succeeded in exploiting all his powers in a
single major poem. *English Bards and Scotch Reviewers* had shown him to
be an able satirist. Such friends as Hobhouse and the poet Tom Moore
already knew him as a humorous and high-spirited companion; the
Byron they knew is still accessible to readers in his incomparable letters.
In 1818, however, those whose acquaintance with him went no further
than his published works could only imagine him as gloomy and somewhat misanthropical. *Don Juan* (1819–24) and *The Vision of Judgment*
(1822) were to convince them that this was only a part of the truth.

By this time Byron thought of himself as having attained middle age;
and this middle-aged man, having discovered in Italy a congenial environment and a congenial mode of life, felt little temptation to persist in
sentimental attitudinizing. He had also found a perfect poetic form for the
total self-expression of which he was now capable. J. H. Frere's *Whistlecraft*, 1 and 2 (1817), had reminded him of the Italian medley poems, by
Luigi Pulci and others, from which it derived. He conceived *Don Juan*
as a medley poem, and both for it and for *The Vision of Judgment* he
adopted the Italian verse form, ottava rima. *Beppo* (1818) was the poem in
which he mastered this instrument.

Don Juan is a vast, unfinished picaresque novel in verse. The hero has
adventures, amatory, nautical, military and social, in Spain, Greece,
Russia and England. These adventures provide Byron with varied opportunities for satirical comedy. Again and again he discloses the realities
which underlie the ideals men profess. Though many of his characters have
all the dramatic life that could be desired, he does not convey his meaning
exclusively through them and their deeds. On the contrary, he regularly
intervenes with his own witty, cynical and worldly comments on the
action. These sometimes develop into full-length digressions on love,
fame, politics and poetry. Both the action and the commentary transmit
Byron's sardonic but finally compassionate sense of the human comedy.

The Vision of Judgment is a satirical attack on Robert Southey and his
official commemoration, as poet laureate, of the dead King George III.
It might almost be an unusually ferocious, though still comic, episode
from *Don Juan* itself.

(See also **Romantic Movement, The.**)

Hours of Idleness: A Series of Poems, Original and Translated, 1807.

English Bards and Scotch Reviewers: A Satire, 1809.
Childe Harold's Pilgrimage: A Romaunt, cantos 1–2, 1812; 3, 1816; 4, 1818; 2 vols., 1819.
The Giaour: A Fragment of a Turkish Tale, 1813.
The Bride of Abydos: A Turkish Tale, 1813.
The Corsair: A Tale, 1814.
Lara, 1814.
Hebrew Melodies, 2 parts, 1815.
The Siege of Corinth, 1816.
The Prisoner of Chillon and Other Poems, 1816.
Manfred: A Dramatic Poem, 1817.
Beppo: A Venetian Story, 1818.
Mazeppa, 1819.
Don Juan, cantos 1–2, 1819; 3–4, 1821; 1–5, 1822; 6–8, 1823; 9–11, 1823; 12–14, 1823; 15–16, 1824.
Marino Faliero, Doge of Venice: An Historical Tragedy in Five Acts, 1821.
Sardanapalus: A Tragedy, 1821.
The Two Foscari: An Historical Tragedy, 1821.
Cain: A Mystery, 1821.
The Vision of Judgment, 1822.
The Age of Bronze; or, Carmen Seculare et Annus Haud Mirabilis, 1823.
Werner; or, The Inheritance: A Tragedy, 1823.
The Deformed Transformed: A Drama, 1824.

Works, ed. E. H. Coleridge (poetry, 7 vols.) and R. E. Prothero (letters, journals, 6 vols.), 13 vols., London: Murray, 1898–1904.
Byron's "Don Juan," ed. T. G. Steffan and W. W. Pratt, 4 vols., Austin: Univ. of Texas Press, 1957.
Correspondence, ed. J. Murray, 2 vols., London: Murray, 1922.   J.D.J.

C

CABELL, James Branch (1879–1958), born in Virginia, was both genealogist and writer of sophisticated romances. His early works had contemporary settings but he turned to historical themes and is best known for the Dom Manuel series set in the mythical medieval province of Poictesme. Of these, *Jurgen* (1919) was initially suppressed on charges of obscenity. The series began with *The Soul of Melicent* (1913; revised as *Domnei*, 1920). In addition to similarly romantic poems and short stories, Cabell also published critical works, some expounding his theory on the use of allegory. *These Restless Heads* (1932), an autobiographical work, appeared under the name Branch Cabell.

Works, Storisende edition, 18 vols., New York: McBride, 1927–1930.

R.W.

CABLE, George Washington (1844–1925) was born in New Orleans and left school at fourteen because of the death of his father. In 1862 he joined the Confederate army and served until the end of the war. He then had a variety of jobs, but during a period of illness began to write humorous sketches. His collection of stories, *Old Creole Days*, appeared in 1879, followed in 1880 by his first novel, *The Grandissimes*, the story of a feud between Creole families. In 1884, after considerable research, he published a history of the Creoles, *The Creoles of Louisiana*. He also wrote a series of antislavery pamphlets, and in his later years returned to fiction.

D.N.C.

CAEDMON. See **Old English Poetry.**

CAIN, James M. (Mallahan) (1892–   ) worked as a journalist and Hollywood scriptwriter, professions which gave his novels social realism and concise, melodramatic plots. His work includes *Serenade* (1937; *f.* 1956), *Mildred Pierce* (1941; *f.* 1945), *The Butterfly* (1947) and *The Moth* (1948), but *The Postman Always Rings Twice* (1934; *f.* 1946) made his name. The adulterous lovers' first embrace draws blood: "I sunk my teeth into her lips so deep I could feel the blood spurt into my mouth." Violence continues to excite them as they plan the murder of the husband. "I'm up awful tight, now," the hero thinks in the death cell. J.L.M.

CALDWELL, Erskine (1903–   ) was born in White Oak, Coweta County (Georgia), the son of a Presbyterian minister who frequently moved from congregation to congregation. Caldwell worked his way through the universities of Pennsylvania and Virginia without graduating, and then led the classic traveling life of preparation for documentary writing. He worked as a mill hand, cotton picker, truck driver, seaman, stagehand, cook and bodyguard, and started his writing career as a newspaper reporter. Moving to Maine, he began to write seriously and his short stories about Maine eccentrics were published in *Scribner's Magazine*. Caldwell's real territory, however, is the ignorance, illiteracy, poverty and human degradation he saw in the poor South. The sociology he learned as a student, his own talent as a sympathetic but critical observer, together with his impressive plain style of writing, which Faulkner admired in his early works, made him a genuinely moving and imaginative reporter, speaking with authority. He is, in this respect, somewhat in the line of earlier regional writers, particularly the Georgian realists, who exploited the dialect, folk wit and humor of the low life of their native soil. The New England sketches of Sarah Orne Jewett or certain aspects of Faulkner's fiction are related to this genre.

Caldwell's first important collection of short stories, *American Earth* (1931), demonstrated at once his mastery of the reportorial fictional sketch. He published two longer short stories, or *contes*, *The Bastard* (1929) and *Poor Fool* (1930), before producing his first important novel and one of his four or five significant works, *Tobacco Road* (1932). This, first in the form of Jack Kirkland's play (*p.* 1933) which ran for over seven years, then in its original book form, pleased the popular taste and started Caldwell off as a best-selling writer. Jeeter Lester, the central character of this book, is one of the sharecroppers who figure largely in Caldwell's fiction and whose problems present for Caldwell all the misery, struggle and squalor he sees in the South. In his best single work, *God's Little Acre* (1933), Ty Ty Walden is another such figure. Caldwell's third significant novel is *Georgia Boy* (1943), an episodic, first-person narrative of growing up in the South.

Caldwell does not spend much time on the construction of his novels, nor, once the reportorial method is assimilated, is he technically inventive. His documentary style had an influence in France, and led to extensive circulation in Russia of translations of some of his works. His later fiction, moving at times into vulgarization of his themes by playing extensive variations on the sexual squalor of his world, does not show any development. Caldwell is, however, not simply a straight reporter, essayist and travel writer. He collaborated with his second wife, the photographer Margaret Bourke-White, in making "picture texts" of great power and interest—*You Have Seen Their Faces* (1937), a gallery of sharecroppers, and *North of the Danube* (1939), the fruit of his extensive European travel. *Say! Is This the U.S.A.?* (1941), another pictures-and-text documentary, is also part of his real achievement, which is confined to but also firmly based on a few stories, three novels and a handful of essays out of his prolific output.

The Bastard, 1929.
Poor Fool, 1930.
American Earth, 1931 (stories).
Tobacco Road, 1932 (*f.* 1941).
God's Little Acre, 1933 (*f.* 1958).
Kneel to the Rising Sun, and Other Stories, 1935.
Journeyman, 1935.
Some American People, 1935 (social criticism).
You Have Seen Their Faces (with M. Bourke-White), 1937.
Georgia Boy, 1943.
Tragic Ground, 1944.
Call It Experience, 1951.
Love and Money, 1954.
Gulf Coast Stories, 1956.
When You Think of Me, 1959 (stories).
Deep South, 1968 (essays).

Complete Stories, New York: Duell, Sloan & Pearce, 1953.   A.M.R.

CALLAGHAN, Morley. See **Canadian Literature.**

CALVERLEY, C. S. (Charles Stuart) (1831–84), after being educated at Harrow, Balliol College, Oxford, and Christ's College, Cambridge, proceeded to the Inner Temple, where he studied law. An accident in 1867 impaired his health severely. Calverley was a deeply read man who wrote serious Latin poetry and translated Theocritus with distinction (1869), but his reading sat lightly upon him and in *Verses and Translations* (1862) and *Fly Leaves* (1872) he parodied then-popular poets with deadly accuracy. He is among the greatest parodists—incisive, witty, spirited and with a bubbling sense of joyous absurdity. (See also **Parody and Nonsense.**)

Complete Works (with memoir), ed. W. J. Sendall, London: Bell, 1901.
                                                                    W.R.

CAMPBELL, Roy (1901–57) was born in Durban, lived in South

Africa, but also spent time in England, France, Spain and Portugal. An individualist, hating conventions, mass thinking and mediocrity, he was a man of action—soldier, torero, cowboy. His great weakness was undisciplined energy and prolixity, but he wrote some terse and telling epigrams, several lyrics remarkable for their realization of natural vigor and beauty, and excellent translations from the Spanish of St. John of the Cross and Lorca which reveal the visionary quality of his imagination. (See also **African Literature; War Poets.**)

Collected Poems, London: Bodley Head; Chicago: Regnery, 1949; 1957; 1960.   s.m.s.

CAMPBELL, Thomas (1777–1844) was born in Glasgow and educated at the university there. His poem *The Pleasures of Hope* (1799) went through four editions within a year of publication and remained popular for several generations, but few know it today, despite the wide currency of its proverbial lines, "'Tis distance lends enchantment to the view," and "Like angel-visits, few and far between." *Gertrude of Wyoming* (1809) had a similar history. Campbell's simple and forceful ballads and war songs have had a longer life than his more ambitious poems.

Complete Poetical Works, ed. J. L. Robertson, London: Oxford Univ. Press, 1907.   j.d.j.

CAMPION (or CAMPIAN), Thomas (1567–1620) was born in Witham (Essex). His father, who died when Campion was nine, was a member of the Middle Temple. In 1581 Campion entered Peterhouse, Cambridge, and four years later, without having graduated, went on to Gray's Inn. He then studied medicine abroad, receiving an M.D. degree at Caen in 1605. He may also have served abroad at Essex's siege of Rouen.

Besides practicing as a physician, Campion was also a distinguished poet and composer, publishing over a hundred songs in five volumes—*A Book of Airs* (1601), in collaboration with his close friend Philip Rosseter, and four independent volumes (the first and second ?1613, the third and fourth ?1617). They constitute the finest body of English songs, the words and music perfectly united. In 1613 Campion provided words for Coperario to set in *Songs of Mourning* on the death of Prince Henry. Three nuptial masques, *Lord Hay's Masque* (1607), *The Lords' Masque* (1613) and *A Masque on St. Stephen's Night* (1614), and two royal entertainments (1613 and 1618) show Campion's interest in music and poetry on a larger scale. Besides his early Latin verses (1595), he published two treatises— *Observations in the Art of English Poesy* (1602), directed against the use of rhyme (a stricture not applied, it seems, to lyrics for music), and *A New Way of Making Four Parts in Counterpoint* (?1613), which has a forward-looking insistence on tonality and became a standard textbook.

Works, ed. P. Vivian, Oxford: Clarendon Press, 1909.
Works, ed. W. R. Davis, New York: Doubleday, 1967; London: Faber & Faber, 1969.
The English School of Lutenist Song Writers, ed. E. H. Fellowes, 32 vols., London: Stainer & Bell, 1920–32, vols. 4, 13.   H.N.D.

CANADIAN LITERATURE. The first Canadian writer of note is a humorist, T. C. Haliburton (1796–1865), whose *The Clockmaker* (1836) is a collection of comic sketches which originally appeared in a Halifax (Nova Scotia) newspaper and have as their central character Sam Slick. Haliburton had a more distinguished successor in Stephen Leacock (1869–1944), one of the best known of Canadian writers. His *Sunshine Sketches of a Little Town* (1912) and *Arcadian Adventures with the Idle Rich* (1914) show him at his best, ridiculing plutocratic, materialistic society, by contrast with his lighter vein in *Literary Lapses* (1910) and *Nonsense Novels* (1911).

The first poet to mention is Charles Sangster (1822–93), but like the first Australians he is heavily, and not even very competently, imitative of the English Romantics. A more important name is that of Sir Charles G. D. Roberts (1860–1943) who, though also influenced by English poets such as Swinburne and Rossetti, was more responsive to local feeling and especially to the intense national excitement in the years that followed Confederation in 1867. His cousin, Bliss Carman (1861–1929), is a poet of melody and atmosphere. Their contemporary, Archibald Lampman (1861–99), at first found relief in the natural environment around him, but at the end there was no relief; his last poems have the quality of nightmare. The last important poet of this period, Duncan Campbell Scott (1862–1947), is a poet of conflict and violence, often expressed through narrative.

In the twentieth century, putting aside the popular rhymes of the merely entertaining Robert Service (1876–1958), whose *Songs of a Sourdough* (1907) show Kipling's obvious influence, the first writer to mention is E. J. Pratt (1883–1964), a master of the long narrative poem through which he expresses the paradox of man, capable of great courage and sacrifice, but also of ferocity and greed. Pratt is a solitary, but a number of his contemporaries—A. J. M. Smith (1902–   ), F. R. Scott (1899–   ), A. M. Klein (1909–   ) and Leo Kennedy (1907–   )—formed the Montreal group, the first organized poetic movement in Canada. The work of Smith and Kennedy is dominated by fear, loneliness and death, whilst that of Klein is affected by his Jewish origins. Earle Birney (1904–   ) has sought to make himself "a clear and memorable and passionate interpreter of Canadians themselves," whilst Irving Layton (1912–) has tried to convey his "double vision" of the glory and horror of life. Louis Dudek (1918–) and Raymond Souster (1921–) are social realists. More recent poetry such as that of James Reaney (1926–) has displayed sophistication, wit and intricacy, whilst Leonard Cohen (1934–) has directed his sensuous and simple early manner into poetry of protest linked with popular music.

Canada has always lived in the shadow of two giants—Britain and the United States, and this has given an urgency and at times a poignancy to her search for identity. The major concerns of Canadian fiction lie in the realistic investigation of the various communities in the country. Examples of this are works such as *A Search for America* (1927), a study of pioneer life by Frederick Philip Grove (1871–1948), and *As for Me and My House* (1941), a later account of life in a small Saskatchewan town by Sinclair Ross (1908–). Hugh MacLennan (1907–) is very sensitive to Canadian national consciousness, as in *Two Solitudes* (1945), about English- and French-Canadian conflict in Montreal. Morley Callaghan (1903–), regarded by Edmund Wilson as "perhaps the most unjustly neglected novelist of the English-speaking world," explores the two cultures of Canada, English and French, in *The Loved and the Lost* (1951). His sensitive understanding of the effect of social attitudes on individuals can be seen in such earlier novels as *They Shall Inherit the Earth* (1935) and *More Joy in Heaven* (1937). Malcolm Lowry (1909–57), though born in England, settled in Canada in 1939 and there wrote his powerful study of alcoholism, *Under the Volcano* (1947), and the short stories in *Hear Us, O Lord, from Heaven Thy Dwelling Place* (1961). His last work, *October Ferry to Gabriola*, edited by his widow, appeared in 1970. Brian Moore (1921–) has written mainly about the effects of loneliness and frustration, as in *The Lonely Passion of Judith Hearne* (1955) and *The Luck of Ginger Coffey* (1960), whilst Mordecai Richler (1931–), though a novelist of laughter, is also a bitter and angry voice—*The Apprenticeship of Duddy Kravitz* (1959); *Cocksure* (1968); *St Urbain's Horseman* (1971).   A.P.

CAPOTE, Truman (1924–) was born in New Orleans but has lived, with frequent sojourns abroad, mostly in New York City, where he was employed, briefly, by *The New Yorker*. His novels include *Other Voices, Other Rooms* (1948), about the painful maturation of a homosexual boy; *Breakfast at Tiffany's* (1958; *f.* 1961), which relates the New York exploits of a wayward young woman, Holly Golightly; and *In Cold Blood* (1966; *f.* 1967), a controversial "nonfiction novel" based on the senseless-seeming multiple murder of a Kansas farm family, the Clutters, by two psychologically disturbed youths. Capote's other writing embraces stories, travel sketches, the book of the 1954 musical *House of Flowers*, television plays and film scripts.   M.G.

CAREW, Thomas (?1595–?1639) was educated at Oxford and, after some time at the Middle Temple, was until 1616 in the service of the ambassador to Venice, Sir Dudley Carleton, and later of Sir Edward Herbert in Paris. From 1630 he held court appointments. He was friendly with Ben Jonson, Suckling, Davenant, George Sandys and Aurelian Townshend among the poets, and with Edward Hyde and James Howell. His masque *Coelum Britannicum* (in collaboration with Inigo Jones) was presented at Whitehall in 1634 and published the same year. His *Poems* appeared in 1640, after his death.

Carew's admiration for Donne was expressed in his "Elegy," an important critical document as well as a fine poem showing clear signs of Donne's influence in its style and movement. Often bracketed with Suckling and Lovelace as a Cavalier lyrist, Carew surpasses them in depth and strength. His most characteristic lyrics, such as "A Deposition from Love," "Ingrateful Beauty Threatened," "Eternity of Love Protested" and "To a Lady That Desired I Would Love Her," combine the smooth music and urbane tone of Ben Jonson with something of Donne's dramatic quality, argumentation and use of conceits. His epitaphs and occasional poems inherit Ben Jonson's kind of civilized and classical poise. His celebration in "To Saxham" of the country house with a paternal responsibility for its neighborhood looks back to Jonson's "Penshurst" and forward to Marvell's "Upon Appleton House" and ultimately to Pope. He could also achieve an impressive rendering of religious feeling, as in his poem on Sandys's translation of the Psalms.

(See also **Masques; Metaphysical Poetry.**)

Poems, 1640 (includes *Coelum Britannicum*); revised and enlarged, 1642; 1651.
Poems . . ., with His Masque Coelum Britannicum, ed. R. Dunlop, Oxford: Clarendon Press, 1949.   R.G.C.

CARIBBEAN LITERATURE. Various nineteenth-century writers (M. G. Lewis, James Montgomery, Lady Nugent, for example) wrote about their experiences in the West Indies, but significant writing by Caribbeans themselves is not found until the interwar period. Of these Claude McKay (1890–1948) with his poems, *Songs of Jamaica* (1912), and novels, *Banjo* (1929) and *Banana Bottom* (1933), is most important, but mention may also be made of H. G. de Lisser (1877–1944), whose historical novel, *The White Witch of Rosehall* (1929), explores voodoo, or obeah, and of C. L. R. James (1901–), whose *Minty Alley* (1936) concerns a West Indian intellectual's discovery of Creole culture.

After the Second World War the first work of importance to appear was *New Day* (1949) by V. S. Reid (1913–)—important first for its sense of Jamaica and her history, covering, as it does, the life of a man from the Morant Bay Rising of 1865 to the Constitution of 1944 (the historical *A Quality of Violence* (1959) by Andrew Salkey (1928–) is also worth noting in this context), and secondly for its use of the Creole dialect, anticipating in this *A Brighter Sun* (1952) and *The Lonely Londoners* (1956), the work of Samuel Selvon (1923–). Roger Mais (1905–55) found angry inspiration in the poverty and violence of the Kingston (Jamaica) slums in his three novels, *The Hills Were Joyful Together* (1953), *Brother Man* (1954) and *Black Lightning* (1955). The best-known and most prolific—too prolific—novelist of these years was the Guyanese Edgar Mittelholzer (1909–65). *A Morning at the Office* (1950) brings out with keen satirical edge the social differences of class and color in Trinidad society. His Kaywana trilogy, *Children of Kaywana* (1952), *The Harrowing of Hubertus* (1954) and *Kaywana Blood* (1958), attempts to trace a family's history in Guyana from 1612 to 1953.

Another Guyanese, Wilson Harris (1921–), has brought a visionary quality to his novels. In them—*Palace of the Peacock* (1960); *The Far Journey of Oudin* (1961); *The Whole Armour* (1962); *The Secret Ladder* (1963); *Heartland* (1964); *The Age of the Rainmakers* (1971)—he reveals a deep sense of what John Hearne has called "the sacramental union of man and landscape" and he is mystically concerned with the deep, empty-forested interior of Guyana. He is also concerned with the dream that takes us behind and beyond the apparent present. History, character, social realism, none of these matter; fable, myth and poetry abound. By contrast with Harris, John Hearne (1926–) himself is a broad and incisive painter of the social scene of his invented island of Cayuna (really Jamaica), not least—and unusually among Caribbean novelists—of the middle classes, as in *Voices under the Window* (1955), *Stranger at the Gate* (1956) and *Land of the Living* (1961). George Lamming (1927–) has written of peasant childhood in Barbados, *In the Castle of My Skin* (1953), which may be compared with other novels of childhood, such as Michael Anthony's *The Year in San Fernando* (1965) and Geoffrey Drayton's *Christopher* (1959). Lamming's *The Emigrants* (1954), like Andrew Salkey's *Escape to an Autumn Pavement* (1960), covers the theme of migration, and he has also written of return—with political corruption back home—in *Of Age and Innocence* (1958), and of political independence in *Season of Adventure* (1960).

The greatest of West Indian novelists is the Trinidadian V. S. Naipaul 1932–), whose *A House for Mr. Biswas* (1961) is a work of Dickensian proportions and vitality. Naipaul has little time or patience for much of what he sees as the stupidity and worse of Trinidadian life—*The Mystic Masseur* (1957); *The Suffrage of Elvira* (1958); *The Mimic Men* (1967)—but he does not seek to reform; he accepts anarchy and laughs at it. Mr Biswas himself is a personification of tragicomedy, and Naipaul often seems to be pointing a finger at the pathetic overseriousness of so many West Indians. He himself has written: "History is built around achievement and creation; and nothing was created in the West Indies", which have "no people in the true sense of the word, with a character and purpose of their own" (*The Middle Passage*, 1962).

Neither English nor African, yet something of both, West Indian culture is absorbed with its search for identity. The appeal of Africa is explored by Denis Williams (1923–) in *Other Leopards* (1963) where Lionel (Lobo) Froad seeks meaning in Africa—in vain. A somewhat similar pilgrimage is described by the poet Edward Brathwaite (1930–) in his threefold work *Rights of Passage* (1967), *Masks* (1968) and *Islands* (1969). Derek Walcott (1930–), however, is a man more than content with the West Indies. In solitude he has discovered ever new wonders and resources of self. Once widely derivative, he has established his own varied and distinct poetic voice with *In a Green Night* (1962), *The Castaway* (1965) and *The Gulf* (1969).

Altogether, West Indian literature since 1948 is a prolific and often remarkable achievement.
                                                                              A.P.

CARLYLE, Thomas (1795–1881) was born in Scotland at Ecclefechan (Dumfriesshire). The moral influence of his devout Presbyterian upbringing never left him despite his eventual defection from orthodox Christianity. He was educated at Edinburgh University, and as a young man corresponded with Goethe, whose influence on him was also ineradicable. He first came to London in 1824 and, apart from the years 1826 to 1834, which he spent in Scotland after his marriage in 1826 to Jane Welsh, never lived elsewhere. His career as a writer developed with translations from Goethe and other German Romantics, and publication of his biography of Schiller. These were followed by *Signs of the Times* and *Sartor Resartus*, but it was not until the publication in 1837 of *The French Revolution*, which established him both as historian and social prophet, that Carlyle achieved a lasting reputation. During the remainder of his long career he devoted himself to further works of history, biography and social analysis. He was elected rector of Edinburgh University in 1865, but after his wife's death in the following year he withdrew from public life, devoting himself to editing her correspondence and to his own *Reminiscences*, which were published in the year of his death.

The volume of Carlyle's prose output is so great as to present formidable problems to the modern reader, and he is now best approached through selected writings. His influence in his own day, however, was considerable: contemporary intellectuals like J. A. Froude and F. D. Maurice testified to its effect, while for Dickens *The French Revolution* was "Mr. Carlyle's wonderful book" and the source book for *A Tale of Two Cities*. The *French Revolution*, like all Carlyle's historical writing, was as much a work of social prophecy as of history, and its thundering prose narrative is typical of its author's passionate interest in issues of social change. Carlyle's major interest today, however, lies in his penetrating analysis of what he saw as the materialistic paralysis that threatened nineteenth-century England. His critical stance throughout his work is that of a Romantic prophet in a utilitarian world: as early as *Signs of the Times* he defined his age as "the age of machinery in every outward and inward sense of that word," and he never ceased to attack the limitations of purely utilitarian perspectives. His social analyses, and above all his critiques of laissez faire economics and of the limitations of nineteenth-century liberalism, ask crucial questions about the nature of the rapidly developing industrial society of his day and (as, for example, in *Chartism*) frequently led him to express extremely radical sympathies with those who suffered from "the supreme triumph of Cash." Carlyle's devotion to German Romanticism led him into both stylistic and theoretical excesses. Prominent among the latter was his cult of the hero with its totalitarian implications. As a social critic, however, he had a capacity for asking fundamental questions about the nature and quality of democracy that in many ways remain unanswered, and it is this quality in his work that has given it lasting interest. (See also **Essays.**)

The Life of Schiller, 1825 (s. 1823–24).
Signs of the Times, 1829.
Sartor Resartus: The Life and Opinions of Herr Teufelsdröckh, 3 vols., 1836 (s. 1833–34).
The French Revolution: A History, 3 vols., 1837.
Chartism, 1839.
On Heroes, Hero-Worship and the Heroic in History, 1841.
Past and Present, 1843.
Oliver Cromwell's Letters and Speeches, 2 vols., 1845.
Latter-Day Pamphlets, 1850.
The History of Friedrich II of Prussia, Called Frederick the Great, 6 vols., 1858–65.
Reminiscences, ed. J. A. Froude, 2 vols., 1881.

Collected Works, Centenary edition, ed. H. D. Traill, 30 vols., London: Chapman & Hall, 1896–99; New York: C. Scribner's Sons, 1896–1901.   A.J.S.

CARMAN, Bliss. See **Canadian Literature.**

"CARROLL, Lewis" was the pseudonym of Charles Lutwidge Dodgson (1832–98), who led an outwardly quiet life as a mathematics lecturer at Christ Church, Oxford. The majority of his published works deal with mathematics and are remarkable for a logical clarity which also gives strength to his famous *Alice's Adventures in Wonderland* (1865; *f.* 1933; 1951) and its sequel, *Through the Looking-Glass* (1872, for 1871). Although originally intended for children, these books continue to intrigue adult readers not only by their rich inventiveness but by their logical conundrums and their open invitation to the Freudian interpreter. Both are works of fantasy in which Alice/Carroll wanders through a hostile world of adults and animals, closely related to Victorian Oxford. Both show a maidenly timidity before the horrors of the grown-up world, which is not unconnected with Carroll's obsessive interest in little girls. Of his other prose works, *Sylvie and Bruno* (1889) and *Sylvie and Bruno Concluded* (1893) are the most interesting, more perhaps for the light they throw on Carroll's mind than for any intrinsic merits.

Carroll was also a writer of parody and nonsense verse. Apart from *The Hunting of the Snark* (1876) all the best examples occur in the Alice books. Probably inspired by Edward Lear (see **Parody and Nonsense**), he indulged in nonsense vocabulary, but his most notable characteristic was the use of "portmanteau" words (words with two meanings packed into one, e.g., frumious = fuming + furious; galumph = gallop + triumph). This technique had an obvious influence on Joyce, especially in *Finnegans Wake*. Carroll's claims to artistic distinction must be based largely on his prose, for his verse is dry and precise, the nonsense carefully calculated. As a poet he was vastly inferior to Lear; as a prose writer he had the distinction of creating a world of his own.

Complete Works, ed. A. Woolcott, New York: Random House, 1936; London: Nonesuch Press, 1939.   E.T.W.

CARTER, Elizabeth. See **Bluestockings.**

CARY, Joyce (1888–1957), born in Ireland, was educated at Clifton and Trinity College, Cambridge, later studying art in Edinburgh and Paris. He saw active service in the Balkan War of 1912–13 and in the latter year he joined the Nigerian political service, fighting on the outbreak of war with the Nigerian Regiment. After being seriously wounded, he returned to the political service and became magistrate and administrative officer in a remote district, there gaining that experience of native life that gives authenticity to his early novels, *Aissa Saved* (1932) and *Mister Johnson* (1939). The belated publication of these novels did not take place till long after his retirement from Nigeria on the grounds of ill health. Because of the dissatisfaction which he felt with his early attempts at writing, he had scrupulously found it necessary to subject himself to a long period of intellectual discipline and training. His later years found him much handicapped by increasingly serious illness.

A prolific writer, Cary is best known for the novels written between 1941 and 1955, but the two novels mentioned earlier are very worthy of note. *Aissa Saved* is a sensitive study of the tribal mind and culture; *Mister Johnson* deals with the West African temperament brought into contact with European colonial civilization. In this latter novel Cary examines with deep compassion and delicacy the relationship between a white official and a subordinate African. He employs for the first time in his work a highly stylized prose, using almost exclusively the present tense and an extremely simple syntax. The result is a tense and dramatic narrative that is very effective in placing the situations and characters before the reader with a minimum of authorial comment.

In the novels that followed he used various modifications of this style, enlarging its scope, but keeping its basic simplicity. After *Mister Johnson* appeared a series of connected novels, *Herself Surprised* (1941), *To Be a Pilgrim* (1942) and *The Horse's Mouth* (1944), concerned with a group of people whose lives cross and recross. In each novel Cary chooses a different character as main figure, through whose eyes the reader generally sees the action; by the end of the series the multiple vision has given the reader a very broad knowledge of the characters. This method obviously owes much to the James Joyce of *Ulysses*, and the nearest approach to him comes in *The Horse's Mouth* where the impressions and resultant thoughts follow each other in a manner strongly reminiscent of the "streams of consciousness" of Stephen and Mr. Bloom. But Cary gives his figures their own individual inner language, which is the full expression of their personalities and ideas, and describes their doings. In these novels Cary shows himself acutely aware of the physical beauty of the world in itself and as expressed in art; at times, to be sure, the attempt to see with the artist's eye does not completely convince us, but, in general, it is highly successful. The social and personal world he depicts is by conventional standards an amoral world, but it exposes sham and empty convention. The novels are a prolonged plea for intellectual and emotional, rather than commercial, honesty. They are, above all, an assertion of the goodness of life, a passionate statement of Cary's belief in sheer existence as worthwhile in itself. This shows itself not only in the constant sense of beauty, but in the exuberant humor; sometimes in bad taste, sometimes even having elements of cruelty, it has superabundant vitality.

Three later connected novels, *Prisoner of Grace* (1952), *Except the Lord* (1953) and *Not Honour More* (1955), show some falling off in vitality, but they have enough of it to be well worth reading. They show, too, the undercurrent of unconventional but genuine religious feeling in Cary's work, his sympathy for the vulnerability of sickness and old age, and his firm conviction that in everything "ripeness is all."

Aissa Saved, 1932.
An American Visitor, 1933.
The African Witch, 1936.
Castle Corner, 1938.
Mister Johnson, 1939.
Charley Is My Darling, 1940.
The House of Children, 1941.
Herself Surprised, 1941.
To Be a Pilgrim, 1942.
The Horse's Mouth, 1944 (*f*. 1958).
The Moonlight, 1946.
A Fearful Joy, 1949.
Prisoner of Grace, 1952.
Except the Lord, 1953.
Not Honour More, 1955.
The Captive and the Free, 1959.
Spring Song and Other Stories, 1960.   C.H.

CASWALL, Isaac. See **Hymns.**

CATHER, Willa (1873–1947) was born in Gore (Virginia). The removal of her family from settled Southern life to Nebraskan wilderness in 1883 marked her and her contrast-haunted fiction indelibly. Aversion to dully materialistic small-town Red Cloud (Nebraska) and attraction to the idealism of pioneering immigrant farmers became obsessions. Educated locally, she graduated from Lincoln (Nebraska). As undergraduate, then journalist and teacher in Pittsburgh, she poured out stories and reviews. The verse of *April Twilights* (1903) and the short stories of *The Troll Garden* (1905) only hinted at that ability to capture in compassionate, lyrical novels the people and places of her youth which she exhibited in parts of *O Pioneers!* (1913) and *The Song of the Lark* (1915) and throughout her masterpiece *My Ántonia* (1918). After 1922, the year she won a Pulitzer Prize for a less distinguished novel, *One of Ours*, her steady retreat from accelerating, abrasive change into elegies on the Old West and shrill satire on the New may be traced in the mildly experimental works, culminating in *Death Comes for the Archbishop* (1927), where her passion for the South West is given fullest rein. Later fiction largely declined into weak recapitulations. She died in New York, her home for many years.

My Ántonia embodies the moral beauty of the frontier experience in the vividly recalled persistent vitality of a Bohemian immigrant's daughter. Surpassed by *A Lost Lady* (1923) in formal economy and by *The Professor's House* (1925) in subtle psychological interest, it triumphs, characteristically, through texture—a naturalism enriched by magically evoked atmosphere, suggestions of myth, a suave and radiant prose.

O Pioneers!, 1913.
The Song of the Lark, 1915.
My Ántonia, 1918.
One of Ours, 1922.
A Lost Lady, 1923 (*f.* 1925).
The Professor's House, 1925.
My Mortal Enemy, 1926.
Death Comes for the Archbishop, 1927.
Obscure Destinies, 1932 (stories).
Not under Forty, 1936 (essays).

Novels and Stories, Library edition, 13 vols., Boston: Houghton Mifflin, 1937–41.
Collected Short Fiction 1891–1912, Lincoln: Univ. of Nebraska Press, 1965.
A.S.

"CAUDWELL, Christopher" was the pseudonym of Christopher St. John Sprigg (1907–37), who was born in Putney. He began his writing career by producing detective fiction and textbooks on aeronautics. By the mid-1930s he had become an ardent Marxist and joined the International Brigade to serve in the war in Spain, where he died in 1937. The ablest and most philosophic of English Marxist critics, he examined the relationship between poetry, politics and economics in two works that were published after his death, *Illusion and Reality* (1937) and *Studies in a Dying Culture* (1938). The first scrutinizes the nature and function of poetry in the light of Marxist dialectic, Caudwell attributing the current low state of poetry to the breakdown of bourgeois society; the second, containing judgments both bizarre and sensitive, detects bourgeois illusions in such writers as Lawrence, Wells and Shaw. O.K.

CAUSLEY, Charles (1917–) was born at Launceston (Cornwall) and educated there and in Peterborough (Northamptonshire). He traveled widely as a young man, serving in the Royal Navy from 1940 to 1946. Later he became a broadcaster, critic and teacher while also publishing several volumes of his own verse. His poems are constructed with a refreshing attention to real detail and often have jaunty ballad rhythms, their apparent spontaneity making an immediate impact. His lilting measures are admirably suited to the vivid and semihumorous sketch, whether drawn from Causley's childhood experience or his life as a teacher. In the more serious of his poems—particularly those written during the Second World War—his lyricism is still evident, but controlled by more urgent speaking tones. (See also **War Poets.**)   O.K.

CAXTON, William (c.1422–91), born in Kent, was apprenticed in 1438 to a London mercer who died in 1441. Caxton went to Bruges and spent the next thirty years trading and traveling in the Low Countries. By 1465 he had become governor of the Merchant Adventurers at Bruges and was involved in negotiating trade in Cologne. In 1476, on returning to England, he set up a press at Westminster. As a printer he was encouraged and patronized by Edward IV, Richard III and by various of the nobility.

Caxton was remarkably industrious both as a printer and a translator, claiming to have translated twenty-one works (mainly from the French) and printing at least eighty, including not only Chaucer, Gower, Lydgate and Malory, but also Cicero and Aesop. His first translation, *The Recuyell of the Historyes of Troye* (1475), is the earliest book printed in English, and the *Dictes and Sayings of the Philosophers* (1477) the first printed in England. Apart from the technological and educational significance of Caxton as printer, his work as translator is important for the development of sixteenth-century English, because his prose, while still structurally mechanical, is clear and idiomatic and because in translating he shows a willingness to interpolate and paraphrase, even at the expense of literal fidelity.

Various of Caxton's translations and publications have been edited in the Early English Text Society series, among them *Caxton's Prologues and Epilogues*, ed. W. J. B. Crotch, 1928.   G.P.

CENTLIVRE, Mrs. Susanna (?1667–1723), actress and dramatist, was supposedly born in Ireland. From 1700 to 1722 she wrote nineteen plays, fourteen of them comedies, and most owing something to other dramatists. She was an enthusiastic Whig and friend of (among other Whigs) Rowe, Steele and Budgell. Her most representative sentimental comedies are *The Gamester* (1705), *The Basset-Table* (1706; *p.* 1705), *Love at a Venture* (1706) and *The Busy Body* (1709), though perhaps her most popular play was *A Bold Stroke for a Wife* (1718). She was a professional dramatist, temperamentally inclined to Restoration rather than sentimental comedy, whose plays succeed in clever, mechanical intrigue and little else. The character of Marplot in *The Busy Body* alone remains memorable.

Works, 3 vols., London: Knapton, 1760–61.
Dramatic Works, 3 vols., London: Pearson, 1872.   P.R.

CHAMIER, George. See **New Zealand Literature.**

CHANDLER, Raymond (1888–1959) was educated in England, served in the First World War and returned to the United States as an oil corporation officer. In Clifton Fadiman's words, Chandler wrote an "image-laden raw-colored prose" in contrast to the "all-bone style" of his master, Dashiell Hammett. The hero of his detective stories lives a lean life amidst the luxury and all-pervading corruption of Southern California. Chandler's best work is *The Big Sleep* (1939; *f.* 1946); *Farewell, My Lovely* (1940; *f.* 1944); *The Little Sister* (1949; *f.* 1969); and *The Long Goodbye* (1954).   J.L.M.

CHAPMAN, George (?1559–1634) was born in or near Hitchin (Hertfordshire), the son of a Protestant yeoman, and may have been to Oxford, and perhaps Cambridge also, after which he may have served in the wars in the Low Countries (1582–91). The most persistent theme of Chapman's life is poverty: he was twice jailed for debt, was involved in various lawsuits, and was consistently unlucky with his patrons (Ralegh, Essex, Prince Henry—who made him a "sewer in ordinary" in 1604—and Somerset). This financial pressure may explain Chapman's career as a dramatist, a career which began unusually late and is varied in a way which suggests real concern to be fashionable. His main literary friends seem to have been Marston, Jonson and Inigo Jones. He died in 1634, apparently back again in Hitchin.

Chapman was an amazingly prolific writer as dramatist, poet and translator. His career began with nondramatic verse, including his continuation of Marlowe's *Hero and Leander* (1598). He seems to have turned to the theater mainly for money, and his first plays—comedies which have been too much neglected—show keen interest in fashion and experiment. *The Blind Beggar of Alexandria* follows Peele; *All Fools* imitates Roman and Greek comedy; *The Gentleman Usher* is romantic; *Eastward Ho!*, in collaboration with Jonson and Marston, is topical. This topical stress recurs in the series of tragedies, based on then recent French history, which began with *Bussy D'Ambois* (1607) and ended with *The Tragedy of Chabot* (1639), and in the course of which Chapman moves from a sense of the paradox that strong passion is a source both of greatness and of danger to an increasingly didactic and static position. He himself regarded his translations of Homer's *Iliad* and *Odyssey* as his greatest achievement. Seven books of the *Iliad* appeared in 1598, the whole in 1611. His versions are not faithful to the letter of the originals—as Chapman's Greek was limited, he called on Latin translations as intermediaries, and he tended to insert moral passages—but his sympathy with Homer and energy of manner give these versions permanent life and value.

Much can be asserted against Chapman. He was widely read in the classics, but is almost entirely without the classical virtues of restraint, balance and sense of form; he lacks literary tact, is extremely prolix, often flat and very uneven; his thought is a cloudy mixture of Christian, Stoic and Neoplatonic doctrines, without Jonson's clarity and consistency; his constant desire to point moral lessons perpetually weakens his awareness and development of the complexities of situations he has begun successfully to imagine. Yet it remains impossible to ignore him. His range is varied and ambitious; he has more humor than is commonly realized; he has great vigor and power of imagination. Above all, his work has remarkable integrity and an urge to try to give form to the chaos of ideas about which he had read and thought. Much of Chapman's difficulty and confusion springs from this integrity and from the strong emotional aspect of his thought. Chapman may have had too much ambition for his talent, but scale and ambition, taken with considerable talent, do provide some counterbalance for his failure to achieve finished masterpieces.

Hero and Leander, 1598.
The Blind Beggar of Alexandria, 1598 (*p.* 1596).
All Fools, 1605 (*p.* ?1599).
Eastward Ho! (with Ben Jonson and John Marston), 1605.
The Conspiracy of Charles, Duke of Byron, 1608 (*p.* c. 1605).
The Tragedy of Charles, Duke of Byron, 1608 (*p.* c. 1605).
Monsieur D'Olive, 1606.
The Gentleman Usher, 1606 (*p.* ?1602).
Bussy D'Ambois, 1607.
Iliad, 1611.
The Widow's Tears, 1612.
The Revenge of Bussy D'Ambois, 1613.
The Whole Works of Homer, Prince of Poets, 1616.
Hesiod's Georgics, 1618.
The Tragedy of Chabot, Admiral of France (with James Shirley), 1639.

Plays, ed. T. M. Parrott, 2 vols., London: Routledge, New York: Dutton, 1910–14.

Plays: Comedies, ed. A. Holaday and M. Kiernan, Urbana: Univ. of
Illinois Press, 1970.
Poems, ed. P. B. Bartlett, London: Oxford Univ. Press; New York:
Modern Language Association of America, 1941.
Chapman's Homer, ed. A. Nicoll, London: Routledge, 1957.   G.P.

CHAPONE, Mrs. Hester. See **Bluestockings.**

CHATTERTON, Thomas (1752–70) was born in Bristol. His father
was a schoolmaster, but his family had long been connected as sextons with
the church of St. Mary Redcliffe, contact with which probably fostered
Chatterton's love of the medieval and provided him with manuscripts
from which he learned to fabricate his own. During his apprenticeship
to a Bristol attorney he began writing imitation fifteenth-century poems.
Despite his prevarications on its origin, Chatterton's prose account of the
opening of the old Bristol bridge "from an ancient MS." (1768) was
accepted as genuine by local antiquarians. His poems interested Horace
Walpole until the latter's friends proved them forgeries. In April 1770,
by threatening suicide, Chatterton escaped his apprenticeship and went to
London. He now tried his hand at writing in the contemporary style, but,
unrecognized and faced with starvation, he committed suicide on 24
August, in his eighteenth year.

Although he wrote satires, songs and an opera in contemporary
English, Chatterton is chiefly remembered for the pseudomedieval
poems he ascribed to a fictitious monk, Rowley. Their language owes
more to Spenser than the fifteenth century, but garbled words from
etymological dictionaries and Speght's *Chaucer* gave a vague air of authenticity. Only one of the Rowley poems was published in Chatterton's
lifetime; the rest circulated in manuscript. They were gathered together
and exposed as forgeries by Thomas Tyrwhitt in 1777 in *Poems Supposed
to Have Been Written . . . by Thomas Rowley in the Fifteenth Century.*

Hazlitt dismissed Chatterton as merely interestingly precocious, and
the unoriginality of the Rowley poems' sentiments might seem to support
this view, but for many Romantics the "Marvellous Boy" became a
prophet and an ideal. Keats particularly owes much to his vivid descriptive
passages, varied rhythms and sensuous language.

Complete Works, ed. D. S. Taylor and B. B. Hoover, 2 vols., Oxford:
Clarendon Press, 1971.   T.W.

CHAUCER, Geoffrey (?1340–1400), son of John Chaucer, a vintner
of some standing, is first mentioned in records in 1357 as a member

of the household—probably a page—of Elizabeth, wife of Prince Lionel. Such bare official records are the sources of information about Chaucer's life as courtier and public servant, but they make no mention of him as a poet. In 1360 Edward III himself contributed to the ransom for Chaucer after his capture near Rheims, and from time to time Chaucer was employed in the service of the reigning king on missions abroad, though the exact nature of these is not always specified. Those which have aroused most speculation were to Genoa and Florence, since it is often thought that it was then that he became acquainted with the works of the Italian writers, Boccaccio, Dante and Petrarch, that influenced his own poems.

Throughout his life Chaucer received royal gifts, among them clothes, a daily pitcher of wine and amounts of money. Probably by September 1366 he had married Philippa, thought to be the daughter of Sir Payne Roet, though mention of her as his wife is not actually found until 1374. After living in royal households for a considerable number of years, in 1374 Chaucer obtained the lease, rent free, for the duration of his life, of the house above Aldgate, and in the same year was appointed controller of the wool custom and wool subsidy in the Port of London. Although the salary was only £10, there seem to have been legitimate means of increasing it. Later the controllership of the petty custom on wines and other merchandise was added, and in both positions he had in due course to have a permanent deputy, but by the end of 1386 both his appointments had been terminated and he had given up his house.

As he had been appointed a justice of the peace for Kent in 1385, Chaucer must already have been living in that county, for which he was also elected knight of the shire in 1386, but he sat for one session only. It has often been thought that in the two and a half years subsequent to this, when his public appointments were ended, Chaucer's fortunes were at a low ebb owing to the hostility of Gloucester and his followers while John of Gaunt was out of the country, but it is uncertain to what extent Gaunt was Chaucer's protector. (It was as an elegy on the death of Gaunt's first wife that Chaucer composed *The Book of the Duchess*, and Gaunt's third wife was Chaucer's sister-in-law.) On her death in 1387 his wife's annuities would cease and for some reason—perhaps to obtain ready money—Chaucer transferred his own Exchequer annuities to John Scalby in 1388. From that year onwards there are records of actions against Chaucer to recover debts.

However, when Richard II came of age in 1389, Chaucer was appointed clerk of the king's works, in which position he had charge of several royal properties. He had to oversee and pay many workmen and, presumably because he was known to have considerable sums, he was robbed twice in 1390. He relinquished this post after only two years, and between

1390 and 1400 held offices relating to the forest of North Petherton, though the precise nature of these is hard to define. Richard II in 1394 granted Chaucer another life annuity, which was confirmed and increased by Henry IV, Gaunt's son, who came to the throne in 1399, but Chaucer died in the next year.

It was as a courtier that Chaucer would first have come in contact with French works, and the *Roman de la Rose* was the French poem that exerted the greatest influence on his writings. It was under French influence that he composed *The Book of the Duchess* (probably soon after September 1369), the earliest work that can be definitely dated. The elegy is cast in the form of a love vision—an unusual use for this form—and not only eulogizes the duchess, but also attempts to console the bereaved husband. Written in octosyllabic couplets, the poem has fairly conventional elements, such as the May morning (when the dreamer awakes) and the singing of the birds or the description of the lady; and the story of the black knight's wooing of his lady is told in courtly-love terms. Nonetheless, Chaucer manages to make real the knight's grief and the sympathy of the dreamer, and through the knight's recalling of his love for his lady and the joys of their relationship the final impression is not one of overwhelming tragedy.

In contrast to this work, which is complete, compact and well proportioned, *The House of Fame*, in the same meter and using also the dream framework, is diffuse and unfinished. If lines 652–53 refer to the time when Chaucer was controller of customs, the date of composition must lie between 1374 and 1386. This poem displays a greater mastery of verse form, and also gives evidence both of Chaucer's interest in scientific matters and of Italian influence on his thought. After examining the Temple of Venus, the dreamer is whirled away by an eagle to the House of Fame to learn more of love as his reward for serving Venus and Cupid so long. The eagle seizes the opportunity to instruct his captive audience in many matters on the way. The House of Fame does not supply the dreamer with the tidings, and in the House of Rumour a pronouncement is about to be made when the poem breaks off. It is more than likely that Chaucer was carried along by his enthusiasm and then abandoned the poem, unable to draw it to a satisfactory conclusion.

Again, in *The Parlement of Foulys*, Chaucer uses the dream framework. Here he is guided into a garden where he sees first the Temple of Venus and then the assembly of birds, gathered on St. Valentine's Day to choose their mates. Three tercel eagles claim the formel eagle sitting on Nature's hand, and the matter is debated in the parliament, though the debate is really a discussion of courtly love. In various ways in the poem many facets of love are shown, though the dreamer himself is presented as merely an onlooker. Of the shorter works, *The Parlement* is undoubtedly the best; in structure and verse form it is the most controlled and has considerable variety and freshness in style. The poem was probably written around 1382, perhaps specifically for St. Valentine's Day.

The prologue (preserved in two versions) to *The Legend of Good Women* has won more praise than the legends themselves, in which Chaucer tells of women faithful in love. He alleges that he has been condemned to write these stories by the god of love for transgressing his law in describing Criseyde's infidelity and translating the *Roman de la Rose* (whether or not any of the existing translation is by Chaucer is uncertain). The dream framework, which reflects contemporary and literary conventions, is well known for its account of the poet's adoration of the daisy, which in his dream turns into Queen Alceste, who defends him. The whole poem shows much classical as well as French influence. It is probable that Chaucer lost interest in the legendary, which is incomplete. The two versions of the prologue were probably composed between 1382 and 1395, but the legends themselves may have been written before or afterwards.

A small number of short poems on various subjects are also preserved. These prove Chaucer's skill in complex verse forms, as does the unfinished *Anelida and Arcite*. He also made a prose translation, probably about 1380, of Boethius's *De Consolatione Philosophiae*, a work which had considerable influence on his own compositions, particularly *Troilus* and *The Knight's Tale*. An interest in science is evident in many of Chaucer's works, and in astronomy specifically in *A Treatise on the Astrolabe* (1391) and the recently discovered *Equatorie of the Planetis* (1392), if this is, as seems likely, attributable to him—it may even be a holograph.

The Canterbury Tales may reveal different qualities, but they do not surpass the long narrative poem, *Troilus and Criseyde*, which was completed probably in 1385–86. This, in its analysis of character and development of plot, is an outstanding achievement. Though Boccaccio's *Il Filostrato* may be its main source, Chaucer has created a highly original work by expanding, contracting or adapting to suit his purpose. Here for the first time Chaucer is dealing with living people, and of the three principal characters Criseyde and Pandarus are the most altered, the former into a very complex and human creature, whose defection the narrator (who becomes emotionally involved in the story) presents with great reluctance. Pandarus, through whose manipulations the love affair is furthered, able to laugh at himself and others, is the source of the poem's humor, and thus relieves what is essentially a tragedy. Unless the poem is read in the light of the code of courtly love, the modern reader cannot fully appreciate the development of the story in which Criseyde was not wrong in yielding to Troilus, but in proving faithless to him.

Although *The Canterbury Tales* was in the main a product of Chaucer's later years—the idea probably being conceived in the late 1380s—some of the tales were written at an earlier period and afterwards fitted into the great plan. Had this plan been carried out, the work would have comprised well over a hundred tales since each pilgrim was to tell two on the journey to Canterbury and two on the return. As it is, it consists of the "General Prologue" (with its remarkable portrait gallery) and twenty-four tales, two of them unfinished, and one by the canon's yeoman who joined the company en route. It comprises several blocks of tales whose order varies in the different manuscripts. Not only is the proper order uncertain, but there are indications in some tales that they themselves were not in their final form.

The idea of the tales within a framework was not new, even though the use of a pilgrimage was unusual. This, by providing an opportunity to bring together men and women of various walks of life, allowed considerable variety in the kinds of tale they told—the knight's chivalric romance, which started the series, the fabliau tale of the miller, the second nun's saint's life, the nun's priest's fable of Chaunticleer. The framework is no mere literary convention, but is given life by the exchanges between the pilgrims, some of which spark off tales told against each other, such as those of the miller and reeve. The pilgrims may represent certain types in society, yet Chaucer has created living people and generally their tales are suited to them. Although most of these are not original to Chaucer, he has as usual made them his own in the telling. What he has read and observed is blended together and presented with the freshness and humor that characterize so much of his poetry; and the descriptive and narrative powers, variety of style, and dramatic ability to be found in *The Canterbury Tales* admirably exemplify the many aspects of his skill.

The Book of the Duchess, 1369.
The House of Fame, ?1374–86.
Boethius: De Consolatione Philosophiae, ?1380.
The Parlement of Foulys, ?1382.
The Legend of Good Women, first version, 1380–86.
Troilus and Criseyde, 1385–86.
The Canterbury Tales, ?1387–1400 (some written earlier).

Works, ed. W. Thynne, London: Godfray, 1532.
The Canterbury Tales, ed. T. Tyrwhitt, London: Payne, 1775–78.

Works, ed. F. N. Robinson, revised 2nd edition, London: Oxford Univ. Press; Boston: Houghton Mifflin, 1957.
Chaucer's Poetry, ed. E. T. Donaldson, New York: Ronald Press, 1958.
Chaucer's Book of Fame, ed. J. A. W. Bennett, Oxford: Clarendon Press, 1968.

The Parlement of Foulys, ed. D. S. Brewer, London: Nelson; New York: Barnes & Noble, 1960.

The Book of Troilus and Criseyde, ed. R. K. Root, Princeton: Princeton Univ. Press, 1926.

The Canterbury Tales, ed. J. M. Manly and E. Rickert, 8 vols., Cambridge: Cambridge Univ. Press; Chicago: Univ. of Chicago Press, 1940.

J.B.

CHEEVER, John (1912–   ) was born in Massachusetts and educated at Thayer Academy. A contributor to *The New Yorker*, he has produced four collections of short stories since the first volume, *The Way Some People Live*, appeared in 1943. He has also written three novels—*The Wapshot Chronicle* (1957), *The Wapshot Scandal* (1964) and *Bullet Park* (1969). *The Wapshot Scandal* opens with snow falling on Christmas Eve but the idyll is comically shattered by modern American neuroses that arrive to perplex the comfortable Wapshot family. *Bullet Park* explores the relationship of nice Eliot Nailles and ambiguous Paul Hammer who meet in a town where the real estate agent is called Hazzard.   J.L.M.

CHESTERFIELD, Philip Dormer Stanhope, 4th Earl of (1694–1773), a notable politician and diplomatist, was ambassador to The Hague and secretary of state (1746–48), but is chiefly remembered in this field for his humanity and astuteness as lord lieutenant of Ireland (1745–46). His literary reputation rests on the letters to his illegitimate son, Philip Stanhope, which he began in 1737 when the boy was five, and later to his godson. Published posthumously, these didactic yet affectionate pieces are elegantly written and contain sensible, if sometimes overworldly, advice as well as considerable learning and experience of life.

Letters . . . to His Son, 1774.
Letters . . . to His Godson, ed. Earl of Carnarvon, 1890.

Collected Letters, ed. B. Dobrée, 6 vols., London: Eyre & Spottiswoode; New York: Viking Press, 1932.   T.W.

CHESTERTON, G. K. (Gilbert Keith) (1874–1936) was born in London, the son of an estate agent. He decided to follow art as a career and studied at the Slade School of Art. However, he began reviewing books and published his first volume, a collection of poems, in 1900. One of his greatest friends was Hilaire Belloc, whose work he illustrated and with whom he edited the periodical *Eye Witness*. His *Autobiography* is an intimate record of his spiritual development. Attracted by the tradition and orthodoxy of Catholicism, he was received into the Roman Catholic church in 1922.

The distinctive personality of G.K.C.—a combination of wit, exuberance, militant but genial faith, and optimism—lies behind his many varied works. He wrote many fictional extravaganzas and fantasies, including *The Man Who Was Thursday* (1908), *Manalive* (1912) and *The Flying Inn* (1914), with reflections on things as they were and as they ought to be, and even in his criticism—upon such diverse figures as Chaucer, Browning, Dickens and Shaw—wit, shrewdness and sympathy are present. As a champion of orthodoxy he wrote many essays and books about contemporary topics in religion and philosophy, and also published a study of St. Francis. The talent of Chesterton succeeds in instilling new life into ancient truths; by temperament a humorist, he animates traditional ideas by the constant unexpectedness of his style, humor and invention. In fiction and nonfiction he usually uses the commonplace as a starting point and then, by means of improvisation and paradox, extracts an important meaning from it.

(See also **Essays.**)

The Napoleon of Notting Hill, 1904.
Heretics, 1905.
The Man Who Was Thursday, 1908.
Orthodoxy, 1908.
The Victorian Age in Literature, 1913.
Autobiography, 1936.

The Father Brown Stories, London: Cassell, 1929; as *The Father Brown Omnibus*, New York: Dodd, Mead, 1933 (*f.* as *Father Brown*, 1954).
Stories, Essays and Poems, London: Dent; New York: Dutton, 1935.

O.K.

CHURCHILL, Charles (1731–64) was educated at Westminster School, married secretly, and so did not proceed to university. Although ordained in 1756 and appointed to the St. John's (Westminster) lectureship to succeed his father, his clerical career was jeopardized by his undisguised affection for theater, tavern and brothel. Having failed to ease his debts by teaching, he began writing in 1760 to support the wife he was to leave in 1761 and the children who were all to die before him.

The Rosciad (1761) rocketed Churchill to fame overnight. It was a directly abusive but clever attack on actors. A wave of replies and defenses appeared, and Churchill's fame was secure. He followed this up with two rather weak poems, *Night* (1761) and *The Ghost* (1762–63). Both are long and tedious, illuminated briefly by occasional pieces of sharp personal satire. About this time Churchill became a contributor to John Wilkes's periodical, *The North Briton*, which attacked Lord Bute's government in particular and Scots in general. These targets also provided the subject of an impressive satire, *The Prophecy of Famine*, in 1763. Churchill added his weight to the battle between Wilkes and Hogarth in *An Epistle to W. Hogarth*. The church authorities could no longer stomach his notoriety as a satirist and as an associate of the Hell-fire group, and he resigned his clerical appointments in 1763. He also published *The Conference* and *The Author*, an incisive attack on minor figures such as William Mason and John Kidgell, and sprang to Wilkes's defense again in *The Duellist*. During the early months of 1764 Churchill was as industrious as ever. He published an ironic eulogy to Lord Sandwich in *The Candidate*, and two dull if lucid discussions, *The Farewell* and *The Times*, concerned among other things with patriotism and homosexuality. *Independence* is a didactic poem on the theory of satire, and *Gotham* a long, moving poem, part satire, part lyric. In late October he set out to meet Wilkes in France, but died suddenly of a fever at Boulogne on 4 November, leaving the fine *Dedication to Warburton* unfinished.

Any poet who wrote so much so quickly, and who volubly scorned correction as Churchill did, was bound to write badly at times. His octosyllabic poems such as *The Ghost* and *The Duellist* are particularly uneven, but he maintained surprising control over the heroic couplet, his favorite medium. Although he owed a great deal to Pope and Dryden, there is in his verse a clear development towards a very individual style. This was more diffuse than that of either of his Augustan masters. By using repeated parallel syntactic structures and complex periodic sentences with numerous parentheses and digressions, he gave his poetry an entirely different rhythm, using the tight self-contained units of Augustan couplet technique to play against this larger movement. There is a corresponding development towards more ironic treatment of his victims, but Churchill remained from first to last a simple and effective moralist. It is unfortunate that his preeminence was so complete. There was no other contemporary satirist to present a worthy challenge and so compel Churchill to explore the full extent of his genius.

Poetical Works, ed. D. Grant, Oxford: Clarendon Press, 1956.
Correspondence of John Wilkes and Charles Churchill, ed. E. H. Weatherley, London: Oxford Univ. Press; New York: Columbia Univ. Press, 1954.   A.W.B.

CHURCHILL, Sir Winston (1874–1965), the elder son of Lord Randolph Churchill, was variously and brilliantly gifted—as statesman, historian, painter, scholar and man of action. He began his career in the army and served in South Africa, India, Cuba and Egypt, a period he recalls in *My Early Life* (1930). Then he held a number of important ministerial positions first as a Liberal and subsequently as a Conservative.

After years in the wilderness predicting the need to rearm against the threat of Hitler's Germany, he became prime minister during the Second World War and again from 1951 to 1955, when he retired. In 1953 he was made knight of the Garter and awarded the Nobel Prize for literature.

He began his writing career as a journalist, then wrote one novel, but finally turned to historical writing, as biographer (e.g., *Marlborough*) and as historian. His two surveys of the First and Second World Wars are important documents, dealing with the tactics and problems involved. Deliberate artistry is everywhere apparent in his writings; an admirer of Macaulay and Gibbon, he believed that history should be made as readable as fiction. Accordingly, his narratives are well plotted, infused with the personality of the author, and his style, though often overornate, ranges from the oratorical to the direct and simple. His best work is both a source of material for the scholar and of great interest to the general reader.

The World Crisis, 1911–1918, 5 vols., 1923–31.
My Early Life, 1930.
Marlborough, 4 vols., 1933–38.
Victory: War Speeches, ed. C. Eade, 1946.
The Second World War, 6 vols., 1948–54.
A History of the English-Speaking Peoples, 4 vols., 1956–58.   O.K.

CHURCHILL, Winston (1871–1947) was born in St. Louis, graduated from Annapolis (1894), and lived mainly in New Hampshire, where he was active in state politics. Churchill's novels reflect both a romantic conception of early American history and a progressive's concern over the political and business corruption of his own day. *The Crossing* (1904), one of his best works, is a historical romance set in frontier Kentucky during the Revolution. *Coniston* (1906) depicts struggles for political power and personal happiness in nineteenth-century New England. His other novels include *The Crisis* (1901), set in the South during and after the Civil War, *Mr. Crewe's Career* (1908), a story of railroad corruption, and *A Far Country* (1915), which is fictionalized muckraking.   J.W.

CIARDI, John (1916–) was born in Boston and has taught at a number of colleges. In 1956 he was appointed poetry editor of *The Saturday Review*. Lively rhetoric and tough wit, often coupled with the use of colloquialisms, endow his poetry with considerable power, yet he has also shown an aptitude for formal lyrics and a more tender mood. His first volume, *Homeward to America* (1940), was followed by *Other Skies* in

1947. Since that date he has produced collections of poems, such as *In the Stoneworks* (1961) and *Person to Person* (1964), nonsense verses for children, and idiomatic verse translations of Dante's *Inferno* (1954) and *Purgatorio* (1961). R.W.

CIBBER, Colley (1671–1757), actor, dramatist and theater manager, was born in London of a Danish father. He joined the United Company at Drury Lane in 1690 and made his mark as Lord Touchwood in Congreve's *The Double-Dealer*. His first play, *Love's Last Shift*, was produced at Drury Lane in 1696, Cibber playing the part of Sir Novelty Fashion. Vanbrugh's sequel, *The Relapse*, saw Cibber create his most celebrated role of Lord Foppington, which gained him a reputation for eccentric parts. A tragedy, *Xerxes* (1699), failed completely. By 1710 Cibber was the virtual manager of Drury Lane. An avid Hanoverian, his *Non-Juror* (1717), exposing Jacobitism, ran for eighteen consecutive days. On the death of Eusden, Cibber was appointed poet laureate (1730). He retired from active management in 1732 and wrote his *Apology*. His last appearance was in his *Papal Tyranny in the Reign of King John* (1745).

Cibber aroused almost universal resentment with a combination of high spirits, good humor and a thick skin. Pilloried throughout his life, notably by Pope in the revised version of *The Dunciad* (1743), his work won praise from Swift and Steele. His dramatic reputation rests on *Love's Last Shift* (1696, the first sentimental comedy), *The Careless Husband* (1705, a clever comedy of intrigue), *The Lady's Last Stake* and *The Provoked Husband* (from Vanbrugh). These demonstrate a facile theatrical technique, fluid and entertaining. Cibber's version of *Richard III* held the stage until 1821. His *Apology* is a valuable account of contemporary theatrical life.

Love's Last Shift; or, The Fool in Fashion, 1696.
The Tragical History of King Richard III, 1700.
She Would and She Would Not; or, The Kind Impostor, 1703 (*p.* 1702).
The Careless Husband, 1705 (*p.* 1704).
The Lady's Last Stake; or, The Wife's Resentment, 1708 (*p.* 1707).
The Provoked Husband; or, A Journey to London, 1728.
Apology for the Life of Mr. Colley Cibber, Comedian, 1740; ed. B. R. S. Fone, Ann Arbor: Univ. of Michigan Press, 1968.

Dramatic Works (with life), ed. D. E. Baker, 5 vols., London: Rivington, 1777. P.R.

CLARE, John (1793–1864), son of a thresher, Parker Clare, and Ann Stimson, was born at Helpston (Northamptonshire) and lived there until 1832, when he "flitted" to the neighboring village of Northborough.

He first went as a very small child to a dame school in his native village, and then, from seven to twelve, to a school at Glinton, where one of his fellow pupils was Mary Joyce, who was to become the center of his emotional life. About 1809 when he worked at the Blue Bell Inn, Helpston, he renewed his friendship with Mary and fell in love with her, but the relationship was broken off, to Clare's great distress. This personal disaster became associated in his mind with the enclosure of his native village, which also helped to destroy his idyllic Garden of Eden in which he and Mary had wandered as Adam and Eve.

After various laboring jobs and with no prospect of permanent employment, he came into contact in 1817 with a bookseller, J. B. Henson of Market Deeping, who showed interest in publishing Clare's poems. Though this scheme proved abortive, it led to a meeting with another bookseller, Edward Drury of Stamford, whose cousin was John Taylor of the London publishing firm of Taylor and Hessey, Keats's publishers. *Poems Descriptive of Rural Life and Scenery* was published in 1820, the year of Clare's marriage to Martha Turner. Within a year the book had gone into a fourth edition, largely as a result of the efforts of Admiral Lord Radstock, a zealous Evangelical, who became Clare's patron. Though the first volume has a good deal of juvenilia in it, there are some poems, such as "Harvest Morning" and "Summer Evening," which reveal Clare's distinctive voice. Three further volumes appeared between 1821 and 1835. In 1837 he entered Dr. Matthew Allen's asylum at High Beech, Epping, as a private patient. There he remained until July 1841 when he escaped and walked back to Northamptonshire, but in December 1841 he was committed to the asylum at Northampton and stayed there until his death in 1864.

Clare's poetry ranges from the lyrical to the satirical, and from the descriptive nature poem to works of an intensely personal kind. He was probably the finest naturalist in English poetry, not excepting Wordsworth or any of the other Romantics, and his knowledge of Northamptonshire birdlife and flora was unparalleled even by experts of his time. This closeness of observation, together with a quality of freshness, has made Clare's poetry best known for his pictures of natural life. His exactness of observation and description reminds one of Crabbe. He has other affinities with this poet in the manner of his tales in *The Shepherd's Calendar* and the satire of *The Parish*. The former of these poems, however, falls principally in the tradition of the eighteenth-century long descriptive poem and shows the influence of Thomson and Cowper. In a few visionary lyrics Clare recalls Blake, but he is never derivative. He speaks with his own distinctive voice, often using his own countryman's vocabulary, except when, to the poetry's loss, it was edited out by his publisher and advisers.

Poems Descriptive of Rural Life and Scenery, 1820.
The Village Minstrel and Other Poems, 2 vols., 1821.
The Shepherd's Calendar, with Village Stories and Other Poems, 1827.
The Rural Muse, 1835.

Poems written after 1835 appear in:
Life and Remains of John Clare, ed. J. L. Cherry, London: Warne, 1873.
The Later Poems of John Clare, ed. E. Robinson and G. Summerfield, Manchester: Manchester Univ. Press; New York: Barnes & Noble, 1964.

Poems, ed. J. W. Tibble, 2 vols., London: Dent; New York: Dutton, 1935.
Prose, ed. J. W. and A. Tibble, London: Routledge, 1951.
Letters, ed. J. W. and A. Tibble, London: Routledge, 1951; reprinted, New York: Barnes & Noble, 1970.   E.H.R.

CLARENDON, Edward Hyde, 1st Earl of (1609–74) was a Royalist statesman who wrote a *History of the Rebellion* (1702–04) and a *Life* of himself (1759). Despite the fact that he was personally involved in many of the affairs of which he wrote, Clarendon achieves a considerable breadth of sympathy and understanding. His character studies, combining classical amplitude with legal purposefulness and incisive statement, serve him admirably.

History of the Rebellion and Civil Wars in England, ed. W. D. Macray, 6 vols., Oxford: Clarendon Press, 1888.   J.D.J.

CLARK, John Pepper. See **African Literature.**

CLARKE, Arthur C. (Charles). See **Science Fiction.**

CLARKE, Marcus. See **Australian Literature.**

CLEAVER, Eldridge (1935–   ) was born in Wabbasaka (Arkansas) and has spent eight years of his life in prison, an experience vividly described in *Soul on Ice* (1968), a powerful and poetic polemic. Released from prison, he was rearrested for parole violation following a shoot-out between the Oakland police and the Black Panthers. A superior court judge ordered his release, ruling that he was a political prisoner. When this ruling was reversed by the higher appellate court, Cleaver fled the country in November 1968 rather than surrender himself. He lived for a time in Cuba before moving to Algeria where he has made his home in Algiers. His *Post-Prison Writings and Speeches* were published in 1969.

C.B.

CLEMENS, Samuel Langhorne. See **"Twain, Mark."**

CLEPHANE, Elizabeth. See **Hymns.**

CLEVELAND, John (1613–58), born at Loughborough (Leicestershire), son of a priest-cum-charity school usher, was educated at Christ's College, Cambridge, becoming lecturer in rhetoric and a fellow of St. John's College (1634). He opposed Cromwell's election for Cambridge in the Long Parliament and, at the outbreak of the Civil War, joined Charles at Oxford, later becoming judge advocate at Newark. In 1655 he was imprisoned at Yarmouth, but was released on appealing to Cromwell. He then went to London, where he died.

Cleveland was a most popular seventeenth-century poet, and although he seems never to have collected or arranged his poems for publication, collections of verse by or foisted on him begin to appear in 1647. By 1700 some thirty editions had come out. Cleveland was the best of the Royalist satirists. It is in this vein that he is most effective, for although there is obscurity, extravagance and structural looseness (pointing back to the Elizabethans), there is also real force and a firm sense of environment, emerging occasionally in couplets worthy of Dryden. Cleveland's carelessness and extravagance are more marked in his occasional and amorous verse, in which Donne's influence seems often just mannered eccentricity. Dryden's comment, that Cleveland provided "common thoughts in abstruse words," is only sometimes unfair.

Poems, ed. B. Morris and E. Withington, Oxford: Clarendon Press, 1967.

G.P.

CLOUGH, Arthur Hugh (1819–61) owed his well-trained mind and oversensitized conscience to the influence of his schoolmaster, Arnold of Rugby. Going up to Oxford in 1837, he was unsettled by the atmosphere of religious debate consequent on the Tractarian movement. After graduation he was elected to a fellowship, but in 1848 he relinquished it, mainly because he could not honestly subscribe to the Thirty-Nine Articles of the Church of England. A Continental tour took him to Paris during the 1848 Revolution and to Rome during its siege in 1849. Then, until 1852, he was principal of the nonsectarian University Hall, London. Following a nine-month search for suitable employment in America, he became an examiner in the Education Office, London, until his health began to fail. His friend Matthew Arnold commemorated him in "Thyrsis."

Much of Clough's poetry records his religious doubts and moral scruples. "Easter Day" has the cruel refrain, "Christ is not risen"; "Dipsychus" (published posthumously, 1869) is a long Faustian dialogue between the spokesmen of tender conscience and of worldly wisdom. This poem contains pungently satirical passages, whilst the well-known "Latest Decalogue" is a compact and memorable protest against the mammonism of the age. Humor is also prominent in *The Bothie of Toper-na-Fuosich* (1848), the long poem in which Clough lightheartedly rejoices on his release from Oxford. But his masterpiece is *Amours de Voyage* (s. 1858). Written, like *The Bothie*, in hexameters, this is a seriocomic psychological study of a young Victorian Prufrock, who cannot commit himself either in politics or in love.

Poems, ed. H. F. Lowry, A. L. P. Norrington, and F. L. Mulhauser, Oxford: Clarendon Press, 1951.
Correspondence, ed. F. L. Mulhauser, 2 vols., Oxford: Clarendon Press, 1957.   J.D.J.

COBBETT, William (1763–1835), born at Farnham (Surrey), son of a farmer, was educated at home and then served with the army in Canada (1784–91). From 1792 to 1800 he lived in America, where he began to write his characteristic brand of political–social–economic journalism. Returning to England, he founded *Cobbett's Political Register* (1802–35), many parts of which were reprinted as books on an enormous variety of subjects. Cobbett wrote an immense amount, and implicit in most of what he did is his vision of himself as a self-educated man of ability offering instruction to those who wish to learn like himself but are less able. He became member of Parliament for Oldham in 1832.

Being equally tireless in observing the life of his day and commenting on it, Cobbett offers an excellent picture of the early nineteenth-century mind at work. However utilitarian his motives might seem, Cobbett never wrote without strength and vigor, and nothing of his is without a rich display of his personal beliefs, prejudices and masculine directness of temperament. Essentially he was a simple man, deeply rooted in eighteenth-century ways and the old order of life in the country.

(See also **Political Pamphlets.**)

The Life and Adventures of Peter Porcupine, 1796.
Cobbett's Political Register, 1802–35.

A Grammar of the English Language, 1818.
Cottage Economy, 1822 (*s.* 1821–22).
Advice to Young Men . . ., 1829 (for 1830).
Rural Rides, 1830 (*s.* 1821–26); ed. G. D. H. and M. Cole, 3 vols.,
London: P. Davies, 1930.

Porcupine's Works, 12 vols., London: Cobbett & Morgan, 1801.
Autobiography, 1933; London: Faber & Faber, 1947 (selections from
works). W.R.

COHEN, Leonard. See **Canadian Literature.**

COLERIDGE, Samuel Taylor (1772–1834) was born at Ottery
St. Mary (Devonshire). After the death of his father (who was vicar and
headmaster of the grammar school) he was sent to Christ's Hospital
and then to Jesus College, Cambridge. During a fit of despair in 1793 he
enlisted as a dragoon. On being discovered and bought out by his brother
some months later, he returned to Cambridge but left shortly afterwards
without taking a degree. With Robert Southey he set up as a public lecturer
in Bristol and planned an ideal community in America, "pantisocracy," to
include twelve men and twelve women. In October 1795 he married Sara
Fricker, who bore him several children including Hartley Coleridge, who
himself became a poet, and Sara Coleridge, who helped to edit her father's
work. On the collapse of the pantisocratic scheme he published a weekly
paper, *The Watchman,* for several months and supported his family by
tutorships and casual journalism. He also became a Unitarian preacher and
was on the point of accepting a permanent appointment when the Wedg-
woods made available a pension which secured his independence. From
1797 onwards he was closely associated with Wordsworth, with whom he
planned and published *Lyrical Ballads,* his own contributions including
"The Ancient Mariner" and "The Nightingale." During this time he also
wrote the first section of "Christabel," the unfinished "Kubla Khan"
(composed, he said, in a semiconscious state) and several fine conversational poems, including "Frost at Midnight."

In September 1798 Coleridge went to Germany with the Wordsworths
and wintered at Göttingen in order to explore recent German learning.
On his return he removed his family to the Lake District, where Wordsworth had set up house. His marriage, which had not been happy, was
further undermined when he fell in love with Sara Hutchinson, sister of
Wordsworth's future wife. The poem "Dejection: An Ode," written first
as a letter to Sara, fully describes his state of mind. He worked as a journalist in London and from 1804 to 1806 as an official secretary in Malta,

after which he started a second journal, *The Friend*, which ran for over a year and was eventually reorganized into book form.

A growing addiction to opium and a final break with Sara Hutchinson made the years round 1810 particularly unhappy for Coleridge, but during the revival of cultural life associated with the Regency he found himself in demand as a lecturer and writer and began to recover. With Byron's encouragement his play *Osorio* (written in 1797) was produced and the still unfinished "Christabel" and "Kubla Khan" were published. From 1816 until his death he made his home at Highgate with the Gillman family, who helped him to control, though not relinquish, his opium addiction and to produce a series of works including *Biographia Literaria, Sibylline Leaves* (a new collection of his poems) and two *Lay Sermons* addressed to his countrymen in the immediate post-Napoleonic period.

The uncertainties, political and social, caused by the combined effects of the war and the Industrial Revolution gave Coleridge a new place as social teacher which, along with his brilliant conversational powers, made Highgate a place of pilgrimage in the following years. His two books, *Aids to Reflection* (a work of theological speculation and comment) and *On the Constitution of the Church and State*, were particularly influential both in England, where disciples of Coleridge became prominent in the Broad Church movement, and in America, where he was much read by the transcendentalists. Newman's disquiet concerning Anglicanism was prompted partly by the popularity of Coleridge's symbolic interpretations of Christianity.

Coleridge's contributions to poetry lay particularly in two directions. As a natural successor to Cowper he perfected the intimate conversational style in English poetry. Poems such as "This Lime-Tree Bower My Prison," "Frost at Midnight" and "Dejection" (which should be read in the long first version as well as the more commonly published one) display his extraordinary mastery of rhythm to convey the natural movement of the mind in informal situations. In his hands this style of poetry finally escapes the demands of decorum, which still shape it in poets like Cowper, and becomes an instrument suited to poets such as Keats and Shelley.

Coleridge's other great contribution is to the poetry of imagination. No poet has succeeded better in rendering the state of "entrancement" (Robert Graves's word): examples appear from time to time throughout his writing (including his manuscript notebooks). Three poems, "The Ancient Mariner," "Christabel" and "Kubla Khan," show this quality to an unusual degree. They display the power of Coleridge's imaginative writing at its intensest. In their subjects also, they reflect his extraordinary interest in the significance of the "visionary" element in human life—the relationship between its operation and problems of good and evil, for example, or metaphysical truth. The preoccupation is evident in the use of symbols such as those of sun, moon, serpent, mist or ice, which, used elsewhere in subordination, become here a part of the poetry itself, adding to its qualities of lucidity and vividness.

Coleridge's further contribution to literature lies in his criticism which, although never fully organized into a system, forms an important part of his *Biographia Literaria* and can also be traced through his lectures, notes and marginal comments. The supreme positions accorded both to the power of the imagination and to the workings of organic nature enable him to see previous writers, and especially Shakespeare, in a new light, free from classicist presuppositions. His criticism of Wordsworth, though exhibiting the gulf of misunderstanding that separates the two poets at some points, is particularly valuable since it is the result of his long and intimate engagement with the mind and personality of the poet as well as with the poems. His criticism, although sometimes uneven in quality, is particularly characterized by occasional brief passages of extreme complexity and profundity, such as the discussion of symbolism in *The Statesman's Manual* or the account of imagination and fancy in the *Biographia*. It is these passages which seem to have most stimulated later poets and critics. Coleridge's "seminal" quality here and elsewhere, first described by J. S. Mill, has become legendary.

(See also **Essays; Romantic Movement, The.**)

Poems on Various Subjects, 1796; new editions, 1797; 1803.
The Watchman, 1796.
Lyrical Ballads (with William Wordsworth), 1798.
The Friend, 1809–10; 3 vols., 1818.
Christabel; Kubla Khan: A Vision; The Pains of Sleep, 1816.
Lay Sermons: The Statesman's Manual, 1816; "*Blessed Are Ye . . .*," 1817.
Biographia Literaria, 2 vols., 1817.
Sibylline Leaves, 1817.
Aids to Reflection, 1825.
Poetical Works, 1828; new editions, 1829; 1834.
On the Constitution of the Church and State, 1830.

Specimens of the Table Talk of the Late S. T. Coleridge, ed. H. N. Coleridge, 2 vols., London: Murray, 1835.
Philosophical Lectures (MS. 1818–19), ed. K. Coburn, London: Pilot Press, 1949.

Poems, ed. J. B. Beer, London: Dent; New York: Dutton, 1963.
Collected Letters, 1785–1819, ed. E. L. Griggs, 6 vols., Oxford: Clarendon Press, 1956–68
Notebooks, ed. K. Coburn, London: Routledge; New York: Pantheon, 1957– .

Shakespearean Criticism, ed. T. M. Raysor, Cambridge, Mass.: Harvard
   Univ. Press, 1936.
Miscellaneous Criticism, ed. T. M. Raysor, Cambridge, Mass.: Harvard
   Univ. Press, 1936.

J.B.B.

COLLIER, Jeremy (1650–1726) was educated by his father, a schoolmaster in Ipswich, and at Gonville and Caius College, Cambridge.
In 1679 he became rector of Ampton (Suffolk) after experience as a private
chaplain. A High Church Tory advocating a return to the 1549 Prayer
Book and association with the Greek church, and strongly loyal to James
II, he was twice imprisoned for opposition to William III and outlawed
in 1696. The *Essays* (1697; 1705; 1709) avoid contention, but *A Short
View of the Immorality and Profaneness of the English Stage* (1698) began a
ten-year controversy in which Congreve and Vanbrugh joined. Though
Collier's attack lacks proportion, the effect was salutary.   H.N.D.

"COLLINS, Tom" (Joseph Furphy). See **Australian Literature**.

COLLINS, Wilkie (1824–89) was born in London, elder son of
William Collins, R.A., and godson of Sir David Wilkie, R.A. He
had vivid childhood memories of Hampstead Heath and of residence
on the Continent. In 1846 he left a tea importer's office for Lincoln's
Inn, being called to the bar in 1851. His first publications were a
biography of his father (1848) and a historical novel, *Antonina* (1850).
Success came through amateur theatricals, friendship with Dickens,
contribution of stories to *Household Words* and serialization of *The
Woman in White* (1860), which drew on a plot in Mejan's *Recueil des
Causes Célèbres*, read while in Paris with Dickens, Scribe and noted
French actors. Collins's best period of fiction ended in 1873 with *The New
Magdalen*. His concentration on propaganda themes, too unconventional
for many readers, and his overmechanical plotting were not good for his
art. When Dickens died, Collins's closest literary friend became Charles
Reade, who was less critically helpful. A reading tour of America
(1873–74), though less impressive than that of Dickens, brought Collins
financial success and many friends. He continued to write methodically
and courageously until his death, while suffering for years from chronic
illness, necessitating excessive doses of laudanum. He did not marry, but he
had a "morganatic" family; and for years he also shared his personal life
with Mrs. Caroline Graves, whose daughter he adopted.
   He gained an important place among mid-Victorian novelists and
dramatists. He collaborated with Dickens in "The Lighthouse" (1861),

"The Frozen Deep" (printed 1866) and *No Thoroughfare* (1867), and he dramatized a number of his novels. He was a great exponent of melodrama, his closest artistic link with Dickens, and held that the novel is a drama narrated and the play a drama acted. Scribe's concept of the well-made play thus applied to the novel of suspense and detection gave to *The Woman in White* and *The Moonstone* an influential achievement in English fiction. In the tradition of Scott and Poe, Collins paid more attention to structure than they. He also created in Cuff a more human professional detective than did Poe in Dupin. The perspective of time has now limited interest to a few novels and stories, but critics like T. S. Eliot and Dorothy Sayers have acclaimed his art in the present age of the popular thriller.

He was exact in description and setting; his main narrators were either ingenious criminals with self-tormenting moral scruples like Miss Gwilt, Magdalen Vanstone and Fosco, or more ordinary people, like Hartright and Marian Halcombe, fired by the passion to save or right the injured. Some of his women characters are among the most attractive of Victorian heroines. He used dreams, sleepwalking, premonitions, madness and other devices to intensify the drama, but his skill in arrangement and dispositions, possibly the product of his legal training, always gave him complete mastery over his story in terms of realistic art.

Antonina; or, The Fall of Rome, 1850.
After Dark, 1856.
The Queen of Hearts, 1859.
The Woman in White, 1860 (s. 1859–60; f. 1948).
No Name, 1862.
Armadale, 1866 (s. 1864–65).
The Moonstone, 1868 (f. 1934).
The New Magdalen, 1873.   I.M.W.

COLLINS, William (1721–59) was the son of a successful hatter and mayor of Chichester (Sussex), who gave his son the traditional education of a young man destined for the Church, first at Winchester, then at Queen's and Magdalen Colleges, Oxford. Despite Collins's manifest ability, the young poet disliked academic life as much as the prospect of ordination. A bequest in his mother's will enabled him to leave for London "to participate of the dissipation and gaiety." Collins's intelligence and genial indolence attracted both Garrick and Johnson, but his literary works were not well received and he destroyed many others in manuscript. He became dependent on the generosity of his nephew, William Payne of Magdalen, Oxford, and on the help of friends such as James Thomson, with whom he lived from 1746 to 1748. In 1751 he began to suffer from lengthening attacks of melancholy and insanity, and in 1754 he was moved for a time to a London asylum under the rigorous care of his sister Anne. He died in Chichester in June 1759.

His first poems were the undergraduate *Persian Eclogues*, published anonymously in 1742. These were a strange admixture of Eastern tale and Popean imitation. What little poetic value they have is the occasional passage of lyrical beauty, when his literary sensibility, constantly at war with his self-conscious sense, triumphs for a time. "Verses on Hanmer's Shakespeare" (1743) are almost as bad as the edition they celebrate, and "Dirge in Cymbeline" (1744) is little better. His reputation as a poet rests squarely on his next poems, the *Odes* of 1746, originally planned as a joint project with Joseph Warton. Half these odes are addressed to personified abstractions such as Fear and Simplicity. It is significant and ironic that Collins should have singled out "Simplicity," for like the other abstract odes it is sabotaged by his excruciatingly deliberate artistry. Again these poems contain fine passages, but only when Collins allows his muted pre-Romantic sensitivity a free rein and writes without an overwhelming consciousness of his Augustan heritage and a conviction of his own emotional inadequacy. Yet in two poems from this volume, the "Ode Written in the Beginning of the Year 1746" ("How sleep the brave") and "Ode to Evening," Collins displayed lyrical talent of the highest order. Both poems show his neo-Romanticism at its best. They make use of Augustan techniques such as classical and Miltonic allusion, tasteful poetic diction and objectifying stock personification to control emotion. Yet delicate observation and lyrical sensitivity transform them into brilliant and atmospheric evocations of mood. It has been justly noted that Collins's detail does not adorn a hollow Augustan moral in these poems; it *is* the moral. His later poetry never again achieved this perfect cohesion. "Ode on the Death of Mr. Thomson" (1749) has something of the same melancholy beauty, but "The Passions" (1750) is as unbalanced as his earliest work. Even the famous *Ode on the Popular Superstitions of the Highlands of Scotland* (1788) is a grossly uneven poem, the rather hysterical culmination of his long interest in neo-Romantic concerns such as the sublime, the picturesque and the horrific. In short, he was too often betrayed by enthusiasm and literary dishonesty in his desire to compensate for what he felt to be his own emotional shallowness; yet at his best he wrote some of the finest atmospheric lyrics in English poetry.

Persian Eclogues, 1742.
Odes on Several Descriptive and Allegorical Subjects, 1746.

The Poems of Thomas Gray, William Collins, Oliver Goldsmith, ed. R. H. Lonsdale, London: Longmans; New York: Barnes & Noble, 1969.

A.W.B.

COLMAN, George (the elder) (1732–94) was born in Florence, the son of the British envoy, and studied at Westminster School, Christ Church, Oxford and Lincoln's Inn. He began to write for the theater in 1760 (*Polly Honeycombe*), producing numerous comedies, farces and adaptations of foreign and classical plays. His most successful play was *The Jealous Wife* (1761). In 1766 he collaborated with Garrick in the comedy, *The Clandestine Marriage*. He became part owner of Covent Garden in 1767 and first produced Goldsmith's *She Stoops to Conquer* there. In 1776 he took over the Haymarket Theatre and ran it till ill health forced his resignation in 1789. Colman was an able manager and a friend of numerous great men of his age. He supplied the epilogue to Sheridan's *The School for Scandal*, translated Terence's comedies (1765) and wrote a new ending for *King Lear*.

Dramatic Works, 4 vols., London: Becket, 1777. **W.R.**

COLMAN, George (the younger) (1762–1836), son of the above, was educated at Westminster School, Christ Church, Oxford (1779–81) and Aberdeen, where he wrote plays which his father produced. He returned to London in 1784 and wrote incessantly, particularly travesties, farces and adaptations, amongst them a musical play, *Inkle and Yarico* (1787), a version of Godwin's *Caleb Williams*, *The Iron Chest* (1796), a musical entertainment, *Blue Beard; or, Female Curiosity* (1798), and a comedy *John Bull; or, The Englishman's Fireside* (1803). Colman lacked his father's business sense and lived recklessly. After imprisonment for debt and other misfortunes he was made examiner of plays by George IV in 1824 and proved notoriously squeamish and difficult. His published work is extensive and miscellaneous.

Dramatic Works (with memoir), ed. J. W. Lake, 4 vols., Paris: Bobée & Hingray, 1827. **W.R.**

COLUM, Padraic (1881–1972) first made his reputation as a playwright. He was a contemporary but not an imitator of Synge. *The Land* (1905), *The Fiddler's House* (1907), and *Thomas Muskerry* (1910) all dramatize in an original and expressive style problems of emigration, pauperdom and oppression in Ireland. The poet went on to explore the resources of the dramatic lyric and reintroduced the medieval Irish idea of the "poet's circuit," in which the poems form a saga of the Irish countryside.

Collected Poems, New York: Devin-Adair, 1953.
The Poet's Circuits: Collected Poems of Ireland, London: Oxford Univ. Press, 1960. **A.N.M.**

COMBE, William (1741–1823), after a dissipated youth, turned to authorship, producing an immense amount of indifferent work. In 1809 he wrote verses for pictures by Rowlandson, "The Schoolmaster's Tour," reprinted as *The Tour of Doctor Syntax in Search of the Picturesque* (1812), a mild burlesque in dull verse based on Gilpin's ideas. The form and content show the influence of Butler's *Hudibras* and the picaresque novel, but there is an essential tediousness, without individuality of places or persons. The ridicule of the picturesque has interest for those concerned with Gilpin's work, but hardly otherwise. Other collaborations with Rowlandson followed, but none had the same popular success.

A.E.

COMPTON-BURNETT, Dame Ivy (1892–1970) was educated at Royal Holloway College, where she made a special study of Greek. Her novels resemble each other, but those of no other writer. Each is a series of conversations, with the barest minimum of comment, description and explanation. The reader gets to know her characters as he does people in actual life and in drama (some of her books have been successfully produced on stage and radio), through their deeds and especially through their language.

Her books explore human relationships and motives in a setting of family life, nominally late-Victorian but essentially timeless. The family is sometimes extended to include the similarly insulated world of school. In scene after scene the exploration proceeds, the characters reveal what they hope to conceal and are remorselessly dissected and exposed. She casts a cold eye on human weakness and worse; without variation of tone she brings to light incest, matricide, infanticide—crimes which are merely the logical result of the wishes and feelings of her characters. Such themes motivate Greek tragedy, but there the Furies avenge blood. In these novels all is worked out and quietly hidden within the family circle. The terror and the tragedy are all the greater for the confinement and the understatement. "Her world is a terrible one. . . . But her survey of her chosen field is a profoundly moral task." (Edwin Muir.)

Dolores, 1911.
Pastors and Masters, 1924.
Brothers and Sisters, 1929.
Men and Wives, 1931.
More Women than Men, 1933.
A House and Its Head, 1935.
Daughters and Sons, 1937.
A Family and a Fortune, 1939.

Parents and Children, 1941.
Elders and Betters, 1944.
Manservant and Maidservant, 1947 (U.S. title: *Bullivant and the Lambs*).
Two Worlds and Their Ways, 1949.
Darkness and Day, 1951.
The Present and the Past, 1953.
Mother and Son, 1955.
A Father and His Fate, 1957.
A Heritage and Its History, 1959.
The Mighty and Their Fall, 1961.
A God and His Gifts, 1963.
The Last and the First, 1971.   A.M.O.

CONGREVE, William (1670–1729) was born in Yorkshire, but was
taken to Ireland by his father, an Army lieutenant. He attended a school at
Kilkenny and in 1686 went on to Trinity College, Dublin. In 1691 he
began to study law at the Middle Temple, though Charles Gildon wrote
that he was "of too delicate a taste, had a wit of too fine a turn, to be long
pleased with that crabbed, unpalatable study." His first publication was a
short novel, *Incognita*, with a preface claiming to have imitated drama in
the "design, contexture and result of the plot." His first stage comedy,
The Old Bachelor, was successfully performed in 1693 after help and encouragement from Dryden. This play also brought him to the notice of
Charles Montague, later earl of Halifax, who was to assist Congreve, a
Whig, in keeping his post of commissioner of the wine licences during the
Tory administration of 1710–14. Swift, too, helped in this way.
  Congreve's second comedy, *The Double-Dealer*, was poorly received,
but a third, *Love for Love*, was a success at the opening of a new theater in
Lincoln's Inn Fields. This year, 1695, also saw his essay, *A Letter concerning
Humour in Comedy* addressed to the critic John Dennis. A tragedy, *The
Mourning Bride*, was again successful and Congreve's reputation stood high
when he was attacked in Jeremy Collier's *A Short View of the Immorality
and profaneness of the English Stage* (1698). Unlike Dryden, Congreve
published an answer. In 1700 his last comedy, *The Way of the World*, was
not well received and he gave up drama, still continuing to write and
translate poetry. Pope dedicated his translation of Homer to him in 1720;
Addison and Steele were his friends. He never married, but he had affairs
with Anne Bracegirdle, the actress, and with Henrietta, duchess of
Marlborough. He died in London, leaving most of his fortune to the
duchess.
  Though *Incognita*, an amusing, mocking piece, is very readable and Dr.
Johnson declared that a passage in *The Mourning Bride* was incomparable,

the stage comedies are most famous. A metropolitan society in pursuit of pleasure, stylish and sophisticated, is reflected in these plays, but Congreve also believed that art must improve upon simple nature. His plays came after the comedies of Dryden, Etherege and Wycherley, and a scene like the one in which Millamant is at last persuaded to dwindle into a wife (*The Way of the World*, 4.1) perhaps marks the peak of achievement in the comedy of wit. Congreve has here created characters who, for all their wit, are capable of giving love and yet retaining their personal integrity. Even more, he has managed to convey a sense of how intelligence and delicacy in personal relations can hold at bay the forces of boredom and decay.

Incognita, 1692.
The Old Bachelor, 1693.
The Double-Dealer, 1694 (*p.* 1693).
Love for Love, 1695.
The Mourning Bride, 1697.
The Way of the World, 1700.

Complete Works, ed. M. Summers, 4 vols., London: Nonesuch Press, 1923.
Complete Plays, ed. H. Davis, Chicago: Univ. of Chicago Press, 1967.

J.C.

CONNOLLY, Cyril (1903–   ) was educated at Eton and Oxford. He is best known as a critic (for *The Observer* and then *The Sunday Times*), but his most notable work in many ways is his novel, *The Rock Pool* (1935), describing the life of a young man of the 1920s, wealthy, leisured and, in the author's own words, "as futile as any" among a group of writers and artists on the French Riviera. After rejection on grounds of possible obscenity by English publishers, it was issued in Paris. Connolly's autobiographical work, *Enemies of Promise*, followed in 1938 and his collection of essays, *The Condemned Playground*, in 1945. He also published a sequence of reflections, *The Unquiet Grave*, under the pseudonym "Palinurus" in 1944–45. It appeared first in *Horizon*, the periodical Connolly founded with Stephen Spender and ran in collaboration with him from 1939 to 1950. His critical work is distinguished for its balanced judgment and broad but discriminating sympathies.   A.P.

CONRAD, Joseph (1857–1924) was born Teodor Józef Konrad Korzeniowski near Berdichev in the Polish Ukraine, the son of a poet and man of letters. In 1862 his father, together with his family, was sent into exile in Russia for his participation in the revolutionary Polish nationalist movement. Conrad's mother died in exile three years later, and his father in 1869. After this isolated childhood passed under the influence of his father's thwarted literary ambitions and gloomy mysticism, Conrad was sent to school in Cracow, but soon determined to go to sea. He traveled alone to Marseilles and based himself there for four years. In *The Mirror of the Sea* (1906) and *The Arrow of Gold* (1919) he described incidents, both at sea and on land, from his romantic adventurous life in those years. In 1878 he came to England and, although he spoke almost no English, joined the merchant navy. He was sent to the Far East, and there on a series of voyages, particularly those made with the *Vidar* between Singapore and Borneo, he became immersed in the landscape and people of isolated trading stations which, together with his knowledge of the sea, were to form the fabric of his first novels and stories. In 1886 he was naturalized as a British citizen and passed the master mariner's examination which allowed him to serve as a captain. Three years later his first novel, *Almayer's Folly*, was begun—but at the time Conrad had no intention of becoming a professional writer. In 1890 he obtained command of a steamboat in the Upper Congo, an ill-fated expedition which in ruining his health forced his retirement from the merchant navy in 1894. From then on he dedicated himself to writing.

A deliberate and painstaking artist, he formed friendships with most of his notable contemporaries—Henry James, John Galsworthy, Edward Garnett, George Bernard Shaw, William Rothenstein, Ford Madox Hueffer (later Ford), Norman Douglas and, for a time, H. G. Wells. It was not, however, until after the publication of *Chance* (1913) that Conrad achieved popular success. The second part of his life was uneventful, being occupied with his writing and broken only by trips to France and Poland, towards which he was increasingly drawn back in his final years—the expression, perhaps, of a conflict that Conrad never resolved between his position as an exile and his deep sense of moral commitment.

In his essay on "Swinburne" (1920) T. S. Eliot remarked that the earlier novels of Conrad were important because the language of them was struggling "to digest and express new objects, new groups of objects, new feelings." While Conrad's stature as a writer is now firmly established, the nature of his achievement, which rises out of the very newness that Eliot praises, involves difficult critical problems. E. M. Forster in *Abinger Harvest* (1936) criticized his obscurity and mistiness: "the secret casket of his genius contains a vapour rather than a jewel." F. R. Leavis, one of Conrad's strongest admirers in other respects, admits in *The Great Tradition* (1948) that he seems intent at times "on making a virtue out of not knowing what he means." In "Heart of Darkness" (1902) and "The Secret Sharer" (1912), for example, some of Conrad's finest work, his language circumscribes feelings and qualities in his characters which by his own admission he cannot find a name for. In *Lord Jim*

(1900), however, Conrad makes use of this indefiniteness in his mind to shape the structure of his fiction and so achieves a modification of the novel as a form.

The mould of Jim's character indicates, too, the area in which Conrad's imagination worked with greatest power and fertility. His central figures —Almayer, Gould, Nostromo, Verloc, Heyst, Kurtz—are characterized at one level by an unwillingness to settle for obvious and immediate horizons. This romantic element in human personality which strikes Conrad, in varying degrees, as emotionally and ethically ambiguous, becomes the focus for his deep moral concern. On the one hand, he admires the human being who has learned while young to hope, to love and to put its trust in life; on the other, he records the incalculable damage that occurs to the individual and to the fabric of human relationships through unrealistic idealism and self-deceit.

In this respect his major achievement may be described as the power to amplify the inner qualities of his characters' lives through the environment in which they live. In *Nostromo* (1904) the Gould Concession of the San Tomé mine acts both as the physical pivot of the book's dramatic action and as a focus for the morally and spiritually deadening effects of obsessively material concerns in the lives of its central characters. At the same time Conrad's vitality in the depiction of the landscape of Costaguana permits this to be seen as a matter of general human significance. But the power of Conrad's imagination in projecting the convergence between the inner and the physical landscapes—of which Kurtz in "Heart of Darkness" provides the clearest example—induces in his fiction a severity which may perhaps have been necessary to the level at which he understood personality, but which is achieved at the expense of those humanizing qualities which exist abundantly, for example, in the last plays of Shakespeare. To borrow Dr. Johnson's distinction, Conrad's characters are easy to admire, but not to love; and even in their waywardness they harbor too much danger to be endearing.

Almayer's Folly, 1895.
An Outcast of the Islands, 1896 (*f.* 1951).
The Nigger of the "Narcissus," 1897.
Lord Jim, 1900 (*f.* 1964).
Youth—a Narrative; and Two Other Stories ("Heart of Darkness" and "The End of the Tether"), 1902.
Nostromo, 1904.
The Secret Agent, 1907 (*f.* as *Sabotage*, 1936).
Under Western Eyes, 1911.
'Twixt Land and Sea Tales (including "The Secret Sharer"), 1912.
Chance, 1913.

Victory, 1915 (f. as *Dangerous Paradise*, 1930).
The Shadow Line, 1917.
The Arrow of Gold, 1919.
The Rover, 1923.

Works, London: Dent; New York: Dutton, 1946–
Letters from Joseph Conrad, 1895–1924, ed. E. Garnett, London: Nonesuch
   Press; Indianapolis: Bobbs-Merrill, 1928.
Letters to R. B. Cunninghame Graham, ed. C. T. Watts, Cambridge:
   Cambridge Univ. Press, 1969.   P.G.M.

COOPER, James Fenimore (1789–1851) was born at Burlington
(New Jersey). His father, William, had made a fortune during the War
of Independence and acquired vast tracts of land west of Lake Otsego in
New York. The experience of creating a settlement there, Cooperstown,
where the family moved in 1790, is described by the father in *A Guide to
the Wilderness* (1810); his son portrayed the settlement and his father in
The Pioneers (1823). James's upbringing combined the rigors of frontier
life with the refinements of a gentleman's education. He went to Yale in
1803 and after being expelled for misconduct in 1805, he became an
ordinary seaman (1806–07) and then a midshipman in the U.S. Navy
(1808). Although he soon retired from active service, Cooper retained a
passionate interest in the sea and the navy throughout his life. In 1811 he
married into the wealthy and well-established De Lancey family and settled
down to the life of a landed proprietor. He became head of the family in
1819, to find that the Cooper estates were heavily in debt. He made a poor
first attempt at fiction, *Precaution* (1820), an imitation of fashionable
English novels of manners, but then had an instant success with *The Spy*
(1821), a skillful "tale of the neutral ground" in the War of Independence,
written on the model of Sir Walter Scott's romances. From then on he
was a dedicated and prolific author; he was to write over thirty novels as
well as books of social and political commentary and of travel, and a vast
History of the Navy of the United States.

His next novel, *The Pioneers* (1823), introduced his most powerful
character, the white hunter Natty Bumppo (also known as Leatherstocking, Deerslayer, Pathfinder, etc.), and the themes which run throughout
Cooper's work—the American frontier experience, the confrontation of
the wilderness, the fate of the Indian, the destinies of class, nation and
race. Two more "Leatherstocking tales" followed in *The Last of the
Mohicans* (1826), his most popular novel, and *The Prairie* (1827), where
Bumppo dies. He published his first sea tale, *The Pilot*, in 1824, to be
followed by the more assured *The Red Rover* (1827) and *The Water-Witch*
(1830) in the same genre. Cooper found the ocean as exciting a theater for

his fiction as the wilderness; these early sea novels combine meticulous description of seamanship with rich romance plotting and atmosphere. His most somber tale of this period is *The Wept of Wish-ton-Wish* (1829), set in an early Puritan settlement.

From 1826 to 1833 he lived in Europe, mainly in France. There he was a close friend of Lafayette, the French Republican leader, and took a keen and sometimes controversial interest in European politics and the comparison of European and American civilization. From this interest came *Notions of the Americans* (1828) and three historical novels set in Europe, *The Bravo* (1831), *The Heidenmauer* (1832) and *The Headsman* (1833), which illustrate the development of forces of social change.

Cooper increasingly devoted himself to the American political scene. He was dismayed at the general crudity, greed and dishonesty he found on his return. His own position was complicated; a landowner, whose guilt of possession was partly assuaged by the notion of stewardship, he believed in the democratic system, but wanted the people to choose their leaders from his own class, which constituted the natural aristocracy of the country. He felt the people were increasingly being misled and manipulated by money oligarchies, corrupt politicians, and their instrument, the popular press.

Cooper's pessimism was increased by press attacks on his books and social position. These finally came to a head when he had trouble with his tenants at Cooperstown, and in the ensuing controversy sued two papers for libel. He was at war with American newspapers for the rest of his life. His work now reflected his social thinking much more openly. *A Letter to His Countrymen* (1834) and *The American Democrat* (1838) are direct political statements. *The Monikins* (1835) was a blatant politieal allegory, and the two novels *Homeward Bound* and *Home As Found* (1838) are directed at the contemporary scene, including in the latter a representation of Cooper's own row with his tenants. *Homeward Bound* turned into a sea and desert tale in the writing.

He returned to the American past and Leatherstocking in *The Pathfinder* (1840) and *The Deerslayer* (1841), and to sea fiction in *Afloat and Ashore* (1844), *Jack Tier* (1848) and *The Sea Lions* (1849). These later sea novels, much changed in tone from the romantic work of the 1820s, together with *The Crater* (1847), a story of an island utopia, powerfully reveal Cooper's increasing pessimism and a growing religious preoccupation. Probably his most substantial achievement of this final period, however, after the completion of the Leatherstocking tales, was the Littlepage trilogy (1845–46) of *Satanstoe*, *The Chainbearer* and *The Redskins*, a family chronicle which brings together most of Cooper's themes and concerns, including the topical antirent controversy. He was busy writing up to his death in Cooperstown in 1851.

The quality of Cooper's work varies considerably, although most of it is still readable. He had a vast international reputation, equal to Sir Walter Scott's. The popularity of the Leatherstocking tales, particularly *The Last of the Mohicans*, is undiminished. His reputation as a literary pioneer is secure—in his use of the American frontier, the development of the historical novel, sea fiction, the family chronicle, even new genres like the courtroom novel. So is his achievement in creating great figures like Leatherstocking or Ishmael Bush (in *The Prairie*), who have a mythic resonance, and in his evocation of the sublimity of wilderness and ocean. The faults are plain enough, too—stilted style, crude comedy, diffuseness, weak characterization, trivial plot, the biased tone of his own gentility and class. He allowed his personal and contemporary concerns to inhibit his fiction's imaginative tolerance and invention.

Although it has become increasingly clear that Cooper's "adventures" cannot be separated from the social and political issues they often intricately symbolize, they can also have an intrinsic value apart from social reference. Cooper's work is full of a profound sense of the littleness of men and their social arrangements against the background of wilderness, ocean and the process of time. It is not surprising that Conrad admired his work. His concern with the fate of the Indian, of ambiguous whites like Leatherstocking who both undertake and oppose American expansion westward, of his own patrician class in decline, is subsumed in a general concern, religious or naturalistic, for human fate, felt most clearly in his later sea fiction. This concern often issues in a sense of the inevitable corruption of the mass of men in the hands of an inscrutable providence, but it also involves a sense of wonder at nature and the spectacle of the human comedy, at the urge to possess, survive and adapt, especially in the early work. Cooper himself never entirely lost his relish for invention and experiment and in his last decade he was engaged in variously successful attempts both at first-person narration and also double narrations combining youth and age, past and present, wonder and despair, contrivance and stoicism. Cooper's strength is often concealed beneath apparent superficiality and tedium, but there is greatness of a kind in the Leatherstocking tales, most of the sea fiction, and the Littlepage trilogy.

The Spy, 1821.
The Pioneers, 1823.
The Pilot, 1824.
The Last of the Mohicans, 1826 (*f.* 1920; 1936; as *Last of the Redskins*, 1949).
The Prairie, 1827.
The Red Rover, 1827.
Notions of the Americans, 1828.
The Wept of Wish-ton-Wish, 1829.

The Water-Witch, 1830.
The Bravo, 1831.
The Heidenmauer, 1832.
The Headsman, 1833.
The Monikins, 1835.
The American Democrat, 1838.
Homeward Bound, 1838.
Home As Found, 1838.
The History of the Navy of the United States, 1839.
The Pathfinder, 1840 (*f.* 1953).
The Deerslayer, 1841 (*f.* 1913; 1943; 1957).
Satanstoe, 1845.
The Chainbearer, 1845.
The Redskins, 1846.
The Crater, 1847.
Jack Tier, 1848.
The Oak Openings, 1848.
The Sea Lions, 1849.
The Ways of the Hour, 1850.

Letters and Journals, ed. J. F. Beard, 6 vols., Cambridge, Mass.: Harvard Univ. Press; London: Oxford Univ. Press, 1960–68.   D.B.H.

CORBET (T), Richard (1582–1635), sometimes referred to as Bishop Corbet as he held the sees successively of Oxford and Norwich, was an unconventional English clergyman of his time. He was a friend of Ben Jonson and a frequenter of the Mermaid Tavern. His attitude in verse, as may be inferred from his life, was strongly anti-Puritan. He is remembered mainly for one poem, "The Fairies' Farewell," a pre-Chesterton lament for a Catholic Merry England which has become blighted and perverted by Puritanism. *Certain Elegant Poems* was published posthumously in 1647.

Poems, ed. J. A. W. Bennett and H. R. Trevor-Roper, Oxford: Clarendon Press, 1955.   C.P.

CORNWALLIS, Sir William. See **Essays.**

CORSO, Gregory (1930–   ) was born in Greenwich Village (New York City) of Italian parents. At the age of seventeen he was sent to prison for three years for theft. Self-educated, he came to Harvard in 1954, and the following year his first book of poetry, *The Vestal Lady of Brattle*, was published. Friendships with Allen Ginsberg and Jack Kerouac helped to win him a wider audience and his second book of poems, *Gasoline*, was published in 1958. Two more volumes, *The Happy Birthday of Death* (1960) and *Long Live Man* (1962), followed. Corso's poems are distinguished by the oxymoronic clarity of his images.   W.D.S.

COTTON, Charles (1630–87), living at Beresford Hall (Staffordshire) by the River Dove, was able to provide a second part ("Instructions how to angle for a trout or grayling") for his friend Walton's *Compleat Angler* in 1676. He wrote "potboilers" and burlesques, such as *Scarronides* (1664–65), a travesty of Virgil's *Aeneid* 1 and 4. As a translator he is more memorable, his *Essays of Montaigne* (1685) preserving the freedom and informality of the original. The posthumous *Poems* (1689) made little impact until some of the pieces were taken up by Lamb and Wordsworth.

Collected Poems, ed. J. Beresford, London: Cobden-Sanderson, 1923; also
   ed. J. Buxton, London: Routledge; Cambridge, Mass.: Harvard
   Univ. Press, 1958.   J.C.

COVERDALE, Miles (1488–1568) was born in Yorkshire and educated at Cambridge, where as an Augustinian friar he formed one of a reforming group of clerics. Encouraged by Thomas Cromwell, he produced his own English version of the Bible (1535), dedicated to Henry VIII, and the first complete text in English. His Great Bible of 1539 was ordered to be used in churches. He became bishop of Exeter in 1551 but fled to the Continent on the accession of Mary. His strong Protestant views militated against his preferment on his return from exile. (See also **Bible, The.**)   A.P.

COWARD, Sir Noël (1899–   ) was educated at the Italia Conti Academy and began his career as an actor before becoming a dramatist and composer. His well-made entertainments fall into two groups, the ironic and the sentimental, though his comedies of the 1920s, matching the contemporary mood of smart sophistication, effectively combine the bitter and the sweet. In his best plays, *Bitter Sweet* (1929; *f.* 1940), *Private Lives* (1930; *f.* 1931) and *Design for Living* (1933; *f.* 1933), the morality of the Mayfair set is treated with amused contempt and represented in brilliant and witty dialogue. He has written two volumes of autobiography, *Present Indicative* (1937) and *Future Indefinite* (1954).

Collected Short Stories, London: Heinemann, 1962; 1969.
Lyrics, London: Heinemann, 1965; New York: Doubleday, 1967.   O.K.

COWLEY, Abraham (1618–67), the posthumous son of a London merchant, was a precocious child, reading Spenser avidly and writing an epic romance of his own at the age of ten. While he was still at Westminster School his first volume of verses appeared, *Poetical Blossoms* (1633), including romances and elegies. A much enlarged edition followed in 1636, and a pastoral play, *Love's Riddle* (1638), also belongs to this period. At Trinity College, Cambridge he became friendly with Crashaw and with William Hervey, who prompted Cowley to write religious verse, probably persuading him to begin his "Davideis." In 1640 Cowley was elected a fellow of his college, but in 1643 he left Puritan Cambridge and joined the royal court at Oxford. A friend of Falkland, he became secretary to Lord Jermyn and probably left England with the queen, becoming her cipher secretary in 1644. He performed confidential, often dangerous, state missions for the exiled court and mixed with such émigrés as Evelyn, Hobbes, Davenant and Waller. In 1654 Cowley was imprisoned in London, apparently apprehended as a spy, but his release in 1655 brought him under Royalist suspicion. He retired to study medicine, was awarded a doctorate of medicine at Oxford in 1657, but at the death of Cromwell rejoined Jermyn. At the Restoration he was reinstated in his Cambridge fellowship, but failing to procure court preferment, he retired to Greenwich and then Chertsey, devoting himself to his botanical writings and his essays. Cowley's literary reputation, however, in the last half-dozen years of his life was enormous. He was a founder member of the Royal Society, a shareholder in Davenant's theater, received an M.D. at Cambridge and was buried with great splendor in Westminister Abbey.

Cowley's literary writings include poems, essays, and plays. His Latin comedy, *Naufragium Joculare*, was performed when Cowley was an undergraduate, and for the visit of Prince Charles to Cambridge (1642) he wrote another comedy, *The Guardian* (1650), which he revised for the Restoration theater in 1661 as *Cutter of Coleman Street*. His first volume of mature poems was *The Mistress* (1647), a cycle of love poems intended to rival Waller's Sacharissa poems, and written and circulated in manuscript in Paris. In 1656 a volume of collected poems appeared that added "Miscellanies," mainly occasional verses, "Pindarique Odes," a form Cowley popularized, and "Davideis; or, A Sacred Poem of the Troubles of David." Later poems included odes celebrating the Restoration and other occasional verses collected in 1663, and Latin poems which include a botanical poem, *Plantarum*, in two books (1662), to which Cowley added another four books. The prose works of greatest interest are his pamphlet *A Proposition for the Advancement of Experimental Philosophy* (1661), *A Vision concerning His Late Pretended Highness Cromwell* (1661), and the essays, published posthumously and including an autobiographical sketch. Cowley's works were collected after his death and went through some fifteen editions before the end of the century.

Cowley's verse ranges in style from his early Metaphysical manner, through Cavalier lyricism to Restoration neoclassicism, but the controlling idea remains constant, that of a universe ordered by divine love acting through natural phenomena. Science, the study of such phenomena, was therefore important and specially relevant for Cowley. His scientific imagery reflects this by being closely integrated with his meaning, and the odes to Harvey, to Scarborough, and to the Royal Society show an intimate knowledge of contemporary scientific advances. In *The Mistress* human love is seen as the parallel of divine love, and in the "Davideis" the theme is the conflict between divine order expressed by the lives of David and Jonathan and the sterile disorder of Satan and his earthly emissary, Saul.

(See also **Essays; Metaphysical Poetry.**)

Poetical Blossoms, 1633.
The Mistress, 1647.
Poems (including "Davideis" and "Pindarique Odes"), 1656.
Cutter of Coleman Street, 1661.
A Vision concerning . . . . Cromwell, 1661.

Works, ed. T. Sprat, 1668 (includes essays).

Works, ed. A. B. Grosart, 2 vols., Edinburgh: for private circulation, Chertsey Worthies Library, 1881.
English Writings, ed. A. R. Waller, 2 vols., Cambridge: Cambridge Univ. Press, 1905–06.   H.N.D.

COWPER, William (1731–1800) was the son of the rector of Great Berkhamsted (Hertfordshire). Early experiences laid the foundation of his later mental troubles. His mother died when he was six, leaving abiding memories of love and deprivation, and he was sent to a local boarding school where persistent bullying brought on nervous troubles. He was happier at Westminster School, but misguidedly went on to study law, for which he was temperamentally unsuited. He loved his cousin Theodora, daughter of Sir Ashley Cowper, and they were engaged for some years, but her father eventually broke off the engagement, as Cowper lacked prospects and was showing signs of mental instability. To this shock was added that of his father's death at about the same time. Cowper's family pressed him to make a career as a clerk in the House of Lords, and the strain of taking an examination brought on insanity and attempted suicide. He became the victim of religious melancholia and a Calvinist certainty of damnation from which he never escaped. For a time he found comfort in the evangelical cheerfulness of the Unwin family at Huntingdon. When Mr. Unwin died, Cowper accompanied Mrs. Unwin to Olney and here became a friend of the Rev. John Newton, with whom he collaborated in *Olney Hymns* (1779). Newton's overzestful personality disturbed Cowper's precarious mastery over his religious terrors and after a dream of final damnation in January 1773 he never doubted he was lost. Newton went to London, and in the years that followed Cowper lived a quiet life in which everyday domestic and country objects assumed great significance as reassurances against the threat of melancholia and his settled belief in ultimate damnation. He was helped by fortunate friendships. Mrs. Unwin turned him to poetry by suggesting the verse satires, and Lady Austen, a neighbor in 1781 and for a year or two afterwards, infected him with enough of her own cheerfulness to inspire "John Gilpin" (1782) and suggested *The Task* (1785), the publication of which brought him widespread popularity. Cowper's last years were rendered needlessly depressing by his misguided decision to translate Homer. After Mrs. Unwin died in 1796 he sank into hopeless melancholia, poignantly suggested in "The Castaway" (1798), his last poem.

Cowper's verse was a refuge from melancholy, providing healthy but soothing exercise for his mind as his country life did for his body. At its flattest, as in the palely Popean opening of *The Task*, it reads like self-diversion, but triviality falls away when his poetry gets out of doors and *The Task* as a whole, moving discursively over a whole range of topics illustrating the superiority and pleasures of a country life, has a quiet naturalness and closeness of observation which shows how carefully its author had studied the countryside. Cowper's nature poetry is the finest the eighteenth century produced, and it enjoyed a high reputation all through the Romantic period. Book 5 of *The Task*, with its description of the countryside under snow, shows him at his best. The unfinished "Yardley Oak" is doubly interesting as a pioneer example of reflective poetry dealing with the Romantic theme of growth and decay and also as the best assimilation of the Miltonic blank verse tradition before Wordsworth's.

The fine gift for treating emotion cleanly, firmly and without hysteria, surprising in view of the terrible record of his life, is evident in Cowper's letters and hymn writing as well as in his best poetry. Tenderness, kindness and sympathy with the weak and unfortunate he could always command (witness the delicate awareness of living fragility in his animal poems). The analogy with his own spiritual helplessness is obvious, and was clear to him. Also, he shares with a very few religious poets, such as Herbert, the ability to record spiritual experiences with complete steadiness of tone. "The Castaway," for instance, rises from his favorite images of shipwreck to a terrible but objectively presented analogy with his own spiritual desolation. But one should not stress unduly the somber side of Cowper's personality. His letters and verses alike show genuine moments of gaiety, and as a recorder of the quiet pleasures of eighteenth-century country life he is virtually without equal.

(See also **Hymns.**)

Olney Hymns (with John Newton), 1779.
Poems, 2 vols., 1782–85.
The Task, 1785.
The Iliad and Odyssey of Homer, 1791.
Translations from Madame Guion [*J. M. Guyon*], ed. W. Bull, 1801.

Works, ed. R. Southey, 15 vols., London: Baldwin & Cradock, 1835–37.
Poems, ed. H. S. Milford, 1905; revised N. Russell, London: Oxford Univ. Press, 1967.
Correspondence, ed. T. Wright, 4 vols., London: Hodder & Stoughton, 1904.
Unpublished and Uncollected Letters, ed. T. Wright, London: Farncombe & Sons, 1925. W.R.

COZZENS, James Gould (1903–), born in Chicago, comes of a family established in New England since the eighteenth century. From his four apprentice novels (the first published while he was still at Harvard) Cozzens's ideal person—an aristocrat (*Michael Scarlett*) who can temper instinct with discipline (Ruth in *Cock Pit*)—emerges as Stellow, a man of "intelligent ruthlessness" in *The Son of Perdition* (1929). Cozzens's first major novel, *S.S. San Pedro* (1931), show what happens to ordinary men when such a natural leader loses his judgment. Yet reason, which a good leader must have, can lead to the inactivity of Herbert Banning in *The Last Adam* (1933) where Cozzens prefers the sensual egoist Doctor Bull. Mr. Lecky in *Castaway* (1934) personifies the incompetent mass, and such "cheap people" are the parishioners of Ernest Cudlipp in *Men and Brethren* (1936). As a "realist" Cudlipp does "the best he can with things as they are," and the lawyer hero of *The Just and the Unjust* (1942) comes to learn that "standing off and saying you don't like the way things are is kid stuff." One of Cozzens's most reasonable realists is Colonel Ross of *Guard of Honor* (1948), who is on hand to save the unreasonable from the consequences of their folly. But, as always, Cozzens knows the limitations of human reason, even though there is no other guide. This is the bitter knowledge of Arthur Winner in *By Love Possessed* (1957). The novel *Morning Noon and Night* appeared in 1968.

Confusion, 1924.

Michael Scarlett, 1925.
Cock Pit, 1928.
The Son of Perdition, 1929.
S.S. San Pedro, 1931.
The Last Adam, 1933 (U.K. title: *A Cure of Flesh*; *f.* as *Doctor Bull*, 1933).
Castaway, 1934.
Men and Brethren, 1936.
Ask Me Tomorrow, 1940.
The Just and the Unjust, 1942.
Guard of Honor, 1948.
By Love Possessed, 1957 (*f.* 1961).
Children and Others, 1964 (short stories).
Morning Noon and Night, 1968.   J.L.M.

CRABBE, George (1754–1832) was born at Aldeburgh (Suffolk), a place which forms the setting for much of his poetry, in particular *The Borough*. The son of a minor customs official, he was initially apprenticed to a surgeon, but in 1780 he decided to seek a literary career in London. After some difficulty he eventually secured the patronage of Burke, who paid for the publication of *The Library* (1781) and introduced him to C. J. Fox, Sir Joshua Reynolds and, through the latter, Dr. Johnson. Crabbe took orders and became curate of Aldeburgh and then chaplain to the duke of Rutland, whose main seat was at Belvoir Castle in Lincolnshire. Crabbe's best-known poem, *The Village*, was published in 1783 and *The Newspaper* in 1785. Thereafter nothing more appeared until 1807, Crabbe having settled down to the life of a country parson and keen amateur botanist. *Poems* (1807) included "The Parish Register." This volume was followed by *The Borough* (1810), *Tales* (1812), *Tales of the Hall* (1819) and a volume of *Posthumous Tales* (1834). He died at Trowbridge (Wiltshire), where he had been rector after leaving Muston (near Belvoir) in 1814.

The *Village* is an antipastoral in reaction to works like Goldsmith's *The Deserted Village*, painting "the cot / As Truth will paint it and as bards will not." It exposes the degradation of a Suffolk coast community with a candid yet also pitying pen. "The Parish Register" with its "simple annals of the village poor" is at once more mature, more varied in tone and more full of understanding. It is the work of a man not only twenty years older, but possessing from these years a wealth of pastoral experience. Its series of pen portraits are expanded into the fuller and more dramatic manner of *The Borough* with characters such as Ellen Orford and Peter Grimes (about whom another native of Aldeburgh, Benjamin Britten, has written his well-known opera). In his portrayal of these characters Crabbe showed his mastery of psychological analysis. The title of his next work, *Tales in Verse*, sufficiently indicates its nature and reminds us that Crabbe has often been considered a short-story writer before that mode existed in prose. In this work he traced what seem to be the infinite variations in the relationships of the sexes. For Crabbe love was usually complicated and often sad. Lovers are infatuated, make mistakes and pay for them by long, usually lifelong, repentance. In the last work he himself published, *Tales of the Hall*, the manner and matter of each tale differs little from the 1812 *Tales*, but the whole is encompassed within a framework of two brothers meeting after years of separation. They recall their own past and the histories of people they have known. In this way they emphasize the poet's strong sense of the irrevocable past. One or two of his poems—"Sir Eustace Grey" and "The World of Dreams," for example—show Crabbe's interest in abnormal states of mind and may even owe something to his own experiences under opium, which he took regularly on medical prescription.

These pieces excepted, most of Crabbe's significant poems are written in the heroic couplet, but especially in the later works, it is a couplet laxer than that of his eighteenth-century predecessors. His vocabulary and grammatical structure are also freer, and the result is that critics have sometimes suggested that, given the nature of his subjects, he might have done better to write in prose. In this respect he resembles Browning, and with both much is lost by even the best of prose paraphrases. It is, above all, a question of tone which only the verse seems able to catch. This "Pope in worsted stockings," as he has been called, was for Byron "Nature's sternest painter, yet the best." It was in the works published after this tribute in 1809 that, as Landor put it, he entered the human heart "on all fours, and told the people what an ugly thing it is inside." Yet he was no mere psychological realist. His aim was always moral; "sparing criminals, attack the crime." He remains a strangely and undeservedly neglected major poet who provides something of a special taste.

The Candidate, 1780.
The Library, 1781.
The Village, 1783.
The Newspaper, 1785.
Poems, 1807.
The Borough, 1810.
Tales in Verse, 1812.
Tales of the Hall, 1819.

Poetical Works (including *Posthumous Tales* and life by his son), 8 vols., London: Murray, 1834.
Poems, ed. A. W. Ward, 3 vols., Cambridge: Cambridge Univ. Press, 1905–07.

New Poems, ed. A. Pollard, Liverpool: Liverpool Univ. Press, 1960. **A.P.**

CRANE, Hart (1899–1932) was born in Garretsville (Ohio). His parents were wealthy, his father being a successful businessman and his mother the daughter of a Chicago industrialist. However, the marriage was never successful and in 1916 they were divorced. What Crane in his poem "Quaker Hill" from *The Bridge* called "the curse of sundered parentage" was to mark his personality irrevocably. He left high school in Cleveland without graduating and received no further formal education. His most significant reading—the Elizabethan and Jacobean dramatists, French symbolists, Whitman, Poe, Melville, Nietzsche, Plato and Ouspensky, as well as the work of contemporary poets, especially Eliot—was largely self-guided. His lack of formal education, however, proved damaging in trying to get work and in 1919, after three years in New York, he was obliged to accept a job in a store in Akron from his father, for whom at that time he felt something close to hatred. His experience there strengthened his growing alienation from the insensitive materialism of modern America. To him the real world was a hell from which he more and more felt he must escape, if not physically, which seemed to him impossible, then spiritually. His life and his poetry came to oscillate between expression of his despair at the world and exultation at his occasional supposed transcendence of it.

Crane had begun to write poetry while at school in Cleveland. Many of the poems of the succeeding years are full of romantic despair—"Porphyro in Akron," "A bunch of smoke-ridden hills" where "poetry's a/ Bedroom occupation." His first collection, *White Buildings* (1926), omitted many of the early poems but included two important sequences, "For the Marriage of Faustus and Helen," and "Voyages." Crane saw "Faustus and Helen" as a reply to the defeatism and death he saw in Eliot, whom he greatly admired but thought had "buried hope as deep and direfully as it can ever be done." He himself felt all too strongly the pressures of his own waste land of Cleveland, Akron and New York, but sought in the rich and elaborate language of his poem to create a vision of the union of Faustus and Helen that would triumph over the triviality, ugliness, and cruelty of the modern world.

The only other volume of Crane's poetry to appear in his lifetime was his long poem, *The Bridge*, which came out in 1930. It was first conceived and begun in 1923, but was written only in fits and starts over the seven years which saw Crane's dissolution under the obloquy resulting from his homosexuality, financial difficulties, increasing alcoholism, and the intermittent crises of the poem's composition. Its intention he described as to make "a mystical synthesis of 'America'," devolving from the central "symbol of our constructive future" provided for him in the delicate arch of the Brooklyn Bridge. Again it was intended as an optimistic poem moving towards a triumphant close in the final section, "Atlantis." The route, however, invoking places and persons from American myth and history—Columbus, Pocahontas, Rip Van Winkle, Edgar Allan Poe—only just emerges from the desperate subway of "The Tunnel" to reach that consummation.

In the remaining two years of his life Crane's personal disintegration became complete. He wrote a number of shorter poems, some of which form "Key West: An Island Sheaf" in the *Collected Poems*, but found it increasingly difficult to write. Returning to the United States from Mexico on the S.S. *Orizaba* he leapt into the sea on 27 April 1932 and drowned.

White Buildings, 1926.
The Bridge, 1930.

Collected Poems, ed. W. Frank, New York: Liveright, 1933; reprinted as *The Complete Poems of Hart Crane*, New York: Doubleday Anchor, 1958.
Complete Poems and Selected Letters and Prose, ed. B. Weber, New York: Liveright, 1966; London: Oxford Univ. Press, 1968.
Letters, 1916–1932, ed. B. Weber, New York: Hermitage House, 1952.

J.P.W.

CRANE, Stephen (1871–1900), was born in Newark (New Jersey), the fourteenth child of a leading Methodist minister, who died when his son was eight. Crane's formal education took him to different establishments, mostly Methodist, including Syracuse University, but his real interest lay in journalism. Both parents had written for the press, and two brothers were professional New York newspapermen. By the age of twenty, when he left Syracuse, Crane had poor grades and little reading, but he was a practiced newspaper writer, working for a brother's news-reporting agency, and he had written a draft of his first short novel, *Maggie*. He worked as a free-lance reporter in and around New York, in financially uncertain conditions, writing urban sketches in a new vogue and immersing himself—partly, it seems, in rebellion against his parental faith and background—in the Bowery world, about which he frequently wrote. In 1893 he brought out *Maggie: A Girl of the Streets* at his own expense, noting in various copies that it "tries to show that environment is a tremendous thing in the world and frequently shapes lives regardless." Crane made his reputation two years later, not from his new type of urban fiction, but from a novel set on the battlefields of the Civil War, *The Red Badge of Courage*. This work can be read as a typically naturalist, or as a modernist, work. Once again its theme is involvement and immersion, the individual captured within a larger, machinelike world; but, unlike other naturalists who employ war as an appropriate metaphor for man's condition, Crane's persistent stress is on the psychology of experience, the fleeting contingency of event, the inconsistent, impressionistic symbolism of the universe.

In 1895 Crane also published a volume of poems, *The Black Rider*, which has increasingly interested critics. Thereafter until his early death his most important work is found in the short story form. There are two poor novels, and a third finished by another hand; he also did some interesting reporting. But it is stories like "The Open Boat," "The Bride Comes to Yellow Sky" (*f.* as *Face to Face*, 1952) and "The Blue Hotel" that sustain his quality as writer through his final harried years. Crane's sense of rebellion against parental and religious morality, his search for adventure, his uneasy, fleeting nature, all left him poised on an uncertain moral edge, evident in work and in life. His Bowery involvements made him unpopular in New York, and he went to Florida, where he met Cora Taylor, the owner of a Jacksonville brothel, whom he later brought to England. He tried gunrunning into Cuba and was war correspondent to the Greco-Turkish War (*Active Service*). In 1897 he moved to England and found himself highly prestigious, his work regarded as experimental by Conrad, Wells, James and others. But he was ill and in debt. He reported the Spanish-American War in 1898, produced largely second-rate work, and in 1900 died at the age of twenty-nine in a German sanatorium.

Always an uneven writer, Crane was also a delicate and significant one. He is significant because he stands at an important moment of transition, moving from a Christian liberalism to a stoic humanism in the face of a frightening prolixity of experience which demanded both immersion and a degree of self-extinction. He was led into uncertainties of perception and language; yet his parodic tone, his uncertainty of style, is in his best writing a complex artistic event. Its parodic, ironic, detached bent is the result of an obvious withdrawal from its opposite, the humanistic, liberal, personally compassionate fiction of the nineteenth century. Crane's subdued symbolism and aesthetic complexity, his concern with exposure and the growth of the awareness of pressure makes him, at best, a very striking modern writer, as Conrad and James saw. His gifts were easily wasted and not always controlled, but they are of great importance.

Maggie: A Girl of the Streets, 1893.
The Black Riders and Other Lines, 1895 (poems).
The Red Badge of Courage, 1895 (*f.* 1951).
George's Mother, 1896.
The Little Regiment and Other Episodes of the American Civil War, 1896.

The Third Violet, 1897.
The Open Boat and Other Tales of Adventure, 1898.
War Is Kind, 1899 (poems).
Active Service, 1899.
Whilomville Stories, 1900.
The O'Ruddy: A Romance (completed by R. Barr), 1903.

Works, ed. W. Follett, 12 vols., New York: Knopf, 1925–26.
Collected Poems, ed. W. Follett, New York: Knopf, 1930.
Stephen Crane: An Omnibus, ed. R. W. Stallman, New York: Knopf, 1952;
London: Heinemann, 1954.
Letters, ed. R. W. Stallman and L. Gilkes, New York: New York Univ.
Press; London: P. Owen, 1960.   M.B.

CRANMER, Thomas (1489–1556), born at Aslacton (Nottinghamshire) and educated at Cambridge, supported Henry VIII in his struggle
against the papacy and was made archbishop of Canterbury in 1533. He
introduced the Bible in English into churches. With the accession of
Edward VI, Cranmer brought out the first English prayer book (1549)
and a more Protestant version in 1552. In the following year he produced
his Forty-Two Articles, and thus completed his threefold contribution
to the church—of Bible, prayer book and confession. The death of
Edward VI and the succession of Mary brought a Romanist reaction, and
with it the imprisonment and ultimately the martyrdom of Cranmer.

Although he wrote more than forty works, Cranmer's lasting monument is the Book of Common Prayer, a judicious combination of the
old medieval liturgy of the Roman church and a new Reformation rite
embodying the changed theological insights of Protestantism. Based upon
biblical phraseology, its sentences move with a flow and dignity that have
done much to determine the characteristic ethos of Anglican worship.
Much of this effect derives from Cranmer's use of parallelisms of words
(e.g., the quasi repetitions, "prayers and supplications") and clauses (e.g.,
"Spare thou them . . . which confess their faults. Restore thou them that
are penitent."), a liberal use of adjectives and adverbs, and complex
syntactical patterns within which each separate part is nevertheless
readily understandable, this because of the completely simple vocabulary
and imagery which are used. Above all, Cranmer had a fine ear;
the cadences of the prayer book are amongst the finest examples of prose
rhythm in the language.   A.P.

CRASHAW, Richard (?1613–49), son of a Puritan divine who
was vigorous in his denunciations of the Roman church, was educated

at Cambridge, where election to the Greek scholarship at Pembroke College encouraged his writing of Latin and Greek verses on scriptural themes. In 1634 he published his first book, a series of Latin epigrams. He was ordained in the Anglican church and served as curate of Little St. Mary's, Cambridge, where he made his name as a preacher. He relinquished his fellowship at Peterhouse in 1643 (he was formally removed from it by the Parliamentarians a year later), left England in 1645 and, although exact details are not known, was converted to the Roman faith during that year. *Steps to the Temple*, sacred poems, with the added secular *Other Delights of the Muses*, appeared in 1646. He lived in Leyden, Paris and Rome, finally securing an appointment at Loreto where he died in August 1649 and was buried *in tumulo sacerdotum*. A last collection of poems, *Carmen Deo Nostro*, was published in Paris in 1652.

Crashaw was a translator of Giambattista Marino, whose baroque ornamentalism and fluidity of sensuous images is strongly evident in Crashaw's own expression. The frank sensuality is transformed in the sacred poems written after his conversion, such as "Saint Mary Magdalene; or, The Weeper," "Upon the Bleeding Crucifix" and "A Hymn to Saint Theresa," into controlled effusions of religious adulation which suggest longings on Crashaw's part for a transcendent, or ultimate, religious experience. The fluid images, characteristic of baroque art, succeed each other with remarkable rapidity. Crashaw's basic images—the flowing of blood and the falling of tears—emphasize the transience of human suffering and faith in a future self-fulfillment to be found in mystical union or death.

(See also **Metaphysical Poetry.**)

Poems, ed. L. C. Martin, Oxford: Clarendon Press, 1927; 2nd edition, 1957.   C.P.

CREELEY, Robert (1926–) was born in Massachusetts. He was educated at Harvard and subsequently lived in New England, France, and Majorca, where he began the Divers Press. He went to Black Mountain College in 1954, edited the influential *Black Mountain Review*, and received a B.A. there in 1955. He has continued to teach and to travel, holding academic appointments at the University of New Mexico and, latterly, the State University of New York at Buffalo.

His first book of poetry, *Le Fou* (1952), was followed by six more volumes, and in 1962 *For Love*, a selection of his poems from the years 1950 to 1960 was published. His association with Charles Olson helped to inspire the latter's essay on the Projective, and his insistent and careful intelligence made Olson's *Mayan Letters* possible. The latter's *Maximus Poems* are dedicated to Creeley.

Creeley's prose is as measured as his poetry, and *The Island* (1963) is a remarkable novel in which relationships are explored through an intense rendering of the spaces in which they occur. In his more recent books of poetry, notably *Words* (1967) and *Pieces* (1969), his work, always intimate and authentic, reaches a maturity which establishes him as the foremost contemporary American poet of the domestic.

Le Fou, 1952.
The Immoral Proposition, 1953.
The Kind of Act Of, 1953.
All That Is Lovely in Men, 1955.
If You, 1956.
The Whip, 1957.
A Form of Women, 1959.
For Love: Poems 1950–1960, 1962.
The Island, 1963.
The Gold Diggers, 1965 (stories).
Words: Poems, 1967.
The Finger (with Bobbie Creeley), 1968.
Pieces (with Bobbie Creeley), 1968.
A Quick Graph, ed. D. Allen, 1970 (essays).
St. Martin's (with Bobbie Creeley), 1971.   w.s.

CRÈVECOEUR, Michel Guillaume Jean de, or J. Hector St. John de (1735–1813) was born in France and settled as a farmer in New York State (1769). Returning from a trip to France (1780–83) during the Revolutionary War, he found his wife dead and his home burned after an Indian raid. After a period as French consul in New York, he returned in 1790 to France, where he died.

Crèvecoeur's best-known work, *Letters from an American Farmer* (1782), falls somewhere between a collection of essays and an epistolary novel. The narrator praises the initiative allowed the American yeoman, attacks the South for its attempt to preserve European social and economic patterns, and finally, unable to choose sides in the impending struggle with England, "lights out" for Indian territory. Further essays and a play were published in 1925 under the title *Sketches of Eighteenth-Century America*.   s.a.f.

CROKER, J. W. (John Wilson) (1780–1857) studied at Trinity College, Dublin, and Lincoln's Inn. A friend of Canning and Peel, he was a member of Parliament from 1807 to 1832 and secretary of the navy from 1809 to 1830. He wrote some youthful poetic squibs, but his main work was as a writer for *The Quarterly Review*, to which he contributed over 250 long articles. He was expert in eighteenth-century history, French affairs and modern politics. Often a severe reviewer, he was responsible for notorious attacks on Keats and on Tennyson's 1832 volume (dated 1833). He knew and corresponded with many of the main figures of his time. In 1831 he edited Boswell's *Life of Samuel Johnson*, too freely for modern tastes though he collected a mass of valuable new material in the process. Disraeli caricatured him in *Coningsby*.

The Croker Papers (correspondence and diaries), ed. L. J. Jennings, 3 vols., London: Murray, 1884; revised, 1885; ed. and abridged B. Pool, London: Batsford, 1967.   w.r.

CROSBY, **Fanny van Alstyne**. See **Hymns**.

CROWNE, **John** (?1640–?1703), born in Shropshire, accompanied his father, an ex-Parliamentary colonel, to America in 1657 and entered Harvard College. After his return to England sometime before 1665, he took up writing to support himself financially, producing eighteen plays between 1671 and 1700. They include his successful two-part *The Destruction of Jerusalem by Titus Vespasian* (1677), adaptations of Shakespeare, and satirical comedies like *City Politics* (1683) and *Sir Courtly Nice; or, It Cannot Be* (1685). His lavish masque, *Calisto* (1675), obtained royal favor, but Crowne died in poverty.

Works, ed. J. Maidment and W. H. Logan, 4 vols., Edinburgh: Paterson, 1873–77.   h.n.d.

CULLEN, **Countee** (1903–46) was born in New York and brought up in Harlem. He developed early as a poet, his first collection of poems, *Color* (1925), being published while he was an undergraduate at New York University. Later collections, including *Copper Sun* (1927), and *The Black Christ and Other Poems* (1929), established him as a leading figure in the "Harlem Renaissance." At his best he was a skillful lyric poet who relied on traditional methods to suggest the poignancy of Negro experience. He also wrote a novel, *One Way to Heaven* (1932), as well as poetry for children. A selection of poems, *On These I Stand*, was published in 1947.   i.w.

CUMBERLAND, **Richard** (1732–1811), a prolific writer, was educated at Westminster School and Trinity College, Cambridge, and began his dramatic career about 1762, succeeding with *The Brothers* (1770; *p.*

1769). His most famous play, *The West Indian* (1771), ran for twenty-eight nights, and follows the tradition of domestic drama established by Lillo. Well known in literary circles, he was satirized as Sir Fretful Plagiary in Sheridan's *The Critic*, allegedly for his behavior on the first night of *The School for Scandal*. After a secret mission to Spain while secretary to the Board of Trade, which ruined him, Cumberland settled in Kent at Tunbridge Wells.

Memoirs, 2 vols., 1806–07.

Posthumous Dramatic Works, 2 vols., London: Nicol, 1813.   P.R.

CUMMINGS, E. E. (e.e.) (Edward Estlin) (1894–1962) was born in Cambridge (Massachusetts). He received his A.B. and M.A. degrees from Harvard and then, in 1917, went to France as a volunteer ambulance driver. Administrative stupidity led to his internment in a French concentration camp, an experience he recorded in *The Enormous Room* (1922). After 1920 he studied art and wrote poetry in Paris, returning to New York in 1924 and receiving the *Dial* Award for distinguished service to American letters in 1926. By 1926 four books of poems—*Tulips and Chimneys; &; XLI Poems;* and *is 5*—had announced his personal style and basic ideas. His paintings were exhibited in several one-man shows, mainly in the 1940s.

The expressionist techniques of his play, *Him* (1927), are still diverting, but his popularity is the result of his poetry, which comprises the lyrical celebration of joy, "innocence" and love, generalized sallies on capitalism and big business, and the arty use of typography. The repetitious nature of his poetic materials and terms (new, spring, April, flowers, balloons) is both reassurance for a mass audience and evidence of a narrow range of attitudes. Cummings's self-reliant anarchism fails to suggest the complexity of human lives. The poet settles instead for a vision of good individual versus bad society ("this busy monster, manunkind").

His documentary novel, *The Enormous Room*, however, is a decent attack on secular and religious authority, exposing the discrepancy between official language and reality and the need to rework language for identity and imagination to survive.

The Enormous Room, 1922.
Tulips and Chimneys, 1923.
&, 1925.
XLI Poems, 1925.
is 5, 1926.
Him, 1927.
Eimi, 1933 (travel).

Collected Poems, 1938.
Santa Claus: A Morality, 1946.
i: Six Nonlectures, 1953.
Poems, 1923–1954, 1954.
73 Poems, 1963.

Complete Poems, 2 vols., London: MacGibbon & Kee, 1968.
Selected Letters, ed. F. W. Dupee and G. Stade, New York: Harcourt,
    Brace & World, 1969; London: Deutsch, 1972.   R.W.

CURNOW, Allen. See **New Zealand Literature.**

CYNEWULF. See **Old English Poetry.**

D

DALLAS, E. S. (Eneas Sweetland) (1828–79), London journalist and critic, wrote two works of literary theory, *Poetics* (1852) and *The Gay Science* (1866), of which the most interesting feature was an attempt to construct a science of criticism based on irrationalistic psychology. Dallas believed that the object of all art was to give pleasure and that this object was achieved by the artist's appeal through "subtle forms, allusions, and associations" to the "unconscious hemisphere" of the mind, which Dallas called the hidden soul or imagination. It was, he believed, the pleasurable connection established between art and the unconscious that criticism as a science should explore. He was, however, unable to develop these ideas and his "theory" resulted in no critical system.

A Century of George Eliot Criticism, ed. G. S. Haight, Boston: Houghton
    Mifflin, 1965; London: Methuen, 1966.   M.S.

DANA, R. H. (Richard Henry), Jr., (1815–82) was born at Cambridge (Massachusetts), of a well-established family. His father was a minor poet. To recover from illness while at Harvard (1831–37), Dana became an ordinary seaman for a voyage to California in the hide trade (1834–36). His account of it, *Two Years before the Mast* (1840; *f.* 1946), was an instant success and is the sole basis for his literary reputation. He devoted his life to law and politics but never with the success of "my boys' book." Matter-of-fact, "a voice from the forecastle" seeking reform, it was also an account of a young man's initiation, and the real sublimity of struggling with the elements. It greatly influenced American sea fiction.

Journal, ed. R. F. Lucid, 3 vols., Cambridge, Mass.: Harvard Univ.
    Press; London: Oxford Univ. Press, 1968.   D.B.H.

DANIEL, Samuel (?1562–1619), born in Somerset, was educated at Magdalen Hall, Oxford, but left without a degree in 1585. Having no private means, Daniel was a poet always dependent on patronage. His distinguished patrons included Mary, countess of Pembroke, Sir Philip Sidney's sister (from 1592 to 1595, and again from 1609), and Charles Blount, Lord Mountjoy, and Fulke Greville. Daniel early gained the favor of James I's queen, for whom he wrote several masques and plays, continuing in her service until her death in 1619, despite the near-disaster of his short-lived appointment as licenser of plays to the Children of the Queen's Revels (1604–05). The plays chosen for performance, including Daniel's *Philotas*, which was believed to refer to the earl of Essex's treason in 1601, were considered seditious by the Privy Council. Always a modest, unassuming man, Daniel spent his last years mostly in retirement, working on his prose *History of England*. He died on his farm at Beckington (Somerset).

Daniel's works illustrate the variety of Elizabethan poetry. The pains and sweets of love and the poignancy of vulnerable mortal beauty are feelingly described in his sonnet sequence, *Delia* (1592), whilst the companion poem of the volume, *The Complaint of Rosamond*, brings sympathetic character study and fashionable Petrarchan diction to the old-fashioned cautionary tale. Sharing his age's fascination with the Wars of the Roses, Daniel wrote a historical epic, *The Civil Wars*, which appeared in installments and revised versions from 1595 to 1609 and remained unfinished. He fails to make history into poetry, becoming dissatisfied with the circumscription his form imposes upon the facts. In *The Civil Wars*, as in *Musophilus* (1599), Daniel's moral seriousness is increasingly stressed. It also underlies his two neoclassical tragedies, *Cleopatra* (1594; extensively revised in 1607) and *Philotas* (1605). The former, undertaken under the auspices of Mary Pembroke, is a closet drama, concentrating on illuminating Cleopatra's character; the latter, designed for theatrical production, observes the unities less rigidly, but lacks cohesion of action. Daniel's two masques, *The Vision of the Twelve Goddesses* (1604) and *Tethys' Festival* (1610) are unimpressive; he disliked the form, and his attitude to it probably occasioned the animosity between himself and Ben Jonson, upholder of the masque (see also **Masques**). The two pastoral dramas also written for the queen, *The Queen's Arcadia* and *Hymen's Triumph*, lack the lightness of touch and fantasy such works required. His essay replying to Campion's pamphlet attacking rhyme, *A Defence of Rhyme*, is one of the incisive critical works of the age, and his *History of England*, unfinished at his death, is a critical, humane document, aiming at a clear representation of the facts.

Daniel's literary qualities are seriousness, moral awareness and sympathetic understanding of human nature. These attributes are present in his early verse, though overlaid with a youthful lyricism. His natural modesty occasioned self-distrust, and his painstaking revisions indicate both self-dissatisfaction and high artistic purpose. Complexity of thought sometimes overwhelms Daniel's poetry, which becomes increasingly a vehicle for reflection. This explains his lack of interest in the ostentatious masque and why his plays fail to come completely to life. His diction, always restrained, approaches the clarity of prose. Indeed, Daniel finally adopted prose and used it with a poet's appreciation of the scope and variety of language.

Delia and *The Complaint of Rosamond*, 1592 (with *Cleopatra*, 1594).
The Civil Wars between the Two Houses of York and Lancaster, 1595–1609.
A Defence of Rhyme, 1603.
Philotas, 1605 (*p.* 1604).
The Queen's Arcadia, 1606 (*p.* 1605).
Hymen's Triumph, 1615.
The History of England, 1618.

Complete Works in Verse and Prose, ed. A. B. Grosart, 5 vols., for private circulation, 1885–96.
Poems and A Defence of Ryme [sic], ed. A. C. Sprague, Cambridge, Mass.: Harvard Univ. Press, 1930; reissued, London: Routledge, 1950; Chicago: Univ. of Chicago Press, 1965.   J.M.P.

DARLEY, George (1795–1846) came to London from Dublin about 1821 to establish himself as a poet. Failing to achieve recognition, he was forced to earn his living largely by journalism, including art and drama criticism. His severe stammer limited human contacts and he became increasingly a recluse. His published poems include *Sylvia; or, The May Queen* (1827) and *Nepenthe* (1835). Darley's lyrics are graceful and often effective. They show his interest in early seventeenth-century poetry. He also has a pleasant vein of fantasy and the grotesque, though limited in subject matter and lacking an individual poetic voice.

Complete Poetical Works, ed. R. Colles, London: Routledge, 1908.   A.E.

DARWIN, Charles (1809–82), grandson of Erasmus Darwin, was appointed as naturalist on an exploratory voyage by H.M.S. *Beagle* to the South American coast (1831–36). On his return he continued his scientific inquiries, which resulted in *The Origin of Species* (1859). The work was of great significance in the light of the debate between science and religious belief and aroused considerable opposition, in spite of Darwin's own assertion that his theories, far from minimizing the divine achievement, emphasized it. It was followed by other scientific publications arising from evolutionary theory.

A Journal of . . . the Voyage of the H.M.S. Beagle . . . , 1839.
Autobiography, ed. N. Barlow, London: Collins, 1958.

The Darwin Reader, ed. M. Bates and P. S. Humphrey, London: Macmillan; New York: C. Scribner's Sons, 1957.   A.J.S.

DARWIN, Erasmus (1731–1802), after qualifying as a doctor in Edinburgh, practiced with success at Lichfield, and later at Derby. A founder member of the "Lunar Society," which included Boulton, Watt, Wedgwood and Priestley, he knew and corresponded with Rousseau. He published two major poetical works, *The Botanic Garden* (part 1, *The Economy of Vegetation*, 1791; part 2, *The Loves of the Plants*, 1789) and *The Temple of Nature* (1803), which showed skill in the writing of couplets to display scientific facts and theories, particularly a theory of evolution contrary to the church's teaching. This brought Darwin into disrepute among those who feared that change of any kind might precipitate an English revolution to match the French. *Zoonomia* (1794–96) was his most important prose work. He was the grandfather of Charles Darwin.

Collected Poems, 3 vols., London: J. Johnson, 1806.
Essential Writings, ed. D. G. King-Hele, London: MacGibbon & Kee, 1968.   P.G.M.

DAVENANT or **D'AVENANT, Sir William** (1606–68) was probably Shakespeare's godson. His claim to be Shakespeare's illegitimate child was, like the aristocratic apostrophe, a publicity gambit. Actually the son of an Oxford innkeeper, Davenant came to London in 1622, eventually entering the service of Fulke Greville. After Greville's death in 1628 Davenant fostered influential friendships at court; he gained the patronage of Henry Jermyn and Endymion Porter and became the boon companion of Suckling. After being gravely ill with syphilis, he killed a tavern servant and fled to Holland in 1633. Soon returning, although not pardoned until 1638, he became an important writer of court masques, succeeding Jonson as poet laureate in 1638 (see also **Masques**). Knighted in 1643 after serving Charles I well throughout the Civil War, he lived in exile before being captured in the Channel in 1650, bound for Maryland. Following his pardon he attempted to revive drama, circumventing legislation against stage plays by presenting opera (1656). After the Restoration he controlled one of London's two licensed theatrical companies.

A theatrical innovator and opportunist of genius, Davenant encouraged the use of elaborate scenery and spectacle, pioneered English opera and established actresses on the public stage. When the theaters reopened, he provided a valuable link with Caroline drama, wrote new plays, adapted old ones to the new taste and trained young actors. His *Love and Honour* (1649; *p.* 1634) proved a seminal play for the heroic drama, though *The Wits* (1636; *p.* 1634) is his best play. His poems include lyrical, occasional and mock-heroic verses mainly published in *Madagascar*

(1638), and an unfinished heroic epic, *Gondibert*, the preface to which caused a celebrated controversy with Hobbes.

The Tragedy of Albovine, King of the Lombards, 1629.
The Temple of Love, 1635 (masque).
The Wits, 1636 (p. 1634).
Madagascar, with Other Poems, 1638.
Love and Honour, 1649 (p. 1634).
Gondibert, 1651.
The Siege of Rhodes, 1656 (opera).
The Rivals, 1668 (p. before 1664).
The Tempest (with John Dryden), 1670 (p. 1667).*
Macbeth, 1674 (p. 1672).*   * Adaptation of Shakespeare.

Dramatic Works, ed. J. Maidment and W. H. Logan, 5 vols., Edinburgh: Paterson, 1872–74.
The Works of the English Poets, ed. A. Chalmers, London: Johnson, 1810, vol. 6.   H.N.D.

DAVIDSON, John (1857–1909), son of a minister of the Evangelical Union, left school at thirteen and took a variety of posts in his native Scotland in and out of teaching, before deciding at the end of the 1880s to go to London to begin a career as a writer and journalist. He had already written a novel, *The North Wall* (1885), and five plays, but it was not until Richard Le Gallienne, reader for John Lane, recognized his talent that Davidson become known. *In a Music Hall, and Other Poems* (1891) and particularly *Fleet Street Eclogues* (2 series, 1893–96) made his name and gave his work some popularity. He knew most of the central figures of the 1890s, being a member of the Rhymers' Club and contributing to *The Yellow Book*, though he was always consciously hostile to the more refined tendencies of the age in which he wrote. His popularity was never such that it could relieve him of the financial burdens which held him to hack journalism for which he was not fitted. He drowned himself in 1909.

Though novelist, critic, translator and a playwright of sufficient talent to impress Shaw, he is remembered for his poems. Both Eliot and "Hugh MacDiarmid" admitted a debt to him. From his earlier lyrics he developed a more assertive, increasingly Nietzschean stance which is expressed in his vigorous "Testaments" (1901; 1901; 1902; 1904; 1908). Though often fine, his poetry is frequently marred by crudity of phrase.

(See also **Romantic Movement, The.**)

Ballads and Songs, 1894.

Selection of Poems, ed. M. Lindsay, London: Hutchinson, 1961.   K.T.

DAVIES, Sir John (1569–1626), son of a lawyer and educated at Winchester and Oxford, entered the Middle Temple, was later attorney general for Ireland and sat in the English and Irish Houses of Commons. He died before he could take up appointment as lord chief justice. Davies wrote on law and politics but is remembered for the airy, ceremonial *Orchestra: A Poem of Dancing* (1596) and the didactic poem *Nosce Teipsum* (1599). His epigrams and "gulling sonnets" have important reference to Elizabethan satire.

Works, ed. A. B. Grosart, 3 vols., Blackburn: for private circulation, Fuller Worthies Library, 1869–76.
Poems, ed. C. Howard, London: Oxford Univ. Press; New York: Columbia Univ. Press, 1941.
Silver Poets of the Sixteenth Century, ed. G. Bullett, London: Dent; New York: Dutton, 1947.   G.P.

DAVIES, W. H. (William Henry) (1871–1940), born in Newport (Monmouthshire) of mixed Welsh and Cornish parentage, left school at thirteen and, finding himself unable to settle to a job, became a tramp. He crossed the Atlantic as a deck hand many times and spent long periods as a hobo till his foot was severed as he was attempting to board a train. Even then, after returning to England, he lived much in dosshouses. He had always had literary ambitions, and *The Autobiography of a Super-Tramp*, with an introduction by Bernard Shaw, made his name but not his fortune. He was befriended by Shaw, Edward Thomas and others who recognized his gifts, and the volumes of Georgian poetry (1911–22) included some of his best work. He has a curiously simple directness which has made his prose and verse often memorable in spite of its lapses into bathos. (See also **Georgians, The.**)

The Autobiography of a Super-Tramp, 1908.
A Poet's Pilgrimage, 1918.
Later Days, 1925.

Complete Poems, London: Cape, 1963.   A.N.M.

DAVIN, Dan. See **New Zealand Literature.**

DAVIS, Richard Harding (1864–1916) was born in Philadelphia, worked for the New York *Sun* (1889–90) and became managing editor of *Harper's Weekly* (1890). The leading correspondent of his day, Davis traveled widely in America and Europe. He covered the Greco-Turkish,

Spanish–American, Boer and Russo-Japanese Wars and, up till his death, the First World War. His graphic and dramatic articles were collected in such books as *Cuba in War Time* (1897), *With Both Armies in South Africa* (1900) and *With the Allies* (1914). Davis's colorful but mediocre novels include *Soldiers of Fortune* (1897), a romantic adventure set in South America, *Vera the Medium* (1908) and *The White Mice* (1909).   J.W.

DAVISON, Francis. See **Elizabethan Miscellanies.**

DAWE, Bruce. See **Australian Literature.**

DAY, John (?1574–?1640), son of a Norfolk "husbandman," was at school at Ely and expelled from Cambridge in 1593 for stealing a book. In the ten years after 1598, when his name first appears in connection with the stage, Day collaborated in numerous plays (now largely lost) and produced several comedies independently, three of which survive. After 1608, the year of his best work, *Humour out of Breath*, his literary output diminished, although his famous verse dialogue, *The Parliament of Bees, with Their Proper Characters*, remained unpublished until 1641. This has grace, melody and a delightful fancifulness, qualities which set him aside from his contemporaries and recall Lyly and the young Shakespeare.

Works, ed. A. H. Bullen, 7 parts, London: Chiswick Press, 1881.   L.S.

DAY(-)LEWIS, Cecil (1904–72), son of an Irish clergyman, was educated at Sherborne School and Oxford. With Auden and Spender he became known as one of the new left-wing poets of the 1930s and his *A Hope for Poetry* (1934) was an important manifesto. He first subsidized his career as a poet by schoolteaching and later by lecturing, poetry readings (especially with his second wife, the actress Jill Balcon), writing detective stories under the pseudonym Nicholas Blake, and by directorship of a publishing house. He was professor of poetry at Oxford from 1951 to 1956 and held visiting professorships at Harvard and other universities. He became poet laureate in 1968.

His wide reading and catholic taste in poetry have distinguished him as an anthologist, a translator and a critic with a flair for popularizing poetry. These qualities, however, allied with an ear unusually sensitive to the poetic idiom of others, perhaps obscured for some readers the strength, originality, technical mastery and genuine feeling in much of his own poetry. A prolific poet by contemporary standards, he showed considerable lyrical range and development. Before and during the Second World

War he spoke for his generation with a sober wisdom and subdued eloquence. He wrote about the intimate tensions of family life with the compassionate honesty of Meredith, and he shared with Hardy a deep feeling for the English countryside.

Collected Poems 1929–33, 1935.
Overtures to Death and Other Poems, 1938.
The Georgics of Virgil, 1940.
The Poetic Image, 1947.
Poems 1943–47, 1948.
The Aeneid of Virgil, 1952.
Collected Poems, 1954.
The Buried Day, 1960 (autobiography).
The Gate and Other Poems, 1962.
The Eclogues of Virgil, 1963.
The Room and Other Poems, 1965.
The Whispering Roots, 1970.   D.W.

DEFOE, Daniel (1660–1731) was born in London, the son of a butcher, and grew up close to the economic and physical realities of the capital. His Nonconformist father intended him for the ministry, but after marrying Mary Tuffley in 1684, Defoe became a partner in a haberdasher's business and started trading in various commodities. His enthusiasm outran his resources and in 1692 he went bankrupt for £17,000. Subsequent success with a tile factory restored his fortunes and paid his creditors. It was at this time that Defoe began to publish economic and political pamphlets, but *The Shortest Way with the Dissenters* earned him a prison sentence in 1703 from the Tory extremists it had duped and led to a second bankruptcy. With his wife and seven children near starvation, Defoe, who described himself as a "constant follower of moderate principles," now began to work for the moderate Tory Harley (to be succeeded by Swift) and undertook the thrice-weekly *Review*, which he wrote unaided for almost ten years. With the advent of the Whigs Defoe found himself discredited (*An Appeal to Honour and Justice* is an apologia for his political conduct), but at Walpole's request he agreed to write for and "disable" the extremist Tory paper *Mist's Weekly Journal*. Defoe was a great reader of travel, trade and historical literature, and it was probably the widely circulated story of Alexander Selkirk's island ordeal that prompted *Robinson Crusoe*, written in retirement in 1719. Defoe exploited its success with two continuations and four more novels, but in his last years reverted to his socio-economic interests, undertaking the three volumes of his remarkable *Tour* and writing guidebooks on trade.

The bulk of Defoe's writing was journalism of immediate relevance to a news-hungry age. His supreme abilities as a narrator of fact were reinforced by his Puritan purposiveness and assurance, and the numerous pamphlets, with their appeal to biblical rather than classical authority, often read like lay sermons. But Defoe also wrote: "Lies are not worth a farthing if they are not calculated for the effectual deceiving of the people they are designed to deceive," and it is his adoption of the "lie direct" as a defensible means of influencing and entertaining his readers that gives him his place in the history of the novel. He had gone to prison for irony; *The Apparition of One Mrs. Veal* declares a new procedure, perfected in that outrageously convincing reconstruction, *A Journal of the Plague Year* (1722); and the novels owe their special quality to this appropriation of fact in the service of fiction. Defoe manufactures detail and circumstance, outflanking skepticism with redundant information (such as the two shoes Crusoe discovers, "that were not fellows") and obliterating authorial intervention with a sustained neutrality of style. The result is that *réalisme indifférent*, prized by later novelists, which has earned Defoe his present reputation. The minuteness of Crusoe's narrative justifies his "editor's" claim—"neither is there any appearance of fiction in it." The noncommittal narration in *Moll Flanders* (1722), the unadapted naïveté of the boy in *Colonel Jacque* (1722)—both books profiting from Defoe's own experiences as London child and Newgate prisoner, both cluttered with names, things, and inventories—satisfy the present documentary ideal. The touch is less sure in *The Fortunate Mistress* (1724), where Defoe goes beyond his own knowledge; and the master of the lie finds his salvation after all in the factuality of *A Tour* and *The Complete English Tradesman*.

(See also **Essays; Political Pamphlets.**)

An Essay upon Projects, 1697.
The True-Born Englishman, 1701.
The Shortest Way with the Dissenters, 1702.
A Review of the Affairs of France and of All Europe, 19 February 1704–11 June
    1713.
The Apparition of One Mrs. Veal, 1706.
The History of the Union of Great Britain, 1709.
An Appeal to Honour and Justice, 1715.
The Family Instructor, 1, 1715; 2, 1718.
The Adventures of Robinson Crusoe, 1719 (*f.* 1954).
The Farther Adventures of Robinson Crusoe, 1719.
The Life, Adventures, and Piracies of Captain Singleton, 1720.
Serious Reflections during the Life of Robinson Crusoe, 1720.
The Fortunes and Misfortunes of Moll Flanders, 1722 (*f.* 1954; as *The Amorous
    Adventures of Moll Flanders*, 1964).

A Journal of the Plague Year, 1722.
The History of Colonel Jacque, 1722.
The Fortunate Mistress, 1724.
A Tour through Great Britain, 1724–27.
The Complete English Tradesman, 1726–27.

Works, ed. G. H. Maynadier, 16 vols., Boston: Nickerson, 1903–04.
Novels and Selected Writings, 14 vols., Oxford: Blackwell, 1927–28.
Letters, ed. G. H. Healey, Oxford: Clarendon Press, 1955.   D.G.

DE FOREST, John W. (William) (1826–1906) was born in Connecticut. A captain in the Federal army during the Civil War, he turned his experiences to good account in *Miss Ravenel's Conversion from Secession to Loyalty* (1867). As a novel depicting scenes of inefficiency and frustration, this work has been regarded by some as a precursor to *The Red Badge of Courage*, but it has none of the underlying pessimism or irony of Crane's masterpiece. It can be seen alternatively as a quasi-allegorical story with obvious political reference. The heroine, betrayed by her Southern lover, recognizes the qualities of her New England admirer and the rightness of the Abolitionist cause. Among other works are *Kate Beaumont* (1872), a local color novel of South Carolina, and novels exposing corruption in Grant's administration.

Miss Ravenel's Conversion from Secession to Loyalty, 1867.
Kate Beaumont, 1872.
Honest John Vane, 1875.
Playing the Mischief, 1875.
Justine's Lovers, 1878.

Novels, Monument edition, ed. J. J. Rubin, State College, Pa.: Bald
    Eagle Press, 1960– .   M.L.

DEKKER, Thomas (?1572–1632), a Londoner probably of Dutch extraction, began writing plays for the Admiral's Men about 1598. During his years of activity he turned out some forty-two plays, only seventeen of which are extant, as well as a variety of prose pamphlets. More frequently than not he wrote his plays with a collaborator. Despite his industry he seems to have suffered considerable hardship and was twice imprisoned for debt—on the second occasion for a period of almost seven years. Though little else is known about Dekker's life, his pamphlets and surviving plays give testimony to one of the most attractive personalities of the age.

His early comedies include *Old Fortunatus* (1600), a dramatized folk tale crammed with adventure interest, *The Whore of Babylon* (1607), a patriotic allegory of the great events of Elizabeth's reign, *Patient Grissil* (1603) and *Satiromastix* (1602), his contribution to the War of the Theatres. They are structurally naïve, unevenly written and unsophisticated in their spectacular effects. *The Shoemaker's Holiday* (1600), however, is more skillfully constructed; its high-spirited glorification of citizen life, as well as the scope it affords for the treatment of important contemporary issues, makes it undoubtedly more worthy of attention. Dekker's next group of plays were citizen comedies, written in collaboration with Middleton and Webster. With Middleton he wrote *The Honest Whore*, part 1 (1604), a sympathetic treatment of regeneration, blending satire, humor and some dreary sermonizing, and *The Roaring Girl* (1611), a comedy of love intrigue portraying the seamy side of London life. With Webster he collaborated on *Westward Ho!* and *Northward Ho!* (both 1607), both satiric treatments of debauchery and cuckoldry in a bourgeois London setting. His late plays, *Match Me in London* (1631), clearly written under the influence of Beaumont and Fletcher, and the domestic tragedy, *The Witch of Edmonton*, written in collaboration with Ford and Rowley, are new departures in a tragic lyrical mode.

Though it is in his underworld and plague pamphlets, particularly *The Wonderful Year*, *The Bellman of London*, *Lanthorn and Candlelight* and *The Gull's Hornbook*, that this intensely humanitarian writer is found at his most pious and compassionate, the domestic virtues of patience, tolerance and forgiveness are prominently celebrated throughout his work. He has other qualities, too—an eye for telling detail, a lively awareness of contemporary city life and an ease in adapting himself to new fashions in drama. But another journalistic quality, his sensitive attunement to the demands of popular taste, perhaps explains the minimal intellectual content of his plays and their many naïvetés. He is also to be criticized for lapses of artistry: structural weakness is common to most of his work, and so far as characterization is concerned, though he shows competence in delineating the externals of his whores and shopkeepers, he seldom perceives deeper. The strengths of his later plays seem ascribable to the superior intellects of his collaborators. Excepting *The Shoemaker's Holiday*, Dekker's extant independent plays have at best only a romantic charm.

(See also **Masques.**)

Old Fortunatus, 1600.
The Shoemaker's Holiday, 1600.
Satiromastix, 1602.
Patient Grissil (with Henry Chettle and William Haughton), 1603.
The Wonderful Year, 1603 (pamphlet).
The Honest Whore, part 1 (with Thomas Middleton), 1604.

News from Hell, 1606 (pamphlet).
The Seven Deadly Sins of London, 1606 (pamphlet).
The Whore of Babylon, 1607.
Westward Ho! (with John Webster), 1607.
Northward Ho! (with Webster), 1607.
The Bellman of London, 1608 (pamphlet).
Lanthorn and Candlelight, 1608 (pamphlet).
The Gull's Hornbook, 1609 (pamphlet).
The Roaring Girl (with Middleton), 1611 (*p. c.* 1606).
The Virgin-Martyr (with Philip Massinger), 1622 (*p.* ?1620).
Match Me in London, 1631.
The Witch of Edmonton (with John Ford and William Rowley), 1658 (*p.* ? 1621).

Dramatic Works, ed. F. Bowers, 4 vols., Cambridge: Cambridge Univ. Press, 1953–61.
Non-Dramatic Works, ed. A. B. Grosart, 5 vols., London: for private circulation, Huth Library, 1884–86.
Plague Pamphlets, ed. F. P. Wilson, Oxford: Clarendon Press, 1925. L.E.P.

DE LA MARE, Walter (1873–1956) was born in Kent, and spent eighteen years in commercial life before devoting himself to literature. As a clerk in an oil company, he published his first book under a pseudonym, but soon established himself as the leading contemporary children's poet. In his later poetry, though he often looks through the eyes of a child, the emotions released are those of the adult; horror, mystery and menace are present as well as wonder and fantasy. Always a good technician, he developed, according to T. S. Eliot, "a conscious art practised with natural ease." (See also **Georgians, The.**)

Stories, Essays and Poems, ed. M. Bozman, London: Dent; New York: Dutton, 1938.
Complete Poems, London: Faber & Faber, 1969; New York: Knopf, 1970.

O.K.

DE LISSER, (H.G.) Herbert George. See **Caribbean Literature.**

DELONEY, Thomas (? 1543–1600), born in Norwich, was a silk-weaver by trade, but became known in the 1580s for his ballads and broadsides. These included three in 1588 on the Spanish Armada, and many others on historical subjects, popular grievances (which came to official notice) and comic material. Most of them have perished, though some survive in *Strange Histories* (?1602) and in nineteenth-century collections. Drayton praised the uneducated Deloney's verse as "full of state and pleasing," although Nashe spoke disparagingly of him as "the balleting silk-weaver of Norwich" who "hath rime enough for all miracles."

But it is Deloney's prose work that commands our attention today. He was the first writer in English to use factual material in a fictional structure, and his three prose narratives, written in a plain style refreshingly different from the "educated" prose of the time, deal at first hand with mercantile life in town and country. *Jack of Newbury* (1597) relates the experiences of a weaver; *The Gentle Craft* (1597–?98) is a work in praise of shoemakers which includes three illustrative stories (one is that of Simon Eyre, the shoemaker's apprentice who became lord mayor—a story taken over by Dekker in *The Shoemaker's Holiday*); and *Thomas of Reading* (?1600), the most substantial of the novels, deals with the adventures of six "gallant clothiers" in the reign of Henry I, interestingly anticipating Scott's manner by grafting historical events on to the story. These narratives, very popular at the time, were reprinted well into the eighteenth century, and they have a definite, if unacknowledged, place in the history of the English novel.

Works, ed. F. O. Mann, Oxford: Clarendon Press, 1912.
Novels, ed. M. E. Lawlis, London: Oxford Univ. Press; Bloomington: Indiana Univ. Press, 1961.   D.G.

DENHAM, Sir John (1615–69) was born in Dublin, the son of the lord chief baron of the Irish Exchequer. The family moved to London (1617) when his father became baron of the English Exchequer. He was educated at Trinity College, Oxford, and attended Lincoln's Inn. Around 1636, to reassure his father, he wrote *The Anatomy of Play* (1651), a tract against gambling; but on his father's death in 1639 he squandered the estate in gaming. As high sheriff of Surrey he surrendered Farnham Castle to the Parliamentarians in 1642, but later fought for the Royalists and served Charles in exile (1648–52), for which he was knighted and made surveyor general of works at the Restoration. After his second marriage in 1665 to a beautiful young girl, his mind was temporarily deranged when she proved unfaithful. She died suddenly in 1667, possibly poisoned.

Denham's reputation was highest in the late seventeenth and early eighteenth centuries, when *Cooper's Hill* (1642), his best-known work, was considered an important poem. From a point overlooking the Thames near Runnymede the poet surveys the valley, the scene suggesting moral, historical and philosophical reflections that show Denham's abhorrence of the chaos of civil war which broke out in the year that the poem was anonymously and piratically published. Denham's satire includes verses on the conduct of the Dutch War, and his occasional verse a fine elegy on Cowley. Early work includes a paraphrase of Virgil's *Aeneid*, book 2 (1656), and a historical tragedy, *The Sophy* (1642; *p.* 1641), an achievement which shattered Denham's early reputation for dreaminess.

Poetical Works, ed. T. H. Banks, London: Oxford Univ. Press; New Haven: Yale Univ. Press, 1928.   H.N.D.

DENNIS, John (1657–1734) is remembered chiefly as a critic, but he also wrote poetry and plays without much success. Born in London, he toured France and Italy (1688) after leaving Cambridge. In London he became friendly with the leading literary figures. He published both *Miscellanies in Verse and Prose* and *The Impartial Critic*, praising Dryden, in 1693, and defended the drama against Collier in 1698. His *Usefulness of the Stage* (1698) complimented Wycherley. By 1706 he had written six plays, seven critical treatises, four long poems, a collection of letters and some translations. After that date he retired from active society, his output declined and he acquired the status of a stock pedant. Pope's satire on him in *An Essay on Criticism* provoked a running fight lasting many years and culminating in Pope's attacks in *The Dunciad*.

Dennis was probably the best critic of his age, especially with regard to drama and poetry. His chief works, *The Advancement and Reformation of Modern Poetry* (1701), *The Grounds of Criticism in Poetry* (1704) and *An Essay upon the Genius and Writings of Shakespear* (1712), insist upon real excellence as a critical priority and adherence to the rules of writing. Dennis's firm assumption was of the importance of literature to religion and to the state. In poetry the essence was passion, and the sublime necessitated imagination, rapture and transport. These ideas, together with a dogmatic gravity, made him vulnerable to ridicule but nevertheless produced criticism of a high quality.

Critical Works, ed. E. N. Hooker, 2 vols., London: Oxford Univ. Press; Baltimore: Johns Hopkins Press, 1939–43.   P.R.

DENNIS, Nigel (1912–   ) returned to England, where he was born, in 1949 and has since written reviews and dramatic criticism, collected as *Dramatic Essays* (1962), novels and plays. *Cards of Identity* (1955) was an unusual satirical novel and *August for the People* (1961) a mordant play. His *Jonathan Swift: A Short Character* appeared in 1965. His novel *A House in Order* (1966) shows sanity and balance being preserved under stress by positive, if obsessive, individuality. This work is shaped with wit and artistry. His *Exotics: Poems of the Mediterranean and Middle East* was published in 1970.   J.C.

DE QUINCEY, Thomas (1785–1859), born in Manchester, showed an early ability in the classics and an enthusiasm for music and books. In 1800 he entered Manchester Grammar School, from which he absconded because of ill health and depression in 1802. He went to Wales and then London, living in great penury and physical misery, until reconciled with his family a year later. He then went up to Oxford, studying in a desultory way (never taking his degree), and pursuing the interests in metaphysics, psychology and moral philosophy which led him on to the German writers, notably Kant. Passionately interested in contemporary poetry, he met Coleridge and Wordsworth in 1807, and became a close friend of their circle after settling at Dove Cottage, Grasmere in 1809, though his marriage in 1816 brought some estrangement. For the relief of neuralgia, brought on by his hardships of 1802–03, De Quincey began to take opium and by 1813 was a confirmed addict, experiencing dreams of intensity and horror. In *Confessions of an English Opium-Eater* (1822, revised from two articles in *The London Magazine*, 1821; enlarged, 1856) he justifies his opium-taking by relating his early life and its effects on his health. Despite his assertion that he had almost given it up, he was addicted to opium for the rest of his life. *Confessions* is far from the sensational revelations suggested by the title; it is a finely written series of digressions strung upon the thread of autobiography. The scenes of his London sufferings are particularly notable and a final section describes some of his opium dreams, which are further rendered in the sketches collected as *Suspiria de Profundis* (1845; and in *Posthumous Works*) and evoked in *The English Mail-Coach* (1849).

From July 1818 to November 1819 De Quincey was editor of *The Westmorland Gazette*, where he was not a success, filling the paper with murder trials—an interest later epitomized in his pieces for *Blackwood's Magazine* in 1827 and 1839, entertaining fantasies in which are mingled the witty, farcical and ferociously macabre, and published together in 1854 as *On Murder Considered As One of the Fine Arts*. The need to support his growing family made him turn to periodical literature. From 1820 he gained a livelihood by essay writing, briefly first in London, but then in Edinburgh for *Blackwood's* and *Tait's Magazines*, and (towards the end of his life) for *Hogg's Weekly Instructor*. Because of this magazine publication, De Quincey's work was largely unavailable in permanent form until the American collected edition (1851–59) began to appear, which prompted De Quincey to produce his own *Selections Grave and Gay* (1853–60), extensively revising everything he wished should survive. His life in Edinburgh was unsettled, and his constitutional dilatoriness combined with the effect of opium led to poverty and debts. Only with his mother's death in 1846, which brought a small additional income, and with increasing financial help from his daughters, did he achieve a secure old age. He died in Edinburgh in December 1859.

A strangely solitary person from his youth, De Quincey nonetheless cultivated the art of conversation, displaying his sense of style as brilliantly as in his writings, drawing on that extensive reading in philosophy, history and literature so valuable to him as a periodical writer. He is excellent at close reasoning and apt illustrations, though his imagination was not strongly developed. His best writings have the quality of good talk, allowing him to wander as his association of ideas takes him, yet always remaining aware of his ultimate goal, as in the essay "On the Knocking at the Gate in Macbeth" (1823). The best of his writings on literature show his preference for critical theory and literary anecdote, most notably in the essays on Coleridge of 1834–35 and the "Lake Reminiscences" essays of 1839–40, in which his recollections caused offense by their frankness about people only recently dead or still alive. In that very frankness their present-day value resides.

(See also **Essays.**)

Writings, ed. J. T. Fields, 24 vols., Boston: Ticknor, Reed & Fields, 1851–59.

Selections Grave and Gay ... Revised and Arranged by Himself, 14 vols., London and Edinburgh: Hogg, 1853–60.

Collected Writings, ed. D. Masson, 14 vols., Edinburgh: A. C. Black, 1889–90.

Posthumous Works, ed. A. H. Japp, 2 vols., London: Heinemann, 1891–93.

A.E.

DEROZIO, Henry. See **Indian Literature.**

DESANI, G. V. See **Indian Literature.**

DE VERE, Aubrey (1814–1902), born into a wealthy Protestant landowning family of county Limerick, was educated at Trinity College, Dublin and was introduced to, and became friendly with, leading English writers and intellectuals. During the Irish famine he worked assiduously throughout Ireland to relieve suffering and in 1851 became a Roman Catholic. He published small volumes of verse at regular intervals throughout his life.

Victim of his own limited experience and victim also of a sentimental tradition in nineteenth-century Anglo-Irish verse, De Vere's writing lacks profundity and originality of expression. His simple statements, best shown in the Irish dirges, are neatly expressed in conventional stanzaic forms. His small poetic virtue is his careful craftsmanship and a quiet seriousness of tone.

Irish Poets of the Nineteenth Century, ed. G. Taylor, London: Routledge; Cambridge, Mass.: Harvard Univ. Press, 1951.　　　　　C.P.

DEWEY, John (1859–1952), philosopher and educator, was born in Vermont, graduated from the University of Vermont (1879) and Johns Hopkins (Ph.D., 1884). He taught philosophy at several universities in the U.S.A., including Chicago where he founded the Laboratory School to test educational techniques. A major figure in the development of progressive education, Dewey emphasized the educational reforms necessitated by industrial and technological growth, the democratic concept and the human adjustments to environment required by modern societies. His most important educational writings include *The School and Society*, in which he stressed "learning by doing," *The Child and the Curriculum, Moral Principles in Education, Interest and Effort in Education* and *Experience and Education*. As a philosopher, Dewey expounded the pragmatism of William James and formulated a view of functional and environmental reality called "instrumentalism," fusing the individualism of James with the social consciousness of Charles Peirce. Since human problems constantly change, truth must itself, Dewey believed, always be hypothetical; the only knowledge is experience, and knowledge is necessarily functional. He developed these ideas in *Outlines of a Critical Theory of Ethics, How We Think, The Influence of Darwin on Philosophy and Other Essays* . . . , *Experience and Nature, The Quest for Certainty* and *Liberalism and Social Action*.

Outlines of a Critical Theory of Ethics, 1891.
The School and Society, 1899; revised, 1915.
The Child and the Curriculum, 1902.
How We Think, 1909.
Moral Principles in Education, 1909.
The Influence of Darwin on Philosophy, 1910.
Democracy and Education, 1916.
Experience and Nature, 1925.
The Quest for Certainty, 1929.
Art As Experience, 1934.
A Common Faith, 1934.

Liberalism and Social Action, 1935.
Experience and Education, 1938.

Early Works, 1882–98, 5 vols., Carbondale: Southern Illinois Univ. Press,
1969– .   J.W.

DICKENS, Charles (1812–70) was the second child of John Dickens,
a clerk in the navy pay office. His father, cheerful and improvident, was
to be his model for Micawber, as was his mother for Mrs. Nickleby.
Charles had a comfortable early childhood. He had an able schoolmaster;
at home he reveled in the novels of Defoe, Fielding, Smollett and others.
But when he was eleven the family's money difficulties became acute.
As soon as he was twelve, he was sent to work in a blacking factory in
conditions that he found degrading. John Dickens was arrested for debts
and confined to the Marshalsea prison, where his wife and younger
children joined him. Charles, who continued in work and lodged outside,
visited his family each Sunday. His intimate acquaintance with London
dated in part from this period. After three months a legacy released
John from the Marshalsea, and some time later he sent his son back to
school, this time under an ignorant and uncongenial master.

Leaving at fifteen, Charles obtained a post in a solicitor's office. For a
year and a half he remained in this work, acquiring a close knowledge of
legal types and ways. Then he learned shorthand and, after developing his
skill in reporting legal cases, became a parliamentary reporter in 1832.
As such, he worked in Parliament when it was in session, and in the
country when it was not, continually extending his observation of English
life.

Meanwhile, he had fallen in love with Maria Beadnell, who rejected
him. She appears as Dora in *David Copperfield* and Flora Finching in
Little Dorrit. In 1836, just as the serial publication of *The Pickwick Papers*
was starting, he married Catherine Hogarth, and late in this same year his
growing success as an independent writer enabled him to give up newspaper employment. Independence did not necessarily mean affluence,
however. Dickens's family responsibilities increased fast, and he was not
the man to shirk them; so he worked himself very hard.

In 1842 he visited America. His sympathy with the common man had
predisposed him favorably towards the republic. But the aggressive
sociability of the Americans exhausted him, he was repelled by much that
he observed, and his urging the need for an international copyright
agreement provoked newpaper abuse. He was glad to leave; and when he
dispatched the hero of *Martin Chuzzlewit* to America, he supplied a
picture of that country which American readers naturally resented. A

second, highly successful, American tour occurred in 1867–68. Dickens also resided for long spells in France, Switzerland and Italy.

During his middle and later years the writing of his novels occupied by no means the whole of his time. His early successes had gained him admission into literary and fashionable society, and he continued to move freely in these spheres. He engaged strenuously in philanthropic work—for example, on behalf of the ragged schools and of a reformatory home for prostitutes. He edited the new radical *Daily News* for a short time, and the weeklies *Household Words* and *All the Year Round* for considerable periods. A talented actor, he threw himself into amateur theatrical ventures in aid of charity. About the time of the separation from his wife (1858), he began to put a good deal of his energy into public readings from his works. These were semidramatic performances. They were immensely popular, but extremely exhausting to the performer. Dickens's friends believed that they shortened his life.

All fifteen of his novels were first published as serials, most of them in monthly numbers unaccompanied by other matter. Initially, he had this form wished on to him by a publisher. Immediately after the appearance of his *Sketches by Boz* (1836) Chapman and Hall invited him to contribute the text to accompany a series of sporting illustrations by Robert Seymour, the work to be brought out monthly in shilling parts. Hablot K. Browne ("Phiz") soon replaced Seymour and so became Dickens's illustrator not only for *The Pickwick Papers* but also for most of his novels.

Dickens quickly perceived the advantages that serial publication had for him, and the monthly number remained his favorite vehicle throughout his life. As author he was normally only one installment ahead of his readers. He would aim to deliver his manuscript to the printer by the twentieth for publication on the last day of the month. He had necessarily to keep in close touch with his illustrator, who might well be working on a scene he had conceived but not yet written.

The "central idea" or master plan of each novel probably existed only in Dickens's head. But from *Dombey and Son* (s. 1846–48) onwards he wrote out a plan for each number. These number plans have survived. Each consists of a sheet of paper, on the left-hand half of which Dickens has jotted down memoranda relating to the number under consideration—doubts regarding such matters as the themes to be introduced in it, the names to be given to new characters, and his decisions on these points. On the right-hand half he has organized his notes under his three or four chapter headings. In each number plan Dickens was sketching the way his book was to go for the next few thousand words; the collected number plans provided him with a brief record of its course so far, a record which he could usefully consult when composing new numbers. This method left him free to modify future developments within the broad and flexible limits of an unwritten master plan, and at the same time supplied him with a concise record which could prevent his losing sight of what had gone before. So his novel might develop unpredictably without lapsing into incoherence.

It was important to Dickens that it should be free to develop unpredictably. He was always highly sensitive to his readers' reactions to the work in progress. These reactions might find expression in critical comments, uttered privately or publicly and communicated directly or indirectly; or they might be implied in rising or falling sales. Occasionally, Dickens's adjustment of his narrative in response to the criticism they conveyed is clearly demonstrable: for example, he developed the role of Sam Weller in *The Pickwick Papers*, he sent Martin Chuzzlewit to America, he decided against using Walter Gay in *Dombey and Son* for a study in moral decline and he altered the ending of *Great Expectations*. Some of these changes of intention were beneficial, others not.

But the value of Dickens's method of composition is not to be assessed merely by examining such particular palpable results of it. Its value to him was that it permitted him to achieve and to maintain the closest intimacy with his readers. More nearly than any other major English novelist, he was in the position of an oral storyteller. A good oral storyteller watches his listeners and allows what he observes to dictate to some extent the tempo of his narrative, its pitch, and at times its course. Moreover, his awareness of his listeners' interest sustains him; and, if he can feel that they share his major beliefs and attitudes, an additional spontaneity and vitality may be imparted to his performance.

This was very much Dickens's position. He watched his readers' changing reactions to each unfolding serial and adjusted his performance to what he observed. He knew his public intimately and was happy to serve it and to be its spokesman. To a considerable extent he shared its attitudes and creed: its Christian sentiment and morality, its humanitarianism, its political individualism and distrust of established authority, its indifference or even hostility to tradition and its love of humor. His closeness to it is clear in his advocacy of social reforms. When he attacked the Court of Chancery in *Bleak House* and the Circumlocution Office in *Little Dorrit*, he was not a lonely pioneer; others had attacked these institutions before him. Nor was he merely a camp follower, pretending to contribute to a victory that was already won; much really was still wrong with the law and the Civil Service. Characteristically, he participated in an already growing awareness of the need for this or that reform; and by giving the movement his assistance he promoted its success. He was all the more effective as a leader of opinion in that he was not too far in advance of the opinion he led.

Dickens's sense that he enjoyed the support of a vast, sympathetic, exacting public, together with his desire to retain its backing, helped to give his work assurance, spontaneity, breadth of appeal and vitality. In the service of this public he exploited his extraordinary gifts—his delighted observation of persons and places, his sharp eye for significant features and mannerisms, his quick ear for genuinely expressive turns of phrase, his irrepressible sense of humor, and the splendidly animated prose in which he fixed unforgettably the observed traits which he had selected to dominate a portrait or a landscape. He exploited these gifts with a view to displaying, to exhibiting, rather than to analyzing, his characters. A typical Dickens novel was written to be read first of all at the rate of three or four chapters a month over a period of a year and a half by a predominantly practical, individualistic, moral, humanitarian and Christian public. The situation called for a Dickensian exhibition, rather than a Jamesian dissection, of the characters and of the moral issues they faced. It favored as bold and emphatic, as vivid and even exuberant, an exhibition as Dickens's genius enabled him to stage. When he fails, we complain of overemphasis and forced exaggeration. But when he succeeds, we enter into the Dickens world.

Everything in the Dickens world is larger than life. Persons, places and things are more odd, more ludicrous, more sinister, more appealing, more somber, more lighthearted and more grotesque than in what we suppose, myopically perhaps, to be reality. Nor does the imagination of Dickens stop at creating this world; it also endows certain of the persons and things in it with a representative, even a symbolic, significance. Examples include Krook, the secretive dipsomaniac who is the lord chancellor's counterpart in *Bleak House*; Bradley Headstone, the desperately repressed exponent of self-help and respectability in *Our Mutual Friend*; the prisons, whether literally or metaphorically such, which throw their shadows over *Little Dorrit*; the slums and the diseases bred in them, which we never quite forget in *Bleak House*; the spreading railway in *Dombey and Son*; the circus in *Hard Times*; the dustheaps in *Our Mutual Friend*; the river in the same novel; and the cathedral in *Edwin Drood*. Whether Dickens deliberately planned that this or that item should carry the weight of significance that we feel it to carry, or whether its significance was the undesigned outcome of his obsessive mode of composition, is an interesting biographical question. A literary critic may be content to say that the significance is certainly there.

Sketches by Boz, 1836.
The Pickwick Papers, 1837 (*s*. 1836–37; *f*. 1952).
Oliver Twist, 1838 (*s*. 1837–39; *f*. 1933; 1948; as *Oliver*, 1968).
Nicholas Nickleby, 1839 (*s*. 1838–39; *f*. 1948).

The Old Curiosity Shop, 1841 ⎱ (both *s*. as part of
Barnaby Rudge, 1841 ⎰ *Master Humphrey's Clock*, 1840–41).
A Christmas Carol, 1843 (*f*. 1935; 1938; as *Scrooge*, 1951; 1970).
Martin Chuzzlewit, 1844 (*s*. 1843–44).
Dombey and Son, 1848 (*s*. 1846–48).
David Copperfield, 1850 (*s*. 1849–50; *f*. 1935; 1969).
Bleak House, 1853 (*s*. 1852–53).
Hard Times, 1854.
Little Dorrit, 1857 (*s*. 1855–57).
A Tale of Two Cities, 1859 (*f*. 1935; 1957).
Great Expectations, 1861 (*s*. 1860–61; *f*. 1934; 1946).
Our Mutual Friend, 1865 (*s*. 1864–65).
Edwin Drood (unfinished), 1870 (*f*. 1935).

The New Oxford Illustrated Dickens, 21 vols., London: Oxford Univ. Press, 1947–58.
The Clarendon Dickens, ed. J. Butt and K. Tillotson, Oxford: Clarendon Press, 1966– .
Letters, Pilgrim edition, ed. M. House and G. Storey, Oxford: Clarendon Press, 1965– .   J.D.J.

DICKEY, James (1923–) was born in Atlanta (Georgia) and educated at Clemson College and Vanderbilt University. In the Second World War and in Korea Dickey served in the U.S. Air Force. After a year in France, he began in 1955 a successful advertising career which he abandoned for writing in 1961. Obsession with his experience as a bomber pilot—a "technical-minded stranger with my hands"—is a significant part of his work, especially in *Buckdancer's Choice* (1965). Also prominent are steady intensity, impressive craftsmanship and a versatile handling of sound. His first volume of poetry, *Into the Stone and Other Poems*, appeared in 1960, and has been followed by *Drowning with Others* (1962), *Helmets* (1964), *Poems 1957–67* (1967), and in 1970 *The Eyebeaters, Blood, Victory, Madness, Buckhead and Mercy*, and a novel, *Deliverance*. Essays first published in *The Suspect in Poetry* (1964) reappeared in an enlarged edition *Babel to Byzantium* (1968). In 1970 he published a prose work drawn from taped conversations, *Self-Interviews*.   J.P.W.

DICKINSON, Emily (1830–86) lived through one of the most traumatically disturbing periods of American history, with the Civil War and its aftermath dividing and dissipating the nation's spiritual, emotional and economic resources. Yet nothing of this appears specifically in her poetry. It is intensely private and personal, a self-examination and analysis as searching and deliberate as any seventeenth-century Puritan's. The vast events mirrored in her poetry lie within the mind and experience of a sheltered woman, moving from kitchen to drawing room to garden, in a New England village.

Emily Dickinson was born and died in Amherst (Massachusetts). She traveled away from home rarely—except for a period at Mount Holyoke Female Seminary—particularly as she grew older. Her mother was a gentle, sickly woman, who later required much nursing care from Emily; her sister, Lavinia, a devoted and loyal friend; her brother Austin, a lawyer and family man like his father. But Edward Dickinson was the dominant figure in the family. Though his daughter Emily said of him, "his heart was pure and terrible," he was not merely a stereotype New England Puritan. A man of great integrity and public virtue, he was a member of Congress and the Legislature as well as a leading lawyer and treasurer of the newly established Amherst College. His profound influence on Emily Dickinson appears both in her letters, and less consciously, in the poetry. Her letters also show the lively and affectionate interest she had in family and friends, which somewhat counterbalances the exaggerated legends of the white-garbed recluse, the "nun of Amherst."

Nevertheless, by 1870 a preference for solitude had become a morbid withdrawal from public life. Some great blow fell upon her about 1862, which inspired a burst of great poetic creativity, but indirectly led to her retirement from the world. Earnest efforts have failed to decide absolutely who was her "lover." Four men had varying degrees of influence upon her: Leonard Humphrey and Benjamin Newton were early friends and mentors; Charles Wadsworth, a distinguished Philadelphia clergyman, entered into a tutelary and pastoral relationship with her; and Thomas Higginson was a later friend and literary adviser. Of these Humphrey and Newton died tragically young (one recalls here Emily Dickinson's early preoccupation with death); Wadsworth accepted a call to minister in California and "left the land"; and Higginson she met on very few occasions. The inevitable conclusion is that Emily Dickinson's passionate love and anguished loss were indeed real, but that the relationship—probably with Wadsworth—was not overt. Like Keats, Emily Dickinson suffered the torments of love; but hers was undeclared.

Emily Dickinson wrote poetry from an early age and showed it to carefully selected persons throughout her life. She refused, however, to publish and kept much of her writing a closely guarded secret even from her family. After her death a box was found containing about 900 poems, from which a selection was made and published in 1890. The total number eventually collected and published was 1,775. Most of her poems are short lyrics, in form and meter much like the eighteenth-century hymns of Isaac Watts and punctuated by her unique, "breathless" method of dashes.

Her period of greatest creativity was in the early 1860s, when the intensity of her spiritual and emotional sufferings gave a magnificent and relentless logic and unity to her poems. Difficulties of obscure ellipses and symbolism are dissipated.

It must inevitably be an artificial exercise to pick out Emily Dickinson's poetic "themes." Her poetry has been well described as "spiritual auto-biography"; all experience available to a woman of her sensibility and background thus became a poetic treasury for her art. Her imagery springs mainly from the natural and domestic world around her, from the Bible, romance, myth and history. It is significant that later in her life she remarked: "Existence has overpowered books." Although her poetry was extraordinarily "modern" for its time, in no sense could it be described as "contemporary." Any comparison with Whitman confirms this. In her poetry Emily Dickinson meditates on her growing experience of life, on friendship and loss of friendship through death, on love and its agonies. She frequently uses the language of Calvinism to describe her passionate love and its transfiguring glory. God and her lover become rivals. Afterwards, despair replaces ecstasy, and gnawing secret pain must be endured.

Death, the greatest mystery, gradually becomes one of her major poetic obsessions, as it cuts a swath through those she loves, young and old. Pondering on the transience of life and fame leads her to note the inevitable decay in nature, reflected above all in the seasonal changes. Occasionally, a certain macabre morbidity creeps in. The imponderables of eternity and immortality are an easy step. Emily Dickinson has an ambiguous relationship with God throughout her poetry. Unlike most of her family and friends, she never underwent the traditional Puritan experience of conversion and commitment, being too clear-eyed to accept what had often become mere formulae. Yet she constantly identifies truth and beauty with God, and especially after her sufferings in love sought a more personal relationship with him. Her attitude to God ranges from that of scornful empress to that of pleading or playful child.

The childlike pose is one which Emily Dickinson seems to enjoy. Whilst it is sometimes engaging, it can also become tedious. It is, however, characteristic of the highly personal tone of her poetry, achieved partly by the subject matter, and partly by techniques like first person narration and use of casual and colloquial speech. She delights in ambiguity, paradox, ellipsis and obscure syntax. Her vocabulary ranges from virtual dialect to theological technicalities, and a number of words like "bee," "purple," "eternity," "noon" and "immortality" recur frequently. Her poetic ear is acute, and she plays with exact and near rhymes, as well as experimenting with the traditional Watts psalmodic meter. Obliqueness, "slantness" and privateness all characterize Emily Dickinson's poetry; the tone can be despairing, ironic, even sentimental.

Her poetic faults can readily be guessed. Unnecessary ambiguity becomes obscurity; elements of whimsy and coyness cloy the palate; too many variants of a single thought or image become monotonous; and the brevity of the lyrics sometimes implies a kind of complacent tidiness of thought. Yet her greatest poems are superbly faceted jewels. Emotion and image are firmly married, and everyday domestic or natural detail gains an often startling profundity of meaning. Emily Dickinson is a bold poet of great originality, whose private drama strengthens the individual excellences of her lyrics. Her latter-day Puritan background makes her poetry as distinctly American as Whitman's.

Poems by Emily Dickinson, ed. M. L. Todd and T. W. Higginson, 1890.
Poems: Second Series, ed. M. L. Todd and T. W. Higginson, 1891.
Letters of Emily Dickinson, ed. M. L. Todd, 2 vols., 1894.
Poems: Third Series, ed. M. L. Todd, 1896.
The Single Hound, 1914.
Further Poems, ed. M. D. Bianchi and A. L. Hampson, 1929.
Unpublished Poems, ed. M. D. Bianchi and A. L. Hampson, 1935.
Bolts of Melody, ed. M. L. Todd and M. T. Binham, 1945.

Poems, Including Variant Readings Critically Compared with All Known Manuscripts, ed. T. H. Johnson, 3 vols., Cambridge, Mass.: Harvard Univ. Press; London: Oxford Univ. Press, 1955.
Complete Poems, ed. T. H. Johnson, Boston: Little, Brown, 1960.
Letters, ed. T. H. Johnson and T. Ward, 3 vols., Cambridge, Mass.: Harvard Univ. Press; London: Oxford Univ. Press, 1958.   s.c.

DISRAELI, Benjamin, 1st Earl of Beaconsfield (1804–81), came of an ancient Sephardi family, the eldest son of Isaac D'Israeli, a scholarly and kindly man now chiefly remembered for his *Curiosities of Literature* (1791–1834). Benjamin as a child was baptized into the Christian church. He read widely in his father's large library and had ambitions to be a writer. Isaac unsuccessfully tried to make him a lawyer. His first novel, *Vivian Grey* (1826–27), published anonymously, is an improbable but lively tale of a young man's efforts to secure a place in political and aristocratic society. He was undaunted by the storm of abuse which broke when London society discovered that the man who wrote with such audacious confidence was an obscure nonentity. With characteristic perseverance he observed, thought and wrote tirelessly. He was always keen for action on a grand scale; his love affairs were colorful and tumultuous, his debts staggering. One of his heroes was Byron. In 1831–32 he went on a Byronic Grand Tour, of which the climax was a visit to Jerusalem, the city he regarded as the source of spiritual life. He saw politics as the perfect sphere for his imagination and ambition. The early satire, *The*

Voyage of Captain Popanilla (1828), is against the utilitarians, whom he regarded as soulless materialists (see **Bentham, Jeremy**). In *A Vindication of the English Constitution* (1835) he pronounced the Tory party "the really democratic party of England" because it supported the country's traditional institutions established for the common good. His early novels are all sentimental romances saved from mawkishness by a lively wit and sardonic humor—*The Young Duke* (1831); *Contarini Fleming* (1832); *Alroy* (1833), a florid historical romance with a Jewish hero; *Henrietta Temple* (1837); and *Venetia* (1837), a fictional account of the lives of Shelley and Byron.

Disraeli entered Parliament in 1837 and organized opposition to Peel with a group of friends who styled themselves "Young England," a Tory ginger group emphasizing the party's social obligations. *Coningsby* (1844) and *Sybil* (1845) propagate Young England ideas, particularly the responsibility of the aristocracy in the country's leadership. Carelessly constructed, with wildly improbable plots, the novels are remarkable in the scope of their social observation and unique in re-creating the business and minutiae of politics. The character of Lord Monmouth, the old-style Tory, is a brilliant satire. Disraeli's lively rhetoric holds the novels together. *Tancred* (1847), an inferior novel, concludes the trilogy: it is a rhapsodic account of spiritual truth revealed in the Jewish faith.

Disraeli's political activity increased and he had no time to write novels. In 1852 he became chancellor of the Exchequer, and prime minister for a few months in 1868. In his enforced leisure he wrote *Lothair* (1870), a romance which is also a study of contemporary revolutionary Europe. He was again prime minister from 1874 to 1880, and in the latter year his last complete novel, *Endymion*, was published. It is a mellower version of contemporary political life than *Coningsby* or *Sybil* and lacks their vigor and wit, but has a certain nostalgic charm. He left an unfinished novel, *Falconet*, at his death in 1881.

Disraeli is a lesser novelist of considerable interest. He was an active politician, never a dedicated literary artist. His descriptions of romantic love are stagy, his novels are badly constructed and take refuge in literary clichés of plot and description, but they are developments of the discursive eighteenth-century novel, not failed attempts at the tightly organized novel later perfected by Henry James. Disraeli was one of the first writers to make the novel a vehicle for serious thought, and his vigorous concern with ideas as well as emotions makes his books invigorating. His command of political satire in self-revealing dialogue has no equal in the English novel.

Vivian Grey, 1826–27.
The Voyage of Captain Popanilla, 1828.

The Young Duke, 1831.
Contarini Fleming, 1832.
The Wondrous Tale of Alroy, 1833.
Henrietta Temple, 1837.
Venetia, 1837.
Coningsby, 1844.
Sybil, 1845.
Tancred, 1847.
Lothair, 1870.
Endymion, 1880.

Novels and Tales, ed. P. Guedalla, 12 vols., London: P. Davies, 1926–27.
S.M.S.

DIXON, R. W. (Richard Watson) (1833–1900), son of a Methodist minister, took Anglican orders after rejecting the dedication to art undertaken by his Oxford friends, Edward Burne-Jones and William Morris, though for some months he studied under D. G. Rossetti. His achievement, six books of verse containing a few successful lyrics, and *Mano* (1838), a narrative poem claimed by some as the finest of its age, and a six-volume *A History of the Church of England* (1878–1902), well researched despite the remoteness of his parishes, is overshadowed by his place with Bridges as the small Victorian audience of Gerard Manley Hopkins to whom Dixon gave diffident but perceptive and encouraging help.

Poems: A Selection, ed. R. Bridges, London: Smith, Elder, 1909.
Letters of G. M. Hopkins to Robert Bridges and R. W. Dixon, ed. C. C. Abbott, 2 vols., London: Oxford Univ. Press, 1935.   K.T.

DIXON, Thomas (1864–1946), novelist and playwright, born in North Carolina, was educated at Wake Forrest College and Greensboro Law School, North Carolina. A Baptist minister and popular lyceum lecturer, he achieved fame with his trilogy of novels depicting Reconstruction in the South. *The Leopard's Spots* (1902), *The Clansman* (1905) and *The Traitor* (1907) reflect a violent hatred of Negroes, depicted as depraved and vicious animals, an admiration for the terroristic Ku Klux Klan, and disgust with the attempt of radical Republicans "to Africanize the ten great states of the American Union." Dixon also wrote *The Flaming Sword* (1939) and the screenplay for the motion picture *The Birth of a Nation* (1915), based on *The Clansman*.   J.W.

DOANE, George W. (Washington). See **Hymns.**

DOBELL, Sydney. See **Spasmodics, The.**

DOBSON, Austin (1840–1921) was born at Plymouth and studied in Strasbourg. He worked at the Board of Trade from 1856 to 1906, for a number of years in the same department as Sir Edmund Gosse. Most of Dobson's energies went into his writing. He was a prolific versifier, mostly in artificial French forms such as the villanelle, and *Old World Idylls* (1883) was long popular. Despite a carefully cultivated urbanity and cosiness of manner he was genuinely expert in eighteenth-century matters and wrote on Hogarth, Fielding, Steele, Goldsmith, Fanny Burney and Walpole. He is at his best in *Eighteenth Century Vignettes* (1892–96).

Complete Poetical Works, ed. A. T. A. Dobson, London: Oxford Univ. Press, 1923.   w.s.

DOMETT, Alfred. See **New Zealand Literature.**

DONLEAVY, J. P. (James Patrick) (1926–   ) was born in Brooklyn, attended Trinity College, Dublin, and lives, elusively, as an expatriate. He created in his first novel, *The Ginger Man* (1955), the figure of Sebastian Dangerfield, whose Dionysian zest leads him to totter on the brink of annihilation. George Smith, the exhausted hero of Donleavy's second novel, *A Singular Man* (1963), lives a life of wary isolation until Eros returns him, temporarily, to humanity. In *The Onion Eaters* (1971) the characters cavort with cold and sometimes calculated lust, but the Donleavy hero, a man of God, knows his demesne. Apart from other novels, Donleavy has written short stories, *Meet My Maker, The Mad Molecule* (1964), and a play, *Fairy Tales of New York* (1961).   w.s.

DONNE, John (1572–1631) was the son of a London merchant of Welsh family, and was related on his mother's side to John Heywood, the dramatist, and Sir Thomas More. Educated as a Catholic, he went to Oxford and subsequently to Cambridge. From 1591 to 1594 he was at Lincoln's Inn and, according to a contemporary at this time, "a great visitor of ladies, a great frequenter of plays, a great writer of conceited verses"; but he was also known to be a wide reader whose studies included controversial theology. In 1593 his brother Henry died in prison for sheltering a seminary priest. In 1595–96 Donne was probably traveling abroad, and he took part in Essex's expeditions of 1596 and 1597 to Cadiz and the Azores. On his return he was made secretary to the lord keeper of the Great Seal, Sir Thomas Egerton, and it is likely that by this time he had become an Anglican. He seemed on his way to a distinguished career in public life, but his prospects were ruined by his secret marriage in 1601 to Anne More, Egerton's ward and niece by marriage. For the next seven years or so Donne lived in poverty, struggling with frustration, ill health and family cares, and he remained dependent on various patrons up to the time of his ordination in 1615. During this period he assisted Thomas Morton in anti-Catholic propaganda, wrote prose works of meditation, controversy and satire (*Biathanatos, Pseudo-Martyr* and *Ignatius His Conclave*) and published the two anniversary poems (1611 and 1612) in memory of Elizabeth Drury, the young daughter of his patron, Sir Robert Drury. Finally, after much hesitation and despite pressure even from the king, Donne was ordained. He became reader in divinity at Lincoln's Inn, a royal chaplain, and in 1621 dean of St. Paul's. In 1617 his wife died, and it was largely to restore his health after this blow that he was sent to accompany Lord Doncaster on his embassy in Germany in 1619–20. During a serious illness in 1623 he composed the prose *Devotions upon Emergent Occasions*. In 1625 he sheltered from the plague at the house of Lady Danvers, an old friend and George Herbert's mother. In his last years he was the most eloquent and famous preacher of his day; and his best-known sermon, *Death's Duel*, was delivered only seven weeks before his own death. His literary friends included Hoskyns, Wotton, Walton, King, Herbert and Jonson.

Most of Donne's poems were not published until the collected volume of 1633, though during his lifetime many had circulated in manuscript among his friends. Exact dating is often difficult—most of the *Songs and Sonnets* belong to the 1590s, while the *Divine Poems* begin with "La Corona" about 1607 and continue to the hymns of his last years, but about many of the best-known poems there is considerable uncertainty.

The *Songs and Sonnets* contain no sonnets in the strict sense of the term and are not songs of the kind we normally expect from an Elizabethan. It is the speaking rather than the singing voice that strikes us here, with its colloquial diction, familiar tone and dramatic directness, not only in arresting openings—

> Busy old fool, unruly sun,
> For God's sake hold your tongue, and let me love.

—but in the whole play of stress and movement throughout a stanza. Donne's rhythm always seems to work through the whole stanza rather than the single line, and his treatment is essentially dramatic. Similarly, his handling of the couplet in the *Elegies, Satires* and *Anniversaries* uses licenses like those of dramatic blank verse, always in the service of expressive emphasis and the driving home of the meaning:

> On a huge hill
> Cragged, and steep, Truth stands, and he that will
> Reach her, about must, and about must go:
> And what the hill's suddenness resists, win so.

Recognizing this dramatic movement, we are no longer so ready as earlier readers to blame Donne for harshness and a "defective ear." Two other distinguishing aspects of Donne's poetry are its argumentative structure and its use of unexpected analogies or "conceits." Neither of these was new in itself, but there had been nothing before like the subtlety, range and force of Donne's thought. It was as though play of intellect tended to become for him an emotional experience, and that, equally, when deeply moved his mind only worked more rapidly. His dialectical habit of mind may be partly due to his Catholic education and his study of scholastic philosophy. His fondness for its terms and ideas led later to the use of the word "Metaphysical" to describe his kind of wit. But Donne's conceits are not merely learned: much of the effect lies in suddenly turning from abstruse philosophizing to homely realism, so that cosmology and alchemy intermingle with powder flask and "bed's feet," and phoenixes and mandrakes with "late schoolboys and sour prentices." What we do not find is the merely ornamental. At its best the wit has the imaginative surprise of the lines on Elizabeth Drury:

> . . . her pure and eloquent blood
> Spoke in her cheeks, and so distinctly wrought
> That one might almost say, her body thought.

Donne's style is of a piece with his choice and treatment of subject. As he avoided Spenser's melodious fluency or the decorative use of classical mythology, so he abandoned the Petrarchan conventions in order to analyze the experience of love, always with the same acute realism, in a variety of moods ranging from cynical sensuality to a profound sense of union. When in later life he turned to religious poetry there was no essential change of style or method: he draws on the same variety and range of reference, and the same dramatic power expresses the emotional intensity of mental conflict. Conflict and anxiety are largely characteristic of the *Divine Poems*, but a more assured faith appears in some of the late hymns. It is for his love poetry and religious poetry that Donne is chiefly known, but his occasional and miscellaneous verse has its rewarding moments, and throughout his work his Metaphysical wit provides the means of bringing all sides of his experience into relation with the immediate subject.

(See also **Metaphysical Poetry**.)

Poems, 1633.

Poems, ed. H. Grierson, 2 vols., Oxford: Clarendon Press, 1912.
Divine Poems, ed. H. Gardner, Oxford: Clarendon Press, 1952.
Elegies and the Songs and Sonnets, ed. H. Gardner, Oxford: Clarendon Press, 1965.
Satires, Epigrams and Verse Letters, ed. W. Milgate, Oxford: Clarendon Press, 1967.
Sermons, ed. G. R. Potter and E. M. Simpson, 10 vols., Berkeley and Los Angeles: Univ. of California Press, 1953–62.
Devotions upon Emergent Occasions, ed. J. Sparrow, London: Macmillan, 1923.   R.G.C.

DONNELLY, Ignatius (1831–1901) was born in Philadelphia, the son of an Irish physician. Having read law for a while, he tried land speculation in the 1850s, buying up land at Nininger (Minnesota), where, after the panic of 1875 left him in debt, he became a farmer. As writer, editor and politician he was considered eccentric and given the titles "Sage of Nininger," and "Prince of Cranks." At the age of twenty-eight he was the Republican lieutenant governor of his state and then went to Congress, but he later became a Democrat and then an active Populist, leading the Farmers' Alliance into that party and being their candidate for vice-president in 1900. In later years he edited *The Representative*. Apart from championing apocalyptic history, Atlantis, and Francis Bacon (as the author of Shakespeare's plays), he wrote his most famous work, *Caesar's Column: A Story of the Twentieth Century* (1891), in which the conflict between the proletariat and the rich oligarchy is seen to end in a vast and bloody war, followed by a savage chaos and the escape of the hero to an idyllic utopia. This book was second only to Bellamy's *Looking Backward* in popularity.   D.C.

DOOLITTLE, Hilda ("H.D.") (1886–1961) was born in Bethlehem (Pennsylvania), went to Europe in 1911, married the English poet Richard Aldington and settled abroad. Early in her poetic career she was acquainted with Ezra Pound and William Carlos Williams, and through them became a confirmed disciple of imagism, a poetic movement advocating the presentation of hard, clear, concentrated images. Her early poems, in such volumes as *Sea Garden* (1916) and *Heliodora and Other Poems* (1924), are elegantly wrought collections of pictures, drawing often on classic Greek themes. More remarkable are some of the novels—*Palimpsest* (1926), *Bid Me to Live* (1960)—and a huge lyrical poem, *Helen in Egypt* (1961). (See also **Imagism.**)   R.W.

DORN, Edward (1929–   ) was born in the prairie town of Villa Grove (Illinois) and educated at the University of Illinois and Black Mountain College. He has edited the poetry journal *Wild Dog*, and has taught at a number of universities in America and at the University of Essex in England. His early books of poetry, from *The Newly Fallen* (1961) to *Geography* (1965), and a long prose work, *Rites of Passage* (1965), are lyric mappings. *The North Atlantic Turbine* (1967) contains the fine long poem, "Oxford," and also the first visitation of Dorn's transubstantiated gunslinger. In *Gunslinger Book 1* (1968) and *Gunslinger Book 2* (1969), Dorn demonstrates smoking "speed."   w.s.

DOS PASSOS, John (1896–1970) was born in Chicago, the son of a successful corporation and criminal lawyer descended from Portuguese and American Quaker stock. He was educated at Harvard, where he contributed to several magazines, some of his college verse being later published in *Eight Harvard Poets* (1917). His father, who had fought in the Civil War, prevented him from joining an American ambulance unit in 1916 by financing a year of architectural study in Spain. When his father died, however, Dos Passos enlisted in the Norton-Harjes unit and served in Italy and France. These experiences provided the background for his first novels, *One Man's Initiation: 1917* (1920) and *Three Soldiers* (1921). Throughout the 1920s he traveled extensively, and wrote about Europe, the Near East and Russia. He found time to write two novels, *Streets of Night* (1923) and *Manhattan Transfer* (1925), two plays, *The Garbage Man* (1926) and *Airways Inc.* (1928), and a defense of Sacco and Vanzetti, *Facing the Chair* (1927). He also helped found and worked for both *The New Masses* magazine and The New Playwrights' Theater.

Throughout the 1930s Dos Passos continued his career as playwright, novelist and political reporter, though his major literary effort went into the writing of the three volumes of *U.S.A.* (1938)—*The Forty-Second Parallel* (1930), *1919*, (1932) and *The Big Money* (1936). During and after the Second World War Dos Passos became increasingly interested in the roots of American culture and produced a number of historical studies relating to the problems of American democracy. At the same time he was at work on his second trilogy of novels, *The Adventures of a Young Man* (1939), *Number One* (1943) and *The Grand Design* (1949)—brought together as *District of Columbia* in 1952. By now he had severed all connections with left-wing political movements, becoming at one period a Goldwater Republican, and, though he continued to publish novels like *Mid-Century* (1961), loosely patterned on *U.S.A.*, much of his work was autobiographical or semiautobiographical, such as *Chosen Country* (1951) and *The Great Days* (1958).

Dos Passos's best fiction has a pessimism different in kind and more profound than that found in the work of any of his American contemporaries. His attitudes to life in general and to American society in particular derive from the naturalists, but his importance in the history of fiction comes from his introduction into naturalistic fiction of a more subtle technique for representing life in its subjective/objective states. Sartre, who comes closer than anyone to understanding the significance of Dos Passos's major novels, maintains that " 'Dos Passos' man is a hybrid creature, an interior/exterior being. We go on living with and within him, with his vacillating individual consciousness, when suddenly it wavers, weakens, and is diluted in the collective consciousness." A growing awareness of the failure of the individual consciousness to resist usurpation by the machine led him to say in 1936—the year of the Spanish Civil War—that the world had arrived at "one of the damnedest tragic moments of history." If the 1920s were years which, for Dos Passos, stripped the bunting off the great illusions of our time and laid bare "the raw structure of history" beneath, they were also the years in which he learned to create a fiction of impassioned objectivity with some of the quality he was later to admire in Fitzgerald's *The Last Tycoon*—the "quality of detaching itself from its period while embodying its period."

The quality of this detachment underwent a radical change at the end of the 1920s, brought about undoubtedly by Dos Passos's political experiences in general, and as Alfred Kazin argues, more particularly as the result of his bitter involvement in the Sacco and Vanzetti affair. Whatever the cause, it made possible the writing of his masterpiece, *U.S.A.*, in which the ineffectual struggles against the world of his earlier aesthete-romantic heroes is superseded by a more complex and subtle dialectic. The phenomenology of *U.S.A.* is unique not only in Dos Passos's work, but in twentieth-century fiction as a whole. To argue, as many critics have done, that Dos Passos mechanically applies the superficial tricks of neomodernist technique to a naturalist novel is to miss completely the point of his structural and stylistic innovations. The relationship between individual characters (there are, of course, no heroes in *U.S.A.*) and the historical and environmental forces they shape and are shaped by does not admit of any but an artificial separation. In contrast, the prose poems of *District of Columbia*, preceding each chapter, are not only crudely written themselves, but are also related to the book's fictional and historical structure in a much cruder way.

One Man's Initiation: 1917, 1920.
Three Soldiers, 1921.

Streets of Night, 1923.
Manhattan Transfer, 1925.
U.S.A., 1938 (*The Forty-Second Parallel*, 1930; *1919*, 1932; *The Big Money*, 1936).
District of Columbia, 1952 (*The Adventures of a Young Man*, 1939; *Number One*, 1943; *The Grand Design*, 1949).
Mid-Century, 1961.
The Best Times, 1966.   B.L.

DOUGLAS, Gavin (? 1474–1522), son of the fifth earl of Angus, was born into a powerful and ambitious family. Educated at St. Andrews University, and possibly also in Paris, he soon received ecclesiastical preferment, and by 1503 had become provost of St. Giles, Edinburgh. After the Battle of Flodden and his nephew's marriage to Margaret, widow of James IV, Douglas was increasingly prominent in political affairs and obtained the important bishopric of Dunkeld (1516). Following the fall of his nephew, he was denounced as a traitor and died, an exile, in London.

Douglas's earliest extant poem, *The Palace of Honour* (written c. 1501), is an allegorical dream, modeled in part on Chaucer's *The House of Fame*. Its ostensible subject is a quest for honor, but Douglas has much to say about love and poetry and his poetic aspirations. Douglas's major work is *The Eneados* (written 1511–12), a verse translation of Virgil's *Aeneid*. Despite its diffuseness and the presence of a thirteenth book (written by Maphaeus Vegius), together with explanatory matter derived from Virgilian commentors such as Servius and Ascensius, *The Eneados* is remarkably accurate and historically important as the first of the great Tudor translations from the classics. Douglas's most original poetry is found in the prologues that precede each book of *The Eneados*; these reveal his ability as literary critic, moralist and landscape poet.

The Palace of Honour, London, c. 1553; Edinburgh, 1579.
The Eneados, 5 MSS. extant; first edition, London, 1553.
Virgil's Aeneid, Translated . . . by Gavin Douglas, ed. D. F. C. Coldwell, Edinburgh: Scottish Text Society, 1957–64.
Shorter Poems, ed. P. J. Bawcutt, Edinburgh: Scottish Text Society, 1967.
                                                                          P.B.

DOUGLAS, Keith (1920–44) was born at Tunbridge Wells (Kent) and educated at Oxford. Edmund Blunden, who was his tutor, helped him to get his early poems published. Called up for active service in 1940, he was posted to North Africa where many of his best poems were written. He was killed in Normandy in 1944. The image of death and the attitude of restrained, even grim acceptance are recurrent in his poems, and memorably combined in "Simplify me when I'm dead." His power lies in the construction of compelling pictorial fables from the fragments of a violent or horrific wartime episode. More limited in feeling than Alun Lewis, he looks death straight in the eye, his tight-lipped restraint serving to deglamorize war. (See also **War Poets.**)

Collected Poems, ed. J. Waller and G. S. Fraser, London: Editions Poetry, 1951.   O.K.

DOUGLAS, Norman (1868–1952), though born in England, was the product of a cosmopolitan culture—brought up in Austria, widely traveled in Europe and resident in Italy. Much of his writing is travel literature, combining realism and exoticism, as in *Old Calabria* (1915), an account of the region surrounding Naples. Though he wrote more than one novel, he is chiefly remembered for *South Wind* (1917), which revives a vanished world of wit, allusive conversation, leisure and indiscreet diversion on the island of Nepenthe. In this novel the method resembles that of Peacock, whose recipe for the novel of ideas is brought up to date.   O.K.

DOUGLASS, Frederick (1817–95), Negro Abolitionist, journalist and orator, was born into slavery in Maryland. He escaped to Massachusetts in 1838 and joined with the Garrisonian Abolitionists, but later broke with them over their doctrinal rigidity on "no union with slaveholders." Favoring political action over moral suasion as the means to secure emancipation, Douglass founded his own newspaper, *The North Star* (1847–64), in Rochester (New York) and did much to alert the North (and Lincoln) to the significance of emancipation. After 1865 Douglass pressed for Negro suffrage and equal rights. He was appointed U.S. minister to Haiti (1888–91). He published the remarkable *Narrative of the Life of Frederick Douglass* (1845) as an answer to those who doubted that he had ever been a slave, and *The Life and Times of Frederick Douglass* (1881; revised, 1892).   J.W.

DOWSON, Ernest (1867–1900), born at Lee (Kent) of a prosperous middle-class family, was educated informally while traveling on the Continent with his parents. There he learnt to speak fluent French, as well as acquiring a love of Latin poetry and the contemporary novel. After an unhappy year at Oxford Dowson decided he would like to take up writing as a career, but necessity compelled him to help in his father's dwindling business. His best work was done in London between 1890 and

1894, while he was active in the *fin de siècle* circle which included Wilde, Beardsley, Lionel Johnson and John Davidson. Many of his finest poems were published first in periodicals such as *The Savoy* and *The Yellow Book*, and later formed two volumes, *Verses* (1896) and *Decorations* (1899). Dowson's notebook also contained a large number of poems (published in Flower's edition). After his father's death in 1894 Dowson went to live in Paris and remained there, except for brief visits to London, until his own death six years later.

Dowson's verse captures a lightness and grace that makes him the creator of some of the most beautiful lyrics in the language. A superficially easy style was achieved by a mastery of metrics and verse forms which his own originality transformed. Influenced by Keats and Swinburne, as well as by his French contemporaries, he achieves a dreamlike remoteness of feeling, toughened by the disillusion of the declining century and by his personal depression. This derived in part from his unrequited love for Adelaide Foltinowicz, but is also characteristic of the spiritual aspiration from which the *fin de siècle* movement gathered such coherence as it possessed.

(See also **Romantic Movement, The.**)

Poetical Works, ed. D. Flower, London: Cassell, 1967.
Stories, ed. M. Longaker, Philadelphia: Univ. of Pennsylvania Press, 1947; London: W. H. Allen, 1949.
Letters, ed. D. Flower and H. Maas, London: Cassell, 1967.   P.G.M.

DOYLE, Sir Arthur Conan (1859–1930), born and educated in Edinburgh, became a medical practitioner in 1885 and, in order to supplement his income, turned to writing fiction. *A Study in Scarlet* (1887; *f.* 1933) was the first in a long series of crime and detection stories set in the late Victorian era, and it introduced the famous gentleman-detective, Sherlock Holmes. Holmes, whose scientific methods of deduction are often as ingenious and eccentric as the crimes he solves, Dr. Watson, his slow-thinking medical friend, and Professor Moriarty, the arch-criminal, were and still are part of a powerful cult. Their stories were serialized in *Strand Magazine* and later collected as *The Adventures of Sherlock Holmes* (1892), *Memoirs of Sherlock Holmes* (1894) and *The Return of Sherlock Holmes* (1905; *f.* 1929), whilst the longer work, *The Hound of the Baskervilles* (*f.* 1932; 1939; 1959), appeared in 1902. So powerful has been the spell of Holmes that what Conan Doyle felt to be his more serious work, his writing on spiritualism and contemporary history, has been largely ignored.

The Annotated Sherlock Holmes, ed. W. S. Baring-Gould, 2 vols., London: Murray; New York: Potter, 1968.   O.K.

DRAYTON, Geoffrey. See **Caribbean Literature.**

DRAYTON, Michael (1563–1631) was born of yeoman stock at Hartshill (Warwickshire). His early life was spent in the service of the family of Sir Henry Goodere of Polesworth, to whose younger daughter Anne, the "Idea" celebrated in his poems, Drayton always remained devoted. A vocational poet, he continued to be dependent on the generosity of the Gooderes and their friends, including, for a while, Lucy, countess of Bedford, patroness of Donne and Jonson. Between 1597 and 1602 Drayton collaborated on plays for Henslowe's company, of which only *Sir John Oldcastle* (1600) survives. He felt resentment when his hopes of gaining James I's patronage in the new reign were disappointed. A genial, loyal man, Drayton numbered amongst his friends leading scholars and literary men of the age, including Shakespeare. He outlived most of his fellow Elizabethans, seeing their ideals which he shared disregarded in Jacobean England.

Drayton's first notable work is *Idea, The Shepherd's Garland* (1593). Initially dependent on Spenserian pastoral, the eclogues have a freshness and youthful enthusiasm sadly missing from the revised version in the pastoral poems of 1605, where bitterness and disappointment darken the technical improvements in style and structure. Similar qualities and weaknesses occur in *Idea's Mirror* (1594), the sonnet sequence which, as *Idea*, Drayton continued to revise until 1619. The beauties of description and psychological insight of the Ovidian *Endymion and Phoebe* (1595) are marred by his inability to keep his material under strict control. The extensive revision this poem later underwent as *The Man in the Moon* (1606) decreased the romantic elements and introduced satire and cynicism. Drayton's "Legends," appearing from 1594 to 1603, demonstrate a typical Elizabethan concern with history, and an interest in the psychology of historical personages first found in Daniel's *The Complaint of Rosamond* and again occurring in Drayton's imitations of Ovid's *Heroides, England's Heroical Epistles* (1597). *Mortimeriados* (1596), his first historical epic, is also in this vein and attempts to relate the disturbances of Edward II's reign to a character study of Mortimer. History and art are more happily reconciled in the revision, *The Barons' Wars* (1603), modeled on Daniel's *Civil Wars.* Although disappointment with the new reign occasions a vein of satire, as in the now obscure *The Owl* (1604), not all Drayton's later poetry reflects such gloom. The epic *Polyolbion* (1622) is a mixture of topographical description, fanciful personification, history and legend, conducting us round the counties of England and Wales; *Nymphidia* (1627) is a delightful fairy poem, whilst *The Muses' Elysium* (1630), graceful and easy in manner, highly ornamented but strictly controlled, is Drayton's final contribution to the pastoral and voices his last regrets for the Elizabethan age.

Rarely an innovator, except in introducing the heroical epistle, Drayton preferred to work in already established genres. His early verse is full of echoes of other poets, but is distinctive in its youthful exuberance of description, emotion, and rhetorical flourishes. Sensitive to criticism, Drayton increasingly disciplined his poetry, removing excesses and developing firmer control over matter and manner. Personal disappointment also dictated a more somber, restrained approach. Little influenced by changing styles, he remained faithful to those of Elizabethan poetry, especially in his devotion to the sonnet and the epic.

Idea, the Shepherd's Garland, 1593.
Endymion and Phoebe, 1595.
Mortimeriados, 1596.
England's Heroical Epistles, 1597.
The Barons' Wars, 1603.
Poems Lyric and Pastoral, 1605.
Polyolbion, 1622.
Nymphidia, 1627.
The Muses' Elysium, 1630.

Works, ed. J. W. Hebel, K. Tillotson, and B. Newdigate, 5 vols., Oxford: Blackwell, 1931–41.   J.M.P.

DREISER, Theodore (1871–1945) was born at Terre Haute (Indiana), the eleventh of twelve surviving children of German immigrants. His father, crushed by financial disaster, retreated from the realities of poverty behind an unbending Catholic morality, and the family was held together precariously by Dreiser's mother, helped by sporadic contributions from her elder son, Paul (Dresser), composer of popular songs and a somewhat raffish man about town. Dreiser was profoundly influenced, as his later themes were to show, by the contrast between the glitter and comfort of Paul's life in New York and the toilsome poverty of life at home. In 1881, after a relatively stable period in Warsaw (Indiana) where Dreiser had attended school and proved himself a promising, intelligent student, he set out for Chicago, a city which then and afterwards fascinated him by its opulence, excitement and freedom from social restraints. His menial jobs—as a dishwasher in a restaurant and as a warehouse hand—brought him experiences which reinforced his feelings about the contrasts of wealth and poverty.

The offer in 1889 of a former schoolteacher, Mildred Fielding, to sponsor him as a student at the University of Indiana was not the stroke of good fortune it seemed. He floundered, inexperienced and friendless, in the fraternity life at Bloomington. During this period he came to recognize what later became a conscious obsession, the connections between low social origins, lack of money and sexual failure. He abandoned the university after a year for journalism, and after a number of temporary jobs, obtained usually through his brother's good offices, he was in 1895 appointed editor of *Ev'ry Month*, a journal founded to exploit the current interest in popular music of the kind Paul Dresser was so successfully writing. Dreiser continued to make a modest living as a journalist and editor of magazines until the success of *Jennie Gerhardt* in 1911 opened for him the career of novelist and essayist.

Jennie Gerhardt was not the first novel he had written. In 1900 he had completed *Sister Carrie*, but this extremely significant work was effectively withheld from the public as a result of bad reviews and the publisher's timidity and received its first real sales in 1907. It is the story of a working-class girl from the suburbs who eventually makes good in the city. It possesses many of the elements which were to become characteristic of Dreiser's later work, the complaisant girl submitting to the strength, wealth and sexual drive and competence of her lovers. But Dreiser's management of his heroine's passive success, taken with Hurstwood's disproportionate failure and sordid death, provides an equation which emphasizes a moral randomness and pessimism characteristic of naturalism. This aspect of the theme is explored particularly through its ingeniously devised central action, which demonstrates the almost accidental nature of Hurstwood's dishonest act. The naturalism is further enhanced by Dreiser's introduction of the notion derived from neo-Darwinian evolutionism, that it is Carrie's rather low-profiled capacity to adapt, amoebalike, to new conditions and Hurstwood's failure to do so which accounts for their disparate success in surviving.

Jennie Gerhardt, together with *The Financier* (1912), *The Titan* (1915) and *The Stoic* (posthumously, 1947), the novels of the Cowperwood trilogy, based on the life of Charles Tyson Yerkes, concern themselves more explicitly with themes in which the potent, ruthless male, accompanied by a succession of passionate but subservient women, pursues a successful career in buccaneering business against entrenched political and corporate interests. Cowperwood's women inspire him by their own passionate desire for affluence and freedom, while Jennie Gerhadt's willingness to sacrifice herself is exploited by her lover.

The underlying moral pattern of these novels can be illustrated by Dreiser's crude use of popular Darwinism in the biological imagery of the lobster and squid, and of the Black Grouper, in *The Financier*. He suggests that the Black Grouper's capacity to adapt to its environment is an example of the "subtlety, chicanery, trickery" of the plan of the forces which made and govern the cosmos. This use of the motif of adaptation is less subtle and satisfactory than in *Sister Carrie*. Dreiser shows little capacity for objectively "placing" his characters, caught up as he seems to be in self-gratifying fantasy, of the kind frequently to be glimpsed in his autobiographical writings, *A Book about Myself* (1922) and *Dawn* (1931). Indeed, most of Dreiser's fiction seems to reflect his own life, real or fantasy, and it is only when he can find a subject more remote, as he does in *An American Tragedy* when he works up a newspaper story he has read, that his themes offer a more than psychoanalytical interest. Like *Sister Carrie*, *An American Tragedy* (1925) uses ambiguous accident as a central plot device. Clyde Griffiths murders as an accidental act at the end of a train of preparations deliberately designed to that end. But, whereas in the earlier novel Dreiser directs us by authorial interventions and evolutionist hints to a naturalistic interpretation, in *An American Tragedy* the theme is somewhat less clear-cut. The stress on class and money seems to invite an interpretation in terms of social or socialist morality. The long religious coda is ambiguous; it may be seen as a psychotheological appendage, or as having an ironic effect when juxtaposed with the social factors which largely condition Clyde's actions.

Besides the autobiographical works mentioned, Dreiser's nonfictional writing includes politico-social essays, the most notable of which are to be found in *Tragic America* (1931), which shows his interest in socialist theory, and *America Is Worth Saving* (1941). The posthumously published *The Bulwark* (1946) represents a further development of his attitude to religion, seen as ambivalent in *An American Tragedy*. After a series of disillusioning shocks the novel's hero, a Quaker, arrives at a broader, sympathetic humanist understanding of the events which have shaped his life.

It can be argued that for Dreiser the naturalism of *Sister Carrie* was not a major intellectual interest, that his gift was not for intellectual analysis. When his instinctive response of compassion is aroused he writes most compellingly and while the label of sentimentality can with some justice be applied to his work, it is sentimentality saved by energy. This leads him beyond conventional attitudes to a vision of glamor or despair, which, in spite of his most commonly acknowledged faults of occasional pornographic involvement or frequent stylistic banality, possesses an individual authority.

Sister Carrie, 1900; 1907 (*f.* as *Carrie*, 1952).
Jennie Gerhardt, 1911 (*f.* 1933).
The Financier, 1912.
A Traveler at Forty, 1913.
The Titan, 1914.

The "Genius," 1915.
Plays of the Natural and Supernatural, 1916.
A Hoosier Holiday, 1916.
Free and Other Stories, 1918.
The Hand of the Potter, 1918.
Twelve Men, 1919 (short stories).
Hey Rub-a-Dub-Dub, 1920.
A Book about Myself, 1922; republished as *Newspaper Days,* 1931.
The Color of a Great City, 1923.
An American Tragedy, 1925 (*f.* 1931; as *A Place in the Sun,* 1951).
Chains, 1927 (short stories).
Dreiser Looks at Russia, 1928.
A Gallery of Women, 1929 (short stories).
My City, 1929.
Dawn, 1931.
Tragic America, 1931.
America Is Worth Saving, 1941.
The Bulwark, 1946.
The Stoic, 1947.

Letters, ed. R. H. Elias, 3 vols., Philadelphia: Univ. of Pennsylvania Press,
1959.   M.L.

DRINKWATER, John (1882–1937), born in Leytonstone (Essex),
was the son of a schoolmaster turned actor. After leaving school he was an
insurance clerk in Nottingham, but, like his father, was attracted to the
theater and spent a long period at the Birmingham Repertory as actor and
manager. A conscientious "Georgian," he wrote poetry with intelligence
and craftsmanship, but without any striking individuality. His contribution to the theater is represented by a series of well-constructed historical
plays, based upon the lives of Lincoln, Robert E. Lee, Cromwell and
Mary Stuart. *Inheritance* (1931) and *Discovery* (1932) are autobiographical
works. (See also **Georgians, The.**)

Collected Poems, 3 vols., London: Sidgwick & Jackson, 1923–37.   O.K.

DRUMMOND, William (1585–1649) belonged to a well-established
landed family, distantly related to the Scottish royal house. After
graduating in 1605 at Edinburgh he studied law on the Continent but
never practiced, since he succeeded to the paternal estate of Hawthornden
in 1610. There he devoted his time to reading both classical and modern
authors, to writing and invention (he patented sixteen devices). He
made and maintained literary contact with London, being a correspondent

of Drayton and having a visit from Jonson in 1619, of which Drummond has left a record.

Apart from the prose works *A Cypress Grove* (1623), a meditation on death, and *The History of Scotland 1423–1542* (James I–V) (1655), Drummond wrote a large body of verse, notably *Tears on the Death of Meliades* (1613), an elegy on Prince Henry; *Poems, Amorous, Funeral, Divine* (1616); *Forth Feasting* (1617), a panegyric on James's visit to Scotland; and *Flowers of Sion* (1623). He wrote English rather than Scots, but his relative isolation from English literary trends is shown both by his use of French and Italian poets who had influenced the Elizabethans and by his kinship with Spenser, which shows in the harmonious sweetness and easy flow of his verse. Drummond uses the sonnet form a great deal, long after the collapse of the Elizabethan sonnet vogue. His verse is marked by a gentle melancholy of tone and a general air of bookishness.

Poems, ed. L. E. Kastner, 2 vols., Edinburgh: Scottish Text Society, 1913.
Works of Ben Jonson, vol. 1, ed. C. H. Herford and P. Simpson, Oxford: Clarendon Press, 1925.   G.P.

DRYDEN, John (1631–1700) was born at Aldwinkle (Northamptonshire), of a Puritan family. He went to Westminster School and to Trinity College, Cambridge, taking his degree in 1654. Little is known of his life during the next few years, though in 1659 he published a poem on the death of Oliver Cromwell in a volume with Sprat and Waller. The following year he "changed with the nation," as Samuel Johnson put it, and celebrated the Restoration of Charles II with a panegyrical poem, *Astraea Redux*. In 1663 he married Lady Elizabeth Howard; they had three sons. About the same time he took up writing for the stage, not hesitating to defend his own plays in prefaces and essays. He also dealt lucidly with other literary forms, topics, authors and works, from both theoretical and practical angles. His finest work, however, was done in poetry, in particular the satires he wrote between about 1678 and 1682—*MacFlecknoe*, *Absalom and Achitophel* and *The Medal*. The last two show most clearly his involvement in the politics of his time, being directed against the earl of Shaftesbury and the Whigs and undertaken as deliberate propaganda on the Tory Royalist side.

About 1685 Dryden became a Roman Catholic, which was to lose him the posts of poet laureate and historiographer royal after the Revolution of 1688. During the uncongenial reign of William and Mary he continued to write, once more composing plays—he had stopped writing them in 1681 —and issuing by subscription his verse translation of Virgil's *Aeneid*, *Georgics* and *Eclogues* in 1697. He also adapted Homer, Ovid, Boccaccio and Chaucer in his *Fables Ancient and Modern, Translated into Verse* (1700).

Throughout his career he turned out commendatory verses, prologues and epilogues, odes to music and prose translations with professional ease and success. At the end of his life he was a leader of London's literary society, friend and adviser of writers like Congreve, Southerne, Addison and Vanbrugh. He seems to have known Milton, whose *Paradise Lost* he made into an operatic entertainment, *The State of Innocence, and Fall of Man*. He collaborated with Henry Purcell, the great composer, in *King Arthur*; and he was acquainted with many leading figures of his time such as Pepys, Evelyn and Kneller.

Dryden's early poetry is surprising. His first published poem, an elegy on the earl of Hastings in 1649, is in the Metaphysical manner of witty and extravagant "conceit." Later poems are much more restrained, though they are still forcefully intellectual, with a strong line of thought or argument binding the lines together. Dryden was quite capable of the lightness and flexibility of a song, but his poetic energies seem best employed when exploiting the resources of the couplet. The mingling of crudity and subtlety can be truly astonishing:

> Got, while his soul did muddled notions try;
> And born a shapeless lump, like anarchy.

These lines from *Absalom and Achitophel* both physically and spiritually lampoon Shaftesbury and his unfortunate son, even as they bring a reminder of a basic impulse of the entire poem (Dryden's abhorrence of civil disorder) in their very last word—the simple simile jerks like a diviner's rod. A series of such couplets, artfully varied in syntax, rhythm and tone, makes up the "portraits" of individual politicians of the day; the "portraits" themselves can vary from the crudely vigorous attack on Titus Oates (Corah) to the sophisticated, gently ironical treatment of Charles II (David) and his private sins. The whole, though told as a biblical allegory, is closely related to actual persons and events of the time and composed about a central statement of political philosophy. It is one of the greatest verse satires in English.

Dryden's poetry is not always satirical. *Annus Mirabilis* is heroic and patriotic, giving a splendid dress to sea battles against the Dutch and the Great Fire of London. *Religio Laici* is a reasoned defense of the Church of England, paradoxically most striking when denying Reason's authority, which "dissolves in supernatural light." *The Hind and the Panther* occasionally achieves a haunting resonance in its defense of Roman Catholicism, though it also devotes considerable satiric attention to other religious positions.

Dryden once wrote that his nature was not fitted for writing comedies, though he produced a good many. A play like *Marriage à la Mode* has been highly praised for the way in which it contains both gaiety and feeling, but Dryden is probably more famous as one of the major writers of rhymed heroic tragedy, his attempt to rival in drama the scope and splendor of an epic poem. *Tyrannic Love* and *The Conquest of Granada* define the genre and reach the limit of majestic eloquence—or rant. In fact, the blank verse *All for Love* is now better thought of than any of the rhymed tragedies. Comparison with Shakespeare's *Antony and Cleopatra* throws some of its qualities into high relief—its observance of the unities of time and place, its restriction of subordinate actions, "every scene in the tragedy conducing to the main design," and a degree of sentimentality in its effects. Dryden's preface draws attention to these features of the play he wrote to please himself.

In literary criticism his clear mind was a distinct advantage, if only that it enabled him to see what he could not agree with in the theories of others. *An Essay of Dramatic Poesy* (1668) proves that for all his neo-classicism he was in practice sensible of the virtues of irregular literature, especially of the drama of the Elizabethan and Jacobean playwrights. Even if they wrote "before the Flood," here was yet a "giant race." Critical flexibility and zest led Dryden into misstatements, restatements and a variety of intellectual contortions deplored by more rigorous critics, but it is not altogether likely that consistency and system will ever be found in a fertile author practicing over a period of thirty-five years, and these inconsistencies are insignificant when set against Dryden's unremitting attention to literature in broadest outline and in smallest detail. Not that the reader feels the strain, for Dryden's prose, easy, fluent, lucid and individual, gives permanent life to topics otherwise sunk dead in their period of history. It was, he wrote in 1681 in the dedication to *The Spanish Friar*, his "ambition to be read." His mental energy, versatility and robust love of literature are sufficient to ensure this for many of his works, in the best of which we encounter the phenomenon of vital creations forming out of the negative material of abuse and politics. Dryden himself, in the last year of his long career, gave an essential clue to the mystery:

Thoughts, such as they are, come crowding in so fast upon me that my only difficulty is to choose or to reject; to run them into verse, or to give them the other harmony of prose: I have so long studied and practised both that they are grown into a habit, and become familiar to me. (Preface to *Fables*.)

(See also **Augustans, The; Essays; Political Pamphlets.**)

Heroic Stanzas, 1659.
Astraea Redux, 1660.
The Rival Ladies, 1664 (play).
The Indian Emperor, 1667 (play, p. 1665).
Annus Mirabilis: The Year of Wonders, 1666, 1667.

Of Dramatic Poesy, 1668.
Tyrannic Love, 1670 (play, *p.* 1669).
The Conquest of Granada, 1672 (play, *p.* 1670).
Marriage à la Mode, 1673 (play, *p.* 1672).
Aureng-Zebe, 1676 (play, *p.* 1675).
The State of Innocence, and Fall of Man, 1677.
All for Love, 1678 (play, *p.* 1677).
The Spanish Friar, 1681 (play, *p.* 1680).
Absalom and Achitophel, 1681.
The Medal, 1682.
MacFlecknoe, 1682.
Religio Laici, 1682.
The Hind and the Panther, 1687.
Don Sebastian, 1690 (play, *p.* 1689).
King Arthur, 1692 (play, *p.* 1691).
The Satires [of Juvenal and Persius], 1693.
The Works of Virgil, 1697.
Fables, Ancient and Modern, 1700.

Works, ed. E. N. Hooker and others, 21 vols., Cambridge: Cambridge Univ. Press; Berkeley and Los Angeles: Univ. of California Press, 1956– .
Poems, ed. J. Kinsley, 4 vols., Oxford: Clarendon Press, 1958.
Dramatic Works, ed. M. Summers, 6 vols., London: Nonesuch Press, 1930–31.
Of Dramatic Poesy and Other Critical Essays, ed. G. Watson, 2 vols., London: Dent; New York: Dutton, 1962.
The Works of Virgil, ed. J. Kinsley, Oxford: Clarendon Press, 1961.
Letters, ed. C. E. Ward, Cambridge: Cambridge Univ. Press; Durham, N.C.: Duke Univ. Press, 1942.   J.C.

DU BOIS, W. E. B. (William Edward Burghardt) (1868–1963), Negro sociologist, novelist and editor, was born in Massachusetts, and educated at Fisk University (1888) and Harvard. As professor of history and economics at Atlanta University (1896–1910), he devoted himself to the study of Negro history and sociology. Du Bois bitterly attacked Booker T. Washington for his racial conservatism and for ignoring the need for the higher education of the "talented tenth" who would provide leaders for the Negro race. He organized the Niagara Movement (1905), a group of militant young Negro intellectuals, and helped to found the National Association for the Advancement of Colored People (1909), the civil rights organization in which he became director of research and editor of *Crisis* magazine (1910–34). Du Bois also organized the Pan-African

Congress (1910) and the First International Conference of Colored Peoples (1918). He finally broke with the NAACP in 1948 over what he regarded as its limited appeal and conservatism, and founded *Phylon*, the Atlanta University Review of Race and Culture. In 1962 he became a citizen of Ghana, where he lived until his death. Among Du Bois's many writings are major historical and sociological studies—*The Suppression of the African Slave Trade, The Philadelphia Negro, The Souls of Black Folk*, his most famous work, and *Black Reconstruction in America*. His novels include *Dark Princess* and *The Black Flame: A Trilogy*, incorporating *The Ordeal of Mansart* (1957), *Mansart Builds a School* (1959) and *Worlds of Colour* (1961). Du Bois described *Dusk of Dawn* as "not so much my autobiography as the autobiography of a concept of race."

The Suppression of the African Slave Trade to the U.S.A., 1638–1870, 1896.
The Philadelphia Negro, 1899.
The Souls of Black Folk, 1903.
John Brown, 1909.
The Quest of the Silver Fleece, 1911.
The Negro, 1915.
Darkwater, 1920.
Dark Princess, 1928.
Black Reconstruction in America, 1935.
Dusk of Dawn, 1940.
The Black Flame, 1957–61.   J.W.

DUDEK, Louis. See **Canadian Literature.**

DUGGAN, Maurice. See **New Zealand Literature.**

DUNBAR, Paul Laurence (1872–1906), was brought up in Dayton (Ohio), the son of former slaves. His early poems, especially those written in Negro dialect, attracted the attention of William Dean Howells who promoted *Lyrics of Lowly Life* (1896), a book which brought Dunbar national fame. Later volumes of poetry—*Lyrics of the Hearthside* (1899); *Lyrics of Love and Laughter* (1903)—consolidated his reputation as a folk poet who expressed the suffering and vitality of his people. He also wrote four mediocre novels, together with several volumes of short stories. I.W.

DUNBAR, William (?1460–?1513). A "William Dunbar" is mentioned in the records of St. Andrews University for 1477 and 1479. If, as seems likely, this is the poet, we have an approximate date for his birth and a clue to the kind of education he received. The little that we know of

Dunbar's career mostly derives from his poetry. He held various posts at the court of James IV, which gave him an intimate acquaintance with life there, even though he seems never to have reached a very high position. Some of his poems celebrate state occasions, such as James's marriage to Margaret Tudor in 1503; several are based on incidents at court; others are appeals to the king for a benefice or a pension. In 1500 he was awarded a pension of £10 a year, which was increased to £20 in 1507 and £80 in 1510. After 1513 there is no further mention of his name in the records, and the probability is that he was dead.

Technically, Dunbar is the most accomplished of the "Scottish Chaucerians." His poems display a variety of form and subject, a brilliance of language and a metrical versatility that cannot be paralleled in Douglas or Henryson. He writes in all the medieval genres: allegorical dream poems in the high style (such as *The Golden Targe* and *The Thistle and the Rose*); debate poems (*The Merle and the Nightingale*); complaints and begging poems (*To the Merchants of Edinburgh* and *The Petition of the Gray Horse, Old Dunbar*); religious poems (his two finest being those on the Nativity and the Resurrection); and moral lyrics (*The Lament for the Makaris* and *Meditation in Winter*). A very large number of his poems are humorous and give comic, sometimes scurrilous, accounts of persons or incidents at court (*Of James Dog, Keeper of the Queen's Wardrobe*). Dunbar's humor is frequently cruel, and there are venomous attacks on lowborn upstarts, with "wavill feit and wirrok tais... lut schulderis and luttard bak, Quhilk natur maid to beir a pak." His humor often takes a wild and fantastic form, as in the grotesque *Dance of the Seven Deadly Sins*, set in Hell. Dunbar's most ambitious poem, *The Treatise of the Two Married Women and the Widow*, is a coarse, bitter but savagely funny account of the "woe that is in marriage."

In an age when most poets sought to "amplify" their material, Dunbar's poems are striking for their brevity. Only two are longer than 500 lines, and Dunbar has a clear preference for lyric forms, in particular those with refrains, which he handles with wit and ingenuity. His poems have the variety of mood that characterizes the lyric poet: just as he may write on a trivial subject such as a headache, so he also writes on the perennial themes, death and mutability. His language sometimes has remarkable compression, achieved in part by the piling up of images. Many of these are drawn from the animal world, but some of the more arresting—an overflowing gutter or the grimaces of a thief in the stocks—are drawn from everyday life in a town. Dunbar's language varies, according to his subject, between a high, ceremonial style, studded with ornate and stylized "aureate" terms, the low, colloquial style of the comic poems and "flytings," and the plain, middle style of the moral lyrics, which perhaps comes closest to Dunbar's own mode of speech.

The chief sources for Dunbar's poems are three great manuscript collections of the sixteenth century: the Asloan, Bannatyne and Maitland Manuscripts, all printed by the Scottish Text Society.

Poems, ed. W. M. Mackenzie, Edinburgh: Porpoise Press, 1932.   P.B.

DUNCAN, Robert (1919–   ) was born at Oakland (California), adopted, and brought up as Symmes. He published under this name in California until 1941 (coediting *The Experimental Review*, 1940–41), when he obtained a psychiatric discharge from the army and went to New York. From 1946 to 1950, back in California, he was associated with Jack Spicer and Robin Blaser and published *Heavenly City, Earthly City* (1947) and *Poems 1948–49* (1949). From the early 1950s he associated himself with the views of Olson and Creeley and taught at Black Mountain College during 1956.

Duncan's study at Berkeley under Ernst Kantorowicz gave him a continuing interest in medieval art and ideas which combines with Platonism in an absorbing interest in "the world of forms." Combined with traditional material and imagery is a concern for technique based on Williams's and Olson's ideas of "composition by field," which allows the materials of the poem to shape it in the process of composition rather than fitting into a preexistent form. His imitations of Gertrude Stein in the early 1950s suggest a concern for local discontinuities and dislocations of syllables for the sake of the emergence of larger continuity, as does the "Structures of Rime" series in *The Opening of the Field* (1960) and *Bending the Bow* (1968). By 1948, in "The Venice Poem," Duncan was moving towards larger-scale musical form ("The multiphasic experience sought a multiphasic form,") stimulated by his experience of Olson, Creeley and the Pound of *Pisan Cantos*. His poetry may be "a ritual referring to divine orders," but this does not preclude political engagement. In "Passages" in *Bending the Bow* (1968) and *Tribunals* (1970), the corporation structure and monopoly capitalism of America are criticized in the context of the values of Duncan's poetry, centering around the vision of beauty in multiple ideal and corresponding forms.

The Opening of the Field, 1960.
Roots and Branches, 1964.
The Years As Catches, 1966.
Bending the Bow, 1968.
The First Decade, 1968.
Derivations, 1968.
Tribunals: Passages 31–35, 1970.
The H. D. Book, Part I: Beginnings, 1971.   D.M.

DUNLAP, William (1766–1839) became enamored of the theater while studying painting in England. On his return to New York and reputedly inspired by the success of Tyler's *The Contrast*, he decided to be a dramatist and first achieved fame with a social comedy, *The Father* (1789; revised, 1806), based on Sterne's *Tristram Shandy*. He catered to popular taste and was responsible for sixty-five plays; many were adaptations but thirty are credited as original. He is now best known for *André* (1798), a historical tragedy in blank verse, and a romantic tragedy, *Leicester* (1806), first produced in 1794 as *The Fatal Deception*. He was also involved in theater management and published two authoritative works, *A History of the American Theatre* (1832) and *History of the Rise and Progress of the Arts of Design in the United States* (2 vols., 1834). R.W.

DURRELL, Lawrence (1912–), born in Darjeeling and educated in England, has pursued a nomadic and expatriate life. As a young man, writing under the name of Charles Norden, he worked for a time in Paris with Henry Miller, his great friend. During and after the Second World War he was a teacher and member of the diplomatic corps, and worked in Greece, Egypt, Argentina, Yugoslavia and Cyprus. The Eastern Mediterranean, where he has spent a large part of his life, forms the background and is the origin of the symbolism in many of his novels.

A writer of considerable variety, he has written novels, poetry, poetic drama, travel books and comic sketches. His first serious novel was *The Black Book* (1938), an account of prewar London. Much of his later poetry and drama, in which the questing figures of Hamlet and Faustus are prominent, rehearse the themes to appear in his most significant work, "The Alexandria Quartet." As a novelist, he is distinctive and experimental, the quartet constituting variant accounts of what might be considered as a single story and being based upon the "relativity proposition." These novels, with their impressive unity of tone, are characterized by a complex treatment of love and identity and by the bewildering arrangement of individual viewpoints. At times Durrell's virtuosity in style and technique obscures rather than clarifies his material.

Prospero's Cell, 1945.
The Trees of Idleness and Other Poems, 1955.
Bitter Lemons, 1957.
"The Alexandria Quartet": *Justine*, 1957.
    (*f.* 1969)   *Balthazar*, 1958.
                  Mountolive, 1958.
                  Clea, 1960.
Collected Poems, 1960; revised, 1968.

An Irish Faustus, 1963.
The Ikons and Other Poems, 1966.
Tunc, 1968.
Nunquam, 1970.   O.K.

DUTT, Michael Madhusudan. See **Indian Literature.**

DUTT, Toru. See **Indian Literature.**

DWIGHT, Timothy (1752–1817), clergyman, schoolmaster, man of letters and president of Yale College (1795–1817), was an influential figure and pillar of society in post-Revolutionary Connecticut, a leading member of the group of Hartford Wits. A devout Federalist and Congregationalist, a substantial section of his writings flay Jeffersonian democracy, atheism and infidelity—as in *The Triumph of Infidelity* (1788). His strength lay not in his largely unoriginal polemical and religious works but in his interesting and still useful travel and descriptive writings. As a poet he favored heroic couplets and the epic style, used in *The Conquest of Canaan* (1785), which was much admired by contemporaries but is unread today.   R.S.

DYER, John (1699–1758), after practicing law in his native Carmarthenshire, studied art under Jonathan Richardson and worked for some years as an itinerant artist. Sensitivity to detail and color—later to attract Wordsworth—is prominent in his best work, notably in his famous "Grongar Hill" (1726), a fine example of the "prospect" poem. *The Ruins of Rome* (1740) is an uninspired pre-Romantic poem. *The Fleece* (1757), castigated by Johnson, lacks the light touch of its original, Philips's *Cyder*, but contains some typically good descriptive passages.

Poems, ed. E. Thomas, Welsh Library, vol. 4, 1903.
Grongar Hill, ed. R. C. Boys, Baltimore: Johns Hopkins Press, 1941.
                                                        A.W.B.

E

EARLE, John (?1601–65) was born in York and educated at Oxford. Charles I appointed him tutor to his son, whom Earle accompanied in exile. He was promoted at the Restoration to the deanery of Westminster, becoming bishop of Worcester (1662) and then of Salisbury (1663). He exercised his influence as a moderate to prevent the persecution of Nonconformists. Clarendon said that he "never had, and never could have, an enemy."

He wrote commemorative verses of some merit when young, but is remembered for one work, *Micro-cosmographie* (1628; enlarged, 1629; 1633; ed. H. Osborne, London: University Tutorial Press, 1933), consisting of fifty-four (later seventy-eight) character sketches after the manner of Theophrastus which throw great light on the social conditions of the time.

D.G.

EBERHART, Richard (1904–) was born in Minnesota and educated at Dartmouth and Cambridge (Massachusetts). His first book, *A Bravery of Earth*, was published in 1930, but his most productive period came after the Second World War. More recent collections have been *Great Praises* (1957) and *The Quarry* (1964). His complicated imaginative poetry, which ranges over many forms, is typified by a sophisticated and precise style. "A motive of the poet" Eberhart says, "is by delving in his senses to clarify his understanding of life, to enlarge it, to mask it, to metamorphose it, to beguile it in metaphor, and to enact its perturbation in the reader in canny cunning manifold ways."

Collected Poems 1930–1960, London and New York: Oxford Univ. Press, 1960.

R.W.

EDGEWORTH, Maria (1767–1849) was the daughter of Richard Lovell Edgeworth, the inventor, educationalist and eccentric. In 1782 the family settled on the paternal estate at Edgeworthstown in Ireland, where Maria spent the rest of her long life (though she traveled widely and met all the leading artists of her time). She was companion and general factotum to her father and governess to the children of his successive marriages. From him she learned precepts of morality, integrity, good sense and feeling, and the importance of educational processes (she was a

Rousseauist in education) which all her fiction exemplifies. Together Maria and her father wrote *The Parent's Assistant* (1795) and followed it with a series of long-celebrated children's books. Maria wrote *Castle Rackrent* during the 1790s and it was published in 1800 after her father had criticized and approved of it. He continued to watch over her writing till his death in 1817 and she completed his *Memoirs* (1820).

Maria Edgeworth was at her best in her lively, realistic stories of life in Ireland (*Castle Rackrent*, *The Absentee*). Her use of peasant characters and local speech to contrast rough honesty with other standards of behavior anticipated Scott (her friend in later years), and her comic sense was always a particular strength. Her books suffer, on the other hand, from their didacticism. Even more, they are almost all weakened by conforming to the three-volume convention of the day. *Belinda* (1801) has unity and improves on Fanny Burney's example of the novel about a girl educated through social experiences, but Maria Edgeworth cared little about structure and her plots are generally no more than an excuse to illustrate some precept which concerns her. She is always better in parts, and the best of them still justify the admiration which Scott and Jane Austen had for her as a writer. Her flexible, strong intelligence shows more effectively in her letters than in her books.

The Parent's Assistant; or, Stories for Children, 1795.
Castle Rackrent, 1800.
Belinda, 1801.
Moral Tales for Young People, 1801.
Popular Tales, 1804.
Tales of Fashionable Life, 1809; 1812.
Patronage, 1814.
Harrington (with *Ormond*), 1817.
Memoirs of R. L. Edgeworth, 1820.

Novels, 10 vols., London: Routledge, 1893.
Tales, ed. A. Dobson, London: Wells Gardner, 1903.
Letters from England, 1813–1844, ed. C. Colvin, Oxford: Clarendon Press, 1972.   W.R.

EDWARDS, Jonathan (1703–58), son and grandson of Congregational ministers, was educated at Yale and followed his forebears into the ministry, first at Northampton (1726–50) and then at Stockbridge. In 1757 he was invited to become president of the college at Princeton, arrived there early in 1758, but died in the same year. As a minister he was rigorous, preaching a return to the old practice of restricting church membership to "visible saints," and as a theologian his works, whatever their methodology, reaffirmed the traditional Calvinistic ideas of election and predestination against the wave of liberal thought present in church circles. Most of his published writings up to the 1750s examine and defend the religious revivals then taking place in America. His account of the revivals at Northampton was issued in England in 1737 by Isaac Watts. Edwards was also a millennialist, spending the last years of his life on a projected "History of the Work of Redemption," a kind of millennial world history. These tendencies in his thought have been emphasized by critics who point out that as a philosopher and theologian his work had little lasting influence, although some of it was well known outside America. More favorable estimates discuss Edwards as the most brilliant mind in colonial America, point to his philosophical studies and his metaphysical skill and seriousness as unrivaled among his contemporaries. There is general accord that *A Treatise concerning Religious Affections* is a pioneering work on the psychology of the religious emotions. His other major treatise is that on freedom of the will. Edwards wrote in a "plain" manner and was capable of passages of lyrical delicacy and vivid pictorial imagery. As a philosopher he made no fundamental contributions, but in the context of the American colonial intellectual life his achievement was very great.

God Glorified in the Work of Redemption, 1731.
A Faithful Narrative, 1737.
Some Thoughts concerning the Present Revival of Religion in New England, 1742.
A Treatise concerning Religious Affections, 1746.
A Careful and Strict Inquiry into the Modern Prevailing Notions of That Freedom of the Will, 1754.
The Great Christian Doctrine of Original Sin Defended, 1758.
Two Dissertations . . ., 1765.

Works, ed. S. E. Dwight, 10 vols., New York: Carvill, 1830.
Works, ed. P. Miller and others, New Haven: Yale Univ. Press, 1957– .

R.S.

EDWARDS, Richard. See **Elizabethan Miscellanies.**

EGGLESTON, Edward (1837–1902), a devout Methodist and ardent reformer, was a native of Indiana who began writing in 1866. He had tried many careers (journalism, farming, bible-selling) before becoming a preacher, though in later life he abandoned Methodism for the New Theology. His novels have a pious, didactic quality, often sentimental but sometimes showing marked realism as in *The Hoosier School-Master*

(1871), which initially brought the author fame. Also popular were *The Circuit Rider* (1874), a faithful account of frontier life, and *Roxy* (1878). He wrote a romantic account of an incident in Abraham Lincoln's legal career, entitled *The Graysons* (1888), some history texts and simple biographies of Indian figures.   R.W.

EKWENSI, Cyprian. See **African Literature.**

"ELIOT, George" **(Mary Ann Evans)** (1819–80), the youngest daughter of a farmer and land agent, Robert Evans, was born near Nuneaton (Warwickshire), where she spent the first thirty years of her life. A lonely and emotional child, she was devoted to her elder brother, Isaac, and to her father for whom she kept house after her mother's death. From an early age she showed signs of extensive intellectual interests; and, in the face of her family's religious conservatism, her enthusiasm for the Evangelical movement, to which she was introduced by her school-mistress, revealed a deeply religious temperament that was to dictate her actions throughout her life. The struggle for intellectual independence, however, led her to reject her formal beliefs altogether and this resulted in temporary estrangement from her father, during which her brother acted as mediator between them. After her father's death in 1849 she came to London where she contributed to *The Westminster Review*, which she helped to edit, and became acquainted with some of the leading literary figures of the day. She developed a particularly close friendship with Herbert Spencer, the pioneer sociologist, who in his turn introduced her to George Henry Lewes, an influential literary journalist. Lewes was separated from his wife and in 1854 Mary Ann Evans, after considerable deliberation, decided to live with him. The partnership proved to be an outstanding success and gave her the confidence that enabled her to become a major novelist under her pseudonym of George Eliot. After Lewes's death in 1878 she was for a while inconsolable; but remarkably, in 1880, six months before her death, she married J. W. Cross, a man twenty years her junior.

It is perhaps characteristic of George Eliot that her first literary achieve-ments were translations of two German works of theology, Strauss's *The Life of Jesus Critically Examined* (1846) and Feuerbach's *The Essence of Christianity* (1854), both of which had considerable repercussions on Victorian belief. The sense of intellectual and moral commitment which led her to undertake such work is evident throughout her novels; she her-self wrote at the height of her career that a "man or woman who publishes writings inevitably assumes the office of teacher or influencer of the public mind." Her intellectualism, however, is tempered by the accuracy and feeling with which she portrays the provincial life that she knew as a child, and she is particularly sensitive to the processes of social change. Her first fictional writing, undertaken at the encouragement of Lewes, was a collection of three stories published under the title of *Scenes of Clerical Life* (1858), and it anticipates the work of her maturity in its preoccupation with characters from provincial life. *Adam Bede* (1859) reveals similar interests, while in *The Mill on the Floss* (1860) George Eliot draws directly on her own childhood and adolescent experience. The quest of the heroine of *The Mill on the Floss*, Maggie Tulliver, for freedom from the restricting attitudes of her family can be directly related to George Eliot's own difficulties and when, in the latter part of the novel, she makes less use of autobiographical experience, there is an element of artificiality. *The Mill on the Floss* was followed by *Silas Marner* (1861), a moralistic fable of humble life, *Romola* (1863), a historical novel set in medieval Florence, and *Felix Holt, the Radical* (1866), a political novel set in the time of the Reform Bill of 1832 in which George Eliot once again shows her understanding of the structure of English provincial life. This understanding achieves its finest expression in *Middlemarch* (1872), subtitled "A Study of Provincial Life," in which the theme of the emancipation of the moral sensibility predominates. The heroine of *Middlemarch*, Dorothea Brooke, is presented as an English Saint Theresa in whose mind "there was a current into which all thought and feeling were apt sooner or later to flow—the reaching forward of the whole consciousness towards the fullest truth, the least partial good." Released by widowhood from a disastrous marriage to the frustrated scholar, Casaubon, Dorothea learns that the application of her sensibility must inevitably be difficult and limited; she nevertheless achieves happiness by her socially inadvisable marriage to the artist Ladislaw. Her experience is paralleled to some extent by that of Lydgate, the gifted medical practitioner, whose altruistic aspirations are frustrated by the social preoccupations of his petty-minded wife, Rosamund Vincy; but for Lydgate there is no release. In its social sensitivity and intellectual control *Middlemarch* is probably unequaled amongst nineteenth-century novels. George Eliot's last novel, *Daniel Deronda*, appears to break new ground in that its characters are drawn from country house society and much of the book is concerned with an analysis of Judaism, in which George Eliot had become interested. The themes of the novel are similar to those of the earlier work, however: Deronda himself, in a quest for identity that leads to his discovery that he is a Jew, is a character in search of moral fulfillment, while the heroine, Gwendolen Harleth, trapped in a marriage that denies her freedom, has close affiliations with Maggie Tulliver and Dorothea Brooke. *Daniel Deronda* is flawed in many ways, particularly in that the study of Judaism will not bear the weight of the significance placed upon it, but its analysis of the psychology of Gwendolen's situation is outstanding and at no point does George Eliot make the concessions to sentimentality that sometimes mar her earlier handling of this theme.

Scenes of Clerical Life, 1858 (s. 1857).
Adam Bede, 1859.
The Mill on the Floss, 1860.
Silas Marner, 1861.
Romola, 1863 (s. 1862–63).
Felix Holt, the Radical, 1866.
Middlemarch, 1872 (s. 1871–72).
Daniel Deronda, 1876.

Collected Works, Cabinet edition, 24 vols., Edinburgh: Blackwood, 1878– [85].
Letters, ed. G. S. Haight, 7 vols., London: Oxford Univ. Press; New Haven: Yale Univ. Press, 1954–56.   A.J.S.

ELIOT, T. S. (Thomas Stearns) (1888–1965), poet, dramatist and critic, was born in St. Louis (Missouri) of a family which was connected on both sides with the Massachusetts Bay Colony. He graduated from Harvard in 1910. He went to Europe and studied at the Sorbonne, in Germany and at Merton College, Oxford. He then returned to Harvard where he was an instructor in philosophy for a year. He left for Europe once more in 1914 and did not return to America until 1932, when he gave a series of lectures at Harvard. He worked in England as a schoolmaster, in a bank and finally as editor and publisher. He became editor of *The Criterion* in 1922 and remained with that journal until it ceased publication in 1939. In 1927 he became a British subject, mainly in recognition of his acceptance of the established church. He was awarded the Nobel Prize for literature and the Order of Merit in 1948 and the Medal of Freedom in 1964.

His admiration for the working relationship of state and church in England can be seen in his collection of essays *For Lancelot Andrewes* (1928). In *The Sacred Wood* (1920) Eliot had already stressed the importance of tradition for the creative artist and critic, and praised those poets from the past who had been most stimulating to him as a poet, particularly the Metaphysical poets of the seventeenth century. In *After Strange Gods* (1934), a series of lectures delivered in the University of Virginia, he reiterated his belief in the value of tradition and stressed the importance of the moral aspects of literature. This balance of art and morality, tradition and individual talent, is best seen in his poetry, which also forms a kind of biography of his maturing into faith as well as into an artist.

Prufrock and Other Observations (1917) showed Eliot's indebtedness to the French symbolists and the English Metaphysicals. The poems are about social life in London and Boston. Often epigrammatic, they present an unflattering view of the world of Henry James. In *Poems* (1919) the despair grows more intense; the characters are old, homeless or displaced and the futility and triviality of modern life, devoid of tradition and values, is stressed. The climax of this feeling was in *The Waste Land* (1922), the poem that gave Eliot a commanding position in English poetry. On the whole, contemporary critics attacked the poem because it was nihilistic and anti-Christian and/or because it was a pointless assemblage of other poets and writers. In retrospect, critics and readers have found signs of hope in the poem (although whether they are sufficient to be reckoned with is doubtful) and have admired the magpie method. Not to know the allusions, often from foreign literature and in foreign languages, demonstrates Eliot's point about our loss of tradition; understanding these implications fulfills in the reader Eliot's intention of writing a dramatic poem.

Ash Wednesday (1930) marks a definite turning point in Eliot's poetic treatment of literature and religion and shows his devotion to Dante. It is a difficult poem because it is so intensely personal and because it is attempting to describe a mystical experience. Eliot was much more successful in *Four Quartets* (1943), where he brings together the problems of a spiritually minded man and those of a poet attempting to record those problems. Knowing the allusions here is less important than responding to the felicities of a private and personal meditation the poet shares with the reader.

His profound belief in the moral quality of literature, combined with his technical demand for dramatic presentation (which can be seen in *The Waste Land* where the characters of the Tarot pack are involved in scenes largely composed of scenery and dialogue), led Eliot to consider writing plays. His first attempt, *Sweeney Agonistes* (1932), remains only as fragments of an Aristophanic comedy, but in 1934 he was asked to write the script for a religious pageant, *The Rock*, the choruses of which survive. He wrote his first play in 1935 for Canterbury Cathedral. *Murder in the Cathedral*, a play on the martyrdom of Thomas à Becket, is remarkable for its use of chorus. For Eliot it was a halfway house. It had the same specialized audience that his poetry had. He began therefore to write plays for the commercial theater. In 1939 *The Family Reunion* appeared, a verse drama which had a speaking chorus, supernatural interventions and a Greek source. It was not altogether successful. His other plays, *The Cocktail Party* (p. 1949), *The Confidential Clerk* (1953) and *The Elder Statesman* (p. 1958), were all commissioned by and performed at the Edinburgh Festival. In all three plays Eliot uses an acceptable stage form, drawing-room comedy or farce, to conceal the religious content and the Greek source. But the characters are shadowy at the best of times, and the verse is scarcely recognizable as such to an unwarned ear. Eliot clearly helped the cause of verse drama in the English theater, but he will be remembered rather as critic and poet than as dramatist.

As critic his fame may well rest upon two phrases: "the objective referring to the correlative," which acts as a means of preventing poetry from becoming a turning loose of emotion, and "the dissociation of sensibility," a phrase descriptive of what happened to English literature at the turn of the seventeenth century. Eliot must be remembered as the major poetic voice and influence in English literature in the first half of the twentieth century.

Prufrock and Other Observations, 1917.
Poems, 1919.
The Waste Land, 1922.
Ash Wednesday, 1930.
Selected Essays, 1917–1932, 1932.
Murder in the Cathedral, 1935 (*f.* 1951).
The Family Reunion, 1939.
Four Quartets, 1943.
The Cocktail Party, 1950 (*p.* 1949).
The Confidential Clerk, 1953.
On Poetry and Poets, 1957.
The Elder Statesman, 1959 (*p.* 1958).
Poems Written in Early Youth, 1967.

Complete Poems and Plays, London: Faber & Faber, 1969.
Collected Plays, London: Faber & Faber, 1969.
The Waste Land: Facsimile and Transcript of the Original Draft, ed. V. Eliot, London: Faber & Faber, 1971.   A.P.H.

ELIZABETHAN MISCELLANIES. Poetical miscellanies were published throughout the reign of Queen Elizabeth (1558–1603). Some were purely a publisher's venture, designed to catch the eye and open the purse of browsing readers at the bookstalls of St. Paul's churchyard; others bear the marks of the individual taste and interests of the compilers. Some miscellanies achieved great contemporary success, others little or no popularity, but all reflect the level and changes of taste of the Elizabethan reading public. To many we are indebted for the earliest printed versions of the poems of the courtier-poets, gentlemen who would not sully their reputations with the stigma of the printing house. Thus, besides providing pleasure for their contemporary readers, the miscellanies supplement our knowledge of Elizabethan poetry and interests in poetry.

Songs and Sonnets (1557), published by Richard Tottel and often known as *Tottel's Miscellany*, is not strictly Elizabethan, since it first appeared in the year preceding Elizabeth's accession. Its influence and continued popularity, however, justify its being included with later anthologies which in many ways it inspired. In 1587 the *Miscellany* was in its ninth and last Elizabethan edition. Like the earlier Tudor anthology, *The Court of Venus, Songs and Sonnets* was a volume chiefly of love poetry. The two major, and best, contributors were the late earl of Surrey (whose poems are given pride of place) and Sir Thomas Wyatt, the first two English poets to introduce the Renaissance poetry of the Continent. The other contributors were either scholars, courtiers, or poets in the service of courtiers, so that the tone of the volume is courtly, reflecting the themes and styles which interested the educated gentleman. A distinguishing feature of the *Miscellany* is the use of the sonnet form, not to reappear again in an anthology to the same extent until *The Phoenix Nest* (1593), which came at the height of the sonneteering vogue. The general standard of the poems is high, and the variety of their forms—quatrains, septenary couplets, "poulter's measure"—marked out the pattern of poetry for the early and middle parts of Elizabeth's reign. Worthy of special mention is Lord Vaux's "When Cupid Scaled the Fort."

If the *Songs and Sonnets* was the most influential of Elizabethan miscellanies, *The Paradise of Dainty Devices* (1576) was the most popular, going through ten editions in thirty years. Compiled by the serious-minded Richard Edwards, the verse is predominantly moral or moralistically religious in tone. The *Paradise* contains both ballad and art poetry, much of which is marred by the dullness of commonplace themes and the pursuit of the more obvious rhetorical devices. Since most of the poems were meant to be sung, the meters are tuneful. The well-controlled pathos of Edwards's "In going to my naked bed," and the unaffected simplicity of Kinwelmarsh's "For Christmas Day" and Heywood's "Easter Day" make these poems outstanding amongst the verse of the "Drab Age" poets. *A Gorgeous Gallery of Gallant Inventions* (1578), unlike its predecessor, was never a popular volume. Archaic in diction, monotonous in style, it could only repeat the themes of *Tottel's Miscellany* and the *Paradise*. Yet the "History of Pyramus and Thisbe" and a version of the "Willow Song" which occurs in *Othello* have an interest of their own. The last anthology of the middle years of Elizabeth's reign was *A Handful of Pleasant Delights* (1584, but probably a reprint of a volume of 1566). This differs from the other miscellanies by being a collection entirely of broadside ballads, possibly compiled by Clement Robinson, an early ballad writer. Their subjects are usually love, and incorporate proverbial sayings and literary allusions. The rhythms are suitably uncomplicated for this kind of verse. One of the ballads, "Greensleeves," has retained its popularity down to the present day.

The remaining anthologies reflect the full flowering of Elizabethan poetry in the last decade of the sixteenth century. In *Breton's Bower of Delights* (1591) this is already to be seen in the inclusion of poems by Ralegh and the earl of Oxford. Although this volume contains some poems by Nicholas Breton, it was fathered on him by the printer, who used his name to promote sales. Though several poems are old-fashioned in diction and style, the majority are less heavily marked by alliteration, more varied and lyrical in rhythm, and frequently Petrarchan in expression. The credit for the most accomplished anthology belongs to R.S., whose *The Phoenix Nest* (1593) was the most courtly anthology since Tottel's and included amongst its contributors the foremost late-Elizabethan lyricists. *The Phoenix Nest* features the then fashionable love sonnet (some of these poems occur in the considerable "Ralegh group" of the anthology) amongst the newly favored forms. Although not reprinted, since so much verse of this kind was being published then, *The Phoenix Nest* was widely read. *The Arbour of Amorous Devices*, which only exists in a second edition of 1597, shows no further advance on the previous miscellany.

England's Helicon (1600) reflects contemporary interest in pastoral poetry, the whole volume being devoted to this verse, with the editor occasionally adapting poems to make them pastorals. The mood is often Petrarchan, delicate, languid and literary. The best poems of this pleasing volume are Marlowe's "Come Live with Me and Be My Love," Ralegh's reply to this poem and the ditty of Phillida and Coridon. The last miscellany, *A Poetical Rhapsody*, was edited by Francis Davison, and in 1602 it was largely retrospective; apart from the editor and his brother, Walter, many of the contributors were then dead. The sophisticated forms of Elizabethan poetry—madrigal, sonnet (already out of fashion), ode—are all included. Most modern of the miscellanies in tone, it succeeded *The Paradise* in popularity, going into four editions in eighteen years, and becoming gradually modified to the taste of the Jacobean reader.

Tottel, Richard, *Tottel's Miscellany*, 1557–87 (ed. H. E. Rollins, London: Oxford Univ. Press; Cambridge, Mass.: Harvard Univ. Press, 1928–29).

Edwards, Richard, *The Paradise of Dainty Devices*, 1576 (ed. H. E. Rollins, London: Oxford Univ. Press; Cambridge, Mass.: Harvard Univ. Press, 1927).

Procter, Thomas, *A Gorgeous Gallery of Gallant Inventions*, 1578 (ed. H. E. Rollins, London: Oxford Univ. Press; Cambridge, Mass.: Harvard Univ. Press, 1926).

Robinson, Clement, *A Handful of Pleasant Delights*, 1584 (ed. H. E. Rollins, London: Oxford Univ. Press; Cambridge, Mass.: Harvard Univ. Press, 1924).

Breton, Nicholas, *Breton's Bower of Delights*, 1591 (ed. H. E. Rollins, London: Oxford Univ. Press; Cambridge, Mass.: Harvard Univ. Press, 1933).
R.S., of the Inner Temple, *The Phoenix Nest*, 1593 (ed. H. E. Rollins, London: Oxford Univ. Press; Cambridge, Mass.: Harvard Univ. Press, 1931).
Breton, Nicholas, *The Arbour of Amorous Devices*, 1597 (ed. H. E. Rollins, London: Oxford Univ. Press; Cambridge, Mass.: Harvard Univ. Press, 1937).
England's Helicon, 1600 (ed. H. E. Rollins, London: Oxford Univ. Press; Cambridge, Mass.: Harvard Univ. Press, 1935).
Davison, Francis, *A Poetical Rhapsody*, 1602 (ed. H. E. Rollins, London: Oxford Univ. Press; Cambridge, Mass.: Harvard Univ. Press, 1931–32). J.M.P.

ELLERTON, John. See **Hymns.**

ELLIOTT, Ebenezer (1781–1849) lived his entire life in the Sheffield (Yorkshire) area. While making his way as a small independent businessman, he published several volumes of verse. Only Southey recognized the merit of his early work, but with the publication of *Corn-Law Rhymes* (1831) Elliott was hailed as a champion of Free Trade and the working classes. Although a Radical all his life, he flirted only briefly with Chartism and the Anti-Corn Law League. His verse seldom rises above honest political fervor, and with the repeal of the Corn Laws, his reputation fell. Ebenezer Elliott, "the Corn-Law Rhymer," is best remembered as an exemplar of the new industrial classes and a faithful advocate of cheap bread.

Poetical Works, ed. E. Elliott (son), 2 vols., London: King, 1876. C.P.

ELLISON, Ralph (1914–), was born in Oklahoma City and educated at Tuskegee Institute. As a young man his primary interests were in music and sculpture, but in 1936 he went to New York, met Richard Wright, and began to write for *The New Masses* and *The Negro Quarterly*. By 1944 his short stories, notably "Flying Home" and "King of the Bingo Game," had revealed an impressive talent struggling to master the theme of racial identity, using the techniques of irony, symbolism and fantasy that were brought to fruition in his novel *Invisible Man* (1952), which remains a substantial contribution to modern fiction. Like much Negro writing in America, *Invisible Man* uses the form of an autobiographical odyssey in which an unnamed Negro boy rejects the humiliating mantle of Uncle Tom, and in his journey from the South to New York he struggles to discover his own identity in an absurd and cruel America ever ready to force him into racial stereotypes and to punish him when he fails to submit. At the end of the novel the hero still defends his integrity by literally going underground to seek illumination. A skillful, serious novelist, Ellison has published no extended fiction since 1952, though he has won acclaim as a teacher, and as a critic with *Shadow and Act* (1964), essays on politics, music and literature, which trace his developing views through two decades.

Invisible Man, 1952.
Shadow and Act, 1964.   I.W.

ELYOT, Sir Thomas (?1490–1546) emerges after an obscure early life as being connected with the law and a landowner, who after holding minor offices became ambassador to the Emperor Charles V and a member of Parliament for Cambridge. A friend of More and Ascham, Elyot shows the influence of Erasmus and other Continental humanists. Though a cultured, widely read man with a clear style, his subject matter is seldom original and his thought sometimes confused. Apart from translations and a dictionary, he wrote *The Book Named The Governor* (1531) and *The Castle of Health* (1534).   G.P.

EMERSON, Ralph Waldo (1803–82) was born in Boston (Massachusetts), fourth son of William and Ruth Emerson. He attended Boston Latin School, Harvard College, and Harvard Divinity School. He was a schoolteacher and, for a time, preached as a Unitarian minister in Boston. In 1829 he married Ellen Louise Tucker, then aged seventeen. When she died just two years later, he resigned his pastorship and sailed for Europe, the first of three such voyages abroad he was to take during his lifetime.

Upon returning to America, he moved to Concord (Massachusetts), where he lived for the rest of his life. In 1835 he married Lydia Jackson. It was after this union that Emerson's intellectual and literary concerns flowered. In 1836 his first son, Waldo, was born, and his essay, *Nature*, was published. In this essay the basic tenets of Emerson's philosophy were presented. He wrote that "the reason why the world lacks unity and lies broken and in heaps is because man is disunited with himself." For Emerson "the whole of nature is a metaphor of the human mind." Emerson's thought, however, is not a closed logical system, but an approach to the spiritual. How to attain, retain, and communicate in language what is essentially a nonverbal experience? This is the core of Emerson's dilemma, and, for him, the task of the poet. For Emerson, true poetry and true philosophy are one.

After the publication of *Nature*, Emerson assumed the role of titular head of a group of New England religious enthusiasts who held weekly meetings at his home. Initial discussions of the communal living experiment which was to be known as "Brook Farm" also took place in Emerson's home, but Emerson himself chose not to participate. "I do not wish to remove from my present prison to a prison a little larger," he said.

In 1839 Lydia gave birth to a daughter whom they named Ellen. In 1842 their son, Waldo, died. In 1844 another son, Edward, was born. By this time Lydia had chosen to occupy herself with concrete realities and turned away from the increasing abstractions of her husband's thought processes. He continued to write, lecture, and travel, and the recognition he had sought throughout his life began to accrue. When, in 1882, Emerson died, he was buried in the family plot in Concord. His tombstone is a large and craggy chunk of white marble.

The most oft-expressed criticism of Emerson's essays is that he lacked "a sense of evil" (Yeats). However, one of Emerson's finest essays, "Fate," addresses itself directly and precisely to this problem. Emerson believes that "evil" exists only in the social sphere. "You have just dined, and however scrupulously the slaughterhouse is concealed in the graceful distance of miles, there is complicity." Nature's inexorable rough wilderness is, Emerson claims, often mistaken by men for that which is evil, but metaphysical evil is, for Emerson, *maia*, illusion. This view, which has much in common with Eastern thought, lies at the heart of Emerson's philosophy.

The man of genius is, for Emerson, the religious man. The greatest teacher, the finest literature, is sacred literature. God is always to be found within man, not external to him, and it is within us all that Emerson's much misunderstood "Oversoul" must be located. Emerson was quick to sense this essentially religious genius in others, and when his wife's sister introduced him to Thoreau in 1836, Emerson saw from the first that he was meeting his most important student. As in any Zen relationship between master and disciple, the student ultimately must transcend not only the teacher, but must pass beyond any fixed concept of "transcendence" as Thoreau finally did. Emerson's address on 9 May 1862, published as the essay "Thoreau," is the finest of its kind in American literature.

Although Emerson was astute enough to recognize, also from the first, the genius of Whitman, his own poetry adheres to more cogent and structured rhythmic patterns. The best of his verse is endowed with a mantralike quality, and indeed Emerson's belief that the poem is a magic amulet which should ideally raise one to a different level of consciousness is precisely what forces him to remain within the bounds of the metrically known and thus causes most of his poems to go flat. But when Emerson's poems do succeed ("Brahma," "Days," the first part of "Merlin," the first stanza of "Hamatreya") they manage to achieve an almost gnostic quality.

Emerson has left over forty volumes of essays, poems, letters, lectures and journal entries, but he remains perhaps the most unread of all classic nineteenth-century American authors. Critics and readers trained in descriptive analysis seem to find that their very orientation is that which makes it difficult to enter imaginatively into Emerson's world. How, for example, to "criticize" a passage like: "Standing on the bare ground,—my head bathed by the blithe air, and uplifted into infinite space, all mean egotism vanishes. I become a transparent eyeball; I am nothing; I see all; the currents of the Universal Being circulate through me; I am a part or parcel of God" (*Nature*)? The persistent question is always how much of Emerson's writing has the ring of spiritual truth and how much is merely the overblown rhetoric of an unconscious desire for psychological withdrawal.

Complete Works, Centenary edition, 12 vols., Boston: Houghton, Mifflin, 1903–04.
Journals, ed. E. W. Emerson and W. E. Forbes, 10 vols., Boston: Houghton Mifflin, 1909–14.
Journals and Miscellaneous Notebooks, vols. 1–5, ed. W. H. Gibson, A. R. Ferguson, M. R. Davis, M. M. Sealts, and H. Hayford, Cambridge, Mass.: Harvard Univ. Press, 1960–65.
Letters, ed. R. L. Rusk, New York: Columbia Univ. Press, 1939.
Early Lectures, ed. S. Whicher and R. E. Spiller, Cambridge, Mass.: Harvard Univ. Press, 1959.
Correspondence of Emerson and Carlyle, ed. J. Slater, New York: Columbia Univ. Press, 1964. w.s.

EMPSON, William (1906–), born in Yorkshire, was educated at Winchester and Cambridge where he studied mathematics and later, under the guidance of I. A. Richards, English literature. In the 1930s he taught in Japan and China and, after returning to England at the outbreak of the Second World War, became Chinese editor for the British Broadcasting Corporation. From 1953 to 1971 he was professor of English literature at Sheffield University.

As a poet and critic he has had considerable influence over a generation of younger writers, encouraging a new interest in the subtleties and ambiguity of poetic language. He has written several critical works, including *Seven Types of Ambiguity*, *Some Versions of Pastoral* and *The Structure of Complex Words*. In these works, by applying to poetry a method of close textual analysis, he aims to show the ambiguities of thought, of which the poets themselves are often unaware, that are revealed in details of language. *Milton's God*, a later critical study, is more polemic and speculative in manner. His output as a poet is restricted to two volumes, *Poems* and *The Gathering Storm*. Much of his poetry is connected with the revival of interest in Metaphysical poetry, and it is often highly logical and allusive, making use of images and the vocabulary of science, puns and paradox. His thought is extremely condensed, his feeling often intense and conveyed with restraint and compression.

Seven Types of Ambiguity, 1930.
Poems, 1935.
Some Versions of Pastoral, 1935.
The Gathering Storm, 1940.
The Structure of Complex Words, 1951.
Milton's God, 1961.

Collected Poems, New York: Harcourt, Brace, 1949; London: Chatto & Windus, 1955.   O.K.

ERVINE, St. John (1883–1971), a native of Belfast, spent his early life in England but returned to Ireland and had his first play, *Mixed Marriage* (1911), performed at the Abbey Theatre, of which he was later to be manager. As an all-round man of letters his literary output is very large and includes drama criticism for *The Observer*, biographies, novels and numerous plays. Of his early plays *John Ferguson* (1915) is very typical; it is a naturalistic "problem" play, set in Protestant Northern Ireland, and dramatizes the Ulsterman's fear of Irish nationalism and Roman Catholicism. His later plays, social comedies written for the London stage such as *The First Mrs. Fraser* (1929), were commercially successful but more conventional. He was a friend and close associate of Æ, Yeats and Shaw, all of them founder members of the Irish Academy. His *Bernard Shaw: His Life, Work and Friends* (1956) is a definitive work.   O.K.

ESSAYS. An essay is a prose piece, relatively short in length, in which the writer discusses or reflects on any aspect of life he may choose, with whatever order or sequence of ideas he pleases. The history of the essay form shows a steady increase in the kinds of material a writer found himself able to treat and a corresponding increase in the variety of artistic means at his disposal, along with more frequent openings for publication of essays whether as works of art or as information.

The essay form developed from the *Essais* (1580) of the French writer Montaigne. Even before these were translated into English by Florio

(1603), they influenced Francis Bacon, whose essays show the personal approach, wide range of subject matter and reproduction of the reflective and discursive thought processes of the writer's mind which characterize fully developed essay writing. Bacon's gentlemanly essays were published in book form, as were the pleasantly personal ones (1600–01) of Sir William Cornwallis (died ?1631) and various other minor writers of the seventeenth century. Cowley's essays (1668) show the qualities of these early essayists at their most companionable, natural and calmly reflective. After the Restoration essays began to be used as a vehicle for theoretical discussion, information and the communication of ideas. Dryden's extended *An Essay of Dramatic Poesy* (1668) and later preface to the *Fables* are early masterpieces in the new manner—easier, less comprehensive and more spontaneous than a treatise, adapting technicalities to the level of a cultivated but nonspecialist audience. A writer such as Sir William Temple (1628–99), Swift's employer, could still cultivate the polished urbanities of gentlemanly discussion at his leisure in the 1690s (providing a model for the essayists of the next generation), but at the same time early forms of newspapers and the growth of journalism were creating a market for the professional essay writing, closely linked to the interests and tastes of the age, which attracted many of the best minds of the eighteenth century. Early journalism like L'Estrange's *The Observator* papers (1681–87) and Ned Ward's *The London Spy* (1698–1700) revealed the public's relish for entertaining disquisitions on current events. Defoe's *Review* (1704–13) succeeded with a mixture of social commentary and satire, moralizing and scandal.

The final establishment of the essay as the generally accepted vehicle for social comment and more fundamental, though still entertaining, criticism of life was achieved by Steele and Addison in *The Tatler* (1709–11), *The Spectator* (1711–12 and 1714) and other papers. Their wide range of subjects was developed according to personal preference by succeeding eighteenth-century writers. Addison's solemn reflectiveness and occasional ventures into critical discussion were carried on with majestic assurance and concision of thought by Dr. Johnson in *The Rambler* (1750–52) and *The Idler* (1758–60), while Steele's sentimentalism was cunningly deepened into a benevolent vision of life by Oliver Goldsmith in a succession of periodical ventures. As the century advanced, the habit of publishing essays weekly, either alone or in groups of two or three, became less common. The magazine evolved, presenting a varied range of contents, and with the proliferation of magazines fresh opportunities for the essayist emerged. In the Regency period steam printing and the increasing size of the reading public led to a mass of periodicals of all kinds, in which essays usually featured. An instance of the essay's popularity and the caliber of the minds working in the form is the fact that John Scott's *The London Magazine*, which first appeared in 1820, had Hazlitt, Lamb, De Quincey and Leigh Hunt among its regular contributors. Coleridge, Hunt and other writers edited magazines or wrote regular series of essays for publication. In these years the essay lost most of its Augustan social consciousness and became, very often, a vehicle for expressing the writer's insights, memories or purely personal interests and enjoyments. Yet at the same time as Lamb and Hazlitt were extending the techniques of the familiar essay to include subjectivism and associational processes, the emergence of the great literary reviews —*The Edinburgh Review* (1802); *The Quarterly Review* (1809)—created a new kind of extended critical essay, running to as many as forty or fifty pages, in which biographical material or general discussion of a topic would be followed by exhaustive examination of the issues raised by the book under review. Sydney Smith, Jeffrey and Scott were among the early reviewers and it became usual for writers to collect their critical essays for subsequent reprinting in volume form. The essays of Carlyle, Macaulay and Matthew Arnold, for example, began life in the great reviews.

As the century advanced the scope of the literary, historical and biographical essay became enlarged. Any attempt to follow it to its present-day forms would soon degenerate into a catalog of names (though an illustrious catalog, taking in the important creative critical work of writers better known in other fields, such as Shaw, Virginia Woolf and Aldous Huxley). The familiar essay developed in the hands of such men as Thackeray and Robert Louis Stevenson to mirror the reflective sentiment, close autobiographical strain and emotional warmth which one associates with the best writing in this form during the Victorian period. Early in the twentieth century the personal essay suffered something of an artistic decline and frequently became a vehicle for preciosity and empty belle-lettrism, but the essay form was far from dead and it regained a healthy fusion of dialectic and private conviction in the work of—among others—Chesterton, D. H. Lawrence and, nearer our own time, George Orwell.

The whole history of the essay has been one of ever-increasing diversity of range, individuality and involvement with the experience and purpose of living. Its vitality as a means of comment and imparting opinion renders it perpetually necessary and valuable.

For bibliography—see under authors named above.   W.R.

ETHEREGE, Sir George (1635–91), son of a Bermuda planter who went into exile with Charles II, also lived in France, but was apprenticed to a London attorney in 1653. At the time of his first play (1664) he became associated with the Court Wits, Rochester, Sedley, Buckhurst and Buckingham. In 1668 he joined the English embassy in Constantinople. Returning in 1671, he resumed a life of libertine pleasures and was involved in a number of serious brawls. Around 1680 he married advantageously and acquired his knighthood. In 1685 he went to Ratisbon on diplomatic service but caused resentment by his scandalous life. This appointment terminated with the 1688 Revolution, and Etherege spent his last three years abroad in continued dissipation, dying in Paris.

Etherege, who admitted being indolent, wrote little, but his three plays initiated the Restoration comedy of manners. *The Comical Revenge* (1664), an uneasy blend of heroic couplet and witty prose, but full of high spirits, was immediately successful. *She Would If She Could* (1668), although initially a failure, is a more considerable achievement, charming and vivacious, and displaying some of the shrewdness that makes his next and last play his best—*The Man of Mode* (1676), in which Dorimant, an accomplished and self-possessed wit, is contrasted with Sir Fopling Flutter, a pretentious idiot. Here Etherege achieves unity and point by thematic parallels and verbal texture rather than by a well-made plot. He also wrote a few graceful and musical lyrics, and some other cleverly handled poems with an amusing or satirical bent.

Dramatic Works, ed. H. F. B. Brett-Smith, 2 vols., Oxford: Blackwell, 1927.
Letterbook, ed. S. Rosenfeld, London: Oxford Univ. Press, 1928.
Poems, ed. J. Thorpe, Princeton: Princeton Univ. Press, 1963.   H.N.D.

EVANS, Caradoc (1883–1945), born in West Wales in a region of Welsh-speaking tenant farmers, went to London as a young man, working as draper's assistant in a large department store and gaining an introduction to literature through a working men's college in Camden Town. He later became a journalist and in 1915 published his first volume of short stories, *My People*. The narrow intense lives of the Welsh peasantry were revealed with a poetic compression in a language which attempted to fashion Welsh idiomatic usage into a type of English prose-poetry. Evans's ability to penetrate the surface of society and his attacks upon the Bible-bound commercialism and sexual hypocrisy of his countrymen gained him increasing notoriety as he developed his insights in the later collections of stories—*Capel Sion* (1916) and *My Neighbours* (1919). He was less skillful as a novelist and dramatist. Some of his finest stories are contained in the posthumous collection, *The Earth Gives All and Takes All* (1946).   C.P.

EVELYN, John (1620–1706), who came of a well-to-do family, was educated at a school in Lewes (Sussex) and at Oxford. He subsequently spent much time traveling on the Continent, to the enrichment of his famous diary. A Royalist, he joined Charles I as a volunteer in 1642, but seems to have been rather inactive during the Civil War. After the Restoration he performed various duties for the government but was mainly settled, with his gardens, at Deptford. Evelyn was one of the founders of the Royal Society.

Although now known mainly as a diarist, Evelyn wrote extensively on such miscellaneous subjects as plantations, smoke prevention, engraving, gardening, and architecture. He also made several translations from French and Greek. The diary runs from 1642 to 1706 and, being a precise and detailed narrative about both England and the Continent, is a most valuable historical document of seventeenth-century life and manners. Although Evelyn is seldom as lively as Pepys, his pure, correct, lucid style has its own attractions and reveals a most appealing personality.

(See also **Political Pamphlets.**)

Diary, ed. E. S. de Beer, 6 vols., Oxford: Clarendon Press, 1955.

G.P.

EXPERIMENTAL POETRY. The 1960s produced a significant revival and development in experimental poetry. Some of the impetus for this work comes from a late but sympathetic response to the achievements of such pioneers of early "modernism" as James Joyce, e. e. cummings and Gertrude Stein. New interest in art movements of the early decades of the twentieth century—particularly dadaism and surrealism, and in the creative possibilities suggested by European poets such as Guillaume Apollinaire, Tristan Tzara, Hans (Jean) Arp, Hugo Ball and Kurt Schwitters—has also helped to encourage the exploration of the expressive possibilities of the basic "elements" of language.

In visual poetry, interest in the way in which letters "perform" on the page (or, indeed, on glass, stone, wood and many other materials) has been shown by several British poets, notably Ian Hamilton Finlay, Simon Cutts, Stuart Mills and Dom Sylvester Houédard. In Finlay's work, in particular, there has been a consistently fine achievement which has earned him international repute.

"Concrete poetry," the much-used term for this kind of work, is a somewhat misleading coinage which fails to do justice to the range of subtle techniques developed by these poets, or to their links with literary and artistic tradition.

In "phonic" poetry, the employment of particles of speech sounds has been interestingly explored by Bob Cobbing and Rosemary Tonks. The British Broadcasting Corporation's radiophonic workshop has helped to project and to realize work by both these British poets, as well as to introduce British listeners to the remarkable performance of the Austrian Ernst Jandl.

Williams, E., ed., *An Anthology of Concrete Poetry*, New York: Something Else Press, 1967.

Bann, S., ed., *Concrete Poetry: An International Anthology*, London: London Magazine Editions, 1967.

Lucie-Smith, E., ed., *A Primer of Experimental Poetry*, London: Rapp & Whiting, 1971.

Bergonzi, B., ed., *Innovations*, London: Macmillan, 1968.   **A.Y.**

EZEKIEL, Nissim. See Indian Literature.

F

FABER, F. W. (Frederick William). See **Hymns.**

FAIRBURN, A. R. D. (Arthur Rex Dugard). See **New Zealand Literature.**

FALCONER, William (1732–69), born in Edinburgh, went to sea at an early age. A shipwreck off Greece, from which only he and two others were saved, gave him the subject of the poem for which he is known, *The Shipwreck* (1762). Heroic in style and structure, this poem of three cantos is written in rhyming couplets. Falconer quite deliberately strove to naturalize sea terms in his verse; "Man the clue-garnets! Let the main sheet fly!" is not untypical. He was also the author of a *Marine Dictionary*, published in the year of his death at sea.

Poetical Works, ed. J. Mitford, London: Pickering, 1836.   J.C.

FANSHAWE, Sir Richard (1608–66), fifth son of a titled family, is best known as the translator of Guarini's *Il Pastor Fido* (1647), *The Lusiad* of Camões (1655) and as the writer of occasional verse. Fanshawe's work displays his patriotism and devotion to the Stuarts, the linguistic ability which equipped him for diplomatic missions in Portugal and Spain, and his literary enthusiasm for Horace and Spenser. His wife's *Memoirs* (ed. H. C. Fanshawe, London: J. Lane, 1907) are interesting.   H.N.D.

FARQUHAR, George (1678–1707), son of an Irish clergyman, was educated at Londonderry and entered Trinity College, Dublin in 1694. After two years he left and became an actor, but following an accident in which he wounded a fellow actor in Dryden's *The Indian Emperor* (by forgetting to use a foil), he resolved to act no more. Encouraged by Robert Wilks, he came to London and wrote his first play, *Love and a Bottle* (1699; *p.* 1698). His autobiographical romance, *The Adventures of Covent Garden* (1699), reveals something of his rakish life in London, and *Love and Business* (1702) his complicated amours. The second play, *The Constant Couple; or, A Trip to the Jubilee* (1700; *p.* 1699), with Wilks as Sir Harry Wildair, was tremendously successful, but the next three plays were less well received and Farquhar became increasingly impoverished. In 1703 he married a penniless widow with three children, supposing her to be wealthy. Attempting to increase his income, he obtained a commission in the Grenadiers and acted in a benefit performance of *The Constant Couple* in Dublin. Sent on recruiting duty in Lichfield and Shrewsbury in 1705, he returned to London with one of his best plays. While writing the other, he became desperately ill. He died dependent upon Wilks's charity during the play's third performance.

The two last plays concern city characters, typical of Restoration comedy, but in a country setting. *The Recruiting Officer* (1706), based on Farquhar's recruiting experiences, has a realism and, in spite of general high spirits, a callousness untypical of Restoration comedy. *The Beaux Stratagem* (1707) returns to artificiality with a dazzling, albeit superficial, brilliance.

Works, ed. C. A. Stonehill, 2 vols., London: Nonesuch Press, 1930.

H.N.D.

FARRELL, James T. (Thomas) (1904–   ) was born in Chicago of a poor Catholic family. He studied at the University of Chicago and has spent much of his working life in the city. It is a recurring theme in his writing. His first novel, *Young Lonigan* (1932), written with the hindsight of its author during the Depression, is a naïvely realistic, stream-of-consciousness, vernacular novel dealing with the experiences of a boy of fifteen among Chicago's teenage gangs. Its setting invites comparison with that of Stephen Crane's Bowery, as does the strong environmental theme, but young Studs Lonigan displays a stronger character than Maggie and, although he succumbs to the pressures of the violent world, he is not yet destroyed. *The Young Manhood of Studs Lonigan* (1934) and *Judgment Day* (1935) follow the hero to his early death, with a picture of increasing bitterness and viciousness. The trilogy presents a realistic treatment of Depression and degradation, and though not obtrusively so, is effectively protest fiction. Cognate with it is *Gas-House McGinty* (1933), which deals with employees in a city express office and again points to social inequalities. Farrell followed the success of the Studs Lonigan books with another series dealing with a proletarian hero, Danny O'Neill.

Among Farrell's critical writings are perceptive defenses of Marxist writing, *A Note on Literary Criticism* (1936), and of realism, *The League of Frightened Philistines* (1945). He has published an account of his devotion to baseball, *My Baseball Diary* (1957), and a volume of *Collected Poems* appeared in 1965.

Young Lonigan: A Boyhood in Chicago Streets, 1932.
Gas-House McGinty, 1933.

The Young Manhood of Studs Lonigan, 1934.
Judgment Day, 1935.
A Note on Literary Criticism, 1936.
No Star Is Lost, 1938.
Father and Son, 1940.
To Whom It May Concern, 1944.
The League of Frightened Philistines, and Other Papers, 1945.
Literature and Morality, 1947.
Reflections at Fifty, and Other Essays, 1954.
My Baseball Diary, 1957.
It Has Come to Pass, 1958.

Studs Lonigan: A Trilogy . . . with a New Introduction by the Author, New
  York: Macmillan Co., 1938 (*f.* 1959; 1964).

Short Stories, New York: Vanguard Press, 1937.
Collected Poems, New York: Fleet Publishing, 1965.   M.L.

FAST, Howard (1914–   ) was born in New York City and attended
the National Academy of Design. Abandoning art, he took a variety of
manual jobs. Experience on an Indian reservation provided material for
The Last Frontier (1941). From 1942 to 1943 he was a member of the
Overseas Staff Office of War Information. Novels and biographies like
Citizen Tom Paine (1943) and *Freedom Road* (1944) are strongly left-wing,
but *The Naked God* (1957) indicates his disillusion with communism.
Spartacus (1958; *f.* 1959) remains an enthusiastic portrayal of the Roman
slave revolt. Work in the 1960s included the play *The Hill* (1963) and
The Hunter and the Trap (1967).   J.L.M.

FAULKNER, William (1897–1962) was born in New Albany
(Mississippi), but grew up—and later elected to live—in Oxford, county
seat of Lafayette (Mississippi), the real-life basis for Jefferson and the
"apocryphal kingdom" called Yoknapatawpha County chronicled in
most of Faulkner's fiction. His region's history and lore were primary
sources of inspiration; for example, Colonel John Sartoris in the episodic
Civil War novel, *The Unvanquished* (1938), was modeled on the exploits
of Faulkner's great-grandfather, William Clark Falkner, a dueling
railroad builder and author of such melodramatic works as *The White
Rose of Memphis* (1880). However, Faulkner was slave to neither fact nor
consistency; though Yoknapatawpha is an identifiable world persisting
in the reader's mind, it changes more or less subtly from book to book.
The works were not intended to form an unchanging saga in the manner
suggested, for instance, by Malcolm Cowley's *The Portable Faulkner*

(1946), a chronological rearrangement of stories and extracts, but should be judged according to their intrinsic merits.

The eldest of four sons born to a moderately successful businessman, Murry C. Falkner, Faulkner was educated in Oxford schools and, briefly, at the University of Mississippi, where his father was business manager. As a young man he liked to draw and his mother, Maud Butler Falkner, encouraged him to read widely, as did his friend and temporary mentor, Phil Stone, a local lawyer. Towards the end of the First World War Faulkner received flying instruction in the Royal Flying Corps in Canada; he remained interested in airmanship, using it as subject matter for *Pylon* (1935) and other works.

In 1920 he worked briefly in a New York bookshop before returning to Oxford as university postmaster. During the next few years he wrote (mostly poems and an unpublished play), read, played golf, hunted, served as scoutmaster, walked and listened. In 1924 (by now Faulkner had incorporated a *u* into his name) his first book, a collection of largely derivative poems, *The Marble Faun*, was published, subsidized by Stone. Soon afterwards he lived in New Orleans, associating with Sherwood Anderson and other contributors to *The Double Dealer* before traveling on to Europe. In February 1926, shortly after his return to Oxford, *Soldiers' Pay*, Faulkner's first novel, a "lost generation" piece about the homecoming of a wounded war veteran, was published at Anderson's request. It was followed by *Mosquitoes* (1927), a satirical Huxleyesque "novel of ideas," and *Sartoris* (1929), carved by the publishers from a longer work, "Flags in the Dust."

Sartoris is important because, in mining his own "postage stamp of native soil," Faulkner made the first version of Yoknapatawpha (we meet, for example, some of the people later to be portrayed in detail—the Snopeses, Peabody, the Benbows, etc.) and fully articulated such major themes as the need to live in harmony with the earth's natural rhythms. Intrinsically, the novel is interesting but uneven. It concerns the return home of Bayard Sartoris, an aristocratic young war veteran, and the tensions caused by his half-willful, half-fated course towards self-destruction. Later, in 1929, *The Sound and the Fury* marked the beginning of Faulkner's major phase, for this study of the disintegrating Compson family is accomplished in every respect. Its four-part structure successfully places the reader within the consciousnesses of three Compson brothers— Benjy, an idiot to whom all time is equally present; Quentin, obsessive, intelligent, a suicide; and Jason, a selfish, prejudiced thief. The final section offers a third person narrative mainly from the viewpoint of Dilsey, the aged but enduring black servant who struggles to keep the family to- gether. *As I Lay Dying* (1930) is a *tour de force* which, through the sixty interior monologues of some thirteen characters, tells the heroic but absurd story of the Bundren family's efforts to bury Addie's corpse in Jefferson. When the book sold as poorly as *The Sound and the Fury*, Faulkner wrote *Sanctuary* (1931). Although toned down in sensation and deepened in meaning at the galley stage at his own expense, this deliberately controversial novel of unnatural rape and unjust fate won Faulkner a reputation for decadence. For more than ten years, though influential in France, he received comparatively little critical attention in the English-speaking world and his sales proved inadequate to sustain the family he had taken on when he married the divorcée Estelle Oldham Franklin in 1929, especially after the birth of his own only surviving child, Jill, in 1933. Consequently, his income derived largely from magazine publication of stories (several later worked into novels) and periods in Hollywood, where he was befriended by Howard Hawks. He received screenwriting credit for such Hawks films as *Today We Live* (1933; based on *Turnabout*), *To Have and Have Not* (1945), *The Big Sleep* (1946) and *Land of the Pharaohs* (1955).

The next decade was highly productive. Faulkner published *These 13* (1931), stories; *Light in August* (1932), about the interlocking lives of Joe Christmas, a man driven by ignorance of his true racial identity, Lena Grove, a simple "earth-mother" seeking the father of her child, and Gail Hightower, an ineffectual minister; *Doctor Martino* (1934), stories; *Pylon* (1935); *Absalom, Absalom!* (1936); *The Unvanquished* (1938); *The Wild Palms* (1939), which in its conjunction of two ostensibly unrelated stories again reveals Faulkner's inveterate experimentalism; *The Hamlet* (1940), a frequently funny examination of the villagers of Frenchman's Bend and the rise to power of Flem Snopes, an unfeeling, incredibly devious and rapacious businessman, mostly told from the vantage of V. K. Ratliffe, an itinerant sewing machine agent; and, in 1942, *Go Down, Moses*.

There is excellence in all these books, especially the stories, but the most important are *Absalom, Absalom!* and *Go Down, Moses*. With great compassion and complexity, both probe the South's shameful racial history. In *Absalom, Absalom!*, against a backdrop of biblical and classical allusions, the reader, piecing together several witnesses' accounts, meets Thomas Sutpen, who in his efforts to found a dynasty prior to the Civil War carved out his plantation and fathered sons of white and mixed blood, who are doomed to clash disastrously. Much later, Quentin Compson, away at Harvard, speculates on the story, assessing its implications, assigning motives and causes. Sutpen's fatal defect is his refusal to acknowledge the essential humanity of others. Faulkner again chose this flaw when he characterized L. Q. C. McCaslin, founder of the family delineated in *Go Down, Moses*: he fathered a daughter on a slave woman and, later, committed incest with that same daughter. Ike McCaslin learns of this act when he reads through the plantation ledgers many years later. He relinquishes his right to the plantation and tries, ineffectually, to make amends towards the black people who farm the land. *Go Down, Moses* also investigates the mysterious forces of nature (Ike learns his morality through hunting), right and wrong relationships towards others, the land and the past.

In 1948, with the publication of *Intruder in the Dust*, his best-selling detective novel about a near-lynching when Jefferson believes a black has murdered a white, Faulkner's fortunes, aided by the publicity given *The Portable Faulkner*, began to rise. In 1950 he received the Nobel Prize. Many other awards, including the Legion of Honor, followed. Always resistant to journalistic exploitation, Faulkner, who claimed he was really only "a farmer," found himself thrust into the public eye. He also addressed himself to and wrote public pieces on controversial issues, especially integration. In these activities Faulkner insisted that man possesses at least the capacity "to prevail"—much to the consternation of critics who had labeled him nihilistic.

Certainly the later fiction is concerned with man's responsibility in society, but perhaps only overtly more so than the major works. *Requiem for a Nun* (1951), which mixes novelistic and dramatic forms and was later staged (by Albert Camus amongst others), forms a sort of sequel to *Sanctuary* and posits a black dope-fiend whore as a moral force in the complex redemption of Temple Drake Stevens. *A Fable* (1954) is a vast philosophical work retelling the Christian Passion story set in the trenches of the First World War. *The Town* (1957) and *The Mansion* (1959) complete the trilogy, begun in *The Hamlet*, devoted to Flem Snopes's career and the frequently impractical interventions of Gavin Stevens. Some of these later works show a decline in intensity; also, in contrast to their earlier appearances, Faulkner's famous long sentences, parentheses, portmanteau words and the like sometimes seem rhetorical, a mannerism. However, in his last book, *The Reivers* (1962), he once more reached the perfect pitch for his subject—a gentle "reminiscence" of a boy's growth towards true "virtue" at the turn of the century. Faulkner died, shortly after a riding fall, on 6 July 1962.

The Marble Faun, 1924 (poems).
Soldiers' Pay, 1926.
Mosquitoes, 1927.
Sartoris, 1929.
The Sound and the Fury, 1929 (*f.* 1959).
As I Lay Dying, 1930.
Sanctuary, 1931 (*f.* as *The Story of Temple Drake*, 1933; 1960).
These 13, 1931 (stories).
Light in August, 1932.

A Green Bough, 1933 (poems).
Doctor Martino and Other Stories, 1934.
Pylon, 1935 (*f.* as *The Tarnished Angels*, 1957).
Absalom, Absalom!, 1936.
The Unvanquished, 1938.
The Wild Palms, 1939.
The Hamlet, 1940 (*f.* as *The Long Hot Summer*, 1957).
Go Down, Moses, 1942.
Intruder in the Dust, 1948 (*f.* 1949).
Knight's Gambit, 1949 (stories).
Collected Stories, 1950.
Requiem for a Nun, 1951 (*f.* as *Sanctuary*, 1961).
A Fable, 1954.
The Town, 1957.
The Mansion, 1959.
The Reivers, 1962 (*f.* 1969).

The Portable Faulkner, ed. M. Cowley, New York: Viking Press, 1946.
Faulkner in the University: Class Conferences at the University of Virginia, 1957–1958, ed. F. L. Gwynn and J. L. Blotner, Charlottesville: Univ. of Virginia Press, 1959.
Essays, Speeches and Public Letters, ed. J. B. Meriwether, New York: Random House; London: Chatto & Windus, 1966.
Lion in the Garden: Interviews with William Faulkner, 1926–1962, ed. J. B. Meriwether and M. Millgate, New York: Random House, 1968.

M.G.

FEARING, Kenneth (1902–61) was born in Oak Park (Illinois) and educated at the University of Wisconsin. He worked as a mill hand and in various types of journalism before becoming a free-lance writer in New York. He published a large amount of poetry, mainly lyric verse which he adapted, by the freest rhythms, for a harsh staccato satire. In such a collection as *Dead Reckoning* (1938) he shows the art of the orator but the work is an uneasy fusion of art and propaganda. He wrote several novels, the finest of which is probably *The Hospital* (1939), a fragmentary but intense work about one hour in a large hospital. A wide variety of characters is handled with poise, authority and wit.   D.V.W.

FENOLLOSA, Ernest (1853–1908) was born in Massachusetts, died in England and was buried in Japan. He taught at Tokyo University before he became curator of the Boston Fine Arts Museum and secured recognition as a leading authority on oriental art and literature. His work included a collection of poems, *East and West* (1893), and *Epochs of Chinese and Japanese Art*, published posthumously in 1911. Ezra Pound, who inherited his manuscripts, edited Fenollosa's translations of Chinese poems in *Cathay* (1915), his versions of Japanese drama, *Certain Noble Plays of Japan* (1916), and *The Chinese Written Character As a Medium for Poetry* (1936), which influenced Pound's ideogrammatic method in the *Cantos*.   R.W.

FERGUSSON, Robert (1750–74), educated at St. Andrews University, brilliantly continued the Scottish vernacular revival begun by Allan Ramsay. His Scots poems (e.g., "The Daft Days," "Leith Races") are vigorous, entertaining and impressive studies of local scene and character. Their themes and artistry captivated and inspired Burns, who movingly acknowledged his debt.

Poems, 1773.
Poems on Various Subjects, 1779.

Poems, ed. M. P. McDiarmid, 2 vols., Edinburgh: Scottish Text Society, 1954–56.   A.M.O.

FERLINGHETTI, Lawrence (1919–   ) was born in Yonkers (New York) and educated at Columbia and the Sorbonne. A poet, painter and book designer, he associated himself with the bookshop and publishing firm of City Lights in San Francisco. He was first noticed with the "Beat" writers such as Kerouac, Ginsberg and Corso, who struck out to capture the openness and outrageousness of experience against what they saw as the oppression of academic formalism. In a collection such as *A Coney Island of the Mind* (1958) Ferlinghetti's work shows an awareness of a crisis in Western values through a style that is witty, colloquial and spontaneous. He rejects the mysticism and political anarchy of other "Beat" writers. His work can be biting and clownish or, when angry, can achieve authentic power; its weakness is that it is sometimes merely smart or shrill. He has written a "labyrinth dream" novel in *Her* (1960).

D.V.W.

FERRIER, Susan (1782–1854), daughter of an Edinburgh writer to the signet, grew up in literary society (her father was a friend of Scott). About 1810 she began *Marriage* (1818), a novel in which Maria Edgeworth's interest in education and the formation of character combines with Mackenzie-like sentimentalism and a tearaway brand of Scottish character comedy which is all Susan Ferrier's own. The comedy survives amid increasing didacticism in *The Inheritance* (1824) and *Destiny* (1831).

She shares with Galt and Scott the distinction of having created the nineteenth-century Scottish novel of regional culture and society.

Works, ed. Lady M. Sackville, 4 vols. (vol. 4, *Memoir* by J. Doyle), London: Grayson, 1928.   W.R.

FIELD, Nathaniel (1587–?1620), son of a Puritan preacher and writer, was forcibly recruited when about thirteen years old as actor in the Queen's Children of the Chapel, and subsequently (c.1616) acted with the King's Men, Shakespeare's old company. A friend of Ben Jonson and George Chapman, he wrote two plays, *A Woman Is a Weathercock* (1612; *p.* 1609) and *Amends for Ladies* (1618; *p.* before 1611), and collaborated in others. His plays, displaying the humor characters of Jonson but without that playwright's moral vision, are tragicomedies of love intrigue, strongest when expressing disgust about human relations.

Plays, ed. W. Peery, Austin: Univ. of Texas Press, 1950.   A.E.

FIELDING, Henry (1707–54) was born in Somerset, son of an army officer, and educated first by a tutor and then at Eton. On leaving school, and after a thwarted love affair, he took to hack writing and committed himself to the pleasures of London life. He was a big man, vigorous and passionate, never prudent, and "more generous than just." The stage offered the quickest return, and *Love in Several Masques* (1728) promised well, even beside *The Beggar's Opera*. Fielding then spent two years studying law in Leyden, but declining family fortunes required his return. A £200 allowance from his mother ceased and Fielding now became a regular playwright, turning out coarse comedies, farces, and burlesques (including *Tom Thumb*) to maintain a day-to-day existence.

In 1734 he married the beautiful heiress Charlotte Cradock and set up house in the West country, but his habitual extravagance quickly swallowed up her small fortune and his own estate. *Pasquin: A Dramatic Satire on the Times* (in which Fielding, though a Whig, attacked the ministry) marked his return to London. *The Historical Register for the Year 1736*, performed the following year, finally precipitated Walpole's Licensing Act of 1737 and Fielding's retirement from the stage. Taking up the law again, he was called to the bar in 1740 and went on the western circuit, but his impulsive temperament hardly served him well in the role of barrister, and he was glad to accept the kindness of Ralph Allen (Allworthy in *Tom Jones*) and Lyttelton in providing for his growing family.

Richardson's *Pamela* appeared in 1740, and provided Fielding—after his coarse parody in *Shamela* (1741)— with the initial idea for *Joseph Andrews* (1742). He feared for his reason when his wife, and two of their children, died in 1743; but the *Miscellanies* appeared, and he was soon committed to political journalism again. He had first tried writing in this genre with James Ralph in the sober *The Champion*, but *The True Patriot* and *The Jacobite's Journal* were calculated to arouse anti-Jacobite feeling and probably exacerbated the feud with Smollett that formed part of the "paper war" enjoyed by Fielding in the person of "Sir Alexander Draw-cansir" in *The Covent Garden Journal* of 1752. In 1747 Fielding married Mary Daniel, who had been his wife's maid; as he said, for "a mother for his children and a nurse for himself." In 1748 Lyttelton secured for him the post of justice of the peace for Westminster. *Tom Jones* appeared in 1749; Fielding received £600 from Millar for the book, and another £100 later on its great success. Millar paid £1,000 for *Amelia* in 1751. Although his health was breaking, and his financial situation was still precarious, Fielding now added pamphlets on crime and poverty to his energetic labors as a magistrate (incidentally prompting Hogarth's "Gin Lane" print) and exhausted himself breaking up a notorious London gang in the winter of 1753–54. He sailed for Lisbon in June, and died there in October 1754. *The Journal of a Voyage to Lisbon*, published posthumously, gives a close account of the last year of his life.

Tom Thumb held the stage for fifty years, has been revived and continues to be reprinted. The satire, too, of *Pasquin* remains accessible to the modern reader, but the staple of Fielding's twenty-seven plays is degraded Restoration repartee, and Fielding himself set no great store by them. The essays, if we except the inflammatory political ones that do Fielding no great credit, witness to his intense awareness of Augustan literary values. He shared the Scriblerus mentality (see, e.g., **Pope, Alexander**) very closely, even to the extent of finding in Cibber a fertile source of fun.

Fielding's novels, too, are imbued with Augustanism, and his prose style shows that verbal and syntactical precision which reflects an artificial and articulate civilization: "He in a few minutes ravished this fair creature, or would have ravished her, if she had not, by a timely compliance, prevented him." His theory of the novel, elaborated within the novels themselves and in the preface to *A Voyage to Lisbon*, did much to establish its status. Fielding proclaimed himself—"I am the founder of a new species of writing"—and proclaimed the novel, which would observe not the inferior Platonic criterion of literal truth (which Fielding considered only proper to a newspaper) but the Aristotelian standard of "artistic truth." Liberated from the factual literalism of Defoe and the moral leading strings of Richardson, the novel could now establish itself in formal terms, as a literary artefact.

Fielding's aesthetic is important and persuasive, and the novels themselves more than fulfill his ideals. *Joseph Andrews* soon forgets its origins in

Pamela and becomes comedy rather than burlesque. The literary impulse is fortified by more immediate moral, social and intellectual concerns as Joseph and the superbly incompetent Parson Adams prompt the self-exposure of a dishonest, punitive and uncharitable society, made up of an abandoned aristocracy, self-seeking stewards, venal magistrates and callous clergymen. The two prose works from *Miscellanies* command less attention: "A Journey from This World to the Next" is a satiric fantasy after the manner of Lucian and Swift (which was much admired by Dickens), and though "Jonathan Wild" has also had enthusiastic devotees, the persistent irony of this biography of a criminal now appears rather flat-footed.

Tom Jones, however, has been awarded as much praise as almost any other English novel, and even at a time when Fielding's reputation has been put rather firmly into perspective, it is still tacitly assumed that it is his best work. Certainly it is his longest and best organized, but it could be argued that for all its apparent dimension the novel is curiously sterile. The clockwork perfection of the plot is partly to blame for this: parts interact so conveniently that the novel becomes insulated in a rarefied world of its own, where Tom can conduct his crude experiments on life without any danger of developing into a moral being, where Sophia can reign like a snow queen (the pale negative of Fielding's dead wife), and where Blifil and Allworthy move mechanically on their black and white squares. The novel travels the road; but mainly at night, and we rarely meet anyone we have not met before. It goes to London, but beyond the provision of a masquerade, a few houses, a theater, a prison and an inn, the capital never impinges on the narrative. The novel is further sterilized by the increasing and ultimately debilitating self-consciousness of Fielding's style, with its translated ironies ("In plain English . . .") and redundant burlesque effects. The best things are certainly concerned with the minor characters—Thwackum, Square, Black George and Partridge.

It is significant that *Amelia* is a more serious work. Fielding declares that it is "sincerely designed to promote the cause of virtue" and seeks to instruct us not in the art of the novel but in "the art of life." It was an innovation for Fielding to base his story on a married couple; Booth inhabits a world of genuine moral alternatives (as well as an oppressive, almost Dickensian prison) and Amelia herself commands real pathos. But the price is paid in the loss of irony and humor. In place of Adams's normative simplicity we have Dr. Harrison's importunate moralizing, and although *Amelia* was Fielding's favorite among his novels, it is unlikely that a modern reader will endorse this choice.

Fortunately Fielding regained his humor in his last, short work. *A Voyage to Lisbon* is indeed a remarkable book, full of sympathetic observation and delightful incongruity (such as the unpalatable tea that turns out to be "a tobacco of the Mundungus species"); and after he has "joyfully" arrived, Fielding announces in a mood of resigned finality, "hic finis chartaeque viaeque."

(See also **Parody and Nonsense.**)

Love in Several Masques, 1728.

Tom Thumb, 1730 (revised as *Tom Thumb . . . The Tragedy of Tragedies; or, Tom Thumb the Great,* 1731).

Pasquin, 1736.

The Historical Register for the Year 1736, 1737.

The Champion (edited with James Ralph, pseud. Capt. Hercules Vinegar), November 1739–June 1741.

An Apology for the Life of Mrs. Shamela Andrews (pseud. Conny Keyber), 1741.

The Adventures of Joseph Andrews and of His Friend Mr. Abraham Adams, 1742.

Miscellanies, 3 vols., 1743 (includes "The Life of Mr. Jonathan Wild the Great" and "A Journey from This World to the Next").

The True Patriot, November 1745–June 1746.

The Jacobite's Journal (pseud. John Trottplaid), December 1747–November 1748.

The History of Tom Jones, a Foundling, 1749 (*f.* 1962).

The Covent Garden Journal, January–November 1752.

Amelia, 1752 (for 1751).

A Proposal for Making an Effectual Provision for the Poor, 1753.

The Journal of a Voyage to Lisbon, 1755.

Complete Works, ed. W. E. Henley, 16 vols., New York: Croscup & Sterling, 1902; London: Heinemann, 1903.

Works, ed. G. Saintsbury, 12 vols., London: Dent, 1893; as Temple edition, 1902.   D.G.

FINLAY, Ian Hamilton. See **Experimental Poetry.**

FINLAYSON, Roderick. See **New Zealand Literature.**

FIRBANK, Ronald (1886–1926), born in London of wealthy parents, was at Trinity Hall, Cambridge (1906–08), and then mostly traveled abroad. He published two short tales in 1905 and then nothing until 1915, after which he wrote about one short novel a year for the rest of his life.

Firbank's imaginative world derives from the aesthetic decadence of the 1890s, but his extreme artificiality is tempered by astringent wit and a strong element of self-mockery. In their ritualistic vision of society his books are perhaps closest to Max Beerbohm, and like Beerbohm he was a perfect stylist. His method of presenting narrative through techniques resembling cinematic montage proved influential, as in the early novels of Evelyn Waugh.

Vainglory, 1915.
Inclinations, 1916.
Caprice, 1917.
Valmouth, 1919.
Sorrow in Sunlight, 1924 (U.S. title and reissued in U.K. as *Prancing Nigger*).
Concerning the Eccentricities of Cardinal Pirelli, 1926.

Collected Works, ed. A. Waley, 5 vols., London: Duckworth, 1929.
The New Rhythum, and Other Pieces, London: Duckworth, 1962. **W.R.**

FITZGERALD, Edward (1809–83), born in Suffolk, spent most of his life in East Anglia, marrying unsuccessfully in 1856. His friendship with Tennyson is fully recorded in Hallam Tennyson's *Memoir* of his father. FitzGerald translated six plays of Calderon from the Spanish but he is best known for his translation, published anonymously in 1859, of the *Rubáiyát of Omar Khayyám*. He tried to capture the spirit of the Persian quatrains rather than the letter, and, although the reliability of his sources was challenged in 1967 by Robert Graves, his work has achieved remarkable popularity and influence.

Poetical and Prose Writings, ed. G. Bentham, 7 vols., New York: Doubleday, Page, 1902–03.
Letters and Literary Remains, ed. W. A. Wright, 7 vols., London: Macmillan, 1902–03. **D.W.**

FITZGERALD, F. (Francis) Scott (1896–1940) was born in the Midwestern city of St. Paul (Minnesota), the son of a salesman for Procter and Gamble. An abortive adolescent romance with Ginevra King, daughter of a rich and influential Chicago family, left him with an ambiguous response to wealth and social success, which he simultaneously denounced and pursued for most of his life. His career at Princeton was an odd mixture of success and failure, but it did result in his first novel, *This Side of Paradise* (1920). The book was an immediate popular success; published in March it had sold nearly 50,000 copies by the end of the year. An imperfect work, the novel combined romantic posturing with a naïve eclecticism. While flawed and even inept, it succeeded in catching the exuberance of the decade before it was fully formed and swept its author into premature prominence. It was a novel which captured and perhaps even helped to form the conviction that his was "a generation dedicated more than the last to the fear of poverty and the worship of success, a generation which had grown up to find all Gods dead, all wars fought, all faiths in man shaken."

His second book, *The Beautiful and Damned*, which appeared first in truncated form in *The Metropolitan Magazine*, was also highly successful and did show improvement on the somewhat callow adolescence of his first novel. It was not until 1925, however, when Fitzgerald's popular reputation was already on the decline and his own self-confidence weakening, that he produced the first of his major works, *The Great Gatsby*. In this story of Jay Gatsby's amoral pursuit of the ideal Fitzgerald at last exercised genuine artistic control and in doing so raised Gatsby's quest to a mythical level.

Gatsby tries desperately to recapture an adolescent dream by winning back the woman he had lost to wealth and power in his youth. Having himself acquired money he sets out to buy the ineffable, blind to the destructive consequence of his demand that the insubstantial should materialize. Daisy Buchanan, married to the rich and philistine Tom Buchanan, who himself has a mistress, is fascinated and not a little enchanted by Gatsby's romantic approach but deserts him without compunction when her own interests are threatened. Gatsby dies at the end of the novel, having kept his own illusions intact at the cost of any ethical structure to his life. Since his whole life had been dedicated to maintaining an illusion, his death has a perverse logic and integrity. Indeed it is precisely this which redeems Gatsby and which creates the subtle ambiguity with which the author leaves us. For while Gatsby is utterly wrong and even dangerous, in that he initiates the chain of events which leads to corruption and death, such total commitment commands respect, the more so when contrasted with the moral equivocation of those who surround him and who destroy and corrupt through their total indifference. Gatsby at least has passion. If it is a passion which can only sustain itself on unreality, it is still preferable to the tawdry lust of a Tom Buchanan or the calculated infidelity of Daisy. Although the narrative voice is not controlled with the finesse or even, finally, the consistency and accuracy of a James or Conrad, this still contains the key to Fitzgerald's new and subtle control of tone and meaning. For the first time he can see the painful poignancy of his own romanticism without justifying himself with cynicism. For the first time he can see that one can be destroyed by virtue as readily as by vice. If he has a new confidence in his own abilities as a writer he also has a new awareness of the limitations and dangers which attend the creative act as clearly as they do Gatsby's own attempt at manipulating truth. He realizes that the cost of reshaping reality to match the elegant structures of the imagination can be high and that it is as likely to lead to individual suffering and the loss of moral integrity as to a victory over an incomplete and unsatisfactory actuality. On this level Gatsby's experience is the American experience and the protagonist's final retreat to the West, after Gatsby's death, an ironical comment on a dangerous mythology rather than a solemn insistence on ethical redemption.

Fitzgerald's moral and artistic maturity in this novel is the more surprising when contrasted with the lack of these qualities in his earlier books. The achievement of this work lies in the success with which he established the connection between the personal dilemma and the public paradox, as indeed it was to be of his next work, *Tender Is the Night*.

The period between the publication of *The Great Gatsby* and *Tender Is the Night* was a difficult one for Fitzgerald. In 1930 his wife, Zelda, suffered a major breakdown while he himself was conscious of the continuing eclipse of his popular reputation. There were new stars in the literary firmament now and, though he could still command impressive fees for his short stories, the real achievement of *Gatsby* had not been adequately recognized.

Tender Is the Night clearly draws on Fitzgerald's own experience and on Zelda's fifteen-month stay in a Swiss sanitarium. It is concerned, as Fitzgerald explained, with a man who is "a natural idealist, a spoiled priest" who is presented as "giving in for various causes to the ideas of the haute Burgeoise [*sic*]" and who "in his rise to the top of the social world" is shown as "losing his idealism, his talent and turning to drink." The novel's protagonist, Dick Diver, sets out as an idealist to reconstruct and redeem. He opposes the terrifying flux of existence with his own constructions. But by degrees he is corrupted and these constructions begin to collapse, destroying their creator. Once again the connection between body and the body politic is convincingly established. The wealth and power which shape Diver's life also mold society in general and the entropic forces revealed in the individual psyche also dominate the social world. Instead of reclaiming shattered minds and reconstructing society Diver ends up teaching the rich the "ABCs of human decency."

Fitzgerald's last novel, *The Last Tycoon*, was never completed and this story of the failure and eventual corruption of the creative mind in the face of the temptations of the material world stands as an appropriate epitaph to a man who was always alive to entropic forces at work in his own life.

Fitzgerald was attracted by romantic notions of revolt. As a writer he wanted to believe that the individual could shape not only his fate but even the nature of his environment by nothing more than an act of will and imagination. But he could never finally convince himself that any of this was possible. His romantics are corrupted and destroyed by a deterministic system. Looking desperately for an order which would grant them some kind of function and identity they found only evidence of dissolution. Even the wealthy who seemed to dictate the terms of their existence, were themselves only victims. The economic crash of 1929, like the dissipation which marked his personal and artistic life and the growing despair which gripped his marriage, was proof of man's inability to retain even a tenuous control over events. A concern with money seems to lie at the very heart of Fitzgerald's work—a confused and vague hatred of its privilege, an envy of its power, an assurance of its corrupting influence, and, finally, an apocalyptic conviction as to its destructive potential. As he increasingly came to feel, the pursuit of money not merely squandered what he saw as an exhaustible supply of talent, it also shattered the fragile constructions of imagination itself. Part of the tragedy of Fitzgerald's life lay in his compulsive need for those very things which destroyed him.

This Side of Paradise, 1920.
Flappers and Philosophers, 1920 (stories).
The Beautiful and Damned, 1922.
The Great Gatsby, 1925 (*f.* 1949).
All the Sad Young Men, 1926.
Tender Is the Night, 1934 (*f.* 1962).
Taps at Reveille, 1935 (stories).
The Last Tycoon, 1941.

The Bodley Head Scott Fitzgerald, 6 vols., London: Bodley Head, 1959–63.
Letters, ed. A. Turnbull, New York: C. Scribner's Sons, 1963; London: Bodley Head, 1964.   C.B.

FITZGERALD, R. D. (Robert David). See **Australian Literature.**

FLECKER, James Elroy (1884–1915), son of a London clergyman, was educated at Uppingham School and Oxford, and after a short period as a teacher entered the consular service in 1908. He was sent to Constantinople in 1910 and became British consul at Smyrna in 1911, but contracted tuberculosis and after long spells of leave died at a sanatorium at Davos in 1915. His poetry has the youthful exuberance of Rupert Brooke, but he was much influenced by the classicism of the French Parnassian school. The rhythms of Tennyson and the Hellenism of Arnold also attracted him. His best-known work is his play *Hassan* (1922), produced in 1923 with music by Delius. (See also **Georgians, The.**)

Collected Poems, London: Secker, 1916.
Collected Prose, London: Bell, 1920.   A.N.M.

FLETCHER, Giles (the younger) (?1588–1623) was born of a distinguished family—his father was an ambassador and minor poet, his elder brother (Phineas) was also a poet, and the dramatist John Fletcher was a cousin—but his life is of no particular interest. He may have been to Westminster School; he graduated B.A. from Trinity College, Cambridge, becoming reader in Greek there in 1615. After holding a college living for a short time, in 1619 he became a country parson at Alderton (Suffolk) where he remained until his death.

Giles Fletcher is now remembered almost solely as author of the poem *Christ's Victory and Triumph* (1610). He considered himself a disciple of Spenser and Du Bartas, and the strong influence of the former is obvious in Giles Fletcher's liking for allegory as well as in the smooth melodiousness of his lines. *Christ's Victory*, however, is Miltonic in matter and conception, and so Giles Fletcher stands as a kind of link between two much greater poets. Despite some clumsiness and tedium, he remains worth reading for the energy of his religious convictions and for his imaginative strength, which in some passages is remarkably powerful. He is also author of the prose work *The Reward of the Faithful* (1623).

Poetical Works of Giles and Phineas Fletcher, ed. F. S. Boas, 2 vols., Cambridge: Cambridge Univ. Press, 1908–09.   G.P.

FLETCHER, John (1579–1625), son of a clergyman who was later to become bishop of London, was born at Rye (Sussex). Until the beginning of his literary career, we know very little of his life. Possibly his uncle, Giles Fletcher, was responsible for his education; possibly he is the John Fletcher who matriculated at Benet (now Corpus Christi) College, Cambridge in 1591. Again it is possible that he married in 1612. Whatever the case, Fletcher made his literary debut with *The Faithful Shepherdess* (?1609), a youthful survey of love in a pastoral setting. Soon afterwards he was collaborating with Francis Beaumont, and in this partnership he rose to a position of prestige and acclaim in the flourishing private theater of the second decade. Only seven plays can be ascribed to the partnership with any certainty, but these contain some of the best writing associated with Fletcher's name, particularly *The Maid's Tragedy*, *A King and No King* and *Philaster*. When Beaumont retired in 1613, Massinger seems to have taken his place as collaborator. Daborne, Field, Rowley and Shirley were other collaborators of lesser distinction, but about half of the canon seems comprised of plays written by Fletcher working alone. He died of plague in 1625.

(For a critical estimate of Fletcher's work, see under **Beaumont, Francis.**)

Plays in collaboration with Francis Beaumont:

Cupid's Revenge, 1615 (*p.* 1612).
The Scornful Lady, 1616 (*p.* 1610).
A King and No King, 1619 (*p.* 1611).
The Maid's Tragedy, 1619.
Philaster; or, Love Lies A-Bleeding, 1620 (*p.* 1611).
Four Plays in One (and with Nathaniel Field), 1647 (*p. c.* 1608).
The Coxcomb, 1647 (*p.* 1612).

Plays in collaboration with Philip Massinger:

Thierry and Theodoret, 1621.
The Elder Brother, 1637.
The Knight of Malta (and with Field), 1647 (*p. c.* 1618).
The Beggar's Bush, 1647 (*p.* 1622).
The Spanish Curate, 1647 (*p.* 1622).
The Lovers' Progress, 1647 (*p.* 1623).
The Custom of the Country, 1647.
The Double Marriage, 1647.
The False One, 1647.
The Honest Man's Fortune (and with Field), 1647.
The Laws of Candy, 1647.
The Little French Lawyer, 1647.
Love's Cure, 1647.
The Prophetess, 1647.
The Queen of Corinth (and with Field), 1647.
The Sea Voyage, 1647.
Sir John van Olden Barnavelt, 1883 (*p.* 1619).

Plays with other collaborators or by Fletcher alone:

The Faithful Shepherdess, ?1609.
The Life of King Henry the Eighth (with William Shakespeare), 1623 (*p.* 1613).
The Two Noble Kinsmen (?with Shakespeare), 1634.
Wit without Money, 1639 (*p.* 1614).
The Bloody Brother; or, Rollo, Duke of Normandy, 1639 (*p.* 1616).
Monsieur Thomas, 1639 (*p.* 1619).
The Night Walker, 1640.
Rule a Wife and Have a Wife, 1640 (*p.* 1624).
The Captain, 1647 (*p. c.* 1612).
Bonduca, 1647 (*p.* 1614).

Valentinian, 1647 (*p. c.* 1617).
The Loyal Subject, 1647 (*p.* 1618).
The Mad Lover, 1647 (*p. c.* 1618).
The Humorous Lieutenant, 1647 (*p.* 1619).
The Island Princess, 1647 (*p.* 1621).
The Pilgrim, 1647 (*p.* 1621).
The Maid in the Mill (with William Rowley), 1647 (*p. c.* 1623).
A Wife for a Month 1647 (*p.* 1624).
The Woman's Prize; or, The Tamer Tamed, 1647 (*p.* before 1625).
The Chances, 1647.
Love's Pilgrimage, 1647.
Women Pleased, 1647.
The Wild-Goose Chase, 1652 (*p.* 1621).

Works of Francis Beaumont and John Fletcher, ed. A. Glover and A. R. Waller, 10 vols., Cambridge: Cambridge Univ. Press, 1905–12.
Variorum Edition, ed. A. H. Bullen, 4 vols. (20 plays), London: Bell & A. H. Bullen, 1904–12.   L.E.P.

FLETCHER, Phineas (1582–1650), son of the elder Giles Fletcher, brother of the younger and cousin of John Fletcher the dramatist, was educated at Eton and King's College, Cambridge, graduating B.A. in 1604 and M.A. in 1608. Phineas's life, like his brother's, was largely uneventful. He seems to have been chaplain to Sir Henry Willoughby for some time and through him became rector of Hilgay in Norfolk, where he worked from 1621 until his death.

He wrote a pastoral play, *Sicelides*, for a visit by James I to Cambridge in 1614 (though the royal party left before the play was ready), a strange work, *Venus and Anchises*, and a group of eclogues, *Piscatory Dialogues* (1633), on which Spenser's *The Shepherd's Calendar* exerts a strong influence, although the shepherds have become fishermen. But Fletcher's major work is the long poem, *The Purple Island* (1633), an allegorical account of man's mind and body, written in seven-line stanzas. Du Bartas's influence is apparent in the poem's didacticism and Spenser's in the diction and use of allegory, but Fletcher handles the allegory clumsily and his personifications are awkward and sometimes absurd. He seems unable to keep the poem moving without recourse to prose notes and the work now survives mainly because in a number of passages the religious feeling and Spenserian influence work together to good effect.

Poetical Works of Giles and Phineas Fletcher, ed. F. S. Boas, 2 vols., Cambridge: Cambridge Univ. Press, 1908–09.   G.P.

FLINT, F. S. (Frank Stewart) (1885–1960), born in London, was largely self-educated, and was particularly fascinated with the study of foreign languages. As a young man he entered the Civil Service as a typist and remained in it for many years, becoming finally a divisional chief. His first book of verse, *In the Net of the Stars* (1909), is romantic in tone and derivative in technique, but he was beginning to rebel against conventional verse structures. He was one of the contributors to the original imagist manifesto (see **Imagism**) but, lacking both the intellectual strength and the technical abilities of Ezra Pound, Flint failed to exploit the new poetic liberation to much advantage. *Cadences* appeared in 1915, *Otherworld* in 1920, and after that time he occupied himself with prose translations.   C.P.

FOOTE, Samuel (1720–77) was born into a wealthy family, from which he inherited and dissipated three successive fortunes. He was educated at Worcester Grammar School and Oxford. While reading for the law, he was driven by poverty to acting. He soon discovered a genius for mimicry and his exploitation of this secured his popularity with audiences at the Haymarket Theatre. Here he offered a mixed bill of entertainments and wrote and acted in a mass of farces which satirized the social abuses, particular follies and even well-known individuals of his day. Though lacking in good feeling and loyalty, Foote retained the friendship of Garrick, and, as a mimic, the admiration of Johnson.

Dramatic Works, 2 vols., London, 1809.   J.P.

FORD, Ford Madox (1873–1939), born Ford Hermann Hueffer at Merton (Surrey), came of a family of artists and writers. He founded and brilliantly edited *The English Review* (1908–09) and *The Transatlantic Review* in Paris (1924). Through his association with authors like Conrad, James, Pound and Joyce, his theorizing about literature and the experiments of his fiction, Ford was an influential figure. During the First World War he was an infantry officer, later making use of his experiences in the four novels—*Some Do Not* (1924); *No More Parades* (1925); *A Man Could Stand Up* (1926); *The Last Post* (1928)—which collectively form the sequence *Parade's End*. He died at Deauville.

Ford turned his hand to most forms of writing, but his greatest achievement was in the novel. Though *Parade's End* is centered on the figure of Christopher Tietjens, son of a Yorkshire landowner, its concerns extend to the actions and careers of a wide range of characters—gentry, business men, officials, social climbers, intellectuals, clergymen, generals and ordinary soldiers. Sexual relationships, in particular, are given very frank treatment. Ford's technical innovations and apparently loose organization can often successfully convey a wide vision of human beings involved in the complexities of a changing society. At the same time his impressionistic prose style gives a vivid sense of particular moments of experience. Despite some unevenness, the quality of his best work is remarkably high.

The Good Soldier, 1915.
Some Do Not, 1924.
No More Parades, 1925.
A Man Could Stand Up, 1926.
Last Post, 1928 (U.S. title: *The Last Post*).
It Was the Nightingale, 1934 (memoirs).
Mightier than the Sword: Memories and Criticisms, 1938 (U.S. title: *Portraits from Life*).

Parade's End, New York: Knopf, 1950.
The Bodley Head Ford Madox Ford, ed. G. Greene, 4 vols., London: Bodley Head, 1962–63.   J.C.

FORD, John (1586–?1639). Very little is known of Ford's life. In all probability he was the second son (christened 17 April 1586) of Thomas Ford of Ilsington (Devonshire). He was admitted to the Middle Temple in 1602, suspended in 1606 (for failing to pay his Hilary term buttery bill), but readmitted in 1608. Two works, the poem *Fame's Memorial* and the pamphlet *Honour Triumphant*, were published during this period of expulsion. Some estrangement from his father may be indicated by the fact that, unlike his brothers, Ford received only £10 when his father died in 1610. He may have begun writing for the stage as early as 1612 with the lost play *An Ill Beginning Has a Good End*, but the attribution is uncertain, while other lost plays which may have confirmed an early interest in the theater cannot be assigned any certain date. Between 1621 and 1624 he collaborated with Dekker on five plays, of which two, *The Witch of Edmonton* and the masque *The Sun's Darling*, survive. Eight extant plays, which may be divided into two groups, followed this period of collaboration: *The Lover's Melancholy*, *The Broken Heart* and possibly *The Queen* were the property of the dramatic company, the King's Men, while the remaining five, presumed to be later, belonged to the companies at the Phoenix with whom he may have made some kind of contract. Virtually nothing is known of Ford himself except that he refers to himself as a scholar. Since the last verses attributable to him appeared in 1638 and his last play, *The Lady's Trial*, was licensed in the same year, it is assumed that he either died or gave up his literary career at that time.

All Ford's plays, with the exception of *Perkin Warbeck*, are concerned with unusual sexual situations involving extremes of emotion. His subjects include bigamy (*The Witch of Edmonton*), consummated and unconsummated adulterous love (*Love's Sacrifice*), forced marriage and jealousy (*The Broken Heart*), supposed impotence (*The Fancies Chaste and Noble*) and incest (*'Tis Pity She's a Whore*). This choice of subject matter has, in the past, earned Ford a reputation for decadent sensationalism, but at his best, notably in *The Broken Heart* and *'Tis Pity She's a Whore*, he is attempting a serious exploration of the situation he presents in a distinctive blank verse characterized by its slow moving dignity, clarity and restraint. The history play, *Perkin Warbeck*, which stands aside from the rest of his work, provides both a late example of a form which enjoyed its chief popularity over twenty years earlier and an unusually sympathetic treatment of the pretender. Throughout his work Ford is profoundly influenced by Shakespeare and draws heavily on Burton's *The Anatomy of Melancholy*.

(See also **Masques.**)

Fame's Memorial, 1606.
Honour Triumphant, 1606.
Christ's Bloody Sweat, 1613 (poem).
The Sun's Darling (with Thomas Dekker), licensed 1624.
The Lover's Melancholy, 1629 (*p.* 1628).
The Broken Heart, 1633.
Love's Sacrifice, 1633.
'Tis Pity She's a Whore, 1633.
Perkin Warbeck, 1634.
The Fancies Chaste and Noble, 1638.
The Lady's Trial, licensed 1638.
The Witch of Edmonton (with Dekker and William Rowley), 1658 (*p.* ?1621).

Works, ed. W. Gifford and A. Dyce, 3 vols., London: Toovey, 1869.
Dramatische Werke, ed. W. Bang and H. de Vocht, 2 vols., Louvain: Louvain Univ. Press, 1908–27.   L.S.

FORESTER, C. S. (Cecil Scott) (1899–1966), born in Cairo, the son of an English government official, was educated in England and, after failing as a medical student, turned to journalism. In 1932 he became a scriptwriter in Hollywood where many of his own books were filmed. He is mainly remembered as the creator of Horatio Hornblower. This naval captain is cast in the heroic mould of Nelson, whose life and times are reconstructed in a series of books with accuracy and pictorial skill.

All of the novels are well-made and picturesque, characterized by their romantic realism, the author's first-hand knowledge of life at sea and by his interest in the psychology of command.

Brown on Resolution, 1929 (*f.* 1933; as *Single Handed*, 1952).
The Gun, 1933 (*f.* as *The Pride and the Passion*, 1957).
The African Queen, 1935 (*f.* 1951).
The General, 1936.
A Ship of the Line, 1939 (with *Happy Return*, 1937 and *Flying Colours*, 1938 formed *Captain Horatio Hornblower*, *f.* 1951). o.k.

FORSTER, E. M. (Edward Morgan) (1879–1970), born in London, son of an architect and a mother whose family had been associated with the Clapham sect, was educated at Tonbridge School (the Sawston School of the novels), which he attended as a day boy, and King's College, Cambridge. Under the influence of liberal teachers such as Nathaniel Wedd (who encouraged him to become a writer) and Goldsworthy Lowes Dickinson he found Cambridge a liberating experience. Until 1907 he lived in Italy, the setting for two early novels, and later visited India twice, in 1912 and 1921, the second time as secretary to the maharajah of Dewas Senior. The last novel published in his lifetime, *A Passage to India* (1924), was begun between the two visits and finished later. After this he devoted himself largely to essays and broadcasts. In 1945 he was elected an honorary fellow of King's College and made his home there.

Forster first wrote short stories, some of which explore the implications of paganism through fantasy. His social comedy, here and elsewhere, is often created by showing a group of middle-class English people, with all their ingrained attitudes and prejudices, in a Mediterranean setting, where their businesslike expedients may prove particularly inadequate to deal with the depths of a human situation. *A Room with a View* (1908), conceived early though published later, shows a young heroine in Italy torn between loyalty to English companions of this sort and her intuitive sense of the liberating power of a more open passion. *Where Angels Fear to Tread* (1905), though another light novel, is a tragic counterpart to the first. In this case an English family sets out to tidy up the results of an "unfortunate" marriage in Italy, hardly grasping that the chief result, a baby, is a human being in its own right. *The Longest Journey* (1907), described by Forster as his "preferred novel," has strong personal overtones. It sets the scene for later work by arguing that there are different sorts of reality, apprehended respectively through reason, imagination and passion.

In *Howards End* (1910), the culminating novel of this group, Forster deals more sympathetically with the suburban middle classes and tries to allow a place to the commercial values that give society its material basis. His final tentative solution to the problem is to leave his cultured and humane heroine married to a businessman, protecting both him and her own values in a small country house close to the earth.

Forster has since admitted that this solution, precarious enough in the novel, has been made steadily less possible by the advance of a technological civilization. *A Passage to India*, published fourteen years later, is set in a different key. Where the earlier novels move towards unity, this one ends in separation. Although often read as a political novel analyzing the British raj, the political picture is incomplete and no more than a subordinate theme in the total work. Forster presents, rather, a picture of the total relationship between Britain and India at a more personal level by showing three different English characters and their methods of approach: Fielding, the administrator, who relies on the head and who succeeds in giving justice but at the expense of general frustration; Mrs. Moore, who lives by the heart and affects particular individuals, but finally suffers extinction; and Adela Quested, whose approach through an undereducated bodily psyche precipitates the main crisis of the novel but who becomes a person through the experience, gaining a better grasp of reality. These interrelated "passages" to India give the novel a complexity which a reader may miss at first sight if he identifies himself too closely with a single character.

Maurice, written in 1913–14 but not published till 1971, is a study of a homosexual's self-discovery. It obviously has autobiographical references, but it lacks the irony, humor and shrewdness of Forster at his best.

Modern critical approaches have often concentrated too closely on the surface texture of Forster's work and its immediate effect. This throws too much emphasis on Forster's use of whimsy and fantasy (admittedly sometimes tiresome), while ignoring the more subterranean effects of his novels. At his best Forster succeeds both in exploring the middle-class world in which he is most at home and in suggesting the existence of other, more passional worlds of human experience which, if not propitiated, take their vengeance by destroying the individual's full sense of reality. Forster's more positive later achievement, his development of an understated style when commenting on society, is often very telling in effect—as in his saying: "Nuclear weapons are not in my line; unfortunately, I am in theirs." It should not, however, obscure the other dimensions of his work.

Where Angels Fear to Tread, 1905.
The Longest Journey, 1907.
A Room with a View, 1908.
Howards End, 1910.

The Celestial Omnibus and Other Stories, 1914.
Pharos and Pharillon, 1923.
A Passage to India, 1924.
Aspects of the Novel, 1927.
Abinger Harvest: A Miscellany, 1936.
Collected Short Stories, 1948.
Two Cheers for Democracy, 1951.
The Hill of Devi, 1953.
Marianne Thornton, 1956.
Maurice, 1971. J.B.B.

FOWLES, John (1926–　) was educated at Bedford and New College, Oxford, where he read French. Before success as a novelist he served in the Marines and was a schoolteacher. *The Collector* (1963; *f.* 1964) defines the interaction of the *aristoi* and *hoi polloi* in the form of a thriller. *The Magus* (1966; *f.* 1969) equates the testing ground that is the universe with the series of mysteries perpetrated on a hapless Englishman on a Greek island. Fowles is a daring experimenter while maintaining an unflagging narrative drive. *The French Lieutenant's Woman* (1969) is a pastiche Victorian novel written with modern hindsight and offering alternative endings. J.L.M.

FOXE, John (1516–87), educated at Oxford, was later tutor to the earl of Surrey's children. A firm Protestant, he fled England in Mary's reign and on returning was ordained and made canon of Salisbury in 1563. *Acts and Monuments* (1563), or *The Book of Martyrs*, Foxe's best-known work and the most popular book of Elizabeth's reign, partly because of its antipapal bias, is written with crude vigor, the work of an industrious but not overscholarly or overscrupulous mind. G.P.

FRAME, Janet. See **New Zealand Literature.**

FRANKLIN, Benjamin (1706–90), born in Boston, was the youngest son of a Oxfordshire tallow chandler who had emigrated to Massachusetts in about 1682. Franklin was apprenticed to an elder half brother in the printing trade because of his "bookish inclination." An avid reader of the works of John Bunyan, Daniel Defoe and Cotton Mather, he tried to educate himself as a writer by imitating the essays in a volume of *The Spectator* which came into his hands. After quarreling with his brother he moved to Philadelphia, arriving there penniless. By hard work, determination and thrift, he rose to become a leading citizen. His experiments with electricity brought him fame as a scientist and membership of the Royal Society. He also invented bifocal spectacles and a slow combustion stove, while a civic zeal led him to promote, in Philadelphia, street lighting, street cleaning, a circulating library, a debating society and the University of Pennsylvania. At the national level he was a drafter and signatory of the Declaration of Independence and the Constitution of the United States and represented his country with distinction as a diplomat in France and Britain.

The success ethic which he exemplified in his career he assiduously promulgated in his writings. The moral aphorisms with which, for twenty-five years, he annually filled *Poor Richard's Almanac* provided the basis of "The Way to Wealth" (1758); sententious, platitudinous, yet naggingly (and sometimes racily) memorable, they survived to irritate writers as diverse as Mark Twain and D. H. Lawrence. The latter's essay on Franklin in *Studies in Classic American Literature* (1923) perceptively, if unsympathetically, highlights Franklin's dualism.

A journalistic pamphleteer, as, for example, in "Information to Those Who Would Remove to America" (1784), Franklin was also the master of an engagingly lighter manner which is best represented in his "bagatelles," composed in the 1770s. His literary reputation, however, rests mainly on his *Autobiography*. This incomplete work comprises four separate sections written between 1771 and 1790; the differences in tone between them reflect his differing interests at the periods of composition. At his death it existed only in manuscript and to what extent some of the corrections received his approval remains conjectural. Its subsequent publication history is too checkered to be detailed here. These factors deny it the unity of a polished work of art, and it is easily denigrated as a philistine careerist's conceited and complacent indulgence. More sympathetically read, it can be recognized as rather the product of a humble man genuinely amazed at his own success, yet so fascinated at the process by which he achieved it as to see the writing of his memoirs as "the next thing most like living one's life over again." He recounts episodes in his career with zest and a disarming candor tinged at times with humor and self-critical irony; his prose is lucid, direct and unaffected; and his criteria of reason and common sense are those of the Enlightenment on both sides of the Atlantic.

If his code of virtue seems to anticipate the principles of pragmatism, his energetic determination to do good and his tendency to find an improving moral in every experience look back to Puritanism and the doctrine of Christian calling. Both Melville ("Franklin was everything but a poet") and Lawrence ("All the qualities of a great man and never more than a great citizen") ignore in their criticisms the standards of Franklin's age, his acceptance of them and the extent to which his vision of America helped to shape the American Dream.

Autobiography, ed. J. Bigelow, 1868 (based on original MS.).

Memoirs, Parallel Text edition, ed. M. Farrand, 1949 (prefers W. T. Franklin's 1818 edition).

Writings, ed. A. H. Smyth, 10 vols., New York: Macmillan Co., 1905–07.

Papers, ed. L. W. Larabee and others, New Haven: Yale Univ. Press, 1959– .   D.W.

FRAZER, Sir James George (1854–1941), born in Glasgow and educated at Glasgow and Cambridge Universities, was a man of wide cultural attainments as well as being an anthropologist of international renown. His greatest work, *The Golden Bough* (1890–1915), is a massively erudite study of the evolution of the primitive religious imagination. Scientific though Frazer's purpose was, his work opened up for the modern world a new mythology of death and rebirth which has influenced religious and literary as well as anthropological thought.

The Golden Bough (abridged), London: Macmillan, 1922.   I.W.

FREDERIC, Harold (1856–98) was born in Utica (New York) of Dutch, French and New England ancestry, his parents being poor and his father dying when he was very young. He eventually worked up to the position of editor-in-chief of the *Albany Evening Journal*, the leading Republican state journal. In 1884 he accepted the job of London correspondent for *The New York Times* and spent the rest of his life in Europe. He investigated the cholera epidemics in France and Italy and the persecution of the Jews in Russia, delivering a sweeping attack on the Russian government. From his European vantage point he wrote local color novels about New York State, historical novels and, towards the end of his life, novels dealing with modern society, both English and American. His greatest success was *The Damnation of Theron Ware* (1896) and it is on this that his reputation largely stands, although claims have recently been made for him to be taken more seriously on the strength of his total output. *The Damnation* deals with the internal conflicts of a Methodist minister, torn between material success within the church and his intellectual doubts. In the end it becomes clear that the hero is essentially a man who is composed of such division and hypocrisies. This is Frederic's central concern, the relationship between a man's knowledge of his own mental processes, and the roles and virtues he is forced to display to the world. Like Howells, Frederic saw a split between the older Puritan and transcendentalist psychology and the drives and ambitions needed to be successful in society. Such success can be a function of self-deception, while self-knowledge and inner purity can lead to weakness and failure.

Seth's Brother's Wife, 1887.
The Lawton Girl, 1890.
In the Valley, 1890.
The New Exodus: A Study of Israel in Russia, 1892.
The Return of the O'Mahony, 1892.
The Damnation of Theron Ware, 1896 (U.K. title: *Illumination*).
Gloria Mundi, 1898.
The Market Place, 1899.   D.C.

FRENEAU, Philip (1752–1832) was born in New York City of a Huguenot family and attended Princeton, providing a poem, *The Rising of Glory of America*, for the graduation ceremony of 1771. After a brief career as a schoolteacher, he began to write satires against the British, until he accepted a private secretaryship to a planter in the West Indies (1776), where he wrote "The Beauties of Santa Cruz" and other Marvellesque meditations on the natural setting. Another journey there was interrupted by a naval engagement and his imprisonment in a British hulk (1780), which led to a bitter poem on the subject and more anti-British satire, all widely disseminated through broadsides and journals, and much appreciated by the Revolutionary troops. From 1784 to 1789 he went to sea as master of various cargo ships. On his return, after editing the New York *Daily Advertiser* (1789–91) and getting married (1790), he became the first editor (1791–93) of the anti-Federalist *National Gazette*, established with Jefferson's help. He retired in 1799 only to be forced through poverty to go to sea again (1801–07). The War of 1812 prompted more anti-British poetry. His last years were spent in poverty. He died of exposure, having lost his way in a snowstorm.

Freneau's polemical poems still appear lively, though they do little to dispel the old view that conservatives make the best satirists. He is now best known for his poems of "romantic fancy," lyrical meditations on nature as an argument for natural religion and the nobility of the savage. "On the Emigration to America," suggesting Marvell's garden poems, describes the West as a promised land; "The Indian Student," having tried college, finds he prefers "nature's god"; "The Indian Burial Ground" is in the tradition of the Wartons or of Collins sentimentalizing Highland superstitions three years after Culloden made Highlanders safe to receive this kind of attention. The best of Freneau's poems in this mode (e.g., "The Wild Honey Suckle") are fine, if slightly fragile, achievements.

The Poems of Philip Freneau, 1786.
The Miscellaneous Works of Mr. Philip Freneau, 1788.
Poems Written between the Years 1768 & 1794, 1795.
Letters on Various Interesting and Important Subjects, 1799.

Poems, ed. H. H. Clark, New York: Harcourt, Brace, 1929.

Last Poems, ed. L. Leary, New Brunswick: Rutgers Univ. Press, 1946.

S.A.F.

FRERE, J. H. (John Hookham) (1769–1846), educated at Eton and Cambridge, was a British envoy in Portugal and Spain during the Napoleonic War. He was one of the founders of *The Quarterly Review* in 1809, and contributed to *The Anti-Jacobin*, the journal founded by his friend George Canning to combat revolutionary principles. In 1817, under the pseudonym of Whistlecraft, he published the first two cantos of a mock-romantic Arthurian poem, which suggested to Byron the verse form and poetic manner which he adopted in *Beppo*, *Don Juan* and *The Vision of Judgment*. He added two more cantos in 1818. The poem is often called *Whistlecraft* after its author's pseudonym and was edited as *The Monks and the Giants* by R. D. Waller, Manchester: Manchester Univ. Press, 1926. Frere also translated a number of Aristophanes' comedies into English verse.

Works, 2 vols., London: Pickering, 1872; revised, 3 vols., 1874.   J.D.J.

FROST, Robert (1874–1963) was born in San Francisco and lived there until the death of his father in 1884, when he moved to Massachusetts. Thereafter, with occasional visits to Europe, Frost lived almost entirely in New England and passed his life writing, teaching and farming. At various times he took teaching posts at Harvard, Amherst, Middlebury and Dartmouth, and served as consultant in poetry to the Library of Congress, poet in residence at the University of Michigan, and Ralph Waldo Emerson Fellow in Poetry at Harvard University. He was undoubtedly the most popular and widely read poet in the history of American letters.

Frost's first two volumes of poetry, *A Boy's Will* (1913) and *North of Boston* (1914), were both published in England, where he had worked under the tutelage of Lascelles Abercrombie and Edward Thomas. The more obvious influences on his early poetry, however, were Bryant, Emerson and Thoreau. In their work he found confirmation of his own views that an original relation with the universe was essentially a matter of the heart rather than the head and that "a poem particularly must not begin with thought first." These ideas are sometimes made the basis of early poems in which he explores the tensions between reason and emotion, usually coming to the conclusion that it is never

> less than treason
> To go with the drift of things,
> To yield with a grace to reason.

More often, though, his early poems are no more than the exploration and objectification of a mood, marred by the archaic diction taken over from nineteenth-century nature poetry.

As early as 1916, at the height of the poetic renaissance, Frost disclaimed all interest in experimentalism, telling Louis Untermeyer that he had already passed through "several phases, four to be exact" and that he now considered himself to be finally formed. "I have myself all in a strong box where I can unfold as a personality at discretion." This literary conservatism led him to reject the work of his contemporaries, and as the poetry of Eliot in the 1920s and MacLeish in the 1930s dominated the academies, Frost continued to cultivate and extend his own themes and techniques, the only radical change—and that a matter partly of his public image—being from the poet of grim naturalism in poems like "Home Burial" and "The Hill Wife" to the amiable, homely and bucolic Yankee of "Something for Hope" or "Happiness Makes Up in Height for What It Lacks in Length." In recent years critics have attempted to rescue Frost from his popular image as a fireside poet affirming the old virtues and pieties. Lionel Trilling, speaking at Frost's eighty-fifth birthday dinner, described the "terrifying universe" of Frost's poetry, and Randall Jarrell explored similar territory in his influential essay "The Other Robert Frost." The poems used to rehabilitate *this* Frost are such works as "Desert Places," "Provide, Provide," "The Witch of Coös," "Design" and "Directive."

Though Frost began his career as a lyric poet, he very quickly developed a unique style of narrative and dramatic poetry. In *North of Boston* he included several dramatic monologues and dialogues including "A Servant to Servants," "The Housekeeper" and "The Death of the Hired Man." He continued to publish similar works throughout his career in which he explores the problems of human isolation and the failures of communication between man and man resulting in estrangement, madness or death. In 1917 he published a short play, *A Way Out*, which, though it has been performed, is an unsuccessful attempt to treat similar themes. In 1945 and 1947 he also produced two masques which are seriocomic commentaries on the biblical stories of Job and Jonah. These "New England Biblicals" are also spoiled by a confusion of tone and feeling, resulting partly from an inability to create fully independent and consistent characters, but also from his ambivalent attitude towards his subject matter.

Despite his mastery of blank verse, it is on his lyric poems that Frost's reputation ultimately rests, for it is here that he achieves both his greatest successes and his worst failures. Though many critics have associated his best poetry with particular themes or attitudes to life, the merits of his poems appear to be unrelated to their particular philosophies, moralities or moods. It is true that the later abstract, metaphysical poetry contains fewer successes than the volumes of his middle years, but both here and in the early nonreflective poetry Frost is just as liable occasionally to substitute manner for matter and to lapse into sentimentality or pompous platitude. His "commitment to convention" and undisputed mastery of traditional techniques sometimes leads him to exert a control over his medium which is damaging to the complexities or subtleties of thought and feeling in the poem. In his famous statement, "The Figure a Poem Makes," Frost brilliantly outlines what he considers true poetry to be, but also indirectly indicates the dangers inherent in such poetry: "It begins in delight and ends in wisdom. The figure is the same as for love. No one can really hold that the ecstasy should be static and still in one place. It begins in delight, it inclines to the impulse, it assumes direction with the first line laid down, it runs a course of lucky events and ends in a clarification of life—not necessarily a great clarification, such as sects and cults are founded on, but in a momentary stay against confusion." Whilst this describes the form of his finest poems such as "After Apple Picking" or "Stopping by Woods on a Snowy Evening," it is an equally good description of those poems like "Mowing," where the wisdom rests all too heavily on the slight facts. Frost's minute observation of the landscape and people of New England is unequaled and he has been deservedly acclaimed as the finest regional poet produced in America. But he is at his best, and his worst, when he becomes something more than this.

A Boy's Will, 1913.
North of Boston, 1914.
Mountain Interval, 1916.
A Way Out, 1917.
New Hampshire, 1923.
West-Running Brook, 1928.
A Further Range, 1936.
A Witness Tree, 1942.
A Masque of Reason, 1945.
A Masque of Mercy, 1947.
Steeple Bush, 1947.
In the Clearing, 1962.

Complete Poems, New York: Holt, 1949; London: Cape, 1951.
Selected Letters, ed. L. Thompson, New York: Holt, Rinehart, 1964; London: Cape, 1965.   B.L.

FROUDE, J. A. (James Anthony) (1818–94), born at Dartington (Devonshire) rectory, was a younger brother of Richard Hurrell Froude, one of the founders of the Oxford movement. Educated, and severely ill-treated, at Westminster School, he went up to Oriel College, Oxford in

1836 and was elected to a fellowship at Exeter College six years later. When, in his novel *The Nemesis of Faith*, he publicized his doubts on the validity of certain religious dogmas, he was compelled to sever his academic connections and devote himself to independent historical research. As the editor of *Fraser's Magazine* from 1860 to 1874 and as the author of a monumental but controversial *History of England* he established his reputation as a major public figure and returned to Oxford as regius professor of modern history shortly before his death.

Famous as the author of a spirited defense of English Protestantism and as the equally contentious biographer of Carlyle, Froude stood at the very center of Victorian England, the epitome of religious and intellectual liberalism in an age characterized by a subtle mixture of doubt and arrogance. His history of Tudor England can still be enjoyed for its engaging prose style, despite alleged inaccuracies, and his close relationship first with Newman and later with Kingsley and Carlyle brought him into contact with many of the seminal ideas of his own time. His stubborn patriotism, which envisaged a mighty English-speaking Commonwealth presided over by the United States, memorably emerges in his *Oceana*, while his general range and scholarship can best be appreciated in the selection of his critical essays entitled *Short Studies on Great Subjects*.

The Nemesis of Faith, 1849.
History of England, from the Fall of Wolsey to the Death of Elizabeth, 12 vols., 1856–70 (retitled . . . *to the Defeat of the Spanish Armada*, 1870).
Short Studies on Great Subjects, 4 series, 1867–83.
Thomas Carlyle, 4 vols., 1882–84.
Oceana; or, England and Her Colonies, 1886.   D.E.P.

FRY, Christopher (1907–   ) received little attention for his work in poetic drama (a genre unsupported except for the unexpected appearance of T. S. Eliot) until the performance in 1946 of *A Phoenix Too Frequent*. The color, vitality and fantasy exactly suited postwar England and several plays followed, apparently more successful in using poetry than Eliot, but wanting his serious concern. *Curtmantle* (1961), though more serious, seemed to lack the earlier poetic fire. Fry's other main works are *The Lady's Not for Burning* (1949; *p.* 1948), *Venus Observed* (1950), *The Dark Is Light Enough* (1954) and *A Yard of Sun* (1970).   A.P.H.

FUCHS, Daniel (1909–   ) was born in New York City. In his late twenties he wrote a trilogy of novels, *Summer in Williamsburg* (1934), *Homage to Blenholt* (1936) and *Low Company* (1937), on Jewish East Side life. The financial failure of these three novels led him to reject the form and he has spent the rest of his creative life on mediocre film scripts and wry short stories. The qualities of Fuchs's trilogy—the warmth, vitality, ironic humor and the ability to create the loves and hatreds of ghetto life without sentimentality—were rediscovered with the renewed interest in Jewish writers of the 1930s such as Nathanael West and Henry Roth.

D.V.W.

FULLER, Henry Blake (1857–1929) was born in Chicago. His early novels, such as his first, *The Chevalier of Pensieri Vani* (1890), project a Europe that is charming and graceful. "He wanted to live and write as a European, and he knew he must live and write as an American." (R. M. Lovett). Though he disliked Chicago, he described its buildings and its inhabitants' greed realistically. In *The Cliff-Dwellers* (1893) a skyscraper symbolizes the impersonal energies of the new business culture. It was followed by *With the Procession* (1895), the story of an ambitious business-man caught up in the Chicago rat race. Later writings include *On The Stairs* (1918) and *Not on the Screen* (1930), a satire on motion pictures.

J.W.

FULLER, Margaret (1810–50) was born in Cambridgeport (Massa-chusetts). Under a rigorous father she became a precocious scholar. After a period spent in teaching, she moved to Boston in 1839 where she met Emerson. In 1840 she became editor of the transcendentalist organ, *The Dial*. She published German translations and wrote and spoke militantly on behalf of women's rights; *Women in the Nineteenth Century* appeared in 1845. Her critical evaluations of contemporaries, displayed in *Papers on Literature and Art* (1846), are uneven, but she is excellent on some authors, such as Goethe. After a period as critic of *The Tribune*, she went to Europe in 1846 where she had an affair with the Marquis Ossoli and became involved in the fight for Italian liberation. She died on the way back from Europe when her ship was wrecked. She has been suggested as a source for the portrait of Zenobia in *The Blithedale Romance* by Haw-thorne.

D.V.W.

FULLER, Roy (1912–   ) was born at Oldham (Lancashire). He left school at sixteen to enter the legal profession. Some of his poems were published in the 1930s, but his reputation was established by those written on active service in the Royal Navy (1941–46). His 1949 volume, *Epitaphs and Occasions*, led the reaction against postwar romantic attitudes in British poetry. Later works, poems and novels, reveal a sensitive, complex and constantly developing artist who still firmly believes that an artist's true concern is with common human experience. He was elected professor of poetry at Oxford in 1968.

The volume of *Collected Poems, 1936–61* (1962) contains most of Fuller's early poetry; *Buff* (1965) and *New Poems* (1968) are more recent verse works. His novels include *Image of a Society* (1956), *The Ruined Boys* (1959), *The Father's Comedy* (1961) and *The Perfect Fool* (1963).   A.Y.

FULLER, Thomas (1608–61) was educated at Cambridge, took orders and became a famous preacher. A strong Royalist, he was chaplain to Charles II after the Restoration. One of the first men to live by writing, Fuller wrote voluminously on theology, morals and history, his books being still attractive because of his shrewdness, wit, narrative ability and compact style. Apart from *The History of the Worthies of England* (1662; ed. and abridged J. Freeman, London: Allen & Unwin; New York: Macmillan Co., 1952), Fuller's best books are *The History of the Holy War* (1639) and *The Holy State, and the Profane State* (1642; ed. M. G. Walten, New York: Columbia Univ. Press, 1938).   G.P.

FURPHY, Joseph ("Tom Collins"). See **Australian Literature.**

G

GALSWORTHY, John (1867–1933), son of a solicitor, was educated at Harrow and Oxford and called to the bar in 1890, though he did not take up practice. Instead, he traveled to the Far East and on this journey met Joseph Conrad who became a lifelong friend. His first success as a writer was with a play, *The Silver Box* (1906), produced in London by Granville-Barker at the Royal Court Theatre. He continued writing until late in life, greatly admired by a large circle of fellow writers, and founded the P.E.N. Club. He was awarded the Nobel Prize for literature in 1932.

A prolific writer of novels, short stories and plays, he set himself the task of chronicling the spirit of his age and of exposing its evils. In numerous plays, such as *Justice* (1910), *The Skin Game* (1920) and *Loyalties* (1922), he examines, thoughtfully and impartially, the shortcomings of social conditions, class prejudice and established beliefs. His first successful novel was *A Man of Property* (1906), the first of a series of novels, collectively entitled *The Forsyte Saga* (1922). This series, extending from late Victorian times to a period after the First World War, traces the evils of acquisitiveness in one family. The solidarity of Galsworthy's novels rests upon his humane curiosity about men in society, his sense of the character of middle-class life and his intelligent understanding and satire of the moral and social problems of his day. The scope and variety of his "chronicles" compensate for the diffuse and often episodic nature of the novels.

The Silver Box, 1906.
The Man of Property, 1906 (first of the series of novels *f.* as *The Forsyte Saga,* 1949).
Fraternity, 1909.
Strife, 1909.
Justice, 1910.
In Chancery, 1920.
To Let, 1921.
Loyalties, 1922 (*f.* 1934).
The White Monkey, 1924.
Swan Song, 1928.

Works, 20 vols., New York: C. Scribner's Sons, 1922; London: Heinemann, 1927.
Plays, New York: C. Scribner's Sons, 1928; London: Duckworth, 1929.

Letters, 1900–32, ed. E. Garnett, New York: C. Scribner's Sons; London: Cape, 1928.   O.K.

GALT, John (1779–1839) was born at Irvine (Ayrshire), the son of a ship's captain, and educated locally. Most of his life was spent in unsuccessful commercial ventures in London, Scotland, the Mediterranean and Canada. His literary output is large and miscellaneous. Galt's best work is unsurpassed for its comedy, delicacy and perceptive treatment of contemporary small-town Scottish characters. His finest achievements are *The Ayrshire Legatees* (1821; s. 1820–21), *Annals of the Parish* (1821) and *The Entail* (1823). He wrote *The Life of Lord Byron* (1830), whom he knew, as well as his own *Autobiography* (1833) and *Literary Life* (1834).

Works, ed. D. S. Meldrum and W. Roughead, 10 vols., Edinburgh: Grant, 1936.   W.R.

GARLAND, Hamlin (1860–1940) was a farm boy from Wisconsin who left home to work in Iowa and South Dakota. He later determined to break away from rural poverty and went to Boston in 1884, where he took a job at the School of Oratory and set out to forge a career as a writer. He read Taine and Henry George, Herbert Spencer and Darwin. His first published work, *Boy Life on the Prairie* (1885), was a collection of stories about the poverty and hardship of the area in which he was raised. He found this a fertile and salable subject for a succession of stories during the next five years. William Dean Howells, sympathetic to his aspirations, encouraged him. In 1891 *Main-Travelled Roads* established Garland as a writer of powerful realistic tales of protest, dealing with the lot of mid-American rural communities. *Crumbling Idols* (1894) is a collection of essays on composition in which he describes his theory of "veritism," a combination of local color realism and social protest.

In his novels *Jason Edwards* (1892) and *A Spoil of Office* (1892) Garland strongly promoted the cause of the Populist movement, while *A Member of the Third House* (1892) exposes the growing power of the railroad lobby. The most striking and accomplished novel, however, is *Rose of Dutcher's Coolly* (1895), in which Garland draws on his own experiences to depict the revolt of the heroine from the deprivations of Wisconsin farm life and the eventual satisfaction of her aspirations to become a poet. It is on the evidence of such novels and tales that Garland is sometimes identified as the father of American naturalism, but his generally optimistic assumptions deny him this distinction. He is rather a local colorist of ability, a writer of clearly meliorist novels and tales.

Among the works produced later in his long life are two conservationist novels, *The Captain of the Gray-Horse Troop* (1902), which deals with the dispossession of the Indian, and *Cavanagh, Forest Ranger* (1910), which describes early attempts by the U.S. government to restrict overgrazing. After a series of memoirs, beginning with *A Son of the Middle Border* (1917) and ending with *Afternoon Neighbors* (1934), he became interested in psychical research and published two works on that subject.

Boy Life on the Prairie, 1885; 1899.
Main-Travelled Roads, 1891.
Jason Edwards: An Average Man, 1892.
A Spoil of Office, 1892.
Prairie Folks, 1893.
Crumbling Idols, 1894 (essays).
Rose of Dutcher's Coolly, 1895.
Ulysses S. Grant: His Life and Character, 1898.
Her Mountain Lover, 1901.
The Captain of the Gray-Horse Troop, 1902.
Cavanagh, Forest Ranger, 1910.
A Son of the Middle Border, 1917.
A Daughter of the Middle Border, 1921.
Roadside Meetings, 1930.
Afternoon Neighbors, 1934.
Forty Years of Psychic Research, 1936.

Diaries, ed. D. Pizer, San Marino, Calif.: Huntington Library, 1968.
M.L.

GARTH, Sir Samuel (1661–1719), friend and physician of Dryden, early encouraged Pope and lives in the latter's tribute, "well-natured Garth" (*An Epistle to Dr. Arbuthnot*), and the felicitous dedication of the "Summer" *Pastoral*, with its theme: "Love, the sole disease thou canst not cure!" *The Dispensary* (1699), a mock-heroic poem designed to heal a contemporary quarrel, and associating supernatural machinery with the follies of society, foreshadows *The Rape of the Lock*.

The Works of the English Poets, ed. A. Chalmers, London: Johnson, 1810, vol. 9.
A.M.O.

GASCOIGNE, George (c. 1530–77) came of a fairly distinguished family, was educated at Cambridge and entered Gray's Inn. Member of Parliament for Bedford from 1557 to 1559, he later saw service in the Low Countries as a refugee from debt. His translation from Ariosto, *The Supposes* (1566), is the earliest English prose comedy and that from Euripides, *Jocasta* (1566), one of the first blank verse tragedies. The nondramatic verse of *The Steel Glass* (1576) and *A Hundred Sundry Flowers* (1572) is better than the neglect of it suggests.

Complete Works, ed J. W. Cunliffe, 2 vols., Cambridge: Cambridge Univ. Press, 1907–10.   G.P.

GASCOYNE, David (1916–   ) was educated in Salisbury (Wiltshire) and London. His early-developing talent, soon strongly influenced by surrealist art, produced some striking poems and translations, as well as an interesting survey of surrealist theory. His later poetry, more disciplined, has little of the power of this early work, but some of his wartime poems, now less influenced by surrealist techniques—though with a strange nightmare imagery—reveal an anguished and compassionate mind deeply concerned with man's spiritual predicament.

A Short Survey of Surrealism, 1935.
Man's Life Is This Meat, 1936.
Poems, 1937–1942, 1943.
Night Thoughts, 1956.

Collected Poems, ed. R. Skelton, London: Oxford Univ. Press, 1965.
Collected Verse Translations, ed. A. Clodd and R. Skelton, London: Oxford Univ. Press, 1970.   A.Y.

GASKELL, Mrs. E. C. (Elizabeth Cleghorn) (1810–65) was born Elizabeth Stevenson, daughter of a Scottish Unitarian minister who had resigned his orders on conscientious grounds. Her mother died when she was thirteen months old, and she spent her childhood and youth under the guardianship of "Aunt Lumb," her mother's sister, at Heathside, Knutsford. This little Cheshire town formed the scene for *Cranford* and others of her works. After school at Stratford-upon-Avon and a girlhood of frequent visits to friends and relatives, she married William Gaskell in August 1832 and settled in Manchester, where her husband was minister at Cross Street Unitarian Chapel, a post he held until his death in 1884. The Gaskells had six children, of whom four—all daughters—survived. It is said that, encouraged by her husband, Mrs. Gaskell took up writing to console her after the death of her only son, an infant of ten months, in 1845.

Her first novel, "a tale of Manchester life," was *Mary Barton* (1848). Her sympathetic treatment of the plight of the textile workers aroused public attention and the book became the center of critical controversy. The literary world noted her gifts as a novelist and she quickly became known in London cultural society. Her next work was *Cranford*, which began as a single contribution in 1851 to Dickens's periodical, *Household Words*, in which the succeeding chapters appeared. She treated another controversial topic, that of the unmarried mother, in *Ruth* (1853), and returned to the theme of masters and workmen in *North and South* (1855). The most intimate of her literary friendships was that with Charlotte Brontë, who died in 1855 and whose *Life* (1857) Mrs. Gaskell was then commissioned to write. Her outspoken sympathies for Charlotte led to threats of legal action against her by some of the people she criticized. During the 1850s she wrote many short stories and a number of *nouvelles*. Her next novel was *Sylvia's Lovers* (1863), a historical work centered on Whitby in the early years of the French Revolutionary Wars. This was followed by the exquisite pastoral idyll *Cousin Phillis* (1864), and her last work, not quite complete in its serial form, was *Wives and Daughters* (1866). Mrs. Gaskell died suddenly on 12 November 1865.

Her strength as a novelist derives principally from her ability to realize a particular setting and then to suggest moral inferences from the situations it contains. In the industrial novels it is the life of Manchester, in *Cranford* and *Wives and Daughters* that of Knutsford. Her creation of setting comes not only from her description of place, but also, and more importantly, from her sense of the way people behave in any given social group. She has an especial awareness of feminine psychology, and some of her young women are among the greatest of her creations. Indeed, her successive heroines provide an indication of her development as a novelist. Her increasing subtlety in realization of character may be measured by a comparison of Mary Barton, Margaret Hale (*North and South*) and Molly Gibson (*Wives and Daughters*). Her concentration upon character compensates for a lack of strength in overall plot construction. Whilst her novels as stories are always adequate, they are more effective in isolated episodes than in total effect. Her work derives considerable power from its firm moral tone, which, whilst always assured, is never oppressive.

Mary Barton, 1848.
Cranford, 1853 (*s.* 1852–53).
Ruth, 1853.
North and South, 1855 (*s.* 1854–55).
Life of Charlotte Brontë, 1857.
Sylvia's Lovers, 1863.
Cousin Phillis, 1864.
Wives and Daughters, 1866 (*s.* 1864–66).

Works, Knutsford edition, ed. A. W. Ward, 8 vols., London: Murray, 1906 (omits *Life of Charlotte Brontë* and *Poems*).
Letters, ed. J. A. V. Chapple and A. Pollard, Manchester: Manchester Univ. Press; Cambridge, Mass.: Harvard Univ. Press, 1966.   A.P.

"GAWAIN POET, The" (second half of the fourteenth century). This anonymous author is credited with the four poems in MS. Cotton Nero A. x, having editorial titles *Pearl, Cleanness* (or *Purity*), *Patience* and *Sir Gawain and the Green Knight*, and less probably, with *St. Erkenwald*. The Nero manuscript dates from the end of the fourteenth century and the poems are held to have been written in the second half of that century somewhere in the English North-west Midlands (South Lancashire, West Derbyshire or North-west Staffordshire). The poet was probably in the employ of an important local family but attempts to reconstruct his biography from the poems are unconvincing.

All four poems show a deep moral concern and owe much to themes and methods of the medieval preaching tradition. *Pearl* is ostensibly an elegy cast in the form of a dream vision, with rich descriptions of the vision world and the lost Pearl maiden. Its lyric stanzas are linked in groups of five (in one case, six) by a repeated word or phrase. The pearl references assume a symbolic religious significance, the vision world account leads to the rich description of the New Jerusalem, and a debate on salvation for innocents, a contemporary theological topic involving other theological issues, is at the center of the poem. *Cleanness* gives three examples of God's punishment on uncleanness—the Flood, the destruction of Sodom and Gomorrah, and Belshazzar's Feast. These are set in a framework of didactic passages which show sermon influence. The poem has extended descriptions of setting and action and, like *Patience*, is written in alliterative long lines marked off in quatrains. *Patience* advocates its titular virtue by the example of Jonah's futile impatience both in adversity and prosperity. Told in a plain style and based upon biblical narrative and contemporary thought, *Patience* has a balanced structure, a fine characterization of the petulant Jonah and some highly original descriptive passages, notably of Jonah's embarkation and of the whale's belly.

Sir Gawain and the Green Knight is a romance combining two plot elements—the beheading (a test of physical courage) and the temptation (a test of chastity). The poem has all the features of a romance, but the prospect of Gawain's death introduces a moral perspective with themes of transitoriness and penance, and the hero falls short of perfection. The poem presents a problem of standards and evaluation which is reinforced by the contrasts of hero and churllike challenger, nature and the court, sexual pleasure and moral standards. It is written in stanzas containing a variable number of alliterative long lines and ending in a "bob and wheel" (i.e. a line of two syllables followed by four short lines). With its subtle variations of tone in dialogue and its highly evocative descriptions of a winter landscape, the poem is the finest English romance.

All four poems are skillfully constructed, subordinating material to theme and avoiding undue elaboration of detail. The poet achieves a wide range of effects within his metrical forms—French syllabic and native alliterative—and draws on the resources of Romance vocabulary and native dialect. This unusual combination and control contribute to the dramatic quality characteristic of his work, but he goes beyond this in the fusion of diverse literary and philosophical traditions in *Pearl* and *Gawain*. In *Gawain* he gives new significance to the romance genre by introducing a moral concern into an action which is ostensibly a run-of-the-mill romance adventure. In *Pearl* he creates a new type of poem in which the unity of setting and debate depends upon the changing motifs, images and symbolism of the pearl.

Pearl, Cleanness, Patience and Sir Gawain (reproduced in facsimile from MS. Cotton Nero A. x), ed. I. Gollancz, London: Early English Text Society, 1923.
Pearl, ed. E. V. Gordon, Oxford: Clarendon Press, 1953.
Purity, ed. R. J. Menner, New Haven: Yale Univ. Press, 1920.
Patience, ed. H. Bateson, Manchester: Manchester Univ. Press, 1912; revised, 1918.
Sir Gawain and the Green Knight, ed. J. R. R. Tolkien and E. V. Gordon, Oxford: Clarendon Press, 1925; revised N. Davis, 1967.
Pearl; Sir Gawain and the Green Knight, ed. A. C. Cawley, London: Dent; New York: Dutton, 1962. A.D.M.

GAY, John (1685–1732), born in Barnstaple (Devonshire) of an old-established family, was orphaned in 1694 and subsequently apprenticed to a London silk mercer, whom he left in 1706. In 1707 he became secretary to his boyhood friend Aaron Hill, who helped introduce him to literary circles. He began writing occasional verse and prose, and after his meeting with Pope in 1711 became established as a member of the rising literary clique. In 1712 he became secretary to the duchess of Monmouth, and in the next year joined his close friends Swift, Pope, Arbuthnot and Parnell in the foundation of the Scriblerus Club, scourge of Grub Street hack writers and pedantry. His first performed play, *The Wife of Bath*, and his poem *Rural Sports* also appeared in 1713, to be followed in 1714 by *The Fan* and *The Shepherd's Week*. Swift then procured for him a post with Lord Clarendon, who was bound on a mission to Hanover, but the queen's death put an end to his hopes and he returned to England unemployed. His repeated efforts to obtain a government post failed, in spite of his popularity with the court ladies, and it was rumored that Addison, by then antagonistic to all Pope's circle, was responsible for his frustration. His second play, *The What D'Ye Call It* (1715), was a popular success, and *Three Hours after Marriage* (1717), written with Pope and Arbuthnot, aroused such interest that it was greeted with riots on the first night. Meanwhile his poetic career advanced with *Trivia* (1716) and the collected *Poems* of 1720, but all his profits were lost in the South Sea crash and he continued to live uncertainly, partly by his pen and partly as the dependent of generous friends. His *Fables* (1727) and *The Beggar's Opera* (1728) were both popular successes, but *Polly*, the sequel to the latter, was banned for political reasons, and the posthumous *Fables* of 1738 were generally judged inferior. When he died in 1732, Pope wrote to Swift: "Would to God the man we have lost had not been so amiable, nor so good! . . . Sure if innocence and integrity can deserve happiness, it must be his."

The sweetness and affability of Gay's disposition may have led critics to underestimate the sharpness of his satirical wit. Though always more genial than Pope, he is extraordinarily clear-sighted in his assessment of human motive and action, and the delightful easygoing surface of his work should not blind us to the firm realistic grasp beneath. As dramatist he soon proved himself a master of burlesque and farce, from the mock-tragic of *The What D'Ye Call It* to the extravagant, sometimes scurrilous absurdities of *Three Hours after Marriage*. *The Beggar's Opera* surpasses all his previous work in range and variety, for it is both comic and touching, and lightheartedly combines burlesque of heroic tragedy with burlesque of Italian opera and contemporary political satire. Swift applauded it for having "placed all kinds of vice in the . . . most odious light," but Dr. Johnson seems truer to its spirit when he recognizes it as above all diverting and original.

As poet, too, Gay was an innovator and displayed a remarkable faculty for introducing forms whose popularity was confirmed by a stream of imitators. *Trivia*, though it owes something to Swift's city poems, adds an amusing element of classical burlesque to lively detailed observation of London streets; and *The Shepherd's Week* is original in its combination of comic, earthy rusticity with real pathos. Goldsmith thought it "hit the true spirit of pastoral poetry" and "more resembles Theocritus than any other English pastoral writer whatsoever." Above all, Gay, out of all the poets who participated in the vogue for fable inspired by La Fontaine, is alone in being wholly original in his invention, consistently subtle in his tone and refreshingly various in his approach.

Wine, 1708.
The Mohocks, 1712.
Rural Sports, 1713.
The Wife of Bath, 1713.
The Fan, 1714.

The Shepherd's Week, 1714.
The What D'Ye Call It, 1715.
Trivia; or, The Art of Walking the Streets of London, 1716.
Three Hours after Marriage (with Alexander Pope and John Arbuthnot),
1717.
Poems, 2 vols., 1720.
Fables, 1727.
The Beggar's Opera, 1728 (*f*. 1953).
Polly . . . Being the Second Part of the Beggar's Opera, 1729.
Fables, vol. 2, 1738.
The Distress'd Wife, 1743 (*p*. 1734).

Poetical Works, ed. G. C. Faber, London: Oxford Univ. Press, 1926.
Letters, ed. C. F. Burgess, Oxford: Clarendon Press, 1966.   R.E.

GELBER, Jack (1932–   ) was born in Chicago and attended the
University of Illinois. His first play, *The Connection*, produced by The
Living Theater in 1959 (*f*. 1962), signaled a new direction in American
drama. The play was not merely an attempt at a new realism; it also
served to raise questions about the substance and function of art and the
nature of the relationship between performer and audience. Gelber
largely avoided that concern for an immediate social and psychological
reality which had dominated the work of O'Neill, Miller and Williams.
Abandoning complexity of plot, he developed an image which, while not
without clear social implications, expressed his notion of metaphysical
truth. *The Connection* was America's *Waiting for Godot*. Gelber's subsequent
work, *The Apple* (1961), *On Ice* (1964, a novel), and *Square in the Eye*
(1966; *p*. 1965) failed to fulfill this early promise.   C.B.

GEOFFREY of Monmouth. See Middle English Literature.

GEORGE, Henry (1839–97), economist, journalist and reformer, was
born in Philadelphia. He worked as a foremast boy, typesetter, prospector,
journalist in California and editor of the Democratic *Oakland Transcript*. His pamphlet *Our Land and Land Policy* (1871) anticipated the
single-tax philosophy he was to elaborate in *Progress and Poverty* (1879).
Regarding land speculation as the cause of human poverty, George
proposed a land tax which would eliminate all unearned income or
speculation and establish economic equality. By 1905 *Progress and Poverty*
had sold over 2 million copies and established George's international
reputation. His other writings include *The Irish Land Question* (1881),
Social Problems (1883) and *Protection or Free Trade* (1886), and his work

influenced the Progressive reform movement of the early twentieth century.

Complete Works, Library edition, 10 vols., Garden City, N.Y.: Doubleday, Page, 1911.   J.W.

GEORGIANS, The. It is important first to recognize the ambiguity of the name. It can refer simply to those writers of the period when George V was on the throne, but more commonly it is used to refer to those poets whose work is primarily associated with the five volumes of the anthology *Georgian Poetry* (1912–22) and to poets of the period roughly from 1910 to 1925 whose work is of a similar kind. The name was coined by Sir Edward Marsh in the first volume, where he wrote that "we are at the beginning of another 'Georgian period' which may take rank in due time with the several great poetic ages of the past,"—a rather too sanguine hope. That the central volumes of the movement were anthologies indicates its popular appeal, an important feature of this poetry; and it is to some extent the accidents of its organization that make Georgian poetry a movement at all.

Edward Marsh, a lover of poetry, though as a civil servant not professionally connected with literature, admired the work of several young poets, particularly Rupert Brooke. With Brooke he conceived the idea of making a collection from their publications of the past two years in order to confront the public with a summary of the best and the latest in poetry and to popularize the work of a group of little-known writers. Marsh's selection was fairly eclectic and his main function was not to demonstrate any other point than that "English poetry is now once again putting on a new strength and beauty," while he freely admitted that "it has no pretension to cover the field." This first volume did indeed seem, as he said in the last, "to supply a want," but the popularity which made it into the first of a series was to prove something of a burden. By the time the fourth volume came out, the collections had become so influential that reviewers were asking who was E.M. "that he should bestow and withhold crowns and sceptres, and decide that this or that poet was or was not to count" (*Georgian Poetry, 1920–22*). Like it or not, and Marsh made it clear in the prefatory note to the fifth volume that he did not, since he felt unqualified for the job, the editor of *Georgian Poetry* had become an arbiter of modern poetry. Worse, it was felt that Marsh was encouraging a small clique of mutually indistinguishable poetasters, which aroused much opposition, for example, in *Wheels* (1916–22), a rival publication established by the Sitwells and devoted to modernism. Marsh wisely stopped the series, which had in any case become out of key with the time. Georgianism had been channeled by opposition into a narrower interpretation of its notions of poetry than that with which it set out; failing to make any significant change to reflect the upheavals in the world during the First World War, it had become something to react against, even to mock.

The easier generalities have tended to obscure the diversity of these anthologies. Forty poets in all were included. The most characteristically Georgian were Lascelles Abercrombie, Gordon Bottomley, Rupert Brooke, W. H. Davies, Walter de la Mare, John Drinkwater, James Elroy Flecker, W. W. Gibson, Harold Monro and J. C. Squire; others, like D. H. Lawrence (who was represented in four of the five volumes), Robert Graves, James Stephens and John Masefield (all represented in three), extended their work beyond the range this implies. But despite variety even within the more coherent central group, some reasonable generalizations can be made. Georgian poetry, unlike the poetry that was to supersede it, was easy to understand. This contributed to, and was perhaps conditioned by, its popularity, as did also what Eliot called a "subject matter which is—and not in the best sense—impersonal; which belongs to the sensibility of the ordinary sensitive person, not primarily only to that of the sensitive poet." It was traditional in form and meter, Marsh disliking much modern work for its "disregard of form." It is further marked off from later poetry by its insularity, its marked "English-ness," intensified by a reaction to the events of the period it covers; and perhaps the same reaction explains the prevailing pastoral atmosphere, which is the most distinctive feature of the school. Robert Ross admits that "even at its best Georgian poetry suffers from a characteristic thinness. It shies away from both the profoundly intellectual and the profoundly emotional; the former tempted the Georgians too much to rhetoric, the latter too much to didacticism."

Despite fairly consistent criticism of these qualities, there are many worthwhile poems in the Georgian canon, apart from those anthology pieces with which the movement is frequently associated. Most have craftsmanship; some, like the occasional poem of Brooke's, have a mild satiric ease that might have provided more strength. Perhaps a clear summary can be gained of the possible qualities and weaknesses of Georgian poetry by seeing the movement as the outcome of Marsh's approach, the enthusiastic amateur whose views seemed modern in 1912 but conservative in 1922. He selected the poems, and he prefaced the first volume with this quotation, which sums up how near he came to easy sentimentality: "What is it to be a poet? It is to see at a glance the glory of the world, to see beauty in all its forms and manifestations, to feel ugliness like a pain, to resent the wrongs of others as bitterly as one's own, to know mankind as others know single men, to know Nature as botanists know a flower, to be thought a fool, to hear at moments the clear voice of God"

(Dunsany). This dangerous definition lies behind the limited success of this group of minor poets.

(See also **Romantic Movement, The.**)   K.T.

GHOSE, Kashiprosad. See **Indian Literature.**

GIBBON, Edward (1737–94), the historian of the Roman Empire, was the son of a Hampshire landowner. After his mother's death he was brought up by his aunt, Catherine Porten, "the true mother of my mind." She supplied the education he was denied because of ill health at Westminster School and through donnish indolence at Magdalen College, Oxford. His conversion to Catholicism ended his college career and his father sent him to stay with a Calvinist minister in Lausanne. His host reconverted him, instructed him and then "wisely left me to my Genius." His wide reading of ancient and modern authors equipped him to defend the study of the former against their neglect by the latter in his first work, *Essai sur l'Étude de la Littérature* (1761), which was partly written in Lausanne in 1758 and finished in England in 1759.

After three years' service as an officer in the Hampshire Militia, Gibbon again visited the Continent, passing through France, Switzerland and Italy. Back in England he published with his friend Deyverdun a journal for the year 1767, *Mémoires Littéraires de la Grande Bretagne*, to which he contributed a review of Lord Lyttelton's *Henry II*. His next publication, *Critical Observations on the Sixth Book of the Aeneid* (1770), was an anonymous attack on Bishop Warburton's assertion that Virgil's theme was an allegory and not a fable. Gibbon lived in Hampshire until his father's death, then moved to London in 1772 and for the next decade was active in both political and literary circles. He served as member of Parliament for Liskeard and for Lymington, and in the debates over America "supported with many a sincere and *silent* vote the rights, though not, perhaps, the interest of the mother country." His support of the government resulted in his becoming a lord commissioner of trade and plantations, a post he held until 1782 when the Board of Trade was abolished. Meanwhile he had become a leading light in Johnson's club, and had published the first three volumes of *The Decline and Fall of the Roman Empire*. His autobiography gives a lucid and candid account of his career. He died in London after spending his last ten years in Lausanne.

The contribution of Gibbon's philosophy, intellect and style to the study of history was immense. Historians seek the causes of events. For centuries historical change had been attributed to supernatural agencies, particularly to divine Providence. More recently scholars had distinguished between primary and secondary causes: God was acknowledged to be the prime mover in history as in other spheres; but historical change was also ascribed to mundane forces. In his controversial explanation of the progress of Christianity Gibbon took this process a stage further: Providence was dismissed in a paragraph, while two chapters (15 and 16) were devoted to a completely secular interpretation of the church's success. His intellectual grasp of argument and evidence was equal to the task. For all the efforts of his outraged detractors, Gibbon succeeded in bringing even the history of religion within the scope of normal historical explanation. His style immortalized his views. Gibbon's prose, oratorical rather than conversational, influenced as much by Montesquieu's French as by Johnson's English, is all the evidence that is needed to demonstrate that history is a branch of literature.

Yet his achievement belongs essentially to the eighteenth century. He was philosophically more at home with the outmoded Deism of Voltaire than with the Romanticism foreshadowed by Rousseau. His scholarly standards have not survived the scrutiny of later historians, especially in his interpretation of Byzantine history. Above all, his style is a stately monument to the Palladian era, an age which has vanished as utterly and as irrevocably as Gibbon himself.

The History of the Decline and Fall of the Roman Empire, 6 vols., 1776–88.

Miscellaneous Works, ed. Lord Sheffield, 2 vols., 1796; enlarged, 5 vols., London: Murray, 1814.

Letters, ed. J. E. Norton, 3 vols., London: Cassell; New York: Macmillan Co., 1956.
Edward Gibbon: Memoirs of My Life, ed. G. A. Bonnard, London: Nelson, 1966; New York: Funk & Wagnalls, 1969.   W.A.S.

"GIBBON, Lewis Grassic" was the pseudonym, adapted from his mother's maiden name, of James Leslie Mitchell (1901–35). The son of peasants, he spent his adolescent years in the Mearns countryside of Scotland. After a stormy interlude at Mackie Academy, Stonehaven, he became a reporter in Aberdeen and, later, Glasgow. At the age of eighteen he joined the army; this satisfied his need for travel and encouraged his efforts at self-education. On his discharge he felt "the compulsion of hunger and unemployment" and joined the Royal Air Force as a clerk. He married in 1925 and published his first book, *Hanno*, in 1928. The following year he completed his air force service and determined to live by his pen. It is likely that overwork largely contributed to his death at the age of thirty-four.

His first novel, *Stained Radiance*, appeared in 1930, but his fictional evocation of Scotland was achieved only in the trilogy, *A Scots Quair*.

In this he broke away from a Latin-structured English and fashioned Scots speech into his own style of poetic English which disregarded conventional grammar in favor of rhythmically flowing narrative periods. *Sunset Song* (1932) is a prose poem evocative of the Mearns countryside— its coarse soil, peasant labor and family penury. *Cloud Howe* (1933) continues the trilogy, dealing with conditions in the 1920s, and *Grey Granite* (1934), the weakest of the novels, shows Gibbon less successful in creating the industrial atmosphere of a Scottish town. His unique quality as a novelist is to bring both compassion and humor to a poetic vision of men toiling futile lifetimes in a universe which in no way recognizes their struggles.

A Scots Quair, London: Hutchinson, 1946.

A Scots Hairst (essays and short stories), ed. I. S. Munro, London: Hutchinson, 1967.   C.P.

GIBSON, W. W. (Wilfred Wilson) (1878–1962) was born in Hexham (Northumberland). His early poetry comprised dreamlike evocations of past ages. In 1910 appeared *Daily Bread*, in which he showed a detailed knowledge of the industrial poor. Two years later he moved to London and was a founder of the Georgian magazine *New Numbers*. Gibson's output was prolific. His plain, almost abrupt language is effective, his perceptiveness adequate but rarely profound.

(See also **Georgians, The**.)

Collected Poems, 1905–25, London: Macmillan, 1926.   C.P.

GIFFORD, William (1756–1826) began life as a shoemaker's apprentice, but was helped to enter Exeter College, Oxford. He grew into a learned but irritable man of strong conservative principles and savage wit. His *The Baviad* (1794) and *The Maeviad* (1795) brilliantly demolished the aesthetically pretentious poetry of an English coterie at Florence called "the Della Cruscans." Gifford edited *The Anti-Jacobin* in 1797 and was *The Quarterly Review*'s first editor between 1809 and 1824. His editions of Massinger (1805), Ben Jonson (1816) and Ford (1827) are still invaluable to scholars.   W.R.

GILBERT, W. S. (Sir William Schwenk) (1836–1911), son of William Gilbert, novelist, was born in London. He began his career in the Civil Service, then transferred to law. He wrote comic verse—*The Bab Ballads* (1869; s. 1866) and *More Bab Ballads* (1873)—and, with Arthur Sullivan, the musician, produced a series of popular comic operas, including

Trial by Jury (1875), *Patience* (1881), *The Mikado* (1885) and *The Yeomen of the Guard* (1888). He was a clever writer of burlesque with remarkable verbal facility and a kindly ironic humor. His comments on contemporary topics, such as aestheticism and women's education, are superficial but entertaining, intended to provoke indulgent laughter.

Savoy Operas, ed. D. Hudson, 2 vols., London: Oxford Univ. Press, 1962–63.
Gilbert before Sullivan: Six Comic Plays, ed. J. W. Stedman, Chicago: Univ. of Chicago Press, 1967; London: Routledge, 1969.　s.m.s.

GILFILLAN, George. See **Spasmodics, The.**

GILPIN, William (1724–1804) was born near Carlisle (Cumberland). After graduating from Queen's College, Oxford, he was ordained and became a schoolmaster. Inheriting an interest in drawing from his father, he toured Great Britain (1768–76), making extensive notes and sketches. Encouraged by friends, he published *Observations on the Mountains and Lakes of Cumberland and Westmorland* (1786), the most important and influential of his works, setting out his ideas on the picturesque. He is not concerned with the artificial picturesque of Pope and the landscape gardeners, but the sublime picturesque of natural scenes. The search for picturesque landscape (ridiculed by Combe) developed that already awakened interest in the Lakes which culminated in the work of Wordsworth and the Lake Poets. Gilpin published accounts of his tours of the Wye (1782), the Scottish Highlands (1786), the New Forest (1791) and the West of England (1798). Gilpin supplies biographical information in *Memoirs of Dr. Richard Gilpin*, ed. W. Jackson, for the Cumberland and Westmorland Antiquarian Society, 1879.　a.e.

GINSBERG, Allen (1926–) was born in New Jersey, son of Naomi Ginsberg, a Russian émigrée, and Louis Ginsberg, schoolteacher and poet. He attended local high schools and Columbia University, interrupting his university career for a year during which he worked at a number of odd jobs including seaman and dishwasher. His journeys throughout the world are well documented, and suffice to say that Ginsberg has traveled more widely than any other writer in the history of America. These travels seemed to culminate in 1965 when he was elected King of the May by Czech students and deported by the Czech government.

His earliest poems were influenced by the ideas of William Carlos

Williams, but in "Howl" (1956) he turned to what he names the "Hebraic-Melvillian bardic breath" as a mode of composition. Ginsberg was also influenced by Kerouac's prose and by his own private illuminations in which he "heard Blake's ancient voice and saw the universe unfold in my brain." Ignored or condemned by critics when it appeared, "Howl" had an immediate impact on a generation of younger Americans and, in retrospect, it is clearly the most striking poem of its decade. Stridently oral, each line of the poem is a single breath unit which carries the Whitman–Jeffers exploration of the rhythmic long line to its extreme. "Kaddish," written in 1959, is an almost Chassidic prayer for the soul of Ginsberg's mother. It begins as a kind of cultural and psychological biography, then lifts itself, slowly, from lament to song. It is perhaps the most lyrically beautiful of all of Ginsberg's poems.

By the early 1960s Ginsberg had become such a conspicuous public presence that he somehow posed a greater threat to his own creative work than to the forces of Moloch against whom he continued to cry, sometimes, as in his poem "America," with wry self-deprecating humor. Then in 1963, on the Kyoto–Tokyo Express, Ginsberg "had a very strange ecstatic experience" which freed him. He attempts to communicate the nature of this epiphany in the poem "The Change," in which he abandons the looseness of the long line and returns, with a newly found assurance, to a more measured speech. "The Change" thus heralds a reawakening, and poems like "Kral Majales" and "Who Be Kind To" confirm that Ginsberg's creative powers are no longer blocked.

Ginsberg returned to America and in the winter of 1965 he composed "Wichita Vortex Sutra," his most carefully structured long poem to date. More firmly and realistically political than any of his other poems, Ginsberg has said that "Wichita Vortex Sutra" is a part of a larger work.

Early in his career Ginsberg wrote that his "message" was to "widen the area of consciousness," and for many years he followed paths charted by William Burroughs (see *The Yage Letters*). Later, however, he chose a more concrete mode of political action. He appeared as a defense witness at the Chicago Conspiracy Trial and compiled what he calls "documents on police bureaucracy's conspiracy against human rights."

Howl, and Other Poems, 1956.
Kaddish, and Other Poems, 1958–1960, 1961.
Empty Mirror: Early Poems, 1961.
Reality Sandwiches: 1953–60, 1963.
The Yage Letters (with William Burroughs), 1963.
Planet News, 1961–1967, 1968.
Indian Journals, 1969.   W.D.S.

GISSING, George (1857–1903), born in Wakefield (Yorkshire), the son of a chemist, showed considerable intellectual ability as an adolescent. However, his academic success at Owens College, Manchester ended abruptly in 1876 when small thefts from a college cloakroom were traced to him. His devotion to a prostitute and his attempts to reform her life had prompted the larcenies. After a lapse of two years he renewed association and made an unhappy marriage with her in 1879. The following year he produced his first novel, *Workers in the Dawn*. It is a long, rambling narrative, overcrowded with characters and crude in its attempts at post-Dickensian humor. Not only urban poverty and the exploitation of the poor by the poor, but also the complacency of the clergy and the indifference of the church are indicted with an intense youthful ardor.

Life in London lodgings with a drunken, illiterate wife darkened Gissing's vision. Employment as a tutor with wealthy families emphasized for him the contrast between rich and poor; he himself belonged to no class, but his life remained divided between several classes. Like Godwin Peake in *Born in Exile*, he shared the cultured interests of the rich, had nothing in common with the dingy environment in which he was forced to live and felt that he had been "born in exile." Gissing's agonizing struggle to earn a living by his pen produced, on average, at least one volume a year between 1884 and 1903. A second marriage in 1891, after the death of his first wife, brought little additional happiness, but he eventually found some degree of domestic comfort during his association with Gabrielle Fleury, a Frenchwoman who had requested his permission to translate *New Grub Street*. Their relationship lasted from 1898 until his death of double pneumonia at St. Jean de Luz.

The uncertainties of his personal and social life provide a dramatic center for many of the young heroes in his novels. Gissing's own emphasis was not on the social commentary and satire in his work; he stated that the most important element is that which deals "with a class of young men distinctive of our time—well-educated, fairly bred, but without money." Those men of talent, but not of genius, who have social ambitions but are unable to rise in a society still too stratified by class concepts, are forced to exist in drudgery and penury, like Reardon and Yule in Gissing's finest novel, *New Grub Street* (1891). Their fates, like those of Arthur Golding in *Workers in the Dawn* (1880) and Godwin Peake in *Born in Exile* (1892), are a type of lingering self-destruction.

Gissing was influenced by Dickens and George Eliot, but he was less successful than Dickens in his use of multiple plots and far cruder in the depiction of unsavory minor figures. Like George Eliot, he was careful in detailing the intellectual and emotional development of his principal characters, but was unable, possibly through insufficient time for revision, to weave a fabric comparable to the subtle and complex material of George Eliot's finest work. To read Gissing is to recognize inventive power and narrative skill, but also to be aware of, and to lament, those social pressures in his life which prevented emergence of the significant artist.

Workers in the Dawn, 1880.
Demos, 1886.
Thyrza, 1887.
A Life's Morning, 1888.
The Nether World, 1889.
New Grub Street, 1891.
Born in Exile, 1892.
The Odd Women, 1893.
In the Year of Jubilee, 1894.
Eve's Ransom, 1895.
The Whirlpool, 1897.
The Private Papers of Henry Ryecroft, 1903.
Will Warburton, 1905.

C.P.

GLAPTHORNE, Henry (1610–?43), fourth son of Thomas Glapthorne, bailiff to Lady Hatton, at thirteen matriculated at Corpus Christi College, Cambridge, but there is no record that he took a degree. He began writing for the stage (whether as amateur or professional is uncertain) in the early 1630s, producing eleven plays in under ten years. In 1639 he published a volume of poems, and another poem, *White-Hall*, appeared in 1643. In his seven extant plays Glapthorne shows limited dramatic resourcefulness. He constantly reuses his own materials and borrows freely from earlier writers. Several of his plays, notably *Argalus and Parthenia*, enjoyed a surprising post-Restoration popularity.

Plays and Poems, ed. R. H. Shepherd, 2 vols., London: Pearson, 1874.

L.S.

GLASGOW, Ellen (1874–1945) was born in Richmond (Virginia), a daughter of a Scotch-Presbyterian ironworks executive. Pretty, destined to deafness, hypersensitive and largely self-educated, she combined "society" with socialism in her youth. Her literary domain, a fictional history of the Commonwealth of Virginia, first emerged in her third novel, *The Voice of the People* (1900). Two unfortunate love affairs between 1900 and 1917 affected her deeply (her later heroes are incredibly weak and selfish). After the First World War she settled down in Richmond with a female cousin as companion and wrote some of her finest fiction. Her last novel,

In This Our Life (1941; *f.* 1942), won a Pulitzer Prize. She died in Richmond.

A prolific popular novelist, Ellen Glasgow succeeded in several books in her ambition to transcend Southern regionalism through ironical subversion of the romantic Southern self-image. *Virginia* (1913), a tragi-comedy of a girl who incarnates the invalid regional ideal, is a splendid example. Grimmer ironies dominate the uneven masterpiece *Barren Ground* (1925). Hardyesque handling of rural setting as fact and symbol raises this study of a woman's long struggle for survival to a poetic level. Meredithian high comedy pervades her Queenborough trilogy— *The Romantic Comedians* (1926); *They Stooped to Folly* (1929); *The Sheltered Life* (1932)—about upper-middle-class Richmond families in decay. The last volume, ambitious and poetic, presents two old families discovering the vulnerability of their "sheltered" life in the alternated perspectives of young Jenny Blair and old General Archbald, her richest characterization.

The Miller of Old Church, 1911.
Virginia, 1913.
Barren Ground, 1925.
The Romantic Comedians, 1926.
They Stooped to Folly, 1929.
The Sheltered Life, 1932.
Vein of Iron, 1935.
A Certain Measure, 1943 (essays).
The Woman Within, 1954 (autobiography).

Works, 12 vols., New York: C. Scribner's Sons, 1938.
Collected Stories, ed. R. K. Meeker, Baton Rouge: Louisiana State Univ. Press, 1963.   A.S.

GLOVER, Denis. See **New Zealand Literature.**

GODWIN, William (1756–1836), born in Wisbech (Cambridgeshire), son of a Dissenting minister, was educated at Hoxton Dissenting College and spent five years as a minister before his faith was shaken by encounters with rationalist philosophy. In 1783 he abandoned the ministry and turned to hack writing and political journalism in London. Inspired by the ferment of idealism occasioned by the French Revolution, he wrote *An Enquiry concerning the Principles of Political Justice* (1793). In 1797 he married Mary Wollstonecraft, the feminist propagandist, who died in childbirth the same year. Afterwards his life was marred by misfortune; his second marriage was ill-advised, he was hounded by poverty and had to resort to hack work and borrowing from friends, notably his son-in-law, Shelley. The latter years of his life were spent in relative obscurity.

Apart from tracts and books on current social and political questions, Godwin also wrote novels, children's books, dramas and historical works. *Political Justice* is, however, the cornerstone of his achievement. Influenced by revolutionary idealism and by his upbringing as a Dissenter, Godwin postulated a theory of human perfectibility that would be manifest in universal political justice. His idealism influenced not only Shelley but also Wordsworth, Coleridge and Southey. Godwin had little skill as a novelist; his best novel, *The Adventures of Caleb Williams* (1794), is basically a crime story with an ingenious plot which Godwin intended as a critique of current social values. Later novels, including *St. Leon* (1799), *Fleetwood* (1805) and *Cloudesly* (1830), are little more than intellectual melodramas.

I.W.

GOGARTY, Oliver St. John (1878–1957) was born and educated in Dublin. His boisterous life as a medical student provided the model for Buck Mulligan in Joyce's *Ulysses*. He later combined his career as a medical specialist with political and literary life. For several years he was a member of the Irish Senate, but his hostility to Sinn Fein became a source of danger to him. From 1939 he lived in America. Among his literary friends were Joyce, of whom he wrote a memoir, Yeats, Moore and Æ. The last-named called Gogarty "the wildest wit in Ireland." An ebullient and irreverent wit is found in his later writings, especially the prose works *As I Was Going down Sackville Street* (1937) and *Tumbling in the Hay* (1939).

O.K.

"GOLD, Michael" was the pseudonym of Irving Granich (1894–1967), who was born in New York City. After leaving school early and having a succession of jobs, he was converted to a lifelong belief in communism, and it was as an editor and party apologist that he is best known. He edited both *The Liberator* and *The New Masses* during the 1930s, and strongly advocated the need for proletarian art. He wrote two plays, *Hoboken Blues* and *Fiesta*, for the New Playwrights.

His only memorable work is *Jews without Money* (1930), a passionate and angry exposure of degradation by poverty in the Jewish East Side and a celebration of the communal life that survived it. Increased isolation and a hardening of his attitudes later in life can be seen in *The Hollow Men* (1941).

D.V.W.

GOLDING, Arthur (?1536–?1605) may have been to Cambridge and possibly served Somerset and Edward de Vere. His translations are tenfold: versions of theological works by Calvin, Beza, etc. (reflecting

Golding's Puritanism), and of classical Latin writers—Seneca, Caesar and Ovid (*Metamorphoses*). This last translation (1565–67), in fourteen-syllable ballad meter and within the medieval tradition of allegorizing Ovid, was extremely popular and was probably used by Shakespeare.

Shakespeare's Ovid, ed. W. H. D. Rouse, London: Centaur Press, 1961.

G.P.

GOLDING, William (1911–   ) spent most of his early life in Marlborough (Wiltshire), interspersed with "long holidays by a Cornish sea." On the evidence of various autobiographical pieces in *The Hot Gates*, it would seem that the two most profound impressions left on him from his childhood and early youth were both connected with his father. One was the sense of difference, of not belonging, that resulted from his being the son of the local schoolmaster at a time and in a place where such a distinction still had meaning. The other was the relationship itself, that contained within it not only the normal ties of deep affection and respect but also the tension between temperaments in many ways very dissimilar. Golding was imaginative and interested in the arts. His father was a practical man and a rationalist in the Wellsian mould, unable to see beyond the simplified notions of his creed and keen for his son to be a scientist.

The reaction of Golding as a child was to escape into a private world of his own, to cultivate the pleasures of the imagination in solitude. In manhood, having taken his degree, served his term in the navy during the Second World War, married and settled down to teach classics and English in a Salisbury (Wiltshire) school, the reaction took a more positive form. In 1954 and 1955 Golding published two books, *Lord of the Flies* and *The Inheritors*, one set on a desert island of the future, the other going back in time to the point when *homo sapiens* finally triumphed over the last of the pre-men. Both were thesis-novels in that they attacked directly the brash, optimistic assumptions about evolution and the blessings of civilization so beloved of nineteenth- and early twentieth-century humanists. In Golding's terms, the loss of innocence and the Fall of Man were seen as a direct consequence of the evolution of civilized society, and in this sense both books strongly reflected the mood of pessimism and disillusionment abroad in the 1950s.

Golding's next two novels, however, turned away completely from the contemplation of man's general development as a race and explored in far greater depth the dichotomy existing within individual man. *Pincher Martin*, an ingenious reconstruction of the afterdeath state of a drowned sailor, and *Free Fall*, the account of an artist searching his life for the point at which innocence was lost, investigated in different ways the central paradox of human experience whereby man's capacity and will to aspire (what Golding has called his sense of "my Godness") are constantly threatened by the "broken-down criminality" of his nature which is the curse he brought from Eden. The theme recurred in *The Spire*, but this time the tortuous searching after certainty experienced by a medieval dean who believed a great spire could be added to his cathedral when all the forces of reason were against him, was linked through a vast complex of associations with the earlier theme of man's general development to form a synthesis so rich in texture as to have the final impact of a dramatic poem rather than a novel. It is probably Golding's finest achievement. His next novel, *The Pyramid*, though constructed with his customary care and ingenuity, was generally less impressive.

Golding has a tendency, unusual in the present age, to overwrite, and he is not at his best when dealing directly with human relationships. Yet his faults are often only the side-effects of his great virtues, the over-writing resulting from the pressure at which he is communicating, and the failure to present people adequately as people arising often from the supreme importance he attaches to the central theme. Of all the novelists in England to emerge since the Second World War, Golding is probably the most ambitious, the most original, the most gifted, and the most likely to be read in one hundred years' time.

Lord of the Flies, 1954 (*f.* 1963).
The Inheritors, 1955.
Pincher Martin, 1956 (U.S. title: *The Two Deaths of Christopher Martin*).
The Brass Butterfly, 1958 (play).
Free Fall, 1959.
The Spire, 1964.
The Hot Gates, 1965 (essays).
The Pyramid, 1967.
The Scorpion God, 1971 (3 short novels).   D.W.C.

GOLDMAN, William (1931–   ) was born in Chicago and educated at Oberlin College and Columbia. His first novel, *The Temple of Gold*, was published in 1957, his best, *Soldier in the Rain* (*f.* 1965), in 1960. *Boys and Girls Together* (1964) is an amalgam of ideas and classes of people, and was followed by *The Thing of It Is* (1967), and *No Way to Treat a Lady* (1968; *f.* 1968). Goldman is an accomplished scriptwriter; among his screen credits are *Masquerade*, *The Moving Target*, and *Butch Cassidy and the Sundance Kid*.   W.D.S.

GOLDSMITH, Oliver (?1730–74), the second son of an Irish clergy-man, went in 1744 to Trinity College, Dublin. His rather irregular and inglorious university career lasted until 1749, when he graduated as a bachelor of arts, returned home and made tentative moves towards ordination, teaching and the law. The money provided for his legal studies was squandered at the Dublin gaming tables. In 1752 he embarked on a medical career, first in Edinburgh and afterwards in Leyden, but by 1755 he had abandoned regular studies for a freer life, traveling round Europe as a happy vagabond, playing his flute and singing, when necessary, for his supper. In 1756 he returned to England to temporary work as apothecary and schoolmaster, and final establishment in London as physician and general literary hack, reviewing, translating, and contributing essays to such periodicals as *The Bee* and *The Weekly Magazine*. Among his best work from this period are the "Chinese Letters," written for Newbery's *Public Ledger* and republished in 1762 as *The Citizen of the World*, giving a new lease of life to the periodical essay. He became a member of Dr. Johnson's circle, though his role within it seems to have been at least partly that of clown and butt, and continued for the rest of his life to fluctuate between momentary prosperity and complete destitution, from which his friends repeatedly rescued him. These financial straits were due not only to personal extravagance—he was notorious for his love of finery—but also to extreme generosity. As he says of the partially auto-biographical Man in Black (in *The Citizen of the World*): "We were perfectly instructed in the art of giving away thousands, before we were taught the more necessary qualifications of getting a farthing." Boswell, who disliked him, describes him as absurdly vain and awkward, but Dr. Johnson said after his death: "Let not his frailties be remembered: he was a very great man."

As author Goldsmith is remarkable for having produced one excellent work in each of three genres—novel, play and poem. *The Vicar of Wakefield* (1766) "found entry," as Thackeray says, "into every castle and every hamlet in Europe," and in spite of the strained melodrama of the latter half of the action it remains delightfully readable, not only for its domestic humor and picture of country life, but also for the delicate subtlety of the tone. The vicar himself is at once good and vain, wise and foolish, complacent and lovable, and in the simple naïve style of his presentation it is hard to determine how far Goldsmith's tone is ironic.

As poet he is master of the unhurried reflective manner, and though his couplets lack Pope's bite and Johnson's weight, they flow smoothly and agree admirably with his subject matter. *The Traveller* (1764), which moves easily over a wide range of his Continental experience, was hailed by Johnson as "a production to which, since the death of Pope, it will not be easy to find any thing equal." *The Deserted Village* (1770) pleads movingly against the destruction of country life and in its blend of firm dignity with honest pathos displays the power of sentiment without sentimentality.

His plays were intended as a wholesome corrective to the sentimental comedy of the day; and they display the virtues of good humor, good sense and good feeling. *The Good Natured Man* (1768) suffers from some strain in the conduct of the action; but *She Stoops to Conquer* (1773), with its farcical, boisterous plot and strong central irony, develops irresistibly from the first scene and has been very frequently revived.

The Citizen of the World, 1762 (*s.* 1760).
The Traveller, 1764.
The Vicar of Wakefield, 1766.
The Good Natured Man, 1768.
The Deserted Village, 1770.
She Stoops to Conquer; or, The Mistakes of a Night, 1773.

Collected Works, ed. A. Friedman, 5 vols., Oxford: Clarendon Press, 1966.
The Poems of Thomas Gray, William Collins, Oliver Goldsmith, ed. R. H. Lonsdale, London: Longmans; New York: Barnes & Noble, 1969.
Letters, ed. K. C. Balderston, Cambridge: Cambridge Univ. Press; New York: Macmillan Co., 1928.   R.E.

GORDON, Adam Lindsay. See **Australian Literature.**

GOSSE, Sir Edmund (1849–1928) reviewed extensively in the periodicals of the 1870s. His *From Shakespeare to Pope* (1885) was attacked on grounds of error of fact by Churton Collins. However, his *Life and Letters of John Donne* (1889) is a pioneer work in the revival of the Metaphysicals. He knew Swinburne and wrote a biography of him (1917), but his main contributions to English literature are his introduction of Ibsen to English readers and his semiautobiographical *Father and Son* (1907), in which he traces the history both of conflict with his father and of the latter's intellectual isolation as a result of his inability for religious reasons to accept the theory of evolution.   A.P.

GOWER, John (?1330–1408) is thought to have come from a well-to-do family holding property in Suffolk and Kent, and was involved in certain property transactions in the 1360s and 1370s. In May 1378 he was given power of attorney by Chaucer during the latter's visit to Italy, and Chaucer's *Troilus* is dedicated to "moral Gower" and "philosophical Strode." On 23 January 1398 a license was granted for his marriage to Agnes Groundolf, which shows Gower to be living at St. Mary Overie Priory, Southwark. Gower had become blind by 1400. He died in 1408 and was buried in St. Mary Overie.

Two ballad sequences by Gower are extant—*Cinkante Balades* and *Un Traitie selonc les Aucteurs pour Essampler les Amantz Marietz*. His fame, however, rests on three long poems. The earliest, in French, is *Mirour de l'Omme*, renamed *Speculum Meditantis*, which is an allegorical study of the vices and virtues. *Vox Clamantis*, in Latin (in three versions, the earliest ?1382), examines the causes of discord in contemporary society, particularly Wat Tyler's revolt. *Confessio Amantis*, in English, is in the form of a courtly love allegory in which carnal love is rejected for divine love. Existing in three versions, the poem was dedicated to Richard II in 1390, but the dedication was transferred to Henry of Lancaster (later Henry IV) in 1392.

Gower is concerned with moral themes, and works within the medieval concepts of sin and society and with an allegorical method. His most original and imaginative achievements are the stories which he tells within his didactic framework.

Complete Works, ed. G. C. Macaulay, 4 vols., Oxford: Clarendon Press, 1899–1902.   A.D.M.

GRANVILLE-BARKER, Harley (1877–1946), born in London, was educated privately and then at drama school. Later he became an actor, dramatist, critic and theater manager. As a producer he was responsible for inaugurating a new type of stage production, in which serious plays—by Shaw, Galsworthy and Barker himself—were performed in a naturalistic manner. Though Barker's own plays, such as *The Voysey Inheritance* (*p.* 1905), are well constructed and deal thoughtfully with social problems, they have neither the wit nor the vitality of Shavian drama. His *Prefaces to Shakespeare* (1927–48) are distinctive criticism, the result of his many years as an actor and producer of Shakespeare's plays. The first of the *Prefaces* was originally printed in a collected edition of Shakespeare in 1923.   O.K.

GRAVES, Richard (1715–1804) was educated at Abingdon and Pembroke College, Oxford, becoming a fellow of All Souls (1736–41) and rector of Claverton (Somerset) from 1749 to 1804. By 1757 Graves had begun *The Spiritual Quixote* (1773), a picaresque novel, cleverly modeled on Cervantes and Fielding, which ridicules the excesses of early Methodism with spirit, perception and genial wit. Lively comedy is linked with interesting social and topographical material. Graves wrote three more novels, verse, essays and translations. His friendship with Shenstone produced the *Recollections of William Shenstone* (1788).   W.R.

GRAVES, Robert (1895–   ), the son of a well-known Irish poet, A. P. Graves, started to write poetry while still a child. On leaving Charterhouse School he enlisted, was involved in active service during the First World War and was deeply disturbed by his experiences of trench warfare. *Goodbye to All That* (1929) is an autobiography as well as a reflection of the postwar disillusionment of his generation. His poetic career after the war was attended by a painful process of self-criticism and conflict. At the same time, despite his growing reputation, he was financially insecure. In 1926 he accepted a post at Cairo University, but in 1929 he went to live in Majorca, where he wrote many works in collaboration with Laura Riding. A series of historical novels brought him financial security and popular success, and he was able to devote all his time to writing. He delivered the Clark Lectures at Cambridge in 1954–55 and was professor of poetry at Oxford from 1961 to 1966.

A versatile and provocative writer, he has published poetry, novels, criticism and works upon mythology, earning a continuously fresh reputation. He began his career by writing poetry, mainly in sympathy with Georgian poets, and the process of making for himself a fresh poetic style was very gradual. His development is seen in eight collections of verse published before 1925, in which the poet seeks an impersonal form for his private feelings. During the 1920s and 1930s he also wrote a number of novels and critical works. His Claudius novels, *I, Claudius* and *Claudius the God*, are remarkable historical reconstructions, told in the form of memoirs by Claudius, and he has written and translated other historical works. His interest in the sources of poetry, psychological and mythological, and in the origin of myth has also produced original books such as *The Common Asphodel* and *The White Goddess*, the latter "a historical grammar of poetic myth." His mature poetry coincides with what appears to be, for him, a working belief in the Muse of poetry who is also goddess of life and death. Though the goddess provides inspiration and subject matter for Graves's more recent poetry, she also demands from the poet honesty, discipline and hard labor.

Graves's self-imposed isolation from English literary life has left him free to develop an uncompromising and critical attitude to his own and others' writing and to work out an individual poetic manner. Though Graves has always emphasized the importance of unconscious inspiration and spontaneity in poetic composition, he has constantly tried to express intense and complex feelings with terseness and masculine strength. Accordingly, many of his poems possess elements of the mysterious and visionary but are also characterized by restraint, irony and urbanity. Using traditional meters and diction, he has explored the complex maladjustments between mind and body, romantic love and sexual appetite, innocence and experience, and between the enjoyment of beauty and forebodings of death. Even in his later poems written about the goddess, the poet still seeks control, directness and "penetrating, often heart-rending sense."

(See also **Georgians, The.**)

Over the Brazier, 1916.
Whipperginny, 1923.
Poetic Unreason and Other Studies, 1925.
Poems, 1914–1926, 1927.
A Survey of Modernist Poetry (with Laura Riding), 1927.
Goodbye to All That, 1929; revised, 1957.
I, Claudius, 1934.
Claudius the God, 1934.
Poems, 1938–1945, 1946.
The White Goddess, 1947.
The Common Asphodel, 1949.
Poems and Satires, 1951.
Man Does, Woman Is, 1964.
Poems, 1965–1968, 1968.
The Crane Bag, and Other Disputed Subjects, 1969.   O.K.

GRAY, Thomas (1716–71), of the twelve children of a violent, financially unreliable, possibly psychopathic scrivener, was the only one to survive infancy. During his schooldays at Eton he formed some of the deepest personal relationships of his life, and with his three close friends, Horace Walpole, Richard West and Thomas Ashton, joined in a precocious, exclusive "quadruple alliance," which held itself aloof from the activities of more athletic schoolfellows. In later life Gray looked back regretfully on these days of youthful happiness in his "Ode on a Distant Prospect of Eton College." At Cambridge he complained of boredom and loneliness, relieved only by visits to London and the letters of friends, with whom he maintained a frequent correspondence all his life. His skill and charm as a letter writer were early recognized, and Cowper, himself a brilliant correspondent, said: "I once thought Swift's letters the best that could be written; but I like Gray's better." In 1738 Gray left Cambridge without taking a degree. For two years he traveled on the Continent with Walpole, but a quarrel between them, not made up till 1745, brought him home in 1741. In the next year he returned to Cambridge, where he remained the rest of his life "like a cabbage," as he put it, studying deeply but without academic advancement until 1768, when he was appointed to the virtual sinecure of professor of modern languages and history. This uneventful life was the effect of a languid, inactive temperament, constantly clouded by apathy and despondency. "Low spirits," he wrote "are my true and faithful companions." His timid fastidious nature often provoked contempt, and although he was capable of deep and enduring friendship, both with his own contemporaries and with young men whom he met at Cambridge, he confessed to "a want of love for general society."

His poetic output was small, and it used to be fashionable to deplore, with Arnold, his misfortune in being a poet fallen upon an age of prose. Wordsworth loathed his "curiously elaborate" and "vicious" poetic diction and made him a special target of attack in the preface to *Lyrical Ballads*, but more recently critics have come to see the heavily "literary" manner of such poems as the "Ode on the Spring" and the "Sonnet on the Death of Richard West" (with their many echoes of such earlier poets as Spenser and Milton) as a means of intensification rather than mere banal pedantry. In contrast to these short lyrical pieces his more vigorous manner is perhaps better represented by the strong satirical lines "On Lord Holland's Seat" than by the frigidly melodramatic, consciously "Gothick" odes which Dr. Johnson described as having "a kind of strutting dignity" and "unnatural violence." Gray's finest poem, *An Elegy Wrote in a Country Church Yard* (1751), displays an interesting tension between personal introspective distress and the public Augustan manner, but it is weakened by Gray's revision and addition of a flaccid, self-indulgent ending. The usual account of the elegy as a masterpiece of "majestic commonplace" does not, however, do full justice to the firm, subtle accuracy of its structure and imagery, which combine to produce in the reader the feeling that, in Johnson's words, "he has always felt" Gray's meaning. In the same way the facile classification of Gray as a "pre-Romantic" can be dangerous, as it tends to distract attention from the technical originality of some of his poems—an originality not followed up by the Romantics—and from the unique quality of his disturbing tone.

Odes, 1757.
Poems, 1768.

The Poems of Thomas Gray, William Collins, Oliver Goldsmith, ed. R. H.
   Lonsdale, London: Longmans; New York: Barnes & Noble, 1969.
Correspondence, ed. P. Toynbee and L. Whibley, 3 vols., Oxford: Claren-
   don Press, 1935.   R.E.

"GREEN, Henry" is the pseudonym of Henry Vincent Yorke (1905–), who was educated at Eton and Oxford. He wrote his first novel, *Blindness* (1926), while still an undergraduate. All his work derives its distinction from the fusion of the prosaic and contemporary with the poetic and symbolic. Using detached observation and an unfailingly accurate dialogue, he explores the problem of happiness and how it is to be attained. His vision is conveyed with freshness, objectivity and accuracy.

Living, 1929.
Party Going, 1939.
Loving, 1945.
Concluding, 1948.
Doting, 1952.   O.K.

GREEN, Matthew (1696–1737), born in a Dissenting family, spent most of his life in the London customhouse. By far his most famous work is *The Spleen* (1737). This most witty and individual long poem was designed to show, writes Green, "What course I take to drive away/ The day-mare Spleen." Its light octosyllabic couplets abound with satire, irony, philosophy and fun. The subtlety and intelligence of his contemplative verse have been admired.

Minor Poets of the Eighteenth Century, ed. H. I'A. Fausset, London: Dent; New York: Dutton, 1930.   J.C.

GREEN, Paul (1894–) was born in Lillington (North Carolina) and educated at the University of North Carolina, where he also subsequently taught. He has worked largely with amateur groups like the Carolina Playmakers and in such ventures as *The Lost Colony* (1937), a historical pageant given annually on Roanoke Island. Green's work is permeated with a sense of defeat and with guilt over the treatment of black Americans in the South. In *In Abraham's Bosom* (1927; *p.* 1926), the mulatto hero, denied by his own father and frustrated in the struggle to make his own way in the world, takes his revenge on his white brother. In *The House of Connolly* (1931), the finest play, a tainted past stands in the way of every attempt on the part of Will Connolly to revive the family fortunes. Green also wrote the antiwar musical *Johnny Johnson* (1936) in collaboration with Kurt Weill.   D.P.M.

GREENE, Graham (1904–) was educated at Berkhamsted School, where his father was headmaster, and at Balliol College, Oxford. He graduated in 1925 and after several false starts became a journalist in Nottingham. He went to London to work on *The Times* until the publication of his first novel, *The Man Within* (1929), when he resigned. Since then he has been a free-lance writer.

Greene was officially a member of the Communist party for only four weeks, but his work is always concerned with social and political situations in the lives of the oppressed. Such problems and characters are, however, primarily influenced by his commitment to the dogma of the Roman Catholic church. Greene was received into that church in 1926, and whether he is writing a spy entertainment or a serious novel (and the early distinction breaks down later in his career), the central theme of the novel is likely to reflect a dogmatic preoccupation which sometimes manages to offend Catholic and non-Catholic alike. *The Power and the Glory* (1940), for example, was condemned by the Holy Office itself. His Catholicism, which is strongly Jansenist, gives an intensity to the material he uses. Its characteristics are seediness, boredom, disgust (particularly in sexual relationships), a preoccupation with hunted men and suicide, and themes of treachery and betrayal. Some critics, also, have found his style too slick. As a journalist Greene certainly learned how to write vividly and powerfully. It seems that his technical expertise and his Catholic dogma can often combine uneasily.

Brighton Rock (1938), which constitutes Greene's first overtly Catholic novel, is the story of Pinkie Brown who has inherited the leadership of a gang of toughs in Brighton. He marries a waitress, Rose, because she can testify to his part in a murder. Pinkie hates sex; and since they are both Catholics, their marriage in a registry office means that they are living in sin. Pursued by justice in the form of Ida Arnold, who represents secular values, Pinkie is finally destroyed by the method he intended for Rose. Greene clearly despises Ida Arnold for her simple morality but some readers are not as certain as he is about this. In any case, Pinkie and Rose are made to carry a theological burden far beyond their abilities as characters. Greene was more successful in *The Power and the Glory* in which the hero is a priest—a whiskey priest, but the last in Mexico—who unwillingly becomes a martyr. In both these novels Greene challenged the conventional definitions of good and evil. Scobie (*The Heart of the Matter*) and Sarah Miles (*The End of the Affair*) continue this exploration of the damned and the saved.

The Quiet American (1955) almost seemed a secular novel, critical of American interference in the East, but its hero, in questioning the "innocence" of the American and his own guilt, gives the novel a strong theological perspective. This novel appeared in the period when Greene wrote two plays, *The Living Room* and *The Potting Shed*, both of which are seriously concerned with religious matters. *Our Man in Havana* (1958), however, a hilarious burlesque of the British Secret Service, treated theology with amusement, a treatment reflected in his next play, *The Complaisant Lover*, which accepted an adulterous situation with some wry compassion. *A Burnt-Out Case* (1961) showed Greene once more in the debate and no nearer an answer. *The Comedians* (1966) and a collection of short stories, *May We Borrow Your Husband?* (1967), show the usual material written about in a tone that combines laughter with the pity and the fear.

England Made Me, 1935.
Brighton Rock, 1938 (*f.* 1948).
The Power and the Glory, 1940 (U.S. title: *The Labyrinthine Ways*; *f.* as *The Fugitive*, 1947; 1962).
The Heart of the Matter, 1948 (*f.* 1953).
The End of the Affair, 1951 (*f.* 1954).
The Lost Childhood and Other Essays, 1951.
The Living Room, 1953 (play).
The Quiet American, 1955 (*f.* 1957).
The Potting Shed, 1957 (play).
Our Man in Havana, 1958 (*f.* 1959).
The Complaisant Lover, 1959 (play).
A Burnt-Out Case, 1961.
Carving a Statue, 1964 (play).
The Comedians, 1966 (*f.* 1967).
May We Borrow Your Husband?, 1967.
Collected Essays, 1969.
Travels with My Aunt, 1969.
A Sort of Life, 1971 (autobiography).   A.P.H.

GREENE, Robert (?1560–92), born in Norwich, went up to St. John's College, Cambridge in 1575, and received his B.A. degree in 1578. He then traveled abroad to Spain and Italy, where he confesses he led a dissolute life. He probably also visited Denmark and Poland before returning to Cambridge where he became an M.A. in 1583. By this time he had already begun to haunt London and had published his first book. In 1585 or 1586 he married "a gentleman's daughter" and lived for a while in Norwich, but, having spent her marriage portion, he deserted his wife on the birth of their child. After a brief period spent in study at Oxford in 1588, Greene settled to a vicious life in London, managing at the same time to keep up a remarkable literary activity. He had published twenty-eight works by the time of his death four years later and ten more appeared posthumously. But he died deserted and in poverty, lodged with a shoemaker; in a last note he charged his wife to reimburse his host, "for if he and his wife had not succoured me I had died in the streets." His death was closely followed by an attack from Harvey in *Four Letters* (1592), which contains grotesque details of Greene's last days. Thomas Nashe retorted, but mainly in order to antagonize Harvey, and offered only a tame defense of Greene. It was the revelations contained in his posthumous confessions that brought him notoriety.

Greene's work was mainly in prose, of two sharply contrasted modes: the euphuistic romance and dialogue on love, for which he was early renowned ("who for that trade was so ordinary about town as Robin Greene?") and the journalistic pamphlet and autobiographical account, the possibilities of which suddenly became apparent to him during his last year. He also wrote five plays, of less interest (apart from their implicit challenge to Marlowe), and is thought to have had a part in the original *Henry VI* plays that Shakespeare took over.

It has been customary to say that the only value in the romances lies in their interspersed lyrics (for which *Menaphon*, to which Nashe wrote a preface, is especially celebrated), but, in fact, the studied movement and alliterative insistence of Greene's prose create a satisfying formality of style ("if virtue draweth one way, vice driveth another way: as profit persuades them, so pleasure provokes them: as wit weigheth, will wresteth …") and the graceful syntax and fluent imagery prompt a comparison with the "uncoined poetry" of Sidney's *Arcadia*. It cannot be denied that the euphuistic manner did contribute to the evolving rhythms of English prose. All Greene's publications up to 1591—twenty in all—were of the romance kind, including a continuation of Lyly's *Euphues* and *Pandosto: The Triumph of Time*, which was particularly popular and which Shakespeare used for the plot of *The Winter's Tale*.

But Greene employed a very different style, direct and unencumbered, for the "coney-catching pamphlets" (1591–92), six pamphlets ostensibly designed to expose the London underworld but actually providing more entertainment than practical information, and thus anticipating the typical provision of sensational journalism. Sensational, too, were the livid and literal accounts of his life of dissipation in London, published shortly after his death, and including admonitions to other writers to mend their "evil ways."

Gwydonius, the Card of Fancy, 1584.
Euphues, his Censure to Philantus, 1587.
Pandosto: The Triumph of Time; or, Dorastus and Fawnia, 1588.
Menaphon: Camilla's Alarm to Sleeping Euphues, 1589.
A Notable Discovery of Cozenage . . ., 1591.
The Second Part of Coney-catching, 1592.
The Third Part of Coney-catching, 1592.
Greene's Groatsworth of Wit, Bought with a Million of Repentance, 1592.
The Honourable History of Friar Bacon and Friar Bungay, 1594.

Complete Works, ed. A. B. Grosart, 15 vols., London: for private circulation, Huth Library, 1881–86.

Plays and Poems, ed. J. C. Collins, 2 vols., Oxford: Clarendon Press, 1905.
Pamphlets, ed. G. B. Harrison, Bodley Head Quartos, London: J. Lane, 1923–27.   D.G.

GREGORY, Isabella Augusta, Lady (1852–1932), born in county Galway (Ireland), became the wife of Sir William Gregory, former governor of Ceylon. From her home at Coole Park she provided inspiration and finance for many young Irish writers, particularly W. B. Yeats, whose efforts she directed towards popular drama and with whom she collaborated. A notable figure in the Irish literary revival, she helped to found the Abbey Theatre, acting as its manager, and as an enthusiastic folklorist she recorded Irish folk tales and legends. Not the least of her services is the series of one-act comedies which she wrote for the Abbey Theatre and which recapture both the prosaic and the poetic qualities of the peasant idiom.

Journals, 1916–30, ed. L. Robinson, New York: Putnam, 1946.
Collected Plays, ed. A. Saddlemeyer, 4 vols., Dublin: Smythe, 1971.
                                                                                    O.K.

GRENFELL, Julian. See **War Poets.**

GREVILLE, Fulke (Lord Brooke) (1554–1628), educated at Shrewsbury and Cambridge, was a close friend of Sidney and Bacon and a favorite of Queen Elizabeth. A Warwickshire member of Parliament, privy councillor and chancellor of the Exchequer (1614–22), he was murdered by a servant. His writings, mainly published after his death, include a biography of Sidney, poems on religious and moral subjects, chamber tragedies and *Caelica* (sonnets). A skeptical thinker rather than stylist, Greville wrote several fine poems which, despite their weight and beauty, have never had due attention.

Poems and Dramas, ed. G. Bullough, 2 vols., Edinburgh: Oliver & Boyd, 1938.   G.P.

GREY, Zane (1875–1939), born in Zanesville (Ohio) was a dentist in New York before he took up writing. His fourth work, *Riders of the Purple Sage* (1912; *f.* 1931; 1941), was a best seller; this and other novels sold 13 million copies in his lifetime.

Keen on historical verisimilitude, Grey was also a mythmaker; his novels often contrast a decadent East with a decent, rugged, morally superior West, where clean-living heroes follow a frontier code of justice. Women appear in these romances, but sex is notably absent; in *The Code of the West* (1934; *f.* as *Home on the Range*, 1935; 1947) the heroine sets out to prove she is really "one of the boys," a Howard Hawks type of woman.

R.W.

GRIEVE, Christopher Murray. See **"MacDiarmid, Hugh."**

GROVE, Frederick Philip. See **Canadian Literature.**

GUNN, Thom (1929–   ) was born and educated in Gravesend (Kent) and later, after two years of national service, completed his education at Cambridge and in California at Stanford University. Since 1954 he has lived in California, though he has spent periods in Paris, Rome, Berlin and Texas. While writing poetry, for which he won a Somerset Maugham Prize in 1958 and an Arts Council Award in 1959, he has also taught English at various universities and worked as a poetry reviewer.

Since the publication of his first volume of verse, *Fighting Terms* (1954), Gunn has steadily established a reputation as a serious writer whose poetic manner is often violent and energetic. Using topical themes, drawn from city life as well as, in his later poetry, the objects of more restrained observation, he presents his distinctive view of the human condition. He is concerned with the meaninglessness of life, the failure of love and desire, and the power of the human will to impose order upon chaos. The manner of his early poetry, which is often tough, cynical and highly metaphorical, has gradually become more restrained, and in *Touch* (1967) the tone of subdued meditation predominates.

Fighting Terms, 1954; revised, 1962.
The Sense of Movement, 1957.
My Sad Captains, 1961.
Positives (with Ander Gunn), 1966.
Touch, 1967.
Moly, 1971.

O.K.

H

HABINGTON, William (1605–54), born into a Roman Catholic family, was educated on the Continent at St. Omer and Paris. On his return to London he formed a wide circle of acquaintances among Catholic writers. He published a successful play, *The Queen of Aragon* (1640), occasional verse and two historical studies, but is remembered for the collection of love poems in *Castara* (1634; enlarged, 1639–40), his name for Lucy Herbert, a distant relative to George Herbert and Habington's future wife. Habington often rises above the general insipidity of the rhetorically conventional and sentimental manner of similar Cavalier poets.

Poems, ed. K. Allott, London: Liverpool Univ. Press, 1948 (includes a biography). H.N.D.

HAGGARD, Sir H. (Henry) Rider. See **African Literature.**

HAKLUYT, Richard (?1553–1616), of Welsh descent, was born in Herefordshire, studied at Westminster School and in 1577 became a clergyman. His clerical life took him to Suffolk, Lincolnshire and finally Westminster, but in his imaginative life he traveled with the English explorers—with Sir Hugh Willoughby in search of Cathay, with Sir John Hawkins on his voyage to Guinea and the West Indies, with John Davys on his Arctic explorations and with Drake on his circumnavigation of the world. His accounts of these and other English voyagers were collected in the two editions of *The Principal Navigations, Voyages, and Discoveries of the English Nation* (1589; enlarged, 1598–1600). Hakluyt's rich, sinewy prose brought dignity and epic splendor to narratives of commercial exploration and mercantile greed. He is among the first of those Anglican clergymen who, devoting themselves patiently to the study and writing of history, held in mind the scholarly intention of bringing "to light many rare and worthy monuments which long have lain scattered in musty corners."

The Principal Navigations, ed. W. Raleigh, 12 vols., Glasgow: MacLehose, 1903–05. C.P.

HALIBURTON, T. C. (Thomas Chandler). See **Canadian Literature.**

HALIFAX, George Savile, 1st Marquess of (1633–95) was educated mainly by his mother, and spent a career close to the center of power. A supporter of Charles II, he was hostile to James II and played an important part in the accession of William III. Politically an honest, conscientious moderate, Savile was a privy councillor, ennobled in 1668, made marquess in 1682, and lord privy seal in 1689. As essayist and pamphleteer Savile has few seventeenth-century equals; his thought is clear and incisive, his style sharply urbane. His best-known work is *The Character of a Trimmer* (1688), which introduced this latter word into English political language. (See also **Political Pamphlets.**)

Complete Works, ed. W. Raleigh, Oxford: Clarendon Press, 1912 (omits *Observations upon a Late Libel*—ed. H. Macdonald, Cambridge: Cambridge Univ. Press, 1940).   G.P.

HALL, Edward. See **Renaissance Humanism.**

HALL, Joseph (1574–1656) came of a poor Leicestershire family. He entered Cambridge, became a doctor of divinity in 1610 and gained a reputation as a scholar. He was successively bishop of Exeter (1627) and of Norwich (1641). He was impeached in 1641 and his revenue sequestrated in 1643. After this he lived in seclusion. His voluminous and varied works have been frequently reprinted, but his Juvenalian satires, *Virgidemiarum Sex Libri* (1597–98), his Theophrastan *Characters of Virtues and Vices* (1608), the first to be written in English, and his satire *Mundus Alter et Idem* (c.1605), translated as *The Discovery of a New World* (c. 1608), are especially remembered.

Works, ed. P. Wynter, 10 vols., Oxford: Clarendon Press, 1863.
Poems, ed. A. Davenport, Liverpool: Liverpool Univ. Press, 1949.
                                                                H.N.D.

HAMMETT, Dashiell (1894–1961) was a writer of detective stories who had been a detective himself. "A little man going forward... through mud and blood and death and deceit—as callous and brutal as necessary..." is how he described a typical detective. His novels like *Red Harvest* (1929), *The Maltese Falcon* (1930; *f.* 1931; as *Satan Met a Lady*, 1937; 1941) and *The Thin Man* (1932; *f.* 1934) sought to reflect this reality and invented the genre of the "hard-boiled" story. During the McCarthy era Hammett went to jail rather than collaborate with forces he felt were antidemocratic.   J.L.M.

HARDY, Frank. See **Australian Literature.**

HARDY, Thomas (1840–1928) was born in Upper Bockhampton (Dorset) and did not go to school until he was eight. He left at sixteen to be articled to an ecclesiastical architect, but was assiduous in educating himself, even at one time studying leaders in *The Times* as part of a plan to improve his prose style. From 1862 to 1867 he lived in London, reasonably successful at architecture but also convinced that his natural bent was for literature, especially poetry. He left London for Dorchester and turned to writing prose fiction. Although his first novel, "The Poor Man and the Lady" (written 1868), was rejected by publishers, George Meredith advised him to drop social satire and write another novel. From *Desperate Remedies* (1871) he was successful as a writer, despite difficulties with prudish Victorian reviewers over his relatively direct treatment of topics usually veiled in euphemism. In 1874 he married Emma Gifford and was able to live by his pen, eventually building himself a house, Max Gate, near Dorchester. Emma died in 1912 and two years later he married Florence Dugdale, who collaborated with him in writing his life.

After *Jude the Obscure* (1896) Hardy returned to the more austere discipline of writing poems, which may never have been widely popular but which have been an acknowledged influence: "Hardy was my poetical father," wrote W. H. Auden (Hardy centennial issue, *The Southern Review*, 1940). Even Hardy's prose fiction, much more frequently read and studied, derives a great deal of its power from his poetic vision and style. Regrets for the defeat of the old rural order in *The Mayor of Casterbridge*, a sense of the difficulties of the human predicament in *Tess of the d'Urbervilles*, feelings of individual loneliness in *Jude the Obscure*, the large, ironic perspective in almost all his work—such aspects of his total vision can control the texture of his writing down to the smallest detail. *The Dynasts* is therefore in some ways the inevitable conclusion: a massive epic drama, an "Iliad of Europe," designed to convey and embody Hardy's philosophy of the individual struggling against what is determined by "the immanent will," a form of writing eccentric, original and unfettered by the realism and probability so often demanded of the novel. Even as a drama, *The Dynasts* was, he wrote, "intended simply for mental performance." Towards the end of his career honors, including the Order of Merit, were heaped upon him and Max Gate became a place of pilgrimage in his lifetime.

Hardy's writing has been considered, with justice, to be a mixture of good and bad. His resort to accident and coincidence in his novels can irritate readers while they are forced to admire the immense significance he communicates; his prose style can be perceptive and crude in a single sentence. An earlier generation of critics, while quite conscious of his greatness, did not hesitate to condemn what they saw as unforgivable faults. More recently a critic like John Holloway asks readers to ignore the almost necessary lack of realism in Hardy's novels in favor of "those larger rhythms which finally expand into the total movement of the novel, transmitting the author's sense of life, the forces that operate through it, the values that chart it out and make it what it is" (*From Jane Austen to Joseph Conrad*, ed. R. Rathburn and M. Steinmann, Jr., Minneapolis: Univ. of Minnesota Press, 1959).

He himself used to emphasize that his art was no simple reflection of life:

> I want to see the deeper reality underlying the scenic, the expression of what are sometimes called abstract imaginings. . . . The exact truth as to material fact ceases to be of importance in art—it is a student's style—the style of a period when the mind is serene and unawakened to the tragical mysteries of life; . . .

His vision was the reverse of suave and assured; his theory of expression insisted upon imaginative realism and the avoidance of the dully documentary. In his writings as a whole we see the transition to a disturbed modern world, but we also perceive his individual wisdom and compassion for human beings in their distress.

(See also **Romantic Movement, The; War Poets.**)

Desperate Remedies, 1871.
Under the Greenwood Tree, 1872.
A Pair of Blue Eyes, 1873 (*s.* 1872–73).
Far from the Madding Crowd, 1874 (*f.* 1966).
The Hand of Ethelberta, 1876 (*s.* 1875–76).
The Return of the Native, 1878.
The Trumpet-Major, 1880.
A Laodicean, 1881 (*s.* 1880–81).
Two on a Tower, 1882.
The Mayor of Casterbridge, 1886.
The Woodlanders, 1887 (*s.* 1886–87).
Wessex Tales, 1888.
Tess of the d'Urbervilles, 1891.
A Group of Noble Dames, 1891.
Life's Little Ironies, 1894.
Jude the Obscure, 1896 (*s.* 1894–95).

The Well-Beloved, 1897 (*s.* 1892).
The Dynasts: A Drama of the Napoleonic Wars, 1903–08.
A Changed Man and Other Tales, 1913.

Novels, Wessex edition, 24 vols., London: Macmillan, 1912–31.
Collected Poems, London: Macmillan, 1919; 4th edition, 1930.
Notebooks, ed. E. Hardy, London: Hogarth Press; New York: St. Martin's
Press, 1955.
Personal Writings, ed. H. Orel, Lawrence: Univ. of Kansas Press, 1966;
London: Macmillan, 1967.   J.C.

HARPUR, Charles. See **Australian Literature.**

HARRIS, Alexander. See **Australian Literature.**

HARRIS, George Washington (1814–69) was born at Allegheny City
(Pennsylvania). His family soon after moved to Knoxville (Tennessee) and
he was later apprenticed to a silversmith. While still in his teens he became
a skilled riverboat pilot and began to write newspaper pieces. Later he
became a postmaster, worked in a foundry and after the Civil War
turned to railway engineering. His only published volume appeared in
1867, *Sut Lovingood: Yarns Spun by a "Nat'ral Born Durn'd Fool."* Mostly a
collection of various earlier newspaper and magazine pieces, it has an
earthy, Rabelaisian flavor, and was immediately popular. Mark Twain
knew the yarns well and was an admirer of Harris.   D.N.C.

HARRIS, Joel Chandler (1848–1908) was born and raised near
Eatonton (Georgia). He worked on various newspapers before joining
the Atlanta *Constitution* in 1876, where he remained for twenty-four
years. It was in the *Constitution* that he published the first Uncle Remus
story, based on the Negro folklore tales he had listened to as a boy.
Immediately successful, Harris continued with "Brer Rabbit, Brer Fox
and the Tar Baby." In 1880 he published *Uncle Remus, His Songs and His
Sayings*, and in 1883 a second series of tales, *Nights with Uncle Remus*.
Other Uncle Remus tales followed, and also numerous other stories and
two novels.   D.N.C.

HARRIS, Wilson. See **Caribbean Literature.**

HART, Moss (1904–61) was born in New York City, and became
famous chiefly for plays written in collaboration with George S. Kaufman,
Once in a Lifetime (1930; *f.* 1932), *Merrily We Roll Along* (1934), *You Can't*

Take It with You (*p.* 1936; *f.* 1938) and *I'd Rather Be Right* (1937). He wrote libretti for some Irving Berlin revues and a sophisticated musical comedy, *Lady in the Dark* (1941), with music by Kurt Weill and lyrics by Ira Gershwin. His own plays, though often full of warmth and humanity, were never quite so successful. They included *Winged Victory* (1943; *f.* 1944), *Christopher Blake* (1946; *f.* as *The Decision of Christopher Blake*, 1948), and *Light Up the Sky* (1948). *Act One* (1959) was a best-selling autobiography. He directed the popular musical *My Fair Lady*.   R.W.

HARTE, Bret (1836–1902), was born at Albany (New York). He left school early, and in 1854 went to San Francisco where he was involved in unsuccessful mining ventures. He began to write humorous sketches, and edited an anthology of Californian verse. In 1867 he published *The Lost Galleon and Other Tales*, and his satirical parody of other writers, *Condensed Novels*. In 1868 appeared "The Luck of Roaring Camp" and in 1869 "The Outcasts of Poker Flat" (*f.* 1937; 1952). In 1871 he moved to Boston, but this was not a success for him artistically, for his subsequent work is not as good as the early stories. Finally he moved to Germany (as U.S. consul) and then to Britain, where he wrote further stories, novels and plays.

Complete Works, 10 vols., London: Chatto & Windus, 1880–1900.
Writings, 20 vols., Boston: Houghton Mifflin, 1902–14.
Letters, ed. G. B. Harte, Boston: Houghton Mifflin, 1926.   D.N.C

HARTLEY, David (1705–57), educated at Cambridge, became a physician instead of a clergyman because of religious scruples. His treatise, *Observations on Man* (1749), interprets human behavior in terms of a mechanistic psychology influenced by Hobbes and Locke, in which mental events are seen as the product of vibrations in the brain ultimately caused by external stimuli. As a consequence the complex of thought and feeling in any person is a network of mental relationships (associations) occasioned by the continuous activation of new and reactivation of old patterns of vibration. Hartley's ideas had a strong influence on utilitarianism (see **Bentham, Jeremy**), for they naturally led to a belief in human perfectibility through favorable alterations in education and environment.
                                                              M.P.

HARTLEY, L. P. (Leslie Poles) (1895–   ), born at Peterborough, was educated at Harrow and Balliol College, Oxford, and served during the First World War with the Norfolk Regiment. He started as a writer of

tales of terror with *Night Fears* (1924) before turning to the novel with
Simonetta Perkins (1925).

Hartley is a prolific and uneven novelist, but his best work is extremely
good and all of it has considerable interest. His first novel to rouse really
widespread interest was *The Shrimp and the Anemone* (1944), followed by
the sequels, *The Sixth Heaven* (1946) and *Eustace and Hilda* (1947) (published together, with an interpolated section, as *Eustace and Hilda* in 1958).
These beautifully written novels trace the relationship between the
retiring and insecure Eustace and his dominant elder sister, Hilda, through
childhood and early adult life. They show a sensitive awareness not only
of character and relationship, but also of the social world; they inquire
into the very nature of individual independence. The next novel to make
a considerable and thoroughly justified impact was *The Go-Between*
(1953). Here Hartley returns to childhood and to Edwardian days; in a
firmly realized social order, that in itself embodies security, he sets a
study of innocence suddenly overwhelmed by experience. In creating the
child, he captures both the conscious and the unconscious essence of
childhood; there is no condescension, no false naïveté, but the reader,
knowing more than the child, nevertheless sees and experiences with him.
The novel leaves the reader with a horrified sense of the reality of evil
akin to that left by some novels of Henry James. Other novels of great
interest are *The Boat* (1950) and *A Perfect Woman* (1955).

Night Fears, 1924 (short stories).
Simonetta Perkins, 1925.
The Shrimp and the Anemone, 1944.
The Sixth Heaven, 1946.
Eustace and Hilda, 1947.
The Boat, 1950.
The Go-Between, 1953 (*f.* 1971).
A Perfect Woman, 1955.
The Hireling, 1957.
Facial Justice, 1960.
The Brickfield, 1964.
The Betrayed, 1966.
Poor Clare, 1968.
The Love-Adept, 1969.
My Sisters' Keeper, 1970.
Mrs. Carteret Receives, 1971.
The Harness Room, 1971.

Collected Short Stories, ed. Lord D. Cecil, London: H. Hamilton, 1968.

C.H.

HAWES, Stephen (?1475–?1523) was educated at Oxford and traveled in Europe before becoming groom of the chamber to Henry VII by 1502. He died sometime before 1530. Hawes continues the aureate style, allegorical mode and admonitory function of poetry, following Lydgate. His earliest work extant is probably *The Example of Virtue*, printed by Wynkyn de Worde in 1512, but his best known is the allegorical pilgrimage, *The Pastime of Pleasure*, completed in 1506 and dedicated to the king. The work contains many medieval themes and conventions and suggests that a poet's task is to veil truth under "cloudy figures."

The Pastime of Pleasure, printed by Wynkyn de Worde, 1509; ed. W. E.
   Mead, London: Early English Text Society, 1928.   A.D.M.

HAWKER, R. S. (Robert Stephen) (1803–75) was educated at Cheltenham Grammar School and Pembroke and Magdalen Colleges, Oxford. In 1834 he became vicar of Morwenstow in North Cornwall and remained there till his death. He was an early and exotic Anglo-Catholic, whose mysticism is found in his poetry. The three main influences upon his work were Cornish scenery, romantic and especially Cornish Arthurian legend, and the Catholic church—in particular, devotion to the Virgin. These combine with his mysticism and philosophy in the single chant he composed of his most ambitious poetic venture, *The Quest of the Sangraal* (1864). Many of his shorter poems are written in ballad measure, of which the best known is his earliest, "The Song of the Western Men" (1826).

Collected Poems, ed. J. G. Godwin, 1879; ed. A. Wallis, London: J. Lane,
   1899.
Life and Letters, ed. C. E. Byles, London and New York: J. Lane, 1905.
                                                              A.P.

HAWKES, John (1925–   ) was born in Stamford (Connecticut) and educated at Harvard. He has held a variety of academic appointments. Hawkes is an uncomfortable and often unpleasant novelist who deals in a world of nightmare, violence and dream in landscapes of inescapable desolation, against which the author opposes only a perfection of style. His first novel, *The Cannibal* (1949), is a death-haunted vision that analyzes the repetitive violence shown in a history of Germany from the First World War to a world of Nazi domination. *The Beetle Leg* (1951) has futile man in the American West failing to affect the inevitable encroachment of desert and hostile land. Hawkes's finest novel, *Second Skin* (1964), is a complex consideration of the disguises that man assumes. Its principal character, Skipper, tries to come to terms with a world where his whole family has either committed suicide or been murdered. Man's powerlessness and his freedom are ironically juxtaposed. Hawkes's is a bleak but honest and powerful vision of man.   D.V.W.

HAWTHORNE, Nathaniel (1804–64) was born at Salem (Massachusetts) of an old Puritan family. One of his ancestors was a judge at the Salem witch trials in 1692. His father, a sea captain, died on a voyage in 1808. After education at Bowdoin College (1821–25) Hawthorne led a withdrawn life at home, developing and testing his literary skill and ambition. He published a novel, *Fanshawe*, at his own expense in 1828, a mild Gothic romance set in Bowdoin College, which he soon after tried to suppress. From 1831 onwards he began to publish tales in magazines, particularly *The Token*, edited by Samuel Goodrich, which included some of his most powerful, such as "My Kinsman, Major Molineux." He also undertook hack magazine and encyclopedia work for Goodrich in Boston (1836–37). His writing was mostly anonymous until the publication of *Twice-Told Tales* (1837) which brought him immediate recognition as a new and important American author. He published widely in magazines, produced several children's books, and a larger edition of *Twice-Told Tales* came out in 1842. A further collection, *Mosses from an Old Manse*, followed in 1846. With literary achievement and success Hawthorne partially emerged from his isolation. He was involved, somewhat skeptically, in the Brook Farm Utopian experiment in 1840; after a long engagement he married Sophia Peabody in 1842; and his need for income beyond what his fiction could earn led him with the help of friends to secure appointments from the ruling Democratic party as weigher and gauger in the Boston Custom House in 1839–40 and then customs surveyor in Salem from 1846 to 1849. Hawthorne dealt with the latter experience in the first part of *The Scarlet Letter*. He became acquainted, while living in Concord, with most of the New England literati, including Emerson and Thoreau, but his most important friendship was with Herman Melville. The relationship cooled in the later 1850s, but by then both men had passed through their most productive periods. Melville dedicated his masterpiece, *Moby-Dick*, to Hawthorne. Hawthorne published his first major novel, and probably his greatest, *The Scarlet Letter*, in 1850. From then on the "romance," as he preferred to call it, was to be his chief genre. A final collection of tales, *The Snow Image*, came in 1851.

The Scarlet Letter, like many of his tales, was set in the New England past. Through his evocation of early Puritan Boston and his story of the consequences of the minister Dimmesdale's adultery with one of his parishioners, Hester Prynne, Hawthorne with characteristic reticence and ambiguity dealt with most of his main themes—the Puritan inheritance, the formation of a distinctive "new world" experience, guilt and isolation, possession, the connection of private process (the "heart") and public, and, above all, the ambiguous need to reveal but not to reveal all. Hawthorne turned to the contemporary world with *The House of the Seven Gables* (1851) and *The Blithedale Romance* (1852). The former deals with the working out of a hereditary curse in a New England family, while *The Blithedale Romance*, his most attractive novel, is based on the Brook Farm experience. It is notable for the exploitation of first-person narration. His best-known children's books also belong to this period; *A Wonder Book* and *Tanglewood Tales* are gentle versions of Greek myth.

After writing a campaign biography of the successful presidential candidate Franklin Pierce, an old college friend, Hawthorne was appointed American consul at Liverpool, a lucrative post, in 1853. He spent the next six years abroad, four of them in England and the other two, after resigning as consul, traveling on the Continent, where he spent a considerable time in Italy in contact with artist exiles, amongst them the Brownings. His last completed novel, *The Marble Faun* (1860), was set in Italy and has an "international" theme of American expatriation and entanglement with European "evil." After his return to America the last four years of his life were rather melancholy. Aware of failing powers, in ill health and worried about the Civil War, Hawthorne made repeated attempts at other novels, all of which were unfinished. A book of impressions of England, *Our Old Home*, was published in 1863. He died in 1864 while on a trip with Pierce to recover health and spirits.

Melville was the first to emphasize the doubleness of Hawthorne's work. Like D. H. Lawrence later (in *Studies in Classic American Literature*), he distinguished a surface, gentle, "babyfaced" Hawthorne from an intense inner Hawthorne who may be glimpsed through that surface, profoundly concerned with the "blackness" and the "diabolism" of life. Such a duality lies at the heart of his fascination and achievement. Whatever the conditioning factors—a Calvinistic sense of doom, a sectional or ancestral guilt or curse, reaction against current optimistic values and inhibitions—the power of his work lies in an obsessive engagement with and evasion of depths of experience. The desperate moral of *The Scarlet Letter*, with its crucial qualification, is characteristic: "Be true! Be true! Be true! Show freely to the world, if not your worst, yet some trait whereby the worst may be inferred!" There is thus a critical "Hawthorne problem"; too much of his work seems thin, haunted trivia, romance and allegorical trappings, surface imagery and ambiguity, not sufficiently connected with inferable truths.

Probably the most perfect work lies in the tales. "Young Goodman Brown" and "My Kinsman, Major Molineux," both early, have a concentrated power and economy never reached by the novels. Both deal with a young man whose simple grasp of life is upset by an appalling opening-up of experience. Many of the tales, however, are weak or incoherent. Again, Hawthorne's humor generally is too labored and whimsical, but there are also fine racy stories such as "Mrs. Bullfrog" and "Mr Higginbotham's Catastrophe." "Molineux" gains some of its power from the interaction of the young man's initiation with the confusion of Revolutionary Boston. It is this feeling for the public resonance of individual crisis which gets its chance in the longer fiction. With length came the opportunity to place both individual psychology and social realities in time, to get at the process of the heart and the process of history. In *The Scarlet Letter* Hawthorne is able to connect the examination of the "interior of a heart," of Dimmesdale and Hester in particular, with the formation of the Puritan state. In what Hawthorne called a "hell-fired" story the couple's "sin" is both productive and alienating, and the horror at their complexities of reaction mixes with a more general horror at the antecedents of community and state. The theme of personal revelation and intrusion and violation, particularly focused through the doctor Chillingworth, substantiates the greater theme of the appalling secrets of history, and the guilt of the characters is matched by the writer's guilt at his means and burden of discovery. Hawthorne's method—the use of a shocked, fascinated authorial voice, of an apparently evasive mixture of ambiguity, alternative explanations, suggestive imagery, allegory, myth, legend, superstition, rumor—is both a defense against and a dramatization of these preoccupations. Inevitably, the strategy breaks down at times, most obviously near the end with its desperate search through the mysterious child Pearl for some kind of cheerful ending. This pressure to find a good result, however, is not merely superficial. In some ways "fortunate falls" as part of the economies of history were the most appalling discoveries of all.

The House of the Seven Gables was a deliberate attempt to write a "sunnier" novel. It has an unambiguously good heroine, Phoebe, who is insulated from the family guilt, and by marrying the descendent of her family's traditional enemies and victims is involved in a generally unconvincing attempt to cancel or redeem the past. The theme is never fully grasped and the novel is burdened with trivial imagery and fancifulness. There is some power in the figure of the young man Holgrave; and the best scenes in the book concern Clifford Pyncheon, a character emerging from seclusion into life too late, desperately pursuing and fleeing its embrace. There is a real vivacity, however, in *The Blithedale Romance*. This is the most naturalistic of the novels, although there are some awkward fanciful elements. A real liberation of expression accompanies the the use of first-person narration. Miles Coverdale's hopes of love, like the ambitions of the Utopian community, are doomed to failure. There is a typical hope for and horror at a new start, a sense of the dust of endless deluded generations, an inescapable but unbearable past. There is a particular concern with the fate of women: Hawthorne created in Zenobia one of the most striking of his "dark ladies," passionate without room for her passion. Her end is tragic, as the novel is in general, yet there is an overall buoyancy of tone, of hope remembered and hope deferred, which make it Hawthorne's most poised achievement, the most truly comic of his fictions.

The Marble Faun, on the other hand, shows clear evidence of a loss of creativity. Much of it is guidebook material—it did, in fact, become a favorite for American tourists. Horror and fascination for the ruins, art and history of Italy are mediated through timid expatriate American sensibilities. The "spotless" New England heroine Hilda, who does copies of the masters better than the originals, rescues an American sculptor from the fatal attraction of Italy. The American couple are contrasted with a European couple who have a real knowledge of and complicity in the "evil" of Europe. Unfortunately, this evil is never convincing; too much of the novel is tired and second-hand. Laboriously, Italy (and Europe), like parts of the American past, are ambiguously cast off, or disinfected and made safe. What is most interesting is the register, insufficiently ironic, of American attitudes to Europe, with its clear influence, as with much of Hawthorne's work, on Henry James. There is also the explicit engagement with the notion of the "fortunate fall" which is finally dismissed as another European horror.

Hawthorne's other work is relatively minor. Versions of the unfinished last romances were published after his death, but far more appealing are the various *Notebooks*, although these first appeared in bowdlerized form.

Fanshawe, 1828.
Twice-Told Tales, 1837; enlarged, 1842.
Grandfather's Chair, 1841 (children's book).
Mosses from an Old Manse, 1846.
The Scarlet Letter, 1850 (*f.* 1926; 1934).
The House of the Seven Gables, 1851 (*f.* 1940).
The Snow Image, 1851.
The Blithedale Romance, 1852.
A Wonder Book for Girls and Boys, 1852.
Life of Franklin Pierce, 1852.
Tanglewood Tales, 1853.
The Marble Faun, 1860 (U.K. title: *Transformation*).
Our Old Home, 1863.

Passages from the French and Italian Notebooks, ed. Mrs Hawthorne, 1872.
Septimius Felton, 1872.
The Dolliver Romance, 1876.

Dr Grimshawe's Secret, ed. J. Hawthorne, 1883; ed. E. H. Davidson,
   Cambridge, Mass.: Harvard Univ. Press, 1954.
The American Notebooks, ed. R. Stewart, New Haven: Yale Univ. Press;
   London: Oxford Univ. Press, 1932.
The English Notebooks, ed. R. Stewart, New York: Modern Language
   Association of America; London: Oxford Univ. Press, 1941.

Complete Works, Riverside edition, ed. G. B. Lathrop, 13 vols., Boston:
   Houghton, Mifflin, 1883.
Works, ed. W. Charvat, R. H. Pearce, and C. M. Simpson, Columbus:
   Ohio State Univ. Press, 1964– .   D.H.

HAYLEY, William (1745–1820) was born at Chichester (Sussex) and
educated at Eton and Trinity Hall, Cambridge. He settled at Eartham
(Sussex) in 1774. After early dramatic and poetic ventures he published *The
Triumphs of Temper* (1781) which was popular long enough to be ridiculed
by Byron years later in *English Bards and Scotch Reviewers*. Hayley was the
friend of Cowper, for whom he secured a pension from William Pitt the
younger, another friend. For a time Hayley assisted Blake, who illustrated
his *Ballads Founded on Anecdotes of Animals* (1805). He wrote lives of Milton
and his friends Cowper and the artist John Romney (1794; 1803; 1809).
He declined the laureateship when Warton died.

Poems and Plays, 6 vols., London: Cadell, 1785.   W.R.

HAZLITT, William (1778–1830) was the son of a Unitarian minister.
He was educated for a time at Hackney College to follow his father's
profession, but changed his mind and returned home in about 1795 to a
life of private study. His father introduced him to Coleridge, whom he
visited at Nether Stowey in 1798, and acquaintance with Wordsworth
and Lamb followed. Hazlitt studied painting for a time, and then
philosophy, and he described the tenor of these early years with memorable vividness in several of his later essays. His first publication was a
ponderous *Essay on the Principles of Human Action* (1805). In 1808 he married
Sarah Stoddart and was soon engaged in writing for London newspapers
and Leigh Hunt's *The Examiner*. His debut as a theater critic coincided
with Kean's first London appearances. He also gave several series of public
lectures.

   The first collection of Hazlitt's essays from *The Examiner, The Round*

Table, appeared in 1817, followed in the same year by *Characters of Shakespear's Plays*. He joined the staff of *The London Magazine* when it started publication and many of his best occasional essays were done for it. *Table Talk* (1821–22), *The Spirit of the Age* (1825), perhaps his best work, and *The Plain Speaker* (1826) collected the essays of these later years. Hazlitt assembled his theater criticism in *A View of the English Stage* (1818) and wasted his last years on a four-volume *Life of Napoleon* (1828–30), which shows the tenacity of his youthful revolutionary enthusiasms and his unhappiness in the reactionary climate of English politics in the 1820s. His first marriage ended in a divorce (1822) and the second was a failure. Emotional torment is painfully evident in his *Liber Amoris* (1823).

Hazlitt's characteristic work mostly belongs to his last fifteen years and is nearly all in essay form. Despite his early interest in philosophy he provides no very clear system of aesthetics. The clue to his approach may rather be found in his painter's eye for effective detail, his love of individuality and his constant habit of returning to the pleasures of memory. He read little in his latter years and loved to write of the enjoyment he recalled from long-past readings of great literature. Consequently, his literary criticism often shows a "filtered" quality, the judgment being primarily of his recollected feelings of early pleasure in a work, so that its characteristics are seen clothed in the mass of his private associations and enjoyment. Yet he was a trenchant critic when necessary; presented with a new book, he responded at once to its special characteristics and clearly identified its particular qualities. His preference for recollected artistic experience was due to personal emotional pressures, not laziness of mind, and it is perhaps significant that his most succinct analytical criticism can be found in the essays on his contemporaries in *The Spirit of the Age* and in the dramatic criticisms, where he was denied easy access to his store of private recollections. As a descriptive critic Hazlitt wrote memorably on every conceivable subject and the autobiographical essays of his last ten years come straight from the heart. His style is vigorous, fresh, discursive and wholly individual.

(See also **Essays.**)

The Round Table, 1817.
Characters of Shakespear's Plays, 1817.
A View of the English Stage, 1818.
Lectures on the English Poets, 1818.
Lectures on the English Comic Writers, 1819.
Lectures Chiefly on the Dramatic Literature of the Age of Elizabeth, 1820.
Table Talk, 1821–22.
Liber Amoris, 1823.
The Spirit of the Age, 1825.

The Plain Speaker, 1826.

The Life of Napoleon Buonaparte, 4 vols., 1828–30.

Complete Works, ed. P. P. Howe, 21 vols., London: Dent, 1930–34.

W.R.

HEARNE, John. See **Caribbean Literature.**

HEBER, Reginald. See **Hymns.**

HEINLEIN, Robert. See **Science Fiction.**

HELLER, Joseph (1923–   ) was educated at New York University and Columbia and was a Fulbright scholar at Oxford. He worked in public relations after serving in the air force during the war. *Catch-22* (1961; *f.* 1970) is a shaggy dog story that constantly starts and stops, as do the lives of its characters, Yossarian, Hungry Joe, Nately and Orr. They are airmen stationed on a Mediterranean island whose quota of flying missions is constantly being raised by the self-seeking generals, Dreedle and Peckem. The novel indicts modern war and commercialism through lunatic humor, the only alternative being total despair.

J.L.M.

HELLMAN, Lillian (1905–   ) was born in New Orleans. Initially, her family was relatively affluent because of her mother's dowry, but after moving to New York, they had to struggle for a time until her father became a successful traveling salesman. She attended New York University briefly (1923–24) before joining Horace Liveright as a publisher's reader. In the 1930s she went to Hollywood where she read film scripts for MGM. Her first play, *The Children's Hour* (1934; *f.* as *These Three,* 1936; as *The Loudest Whisper,* 1962) was followed by *Days to Come* (1936), *The Little Foxes* (1939; *f.* 1941) and *Watch on The Rhine* (1941; *f.* 1943). She has also written a number of film scripts, the book of a musical, *Candide* (1956), and an autobiography, *An Unfinished Woman* (1969). Her last dramatic work was *Toys in the Attic* (1960; *f.* 1963).

Her reputation rests on a relatively small number of works, primarily *The Children's Hour* and *The Little Foxes,* but these are, nevertheless, enough to establish her as one of the more important American dramatists. Her view of the world and of human conduct is bleak and pitiless, if not quite despairing. The motives that figure prominently in her work are petty, and seldom pretty—spite, envy, malice and a brutal indifference to the feelings of others. Although social themes frequently recur—for example, the framing of a labor leader for murder in a strike-ridden town in *Days to Come*, or the ruthless exploitation of the South by Northern industrialists in *The Little Foxes*—she presents less a critique of society than an analysis of the way in which individuals allow themselves to become the accomplices, willing or unwilling, of evil.

Six Plays, New York: Modern Library, 1960.   D.P.M.

HEMANS, Mrs. Felicia Dorothea (1793–1835), née Browne, showed her precocity as an author in her *Poems* (1808). In 1812 she made an unhappy marriage which broke up six years later. Much of her life was spent in Dublin and she produced practically a volume a year of fluent, limpid, "sensibilitous" but unmemorable poetry. In *Modern Greece* (1817), for example, she shows the Romantic love of picturesqueness and sentiment. At her best she has a little of Campbell's and Scott's ability to write plainly but strongly about masculine emotion. The second edition of *The Forest Sanctuary and Other Poems* (1829) contains "Casabianca" ("The boy stood on the burning deck"). Mrs. Hemans was immensely popular and Victorian reprints of her poems are common.

Works, ed. H. Hughes (sister) (with memoir), 7 vols., Edinburgh: Blackwood, 1839.   W.R.

HEMINGWAY, Ernest (1899–1961) was born in Oak Park, a middleclass suburb of Chicago; his father was a doctor, his mother educated, musical, religious. He grew up there and, in summer, in the Michigan woods, where his ideal of a physically active, natural life began to form. After school he entered journalism on the Kansas City *Star*, a training that was to shape his precise, factualized literary style. In the First World War, rejected for active service, he went to the Italian front as an ambulance driver and was severely wounded; this experience he saw as a bleak initiation, and around it he focused many of his presumptions about man's vulnerability, isolation and exposure and his need for courage and control. Returning disenchanted to postwar America, he joined the Toronto *Star*, managed a free-lance assignment in Paris, and began writing seriously there. He entered the large literary expatriate enclave (see his *A Moveable Feast*); contact with Gertrude Stein, Fitzgerald, Pound and Ford helped to confirm the stylistic authority of the pared-down, puristic, exposed style he was maturing. His first books, from expatriate presses, were stories and poems, the former largely about his surrogate, Nick Adams, dealing with the Michigan woods and war. In 1926 he followed a savage, comic, ungenerous parody of his friend Sherwood Anderson, *Torrents of Spring*, with *The Sun Also Rises*, the "lost generation" novel about expatriate Paris which made his name. This, the stories of *Men without Women* and his novel about the Italian front, *A Farewell to Arms*, established him as a classic explorer of modern experience and disturbance, a kind of self-taught existentialist of the stark, bleak, cultureless world the war had left. His writing, ranging in setting from the exposure to natural power and cruelty in the Michigan woods to his postwound, postwar vision of anxiety, tension and deprivation around the battlefield or in the city, was a stoic tragedy of modernity.

As two following books of reportage, *Death in the Afternoon* and *Green Hills of Africa*, indicated, Hemingway saw life and writing as intimately connected. The writer, like the journalist or bullfighter, faced the intenser moments of reality and responded with appropriate control, accuracy and integrity. Hemingway was not the writer as intellectual but as doer; and the authenticity of his writing had to derive from the authenticity of his living. He traveled widely, constantly seeking experience, exploring a distinctive terrain (Spain, Florida, Italy, Africa) appropriate to the challenges from nature he wished to encounter, fishing, flying, hunting, fighting, drinking and—four times—marrying. In the 1930s he settled at Key West, and later in Cuba, but he managed to report the Spanish Civil War and then, after a campaign hunting U-boats in the Caribbean, to report the European front during the Second World War and liberate the Paris Ritz. Hemingway now became his own best hero; his fiction itself became more romantic, less sparse and comic. In the postwar years, with the autobiographical bravura of *Across the River and into the Trees* and the rather sentimental perfection of *The Old Man and the Sea*, Hemingway, now famous and in 1954 a Nobel Prize winner, seemed a grand old man of letters. In fact, as is now evident from *Islands in the Stream*, one of perhaps several pieces of fiction arising from a burst of creativity in the early 1950s, which has appeared posthumously, his romantic self-aggrandizement was of a piece with his intensifying desperation. For Hemingway's basic psychic oscillation, between confident physical energy and "black-assed" depression, was sharpened by age, his expulsion from Cuba by Castro, the physical deterioration consequent on several severe accidents (one, a plane crash, led to worldwide reports of his death), and the consequent weakening of his moral assurance, so closely tied to the physical. His last years were disturbed, and he died, like his father, by suicide.

Hemingway is one of the great American novelists, a central figure in the coming of age of American writing in the 1920s and an inestimable influence in American fiction since. His assault on the prolix and sentimental language of previous writers and his own distinctive, deceptively simple discourse represents a small cultural revolution. Hemingway stressed the realism of his aim, his concern with reportorial truth and accuracy, but his style is, in fact, an extremely complex and supple instrument. The truth he was after was not simply factual but moral; it was the truth about what was revealing and enlarging in experience. His characters are modern men and women, deprived of values and often anxious and febrile, members of a pained new generation in a dislocated, contingent world, linked by the cameraderie of "those who had fought or been mutilated" (*Across the River* . . .). In this world where most things are lost, life becomes a steady series of personal rituals, of locally and instantaneously significant encounters with experience. Because a certain element of grace and recovery is possible, it can contain the concept of heroism, of comedy and tragedy. The same idea of a continuous personal integrity of style which is applied to life Hemingway applies to the style of his own writing.

In many respects Hemingway's universe seems bleakly naturalistic, a world of battlefield and jungle in which man is conditioned and limited by external determinants. What mitigates this is the notion of some authentic act of address to experience by which the universe is stripped of contingency and falsity and reduced to its essence. Because of this, because he is primarily concerned with action, and because he postulates a world arbitrary and contingent, he has often been called "existential." The term is apt if it describes a pace of style and perception rather than a philosophy. In Hemingway's prose, with its limited number of subordinate clauses, its severely restricted use of adjectives, its minimal landscapes, its use of significant repetition, Hemingway seems to sustain a concept of active truth; his language claims authenticity, as well as aesthetic elegance. He is less a naturalist than a muted symbolist, especially in some of the earlier stories which represent some of his most perfect work. In this and in his creation of that distinctive Hemingway universe, knowing, élitist and puritan, Hemingway undoubtedly invented a genuine, distinctive and living modern style, a style which meets his own prescription of not going bad afterward.

Three Stories and Ten Poems, 1923.
In Our Time: Stories, 1924; revised, 1925.
The Torrents of Spring, 1926.
The Sun Also Rises, 1926 (U.K. title: *Fiesta*; f. 1957).
Men without Women, 1927 (stories).
A Farewell to Arms, 1929 (f. 1932; 1957).
Death in the Afternoon, 1932 (nonfiction).
Winner Take Nothing, 1933 (stories).
Green Hills of Africa, 1935 (nonfiction).
To Have and Have Not, 1937 (f. 1944; as *The Breaking Point*, 1950).
The Fifth Column [play] and the First Forty-Nine Stories, 1938.

For Whom the Bell Tolls, 1940 (*f.* 1943).
Across the River and into the Trees, 1950.
The Old Man and the Sea, 1952 (*f.* 1957).
A Moveable Feast, 1964 (nonfiction).
Islands in the Stream, 1970.

Works, 15 vols., New York: C. Scribner's Sons, 1953.
By-Line (journalism), ed. W. White, New York: C. Scribner's Sons, 1967; London: Collins, 1968.   M.B.

HENLEY, W. E. (William Ernest) (1849–1903), eldest of six children of an impecunious Gloucester bookseller, lost a leg at sixteen and suffered considerable hardship in youth and early manhood. After a brief period as a hack journalist in London, he was obliged to seek Lister's surgical skill at Edinburgh Royal Infirmary where he was lucky enough to meet Robert Louis Stevenson and gain an introduction to London's literary élite. Editor of several ephemeral journals, he collaborated with Stevenson on four plays and in 1890 helped to launch Kipling to immediate fame by publishing the first of the *Barrack-Room Ballads* in *The National Observer.* After a stormy career as a generous but irascible man of letters he died at Woking (Surrey) in July 1903.

Now totally neglected or condemned for his brash imperialism, Henley was one of the key figures of the 1890s in his various roles as editor, poet and critic. He encouraged other better-known writers in what was dubbed the "Henley Regatta" and himself produced work that still reads as freshly as when it was written. Often identified only with poetic clichés like "I am the master of my fate / I am the captain of my soul," he was, in fact, capable of achieving genuine tenderness and warmth in, for example, his *London Voluntaries* or *Echoes.* His prose style, easy and casual yet always vigorous and perceptive, makes him a supremely readable critic and the first volume of his *Views and Reviews* contains some of the most stimulating literary assessments in the whole of Victorian journalism.

A Book of Verses, 1888.
The Song of the Sword, 1892.
London Voluntaries, 1892.
Views and Reviews (first series), 1890.

Collected Works, 5 vols., London: Macmillan, 1921.   D.E.P.

"HENRY, O." was the pen name of William Sydney Porter (1862–1910). Born in North Carolina, he became a bank teller in Texas (1891–94). Charged with embezzling, he fled to Honduras but upon returning to

Texas where his wife was dying, he was convicted and jailed for three years. A prolific writer, Porter began his literary career with exciting tales set in Latin America, *Cabbages and Kings* (1904). His sentimental, humorous short stories of ordinary New Yorkers often employ irony and unexpected endings. Henry's best-known collection is *The Four Million* (1906), which contains "The Gift of the Magi," (*f.* in *Full House*, 1952), in which a wife sells her hair to buy her husband a watch fob at the moment he sells his watch to buy her combs.

Complete Works, 2 vols., foreword by H. Hansen, Garden City, N.Y.: Doubleday, 1953. J.L.M.

HENRYSON, Robert (c. 1430–?1506), one of the so-called "Scottish Chaucerians," was the older contemporary of Dunbar and Douglas. The precise date of his birth is uncertain, and little is known of his life except the tradition that he was a schoolmaster at Dunfermline. Although there is no record of his attendance at the universities of St. Andrews or Glasgow, Henryson is regularly given the title "maister," which implies that he was a graduate; probably, like many other medieval Scots, he studied abroad. Henryson's works show his familiarity with the arts course of a medieval university, and some of his *Fables* reveal a knowledge of legal procedure that supports the conjecture that he may be the "magister Robertus Henrisone in artibus licentiatus et in decretis bacchalarius" who was incorporated in Glasgow University in 1462, probably to lecture in law. He is mentioned as dead in Dunbar's *Lament for the Makaris* (dated c. 1506). Henryson wrote a number of short poems, but his two major works are *The Testament of Cresseid* and *The Moral Fables of Aesop*. None of his poems can be dated precisely.

The Testament of Cresseid, though not strictly a sequel to Chaucer's *Troilus*, requires to be read in the context of Chaucer's poem. Henryson tells how the prostituted Cresseid returns to her father, and while "chiding" against the gods is struck with leprosy. Cresseid at first disclaims any responsibility for her sin, and the poem traces the progression from this first arrogance and spiritual blindness to her final state of insight and contrition: "Nane but myself as now I will accuse." Although Henryson is more concerned to make moral judgments than was Chaucer, his portrait of Cresseid is not harsh but compassionate. *The Testament* is not conceived on the grand scale of *Troilus*, but it has great compactness and something of the intensity of a ballad. Images of frost and hail occur repeatedly, now as attributes of the planet Saturn, now symbolizing the coldness of dead love. The poem exemplifies Henryson's own stylistic ideal—"in breif sermonei and pregnant sentence wryte."

The Fables is a highly original work, even though most of the stories are traditional, some deriving from the collection attributed to Aesop, others from the medieval cycle of Reynard the Fox. Henryson is a master of the fable and knows how to maintain the precarious balance between the human and the animal in his characters, from which much of the humor and significance of a fable derive. His deft and original handling of traditional themes may be seen in "The Taill of the Uponlandis Mous and Burges Mous" and "The Taill of Schir Chantecleir and the Foxe." His humor, "saturated with irony," his easy colloquial dialogue and his sheer storytelling power bring Henryson very close to Chaucer. He has a remarkable capacity for comic invention, and the imagination to present the world through a small animal's eyes. At the same time Henryson writes always as a professed moralist, and his concern for "guid morall edificatioun" is especially marked in *The Fables* (traditionally the vehicle for satirical or moral comment), each of which is followed by a short expository "moralitas." Henryson, like Langland, frequently attacks the social injustices of his day, and sympathizes warmly, "if not uncritically," with the "pure commounis that daylie ar opprest."

The Testament of Cresseid, first printed in Thynne's edition of Chaucer, London, 1532.
The Moral Fables of Aesop, Edinburgh: Charteris, 1570.

Poems, ed. G. Gregory Smith, 3 vols., Edinburgh: Scottish Text Society, 1906–14.
Poems and Fables, ed. H. H. Wood, Edinburgh: Oliver & Boyd, 1933; 1958.   P.B.

HENSLOWE, Philip (died 1616), was a farsighted and ambitious businessman who built the earliest Bankside theater, the Rose, in 1587, and in due course controlled the Fortune and the Hope playhouses. His stepdaughter married the actor Edward Alleyn. Henslowe's so-called *Diary*, an account book and memorandum book for the period 1592–1603, is a main source of our knowledge of Elizabethan theater management and stage history.

Diary, ed. W. W. Greg, 2 vols., London: Bullen, 1904–08; ed. R. A. Foakes and R. T. Rickert, Cambridge: Cambridge Univ. Press, 1961.   J.D.J.

HERBERT, George (1593–1633), fifth son of Richard and Magdalen Herbert and younger brother of Edward, later Lord Herbert of Cherbury, came of an ancient and notable Welsh border family. His father died in 1596 and his mother, a friend of Donne, married Sir John Danvers in 1609. Educated at Westminster School and Trinity College, Cambridge, of which he became a fellow, he was from 1620 to 1627 public orator to the university. He appears to have had hopes of a career in public service or the court, but these were partly checked by the death of certain of his patrons and of King James I. By July 1626 he was already in deacon's orders and for some two or three years he lived with friends in an unsettled state of mind and poor bodily health. In 1629 he married Jane Danvers, and in 1630 he was appointed to the living of Bemerton near Salisbury (Wiltshire) and ordained priest. In the three remaining years of his life he acquired a reputation for saintly living and great devotion to his parish. Shortly before his death he sent his poems to his friend Nicholas Ferrar to deal with as he thought best, and they were published as *The Temple* at Cambridge in 1633. The prose "character" of the country parson, *A Priest to the Temple*, was printed in 1652. *The Temple* was very popular in the seventeenth century but survived in the eighteenth rather as piety than poetry, until Coleridge once more insisted on its literary merits and founded Herbert's modern reputation.

It is natural to compare Herbert's work with the religious poetry of Donne, and there seems to be an obvious affinity in the use of wit and the conceit. At the same time there are marked contrasts: Herbert shows neither Donne's passionate casuistry nor his aggressive unconventionality of style. His simple, urbane language, his varied and smoothly musical verse forms and a certain neatness and point suggest links with the courtly poets and Ben Jonson. Because it tends to draw on ordinary experience and practical affairs, Herbert's wit has been patronizingly described as "homely" or "quaint." Though there are occasions when it seems merely a matter of fanciful ingenuity, in his best work the wit has emotional intensity and an effect of imaginative illumination, as when he brings home the seriousness of inactivity with "So we freeze on, Until the grave increase our cold!," or vividly defines his state of despair with "a blunted knife Was of more use than I." Often the sense of mental alertness tempers what might have become emotional excess, as in "Love bade me welcome . . ." Here there are no conceits but an effect of wit arises from the carefully controlled tone of the urbane dialogue. Sometimes the conceit lies in the title ("The Collar," "The Pulley"), sometimes it is expanded into a short allegory ("Redemption," "The Pilgrimage"). But there is always a controlling play of mind and a vivid dramatic sense. Herbert's general purity of diction does not exclude racy colloquialisms like "*snudge* in quiet*," and the musical quality of his rhythms still permits an expressive relation to the meaning. In "The Collar," for example, the movement renders vividly both the rebellious mood and the way it subsides.

The realistic strength underlying Herbert's grace of style is related to the maturity of his emotional and religious life. The intense honesty with which he expresses suffering and conflict adds conviction to their resolution in faith and acceptance which is never felt as mere resignation. His best poetry embodies the religious temper of the age at its finest and most humane.

(See also **Hymns; Metaphysical Poetry.**)

The Temple, 1633.

Works, ed. F. E. Hutchinson, Oxford: Clarendon Press, 1941.   R.G.C.

HERBERT OF CHERBURY, Edward, Lord (1st Baron) (1583–1648), eldest brother of George Herbert, frequented the company of Jonson, Donne and the Wits, and traveled widely on the Continent. In 1619 he was made ambassador to France, and in 1629 created Baron Herbert of Cherbury. His submission to Parliament during the Civil War labeled him in his last years as "treacherous Lord Herbert."

His poetry combines something of the argumentativeness of Donne and the polish of Jonson. These influences can be seen at their best in "Ode upon a Question Moved: Whether Love Should Continue for Ever?," a poem which has strong affinities with Donne's "Extasie." The argumentative tone of Herbert's poetry has none of the toughness of Donne's and he tends to round off a lyric statement with a scholastic maxim which reduces the effectiveness of his work. The dryness of his tone can be seen by comparing his elegy on the death of Donne with that of Thomas Carew. Herbert's originality can be seen most clearly in his religious treatises, *De Veritate* (1624) and *De Religione Laici* (1645). His attempt to establish some level of certainty in the "natural instinct" and "common notions" of mankind foreshadows eighteenth-century Deism. The Deist's position in Dryden's *Religio Laici* echoes Herbert's ideas and the very title of the poem implies the influence of Herbert.

Courtier, poet, philosopher, historian and autobiographer, Lord Herbert possessed an impressive range of talents. A lack of discipline tended to limit the quality of his literary output, but nonetheless his work suggests both the literary continuity and change in his age.

Poems, English and Latin, ed. G. C. Moore Smith, Oxford: Clarendon Press, 1923.
De Veritate, ed. M. H. Carré (with translation), Bristol: J. W. Arrowsmith (Univ. of Bristol Studies, no. 6), 1937.   G.A.K.

HERBERT, Xavier. See **Australian Literature.**

HERBST, Josephine (1897–1969) was born in Iowa and first established her reputation as a proletarian novelist, writing about working-class

people with insight and first-hand detail. She is best known for a trilogy—
Pity Is Not Enough (1933), which begins after the Civil War, *The Executioner Waits* (1934), set in the present, and *Rope of Gold* (1939), which draws attention to international issues. The trilogy, never published as such, is both didactic and documentary: "The whole trilogy was an attempt to relate the urgency of the issues which projected the nation into the world." Later books were *Satan's Sergeants* (1941), *Somewhere the Tempest Fell* (1947), *New Green World* (1954) and *The Watcher with the Horn* (1955).

E.M.

HERRICK, Robert (1591–1674), seventh child of a prosperous London goldsmith, probably spent his childhood in or near London. Although his father was killed in a fall, suspected to be suicide, when Herrick was fourteen months old and another baby was expected, the family was left well provided for. At sixteen years of age Herrick was apprenticed to his goldsmith uncle, Sir William Herrick, but before completing this apprenticeship entered St. John's College, Cambridge, later transferring to Trinity Hall and graduating in 1617. Little is known about his next twelve years, though there are records of his becoming master of arts (1620), his ordination (1623) and his appointments as chaplain to the duke of Buckingham (1627) and to the living of Dean Prior (Devonshire) (1629). During most of this time Herrick was probably living in London and enjoying the convivial friendship of such men of letters as Jonson, Endymion Porter, Mildmay Fane, Selden and the Lawes brothers, all of whom are named in his verses. The ode beginning "Ah, Ben!" recalls the delights of this society. In 1630 Herrick removed to his Devonshire parish where he spent the next decade being cared for by his housekeeper, Prue, and gaining a reputation with the gentry "for his florid and witty discourse." He found country life delightful at times (see "His Content in the Country") and frustrating at others ("Discontents in Devon"), but besides providing material for some poems and prompting nostalgic memories of metropolitan life for others, it gave Herrick leisure to compose his best work. Around 1640 he was again in London, but the story that he fathered an illegitimate child there is unwarranted. His Royalist sympathies caused his ejection from Dean Prior in 1647, though in 1660 he returned there for the remainder of his life.

By 1648, when Herrick was fifty-seven, only ten poems had been published in seven different books, of which the earliest was Stow's *A Survey of London* (1633), which included a transcription of an epigraph from a niece's memorial. Most of Herrick's poems were collected in his only book, *Hesperides* (1648), and arranged in two sections, the first of secular poems, the second, subtitled "His Noble Numbers," of sacred poems. Although only the obituary verses for Lord Hastings and an epitaph in Dean Prior church are known to have been written after 1648, Herrick continued to polish his earlier poems. A number of poems probably written before 1648, though not included in *Hesperides*, have come to light since Herrick's death, some preserved by oral tradition until recorded in Devonshire in 1809.

Herrick's present reputation dates from the nineteenth century. In his own time he was held in high repute around 1625, but by 1648 taste had changed and *Hesperides* sold slowly. Henry Lawes had set a number of the poems to music, and some of these, notably "Gather ye rosebuds while ye may," continued to be sung. No edition of Herrick's poems appeared between 1648 and 1810, when his reputation began to grow. By 1894 Swinburne was able to write of "the greatest songwriter . . . ever born of English race." Recent opinion is less eulogistic, though the delicacy and artistry, which may be compared with that of the goldsmith Herrick, might have been—indeed are—admired, particularly in the more tightly constructed poems. Charges of grossness have been dropped and an awareness of Herrick's models and conventions has shown the danger of supposing Anthea, Julia, Corinna, Electra and the others of his poetical mistresses to have been his mistresses in real life.

Poetical Works, ed. L. C. Martin, Oxford: Clarendon Press, 1956.

H.N.D.

HERRICK, Robert (1868–1938) was born in Cambridge (Massachusetts), the son of a lawyer member of an old New England family. A Harvard graduate, Herrick taught English at the University of Chicago from 1893 to 1923. His realistic novels, such as *The Memoirs of an American Citizen* (1905), deal predominantly with the pressures of an industrial society, which he came increasingly to detest, on a series of heroes of varying sensitivity and talent. His treatment evolves from an early deterministic environmentalism through more explicitly political protest to an interest in the problems, psychological and domestic, of personal relations in an increasingly mechanistic society. His last novel, *Sometime* (1933), is a satiric utopian work, which criticizes contemporary society and looks forward to improved conditions when men turn away from materialism to the cultivation of their own personalities.

The Memoirs of an American Citizen, 1905.
The Master of the Inn, 1908 (short stories).
One Woman's Life, 1913.
Waste, 1924.
The End of Desire, 1932.
Sometime, 1933.

M.L.

HEYWOOD, John (?1497–?1580) was possibly born in London or Hertfordshire and educated at Oxford, but little is known of his early life. He gained Henry VIII's favor through his friend Sir Thomas More and was a musician and professional wit at Henry's court. A Roman Catholic, he found favor also under Mary, but left England at the accession of Elizabeth and went to Mechlin, his probable place of death.

Heywood was the only sixteenth-century dramatist to make real use of the French fabliau tradition and his interludes—entertainments halfway between morality plays and secular drama—have an important place in the development of English theater. They show some skill in structure, less didactic emphasis than most Tudor plays, a broad sense of humor, and in characterization a movement from abstraction to individuality. *Johan Johan, The Play of the Weather, The Play of Love* and *The Pardoner and the Friar* were all published in 1532–33 and *The Four PP* about 1545. Heywood was in his time a famous writer of epigrams and also wrote an odd allegorical religious poem, *The Spider and the Fly* (1556).

Dramatic Writings, ed. J. S. Farmer, London: Early English Drama Society, 1905.
Works and Miscellaneous Short Poems, ed. B. A. Mulligan, Urbana: Univ. of Illinois Press, 1956.   J.P.

HEYWOOD, Thomas (?1573–1641) was born in Lincolnshire, possibly the son of a clergyman, and entered Cambridge in 1591. In 1596 he was writing plays and acting for the Admiral's Company; later he transferred to Derby's Men and in 1601 was a sharer in Worcester's Company. He continued acting up to 1622 and in his *An Apology for Actors* (1612) defended this calling against opponents of the theater. His dramatic output is astonishing; he claimed to have had a share in some 220 plays, but of these relatively few have survived. *Edward IV* and *If You Know Not Me, You Know Nobody*, both in two parts, the second a dramatization of the reign of Elizabeth, are in the chronicle history mode. *The Four Prentices of London, The Fair Maid of the West* (2 parts), *Fortune by Land and Sea* (with William Rowley, 1655) and *Dick of Devonshire* (first collected 1883) are bustling romances full of extravagant adventure. In *The Rape of Lucrece, The Captives* and the five plays collectively named *The Four Ages*, Heywood drew heavily on his classical learning, yet succeeded in popularizing it with spectacle, farce or long explanations of the myths to accord with the taste of his audience. With *The Wise Woman of Hogsdon* (1638) he made a new and successful departure in satiric intrigue comedy. He achieved his most assured successes, however, with his domestic dramas, *A Woman Killed with Kindness* (1607) and *The English Traveller* (1633), both of which treat of human relationships disfigured by adultery. Heywood collaborated frequently, Brome, Day, Dekker and Rowley being among his associates. Apart from drama and his prose works, Heywood has a number of poems to his credit. They are generally lengthy and erudite works and range from his erotic minor epic, *Oenone and Paris*, to his scholarly religious poem, *The Hierarchy of the Blessed Angels* (1635). In the 1630s he provided a series of civic pageants and also a masque for the royal household. He died in London in 1641.

Undoubtedly the most prolific of the Elizabethan dramatists, Heywood was also one of the most popular. Part of his success must be attributed to his keen sensitivity to the changing demands of his audience, part to his intelligent interest in current events and his urgent topicality, and part to his versatile handling of all the popular tricks of the theatrical trade. His flair was clearly for domestic themes, and in scenes of domestic pathos he achieved his most powerful dramatic effects. The fallen wife situation, apparently a favorite with him, appears in various permutations in no fewer than six extant plays. Sympathetic female portraiture is characteristic of Heywood (he wrote two prose works in defense of women), and whether vigorous and attractive like Bess Bridges or frail and peccant like Nan Frankford, his women are his most memorable creations. Glorification of the mercantile classes and a robust patriotism are other recurring features. Though without intellectual pretensions and all too frequently geared to the lower levels of popular taste, Heywood's plays are workmanlike and well-plotted structures, which rise in the occasional scene to a high pitch of dramatic tension.

Edward IV, 2 parts, 1599.
If You Know Not Me, You Know Nobody, 1605; part 2, 1606.
A Women Killed with Kindness, 1607 (p. 1603).
The Rape of Lucrece, 1608.
The Four Prentices of London, 1615 (p. 1600).
The Fair Maid of the West; or, A Girl Worth Gold, 2 parts, 1631 (p. 1617).
The English Traveller, 1633.
The Hierarchy of the Blessed Angels, 1635 (poem).
The Wise Woman of Hogsdon, 1638.
The Captives, ed. A. C. Judson, New Haven: Yale Univ. Press, 1921 (p. c. 1624).

Dramatic Works, ed. R. H. Shepherd, 6 vols., London: Pearson, 1874.

L.E.P.

HIMES, Chester (1909–) was born in Jefferson City (Missouri). He is best known for his crime fiction, such as *Cotton Comes to Harlem* (1965; *f.* 1969), which features two black detectives, Cotton Ed and Grave

Digger, and is important for its graphic descriptions of Harlem, its cynical humor and elaborate set pieces of violence. In his more seriously intentioned novels Himes belongs to the Wright school of naturalism. *If He Hollers Let Him Go* (1945) details the humiliations and racial insults suffered by a black youth in a shipyard during the Second World War. *Pinktoes* (1965) is a lightly satirical novel about sexually integrated parties.   R.W.

HOBBES, Thomas (1588–1679) was the son of a Wiltshire clergyman. Precociously learned, he was educated at Magdalen Hall, Oxford, and later became tutor and secretary in the household of the earls of Devonshire. His *Leviathan; or, The Matter, Form and Power of a Commonwealth Ecclesiastical and Civil* was a deliberate attempt to be realistic about the nature of man and society, in a style both forceful and chillingly effective. It would be hard to overestimate the effect of his writings upon philosophers, scientists and men generally; in his own time he was regarded as a liberator from dark ignorance and superstition, but also as an atheist and a vilifier of human nature. Hobbes always denied the charge of atheism.

For Hobbes, thinking and knowing began in sensation, and even imagination is "decaying sense," but "when we would express the decay, and signify that the sense is fading, old and past, it is called memory." His general distrust of metaphorical language is part of the wider movement in the century towards cool rationality. In his long life he seems to have known most men of note, from Jonson to Waller and from Bacon to Selden.

Leviathan, 1651; ed. M. Oakeshott, Oxford: Blackwell, 1946.

English Works, ed. W. Molesworth, 11 vols., London: Bohn, 1839–45.

J.C.

HOGG, James (1770–1835) ("the Ettrick Shepherd") spent most of his life in the Border country. Brought up on pure folk tradition which, together with the poems of Burns, influenced all his work, Hogg was self-taught. He helped Scott to gather ballads for the *Minstrelsy* and then, beginning with the poems in *Scottish Pastorals* (1801), he wrote profusely in prose and verse. Hogg's best poetry exploits folk traditions and a strong sense of atmosphere. "Bonny Kilmenny" in *The Queen's Wake* (1813) is particularly fine. *The Private Memoirs and Confessions of a Justified Sinner* (a novel, 1824) interestingly dramatizes the bitter vision of a Scottish Calvinist. Hogg wrote for *Blackwood's Magazine* and was frequently introduced into its "Noctes Ambrosianae."

Poetical Works, 4 vols., Edinburgh, 1822.
Selected Poems, ed. D. S. Mack, Oxford: Clarendon Press, 1971.   W.R.

HOLCROFT, Thomas (1745–1809), son of a shoemaker and self-taught, began his literary career as a journalist. First a schoolmaster, he later became an actor, translator and dramatist. In the last of these roles his main work was in comedy and comic opera. Working in the tradition of the comedy of manners, he reveals considerable skill in plot construction, characterization and dialogue. His plays show the influence of sentimentalism and a strong moral intention, not least his belief in human perfectibility. This is also demonstrated in his novel *Anna St. Ives* (1792).

Memoirs, ed. W. Hazlitt, 3 vols., London: Longman, 1816; ed. E. Colby, 2 vols., London: Constable, 1925. A.P.

HOLINSHED, Ralph (?1529–?1580), possibly from Cheshire, possibly a graduate, was a hack for the London printer Wolfe. The famous *Chronicles* are something of an accident, a recension of Wolfe's proposed universal history. The "author," Holinshed, received much help in the first version (1577) and the revised (1586) edition with further material by John Hooker. The *Chronicles*, for which medieval chronicles and Leland are important authorities, convey much useful information in a lively, unelevated style and with a Protestant-patriotic bias. They are an important source for Shakespeare.

Holinshed's Chronicles As Used in Shakespeare's Plays, ed. A. and J. Nicoll, London: Dent; New York: Dutton, 1927. G.P.

HOLMES, Oliver Wendell (1809–94) was born in Cambridge (Massachusetts), the son of the Rev. Abdiel Holmes. He was educated at Harvard, where he abandoned law for medicine, and after studying in Boston and Paris, he graduated M.D. in 1836. He briefly practiced as a doctor, but his chief medical work was as a famous teacher of anatomy and physiology, first at Dartmouth, then at Harvard Medical School. Holmes was born into and became a leading member of the group of thinkers, conversationalists and writers, the Boston "Brahmins," whom he described as a "harmless, inoffensive, untitled aristocracy." Clustered round Harvard, they made New England and their own city in particular the center of American intellectual life in the first two-thirds of the nineteenth century. From his undergraduate days, when the publication of "Old Ironsides" (1830) was instrumental in saving the old frigate *Constitution* from destruction, Holmes was a successful writer of occasional verse, witty and slightly sentimental. Only a few pieces are now read, such as the parody "The Ballad of the Oysterman" (1830) and "The Deacon's Masterpiece; or, The Wonderful 'One-Hoss Shay' " (1858), a satire on the strict Calvinism which had caused his father's displacement and still remained part of New England religious life.

Holmes achieved reputation as a lecturer, man of letters and prominent contributor to *The Atlantic Monthly* (the Brahmin periodical founded in 1857, and first edited by John Russell Lowell). The title of the magazine, an example of Holmes's own verbal style, shows the essentially European, indeed English, provenance of Boston culture. Holmes's most famous work, *The Autocrat of the Breakfast Table* (1858), took the form of papers to *The Monthly*. These are sub-Addisonian essays, including dramatic fiction, in the form of conversations in a Cambridge boardinghouse, giving excellent scope for Holmes's wit, wide range of information, anecdotes and jokes. They are also a platform for the cultured, scientific optimism which was the basis of his militant reformism. Holmes also wrote three novels, of which the earliest and best, *Elsie Venner* (1861), is a good example of the use of "abnormal psychology" not to explore the depths of human nature, but, as in the old Gothic novels, to simplify through the agency of science.

(See also **Hymns.**)

Poems, 1836.
Homeopathy and Its Kindred Delusions, 1842.
The Autocrat of the Breakfast Table, 1858.
The Professor at the Breakfast Table, 1860.
Elsie Venner: A Romance of Destiny, 1861.
Soundings from the Atlantic, 1864 (essays).
The Poet at the Breakfast Table, 1872.
Pages from an Old Volume of Life, 1883 (essays).

Works, 13 vols., Boston: Houghton, Mifflin, 1892.
Life and Letters, ed. J. T. Morse, Jr., 2 vols., Boston: Houghton, Mifflin, 1896.   A.M.R.

HOOD, Thomas (1799–1845), son of a London bookseller and educated locally, entered a countinghouse in 1812. Ill health soon necessitated a stay with his father's relatives in Dundee, where he learned engraving. In 1817 he returned home to work as an engraver (he designed the illustrations for much of his own published work). Joining *The London Magazine* in 1821 as a writer and assistant editor, he got to know Lamb, Clare and De Quincey. He describes these friendships in his "Literary Reminiscences" in *Hood's Own* (1839).

In 1825 Hood and John Hamilton Reynolds, whose sister Hood married in 1824, published *Odes and Addresses to Great People*, a lively volume of verse satire. Hood's first collection of his magazine pieces, *Whims and*

Oddities (first series, 1826), succeeded while a volume of serious poetry failed, so thereafter he mostly wrote comic verse, publishing *The Comic Annual* from 1830 to 1839 (and in 1842) and editing *The New Monthly Magazine* (1841–43) and *Hood's Magazine* (1844–45). He made various collections of his periodical contributions. Financial problems forced him to live abroad from 1835 to 1840. His whole career was plagued by problems of money and health.

Hood is best remembered for the serious poems on social inequality and injustice which he wrote at the end of his life and for the clever punning and metrical dexterity of his best comic verses. He overproduced, but possessed real ability; his serious poetry shows a genuine gift of Romantic sensitivity and imagination.

(See also **Political Pamphlets.**)

Works, ed. T. Hood (son) and F. F. Broderip (daughter), 11 vols. (includes memoir), London: Ward, Lock, 1882–84.

Poetical Works, ed. W. Jerrold, London: Oxford Univ. Press, 1906.

Selected Poems, ed. J. Clubbe, London: Oxford Univ. Press; Cambridge, Mass.: Harvard Univ. Press, 1970.

Letters, ed. L. A. Marchand, New Brunswick, N.J.: Rutgers Univ. Press, 1945.   W.R.

HOOKER, Richard (1554–1600) was born in Exeter and educated at Corpus Christi College, Oxford, where he remained until 1580 when he removed to London, becoming master of the Temple in 1585. There he came into conflict with the Puritan lecturer Travers, and out of this controversy emerged Hooker's great work, *Of the Laws of Ecclesiastical Polity*, which was incomplete at his death. The first five books appeared in Hooker's lifetime, the last three not until nearly fifty years later. Doubts have been cast on the authenticity of these latter.

Hooker had to counter the Puritan appeal to Scripture and its refusal of man-made authority. He began with a discussion of law and its purpose in relation to the will, appetite and reason of man. God is law, and he is above Scripture; he is not the slave of his own message. He has given man reason to understand him. The great fifth book is the apology for the Church of England, its doctrine and practice. Hooker appeals to the arguments of reasonableness, antiquity, the authority of the church and its power to prescribe change when change is necessary. Thus he safeguards authority without denying reformation. In the latter part of the book he considers the relation of church and state and goes on to show that the Puritan attack threatens not only the church but also the monarchy.

Hooker is one of the great English prose stylists. His sentences move in majestic, controlled, developing periods, a mirror of the mighty mind they express. He is a model of the Ciceronian manner in English.

Works, ed. J. Keble, 3 vols., 1836; revised R. W. Church and F. Paget, 3 vols., Oxford: Clarendon Press, 1888.   A.P.

HOOPER, J. J. (Johnson Jones) (1815–62) was born in Wilmington (North Carolina), the son of a prominent state family. He flirted with the law but spent most of his early years in drifting and journalism. He wrote for many newspapers, the most famous of which was the Montgomery *Mail*, which he established in the early 1850s and edited until 1861. He created the character of Simon Suggs in *Some Adventures of Captain Simon Suggs* (1846). Suggs is a comic creation showing many facets of the early Southern frontier rogue. He has one principle that "It is good to be shifty in a new country," and his adventures are described with lively dialogue and rowdy humor, but not infrequent irony and some delicacy of touch. Later Hooper regretted his humorous writing, feeling that it kept him from high office. He did become the secretary of the Provisional (Confederate) Congress.   D.V.W.

HOPE, A. D. (Alec Derwent). See **Australian Literature.**

HOPKINS, Gerard Manley (1844–89), born near London into a family with considerable artistic talent, was educated at Highgate School, where he produced prize poems, and then at Balliol College, Oxford. While at Oxford he came under the tutorial influence of Pater, a relationship that developed into a personal friendship. By birth a High Anglican, Hopkins was attracted, while an undergraduate, by the Oxford movement and was received into the Roman Catholic church by Newman in 1866, a decision which alienated him from his family. After taking first class honors in classical moderations, and in Greats in 1867, Hopkins taught temporarily at Newman's Oratory School in Birmingham before making the final decision to become a Jesuit priest in 1868. On commencing his novitiate he resolved to write no more poetry and he destroyed what he had written up to that time. In 1875, however, a hint from his religious superior encouraged him to begin work on a poem commemorating five Franciscan nuns, exiled from Germany, who had died in a shipwreck off the east coast. "The Wreck of the Deutschland" was the result. Following this, Hopkins produced a series of poems predominantly concerned with nature. He was ordained in 1877 and from 1878 to 1881 was engaged in parish work, first in London and then in Oxford and Liverpool. After the final retreat required of him by his order in 1881, he became a teacher of classics, first at Stonyhurst College and then, as professor of classics, at

University College, Dublin. While in Ireland he suffered from periods of intense depression and considerable ill health, and he eventually died there of typhoid fever. During his lifetime he never published his poetry, but sent it to his friends, Robert Bridges, whom he had met at Oxford, Coventry Patmore and Canon Dixon. After Hopkins's death Bridges began to insert some of his poetry, extremely selectively, in anthologies, and it was not until 1918 that a complete edition, edited by Bridges, appeared.

The unusual circumstances of the publication of Hopkins's poetry, together with his enthusiasm for technical experiment, carried on in comparative literary isolation, have led many commentators to regard him as a modern poet, and it is not unusual to find his work included in anthologies of modern poetry. It should be remembered, however, that Hopkins's earliest poetry shows signs of a post-Romantic aestheticism that has affiliations with the Pre-Raphaelite movement and that the emphasis on his awareness of physical beauty, while it takes on a strongly religious significance after his conversion, is consistent with his friendship with Pater and his reading of Ruskin. Furthermore, his religious experience is very much of his time, the spirit of the Oxford movement, in Newman's words, acting as "the practical safeguard against atheism in the case of scientific enquirers."

Hopkins's early poetry, written before his conversion, shows little sign of the technical achievement to be found in "The Wreck of the Deutschland," where his startling control of unusual linguistic effects, coupled with his handling of what he called "sprung rhythm," produces a particularly compelling effect. This poem, which celebrates the self-sacrifice of the drowned nuns, celebrates also the poet's own conversion. Its sheer unusualness prevented its publication in the Catholic magazine, *The Month*, for which it was originally intended. The technical innovations discussed in detail by Hopkins in his correspondence with Bridges continue to appear in the poems which follow "The Wreck of the Deutschland." Many of these affirm the physical beauty of nature as evidence of the beneficence of God, thus allowing Hopkins to combine his aesthetic and his religious impulses. The claim in "God's Grandeur" that "The world is charged with the grandeur of God" might well be taken as a motto for Hopkins's nature poetry. An interesting foretaste of Hopkins's perception of God in the individual characteristics of observed nature is provided by the commentary running through the *Journals* which he kept during his period of poetic silence.

While a parish priest Hopkins wrote poetry arising directly out of his work and seems, as in poems like "The Bugler's First Communion," to have been particularly concerned with the theme of the potential contamination of innocence. Other poems of this period of Hopkins's life concern his liturgical interests and often display an emblematic delight in the details of Roman ritual. Hopkins's last poems, the so-called "terrible sonnets," written in Dublin, deal with the sense of spiritual desolation that oppressed him in his last years. His unusual mode of expression, in that it frequently approaches the barriers of coherence, is particularly effective in evoking his mental distress. The intensity of expression in these last poems parallels that of the climaxes of "The Wreck of the Deutschland," and it is Hopkins's achievement in such poetry that he manages to universalize what is essentially a private and religious experience. His last great poem, "That Nature Is a Heraclitean Fire and of the Comfort of the Resurrection," demonstrates that Hopkins's faith finally sustained him. This poem is both a final celebration of nature and an assertion of its ultimate insignificance in the face of the widest spiritual perspectives.

Poems, ed. R. Bridges, 1918; 4th edition (with additional poems), ed. W. H. Gardner and N. H. Mackenzie, London: Oxford Univ. Press, 1967.

Notebooks and Papers, ed. H. House, London: Oxford Univ. Press, 1937; 2nd edition, revised and enlarged, 2 vols.; *Journals and Papers*, ed. H. House and G. Storey; *Sermons and Devotional Writings*, ed. C. Devlin, 1959.

Letters to Robert Bridges, ed. C. C. Abbott, London: Oxford Univ. Press, 1935.

Correspondence . . . with R. W. Dixon, ed. C. C. Abbott, London: Oxford Univ. Press, 1935.

Further Letters, ed. C. C. Abbott, London: Oxford Univ. Press, 1938; 2nd edition, revised and enlarged, 1956.   A.J.S.

HOSMER, F. L. (Frederick Lucian). See **Hymns.**

HOUSMAN, A. E. (Alfred Edward) (1859–1936), born at Fockbury (Worcestershire), the eldest of seven children of a Bromsgrove solicitor, showed a precocious talent for verse. In 1870 he entered Bromsgrove School, where after a conventional career he went up to Oxford in 1878. His excellence in textual scholarship did not atone for studied indifference to the rest of the curriculum and he failed in Greats in 1881. For eleven years he worked as a clerk in the Patent Office, meanwhile producing a series of learned articles on the Greek and Latin poets, till in 1892 he was elected to the chair of Latin at University College, London. After nineteen years there he became Kennedy Professor of Latin at Cambridge in 1911, a post he held until his death.

His greatness lies rather as a scholar than as a poet, but his editions of

Manilius, Juvenal and Lucan show a sure instinct and taste for a poet's language, and his love of poetry added another dimension to his work on the Latin poets. His output is limited because he rigorously subdued his inspiration and wrote only when his feelings compelled him. His Leslie Stephen Lecture in 1933 on *The Name and Nature of Poetry* concludes with an account of his method of composition. (See also **Romantic Movement, The.**)

A Shropshire Lad appeared in 1896 and *Last Poems* in 1922. Most of the latter had been written between 1895 and 1910. In 1936 Laurence Housman printed several of the poems which Alfred had suppressed because of imagined imperfections, and yet more appeared in the *Collected Poems* in 1939. This pursuit of perfection is apparent in all the poems, which use lapidary classical phrases in a sturdy, forthright Saxon syntax. The Shropshire Lad is a mythical figure, whose preoccupation with soldiers and death reflects Housman's own outlook. The poems have had a mixed reception, being praised or blamed by critics for opposite and irreconcilable qualities such as anonymity and autobiographical exactness. They are written in direct, simple meters and their perfection within a narrow compass is seldom questioned.

A Shropshire Lad, 1896.
Last Poems, 1922.
The Name and Nature of Poetry, 1933.
More Poems, ed. L. Housman, 1936.

Collected Poems, London: Cape, 1939; new edition, 1960.
Letters, ed. H. Maas, London: Hart-Davis, 1970.   A.N.M.

HOW, W. (William) Walsham. See **Hymns.**

HOWARD, Bronson (1842–1908) was America's first professional dramatist. He worked as a journalist in his native Detroit, then for *The Tribune* under Horace Greeley before his first play, *Saratoga* (*p.* 1870), a farcical comedy, was accepted by Augustin Daly and enjoyed a great success. Although Howard is best known for his spectacular drama of a family divided by the Civil War, *Shenandoah* (*p.* 1888), he is essentially a moralist and his work is still of interest for the light it sheds on the values of the Gilded Age. In *Young Mrs. Winthrop* (1882) he showed the damaging impact on family life of the husband's absorption in business and the wife's immersion in the frivolities of fashionable society, whilst in *The Banker's Daughter* (1878) he criticized the marriage of convenience. Even the Church did not escape his censure in the attack on big business and the Protestant ethic in his melodrama *Baron Rudolph* (*p.* 1881). In *One of Our*

Girls (*p.* 1885) and *Aristocracy* (*p.* 1892) he turned to the international theme in a staunch defense of American democratic values. Howard always saw things in black and white, but he was a trenchant critic of his age.

D.P.M.

HOWARD, Sidney (1891–1939) was born in California and studied in George Pierce Baker's Drama Workshop at Harvard. His action plays may border on melodrama, but they contain strong characters and an interest in society. *They Knew What They Wanted* (*p.* 1924; *f.* 1940), the story of an elderly Italian immigrant who marries a young woman, became the model for the Frank Loesser musical *The Most Happy Fella* (*p.* 1956). The selfish love of a possessive mother is the theme of *The Silver Cord* (*p.* 1926), and *Yellow Jack* (1934; *f.* 1938) vividly re-creates the personal and practical difficulties of men involved in combating yellow fever in Cuba. Howard was the main scriptwriter for the screen version of *Gone with the Wind* (*f.* 1939). R.W.

HOWE, E. W. (Edgar Watson) (1853–1937) was brought up in Missouri and Nebraska. The son of a fanatical Methodist, he too was very religious. He owned and edited *The Daily Globe*, Atchison (Kansas) (1877–1911) and published his first novel, *The Story of a Country Town* (1883), privately. The book was highly praised by William Dean Howells for its realistic presentation of rural life and is still widely regarded. He wrote several other books but is better known for his concise editorial articles which appeared in *E. W. Howe's Monthly* from 1911 onwards. These revealed his Puritan materialism and faith in individual advancement. His autobiography, *Plain People*, was published in 1929. R.W.

HOWE, Julia Ward. See **Hymns**.

HOWELLS, William Dean (1837–1920) was born in Martin's Ferry (Ohio), the son of a journeyman printer and newspaper man. He had little formal education, but was already contributing to various newspapers during his boyhood. By the age of twenty-three he had published two books, one of which—a campaign life of Lincoln—helped him secure the post of U.S. consul in Venice. He returned to America at the end of the Civil War and was appointed first assistant editor, and later editor of *The Atlantic Monthly*. In 1886 he began his long association with *Harper's Monthly*, to which he contributed the "Editor's Study." Howells used his influential editorial positions and his growing reputation as a novelist to encourage the work of new writers. He was especially hospitable to Henry

James, Mark Twain, the local color writers, and the early naturalists. His own theories of fiction, developed in *Criticism and Fiction*, centered upon the possibility of creating a "realism of the commonplace," and his early fiction can be seen as a continuation of the tradition of the novel of manners. In the 1880s, however, resulting directly from his emotional involvement in the Haymarket Riot and its aftermath, but also partly due to the influence of Tolstoy and certain American socialists, Howells entered upon a period of militant liberalism. His changing political views and his growing pessimism are reflected in his fiction of this period, particularly in *A Hazard of New Fortunes* (1890), but also in his other "economic" novels. He had earlier claimed that the quality of American life was such that her novelists need deal only with the "smiling aspects," but, in common with many of his contemporaries, he was proved wrong by the political events of the 1880s and 1890s. Though his militant period did not last long, Howells continued to champion the cause of naturalism and was one of the first to recognize the merits of Stephen Crane and Frank Norris. In 1908 he was elected to the presidency of the American Academy of Arts and Letters.

In spite of his prolific output—thirty-five novels, thirty-five plays, six critical books, four volumes of poetry, thirty-four miscellaneous books—and the high quality of his best fiction such as *The Rise of Silas Lapham* (1885), *A Modern Instance* (1882) and *A Traveler from Altruria* (1894), Howells's significance in the history of American literature has more to do with the causes he championed and the critical battles he fought than with his own work. Howells's career has often been seen as a mirror reflecting the state of American literature during its most eventful period. His acceptance by the New England literati was seen by one of its members—Holmes—as an apostolic succession involving the shift from what had hitherto been a New England literature to an American literature. Howells's subsequent move from Boston to New York in 1888 marked another stage in the rejection of literary provincialism, and when he died, even his most hostile critic, H. L. Mencken, who had characterized him formerly as "a contriver of pretty things," admitted that there was no longer anyone who could serve as the representative of American letters.

A Chance Acquaintance, 1873.
The Lady of the Aroostook, 1879.
A Modern Instance, 1882.
The Rise of Silas Lapham, 1885.
Indian Summer, 1886.
A Hazard of New Fortunes, 1890.
A Boy's Town, 1890.
Criticism and Fiction, 1891.

The World of Chance, 1893.
A Traveler from Altruria, 1894.
The Kentons, 1902.
My Mark Twain, 1910.

Selected Edition of Works, 36 vols., ed. E. H. Cady, R. Gottesman, and others, Bloomington: Indiana Univ. Press, 1968.
Complete Plays, ed. W. Meserve, New York: New York Univ. Press, 1960.
Life in Letters, ed. M. Howells, 2 vols., Garden City, N.Y.: Doubleday, Doran, 1928.   B.L.

HUDSON, W. H. (William Henry) (1841–1922) was born in Argentina, settled in England in 1869 and began a career as novelist, essayist and naturalist, drawing upon his reminiscences of South America and his observations of the English countryside. In most of his books, as *Nature in Downland* (1900) and *A Shepherd's Life* (1910), the interest is in plant and animal life and in natural beauty unspoiled by civilization. A careful observer and stylist, he shows considerable skill in depicting the rural life of the downlands, while his treatment of South America is often romantic and exotic, as in *Green Mansions* (1904).

Collected Works, 24 vols., London: Dent, 1922–23.
Letters . . . to Edward Garnett, London: Dent, 1925.   O.K.

HUGHES, Langston (1902–67) was born in Joplin (Missouri) and educated at Lincoln University. In a career which covered half a century Hughes produced more than fifty books. In doing so he reflected and in large part forged the changing moods of the Negro intellectual. A leading figure of the Negro Renaissance of the 1920s (*The Weary Blues*; *Fine Clothes to the Jew*), who also voiced with equal force the bitterness of the 1930s in his play *Mulatto* (p. 1935), Hughes proved no less capable of capturing the brooding frustrations of the 1950s (*Montage of a Dream Deferred*). Rarely resorting to the brutal contours of the racial stereotype, he nonetheless eloquently expressed the barely suppressed anger as well as the cultural resources of the black community.

Justifiably famous for his creation of Jesse B. Simple, a comic character through whom Hughes commented on the vagaries of American society in general and the Negro community in particular—*Simple Speaks His Mind* (1950); *Simple Stakes a Claim* (1957); *The Best of Simple* (1961)—he was the most influential Negro writer of his generation. A poet, a novelist, a dramatist, and an anthologist, by his example and professional commitment he played a central role in the development of black writing in

America. Hughes's interests spanned the whole range of black culture, from music (*The First Book of Jazz*, 1955) and mythology (*The Book of Negro Folklore*, 1958) to racial protest groups (*Fight for Freedom: The Story of the NAACP*, 1962). His autobiography was published in two parts as *The Big Sea* (1940) and *I Wonder As I Wander* (1956).

The Weary Blues, 1926 (poems).
Fine Clothes to the Jew, 1927 (poems).
Not without Laughter, 1930 (novel).
The Negro Mother, 1931 (poems).
Scottsboro Limited, 1932 (poems and verse play).
A New Song, 1938 (poems).
Shakespeare in Harlem, 1942 (poems).
Fields of Wonder, 1947 (poems).
One-Way Ticket, 1949 (poems).
Montage of a Dream Deferred, 1951 (poems).
Selected Poems, 1959.
Ask Your Mama, 1961 (poems).
The Best of Simple, 1961.
Five Plays, 1963.
The Panther and the Lash, 1967 (poems).   C.B.

HUGHES, Ted (1930–   ) was born at Mytholmroyd (Yorkshire) and educated at Mexborough Grammar School and Cambridge, where he met the American poet Sylvia Plath. They were married in 1956.

In *The Hawk in the Rain* (1957) and *Lupercal* (1960) there are poems of such violent imaginative power that they were seen by many readers as a necessary breakthrough in a postwar literary scene which had become too careful, analytic and respectable. In much of this early poetry Hughes is an unsentimental nature poet who is at once fascinated and horrified by the instinctive sureness and the pointlessness of the violence in animal life, and, by analogy, in men. In his best poems his control of strong rhythms and startling imagery is without equal in contemporary poetry. *Wodwo* (1967) is more experimental and uneven, but there are some fine poems and impressive stories. *Crow* (1970) achieves a superb fusion of fierce terrifying image and grim, equally terrifying humor. Hughes's strange and powerful imagination has sometimes relaxed to produce excellent books for children, revealing a delightful whimsy as well as a gift for storytelling. Through broadcasts and anthologies he has done much to stimulate imaginative response and creative writing in schools.

The Hawk in the Rain, 1957.
Lupercal, 1960.

Meet My Folks!, 1961 (children).
How the Whale Became, 1962 (children).
The Earth-Owl and Other Moor People, 1963 (children).
Poetry in the Making, 1967 (children).
Wodwo, 1967.
The Iron Man, 1968 (children).
Crow, 1970.   A.Y.

HULME, T. E. (Thomas Ernest) (1883–1917) was a theorist of aesthetics and occasional poet whose reputation depends as much on the enthusiasm expressed for his ideas by writers like Pound, Wyndham Lewis and, notably, T. S. Eliot as on his published work, which is fragmentary in nature. Hulme's thinking was frankly authoritarian, involving the rejection of humanism, particularly in its manifestations as liberalism in politics and romanticism in the arts. His neoclassical positives, however, are ill-defined, depending on allusions to tradition which, while religious in concept, are not formulated in terms of a specific religious belief. (See also **Imagism; Romantic Movement, The.**)

Speculations: Essays on Humanism and the Philosophy of Art, ed. H. Read, London: Kegan Paul, 1924.   A.J.S.

HUME, David (1711–76) was born in Edinburgh and educated at the university there. After studying law and starting a career in commerce, he went to France at the age of twenty-three and spent three years with the Jesuits at La Flèche. In 1739 he published anonymously the first two volumes of *A Treatise of Human Nature* and completed it with a third volume in the following year. The book attracted little attention; in his own words, "it fell dead-born from the press," but in fact it was the beginning of a radically new approach to philosophy. In 1741–42 he published *Essays Moral and Political*, which, though they roused more interest, brought him no prospect of financial independence, and so in 1746 he accepted an appointment as secretary to General St. Clair, whom he accompanied on the expedition to Port L'Orient in 1747 and on a mission to Vienna and Turin in 1748. In 1748 he produced *An Enquiry concerning Human Understanding* and in 1751 *An Enquiry concerning the Principles of Morals*, both of these being a reformulation of the philosophy contained in his earlier *Treatise*. These were followed by *Political Discourses*, which were translated into French and gave him a reputation on the Continent. In the same year he was appointed keeper of the Advocates' Library in Edinburgh and now turned to the writing of history. His *History of Great Britain* appeared in six volumes between 1754 and 1762. From 1763 to 1765 he was secretary to the British Embassy in Paris, where he became a leading figure in the literary and intellectual circles of the day. A short period as undersecretary of state (1767–68) was followed by retirement in Edinburgh. His autobiography was published posthumously in 1777, and in 1779 *Dialogues concerning Natural Religion* appeared, which Hume's friends, alarmed by the skeptical tone, had advised him not to publish in his lifetime.

Hume's philosophy was marked by an extreme skepticism which questioned the assumptions made by the empiricism of Locke and the early Berkeley. His separation of the ideas impressed on the human mind by the external world from the absolute existence of that world itself left him free to demonstrate that we can know little of the external world with anything approaching certainty. The idea of causality, for instance, according to Hume, is no more than a habit of mind which expects one event to follow another simply because it has generally done so in the past. It was this skepticism and the need to challenge it which first aroused Kant from his "dogmatic slumbers." Positivism, whether of the nineteenth-century kind or in its more recent forms, has generally been indebted to Hume. He was regarded as a dangerous infidel by many of his contemporaries, who were scandalized especially by *An Essay on Miracles* (see Boswell's *The Life of Samuel Johnson*).

A Treatise of Human Nature, books 1–3, 1739–40.
Essays Moral and Political, 2 vols., 1741–42.
Philosophical Essays concerning Human Understanding, 1748.
An Enquiry concerning the Principles of Morals, 1751.
Political Discourses, 1752.
History of Great Britain, 6 vols., 1754–62; 8 vols., 1763.
Dialogues concerning Natural Religion, 1779.

Philosophical Works, ed. T. H. Green and T. H. Grose, 4 vols., London: Longmans, 1874–75.
Letters, ed. J. Y. T. Greig, 2 vols., Oxford: Clarendon Press, 1932.
New Letters, ed. R. Klibansky and E. C. Mossner, Oxford: Clarendon Press, 1954.   R.L.B.

HUNT, Leigh (1784–1859), educated at Christ's Hospital, London, was a precocious writer, producing his first volume of poems at seventeen. His journalistic and literary output was vast. After writing theater criticism for *The News*, he started *The Examiner* with his brother John in 1808 and was its main writer till 1821. From 1813 to 1815 the brothers edited the paper from prison, having attacked the Regent once too often in its pages. Hunt's interest in politics, however, soon declined and most of his journalism is literary and occasional. His liberalism and his fanciful poetry, like *The Story of Rimini* (1816), made him many friends among young writers, and for a time Keats was an admirer. After Hunt's paper *The Indicator* (1819–21) had died, Shelley and Byron sent for him to conduct *The Liberal* from Italy (1822–23), and in later years he edited a succession of other journals, besides contributing copiously to those run by other people.

Hunt's best journalism, and probably his best work, is to be found in *The Examiner*, *The Indicator* and *The Companion* (1828). Behind most of his writing lies the desire to communicate enjoyment, and while this can be attractive, both his poetry and his occasional essays are often weakened by overmuch sweetness of tone and genteel fancifulness. In literary and dramatic criticism he shows a welcome trenchancy in addition to his habitual perceptiveness. He knew many great literary figures and his *Autobiography* (3 vols., 1850; revised, 1860), though unreliable in detail, is interesting. This may also be said of his *Lord Byron and Some of His Contemporaries* (1828).

(See also **Essays.**)

Correspondence, ed. T. Hunt (son), 2 vols., London, 1862.
Poetical Works, ed. H. S. Milford, London: Oxford Univ. Press, 1923.
Autobiography, ed. J. E. Morpurgo, London: Cresset Press; 1949.
Dramatic Criticism 1808–1831, ed. L. H. and C. W. Houtchens, New York: Columbia Univ. Press, 1949; London: Oxford Univ. Press, 1950.
Uncollected Literary Criticisms, ed. L. H. and C. W. Houtchens, New York: Columbia Univ. Press; London: Oxford Univ. Press, 1956.
Political and Occasional Essays, ed. L. H. and C. W. Houtchens, New York: Columbia Univ. Press, 1962.   W.R.

HURD, Richard (1720–1808), bishop of Worcester, wrote prolifically on politics, history, ethics and criticism throughout a distinguished clerical career. His *Moral and Political Dialogues* (1759) was admired by Johnson and his historical acumen praised by Gibbon. His most influential work, *Letters on Chivalry and Romance* (1762), is often cited as seminal neo-Romantic criticism, but Hurd was really interested in "Gothic" subjects, particularly Spenser's *The Faerie Queene*, as material for neo-classical poetry. His basically Augustan concerns are reflected by his decorous prose style.

Works, 8 vols., London, 1811.
Letters on Chivalry and Romance, ed. E. J. Morley, London: Oxford Univ. Press, 1911.
Correspondence of Richard Hurd and William Mason . . . and Letters to Thomas Gray, ed. E. H. Pearce and L. Whibley, Cambridge: Cambridge Univ. Press; New York: Macmillan Co., 1932.   A.W.B.

HUXLEY, Aldous (1894–1963), born in Godalming (Surrey), belonged to a family of great talent. He was brother of Sir Julian Huxley; their father was Leonard Huxley, editor of *The Cornhill Magazine*, and their grandfather was Thomas Huxley. Educated at Eton and Oxford, Aldous entered the literary world as a journalist and critic, instead of becoming a doctor as he had intended. His physical difficulties and spiritual depression lie behind his early work, which reflects the author's disillusioned view of a decaying postwar society. In middle and later life the desire for a satisfying philosophy of life brought him into contact with varied people and places. He met and became a disciple of D. H. Lawrence (who is a model for Rampion in *Point Counter Point*), lived for a time in Italy and traveled widely in America and Mexico. By 1936 Huxley was a pacifist and convert to what he calls the "perennial philosophy," finding intellectual and emotional satisfaction in the meditative practices of Eastern religions. In later life he lived in America and continued writing until his death.

A writer whose talent was vigorous and many-sided, he wrote poetry, novels, critical essays, short stories and works of ethical and philosophic character, all of which reflect, in a most illuminating way, the intellectual climate from 1920. His first success was *Limbo*, a book of stories, and this was followed by three novels written in a Peacockian manner, *Crome Yellow* (1921), *Antic Hay* (1923) and *Those Barren Leaves* (1925). In these the author, with a combination of learning and satire, speaks his opinions under the guise of different characters. His three best novels are *Point Counter Point* (1928), *Brave New World* (1932) (see **Science Fiction**) and *Eyeless in Gaza* (1936), the first a seriocomic exposure of a decaying society, the second a fantasy and satire of the future as planned by the scientist, and the third showing the hero, Anthony Beavis, finding his way to pacifism. Although he continued to write satirical novels after 1936, Huxley also wrote semiphilosophical works: *The Perennial Philosophy* is an anthology of mystical writings, while *Ends and Means* is an examination of the ethical basis of pacifism. He was also a versatile essayist and wrote several volumes upon such diverse subjects as architecture, criticism, science, education, economics and political democracy.

The vitality of his novels derives principally from the play of the author's brilliant, if somewhat cynical, intelligence as it exercises itself on the intellectual and social attitudes of a variety of characters. As a "novelist of ideas" he so fashions his narratives that they become a framework for the exposition, rather than the dramatization, of ideas, and he often uses his characters as mouthpieces for conflicting ideas. Ignoring fine shades of character, he strives to present an anatomy of the popular intellectual obsessions of his time in social, political, literary and scientific circles.

Though Huxley is often charged with pessimism, his seriousness is not irreconcilable with wit and sympathy. There are varying types of characterization in his novels, ranging from caricature to sympathetic exposition, and his ideas, though often disturbing, are animated by means of comic satire, parody and farce.

Crome Yellow, 1921.
Antic Hay, 1923.
Those Barren Leaves, 1925.
Point Counter Point, 1928.
Brave New World, 1932.
Eyeless in Gaza, 1936.
Ends and Means, 1937.
After Many a Summer, 1939.
The Perennial Philosophy, 1946.
Ape and Essence, 1949.
The Doors of Perception, 1954 (essays).
Brave New World Revisited, 1958.

Collected Short Stories, London: Chatto & Windus; New York: Harper, 1957.
Collected Essays, London: Chatto & Windus; New York: Harper, 1959.
Letters, ed. G. Smith, London: Chatto & Windus; New York: Harper & Row, 1969.
Collected Poetry, ed. D. Watt, London: Chatto & Windus; New York: Harper & Row, 1971.   O.K.

HUXLEY, T. H. (Thomas Henry) (1825–95) was scientist, essayist, and educationalist. From 1846 to 1850 he was surgeon on H.M.S. *Rattle-snake*'s voyage to Australia on a scientific survey. He later made important contributions to zoology, comparative anatomy and palaeontology, Known as "Darwin's bulldog" in the public controversy over *The Origin of Species* (1859), he attacked orthodox theological beliefs. He wrote *Evidence of Man's Place in Nature* (1863) to illustrate anatomical similarities between man and the apes. He invented "agnosticism" to describe his religious position and pleaded for humanist ethics. He was president of the Royal Society.

Collected Essays, 9 vols., London: Macmillan, 1893–94.
Scientific Memoirs, ed. M. Foster and E. R. Lankester, 5 vols., London: Macmillan, 1898–1903.   P.G.M.

"HYDE, Robin." See **New Zealand Literature.**

HYMNS. The Church has always used hymns in its worship from biblical times onwards, but it was in the eighteenth and more especially the nineteenth centuries that hymns gained such a hold on the religious consciousness of the English nation. In part, this was due to the prominence given to hymns in the worship of Nonconformists and especially of the Methodists. For the followers of Wesley the hymn must have had the same place as the popular ballad of all ages, forming in fact a kind of religious folk poetry.

The best hymns are usually composed in one of a few simple measures (8.6.8.6 or 8.8.8.8 syllables per line). Simple rhythm supports bold and simple statement. This manner characterized the Elizabethan translation of the Psalms under the direction of Sternhold and Hopkins, of which Kethe's "All people that on earth do dwell" is an example. It characterizes also the Scottish metrical Psalms (e.g., "The Lord's my shepherd") and, though diluted by Augustan demands for more decorous and more abstract statement, the Tate and Brady version of the Psalms (1696) (e.g., "Through all the changing scenes of life").

It will be noticed that the main activity of hymn writers to the end of the seventeenth century lay in versifying the Psalms. One of the greatest of English hymn writers, Isaac Watts, began in the same way, but with the important innovation that he deliberately set out to Christianize the Psalms. There were writers in the seventeenth century, like Crossman and George Herbert, who produced hymns, but what of theirs are now used as hymns were often in the first place written as poems.

Charles Wesley exploited the freedom that Watts ventured upon to write hymns which were original compositions and not just metrical versions of something else. Together these two writers cover a very broad range of religious experience, Watts stressing the austere dignity and strength of God, Wesley his love and care. A later writer of the century, William Cowper, presents a strongly introspective view of the religious condition, and he too is in contrast, in this case with his collaborator in the *Olney Hymns* (1779), the converted slave trader and confident evangelist, John Newton. The contrast here is illustrated by the former's "O for a closer walk with God" and the latter's "Glorious things of Thee are spoken."

Nineteenth-century hymnody shows the influence of general poetic attitudes. There is something Romantic in the colorfulness and subjectivism to be found in the work of men such as Reginald Heber (1783–1826), Francis Lyte (1793–1847) and F. W. Faber (1814–43). The last-named was one of a group inspired by the revival of Catholic belief and practice. Others were Newman, Keble and the translators of Latin and

Greek hymns, J. M. Neale (1818–66) and Isaac Caswall (1814–78). Greater than any of these early nineteenth-century writers, however, was James Montgomery (1771–1854), who is remarkable both in his range and power.

The later nineteenth century saw the introduction and proliferation of hymnbooks, the best of which, such as *Hymns Ancient and Modern*, still survive. Demand stimulated supply, and important names such as Sabine Baring-Gould (1834–1924), Walsham How (1823–97) and John Ellerton (1826–93) belong to this period; and even into our own century there are some considerable hymn writers, such as G. W. Briggs (1875–1959). In general, however, the art was well past its best by about 1850.

As in Britain, so also the nineteenth century was the golden age of hymnody in America. Partly no doubt under the influence of European Romanticism but partly also because New England Puritanism was emerging from the gloomy emphases of its earlier years, there came an outburst of hymn writing connected with such names as Samuel F. Smith, William Cullen Bryant, Ray Palmer, George W. Doane and E. H. Sears. Later in the century there was a notable group of Harvard men, most of them Unitarians, and including Oliver Wendell Holmes, J. Russell Lowell, Henry Longfellow, Samuel Johnson and F. L. Hosmer. Probably the best known and the best of American hymnists, however, was the New England Quaker, J. G. Whittier, who wrote with awe, tenderness and humility about religious experience. Elizabeth Clephane and Fanny van Alstyne Crosby were notable women writers, stressing the evangelical experience of Christianity, and another woman, Julia Ward Howe, was the authoress of the great "Battle Hymn of the Republic," "Mine eyes have seen the glory of the coming of the Lord."

Hymns Ancient and Modern, 1861; 1904; revised, 1950.
The Methodist Hymn Book, 1876; 1904; 1933.   A.P.

I

IMAGISM was an Anglo-American poetic movement, with which Ezra Pound, F. S. Flint, T. E. Hulme, Amy Lowell and Edward Storer were associated. The word "imagist" appears to have been coined by Ezra Pound in 1912 and it was he who brought Richard Aldington and Hilda Doolittle ("H.D.") within the imagist circle. Collections of poetry by these and others appeared as *Some Imagist Poets* in 1915, 1916 and 1917, but by this latter date Pound was dissatisfied with the development of the movement and left. Lawrence, Joyce and William Carlos Williams were among the contributors. After 1918 the group lost its coherence, though some of its members, notably "H.D.," continued to write in the imagist manner.

That manner may be summarized as a concentration upon the image and, in Hulme's words, "absolutely accurate penetration and no verbiage." Pound's "A Few Don'ts" in the March 1913 issue of Harriet Monroe's review *Poetry* and Aldington's preface to the 1915 imagist volume have both been described as imagist manifestoes. Aldington set out six "essentials of all great poetry," namely, "1. To use the language of common speech, but to employ always the *exact* word ... 2. To create new rhythms—as the expression of new moods ... 3. To allow absolute freedom in the choice of subject ... 4. To present an image ... We believe that poetry should render particulars exactly ... 5. To produce poetry that is hard and clear, never blurred nor indefinite. 6. .... Concentration is of the very essence of poetry." More succinctly, Pound had written: "An 'Image' is that which presents an intellectual and emotional complex in an instant of time." Fundamentally, imagism was a recall to economy and discipline: "Poetry should be burned to the bone by austere fires and washed white with rains of affliction" (Aldington).   A.P.

INDIAN LITERATURE in English or Indo-Anglian, as it is sometimes called, has a comparatively short history. Little English was taught in India until after the government took over the administration of the subcontinent from the East India Company following the Indian Mutiny in 1857, but even since then the writing of English has taken place on only a very limited scale. There are good reasons for this. By contrast with other areas of British imperialism, India is the repository of ancient civilizations with their own religions, cultures, languages and literature, and all continued to function under British rule. Even where by

351

translation or original writing in English attempts have been made to convey the aura of India, there has always been the difficulty of expressing a sophisticated and complex culture to English readers totally ignorant of it and, what is more important, simply incapable of imagining its significance to native readers.

Some of the earliest work in English, the poetry of Henry Derozio (1809–31), Kashiprosad Ghose (1809–73) and Michael Madhusudan Dutt (1827–73) is very derivative of the English Romantics, especially of Byron. In *A Sheaf Gleaned in French Fields* (1875)—translations of French poems—Toru Dutt (1856–77) shows a delicate sensibility that is missing, for instance, in *The Golden Threshold* (1905), *The Bird of Time* (1912) and *The Broken Wing* (1917), the work of Sarojini Naidu (1879–1949). Mrs. Naidu knew members of the Rhymers' Club in the 1890s, and we remember the appeal of the East to some of these. W. B. Yeats wrote of Tagore, for example: "These lyrics . . . display in their thought a world I have dreamt of all my life long."

Two figures dominate the next phase of Indian literature—Tagore and Sri Aurobindo. Rabindranath Tagore (1861–1941) wrote mainly in Bengali, but he also translated his work (often abbreviated) into English, as in *Collected Poems and Plays* (1936). He wrote not only poems, plays and novels, but also philosophical and religious work, including the Hibbert Lectures for 1932, *The Religion of Man*. The words of Yeats above come from the introduction to *Gitanjali* (1912), a collection in which we see Tagore dealing with a double world of the phenomenal and the supernatural in an awareness of the simultaneously temporal and spiritual that produces conflict in some of his plays (e.g., *Natir Puja*). Sri Aurobindo (1872–1950) is even more mystical in *Collected Poems and Plays* (1942). His metaphysical treatise, *The Life Divine* (1939–40), has its poetical equivalent in the long *Savitri*, which traces the course of events up to and during the day on which Satyavan must die and sees in these events an allegory of the spiritual conquest of death through the emergence of the soul into divine or superconscient life.

More recently, the novel has been the dominant literary form. The political activities of Mahatma Gandhi undoubtedly inspired such novels of social consciousness as Shanker Ram (T. L. Natesan)'s *The Love of Dust* (1938), K. S. Venkataramani's *Murugun the Tiller* (1927) and *Kandan the Patriot* (1932), and Kamala Markandaya's *Some Inner Fury* (1956), whilst K. Nagarajan has written a historical novel of the 1930s in *Chronicles of Kedaram* (1961). Here Gandhi appears as a character, as he does also in the work of two better-known novelists, Mulk Raj Anand (1905–) and R. K. Narayan (1907–).

Anand, who comes from the North-West Frontier, concerned himself in his first two novels—*Untouchable* (1935) and *Coolie* (1936)—with two of

India's depressed classes. His next novel, *Two Leaves and a Bud* (1937), examined relationships on a tea plantation and is, in some ways, an Indian version of E. M. Forster's view of the communities there. After the trilogy of Lalu Singh—*The Village* (1939), *Across the Black Waters* (1940) and *The Sword and the Sickle* (1942)—Anand turned to the conflict of craft economy and capitalist manufacture in *The Big Heart* (1945). Later work, *The Private Life of an Indian Prince* (1953), *The Old Woman and the Cow* (1960) and *The Road* (1961), retains the vitality but lacks the power of the earlier. Narayan—*Swami and His Friends* (1935); *The Bachelor of Arts* (1937); *The English Teacher* (1945); *Mr. Sampath* (1949); *The Financial Expert* (1952); *Waiting for the Mahatma* (1955); *The Guide* (1959); *The Man-Eater of Malgudi* (1961)—writes with a wit and irony rare in Indo-Anglian literature, often about the imaginary Malgudi, which provides in his novels the type of small society in which everybody is recognizable and recognized. In the course of his work he has brought Malgudi into the contemporary world of financiers and film stars, and it is no better for that.

Raja Rao in his small output—*Kanthapura* (1938) and *The Serpent and the Rope* (1969)—tries to produce an English equivalent of Indian rural speech. The first of these novels is about the impact of Gandhi on a South Indian village; the second traces the relations of its Indian hero with his French wife and two Indian women, but, as with other Indian writings, behind the personal and sociological lie the metaphysical and even mystical questionings of the hero's soul.

Other authors who must be mentioned include, in the novel, Bhabani Bhattacharya, with *So Many Hungers!* (1947), *He Who Rides a Tiger* (1954) and *A Goddess Named Gold* (1960); Khushwant Singh, with *Train to Pakistan* (1956); G. V. Desani, with *All about Hr. Hatterr* (1948); and Balachandra Rajan, with *The Dark Dancer* (1959) and *Too Long in the West* (1961). In poetry, attention should be drawn to Nissim Ezekiel's *A Time to Change* (1951), *Sixty Poems* (1953) and *The Unfinished Man* (1960); to *Poems* (1960) and *Poems, 1955-65* (1966) by Dom Moraes (1938-); and to *Graffiti* (1962) and *Kanchenjunga* (1966) by Lawrence Bantleman (1943-).   A.P.

INGE, William (1913-) was born in Independence (Kansas) and attended the State University there. He has been a teacher, lecturer at Washington University and drama critic of the St. Louis *Star-Times*. In his work he has depicted the stifling conventionality of smalltown life, the frustrations and craving for excitement, the restricted horizons of characters like Cherie, the night club singer of *Bus Stop* (*p*. 1955; *f*. 1956), for whom Joplin (Missouri) is a "*big*" town." With Tennessee Williams, Inge helped to set the tone of Broadway in the 1950s, for both dramatists focused on individual loneliness and espoused a melodramatic sexuality, but Inge's world always seemed cosier and more confined. His concern with the dangers of alcoholism in *Come Back, Little Sheba* (1950; *p.* 1949; *f.* 1952) and of smooth talking, unemployed, attractive strangers in *Picnic* (1953; *f.* 1955) reflected the puritanism of the Middle West and revealed little psychological insight. *The Dark at the Top of the Stairs* (1958; *p.* 1957; *f.* 1960) and *A Loss of Roses* (1960; *p.* 1959; *f.* as *The Stripper*, 1963) deal with destructive family relationships.   D.P.M.

IRVING, Washington (1783–1859) was born in New York City of a trading family. Rather scrappily educated, he took up law in 1801. His early life was one of pleasure and fashionable pursuits, including contributions to his brother's *Morning Chronicle* (1802–03) as "Jonathan Oldstyle." After an exciting tour of Europe (1804–06), partly to recover his health, he returned to pass his law examination and to be involved in *Salmagundi* (1807–08), a satirical periodical. In 1809 his fiancée Matilda Hoffman died at seventeen; Irving was to remain a bachelor for the rest of his life. The same year saw the appearance of one of his best works, the burlesque *A History of New York, from the Beginning of the World to the End of the Dutch Dynasty* by "Diedrich Knickerbocker." Irving became increasingly involved in the family business, and this entailed a trip to Liverpool in 1815. He remained abroad until 1832. The firm became bankrupt in 1818, and Irving, encouraged by Sir Walter Scott, turned to writing for a living. He made an immediate success with *The Sketch Book of Geoffrey Crayon, Gent.*, a collection of essays and tales including the famous "Rip Van Winkle" and "The Legend of Sleepy Hollow." From then on Irving had a great European and American reputation for the charm of his work and for being the first major American author. Two other collections, *Bracebridge Hall* (1822) and *Tales of a Traveller* (1824), were followed by more serious attempts at narrative and history while living in Spain (1826–29), in particular *A History of the Life and Voyages of Christopher Columbus* and *The Conquest of Granada*. But "the Spanish sketch book," *The Alhambra* (1832), was the most popular work of the period. After a triumphant return to America, Irving's remaining literary life was rather an anticlimax, although his public honors increased, including diplomatic appointments in Spain and England. His most interesting work was about the West—*A Tour on the Prairies* (1835) and *Astoria* (about the fur trade, written at the request of John Jacob Astor, 1836). Irving, however, increasingly concentrated on biography and history, typified by *Oliver Goldsmith* (1840), a very congenial subject, and the monumental *Life of Washington* in five volumes, which occupied him until his death.

Irving's achievement was to become the first respected American writer, an achievement based on the mastery of a moderate gentlemanly tone. This had its sources in the English tradition of *The Spectator* essayists, but at his best Irving could also include the racier tradition of Sterne and the freshness of local tones. His success owed something to the confidence of New York ("Knickerbocker") culture and the mild mediation of romanticism (see "The Voyage" in *The Sketch Book*). Irving was never a very original writer—"Rip Van Winkle" was European legend Americanized—and he spent his literary life in search of adaptable materials on which he could exercise "the play of thought, and sentiment and language." At his most interesting his subject is being in search of a subject as in "The Stout Gentleman" (*Bracebridge Hall*). He burlesques and parodies serious forms, including history and biography, and his best work, his tales of the supernatural (e.g., "The Spectre Bridegroom" in *The Sketch Book*), manage both a mockery of superstition and a place for its excitements. His tone was remarkably assimilative, and though to later readers there is something slight, even hollow, in it, in its own context it has a resilience, a tone of poise and survival before the diverse pressures of American experience, which could also claim a place, even a preeminent cosmopolitan one, in the larger world of letters and culture.

Salmagundi, 1807–08.
A History of New York, 1809.
The Sketch Book of Geoffrey Crayon, Gent., 1820.
Bracebridge Hall, 1822.
Tales of a Traveller, 1824.
A History of the Life and Voyages of Christopher Columbus, 1828.
A Chronicle of the Conquest of Granada, 1829.
Voyages and Discoveries of the Companions of Columbus, 1831.
The Alhambra, 1832.
A Tour on the Prairies, 1835.
Astoria, 1836.
The Rocky Mountains; Digested from the Journal of Capt. B. L. E. Bonneville, 1837 (U.K. [and later U.S.] title: *The Adventures of Captain Bonneville . . . in the Rocky Mountains . . .*).
Oliver Goldsmith, 1840; revised, 1849.
Mahomet and His Successors, 1850.
Wolfert's Roost, and Other Papers, 1855 (sketches and tales).
Life of George Washington, 5 vols., 1855–59.
Works, 21 vols., New York: Putnam, 1860–61.
Complete Works, ed. H. Pochman and others, Madison: Univ. of Wisconsin Press, 1969– .
Life and Letters, ed. P. M. Irving, 4 vols., New York: Putnam, 1862–64.

D.B.H.

ISHERWOOD, Christopher (1904–), born in Disley (Cheshire) and educated at Repton and Corpus Christi College, Cambridge, taught in

London and Berlin, and later became a journalist. His first novels, *All the Conspirators* (1928) and *The Memorial* (1932), show his debt to E. M. Forster and Virginia Woolf, writers he much admires. He has written several novels, but the best of them are *Mr. Norris Changes Trains* (1935) and *Goodbye to Berlin* (1939), in which acutely observed social comedy conveys the horror of corruption and threatening disaster in Western Europe in 1938. He collaborated with W. H. Auden in plays of social comment, combining verse and prose. *The Dog beneath the Skin* (1935), a Freudian entertainment mingling pantomime, charade and musical comedy, is self-consciously clever but has its moments of gruesome gaiety. As the Chorus remarks, "We show you man caught in the trap of his terror, destroying himself." *The Ascent of F6* (1936), also heavily indebted to Freud, is more solemn. *On the Frontier* (1938) is an attempt to assert the dignity of man in the face of encroaching political corruption. These plays have their effective moments, but none of them solved the problem of reinstating poetry in the modern theater. Isherwood writes best as a detached, witty observer of men and manners, as in the novels about Berlin and in *The Condor and the Cows* (1949), a diary of a trip to South America. When his writing is more personal, it parades a bruised vulnerability which limits its appeal as, for example, in the novel *The World in the Evening* (1954). Isherwood emigrated to America in 1939 and became an American citizen in 1946. His work also includes *The Bhagavad-Gita* (1944) and *How to Know God: The Yoga Aphorisms of Patanjali* (1953), both translated with Swami Prabhavananda, and the biographical memoir of his parents, *Kathleen and Frank* (1971).

All the Conspirators, 1928.
The Memorial, 1932.
Mr. Norris Changes Trains, 1935 (U.S. title: *The Last of Mr. Norris*).
The Dog beneath the Skin (with W. H. Auden), 1935 (play).
The Ascent of F6 (with Auden), 1936 (play).
On the Frontier (with Auden), 1938 (play).
Lions and Shadows, 1938 (autobiography).
Journey to a War (with Auden), 1939.
Goodbye to Berlin, 1939.
Prater Violet, 1945.
The Condor and the Cows, 1949.
The World in the Evening, 1954.
A Single Man, 1964.
A Meeting by the River, 1967.
Kathleen and Frank, 1971.   S.M.S.

J

JACOBSON, Dan. See **African Literature.**

JAMES, C. L. R. See **Caribbean Literature.**

JAMES, G. P. R. (George Payne Rainsford) (1799–1860) was born in London. He was historiographer royal to William IV and afterwards held posts in the consular service in Massachusetts (1850–52), Virginia (1852) and Venice (1856–60). Besides historical writings, such as *The Life of Edward the Black Prince* (1836), he also wrote historical novels, which show the influence of Scott. The first of these, *Richelieu* (1829), has affinities with *Quentin Durward*. Subsequent novels included *Darnley* (1830), *Philip Augustus* (1831) and *Mary of Burgundy* (1833) amongst an output prolific both in number and length. His characters are conventional and the interest of his novels lies in their intrigue. His pompous style was parodied by Thackeray in "Novels by Eminent Hands."   A.P.

JAMES, Henry (1843–1916) was born in New York City, second son of Henry James, Sr., who believed that his children were to be citizens of the world, and to this end insisted that they go to Europe where they would get the "sensuous education" America could not provide. Though James entered Harvard Law School in 1862 and also considered a career as a painter, he finally chose to be a writer and expatriate. After 1886, whether for reasons of health, economy or literature, he lived mainly in Europe. After a short stay in Paris where he met distinguished writers like Turgenev and Flaubert, he settled in London in 1876. His output was tremendous and financially rewarding, but in his later years he seems to have felt neglected by the public. His attempts to win a larger recognition in the theater were disastrously unsuccessful. The death of his brother William and of several other friends darkened his life and the coming of the First World War particularly distressed him. When America did not immediately enter the war, James made the solemn gesture of becoming a British citizen. He was given the Order of Merit a month before his death.

James's choice of Europe was scarcely surprising in view of his upbringing. It also reflected his feeling that America was hostile to art and deficient in the social strata necessary for novel writing. He demonstrates this in his biography of Hawthorne (1879), whom he much admired but whom he portrays struggling to create works of art out of the thin American scene. Where Hawthorne created emblematic fables, James, by choosing Europe, gained more than a *mise en scène* for his novels; he found his major theme and moral dilemma—the passionate pilgrim, attracted by the alluring but perilous society of Europe. He began his long investigation of this problem in *Roderick Hudson* (1876).

Hudson, a New England sculptor of some potential, must go to Italy if he is to develop as an artist. Unfortunately, in Rome he falls in love with a young girl and is distracted from his work and his faithful fiancée back in America. Moreover, the girl's mother will be satisfied with nothing less than a prince for her daughter. The novel ends with the destruction of Hudson in a storm in the Swiss Alps (whether by suicide or accident is not made clear). Even at this stage James is more complex than the equation America/innocence versus Europe/experience suggests. With or without Europe Hudson is doomed; and the girl he falls in love with is herself American. Most of James's characters, in fact, are Americans, the crucial distinction possibly being between expatriates (sophisticated but corrupt) and natives (innocent but socially ignorant).

James saw that the artist was very much a special case. In *The American* (1877) and *Daisy Miller* (1879) he brought an American businessman and a young girl to Europe with similar consequences, but his first mature treatment of the dilemma was in *The Portrait of a Lady* (1881). In this novel he finally mastered the technique of using relationships with other people to objectify his heroine's maturing moral sense. In *Washington Square* (1881) and *The Bostonians* (1886) he continued to evaluate the American character, but this time in its native environment. In all these novels his characters belong to the leisured upper class. *The Princess Casamassima* (1886), a story of anarchists in London, showed James exploring working-class characters with questionable success, since men and women who have to work have less time and energy for the niceties of moral choice. Throughout his novels money is, however, a prime motive, whether the character has too much (Isobel or Milly) or not enough (Kate or Hyacinth Robinson).

What Maisie Knew (1897), a story of immorality seen through the eyes of a child, and *The Awkward Age* (1899), written in dialogue, showed James perfecting his final style. His interest in the theater was no accident, but part and parcel of his urge to render events more dramatically in his novels. At the same time the metaphoric content of his style, always high, was intensified to produce his most baffling novel, *The Sacred Fount* (1901). This is apparently a satire on his own methods, but it also ushers in the "symbolic" period of the last three novels—*The Wings of the Dove* (1902), *The Ambassadors* (1903) and *The Golden Bowl* (1904). Critics have divided sharply in their estimates of these works, and many readers have found James's style, possibly as much due to the habit of dictation as to the search for the right word, unrewarding.

James's remarkable concern with texture and structure can be seen in his revisions, notebooks, prefaces and critical essays which alone would give him a considerable reputation. In psychological realism, structure, use of metaphor and the depiction of moral shades he is without equal, but the consistently conscious artist seems at times, according to some critics, to have left life behind. In 1903 James visited America again and wrote *The American Scene* (1907) and the unfinished novel *The Ivory Tower*, which would seem to deny this view.

A Passionate Pilgrim and other Tales, 1875.
Roderick Hudson, 1876 (*s.* 1875).
The American, 1877 (*s.* 1876–77).
French Poets and Novelists, 1878.
The Europeans, 1878 (*s.* 1876).
Daisy Miller, 1879 (*s.* 1878).
Hawthorne, 1879.
Washington Square, 1881 (*s.* 1880; *f.* as *The Heiress*, 1949).
The Portrait of a Lady, 1881 (*s.* 1880–81).
The Bostonians, 1886 (*s.* 1885–86).
The Princess Casamassima, 1886 (*s.* 1885–86).
Partial Portraits, 1888.
The Tragic Muse, 1890 (*s.* 1889–90).
The Lesson of the Master, 1892.
The Spoils of Poynton, 1897 (*s.* 1896).
What Maisie Knew, 1897.
The Two Magics, 1898 (including "The Turn of the Screw," *s.* 1898; *f.* as *The Innocents*, 1961).
The Awkward Age, 1899 (*s.* 1898–99).
The Sacred Fount, 1901.
The Wings of the Dove, 1902.
The Ambassadors, 1903.
The Golden Bowl, 1904.
Views and Reviews, 1908.
A Small Boy and Others, 1913.
Notes on Novelists, 1914.
The Ivory Tower, 1917.
The Sense of the Past, 1917.

Novels and Stories, 35 vols., London: Macmillan, 1921–23.
Complete Plays, ed. L. Edel, Philadelphia: Lippincott; London: Hart-Davis, 1949.

Complete Tales, ed. L. Edel, 12 vols., Philadelphia: Lippincott; London: Hart-Davis, 1962–65.
The Art of the Novel (critical prefaces), ed. R. P. Blackmur, New York: C. Scribner's Sons, 1934.
Letters, ed. P. Lubbock, 2 vols., London: Macmillan, 1920.
Notebooks, ed. F. O. Matthiessen and K. B. Murdock, New York: Oxford Univ. Press, 1947; London: Oxford Univ. Press, 1948.   A.P.H.

JAMES, William (1842–1910), psychologist and philosopher, brother of Henry James, was born in New York City, educated abroad and at the Lawrence Scientific School (1861–64) and Harvard (M.D., 1869). James lectured in physiology at Harvard (1872–80), but an increasing interest in psychology and philosophy—in particular, the hypothesis of Darwin and Spencer—led him to join the Department of Philosophy and to give his celebrated lectures on "The Philosophy of Evolution." As early as 1896 James used the term "pragmatism"—the testing of truth by practical consequences—to characterize his philosophic attitude and method. In 1890 he published *The Principles of Psychology*, a carefully documented account of contemporary psychological knowledge together with his own hypothesis that mind and body are basically inseparable, with mind a function of the physical organism causing the individual to adjust to the environment. *The Will to Believe* (1897), a collection of essays, defined James's position as a "radical empiricist" and asserted that in matters of faith beyond the possibility of experimental proof, the yardstick for acceptance must be "the will to believe." Appointed Gifford Lecturer on Natural Religion at the University of Edinburgh (1901–02), James published his lectures in *The Varieties of Religious Experience* (1902), in which he indicates the practical values of religious belief while denying any necessary conflict between religion and the apparently deterministic implications of science. His other philosophic writings include *Pragmatism* (1907), *A Pluralistic Universe* (1909), and *Essays in Radical Empiricism* (1912). The most distinguished American philosopher of his day, and a writer of great clarity and verve, James also opposed the Spanish–American War and American imperialistic ventures, and attacked discrimination against spiritualists and Christian Scientists.

The Principles of Psychology, 1890.
The Will to Believe, 1897.
The Varieties of Religious Experience, 1902.
Pragmatism, 1907.
A Pluralistic Universe, 1909.
The Meaning of Truth, 1909.
Memories and Studies, ed. Henry James, 1911.

Some Problems of Philosophy, 1911.
Essays in Radical Empiricism, ed. R. B. Perry, 1912.

Collected Essays and Reviews, New York: Longmans, 1920.
Letters, ed. H. [Henry] James, 2 vols., Boston: Atlantic Monthly Press;
London: Longmans, 1920.   J.W.

JARRELL, Randall (1914–65) was born in Nashville (Tennessee), but spent most of his childhood in California. He graduated from Vanderbilt University in 1935, where he was regarded as a brilliant student, and took his Master's degree there in 1938. Although Vanderbilt's intellectual atmosphere was then dominated by Allen Tate and the Fugitive group, Jarrell remained largely uninfluenced by their ideas. He did, however, in 1938 follow John Crowe Ransom to Kenyon College for a short time, but in 1939 he moved to the University of Texas. In 1942 he entered the Army Air Force, where he was a "celestial navigation tower operator"; the title at least pleased him. Several of his finest and best-known poems, "Transient Barracks," "Eighth Air Force," "The Death of the Ball-Turret Gunner," arise out of this experience. After the war he taught briefly at Sarah Lawrence College, New York, before moving to the Women's College of the University of North Carolina at Greensboro where he taught English and imaginative writing. He was killed in a car accident.

Besides poetry, Jarrell is noted for his critical writing, especially the essays collected in *Poetry and the Age*. He was at different times poetry editor of *Partisan Review*, literary editor of *The Nation*, and a frequent contributor to *The Sewanee Review*, *The Kenyon Review*, *Poetry* and *The New York Times Book Review*. As a reviewer he gained a reputation for stringency, and even cruelty, for the rigor and occasional dismissiveness of his assessments. His criticism, somewhat influenced by that of William Empson, is precise and linguistically detailed. His essay on Robert Frost containing his analysis of "Design" is an excellent example of this.

The Rage for the Lost Penny (in *Five Young American Poets*), 1940.
Blood for a Stranger, 1942.
Little Friend, Little Friend, 1945.
Losses, 1948.
The Seven-League Crutches, 1951.
Poetry and the Age, 1953 (essays).
Pictures from an Institution, 1954 (novel).
Selected Poems, 1955.
The Woman at the Washington Zoo, 1960.
A Sad Heart at the Supermarket, 1962 (essays).

The Lost World, 1965.

Complete Poems, New York: Farrar, Straus, 1969.   J.P.W.

JEFFERIES, Richard (1848–87), son of a Wiltshire farmer, lived in rural obscurity and wrote about the English countryside. His early works, including *The Gamekeeper at Home* (1878), reveal the naturalist's keen and loving eye for country life and rural husbandry and an ear for regional dialect. Description is increasingly suffused with an atmosphere of magic and wonder in later writings such as *Wood Magic* (1881) and *Bevis* (1882). The author's imaginative survey of Wiltshire is made poignant by his realization of encroaching industrialism. *The Story of My Heart* (1883) is his spiritual autobiography.   O.K.

JEFFERS, Robinson (1887–1962) was born in Pittsburgh, the son of a Presbyterian minister and professor of Old Testament literature. At five years old Jeffers was learning Greek. During childhood he traveled much in Europe with his parents, but in 1903 they moved to California which became Jeffers's permanent home. He graduated from Occidental College, studied medicine for three years, followed by forestry. In 1912 a legacy made him financially independent and he published his first volume of poetry, *Flagons and Apples* (1912), followed by *Californians* (1916). Neither volume received much attention, even from the author himself, who included nothing from them in his *Selected Poetry* (1938). Eight years were dominated by Jeffers's love for a married woman, Una Call Kuster, who finally became his wife in 1913. The hawklike woman and the house he built for her above Carmel Bay, quarrying the granite and raising the stone with his own hands, were among the few but inexhaustibly potent symbols essential to the articulation of Jeffers's vision. The isolated tower on the continent's rock edge was a symbol of heroic individualism, deepening through misanthropy to a final rejection of human existence.

"Tamar" (1924) and "Roan Stallion" (1925), followed by "Cawdor" (1928), were immediate critical and popular successes. Contemporaries saw in them a force comparable to Aeschylus and Sophocles. "The Tower beyond Tragedy" indeed handles the theme of the *Oresteia* in language which aspires to a Homeric quality. Other poems are narratives achieving a fusion of contemporary realism and archetypal myth, with its complex patterns of incest and murder. Jeffers found the timelessness which he considered the essential quality of poetry in the Monterey coast mountains, where he saw people still living as they did in the sagas or Homer's Ithaca. The dramatic poem "Dear Judas" (1929) reinterprets the suffering of Jesus as a source not of atonement but of power. *Medea* (1946) was a free adaptation of Euripides; "The Double Axe" (1948) is closely related to the Book of Job; "Hungerfield" (1954) shows a modern Hercules whose wrestling with death reaps a bitterly futile success. "Thurso's Landing" (1932) and "Give Your Heart to the Hawks" (1933) are realistic novels in verse, but in the latter poem, the fratricide, Lance Fraser, whose self-lacerating remorse drives him to tear his hands on barbed wire, has affinities with the Jesus of "Dear Judas" and the complex Hanged God, part Prometheus, part Odin, in "At the Birth of an Age."

Jeffers's sense of man's cosmic insignificance led him to a philosophy of "inhumanism," involving a renunciation of human individuality and consciousness. It was a renunciation of the "introversion" or excessive self-awareness of modern life, for which incest was his rather overworked symbol. Inhumanism may be an attempt to intellectualize what, elsewhere in his poems, is simply an infatuation with death. Against these images of annihilation his self-destroying characters achieve heroic stature not through the catharsis proper to tragedy but through sheer intensity. Jeffers's style is often conspicuously reminiscent of Whitman's, while his thought, antidemocratic and isolationist, is in ironic contrast. Jeffers modeled his verse rhythms on the movement of waves, the pulse of blood, the cadences of speech. His chosen images were the stallion and the mountain lion, the broken-winged hawk and the trapped falcon. A woman's fiery hair is a flag of life; a man falls like a cleft redwood. Jeffers's violent narratives now seem escapist rather than realistic and his rhetoric flabby; his evocation of landscape and action remains impressive.

Flagons and Apples, 1912.
Californians, 1916.
Tamar and Other Poems, 1924.
Roan Stallion, Tamar and Other Poems, 1925.
The Women at Point Sur, 1927.
Cawdor and Other Poems, 1928.
Dear Judas, and Other Poems, 1929.
Thurso's Landing and Other Poems, 1932.
Give Your Heart to the Hawks and Other Poems, 1933.
Solstice and Other Poems, 1935.
Such Counsels You Gave to Me and Other Poems, 1937.
Be Angry at the Sun, 1941.
Medea, Freely Adapted from the Medea of Euripides, 1946.
The Double Axe and Other Poems, 1948.
Hungerfield and Other Poems, 1954.

Selected Poetry, New York: Random House, 1938.
Selected Letters, 1897–1962, ed. A. N. Ridgeway, Baltimore: Johns Hopkins Press, 1968.   M.T.

JEFFERSON, Thomas (1743–1826), third president of the United States, was born in Virginia, graduated from William and Mary College (1762) and practiced law (1767–74). He served in the House of Burgesses (1769–95) and was governor of Virginia (1779–81). Jefferson made a valuable contribution to Revolutionary theory with *A Summary View of the Rights of British America* (1774). A delegate to the Continental Congress, Jefferson drafted the Declaration of Independence (1776), his greatest literary and political achievement. The formal announcement of the thirteen colonies' separation from Great Britain, the Declaration drew upon prevailing natural rights philosophy and was expressed in Jefferson's felicitous style, a combination of precision, clarity and elegance. While minister to France (1785–89), he published *Notes on the State of Virginia*, a compendium of social, political, geographic and natural characteristics of the region. Washington's first secretary of state, Jefferson resigned in protest over Hamilton's fiscal and centralizing policies. Leader of the Democratic Republican party, and vice-president under John Adams, Jefferson was chosen president in the tied election of 1800 by the House of Representatives. His administration (1801–09) was marked by the Louisiana Purchase (1803), the Lewis and Clark and Pike expeditions (1807), the Embargo Act (adopted 1807, repealed 1809) and by simplicity and economy in government. In retirement, Jefferson founded the University of Virginia and contributed to the revival of classical architecture in America. Philosophically, he favored an agrarian society of independent farmers in a politically decentralized republic. He composed his own epitaph: "Here was buried Thomas Jefferson, Author of the Declaration of American Independence, of the Statute of Virginia for Religious Freedom, and Father of the University of Virginia."

Papers, ed. J. P. Boyd and others, Princeton: Princeton Univ. Press, 1950– , and in progress (60 vols. projected).   J.W.

JEFFREY, Francis, Lord (1773–1850), son of an Edinburgh lawyer, was educated at Glasgow and Edinburgh Universities and for a short time at Oxford. Called to the Scottish bar in 1794, he was the first editor of *The Edinburgh Review* (1802–29). He was lord advocate (1830–34), a judge in the Court of Session (1834) and member of Parliament (1832).

Jeffrey is a discerning and stimulating critic of literature within his limits, which are basically those of the orthodox good taste of his day. On contemporary works he is always worth examining. He knew most of the Edinburgh literary figures of its great age and was friendly with younger writers such as Carlyle and Dickens.

(See also **Essays.**)

Contributions to The Edinburgh Review, 4 vols., London: Longman, 1844.
W.R.

JENNINGS, Elizabeth (1926–), born in Boston (Lincolnshire) and educated at Oxford, worked in advertising and in the Oxford City Library before devoting herself to writing. She has published several volumes of verse, including *Poems*, which won an Arts Council Award in 1953, *Collected Poems* (1967) and *The Animals' Arrival* (1969). She has sought by means of analysis and meditation to convey her intensely personal feelings. Her poems, though occasionally remote and elusive, avoid artificiality and affectation and make their effect by quietly conversational, yet accurate, language.
O.K.

JEWETT, Sarah Orne (1849–1909) was born in South Berwick (Maine), a doctor's daughter. Her grandfather's legacy gave her leisure for writing. W. D. Howells advised her to collect her stories about Maine; the result was *Deephaven* (1877), local color sketches tenuously connected by a visitor's viewpoint. This pattern was perfected in that supreme distillation of her region, *The Country of the Pointed Firs* (1896). Three novels, verse, essays and many early tales are negligible beside the stories, subtly exploring New England experience, which she published between 1886 and 1896. Friend and companion of Mrs. Annie Fields, the Boston hostess, she had many literary acquaintances and admirers.

Best Stories, ed. W. Cather, 2 vols., Boston: Houghton Mifflin, 1925.
Letters, ed. R. Cary, Waterville, Me.: Colby College Press. 1956; revised, 1967.
A.S.

JOHNSON, James Weldon (1871–1938) was born in Jacksonville (Florida) and distinguished himself by becoming the first Negro to be admitted to the bar in that state since Reconstruction. Johnson served as United States consul in Venezuela and Nicaragua and was professor of creative literature at Fisk University. His first book, *The Autobiography of An Ex-Colored Man* (1912), was an impressive novel, though at the time it was widely accepted as a genuine autobiography. The editor of two collections of Negro spirituals and *The Book of Negro Poetry*, he published an autobiography, *Along This Way* (1933), in addition to several volumes of poems and essays, such as *God's Trombones* (1927), *Black Manhattan* (1930) and *Saint Peter Relates an Incident of the Resurrection Day: Selected Poems* (1930).
C.B.

JOHNSON, Lionel (1867–1902), born at Broadstairs (Kent), won scholarships to Winchester in 1880, and in 1886 to New College,

Oxford, where he knew Pater and took a first. In 1890 he began a lifetime's reviewing, though his wish was to be known as a poet, and his first book was *The Art of Thomas Hardy* (1894). A member of the Rhymers' Club, he was associated with the group connected with *The Yellow Book* and *The Savoy*, and concerned also, though Irish more by desire than descent, in the Irish literary revival. Yeats, who learned from Johnson the value of scholarship, weaves him into his myths in *Autobiographies* and "In Memory of Major Robert Gregory," as does Pound in "Monsieur Verog."

His poems are precise and meticulous, showing a love of tradition and the influence of Celticism, the classics and Roman Catholicism, his adopted religion. He is frequently cited among "typical decadents," yet the most "ninetyish" feature of his poetry is a Pateresque attempt to achieve a musical effect through repetition. Always skillful, the poems can be cold or academic, but can also rise to an austere perfection. His criticism, largely ignored though frequently illuminating, is of the school of Arnold and Pater and shows a vast range of reference. Though often written hastily for a review, it is always the calm and fair judgment of an educated and refined taste.

(See also **Romantic Movement, The.**)

Poems, 1895.
Ireland, with Other Poems, 1897.
Post Liminium: Essays and Critical Papers, ed. T. Whittemore, 1911.
Some Winchester Letters, 1919.
Reviews and Critical Papers, ed. R. Shafer, 1921.

Complete Poems, ed. I. Fletcher, London: Unicorn Press, 1953.   K.T.

JOHNSON, Pamela Hansford (Lady Snow) (1912–   ) was born and educated in London. Her work is often witty, often comic, but at the same time she is concerned with moral problems and especially with the effect of circumstances that alter cases. She often leads us uncomfortably to refuse the orthodox judgment and yet unsurely to suggest another. Her own concern about social reaction to criminal behavior was shown in her forthright comments on the Moors murder trial, *On Iniquity* (1967). Of an output of some twenty novels the following deserve particular mention: *This Bed Thy Centre* (1935); *The Trojan Brothers* (1944); *An Avenue of Stone* (1947); *The Unspeakable Skipton* (1959); *The Humbler Creation* (1959); *An Error of Judgment* (1962); *Cork Street, Next to the Hatter's* (1965); *The Honours Board* (1970); and *The Holiday Friend* (1972).
A.P.

JOHNSON, Samuel (1709–84) was the son of a bookseller in Lichfield (Staffordshire). Both parents were elderly and he was a sickly child.

An attack of scrofula affected his eyesight and nerves generally. Throughout his life he was rarely free from pain, and to his damaged nervous system must be attributed some at least of the emotional instability (manifesting itself through alternations between near-hysteric gaiety and deep despair), which he waged a lifelong struggle to control.

Johnson was a voracious reader in childhood, and after attending local schools, he entered Pembroke College, Oxford in 1728, astonishing his tutor at their first meeting with the extent of his classical scholarship. He was extremely poor and his departure from Oxford in December 1729 may have been due to poverty, but it may equally have been caused by mental distress. His nervous illness was increasing and he suffered from obsessive neuroses, melancholia and a complicated sense of unworthiness and guilt. He fought determinedly against them, and after his father's death in 1731 took a teaching post at Market Bosworth (Leicestershire), which proved intolerable. He went to stay with a friend, Edmund Hector, at Birmingham and there began to write for publication (newspaper essays and a translation of Father Lobo's *A Voyage to Abyssinia*). In 1735 Johnson married Mrs. Henry Porter ("Tetty"), a widow twenty years his senior, and used her money to start a school near Lichfield, which soon failed. David Garrick was one of his few pupils, and in 1737 master and pupil went to London together to seek their fortunes.

For fifteen years Johnson led a life of drudgery for the London booksellers, the flavor of which can be caught in his moving *Life of Mr. Richard Savage* (1744). He did brilliant hack work for Edmund Cave's *The Gentleman's Magazine*, covering every conceivable topic, including parliamentary reports invented from brief notes supplied by eyewitnesses of the debates. When he learned that people took his reports for gospel, he characteristically refused to write any more. Apart from the satires in imitation of Juvenal, *London* (1738) and its majestic successor, *The Vanity of Human Wishes* (1749), the chief literary milestones of these years are *A Life of Mr. Richard Savage* and the production by Garrick of Johnson's classical tragedy, *Irene* (1749). From 1747 to 1755 Johnson labored at *A Dictionary of the English Language*, the publication of which brought widespread acclaim. From 1750 to 1752 he wrote the twice-weekly essay paper, *The Rambler*. He also contributed to *The Adventurer* (1753–54) and wrote a weekly essay paper, *The Idler*, from 1758 to 1760. These were shorter essays than those in *The Rambler*, but as powerful in thought and agreeably varied in content. *Rasselas* (1759), an Abyssinian moral tale, was written in the evenings of a single week to pay the expenses of his mother's funeral.

Following this phase of literary activity Johnson seems to have gone through a period of terrible depression and religious despair in the early 1760s. In spite of this his edition of Shakespeare (with its splendid preface) was finished in 1765. His financial and social situation, too, was improving. In 1762 he received a government pension and in 1764 he met the Thrales, in whose comfortable and cultured household at Streatham he was to spend long periods. Boswell met Johnson in 1763 and began the records of his conversation which were later to be worked up in the *Life*. In 1773 Boswell and Johnson visited the Highlands and Skye, and the tour is recorded in Johnson's *A Journey to the Western Islands of Scotland* (1775) and Boswell's *Tour* (1785). In 1779–81 Johnson wrote *The Lives of the Poets* at the request of the London booksellers. His social life blossomed in his later years and his fame was far-reaching. On his death in 1784 he was buried in Westminster Abbey.

It has been truly said that "the Christian and humanist traditions meet in Johnson and he draws his strength from both." In all his work he imparts a sense of awe and humility in the face of eternity and a marveling awareness of the dignity accorded to man by his capacity for reason. For him the eighteenth-century belief in reason was achieved not by easy optimism but through a desperate battle against his own mental infirmities; the power of reason seemed to be the ultimate salvation of his personality and the greatest gift of God. Johnson is a writer whose primary aim is to discover and codify truth. He was interested in science and his writing constantly reveals a process of examining, clarifying and resolving problems, leading to a powerfully compressed final aphorism in which general truth is revealed, a process which has direct analogies with scientific methods. But Johnson's humanity and sense of the tragic element in human life, together with the inevitability of suffering, ensure that his reasoning is suffused with passion and vivid psychological insights. Even a long poem like *The Vanity of Human Wishes* combines reasoned clarity and orderliness of structure with a somber awareness of human ills and a pathetic sense of this inevitability. In *Rasselas* similar themes are more fully examined. This work explores literary and ideological conventions such as pastoralism, romance and the eighteenth-century optimistic dreams of Pope's *An Essay on Man*, because to Johnson all fiction encourages the growth of stock attitudes to existence, softening the hardships, but reducing man's ability to appreciate life's true reality. Johnson sincerely held that all thinking men must prefer realism to invention, since the business of literature is to illuminate and help the reader to evaluate life. His criticism is moralistic in the most sympathetic, informed and compassionate sense of that term. His major works are all attempts to define and establish truth. The *Dictionary* removed the linguistic uncertainty which writers like Swift and Pope feared and lamented. It created new standards for understanding language in its historical development and numerous shades of meaning. The preface to *The Plays of William Shakespeare* brilliantly defines the principles of true textual editing and the concept of historical criticism. In *The Lives of the Poets* (a series of prefatory essays for a collection of seventeenth- and eighteenth-century poetry) Johnson created a new kind of literary biography in which the author's life and times were fully considered in understanding and appraising his work. Johnson's strong classical scholarship and his own accomplishment as an exponent of serious couplet poetry make him a powerfully discerning critic of Dryden, Pope and the Augustan versifiers. On the Metaphysicals and Milton his certainty of the superiority of the neoclassical tradition causes difficulties, but even here he discerns and skillfully defines many things he disapproves of, and as in all his criticism he is refreshingly able to fly from the authority of the "rules" to that of nature when he feels that an unorthodox piece of writing has quality.

Johnson's prose style was latinate and dignified during most of his his career, then agreeably simpler and direct in *The Lives of the Poets*. His formal style with its periods, antitheses and inversions was long imitated and had, on the whole, no very good influence. There was a reaction later (see the opening of *Vanity Fair* for an amusing instance), but today it is generally understood how appropriate "Johnsonese" was for that ordered examination of experiences which operates ceaselessly throughout Johnson's work.

As a poet Johnson gave the heroic couplet a quality of sheer weight and emotion in expressing his somber view of the inevitability of suffering which points forward to Crabbe and, in another style, to Wordsworth—though Wordsworth would have been annoyed by the comparison. Johnson's long couplet poems have a rhetorical urgency and tendency to build up into dramatic verse-paragraphs, a mode quite unlike Pope's and one that again points forward to Crabbe. In shorter pieces he could achieve the same weight and humanity of feeling, as the moving "Elegy on the Death of Dr. Robert Levet" reveals.

Johnson's fascination is twofold. First, the nobility of his character and the depth and pithiness of his judgments are unforgettable. Secondly, thanks to Boswell's biography with its immense re-creation of Johnson's conversations in their social environment, we know more of the man than of any other English writer (save possibly, now that his journals have been rediscovered, of Boswell himself). For Johnson in his relaxation, Fanny Burney's *Diary* and Mrs. Thrale's *Anecdotes* (1786) have interesting details to add. Johnson was a man of splendidly large views, with comparable idiosyncrasies and prejudices. No man has written with a truer sense of human weakness allied to a broad vision of the dignity of human intelligence.

London: A Poem in Imitation of the Third Satire of Juvenal, 1738.
The Account of the Life of Mr. Richard Savage, 1744.

The Plan of a Dictionary of the English Language, 1747.
Irene: A Tragedy, 1749.
The Vanity of Human Wishes: The Tenth Satire of Juvenal Imitated, 1749.
The Rambler, 1750–52.
A Dictionary of the English Language, 2 vols., 1755.
Proposals for Printing the Dramatic Works of Shakespeare, 1756.
Rasselas: The Prince of Abyssinia, 1759.
The Idler, 1758–60.
(ed.) *The Plays of William Shakespeare,* 8 vols., 1765.
A Journey to the Western Islands of Scotland, 1775.
The Lives of the Poets, 1779–81.

Works, ed. A. T. Hazen, H. W. Liebert, and others, 9 vols., New Haven:
   Yale Univ. Press, 1958– .
Poems, ed. D. Nichol Smith and E. L. McAdam, Oxford: Clarendon
   Press, 1941.
The Lives of the English Poets, ed. G. B. Hill, 3 vols., Oxford: Clarendon
   Press, 1905.
Letters, ed. R. W. Chapman, 3 vols., Oxford: Clarendon Press, 1952.

W.R.

JOHNSON, Samuel (hymn writer). See **Hymns.**

JONES, Ebenezer. See **Spasmodics, The.**

JONES, Henry Arthur (1851–1929), a farmer's son, left the drapery
business in 1879 to write for the theater. *The Silver King* (p. 1882), a melodrama, established his position and, though he was to write over sixty
plays of various types, all with great technical skill, melodramatic effects
taint even his best work—serious drama like *Michael and His Lost Angel*
(p. 1896) and comedies like his most memorable play, *The Liars* (p.
1897). Though he later indulged in controversial arguments, his fame
rests on the creation with Pinero of a new thoughtful drama in England.

The Renascence of the English Drama: Essays, Lectures and Fragments, 1883–94,
   London: Macmillan, 1895.

Representative Plays, ed. C. Hamilton, 4 vols., Boston: Little, Brown, 1926.
Life and Letters, ed. J. D. Jones, London: Gollancz, 1930.   K.T.

JONES, James (1921–   ) was born in Illinois. He served in the army
during the Second World War and was inspired to write after reading
Thomas Wolfe. Latterly he has lived in Paris. *From Here to Eternity* (1951; *f.*
1953) documents the brutality of a peacetime army stationed in Hawaii.

Some Came Running (1957; *f.* 1958) concerns an ex-soldier hoping to write, and his friend, a professional gambler. Set in a small Illinois town, the novel recounts its hero's drinking and fornications as well as his philosophic discussions. The twin concerns indicate the scope of Jones's pretensions and his very marketable sensationalism. *The Thin Red Line* (1962; *f.* 1964) is a brilliant examination of the true nature of war and killing. His later work includes *Go to the Widow-Maker* (1967), *The Ice-Cream Headache and Other Stories* (1968) and *The Merry Month of May* (1971).   J.L.M.

JONES, LeRoi (1934–   ) received his A.B. from Howard University in 1954 and M.A.s from Columbia University and the New School for Social Research, where he also worked as an instructor.

Jones spent his early twenties in Greenwich Village, founding *Jugen* magazine in 1958. His first book of poems, *Preface to a Twenty Volume Suicide Note*, was published three years later. To many it seemed that he was on the verge of a successful and prestigious literary career. Another volume of poems, *The Dead Lecturer*, appeared in 1964, followed by an experimental novel, *The System of Dante's Hell*, in 1965, while two brilliant one-act plays, *Dutchman* and *The Slave*, had been produced in 1964. But at this point there occurred an abrupt caesura in Jones's life. In April 1964 he founded the short-lived but seminal Black Arts Repertory Theater in Harlem. Though this experiment in black theater was rapidly closed down, as a result of the withdrawal of federal funds, it proved profoundly important both to Jones and to the development of a genuine black culture in the United States. In 1965 Jones divorced his white wife, subsequently changing his name to Amiri Imamu Baraka and moving to Newark, New Jersey, where he established Spirit House. Constantly harassed by officialdom, Baraka has embraced an understandably violent rhetoric in creating powerful rituals of racial conflict avowedly intended solely for a black audience (see *Four Black Revolutionary Plays*).

Baraka is an impressive poet and a dramatist of genuine originality and power. His work stands as a constant reminder of the perhaps ineluctable connection between ethics and aesthetics.

Preface to a Twenty Volume Suicide Note, 1961.
Blues People: Negro Music in White America, 1963.
(ed.) *The Moderns: An Anthology of New Writing in America*, 1963.
The Dead Lecturer, 1964.
Dutchman and The Slave, 1964 (plays; *Dutchman f.* 1967).
The System of Dante's Hell, 1965.
Black Art, 1966.
Home: Social Essays, 1966.
The Baptism and The Toilet, 1967 (plays).

Tales, 1967.

Black Music, 1967.

(ed., with Larry Neal) *Black Fire: An Anthology of Afro-American Writing*, 1968.

Black Magic: Collected Poetry, 1961–1967, 1969.

Four Black Revolutionary Plays, 1969.

In Our Terribleness (with Billy Abernathy), 1970.

C.B.

JONSON, Ben (1572–1637) was educated at Westminster School under William Camden, the antiquary. He was in turn a bricklayer (with his stepfather), a soldier in the Netherlands, and an actor and playwright for Henslowe. During his career as an author, he twice suffered imprisonment for causing matter offensive to the authorities to be uttered on the stage. He was also held in 1598 for having killed a fellow actor in a duel and escaped death only by benefit of clergy. In this same year his comedy *Every Man in His Humour*, with Shakespeare in the cast, was successfully performed. *Every Man out of His Humour* followed it a year later.

Jonson's finest comedies belong to the years 1606 to 1616: *Volpone* (*p.* 1606), *Epicoene* (*p.* 1609), *The Alchemist* (*p.* 1610), *Bartholomew Fair* (*p.* 1614) and *The Devil Is an Ass* (*p.* 1616). In 1616 he became in effect the first poet laureate. Three years later he visited William Drummond of Hawthornden and his host set down his conversation for posterity. Jonson continued to write plays, though with less success, and by the 1630s he was something of a literary dictator. To be admitted to the Apollo Room in the Devil Tavern, where he presided, was to be "sealed of the tribe of Ben." Many of the younger writers—Herrick and Suckling, for example—considered themselves his literary "sons."

In addition to his comedies, Jonson wrote two tragedies, *Sejanus* (1605) and *Catiline* (1611). These are classically constructed plays on subjects from Roman history. Satire has an important place in each of them. In addition to his plays, he wrote many elegant and fanciful court masques (see **Masques**), a body of literary criticism that manages to be both neoclassical and sturdily independent, and a considerable volume of poetry, combining classical urbanity with idiomatic toughness.

Jonson's comedies constitute his main achievement. In them he opposed the dominant trends of his time. Shakespeare, the leading comic writer of the 1590s, favored a kind of comedy that was exotic in setting, accommodated absurdities with a minimum of satire, enabled a happy ending to supervene on perils and misfortunes, and recognized the supremacy of romantic love. Jonson set all but one of his major comedies in England, was nothing if not satirical, preferred poetic justice to happiness in his endings (and was not too scrupulous even about justice), and showed little or no interest in romantic love.

His models were the Latin comic writers, Plautus and Terence. Following them, he liked to operate within the limits of the classical unities of time, place and action. He borrowed stock characters from them: the boastful soldier, for example, and, more important, the quick-witted and unscrupulous servant or parasite, who functions as the mainspring of many of his plots. The intrigues initiated by a Mosca or a Face, confined within the narrow bounds of the three unities, develop an enormous complexity and pace. By act 3 the spectator has probably lost all recollection of how the situation arose; he dares not distract himself by speculating about its outcome; he is fully extended in apprehending it in its intricacy. As a result, no recollection or expectation takes from his astonishment when a further complication proves to be the very development that ludicrously unties the whole knot.

The characters who participate in such an action need to be severely simplified. Jonson formulated a theory of caricature in his doctrine of humors and showed himself a brilliant artist in caricature in his comedies from *Every Man in His Humour* onwards. In his greatest comedies the leading characters transcend caricature; but around Volpone and Mosca there are still the caricatured secondary figures, Corbaccio, Corvino, Voltore and the rest.

Jonson presents his characters with all the realism that their status as caricatures allows. In *Epicoene*, *The Alchemist* and *Bartholomew Fair* he reproduces the very language of various social classes and groups in contemporary London. His dialogue is packed with allusions to contemporary customs, habits and institutions. We see his persons engaged in their normal pursuits and enjoying their normal recreations. We see all this through Jonson's eyes, that is, through the eyes of a robustly satirical observer. As a result, each of the major comedies has its distinct unity of feeling and collectively they introduce us to the Jonson world. This world is the scene of a conflict between predators and the would-be predators upon whom they feed. Its denizens think of little except how to outwit or "outsmart" one another; with a truly obsessive fury they give themselves up to cheating and grabbing. Those who are stronger and more skillful become the predators, those who are feebler and more gullible become the prey. Morally, there is little to choose between the two parties. But in a world in which love and friendship hardly exist, in which almost everybody is ruthlessly self-seeking, the successful predators in their boldness and resourcefulness cut more impressive figures than do their victims; seizing upon the imagination of the beholder, they command his respect and at times perhaps even his sympathy.

From this derives the morally ambiguous effect of some of Jonson's comedies. There is no doubt that he hates the vices that he satirizes, acquisitiveness, perhaps, above all. But he laughs and he wishes us to laugh; and our gratitude to the characters whose brilliant swindling provides butts for our laughter—to Mosca and Face, for example—can inhibit the disapproval which the moralist would have us feel.

Every Man out of His Humour, 1600 (*p.* 1599).
Every Man in His Humour, 1601 (*p.* 1598).
Cynthia's Revels, 1601 (*p.* ?1600).
The Poetaster; or, The Arraignment, 1602.
Sejanus, 1605 (*p.* 1603).
Volpone; or, The Fox, 1607 (*p.* 1606; *f.* 1947).
The Case Is Altered, 1609 (*p.* 1598).
Catiline, 1611.
Epicoene; or, The Silent Woman, 1612 (*p.* 1609).
The Alchemist, 1612 (*p.* 1610).
Epigrams and *The Forest* in *Works,* first folio, 1616.
The Devil Is an Ass, 1631 (*p.* 1616).
The Staple of News, 1631 (*p.* 1626).
The New Inn, 1631 (*p.* 1629).
Underwoods and *Timber; or, Discoveries upon Men and Matter* in *Works,*
    second folio, 1640.
Bartholomew Fair, ed. C. S. Alden, 1904 (*p.* 1614).

Works, ed. C. H. Herford and P. Simpson, 11 vols., Oxford: Clarendon Press, 1925–52.   J.D.J.

JOYCE, James (1882–1941) was the eldest son of a reckless and charming father, who in the course of Joyce's childhood managed to steer the family from bourgeois prosperity to a very shabby gentility. Joyce was educated at Clongowes Wood College, Belvedere College and University College, Dublin. Clongowes was the most influential, for Joyce retained "the Jesuit strain" for most of his life. Early dissatisfied and disillusioned with Ireland, its religion, its politics and its literature, and nursing a sense of betrayal by his friends, he cut himself off from family, church and country by escaping first to Paris (1903–04) where he followed some desultory studies, and then, with Nora Barnacle, whom he subsequently married, to Trieste, with spells in Pola and Rome, teaching English and acting for a time as a bank clerk. He had published in Ireland some of the stories of *Dubliners* and a collection of slight lyrics, *Chamber Music.* After nine years of frustrating battles with publishers and printers, *Dubliners* finally appeared in 1914. *A Portrait of the Artist As a Young Man* appeared serially in *The Egoist* under the editorship of Ezra Pound, who greatly admired the novel; it was published in book form in 1916. In

1914, too, Joyce started writing *Ulysses*. During the First World War he was at first under "free arrest" in Austria, but was later allowed to go to Zurich, where his eyesight, never good, started to give him serious trouble; in his later years he was all but blind. In 1918 his rather ineffective play, *Exiles*, was published. From 1918 to 1920 excerpts from *Ulysses* appeared in the New York *Little Review* until they were banned as "vicious." In 1920 Joyce and his family "went to Paris to stay a week and remained for twenty years." *Ulysses* was published by The Egoist Press, England, and Shakespeare and Co., Paris, in 1922, but was banned from circulation in England and the United States. This ban certainly gave it notoriety and helped its sales, but the book steadily achieved recognition as a major work of art on its own merits. There were further battles, with a pirate publisher and the law, before it was finally declared fit for public reading and released in the United States (1934) and in England (1936). From 1927 onwards sections of *Work in Progress* appeared in various forms, finally to be published complete as *Finnegans Wake* in 1939. During this time Joyce's fame and prosperity increased; he became one of the major figures of the literary world, but his last years were tortured by the growing insanity of his daughter Lucia, which he refused to admit. He died of a perforated duodenal ulcer on 13 January 1941 in Zurich.

The whole of Joyce's work could be titled "Dubliners"; he escaped from Dublin only to spend his whole life re-creating it, and his works, taken together, form a graduated and interrelated whole. *Dubliners* and *Finnegans Wake* seem widely disparate, but the latter is the logical end-product of the former. *Dubliners* consists of studies of Dublin life; the method ranges from the photographic realism of "Counterparts," written in "a style of scrupulous meanness," to the elaborate symbolism of "The Dead." Whatever the style, all the stories are based on Joyce's idea of "epiphany," the sudden intuitive revelation afforded by an incident trivial and perhaps even squalid in itself. The stories move from childhood to death, and cover most of the aspects of Dublin life. Comic as some of them are, the prevailing impression remains one of a stagnant and decaying society. *A Portrait of the Artist As a Young Man* concentrates on one person, Stephen. It is superficially simple, but closer reading reveals it as extremely complex. There is a strong autobiographical element, but Stephen is not the young James Joyce, however many of his characteristics he may share. Though the reader's interest is focused entirely on the central character, the author's attitude is detached and ironic. The fusion of intimate inner knowledge and amused yet critical scrutiny make this one of the most puzzling of novels.

The techniques of *Ulysses* are more varied and complex, and at first present an awkward barrier to the reader. Their difficulties should not obscure the fact that the novel, for all its experimentation, is essentially within the classical European tradition: it investigates the inner lives of certain characters, sets them in relationship with each other, and places them firmly in a real society. All that Joyce does is to go further than any previous novelist along the same road, but by different means. The most extensively used technique is that of the "stream of consciousness," when Joyce attempts to take his readers into the minds and feelings of his characters. The reader sees with the character, responds with him, and, sharing his memories, is enabled to reconstruct the past; in his different manner Proust does the same. The stylized chapters are more difficult, parts of a mosaic that can only be understood if they are seen as parts of a whole. Joyce in these chapters tries to make the language by its very form re-create the object under consideration—Mr. Bloom and Stephen, tired and worn out, are conveyed in a chapter composed entirely of jaded clichés. In the brothel chapter Joyce goes further afield. In most of the novel he is trying to give the impression of the conscious mind at work; here he is trying to show the subconscious and unadmitted fears, desires and intentions of his two principal characters. The whole novel is held together by a series of cross-references; identical phrases recur repeatedly, acquiring a symbolic quality and uniting past and present. The Homeric parallel is only important in general: the unheroic Mr. Bloom *is* the heroic Ulysses, the wily one who symbolically finds his son, slays his rivals, and comes into his own. Highly self-conscious as the craftsmanship is, it serves a warm and rich humanity. Joyce is the novelist of the ordinary and the commonplace; tragedy and comedy lie for him in very humble places. *Ulysses*, with its exuberant vitality, is one of the great comic masterpieces of European fiction, and, like all great comedy, is very near to pathos and tragedy.

Finnegans Wake carries further the attempts of *Ulysses* to make language, like music, be what it expresses. There are layers upon layers of references and connotations in the multilingual puns, and it helps if one can recognize them; but finally it is the words themselves, the sounds themselves, that matter. There is plot of a kind, but it is the plot of dream; its only logic is its own. *Ulysses* explores the world of day, *Finnegans Wake* the world of night. It is a wildly funny and a deeply moving book; the crossword puzzle element in it is certainly daunting, but fascinating in its own right. It is doubtful if *Finnegans Wake* will have any legitimate issue, though both it and *Ulysses*, directly and indirectly, have had a very great influence on much that has been written subsequently, both in poetry and prose.

(See also **Imagism; Parody and Nonsense.**)

Chamber Music, 1907.
Dubliners, 1914.

A Portrait of the Artist As a Young Man, 1916.
Exiles, 1918 (play).
Ulysses, 1922 (*f.* 1966).
Pomes Penyeach, 1927.
Finnegans Wake, 1939 (*f.* 1969).

Stephen Hero, ed. T. Spencer, London: Cape, 1944; revised edition, 1956.
Giacomo Joyce, ed. R. Ellmann, London: Faber & Faber; New York: Viking Press, 1968.

Letters, ed. S. Gilbert, 3 vols., London: Faber & Faber; New York: Viking Press, 1957–66.   C.H.

K

KAUFMAN, George S. (Simon) (1889–1961), born in Pittsburgh, wrote many successful comedies in collaboration with other authors and was renowned for his witty, wisecracking style. His co-writers included Marc Connelly, in *Beggar on Horseback* (*p.* 1924; *f.* 1925), Ring Lardner and Edna Ferber.

Of Thee I Sing (*p.* 1931), set during a fictitious presidential campaign, was written with Morrie Ryskind and George Gershwin and received a Pulitzer Prize. Kaufman and Moss Hart produced several very popular plays, including *Once in a Lifetime* (1930; *f.* 1932), a satire on Hollywood, *You Can't Take It with You* (*p.* 1936; *f.* 1938), a zany farce in favor of individualism, and *The Man Who Came to Dinner* (1939; *f.* 1941), based on the personality of author Alexander Woollcott.   R.W.

KEATS, John (1795–1821) was a Londoner. Both parents died before he was fifteen and his guardians apprenticed him to an apothecary at Edmonton. He later became a dresser at Guy's Hospital, but gave it up to concentrate upon poetry. In 1817 he took lodgings in Hampstead with his brothers George and Tom, having published his first volume of verse in the same year. He received encouragement from writers like Leigh Hunt and Charles Cowden Clarke, yet reviewers were often unfavorable. So was Keats himself, who in the preface to his next volume, *Endymion*, admitted to "great inexperience, immaturity, and every error denoting a feverish attempt, rather than a deed accomplished." He was highly conscious of his need to develop as man and as artist; this shows quite clearly in his letters. In one dated 8 October 1818 he writes that even the thousands of lines of *Endymion* were little more to him than a trial of his powers of continuous invention.

In 1818 his brother Tom died of consumption, a disease soon to attack Keats himself. He was helped by many friends, especially Charles Armitage Brown, who collaborated with him in writing a verse tragedy (*Otho the Great*) and two artists, Benjamin Haydon and Joseph Severn. It was Haydon who introduced Keats to Lamb and Wordsworth. Severn was to nurse him in his last illness. The progress of the disease was inexorable and in the winter of 1820–21 Keats left for Italy in a futile attempt to regain his health, wretched at leaving his fiancée Fanny Brawne. He died in Rome in February and was buried there.

Such a brief and outwardly uneventful life must be appreciated in its particular intensity—the hectic passion for Fanny Brawne, the strong opinions and friendships and, above all, the devotion to poetry. His letters openly reveal the progress of his inner life, to such an extent that it has taken on the power of an incandescent myth for later generations. They also show very clearly that he thought vigorously about his art. His words in a letter of 27 February 1818, "If poetry come not as naturally as the leaves to a tree, it had better not come at all," are not a plea for uninhibited spontaneity and should be read in the larger context.

The poems in the 1817 volume are usually criticized, sometimes for just plain silliness. The many successes, however, are often to be related to the failures, both springing from joy in the actual and tangible ("A pigeon tumbling in clear summer air") and products, too, of a belief that poetry's "touches of beauty should never be half-way, thereby making the reader breathless, instead of content." Such a feat is in practice a hair's breadth from bathos. The long narrative poem *Endymion* is luxuriantly fanciful, full of symbolism, but disjointed and obscure. The poems of the 1820 volume are much more controlled in the technical sense: *Isabella* is highly sentimental and mawkish, but it hangs together and the stanzas are often beautifully managed.

The 1820 volume contains verse that marks a radical change of style. The loosely "pleasant smotherings" of the earlier poems are flaccid in comparison with the more assured texture of the later work and its constant stressing of pain that is sometimes unavoidable in human existence, "Where youth grows pale, and spectre-thin, and dies," sometimes as the necessary condition of rebirth into "knowledge enormous" (*Hyperion*, 3). The clash between dream and harsh reality is a shaping factor in "The Eve of St. Agnes" and in the "Ode to a Nightingale," though the seventh stanza of the ode offers a kind of permanent happiness. The "Ode on a Grecian Urn" brings out this stanza's underlying meaning by emphasizing the permanence of art, to be set against the transience and imperfection of life. Keats's maturity is manifest at the end of the ode, where his chilling words about the work of art, "Cold Pastoral," prevent us from reading this poem too simply.

Other poems in the 1820 volume are great achievements of their kind. The dense richness and full sonorities of three odes, "On Melancholy," "To Psyche" and "To Autumn," are successful in a way that more ambitious poems are not. "To Autumn" is generally considered the most perfect and thoroughly realized, a celebration of fruition and ripeness given just the touch of contrast needed to define quality. Its artistic wholeness makes the unfinished *Hyperion* seem even more disappointing, since in detail this poem is often very fine. Leaving aside the more obtrusive Miltonisms, which Keats himself came to reject, it contains passages of assured artistry. Clymene's speech in book 2, for example, expresses a piercing apprehension of beauty. The larger themes, the tragic dignity and agony of the gods, the blank verse which can surge forward or cease its movement at Keats's bidding—all these aspects combine to make *Hyperion* extraordinary in the subtle variety of its effects. A poem like "The Eve of St. Agnes," which admittedly remains memorable for its sensuousness, seems slight in comparison.

Keats returned to *Hyperion* in an attempt to revise it. The second version, still unfinished, was published posthumously and entitled *The Fall of Hyperion*. The changes he made are fascinating, but more important is the long new induction. There are passages quite unlike his earlier work, such as the description of Moneta. Straining to convey his belief in the uniqueness and importance of intuitive powers, Keats found a sinewy directness of style that is unmatched in his previous poetry.

He was nothing if not in earnest. His letters, in particular, are the record of a mind positive about its own discoveries yet forever trembling upon the brink of new knowledge and poised to follow its slightest signs:

> I have made up my mind never to take anything for granted—but even to examine the truth of the commonest proverbs.
>
> Man should not dispute or assert, but whisper results to his neighbour.
>
> ... *Negative Capability*, that is when man is capable of being in uncertainties, mysteries, doubts, without any irritable reaching after fact and reason ...

Keats's early death may have prevented an astonishing maturity, but at least advancing years did not bring on the inevitable hardening of the spiritual arteries. The letters stand in English literature without parallel. The reputation of his poetry remains at a consistently high level, only fluctuating as critics understandably mistake extraordinary promise and exceptional achievement for substantial, unqualified excellence.

(See also **Romantic Movement, The.**)

Poems, 1817.
Endymion: A Poetic Romance, 1818.
Lamia, Isabella, The Eve of St. Agnes and Other Poems, 1820.

Life, Letters and Literary Remains, ed. Lord Houghton, 2 vols., 1848.

Poems, ed. M. Allott, London: Longmans, 1971.
Letters, ed. H. E. Rollins, 2 vols., Cambridge, Mass.: Harvard Univ. Press, 1958.
The Keats Circle: Letters and Papers, 1816–78, ed. H. E. Rollins, 2 vols., Cambridge, Mass.: Harvard Univ. Press, 1948; *More Letters and Poems*, 1955.

J.C.

KEBLE, John (1792–1866), with Newman and Pusey, was eminent in the High Church Tractarian movement, the beginnings of which are often traced to his 1833 sermon on national apostasy. His collection of religious verse, *The Christian Year* (1827), was extremely successful. From 1831 to 1841 he was professor of poetry at Oxford. His lectures were published as *De Poeticae Vi Medica* (1844), sometimes referred to as *Praelectiones Academicae*. He also published another collection of verses, *Lyra Innocentium* (1846), and several volumes of sermons. He is now remembered for his firm Anglican High Churchmanship, never attracted to Rome, and for a few hymns; but his theories about poetry as cathartic veiled self-expression deserve more attention than they have received.

A.P.

KENDALL, Henry. See **Australian Literature.**

KENNEDY, John Pendleton (1795–1870), was born in Maryland, and was primarily a man of public affairs, first entering politics in 1820. He contributed to *The Red Book*, a satirical periodical, and in 1832 published *Swallow Barn*, a series of sketches of Virginia country life depicted as full of pastoral charm. His most successful novel, *Horse-Shoe Robinson* (1835), is a romantic tale of lovers and patriots towards the end of the Revolutionary War. His second novel, *Rob of the Bowl* (1838), includes a realistic account of the Protestant uprising in colonial Maryland. Much of his literary work was political and included his *Defense of the Whigs* (1844) and a biography of William Wirt (1849).

Collected Works (includes life by H. T. Tuckerman), 10 vols., New York: Putnam, 1871.

R.W.

KENNEDY, Leo. See **Canadian Literature.**

KEROUAC, Jack (1922–69), born Jean-Louis Kerouac in Lowell (Massachusetts) of French-Canadian parents, reports in *Lonesome Traveler* that once in London (by way of Morocco and France) he went to the British Museum and managed to locate his family's roots in Brittany. Their coat of arms read "Work, love, suffer."

When Kerouac was four, his brother (celebrated in *Visions of Gerard*) died. At the age of eight, Kerouac produced comic strips, and at eleven, he wrote little novels which he kept in notebooks. He attended St. Joseph's Parochial School, and the Horace Mann School for Boys. A sports fan, inventor of sports games, and a good athlete, he played football at Lowell High School and won a scholarship to Columbia University. His first "serious" writing began when he was seventeen, but it was not until a decade later that he discovered the freewheeling prose style of Neal Cassady's letters which Kerouac adopted as his métier to shape a "new literary movement aimed at freer expression of highly personal experiences" and which he, in response to the emerging rhythms of be-bop, named "Beat." His friends whose lives he chronicled became known as the "Beat Generation."

But Kerouac himself, a "strange solitary crazy Catholic mystic," a "madman bum and angel" (see *The Dharma Bums*), finally removed himself from the world of Duluoz, his first-person narrator, and retired to the peace of his mother's home (as described in *Desolation Angels*). The vibrance of *On the Road*, the intensity of *The Subterraneans*, the vision of his poetry, are testament to his wisdom.

The Town and the City, 1950.
On The Road, 1957.
The Subterraneans, 1958 (*f.* 1960).
The Dharma Bums, 1958.
Doctor Sax, 1959.
Maggie Cassidy, 1959.
Mexico City Blues, 1959 (poems).
Visions of Cody, 1959.
The Scripture of the Golden Eternity, 1960 (poems).
Lonesome Traveler, 1960.
Rimbaud, 1960 (poems).
Tristessa, 1960.
Book of Dreams, 1961.
Pull My Daisy, 1961 (filmscript).
Big Sur, 1962.
Visions of Gerard, 1963.
Desolation Angels, 1965.

W.S.

KESEY, Ken (1935–) was born in Colorado and moved with his parents to Oregon when he was nine. His first published novel, *One Flew over the Cuckoo's Nest* (1962), a visionary tale of psychic liberation, was followed by *Sometimes a Great Notion* (1964), which explored the nature of heroism. Together with Neal Cassady and The Merry Pranksters, Kesey tripped across America. He was arrested in California, fled the country, and returned to be taken into custody by the FBI in 1966. Some of his prison writings have since been printed. Tom Wolfe examined the subject of Kesey and his followers in *The Electric Kool-Aid Acid Test* (1968).

W.S.

KEYES, Sidney (1922–43) was born at Dartford (Kent) and educated at Tonbridge and Oxford where, as a sensitive and introspective young man, he wrote his first book of poems, *The Iron Laurel* (1942). He enlisted in the army in 1942 and was killed in the Tunisian campaign after only a fortnight's active service. His poems, most of which were written whilst he was at Oxford, have a youthful but mannered intensity. He is ambitious in his attempt to see war in relation to suffering, death and the "inner war" of the individual, and is also self-consciously the spokesman for his own generation. Yet his verse is uneven in tone and feeling, partly derivative in its echoing of Yeats, Eliot and Rilke, and frequently overburdened with apocalyptic or legendary symbolism. His poems show most promise when he depicts extremities of experience with some attempt at visual and pictorial sharpness. (See also **War Poets.**)

Collected Poems, ed. M. Meyer, London: Routledge, 1945; New York: Holt, 1947.   O.K.

KEYNES, John Maynard, Lord (1883–1946), son of the registrary of Cambridge University, was educated at King's College, where he later became a fellow. This distinguished economist held a number of public appointments, besides editing *The Economic Journal* from 1911 to 1944. He represented the Treasury at the Versailles Treaty negotiations after the First World War. In *The Economic Consequences of the Peace* (1919) he gave a devastating analysis of the effect that the huge reparations demanded of Germany would have on European economic life. A brilliant and versatile thinker, he had considerable influence on modern economics, especially in advocating more efficient planning during the economic crises of the 1920s and '30s. His most influential work is *The General Theory of Employment, Interest and Money* (1936). As well as being the leading economist of his day, he was a man of wide cultural interests and became first chairman of the Arts Council.

Collected Writings, 24 vols., London: Macmillan (for the Royal Economic Society), 1970– .   O.K.

KING, Henry (1592–1669) was educated at Westminster School and Oxford. He rose steadily in the Church to become in 1642 bishop of Chichester, but was ejected a year later. After a period of dependence on friends he was reinstated at the Restoration. A friend, executor and elegist of Donne, he also contributed to the memorial volume on Ben Jonson; his own verse has affinities with both these poets. Apart from a few graceful lyrics, he is chiefly remembered for the "Exequy" upon his young wife, a poem in which personal feeling informs the witty conceits and gives an impressive gravity of movement to the simple tetrameter line.

Poems, Elegies, Paradoxes and Sonnets, 1657.

Poems, ed. M. Crum, Oxford: Clarendon Press, 1965.   R.G.C.

KINGIS QUAIR, The (or "King's Book") (?1423; ed. W. Tytler, 1783) is traditionally attributed to James I of Scotland (1394–1437), and certain episodes in the poem have parallels in James's early career, notably his capture by the English and subsequent imprisonment. It is partly a love poem, celebrating a love "ground and set in Cristin wise," partly a meditation on the means of defeating the vicissitudes of fortune. The style and phrasing are full of echoes of Chaucer, especially of the dream poems and *Troilus and Criseyde*; the thought owes much to Boethius's *De Consolatione Philosophiae*.

The Kingis Quair, ed. W. M. Mackenzie, London: Faber & Faber, 1939.
                                                                    P.B.

KINGLAKE, A. W. (Alexander William) (1809–91), born in Taunton (Somerset), was educated at Eton and Trinity College, Cambridge. Deficient sight prevented him entering the army but in no way limited his perceptiveness as a traveler. His career as a barrister was subordinated to travel and writing. In 1834 he visited the Near East, and for several years afterwards revised the account of his experiences before publishing *Eothen* (1844). These impressions of an Englishman writing "from the East" (Eothen) are conveyed with elegant wit in sentences showing fine structural control. Kinglake's emphatic egotism "of refusing to dwell upon matters which failed to interest my own feelings" does not appear offensive, because the delicate rhythms of his prose prevent ponderous self-assertiveness. His concern with factual and stylistic perfection caused him to devote thirty-one years to writing a history of *The Invasion of the Crimea* (8 vols., 1863–87). Although the subject combined knowledge acquired from further travels with Kinglake's interest in military affairs, the work is exhausting in its detail and is largely forgotten today.   C.P.

KINGSLEY, Charles (1819–75), the son of an Anglican clergyman, was educated first at King's College, London and then, in 1838, went to Magdalene College, Cambridge. The story of his religious doubts is recorded in the correspondence with his future wife, Fanny, whom he met in 1839 and married in 1844. He was ordained in 1842 and in 1844 received the living of Eversley in Hampshire. He set himself to reform the chaotic state of his parish with tremendous energy, but only at a serious cost to his health, which was further weakened after 1848 by his energetic efforts for the Christian Socialist movement As part of his response to the social problems of his day Kingsley wrote his novel *Yeast*, which was published in *Fraser's Magazine* in 1848 but had to be discontinued because of protests at its apparent radicalism. This reaction was a partial cause of the complete breakdown in Kingsley's health which then followed. A similar reaction was aroused by *Alton Locke*, but it became increasingly clear that Kingsley's interest in the Chartist movement was the result of an emotional sympathy with the poor rather than a convinced political radicalism. The emergence of his essential Toryism may be seen in his appointment as chaplain to Queen Victoria in 1859 and his chauvinistic acceptance of the Crimean War as a regenerative force in the life of the nation.

Kingsley is mainly known today for works such as *The Water-Babies*, which have become children's books. His historical novels, *Westward Ho!* and *Hereward the Wake*, are the vehicles of a fervent nationalism which is of interest for its revelation of the optimistic strand in Victorian thought, but the works themselves have little imaginative appeal for the modern adult. Kingsley's social novels, however, hold an important place as part of the Victorian response to the "condition of England" question and deserve to be more widely known. *Yeast* was designed to draw attention to the condition of the rural poor, but its documentary interest is not matched by a corresponding literary power in its characterization or structure. The center of Kingsley's achievement here is *Alton Locke*, a novel of great power and compassion. The story, told in the first person, is of the self-education of a working-class tailor–poet who moves from an involvement with Chartism to an eventual quietist Christianity through the offices of an upper-class saver of souls. The novel contains many scenes of documentary horror on the lives of the London proletariat and is memorable also for the character of Sandy Mackaye, an old Scottish bookseller, who is based on Carlyle and whose doctrines the novel helped to popularize. But the novel is of artistic as well as social significance and it gains this from Kingsley's extraordinary imaginative penetration of the class consciousness that constantly humiliates Alton. The work is perhaps unique in English literature for its power of embodying the sufferings of those who feel themselves humanly slighted by an alien social system.

(See also **Political Pamphlets; Sermons; Spasmodics, The.**)

Alton Locke, Tailor and Poet, 1850.
Yeast, a Problem, 1851 (*s.* 1848).
Hypatia; or, New Foes with an Old Face, 1853 (*s.* 1852–53).

Westward Ho!, 1855.
Two Years Ago, 1857.
The Water-Babies: A Fairy Tale for a Land-Baby, 1863.
Hereward the Wake, 1866.

Life and Works, 19 vols., London: Macmillan, 1901–03.   G.S.

KINGSLEY, Henry. See **Australian Literature.**

KINGSLEY, Sidney (1906–   ) was born in New York City. His first plays appeared during the Depression. Despite a melodramatic style, his concern with social conditions is apparent. He was awarded a Pulitzer Prize for *Men in White* (1933; *f.* 1935), a love triangle with a hospital background. His most powerful social drama was *Dead End* (1935; *f.* 1937) which vigorously portrayed the life of New York slum kids. The following year he wrote an antiwar drama, *Ten Million Ghosts*, and in *The Patriots* (1942), written with his wife, Madge Evans, compared the ideologies of Thomas Jefferson and Alexander Hamilton. Later work includes *Detective Story* (1949; *f.* 1951) and a dramatization of Arthur Koestler's novel *Darkness at Noon* (1951), and *Night Life* (1962).   R.W.

KIPLING, Rudyard (1865–1936), born in Bombay, spent half his childhood in India and half in England, where he suffered five years of intense unhappiness at Southsea in the unloving care of an authoritarian guardian, whose severity was to distort Kipling's whole view of life. As a young journalist in India, he wrote copiously on Anglo-Indian themes, and when he returned to London in 1890 and published an accumulation of verses and short stories, as well as a novel, *The Light That Failed*, he achieved immediate and sensational celebrity. From the 1890s onwards he produced a stream of popular verse and hundreds of short stories, steadily maintaining his best seller status in the face of growing critical disparagement. Scorning his critics, he became a kind of unofficial poet laureate who enjoyed the patronage of monarchs and common readers while he enraged liberal intellectuals. Awarded the Nobel Prize for literature in 1907, he played an actively patriotic role in both the Boer War and the First World War (see **War Poets**), in which he lost his only son. When he died in 1936, his critical reputation was probably at its lowest ebb.

Kipling is beyond doubt one of the greatest short-story writers in the English language; his verses are better known and more widely quoted by a greater variety of men than those of any of his contemporaries; his books have never failed to attract new readers. Where they previously saw only crude jingoism and tub-thumping doggerel, his critics now detect hidden virtues and layers of meaning hitherto obscured by verbal mannerisms. Kipling's range extends from his children's fairy tales through the classic adventure story of *Kim* to the complex and often moving subtleties of "The Wish House" and "Mrs. Bathurst"; so fruitful a subject for psychological interpretation could not remain unexplored and unexploited. As the sun set upon the British Empire, Kipling's imperialism seemed irrelevant and his real achievement could be assessed without prejudice. George Orwell and T. S. Eliot revealed the merits of his infinitely memorable verse and thus confounded skeptics who failed to appreciate that even the *Barrack-Room Ballads* combined popularity with genius.

The truth was that Kipling's work had always displayed those qualities which his critics so long ignored. He was popular, not simply because he reflected an imperialist mood (his great "Recessional" was a warning rather than a compliment), but because he wrote in a way that aroused some of the deepest emotions in the human heart—jealousy, suppressed passion, revenge, all the less agreeable manifestations of human infirmity. Yet beneath his stoical and often callous devotion to "the God of things as they are" lay a profound awareness of the importance of pity and terror in the average man's experience of life, whether he be Tommy Atkins, the long-suffering British soldier of the *Ballads*, or Dick Heldar, the frustrated virtuoso of *The Light That Failed*. In stories like "The Gardener" and "On Greenhow Hill" Kipling showed the other side of the coin—the love that redeems hate and the truth that kills the lie.

Plain Tales from the Hills, 1888.
Soldiers Three, 1888 (*f.* 1951).
Wee Willie Winkie, 1888 (*f.* 1937).
The Light That Failed, 1890 (*f.* 1939).
Barrack-Room Ballads, 1892.
The Jungle Book, 1894 (*f.* 1966).
The Second Jungle Book, 1895.
The Seven Seas, 1896.
Captains Courageous, 1897 (*f.* 1937).
Kim, 1901 (*f.* 1949).
Puck of Pook's Hill, 1906.
Actions and Reactions, 1909.
Debits and Credits, 1926.
Limits and Renewals, 1932.
Something of Myself, 1937.

Complete Works, Sussex edition, London: Macmillan, 1937–39.   D.E.P.

KLEIN, A. M. (Abraham Moses). See **Canadian Literature.**

KOCH, Kenneth (1925–   ) was born in Cincinnati (Ohio), served in the army from 1943 to 1946, and was educated first at Harvard and then Columbia where he later returned to teach. French poetry stimulated him during a period in Europe and he has written of its effect on his work as comparable only to "the influence of John Ashbery and Frank O'Hara." His *Poems* was published in 1953, *Ko, or A Season on Earth* in 1959 (a mock epic whose large cast includes an Achai poet and a Japanese baseball star). In *Permanently* (1960) and *Thank You and Other Poems* (1962), shorter pieces, he still engages in fantastic word play. *The Pleasures of Peace* and *When the Sun Tries to Go On*, which is illustrated by Larry Rivers, both appeared in 1969. Koch has also published *Bertha and Other Plays* (1966), and two plays in *Theatre Experiment* (ed. Michael Benedikt, 1967). In 1970 he published *Wishes, Lies and Dreams: Teaching Children to Write Poetry*, with the children of a New York school.   J.P.W.

KOESTLER, Arthur (1905–   ) was born in Budapest and attended the University of Vienna. He was foreign correspondent for German and British publications and during the Spanish Civil War was captured by the Fascists and condemned to death. Saved by British protests, he wrote *Spanish Testament* (1938). During the Second World War he was held in a French detention camp, described in *Scum of the Earth* (1941). *Darkness at Noon* (1941) discusses dictatorship and imprisonment in the form of a novel. *Thieves in the Night* (1946) describes the foundation of Israel. Koestler's later work includes philosophy, in *The Sleepwalkers* (1959), and scientific journalism, in *The Case of the Midwife Toad* (1971).   J.L.M.

KOPIT, Arthur (1937–   ). Following the success of his fantasy *Oh Dad, Poor Dad, Mamma's Hung You in the Closet and I'm Feeling So Sad* (1960; *f*. 1966), a play which uses absurdist methods to mock absurdist assumptions, Kopit produced a number of effective but lightweight works in the same vein such as *The Day the Whores Came Out to Play Tennis* and *Chamber Music*. In 1968, however, he achieved considerable popular and critical success with *Indians*, a play which traces the contours of American-Indian relations through the medium of a mock wild west show. An impressive work, *Indians* demonstrated a sensitive appreciation of the power of spectacle combined with a powerful, though sometimes awkwardly poeticized, articulateness.   C.B.

KUNITZ, Stanley (1905–   ) was born in Worcester (Massachusetts) and graduated from Harvard. His first book of poems, *Intellectual Things*, appeared in 1930. He completed three years of military service in the

Second World War, and in 1944 published his second book, *Passport to the War*. His earlier tragic poetry, expressing horror through surrealistic images, has given place to a more affirmative poetry, resisting defeatism through joyous love poetry and enthusiastic verses on teaching. Robert Lowell has described his *Selected Poems, 1928–58* as written "in the toughest and densest style of the thirties and forties." *The Testing-Tree*, a volume of poems in a much simpler, more straightforward manner, was published in 1971.

Selected Poems, 1928–58, Boston: Little, Brown, 1958.   J.P.W.

KYD, Thomas (1558–94), educated at the Merchant Taylors' School, London, achieved success as a playwright during the 1580s. In 1591 he was in close association with Marlowe, and in 1593, when he was in trouble with the authorities, he alleged that certain heretical documents found in his possession were not his but Marlowe's.

The Spanish Tragedy (?1592) is his one important extant play. *The First Part of Hieronimo* (anonymously, 1605) was evidently designed to precede it. But the corrupt state of the text of *1 Hieronimo* makes conjectures regarding its authorship very hazardous. At one time the view found favor that Kyd was the author of a lost *Hamlet* upon which Shakespeare had based his tragedy, but some recent investigators see no reason why Shakespeare should not himself have written the early version. Apart from *The Spanish Tragedy*, the only play certainly by Kyd is the rather dull translation, *Cornelia* (1594).

Kyd was one of the most influential pioneers of Elizabethan drama. *The Spanish Tragedy* enjoyed an extraordinary popularity. Its elaborate plot, propelled by devious and even Machiavellian scheming on the part of individual characters, its complicated romantic intrigue, and its powerful revenge theme, reinforced by a choric commentary uttered by Revenge itself and a ghost—all these make the play, despite occasional heavy-handedness, unmistakably "good theater."

The Spanish Comedy; or, The First Part of Hieronimo; and The Spanish Tragedy; or, Hieronimo Is Mad Again, ed. A. S. Cairncross, London: Arnold; Lincoln: Univ. of Nebraska Press, 1967.   J.D.J.

L

LAMB, Charles (1775–1834) was born in London and educated at Christ's Hospital, where he met Coleridge. In 1790 he began work as a clerk, proceeding to the South Sea Company in 1791 and the East India Company in the following year. During 1795–96 he was mentally ill and in September 1796, shortly after his recovery, his sister Mary killed their mother in a fit of insanity. For the rest of his life Lamb acted as Mary's guardian and companion. Together they wrote *Tales from Shakespear* (1807) and other works for children. As a young man Lamb wrote verse and attempted both drama and the novel, but after editing the *Specimens of the English Dramatic Poets* (1808), which influenced the Romantic rediscovery of the older drama, he mostly wrote essays and occasional reviews. He collected the most celebrated series in the *Essays of Elia* (1823) and the *Last Essays of Elia* (1833).

Lamb loved the Elizabethans and the seventeenth century, and his sly, quaint, quirky and intensely personal style shows this. His individuality of taste and approach causes him always to be linked with Hazlitt, and they share a common fondness for the pleasures of memory and the gentle sadness of time past. But he is perhaps closer to Leigh Hunt in so frequently choosing small, quiet experiences which are savored to the full against a mature palate of recollected childhood happiness and personal enjoyments. Lamb had numberless friends and his letters are admirable.

(See also **Essays.**)

Works, ed. E. V. Lucas, 7 vols., London: Methuen, 1903–05.
Letters, ed. E. V. Lucas, 3 vols., London: Dent/Methuen; New Haven: Yale Univ. Press, 1935.   W.R.

LAMMING, George. See **Caribbean Literature.**

LAMPMAN, Archibald. See **Canadian Literature.**

LANDOR, Walter Savage (1775–1864), son of a doctor, was born at Warwick. His unruly temper and quarrelsome nature caused him to be removed from Rugby School and rusticated whilst an undergraduate at Oxford. Proud, with stubborn prejudices, he was also a contemplative man of strong feeling and deep tenderness. He was an aristocratic republican, like his hero Milton, and devoted to classical literature. In 1808 he fought in Spain against Napoleon. He married Julia Thuillier in 1811. His attempt to develop a large estate at Llanthony (Monmouthshire) failed and he left England in 1814. He lived first in France, then in Italy, remaining there until 1835 when he returned alone to England. During this period he made friends with John Forster and Dickens, whose portrait of Landor is Boythorn in *Bleak House*. Because of a libel action he left England in 1858 and lived in Italy, chiefly in Florence, until his death.

Landor's literary achievement is as a writer of prose rather than as a poet. His most important work is *Imaginary Conversations of Literary Men and Statesmen* (3 vols., 1824–28; second series, 1829). Next in value are *Pericles and Aspasia* (1836) and *The Pentameron* (1837), a conversation between Boccaccio and Petrarch. His prose is formal and ceremonious, yet has considerable range and flexibility, sometimes colored by a Romantic imagination. He excels in detailed effect, but lacks organized unity and breadth of vision. His best poetry has a controlled passion like a lesser version of Ben Jonson's lyrics. He produced some excellent epigrams.

Gebir: A Poem in Seven Books, 1798.
Count Julian: A Tragedy, 1812.
Imaginary Conversations of Literary Men and Statesmen, 3 vols., 1824–28; second series, 1829.
Citation and Examination of William Shakespeare Touching Deer-Stealing to Which Is Added a Conference of Edmund Spenser with the Earl of Essex, 1834.
Pericles and Aspasia, 2 vols., 1836.
The Pentameron and Pentalogia, 1837.
The Hellenics of Walter Savage Landor, Enlarged and Completed, 1847.
Poemata et Inscriptiones, 1847.
The Italics of Walter Savage Landor, 1848.
Imaginary Conversations of Greeks and Romans, 1853.
Heroic Idylls, with Additional Poems, 1863.

Complete Works, ed. T. E. Welby (prose, 12 vols.) and S. Wheeler (poetry, 4 vols.), 16 vols., London: Chapman & Hall, 1927–36.
Poems, ed. S. Wheeler, 3 vols., Oxford: Clarendon Press, 1937.
Letters, ed. S. Wheeler, London: Bentley, 1897.   S.M.S.

LANG, Andrew (1844–1912) was born at Selkirk and educated at St. Andrews University and Balliol College, Oxford. He was elected fellow of Merton, but in 1875 settled to a life of journalism and letters in London. His output was immense and varied. Books on the relationship between myth, folklore and modern culture (e.g., *Custom and Myth*, 1884; *Myth, Ritual, and Religion*, 1887) bear witness to his important studies in this field (as do his children's books). He wrote poetry in revived old French forms, translated Homer's *Odyssey* (1879) with S. H. Butcher, and *Iliad* (1883) with W. Leaf and E. Myers, and wrote a great deal on Scotland and its history (e.g., *A History of Scotland from the Roman Occupation*, 4 vols., 1900–07). He was an accomplished biographer, perhaps seen at his best in *The Life and Letters of J. G. Lockhart* (1896).

Poetical Works, ed. Mrs. Lang, 4 vols., London: Longmans, 1923.

W.R.

LANGHORNE, John (1735–79) was born at Winton, near Kirkby Stephen (Westmorland), took orders and became rector of Blagdon (Somerset) in 1776. With his brother William he translated Plutarch's *Lives*. There is much of the conventional eighteenth-century manner in his verse, but there are also flashes of feeling—for nature in *The Fables of Flora* (1771) and for the common people in *The Country Justice* (1774–77) —that foreshadow subsequent developments. This latter poem, in particular, reminds us of what Crabbe would do a decade later in *The Village*.

Poems, 2 vols., 1766; ed. J. T. Langhorne, 2 vols., London: Mawman, 1804 (with additions).
The Works of the English Poets, ed. A. Chalmers, London: Johnson, 1810, vol. 16.

A.P.

LANGLAND, William (?1330–?1400) is the name usually given to the author of the fourteenth-century *Piers Plowman*, of which some fifty manuscripts exist, containing between them three basic forms (texts "A," "B" and "C") of the poem to which W. W. Skeat gave the cumbersome but usefully accurate title *The Vision of William concerning Piers the Plowman, Together with Vita de Dowel, Dobet, et Dobest, Secundum Wit et Resoun*.

Little is known about the poet's life. The danger of trying to draw biographical inferences from "unsigned" medieval poems is well known, and about all that cautious scholars are willing to surmise is that Langland was probably born in the West Midlands, became a priest in minor orders and spent much of his adult life in London. He apparently wrote only this one work. Textual references to topical events suggest the dates 1362 for the composition of the "A" text, 1377 for that of the "B" text, and 1393 for that of the "C" text.

The "A" text, as designated by Skeat, contains only the vision concerning Piers the Plowman, which has been seen as satire, as a document for the study of fourteenth-century social history, and as the polemics of a medieval precursor of the Reformation movement. All these are, in fact, aspects of a poem primarily concerned with the salvation of the soul of man. Piers Plowman is presented as a type of the honest, hardworking Christian laborer; by following his precepts a regenerate society may make amends for the manifold sins of which it has been guilty, and thus "do well" in carrying out the work of God in this world.

The "B" and "C" texts also contain versions of this vision concerning Piers the Plowman, but these are followed by versions of the life of Do-Well, Do-Better and Do-Best. Although these are the respective titles of three subdivisions of this second part of the poem, they are, as spiritual concepts, never entirely separated, but are, rather, three related aspects of the established theme of the means of gaining eternal life. At a supreme moment in the vision concerning Dobet, Piers the Plowman is presented in the person of Christ Himself. In the earlier vision concerning Piers the Plowman, Truth (God the Father) had been shown to reside in the heart of man made in God's image; now, in the equation of Piers with Christ, we have a more explicit realization of the role of man as son of God. The poem ends where it began—on the Malvern Hills, in the real world of men. Although man's search for Truth has to begin all over again, he has now been shown the Way.

The poem is a notable example of the latest known medieval English poetry written in alliterative verse. Although such stylistic features as sound effect, the use of figurative language, vivid portraiture (as exemplified particularly in the Passus portraying the seven deadly sins) and word play are all present in the poem, it is altogether more plain, rugged and rambling in structure and style than alliterative works such as *Pearl* and *Sir Gawain and the Green Knight*. Langland knew the conventions of his art—witness his use of the dream framework within which the poem is written, his use of an allegory whose levels are manifold and his indebtedness to the medieval manuals of sermon composition. But, following the precepts of these manuals, he regarded himself as a spiritual teacher first, an artist second, and whenever a conflict arose between the claims of lucidity of doctrinal exposition on the one hand and those of artistry on the other, it was always the latter that had to be denied.

The Vision of William concerning Piers Plowman, ed. W. W. Skeat, London: Early English Text Society, Text "A," 1867; Text "B," 1869; Text "C," 1873.

Piers the Plowman: A Critical Edition of the "A" Version, ed. T. A. Knott and D. C. Fowler, Baltimore: Johns Hopkins Press, 1952.

Piers Plowman: The "A" Version, ed. G. Kane, London: Athlone Press; New York: Oxford Univ. Press, 1960.   D.P.

LANIER, Sidney (1842–81) was born in Georgia and served in the Civil War, contracting tuberculosis—see his only novel, *Tiger-Lilies* (1867). A talented musician, he believed music and poetry obeyed the same artistic laws and he presented this idea in *The Science of English Verse* (1880). His widow edited *Poems of Sidney Lanier* in 1884. Lanier has been compared with Poe and Tennyson, but his own particular skill lay not only in the imaginative and sensuous use he made of sound patterns, but also in the articulating of his regional preoccupations. His weaknesses were occasional obscurity and a lack of intellectual depth. His most successful poems are "The Symphony" (1875) and "The Marshes of Glynn" (1878).

Works, 10 vols., ed. C. R. Anderson, Baltimore: Johns Hopkins Press, 1945.   R.W.

LARDNER, Ring (1885–1933) was born in Niles (Michigan). When he was sixteen, his family lost its fortune. Abandoning his education as an engineer, he drifted until, in 1907, he became a journalist in Chicago. On the *Tribune* he wrote the column "In the Wake of the News" (1913–19), gradually leavening the style of the day with demotic crackle. A baseball fanatic, he wrote his first stories about a sports hero, Jack Keefe; the success of "A Busher's Letters," originating in the *Saturday Evening Post* and collected as *You Know Me, Al* (1916), led to two more volumes. But dialect and baseball were left behind as Lardner, who removed to New York to write a syndicated column, concentrated in *Gullible's Travels* (1917) and *The Big Town* (1921) on the social-climbing games of provincial bumpkins. He wrote unsuccessfully for Broadway but created marvelous unplayable nonsense dramas and stories inspired by his mania for vaudeville and theater. Helped initially by Scott Fitzgerald, he collected his magazine tales in *How to Write Short Stories* (1924) and other volumes. He had become a heavy drinker and threatened suicide, but went on churning out hack work to support his wife and four sons. Stricken with tuberculosis, he spent his last seven years virtually confined to hospital. Beginning with the finest humorous dialect stories since Twain, he had developed a brilliant vernacular medium for his bitter satire on middle-class stereotypes. His best stories (e.g., "Haircut" or "The Golden Honeymoon") are generated by a hatred of sham and shallow feeling.

You Know Me, Al, 1916.
Gullible's Travels, 1917.
Treat 'Em Rough, 1918.
The Real Dope, 1919.
The Big Town, 1921 (*f.* as *So This Is New York*, 1948).

How to Write Short Stories, 1924.
What of It?, 1925 (plays).
The Love Nest and Other Stories, 1926.
The Story of a Wonder Man, 1927 (autobiography).
Round Up, 1929.

The Ring Lardner Reader, ed. M. Geismar, New York: C. Scribner's Sons,
1963.   A.S.

LARKIN, Philip (1922–   ) was educated at King Henry VIII School,
Coventry, and St. John's College, Oxford. He then held various library
positions in the Midlands and Belfast before becoming librarian at
Hull University. He has published three collections of poetry—*The
North Ship* (1945; reissued 1966 with an autobiographical introduction),
The Less Deceived (1955) and *The Whitsun Weddings* (1964). The early
poems show a Yeatsian lyricism and the beginnings of his characteristic
kind of long poem of personal reflection. Hardy was a later and more
permanent influence and some of the more important poems (such as
"Church Going" or "1914") reflect his admiration for John Betjeman's
serious work. Both poets are at home in the kind of personal writing in
which some scene, place or stirring of memory stimulates them to reflect
upon the way in which old associations or some private opinion have
been altered, given a new depth (or perhaps simply reasserted) by later
experience. Larkin's work shows great sensitivity to the effects of time,
the ironies of experience and the changing qualities of English life as he
sees it all about him. His poetry is "popular" in that it is clearly expressed
and aims to share its experience with the reader as easily as possible. It
conveys a strong sense of its author's personality, private viewpoint and
quiet wit. Larkin has also written two novels, *Jill* (1946; reissued 1964 with
autobiographical preface), which is set in wartime Oxford, and the lyrical
A Girl in Winter (1947).   W.R.

LATIMER, Hugh (?1485–1555) was a controversial character in a controversial age. After graduating from Cambridge he took priest's orders
and around 1521 joined the reforming group of English clergy, who
criticized the dogma and practices of the church and emphasized the
importance of a direct appeal to the Bible. From 1535 to 1539 he was
bishop of Worcester but resigned as a result of the reactionary ascendancy
of Bishops Gardiner and Bonner. On the accession of Edward VI in 1547
Latimer became an important influence in the renewed drive towards
Reformation, but he was thrown into prison by the Catholic Queen
Mary and martyred in 1555. Latimer was impulsive, vigorous and enthusiastic. All these qualities are to be found in his racy sermons, which

are still very readable and of which the best are those on the card and the plough. (See also **Renaissance Humanism.**)

Sermons, ed. H. C. Beeching, London: Dent; New York: Dutton, 1906.

A.P.

LAW, William (1686–1761), theologian and mystic, after becoming a nonjuror on the accession of George I, resigned his Cambridge fellowship and engaged in theological controversy. He followed Jeremy Collier in attacking the stage, and became tutor to Gibbon's father (see Gibbon's *Autobiography*). In 1728 he produced his most influential work, *A Serious Call to a Devout and Holy Life*, which formed Dr. Johnson's religious views at Oxford. In later life he was much influenced by the works of Jacob Boehme and produced his own mystical works, *The Spirit of Prayer* (1749) and *The Spirit of Love* (1752). A good contemporary account of him appears in John Byrom's *Journals*.

Complete Works, 9 vols., London, 1753–76.
Selected Mystical Writings, ed. S. Hobhouse, London: Daniel, 1938.

P.G.M.

LAWRENCE, D. H. (David Herbert) (1885–1930) was born at Eastwood (Nottinghamshire), son of a coal miner and a schoolteacher. He was educated at Nottingham High School and University College, Nottingham. He was a clerk for a time, and then became an unhappy but efficient schoolmaster. In 1911 he published his first novel, *The White Peacock*, an uneven, interesting book, and in 1913 his first really important novel, *Sons and Lovers*, a reenactment of his own family relationships and his adolescence and early manhood generally. In between he eloped with the wife of Professor Ernest Weekley, Frieda, a member of the aristocratic German family von Richthofen; and he remained with her for the rest of his life. After sojourns in Germany and Italy, he became a member, though a rebellious and remarkably touchy member, of the English literary world, the more or less intimate acquaintance of Aldous Huxley, Edward and David Garnett, Lady Ottoline Morrell, Richard Aldington and, more importantly, John Middleton Murry and Katherine Mansfield. The hostile reception of his deeply felt novel, *The Rainbow*, in 1915 combined with his horror of the war to cement his hatred of modern industrialized materialistic society. This resentment found full expression in *Women in Love* (1920). He sought refuge intellectually and emotionally in a mystical primitivism, and physically in flight from England, wandering on the continent of Europe, and in Ceylon, Australia, the United States and Mexico. Impressed by his reading of the Aztec civilization, he formulated an intuitive religion on the fundamental instincts of man and expressed it in the novel *The Plumed Serpent* (1926). All this time he was writing some good poetry, excellent idiosyncratic travel books, stories, and critical and paraphilosophical essays. The best of this work is to be found in *Sea and Sardinia* (travel, 1921), *England, My England* (stories, 1922), *Fantasia of the Unconscious* (essays, 1922), *Studies in Classic American Literature* (essays, 1923), *Birds, Beasts and Flowers* (poems, 1923), and *St. Mawr* (story, 1925). In 1928 appeared *Lady Chatterley's Lover*, in which his descriptions of sexual activity in language then banned from polite usage brought about its suppression. He died on 2 March 1930 at Venice of the tuberculosis from which he had suffered for many years.

Lawrence's first important novel, *Sons and Lovers*, although it is a highly personal work, manages to achieve a very adequate measure of critical detachment. Some of his recurrent characteristic themes appear for the first time, but there are also simpler, more direct qualities that his later work obscures. There is humor; a working class environment is described at first hand with complete authority; and there is a freshness and immediacy of vision. The book's strength is in the presentation and analysis of human relationships between children and parents and between young men and women. Lawrence cared little for "character" in the accepted critical sense; he was more interested in what went on between people's personalities than within people or personalities themselves. This interest, oversubtilized in the later novels, can make for a lack of concrete substance. He deals passionately with the theme of the emotional dominance of one person over another, stressing the need for the individual, particularly the male individual, to remain free.

The next novel, *The Rainbow*, perhaps Lawrence's greatest, is more ambitious. It is a study of three generations of a family, and in its complex course it presents a powerful case for the value of the life of the instincts and intuitions, which are to find their fulfillment through sexuality. The book was considered obscene; it most certainly is not. Obscenity profanes sexuality; Lawrence approaches it with reverence. He creates a series of situations illustrating the deep need for the mutual surrender of man and woman, each to the other, which nevertheless leaves both free. Sex is not seen as an end in itself, but as a means to an end. There is here, too, a powerful expression of Lawrence's vision of modern society as not only intolerably ugly in every way, but as crippling and destructive; both it and the people caught up in it are seen as blasphemously denying life. The prose, though sometimes tiresomely repetitive, is poetically suggestive and subtle; there is a superb fusion of delicate perceptiveness and powerful statement. *Women in Love* explores further the nature of society and the relationship between individuals; the condemnation of society is more bitter and the theory of the nature of human relationships more recondite. The novel is marred by overinsistence and Lawrence's too obvious self-identification with Birkin, the central male character, but it is still a very considerable achievement.

From this time on, the novels are more patchy. All of them offer much that is beautiful and admirable, but Lawrence is often strident, the propagandist rather than the artist. This process of preaching a new gospel culminates in *The Plumed Serpent* (1926), in which Lawrence adumbrates a mysterious and mystical new religion (*locus* Mexico), realizing the age-old instincts of man and the truths contorted, forgotten or destroyed by degenerate modern civilization, and completely satisfying all physical and spiritual needs. His last novel, *Lady Chatterley's Lover*, is altogether simpler, and its real and many virtues have been blurred by Lawrence's misguided belief that he could purge certain words of the meaningless rather than vicious obscenity they have acquired over the course of centuries.

In these later years, it is safe to say, his finest creative work is to be found in the stories. They have a surprising range, are economical in style and structure and are content to present their themes in the terms of literature without the intrusion of homily. The poems, by conventional standards formless, often capture subtle scenes, incidents, moods and feelings with very great success. Lawrence's essays vary widely in quality, but they are intelligent and sensitive, and well repay an attempt to overcome the irritation they (sometimes deliberately) cause. All Lawrence's work is serious. His morality is not that of the puritan, but his spirit is; he is entirely concerned with the quality of life, and the need and duty of man at all costs to achieve his full physical and spiritual potentialities.

(See also **Essays; Georgians, The; Imagism.**)

The White Peacock, 1911.
The Trespasser, 1912.
Sons and Lovers, 1913 (*f.* 1960).
Love Poems and Others, 1913.
The Prussian Officer and Other Stories, 1914.
The Widowing of Mrs. Holroyd, 1914 (play).
The Rainbow, 1915.
Twilight in Italy, 1916 (travel).
New Poems, 1918.
Women in Love, 1920 (*f.* 1969).
The Lost Girl, 1920.
Sea and Sardinia, 1921.
Psychoanalysis and the Unconscious, 1921.
Fantasia of the Unconscious, 1922.
Aaron's Rod, 1922.
England, My England, 1922.
Birds, Beasts and Flowers, 1923.

The Ladybird and Other Stories, 1923 ("The Fox" *f.* 1968).
Studies in Classic American Literature, 1923.
Kangaroo, 1923.
St. Mawr; Together with The Princess, 1925.
The Plumed Serpent, 1926.
David, 1926 (play).
The Woman Who Rode Away and Other Stories, 1928.
Lady Chatterley's Lover, (privately) 1928 (*f.* 1956).
Pansies, 1929 (poems).
Pornography and Obscenity, 1929 (essays).
Nettles, 1930 (poems).
The Virgin and the Gipsy, 1930 (*f.* 1970).
The Man Who Died, 1931 (originally *The Escaped Cock*, 1929).
Last Poems, ed. R. Aldington and G. Orioli, 1932.
The Lovely Lady, 1932.
A Collier's Friday Night, 1934 (play).
A Modern Lover, 1934.

Phoenix: Posthumous Papers, 1, ed. E. D. MacDonald, 1936; 2, ed. H. T. Moore and W. Roberts, 1968.

Works, 33 vols., London: Heinemann, 1936–39.
Complete Plays, London: Heinemann, 1965; New York: Viking Press, 1966.
Complete Poems, ed. V. de S. Pinto and W. Roberts, 2 vols., London: Heinemann; New York: Viking Press, 1964.
Complete Short Stories, 3 vols., London: Heinemann, 1955.
Collected Letters, ed. H. T. Moore, 2 vols., London: Heinemann; New York: Viking Press, 1962.
Lawrence in Love: Letters to Louie Burrows, ed. J. T. Boulton, Nottingham: Univ. of Nottingham Press, 1968.   C.H.

LAWRENCE, T. E. (Thomas Edward) (1888–1935), born at Tremadoc (Caernarvonshire), the second son of an Anglo-Irish Protestant, lived in Oxford from his eighth year. He took a first in history at Oxford in 1910, having written a thesis on Crusader castles in Syria. From 1910 to 1914 he was with Hogarth and Woolley digging at Carchemish. His exploits in Arabia in the First World War are legendary. Lawrence never settled down to civilian life and after an unsuccessful spell under the name of Ross in the army, he finally found his niche in the air force, where he did a great deal to develop speedboats. He was killed in an accident on his motor cycle. His *Seven Pillars of Wisdom*, an account of his experiences in Arabia, contains much fine writing, and *The Mint* is a self-consciously realistic account of his experiences in the air force. His translation of the *Odyssey* has the authentic ring of a man who had lived a life of heroic courage and hardship and dangers. In all his writings there is a conscious reaching for effect which has perhaps led to their being overrated.

Seven Pillars of Wisdom, (privately) 1926 (*f.* as *Lawrence of Arabia*, 1962).
Revolt in the Desert, 1927.
The Odyssey of Homer, 1932.
The Mint, 1955.

Letters, ed. D. Garnett, London: Cape, 1938.   A.N.M.

LAWSON, Henry. See **Australian Literature.**

LAWSON, John Howard (1895–), born in New York City, was one of the "Hollywood Ten" imprisoned for communist activities. He considers the overthrow of capitalism as the principal function of theater. His expressionistic drama *Roger Bloomer* (1923) was his first major success; his lively *Processional* (1925), similarly devised, and *Loud Speaker* (1927) both earned praise by Marxist critics. After *The International* (1928), his plays show more concern with the individual in society—*Success Story* (1932), *The Pure in Heart* (1934) and *Gentlewoman* (1934). He went to Hollywood after writing his last play, *Marching Song* (1937), about a factory strike. His critical works include *Theory and Techniques of Playwriting* (1936; revised, 1949) and *Film: The Creative Process* (1964).   R.W.

LAYTON, Irving. See **Canadian Literature.**

LAZAMON. See **Middle English Literature.**

LEACOCK, Stephen. See **Canadian Literature.**

LEAR, Edward. See **Parody and Nonsense.**

LEAVIS, F. R. (Frank Raymond) (1895–) was born in Cambridge and educated there at the Perse School and Emmanuel College, where he read history and English. His studies were interrupted by service with the Friends' Ambulance Unit during the First World War. He began teaching in Cambridge and was one of the "outlaws" (as he called them) who started the rigorous and combative journal, *Scrutiny*, in 1932. He contributed regularly to it until it ceased publication in 1953. He became fellow of Downing College in 1935, university lecturer in 1936 and reader in English from 1959 to 1962.

From the first, inspired by his own social studies, equipped by I. A. Richards's scientific or "textual" approach to poetry and stimulated in particular by the early criticism of T. S. Eliot, Leavis insisted on the cultural function of literature; he invoked "moral significance" as a criterion of literary worth (in the spirit of Arnold) and discounted the amateur and academic criticism that would obscure these values. In *New Bearings in English Poetry* he claimed that poetry "can communicate the actual quality of experience," citing T. S. Eliot, Ezra Pound and Hopkins. Sensitive analytic studies of earlier poetry (notably Shakespeare, Pope and Keats) further defined this principle, which hardens, however, in Leavis's purposive reading of the English novel to an assertion that "ethical sensibility" is the essential characteristic of the great writer. For all their subtlety, the persuasive studies of George Eliot, James and Conrad (in *The Great Tradition*) and Lawrence refer ultimately to this truistic position, which elides whole areas of discussion at the theoretical level. Leavis persistently stresses the moral at the expense of the imaginative faculty in matters both of literary creation and response and, where the complex problems of "function" are short-circuited with simple effective assumptions, the critical vocabulary used betrays its inadequacy. But despite this, and even because of its contentious nature, Leavis's criticism has been widely read and widely, if sometimes doubtfully, influential. He must be recognized as one of the foremost teachers of literature in the modern English-speaking world.

Mass Civilization and Minority Culture, 1930.
New Bearings in English Poetry, 1932.
Culture and Environment (with Denys Thompson), 1933.
Revaluation. Tradition and Development in English Poetry, 1936.
The Great Tradition: George Eliot, Henry James, Joseph Conrad, 1948.
The Common Pursuit, 1952.
D. H. Lawrence, Novelist, 1955.
"Scrutiny": A Retrospect, 1963.
Anna Karenina and Other Essays, 1967.
Lectures in America (with Q. D. Leavis), 1969.
Dickens the Novelist (with Q. D. Leavis), 1970.

A Selection from "Scrutiny," 2 vols., Cambridge: Cambridge Univ. Press, 1968.   D.G.

LEE, Nathaniel (?1649–92), son of a politically dexterous clergyman, was educated at Westminster School and Trinity College, Cambridge. Unsuccessful as an actor, he turned to writing, and a dozen plays, two in collaboration with Dryden, were staged between 1674 and 1683. *The Rival Queens* (1677) held the stage for nearly two centuries, but *Lucius Junius Brutus* (1681; *p.* 1680), censored at the time, is now considered his best play and shows characteristic flamboyance. Lee was an alcoholic, and after four years in Bedlam and four years of poverty and obscurity, he died drunk in the street.

Works, ed. T. B. Stroup and A. L. Cooke, 2 vols., New Brunswick, N.J.: Scarecrow Press, 1954–55. H.N.D.

"LEE, Vernon" was the pen name of Violet Paget (1856–1935), who was born in Boulogne and brought up on the Continent. After an intellectually precocious adolescence she wrote *Studies of the Eighteenth Century in Italy* (1880), the first significant study of this period in English. The insight and erudition displayed in this book was repeated in *Euphorion* (1884), a study of Renaissance art, and various inquiries into aesthetics and art criticism, including *The Beautiful* (1913). A cosmopolitan literary figure, her best work is on Italy and aesthetics, though she also wrote fiction and books on sociology, philosophy and travel. I.W.

LE FANU, Sheridan (1814–73) was educated at Trinity College, Dublin. He became a barrister but did not practice, preferring to work as a writer and editor. His stories take in ghosts and murder, guilt and retribution, mystery and the supernatural. They are often set within Anglo-Irish society. Though the novels are competently constructed and controlled, they lack the brilliance of his short stories. The best of the latter are found in *In a Glass Darkly* (1872) (one of these, "Carmilla," *f.* as *The Vampire Lovers*, 1970), whilst his most successful novels were *The House by the Churchyard* (1863) and *Uncle Silas* (1864). A.P.

LE GALLIENNE, Richard (1867–1947) lived in England until 1902 and then in America and France. As poet, critic and belle-lettrist he wrote copiously throughout his life, but his name is rightly connected most commonly with the work he did in the 1890s and his reminiscences of *The Romantic '90s* (1926). His facility in prose and verse is marred by lack of scholarship and self-criticism, and he is at his best praising those greater than himself. *English Poems* (1892), *Retrospective Reviews: A Literary Log* (1896) and *The Quest of the Golden Girl* (1896) sum up his achievement. K.T.

LEHMANN, John (1907–) was educated at Eton and Cambridge. He was an important background figure in the literary culture of the 1930s, a friend and mentor to both unknown and established writers, especially Auden, Isherwood and Spender. His three-volume autobiography, beginning with *The Whispering Gallery* (1955), is also an illuminating record of that decade. The other two volumes are *I Am My Brother* (1960) and *The Ample Proposition* (1966). His own poetry written during that period and included in *Collected Poems* (1963) makes a minor contribution in the movement towards a socially conscious verse. As an editor and publisher he has had a long and distinguished career. First associated with the Hogarth Press (from 1931 to 1946), he also edited various magazines, including *Penguin New Writing* and later *The London Magazine*.   O.K.

LEHMANN, Rosamond (1903–), born in London, the sister of John Lehmann, was educated at Cambridge which provides the setting for her first, very successful novel, *Dusty Answer* (1927), in which there is also a large autobiographical content. Her fiction is characterized by the persistent backward glance towards childhood and youth, interest in the inner difficulties of a young woman approaching maturity and by the lyrical delicacy of her style. Her two finest books are probably *The Ballad and the Source* (1944), the story of a domineering old lady as seen through the eyes of a young child, and *The Echoing Grove* (1953) in which a triangular love affair is played out against a shifting social and political background. Her autobiography is *The Swan in the Evening* (1968).

O.K.

LELAND, John (1506–52) was educated at St. Paul's School and Cambridge, Oxford and Paris, later becoming librarian to Henry VIII and king's antiquary. His long journey through England (c. 1534–43) included the examination of many documents and other historical remains. His notes were of great importance to later antiquaries and topographers. Leland published little, but his *Itinerary* and *Collectanea* were printed in the eighteenth century (1710–12; 1715). They illustrate his industry and powers of observation, although their style is somewhat rough.

Itinerary, ed. L. Toulmin Smith, 5 vols., London: Bell 1906–10; London: Centaur Press; Carbondale: Southern Illinois Univ. Press, 1964.

G.P.

LESSING, Doris. See **African Literature.**

L'ESTRANGE, Sir Roger (1616–1704), the son of a Norfolk baronet, was an energetic censor on the unashamedly political grounds which he argued in *Considerations and Proposals in Order to the Regulation* of the Press (1663). He was alternately lauded and persecuted for his life-long championing of royalist and conservative causes in scores of polemics, notably the *Citt and Bumpkin* pamphlets (1680) and in *The Observator* (1681–87), an early newspaper of considerable literary historical signifi-cance. Such ventures were supported by his many accomplished and lively translations of Latin and modern European texts (on which he contrived to engraft his "foreign" political bias) such as Quevodo's *Visions* (1667) and the popular *Fables of Aesop* (1692). (See also **Essays; Political Pamphlets.**) A.W.B.

LEVER, Charles (1806–72), the Dublin-born son of an English architect, was educated privately and at Trinity College, Dublin. He was successively doctor under the Irish Board of Health (1831–42), editor (1842–45) of the influential *Dublin University Magazine*, in which his first novels were serialized, and later British consul in Spezzia (1857) and Trieste (1867–72). His early novels—*The Confessions of Harry Lorrequer* (1839; s. 1837); *Charles O'Malley, the Irish Dragoon* (1841; s. 1840); *Tom Burke of "Ours"* (1843); and *Arthur O'Leary* (1844; s. 1843)—are ill-disciplined and racy portrayals of the more exuberant side of Irish life, hilarious, crude in characterization, vivid and not without fidelity to their models in real life. His later novels—*Roland Cashel* (1850; s. 1848); *The Fortunes of Glencore* (1857; s. 1855); *Lord Kilgobbin* (1872; s. 1870)—show greater depth and maturity, but lack the immortal passages that light up their predecessors, notably *Charles O'Malley*. O.E.

LEVERTOV, Denise (1923–) was born at Ilford (Essex) and educated privately. She served as a civilian nurse in London during the Second World War and lived in Europe in the years immediately follow-ing. In 1948 she settled in New York with her husband, Mitchell Good-man. Her first American publication was *Here and Now* (1957). She spent the years 1956 to 1958 in Mexico, was poetry editor of *The Nation* for eight months in 1961 and returned in the fall of 1963. Her books of poetry, in which, like W. C. Williams, she celebrates the discovered splendors of ordinary existence, include *The Jacob's Ladder* (1962), *O Taste and See* (1964), *The Sorrow Dance* (1968) and *Relearning the Alphabet* (1970). W.S.

LEWIS, Alun (1915–44), born at Aberdare (Glamorgan), was educated at Aberystwyth University College and, after a further two years' postgraduate research at Manchester University, took up a teaching post near his birthplace. He was called up for army service in 1940, being posted to India where he was killed in 1944. The meaning of war, both as a particular and demoralizing reality as well as part of a permanent human condition, forms the material for Lewis's best poems. Suspended between protest and resignation, he explores the plight of the soldier as a solitary and forgotten exile. He often renders this predicament in poems that are dignified and elegiac, using Indian scenes and figures to universalize his sense of futility; but his most moving poems are simple and personal, drawing upon intense moments of experience—his memories of human relationships and the inviolate natural world that seemed threatened. (See also **War Poets.**)

Selected Poetry and Prose ed. I. Hamilton, London: Allen & Unwin, 1966.

O.K.

LEWIS, C. S. (Clive Staples) (1898–1963), scholar and critic of English literature, Christian apologist and writer of fantasy novels both of science fiction and fairy tale, prided himself on his ability to reach a wide audience. Apart from the theological *The Screwtape Letters* (1942), his most popular work is probably the seven children's books which make up the *Chronicles of Narnia*, a series of magical adventures containing pervasive Christian analogies. Though always lucid, persuasive, highly readable and brilliant in his imaginative creation of otherworldly vegetation and atmosphere, Lewis is less satisfactory with his fictional human beings; and W. W. Robson has detected a debilitating strain of boyish romantic taste and emotional immaturity, as well as some lapses into the moralizer, as distinct from moralist, in his work. His literary criticism, always backed by sound scholarship, is notable for its lucidity, wit and obvious enjoyment of its subject.

The Allegory of Love, 1936.
Out of the Silent Planet, 1938.
A Preface to Paradise Lost, 1942.
The Screwtape Letters, 1942 (with *Screwtape Proposes a Toast*, 1961).
Perelandra, 1943.
The Lion, the Witch and the Wardrobe, 1950.
Mere Christianity, 1952.
Surprised by Joy, 1955 (autobiography).
The Last Battle, 1956.
An Experiment in Criticism, 1961.

Letters, ed. W. H. Lewis, London: Bles, 1966.   R.E.

LEWIS, M. G. (Matthew Gregory) ("Monk") (1775–1818), born in London, was educated at Westminster School and Oxford. He was in Weimar (1792–93) and then went as attaché to the British embassy at The

Hague, where he wrote *The Monk* (1796), a novel in the Mrs. Radcliffe vein of Gothic horror, spiced with new elements of sex and religious sensationalism which gained it immediate notoriety. It is the wildest and most lurid of the Gothic romances. Also sensational are the six romantic melodramas, two versions of German romances and two tragedies which followed. Lewis's more sensible side is seen in his humane and delightful *Journal of a West Indian Proprietor* (1834). His ballad poems and personal friendship influenced Sir Walter Scott's early verses. Lewis collected his own *Poems* (1812).

Life and Correspondence, ed. M. Baron-Wilson, 2 vols., London: Colburn, 1839.   W.R.

LEWIS, Sinclair (1885–1951) was born in Sauk Center (Minnesota), youngest son of a country doctor. An unloved, awkward red-haired youth (nicknamed Red), he dreamed of escape from small-town drabness. He was educated at Yale (1902–08), writing for the *Literary Magazine*, making two trips to Europe and, during a truant year, taking various jobs including one at the community experiment of Upton Sinclair. In 1914 he published *Our Mr Wrenn* and married. Although stories for *The Saturday Evening Post* allowed him to write full time, four more lightweight novels preceded the realization of his cherished project "The Village Virus" as *Main Street* (1920). His early revulsion from crass materialism and philistinism in American provincial life informs Carol Kennicott's vague, futile effort to bring culture to smug, hypocritical Gopher Prairie. The novel made history with its frenzied denunciation and systematically accumulated detail, but its satire was blunted by the final endorsement of the values of the heroine's hard-working, thrifty doctor-husband. Launched on a career of research into middle-class manners, Lewis made his major contribution to satirical social categorization in *Babbitt* (1922), but his assiduous assemblage of fact is far from realism. As in much of *Elmer Gantry* (1927), his raucous, controversial exposure of hypocritical and hysterical evangelicalism, he fabricates impressively a gruesomely comic nightmare. He attempted a soberly naturalistic hero with positive vision in *Arrowsmith* (1925), his tribute to medical researchers, and in *Dodsworth* (1929), about a richer, more sensitive Babbitt and his snobbish wife. In 1930 he was awarded the Nobel Prize specifically for *Babbitt* and, as his notable acceptance speech confirms, in European acknowledgment of America's coming-of-age. Ironically, the ex-socialist's modest literary iconoclasm was ended. The best of his later mediocrity was inspired either by his second wife, Dorothy Thompson, the newspaper woman—*Ann Vickers*, (1933), about a career woman; *It Can't Happen Here*, (1935), an antifascist fantasy set in America—or by his affair with a young actress—*Cass Timberlane* (1945). Roughly treated by the critics, he was remarkably generous to other writers. Wolfe and Hemingway responded to his encouragement with, respectively, sympathetic and vicious caricatures in *You Can't Go Home Again* (1941) and *Across the River and into the Trees* (1951). Lewis died in Rome.

George F. Babbitt is Lewis's freshest, perhaps only enduring comic type, the "boob" as booster of real estate in Zenith, a medium-sized Midwestern city partly modeled on Cincinnati (Ohio). A deluge of horrendous detail nearly swamps the meager plot of his story. Structurally weak, though clearly following Lewis's usual pattern (the hero has some success in his impulsive attempt to escape from routine, then returns under pressure, only half-reluctantly, to the fold), *Babbitt* lives in the virtuoso comic ventriloquism and the innumerable grotesques, such as Chum Frink and Vergil Gunch, that embellish episodes in two crucial years of the hero's life. Babbitt himself, ridiculous and pathetic by turns, is not finally in focus—his serious gestures are too ambiguously rendered; but the negative vision of Zenith, a gross parody of Dante's *Inferno*, is dauntingly vigorous.

Main Street 1920 (*f.* 1923; as *I Married a Doctor*, 1936).
Babbitt, 1922 (*f.* 1934).
Arrowsmith, 1925 (*f.* 1931).
Elmer Gantry, 1927 (*f.* 1960).
The Man Who Knew Coolidge, 1928.
Dodsworth, 1929 (*f.* 1936).
Ann Vickers, 1933 (*f.* 1933).
It Can't Happen Here, 1935.
Cass Timberlane, 1945 (*f.* 1947).
Kingsblood Royal, 1947.

The Man from Main Street: Selected Essays and Other Writings, 1904–1950, ed. H. E. Maule and M. H. Cane, New York: Random House, 1953; London: Heinemann, 1954.   A.S.

LEWIS, Wyndham (1884–1957), born in America and educated in England, trained as an artist before turning to literature and journalism. As editor of a number of reviews (notably *Blast*, with Ezra Pound, 1914–15) and in a series of forceful books, *Time and Western Man* among them, he attacked the decay of modern life and letters, and especially the decadent Romanticism (as he saw it) of Joyce, Bergson, whose theory of "flux" he considered dangerous to the idea of stability, Spengler and Einstein. He also attacked behaviorist theories in psychology. His satire and fable, exemplified by *Monstre Gai* (1955), has a strong intellectual cast that tends to overshadow the imaginative element. In a critical work, *The Lion and* *the Fox*, he cast Shakespeare in the role of artist-hero, illustrative of his view that the intellectual should be a leader of society.

Tarr, 1918 (novel).
The Lion and the Fox, 1927.
Time and Western Man, 1927.
The Childermass, 1928 (novel).
The Apes of God, 1930 (novel).
Blasting and Bombardiering, 1937.

Letters, ed. W. K. Rose, London: Methuen, 1963.   A.P.

LIDDON, H. P. (Henry Parry). See **Sermons.**

LILBURNE, John. See **Political Pamphlets.**

LILLO, George (1693-1739), born in London, son of a Dutch jeweler, began writing late in life. A tragedy, *The London Merchant; or, The History of George Barnwell* (1731), made him famous and popularized the domestic drama in England by seriously presenting bourgeois and mercantile material. The play was a great success, commended by Pope, patronized by royalty and warmly applauded by the city merchants, for it suggested the nobility of their trade. It held the stage for more than a century. His other works, apart from *Fatal Curiosity* (1737; *p.* 1736), were unsuccessful.

Works, 2 vols., London: Davies, 1755.   P.R.

LINCOLN, Abraham (1809-65), sixteenth president of the United States, was born in Kentucky, then moved to Indiana and to Illinois. A captain in the Black Hawk War (1832), he served as postmaster at New Salem (Illinois), studied law and served in the state legislature (1834-41). Moving to Springfield in 1837, he practiced law and served in Congress (1847-49) as a Whig. Lincoln joined the Republican party in 1856; he ran unsuccessfully for the Senate in 1858, but established a national reputation. His nomination as Republican presidential candidate in 1860—largely because of his conservative views on slavery—and subsequent election provoked the Southern secession movement, which he considered illegal. Following the Confederate attack on Fort Sumter, Lincoln resolved to restore the Union by force. Declaring that "My paramount object is to save the Union and not either to save or destroy slavery," he issued his famous Emancipation Proclamation (1863) as a war measure, but one which gave a high moral purpose to the struggle. Reelected in 1864, Lincoln favored the prompt restoration of the Confederate states to the

Union ("with malice toward none"). He was shot in Ford's Theater, Washington and died the following day (15 April 1865).

A great president, who vastly extended the powers of the executive office, Lincoln also quickly achieved symbolic status as the Great Emancipator and Savior of the Union. His greatest achievement was his identification of the Union cause with that of human liberty, his two inaugural addresses and the Gettysburg Address being notable expressions of Lincoln's fundamental beliefs and almost mystical concept of the American Union. Lincoln's collected papers and letters, couched in prose of remarkable lucidity, reveal his profound intellect and compassion.

Collected Works, ed. R. P. Basler, 8 vols. and index, New Brunswick: Rutgers Univ. Press, 1953–55.   J.W.

LINDSAY, Vachel (1879–1931) was born in Springfield (Illinois), the son of a country doctor. Unrecognized until 1913 when "General William Booth Enters into Heaven" appeared in the fourth number of *Poetry*, Lindsay became immediately famous with his electrifying public recitations of this poem, whose revolutionary sound effects were based on Salvation Army hymns. Other startlingly successful celebrations of American popular culture were the fairground steam organ whistles of "The Kallyope Yell," the motor horns of "The Santa Fe Trail" and "The Congo," based on Negro sermons and cakewalk, ragtime and blackface routines. Lindsay's career thereafter was "the higher vaudeville," performing these poems to audiences which at first included Yeats and Masefield, but later seemed to consist of Rotarians' wives who disgusted him by ignoring everything in his work except its supposedly jazz elements. Lindsay, who regarded jazz as diseased, and who was a teetotaler, an Anti-Saloon League orator, a YMCA lecturer and a virgin until his marriage in 1925, was an idealist, whose "Gospel of Beauty" meant spiritual and social regeneration, not aesthetic experiment. His spiritual center was Springfield, his birthplace and Lincoln's city. A faith in the people, more artless than Lincoln's, inspired his early hikes through the west (1906; 1908; 1912) when, as the peddler of dreams, he recited his poems to farmers in return for a night's lodging. "Bryan" commemorates the presidential campaign of a reformer whose hatred of capitalism and belief in self-improvement sparked by flamboyant whistle-stop oratory was akin to Lindsay's own. "The Proud Farmer" and "Alexander Campbell," the prophet of an American millennium, were spiritual predecessors, while "Johnny Appleseed," the Swedenborgian pilgrim who sowed orchards in the western wilderness, is Lindsay's truest image of his art's purpose.

Rhymes to Be Traded for Bread, 1912.
General William Booth Enters into Heaven and Other Poems, 1913.
Adventures While Preaching the Gospel of Beauty, 1914.
The Congo and Other Poems, 1914.
The Art of the Moving Picture, 1915.
A Handy Guide for Beggars, 1916.
The Chinese Nightingale and Other Poems, 1917.
The Golden Whales of California, 1920.
The Golden Book of Springfield, 1920.
Going-to-the-Sun, 1923.
Going-to-the-Stars, 1926.
The Candle in the Cabin, 1926.
The Litany of Washington Street, 1929.
Every Soul Is a Circus, 1929.

Collected Poems, New York: Macmillan Co., 1923; 1925.
Letters, ed. A. J. Armstrong, Waco, Tex.: Baylor Univ. Press, 1940.

M.T.

LOCKE, John (1632–1704) was educated at Westminster School and Christ Church, Oxford, where he studied medicine and held several academic posts. He became acquainted with the Shaftesbury family when he carried out a surgical operation on the first earl, and subsequently joined the great Whig household—initially as physician, but then as tutor, adviser and general confidant. In 1672 Shaftesbury became chancellor and Locke was made secretary to the Board of Trade, but in 1682, when Shaftesbury fled to Holland as a result of the plots connected with the Exclusion Bill and the Monmouth Rebellion, Locke followed him and remained in exile for five years. Holland at that time was a center of liberal thought in religion and politics and Locke spent his years there in developing his philosophical and political doctrines. It was in Holland that he completed his most important work, *An Essay concerning Human Understanding*, which was published in 1690. By this time the Revolution of 1688 had occurred and Locke, now returned to England, was regarded as the foremost defender of the principles embodied in the new political settlement. His health was never robust and in 1691 he retired from public life to the home of Lady Masham at Oates in Essex, where he spent his remaining years in writing and study.

While in Holland Locke had written (in 1685) *Epistola de Tolerantia* and on his return to England this was translated into English. It was followed in 1690 by *Two Treatises on Government*. These works were pleas for the liberty of the individual; *An Essay concerning Human Understanding* was an extension of the argument, defending the right of the individual to determine his beliefs according to his own experience. The central concern of the *Essay* is to describe the limits of human understanding and knowledge. Our knowledge nearly always falls "far short of perfect comprehension," but, nonetheless, it is "sufficient for our state." Locke discounts the notion that we have any knowledge prior to experience and argues strongly against the Cartesian theory of "innate ideas."

Locke's empiricism, or what he called the "new way of ideas," had a pervasive influence upon the thought of the eighteenth century and therefore upon its literature. Where literature comes close to philosophy in the eighteenth century, as in Swift, Pope and Thomson, this influence is manifest. Locke's account of how our ideas become connected by association played its part in the narrative technique of Sterne, in Addison's *The Spectator* essays on the "Pleasures of the Imagination," and, indirectly, in Wordsworth's Preface to *Lyrical Ballads*. By the end of the century a reaction set in, and for Romantic writers such as Blake and Coleridge, Locke's influence was seen as inimical to the poetic imagination.

(See also **Romantic Movement, The.**)

An Essay concerning Human Understanding, ed. A. C. Fraser, 2 vols., Oxford: Clarendon Press, 1894.   R.L.B.

LOCKHART, J. G. (John Gibson) (1794–1854) was born in Glasgow and educated at the university there and at Balliol College, Oxford. In 1815 he went to study law at Edinburgh, where in 1817 he and John Wilson founded and edited *Blackwood's Magazine*, composing savage attacks on the "Cockney School" of Romantic poets. In 1820 Lockhart married Sir Walter Scott's eldest daughter Sophia, and after Scott's death he produced his *Memoirs of the Life of Sir Walter Scott, Bart.* (1837–38), the first major biography to embody Romantic theories about the influence of environment and childhood experience on the growth of genius. Lockhart wrote biographies of Burns and Napoleon (1828 and 1829) and his *Peter's Letters to His Kinsfolk* (1819) contains racy but discerning criticism of Edinburgh intellectual life of the time. From 1826 to 1854 Lockhart edited *The Quarterly Review*. He translated from German and Spanish and wrote four novels. *Some Passages in the Life of Mr. Adam Blair* (1822) is a study in Scottish Calvinism.

Literary Criticism, ed. M. C. Hildyard, Oxford: Blackwell; New York: P. Smith, 1931.   W.R.

LODGE, Thomas (?1558–1625), born in London, the son of a lord mayor, and educated at Merchant Taylors' School and Oxford, became a Catholic and later a doctor. He made a bid for literary fame in many fashionable genres, including the Ovidian poem *Scilla's Metamorphosis* (1589), the sonnet sequence *Phillis* (1593), and formal satire, *A Fig for Momus* (1595). His verse is musical and competent in a minor key, heavily but honestly reliant on foreign models. His prose includes an untitled defense of poetry (1577); and, amongst other romances, *Rosalynde*; *Euphues Golden Legacy* (1590), a pastoral of delicate artifice. Lodge's last writings were philosophical and medical.

Complete Works, ed. E. W. Gosse, 4 vols., Glasgow: Hunterian Club, 1883.

J.M.P.

LONDON, Jack (1876–1916), born in San Francisco, seems to have been the illegitimate son of an itinerant astrologer, William H. Chaney. His mother married John London, an earnest, optimistic but luckless businessman. The boy, left very much to his own devices, grew up tough, enterprising and lawless among the longshoremen and oyster pirates of Oakland. He also had an unusual taste for reading and is said to have haunted the reading room of the Oakland public library, devoting himself first to adventure stories and later to the then fashionable writings of Herbert Spencer and his popularizers and the works of Nietzsche and Karl Marx, the sources of his later pseudoscientific social ideas.

In 1893 he signed on for a sealing voyage in the Pacific. Shortly after his return from sea and after a tramping expedition through the Northern states into Canada, he entered the University of California, where he completed only one semester before joining the Klondike gold rush in 1897. It was there that he encountered the primitive scenes and hardly less primitive personages which were to provide him with material for his writing. On his return he seized the opportunity to work up into short stories his experiences in the Northern wastes. They suited the public demand for "strong" exotic tales and were accepted not only by the now waning *Overland Monthly*, but also by *The Atlantic Monthly*. When he published a collection of such tales in *The Son of the Wolf* (1900) he received national and, later, international acclaim for his racy treatment of exciting subjects, embodying powerful atavistic themes.

A man of great energy, London wrote prolifically. In a short life he published some fifty volumes—novels, essays, plays and tales, reflecting his none too subtle "philosophy" of evolutionism and crude Marxian analysis. As a journalist he covered the Russo-Japanese War for Hearst. He became involved in Mexican revolutionary politics, made a number of voyages through the South Seas and the Caribbean in a yacht that told of his growing financial success, and built himself a grandiose mansion which was destroyed by fire shortly after its completion. As an early addiction to liquor extended into alcoholism, he made a fortune and spent it with equal swiftness. After a disappointing first marriage, on which he draws in *Martin Eden* (1909), he married Charmian Kittredge, treating her as "mate" to balance his fantasy of himself as "wolf."

The fiction which followed London's early success, fashioned to a market for romantic adventure, contained references to "superior" men and women and catered to the daydreams of author and immature readers alike. Typical are *A Daughter of the Snows* (1902) and *The Sea-Wolf* (1904). The latter invites comparison with Frank Norris's *Moran of the Lady Letty*, published a year earlier—to London's disadvantage. The earlier sections of both novels are similar, but in place of Norris's wistful ending which is consistent with the naturalism of the whole, London settled for a titillating, if somewhat moralistic, South Seas romance. A similar sentimentality attends *A Daughter of the Snows*, a novel of Nordic superiority. It is only in the animal stories, *The Call of the Wild* (1903) and *White Fang* (1906), that London's atavistic themes avoid silliness, the animal heroes providing a more suitable vehicle for their creator's fantasies.

London's Marxist enthusiasms expressed themselves, outside his pamphlets, in a revolutionary novel, *The People of the Abyss* (1903), set in the slums of London, and *The Iron Heel* (1907), in which oppressive totalitarian capitalism defeats socialist revolution, only to be superseded after some three hundred years by a millennial era of collective socialism. Apart from *Martin Eden*, London's other excursion into autobiography— if we except the overt wish-fulfillment of his wolf-men and women— was in *John Barleycorn* (1913), where he draws a passionate, horrific picture of his experiences as an alcoholic.

Although it is common to see London as a naturalist, he rarely hits the note of pessimistic determinism of Crane's naturalist tales. More often he emphasizes atavistic power and the morality of cleanliness and strength as rather simplistic bases for his melioristic themes.

The Son of the Wolf, 1900.
Children of the Frost, 1902.
A Daughter of the Snows, 1902.
The Call of the Wild, 1903 (*f.* 1935).
The People of the Abyss, 1903.
The Sea-Wolf, 1904 (*f.* 1930; 1941; as *Wolf Larsen*, 1959).
White Fang, 1906 (*f.* 1936).
The Iron Heel, 1907.
Martin Eden, 1909 (*f.* as *Adventures of Martin Eden*, 1942).
Revolution and Other Essays, 1910.
South Sea Tales, 1911.
The Valley of the Moon, 1913.

John Barleycorn, 1913.
The Strength of the Strong, 1914.
The Scarlet Plague, 1915.

The Bodley Head Jack London, ed. A. Calder-Marshall, 4 vols., London: Bodley Head, 1963–66.
Letters, ed. K. Hendricks and I. Shepard, New York: Odyssey Press, 1965; London: MacGibbon & Kee, 1966.   M.L.

LONGFELLOW, H. W. (Henry Wadsworth) (1807–82) was born at Portland (Maine), a lawyer's son. After private schools he graduated from Bowdoin College in 1825 in the same class as Hawthorne. Following three years' travel in Europe he returned to teach at Bowdoin as professor of modern languages. He returned to Europe in 1835 where his wife, whom he had married in 1831, died. In 1836 he took the chair of French and Spanish at Harvard, and remained there for sixteen years. His first books were *Outre-Mer: A Pilgrimage beyond the Sea* (1834–35) and then an unsuccessful novel, *Hyperion* (1839). His first volume of verse was *Voices of the Night*, but it was *Ballads and Other Poems* that established his popularity, including, as it did, "The Wreck of the Hesperus" and "The Village Blacksmith." The untypical *Poems on Slavery* (1842) was his only political venture. In 1843 he married Frances Elizabeth Appleton and published *The Spanish Student*, a poetic drama. *The Belfry of Bruges and Other Poems* (1845) contained "The Bridge" and "The Old Clock on the Stairs." There followed the long narrative poem, *Evangeline* (1847), and other works, notably *Hiawatha* (1855). He continued the exploration of America's past in *The Courtship of Miles Standish* and *Tales of a Wayside Inn*, in which a collection of stories about different countries is told around the fireside of a New England inn. His translation of Dante's *Divine Comedy* was published between 1867 and 1870, a work originally undertaken as "refuge" after his second wife was burnt to death in 1861.

Longfellow's immense popularity during his lifetime stemmed from his view of poetry, shared by his readers, as an escape from the realities of the present. The past, made suitably unreal and sentimental, was his main inspiration, and his audience found the affirmation and indulgence they wanted, protected from a critical view of past or present by the skillful web of the verse. (See also **Hymns.**)

Voices of the Night, 1839.
Ballads and Other Poems, 1841.
Poems on Slavery, 1842.
The Spanish Student, 1843.
The Belfry of Bruges and Other Poems, 1845.

Evangeline, 1847.
Kavanagh, 1849 (novel).
The Song of Hiawatha, 1855.
The Courtship of Miles Standish, 1858.
Tales of a Wayside Inn, 1863; 1874.
Kéramos and Other Poems, 1878.
Ultima Thule, 1880.
In the Harbor, 1882.

Writings, 11 vols., London: Routledge, 1886.   D.M.

LONGSTREET, Augustus (1790–1870), born in Georgia and educated at Yale, became a Methodist clergyman and president successively
of Emory College (1839–48), Centenary College (1849), the University of
Mississippi (1849–56) and the University of South Carolina (1857–65).
He is best known for eighteen comic pieces which first appeared in the
Augusta Sentinel, and were collected as *Georgia Scenes, Characters, Incidents,
etc.* (1835). These tales of "gander-pulling," horse racing and country life
are realistic but safely sanitized by being placed in the past. Devoted to
low life, they illustrated "the manners, customs, amusements, wit and
dialect" of his native state and are in the tradition of "the old South
West" sketches that are important in the background of Mark Twain.
Longstreet skillfully employed an "eye and ear" color which made him
the forerunner of the Georgia Realists, of whom the most famous is
Erskine Caldwell.   A.M.R.

LOVELACE, Richard (1618–57), inheriting at the age of eleven
extensive estates in Kent, was educated in London at the Charterhouse
before going up both to Oxford, where he received an honorary M.A.
after only two years' residence (1636), and, briefly, to Cambridge. He then
began a military career, serving in Scotland (1639–40) and, after a brief
period in prison (1642), as a colonel in England and Holland (1642–46).
Simultaneously, he was leading, like a Renaissance courtier, an active
cultural life. Remarkable for his fine appearance and manners, he included
amongst his many friends the poets Marvell, Suckling and Cotton, the
musician Henry Lawes, and the painter Lely. His fortunes declined after
1647 and he died poor.
    Apart from commendatory verses and two lost plays, all Lovelace's
work is contained in two volumes of poems, mainly addressed to friends
and mainly love lyrics: *Lucasta* (1649), which he prepared for publication
during a second term of imprisonment, and *Lucasta: Posthume Poems*
(1660), published by his brother after Lovelace's death. Lucasta has sometimes been identified with Lucy Sacheverell, said to have been betrothed

to Lovelace but married to another on the false report of his death at the siege of Dunkirk (1646). The poems have a careless ease, characteristic of Cavalier poetry, but the finest, like "To Althea, from Prison" and "To Lucasta, Going to the Wars," are admired for their controlled strength of tone, their dignity of sentiment, and the neat elegance and lucidity of expression. Other poems display an engaging playfulness, an ability to pursue a conceit with Metaphysical thoroughness, and occasionally some satire.

(See also **Metaphysical Poetry.**)

Poems, ed. C. H. Wilkinson, 2 vols., Oxford: Clarendon Press, 1925.

H.N.D.

LOVER, Samuel (1797–1868) was born in Dublin of well-to-do Protestant parents. Regarded by his family as a prodigy, he lost their sympathy when he abandoned a professional career to become an artist. His work as a portrait painter, miniaturist and engraver led to his becoming secretary of the Royal Hibernian Society and having work accepted by the Royal Academy. He gained a reputation as a singer and songwriter, and, on settling in London, moved in the same Whig society as his friend Tom Moore. He wrote plays, musicals, opera libretti; and he helped found *The Dublin University Magazine* and *Bentley's Miscellany*.

His novels *Rory O'More* and *Handy Andy* were popular for half a century. Like Carleton, he wrote of the Irish peasants, their heritage and their history of suffering; like Lever, he used them as figures of whimsy and farce. Much as he loved and understood them, he helped to establish Paddy the illiterate clown, the light-hearted, impractical, out-at-elbow butt of Victorian England.

Legends and Stories of Ireland, 1831; second series, 1834.
Rory O'More, 1837.
Songs and Ballads, 1839.
Handy Andy, 1842 (s. 1839).

G.G.U.

LOWELL, Amy (1874–1925), born in Brookline (Massachusetts), became a literary legend partly through the luster of her family name. The public image was often unfair to a clever, highly sensitive, if eccentric, woman. She befriended many writers, including D. H. Lawrence, and through her enthusiastic espousing of imagism she exercised considerable influence. Her first important collection of poems was *Sword Blades and Poppy Seed* (1914). *What's O'Clock?* (1925) contains the best of her later work. In her verse, which ranges from romantic lyric to Frost-like dramatic monologue, mild satire and, in *Fir-Flower Tablets* (1921), "translation" from the Chinese, the dominant characteristics are precision and a delight in color and texture. She experimented with so-called "polyphonic prose," but her main prose achievements were a biography of Keats, which she fought to complete despite increasing ill health, and a book of essays, *Tendencies in Modern American Poetry* (1917). (See also **Imagism.**)

Complete Poetical Works, ed. L. Untermeyer, Boston: Houghton Mifflin, 1955.   S.C.

LOWELL, James Russell (1819–91) was born at Cambridge (Massachusetts). He came from an eminent New England family and was educated at Harvard. A versatile man of letters, Lowell reflected in his work most of the literary and social concerns of a complex period of American life. Poet, essayist, literary critic, editor—notably of *The Atlantic Monthly* (1857–61) and, with others, of *The North American Review* (1863–72)—he was also professor of French and Spanish, and of belles-lettres, at Harvard from 1855 to 1872, and American ambassador to Spain (1877–80) and to Great Britain (1880–85).

The facility of his work, his central position in the literary world, and his articulation of current values made him, for later critics, the embodiment of "the genteel tradition" of New England letters. The writing is not always superficial and complacent. The best of his verse is humorous, as in *A Fable for Critics* (1848), a collection of portraits, mostly satirical, some approving, of contemporary writers including himself, and in *The Biglow Papers* (1848 and 1867), antislavery and political satires written in Yankee dialect. The more serious verse has moments of power (e.g., in "Columbus," "The Vision of Sir Launfal" and "Agaziz"), but it is generally too vague in its attempted nobility. Lowell's best work is his literary criticism. On Gray, Dante, and *Hamlet* (in "Shakespeare Once More") he is both fluent and perceptive, drawing on one of his most persistent concerns (a typical Victorian one), the rise of modern skepticism and self-doubt.

(See also **Hymns.**)

A Year's Life and Other Poems, 1841.
Poems, 1844.
Conversations on Some of the Old Poets, 1845.
A Fable for Critics, 1848.
The Biglow Papers, 1848; second series, 1867.
The Vision of Sir Launfal, 1848.
The Ode Recited at the Harvard Commemoration, 1865.
Under the Willows, 1868 (poems).
Among My Books, 1870; second series, 1876.
The Cathedral, 1870 (poem).

Three Memorial Poems, 1877.
Heartsease and Rue, 1888 (poems).
Latest Literary Essays and Addresses, 1891.

Writings, 11 vols., Boston: Houghton, Mifflin; London: Macmillan, 1890–92.
Uncollected Poems, ed. T. M. Smith, Philadelphia: Univ. of Pennsylvania Press; London: Oxford Univ. Press, 1950.
Letters, ed. C. E. Norton, 3 vols., New York: Harper, 1904.   D.B.H.

LOWELL, Robert (1917–   ) was born in Boston (Massachusetts). He belonged to a distinguished New England family, grew up among "autochthonous Boston snobs," attended St. Mark's School and spent a year at Harvard. Then, attracted by the reputation of the "Fugitive Poets," John Crowe Ransom and Allen Tate, he went to Kenyon College, read classics and graduated *summa cum laude*. In 1940 he became a Roman Catholic. In 1943, as a protest against allied bombing of civilians, he refused to report for military service and was sentenced to a year's imprisonment. Lowell remains a "fire-breathing" pacifist. He has taught at several colleges and has received many prizes and awards.

His first volume of poems, *Land of Unlikeness* (1944), has never been reprinted and is virtually unobtainable. Seven of its poems, however, appear, revised, in *Lord Weary's Castle* (1946). Four others are printed in W. J. Martz's *The Achievement of Robert Lowell* (1966). *Poems: 1938–1949* (1950) contains the whole of *Lord Weary's Castle* and *The Mills of the Kavanaughs* (1951), with the exception of the latter's title poem, which is printed as an appendix to H. B. Staples's *Robert Lowell* (1962). Lowell describes his early poems as forbidding and clotted:

> I wanted an art as disciplined
> and dark as Calvin in his *Institutes*.

Modeled on the seventeenth-century Metaphysical poets in their formal prosody, ambiguities, puns and outrageous conceits synthesizing apocalyptic imagery with slang—

> only Armageddon will suffice
> To turn the hero skating on thin ice

—they are ostentatiously repellent and obscure. Allen Tate's influence is apparent in the passionate yet impersonal rhetoric, the preoccupation with history and tradition, the densely wrought verbal texture. Lowell saw his work as continuing a tradition established by Pound and Eliot, but composed in formal meters that both looked, and were, hard to write. "The Mills of the Kavanaughs" resembles *The Waste Land* as a synthesis of many cultures, containing allusions to myth, dogma, Ovid, Dante and contemporary events and such *double entendres* as "jelly-roll." Written entirely in rhymed sixteen-line stanzas, it incorporates also an occult metaphysic and a melodramatic plot. An ambitious amalgam of incompatible elements, it defeats most readers.

The autobiographical *Life Studies* (1959), written in free or loosely rhymed verse, is Lowell's most popular work. Acclaimed as a new genre, "confessional verse," these ironic poems are actually less ingenuous than they seem. "Waking in the Blue," for example, looks like a personal recollection of insanity, but the madman who mimics Louis XVI and "horses" about is compounded of images from two earlier poems, "1790" and "The Fat Man in the Mirror," while these in turn are based on the work of other writers. Lowell describes madness not to reveal himself but as a device to liberate images from habitual contexts. The unifying theme of *For the Union Dead* (1964) seems to be an exploration of the Satanic element both in the artist ("Hawthorne") and, in the poems about cities, in modern society. Themes of war and the city reappear in *Near the Ocean* (1967). *Notebook* (three versions, May 1969; July 1969; 1970), a sequence of unrhymed sonnets, is much concerned with aggression, from "the Piltdown Man, first carnivore to laugh," through the monsters Clytemnestra, Caligula, Attila, Mussolini, Stalin and Hitler, concluding with the Pentagon, "Dies Irae" and "Closing." It reiterates therefore the apocalyptic terror of *Land of Unlikeness*. To these images of violence, the translations in *Imitations* (1961) and *Near the Ocean* implicitly oppose the image of the artist: Juvenal replies to Caligula, Hugo and Rimbaud to Napoleonic militarism, Montale to Mussolini and Pasternak to Stalin.

Land of Unlikeness, 1944.
Lord Weary's Castle, 1946.
Poems: 1938–1949, 1950.
The Mills of the Kavanaughs, 1951.
Life Studies, 1959; 2nd (enlarged) edition, 1968.
Phaedra, Racine's Phèdre, 1961.
Imitations, 1961.
For the Union Dead, 1964.
The Old Glory, 1965 (drama).
Near the Ocean, 1967.
Prometheus Bound, 1969 (prose drama).
Notebook, 1967–68, 1969.
Notebook, 1970.   M.T.

LOWRY, Malcolm. See **Canadian Literature.**

LYDGATE, John (?1370–?1450), born at Lydgate (Suffolk), was a member of Bury St. Edmunds Abbey from the age of fifteen, although he was also for a time prior of Hatfield. As a court poet he wrote mummings and other dramatic compositions for court and state occasions which give him an important position in the history of drama. He developed and transmitted the allegorical and rhetorical traditions of Chaucer and Gower and gave vogue to the aureate style, highly elaborate, decorative and verbose. His characteristic works are moral "epics"— *Troy Book* (c.1412–20), *The Story of Thebes* (c.1420–22) and *Falls of Princes* (c.1431–39)—but he also wrote a number of short religious poems.

The Temple of Glass, Caxton, ?1477; ed. J. Schick, London: Early English Text Society, 1891.

The Fall of Princes, Pynson, 1494; ed. H. Bergen, 4 parts, Washington: Carnegie Institution of Washington, 1923–27; London: Early English Text Society, 1924–27; additions and corrections, Washington, 1936.

The Siege of Thebes, de Worde, c. 1500; ed. A. Erdmann and E. Ekwall, 2 vols., London: Early English Text Society, 1, 1911; 2, 1930.

The History, Siege and Destruction of Troy [*Troy Book*], Pynson, 1513; ed. H. Bergen, 4 parts, London: Early English Text Society, 1906–35.

Poems, ed. J. Norton-Smith, Oxford: Clarendon Press, 1966.   A.D.M.

LYLY, John (?1554–1606), grandson of the author of *Lily's Grammar*, was brought up in Canterbury where he probably attended the King's School. He matriculated at Magdalen College, Oxford and by 1579 was M.A. at both Oxford and Cambridge. Failing to obtain a fellowship, he resorted to writing, and in 1578 made a debut of unprecedented success with *Euphues: The Anatomy of Wit*, a prose treatise on wit and wisdom in the form of a cautionary tale. Two years later he published a lengthy sequel, *Euphues and His England*, dedicated to his new patron, the earl of Oxford. In 1583 he married Beatrice Browne, a Yorkshire heiress, and during this same period, with Oxford's support, presented two plays at court. These, *Campaspe* (1584), a dramatization of the conflicting claims of love and honor on a magnanimous ruler, and *Sappho and Phaon* (p. 1584), an investigation into the feasibility of love between a menial and a monarch, were performed by a combination of boys' acting companies. Lyly's next work, *Galatea* (1592), a pastoral intrigue comedy in which he examined the problem of evading destiny, was given a court performance in 1588. A month later *Endymion* (1591) was performed. The classical myth is delicately transformed here into an allegory of the relationship between a courtier and his monarch. Lyly's later plays are more difficult to date. They are alike in a tendency to strike out in new directions and to adapt to changes of taste. In *Midas* (1592), which was given a court performance, Lyly exchanges his usual love-centered plot for a devastating lampoon on Philip II. *Love's Metamorphosis* (1601), a highly stylized "anatomy" of love, is perhaps an experiment with a shorter form. In *Mother Bombie* (1594) he makes his closest approach to classical Roman comedy. It is a convivial intrigue play set against a realistic social background. *The Woman in the Moon* (1597), performed at court, is his only play in verse. Its intrigue structure, an element of slapstick farce and some details of its staging suggest that it was designed for an adult company. Between 1589 and 1601 Lyly was member of Parliament for Hindon, Aylesbury and Appleby, and during this same period he contributed to the Marprelate controversy in support of the bishops. He died in poverty in 1606.

Lyly's two prose treatises and his eight plays are refined coterie works designed to appeal to a cultural and aristocratic élite. The delicate observation of manners which is a central concern is thus a reflection of the decorous manners of his audience and at the same time a pattern of courtly behavior. An emphasis is laid on elegance, symmetry and sophistication, and the outlook of his works is clearly intellectual and complimentary. Concerned less with character and the tensions of human relationships than he is with the propriety or significance of relationships, his actions fall naturally into series of static tableaux. These reflect in miniature the debate structure which Lyly employed so frequently as an ordering principle in his works. Structural symmetry is an important feature of his so-called euphuistic style. Perfected in *Euphues*, this idealization of polite conversation is characterized by its exquisite balancing of clauses and by a very individual brand of precious imagery. Although this style precludes the individualizing of characters by means of speech, it epitomizes the minute and flawless craftsmanship of Lyly's métier.

Works, ed. R. W. Bond, 3 vols., Oxford: Clarendon Press, 1902.   L.E.P.

LYNDSAY, Sir David (?1486–1555), eldest son of David Lindsay of the Mount, Fifeshire, entered James IV's court before 1511 and was appointed usher to Prince James in 1512. Out of favor at court from 1524 to 1528, he later returned there, went on embassies abroad and rose to the position of Lyon king of arms. He wrote in the traditions of allegory and social complaint, but was remembered for his criticisms of ecclesiastical abuses. The earliest of these is *The Dream* (c. 1528), a vision of contemporary evils. His most famous work is *A Pleasant Satire of the Three Estates* (p. 1540), a social morality play.

Poetical Works, ed. D. Hamer, 4 vols., Edinburgh: Scottish Text Society, 1931–36.

A.D.M.

LYTE, Francis. See Hymns.

LYTTON, Lord (Edward Bulwer-Lytton, 1st Baron) (1803–73), born in London, the son of General Bulwer, had an outstanding career as a writer, orator, politician and scholar. Acutely susceptible to literary fashions, he was the most popular and prolific author of his day. His novels include *Pelham* (1828), a study of high society, *The Caxtons* (1849), a panorama of contemporary life, and *The Last Days of Pompeii* (1834), the best of his many historical romances. His mediocre verse was also popular, as were two of his plays, *The Lady of Lyons* (1838) and *Richelieu* (1839).

I.W.

M

MACAULAY, Rose (1881–1958), daughter of a lecturer at Cambridge, was brought up in Italy, then educated in Oxford. Her writings are copious and in a variety of forms. As a novelist her characteristic fusion of sensitivity, comic sharpness and concern for the deepest issues of personal spiritual life can be discerned in *Potterism* (1920), *Dangerous Ages* (1921), *Orphan Island* (1924), *Going Abroad* (1934) and her finest book, *The Towers of Trebizond* (1956). She wrote critical works on Milton (1933) and E. M. Forster (1938) and the valuable *Some Religious Elements in English Literature* (1931). She loved traveling and wrote excellent travel books. Since her death three collections of her letters have appeared.

Letters to a Friend, 1950–1952, ed. C. Babington-Smith, London: Collins, 1961.
Last Letters to a Friend, 1952–1958, ed. C. Babington-Smith, London: Collins, 1962.
Letters to a Sister, ed. C. Babington-Smith, London: Collins 1964.

W.R.

MACAULAY, Thomas Babington, Lord (1st Baron) (1800–59), born at Rothley Temple (Leicestershire), showed prodigious powers of memory as a young child. He studied at Cambridge, and his public life after graduation was a series of successes—as member of Parliament, member of the Supreme Council for India, secretary for war, and paymaster of the forces. His ponderous oratorical style, so praised by contemporaries in his parliamentary speeches, can be studied today in his essays and historical writings. In his *History of England* (1849–61), covering only the latter years of the seventeenth century, his facts are often inaccurate and his interpretations unoriginal, but as examples of a use of language which matured in the nineteenth century his *Critical and Historical Essays* (3 vols., 1843) should still be read. *Lays of Ancient Rome* (1842) shows Macaulay's gift as a narrative poet. (See also **Essays.**)

Works, ed. T. F. Henderson, 9 vols., London: Routledge (New Universal Library), 1905–07.

C.P.

McAULEY, James. See **Australian Literature.**

McCARTHY, Mary (1912–   ) was born in Seattle and orphaned at an early age; her recollections appear in *Memories of a Catholic Girlhood* (1957). After graduating from Vassar she became drama critic of *The Partisan Review*. Her highly regarded theater reviews are collected in her *Theatre Chronicles 1937-62*. She is chiefly known for her novels, which often satirize the intelligentsia in a style that is both skillful and witty: *The Company She Keeps* (1942), *The Oasis* (1949), *The Groves of Academe* (1952), *A Charmed Life* (1955) and the very successful *The Group* (1963; *f.* 1965), which records thirty years in the lives of eight Vassar alumnae since graduating in 1933. *Birds of America* (1971) satirizes the American tourists encountered by a young New England bird watcher in Rome and Paris.   R.W.

McCULLERS, Carson (1917–67) was born Carson Smith in Georgia, the setting for nearly all her writing, though her adult life, especially after marriage to Reeves McCullers in 1937, was spent mostly in New York. *The Heart Is a Lonely Hunter* (1940), her first novel, records with extreme sensitivity how a deaf mute, Singer, receives the love and confidence of a range of characters in a small Southern town, including a black doctor, a young radical and a lonely girl. But the mute is himself dependent on communication with another, Antonapoulos, who has been institutionalized. When Antonapoulos dies, Singer kills himself and all their worlds collapse. These themes, the quest for love and the pain of isolation, recur. *Reflections in a Golden Eye* examines the misplaced love of each of a group of "grotesques," and the consequent violence. *The Member of the Wedding* captures the anguish of adolescence when Frankie, a motherless girl, mistakenly believes that she will be joining her brother's honeymoon. McCullers successfully dramatized the book in 1950, with Julie Harris and Ethel Waters in leading roles. *The Ballad of the Sad Café*, a novella about a strange love triangle, was staged by Albee in 1963. McCullers' own theater work includes *The Square Root of Wonderful* (1958). She was never healthy, and her final years were marred by constant illness. *Clock without Hands* (1961), a novel overtly confronting Southern race relations, won only a mixed reception.

The Heart Is a Lonely Hunter, 1940.
Reflections in a Golden Eye, 1941 (*f.* 1967).
The Member of the Wedding, 1946 (*f.* 1952).
The Ballad of the Sad Café, 1951.
The Square Root of Wonderful, 1958 (play).
Clock without Hands, 1961.
Sweet As a Pickle and Clean As a Pig, 1964 (poems).   M.G.

"**MacDIARMID, Hugh**" is the pseudonym of Christopher Murray Grieve (1892–   ), who was born at Langholm (Dumfriesshire), the son of a postman, and educated there and at Edinburgh University. He served in the First World War, and in the early 1920s associated himself with, and inspired, the Scottish Renaissance movement. His three anthologies, *Northern Numbers*, were intended to achieve for Scottish verse what Edward Marsh's anthologies had achieved for English (see **Georgians, The**). An increasing national awareness characterized the successive volumes, and MacDiarmid's first collection of poems, *Sangschaw* (1925), revealed a genuine lyric impulse and the attempt to reform Scottish poetry by the fashioning of a new poetic diction. In 1926 he published *A Drunk Man Looks at the Thistle*, which is considered by a majority of critics to be his finest sustained achievement. In the late 1920s he left Scotland, lived in London and Liverpool, then, after experiencing the depths of poverty, returned to Scotland and took up residence for nine years on the Shetland island of Whalsay. In 1933 he stated: "I turn from the poetry of beauty to the poetry of wisdom," and the period of his residence on Whalsay marks a profound change in his development—through and beyond Scottish nationalism to a global internationalism, through and beyond a synthetic Scots language to awareness of an emergent world consciousness and of the need to find a language to express this new phenomenon.

MacDiarmid's extensive reading continued during these years and evidence of its scope, if not always of its intellectual depth, is found in his autobiography, *Lucky Poet* (1943). During the Second World War he was conscripted and given industrial work. In 1955 appeared *In Memoriam James Joyce*, a poem expressing the world-vision which had been forming for the previous twenty years. Although the poem is not successful as a whole, it contains magnificent passages of visionary fervor and lyric power. He became a member of the Communist party in 1956, seeing in the national Communist movements an evolutionary force towards human brotherhood and world unification. His *Collected Poems*, published on American initiative, appeared in 1962. Although offering a comprehensive survey of his work, this is not a complete edition.

MacDiarmid is a rare combination—lyric poet, visionary idealist, a severe, sometimes petty, critic and pamphleteer, nationalist and internationalist. His lyric utterances with their delicate perceptiveness and humane comic spirit are unique; his struggle to forge not only a new tradition out of Celtic and non-English elements, but also a new language to express Scottish and world consciousness has been the effort of a major poet and visionary thinker. His later internationalist and linguistic ideas, propounded in the diffuse and clumsy autobiography and clarified in parts of *In Memoriam James Joyce*, are sometimes profound, sometimes absurd, but invariably stimulating.

Lucky Poet, 1943.
A Lap of Honour, 1967.
A Clyack-Sheaf, 1969.

Collected Poems, 1920–61, Edinburgh: Oliver & Boyd; New York: Macmillan Co., 1962; revised, New York, 1967.
Selected Essays, ed. D. Glen, London: Cape, 1969.   C.P.

MACDONALD, George (1824–1905) was educated at King's College, Aberdeen. He was intended for the Congregational ministry, but spent most of his life as a writer and lecturer. His early poem *Within and Without* (1855) was admired by Tennyson, but MacDonald soon turned to fiction, in which most of his work was written. The only other poem of note is his *Diary of an Old Soul* (1880), a religious piece. His writings are reflective and philosophical, and even at times mystical, as in *David Elginbrod* (1863). He also wrote for children, but his abiding fame will rest on his novels of Scottish life such as *Alec Forbes* (1865), *Robert Falconer* (1868), *Malcolm* (1875), *St. George and St. Michael* (1876), *The Marquis of Lossie* (1877) and *Paul Faber, Surgeon* (1879).

Poetical Works, 2 vols., London: Chatto & Windus, 1893.
George MacDonald: An Anthology, ed. C. S. Lewis, London: Bles, 1946; New York: Macmillan Co., 1947.   A.P.

McKAY, Claude (1890–1948), was born in a village in Jamaica. Educated locally, he went to America in 1912 and established himself as a poet and editor in Harlem. His most important book, *Harlem Shadows* (1922), is a collection of sonnets and lyrics pervaded by anger, frustration and lament. His novel *Home to Harlem* (1928) celebrates the exotic qualities in Harlem life, and it became a best seller. His later fiction, *Banjo* (1929), *Singertown* (1932) and *Banana Bottom* (1933), is both sentimental and sensational. He also wrote an autobiography, *A Long Way from Home* (1937), and an impressionistic study, *Harlem: Negro Metropolis* (1940). His volume of *Selected Poems* was published in 1953. (See also **Caribbean Literature**.)   I.W.

MACKENZIE, (Sir) Compton (1883–1972), son of the actor Edward Compton, began his literary career by writing poetry and for the theater, but later published novels, of which he was to write over twenty-five. A professional craftsman and writer of talent, he combined picturequeness, humor and psychological insight in his best work. This is particularly true of *Sinister Street* (1913), an early semiautobiographical novel which is a vivid account of Oxford life. He later preferred to write on more popular themes in a semicomic manner, not always with great success. His autobiography, *My Life and Times*, appeared in ten octaves (1963–71).   O.K.

MACKENZIE, Henry (1745–1831) was born in Edinburgh, educated at its university and became prominent in its public life. He edited and frequently contributed to two periodicals, *The Mirror* (1779–80) and *The Lounger* (1785–87), and though he practiced law, also found time to write three novels and four plays. *The Man of Feeling* (1771) is an extreme example of the novel of sentiment. His last novel, *Julia de Roubigné* (1777), displays an interesting mingling of the cults of sensibility and of the noble savage.   J.C.

MACKENZIE, Kenneth. See **Australian Literature.**

MacLEISH, Archibald (1892–), the Illinois-born poet, lived in Europe between 1923 and 1928. His early work reflects postwar disillusionment and shows the influence of Pound and Eliot. The poems which followed are marked by a greater geographical and cultural awareness. *Conquistador* (1932; Pulitzer Prize) uses powerful imagery to describe Cortes's conquest of Mexico, and *Frescoes for Mr Rockefeller's City* (1933) is devoted to the American peoples. His radio verse plays, like *The Fall of the City* (1937), dealt with social issues. He was awarded a Pulitzer Prize in 1952 for his *Collected Poems 1917–52* and also for *J.B.* (1958), a "successful" treatment of the Job story, preaching acquiescence and religious faith.   R.W.

MacLENNAN, Hugh. See **Canadian Literature.**

MacNEICE, Louis (1907–63), son of the bishop of Down, Connor and Dromore, was born in Belfast. From Marlborough he went to Oxford where he read classics. During the 1930s he lectured at Birmingham University and at Bedford College, London. Although always the least politically committed of its contributors, his name was linked with the New Verse Group, and he did visit Spain in 1936. Later that year he went with Auden to Iceland and together they produced *Letters from Iceland* (1937). From 1941 to 1949 he was a BBC scriptwriter and producer, and throughout his life he wrote regularly and most effectively for radio.

MacNeice's poetry varies from the casual and sometimes playfully trite to a classical tautness; the more carefully controlled style is present chiefly in his later work, but he never became overserious about his art. Such an attitude is inherent in his celebration of the sensual richness of commonplace experience through a vivid and witty use of language. A steadfast rejection of orthodoxies and abstractions of all kinds is consistent both with his political liberalism and with his poet's vision of the para-doxical plurality and uniqueness of all experience.

Poems, 1935.
Modern Poetry, 1938.
The Earth Compels, 1938.
Autumn Journal, 1939.
The Dark Tower, and Other Radio Scripts, 1947.
Holes in the Sky, 1948.
Autumn Sequel, 1954.
Visitations, 1957.
The Burning Perch, 1963.
The Strings Are False, ed. E. R. Dodds, 1965 (unfinished autobiography).

Collected Poems, ed. E. R. Dodds, London: Faber & Faber, 1966: New York: Oxford Univ. Press, 1967.   A.Y.

MACPHERSON, James (1736–96), son of a poor farmer of Inver-ness, was intended for the Church, but became a schoolmaster when he left King's College, Aberdeen at the age of twenty. In 1758, almost unnoticed, his poem *The Highlander* was published. Two years later, under the influence of John Home, the playwright, he published some pieces he had translated as *Fragments of Ancient Poetry Collected in the Highlands of Scotland, and Translated from the Gaelic or Erse Language*. Gray and the antiquarian Blair were impressed, and the latter helped to finance Mac-pherson for an expedition to the Highlands to find more poetry. The result was *Fingal*, claimed as a complete epic poem. In London the genuineness of the poem was immediately challenged, but many men of taste and intelligence were enthusiastic, among them Horace Walpole. A second epic, *Temora*, attributed by Macpherson to the poet Ossian, was more coolly received. In 1780 he became member of Parliament for Camelford and ended his days comfortably on his estate in Invernessshire.

Although an undistinguished Gaelic scholar, Macpherson had literary ability, and the "epics"—prose paraphrases of genuine poetic fragments joined together by material of his own composition—have at their best an imposing sonority of style, a romantically mysterious setting and overtones of elegiac nostalgia for past glories. Scottish national pride and a new enthusiasm for ancient literature also contributed to an immense popularity in Britain and abroad, which lasted, despite Dr. Johnson's unyielding contempt for the poems and their "editor," until the advent of Scott's historical novels.

Fragments of Ancient Poetry Collected in the Highlands of Scotland, 1760.
Fingal, with Other Poems, 1762.
Temora, with Other Poems, 1763.

Works of Ossian, ed. O. L. Jiriczek, 3 vols., Heidelberg, 1940.   T.W.

MAGEE, William Connor. See **Sermons.**

MAILER, Norman (1923–) was born in New Jersey, grew up in Manhattan, received his education at Harvard and served in the 112th Cavalry in the Pacific during the Second World War as a rifleman. His earliest writings, while still at college, concern his lifelong obsession with the individual man surviving within the confines of a predatory sphere of action—Pacific jungle, the battlefield, the city jungle, the warfare of ideology, and the civil war of America in the 1960s. His career has become characteristic of the writer's function in later twentieth-century culture: he must embody in his actions, as a citizen and as an artist, the necessary and continuous war against the erosion of life-fulfillments by the Establishment or the military-industrial-media complex. His career extends from the Second World War through the Korean War into the Vietnamese War and reflects America's involvement in global catastrophe. His typical hero is therefore the wary man who tries to live out his life while answering the intrusions of society and at the same time creating his experience.

Mailer's Pacific experience enabled him to write *The Naked and the Dead* (1948); his first novel, but there are stories before this in which his main themes appear, for instance, "A Calculus at Heaven." *The Naked and the Dead* cuts typical scenes from American life into the lives of soldiers engaged in battle against the Japanese, in order to show the essential continuity of the class structure and the army which exacts sacrifice from men under self-assumed leadership. General Cummings is the archetype of the American leader who believes in a global destiny for his country and for men of authoritarian power universally. *Barbary Shore* (1951) employs a less naturalistic, more allegorically fantastic style to project the conflict between Left and Right in America and the possibilities of change away from capitalism. Again, the center is the nature of the leader and his responsibilities. *The Deer Park* (1955) sets up a structure of conflict between three men of ambition, operating in Hollywood—an air force veteran's attempt to find meaningful work in postwar America, a politically committed film director trying to work within a film industry pressurized from the anti-Communist anti-intellectualist Right, and a Faustian pimp with existential yearnings who exemplifies Mailer's criticism of egotistic and erotic power in any age. The diseased society again features prominently in *An American Dream* (1965), but here the hero is driven to flight from America as its dream of corrupt affluence takes on cosmic dimensions of evil, an almost "gothic" intensity of glittering surfaces and relationships of power. *Why Are We in Vietnam?* (1967) is the outpouring of a hallucinatory disc-jockey telling, in high camp style, of the masculinity trials between himself and his father on a bear hunt in Alaska, itself the parody of all organized killing expeditions, including the Asian war. Mailer has backed these major novels with nonfiction works of equal exploratory significance, providing a unique panoramic perspective on American life over a crucial decade in its history. Mailer's stories are collected in *The Short Fiction* (1969); *Deaths for the Ladies and Other Disasters* (1962) is a volume of poems; *The Deer Park* was made into a successful play in 1967. The best introduction to Mailer's whole career is *Advertisements for Myself* (1959), a brilliant running self-commentary.

The Naked and the Dead, 1948 (*f.* 1958).
Barbary Shore, 1951.
The Deer Park, 1955.
Advertisements for Myself, 1959.
Deaths for the Ladies and Other Disasters, 1962.
The Presidential Papers, 1963.
An American Dream, 1965 (*f.* as *See You in Hell, Darling*, 1966).
Cannibals and Christians, 1966.
Why Are We in Vietnam?, 1967.
The Idol and the Octopus, 1968.
The Armies of the Night, 1968.
Miami and the Siege of Chicago, 1968.
A Fire on the Moon, 1970.
The Prisoner of Sex, 1971.

Short Fiction, New York: Dell, 1967.   E.M.

MAIS, Roger. See **Caribbean Literature.**

MALAMUD, Bernard (1914–) was born in Brooklyn, graduated from Columbia and did clerical work and teaching before writing his first full-length novel, *The Natural* (1952). This, the least representative of

Malamud's novels, is an uneasy yoking of a baseball story with the Grail quest. In subject matter it gives an indication of Malamud's later work only in the theme of redemption through suffering, but the realistic and symbolic levels fail to coalesce.

His second novel, *The Assistant* (1957), generally considered his most successful, achieves that success by showing the redemption of its principal character, Frankie Alpine, in a book of suffocatingly intense realism. Alpine, an Italian, learns the nature of misery in the overwhelming poverty of the New York Jewish grocer's store that he has previously robbed. The symbolic potency of Frankie's agony is not reduced because of the inescapable power of the naturalistic setting.

In *A New Life* (1961) Malamud attempts to invest the journey west of a former drunkard academic, S. Levin, to a North Western university with symbolic significance. The novel rests uneasily between antiacademic satire and an oversignificant love story. More successful is the epic *The Fixer* (1966), where Malamud can unite the disparate aspects of his writing in the distant world of Russian nineteenth-century anti-Semitism. The book's hero, Yakov Bok, is the nearest that Malamud has got so far to an acceptable portrait of the Jew as victim. The story has grandeur and nobility. *The Tenants* (1971) traces the destructive relationship of two writers, one black, the other white.

Malamud has published a wide variety of short stories ranging from the directness and compassion of *The Magic Barrel* (1958) to the rather flat comedy of *Pictures of Fidelman* (1969).

The Natural, 1952.
The Assistant, 1957.
The Magic Barrel, 1958.
A New Life, 1961.
Idiot's First, 1963.
The Fixer, 1966 (*f.* 1968).
Pictures of Fidelman, 1969.
The Tenants, 1971.   D.V.W.

MALORY, Sir Thomas (?1410–71), a landowner of Newbold Revell (Warwickshire), owed allegiance to the earls of Warwick under whom he fought at Calais in 1436, in Northumberland in 1462 and at the siege of Alnwick in 1463. In 1456 he represented Warwickshire in Parliament. From 1450 he is cited in lawsuits, charged with rape, robbery, cattle-stealing and twice breaking into the Abbey of Blessed Mary of Coombe. Malory served at least four prison sentences (from 1460 to 1462 in Newgate) and it seems to have been in prison that his only known book, *Morte d'Arthur* (*f.* as *The Knights of the Round Table*, 1954), was written. In 1466

Malory was excluded from two general pardons and was probably not finally released until the year before his death. He was buried near Newgate at Grey Friars.

Malory's *Morte d'Arthur*, a compilation of Arthurian material from many sources telling the story of this legendary king of Britain and his company of knights, was printed by Caxton (1485) from a manuscript in his possession. This printed version of *Morte d'Arthur* was for the following 450 years the only version known, and its remarkable popularity is attested by its being frequently reprinted and by the strong influence it exerted over many writers, Tennyson, Charles Williams and T. H. White among them. In 1934 it was found that a fourteenth-century manuscript at Winchester College was a much fuller version than Caxton's, and contained in its unique explicits, which followed the separate sections of the work, sufficient biographical information to establish the author's identity. Although this manuscript is probably two stages removed from Malory's original, it is closer to what Malory wrote than is Caxton's edited version, and with the publication of Professor Vinaver's edition of *The Works of Sir Thomas Malory* (1947) a reappraisal of *Morte d'Arthur* was necessary and possible.

The title chosen by Vinaver reflects his view that what had been thought of as a single work, *Morte d'Arthur*, was eight quite separate tales. His case rests on the difficulty of compiling a satisfactory time-scheme for the work as a whole, on inconsistencies such as the reappearance in later tales of knights killed in earlier ones, and Malory's advice in the explicit to the first tale that readers wishing to know more about Arthur and his knights should read about them elsewhere. This thesis has been strongly contested by many scholars who have shown that Malory had a synoptic knowledge of Arthurian legend and romance before writing the first tale, and, more significantly, that he adapted his varied sources with marked consistency to conform to an original concept of the Arthurian legend. Allowing for the difficulties under which Malory must have written most of his book, the probability that he had no opportunity to revise it and that its unity is of a sort characteristic of medieval literature, *Morte d'Arthur* is a sophisticated and coherent whole, telling the tragedy of Arthur's court, of a society noble in conception and ideals but containing within itself from the outset the causes of its downfall. Malory's greatness lies not only in his local narrative skill, but also in his ability to organize a large and varied body of legends into a coherent whole.

Works, ed. E. Vinaver, 3 vols., Oxford: Clarendon Press, 1947.   H.N.D.

MALTHUS, T. R. (Thomas Robert) (1766–1834) was educated at Jesus College, Cambridge, elected to a fellowship and ordained to a curacy in Surrey. In 1804 he was appointed professor of modern history and political economy at the East India College, Haileybury, and so became the first incumbent of a chair in political economy in England. He was elected a fellow of the Royal Society in 1819.

He is best known for his work concerning population and the standard of living, which, together with his discussion of rent, forms part of the body of classical political economy. His most important contribution to economic thought, however, is critical of the classical system. Malthus differed from the classical school in denying the self-regulating character of the economic system taken as a whole and hence in being concerned to find policies for ensuring adequate effective demand. His first *Essay on the Principle of Population As It Affects the Future Improvement of Society* (1798) argued against the theory of the perfectibility of man and the human condition put forward by Condorcet in France and, following him, Godwin in England. The essay asserted "that the power of population [to increase] is indefinitely greater than the power in the earth to produce subsistence for man." The checks on the tendency for population to outstrip subsistence were vice and misery, which included war, famine and disease.

After the publication of his first *Essay* Malthus traveled to Scandinavia, Russia, France and Switzerland, collecting factual material about population which he used in a second edition (1803) to give a more empirical and inductive character to his work compared with the generally a priori approach of the earlier version. The second *Essay* introduced "moral restraint" as a third check on population, and it is possible to view this as a concession to the perfectibility thesis of Godwin, though Malthus himself did not do so. Darwin found in Malthus's *Essay* the inspiration for his theory of natural selection, and Herbert Spencer applied the evolutionary implications of Malthus's principle to human society. From the struggle for survival and the elimination of the less fit he derived a theory of human progress—not without an element of paradox in view of Malthus's position in relation to Godwin.

Principles of Political Economy, 1820.

Travel Diaries, ed. P. James, Cambridge: Cambridge Univ. Press, 1966.
R.H.B.

MANDER, Jane. See **New Zealand Literature.**

MANDEVILLE, Bernard de (1670–1733), a Dutch immigrant who came to London as a physician, quickly found his way into literary circles and began to publish satirical books and pamphlets, including the notorious *The Fable of the Bees*, in which he demolishes the supposed moral basis of society by a Hobbesian demonstration that civilization depends on vice. This provoked an outcry, but Dr. Johnson, without accepting its conclusions, said it "opened my views into real life very much." Mandeville's other works, all written in vigorous, coarse, fluent style, include fables in burlesque imitation of La Fontaine and lively examinations of capital punishment and prostitution.

The Fable of the Bees: or, Private Vices, Public Benefits, 1714 (first published as *The Grumbling Hive: or, Knaves Turn'd Honest*, 1705); ed. F. B. Kaye, 2 vols., Oxford: Clarendon Press, 1924.
A Modest Defence of Public Stews, 1724.
An Enquiry into the Causes of the Frequent Executions at Tyburn, 1725.

R.E.

MANGAN, J. C. (James Clarence) (1803–49), born in Dublin, the son of a grocer, was brought up to speak English. He later acquired a knowledge of Latin, French, Spanish and Italian, but never learnt Irish. His life as clerk-copyist in various Dublin offices offered little escape from tedium except in alcoholism and, later, drugs. He was a prolific journalist but is best known for a few poems, some of which purport to be translations from the Irish. The most famous of these, "Dark Rosaleen," is rich in harmonious sounds and lyrical rhythms, but far from capturing the vigor of the original Irish "Roisin Dubh." It can be seen today as an example of the lyrical sentimentality characterizing most Anglo-Irish verse of the nineteenth century.

Poems, 1859.

Irish Poets of the Nineteenth Century, ed. G. Taylor, London: Routledge; Cambridge, Mass.: Harvard Univ. Press, 1951.   C.P.

MANING, F. E. See **New Zealand Literature.**

MANN, Leonard. See **Australian Literature.**

MANNYNG, Robert. See **Middle English Literature.**

"MANSFIELD, Katherine" was the pseudonym of Katherine Beauchamp (1888–1923). She spent her childhood in the comfortable but disciplined atmosphere of a New Zealand ruling-class family at the turn of the century. She came to Queen's College, London in 1903. After several years of study she returned to New Zealand, lived there for eighteen months, and then begged her father to let her return to London, confident she could succeed in the literary world. In 1908 she arrived in England for the second time.

She published in 1911 a collection of her early stories, *In a German Pension*. In 1912 she met John Middleton Murry, who became a lodger at her flat and, six years later, her second husband. An emotional insecurity, resulting partly from rebellion against authoritarian parents, characterized many of her relationships. From this uncertainty there arose a tendency to idealize love which, consequently, could never be grasped in any entirety. A dichotomy between this idealism and the bitterness of realizing the cruelty of life is, suggests Murry, an underlying tension in her work.

A second collection of stories, *Bliss*, appeared in 1920. This contained "Prelude," one of her finest achievements and a remarkable evocation of childhood attitudes and preoccupations. *The Garden Party* (1922) is her most sustained single achievement. Her health steadily deteriorated, although she impelled herself to further writing. She finally sought release from what she regarded as her spiritual and physical imperfections at at Gurdjieff's Institute for the Harmonious Development of Man at Fontainebleau, where she died of pulmonary tuberculosis in January 1923.

In her weaker work close observation of individuals and relationships is tinged with an acerbity that is frequently unconvincing. Her essential theme is isolation and loneliness and in her later stories it is conveyed in a complex attitude of pathos, humor and affection. Although her achievement is limited, her control of form and subtlety of mind promised a greatness which was never fully realized.

In a German Pension, 1911.
Bliss and Other Stories, 1920.
The Garden Party and Other Stories, 1922.

Collected Stories, London: Constable, 1945.
Journal, ed. J. M. Murry, 1927; enlarged, London: Constable, 1954.
Letters, ed. J. M. Murry, 2 vols., London: Constable, 1928.   C.P.

MARKANDAYA, Kamala. See **Indian Literature.**

MARLOWE, Christopher (1564–93), son of a fairly prosperous shoemaker, was educated at the King's School, Canterbury and at Corpus Christi College, Cambridge. While still a student, he engaged in confidential work for the government. For a time he probably meant to enter holy orders, but he must have given up this intention by 1587, when he left Cambridge for London. Before the end of the year *Tamburlaine* brought him great success as a playwright, and he exploited this success by at once adding a second part. A year or two later, in 1589 or

1590, he wrote *The Jew of Malta*, and in 1592 *Edward II*. His other major play, *Doctor Faustus*, is of uncertain date, though recent investigators incline to think of it as following *Edward II*. His principal nondramatic work, also of uncertain date, is the long, unfinished erotic poem, *Hero and Leander* (completed by George Chapman).

Marlowe appears to have been of a turbulent disposition. In 1589 he was involved in a sword fight in which a man was killed; within three years a constable and underconstable were seeking the protection of the law against him; and in May 1593 he became implicated in a brawl about the payment of a tavern bill and was stabbed to death.

Contemporaries sometimes spoke of Marlowe as an atheist, but, even if he uttered the statements they ascribed to him, he may well have done so merely to shock them. Moreover, the term "atheist" was often used loosely in the sixteenth century. If we understand it in a strict sense, we shall be puzzled by the fact that Marlowe wrote, in *Doctor Faustus*, the most obviously Christian document in all Elizabethan drama.

The two parts of *Tamburlaine* stage the career, partly historical and partly imaginary, of a man who sets out to conquer the world. Marlowe defies conventional susceptibilities by taking this conqueror's side. In his hands Tamburlaine becomes an attractive, eloquent and intrepid leader of men; his atrocities become demonstrations of his firmness of mind in discharging the responsibilities of power; and of his victims only Bajazeth and Zabina are allowed to claim much of our pity. Marlowe's powerful and melodious blank verse—his "mighty line," as Ben Jonson called it—compels us to admire the conqueror's manly prowess and ruthless ambition. Humane feelings are ridiculed by association with the contemptible weaklings Mycetes and Calyphas. In part 2, admittedly, certain incidents serve to define the limits of Tamburlaine's power. He cannot instill courage into a cowardly son or prolong Zenocrate's life or prevent his own death. But within these natural limits he continues to carry everything before him and is at his most victorious immediately before he dies. While there have been some attempts to describe the two-part play as a tragedy in which Tamburlaine's pride leads to his fall, these have not won general assent.

Like *Tamburlaine*, *The Jew of Malta* has a protagonist who embodies an insatiable craving for power. Barabas is a disciple of Machiavelli, whom many Elizabethans thought a mere cynical advocate of ingenious and ruthless self-seeking. But the men whom Barabas robs and destroys are just as self-seeking as he is. Morally, there is nothing to choose between him and them. Aesthetically, however, Barabas's subtlety, resourcefulness and energy gain him an admiration withheld from his opponents. In addition, Barabas is highly entertaining, both in his infectious enjoyment of his own villainy and in his lively mockery of his enemies. His death, taking almost the form of a public execution, excites sharply conflicting feelings. *The Jew of Malta* comes closer to black comedy than to orthodox tragedy.

Edward II, too, is set in a world in which men have little or no awareness of any higher purpose than that of looking after their own interests, getting their own way and gratifying their own desires. Edward knows what he wants—to be left to enjoy his passionate friendship with his favorite—but has not the strength to secure it. Weak and petulant, he is opposed by his insubordinate and ruthless barons. As they conquer and destroy him, he grows increasingly pathetic. *Edward II* differs from its predecessors in that Marlowe has tried to dramatize a sustained struggle between two fairly evenly balanced parties; it differs from Shakespeare's history plays in that the struggle is almost entirely personal and nonpolitical.

The hero of *Doctor Faustus* is one more seeker after power. The world in which he lives, however, is not one in which the highest purpose known to man is that of getting his own way. Naturally, the creator of Tamburlaine and Barabas felt a profound sympathy with one who sought by magic to make himself a "demigod." But, while writing *Doctor Faustus*, he recognized that a man who presumptuously attempted to raise himself above humanity would infallibly isolate himself both from God and from his fellow men and so consign himself to the hell so powerfully evoked early in the play by Mephistophilis. The eventual abduction of Faustus to the fiery hell of tradition symbolizes the completion of this process of willful self-commitment to damnation.

Two speeches near the end of the drama exemplify the range of Marlowe's verse at this stage. The rhapsody to Helen of Troy, Faustus's last assured speech in his aspiring vein, is in a lyrical and rhetorical style reminiscent of *Tamburlaine*; whilst the final soliloquy, giving flexible, unpredictable and disconcerting expression to Faustus's despair, shows Marlowe's verse at its most dramatically expressive.

(See also **Elizabethan Miscellanies.**)

Tamburlaine the Great, 2 parts, 1590 (part 1, *p.* ?1587; part 2, *p.* ?1588).
Edward the Second, 1594 (*p.* ?1592).
Dido, Queen of Carthage (with Thomas Nashe), 1594.
Hero and Leander (completed by George Chapman), 1598.
Doctor Faustus, 1604; 1616 (*p.* ?1589; *f.* 1966).
The Jew of Malta, 1633 (*p.* ?1589).

Works and Life, ed. R. H. Case and others, 6 vols., London: Methuen; New York: Dial Press, 1930–33.   J.D.J.

"MARPRELATE, Martin" is the pseudonym of the author of seven pamphlets published in 1588 and 1589 on behalf of the Puritans against the Anglican episcopacy. The authorship has never been established, although the names of some men connected with Martin are known. The immediate impulse to the Marprelate pamphlets was Whitgift's 1586 Star Chamber decree, extending his control over printing in an attempt to curb increasing Puritan pamphleteering. This decree sharpened Puritan animosity towards the bishops, and the publication of these seven pamphlets, printed in five different places under conditions of extreme secrecy and difficulty, seems to have been the result. Other pamphlets, of varying closeness to the Marprelate Tracts proper, were published in this Anglican-Calvinist dispute, but by 1593 several of the men connected with Martin had been arrested and one, John Penry, hanged. From the controversy came more stringent press restrictions and censorship of sermons.

The Marprelate tracts have status as literature because of their boisterous satire: a spontaneous and natural feeling for invective, a force and liveliness of mind make them still accessible to us. The lampoon method of these tracts is found in other works on both sides of the controversy, but Martin's prose has a vitality and a feeling for popular speech which is his own, particularly when taken with his liking for pun and local allusion.

The Marprelate Tracts, ed. W. Pierce, London: Clarke, 1911.   G.P.

MARQUAND, John P. (Phillips) (1893–1960), born in Wilmington (Delaware), grew up in Massachusetts and graduated from Harvard. He started writing on *The Boston Transcript* in 1915, but his journalistic career was interrupted by service in Europe with the Field Artillery. On his return he began again on *The New York Tribune*, moving into advertising a little later. Marquand began to have some success as a writer of fiction with adventure stories, which became popular in *The Saturday Evening Post*, and he turned professional. His first books were romances like *The Black Cargo* (1925), and he also wrote a number of successful tales involving a Japanese detective, Mr. Moto, which exploited the current taste for offbeat sleuths, such as the inscrutable Charlie Chan. In 1937, however, with his novel *The Late George Apley* (Pulitzer Prize) he took over the fictional territory which he made his own, the life of upper-class New York and New England business and professional men, as well as establishing his place as a satirist and ironist. Marquand's subjects are Boston Brahmins like Apley, New England "clans" as in *Wickford Point*, and businessmen like *H. M. Pulham, Esq.*, which made his best book. His novels are comedies of manners with a Jane Austen-like use of the tension between the inner life of will and personal inclination and a powerful social code. In *So Little Time* a play doctor regrets his stultifying, uncreative job, and in *B. F.'s Daughter* a tycoon's daughter struggles to subdue her husband's doomed individuality. Marquand's main characters are often stranded in middle age. The satire is a gentle but ineffective gesture against a resigned and ingrained determinism. Marquand's later writing career was a repetitious, if skillful, quartering of his chosen tract of life.

The Unspeakable Gentleman, 1922.
Warning Hill, 1930.
Ming Yellow, 1935.
No Hero, 1935.
Thank You Mr. Moto, 1936 (*f.* 1937).
Think Fast, Mr. Moto, 1937.
Mr. Moto Is So Sorry, 1937.
The Late George Apley, 1937 (dramatized with George S. Kaufman; *p.* 1944; *f.* 1947).
Wickford Point, 1939.
H. M. Pulham, Esq., 1941 (*f.* 1941).
So Little Time, 1943.
B. F.'s Daughter, 1946 (*f.* 1949).
Melville Goodwin, U.S.A., 1951 (*f.* as *Their Secret Affair*, 1956).
Sincerely Willis Wayde, 1955.
Stopover: Toyko, 1957 (*f.* 1957).
Life at Happy Knoll, 1957.
Women and Thomas Harrow, 1958.

Thirty Years, Boston: Little, Brown, 1954 (collected stories and essays).

A.M.R.

MARRYAT, Frederick (1792–1848) was born in London and served in the navy, rising to the rank of captain before retiring in 1830. He used his naval experiences in many of the novels which have placed him so high among tellers of sea stories. These include *Peter Simple, Jacob Faithful* (both 1834) and *Mr. Midshipman Easy* (1836). Though his work is ill-constructed, it gives the sense of being true to life, possesses clarity, vitality and a certain broad humor, and celebrates the masculine virtues of loyalty, courage, patriotism and the like. He also wrote for children— *Masterman Ready* (1841), *The Settlers in Canada* (1844) and *The Children of the New Forest* (1847). A.P.

MARSTON, John (1576–1634), son of a Shropshire lawyer and his Italian wife, was at Brasenose College, Oxford (1591–94) before entering the Middle Temple (1594–1606). His first poetic works, *The Metamorphosis of Pygmalion's Image, and Certain Satires*, the former in the Ovidian erotic vein, and another collection of satires, entitled *The Scourge of Villainy and Certain Satires*, made their controversial appearance in 1598. His earliest dramatic writings, *Histrio-mastix*, *Jack Drum's Entertainment* and *What You Will*, containing satiric tilts at certain fellow writers including Ben Jonson, initiated the notorious War of the Theatres. Jonson rejoined in *Cynthia's Revels* and *The Poetaster* with satiric portraits of Dekker, Marston's ally, and of Marston himself. *Antonio and Mellida*, a heroic love comedy in an Italian court setting, and its sequel, *Antonio's Revenge*, a bloody melodrama, reveal a youthful Marston eagerly exploiting the successful theatrical formulae of his predecessors. Working within a similar revenge framework, Marston indulged his penchant for satiric observation in *The Malcontent* to provide his most assured achievement. The disguised Duke Altofront, who is at once the prime mover of the action and the play's main source of satiric commentary, became the prototype for a number of later Jacobean heroes. *Eastward Ho!*, a city comedy, brought trouble to Marston and his collaborators, Chapman and Jonson. All three were imprisoned for having insulted King James. His next venture, *The Dutch Courtesan*, which traces the sapping of an overscrupulous morality under pressure of a lustful passion, is chiefly celebrated for its powerful portrait of Franceschina, the courtesan, and for its lively underplot. *Parasitaster; or, the Fawn* employs the disguised duke device again, but within a love-centered intrigue plot. His final works, *Sophonisba* and *The Insatiate Countess*, are less distinguished efforts in a tragic vein. He was ordained priest in 1609 and secured a living at Christchurch (Hampshire) in 1616. He married Mary Wilkes, a chaplain's daughter, in 1619. He resigned his living in 1631 and died in 1634.

Marston is a powerfully individual personality with a violent exuberance of style which is his particular trademark. His strength lies clearly in the energetic satirical bias of his writing, especially where he is surveying the manners and morals of a decadent society such as is found in *The Malcontent*. He is the first English dramatist to exploit an Italian setting as an appropriate milieu for scenes of treachery, vice and carnage, and he reveals in his Italian plays some definite interest in the machinery of political power. On the other hand, he has genuine comic gifts which are seen at their best in the boisterous Cockledemoy episodes of *The Dutch Courtesan*. Though negligible in their intellectual content, his plays are full of interesting experiments and reveal a definite theatrical instinct which assured his success with his first audiences but led him on occasion to the sacrifice of artistic integrity for the sake of immediate theatrical effect. Such is the case in the notorious final scene of *Antonio's Revenge*.

The Metamorphosis of Pygmalion's Image, and Certain Satires, 1598.
The Scourge of Villainy, and Certain Satires, 1598.
Antonio and Mellida, 1602 (p. 1599).
Antonio's Revenge, 1602.

The Malcontent, 1604.
The Dutch Courtesan, 1605 (*p.* ?1603).
Eastward Ho! (with George Chapman and Ben Jonson), 1605.
Parasitaster; or, The Fawn, 1606 (*p.* ?1605).
The Wonder of Women; or, Sophonisba, 1606.
What You Will, 1607 (*p.* 1601).
The Insatiate Countess, 1613.

Plays, ed. H. H. Wood, 3 vols., Edinburgh: Oliver & Boyd, 1934–39.
Poems, ed. A. Davenport, Liverpool: Liverpool Univ. Press, 1961.

L.E.P.

MARSTON, John Westland. See **Spasmodics, The.**

MARTIN, Gregory. See **Bible, The.**

MARTINEAU, Harriet (1802–76), born in Norwich (Norfolk), the daughter of a cloth manufacturer, became, despite her notorious ill health, a popular and influential spokeswoman for Victorian radicalism. Primarily a journalist, her prolific output covers many of the social and economic issues of the day. Apart from journalism, she wrote numerous books on public affairs and economics, didactic novels like *Deerbrook* (1839) and *Forest and Game-Law Tales* (1845), children's tracts, works on history like *British Rule in India* (1857), and travel like her *Guide to Windermere* (1854). The best of them are her two controversial books on America—*Society in America* (1837) and *Retrospect of Western Travel* (1838). Her *Autobiography* (1877), published posthumously, contains valuable insights into Victorian life.

I.W.

MARVELL, Andrew (1621–78), son of a clergyman at Hull (Yorkshire), was at Cambridge from 1633 to 1641 and, while there, had a brief Catholic period. From 1642 to 1646 he traveled abroad and in 1651–52 he was tutor to Lord Fairfax's daughter at Nun Appleton House in Yorkshire. He seems at first to have had Royalist sympathies (in 1649 he published a complimentary poem to Lovelace's "Lucasta"), but by 1650, the probable date of "An Horatian Ode," he had apparently become a moderate supporter of the Parliament. In 1653 he became tutor to William Dutton, a ward of Cromwell's, and from 1657 to 1659 was Milton's assistant in the Latin secretaryship. In 1659 he was elected member of Parliament for Hull; and, elected again in the Convention of 1660 which invited Charles II to return, he used his influence at this time to protect Milton from reprisals. Reelected in 1661, he continued as member for Hull until his death. In 1662 he visited Holland and from 1663 to 1665 traveled in

Russia, Denmark and Sweden as secretary to the embassy of the earl of Carlisle. During the latter part of his life Marvell increasingly opposed the methods of Charles II and his ministers, writing verse satires and prose pamphlets in defense of toleration and against arbitrary government. As a pamphleteer he earned the later admiration of Swift.

The poetry for which Marvell is chiefly remembered was mostly written before the Restoration, much of it probably at Nun Appleton, but not published until after his death, in the 1681 *Miscellaneous Poems*. It gathers together many strands of seventeenth-century thought, feeling and style—the imaginative surprise of Donne and the civilized grace of Jonson, the gallantry of Carew and the grave delicacy of Herbert, Herrick's feeling for natural beauty and something of Milton's Puritan sobriety. His wit mingles levity and seriousness in an inseparable blend, and this makes possible surprising transitions, from light pastoral to religious allegory, as in "Clorinda and Damon," from the fanciful figure of garden flowers as soldiers on parade to serious reflections on the Civil War, as in "Upon Appleton House." At his most Metaphysical, in "The Definition of Love," he draws on geometry and astronomy as well as vividly presenting Fate driving its "iron wedges"; elsewhere he conducts an elaborately pseudological argument against the hesitations of his "coy mistress," which can suddenly evoke "Time's winged chariot" and the "deserts of vast eternity." It was largely Marvell's feeling for the countryside and natural beauty which brought him back to favor in the nineteenth century somewhat sooner than other Metaphysical poets; his poetry on themes of this kind has freshness and intimacy as well as sophistication. In such a poem as "The Garden," nature and artifice are no more felt as opposed or exclusive than are the sensuous enjoyment and intellectual contemplation which unite in the famous conceit of "a green thought in a green shade." Marvell's specifically religious poems have the Metaphysical quality of remaining in touch with many sides of life and experience; characteristically, his "Dialogue between the Resolved Soul and Created Pleasure" is conducted in a manner of urbane, epigrammatic wit. His classical qualities of precision, economy, restraint and a balanced sense of human limitations appear in "An Horatian Ode upon Cromwell's Return from Ireland," where he has almost the detachment of a European spectator, combining sympathy for Charles I, admiration for Cromwell as a national leader and a clear-sighted awareness that "the same arts that did gain/A power must it maintain." Politics and public affairs were ultimately to crowd poetry out of Marvell's life; and after the Restoration he used verse only in a rough doggerel form for political satire.

(See also **Metaphysical Poetry**.)

Miscellaneous Poems, 1681.

Poems and Letters, ed. H. M. Margoliouth, 2 vols., Oxford: Clarendon
Press, 1927.   R.G.C.

MASEFIELD, John (1878–1967) was born near Ledbury (Hereford-
shire). His love of the countryside, shown in *The Land Workers* and
Wonderings, is as important a part of his creative life as his love of the sea.
He served as deck hand in his adolescence, worked in the United States
and achieved notoriety in England with publication of *The Everlasting
Mercy* (1911). He became poet laureate in 1930.

His skill as a writer of narrative is best shown in the poem *Reynard the
Fox* (1919) and the novel *Dead Ned* (1938). Although an attempt at profundity is made in the *Sonnets and Poems* (1916), Masefield's work lacks
depth and frequently shows inadequate artistic control. A section of
autobiography is revealed in *So Long to Learn* (1952).
(See also **Georgians, The.**)

Collected Works, Wanderer edition, 10 vols., London: Heinemann,
1935–38.   C.P.

MASON, R. A. K. See **New Zealand Literature.**

MASON, William (1724–97) was born at Hull (Yorkshire) and educated
at St. John's College, Cambridge. There he formed a lifelong friendship
with the poet Gray, whose *Life and Letters* he published in 1774. He wrote
two tragedies, *Elfrida* (1752) and *Caractacus* (1759), together with four
bombastic *Odes* (1756), but his best works are the didactic poem *The
English Garden* (in 4 books, 1772–82) and his satirical "An Heroic Epistle to
Sir William Chambers" (1773, under the pseudonym of Malcolm
Macgregor). Mason always shows a perfect control of his medium, but this
is not often enough accompanied by any great liveliness. His satires,
however, do not suffer from this defect; they are neat, economical and
sharp in their effects.

The Works of the English Poets, ed. A. Chalmers, London: Johnson, 1810,
vol. 18.   A.P.

MASQUES were the late Elizabethan and early seventeenth-century
equivalents of modern theatrical extravaganzas—splendid combinations
of song, dance, poetry and sumptuous spectacle. Jonson's *Oberon*, for
instance, cost over £2,000 to stage in 1611. His *Love Freed from Ignorance
and Folly* (1611) cost the Exchequer less than half this sum; even so, the
great Inigo Jones was responsible for décor and production, Alfonso Ferra-
bosco and Robert Johnson provided the music, which was performed by

no less than sixty-six musicians on a variety of instruments, and other experts saw to the dances and taught choreography to Queen Anne and her ladies. Their pains were not wasted, since Jonson successfully developed this masque's dramatic elements and managed to preserve "the standards of decorum, hierarchical unity and moral truth which he held to be the governing principles of the masque as a literary form" (N. Sanders, in *A Book of Masques*).

One must also note more external features of the form, such as the group of amateur masquers, who appeared for their dances in the most striking ways that could be devised. The *Masque of Heroes* (1619) discovers them sitting in arches of clouds; the *Masque of Blackness* (1605) has them lifted forward in a concave shell upon an artificial sea, and so on. Scenic and mechanical inventiveness was highly prized. After their main dances the masquers would "take out" members of the audience for livelier "revels," a very distinctive and important feature of the form. In the light of Stuart developments one should also stress the prefacing of the main masque by an antimasque, disorder preceding order. In Jonson's *Masque of Queens* (1609), Mischief and eleven witches came from an ugly stage Hell with rats and vipers, uttering confused noises and (equally symbolic) "dancing back to back, hip to hip, their hands joined, and making their circles backward, to the left hand, with strange fantastic motions of their heads and bodies." This bizarrely fascinating spectacle was intended as a foil to the beauty of Queen Anne and her ladies, who suddenly appeared on a throne triumphal "circled with all all store of light." Eventually the antimasque became highly elaborated and the more popular part of the whole.

Historically considered, masque is a protean form, changing with time and place, though its finest English examples are notable for the powerful tension between an inner, serious meaning expressed by a complexity of outward show, and that show created as complicated entertainment for its own sake. Jonson had no doubt that mere spectacle had come to smother moral and intellectual truth; his bitterness is evident in the mordant couplets of "An Expostulation with Inigo Jones" (1631):

> Oh, to make boards to speak! There is a task!
> Painting and carpentry are the soul of masque!
> Pack with you peddling poetry to the stage!
> This is the money-get, mechanic age.

This marked the end of their extraordinary collaboration and court masques were henceforth written by others—Townsend, Carew, Shirley and Davenant.

In fact, not many years remained. Davenant's *Salmacida Spolia* (1640), last and most magnificent of the court series, was produced on the eve of civil war. The optimism of its concluding song to the king and queen,

> All that are harsh, all that are rude,
> Are by your harmony subdued.

was to prove utterly ironical; fancy bore no relation to sad reality. It was not the last masque ever written, since Shirley's *Cupid and Death* was presented in 1653 and 1659 and there are later examples, but their place was really taken by the professional theatrical performances of the Restoration, which were often operatic in nature.

Besides the court series, masques were given in great houses and the halls of City companies, though few have survived. The masque form exerted a strong pressure upon contemporary drama. Sometimes there was actual coalescence: Dekker's *Old Fortunatus*, Ford's *The Sun's Darling* and Nabbes's *Microcosmus* are examples of "eclectic forms," kin to Milton's *Comus*. Very often plays would contain masques, simplified but usually very relevant. Probably the most famous of this kind is Shakespeare's *The Tempest*, where a masque of spirits is used to sum up some of the deepest themes of the drama and then related to the very nature of existence:

> ... the great globe itself,
> Yea, all which it inherit, shall dissolve,
> And like this insubstantial pageant faded,
> Leave not a rack behind. (4, 1)

This time fancy and sad reality meet, where inevitable change knows no distinctions.

Sidney, P., *The Lady of the May*, 1598 (p. 1578).
Daniel, S., *The Vision of the Twelve Goddesses*, 1604.
Jonson, B., *Hymenaei*, 1606.
   The Masque of Beauty, 1608.
Daniel, S., *Tethys' Festival; or, The Queen's Wake*, 1610.
Chapman, G., *The Masque of the Middle Temple and Lincoln's Inn*, ?1613.
Anon., *The Masque of Flowers*, 1614.
Jonson, B., *The Masque of Augurs*, 1621.
   Neptune's Triumph for the Return of Albion, ?1624.
   The Fortunate Isles and Their Union, 1624.
Townsend, A., *Albion's Triumph*, 1632.
Shirley, J., *The Triumph of Peace*, 1634.
Carew, T., *Coelum Britannicum*, 1634.
Kynaston, F., *Corona Minervae*, 1636.
Nabbes, T., *The Spring's Glory*, 1638.
Jonson, B., *News from the New World Discovered in the Moon*, 1640 (p. 1621).
Cokayne, A., *The Masque at Bretby*, 1658 (p. 1640).

Crowne, J. *Calisto*, 1675.

Davison, F., *The Masque of Proteus and the Adamantine Rock*, 1688 (p. 1595).

Congreve, W., *The Judgement of Paris*, 1701.

Browne, W., *The Inner Temple Masque*, 1772 (written for performance in 1615).

Nichols, J., *The Progresses. . . of Queen Elizabeth*, 3 vols., 1823.
The Progresses . . . of King James I, 3 vols. in 4, 1828.

English Masques, ed. H. A. Evans, London: Blackie (Warwick Library), 1897.

A Book of Masques, Cambridge: Cambridge Univ. Press, 1967. J.C.

MASSINGER, Philip (1583–1640) was born in Salisbury (Wiltshire) and educated at Oxford. He may well have become a Roman Catholic. After Beaumont's retirement in 1613, Massinger collaborated with Fletcher so frequently that he appears to have contributed to more of the "Beaumont and Fletcher" plays than did Beaumont himself. When they were working together, Massinger seems generally to have undertaken the more forensic scenes and Fletcher those of a more pathetic cast. Massinger collaborated also with other writers.

His career as an independent playwright began during Fletcher's lifetime. In 1629 he described his tragedy *The Roman Actor* as "the most perfect birth of my Minerva." No one can say whether any of the plays of his last decade would have made him change his mind. But, in speaking when he did, he was preferring *The Roman Actor* to such exciting tragicomedies as *The Bondman* and *The Renegado*. In his tragedies and tragicomedies Massinger lacks profundity and originality. His indebtedness to Shakespeare and others is notorious. But he dramatizes interesting plots with some skill and is a most workmanlike and dependable writer.

Fifteen plays survive as Massinger's unaided work, and approximately twenty have perished. Only two of the fifteen are comedies, and the quality of these two is such that the possible loss of one or more comedies among the other twenty is especially regrettable. *A New Way to Pay Old Debts*, his masterpiece, is a satirical comedy in the line of descent from Ben Jonson's *Volpone* and *The Alchemist*. Like them, it is an anti-acquisitive play. Sir Giles Overreach, a greedy and Machiavellian usurer, schemes to ennoble his family by obtaining possession of landed estates and marrying his daughter to an aristocrat. When his schemes collapse, he goes mad. Massinger is a less humorous and less complex satirist than Ben Jonson, but he is quite as ferocious. Thanks to the power with which he presents its leading character, *A New Way* kept its place in the eighteenth-century and nineteenth-century theatrical repertoires on both sides of the Atlantic.

The City Madam also owes a good deal to Jonson. This time Massinger's satire is directed against the ludicrous vanity displayed by Lady Frugal and her daughters and the dangerous hypocrisy practiced by Luke Frugal. Luke is permitted to castigate the affections of the women before his hypocrisy is exposed by his brother, Sir John. As a former spendthrift who has developed into a miser, and a monster of humility whom opportunity can transform into a despot, Luke is plausible, ominous and memorable.

The Virgin-Martyr (with Thomas Dekker), 1622 (*p*. ?1620).
The Duke of Milan, 1623 (*p*. ?1622).
The Bondman, 1624 (*p*. 1623).
The Roman Actor, 1629 (*p*. 1626).
The Picture, 1630 (*p*. 1629).
The Renegado, 1630 (*p*. 1624).
The Emperor of the East, 1632 (*p*. ?1631).
The Fatal Dowry (with Nathaniel Field), 1632.
The Maid of Honour, 1632 (*p*. ?1621).
A New Way to Pay Old Debts, 1633 (*p*. ?1621).
The Unnatural Combat, 1639 (*p*. ?1624).
Three New Plays [*The Bashful Lover, The Guardian, A Very Woman*], 1655.
The City Madam, 1658 (*p*. ?1632).

Plays, ed. W. Gifford, 4 vols., London, 1805.   J.D.J.

MASSEY, Gerald. See **Spasmodics, The.**

MASTERS, Edgar Lee (1869–1950) was born at Garnett (Kansas). While working as a lawyer in Chicago until 1920, he educated himself by reading literature, philosophy and the classics, and published his first verses in 1898. He achieved popularity with the publication in 1915 of *Spoon River Anthology*, in which, in imitation of Greek epigrams, he had village dwellers of the past—"characters interlocked by fate"—present their lives trenchantly in free verse. After this his popularity declined and he never regained his original sympathy and insight, becoming increasingly bitter about his public neglect. *The New Spoon River* (1924) attacks the changes caused by American urbanization. During the 1920s and '30s he wrote five novels, some verse plays, his autobiography *Across Spoon River* (1936) and controversial biographies of Lincoln, Vachel Lindsay, Whitman and Twain.   D.M.

MATHER, Cotton (1663–1728), a member of a leading Massachusetts clerical family, succeeded his father, Increase, as pastor of the North Church, Boston in 1723 but not, to his sorrow, as president of Harvard

College. Mather's life coincided with a period of diversification in the traditional Puritanism of New England. In theological and ecclesiastical terms he was a conservative. His greatest work, *Magnalia Christi Americana*, an ecclesiastical history of New England with valuable biographical portaits of numerous Puritan leaders, has also been judged old-fashioned compared with the emerging rationalist history writing of his time, and Mather is often condemned as unable to adapt himself to the new currents of his own age. His writings on natural history, medicine and science (he was elected F.R.S. in 1713) have therefore attracted considerable attention as test cases of the ability of New England Puritanism to adapt itself to the Enlightenment, particularly his tracts in favor of smallpox inoculation. Similarly, his role in the Salem witch trials of 1692 has been debated. Mather's prose style has some admirers. It is prolix, florid, perfervid, rhetorical and given to archaisms. He was one of the most learned and productive American authors, writing over 500 tracts and books and with a considerable private library.

Memorable Providences, Relating to Witchcrafts and Possessions, 1689.
The Way to Prosperity, 1690.
The Wonders of the Invisible World, 1693.
Magnalia Christi Americana; or, The Ecclesiastical History of New England, 1702.
Bonifacius (Essays to Do Good), 1710.
The Christian Philosopher, 1721.
Some Account of . . . Inoculating . . . the Smallpox, 1721.
Parentator, 1724.
Manuductio ad Ministerium, 1726.

Diary, 2 vols., Boston: Massachusetts Historical Soc., 1911–12.
Selections, ed. K. B. Murdock. New York: Harcourt, Brace, 1926.   R.S.

MATURIN, C. R. (Charles Robert) (1782–1824), born in Dublin, was educated at Trinity College before taking holy orders. His fascination with Gothic melodrama is evident in all his fiction. *The Fatal Revenge* (1807) owes much to the example of Mrs. Radcliffe and "Monk" Lewis; so does his drama *Bertram*, produced in 1816 by Kean. His best novel, *Melmoth the Wanderer* (1820), is a high point of Gothic romance. Based on the Faust legend and using an intricate plot structure, it is at times a compelling study of mental torment.   I.W.

MAUGHAM, W. (William) Somerset (1874–1965), son of a solicitor, lived in Paris until he was ten and was subsequently educated at Canterbury, Heidelberg University and as a medical student at St. Thomas's

Hospital in London. The success of his first novel, *Liza of Lambeth* (1897), started his career as a writer and by 1920 his reputation as a novelist was secure. From 1930 he lived at Cap Ferrat on the Riviera, though he also traveled widely.

A prolific writer, he was equally competent as a novelist, short-story writer and dramatist. He began by writing novels in a naturalistic manner, but in the 1920s he concentrated mainly upon writing for the theater and also maintained a steady output of short stories, which form more than ten collections. He is an accomplished professional artist who, without any original vision or any great distinction of style, has modestly offered his work as entertainment rather than as creative art. In his plays, in particular, the best of which include *The Circle* (1921), *Our Betters* (1923) and *The Constant Wife* (1927), there is a skillful combination of wit and satire, which is designed to suit the tastes of the commercial theater audience. His fiction offers a synthesis of pleasures—realism, exoticism, shrewd and ironic observation, careful craftsmanship and characterization.

Of Human Bondage, 1915 (*f.* 1934; 1963).
The Moon and Sixpence, 1919 (*f.* 1942).
Ashenden; or, The British Agent, 1928 (*f.* as *Secret Agent*, 1936).
Cakes and Ale, 1930.
The Razor's Edge, 1944 (*f.* 1946).
A Writer's Notebook, 1949.

Collected Edition, 21 vols., London: Heinemann; Garden City, N.Y.: Doubleday, 1934–51.
Collected Plays, 3 vols., London: Heinemann: Garden City, N.Y.: Doubleday, 1952.
Complete Short Stories, 3 vols., London: Heinemann, 1951; Garden City, N.Y.: Doubleday, 1952.   O.K.

MAYHEW, Henry (1812–87), son of an attorney, was born in London and educated at Westminster School. After several years of wandering on land and sea, he established *Figaro in London* (1831–39), a precursor of *Punch* (1841). His knowledge of the poor in London led to an appointment with *The Morning Chronicle*, out of which came his account of *London Labour and the London Poor* (1851; enlarged, 1861–62). In this work he documented the lower-class life of the capital, at once sad and funny, squalid and grotesque, in massive and intimate detail.   A.P.

MELVILLE, Herman (1819–91) was born in New York City. His father went bankrupt in 1830 and died, a madman, two years later.

Herman also was to experience money problems and to be suspected by his relatives of madness. After a variety of land occupations he took to sea in 1839. In 1842 he deserted the *Acushnet* in the Marquesas Islands, lived among the Typee for some weeks and later became an omoo or beachcomber. After the success of *Typee* he married, in 1847, Elizabeth Shaw. They settled in New York where Evert Duyckinck, an editor and man of letters, introduced Melville to literary society. *Omoo* (1847) proved as successful as *Typee*; Melville was to confide in Hawthorne his apprehension that he would be known only as "a man who had lived among the cannibals." But following the critical and commerical failure of the allegorical *Mardi* (1849), Melville returned to the shipboard experiences of his youth for *Redburn* (1849) and *White-Jacket* (1850). In 1849 he visited Europe and in the following year moved to Pittsfield (Massachusetts), a mere seven miles from Lenox where Hawthorne lived. Inspired by Hawthorne's tales, Shakespeare's plays and Milton's *Paradise Lost*, Melville completed, in the summer of 1850, the first draft of *Moby-Dick*, an epic romance of overwhelming power. The mixed reception accorded *Moby-Dick* was succeeded by the rejection of *Pierre* (1852), his "bowl of rural milk." During the 1850s he farmed and wrote stories for magazines, These short narratives, the best of which were collected in *The Piazza Tales* (1856), and his bitter prose satire *The Confidence-Man* (1857) reveal his mood as he approached middle age, sardonic, alienated, enraged. Yet he remained continuously inventive and persistently curious. After a visit to the Holy Land (1856–57), engineered by his apprehensive family, Melville embraced poetry and comparative obscurity. In 1866 he became a New York customs officer and also published his first volume of poetry, *Battle-Pieces*, consisting of his compassionate meditations on the Civil War. His greatest poetic achievement was the long philosophical and religious poem, *Clarel* (1876), in which he drew upon the spiritual feelings produced by his trip to the Near East. In 1888, having retired from the Customs House, Melville began *Billy Budd, Sailor*, a symbolic novella, completed shortly before his death in 1891 but not published until 1924.

Working with Romantic materials of primitivism, individualism, nature and the Gothic, Melville produced a body of fiction which analyzed reality in both its social and metaphysical dimensions. Local attacks on Western attitudes and activities in the nineteenth century are manifold: in *Typee* and *Omoo* he exposes American imperialism; in *White-Jacket* he indicts the naval laws which sanctioned inhuman brutality; in *The Confidence-Man* hypocrisy and deceit are seen to be normal in a commercial society. It is in the short stories of the 1850s that Melville's social preoccupations are clearest: "Benito Cereno" reveals the dangerous naïveté of the liberal Yankee and the circle of violence initiated by slavery;

"The Tartarus of Maids" makes striking use of images of female sexuality to show the dehumanization caused by industrial technology; and in "Bartleby the Scrivener" (*f.* 1970), Melville shows what happens to the individual, supported by well-meaning liberals, who refuses to compete within the capitalist system. Melville's radicalism, however, is tempered by fears of mob violence and by the attraction of paternalistic charismatic leaders, such as Lord Collingwood in *White-Jacket* and Nelson in *Billy Budd, Sailor*.

Melville's social critique was buttressed by his view of Christianity. He saw plainly how Christian myths were used to justify secular purposes, such as the pursuit of money and "progress," and the prosecution of war. In "Hawthorne and His Mosses" he referred to "that Calvinistic sense of Innate Depravity and Original Sin, from whose visitations, . . . no deeply thinking mind is always and wholly free." This Calvinistic sense enabled him to perceive the social dangers of religious power structures, with gods and saints created as myths for emulation by Promethean individualists. But if man was irresponsible, so too was God or nature or whatever Platonic force oppressed man: "de god wat made shark must be one dam Ingin."

Melville's first novel, *Typee*, counterposes the predatory culture of the West against the flawed paradise of natural man, the "Happy Valley." Already Melville is challenging the practice and viability of Christianity. Here, and in *Omoo*, he attacks Western "snivelization" which through its missionaries has opened up the South Sea islands to vice, disease and alienation. Moreover, Typee religion, like nineteenth-century New England Puritanism, lacks spiritual substance, and the Typeean beats the silent, wooden god, who, like the sperm whale in *Moby-Dick*, refuses to acknowledge human claims and existence.

Mardi begins with a sea voyage, but soon becomes a social, political and religious allegory. A dense, rewarding work, *Mardi* touches on sin, guilt, "innocence," quest, myths and ideals; it concludes with one of the most haunting images in modern literature.

Moby-Dick is true to the notion of travel as adventure, as excitement, as conquest and confrontation with the unknown, notions which express the aggressive confidence and optimism of Victorian society. But in this work which is at different times novel, eyewitness journalism, Shakespearean play and scientific textbook, Melville is fruitfully ambivalent towards Romantic energy and expresses his standpoint through the Ishmael-Ahab polarity. Ishmael learns love and "sociality" from his association with Queequeg, so he earns survival and the right to tell his story. Ahab, the "grand, ungodly, godlike man," dies mad, defiant and lonely, insisting on personal expression and integrity at the cost of the lives of those he commands. Ahab deifies nature, defining the White

Whale as Evil, allegorizing in a symbolic universe where whiteness is mysterious and multivalent. Moby Dick is part of nature, but so too are the mother whales and their infants in "The Grand Armada." And in executing his monomanical desire, his egotistical idealism, Ahab grows to resemble his monstrous version of Moby Dick. Prometheus imitates God: Ahab dies bound to Moby Dick, his tragic grandeur and his social dess-tructiveness inextricable functions of his fascist will to power.

The greatness of *Moby-Dick* is the greatness of Melville's gifts: the verbal richness of his prose, the buoyancy of his humor, the aptness of his symbolism, the quality of his mind, the realism and force of his description and his sense of pace. There are, as in Cooper, splendid set pieces, but they are held together by the swelling narrative and by Melville's imagina-tive vision. We are spectators at a version of tragedy, but, as Pavese reminds us, we "leave the theater each time with a sense of increased vitality."

Pierre has rarely been a favorite with critics, but it has its own kind of uniqueness. It is, in its allusions and structure, Melville's most literary work; it is stylistically the most extravagant and the most inclined towards parody, and it is his only major novel set entirely on land. It lacks the epic sweep of *Moby-Dick*, but the lyricism, romantic fervor and intellectual energy of that earlier masterpiece operate again to create a mysterious melodrama of character and action in country and city societies. Pierre, the eponymous hero, lacks Ahab's grandeur, but partakes of his myopic pride and single-minded recklessness. Like Ahab, he functions partly to articulate Melville's own angry protest, directed yet again at the meta-physical and social arrangements that are revealed when Christian fictions and liberal assumptions are challenged and penetrated.

Melville maintained his bitterness in *The Confidence-Man*, which takes place on a steamboat sailing down the Mississippi, a ship of fools and swindlers. The Confidence-Man himself in his humorous disguises represents both human chicanery and divine mystery. As first cause, is he God or the devil? His actions suggest God is amoral, beyond concepts of value and notions of good and evil, and that nature is inscrutable; neither should be trusted. The Confidence-Man cannot simply be equated with wickedness; his is the ambiguity of the White Whale. When the duped misplace their confidence (faith), they blame the duper completely, rather than acknowledge their error, their part in their own destruction. It is the moral nature of a money-mad cannibalistic civilization that Melville seeks to reveal in this romance.

As a poet Melville lacked the radical originality of Whitman and the synthesizing skills of Emily Dickinson. He was obliged to rely too much on the confining rhythms and poeticisms of the sentimental tradition, but there are often intimations of a sinewy, resonant style struggling to emerge. His long poem, *Clarel*, is now seen as a major work, mature and complex, part of that Victorian debate about faith and doubt, religion and science in which Clough, Tennyson and Arnold were engaged. Melville uses the voyage structure of *The Confidence-Man*, enabling him to introduce and withdraw characters, shuffling at will the voices discussing the future of Western civilization. The final humanistic note is one of guarded optimism affirming life in the face of death.

Melville's last prose work, *Billy Budd, Sailor*, is notable for its cool, restrained style and its obtrusive religious symbolism. But in this sea story, set in the period of the Napoleonic Wars and the Nore Mutiny, Billy Budd, the victim of the logic of naval law, is an ironic Christ. His death is wasteful and futile; too simple-minded to have a concept of natural rights, he is no revolutionary martyr, so the ballad "Billie in the Darbies" expresses social impotence as surely as a British music-hall song. Melville's treatment of Captain Vere is unequivocal. Overcivilized, imperceptive, prudent, Vere is a Burkean Conservative, part of the God-King-Captain hierarchy of authoritarian power. He relies upon law and the "measured forms" of institutions. In the epilogue history is distorted for the convenience of the state; Melville's posture towards state tyrannizing of the individual freezes in irony.

American literature is the first modern literature; no writer exemplifies this truism better than Melville. Admired by a variety of modern artists—Picasso, Hart Crane, Wells, Camus—he is one of the first explorers of the existential condition, weighing the penalties and glories of vulnerable individualism within the chaotic modern multiverse.

Typee, 1846 (*f.* as *Enchanted Island*, 1958).
Omoo, 1847.
Mardi, 1849.
Redburn, 1849.
White-Jacket, 1850.
Moby-Dick, 1851 (*f.* as *The Sea Beasts*, 1930; 1954).
Pierre, 1852.
Israel Potter, 1855.
The Piazza Tales, 1856.
The Confidence-Man, 1857.
Battle-Pieces, 1866.
Clarel: A Poem and Pilgrimage in the Holy Land, 1876.
John Marr and Other Sailors, 1888.
Timoleon, 1891.
Billy Budd and Other Prose Pieces, 1924 (*f.* as *Billy Budd*, 1962).

Writings, Northwestern–Newberry edition, ed. H. Hayford and others, Evanston, Ill.: Northwestern Univ. Press, 1967– .   R.W.

MENCKEN, H. L. (Henry Louis) (1880–1956) was born in Baltimore, where he began his newspaper career in 1899. He was editor of *The Evening Herald* (1905–06), *The Evening Sun*, and literary critic of *The Smart Set* from 1908, which he coedited with George Jean Nathan from 1914 to 1923. Together they founded in 1924 a similarly lively publication, *The American Mercury*. Mencken was an outrageously iconoclastic and influential writer, who encouraged many new authors, including Dreiser and Sherwood Anderson. He is justly famed for his scholarly work on American English, *The American Language*, originally published in 1919, revised three times and supplemented in 1945 and 1948. His collection of essays in *Prejudices* (6 vols., 1919–27) exemplify his rumbustious style.

R.W.

MEREDITH, George (1828–1909) was born at Portsmouth (Hampshire), the son and grandson of naval tailors. He used and concealed his family history in several novels (e.g., *Evan Harrington*). Educated privately and at a Moravian school in Neuwied, he was articled to a solicitor and then became a journalist. In 1849 he married Mary Ellen Nicholls, widowed daughter of T. L. Peacock, by whom he had one son, Arthur, and who left him in 1858. Three years after her death in 1861 he married Marie Vulliamy, who gave him three children. Much of his writing career was spent at Box Hill, Dorking (Surrey). He also worked as publisher's reader, going up to London once a week. He traveled widely on the continent of Europe, the cultural life of Germany and Alpine scenery being strong inspirations. In old age he was a much admired literary figure, whose opinions on art and matters of the day were sought by other authors, including R. L. Stevenson and Henry James.

Meredith wrote both poetry and fiction. His best poem, "Modern Love" (1862), was written after the death of Mary. His first full-length novel, *The Ordeal of Richard Feverel* (1859), written during the breakup of that marriage, concerns a father's attempt to educate his son according to a new system; it satirizes social Darwinism, Carlyle's doctrine of work and other contemporary topics. *The Adventures of Harry Richmond* is an appealing romance, describing a young man's growth away from the Royalist fantasies of his pretender father and into maturity. Meredith's most famous novel, *The Egoist* (1879), describes the breakup of a conventionally appropriate engagement; it wittily and poignantly examines the psychological comedy of relationships between the sexes. *The Tragic Comedians* (1880) is based on the love of Ferdinand Lassalle and Helene von Dönniges. *Diana of the Crossways* (1885) had an immediate success, partly because it was based on a well-known scandal concerning Mrs. Caroline Norton, who was reputed to have sold a cabinet secret to the editor of *The Times*.

After this novel Meredith's writing was increasingly highly wrought. *The Amazing Marriage* (1895) his last published novel, was written over the preceding fifteen years. It is a final attempt to combine the elements of romance and realism which are frequently at odds in his work.

Meredith's strength as a novelist lies principally in his evolution of techniques to express the subconscious. The late style, though obscure, foreshadows that of James and shows the possibilities for the novel of making an idiosyncratic sensibility the central narrative voice. His *Idea of Comedy* (1897) expresses his belief in the power of reasoned wit to exercise a moral control over human passion, a belief which partly explains the alternations between irony and lyricism in his novels and poems, and which (although made unfashionable by the growth of psychoanalysis) is central to his whole achievement.

The Shaving of Shagpat, 1856.
The Ordeal of Richard Feverel, 1859.
Evan Harrington, 1861 (s. 1860).
Modern Love, and Poems of the English Roadside, 1862.
Rhoda Fleming, 1865.
Vittoria, 1867 (for 1866).
The Adventures of Harry Richmond, 1871.
Beauchamp's Career, 1876 (for 1875).
The Egoist, 1879.
The Tragic Comedians, 1880.
Diana of the Crossways, 1885 (in part s. 1884).
One of Our Conquerors, 1891.
Lord Ormont and His Aminta, 1894.
The Amazing Marriage, 1895.
The Idea of Comedy and the Uses of the Comic Spirit, 1897 (lecture delivered 1877).
Celt and Saxon (unfinished), 1910.

Novels, Memorial edition, 27 vols., London: Constable, 1909–11; New York: C. Scribner's Sons, 1909–12.
Poetical Works, ed. G. M. Trevelyan, London: Constable, 1912.
Collected Letters, ed. C. L. Cline, 3 vols., Oxford: Clarendon Press, 1970.

G.B.

MERWIN, W. S. (William Stanley) (1927–) was born in New York City, the son of a Presbyterian minister, and educated at Princeton. He has lived much of his life in Europe. His work includes poetry, plays and a considerable amount of translation, mainly from Spanish. *A Mask for Janus* (1952) established him as a poet who could write in a variety of forms, technically assured, eloquent and inventive. Subsequent collections, particularly *The Drunk in the Furnace* (1960), have used much freer verse forms and are noticeable for particularly startling imagery. Merwin has been praised by W. H. Auden as a new "mythological" poet, universal and impersonal. Recent work has shown considerable interest in animals as figures of contrast with man, and in a poem like "Leviathan" he uses a massive grandeur of language and imagery to exhibit a view of the universe emerging from chaos.

D.V.W.

METAPHYSICAL POETRY is the term used to refer to a trend in seventeenth-century English verse. More than anyone else, John Donne initiated this trend; and George Herbert, Richard Crashaw, Andrew Marvell and Henry Vaughan were his chief successors. The Cavalier lyrists—Thomas Carew, John Suckling and Richard Lovelace—felt its influence, as did occasionally certain other poets whose principal works were of an entirely different sort. Abraham Cowley represents the final stage in its history.

It came to be known as "Metaphysical" long after the deaths of these poets. Admittedly William Drummond complained, while Donne was still alive, of new "metaphysical ideas and scholastical quiddities," but it was Dryden later in the century who declared that Donne "affects the metaphysics, not only in his satires, but in his amorous verses, where nature only should reign; and perplexes the minds of the fair sex with nice speculations of philosophy, when he should engage their hearts, and entertain them with the softnesses of love." It was left to Dr. Johnson, in the following century, to affix the label. In his "Life of Cowley" he stated: "About the beginning of the seventeenth century appeared a race of writers that may be termed the metaphysical poets . . . [These] were men of learning, and to show their learning was their whole endeavour."

It might be supposed that a "metaphysical" poet would be concerned above all with putting forward a particular philosophical world view. Thus Lucretius in *De Rerum Natura* formulates classical materialism, Dante in *La Divina Commedia* gives poetic substance to the medieval Christian view of the cosmos and of man, Wordsworth in *The Prelude* reveals his preoccupation with questions of being and knowing, Eliot in *Four Quartets* examines concepts of time and eternity, and Wallace Stevens in *Notes toward a Supreme Fiction* seeks a "supreme fiction" which will be valid for life in a changing godless universe. These are all "metaphysical" poets in a perfectly straightforward sense of the word.

The sense in which Donne and his successors are "metaphysical" is altogether less obvious. Donne's main themes are himself in relation to women and himself in relation to God; Herbert writes as a gentle and earnest parish priest who sometimes allows us to share in imagination the crises of his spiritual existence; Vaughan craves to return to "the world of light," his heavenly home; Crashaw experiences fervors of adoration and self-surrender; and Marvell achieves the detached, complex attitude of one who can meet the claims of contemplation and action, of solitude and society, of Puritan earnestness and Cavalier grace. But these are all personal stances, personal experiences and personal relationships. In what sense are the poems embodying them "metaphysical" poems?

Dryden and Johnson both insist that the poets with whom they are concerned are nothing if not learned. At the same time, they do not suggest that these poets write to put forward particular philosophies. What the poets have in common appears to be simply a learned poetic style and a learned fashion of thinking.

In practice, readers today classify as "Metaphysical" those seventeenth-century poets who have (1) a taste for strenuous argument in poetry, (2) a dramatic and colloquial mode of utterance, and (3) what is termed "Metaphysical wit." Strenuous argument characterizes Donne's "The Ecstasy" and Marvell's "The Definition of Love"; the arresting openings of many of Donne's and Herbert's poems exemplify the taste for dramatic and colloquial utterance. But "Metaphysical wit" calls for fuller discussion.

As found in Donne's work, it is a serious wit, the product at its best of urgent feeling and agile thought, manifesting itself above all in pun, paradox and conceit. Donne puns on his own name in the lyric, "To Christ," and concludes his sonnet, "Batter my heart, three-person'd God," with an outrageous paradox. But his conceits—figures of speech establishing striking and usually elaborate parallels between apparently dissimilar things—constitute the most famous expression of his "Metaphysical" wit. While we must not draw a hard-and-fast line between Elizabethan and "Metaphysical" conceits, we may say that by Donne's time the conceits which poets had inherited from Petrarch had become conventional and hackneyed. Donne took fresh material for his conceits from widely varied fields of knowledge, including metaphysics, and made comparisons that are simply startling at first acquaintance but, at their best, are seen in due course to be also startlingly successful. At first, his well-known comparison of lovers' souls to stiff twin compasses seems to be merely an exercise in incongruity; on further reflection, guided by the poet's elaboration of his parallel, we discover it to be relevant, suggestive, and at last completely effective in defining a relationship and expressing the feelings that animate it.

Donne's followers employ "Metaphysical" wit and "Metaphysical" conceits in varying manners and degrees. We must not exaggerate their likeness to one another. The best of them were highly individual artists. The fact that they were all more or less affected by a trend which posterity has chosen to label "Metaphysical" does not convert them into members of a disciplined and self-conscious school or movement.

Metaphysical Lyrics and Poems of the Seventeenth Century, ed. H. J. C. Grierson, Oxford: Clarendon Press, 1921.
The Metaphysical Poets, ed. H. L. Gardner, London: Oxford Univ. Press, 1961.   J.D.J.

MICHAEL of Northgate. See **Middle English Literature.**

MIDDLE ENGLISH LITERATURE. The bulk of early Middle English literature is anonymous; even where an author's name is identified, so little is known of his life that his work may be treated as if it were anonymous. By modern standards the literature is sparse, but what has survived must represent only a small proportion of the literary and oral composition of the age. Latin and Anglo-Norman writings form an important background to the period and many works in these languages were composed in England. Many English works are translations or adaptations of known Latin or Anglo-Norman originals. Indeed, much of the literature is learned, depending on cultivated literary traditions, and one must guard against supposing that early English literature is naïve or "primitive."

The surviving literature exhibits wide variation in literary merit as well as a surprising variety of style, genre and subject matter. In verse, the main division lies between the native alliterative meter, with its strong stress accent and attendant features, and rhymed syllabic verse of combined French and native origin. The alliterative verse (typified in Laȝamon's *Brut*, c. 1200) is characterized by a looser structure than the Old English meter and a much more frequent use of rhyme and assonance. Syllabic rhymed verse appears sporadically in works which are otherwise alliterative, but already by 1200 it is being used consistently with considerable skill in the octosyllabic couplets of *The Owl and the Nightingale*.

A great deal of the surviving literature is devotional in purpose and broadly religious in subject matter. In the twelfth century, homilies in Old English continued to be transcribed, and the Middle English Lambeth and Trinity homilies, with the *Poema Morale*, witness a continuation of the Old English homiletic tradition. Devotional themes were explored in saints' lives, versified biblical narrative and literature of moral edification and instruction. Legendary matter is used for devotional purposes in such works as *The History of the Holy Rood Tree*, based on Eastern legends of the Cross, and *The Bestiary*, based on traditional animal lore first used for homiletic purposes in Alexandria in the early centuries

A.D. The religious preoccupations of the age are evident in the large amount of surviving devotional literature, and even secular works normally bear some trace of religious or ecclesiastical influence.

Early Prose. Historical writing is represented by the Peterborough continuation of *The Anglo-Saxon Chronicle*. The annals for 1132–54 are in Middle English, composed in retrospect after 1154. The annal for 1137, describing the anarchy of Stephen's reign, is the most famous. The language and style deviate considerably from late Old English literary usage, and it may be its closeness to speech rhythms and sentence structure that gives the work of this continuator its undoubted vividness and force. After this time historical writing in Middle English is mainly in verse. The next notable historian is Robert of Gloucester, who completed his versified chronicle early in the fourteenth century. Barbour's *Bruce*, a very long Middle Scots poem of the later fourteenth century, is also a versified chronicle.

The most remarkable prose of the early period is found in a group of South West Midland devotional texts. The best of them, the *Ancrene Riwle*, was originally written as a series of instructions for anchoresses and later adapted for use by a male community as the *Ancrene Wisse*. Although Latin and French versions exist, there is no doubt that the English version is original. The first and last sections deal with the "outer rule," the central six with the "inner rule." While the outer parts give sidelights on the life of the times and so appeal immediately to the modern reader, the inner sections, which deal with the mind and the soul, are written with greater feeling. The author is notable for his delicate use of imagery, much of it traditional in nature but powerful in its effect. Christ is likened to the pelican that feeds its young with blood from its own breast, and to the knightly lover who woos a hardhearted maiden in an earthen castle and is rejected by her.

Related in language and style are the texts of the "Katherine Group." All of these are written in a rhythmic, alliterative prose, and all except one are adaptations of known Latin originals. The three saints' lives in the group (those of Katherine, Margaret and Juliana) suffer from many of the worst features of medieval hagiology—for example, lists of the tortures and temptations visited upon the saints—but they are partly redeemed by the authors' mastery of style. Of the two homilies, *Hali Meidenhad* (for which no Latin original is known) praises virginity at the expense of married life, with many vivid and homely touches, and *Sawles Warde*, which presents man's mind allegorically as a house, is concerned with the protection of the greatest treasure of that house, the soul. Sometimes associated with these are three lyrical prose pieces, of which the best known is *The Wooing of Our Lord*. These pieces have much in common with the lyrics.

Devotional prose writing is continued in the fourteenth century in the work of Richard Rolle and his followers. These works are characterized by emphasis on the contemplative life; they are emotional and inspirational, and their style is highly elaborate and mannered. Some critics argue that this school of writing owes much to the *Ancrene Riwle*.

Other Religious and Didactic Works. The main repository of saints' lives is the Southern English Legendary, extant in manuscripts from the thirteenth to the sixteenth century. Personages treated include St. Michael, St. Patrick and St. Thomas à Becket. The life of St. Kenelm, the child martyr, depends on local traditions that go back to Old English times.

Much homiletic literature is extant in early Middle English. The Old English homiletic tradition is continued in such works as *Vices and Virtues*; others (e.g., the *Kentish Sermons*) are translations from French. The *Ormulum* (c. 1200) is a versification of the gospels read at Mass, in which the Bible story is expanded to tedious length. Clearly composed for the instruction of the laity, it is of little interest as literature. The *Proverbs of Alured* is a repository of folk wisdom, attributed to the famous Saxon monarch. In it we are advised that friendship is better than wealth, that a wife should not be chosen for her pretty face, and so on. Similar, but less religious in tone, are the *Proverbs of Hendyng*. The *Bestiary* is the only Middle English adaptation of the ancient and ubiquitous *Physiologus*, extant in thousands of Latin and vernacular MSS. from very early times. In it habits attributed to certain animals are described and religious morals drawn from their behavior. The whale, who dives to the sea depths with stranded mariners on his back, represents the devil, and his treacherous act teaches men not to trust in the devil. This traditional lore is widely influential in literature until modern times. The *Cursor Mundi* (c. 1300), an encyclopedic work of nearly 30,000 lines, treats the principal incidents of the Bible and religious topics of current interest. The material is skillfully handled and well ordered. This work probably influenced the subject matter of the medieval drama.

One of the best didactic works of the fourteenth century is Robert Mannyng's *Handlynge Synne*, a versified treatment of such religious matters as the Commandments, the sins and the Sacraments. It is rich in lively detail drawn from contemporary life. Much less effective is Michael of Northgate's *Ayenbite of Inwit*, a tedious and unenlivened prose treatment of similar themes.

Popular tales. The French fabliaux, humorous tales of a popular type, have much general influence on Middle English literature, but the only pre-Chaucerian example of the genre is *Dame Sirith*. Beast tales, in which animal characters are invested with human attributes, must also have been well known, but only two survive—*The Vox [Fox] and the Wolf* and *The Nun's Priest's Tale*.

The Owl and the Nightingale. Composed just before 1200, this is the finest monument of early Middle English literature. The theme of the poem is an ill-tempered debate between an owl and a nightingale, in which each maligns the song and the habits of the other. It ends with the birds flying away to have their debate adjudicated by one Nicholas of Guildford. It has an easy, informal tone; the images are natural and drawn from everyday life; there is nothing of the pedantic flavor of the traditional medieval Latin debate form, although precise legal vocabulary is evident. The meaning of the allegory has been much discussed. Since the purpose of the poem is to bring Nicholas to the notice of his ecclesiastical superiors, the owl and nightingale may represent older and newer forms of religious observance, but it has been argued that the subject of the debate is literary.

The Lyric. Large numbers of short lyrical poems are extant from the thirteenth century onward, and the best of them are amongst the highest achievements of the period. Most are religious, but secular lyrics are known to have existed in the twelfth century. Undoubtedly, the secular lyric has largely popular origins in folk song and dance, but one must not imagine that the lyrics are naïve and simple manifestations of the "folk," for they often display considerable learned influence, and many, especially later ones, are affected by the French *chanson courtois* and courtly love. The musical setting of the early "Sumer is icumen in" is complicated, and it is also accompanied by Latin words.

The conventional lyric opens with a description of spring and then contrasts the narrator's pangs of unrequited love with nature's freshness:

> when þe nyhtegale singes þe wodes waxen grene . . .
> ant love is to myn herte gone wiþ one spere so kene.

Some lyrics that use popular refrains may also display learned rhetoric in their catalogs of the beloved's charms. Some are in debate form, in which a man attempts to persuade a woman to be his beloved, and this type too (e.g., "De Clerico et Puella") tends to show learned influence in its diction. Some lyrics have an immediate appeal, but many make difficult reading because of their complicated diction and word play.

Religious lyrics owe much to Latin hymns and religious verse, and such traditional themes as the transience of earthly life. The most famous are those which celebrate and describe with great tenderness the important Christian events such as the birth and Passion of Christ and the joys of the Virgin. Many are songs of praise—to God, to Christ and especially to the Virgin. The division between secular and religious is not in every way clear-cut. Popular forms, such as descriptions of spring, are used in devotional lyrics, and secular lyrics contain religious allusions. In particular, the Virgin may be apostrophized in terms appropriate to an earthly beloved, and vice versa. Some of the finest devotional lyrics (e.g., "I sing of a maiden þat is makeles") date from the fifteenth century.

Political and Social Commentary. Before 1350 political and social commentary is scattered in different types of work. The earliest is the Peterborough continuation of *The Anglo-Saxon Chronicle*. From the thirteenth and early fourteenth century come a number of political songs, such as the *Song on the Times of Edward II*, a complaint against current lawlessness and oppression, which makes use of animal fable and ends with religious exhortation. The eleven poems of Lawrence Minot on the wars of Edward III date from 1333 to 1352. Of prophetic writings, the best known are those attributed to Thomas Rymour of Erceldoune (died 1294), of which the chief example, *Thomas of Ersseldoune* (extant only in late MSS.), relates how future events are revealed to Thomas in a super-natural adventure. *The Land of Cockaygne* is satirical and takes the form of a fantasy about the Land of Fair Ease, where rivers flow with wine and honey and the monks have high jinks with the nuns. An excellent complaint poem, "The Blacksmiths," in alliterative lines, although in a thirteenth-century MS., is a late addition to it.

The most important moral and social commentary of the age is found in the poems of the alliterative revival in the West Midlands and in the prose of John Wyclif and his followers. *The Parlement of the Three Ages* and *Wynnere and Wastoure* (c. 1350) are precursors of *Piers Plowman* and similar to it in many respects. Both are allegorical dream visions. In *The Parlement* the dreamer witnesses a debate between Youth, Middle Age and Old Age. *Wynnere*, although unfinished, is a well-constructed piece, full of social and political satire on questions of labor, prices, wages and so on, much in the manner of Langland. Both are notable for their effective descriptive passages. *Richard the Redeless*, written later than *Piers Plowman*, is a satirical attack on the times of Richard II. *Pierce the Ploughmans Crede* (c. 1394) relates how the narrator learns his creed from the poor plough-man rather than from the vicious friars, whose wickedness is satirized in passages of vivid description.

The writings of Wyclif and his school are characterized by strong attacks on the Pope, the church hierarchy and abuse of ecclesiastical powers, and by insistence on the fundamental importance of preaching and clerical poverty. Wyclif is best known for a translation of the Bible, which was probably carried out under his supervision, and which was completed about 1382. (See also **Wyclif(fe), John**.)

Romance. Romance in English differs from the earlier epic in its emphasis on action rather than psychology, and the hero typically wins a series of battles against overwhelming odds. Women provide a "love interest" of varying degrees of superficiality. English romance is more popular in tone than the French, which usually supplies the model.

Continental romance relied on themes connected with the courts of

Arthur and Charlemagne and heroes of classical antiquity. Interest in exotic matter is already displayed in the Old English *Apollonius of Tyre* (see **Old English Prose**). Charlemagne romance is poorly represented in England; Arthurian matter, on the other hand, is plentiful. It first appears in Laʒamon's *Brut* (c. 1200), not itself a romance, but a legendary history of Britain based on Wace's Anglo-Norman translation of the *Historia Regum Britanniae* of Geoffrey of Monmouth (c. 1137). Laʒamon presents Arthur as a Germanic hero rather than a knight of chivalry, and the *Brut* has no direct influence on later Arthurian romance, which reappears in the fourteenth century in adaptations of French originals. In some poems Arthur's life is the main subject, but Gawain, Tristram and other heroes tend to displace him as protagonist as time goes on. Many of the best romances come from the alliterative revival in the North of England and Scotland. Apart from *Sir Gawain* (see **"Gawain Poet, The"**), we may mention *The Avowing of Arthur*, *The Awntyrs [Adventures] of Arthur* and the alliterative *Morte Arthur*, and the fifteenth-century *Golagrus and Gawain* and *Sir Gawain and the Carl of Carlisle*.

But already in the thirteenth century, native Germanic themes appear in long narrative poems of a "romance" type. The best known are *King Horn*, *Havelok the Dane* and *Guy of Warwick* (c. 1300), the last-named extremely popular in medieval times. Their subject matter is very strongly influenced by standard folklore motifs. Eastern matter based on the Crusades provides the theme of the love story, *Floriz and Blaunche-flour*, adapted from French about 1250.

In the fourteenth century appear poems based on Breton lays, such as *Sir Launfal*, *Sir Degare*, *Sir Orfeo*, the last-named a medievalization of the legend of Orpheus and Eurydice. Among the most influential classical stories were those of Alexander the Great and the fall of Troy. The latter, derived from Dares and Dictys rather than Homer and favoring the Trojans rather than the Greeks, is represented in the fourteenth-century *Geste Historiale of the Destruction of Troy* and later in Lydgate's *Troy Book*.

Although it is true that few English romances rise to great heights as literature and are generally inferior to their French models, many of the best have been unjustly neglected. In particular, some of the alliterative ones are of high quality, and *Sir Gawain and the Green Knight* is to be numbered amongst England's great poetic achievements.

The Owl and the Nightingale, ed. E. G. Stanley, London: Nelson; New York: Barnes & Noble, 1960.

Medieval English Lyrics, ed. R. T. Davies, London: Faber & Faber, 1963; Evanston, Ill.: Northwestern Univ. Press, 1964 (includes modern versions).

Early Middle English Verse and Prose, ed. J. A. W. Bennett and G. V. Smithers, Oxford: Clarendon Press, 1966.

Middle English Verse Romances, ed. D. B. Sands, New York: Holt, Rinehart, 1966.

Middle English Romances of the Thirteenth and Fourteenth Centuries, ed. D. Mehl, London: Routledge; New York: Barnes & Noble, 1969.

J.M.

MIDDLETON, Thomas (?1580–1627), like his fellow dramatist and contemporary, Jonson, derived from a family associated with the bricklaying trade. His father died in 1586, leaving a small but comfortable estate. In 1598 Middleton matriculated at Queen's College, Oxford, but there is no evidence that he took a degree. Before the turn of the century he was already engaged in literary activities, having produced three poems: *The Wisdom of Solomon Paraphrased* (1596), *Micro-Cynicon* (1599) and *The Ghost of Lucrece* (1600). In 1602 his name first appeared in Henslowe's diary, where he is recorded as collaborating on the lost play, *Caesar's Fall* (see **Webster, John**). At an unknown date Middleton had married Maria Marbeck and a son, Edward, was born in 1604. In the same year he published two further nondramatic works, *The Black Book* (prose pamphlet) and *Father Hubburd's Tales* (prose and verse). About this time he began a series of citizen comedies for the boys' companies, for which he wrote until 1608. From 1613, in addition to his dramatic work, he wrote entertainments for civic events, producing at least five before his appointment to the post of city chronologer in 1620. He had begun writing for the King's Company in 1615, and the period 1615–24 was an extremely productive one in both theatrical and civic spheres of activity. In 1624 his dramatic career was interrupted and possibly terminated as a result of conflict with the authorities over his political play, *A Game at Chess*. He died in the summer of 1627.

Although the exact canon of Middleton's work has yet to be established (some fifty plays and entertainments have been associated with his name), there is, nevertheless, a considerable corpus of well-attested work which falls into two groups. Prior to 1615 his extant work is wholly comic; after 1615 (when he began writing for the King's Company) tragedy and tragicomedy predominate.

Middleton's numerous London comedies center on the conflict of wits and wills waged between avaricious citizen and amorous gallant. Notable among them are *A Mad World, My Masters* and *A Trick to Catch the Old One*, both lively comedies of intrigue, and *A Chaste Maid in Cheapside*, in which humor arises from the complete reversal of the conventional attitudes of husband, wife and lover in the traditional triangular situation. All three plays demonstrate Middleton's distinctive dramatic realism. A number of the plays Middleton produced after 1615 were the result of collaboration with William Rowley, with whom he wrote his masterpiece, *The Changeling* (p. 1622). This play traces the gradual process by which the heroine unwittingly commits herself to, grows accustomed to, and eventually embraces an evil from which she initially shrank. Two other plays of a very high order were produced during this second period— the tragedy *Women Beware Women* (p. ?1621) and the political satire *A Game at Chess* (p. 1624). Middleton's style lacks conventional poetic "beauties," but it has a strength and directness which permit extremely effective dramatic passages.

Blurt Master-Constable, 1602 (p. 1601).
Father Hubburd's Tales, 1604.
The Honest Whore (with Thomas Dekker), part 1, 1604.
Michaelmas Term, 1607.
The Phoenix, 1607.
The Family of Love, 1608 (p. ?1602).
A Mad World, My Masters, 1608 (p. ?1604).
A Trick to Catch the Old One, 1608 (p. ?1605).
Your Five Gallants, 1608 (p. ?1605).
The Roaring Girl (with Dekker), 1611 (p. c. 1606).
A Fair Quarrel (with William Rowley), 1617 (p. ?1616).
A Game at Chess, 1625 (p. 1624).
A Chaste Maid in Cheapside, 1630 (p. ?1611).
The Widow (with Ben Jonson and John Fletcher), 1652 (p. ?1616).
The Changeling (with Rowley), 1653 (p. 1622).
Women Beware Women, 1657 (p. ? 1621).

Works, ed. A. H. Bullen, 8 vols., London: Nimmo, 1885–86.   L.S.

MILL, John Stuart (1806–73), son of James Mill, an ardent Benthamite, underwent a rigorous utilitarian education at the hands of his father. At the age of twenty he suffered a nervous collapse, from which he emerged making radical adjustments to orthodox utilitarian philosophy. For a large part of his life he worked as an official at India House, his literary work being done in his leisure time. He founded the Utilitarian Society, and was one of the founders of the Women's Suffrage Society. In 1851 he married Mrs. Harriet Taylor, with whom he had conducted a platonic relationship for twenty years. In 1865 Mill was elected member of Parliament for Westminster, but his championship of the more radical forms of civil liberty led to his defeat at a subsequent election, after which he left England to live in Avignon—where Mrs. Taylor, who had died in 1858, was buried.

Mill's intellectual method retained the empiricism of eighteenth-century utilitarianism, but he substituted the concept of altruism for Bentham's emphasis on individual happiness and furthermore insisted on "the internal culture of the individual." His arrival at the need for these qualifications is described in his *Autobiography*, a particularly illuminating nineteenth-century document, while his essays on Bentham and on Coleridge exemplify the duality in his thinking. Mill himself considered *A System of Logic* to be his greatest achievement, but the *Essay on Liberty*, in which he argued for the freedom of the individual not only from political interference, but also from the restrictions of social convention, is now generally regarded as his masterpiece. The philosophical basis of his thinking is outlined in *Utilitarianism*, and he published other essays on the social issues of his time.

A System of Logic, 1843.
Principles of Political Economy, 1848.
On Liberty, 1859.
Considerations on Representative Government, 1861.
Utilitarianism, 1863.
The Subjection of Women, 1869.
Autobiography, 1873.

On Bentham (1838) *and Coleridge* (1840), ed. F. R. Leavis, London: Chatto & Windus, 1950; New York: Stewart, 1951.

Collected Works, ed. F. E. Mineka, F. E. L. Priestley, J. M. Robson, and others, 25 vols., Toronto: Univ. of Toronto Press, 1963– .   A.J.S.

MILLER, Arthur (1915–) was born in New York City. His father, Isidore Miller, a clothing manufacturer, lost his money in the Great Crash of 1929. After leaving high school during the Depression (1932) Miller worked for two years in an automobile parts warehouse, an experience which was later reflected in his one-act play, *A Memory of Two Mondays*. He then entered the University of Michigan, maintaining himself with aid from the National Youth Administration and by working as night editor for the *Michigan Daily*. At college he won several prizes for playwriting and after graduating he worked briefly with the Federal Theater Project. In 1940 he married Mary Slattery. Rejected for military service on medical grounds, he worked for a year as a fitter in Brooklyn navy yard. At the same time he wrote plays for radio, although he found the restrictions of the medium irksome. In 1944 he published *Situation Normal*, a report on his experience of collecting material for a film on army training, and won a Theater Guild Prize for his play, *The Man Who Had All the Luck*, which had closed after only four performances. *Focus*, a novel about anti-Semitism appeared in 1945. With *All My Sons* (1947) and *Death of a Salesman* (1949), both of which won New York Drama Critics' Awards, Miller became a leading figure in the postwar dramatic revival. *The Crucible* (1953) struck a note of opposition to McCarthyism before it was either fashionable or safe to do so and Miller subsequently became a target when, in 1956, his refusal to denounce associates before a House Un-American Activities Committee led to a fine of $500 and a prison sentence of thirty days until he was successful in an appeal. In the same year he was divorced from Mary Slattery and married Marilyn Monroe. Miller wrote the screenplay for *The Misfits*, which appeared in 1961, the year of his divorce from Marilyn Monroe. This film provided her last starring role. The experiences of this period entered into the semiautobiographical *After the Fall* (1964). In 1962 he married Ingeborg Morath.

Miller's dramatic work has been strongly influenced by his experience of the Depression. Because he was aware of the degree to which the lives of individuals could be shaped by factors over which they had no control, because he saw how necessary it was for people to compromise and to accommodate themselves to changing circumstances in order to survive, because he has realized that people often act short-sightedly without fully considering the implications of what they are doing, he has inclined to be tolerant of his characters and to refrain from passing judgment upon them. He tends to imply that anyone who has had to contend with the sharp vicissitudes and rapid changes in American life has fully earned the right to our sympathy, but his vision stops short of the sentimental because of his insistence on moral responsibility and his refusal to exonerate or condone. If Miller focuses on the discrepancy between what America seems to promise and what she actually delivers to those who have internalized the ethic of success, he is by no means an unqualified critic of the American dream. Society is censured, not for filling them with false hopes, but for subtly betraying them.

Miller's departure from the Ibsenite drama of social criticism is already evident in *All My Sons*, despite its debt to *Pillars of Society* in its theme of the small manufacturer (Joe Keller) who knowingly sends young fliers to their death by supplying the army with defective cylinder heads. Keller, far from standing for organized social hypocrisy, emerges as a pathetic, alienated "little man," whose error of judgment is seen as stemming from short-sightedness, self-absorption, a background of instability, and sheer panic, rather than from any callous devotion to the profit motive. Keller emerges as a prototypical Miller figure—a man who acts with a reckless disregard for the consequences of his actions for others, whose insensitiveness and lack of knowledge lead him to make mistakes which are more serious than he himself is capable of recognizing. In *Death of a Salesman*

Miller's attitude to Willy Loman is ambivalent. He has nothing but compassion for Willy the salesman, who can no longer justify his existence once he loses his ability to sell and whose fate reflects a world in which "the absolute value of the individual human being is believed in only as a secondary value"; his criticism is reserved for the web of deception and self-deception which Willy has woven around his own life and the lives of his sons, Happy and Biff. The paradox of Miller's work is that he retains the traditional emphasis on the moral responsibility of the individual, yet largely dispenses with the capacity to gain self-knowledge with which it has been associated. At the same time he persists with this emphasis, despite his own clear recognition of the social factors that tend to undermine the individual's moral responsibility.

Miller's social concern, true to the spirit of American individualism, of which his drama constitutes a critique from within, expresses itself primarily through an emphasis on the obligations which each man owes to others. Thus in *The Crucible*, where Miller found in the Salem witch trials a historic analogue for the contemporary hysteria and compulsion to conform, he characteristically portrayed his hero, John Proctor, as a deeply compromised character, who refuses to confess, not because he objects to lying but because he is unwilling to implicate others. For Miller the dangers of the witch hunt lay not so much in its fanatical idealism as in the way it could become a screen onto which private hatreds, resentments and ambitions could be projected. At the time Miller's essay, "On Social Plays," which accompanied *A View from the Bridge*, was taken as a criticism of the psychological drama of Tennessee Williams, yet it was written more to clear up misconceptions about himself. He significantly invoked the example of Greek drama rather than Ibsen and insisted that the social drama was "only incidentally an arraignment of society." In *A View from the Bridge* the incestuous and possessive regard of Eddie, the longshoreman, for his niece, separates him even from those who love him, distorts all his relationships and leads him to violate the taboos of his community by betraying Rodolpho and Marco to the immigration authorities. The social perspective explicitly presents itself as criticism of the *individual*.

Incident at Vichy (1965) found grounds for hope in the limited but highly significant gesture of the aristocrat Von Berg, in handing over his pass to a Jewish detainee. But in his more recent work Miller has been more concerned with probing the conflict between the individual's obligation to himself and to others. In *After the Fall* Quentin tells Maggie, "I have to survive too, honey"; yet in *The Price* Miller is by no means certain that Victor was wrong to support his father. Thus Miller rejects universal categorical imperatives: only the individual can decide what price he is prepared to pay.

The Man Who Had All the Luck, 1944.
Situation Normal, 1944.
Focus, 1945.
All My Sons, 1947 (*f.* 1948).
Death of a Salesman, 1949 (*f.* 1951).
The Crucible, 1953 (*f.* as *Les Sorcières de Salem*, 1957).
A Memory of Two Mondays, 1955.
A View from the Bridge, 1955 (*f.* 1962).
The Misfits, 1961 (*f.* 1961).
After the Fall, 1964.
Incident at Vichy, 1965 (*p.* 1964).
The Price, 1968.
The Creation of the World and Other Business, *p.* 1972.

Collected Plays, New York: Viking Press, 1957; London: Cresset Press, 1958.
                                                              D.P.M.

MILLER, Henry (1891–   ) was born in New York City, the son of a tailor, and was a student at City College, N.Y. and at Cornell. Although he wanted to be a writer from childhood, he drifted through a long series of odd jobs until, in 1930, he left America for Paris where he lived for nine years, acting as the European editor of *The Phoenix* and as editor of the revolutionary *Volontes*. Here he produced his first major work, *Tropic of Cancer* (1934), which deals with his early experiences in Paris. From then on, his major works recapitulate sections of his life prior to this time, and from these we learn in *Tropic of Capricorn* (1939) about the New York of the 1920s and from *The Rosy Crucifixion* trilogy—*Sexus* (1949); *Plexus* (1953); *Nexus* (1960)—about the marriages and tribulations which had led up to his departure for France to make his mark as a novelist. His best novels, then, are autobiographical and discuss the nature of literature and creative ability, but he has written much besides, the most important being his critique of American society, *The Air-Conditioned Nightmare* (1945), with its sequel, *Remember to Remember* (1947).

   Miller's reputation is hard to establish, despite his impressive body of work and his longevity, since his books are anti-intellectual in the sense that they deal with sexual and emotional reality and so build up structures which are subjective and personally symbolic, instead of being controlled by formal demands or the working-out of ideas. They travesty traditional literary language and the stance of the narrator by demonstrating the ways in which such techniques rationalize personal needs. Consequently, the language follows every shift of mood and situation, working out a psychological pattern of growth which is confusing to literary analysis. Nevertheless, he has influenced American writing enormously, most directly in the case of the "Beat" poets, and could well in time assume a greater stature than he has so far attained.

Tropic of Cancer, Paris, 1934; New York, 1961 (*f.* 1970).
Black Spring, Paris, 1936; New York, 1963.
Tropic of Capricorn, Paris, 1939; New York, 1962.
The Cosmological Eye, 1939.
The Colossus of Maroussi, 1941.
Sunday after the War, 1944.
The Air-Conditioned Nightmare, 1945.
Remember to Remember, 1947.
The Books in My Life, 1952.
Big Sur and the Oranges of Hieronymus Bosch, 1957.
The Rosy Crucifixion (trilogy): *Sexus*, 1949.

Plexus, 1953.

Nexus, 1960.   D.C.

MILLIN, Sarah G. (Gertrude). See **African Literature.**

MILTON, John (1608–74), poet and controversialist, was born in Bread Street, Cheapside, in the City of London. He was the son of a well-to-do scrivener, who had broken with his family over his profession of the Reformed faith. Milton's father also composed music and loved the arts; he fostered his son's musical talent and his appetite for learning, as well as his aspirations from an early age to be a poet. The son, who fully acknowledged his debt to his father, was sent in 1620 to St. Paul's School, where the humanist education program of Erasmus (see **Renaissance Humanism**) was still dominant, and where he was thoroughly grounded in Latin and Greek. English poetry was not neglected in the school, and Milton also studied Hebrew privately with a Scottish Puritan friend of his father's, Thomas Young, later a member of the Smectymnuus group of controversialists. In 1625 he matriculated at Christ's College, Cambridge. His manners and appearance at first earned him the nickname of "the lady," but he became known for his mental toughness and ability. He kicked against the fossilized, partly medieval, university curriculum of disputation, and sought to extend himself in the broader fields of humanist education. During his seven years at Cambridge Milton's output of writing was impressive. His rhetorical exercises, which he approved well enough to publish late in life, contain in formal arrangement many of the ideas, principles and even symbols which are important in his greatest poetry—attacks on Scholastic philosophy, praise of the English language as an instrument for great poetry, the music of the spheres as a symbol for God's (and hence the artist's) ordering power. In poetry he tried his hand at

English versions and paraphrases of the Psalms and at pastiche Jacobean wit such as "An Epitaph on the Marchioness of Winchester" and "On the University Carrier." The latter was the only poem of Milton's which gained any contemporary popularity. He also wrote Latin verse in Ovidian elegiacs and in Horatian forms, as well as a group of Italian sonnets.

In 1629, the year of his graduation, Milton wrote his first great poem, "On the Morning of Christ's Nativity," which he placed first in his two collections of *Poems*. This work consists of a poem and a hymn. The function of the poem is to frame the hymn by defining the poet's divine status and his place in a tradition as both learned and inspired. If any poem in English is of the Renaissance, this is. The hymn is an amalgam of classical learning and Christian doctrine, though, as usual with Milton, the religious doctrine does not drive out the pagan poetry and splendor but absorbs it. By 1632 Milton had for some reason abandoned his original purpose of becoming a priest, probably for "political" reasons of objection to the state-organized aspects of the Anglican church. Most likely in this year, too, he wrote the highly formalized companion pieces in octo-syllabics, "L'Allegro" and "Il Penseroso," the active man and the man of contemplation. The poems are obviously attractive on the surface, but also contain complexities of philosophical doctrine (specifically the Platonism of the latter) not easy to grasp. From 1632 to 1638 he lived in his father's house at Horton (Buckinghamshire), engaged in the severe and extensive program of private study and meditation which he felt was the necessary preparation for writing great poetry. From this period dates, for example, the so-called Cambridge or Trinity MS., which among other things contains a list of possible subjects for noble poems and tragedies. Milton's musical interests involved him with Henry Lawes, the composer, in producing two masques, "Arcades" (1633), written for the dowager countess of Derby, and *Comus* (1634), written for the installation of the earl of Bridgewater at Ludlow Castle as lord president of Wales. The former is a skillful example of this cultivated form, celebrating the innocent delights of rural life, but in his second and final attempt at such a sophisticated entertainment Milton forces the doctrine of the work, however important in earlier masques, to a position of such preeminence that it drives the slender dramatic and competing musical contexts off the stage. *Comus* must be read as Christian apologetic about temperance and virtue united with Platonic speculation about evil and beauty, the whole rhetorically presented as a work of contemplation which contains some excellent poetry. It is ironic that the masque should have derived its title from Comus, the antimasque figure in it, the protagonist of evil, if beguiling, sensuousness.

In 1637 Milton wrote one of the greatest short poems in English,

"Lycidas." This takes the form of a pastoral elegy on a fellow student, Edward King, who was drowned in the Irish Channel. The poem, however, only starts here. It is a complex exploration of Milton's own feelings about a world where the good and virtuous are apparently abandoned to death and oblivion by the God they set out to serve. The intense feeling of the poem, not for King (here the "personal" explanation is beside the point) but for the apparent injustice of life to the poet, is beautifully disciplined by the formal perfection of the tradition of pastoral writing, which allows metaphysical speculation to be presented symbolically with great power and economy. In 1638 Milton ended what has always been regarded, both biographically and in achievement, as his period of "preparation" by setting out to travel in Italy and Greece, the scenes of the classical civilization and culture he admired so much and strove so hard to belong to. He visited Grotius, the learned civil lawyer in Paris, became the friend of virtuosi in Italy, such as G. B. Manso, (himself the friend of Tasso, to whom Milton wrote an important Latin poem on his aspirations as a poet), and spoke to Galileo. The outbreak of the Civil War recalled him prematurely from Italy. His return was marked by his greatest Latin poem, the "Epitaphium Damonis" to his close friend Diodati, who had died in his absence. This is the personal counterpart of the more formal "Lycidas," and is again about the poet's destiny. Milton's life "is all of a piece throughout." In this preparatory stage may be seen the great themes which, with variations, make up the rest of his career—his notion of education as repairing the ruins of time and assisting to restore the disorder caused by the Fall, his idea of the sacred and constructive art of poetry, his deep religious belief, his collateral conviction that high ideals must be localized in resolute action.

On his return to London Milton at first settled down as a teacher with his nephews, Edward and John Phillips (the former the author of a valuable early biography of the poet), and other pupils. As the momentum towards civil war grew, Milton became, as befitted his principles and ambitions, more engaged in public affairs, and for the next twenty years, the second era of his life, he produced the mass of his prose works, chiefly in religious and political controversy. In 1641 he began publishing a series of anti-episcopal pamphlets. The first was the anonymous *Of Reformation Touching Church Discipline in England*, notable for the development of a kind of nationalist religious tone, reminiscent of the Hebrew prophets, indicating that Milton was more and more identifying himself with what he believed to be God's purpose in finishing the Reformation through his chosen people in England. *The Reason of Church Government Urged against Prelaty* (1642) was the first published controversial tract with his name, and book 2 of this work is one of Milton's most important statements about his own aims and status as a thinker and controversial writer, as well as of his views of rhetoric and poetry. *An Apology against a Pamphlet ... against Smectymnuus*, printed in the same year, also has a valuable autobiographical passage. Such passages, as well as the next series of pamphlets he wrote, are the center of problems about how Milton's biography is to be related to criticism of his works. More is known about him personally than about any previous major English writer, but such information (much of it provided by himself) only very crudely gives an "explanation" of what he wrote. Milton was what may be described as an ideological writer, with a powerful drive to make his life, actions, thought and writing all consistent and, in the circumstances of seventeenth-century controversy, justifiable. So, in his controversial works or in the proems to books 1 and 7 of *Paradise Lost*, for example, personal passages are part of the total statement, not merely reminiscent chitchat.

In 1642 Milton married Mary Powell, the seventeen-year-old daughter of a Cavalier. She seems to have left him after six weeks, though she returned to him in 1645, and before her death in 1652 they had three daughters. Beginning with *The Doctrine and Discipline of Divorce* (1643), he published a series of four tracts on divorce, in which he argued, rather dubiously, that divorce was consonant with, or even enjoined by, primitive and later Christian teaching, and also (more convincingly to modern readers) that a total and worthy view of marriage means that intellectual and spiritual incompatibility is an obvious ground for severing the bond. Here again Milton is presenting an "ideological" view, a powerful fusion of intense feeling, personal experience, learning and action, though the argument itself is now stale. Viewed in another way, however, it appears as if Milton is firing off his heavy guns for less worthy personal reasons and mixed-up notions of chastity and other doctrines (see, e.g., Robert Graves's romanticized psychologizing in *Wife to Mr. Milton*, 1943). Two other works appeared in 1644: the tractate *Of Education*, which again sets out Milton's humanist ideal of education for an élite of "scholars on horseback," but also contains important formulations of his views on rhetoric and poetry; and his now most widely read work in prose, *Areopagitica*. This is an eloquent plea for unlicensed printing, and an attack on a government censorship law which Milton had fallen foul of with his divorce pamphlets. It is addressed to the "Lords and Commons of England" in imitation of a speech by the famous orator, Isocrates, to the Areopagus, the highest court of the Athenian state. It unites Milton's Protestant patriotism, his belief in the invincibility and unity of truth, and his trust in "good" rhetoric, practiced by virtuous men. Milton's prose is an eloquent and subtle form of writing. His long, carefully built-up sentences allow the meaning to reverberate among the complexities of his tightly packed arguments, backed up by a close reading of ancient and modern history. Such prose is more akin to his own poetry than to the simplistic rhetoric of successful political pamphleteers such as Swift.

During the trial of Charles I Milton prepared a pamphlet, *The Tenure of Kings and Magistrates*, justifying the king's arraignment and the Puritans' rebellion. This was published in February 1649, a month after the king's execution. In the following month Milton was appointed secretary for foreign tongues to the executive body of government, the Council of State. This was an important and onerous diplomatic job, in which Milton drafted the Latin letters to foreign governments and for which he had to some extent to be in the close confidence of Cromwell and his group. He also became the principal apologist for the Protectorate in the international debate about the legality of the King's execution and produced a series of Latin works for foreign consumption in answer to the celebrated Salmasius and others. These include the *Pro Populo Anglicano, Defensio Prima* and *Secunda*, and they also contain self-justificatory autobiographical passages of general interest. Their often coarse and personal tone is more reminiscent of the abuse in modern communist controversy than of the liberal politeness expected by nineteenth-century critics, who found the more "literary" *Areopagitica* a closer reflection of their own approach to politics. In February 1652 Milton became totally blind after a period of partial loss of sight. He had the assistance of Andrew Marvell and others in his secretary's duties and in 1655 gave most of them up. As the Protectorate became more unstable and finally foundered with the death of Cromwell in 1658, Milton again entered the lists of political controversy, though now prophesying to a diminishing audience, soon to grow hostile. *A Treatise of Civil Power in Ecclesiastical Causes* (1659) is an attack on the state establishment of the church. Milton had reached an extreme left-wing position in ecclesiastical affairs, which is mirrored in the radical theological position he develops in his idiosyncratic *De Doctrina Christiana*, begun some time in the 1640s but not published until 1825. In the face of the general swing towards the restoration of the monarchy and consequently of episcopacy, Milton published *Considerations Touching the Likeliest Means to Remove Hirelings out of the Church* (1659) (by denying them state-supported stipends), and a last defiant Puritan statement, *The Ready and Easy Way to Establish a Free Commonwealth* (March 1660).

Charles II entered London in May. Milton's seizure was ordered; he went into hiding, but was freed from official persecution by the Act of Indemnity after a brief period of arrest. During the twenty years of this part of his life he published his collected *Poems* (1645) but wrote little new poetry except sonnets. These, however, including the famous piece on his blindness and that on the death of his wife, are among the triumphs of his art. The discipline of the traditional, tight Italian form, united with its possibilities for concentrated nobility, allowed Milton to produce not small-scale works, but short works of true greatness, in which the splendid protest of the political lines "On the Late Massacre in Piedmont" (1655) is found alongside the more relaxed urbanity or personal compliment. In 1656 he had married Catherine Woodcock, who died two years later. In 1663 he was married for a third time, to Elizabeth Minshull, who survived until 1727.

For the remaining fourteen years of his life Milton lived retired from Restoration society, "the sons of Belial, flown with insolence and wine," in Bunhill Fields, London, perhaps more famous abroad than at home, but never without friends. He took up the epic *Paradise Lost*, which he had started in 1656, and finished it in 1664. It was published three years later. This is a work dealing partly with an allegory of the biblical Creation story, but it is also set in a wide cosmic setting involving metaphysics and contemporary cosmology. It opens with a great debate among the fiends in Hell, contains angelic disputations and makes use of ancient techniques, such as the allegorical figures of Sin and Death, reminiscent of Spenser. The hero of the epic is not God or Christ, but surely Adam, and the justification of God's ways to man involves placing man's ways and suffering in true perspective. Thus, besides allegory, Milton is constrained to use biblical teaching, history and his own aesthetic and psychological sensibility, all on a vast scale. The variety demanded is the power behind the remarkable and elaborate similes. Man's reason and virtues and, after the Fall, his weaknesses, but also his strength, are movingly presented. The poem is written in a blank verse which is not uniform or uniformly stiffly elevated. Much of the poem consists of speeches or thoughts presented rhetorically as speeches. It is a "dramatic" epic, unlike later long poems such as Wordsworth's *Prelude* which are monologues or "contemplative" structures. Thus in Milton's poem a close watch must be kept on the rhetoric of each particular speaker. Whatever reservations may be made about Milton's heterodoxy or his doctrinaire views or his outdated learning or the sometimes daunting and counterproductive elaboration of his art, *Paradise Lost* is a monument to poetic daring. He could never fulfill his vast program, but his achievement remains staggering. It is not a work of disillusion but surely, in its success, of qualified hope.

Paradise Regained is a much sparer work about the temptation of Christ. In the dialogue Satan is given an ornate rhetoric and Christ speaks almost flatly. The contrast is between the lures of public action and the virtues of private life. It is too easy, however, to see this also as Milton's soured view of his own part in unsuccessful political action. Along with this second epic in the 1671 volume was *Samson Agonistes*, a treatment of the biblical story of the betrayal of Samson by Delilah (in Milton's poem Dalila) and his consequent imprisonment and death. This is the kind of biblical tragedy which Milton had earlier suggested as a valuable art form for a Christian society. Samson is more than a convenient figure for Milton's own experiences, though he is that also. In his series of dialogues with visitors to his prison he regains composure from despair, and finally reaches resignation and penitence, before his self-caused, but not self-sought, death. He is a type of human ambition, action, and finally moral regeneration. The dialogues are interspersed with comments by the chorus, and their famous concluding lines

> All is best, though we oft doubt,
> What th' unsearchable dispose
> Of highest wisdom brings about . . .

are generally taken as Milton's final view of man's lot. The work is not perhaps, with its Christian resignation (and presumably heavenly reward to Samson), truly tragic.

Milton's influence on later English poetry is incalculable. There is no adequate account of it, but no reader of Pope, Thomson, Wordsworth, Carlyle and many others can be ignorant of its reach. Some thirty or forty years ago it was fashionable to belittle Milton as an apparently necessary process in praising Donne, but there has never been a time when his works were not read and justly valued by some. Unfortunately, the richness and complexity of his thought allows pedantry to flourish freely, just as his personal stylization was often fatal to imitators. Most readers of Milton's works themselves, however, will agree that

> Samson hath quit himself
> Like Samson

(See also **Political Pamphlets**.)

A Mask Presented at Ludlow Castle [*Comus*], 1637.
"Lycidas," in *Iusto Edouardo King*, 1638.
Epitaphium Damonis, 1640.
Of Reformation Touching Church Discipline in England, 1641.
Of Prelatical Episcopacy, 1641.
Animadversions upon the Remonstrant's Defence against Smectymnuus, 1641.
The Reason of Church Government Urged against Prelaty, 2 books, 1641.
An Apology for Smectymnuus, 1642.
The Doctrine and Discipline of Divorce, 1643; revised, 1644.
Of Education, 1644.
The Judgement of Martin Bucer concerning Divorce, 1644.
Areopagitica, 1644.
Poems . . . Both English and Latin, 1645.
The Tenure of Kings and Magistrates, 1649.
Eikonoklastes, 1649.

Pro Populo Anglicano Defensio, 1651.
Pro Populo Anglicano Defensio Secunda, 1654.
Pro Se Defensio, 1655.
A Treatise of Civil Power in Ecclesiastical Causes, 1659.
Considerations Touching the Likeliest Means to Remove Hirelings out of the Church, 1659.
The Ready and Easy Way to Establish a Free Commonwealth, 1660.
Paradise Lost, 10 books, 1667; 12 books, with minor corrections, 1674.
The History of Britain, 1670.
Paradise Regained and *Samson Agonistes,* 1671.
Of True Religion, Heresy, Schism, Toleration, 1673.
Epistolae Familiares, 1674.
De Doctrina Christiana, 1825.

Works, Columbia edition, ed. F. A. Patterson and others, 20 vols., New York: Columbia Univ. Press, 1931–40.
Complete Prose Works, ed. D. M. Wolfe and others, 8 vols., New Haven: Yale Univ. Press, 1953– .

A.M.R.

MINOT, Laurence. See **Middle English Literature.**

MIRACLE PLAYS. Though often applied to the medieval religious drama as a whole, the term "miracle" properly refers only to plays concerned with the lives, miracles and martyrdom of the saints. Records dating from the twelfth to the sixteenth centuries show that such plays were performed all over the British Isles, and at York there was a creed play which may have dealt with the missionary adventures of the twelve apostles. But the only English texts to survive are a *Play of the Sacrament,* on the miraculous conversion of a Jew who abused a consecrated Host, and a *Mary Magdalene,* apparently elaborated from an earlier mystery play. The surviving mystery plays, too, can only be a random example of those which once existed. Based on biblical matter and covering everything from the Creation to the Last Judgment, their appeal was universal. But though we have records from places as far apart as Aberdeen and Cornwall, from Dublin, Kendal, Preston, Beverley, Oxford, Canterbury and many other towns, only a few texts have survived. Amongst them are four full mystery cycles, from Chester, York, Wakefield (Towneley MS.), and from an unidentified North East Midland town, possibly Lincoln (Hegge MS., misleadingly labeled *Ludus Coventriae*). Manuscripts containing one or two plays only indicate that other towns once had cycles also: Coventry is represented by its Shearmen and Tailors' pageant of *The Nativity* and its Weavers' pageant of *The Presentation in the Temple*;

Norwich by its Grocers' play of *The Creation of Eve*; Newcastle-upon-Tyne by its Shipwrights' play of *Noah*. There are also a number of single plays which seem not to have formed part of a cycle: two plays of *Abraham and Isaac*, a *Conversion of St. Paul*, a *Slaughter of the Innocents* and a *Burial and Resurrection*.

These chance survivals, though they may well be unrepresentative, suggest the distinctive character of Middle English drama. After the Dark Ages, drama in Western Europe was spontaneously reborn within the church, in dramatic elaborations of the liturgy for the Easter and Christmas services—hence the generic title "mystery," derived from the Latin *ministerium*, meaning service. By the end of the thirteenth century the liturgical drama, grown too complex for its original function, had passed from the church into the street, from Latin into the vernacular, from the care of clerics to that of laymen organized in religious confraternities or minstrel guilds, from the ritual and symbolic setting of the choir to an open playing place about which were grouped the necessary scenic locations or the seats of prominent characters. But though biblical sources were now supplemented by apocryphal material, sacred legend and pure invention, the thematic principle remained the same, numerous short scenes being organized about the focal points of the liturgical year. Plays of this type were undoubtedly performed in England. London and other towns had plays of the *Passion*, others had *Nativity* or *Resurrection* sequences; the Cornish *Creation*, *Passion* and *Resurrection* were played "in the round," and so, apparently, were the *Passion* and *Resurrection* at New Romney and the *Conversion of St Paul*; the London plays were performed by clerics and the Hegge plays possibly by a guild formed for the purpose. But most of the surviving texts and records, originating predominantly in the North and East of England, indicate a different tradition. There the mysteries, organized and regulated by the city authorities, were performed by the trade guilds, to which individual plays were assigned as appropriate to their professional skills, the Waterdrawers playing *The Deluge*, the Bakers *The Last Supper*, the Ironmongers *The Crucifixion*, and the Cooks *The Harrowing of Hell*. The performances were originally given on Corpus Christi Day and, perhaps because the feast was marked by a religious procession, were played processionally at a number of sites through the town, to which the "pageants" or wagons were drawn in turn. Later, so as not to conflict with the sacred procession, the greatly expanded cycles were moved to other summer feast days. But the association with Corpus Christi had already determined their thematic unity. The feast celebrated the institution of the Holy Sacrament and the Corpus Christi cycles not only commemorated Christ's sacrifice, as the more limited Passion plays did, but demonstrated the whole sweep of God's design for his creation, from the sin of Adam and Eve, which made that sacrifice necessary, to the Last Judgment at which the innocent experience its redeeming power.

Such a conception compels respect. A serious dramatic project, larger than anything attempted since, which held the stage from the early fourteenth century well into the reign of the Protestant Elizabeth and which inspired clerics "to fortify the unlearned in their faith" by constantly revising and expanding the texts, led the trade guilds to vie with each other in lavishing money on the production of their plays and induced audiences to stand in the streets from dawn to dusk while some forty pageants passed before them. But modern critics, though they admire the social phenomenon, have rarely appreciated the mysteries at their true value. Discounting their cyclic structure, they admire individual plays amongst many which they find dully didactic; yet the emotional power which they recognize in *Abraham and Isaac* partly derives from its prefiguration of the divine sacrifice which is at the core of the Corpus Christi drama, and many less dramatic episodes had a similar relevance for medieval audiences. Critics often praise what is incidental rather than essential in the plays—the vigorous naturalism of Noah's nagging wife, whose refusal to enter the ark makes her the type of sinful humanity resistant to God's will, or the farcical byplay of the stolen lamb concealed in a cradle in which the Wakefield cycle parodies the Nativity, giving intense conviction to the brief epilogue in which the shepherds kneel in simple humility before the crib. All too often the plays have been viewed as merely preparatory to the Elizabethan drama, naïve and fumbling exercises in tragedy and comedy. But the classical categories are largely irrelevant to the cosmic theme of the mystery cycles which evolved a dramatic technique, partly realistic, partly symbolic, appropriate to their purpose. Much of that technique has recently been rediscovered in the theater of Brecht, Ionesco and Beckett, and audiences accustomed to the theater of illusion have learnt to accept that a few yards of bare planking may separate Heaven from Earth, Jerusalem from Calvary. For them the didactic structure of the cycles cannot have full significance, but they are unconsciously affected by the dramatic talent which evokes the horror of mankind's crowning sin by contrasting the violence and blasphemies of Christ's torturers in the *Flagellation* and *Crucifixion* with the silence of the central figure. With the revival of the cycles at Chester and York, with improved editions and translations which recognize the need for a colloquial medium to render the regional dialects of the originals and respect their vigorous, if occasionally incoherent, verse forms, the English mystery cycles are beginning to find new audiences.

The Chester Plays, ed. H. Deimling and Dr. Matthews, 2 vols., London: Early English Text Society, vol. 1, 1893; vol. 2, 1916.

Two Coventry Corpus Christi Plays, ed. H. Craig, London: Early English Text Society, 1902.

The Towneley Plays, ed. G. England and A. W. Pollard, London: Early English Text Society, 1897.

Ludus Coventriae, ed. K. S. Block, London: Early English Text Society, 1922.

The Plays Performed by Crafts or Mysteries of York, ed. L. T. Smith, Oxford: Clarendon Press, 1885.

R.B.

MITCHELL, James Leslie. See **"Gibbon, Lewis Grassic."**

MITCHELL, Margaret (1900–49), a novelist and journalist, was born in Georgia and died in Atlanta after a road accident. Her monumental novel, *Gone with the Wind* (1936; *f.* 1939), traces the romantic career of Scarlett O'Hara. Set in Georgia during the Civil War and Reconstruction, the narrative is told entirely from the viewpoint of the upper class in the Old South. Its sentimentality is chiefly political, portraying through stereotypes a benign, slaveholding South and the brutalities and excesses of Reconstruction. Despite Miss Mitchell's assertion: "I know good work and I know good writing and I didn't think mine good," her novel sold over 500,000 copies in its first year, winning an unprecedented popularity throughout the United States.

J.W.

MITFORD, Mary Russell (1787–1855), poet, dramatist and novelist, was born in Hampshire and lived for most of her life near Reading (Berkshire). Macready and Kemble acted in her verse tragedies at Covent Garden, but her greatest literary work is *Our Village* (1824–32; *s.* 1819), written for money to pay her father's debts. These goodhumored and faithful records of ordinary country life were a new kind of literature. She was a good conversationalist and knew many writers of the day, including Elizabeth Barrett Browning who described her as "a sort of prose Crabbe in the sun." Her *Recollections of a Literary Life* (1852) is of some interest.

Letters, ed. R. B. Johnson, London: J. Lane, 1925.

S.M.S.

MITTELHOLZER, Edgar. See **Caribbean Literature.**

MONRO, Harold (1879–1932), poet, editor, and bookseller, was born near Brussels, where he lived for seven years. After Cambridge and various projects, including the Samurai Press which published W. W.

Gibson and John Drinkwater, Monro's life, except for his First World War service, centered on poetry. He founded and edited *The Poetry Review* (1912), *Poetry and Drama* (1913–14) and *The Monthly Chapbook* (1919–25), and opened the influential Poetry Bookshop in 1913, all of which ventures provided a focal point for, and encouraged the un-economic business of, poetry. His influence is of more significance than his own poetry, which Eliot called "honest and bitter." (See also **Georgians, The.**)

Collected Poems, ed. A. Monro, with biographical sketch by F. S. Flint and critical note by T. S. Eliot, London: Cobden-Sanderson, 1933.

K.T.

MONTAGU, Mrs. Elizabeth. See **Bluestockings.**

MONTGOMERY, James. See **Hymns.**

MOODY, William Vaughn (1869–1910) was born in Indiana, studied at Harvard and taught at the University of Chicago. *Poems* (1901) contained lyrical verse commenting on the state of mankind, and included the famous anti-imperialistic "An Ode in Time of Hesitation" (1900). In 1904 he wrote *The Fire-Bringer*, the second verse drama of a projected trilogy. Both this play and his earlier *The Masque of Judgment* (1900) deal with man's alienation from God. *A Sabine Woman* (1906) was first staged in Chicago and was revised, retitled and published as *The Great Divide* (1909; f. 1930). This prose play contrasts the Puritan East with the pioneering West.

Poems and Plays, 2 vols., ed. J. M. Manly, Boston: Houghton Mifflin, 1912.

R.W.

MOORE, Brian. See **Canadian Literature.**

MOORE, George (1852–1933), born in county Mayo (Ireland), the son of a member of Parliament, was educated in England and at art schools in Paris, where he met most of the leading French writers and artists. Deeply impressed by Zola, he returned to England and applied the methods of the French naturalistic writers to English life. In 1901 he returned to Ireland and collaborated with Yeats in forming the Irish National Theatre, a period of his life which he recalls in *Hail and Farewell*. Later he returned to England and continued to write until the time of his death.

It is difficult to define the special quality of his work which, in its variety, reflects the literary developments of half a century. His early work is influenced by French writers, particularly in a series of naturalistic novels, culminating in *Esther Waters*. In middle life, in such works as *The Untilled Field* (1903) and *The Lake* (1905), he aspired to be the "Irish Turgenev," and finally turned to historical and philosophic romance. Though he has been called the "chameleon of novelists," Moore possesses both individuality and integrity. Beginning with the desire to observe and record accurately, he became a personality filled with apprehension of beauty and ecstasy. At best, he is a penetrating, compassionate observer of human nature and embodies his impressions in original narratives. His refined style is a distinctive blend of the written and spoken word.

Confessions of a Young Man, 1888 (autobiography).
Esther Waters, 1894.
Evelyn Innes, 1898.
Hail and Farewell, 1911–14 (*Ave*, 1911; *Salve*, 1912; *Vale*, 1914: auto-
    biography).

Works, Ebury edition, 20 vols., London: Heinemann, 1936–38.   O.K.

MOORE, Marianne (1887–1972) was born in St. Louis (Missouri). She was brought up in the Presbyterian home of her maternal grandfather, the Rev. John R. Warner, and educated at Metzger Institute in Carlisle (Pennsylvania) and then at Bryn Mawr. After a year at Carlisle Commercial College she taught from 1911 to 1915 at Carlisle Indian School. From 1915 she had begun to contribute poems to *The Egoist* in London where much imagist work was then appearing, and to *Poetry*. Her first volume, *Poems* (1921), was brought out by friends, including "H.D.," without her knowledge. By this time she was living in New York, working first for the New York Public Library and then as acting editor of *The Dial* until it closed in 1929. Alfred Kreymborg, William Carlos Williams, "H.D." and Marsden Hartley were all among her friends, and were people whom, together with Eliot, Pound and Richard Aldington among others, she named as giving her advice and encouragement. Marianne Moore never married and lived, in her own phrase, "a metropolitan recluse," in a Brooklyn apartment from 1929 until 1965, and thereafter in Manhattan. Since the early appreciation of her contemporaries she achieved increasing public recognition, and following the publication of her *Collected Poems* in 1951 she was awarded the Bollingen Prize and in 1952 the National Book Award and Pulitzer Prize for poetry.

Describing her poetry, Stanley Kunitz in *Twentieth Century Authors* (1942) referred to her working in mosaic, getting many of her most apt comparisons from clippings, scientific books, or passing conversation. Her poems are often difficult not because they are obscure, but because they are so compact, and she herself said that in poetry "understatement is emphasis . . . metaphor substitutes compactness for confusion."

Poems, 1921.
Observations, 1924.
Selected Poems, 1935.
The Pangolin and Other Verse, 1936.
What Are Years?, 1941.
Nevertheless, 1944.
Collected Poems, 1951.
The Fables of La Fontaine, 1954 (translation).
Predilections, 1955 (essays).
Like a Bulwark, 1956.
O to Be a Dragon, 1959.
The Arctic Ox, 1964.
Tell Me, Tell Me: Granite, Steel, and Other Topics, 1966.

A Marianne Moore Reader, New York: Viking Press, 1961.
Complete Poems, New York: Macmillan Co. and Viking Press, 1967; London: Faber & Faber, 1968.
                                                          J.P.W.

MOORE, Thomas (1779–1852), the son of a Dublin grocer, was educated at Trinity College, Dublin and entered the Middle Temple. He spent most of his adult life in England, where his gifts as a poet and a musician, together with his social accomplishments, gained him a welcome in both literary and aristocratic circles. He was a loyal and intimate friend of Byron.

Moore's *Irish Melodies* made him the national lyrist of his native country, and he is still most widely remembered as the author of a large number of patriotic and other popular songs. His lyrics are easy, melodious, sentimental and singable; well-known examples include "The Minstrel Boy," "'Tis the last rose of summer," "The harp that once through Tara's halls," and "Believe me, if all those endearing young charms." He also had a lively wit. *The Twopenny Post-bag*, purporting to be a collection of intercepted letters versified for publication, exhibits the Prince Regent and his supporters in a ludicrous light. But perhaps Moore's most pointed satirical poem is "'The Living Dog' and 'The Dead Lion'"; it deserves recognition as one of the finest protests by an admirer of a great man—in this case, Byron—against the posthumous defilement of his reputation by the issuing of ungenerous and disparaging "Reminiscences." Moore's best long work is *Lalla Rookh*, an exercise in Regency orientalism. This quickly acquired a European reputation but has failed to maintain it. Moore also wrote biographies of Sheridan (1825), Byron (1830), and Lord Edward Fitzgerald (1831). His memoirs give a detailed picture of the aristocratic Whig society of his time.

Irish Melodies, 10 parts, 1808–34.
Intercepted Letters; or, The Twopenny Post-bag, 1813.
Lalla Rookh, 1817.

Memoirs, Journal and Correspondence, ed. Lord J. Russell, 8 vols., London, 1853–56; abridged, 1860.

Poetical Works, ed. A. D. Godley, London: Oxford Univ. Press, 1910.

J.D.J.

MORAES, Dom. See **Indian Literature.**

MORALITY PLAYS. From the time of St. Paul's injunction to the Ephesians to "take unto you the whole armour of God" the life of the Christian in this world has been consistently seen in allegorical terms as a battle against the forces of evil. As early as the *Psychomachia* of Prudentius (fl. 400), Christian literature employed what was to be the central mode of the morality play, the representation of man's mental struggle for righteousness as a physical combat between personified vices and virtues. The device was one which naturally recommended itself to the pulpit, being a readily apprehended means of communicating spiritual truths, and, since conflict was its essence, it invited dramatic representation. Hence from the homily developed first the Paternoster play (the Paternoster being conceived as seven petitions, each against a separate vice) and thence the morality play.

The first surviving drama of the genre, the fragmentary *The Pride of Life* (late fourteenth century), has characteristics in common with all four extant fifteenth-century plays, *The Castle of Perseverance* (1405–25), *Mankind* (1465–70), *Mind, Will, and Understanding* (1450–1500) and *Nature* (Medwall, c. 1490–c. 1501), and, to a lesser extent, with *The Summoning of Everyman*, published early in the sixteenth century. These plays are allegorical in mode, homiletic in aim and eschatological in emphasis. They present a struggle between vices and virtues for the confidence and thus the soul of a representative human figure—Humanum Genus, Mankind, Everyman, etc. The mode of operation of the vices is twofold, mental (persuasion and deception) and physical (violence). For example, in *The Castle of Perseverance* the vices first besiege the castle in which Humanum Genus has taken refuge and then, being repulsed, persuade him to come out of it. Since these plays inculcate that the fate of the soul depends on the type of life led on earth, interest being focused on the outcome of the action in the life to come, the sense of the imminence of death is all important. Thus in *The Pride of Life* Rex Vivus challenges Death to a wrestling match, in *The Castle of Perseverance* Humanum Genus dies in the midst of sin, while the whole action of *Everyman* takes place after the hero has received Death's summons. The gravity of tone this type of drama implies is relieved by the bawdiness, quarrels, antics and discomfitures of the vices (cf. particularly *Mankind*). The humor they provide is functional, both amusing the audience and demonstrating the inferiority of the vices to the exalted, self-controlled virtues. *Everyman*, possibly because it may be a translation of the Dutch *Elckerlijk*, is in some respects untypical in that it lacks the humor and the elements of conflict and seduction prominent in the other plays mentioned. The action simply demonstrates the futility of worldly concerns when man faces death.

The second phase of the history of the morality play extends from 1500 to after 1550. During this period the allegorical method and homiletic function remain constant, but the emphasis shifts both structurally and thematically. The physical aspect of the battle for the soul virtually disappears (surviving vestigially in the dagger of lath traditionally carried by the Vice), while the mental aspect, seduction, is proportionately increased with the use of disguise (already foreshadowed in *Mind, Will, and Understanding*) becoming the central mode of deception. Dramatists recognized that man blinds himself to the nature of his vices by assuming the names of virtues similar to, but essentially different from, their own natures (cf. *Respublica*, 1533). With the growth of the element of seduction requiring an organizing intelligence, the figure of the lighthearted, quick-witted Vice emerged from the earlier large group of barely distinguished vices. His complex role uniting intrigue and villainy with humor and homiletic instruction forms the ultimate stage of development in the medieval comedy of evil. Equally radical changes take place thematically. After 1500, with the new concerns of the Renaissance, the central interest shifts from the fate of the soul after death to worldly success or failure consequent upon right or wrong conduct in secular spheres. For example, in Skelton's *Magnificence*, which is concerned with the right use of wealth, a prince falls prey to disguised vices, becomes impoverished, but is restored to his former affluence when he submits to the guidance of the virtues. There is also a narrowing of focus in the partisan productions which resulted from the religious controversies of the period (cf. Wever, *Lusty Juventus*, 1547–53).

Further developments take place in the closing decades of the century. The issues displayed become increasingly limited while the central figure loses his universal quality, frequently undergoing fragmentation into a number of contrasting types (cf. Fulwell, *Like Will to Like*, 1568). At the same time the morality play structure, aspects of its technique, and often simply the character of the Vice are incorporated into otherwise naturalistic dramas, as in *Appius and Virginia* (1567) and *Clyomon and Clamydes* (c. 1570–83), forming a sometimes uneasy, occasionally triumphant combination of allegorical and literal modes.

The morality play retained its popularity for over two centuries (Queen Elizabeth watched a performance of *Liberality and Prodigality* as late as 1601) and its influence on the subsequent drama was great. It has been suggested that such characters as Shakespeare's Richard III, Falstaff and Iago derive from the Vice and that the form lies behind many Elizabethan history plays and tragedies, including Shakespeare's *Henry IV* and Marlowe's *Dr. Faustus*.

Old English Plays, coll. R. Dodsley, 12 vols., 1744; 4th edition, revised W.C. Hazlitt, 15 vols., London: Reeves & Turner, 1874–76.

Recently Recovered "Lost" Tudor Plays, ed. J. S. Farmer, London: Early English Drama Society, 1907.

Magnyfycence, ed. R. L. Ramsay, London: Early English Text Society, 1908.

The Macro Plays, ed. M. Eccles, London: Early English Text Society, 1969.

The Pride of Life, ed. N. Davis, *Non-Cycle Plays and Fragments*, London: Early English Text Society, 1970.   L.S.

MORE, Hannah. See **Bluestockings.**

MORE, Henry (1614–87), Neoplatonic poet and philosopher, was born of Calvinist parents at Grantham (Lincolnshire). He spent most of his life at Christ's College, Cambridge, which he entered in 1631, becoming a fellow from 1639. Always ardently Anglican, his theology took a mystical turn through his Platonic preoccupations; it is expressed in verse or in a prose often poetical. The preface to his *Opera Omnia* (1675–79) and his philosophical poems reveal much of his life and interests, which included the study of the Jewish Kabbalah. His influence lasted into the eighteenth century, certainly affecting Coleridge and probably Blake.

Divine Dialogues, 1668.

Theological Works, 1708.

Philosophical Writings, ed. F. I. MacKinnon, London and New York: Oxford Univ. Press, 1925.

Philosophical Poems, 1647; ed. G. Bullough, Manchester: Manchester Univ. Press, 1931.   D.H.

MORE, Sir Thomas (St.) (1478–1535) was born in London and, after his early schooling, placed in Archbishop Morton's household, his formal education being completed at Oxford and the Inns of Court. His love for the "new learning," which produced friendships with Colet and Erasmus, never left him, but his ambition for a Church career gave way to his political interests. In 1504 he was returned to Parliament and soon found favor with Henry VIII and Wolsey. He was Speaker in 1523, chancellor of the duchy of Lancaster in 1525 and, on Wolsey's fall, lord chancellor in 1529. He resigned this last post in 1532 because of Henry's ecclesiastical policy and the proposed royal divorce. Refusal to sign an oath approving the Boleyn marriage led to More's imprisonment and execution.

More's direct influence on English literature is not great, although his English prose is vivid and humorous, but as a man, a humanist and as author of *Utopia* (1516) he is one of the century's great figures. By 1551 *Utopia* had been translated from Latin into four European vernaculars and in its idealism (following Plato in the imaginative construction of an ideal state) makes a perfect contrast with Machiavelli's realism. More's book is essentially a restatement of Christian sociopolitical ideals against what seemed to More pernicious modern developments.

(See also **Renaissance Humanism.**)

Complete Works, Yale edition, ed. R. S. Sylvester and others, 13 vols., New Haven: Yale Univ. Press, 1963– .

English Works, ed. W. E. Campbell and A. W. Reed, 2 vols. from incomplete edition, London: Eyre & Spottiswoode; New York: Dial Press, 1931 (based on W. Rastell's edition of 1557).

Correspondence, ed. E. F. Rogers, Princeton: Princeton Univ. Press, 1947.

G.P.

MORGAN, Charles (1894–1958), son of an eminent railway engineer, became a naval cadet, volunteered during the First World War and studied at Oxford from 1919, when he also published his first novel, *The Gunroom*. After graduating, he became a novelist and drama critic for *The Times*. He is a writer of some seriousness, whose novels usually take the form of philosophic romances; often, as in *Portrait in a Mirror* (1929) and *The Fountain* (1932; *f.* 1934), a passionate love story is interwoven with the author's meditations and mysticism. His emotional searchings are also combined with symbolism and a chastened style.

O.K.

MORRIS, William (1834–96), a Londoner educated at Marlborough and Oxford, came under the influence of Rossetti and Pre-Raphaelitism, abandoned architecture for painting, and in 1861 founded a firm of decorators and furnishing designers to implement his doctrine, "Have nothing in your home which you do not know to be useful and believe to be beautiful." He enunciated such principles in lectures on the social reforms necessary for an artistic renaissance and was a founder of the Socialist League. In 1890 he established the Kelmscott Press to improve the aesthetic standards of book production.

Morris's Socialism, like his work in literature and in design, originated in the free, creative craftsmanship he associated with Gothic architecture and the Middle Ages. His earliest poetry (*The Defence of Guenevere*) handled medieval themes and forms with freshness and vigor, but in work like *The Earthly Paradise* he attempted a neo-Chaucerian narrative verse for retelling stories from classical and Scandinavian mythology. Despite a pictorial vividness, the facility of these long poems has an enervating effect, as do the prose romances on which he lavished so much of his abundant energy. The past is similarly idealized in the prose political parable, *A Dream of John Ball*, and the Utopian romance, *News from Nowhere*. The theories of art and socialism in his lectures are more stimulating, though no less visionary, than his imaginative fiction.

(See also **Romantic Movement, The.**)

The Defence of Guenevere and Other Poems, 1858.
The Life and Death of Jason, 1867.
The Earthly Paradise, 1868–70.
The Story of Sigurd the Volsung and the Fall of the Niblungs, 1877 (for 1876).
Art and Socialism, 1884.
A Dream of John Ball, 1888.
Gothic Architecture, 1893.
News from Nowhere, 1891.

Collected Works, ed. M. Morris (daughter), 24 vols., London: Longmans, 1910–15.

D.W.

MORRIS, Wright (1910–   ) was born in Nebraska and traveled in Europe before writing his first novel, *My Uncle Dudley* (1942). He is probably best known for *The Home Place* (1948), which, like many of his other books, focuses on Nebraska. Through the study of a family returning to that state, he expresses his ambivalent feelings towards America. Morris maintains, however, that *The Works of Love* (1952) is the key to all he has written. Among his witty, ingenious novels, which often combine comedy with the macabre, are a sharp dissection of the monstrous American matriarch, entitled *Man and Boy* (1951), and the description of people on a car journey from California to Nebraska, *Fire Sermon* (1971).

R.W.

MUIR, Edwin (1887–1959), after leaving the Orkneys where he was born, worked as a journalist and translator of Kafka, and produced works of fiction, poetry, criticism, travel and biography. His own autobiography, *The Story and the Fable*, appeared first in 1940 (revised and enlarged, 1954). As a poet Muir is in the Romantic tradition, influenced by Blake and Wordsworth. He attempts the largest themes, giving them a symbolic and mythic extension.

Collected Poems, 1921–58, ed. W. Muir and J. C. Hall, London: Faber & Faber, 1960.   J.C.

MULGAN, John. See **New Zealand Literature.**

MUMFORD, Lewis (1895–   ), born in New York, editor of *The Dial* in 1919, acting editor of *Sociological Review* in London in 1920, settled in New York as a free-lance writer. He wrote numerous wide-ranging books on architecture, literature and urban civilization and held several professorships both in the humanities and in regional planning.

In *Sticks and Stones* (1924), on American architecture, *The Golden Day* (1926), on American literature, and *The Brown Decades* (1931), on American arts in the second half of the nineteenth century, he set the arts in their social context. Before 1930, influenced by Ebenezer Howard's garden cities, he made proposals for regional and city development which were to be accepted by many planning authorities. The example of Patrick Geddes was the stimulus to the writing of the Renewal of Life series. In *Technics and Civilization* (1934), *The Culture of Cities* (1938), *The Condition of Man* (1944) and *The Conduct of Life* (1951) he produced a unifying study of the interaction through history of urban man and the man-made environment. The series expresses an ardent conviction that domination by technology or romantic revolt against it can be transcended by faith in the emergence of a biotechnic civilization in which the machine and the city can subserve the development of fuller life and personality. In his later works the advent of totalitarian regimes and the Second World War increased his awareness of the greater urgency and difficulty in realizing Ruskinian hopes.

The Story of Utopias, 1922.
Sticks and Stones, 1924.
The Golden Day, 1926.
Herman Melville, 1929; revised, 1963.
The Brown Decades, 1931.
Technics and Civilization, 1934.
The Culture of Cities, 1938.

The Condition of Man, 1944.
The Conduct of Life, 1951.
Art and Technics, 1952.
The Transformations of Man, 1956.
The City in History, 1961.
The Myth of the Machine, 1967.
The Urban Prospect, 1968.

R.V.O.

MUNFORD, Robert (c. 1730–84) was a gentleman planter, legislator, soldier and playwright. Born in Virginia, he was educated in England and his plays, in both plot and characterization, display the influence of eighteenth-century English comedy. *The Candidates*, written in 1770, is a farcical treatment of a local election, but the farce does not weaken the play's documentary quality. Its serious theme is aristocratic responsibility, the duty of "natural" leaders to stand for election. *The Patriots* (1776) takes for its theme the distinction between true and false patriotism. Munford ultimately supported Independence but was apprehensive about the xenophobic excesses of the Revolutionaries.

R.W.

MURDOCH, Iris (1919–), born in Dublin (her mother being a Dubliner and her father a native of Belfast), was educated at the Froebel Educational Institute, Badminton School and Somerville College, Oxford. She worked as an assistant principal with the British Treasury (1942–44) and with UNRRA in London, Belgium and Austria (1944–46). After the war she taught philosophy at St. Anne's College, Oxford, and then lectured at the Royal College of Art, London. In 1956 she married John Bayley, fellow of New College, Oxford.

Iris Murdoch has been particularly influenced by French literature and philosophy. Her first published book was a study of Jean-Paul Sartre, whom she particularly admires. Her first novel, *Under the Net*, a picaresque narrative involving a rootless young man who is looking for truth in post-war London, owes something, she says, to Beckett's *Murphy* and Queneau's *Pierrot*. *Under the Net*, though largely comic in tone, is also the most tightly argued of the novels. It shows a three-cornered relationship between Jake, the seeker, Dave, the withdrawing rationalizer, and Hugo Belfounder, the character who seems to offer Jake reality but who disappoints him finally by becoming a watchmaker and telling him that "God is little things." A key phrase from this novel, "All theorizing is flight," gives a clue to the theme of the second, *The Flight from the Enchanter*, which contains at its center an all-powerful figure who cannot face the effects of his power, who delegates cruelty while himself suffering.

The resonant imaginative quality which haunts these novels has declined in later work. *The Sandcastle* is more simplistic: it drives inexorably to a situation which, though existential in character, does not differ greatly from similar situations in Victorian novels. *The Bell*, overpraised by critics who welcomed its concessions to the traditional form of the novel, gives the pattern of the later novels—interesting in the opening situations, but disappointing in development. The use of sexual perversity in several of the novels has helped them to a commercial success which distorts their reception. The author's interests are, in fact, basically serious and show a growing preoccupation with religious questions. Though an agnostic, she believes that Christianity contains "all the wisdom one requires, if one can only get hold of it." *The Unicorn*, which has a strong religious content, owes something to Simone Weil, another writer whom she admires.

Iris Murdoch's philosophical enthusiasms have given her a strong sense of the relationship between the "contingent" and the "necessary," which she sometimes uses with comic effect (as of London: "Everywhere west of Earl's Court is contingent except for a few places along the river)." Her central ideas about the novel are set out in her article "Against Dryness," in which she argues that twentieth-century fiction has alternated between the "crystalline novel" and "a large, shapeless quasi-documentary object." Both, she argues, give too shallow and flimsy an idea of human personality, which is, in fact, "substantial, impenetrable, individual, indefinable and valuable." Further light on her position is given in her Leslie Stephen Lecture of 1967, where she argues for a conception of good which overcomes "the powerful energy system of the self-defensive psyche" by a process of "unselfing."

All the novels display sharp intelligence colored by imagination. So far, however, Iris Murdoch has not succeeded in finding a form for her work which reconciles her intellectual concerns with the demands of fiction as an art, her chief defect, perhaps, being that her distrust of fantasy undermines what is one of her own best gifts.

Sartre: Romantic Rationalist, 1953.
Under the Net, 1954.
The Flight from the Enchanter, 1956.
The Sandcastle, 1957.
The Bell, 1958.
A Severed Head, 1961 (*f.* 1971).
An Unofficial Rose, 1962.
The Unicorn, 1963.
The Italian Girl, 1964.
The Red and the Green, 1965.

The Time of the Angels, 1966.
The Nice and the Good, 1968.
A Fairly Honourable Defeat, 1970.
An Accidental Man, 1971.

J.B.B.

MURRY, John Middleton (1889–1957), son of a clerk and educated at Oxford, began his career as a journalist and critic. From the appearance of the quarterly *Rhythm* in 1911 to his resignation from the editorship of *The Adelphi* in 1948, he was responsible for much distinctive reviewing. His criticism and biography—upon Shakespeare, Swift, Keats, D. H. Lawrence (his friend) and Katherine Mansfield (his first wife)—has a strongly marked emotional and speculative bias. Starting from the assumption that the key to a writer's work is his "mental hinterland," Murry is often led to an intense and personal identification with the writer and his work.

The Problem of Style, 1922.
Keats and Shakespeare, 1925.
Son of Woman: The Story of D. H. Lawrence, 1931.
Jonathan Swift, 1954.

O.K.

MYERS, L. H. (Leopold Hamilton) (1881–1944), born at Cambridge, son of the philosopher F. W. H. Myers, was educated at Eton and Trinity College, Cambridge. Myers is an inexplicably neglected novelist. His connected novels, *The Near and the Far* (1929), *Prince Jali* (1931), *The Root and the Flower* (1935) and *The Pool of Vishnu* (1940), were published as a series in 1943 under the title *The Near and the Far*. This series, Myers's principal work, does not fit into any simple classification. It is philosophical, satirical (the Bloomsbury Group suffers heavily), romantic, adventurous, horrifying, comic, fantastic and realistic. It is throughout highly intelligent and serious; the events and characters, set in a half-imaginary India, are used with splendid control to express the need to connect the practical and the ideal, the worldly and the spiritual, hope and actuality.

C.H.

N

NABBES, Thomas. See **Masques.**

NABOKOV, Vladimir (1899–   ) was born in St. Petersburg and emigrated in 1919. After graduating from Trinity College, Cambridge in 1922, he lived in Berlin and Paris, writing novels, stories and poems in Russian. He emigrated to the U.S.A. in 1940 and was naturalized in 1945. He is a lepidopterist, and was research fellow in entomology at Harvard Museum from 1942 to 1948. After teaching at Wellesley College, he was appointed professor of Slavic literature at Cornell University, a post he held from 1945 to 1959. He now lives in Montreux.

The novels in Russian translated into English include *Laughter in the Dark,* which uses cinema devices in depicting the tragic deterioration of an infatuated Berlin art critic; *The Defense,* which moves into fantasy in tracing the pattern of self-destruction of a chess genius; *Invitation to a Beheading,* which by surrealistic scenes in the cell of a condemned individualist makes grotesque the tyranny of a totalitarian state; and *The Gift,* a fictional account of a poet's development, which incorporates a critical biography of Chernyshevsky and a history of Russian literature.

The Real Life of Sebastian Knight, written in English in Paris in 1938, is narrated by the half-brother preparing a biography of novelist Sebastian, and Nabokov takes the opportunities of parodying novels and forms of critical biography. Contempt for tyranny informs *Bend Sinister* in which a philosopher and a dictator are opposed. *Pnin,* four chapters of which first appeared in *The New Yorker,* contains a character, a Russian émigré professor, simultaneously comic, pathetic and admirable, and some good-humored comment on language, college and psychotherapy.

Nabokov was not widely known until *Lolita,* published in Paris in 1955, acclaimed in England in 1956, was eventually published in the U.S.A. in 1958. The narration by Humbert Humbert, who has seduced his nymphet foster daughter and murdered the man who took her away, is a good medium for Nabokov's rich vocabulary, sharp style, accurate parodies and witty panorama of American life and popular culture, ranging over schools, camps, advertisements, magazines, motels and hotels. Nabokov's writing is often paradoxically effective. The superficially comic treatment of the murder increases its horror, and the comic irony of the contrast of innocence in the romanticism of Humbert and experience in the

493

nonchalant young Lolita reinforces the expression of an intense and lasting affection.

The structure of *Pale Fire* is that of a poem and an extensive critical commentary by an émigré professor who interprets the poet, the poem and the situation through his distorting obsession with his former kingship of fictional Zembla. Nabokov's use of dramatic narration fosters a vivid awareness of the narrator, egocentric, erudite, obsessed or deranged, as the reader actively seeks the actual within the subjective version.

Nabokov creates fictional worlds. *Ada* has its own geography, with an Amerussia governed by Abraham Milton. The novel is full of allusions, puns and linguistic play, and it seems appropriate that the concluding parody of publisher's blurb has been used as publisher's blurb. Throughout the book there is cumulative reference to the evolution of the novel form. The protagonist, Van Veen, acknowledging Jorge Luis Borges, proposes a theory of pure time which is textured, not chronometric. *Ada*, too, is an unusual love story in which the incestuous relationship of Van and his sister, interrupted by her marriage and his amours, remains a constant love.

Nabokov's enjoyment of pun, fun and parody, his irony, wit and play with pompous readers, the intricate construction and oblique effects and his disdain for literature of ideas have prompted criticism of his work as the stylistically clever surface of a cynical aesthete, but such criticism misses the underlying strength of feeling, the hatred of tyranny and cruelty, the concern for art and sharp sense of the meretricious, and the desire for texture in life.

Camera Obscura, 1936 (as *Laughter in the Dark*, 1938; *f.* 1969; translated from Russian).

Despair, 1937; revised, 1966 (translated from Russian).

The Real Life of Sebastian Knight, 1941.

Bend Sinister, 1947.

Nine Stories, 1947.

Conclusive Evidence, 1951 (U.K. title, and revised U.S. 1966: *Speak, Memory*).

Lolita, 1955 (*f.* 1962).

Pnin, 1957.

Nabokov's Dozen, 1958 (short stories).

Invitation to a Beheading, 1959 (translated from Russian).

Poems, 1959.

Pale Fire, 1962.

The Gift, 1963 (translated from Russian).

The Defense, 1964.

The Eye, 1965 (translated from Russian).

Quartet, 1966 (U.K. title: *Nabokov's Quartet*; short stories).
King, Queen, Knave, 1968 (translated from Russian).
Nabokov's Congeries, 1968 (short stories).
Ada; or, Ardor: A Family Chronicle, 1969.
Mary, 1970 (translated from Russian).
Glory, 1971 (translated from Russian).   R.V.O.

NAGARAJAN, K. (Krishnaswami). See **Indian Literature.**

NAIDU, Sarojini. See **Indian Literature.**

NAIPAUL, V. S. (Vidiadhar Surajprasad). See **Caribbean Literature.**

NARAYAN, R. K. (Rasipuram Krishnaswami). See **Indian Literature.**

NASH, Ogden (1902–71) was born in Rye (New York) and attended Harvard briefly. After early careers in advertising and publishing, he was able by 1935 to spend his whole time writing verse. Disregarding poetic convention, he created his own unique, technically accomplished form, composed of uneven lines often ending in outrageous rhymes and unexpected puns. His urbane, often astringent wit is well represented in two selections, *The Face Is Familiar* (1940) and "One Man's Opiate" (*The New Yorker*, 1970). He was responsible for the memorable

> Candy
> Is dandy
> But liquor
> Is quicker;

he lived long enough to add "Pot/Is not."   R.W.

NASHE, Thomas (1567–1601) was born at Lowestoft (Suffolk), the son of a curate. He matriculated at St. John's College, Cambridge in 1582 and took his B.A. in 1586. Though a good classical scholar and well versed in modern letters, Nashe decided against a fellowship and after brief travels in France and Italy settled in London in 1588, resolved to live by his pen. But his bitter sarcasm and invective (which earned him the description "young Juvenal" from Greene) alienated friends and patrons, and as a result Nashe remained in poverty. The spirit of controversy involved him (as "Pasquil") in the "Martin Marprelate" pamphleteering against the Puritans, and a protracted feud with Gabriel Harvey, whose

Trimming of Thomas Nashe (1597), in reply to Nashe's *Have with You to Saffron Walden*, prompted official proscription of the quarrel.

Nashe had a sophisticated literary sense, and his enthusiastic admiration for Surrey, Sidney, and Spenser was coupled with an intolerance of mediocrity. His preface to Greene's romance *Menaphon* (1589) attacks bad poets in the spirit of *The Dunciad* and proposes an "Anatomy of Absurdities" to probe the "diseases of Art." He scorned the affectations of Euphuism (see **Lyly, John**) and his vigorous prose was memorably employed in his one novel, *The Unfortunate Traveller*—a genuine antecedent of Fielding and Smollett in the picaresque manner, a truculent compound of farce, horror and occasional lyricism as squire Jack Wilton tells "his own tale" of domestic service abroad.

Pierce Penniless His Supplication to the Devil, 1592.
Christ's Tears over Jerusalem, 1593.
The Terrors of the Night, 1594.
The Unfortunate Traveller; or, The Life of Jack Wilton, 1594.
Have with You to Saffron Walden, 1596.
Summer's Last Will and Testament, 1600 (play).

Works, ed. R. B. McKerrow, 5 vols., London: A. H. Bullen, 1904–10; revised F. P. Wilson, Oxford: Blackwell, 1958.
For the Nashe-Harvey pamphlets, see *Elizabethan Critical Essays*, ed. G. G. Smith, Oxford: Clarendon Press, 1904, vol. 2.   D.G.

NEALE, J. M. (John Mason). See **Hymns.**

NEWBY, P. H. (Percy Howard) (1918–) was born at Crowborough (Sussex) and joined the British Broadcasting Corporation in 1949. His comic novels, *The Picnic at Sakkara* (1955) and *A Guest and His Going* (1959), derive from his experiences as a wartime academic in Cairo. Behind the comedy lies a clash of race and culture. Others of his novels, such as *A Step to Silence* (1952), *The Retreat* (1953) and *The Barbary Light* (1962), take a more straightforwardly serious view of the human predicament, of individuals isolated in a life that has no meaning. Newby also possesses a fine capacity for noticing common scenes in an uncommon light, a faculty reminiscent at times of D. H. Lawrence.   A.P.

NEWMAN, J. H. (John Henry), Cardinal (1801–90) became vicar of St. Mary's, Oxford in 1827 after an Oxford education leading to a fellowship of Oriel College. He helped to found the Oxford movement and resigned his Anglican living in 1843, entering the Roman Catholic church in 1845. He was ordained priest in 1846 and devoted the rest of his life to Catholic education, first at the Oratory, Birmingham, and then for a short time as rector of Dublin University. He was created cardinal in 1879.

Newman was the most eloquent voice of the Oxford movement, which, while it had strong aesthetic attractions for some nineteenth-century intellectuals, is of major importance for the stand that it made against the development of rationalist intellectual trends. Newman's own conversion was not spontaneous, but the result of a gradual realization that the established church did not offer a dogmatic defense against liberal intellectual speculation. Newman argued that there were only two alternatives: "the way to Rome, and the way to Atheism: Anglicanism is the half-way house on the one side, and Liberalism is the half-way house on the other" (*Difficulties Felt by Anglicans in Roman Catholic Teaching*). Of particular interest amongst his considerable prose output are his contributions to *Tracts for the Times* (1833–41), *Apologia pro Vita Sua* (1864) and *The Idea of a University Defined* (1873). Some of his poems have also found popularity as Anglican hymns.

(See also **Sermons.**)

Parochial Sermons, 6 vols., 1834–42.
Apologia pro Vita Sua, 1864.
The Dream of Gerontius, 1866 (*s.* 1865).
A Grammar of Assent, 1870.
The Idea of a University Defined, 1873.

Collected Works, 40 vols., London: Longmans, 1874–1921.
Letters and Diaries, ed. C. S. Dessain, London: Nelson, 1961– .   A.J.S.

NEWTON, John. See **Hymns.**

NEW ZEALAND LITERATURE. One of the earliest pieces of writing from New Zealand is the Englishman Samuel Butler's (1835–1902) letters edited by his father as *A First Year in Canterbury Settlement* (1863), whilst F. E. Maning (1811–83) mixes biography and fiction in *Old New Zealand* (1863) and George Chamier's *Philosopher Dick* (1891) sums up a whole class of fiction and memoirs with its stock characters, loose construction and mixture of the sincere and pretentious. Alfred Domett (1811–87) wrote a long narrative poem of Maori life, *Ranolf and Amohia* (1872), which contains some good description of New Zealand scenery.

In the early twentieth century Jane Mander (1877–1949)'s *The Story of a New Zealand River* (1920) relates to the timber industry and in its feminist and colonial artist concerns recalls Olive Schreiner's *The Story of an African Farm*. William Satchell (1860–1942) is reminiscent of Hardy in *The Land of the Lost* (1902), but there is also plenty of local color in his description of settings and occupations. Much the most important name in this period, however, is that of "Katherine Mansfield" (1888–1923); among her short stories "Prelude," "The Garden-Party," "At the Bay" and "The Young Girl" show the pull that New Zealand and her own childhood there exercised upon her. There is also some autobiographical reminiscence in the middle-class aura of *The Godwits Fly* (1938) by "Robin Hyde," the pen name of Iris Guiver Wilkinson (1906–39), whilst *Passport to Hell* (1936) and *Nor the Years Condemn* (1938) cover New Zealand life from 1900 to 1935. Roderick Finlayson (1904–) writes of the Maoris in his stories, *Brown Man's Burden* (1938), and, less sympathetically, in *Sweet Beulah Land* (1942). One of the most powerful novels of the interwar period was *Man Alone* (1939) by John Mulgan (1911–45), a study of the "world of the underdog and the fugitive" (E. H. McCormick). These last three writers all came from Auckland, and so did Frank Sargeson (1903–), one of that list of distinguished New Zealand short-story writers which also includes Maurice Duggan (1922–), with *Immanuel's Land* (1956), Maurice Shadbolt (1932–) with *The Presence of Music* (1967), and Janet Frame (1924–). Sargeson's short stories are often told by a semiliterate narrator and derive a sense of authenticity from this device. His studies of childhood and of women are particularly good—see his *Collected Stories* (1964). Besides her short stories, *The Lagoon* (1952) and *The Reservoir* (1966), Janet Frame has also written *Owls Do Cry* (1957), a novel examining the life of a family within the community in which it is situated, and *Intensive Care* (1971), in which, as elsewhere, she considers the power and effects of loneliness. Dan Davin (1913–), with *The Gorse Blooms Pale* (1947) and *Roads from Home* (1949), is often occupied with the problems of Irish Catholics in New Zealand.

In poetry the early years of New Zealand (in terms of literary history, up to about 1920) have even less to boast than those of Canada and Australia. Besides Domett, Sir Charles Christopher Bowen (1830–1917), in his *Poems* (1861), faintly recalls the romantic Byron, whilst W. P. Reeves (1857–1932), with *New Zealand and Other Poems* (1898), and Edward Tregear (1846–1931) have some slight appeal as nature poets. The first major names, allowing that Mary Ursula Bethell (1874–1945) delayed publication, are those of R. A. K. Mason (1905–), whose work—see his *Collected Poems* (1962)—is tense, skeptical and pessimistic, and A. R. D. Fairburn (1904–57), who is more relaxed, though with no loss of vigor or, when necessary, satiric power—*Strange Rendezvous* (1952); *Three Poems* (1952). These two came from Auckland. At the same time in the South Island at Christchurch work of note included *The Land and the People* (1939) and *The Estate* (1957) by Charles Brasch (1909–); *Islands and Time* (1941) and *Poems 1947–57* (1957) by Allen Curnow (1911–); *Collected Poems* (1950) by Ursula Bethell; and *The Wind and the Sand* (1945),

Sings Harry (1951) and *Enter without Knocking* (1964) by Denis Glover (1912–). Brasch founded and edited the important periodical, *Landfall*, from 1947 to 1966. In the work of all these poets from South Island there is much attraction to landscape and then from it to meditation on the relation of people to place and to time. In the postwar generation J. K. Baxter (1926–)—*The Fallen House* (1953); *In Fires of No Return* (1958); *Pig Island Letters* (1966)—in his spare manner has seen in New Zealand a bleak landscape and an empty past, whilst Kendrick Smithyman (1922–) —*The Blind Mountain* (1950); *The Gay Trapeze* (1955)—has struggled with words to obtain a rigorousness of meaning rarely found in New Zealand poetry.

A.P.

NGUGI, James. See **African Literature.**

NICHOLSON, Norman (1914–), born in Cumberland, and educated at local schools, became a teacher in his native county. He established himself as a poet during the Second World War with his volume, *Five Rivers* (1944). Since then he has written other volumes of poetry and religious verse drama. He is often called, somewhat unfairly, a "regional" poet because he writes about the people and places of Cumberland. One of the virtues of his poetry is its particularity, the feeling it gives of palpable country life; but equally important is the religious feeling of his verse.

Rock Face, 1948.
The Pot Geranium, 1954.

O.K.

NORRIS, Frank (1870–1902), the naturalist novelist, was born in Chicago, then a great shock-city of American expansion, son of a well-off jeweler and an artistic mother. The family moved to San Francisco when Norris was fifteen; his parents then took him to Paris where he studied art. At this time the main artistic and literary influences were medieval-gothic ones; it was when he returned to study at Berkeley (1890–94) that he read Zola and was influenced by his literary ideas and the social theories of the Darwinists and Le Conte. In 1894, aided by his mother, he moved to Harvard to Professor Lewis Gates's writing class, working on two naturalistic novels, *McTeague* and *Vandover and the Brute*. From there he went as a correspondent to South Africa and then returned to San Francisco to join the staff of the literary journal, *The Wave*, for which he wrote pieces revealing his fashionable concern with theories about social advance and degeneration, evolution and the stratified, higher-and-lower nature of man and society. *McClure's* magazine sent him to report the Spanish-American war, and after this he returned to New York to work for Doubleday, the publishers. By this time he had published several novels, *Moran of the Lady Letty* (1898), *McTeague* (1899) and *Blix* (1899), mixing the stern naturalism of the second with the romance of the first and third. But after *A Man's Woman* (1900), a poor book, he reavowed naturalism: "I am going back *definitely* to the style of *McTeague* and stay with it right along." This led to his plan for a trilogy about the cultivation, marketing and consumption of wheat, a book that would cover California, Chicago and Europe and be concerned with global movements of life and force, the model of the aspiration being obviously Zola. *The Octopus* appeared in 1901; but in the following year Norris died of peritonitis. The second of the trilogy, *The Pit*, appeared posthumously (1903); the third, *The Wolf*, was never written. His early manuscript of *Vandover and the Brute* was rediscovered and also published posthumously, in 1914.

Norris's was an uneven yet startling achievement, an important contribution to the underlying vein of naturalism so powerful in the modern American novel. For this Norris and Dreiser, whom Norris discovered while working at Doubleday, are undoubted prime sources. His most important work lies in the two naturalist novels, *McTeague* and *Vandover and the Brute*, and the two volumes of the wheat epic. The first two—with their schematic plots of man's doubleness, their division of the world into civilized man and sensual counterpart, reason and instinct, upward striving and downward lapsing—distill Norris's naturalism. The wheat books are epic and social, rather than psychological and instinctual; they contrast individual lives with the larger operational processes of which they are a part, processes both inhuman and vitalistic (significantly, Norris sees the dynamic process as being not history, but nature itself in its regenerative cycle). All four are concerned with the naturalist obsession of relating men to large-scale, morally ambiguous fields of force; Norris was at one with many contemporaries in sensing a yielding of individualism and a consequent formal difficulty for art, which he discussed in *The Responsibilities of the Novelist*. He stressed the need for life, not art; the stress was both antiaesthetically concrete (like many naturalists he was a close documenter) and theoretical (life was particular sectors of human experience observable in certain appropriately scientific-experimental ways). Norris's best novels offer striking explorations of human sexuality and psychology (*McTeague, Vandover*) and of the social process, as shown in the struggles of the California farmers and the Chicago wheat traders (*The Octopus, The Pit*) in a time of entrepreneurial expansion, ruthless competition and the growth of impersonal technology like the railroad. They demonstrate an undercutting of human hope and pretension, yet, at the same time, a buoyant optimism and an Anglo-Saxon dream of a higher civilization, the processes controlled, the instincts commanded. His lighter novels show this last mood especially; in this respect he embodies an essential part of the expansionist spirit of the American 1890s. But so he does in the bleaker implications of the process-ridden naturalism for which he is now best remembered.

Moran of the Lady Letty, 1898.
McTeague, 1899 (*f.* as *Greed*, 1923).
Blix, 1899.
A Man's Woman, 1900.
The Octopus, 1901.
The Pit, 1903.
The Responsibilities of the Novelist, 1903.
A Deal in Wheat, 1903 (stories).
The Third Circle, 1909 (stories).
Vandover and the Brute, 1914.

Complete Works, 10 vols., Garden City, N.Y.: Doubleday, 1928.
Literary Criticism, ed. D. Pizer, Austin: Univ. of Texas Press, 1964.
Letters, ed. R. Walker, San Francisco: Book Club of California (limited edition), 1956.

M.B.

"NORTH, Christopher." See **Wilson, John.**

NORTH, Sir Thomas (?1535–?1601), second son of the first Lord North, may have been to Cambridge, was admitted to Lincoln's Inn (1557), later becoming a Cambridgeshire justice of the peace. One of the first great English translators and prose writers, North's earliest work was *The Dial of Princes* (1557), his version of Guevara's *Libro Aureo*. It was followed by *The Moral Philosophy of Doni* (from an Italian version of an Arabic book of fables) and *Plutarch's Lives*, one of the most influential sixteenth-century books and extensively used by Shakespeare. (See also **Renaissance Humanism.**)

Plutarch's Lives, ed. C. F. Tucker Brooke, 2 vols., London: Chatto & Windus (Shakespeare Library), 1909.

G.P.

NORTON, Thomas (1532–84), son of a wealthy citizen, may have studied at Cambridge, was at the Inner Temple (1555) and from 1558 was frequently a member of Parliament. He held several legal and political posts, sometimes overzealously. Norton's literary work includes Latin and English verse and a translation from Calvin, but he is remembered as coauthor (with Sackville) of the monotonous but historically important blank verse tragedy *Gorboduc* (1565; *p.* 1561), taken from Geoffrey of Monmouth and showing Seneca's influence.

Five Elizabethan Tragedies, ed. A. K. McIlwraith, London: Oxford Univ. Press, 1938.   G.P.

O

O'CASEY, Sean (1884–1964), youngest child of a Dublin family of seven, had three years of schooling in a Protestant school, but claimed to have been truly "educated in the streets of Dublin." He then became in turn errand boy, dock worker, building laborer, janitor and plasterer. At first interested in the Gaelic League, he learnt Irish and was known as "Irish Jack." He then became involved in the political struggles of the workers and joined the Irish Transport and General Workers' Union. In the Transport Workers' Strike of 1913 he ran a soup kitchen and became a close friend of Jim Larkin, the union leader. After this he enlisted in the Irish Citizen Army and as its secretary helped to formulate its constitution. A pamphlet, *The Story of the Irish Citizen Army* (1919), seriously began his literary career, while his experiences of the Easter Rebellion in 1916, when he himself narrowly escaped execution, provided the subject matter of his earliest and most successful plays. He began his association with the Abbey Theatre in 1919, but it was not until 1923 that the Abbey produced his play *The Shadow of a Gunman*, and in the next year *Juno and the Paycock*. The latter play deals with the civil war which followed the creation of the Irish Free State. In his third full-length play, *The Plough and the Stars*, he returned to the Rebellion of 1916 and brought upon himself all the prejudices of the different parties in Dublin society who refused to see themselves as O'Casey painted them. These plays were the finest ever produced by the Irish movement and probably the best that O'Casey himself wrote, but they caused such vilification of the playwright that in 1927, after marrying an actress of the Abbey, Eileen Reynolds, he left Ireland and went to England where he passed the rest of his days in voluntary exile.

Unfortunately the move from Ireland impaired the sense of immediacy in his plays and O'Casey now came to be for a time a symbolist playwright in the tradition of Strindberg and O'Neill. His political position moved further to the Left, he became a violent propagandist for pacifism, and his next play, *The Silver Tassie*, was rejected by the Abbey Theatre in 1928, largely on the advice of W. B. Yeats, who saw it as mere propaganda and badly constructed at that. O'Casey now turned his back on Ireland and *Within the Gates* (1933) provided him with the opportunity to expose the moral confusion of the European world in general. In still later plays O'Casey returned to the Irish scene and once more employed his great comic talents in ridiculing the sterility of Irish religious life (e.g., *Cock-a-*

Doodle Dandy and *The Bishop's Bonfire*). Against narrowness of religious and political creeds he constantly set the ideal of the full life lived in freedom and joy. *Behind the Green Curtains* (1961) attacks Dublin cultural life and different kinds of humbug. From 1939 onwards O'Casey produced a series of autobiographical volumes which are full of the flavor of Dublin and show the experimental character of O'Casey's writing, ranging from dramatic dialogue to nonstop soliloquy. Though there is a good deal of rant in these books and a fair amount of sentimentality, they never lack vitality and are in themselves important social documents for the period and for O'Casey's plays. Similar characteristics are shown in his critical essays, *The Flying Wasp* (1937) and *The Green Crow* (1956), which always have punch, though they often seem to be limited by the particularity of their reference.

The Story of the Irish Citizen Army, 1919 (political pamphlet).
The Shadow of a Gunman, 1925 (p. 1923).
Juno and the Paycock, 1925 (p. 1924).
The Plough and the Stars, 1926.
The Silver Tassie, 1928.
Within the Gates, 1933.
The Flying Wasp, 1937.
The Star Turns Red, 1940.
Red Roses for Me, 1942.
Cock-a-Doodle Dandy, 1949.
The Bishop's Bonfire, 1955.
The Green Crow, 1956.
Behind the Green Curtains, 1961 (3 plays).

Collected Plays, 4 vols., London: Macmillan, 1949–51.
Autobiographies (6 vols., 1939–54), 2 vols., New York: Macmillan Co., 1956; London: Macmillan, 1963.

E.H.R.

OCCLEVE, Thomas (?1368–?1450), was the most prominent, with Lydgate, of the Chaucerian school of poets. His work was printed less often and its full extent remains uncertain. His debt to Chaucer and Gower is acknowledged in the preface to his *De Regimine Principium*, a poem addressed to Henry, Prince of Wales (later Henry V). It is a partly political, partly ethical work with obvious debts to Aristotle and Solomon. Occleve also translated tales from the *Gesta Romanorum*, a kind of verse confession called *La Male Règle*, and an *Ars Sciendi Mori*, his finest poem. His most attractive trait is his propensity to self-revelation, which redeems his work from the tedious flatness of Lydgate.

Works, ed. F. J. Furnivall and I. Gollancz, 3 vols., London: Early English Text Society, 1892–1925.

A.N.M.

O'CONNOR, Flannery (1925–64) was born in Savannah (Georgia) and was educated in her native state and at the University of Iowa where she studied creative writing. Her first story, "Accent," was published in *The Kenyon Review* in 1946, and this was followed by regular appearances in prestigious journals. In her lifetime she published two novels—*Wise Blood* (1952) and *The Violent Bear It Away* (1960)—together with a collection of shorter fiction, *A Good Man Is Hard to Find and Other Stories* (1955). A further collection of short fiction, *Everything That Rises Must Converge*, appeared posthumously in 1965.

An orthodox Roman Catholic, she produced fiction that is God-ridden, grotesque and violent. Her range is narrow and her themes repetitious, but within her limitations she has a fine control of dialogue and symbol. She writes about man cut off from God's grace in a tawdry world, yet yearning for God and finding him through grotesque torments, sometimes comic in their extremes, and paradoxes (Hazel Motes, for example, in *Wise Blood*, burns out his eyes with quicklime in order that he might see). She writes about a world of fools, charlatans, killers and lunatics, in some ways reminiscent of Poe, yet her characters are always liable to be saved by God's inexplicable mercy.   I.W.

ODETS, Clifford (1906–63) was born in Philadelphia into a lower-middle-class Jewish family which later settled in the Bronx. A melancholy child, he left school at fourteen to become an actor. After working with the Theatre Guild, he became in 1930 a founder member of the Group Theatre. Odets needed a body of people to whom he could offer his talent, and his best work was written for the Group between 1932 and 1940.

He belonged to the Communist party for a mere eight months: he was neither a strictly Marxist writer nor a proletarian one, even in *Waiting for Lefty* (1935). Based on the New York taxi-drivers' strike of 1934, this fifty-minute play drew on agitprop and minstrel shows to express bitter feelings of frustration and oppression: ideology is subsidiary to the Constitutional demand for a better life. The cry of "Strike" at the end of the play was enthusiastically taken up by audiences; *Lefty* was banned in seven cities. In the same year Odets's *Awake and Sing!* focused on "a struggle for life amid petty conditions." Set in the Bronx during the Depression, it presented a decaying Jewish family, the Bergers, bewildered by contemporary dislocations and deprivations. Its members impinge on one another; social discontent emerges as personal animosity. But Jacob, the old Marxist, manages to inspire his grandson Ralph, not with party dogma, but with a vision of change and community. In this play, and in the similar *Paradise Lost*, Odets invokes the mythic world of comic strips and movies to express his sympathy for those anguished classes who, trapped by city and capitalism, cannot make dream and reality converge.

In 1936 Odets himself visited Hollywood and began an ambivalent relationship with the movie capital. He directed two feature films and adapted a number of works for the screen. Of the films he wrote, the best known are *Humoresque* (1947) and *Sweet Smell of Success* (1957). Several of his plays have been filmed, including *Golden Boy* (*f*. 1938) by Mamoulian. The original play traced the career of Joe Bonaparte, pulled between two careers as musician and boxer. His absurd belief in violence and total freedom ends logically in death—but the film ends happily. Odets's tense study of the desperate members of an emotional triangle, *Clash by Night* (1941), was filmed by Fritz Lang in 1952. Films were also made of the plays *The Country Girl* (produced in Britain as *Winter Journey*; *f*. 1954) and *The Big Knife* (*f*. 1955), itself a commentary on Hollywood as an industry with people as commodities. The play was incisive, but concluded in weary impotence, and in 1958 its author was writing the eulogy for Harry Cohn's funeral. Furthermore, in 1952, Odets had collaborated with the House Un-American Activities Committee.

His last play, *The Flowering Peach* (1955, abridged; *p*. 1954), used the legend of Noah to counsel compromise and acquiescence. After his last film in 1961 Odets moved into television work. He died in a Los Angeles hospital in 1963, nearly a year after telling a young journalist: "Don't do what I did. Don't screw it up." The achievement of the 1930s, some of the finest plays written in the U.S.A., remains.

Odets's plays, which show, in E. Mottram's words, "the awakening from loneliness into companionship and love," were not the work of a radical experimentalist. Like O'Casey, he owed something to the tradition of melodrama; his simple plots were vehicles for showing human feelings. Perhaps his greatest gift was his ear for language; he reproduced with accuracy the rapid, inventive, cynical talk of the city, yet he could also bring off the pious, sentimental insincerities of Marcus Hoff, the vicious, tyrannical producer in *The Big Knife*.

Six Plays, New York: Random House, 1939.

R.W.

O'HARA, Frank (1926–66) was born in Baltimore (Maryland) and educated at Harvard and University of Michigan. From 1951 he lived in New York where he worked as a curator at the Museum of Modern Art. His primary work was as a poet—*A City Winter and Other Poems* (1952), *Meditations in an Emergency* (1957), *Second Avenue* and *Odes* (both 1960), and *Lunch Poems* (1964). The long poem *Second Avenue* is typical: uninhibited, energetic, delighting in colloquialism and "deep images." O'Hara also published two plays, *Try! Try!* (1960) and *The General Returns from One Place to Another* (1966). His writings on art are also important, especially his book *Jackson Pollock* (1959) and his work in Museum of Modern Art exhibition catalogs on *Nakian* (1966), *New Spanish Painting and Sculpture: Rafael Canogar and Others* (1960) and *Robert Motherwell* (1965). He was killed by a car in 1966, "an innocent victim," said his friend, the painter Larry Rivers, "in someone else's war." J.P.W.

O'HARA, John (1905-70) was born in Pottsville (Pennsylvania) and worked on a variety of newspapers and magazines. Considerable expectations were aroused by his early novels like *Appointment in Samarra* (1934). This remains his most effective work in its painstakingly thorough creation of the world of the best families of Gibbsville, Pennsylvania. Its weakness, symptomatic of much that is wrong in O'Hara's later fiction, is the absence of any real complexity in its central character, Julian English. His later books, such as *Ten North Frederick* (1955; *f.* 1958), show some vitality as social commentary. They have vigor and life, but lack organized form and real human insight. Many critics feel that his short stories represent his finest work. D.V.W.

OKIGBO, Christopher. See **African Literature.**

OLD ENGLISH POETRY (before 1100). The reader who turns to Old English poetry for the pagan utterance of primitive Germanic forefathers will be disappointed. What has survived of the literature of the period is largely the product of one of the most civilized societies of the Europe of its day, and poets involved in its composition were both literate, in that they committed their work to writing, and Christian. For their poetic forms and some of their material, they drew, it is true, on the oral poetry of their Germanic heritage, but they blended with these the ideas and ideals of Christianity which had also formed part of their cultural heritage for some centuries. The mixture varies; in some poems—for example, the tale of Judith the tyrant slayer—the story is biblical and the telling very Germanic; in others—for example, that of Beowulf the giant slayer—the story is Germanic and the telling Christian.

The meter used, like that of English poetry of all centuries, is based on stress. The basic line has four main beats with a variable number of unstressed syllables; the line is divided centrally by a strong caesura, each half being linked again by alliteration of the stressed syllables. The half line normally contains a single syntactic unit, while long sentences of complicated structure bind together the otherwise disjointed and slow-moving verse. Many of the half lines are traditional, having been passed down for perhaps many centuries, and special effects may be gained by altering one element of a traditional phrase. Imagery is provided mainly by *kennings* or circumlocutory compounds—for example, "whale-road" for "sea."

Most of the poetry has been fortuitously preserved in four great codices copied around the year 1000. Opinions vary as to the date of composition, but it is unlikely to have been less than one century or as much as three centuries earlier. Few poems survive in more than one copy, and the inference of this, that a great many more have been lost, is borne out by the unlikelihood of poetry of the standard of the best of what remains having been composed in a vacuum. The poems fall somewhat uneasily into the categories "heroic," "religious" and "historical."

Characteristic of the heroic group is the reworking of traditional stories of the Germanic homeland. The width of knowledge of Germanic legend is indicated by *Widsith*, the listing by a minstrel of the famous heroes of the past he has figuratively seen and the many tribes he has visited in his imagination. In *Deor* similar material is used more constructively. The poet adopts the persona of a displaced minstrel and reminds his audience briefly of a series of Germanic figures, all of whom, with their physical and emotional suffering, have perished; so, the minstrel consoles himself, all hardship including his own is transitory and God-ordained. The power of the poem lies in its extreme brevity and in the refrain "That passed; this will too," which is repeated after each section except the one telling of God's power.

Beowulf is a narrative on epic scale, telling the story of the Geatish prince whose name gives the poem its title. The Geats were a Germanic tribe inhabiting what is now Götaland, the southern part of Sweden, and the tale is also concerned with the two neighboring tribes, the Swedes and the Danes. The action is built around the three fearsome single combats of Beowulf's life, the poem falling naturally into three sections: the first describes the growth of stability in the Danish state, the disruption of that stability by a monster, Grendel, and the killing of Grendel by the already famed warrior, Beowulf; the second tells of the revenge exacted by Grendel's mother, also monstrous, the terrible journey to seek her at her weird lair, her death encompassed by Beowulf with supernatural aid, and the triumphant return of the hero to his homeland; the final section concerns Beowulf's old age, when a dragon suddenly attacks the Geats after a long peaceful rule by Beowulf, now their king. In killing it he receives his death wound.

The structure of the poem is extremely involved, each section fitting into a closely organized and highly complex pattern. For example, the rest of the life story of Beowulf is revealed during the course of the very limited action through so-called digressions, principally speeches of the protagonists. These also tell of the lives of other Germanic heroes and villains, many of whom are mentioned in *Widsith* and *Deor*, and thus the poet dramatizes and quietly comments upon many facets of heroic society which survived in Anglo-Saxon England—honor, treachery, pride, folly, divided loyalties, noble deaths, disastrous warfare. Although the whole social structure of the "heroic age" is realized for an audience whose own civilization was already far removed from that described in Tacitus's *Germania*, it is also cunningly modernized. Many of the characters involved in the action are historical figures of the early sixth century who in their day were pagan, as the poet is quite well aware, though he makes them Christian. Grendel is a fiend from Hell, the enemy of God as well as of mankind, and Beowulf defeats him with God-given strength. "The Lord giveth and the Lord taketh away," starkly expressed in *Deor*, is a motif running through the whole of *Beowulf*. As in *Deor*, the poet is giving traditional material universal significance; he draws together countless threads of the Germanic legend clearly familiar to his Anglo-Saxon audience, and out of them weaves a tale of how a man is to live in the world. Beowulf uses his superhuman strength to fight supernatural creatures, and the merely human reader, whether ancient or modern, gains from his story something of what he gains from that of Achilles or of Lear.

The *Fight at Finnsburg* is a mere fragment of a heroic poem, the tragic subject of which is mentioned in *Beowulf* also. The fragment gives us a glimpse of a very exciting battle scene, perhaps the liveliest and fastest-moving of all the fight descriptions in Old English.

The "lyrical elegies" are a group of short poems on the themes of exclusion and transience; they utilize a heroic background for homiletic comments on the lot of the Christian and invite comparison with *Deor*. All offer some difficulties of interpretation but the more famous of them, *The Wanderer* and *The Seafarer*, contain lyric passages which even after the lapse of a thousand years make an immediate impact on the reader. These two poems portray most vividly the lot of a man thrust voluntarily or involuntarily outside the bounds of society, *The Wanderer* telling of the sufferings of a man excluded from the social system by the loss of his lord and protector, a situation which should encourage men to turn to the protection of the eternal Lord, and *The Seafarer* showing a man embracing the difficulties of the solitary life at sea since the joys on land, like all earthly joys, are transitory. Reminiscent of these is *The Ruin*, a moving description of a decayed city. Here, however, the poet's imaginative realization of the city alive and peopled introduces a regret at the ravages of time which also appears in passages of *Beowulf* but which is not so evident in the other elegies.

Rather more obscure are the two poems, *The Wife's Complaint* and *The*

Husband's Message. The first is the bewailing of a woman separated from her loved one; the second is a message of comfort to a loved one from someone far away. Some of the difficulties may be explained if we take the poems as types of riddle and assume that the surface meaning is not the most important. Nearly a hundred Anglo-Saxon poetic riddles survive; they are for the most part literary exercises, probably in imitation of Latin riddles, but the obvious popularity of the form may have had an effect on other genres. The enigmatic poem, *Wulf and Eadwacer*, has been interpreted as a riddle, but appears to be a dramatic monologue. It is related to *The Wife's Lament* and *The Husband's Message* by its apparent subject matter, a woman separated from her husband, and to *Deor* by the slight appearance of a refrain.

Two distinct groups of religious poems are evident, named after the two poets of the period known to us by name: Caedmon and Cynewulf. Caedmonian poetry seems to have evolved earlier, since Bede tells, in his eighth-century *Historia Ecclesiastica Gentis Anglorum*, that the first poet to sing of God in English was Caedmon, an otherwise undistinguished lay-brother in a seventh-century monastery at Whitby. Only nine lines of Caedmon's poetry survive, but we are told that he specialized in versifying biblical paraphrase. Such paraphrase does survive in poems like *Genesis*, *Exodus* and *Daniel*, called "Caedmonian," though not now felt to be by Caedmon himself. They are not close paraphrases, the poets having selected and expanded themes from the Old Testament which appealed to them, particularly descriptions of battles and the sea. One section of *Genesis* is an interpolated translation of an Old Saxon poem; officially called *Genesis B* or *The Later Genesis*, it is better known in its anthologized form as *The Fall of the Angels*, and tells of the war in Heaven and the creation and fall of Adam and Eve. The story has a superficial affinity with that of *Paradise Lost*, as both are based on the exegetical tradition. As in Milton's poem, the personality of Satan is of great importance, and he appears here as one of the best delineated characters of Old English poetry. Associated with Caedmonian poetry is the late (perhaps tenth-century) poem, *Judith*, of which only the last part remains. Here a Hebrew story has been retold in Germanic guise, with Judith herself awarded the attributes of a Germanic heroine. Again a battle scene is very prominent.

Proof of the literacy of Old English poets is offered by Cynewulf. Four poems exist "signed" with this name in an acrostic of runes, the pre-Christian letters used by the Germanic peoples, but we have no further knowledge of the poet's life or works. Whereas Caedmonian poets were fired by Hebrew stories to which Christianity introduced them, Cynewulf's poetry with its more mystic element is concerned with Christ and his followers. Of the signed poems, *Christ*, in the section definitely written by Cynewulf, deals with the Ascension; *The Fates of the Apostles* is a brief versified catalog of the lives of the Apostles; and the last two are lives of Saints Juliana and Helena (spelt *Elene* in Old English). Many other poems with similar characteristics form the Cynewulfian school. There are, for example, lives of two more saints: *Andreas* (St. Andrew), the most interesting feature of which is the occurrence of close verbal parallels with *Beowulf*, and *Guthlac*, the life of a popular native saint, a number of versions of which exist in verse and prose.

But the pride of the poetry of Cynewulfian spirit is *The Dream of the Rood*, an account of a vision in which Christ's Cross appears to tell its own story. The contemporary interest in the Cross is suggested by *Elene*, which tells of the finding of the true Cross by the saint, but Cynewulf's signed poem shows far less imagination and has a much more limited appeal today than *The Dream of the Rood*. A large part of the latter's success lies in its essential simplicity. The dreamer is a modest man of humble status, in need of "friends in high places," telling his "most extraordinary dream" in simple, unadorned language. The Cross, too, shows itself of humble origin, yet honored above other trees; through its speech, the longest part of the poem, it offers the reaction of an honest, open individual to the earthshaking events of the Crucifixion. Thus, linguistically, the poem is one of the easiest of the Old English remains to understand, the poet's conception giving the mundane phraseology great poetic force.

Of the many other religious poems which survive, the one most deserving of mention is perhaps *The Phoenix*, a quiet and graceful allegorical tale adapted from a classical source and infused with the mixture of heroic and Christian ideals so typical of the period.

Poetry on historical themes offers external evidence of dating, and mainly survives from the tenth century. Most of the poems in this category are incorporated in *The Anglo-Saxon Chronicle* (see **Old English Prose**); they are for the most part eulogies on dead kings, but a notable exception is *The Battle of Brunanburh*, which celebrates with great exuberance the English victory of 937 over the Scots and the Norse Vikings. In contrast is a late poem outside the *Chronicle* tradition "celebrating" an English defeat by Danish Vikings in 991. *The Battle of Maldon*, surviving in imperfect form, attempts to salvage a moral victory from a disastrous battle by portraying heroism in defeat. The English leader, Byrhtnoth, having cornered the Danes, allows them to move into a more favorable position and is slain in the subsequent battle. Many of the English flee, but the more heroic stay to die in the attempt to avenge their lord. The poet is torn between the nobility of Byrhtnoth's action and its tactical folly, but his condemnation of those who flee is unequivocal and his celebration of the qualities of the faithful provides the last and most complete exposition in Old English of the Germanic heroic relationship between lord and retainer.

With the defeat at Maldon Old English poetry died symbolically. Very little verse has survived from the eleventh century, and with the coming of the Normans the English-speaking aristocratic class, for whom poetry was composed, was destroyed. The form, like the language, survived the conquest, to be used with such consummate skill centuries later by the writers of *Piers Plowman* and *Sir Gawain and the Green Knight*, but the stately, laconic, convoluted verse was never successfully repeated after 1066.

Anglo-Saxon Poetic Records, ed. G. P. Krapp and E. van K. Dobbie, 6 vols., London: Routledge; New York: Columbia Univ. Press, 1931–53.
Beowulf, ed. Fr. Klaeber, Boston: Heath, 3rd edition, revised, 1950.

There is a close translation of *The Battle of Maldon and Other Old English Poems* by K. Crossley-Holland, ed. B. Mitchell, London: Macmillan; New York: St. Martin's Press, 1965, and a freer one, *The Earliest English Poems*, by M. Alexander, Harmondsworth: Penguin, 1966. *Beowulf* is also translated by E. T. Donaldson, New York: Norton, 1967 and G. N. Garmonsway and J. Simpson, London: Dent, 1968; New York: Dutton, 1969.

D.G.S.

OLD ENGLISH PROSE (before 1100).

The earliest extant English prose was composed in the reign of, and under the auspices of, Alfred, king of Wessex from 871 to 899. In a letter circulated to his bishops about 896, Alfred bewailed the decline of Latin scholarship in England, and told of his plans to revive learning by translating into English certain books which he considered "most necessary for all men to know." Six major translations survive from this period, and a number of fragments. Alfred himself certainly translated Gregory the Great's *Regula Pastoralis* and Boethius's *De Consolatione Philosophiae*, was probably responsible for St. Augustine's *Soliloquia*, and possibly for Orosius's *Historia*; the others are Gregory's *Dialogi*, translated by Bishop Werferth of Worcester, and Bede's *Historia Ecclesiastica Gentis Anglorum*. The translations are by and large free, with numerous omissions and interpolations. Though the prose is immature, often stilted and cumbersome, it has lively intervals and offered a firm foundation for the great masters who were to acknowledge their debt to Alfred a century later.

Another important prose work associated with Alfred, since it appears to have been founded in his reign, is *The Anglo-Saxon Chronicle*, an annalistic history of the English which becomes a contemporary or near-contemporary account from the end of the ninth century to the middle of the twelfth. Five versions survive from different parts of the kingdom, each containing some common material but with individual entries relating more specifically to the area of origin. The work of the many anonymous writers involved shows something of the development of prose style during the Old English period, from the stark, factual entries of the earliest phase and the first attempts at storytelling (as in 755 with its unfortunate ellipsis and ambiguity of pronouns) to the clear narrative style of the tenth century and the polished elegance of the eleventh. Under the surface narration of events one feels the pride in the victories of Alfred, the impotence in the calamities under Ethelred, the anger at the indignities offered to Englishmen under the Confessor and the Conqueror. The passion, narrative power and subtlety of tone of much Old English didactic prose reappear in the *Chronicle* entries with the added force of a subject based on contemporary events.

Most of the extant Old English literature, copied and preserved as it was within the monasteries, is religious, and, not unnaturally perhaps, translations of the Bible are prominent. One of the most effective is a late tenth-century version of the Gospels, a powerful and majestic rendering, not at all oppressed by the Latin original. From this period also survive translations of many of the books of the Old Testament, some of them by Abbot Aelfric, the greatest of the Old English prose writers.

Aelfric's name survives as a homilist rather than a translator, by far the majority of the many hundreds of homilies still extant from the period being his. Born early in the second half of the tenth century, educated at Winchester, he spent the years from about 987 to 1005 writing in the monastery of Cerne Abbas (Dorset) and was then made first abbot of Eynsham (Oxfordshire). He died between 1010 and 1020. The earliest of his extremely popular homilies were arranged in two series with about forty in each (the *Catholic Homilies*), the first completed at Cerne about 991, the second probably in 992. A third somewhat shorter series, *The Lives of the Saints*, was issued about 998, and more followed. His style developed considerably during his lifetime, the alliterative technique so much associated with him appearing as an ornamental feature in the second series and becoming a regular and most effective part of the rhetoric in *The Lives of the Saints*. Outside homiletic writing Aelfric's work is very varied, his best known being two works designed to teach pupils Latin—a Latin grammar in English, and a *Colloquy* or series of conversations in Latin which was later provided (not by him) with an English gloss which has become a famous example of Old English dialogue.

Aelfric's prose is elegant, mature, restrained, invariably unambiguous, and free from the awkward Latinisms which bedevil the Alfredian translations. Throughout his work Aelfric is teaching, explaining, expounding, yet he does so without condescension, and with a moderation and humanity which make him and his work most attractive, even today when didacticism and his particular religious attitudes are out of favor.

A number of pre-Aelfrician homilies survive, notably in two manuscripts, the Vercelli Book and the Blickling Manuscript. All are anonymous and show no consistency of style, although those in Blickling are mainly admonitions which dwell on the horrors of Hell and the Day of Judgment. Other than Aelfric himself, the only great homilist of the period known to us by name is his contemporary, Wulfstan. Less prolific than Aelfric, being known for a mere twenty-two homilies (perhaps because he was so much engaged in active politics), Wulfstan was trained as a Benedictine monk, became bishop of London in 996, and held the archbishopric of York in plurality with Worcester from 1002; he died in 1023. Though he served the Dane Canute as adviser when the latter became king of England in 1016, Wulfstan is best remembered as a champion of English defense against the Danish attacks in the reign of Ethelred the Unready, and his principal surviving monument is the classic *Sermo Lupi ad Anglos*, a raging torrent against the cowardice, treachery and ungodliness which was allowing the English state to be brought to its knees.

Prose works in many fields survive from eleventh-century England, demonstrating the versatility and vitality of the medium. Of particular interest to students of literature is *Apollonius of Tyre*, the earliest telling in English of the story which Shakespeare was to use in *Pericles*. *Apollonius* is a tale of love and adventure of the type which was popular in verse in later centuries. Written with delicacy, humor and sureness of touch, it links the literature of the Old English period firmly with that of later centuries, and contributes to the view that native prose before the Norman Conquest had a greater range and subtlety of expression than English prose was again to display for over half a millennium.

The Early English Text Society has published most of the Alfredian and much Aelfrician material.

The Homilies of the Anglo-Saxon Church, trans. and ed. B. Thorpe, 2 vols., London: Aelfric Society, 1844–46.
The Anglo-Saxon Chronicle, trans. and ed. B. Thorpe, 2 vols., London: Rolls Series, 1861.
The Wulfstan Canon, ed. D. Bethurum, Oxford: Clarendon Press, 1957.
Apollonius, ed. P. Goolden, London: Oxford Univ. Press, 1958.   D.G.S.

OLDHAM, John (1653–83), son of a clergyman, was educated at Tetbury (Gloucestershire) and at St. Edmund Hall, Oxford. After graduating in 1674 he spent a year with his father before reluctantly holding a succession of teaching posts, first at Whitgift's School, Croydon, and subsequently in the households of Sir Edward Thurland and Sir William Hicks. After a period of living independently in London and studying medicine, his health deteriorated and Oldham accepted the

Nottinghamshire hospitality of the earl of Kingston. At his early death from smallpox the many tributes included Dryden's fine elegy, justly commending the satirical verses which earned Oldham the title of "the English Juvenal."

Poems, ed. B. Dobrée, London: Centaur Press; Carbondale: Southern
Illinois Univ. Press, 1960.   H.N.D.

OLSON, Charles (1910–70) was born in Worcester (Massachusetts). His family moved to Gloucester, on the coast, while the poet was still a child, and it is from this old seaport town that his work radiates as from a steady location of his basic geography and history. His university studies accumulated at Wesleyan, Yale and Harvard, and he taught at various colleges and held a number of mainly outdoor jobs, as well as working for the Democratic party during the F. D. Roosevelt campaign for a fourth term.

His dedication to literature begins with research into the work of Herman Melville, a writer whose work deeply concerned him for the rest of his career. Olson recovered a major part of Melville's library and studied materials which had hitherto been ignored. The results are mainly recorded in *Call Me Ishmael* (1947), a major work on the great author. In the 1940s Olson began his important teaching at Black Mountain College, North Carolina, of which he later became rector. Here he instigated programs of education designed to place poetry centrally in any curriculum of the media and the arts. In 1950 he began field researches in Yucatan, the results of which may be seen in *Mayan Letters* (1953), a work which moves from Mayan culture to general cultural considerations. From these years also dates the correspondence with Cid Corman on the nature of a poetry magazine, which appeared in 1969 as *Letters for Origin*, and a highly influential collection of essays, including the important "Projective Verse," published in 1965 as *Human Universe and Other Essays*. His poetry, at once deeply personal and committed to an epic scope which includes the migratory movements and the mythologies of the earth's peoples, is found in *In Cold Hell, In Thicket* (1953), *The Distances* (1960), *The Maximus Poems* (1960), *The Maximus Poems IV, V, VI* (1968) and *Archaeologist of Morning* (1970). Olson was not only a major poet but a theorist and teacher of penetrating influence.

A Bibliography on America for Ed Dorn, 1964.
Charles Olson Reading at Berkeley, 1966.
The Special View of History, ed. A. Charters, 1970.
Poetry and Truth: The Beloit Lectures and Poems, 1971.

Selected Writings, ed. R. Creeley, Norfolk, Conn.: New Directions, 1967.
                                                                   E.M.

O'NEILL, Eugene (1888–1953) was born in New York City, the son of the actor James O'Neill, originally a competent Shakespearean but eventually typecast in a dramatic version of *The Count of Monte Cristo*. In his early years Eugene moved between the family home in New London (Connecticut), preparatory school and his father's road companies. He left Princeton after a short time and was early introduced to New York City bohemian life by his older brother. His first marriage was opposed by both families and ended quickly in an arranged divorce, after which O'Neill shipped out and gained the experience of the sea he exploited in his early plays. In New York in 1912 he was present at the performances given by the Abbey Theatre of Dublin on their first American tour, and during a period of convalescence at a tuberculosis sanatorium his aspirations as a playwright crystallized. He was accepted as a special student at Harvard, where he attended Professor George Pierce Baker's famous Drama Workshop. Still living on the fringes of Greenwich Village artistic life, O'Neill was introduced to a small band of theatrical devotees hoping to develop a season of avant-garde theater in the summer resort town of Provincetown (Massachusetts). O'Neill became their great discovery, and as the Provincetown Players the group also established itself in New York City. O'Neill's earlier works, of which the best is *Bound East for Cardiff*, were one-act plays in a theatrical tradition of mixed naturalism and expressionism; Strindberg was his master. Many were set at sea or in New England farm communities and exploited provincialism and characters from the lower depths.

Gradually, from *Beyond the Horizon* (written 1918) to *The Hairy Ape* (written 1921), *Desire under the Elms* (written 1924) and *Strange Interlude* (written 1926–27), his plays lengthened until he was conceiving immense sagas of New England family history, like *Mourning Becomes Electra* (1931), a trilogy of plays, and the vast uncompleted cycles of his later years, of which *Long Day's Journey into Night* (1956) and *A Touch of the Poet* (1957) are examples. During these years O'Neill was indisputably the major writer of American drama and, though his stature as a "literary" figure was much in dispute, he was possibly the only American dramatist before the Second World War who stands comparison with contemporary European figures from Kaiser and Toller to Samuel Beckett. In 1930 he became the first American to receive the Nobel Prize for literature, which he accepted graciously as the European recognition of American art generally. In 1927 O'Neill left his second wife, Agnes Boulton, for the actress Carlotta Monterey, whom he married; together they lived in deepening seclusion. This phase of detachment was marked by the writing of some of his most grandiose dramas, by a gradual withdrawal from theater life—there was no new play by O'Neill produced between

1935 and 1946—and by the onset of the long disease which progressively reduced his motor activity.

The early one-act plays are characterized by their down-and-out settings and by the sharp contrast between the sordid existences and half-inarticulable transcendental longings of the protagonists. In a characteristic play they reminisce in agony over wasted chances and make promises one knows they cannot keep. *Anna Christie* (1922) has as its subject the maunderings of a self-deluding Scandinavian scow captain who does not realize that the daughter who has returned to him has declined from housemaid to prostitute. Anna herself is a character of great vitality, as are others of O'Neill's women characters—Abby in *Desire under the Elms*, Nina Leeds in *Strange Interlude* and Lavinia Mannon in *Mourning Becomes Electra*. Each has a streak of self-destructiveness and the conditions of their lives are never sufficient to assuage their passionate undirected intensity. Like Samson, they "grope the temple's posts in spight." O'Neill's men are often weaker characters, whose regressive search for oblivion is seen in returns to the mother or the bottle. O'Neill is a romantic tragedian to the extent that his protagonists, men and women, live in a universe where life is itself the crime, where some essential organic bond has been shattered by the advent of self-consciousness (or of consciousness itself) and where lives are lived in agonies of incompleteness and cross-purposes. There is only a nirvana that never comes as the promised end. It is difficult to determine whether O'Neill was himself categorically possessed of this myth or whether his plays are pointing to the tragic frustrations of life lived by characters who themselves believe it.

Arguments about O'Neill's more narrowly literary abilities have often centered on his structural capabilities and his use of language. He has been disparaged for the gigantism of many of his later plays, both in structural and philosophical pretension. A domesticated, realistic theater was uneasy with plays patently about the secrets and meaning of life, like *Lazarus Laughed* (1927) and *Days without End* (1934). It is well to remember, however, his mastery of the short form from *Bound East* to the late play, *Hughie* (1959), a masterpiece of controlled vernacular poetry. Whether he dealt with the semiarticulate or the philosophizing intellectual, O'Neill was dogged by critical opinion that he was a clumsy stylist. The halting speech, however, is a function of characterization. Though some awkwardness will always hang over this aspect of O'Neill's work, there are also incandescent verbal occasions as when Lavinia Mannon says, "I forgive myself." *The Emperor Jones* (1921) has a consistent verbal pattern of imagery concerning money and chicanery which is in poetic service to the thematic material. *Hughie* also refutes arguments about O'Neill's supposed inability to use language with poetic intensity, beyond that implied by the phrase, "the purple patch." It is necessary to realize that words were understood by O'Neill as only one of many dimensions of the dramatic, which included situation, atmosphere and action, and at times words are less relevant to the theatrical experience than the drama of tortured and anguished interpersonal and intrapsychic encounters.

Bound East for Cardiff, 1916.
The Long Voyage Home, 1917 (*f*. 1940).
The Moon of the Caribbees, 1918; revised, 1919.
Beyond the Horizon, 1920.
The Emperor Jones, 1921 (*p*. 1920; *f*. 1933).
Anna Christie, 1922 (*p*. 1921; *f*. 1923; 1930).
The Hairy Ape, 1922 (*f*. 1944).
Welded, 1924.
All God's Chillun Got Wings, 1924.
Desire under the Elms, 1925 (*p*. 1924; *f*. 1957).
The Great God Brown, 1926.
Lazarus Laughed, 1927 (*p*. 1928).
Strange Interlude, 1928 (*f*. 1932).
Mourning Becomes Electra, 1931 (*f*. 1948).
Ah, Wilderness!, 1933 (*f*. 1935).
The Iceman Cometh, 1946 (written 1939).
A Moon for the Misbegotten, 1952 (*p*. 1947).
Long Day's Journey into Night, 1956 (*f*. 1962).
A Touch of the Poet, 1957.
Hughie, 1959 (*p*. 1958).

Plays, 16 vols., London: Cape, 1922–62.   A.G.

ORD, Mrs. See **Bluestockings.**

ORTON, Joe (1933–67) was born in Leicester. A short but checkered career included a prison sentence for defacing library books. He wrote three full-length comedies, *Entertaining Mr. Sloane* (1964), *Loot* (1967: *p*. 1966) and *What the Butler Saw* (1969), as well as *The Ruffian on the Stair* (1964) for radio and *The Erpingham Camp* (1966) for television, both of which were adapted in 1967 for the stage. All Orton's plays bear his own distinctive style, part shocking, part deceptively innocent and often very funny. His characters discuss violence, perversion and death in tones that vary between naïve amorality and genteel outrage. If the absence of overt social comment is a marked one, his lasting quality may well lie in the uncritical picture that he offers of his time, distorted certainly but eminently recognizable.   J.M.W.

"**ORWELL, George**" was the pseudonym of Eric Arthur Blair (1903–50). Born in Bengal of middle-class but not rich parents, on returning to England he was sent to a preparatory school on a semicharitable basis. He loathed the situation, a loathing that comes out clearly in a later autobiographical work, *Such, Such Were the Joys*. Nevertheless, he duly won the scholarship expected of him and moved on to the more congenial atmosphere of Eton. Always a strange mixture of opposites and always doing the unexpected, he went—an Eton king's scholar—not to Oxford or Cambridge, but to Burma as a policeman in the Imperial Service that both repelled and fascinated him. The fascination is indicated in the love-hate relationship he had for most of his life with writers like Rudyard Kipling, the repulsion in the fine essays "Shooting an Elephant" and "A Hanging," and in the character of one of his many *alter egos*, Flory, the hero of *Burmese Days*. In 1927 he came home on leave and never went back.

For the next few years he led a rootless existence, sometimes making brief excursions into the money world—working in a bookshop and school, writing the occasional poem, article or review—but never getting more than a step or two from utter destitution. Why this happened to him is a matter of debate, and Orwell himself provided more than one explanation; but what is certain is that, without the experience, *Down and Out in Paris and London* and the novels *A Clergyman's Daughter* and *Keep the Aspidistra Flying* would never have been written.

By 1936 Orwell, better known but as unpredictable as ever, was commissioned to report on the depressed social conditions in the northern industrial areas. He produced *The Road to Wigan Pier*, a work so critical of the left-wing intelligentsia that it became one of the strangest books ever to come from the politically active Left Book Club. His next assignment was as a reporter in the Spanish Civil War. Orwell stayed to fight; he was wounded, and he wrote, on his return, *Homage to Catalonia*, a book which still has power to move by its idealism and the quality of its first-hand reporting.

Convinced, after Spain, that the forces of totalitarianism were on the move and that the larger war was coming, Orwell had time to write one more novel, *Coming Up for Air*, full of nostalgia for the past and forebodings for the future. Yet, ironically, the Second World War was to be Orwell's most productive period. He reported and reviewed for many papers, including *The Manchester Evening News* and *The Observer*; he contributed to many journals; he broadcast in the BBC's foreign service; he produced some of his most memorable literary and popular essays; and he wrote his one undoubted masterpiece, *Animal Farm*, a satire on the lure of totalitarianism so taut in construction, so perfect in the working out of the fable, as to ensure his survival on the strength of this work alone.

By the end of the war Orwell's health, always precarious, began to break down and this, as he himself admitted, was partly responsible for the unrelieved gloom and pessimism of his final work, *Nineteen Eighty-Four*, a horrifying vision of the future world of violence and power in which the individual spirit is completely crushed. The book had some importance in crystallizing the immediate postwar mood, but it is not the most typical of Orwell's works. He died of tuberculosis in 1950.

By both what he stood for as a man and a writer, Orwell became an important influence after his death. The simple directness of his style, his honesty, nonconformity, commonsense approach to life, distrust of intellectual pretension, ability to expose the sham and meretricious, were all qualities much admired, particularly in the 1950s.

(See also **Essays; Political Pamphlets; Science Fiction.**)

Down and Out in Paris and London, 1933.
Burmese Days, 1934.
A Clergyman's Daughter, 1935.
Keep the Aspidistra Flying, 1936.
The Road to Wigan Pier, 1937.
Homage to Catalonia, 1938.
Coming Up for Air, 1939.
Inside the Whale, 1940.
Animal Farm, 1945 (*f.* 1954).
Critical Essays, 1946.
Nineteen Eighty-Four, 1949 (*f.* 1956).
Shooting an Elephant, 1950.
Such, Such Were the Joys, 1953.

Collected Essays, Journals and Letters, ed. S. Orwell and I. Angus, 4 vols., London: Secker & Warburg; New York: Harcourt, Brace, 1968.

D.W.C.

OSBORNE, John (1929–   ) turned to acting as a career after brief spells as a journalist and tutor. While working in provincial repertory theaters he wrote several plays in collaboration before *Look Back in Anger* was accepted for production in May 1956 by George Devine's English Stage Company at the Royal Court Theatre, where the majority of Osborne's later plays received their first London performances. He subsequently wrote for television (*A Subject of Scandal and Concern*), worked with Tony Richardson in Woodfall Films and has continued to act and direct from time to time.

Osborne's work is uneven and he is less of an innovator than has sometimes been supposed. Although *Look Back in Anger* certainly provided the initial impulse for the fitful renaissance in English drama which is still in progress, it has, in retrospect, the ill-disguised features of a "well-made play," as Osborne subsequently acknowledged. When he has been influenced by current vogues, such as Brechtian or "epic" theater (in *The Entertainer* and *Luther*), the influences have not always been well assimilated and do not seem to have persisted. *Time Present* and *The Hotel in Amsterdam* are little more than conversation pieces which the actors must labor to support; *A Patriot for Me*, his most formal play, verges on the melodramatic; *The World of Paul Slickey* was a disastrous attempt at contemporary satire, noteworthy for a number of extremely banal lyrics. What distinguishes all Osborne's work, however, is honesty of purpose and vehemence of attack. Belligerent, quixotic, contradictory, Osborne has charged most of the windmills of emotional complacency in an effort to give his audiences "lessons in feeling," and his battles with the press, the "establishment" and the censor have helped to perpetuate the cant title of "Angry Young Man" earned for him by *Look Back in Anger*. Despite its traditional form, this play shattered most of the then received ideas about the scope of English drama and it lambasted precisely that Aunt Edna whom Rattigan had elevated as the doyenne of the middle-class audience. With *The Entertainer*, *Look Back in Anger* remains, perhaps, its author's most memorable work, certainly his most influential. Both plays center upon powerful studies of character. Jimmy Porter and Archie Rice are preeminent in the catalog of Osborne's creations; they are immediate and vital, and above all else they exhibit on-stage that sort of authenticity which is the hallmark of dramatic writing of the highest quality.

Look Back in Anger, 1957 (*p.* 1956; *f.* 1959).
The Entertainer, 1957 (*f.* 1960).
Epitaph for George Dillon (with Anthony Creighton), 1958 (*p.* 1957).
The World of Paul Slickey, 1959.
Luther, 1961.
A Subject of Scandal and Concern, 1961 (*p.* TV 1970).
Plays for England (*The Blood of the Bambergs; Under Plain Cover*), 1963 (*p.* 1962).
Inadmissible Evidence, 1964 (*f.* 1969).
A Patriot for Me, 1965.
A Bond Honoured, 1966.
Time Present (*p.* 1967) and *The Hotel in Amsterdam*, 1968.
West of Suez, 1971.

D.H.R.

OTWAY, Thomas (1652–85) was born in Sussex, where his father was curate at Trotton. In 1654 the family probably moved to Yorkshire, but returned at the Restoration and in 1668, after trying for three years, Otway entered Winchester College, proceeding to Christ Church, Oxford in 1669. Although well thought of, he had to leave after the death of his father in 1671, and a life of hardship and despondency followed. In London he wasted at least two years before turning to writing for the stage; his first play, *Alcibiades*, appeared in 1675. He failed as an actor, and military service in Flanders (1678–79) proved financially unrewarding. The final years of hardship, sickness and mounting debts, probably aggravated by excessive drinking and debauchery, culminated in an early death, of which there are many contradictory accounts.

Elizabeth Barry's and Rochester's treatment of Otway contributed to his misery. Otway's unrequited love for Mrs. Barry, who acted in many of his plays, is revealed in his passionate love letters. She was Rochester's mistress, and although Otway dedicated two plays to Rochester, the latter ruthlessly satirized him. Otway replied in his autobiographical *The Poet's Complaint*.

Otway's ten plays include comedies and adaptations from Racine and Molière, but better known are three tragedies—*Don Carlos, Prince of Spain* (1676), acclaimed at the time and reminiscent of *Othello, The Orphan* (1680), a domestic tragedy tending towards the sentimental, and *Venice Preserved* (1682), a grandiose, somber and compelling play. The last two remained in the repertoire into the nineteenth century.

Alcibiades, 1675.
Don Carlos, Prince of Spain, 1676.
The Orphan; or, The Unhappy Marriage, 1680.
Venice Preserved; or, A Plot Discovered, 1682.

Works, ed. J. C. Ghosh, 2 vols., Oxford: Clarendon Press, 1932. H.N.D.

OVERBURY, Sir Thomas (1581–1613) was murdered for his opposition to the marriage of his patron Robert Carr, viscount Rochester, and the countess of Essex. His poem *A Wife* (1614) is mainly valued for the *Characters* appended to the first and expanded in succeeding editions. While retaining many features of the rhetorical Theophrastan "character," his work was less objective, more dramatic and occasionally overdependent on wit and innuendo. Yet his strong sense of fact and locality was instrumental in directing the development of the English "character" towards its use as a sociopolitical propaganda weapon in the Civil War.

The Overburian Characters, ed. W. J. Paylor, Oxford: Blackwell, 1936.
A.W.B.

OWEN, Wilfred (1893–1918), born at Oswestry (Shropshire), was educated at the Birkenhead Institute and London University. He lived in France for some time, and was a private tutor with a French family. He enlisted in the Artists' Rifles in 1915, was commissioned in the Manchester Regiment and saw much action before he was invalided home in June 1917. He spent four months at Craiglockhart military hospital, where Siegfried Sassoon encouraged his already growing feelings against the war and his desire to write about them. Towards the end of the war he returned to France as a company commander, was awarded the Military Cross in October and killed on 4 November 1918.

Owen's war poetry is a powerful indictment of modern warfare. This power stems from a horrified imagination which never overwhelms a selfless compassion or a growing mastery of the resources of language. In poems such as "Exposure" and "Strange Meeting" Owen found a maturity of expression which readers of his talented but ordinary pre-war verse could never have foreseen. Few of his poems were published during his lifetime, and no collected volume appeared until Sassoon's 1920 edition, but they have made a lasting impression on readers ever since.

(See also **War Poets.**)

Poems, with introduction by S. Sassoon, 1920.

Collected Poems, ed. C. Day Lewis, memoir by E. Blunden, London: Chatto & Windus, 1963; Norfolk, Conn.: New Directions, 1964.

A.Y.

P

PAGE, Thomas Nelson (1853–1922) was born in Virginia. He employed Negro dialect, not only in early poems (such as "Uncle Gabe's White Folks") but also in prose works. "Marse Chan" (1881) is a typical example of his many sentimental tales of plantation life, collected in *In Ole Virginia* (1887). The relationship between the white and Negro races and his belief in white supremacy represent the principal materials of his writings and lecture tours. *Red Rock* (1898), a novel, gives a Southern view of Reconstruction, but is marred by vicious stereotyping. He led an active social and political life, later being ambassador in Italy from 1913 to 1919.

Novels, Stories, Sketches and Poems, Plantation edition, 18 vols., New York: C. Scribner's Sons, 1906–12.

R.W.

PAINE, Thomas (1737–1809) was born at Thetford (Norfolk) into a Quaker family. Dissatisfied with conditions in England, in 1774 he went to America and there wrote *Common Sense* (1776), advocating American independence. On his return to England he wrote *The Rights of Man* (1791–92), a controversial radical appeal for human equality. Paine was moved to write by his opposition to Burke's views in *Reflections on the Revolution in France*. He rejected the idea of an established constitution, asserting that, at best, government was based only on precedent. He attacked the concept of succession, deriving, as he claimed, from "a French bastard landing with an armed banditti" (William the Conqueror). By *The Rights of Man* Paine ranks among the earliest advocates of class war philosophy, seeing government in his time as oppression and taxation as robbery. In the famous fifth chapter of the second part he extolled representative government, attacked colonialism and the penal code and put forward schemes for graduated income tax, poor relief, old age pensions, family allowance and educational provision. Because of his views he was forced to escape to France, where he wrote *The Age of Reason* (1794–96), a crude but passionate tract taking a broadly Deistic view of religion. With his combination of political radicalism and religious free-thinking Paine was regarded as a dangerous influence in his day. His idealism, rationalism and clear vigorous prose style made him an important influence on English radical movements in the nineteenth century. (See also **Political Pamphlets**.)

Complete Works, ed. P. S. Foner, 2 vols., New York: Citadel Press, 1945.

A.P.

PALGRAVE, F. T. (Francis Turner) (1824–97), son of a historian, was educated at Oxford. He entered the Education Department of the Civil Service in 1849 (the year he met Tennyson) and retired in 1884. He then became professor of poetry at Oxford (1885–95). He published original verse (including hymns) of no great merit, and critical writings on art and literature. He conceived the idea of *The Golden Treasury of Songs and Lyrics* (1861; revised and enlarged, 1891; second series, 1896), in compiling which he consulted Tennyson closely. Its popularity helped to establish the lyric as the chief poetic form of the late nineteenth century.   A.E.

PALMER, Ray. See **Hymns.**

PARKMAN, Francis (1823–93), American historian, was born in Massachusetts, graduated from Harvard (1844) and Harvard Law School (1846). In 1846 he made a strenuous expedition to the Far West, which he recorded in *The Oregon Trail*. The journey induced a physical and nervous breakdown and Parkman was a semi-invalid for the remainder of his life. He soon, however, became the leading American historian of his day, working from manuscript materials and employing an evocative and gracious prose style. His writings include *History of the Conspiracy of Pontiac* (1851), *Pioneers of France in the New World* (1865), *The Discovery of the Great West* (1869), *The Old Regime in Canada* (1874) and *A Half-Century of Conflict* (2 vols., 1892).

Journals, ed. M. Wade, New York: Harper, 1947.   J.W.

PARNELL, Thomas (1679–1718) was born in Dublin and educated there at Trinity College. He was an archdeacon in the Irish church, but also spent time in England where he became a member of the Scriblerus Club. His poems were admired by contemporaries for their "ease and sweetness" and in his "The Third Satire of Dr. Donne, Versified" he undertook, like Pope, to refurbish an older poet. Amongst mock-heroics, pastorals and occasional poems "A Night-Piece on Death" is gloomy yet charming, while "The Book-worm" is neatly satirical. He contributed to *The Spectator*.

Poetical Works, ed. G. A. Aitken (with memoir), London: Bell (Aldine edition of the British Poets), 1894.   J.C.

PARODY AND NONSENSE. Parody is an imitation of an author which exaggerates his idiosyncrasies in order to produce a ludicrous disparity between style and content. Like satire it is basically conservative. It punishes new departures and usually leaves conventional works unscathed. Thus Wordsworth was one of the most popular targets for parodists, while his inferior contemporaries—Moore, Campbell and Rogers—escaped almost untouched. Its value as literary criticism is therefore strictly limited. However, it is not always destructive but often takes on a life of its own. Much of our pleasure in reading it is often only marginally related to a sense of the deficiencies of the original.

English parody probably had its source in medieval travesties of the liturgy. There were few successful parodies before the eighteenth century, although Chaucer's *Sir Thopas* and John Philips's *The Splendid Shilling* (1705; though first published in a miscellany, 1701) deserve mention. Henry Fielding was perhaps the first great English parodist. In *Shamela* and *Joseph Andrews* he parodied Richardson's *Pamela*, particularly Pamela's combination of maidenly modesty with an eye for the main chance. *Joseph Andrews* is especially interesting because it is an example of a work which began as a parody but ended as an artistic creation in its own right. A similar result was achieved by two other novelists, Swift and Sterne, who in *Gulliver's Travels* and *Tristram Shandy* parodied respectively the traveler's tale and the conventional narrative method. These three prose writers were exceptional; most of the great parodists have worked in verse. From 1790 England enjoyed a period of great verse parody, beginning with Canning's *Anti-Jacobin*. This journal and *Rejected Addresses* (1812) by James and Horace Smith satirized the excesses and singularities of Romantic poetry. The line of parody continued through the *Bon Gaultier Ballads* (1845), Calverley, Lewis Carroll, Hood, Traill and J. K. Stephen. In this century prose has reappeared as the most successful medium. The greatest achievements are Max Beerbohm's *A Christmas Garland* (1912) and, more creatively, the Oxen of the Sun episode in James Joyce's *Ulysses* (1922).

Parody sometimes verges on the borderline of **Nonsense**. For example, Carroll's parody of Wordsworth's "Resolution and Independence" is partly a parody of certain elements in Wordsworth's poem but it also includes lines like these:

> He said "I look for butterflies
> That sleep among the wheat:
> I make them into mutton-pies,
> And sell them in the street."

Clearly Carroll is no longer concerned with satirizing Wordsworth.

Here as in many of his parodies he is mainly interested in building something of his own on the ruins of an original, which is why he is often content to parody a little-known poem. Carroll also wrote a number of nonsense poems, most notably "Jabberwocky" (in *Through the Looking-Glass*) and *The Hunting of the Snark* (1876), but the real originator of nonsense verse was Edward Lear (1812–88). Much of Lear's nonsense appears in his limericks, a form he largely created, but he also wrote some successful longer poems (e.g., "The Dong" and "The Jumblies"). Unlike some of Carroll's nonsense, these poems are not mere gibberish. There is an emotional intensity, coupled with a disparity between sound and meaning, which marks Lear as the last of the Romantics and the contemporary of Tennyson and Swinburne. Lear and Carroll both created their nonsense worlds as a refuge from the harshness of the real world and both provide fascinating subjects for the psychologist and the symbol hunter.

Parodies of the Works of English and American Authors, ed. W. Hamilton, 6 vols., London: Reeves & Turner, 1884–89.

A Parody Anthology, ed. C. Wells, New York: C. Scribner's Sons, 1904.

A Century of Parody and Imitation, ed. W. Jerrold and R. M. Leonard, London: Oxford Univ. Press, 1913.

The Complete Nonsense of Edward Lear, ed. H. Jackson, London: Faber & Faber, 1947.

Parodies, ed. D. Macdonald, New York: Random House, 1960; London: Faber & Faber, 1961.

E.T.W.

PASTON LETTERS, The (c.1420–c.1500) were written by or to three generations of the Paston family, originally of Paston (Norfolk) and deal mainly with the property transactions which mark the rise of the Pastons from virtual obscurity to a position of prominence during the fifteenth century. Although many are business letters, they also contain personal details and accounts of social and national events. They are written in a plain prose style with few literary embellishments, quite distinct from the earlier literary prose tradition, and exemplify a practical use of prose which may have been developing before the fifteenth century.

Paston Letters, ed. J. Gairdner, 6 vols., London: Chatto & Windus, 1904.

A.D.M.

PATCHEN, Kenneth (1911–72) was born in Niles (Ohio) and educated at the University of Wisconsin. He was a writer of prose and poetry and an artist working in the graphic arts and the originator of his own limited-edition books. Representative of his work is *First Will and Testament* (1939), a collection that derives its power from the force of the disgust in its representation of humanity as degraded and animal. In the *Journal of Albion Moonlight* (1941) Patchen mixes poetry and prose to create a surrealist nightmare, a representation of a journey through chaos. He possibly failed to reach his full potential because of his tendency to publish too frequently and hastily.

D.V.W.

PATER, Walter (1839–94) was educated at the King's School, Canterbury and at Queen's College, Oxford, and became a fellow of Brasenose. He formulated a number of the aesthetic doctrines to which Oscar Wilde was to give a wider popularity.

His two important manifestoes are "The Preface" and "The Conclusion" to *The Renaissance* (1873). In "The Conclusion" he recommends "the supreme, artistic view of life." The fact that he speaks of a "view" and not a "way" of life is indicative. According to him, the best life is one of discriminating receptiveness to pleasurable sensations; and the most pleasurable sensations are, in his opinion, those obtained from works of art. The brooding contemplation of works of art becomes for him a sort of religion, and he carries over into everyday life the habits of detached and fastidious appreciation which it fosters. As a result, he is able to list, as being indifferently the objects of "the supreme, artistic view of life," "strange dyes, strange colours, and curious odours, or work of the artist's hands, or the face of one's friend."

In "The Preface" he defines the task of the aesthetic critic as being to discriminate between and to define the kinds of pleasure produced in him by the various works of art and other objects by which he is confronted. The active formulating of critical judgments is not included among his functions.

The studies composing the main part of *The Renaissance* and the essays contained in *Appreciations* (1889) show Pater's literary and art criticism in a most attractive light. But creative impulses seem at times to be seeking expression through critical forms; and when Pater turned to write studies of imaginary subjects he produced his most freely creative works, his novel, *Marius the Epicurean*, and *Imaginary Portraits*. All of these are written in Pater's characteristic prose, with its slow, deliberate and fastidious movement, its languid air and its brooding tone.

(See also **Romantic Movement, The.**)

Studies in the History of the Renaissance, 1873; with revised Conclusion, 1888.
Marius the Epicurean, 1885.
Imaginary Portraits, 1887.
Appreciations, 1889.

Works, New Library edition, 10 vols., London: Macmillan, 1910.

Letters, ed. L. Evans, Oxford: Clarendon Press, 1971.   J.D.J.

PATERSON, A. B. (Andrew Barton) ("Banjo"). See **Australian Literature.**

PATMORE, Coventry (1823–96), born in London, had no formal education but was encouraged by his father to read widely. After his father fled from creditors, he himself was in poverty till he was nominated to a minor appointment at the British Museum, where he stayed from 1846 to 1865. He was three times married—to Emily Andrews in 1847 (his love and courtship form the basis of his longest and most popular poem, *The Angel in the House*); after Emily's death in 1862, to a Catholic, Caroline Byles, whose fortune enabled him to be independent after 1865; and after Caroline's death in 1880, to Harriet Robson. His deepest friendship in his last years was with Alice Meynell. The marriages were a major influence upon his poetry.

Patmore is important as being the first to achieve recognition of a group of poets of Catholic and mystical tendencies, who owed allegiance to seventeenth-century religious poetry. Hopkins, Christina Rossetti and Bridges were all influenced by him. His first volume, *Poems* (1844), consists of four narratives of tragic or unrequited love, in lyrical measures that are reminiscent of Coleridge, Wordsworth and particularly of Tennyson. The second volume, *Tamerton Church Tower* (1853), shows Patmore attempting to treat love in a mystical and sacramental way, and *The Angel in the House* treats of married love in a contemporary realistic setting strongly influenced by Tennyson and Crabbe, risking pathos and dullness but usually avoiding it.

Patmore is one of the few poets who have written scientifically and authoritatively on prosody and metrical law, which he covers in the preface to *Amelia* (1878).

Poems, 1844.
Tamerton Church Tower and Other Poems, 1853; revised, 1854.
The Angel in the House, 1854–56; revised; 6th edition, 1885.
The Unknown Eros, 1877.
Amelia, 1878.   A.N.M.

PATON, Alan. See **African Literature.**

PEACOCK, Thomas Love (1785–1866), son of a glass merchant, was born in Dorset. He went to a private school and in 1800 became a clerk in a London business house (which he disliked). He published

Palmyra and Other Poems (1806) and some later verses, besides those in his novels. In 1812 he met Shelley and they became close friends. *Headlong Hall*, his first novel, appeared in 1816, *Melincourt* in 1817 and *Nightmare Abbey* in 1818. In 1820 he married Jane Gryffydd. His half-serious essay *The Four Ages of Poetry* (1820), which asserts that in an age of increasing enlightenment poetry has buried its head in mystery and the irrational, is doubly interesting for what it shows of his own attitudes and for the fact that it inspired Shelley's *A Defence of Poetry*. Peacock published further novels, including *Crotchet Castle* (1831) and *Gryll Grange* (s. 1860). In the latter year he wrote reminiscences of Shelley for *Fraser's Magazine*.

The standard pattern for his novels was established by the first one, *Headlong Hall*. The book is short and its plot relatively unimportant. Squire Headlong has gathered together a Christmas house party at his home in Wales and the "humor" characters of his acquaintance, representing popular opinions of the day, discuss craniology, deteriorationism, landscape design, human perfectibility and novels. Peacock was always primarily interested in ideas. Himself an agnostic with an epicurean acceptance of reality, he stands on a firm basis of solid comprehensible attitudes to attack "the march of mind," optimism and the whole romantic climate of the day as seen through its popular fads and opinions. The novels endlessly discuss ideas with the most exquisite absurdity; agreement is never possible, for each character is walled off in the prison of his own obsessive opinions. *Melincourt* introduces characters dramatizing the ideas of Southey, Scott, Coleridge and lesser writers. *Nightmare Abbey* sports another Coleridge figure in Mr. Flosky, Byron (Mr. Cypress) and Scythrop, a Shelleyan hero, whose characteristic dilemma between two attractive heroines supplies much of the book's plot—which is stronger than usual. *Nightmare Abbey* is Peacock's best novel. The satire of romantic figures is accurate, and the atmosphere of ironically described melancholy (compare Jane Austen's *Northanger Abbey*, published in the same year) gives the book effective unity.

It is noticeable that Peacock's novels always satirize ideas which were immediately contemporary. *Crotchet Castle* (1831) pounces on what he considered the canting optimism of Brougham and his very powerful Society for the Diffusion of Useful Knowledge. It shows something of Peacock's worries about the Reform Bill, which was then before Parliament, and lacks the unforced satiric humor of his last work, *Gryll Grange*. Here the ubiquitous classical conversation which Peacock loved is inspired by Mr. Falconer with his passion for the Greeks and his tower full of damsels. The Peacockian colloquies on food and drink are exactly right, and all the characters refine on the "humor" figures in the earlier books from which they derive. As always, progress is satirized, but the whole novel reaches a unique geniality of criticism and mellow warmth.

Peacock stood outside his period, satiric but not intolerant. His early verse is unimportant, but the sharp parodies of contemporary poetry in his novels are frequently excellent (e.g., the Byronic "There is a fever of the spirit" in *Nightmare Abbey*) and his light lyrics consistently good. His critical pieces repay examination and *The Four Ages of Poetry* is a stimulating performance.

Headlong Hall, 1816.
Melincourt, 1817.
Nightmare Abbey, 1818.
The Four Ages of Poetry, 1820.
Maid Marian, 1822.
The Misfortunes of Elphin, 1829.
Crotchet Castle, 1831.
Gryll Grange, 1861 (s. 1860).

Works, Halliford edition, ed. H. F. B. Brett-Smith and C. E. Jones, 10
vols., London: Constable; New York: Wells, 1924–34.   W.R.

PEELE, George (?1557–96), educated at Christ's Hospital and Oxford, worked in London from c.1581 as writer and, possibly, actor. Although many doubtful attributions have been made to him, Peele's writings were many and various, including several fine lyrics and five plays accepted as his, among them the chronicle history *Edward I* (1593), the folk comedy *The Old Wives' Tale* (1595) and the biblical *The Love of King David and the Fair Bethsabe* (1599). His work has melody and variety of imagery, but is weak in structure and suffers from verbal extravagance.

Works, ed. A. H. Bullen, 2 vols., London: Nimmo, 1888.
Life and Works, ed. C. T. Prouty and others, New Haven: Yale Univ.
Press, vol. 1, 1952; London: Oxford Univ. Press, 1953; vol. 2, New
Haven, 1961.   G.P.

PEIRCE, C. S. (Charles Sanders) (1839–1914), philosopher and logician, was born in Cambridge (Massachusetts), graduated from Harvard and was a member of the U.S. Coast and Geodetic Survey (1861–91). An original thinker and prolific writer, Peirce published little in his own lifetime and was relatively unknown outside philosophic circles. He made basic contributions to scientific methodology, formal logic, and, in such works as *Existential Graphs*, semiology, probability theory and induction. A founder of the school of pragmatism, he first outlined the concept in *The North American Review* (October 1871) and refined and amplified it in subsequent articles, calling his doctrine "pragmaticism," to distinguish it from that of William James. *Chance, Love and Logic* (1923) was compiled from his manuscripts.

Collected Papers, ed. C. Hartshorne and P. Weiss, 8 vols., Cambridge, Mass.: Harvard Univ. Press, 1931–1958.   J.W.

PEPYS, Samuel (1633–1703), a great naval administrator, is now best known as the author of the *Diary* which he kept from 1660 to 1669. Employing a form of shorthand and showing his manuscript to nobody, he wrote for himself alone. As a result he felt free to depict himself and his times in minute detail and with exceptional honesty. His accounts of the Plague (1665) and Fire (1666) of London are the most famous products of his extraordinary powers of observation and selection. (See also **Ballads.**)

Diary, ed. H. B. Wheatley, 10 vols., London: Bell, 1893–99; ed. R. Latham and W. Matthews, 8 vols., London: Bell; Berkeley and Los Angeles: Univ. of California Press, 1970– .
Letters, ed. J. R. Tanner, 3 vols., London: Bell; New York: Harcourt, Brace, 1926–29.   J.D.J.

PERCY, Thomas (1729–1811) was born at Bridgnorth (Shropshire) and went to Christ Church, Oxford in 1746. He was ordained in 1753 and became bishop of Dromore in 1782.

He participated actively in the literary life of his day, and was a close friend of Shenstone, Gray, Johnson and Goldsmith. With his *Five Pieces of Runic Poetry from the Icelandic Language* (1763) and his translation of Mallet's history of Denmark as *Northern Antiquities* (1770), he was probably the first writer to stimulate an interest in Old Norse literature in Britain, but his main reputation in literary history derives from his *Reliques of Ancient English Poetry* (1765). The basis of this anthology was a seventeenth-century folio volume of nearly two hundred songs and ballads which Percy possessed (see also **Ballads**). A selection of these was supplemented by material from other sources, such as the Pepys and Ashmolean libraries, and arranged to show the "gradual improvements" of English language and poetry. Various essays were interspersed on such subjects as "Minstrels" and the origins of the English stage. Specimens were chosen not primarily for artistic worth but to illustrate "manners and customs." Some contemporary imitations were admitted, and with the prejudice of his age Percy did not scruple to alter ballads for their "improvement" by eighteenth-century standards. Nevertheless, the true ballad style and spirit made itself felt through the collection and influenced literary taste obscurely and gradually, becoming prominent with the Romantics—notably Words-worth and Coleridge, who, though not always preserving the original spirit of the traditional ballad, were stimulated to fresh imaginative achievements by their study of the form.

Reliques of Ancient English Poetry, 3 vols., 1765; ed. H. B. Wheatley, 3 vols., London: Sonnenschein, 1891.
Letters, ed. D. Nichol Smith, C. Brooks, and others, 6 vols., London: Oxford Univ. Press; Baton Rouge: Louisiana State Univ. Press, 1944– .   T.W.

PERCY, Walker (1916–) was born in Alabama and graduated B.A. from University of North Carolina and M.D. from Columbia (1941). His literary career began when ill health forced him to give up medicine. He won a National Book Award for his novel *The Movie-goer* (1961), whose hero seeks a normal life in a society from which he is alienated. In *The Last Gentleman* (1966) the central character creates his own hermeti-cally sealed world which he occasionally, but unconvincingly, pierces. *Love in the Ruins* (1971), set in the near future, concerns a degenerate doctor finally shocked into leading a quiet, industrious existence.   R.W.

PERELMAN, S. J. (Sidney Joseph) (1904–) was born in Brooklyn. He was educated at Brown University where he knew Nathanael West, whose sister he married. The burlesque *Dawn Ginsbergh's Revenge* (1929) made him famous, and he went on to write filmscripts for the Marx Brothers, including such lines as "Leave a sample of your handwriting and above all, don't worry" and "Don't point that beard at me, Gottlieb, it's loaded." His collections of humor include *Crazy Like a Fox* (1944), *The Road to Miltown; or, Underneath the Spreading Atrophy* (1957) and *The Rising Gorge* (1961).   J.L.M.

PHILIPS, Ambrose (1674–1749) was born in Shropshire and educated at Cambridge, where he held a fellowship at St. John's College from 1699 to 1708. His epistle "To the Earl of Dorset" was published in *The Tatler*, no. 12, and his six "Pastorals" were published with Pope's in Tonson's *Poetical Miscellanies* (1709). On his return from Denmark he became one of Addison's circle. His play *The Distrest Mother* (1712) was heralded by Steele in *The Spectator*, no. 290 (in no. 335, Sir Roger de Coverley is taken to see it). In five papers of *The Guardian* (1713), Philips's *Pastorals* (1710) were praised and Pope's ignored. Pope's *The Guardian*, no. 40 ironically compared the two sets of pastorals, giving preference to Philips's, but for absurd reasons. As a result Philips is said to have kept a switch at Button's to chastise Pope. Philips became secretary to the Hanover Club, formed to ensure the Succession. He subsequently became a justice for Westminster and in 1717 a commissioner for the lottery. From March 1718 until July 1721 he ran *The Freethinker* in imitation of *The Spectator* and in support of the government. In 1724 he went to Ireland as secretary to Archbishop Boulter, represented Armagh in the Irish Parliament and became secretary to the lord chancellor in 1726. In 1748 he returned to London and his collected poems were published. He was nicknamed "Namby-Pamby," originally by Carey in a parody of Philips's diction in complimentary verses to the infant daughter of Lord Carteret (1725).

Poems, ed. M. G. Segar, Oxford: Blackwell, 1937.   P.R.

PHILIPS, John. See **Parody and Nonsense.**

PHILLIPS, David Graham (1867–1911), journalist and novelist, was born in Indiana. Associated with the muckraking movement, his articles on "The Treason of the Senate" in *Cosmopolitan* (1906) helped to secure the passage of the Seventeenth Amendment for the direct election of senators in 1913. Phillips wrote twenty-three novels, some dealing with social issues and political corruption, including *The Great God Success* (1901), *The Cost* (1904) and *The Deluge* (1905), others with the position of women in society, *The Worth of a Woman* (1908), *The Husband's Story* (1910) and *The Price She Paid* (1912). His greatest novel, *Susan Lenox* (1917, written 1908; *f.* 1931), describes a country girl forced into prostitution through environmental, economic and personal circumstances. He was murdered by a lunatic claiming that Phillips was "trying to destroy the whole ideal of womanhood."   J.W.

"PETER PINDAR." See **Wolcot, John.**

PINERO, A. W. (Sir Arthur Wing) (1855–1934), son of a solicitor of Portuguese origin, gave up the law for acting and then acting for writing. He became the most successful English playwright for many years, being knighted in 1909. Early farces like *The Magistrate* (1885; *f.* as *Those Were the Days*, 1940) and *Dandy Dick* (1887) were followed by more serious work like *The Profligate* (1889) and *The Second Mrs. Tanqueray* (1893; *f.* 1952), which established Pinero's position with Henry Arthur Jones in creating a serious modern drama. In *Trelawny of the "Wells"* (1898) he turned to comedy of sentiment with the story of an actress who marries and moves from the tawdry little world into the great world—and finds herself bored to death. Of his more than fifty plays, the best are realistic and owe much to Ibsen, though all reflect Pinero's own technical mastery.

The Social Plays, ed. C. Hamilton, 4 vols., New York: Dutton, 1917–22.

K.T.

PINTER, Harold (1930–) was born in Hackney (East London) of Jewish parents and began his career as an actor under the name of David Baron. After writing poetry and a semiautobiographical novel (which later became the basis for a radio play, *The Dwarfs*) he turned to drama. His first play, *The Room*, was produced at Bristol University in 1957. On the strength of this, a commercial production of his first full-length play, *The Birthday Party*, was mounted in London in 1958, but was a disastrous failure. The breakthrough came with *The Caretaker* (1960), possibly prepared for by his work in television. *The Birthday Party* was revived in 1965 and hailed as a great play. Pinter has also written several filmscripts —in particular for Losey in *The Servant, Accident* and *The Go-Between*.

The basic situation of his early plays is identical—battle for possession of a room, albeit a shabby one, carried out with both physical and verbal violence (though noticeably the excessive use of violence in his first play, *The Room*, has been dropped). During this battle we see the dangers and difficulties of communication which, with the absence of any political commitment at all, makes Pinter a dramatist in the theater of the absurd. These plays have been aptly called "comedies of menace" and Pinter's themes and dialogue coupled with rather depressing décor have invited comparison with Beckett, whom Pinter acknowledges as an influence. But it was the novels of Beckett rather than his plays that Pinter first admired, and there is little suggestion of existentialist philosophy in Pinter's plays, except perhaps in *The Dwarfs*. His characters are not isolated in a cosmic void or buried in urns. Although outside society, they are recognizably fugitives from it and very indigenous. Their language, although ultimately "poetic" in effect, reads like a tape recording of normal inarticulate people. Pinter makes a significant use of silence in his dialogue which has been described by one critic as "orchestrated naturalism."

After *The Caretaker* the sense of claustrophobia disappears. This was possibly a result of television, where there is greater mobility on the part of the camera. His characters come from a higher class of society and are more elegant and articulate. Their concern now is with something the earlier plays had not contained—sex. From his early television play *Night School* (p. 1960) to *The Homecoming* (1965) Pinter seems to have been investigating the role of woman in society and male attitudes towards her. His technical control is now so perfect that he has been accused of heartlessness and self-parody, but this assured treatment in *Tea Party* and *The*

Homecoming seemed to indicate that the theme was now complete, just as *The Caretaker* completed the examination of the early plays.

The Birthday Party, 1959 (p. 1958; f. 1968); .... *and Other Plays* ("The Room" and "The Dumb Waiter" p. 1957), 1960.
A Slight Ache and Other Plays, 1961 ("A Slight Ache" p. radio 1958).
The Caretaker, 1960 (p. 1959; f. 1963).
The Collection; and The Lover, 1963 ("The Collection" p. TV 1961).
The Homecoming, 1965.
Tea Party and Other Plays, 1967 ("Tea Party" p. TV 1964).
Landscape; and Silence, 1969 ("Landscape" p. radio 1968).
Five Screen Plays, 1971.
Old Times, 1971.

A.P.H.

PLATH, Sylvia (1932–63) lived in New England until her marriage to Ted Hughes in 1956. Thereafter they divided their time between England and America until the birth of their daughter in England in 1960. She was of German–Austro–American parentage, her father, a biologist, dying in 1940. She graduated from Smith College in 1955, having recovered from severe depression leading to attempted suicide in 1953. This followed a hectic month in New York as a winner of *Mademoiselle* College Board contest, experiences she used in her only novel, *The Bell Jar* (1963). Poetry had been a major interest since childhood and her first volume, *The Colossus*, appeared in 1960. Frequent bouts of ill health perhaps contributed to her suicide in February 1963.

All this helps in understanding Sylvia Plath's poetry, though it would be facile to call it "confessional," for there is little self-dramatization or opportunity for poetic voyeurism. Her style is terse, lyrical, frequently witty, and revealing a fine ear, with remarkable metrical skills. She writes about the external world—places, animals, plants, about her children, motherhood, an appendectomy—everyday things made extraordinary by a sense of hidden nightmare as well as newly discovered beauty. Her vision edges on the abyss of madness, pain and death; yet this is counterbalanced by a delight in the richness of life, and particularly the natural world. When the horror becomes an artificial mannerism, Sylvia Plath's poetry fails. Her finest work, however, reveals a strong intellectual, emotional and imaginative discipline.

The Colossus and Other Poems, 1960.
The Bell Jar, 1963.
Ariel, 1965.
Uncollected Poems, 1965.
Crossing the Water, 1971.
Winter Trees, 1971.

S.C.

PLOMER, William. See **African Literature.**

POE, Edgar Allan (1809–49) was born in Boston, the son of impoverished actors. His father died in 1810 and after the death of his mother in 1811 in Richmond (Virginia) he was taken into the home of John Allan, a wealthy local merchant. He was educated at schools in Richmond and in England, where the Allan family lived from 1815 to 1820, and then briefly at the University of Virginia. After quarreling with John Allan over debts incurred at the university, he left for Boston where in 1827 he joined the U.S. Army and published, at his own expense, *Tamerlane and Other Poems*. This slight volume made no impression on the critics or the reading public, but, undeterred in his ambition to become a poet, he produced two further volumes of lyric verses in 1829 and 1831. His early poetry brought him neither fame nor reward, so he turned to writing fiction and literary reviews. In 1833 his story "MS. Found in a Bottle" won a prize in Baltimore, and this success helped him to an editorial position with the *Southern Literary Messenger* of Richmond. There he found an outlet for his tales and poems, but it was his work as a reviewer that gave the *Messenger* its distinctive tone and established him as a significant literary personality. His slashing reviews of overrated American poets and novelists made him notorious and brought him into controversy with the established literary cliques of his day. In 1837 his editorial connection with the *Messenger* came to an end, and in an attempt to expand his horizons he moved on to Philadelphia and New York, editing and writing for *Burton's Gentleman's Magazine* (1839–40) and *Graham's Magazine* (1841–42), but his plans to own and edit a superior literary journal based on his own élitist principles came to nothing. In 1838 he published his only novel, *The Narrative of Arthur Gordon Pym*, and this was followed by 1839 by his collected *Tales of the Grotesque and Arabesque*.

His literary endeavors brought little financial return, and he and his family (he had married his thirteen-year old cousin, Virginia Clemm, in 1836) were haunted by poverty and ill health. After moving to New York in 1844 his fame as a "magazinist" grew, and by 1845 he was at the peak of his career. His rhythmic narrative poem, "The Raven," was a brief sensation in America and in England. For a short time he owned the weekly *Broadway Journal*. A new collection of *Tales* appeared, and also his last and most successful volume of poems, *The Raven and Other Poems*. After his wife Virginia's death in 1847, however, his life began to disintegrate. His health was poor, and acrimonious journalistic disputes, especially that concerning Longfellow's alleged plagiarism, made him many enemies. Yet, despite his confused personal life, he continued to write important poetry and criticism and to explore new areas of thought. His last published work, *Eureka* (1848), a long prose poem on the nature and destiny of the universe, was considered by Poe to be the greatest achievement of his career, though it made little impression on its small audience. He died in October 1849 in miserable circumstances in Baltimore, probably from the effects of a heart attack.

From the beginning of his career Poe thought of himself primarily as a poet. The themes of the loss of the visionary world of childhood, alienation and despair that run through his early poetry are commonplace Romantic attitudes, but he uses them with considerable skill and they have a genuine significance in his life. The collection of 1829 is dominated by the long poem, "Al Aaraaf," which marks a new departure in his work; it is less concerned with the poet's private emotions than with celebrating the unity of Truth and Beauty—a doctrine which Poe elaborated in his critical essays on poetry and in poems such as "Israfel" and "To Helen" from the collection of 1831. His later poetry, especially "The Raven," "Annabel Lee," "Ulalume" and "To Annie," is technically more complex and dominated by an agonized sense of death and loss. Poe was the first American poet to write seriously and with originality on the nature and function of poetry. In essays like "The Philosophy of Composition" (1846) and "The Poetic Principle" (1850) he argued that genuine poetry was the record of a mystical, aesthetic experience, and as such must be "indefinite," musical, symbolic and brief.

His harsh reviews of contemporary authors brought him notoriety, but he also thought carefully about the structures of fiction from which he demanded unity and psychological integrity. His review of Hawthorne's *Twice Told Tales* (1842) is perhaps his best definition of the formally unified and economical short story. Poe's own fiction is remarkably varied, though he is best remembered for his tales of psychological terror like "Ligeia" (1838; *f.* as *The Tomb of Ligeia*, 1964), "The Fall of the House of Usher" (1839; *f.* 1929; 1950; 1960), "William Wilson" (1839), "The Pit and the Pendulum" (1843; *f.* 1931; 1961), "The Tell-Tale Heart" (1843; *f.* 1942; 1950; 1954; 1960), "The Black Cat" (1843; *f.* 1931; 1933; 1941; as part of *Tales of Terror*, 1962) and "The Cask of Amontillado" (1846) and for such skillfully constructed detective stories as "The Murders in the Rue Morgue" (1841; *f.* 1914; 1942; as *The Phantom of the Rue Morgue*, 1954) and "The Purloined Letter" (1845). Poe largely avoided the supernatural and the sentimental in his serious fiction, and his tales of terror are remarkable for their psychological realism. Here he explores through his first person narrators an inner world of nightmare, repression, sadism and self-destruction with economy and symbolic intensity. His narrators, like the hero of *The Narrative of Arthur Gordon Pym* go on symbolic voyages to seek the dimensions of their own minds. Poe also wrote hoaxes, as "Von Kempelen and His Discovery" (1849), parodies ("A Predicament," 1838), science fiction ("The Conversation of Eiros and Charmion," 1839), and social satire ("Mellonta Tauta," 1849).

For many years after his death Poe's significance was obscured by the calumnies of his literary executor, R. W. Griswold. In France Baudelaire defended his insights, but only in the last half-century has his art been appreciated in America.

Tamerlane and Other Poems, 1827.
Al Aaraaf, Tamerlane, and Minor Poems, 1829.
Poems, 1831.
The Narrative of Arthur Gordon Pym, 1838.
Tales of the Grotesque and Arabesque, 1839 (dated 1840).
Tales, 1845.
The Raven and Other Poems, 1845.
Eureka, 1848.

Complete Works, ed. J. A. Harrison, 17 vols., New York: Crowell, 1902.
Poems (vol. 1, *Collected Works*), ed. T. O. Mabbott, Cambridge, Mass.: Harvard Univ. Press, 1969.
Letters, ed. J. W. Ostrom, Cambridge, Mass.: Harvard Univ. Press, 1948.

I.W.

POLITICAL PAMPHLETS. The term "pamphlet" came to be used from Tudor times for a small unbound book or broadsheet of contemporary interest and often controversial views. Under the influence of emblem literature it was sometimes adorned with cuts and was in verse as well as prose, and in this and its political slant it was akin to the popular ballad. It preceded newspapers, was closely associated with them from the seventeenth century and even today this can be seen, for example, in *Tribune* pamphlets. The first serious historian of the pamphlet, Myles Davies, traced its origin to the end of Queen Elizabeth's reign. For Elizabethans the first popular series of political pamphlets consisted of John Penry's anonymous "Martin Marprelate" tracts (1588–89), attributed to Job Throckmorton (Neale, *Elizabethan Pamphlets, 1584–1601*) or to other Puritan associates, attacking the bishops generally and Archbishop Whitgift in particular. The latter was engaged in a book warfare with Thomas Cartwright, the Puritan leader. Politics and religion were to be involved with each other, and a source of strong popular feeling for two centuries and more, over order and freedom as differently interpreted by writers and readers of various parties in church and state. "Martin's" wit was scurrilous and daring, his presses unlocated; the government had to repay in kind, and "Pasquil" (variously identified as Lyly, Nashe and other court journalists) lampooned "Martin" until Penry was arrested.

Political pamphleteering made great advances from 1638 to 1660 and from 1679 to the end of the century, periods when press licensing was ineffective and controversial writings abounded. A number of devices were employed: dialogues, familiar letters, trials, last speeches, wills. The tone was either one of satire and ridicule, or a pretense of truthful narration. To ridicule Parliament there was a dialogue between Prince Rupert's poodle, Puddle, and Toby, the Parliament dog, who was brought over to the Royalists. When the Royalists needed morale for the second Civil War, a pamphlet described Cromwell's deathbed directions to his officers (July 1648) in convincing language. Arbuthnot's *The Art of Political Lying* (1715) presented a much practiced philosophy, and the subtle prevarications and ironies of Defoe and Swift had been prepared for in such pamphlets as L'Estrange's *Citt and Bumpkin* dialogues, where the plotting of two Whigs is dramatically ridiculed while overheard in a tavern (1680). A more elevated style in the rhetorical tradition is represented by Milton's *Areopagitica* (1644)—on licensing the press. It made little contempory impact, though Milton's ideas were used again by Charles Blount in two pamphlets in 1679 and 1693 in a more familiar style, and Richard Janeway defended the press as "a mint of solid worth" in *The Tears of the Press* (1681).

Some of the most politically interesting of Puritan pamphlets are those of the Levellers under the leadership of John Lilburne, who has been described as the first English radical and democrat, because he stood for the principle of an elected parliament with equal electoral rights for all citizens without property qualification. In association with John Wildman, William Walwyn, Richard Overton and John Williams, he wrote popular pamphlets bringing him into conflict with Cromwell's policies to establish a stable government under his own control. Equally disapproved were the Diggers, led by visionary Gerrard Winstanley, whose *Law of Freedom . . . or True Magistracy Restored* was addressed to Cromwell in 1641: "I have set the candle at your door; for you have power in your hands . . . to act for common freedom if you will; I have no power." He advocated land-sharing schemes, annual parliaments, elected magistrates, a society based on peace and brotherhood, and he spoke of it prophetically: "Every freeman shall have a freedom in the earth, to plant or build, to fetch from the storehouse anything he wants, and shall enjoy the fruits of his labours without restraint from any."

Government was less ideal and the struggle seemed always against the tyrant. For Milton, in *The Tenure of Kings and Magistrates* (1649), the tyrant was the king; for Colonels Sexby and Titus in *Killing No Murder* (1657) he was Cromwell, attacked in a clever ironical address by disillusioned army officers. Under the stress of the "troubles" pamphleteers were hammering out principles in ever-changing situations. In 1659

Milton made his bid for a free commonwealth; the army issued its plea for the mode of government then prevailing; in answer Evelyn published *An Apology for the Royal Party* in an impassioned style; L'Estrange's *A Plea for Limited Monarchy* addressed General Monk in a sober, lucid manner declaring the prewar constitution had "included the perfections of a free state, and was the kernel... of a commonwealth, in the shell of monarchy." The interpretation of that shell of monarchy was in debate during the Succession dispute. In 1681 the king, as the champion of law and order, issued a proclamation which was attacked by a Whig pamphlet, to which replies were written by moderate Tories—Halifax, in *Observations upon a Late Libel*, and Dryden, in *His Majesty's Declaration Defended*, which preceded the more devastating poetic tract, *Absalom and Achitophel*, the perfection of fine raillery and yet a serious, carefully argued political statement, thus reaching the high-water mark of literary and political art in the pamphlet.

The development of party newspapers in the late seventeenth and eighteenth centuries drew away some political fire from the pamphlet, but Defoe and Swift found it a valuable adjunct to *The Review* and *The Examiner*, the one in *The True-Born Englishman* (1701) and *The Shortest Way with the Dissenters* (1702), and the other in *The Conduct of the Allies* (1711) and *A Modest Proposal* (1729). The dangers involved in political journalism under the developing party system made irony a convenient weapon, but it could be double-edged, as Defoe found from *The Shortest Way*. He therefore chose plain satire in *A Hymn to the Pillory*, which he claimed "sold beyond the best performance of any ancient or modern poet." Both writers believed that one party had no more right than any other to publish its views or to suppress the writers of another; but parties in power did not subscribe to this view, though at the expiration of the Licensing Acts at the end of the previous century the Queen Anne writers had greater scope. *The Englishman* (in opposition 1713–14, for the government 1715) was Steele's contribution in newspaper form to the political war. Henceforward the newspaper took over the previous role of the pamphlet in the discussion of such issues in the eighteenth century as the Hanoverian Succession (1714), the Continental Wars, the South Sea Bubble (1720), the French Revolution (1789) and the industrial problems. In the later decades of the century the American colonial situation called forth pamphlets from men as different as Burke and Paine, the first trying in *Thoughts on the Cause of the Present Discontents* (1770) to reconcile, the second in *Common Sense* (1776) to encourage a separation and taking the revolutionary view that government is of necessity evil, not that it needs devolution, as Burke suggested. Burke's *Letter on a Regicide Peace* (1796) (with France) shows the popular fear of "revolution," which was to be hailed so enthusiastically by Wordsworth as the dawn of liberty. The Romantic poets made no great use of the pamphlet, but Shelley's contributions are interesting. His *Proposals for Putting Reform to the Vote* and *Address on the Death of Princess Charlotte* (1817) advocated disfranchisement of rotten boroughs in favor of unrepresented urban areas. The horror of the Peterloo Massacre produced both *The Mask of Anarchy* and the constructive pamphlet *A Philosophical View of Reform*, with its appeal "from the passions to the reason of men" and advocacy of a secret ballot, a topic taken up again after the Reform Act of 1832.

The nineteenth century has so many political issues that it is impossible to examine them all, and while pamphlets continued to be written, they were less important than books, speeches and periodical contributions. Even Cobbett, writing for the working and middle classes, preferred books or his *Political Register*, nicknamed "Twopenny Trash," for the diffusion of ideas, but no. 18 reappeared in pamphlet form as *Addresses to the Journeymen and Labourers* and made him a great working-class leader— 200,000 copies sold in two months. The Chartists had O'Connor's *The Northern Star* and Hetherington's *The Poor Man's Guardian*, and less use was made of pamphlets, but at irregular intervals William Carpenter published, as Cobbett had done, open letters addressed to individual politicians. These sold well, as did the anonymous *The People's Charter* (1832) and Cobden's *England, Ireland and America* against the Corn Laws (1835). Charles Kingsley's *Cheap Clothes and Nasty* by "Parson Lot" in *Tracts by Christian Socialists* (1850) was popular. Hood's poem, "The Song of the Shirt," which appeared in a *Punch* Christmas number, had the impact of the pamphlet on the public, as did an analysis of London poverty, probably by George R. Sims, *The Bitter Cry of Outcast London* (1883). Gladstone's most famous pamphlet, *Bulgarian Horrors* (1876), attacking Turkish misrule, sold 76,000 copies in three months. Catholic emancipation, the Irish question, women's suffrage, prison reform were keenly debated, as in the twentieth century, pacifism, the World Wars, race prejudice have been since. From time to time special pamphlets are issued apart from those by societies, such as Fabian pamphlets from 1884. We may note Edward Carpenter on prisons in *Non-Governmental Society* (1911), Laurence Housman in defense of women, *The Bawling Brotherhood* (1913), George Orwell's independent views in *The Lion and the Unicorn: Socialism and the English Genius* (1941), and other essays. It is difficult to select from more recent party pamphleteers, but mention may be made of John Strachey's *The Challenge of Democracy* (no. 10 of *Encounter Pamphlets*, 1963) and Michael Foot's *Parliament in Danger* (1959). Michael Foot has been influenced by Hilaire Belloc's broadside of 1911, *The Party System* (written in collaboration with Cecil Chesterton), and has recognized the problem of individual opinion versus party policy. He has expressed his views with brilliant trenchancy and wit and has recalled some of that skill Swift used in one of the greatest periods of the English pamphlet.

A Collection of State Tracts . . . Privately Printed in the Reign of King Charles II, 1689.

The Harleian Miscellany, ed. W. Oldys and T. Park, 10 vols., London, 1808–13.

A Collection of Scarce and Valuable Tracts ("the Somers Tracts"), ed. [Sir] W. Scott, 13 vols., London, 1809–15.

The Marprelate Tracts, ed. W. Pierce, London: Clarke, 1911.

Tracts on Liberty in the Puritan Revolution, 1638–1647, ed. W. Haller, 3 vols., London: Oxford Univ. Press; New York: Columbia Univ. Press, 1934.

Winstanley, G., *Works*, ed. G. H. Sabine, London: Oxford Univ. Press; Ithaca, N.Y.: Cornell Univ. Press, 1941.

The Leveller Tracts, 1647–1653, ed. W. Haller and G. Davies, London: Oxford Univ. Press; New York: Columbia Univ. Press, 1944.

British Pamphleteers, ed. G. Orwell and R. Reynolds, 2 vols., London: Wingate, 1948–51.

Dryden, J., *His Majesty's Declaration Defended, 1681*, ed. G. Davies, Augustan Reprints, no. 23, Berkeley and Los Angeles: Univ. of California Press, 1950.

Evelyn, J., *An Apology for the Royal Party, 1659*, ed. G. Keynes, Augustan Reprints, no. 28, Berkeley and Los Angeles: Univ. of California Press, 1951.

Political Tracts of Wordsworth, Coleridge and Shelley, ed. R. J. White, Cambridge: Cambridge Univ. Press, 1953.

Davies, M., *Selections from Athenae Britannicae, 1716–1719*, ed. R. G. Thomas, Augustan Reprints, no. 97, Berkeley and Los Angeles: Univ. of California Press, 1963.

L'Estrange, Sir R., *Citt and Bumpkin, 1680*, ed. B. J. Rahn, Augustan Reprints, Berkeley and Los Angeles: Univ. of California Press, 1965.

I.M.W.

POMFRET, John (1667–1702), minor poet and parson, is now remembered for one poem from his small output, "The Choice," which secured his inclusion in Johnson's *Lives of the Poets*. It is in the tradition of Horatian poems praising the happy life—"such a state," in Johnson's words, "as affords plenty and tranquillity, without exclusion of intellectual pleasures." His other poems include a pastoral elegy on Queen Mary and "Dies Novissima," which together with "A Prospect of Death" in some ways foreshadows the eighteenth-century "Graveyard Poets."

The Works of the English Poets, ed. A. Chalmers, London: Johnson, 1810, vol. 8.

A.P.

POPE, Alexander (1688–1744) was born in London of Roman Catholic parents in the year of James II's deposition. He was debarred by his religion from university and public life. Wretched health made his existence a "long disease." He lived in retirement with his parents in Windsor Forest, later at Chiswick, and after his father's death in 1717 removed with his mother to Twickenham, where his garden and grotto were a major and increasing delight.

He undertook his own education in languages and letters, and began early to translate and imitate classical and earlier English poets and to write original work. He was encouraged by his father and by the writers whom he salutes in *An Epistle to Dr. Arbuthnot,* "great Dryden's friends before." One of these was Swift, with whom and with Arbuthnot, Gay, Parnell, Congreve, Atterbury and Robert, earl of Oxford, he formed the Scriblerus Club (?1713). Although the club was broken up by Queen Anne's death, the friendships were lifelong. There was a second, and fruitful, gathering of the club in 1726, when Swift came from Ireland to visit Pope.

Pope interrupted his creative work to produce, with much labor, his translation of Homer. "When I translate again I will be hanged," he wrote to Caryll in 1725. Homer secured for him fortune, independence, friends. He now had the entrée to the world of "the great," opportunity to observe the whole social scene, to

> Eye Nature's walks, shoot folly as it flies,
> And catch the manners living as they rise.

Bound to no patron, he was free to make and pronounce his own criticism of life—"The proper study of mankind is man." From the first version of *The Dunciad* to its final form in the year before his death, Pope's poems are a series of brilliant reports on this study. To the end he was revising and repolishing them, achieving effects which make him the most quoted of our poets after Shakespeare. He was engaged on "Epistles to Several Persons" when he died.

Pope "lisp'd in numbers, for the numbers came." At first he had little to say, but said it, nonetheless, with felicity and grace. The early poems are a series of experiments in traditional and modish forms— pastoral, didactic, mock-heroic, descriptive, heroic epistle. Johnson justly says that "his early pieces show, with sufficient evidence, his knowledge of books." They show, too, that he was not a mere sedulous ape. He takes boldly and transmutes with authority. One may compare Waller's "At Penshurst" with the lines in Pope's "Summer" Pastoral which inspired Handel's "Where'er you walk." He was to carry this process a stage further when he parodied Addison's "angel" simile in "Immortal Rich! How calm he sits at ease," and Denham's celebrated invocation to the Thames in "Flow, Welsted, flow, like thine inspirer beer." *An Essay on Criticism*, in its firm construction, its memorable phrasing, its impassioned invocation to the ancients, and its didactic, coolly authoritative tone, demonstrates the Augustan virtues which it preaches. It is, with one exception, the most characteristic among the early works of Pope as he was to mature and develop. The exception is *The Rape of the Lock*. Here Pope for the first time turns to what Hobbes had prescribed as the subject of poetry, "the manners of men," the subject to which he was to devote nearly all his creative writing. In the marvelous decade of the 1730s he would explore this subject more widely and at greater depth, but never again with such gaiety and charm. The common reader agrees with Johnson in judging it "the most airy, the most ingenious, and the most delightful of all his compositions."

He translated Homer (Dryden, with whom he matched himself, had translated Virgil) and had reason to be pleased with the financial result. (Bentley described it as a pretty poem but one not to be called "Homer," and Bentley was not forgiven; see *The Dunciad*, 4, 201–74.) Bolingbroke, who really was a "guide, philosopher and friend," warned Pope (18 February 1724): "You must not look on your translations of Homer as the great work of your life. You owe a great deal more to your self, to your country, to the present age, and to posterity . . . It is incumbent upon you that you write, because you are able to write, what will deserve to be translated three thousand years hence into languages as yet perhaps unformed." Pope replied, "To write well, lastingly well, immortally well, must not one leave Father and Mother and cleave unto the Muse? . . . 'Tis such a task as scarce leaves a man time to be a good neighbour, an useful friend, nay to plant a tree, much less to save his soul."

This task he undertook and achieved while continuing to plant trees and perform all the offices of devoted friendship. The early experiments had shown him where his true strength lay. In *The Dunciad* he magnificently deploys it. Dryden's *MacFlecknoe* was a witty attack on one dull poet; *The Dunciad* attacks the whole breed. Pope shared Swift's fear of the extinction of genius by cold pedantry and dullness, and *The New Dunciad* a dozen years later shows him at war with dullness, not only in writing, but in every field of life. Its closing passage is one of his most sustained and moving pieces, far more truly characteristic of his thought than is the facile optimism of *An Essay on Man*.

He composed this verse essay, he writes, with "honest and moral purposes," and with a "great heap of fragments and hints" before him. This fragmentary character marks the poem, of which the parts are better than the whole. His strength lay in poems of a more concrete, less philosophic nature. The rest of his work in the 1730s demonstrates this. The *Imitations* of Horace's satires, and the poems ("Epistles to Several Persons," *An Epistle to Dr. Arbuthnot*, "Epilogue to the Satires," which may all be described, as indeed the last was, as "something like Horace") are the crown of Pope's achievement. He modulates his couplet as Horace had varied his hexameter, relaxing it for familiar talk, bracing it for serious or impassioned utterance. Variety in method, rhythm, tone and content is the outstanding quality of these poems, which express all his feelings from filial love and deep friendship to anger, disgust and scorn. Of the greatness of Pope the satirist there has never been any dispute. To Byron he was "the great moral poet of all times, of all climes, of all feelings, and of all stages of existence." He found him "the most *faultless* of poets, and almost of men," and Tennyson, quoting *The Dunciad*, remarked, "The perfection of that brings tears to one's eyes."

Pope the craftsman, too, has never lacked intelligent admiration. One may or may not care for the measure as such, but every fit reader is awed by the brilliance and endless variety of Pope's heroic couplet. Walsh had early advised Pope to make "correctness" his aim, and Pope spared nothing in his constant, ceaseless labor to polish and perfect. Even such a lukewarm admirer as Cowper had to admit, in *Table Talk* (1781),

> his musical finesse was such,
> So nice his ear, so delicate his touch . . .

and it was not Pope whom Cowper was here attacking—it was his imitators, a very different matter.

Perhaps the side of Pope which has had least recognition is that which is everywhere present in his letters, but which emerges more rarely in his poetry—his capacity for love and friendship. The very preponderance of satirical attack makes the offerings of friendship the more precious. One thinks of the dedication of *The Dunciad* to Swift, the closing passage of the second "Moral Essay," the superb and perfectly timed *An Epistle to Dr. Arbuthnot*. Even more moving is his dedication of Parnell's works, the collection of which had been a labor of love, to a third member of the Scriblerus Club, once great, now fallen—Robert, earl of Oxford. Hazlitt was right; Pope's compliments are worth an estate.

(See also **Augustans, The; Romantic Movement, The.**)

Pastorals, 1709 (in Tonson's *Poetical Miscellany*).
An Essay on Criticism, 1711.
The Rape of the Lock, 1712; revised, 5 cantos, 1714.
Windsor Forest, 1713.
"Verses to the Memory of an Unfortunate Lady"; "Eloisa to Abelard," in
   Works, 1717.

The Iliad, 1715–20.
The Odyssey (with collaborators), 1725–26.
The Works of Shakespear, 6 vols., 1725.
The Dunciad, books 1–3, 1728; revised as *The Dunciad Variorum, with the Prolegomena of Scriblerus,* 1729; book 4 entitled *New Dunciad,* 1742; books 1–4 in final form, 1743.
An Essay on Man, 1733–34.
Epistles, 1733–35 (called by Warburton "Moral Essays").
Imitations of Horace (under various titles), 1733–38.
An Epistle to Dr. Arbuthnot, 1734; as "Prologue to the Satires," 1735.
"Epilogue to the Satires," in *One Thousand Seven Hundred and Thirty-Eight,* 1738.

Poems, Twickenham edition, ed. J. Butt and others, 6 vols., London: Methuen; New Haven: Yale Univ. Press, 1939–62; 1 vol. edition, 1963.
Homer, Twickenham edition, ed. M. Mack and others, 4 vols., London: Methuen; New Haven: Yale Univ. Press, 1967.
Correspondence, ed. G. Sherburn, 5 vols., Oxford: Clarendon Press, 1956.

A.M.O.

PORTER, Katherine Anne (1890–) was born at Indian Creek (Texas), a descendant of Daniel Boone. Educated in convent schools in Texas and Louisiana, she is a nonpracticing Catholic and a Southern liberal. Her stories were first published by Carl Van Doren in *The Century* in the 1920s. The first collection *Flowering Judas* (limited edition, 1930; enlarged, 1935) won her a Guggenheim Fellowship, enabling her to sail from Mexico for Germany in 1931. She has been married twice. Rescued from straitened circumstances by a Book-of-the-Month Club Special Award (1937) and a second Guggenheim Fellowship (1938), she published in 1939 her masterpiece *Pale Horse, Pale Rider,* comprising three short novellas—"Old Mortality" (1937); "Noon Wine"; and "Pale Horse, Pale Rider" (1938). The collection *The Leaning Tower* (1944) was less successful. Her only novel, conceived in 1940 and based on the 1931 voyage, appeared piecemeal in magazines until published entire as *Ship of Fools* (1962); it was a best seller.

The distinction of Katherine Anne Porter's comparatively slender output lies in her long short stories and short novels. In her novel, short-fiction technique drained her panoramic subject of narrative energy, but *Pale Horse, Pale Rider* is typically stylish and sensitive in transposing autobiography. She uses Miranda, the young heroine of two of the stories (and of other collected tales) and probable author of the best ("Noon Wine"), to explore, in a moving manner, her favorite themes—a modern sense of disorientation, self-deception, thwarted love, stoic renunciation.

Flowering Judas and Other Stories, 1930; 1935.
Pale Horse, Pale Rider: Three Short Novels, 1939.
The Leaning Tower and Other Stories, 1944.
The Days Before, 1952 (essays).
Ship of Fools, 1962 (*f.* 1965).

Collected Short Stories, new edition with three additional stories, New York: Harcourt, Brace, 1965; London: Cape, 1967.   A.S.

PORTER, William Sydney. See "Henry, O."

POUND, Ezra (1885–1972) was educated at Pennsylvania State University where he took a master's degree in Romance languages. He was appointed lecturer in French and Spanish at Wabash College in 1907, but was dismissed from this post ostensibly for disapproving of the narrowness of the academic discipline. He left for Europe and his first book, *A Lume Spento*, was published in Italy in 1908. He spent the years from 1908 to 1920 in London, marrying in 1914. He moved to Paris (1920–24) and then to Italy again, settling finally in Rapallo. During all this time he was constantly helping other artists (Joyce, Eliot, Antheil, Tagore, Gaudier-Brzeska, for example) as well as writing poetry and criticism. During the Second World War he made several unfortunate broadcasts from Italy, was arrested in 1945, put in the stockade at Pisa, flown to Washington and tried for treason. Declared unfit to plead, he was imprisoned in St. Elizabeth's Hospital from which he was released in 1958. He returned to live with his daughter in the Italian Tyrol.

As G. S. Fraser has said, Pound is probably *the* controversial figure of the century. His long poem *The Cantos*, left unfinished, has been immensely praised and condemned; his views on economics and politics have been mainly deplored whilst his qualities as a poet have been mainly undeniable. Though possibly the finest poet America has produced, many Americans think of him as having been a madman and a traitor. Yet, setting aside Pound's own writing, his active aid for other artists (and not simply poets) would have made him important and remarkable. His own work is far from negligible but, like the man, always controversial; and his habit of taking rather brash short cuts to specialized knowledge has not endeared him to critics or readers. But if his translations are inaccurate from the scholar's viewpoint, they capture the spirit of the original often better than scholars can or do; they fulfill, in short, Pound's maxim: "Make it new." Similarly, if Pound's view of the ideogram is inaccurate, as a poetic device it works extremely well. From the very beginning Pound had a clear idea of a poet's duty and stuck to this idea consistently throughout his career. His criteria were simple: *melopoeia* (melody-making), *phonopoeia* (image-making) and *logopoeia* (word- or thought-making). He was a powerful, vigorous imagist poet who learned a great deal from the Japanese *haiku*, which combines thought and picture in highly concentrated form.

Hugh Selwyn Mauberley (1920), Pound's farewell to London, is also Pound's farewell to a purely "aesthetic" attitude to poetry. Some critics think it finer as a study of general culture than Eliot's *The Waste Land*. It was followed by a "translation," "Homage to Sextus Propertius," which is also a poem about Pound, poetry and the general state of culture. It should be read not as a bad translation, but as significant misquotation would be read in Eliot. Pound's main poem is, of course, his great statement on civilization, *The Cantos*, begun in the second decade of this century and left untitled as well as unfinished. At the time of Pound's death, *The Cantos* had long since passed the hundred predicted, hopefully, by critics as the structure of the poem, but the survey, in epic form, of world history was not yet complete. It is, however, a very selective view of history, in spite of its far-ranging material, allusions and foreign languages. To understand the poem the reader should begin at the beginning and also read everything Pound ever read. The references have been indexed, but Pound's elliptical style and the enormous length and amount of recondite reference remain a difficulty. *The Pisan Cantos* (74–84) are an exception. Written during Pound's incarceration in the stockade, when, significantly, he was not merely suffering great physical discomfort but also deprived of books from which to quote, these cantos seem more immediately beautiful, compassionate and good. Ironically, they also illustrate Pound's uncritical admiration of Mussolini, as well as containing some of his strongest statements of economic policy. His oversimplified views, especially about money supply, were influenced by the social credit theories of Major Douglas. If *The Cantos* are finally judged as an overall failure, they have too many moments of "great poetry" to be dismissed. It is in these moments that we see Pound as *il miglior fabbro*, as Eliot called him.

(See also **Imagism.**)

Hugh Selwyn Mauberley, 1920.
A Draft of XVI Cantos, 1925.
Personae: Collected Poems, 1926.
A Draft of XXX Cantos, 1930.
The Pisan Cantos [74–84], 1948.
The Cantos of Ezra Pound [1–84], 1948.

Section: Rock-Drill, 85–95 de los Cantares, 1956.
Thrones: 96–109 de los Cantares, 1959.
Drafts and Fragments of Cantos CX to CXVII, 1969.

Letters, 1907–1941, ed. D. D. Paige, New York: Harcourt, Brace, 1950; London: Faber & Faber, 1951.
Literary Essays, ed. T. S. Eliot, London: Faber & Faber; Norfolk, Conn.: New Directions, 1954.
Annotated Index to the Cantos (1–84), ed. J. H. Edwards and others, Berkeley and Los Angeles: Univ. of California Press, 1957; Cambridge: Cambridge Univ. Press, 1958.
Letters to James Joyce, ed. F. Read, Norfolk, Conn.: New Directions, 1967; London: Faber & Faber, 1968.

A.P.H.

POWELL, Anthony (1905–   ), born in London and educated at Eton and Oxford, worked for a London publisher until 1935 and then, temporarily, as a scriptwriter. His writing career was interrupted by the Second World War, when he served in the Intelligence Corps, but afterwards he began a sequence of novels entitled *The Music of Time.* While writing novels, he has also been an active journalist and reviewer and from 1952 to 1958 he was literary editor of *Punch.*

Though he has written many novels since 1930, he has been recognized only relatively recently as an original writer. Before the war he wrote a number of comic novels—anatomies of the futility and boredom of fashionable London and artistic Bohemia. In his postwar sequence the social comedy is still present but becomes more thoughtful and analytic. The novels begin in the 1920s and trace the career of Nicholas Jenkins, though the scores of characters he meets are as important as the central figure. Powell's principal achievement lies in his ability to combine the methods of the comic writer with the seriousness of the social observer. He has created a world of characters who, though extravagant and grotesque, are ultimately credible and representative of their period. His humor depends more on the characteristics of normality than on eccentricity, so that in *The Music of Time* there is a serious awareness of social change and the passage of time.

Afternoon Men, 1931.
John Aubrey and His Friends, 1948.
A Question of Upbringing, 1951.
A Buyer's Market, 1952.
The Acceptance World, 1955.
At Lady Molly's, 1957.
Casanova's Chinese Restaurant, 1960.
The Kindly Ones, 1962.

The Valley of Bones, 1964.
The Soldier's Art, 1966.
The Military Philosophers, 1968.
Books Do Furnish a Room, 1971.   O.K.

POWERS, J. F. (James Farl) (1917–) was born in Jacksonville (Illinois) and educated at Northwestern University. He has taught literature at Marquette and Michigan Universities, has been writer-in-residence at Smith College and has been awarded several fellowships. Two volumes of stories, *The Prince of Darkness* (1947) and *The Presence of Grace* (1956), were followed by the award-winning novel, *Morte d'Urban* (1962). His stories explore the predicament of Roman Catholicism in the wilderness of the Midwestern United States, evoking with meticulous accuracy the muted comedy of souls wrestling with the shabby devils of mediocrity, isolation, boredom and penny-wise fund-raising. Witty, detached and compassionate, his ironic fables hint, however, at the persistent "presence of grace."   M.T.

POWYS BROTHERS—POWYS, John Cowper (1872–1963), **POWYS, Llewelyn** (1884–1939), **POWYS, Theodore Francis** (1875–1953) were the three most famous brothers of a family of eleven, closely associated with the West country, where their father was a clergyman. John and Llewelyn were given a formal education at Cambridge and then followed a nomadic life of travel—John lecturing for many years in America, Llewelyn traveling to Greece, Italy, Kenya and America. Theodore attended a private school in East Anglia and in 1905 settled in Dorset, which was to provide the rural background for all his novels.

The brothers were to develop their gifts in quite different ways. John's temperament was romantic, philosophic and introspective and his works are more autobiographical than those of the other two brothers. He also uses ancient legend and myth in his novels, as in *A Glastonbury Romance* (1932). Llewelyn's gift for fiction was not great; he excels in the evocation of nature and in half-fictional, half-reminiscent sketches. Theodore is, in many ways, the most original of the three. Like Hardy's, his narrative methods are close to those of the folktale, though in his case the allegorical element is stronger and his prose style simpler, deriving much of its flavor from Bunyan and the Bible. His most important works —*Mr. Weston's Good Wine* and *Unclay*—are pastoral allegories, in which the central figures—Mr. Weston and John Death—have a symbolic role.

John Cowper Powys
Wolf Solent, 1929.
A Glastonbury Romance, 1932.

John Cowper Powys, 1934 (autobiography).
Owen Glendower, 1941.

Llewelyn Powys.
Confessions of Two Brothers (with J. C. Powys), 1916.
Ebony and Ivory, 1923.
Earth Memories, 1934.

Theodore Powys.
Mr. Tasker's Gods, 1925.
Mr. Weston's Good Wine, 1927.
Fables, 1929; as *No Painted Plumage*, 1934.
Unclay, 1931.   O.K.

PRAED, W. M. (Winthrop Mackworth) (1802–39) was born in London, educated at Eton and Cambridge and called to the bar in 1829. He was a member of Parliament and in 1834–35 secretary to the Board of Control. He died of tuberculosis in 1839. His verse, consisting mainly of light satire and occasional poems, appeared in periodicals and was not collected until after his death. The political poems illustrate his gift for witty satire on contemporary incidents and personalities, whilst his *vers de société* is always elegant and sometimes pleasantly ironical.

Selected Poems, ed. K. Allott, London: Routledge, 1953; Cambridge,
    Mass.: Harvard Univ. Press, 1954.   A.P.

PRATT, E. J. (Edwin John). See **Canadian Literature.**

PRIESTLEY, J. B. (Joseph Boynton) (1894–   ), born in Bradford (Yorkshire), was educated locally and at Cambridge before starting his career as a reviewer and critic. He has since written many works of criticism, plays and novels, first achieving popular success with his third novel, *The Good Companions* (1929; *f.* 1933; 1957). His early plays were conventional, realistic dramas and reached a wide audience, though later, as in *Johnson over Jordan* (1939), he experimented with dramatic form and popular theories of time. His novels justify the claim he makes for himself as an entertainer; they are robust, colorful and humane interpretations of English middle-class life.

Plays, 3 vols., London: Heinemann; New York: Harper, 1948–50.
Essays of Five Decades, ed. S. Cooper, London: Heinemann, 1969.   O.K.

PRINGLE, Thomas. See **African Literature.**

PRIOR, Matthew (1664–1721) was the son of a Wimborne (Dorset) joiner. His precocious classical learning prompted Charles Sackville, earl of Dorset, to patronize his education at Westminster School. After further study at St. John's College, Cambridge, he progressed to important diplomatic appointments at the Hague under the Whigs, then after a change of political heart, in Paris under Harley. He was imprisoned (1715–16) by the Whig government which attempted unsuccessfully to use him as a lever against the fallen ministers. On release, a subscription volume and a £4,000 gift from Lord Hervey enabled Prior to buy Down Hall in Essex. He died suddenly of cholera in September 1721.

Prior wrote some of the finest occasional verse in the language. His tales, epigrams, pastorals, lyrics and amorous verses display all the qualities of his favorite mentors, the urbane strength of Horace, the vitality of Restoration poetry and the delicate artistry of the French *petits poètes sur les sujets légères*. He also wrote fine clear hudibrastic (see **Butler, Samuel** 1612–80) poems such as "Alma" (composed in 1716), a skeptical burlesque of contemporary philosophy. In addition, he attempted Spenserian and Chaucerian imitations, which like "Solomon" (1719), a poem prefiguring Johnson's *The Vanity of Human Wishes* in form and content, were significant if unsuccessful experiments. His prose adds little to the scope of his literary achievement, but it does have the strength and grace of his verse.

Literary Works, ed. H. B. Wright and M. K. Spears, 2 vols., Oxford: Clarendon Press, 1959; 2nd edition, 1972.   A.W.B.

PROCTER, Thomas. See **Elizabethan Miscellanies.**

PURDY, James (1923–), who was born in Ohio, reveals in his fiction a prevalent contemporary preoccupation with the nature of reality. His first novel, *Malcolm* (1959), relates in picaresque fashion the adventures of a beautiful boy, abandoned by his father and led by an astrologer in his quest for identity. In *The Nephew* (1960) a schoolteacher discovers the true characteristics of her nephew, killed in war, when she writes a memorial to him. A celebrated rapist, trying to learn about himself through his biographers, is the subject of the satirical *Cabot Wright Begins* (1964). *Color of Darkness* (1957) collects short stories and *Children is All* (1962) stories and plays. Purdy's characteristic themes are repeated in *Eustace Chisholm and the Works* (1967), set in Depression Chicago.   R.W.

PYNCHON, Thomas (1937–) born in Long Island, studied engineering at Cornell before becoming a full-time writer. His challenging novels combine a fertility of invention with philosophical and scientific erudition; he is particularly interested in entropy (the title of one of his short stories) and the quantum theory, which rejects linear causality. His first novel, *V*, which won the William Faulkner award for the best new novel in 1963, interweaves three tales—the first, the career of Benny Profane, a rootless street-man whose life is fragmented, without direction; the second, the story of Herbert Stencil, who searches for the meaning of V; and the third, Victoria Wren's history (1898–1942), full of espionage, revolution and sexual episodes. Victoria is only part of what V means, but Stencil finds versions of V everywhere; if V means everything, it means nothing, or rather an entropic condition without distinctions. Stencil suspects an ultimate plot of "ominous logic," but the plots men see may be solipsistic creations. This problem is reexamined in *The Crying of Lot 49* (1966), a funnier, more controlled, more compassionate novel with a strong sense of loss and waste. It follows the adventures of Oedipa Maas as she carries out her task as executrix of an estate and lights upon the alternative society of the Tristero system. But the dilemma of *V* remains; if there is no meaning beyond chaos and contingency, Tristero is a paranoid fantasy; if there is an ordered pattern, it is invented, and invites narcissism and madness.   R.W.

Q

QUARLES, Francis (1592–1644), born near Romford (Essex), was at Cambridge and entered Lincoln's Inn. He was in Germany (1613–20) in the suite of Princess Elizabeth after her marriage to the elector Palatine, and in Ireland (1626–30) as secretary to Archbishop Ussher. From 1620 he published devotional poetry, including *Divine Fancies* (1634), his very popular *Emblems* (1635), and *Hieroglyphics of the Life of Man* (1638). His loyalty to Charles I, expressed in his pamphlet *The Loyal Convert* (1644), led to Puritan reprisals. The consequent destruction of his books and papers hastened his death.

Works, ed. A. B. Grosart, 3 vols., Chertsey Worthies Library, 1880–81.

H.N.D.

R

"R.S." of the Inner Temple. See Elizabethan Miscellanies.

RADCLIFFE, Mrs. Ann (1764–1823), born in London, daughter of William Ward, a merchant, came into early contact with artists at the home of Thomas Bentley, a partner of Josiah Wedgwood. After her marriage in 1787 to William Radcliffe, a newspaper proprietor, she lived quietly except for regular holiday tours in and outside England. Foreign travel and the experience of keeping a travel journal (published in 1795 as *A Journey . . . through Holland and the Western Frontier of Germany*) completed Mrs. Radcliffe's art-inspired tendency to combine sensuous, spatial and emotional impressions in a single description, so that the scene described makes a compelling visual-emotional effect on the reader's sensibility. This is her greatest gift to the Romantic aesthetic; it emerges clearly after her two early novels, *The Castles of Athlin and Dunbayne* (1789) and *A Sicilian Romance* (1790), and can be felt in *The Romance of the Forest* (1791) and her best novel, *The Mysteries of Udolpho* (1794; ed. B. Dobreé, London: Oxford Univ. Press, 1966).

Mrs. Radcliffe's influence may be detected behind much of the Gothic writing of the age, and her use of apprehension to sensitize the reader's awareness is a procedure of some significance. Both Coleridge and Keats benefit from it. Her rationalistic timidity in relying on supernatural effects has caused critical amusement: she was, essentially, more concerned to stimulate than merely to astonish, though it was the more sensational parts of her novels which most impressed her first readers.   W.R.

RAINE, Kathleen (1908–   ), the daughter of a schoolmaster, read natural sciences at Girton College, Cambridge. Her marriage to the poet Charles Madge was dissolved. Her poetry reflects deep impressions from childhood years spent with relatives in Northumberland. "The noble country and dignified way of life among the still feudal community of farmers and shepherds" remains her ideal world, and life, since her return to the suburb where her father was teaching, has seemed an exile. Her work on William Blake and Neoplatonism, for which she held a research fellowship at Girton, was the subject of the Andrew Mellon lectures which she delivered in Washington in 1962—they were published as *Blake and Tradition* (1969).

Stone and Flower: Poems 1935–43, 1943.
Living in Time, 1946.
The Pythoness and Other Poems, 1949.
The Year One, 1952.
The Hollow Hill and Other Poems, 1960–1964, 1964.

Collected Poems, London: H. Hamilton, 1956.   D.H.

R A J A N, Balachandra. See **Indian Literature.**

RALEGH, Sir Walter (?1552–1618), soldier, sailor, courtier and
explorer, held and lost the favor of Queen Elizabeth, was imprisoned by
James I and executed after an ill-fated expedition to Guiana. Reputedly an
atheist, he was probably connected with the "School of Night." His
writings reflect his life and interests. Many poems, plaintive and passionate, are addressed to the queen. Disillusionment and suppressed violence
mark the later verse. His prose ranges from simple narrative to polemic
and the dignified, poignant cadences of the unfinished *History of the
World* (1614). (See also **Elizabethan Miscellanies.**)

Works, ed. W. Oldys and T. Birch, 8 vols., Oxford: Oxford Univ. Press,
    1829.
Poems, ed. A. M. C. Latham, London: Routledge; Cambridge, Mass.:
    Harvard Univ. Press, 1951.   J.M.P.

RAM, Shanker. See **Indian Literature.**

RAMSAY, Allan (1685–1758), a Scottish wigmaker who became a
bookseller and poet, did much to preserve the continuity and vitality of
the Scottish poetic tradition, both by his own verse and by his editions of
earlier Scottish poetry. His most celebrated work is *The Gentle Shepherd*
(1725), which was produced on the London stage and described by Burns,
who frequently acknowledged his debt to Ramsay, as "the noblest
pastoral in the world." The fresh, boisterous, even racy quality of Ramsay's Scottish verse is less apparent in his English poetry, but he is always
distinguished by good humor and liveliness.

Works, ed. B. Martin, J. W. Oliver, and others, 5 vols., Edinburgh:
    Scottish Text Society, 1951–71.   R.E.

RAND, Ayn (1905–   ), novelist and philospher, is a naturalized American who left her native Russia in 1926. Her two most successful novels are
The Fountainhead (1943; *f.* 1949 by King Vidor), ostensibly based on the

life of Frank Lloyd Wright, and *Atlas Shrugged* (1957), a fantasy in which a colony of geniuses dedicate their lives to self-interest. *For the New Intellectual* (1961) and *The Virtue of Selfishness* (1964) contain essays and philosophical excerpts from her novels which advance her theory of objectivism founded on a defense of capitalism, unadulterated by any altruistic motives, and an unfettered individualism.

R.W.

RANDOLPH, Thomas (1605–35), son of Lord Zouch's steward, was educated at Westminster School and Trinity College, Cambridge. A friend of Jonson and Shirley, Randolph spent his last dissipated years in London. Author of six plays marked by condensed learning and a clear, cool style, of which the best are *The Jealous Lovers* (1632) and *The Muse's Looking-Glass* (1638; p. 1630), Randolph also wrote pastorals, elegies and epithalamia in which the wit, clarity and melodiousness are reminiscent of Jonson's lyrics, although Randolph is quite without Jonson's moral strength.

Works, ed. W. C. Hazlitt, 2 vols., London: Reeves & Turner, 1875.
Poems, ed. G. Thorn-Drury, London: Etchells & Macdonald, 1929.   G.P.

RANSOM, John Crowe (1888–   ), a minister's son, was born in Tennessee and educated at Vanderbilt and Oxford. He taught English at Vanderbilt (1914–37) and, with others, edited *The Fugitive* (1922–25), which championed Southern regionalism and published the bulk of his own finest poems. He wrote the "Statement of Principles" for *I'll Take My Stand* (1930), in which he and other Southerners argued for cultural values they associated with the prewar South's agrarian economy. His famous poem "Antique Harvesters" is an ironic expression of similar nostalgia. He then taught until retirement at Kenyon College (1937–58) and founded *The Kenyon Review* in 1939, partly to publish examples of the New Critics' close textual analysis. He helped to formulate their guiding principles in two works, *The New Criticism* (1941), itself an elaboration of *God without Thunder* (1930), an attack on scientism, and *The World's Body* (1938), an apology for poetry as "nothing short of a desperate ontological or metaphysical manoeuvre." Critics should concentrate on a poem's particular "structure" and "texture."

A friendly mentor to more ambitious writers such as Tate and Warren, Ransom can claim an intrinsic importance for his own poetry. *Poems about God* (1919) contains attempts to forge his own style, which he certainly achieved in his *Fugitive* period poems, *Chills and Fever* (1924) and *Two Gentlemen in Bonds* (1927). These are precise, witty, often deliberately archaic in diction, scholarly, full of ironies concerning death, childhood and man's contrarieties. Ransom has since composed few new poems, but has revised, rejected and reaccepted old poems for various selections. The latest appeared in 1970.

Selected Poems, 1945.
Poems and Essays, 1955.
Selected Poems, 1963.
Selected Poems, 1970.   M.G.

RAO, Raja. See **Indian Literature.**

RATTIGAN, Sir Terence (1911–) was educated at Harrow and Trinity College, Oxford. His first play was *First Episode* (1934) and since then he has been one of the most prolific writers for stage and screen of his generation. Two of his plays, *French without Tears* (1936; *f.* 1940) and *While the Sun Shines* (1943; *f.* 1947), each had runs of over 1,000 performances. An old-fashioned playwright, unaffected by ideas of the absurd or the theater of the "angry young men," Rattigan stresses the qualities of craftsmanship and understatement in writing for the stage and screen, and even in his slightest comedies these professional qualities are always apparent. However, *Flare Path* (1942), *The Winslow Boy* (1946; *f.* 1949), *The Browning Version* (1948; *f.* 1951), *The Deep Blue Sea* (1952; *f.* 1955), *Ross* (1960) and *Man and Boy* (1963) all point to a more serious and dramatically intense side to Rattigan's supposed "middle-brow" attitudes.

Collected Plays, 3 vols., London: H. Hamilton, 1953–64.   G.A.K.

READE, Charles (1814–84) was born in Oxfordshire, educated at Magdalen College, Oxford, and called to the bar in 1843. He sacrificed his academic and legal career to his passionate interest in the drama and in social reform. When he published his novel *Peg Woffington* in 1853, he slowly began to reap the reward for long and obscure years of pre-paratory labor, and during the 1850s and 1860s created a reputation as a crusading reformer whose steady stream of plays and novels reflected his warm-hearted indignation with social injustice of every description, from official brutality in prisons and asylums to abstruse legal anachronisms. Worn out by hard work and constant litigation, he died in London in 1884.

Steeped in melodrama, painstakingly documented and generally weak in characterization, Reade's novels are unique in Victorian fiction. Superficially propagandist and forbidding, they have a strange power to seize and hold the reader's imagination, even when their artistic inade-quacy seems overwhelming. As with Dickens, whom Reade greatly admired, fundamental generosity of spirit transcends gross errors of taste and judgment. *It Is Never Too Late to Mend, Hard Cash* and *Griffith Gaunt* are all impressive examples of the "social problem" school of Victorian literature. The last has been acclaimed (by Henry James among others) as one of the neglected masterpieces of the period, but Reade's medieval reconstruction, *The Cloister and the Hearth*, remains his best-known if not necessarily his most accomplished work.

Peg Woffington, 1853.
Masks and Faces (with Tom Taylor), 1854 (*p.* 1852).
It Is Never Too Late to Mend, 1856.
The Cloister and the Hearth, 1861.
Hard Cash, 1863.
Griffith Gaunt; or, Jealousy, 1866 (*s.* 1865–66).
Put Yourself in His Place, 1870 (*s.* 1869–70).

Collected Works, Uniform Library edition, 17 vols., London: Chatto & Windus, 1895.

D.E.P.

REANEY, James. See **Canadian Literature.**

REEVE, Clara (1729–1807), a clergyman's daughter, was born in Ipswich (Suffolk) and educated at home. After her father's death in 1755 the family moved to Colchester (Essex), where her life was spent quietly. She published a miscellaneous collection of works, including *The Progress of Romance* (1785), which gives an interesting account of contemporary vogues in fiction and critical attitudes towards it. *The Old English Baron* (1772), a novel, connects the Gothic historical fiction of Walpole with that of Mrs. Radcliffe. A moderate element of the supernatural is introduced into a tale of a basically Richardsonian kind, dealing with conduct and common life. The historical coloring is also relatively restrained and limited, and Clara Reeve tries hard to use emotionalism to extend the limits of everyday experience.

W.R.

REEVES, W. P. (William Pember). See **New Zealand Literature.**

REID, V. S. (Victor Stafford). See **Caribbean Literature.**

RENAISSANCE HUMANISM was essentially a devotion to the *studia humanitatis*, a shift from the medieval schoolmen's arguments about doctrine to studies whose basis was linguistic and literary. It originated in Italy, in response to the practical need for men versed in eloquence and statecraft to conduct the affairs of the prospering city-states. The humane disciplines were grammar, rhetoric, history, poetry, moral philosophy; and the fresh appraisal of them initiated by Petrarch (1304–74) signals a revolution in human consciousness. The leading humanists were not theologians but state officials and scholars such as Salutati, Bruno, Alberti and Poliziano, who stood close to power in republican Florence. They wanted to justify the active life of men in secular society as against the ascetic ideal of retired contemplation.

A sharper civic awareness helped change men's attitudes to classical literature and the idea of the ancient world. Diplomats like Poggio Bracciolini (1380–1459) hunted down lost writings in the belief that they were disinterring Rome itself. They revered Cicero and Virgil as repositories of a civic wisdom which had matured in the exigencies of state. Humanists saw that ancient authors are not timeless authorities but men whose writings related to their circumstances and survived fortuitously in corrupt texts. This critical understanding made a codex a priceless human testimony; by establishing a better text, one got nearer to the realities of ancient civilization and of man's moral nature in society.

To place a text critically is to measure its distance from one's own times. Humanist scholars understood that the ancient civilizations were dead, separated from them by a thousand years of barbarism, but the literature survived and showed the way to a new birth, not of learning only but of civilization itself. Linguistic analysis was the solvent, proving the documents, purging the accretions of uncritical centuries, cutting philosophical knots. Valla's exposure of the false Donation of Constantine (1444) and the pseudo-Dionysius Areopagus vindicated humanist faith that all authorities, including the Scriptures, were open to critical scrutiny as literary texts.

Secular history was necessarily revalued. Ancient civilizations presented a perfected model of every kind of political institution in a discernible pattern of change, growth and decay. Implicit in humanist historiography was the idea of a consummate moment which once achieved might be reevoked but not surpassed. Roman history culminated with the decades which fostered Virgil, Horace and Ovid, and ushered in the birth of Christ—the Augustan peace; or alternatively, as one valued political freedom, with the republican Rome of Cicero. Domestic politics in Italy from Cola di Rienzi's rising (1347) to Mussolini show what practical power lay in the dream of re-creating the Roman *civitas* at the precise moment of its perfect realization.

Humane studies were the civilizing agents themselves. They fostered the qualities which specifically distinguish men from beasts and barbarians, perfecting speech and language, inculcating self-knowledge and offering models of civic conduct. An elegant purity of style, which one sought by imitating the best Latin models, was a supreme moral grace. Rhetoric, the art of eloquence and persuasion, held the key; the Orpheus myth shows how poets and orators first drew men from bestial anarchy into the harmony of cities. Cicero had said that eloquence was articulate wisdom, and some celebrated humanist controversies grew out of his corollary that without wisdom eloquence is a weapon in the hands of a madman.

In the end humanism comes back to humanity itself, to the qualities which fulfill one's human nature and relate one to one's fellows by a bond of mutual need. Human life is not a prolonged mortification but has worth and dignity in virtue both of man's middle position between beasts and angels, and of his unique—and perilous—freedom to will his own station in the scale of existence. The final use of humane studies is to fit men to make the proper choice as men and move the right way towards their ultimate bliss.

Humanism was an attitude, not a creed, and its pieties were scholarship and education. The accessory development of printing in Venice by the humanist Aldus Manutius (1449–1515) gave it European currency and promoted the ideal of a Christian community of scholar-statesmen, an aristocracy of intellect. Princes sent promising men to study Greek with Poliziano and Ficino. But there were also great humanist educators in a larger sense, and some outstanding pedagogues. Such men as Guarino da Verona, Vittorino da Feltre, Vives, Sturm and Ascham set before mentors the ideal of training a gentleman in virtue and courtesy through the languages of the two great civilizations, and they implanted in European education its characteristic faith in the moral value of linguistic disciplines. The tangible progeny of Renaissance humanism were the scholastic foundations endowed in this spirit.

Humanist ideas reached England during the fifteenth century and their royal patron, Duke Humphrey of Gloucester, enlarged the university library at Oxford to house collections of codices. But the true English humanists were the scholars who flourished around 1500, some of them pupils of the great Italians: Grocyn, Colet, More, Linacre, Latimer and Lily. Theirs was a Christian humanism, not because Italian humanism was pagan but because their studies had a religious and ethical focus. Like their associate Erasmus, they were Greek scholars because they wanted to understand the New Testament in its essential purity; and they valued civil life as the field of an active piety, the arena of the Christian knight. An ideal of Christian society is implicit in the social criticism of More and Erasmus; writers as different as Foxe and Hooker would appeal to it.

Tudor humanism was institutionalized and perpetuated in the grammar schools and colleges whose foundation was an act of statesmanship in the sixteenth century. Colet himself refounded St. Paul's School in 1510 with the philologist Lily as high master. At the Reformation English humanism entered a narrower pedagogic phase, represented by Cheke and Ascham. Concern for pristine purity sometimes hardened into the equation of truth with simple plainness, in incipient puritanism far from the humanist spirit. Yet Virgil and Ovid had become standard texts, and Terence and Plautus were performed; Ascham thought pagan literature a treasury of wisdom second only to the Bible, a view often disputed in England.

The academic curriculum was reflected in the published output of English works on oratory. But rhetoric and poetry came under attack together as arts of blandishment and lies. Sidney's *An Apology for Poetry* (1595), the most humane-spirited of Tudor prose, made the humanist reply that there is no moral agent more powerful than the eloquent presentation of an ideal world.

Translation diffused humane culture more widely and became a Tudor art. Influential in English renderings were those contemporary European books of nurture and courtesy, such as Castiglione's *Il Cortegiano* (1528), which made style a criterion of civil conduct. Elyot's *The Book Named the Governor* (1531) was the characteristic northern version, taking courtesy to mean the nurturing of a ruler in civic understanding. Elyot's appeal to history for models of worldly wisdom was typical: North presented Plutarch so, and a succession of Tudor chroniclers read our native history as a mirror for statesmen. Edward Hall, with his *Chronicle* (1542), found in it a pattern of providential development towards civic accord and national unity under the Tudors, a reading Shakespeare would transform.

In the sixteenth century humanist attitudes prevailed, but inflexibly and piecemeal. Imitation ossified into Ciceronianism or Petrarchism (the notion that good writing consists in redeploying the features of Cicero's prose or of Petrarch's love poetry); and the unifying vision of humane polity was uncertainly glimpsed. Spenser and Sidney are scions of humanism rather than humanists; their poetry looks to Renaissance ideals but is essentially unclassical. Milton was the one English Poliziano and the last, belated, European humanist. But if the spirit of Renaissance humanism is a celebrating of what it is to be human, with a care for the bond of kind that hallows civil harmony, then the flower of English humanism is William Shakespeare. J.S.

REXROTH, Kenneth (1905–) was born in Indiana but has lived most of his working life in San Francisco where he has long been a powerful center of letters and the arts. His extraordinarily packed and exciting early life is brilliantly recorded in *An Autobiographical Novel* (1966). His excellent critical essays on literature, art and philosophy are collected in *Bird in the Bush* (1959) and *Assays* (1962). His translations include works from the Greek, the Japanese and Chinese—the latter are collected in *One Hundred Poems from the Chinese* (1956). *Beyond the Mountains* (1951) is four verse plays. His connections with the surrealists and objectivists are apparent in *The Art of Worldly Wisdom* (1949) and *The Phoenix and the Tortoise* (1944) respectively; these were followed by other volumes of verse at regular intervals. Much of Rexroth's large output of mainly autobiographical and lyrical poems continuously reasserting aesthetic and ethical values was published in the 1960s and is still being collected.

The Phoenix and the Tortoise, 1944.
The Art of Worldly Wisdom, 1949.
The Signature of All Things, 1950.
Beyond the Mountains, 1951.
The Dragon and the Unicorn, 1952.
In Defense of the Earth, 1956.
One Hundred Poems from the Chinese, 1956.
Bird in the Bush, 1959.
Assays, 1962.
Natural Numbers: New and Selected Poems, 1963.
An Autobiographical Novel, 1966.

Collected Shorter Poems, Norfolk, Conn.: New Directions, 1967.
Collected Longer Poems, Norfolk, Conn.: New Directions, 1968.
The Kenneth Rexroth Reader, ed. E. Mottram, London: Cape, 1972.

E.M.

RICARDO, David (1772–1823) was born in London of Dutch Jewish parents. He followed his father, from whom he became estranged on a point of religious faith, in making a sizable fortune as a member of the London Stock Exchange and in enjoying the respect and confidence of financial circles. He bought a landed estate and in 1819 became a member of Parliament; and, although not a Whig, he was continuously on the side of parliamentary and social reform. His friends included the elder Mill, Malthus and Bentham, and without them he might never have published anything, since his background, though cultured, was not scholarly. This may account for the disorderly arrangement, if not the atrocious style, which marks his writings; their severely logical power proceeds from his natural endowment. His *Principles of Political Economy and Taxation* (1817) made him the supreme political economist of his time, both in England and abroad, and his influence is not yet spent. He is chiefly notable for the celebrated theory of rent to which his name is often applied. According to this, rent was not a cost of production but a surplus. The theory became a powerful weapon against the landowning class.

Works and Correspondence, ed. P. Sraffa and M. H. Dobb, 10 vols., Cambridge: Cambridge Univ. Press (for Royal Economic Society), 1951–55.

R.H.B.

RICE, Elmer (Elmer Leopold Reizenstein) (1892–1967) was born in New York City and took a law degree at New York University. He made use of his legal background in his first theatrical success, *On Trial* (1914), in which he employed the then novel technique of flashbacks in the dramatization of a murder inquiry. His reputation as an innovator was confirmed by *The Adding Machine* (1923), his most important work, which was the first genuine American transplantation of expressionism. Through his figure of Zero, the clerk who is to be replaced by a machine, Rice developed an indictment of the alienation and monotony of life in a mass society and of the gospel of progress. With *Street Scene* (1929; *f.* 1931) he portrayed everyday scenes in a New York apartment house with a Chekhovian poetic realism that was to prove influential, but his subsequent populist dramas, *Counsellor-at-Law* (1931) and *We, the People* (1933) were more conventional in style. His autobiography is *Minority Report* (1963).

D.P.M.

RICHARDS, I. A. (Ivor Armstrong) (1893–) was born at Sandbach (Cheshire) and educated at Clifton and Magdalene College, Cambridge, of which he became a fellow. From 1922 to 1929 he was a university lecturer in English, and during these years produced his most important works in semantics and criticism. During the 1930s he conducted research and taught variously in China and America, returning to Harvard in 1939, first as director of the Harvard Commission on English Language Studies and later (1944) as professor of English literature.

Richards's work has been firmly rooted in the broad field of communications, from philology to politics (*Basic English and Its Uses* set better international understanding as its goal), and is characterized by a deliberate disregard for traditional barriers between branches of study. *The Meaning of Meaning* (written with C. K. Ogden) ventures on "the peculiarly difficult borderlines of linguistics and psychology" in elaborating a more efficient science of symbolism, and in *The Principles of Literary Criticism* Richards submits criticism to psychological scrutiny. The value of a poem resides in its capacity to organize our impulses "for freedom and fullness of life"; thus "the critic . . . is as much concerned with the health of the mind as any doctor with the health of the body." The limitation of this theory of value becomes apparent when a "bad" poem can effect this organization as successfully as a "good" one: discrimination becomes superfluous, and literature itself baffled by relativistic inclusiveness.

Ironically enough, *Practical Criticism*, the later book which drew these conclusions, also set the fashion for close textual analysis and the very identification of technique with value that Richards deplored; hence the contradictions in his influence on subsequent criticism.

The Foundations of Aesthetics (with C. K. Ogden and James Wood), 1922.
The Meaning of Meaning (with C. K. Ogden), 1923.
Principles of Literary Criticism, 1924.
Science and Poetry, 1926.
Practical Criticism, 1929.
Coleridge on Imagination, 1934.
The Philosophy of Rhetoric, 1936.
Basic English and Its Uses, 1943.
Speculative Instruments, 1955.   D.G.

RICHARDSON, Dorothy (1873–1957), after a lonely and uneventful childhood, became a teacher and later a clerk, before marrying Alan Odle, the artist. She devoted nearly all her time to a single work of narrative, *Pilgrimage*, published as a series of novels between 1915 and 1938. This is an "adventure of personality" of Miriam Henderson, from girlhood to womanhood. It is chiefly remarkable as an early example of the stream of consciousness method of characterization; traditional methods of narration are replaced by the ebb and flow of the consciousness of the heroine, whose half-formed impressions of life are recorded with delicacy and single-mindedness.   O.K.

"RICHARDSON, Henry Handel." See **Australian Literature**.

RICHARDSON, Samuel (1689–1761), born in Derbyshire, the son of a reduced tradesman, received little formal education and was apprenticed to a printer at seventeen. By this time, however, he had already exercised his moralistic, narrative and epistolary gifts. At eleven he wrote a cautionary treatise to a scandalmonger; he was sought after by his friends as a storyteller; and he used to assist young ladies in the composition of their love letters. He served his exacting master dutifully, and having worked as a compositor and corrector, in 1719 set up his own business in London, publishing much official and journalistic material. In 1724 he married Martha Wilde, who died in 1731, and all their six children died in childhood (Richardson writes movingly of his domestic misfortunes in his *Correspondence*, 4, 226 ff.). He married again, his second wife being Elizabeth Leake, sister of a Bath bookseller, and four daughters of this second marriage survived him.

Richardson wrote readily in his professional capacity "indexes, prefaces, and sometimes . . . *honest* dedications," but it was only when a request to compile a letter-writing manual called to his mind the story of a servant girl who had resisted her master's advances and eventually married him, that he "slid into the writing of *Pamela*" at the age of fifty-one. The novel was immediately successful. Richardson disdained the praise of Pope and the advice of Warburton, and his break with the aristocratic literary values of the Augustans became complete after Fielding's parody in *Joseph Andrews*, which Richardson, narrow-minded for all his generosity, never forgave. *Clarissa* brought Richardson more certain and more general fame, and a reverential following in England and Europe, especially among women, whose company Richardson always preferred to that of the typically boisterous eighteenth-century gentleman. *Sir Charles Grandison* was eagerly awaited and seemed on publication to offer a hero worthy of comparison with Clarissa. Richardson became master of the Stationers' Company in 1754, the final reward for a life of middle-class virtue; new enterprises, correspondence and fatigue distracted him from any further writing.

Richardson's person and career contradict the traditional idea of the artist (he said of himself that he was "guilty of a very great presumption in daring to write at all"), and his loosely constructed novels run counter to the traditional "rage for order," but they caught the imagination of the age. Johnson acclaimed Richardson as a writer who had "taught the passions to move at the command of virtue," and his method of composition emphasizes this didactic ideal. Richardson would read his "work in progress" to a reverent, mainly feminine, audience, and discuss with them his moral and formal problems, such as the danger of Lovelace's attractiveness as Clarissa's seducer—hence the doubtful idea of appending footnotes to guide the reader's moral discrimination. The readers of *Pamela* and *Clarissa* identified themselves with their heroines in a way that was not possible before. Pamela's claim, "my soul is of equal importance with a princess," contained the aspirations of a new class, and the two heroines became almost mythical embodiments of feminine virtue for the age.

Pamela is in some ways a crude work. Besides the evident facility of its moral lesson, and the sentimentality, there is no exchange of letters, and as a result the epistolary form degenerates into a journal. The best thing in the novel is Pamela's dawning awareness of her feeling for Mr. B—, which "crept like a thief upon me; and before I knew what was the matter, it looked like love." Richardson's understanding of women is based on their not understanding themselves. He was hurried into writing a second part (*Pamela in High Life*) and this continuation, though it contains some good scenes of social comedy (Lady Davers is an early Lady Catherine de Bourgh), suffers from Pamela's parade of self-righteousness.

F. R. Leavis has said that life is too short for *Clarissa*, and certainly

Richardson's prolixity is a serious obstruction to the modern reader. "With you, verbosity becomes a virtue," wrote Aaron Hill to its author; we may not be so convinced, but it is this work that defines his genius, and many are prepared to tackle its 2,000 pages for the reward of Richardson's sensitive psychological insights. "I have no plan," Richardson confessed, and it may be that the steady process of accretion is best suited to the patient exploration of subtly shifting states of mind. It is an art of exhaustive inclusion rather than of discriminating selection; Richardson discovers Clarissa as he writes—profiting from the flexibility of the present tense: "How *much more* lively and affecting . . . must her style be, her mind tortured by the pangs of uncertainty . . . *than* the dry narrative, unanimated style of a person relating difficulties and dangers surmounted," writes Belford to Lovelace. The novel seems to have evolved rather than endured the rigors of formal composition. But Richardson also said, "It is the execution must either condemn or acquit me." Acquittal is assured by his artistic use of the epistolary technique. The exchange of letters is an essential part of the action, and Richardson arouses tension and excitement by simple means, as when Lovelace has monopolized the narrative at the time of the actual rape, and then Clarissa's letters come with her story from a wilderness of silence and isolation. Her slow, certain tragedy is one of the most powerful things in eighteenth-century literature, easily surviving the book's frequent clumsiness. Richardson is capable of other effects besides pathos, as is shown by the description of the sexually repulsive Solmes and the grotesque death of Mrs. Sinclair, the latter a scene of gross physicality which Abbé Prévost saw fit to exclude from his French translation of the novel.

Sir Charles Grandison, equally long, more polished, but far too studied, has less central interest; the nearest thing to a dramatic occurrence is that Sir Charles almost fights a duel. It is only the social comedy of Harriet Byron's introduction into the world, with her minute apprehensions and exquisite embarrassments (a theme that was taken up with delight by Fanny Burney, and later by Jane Austen), that saves Richardson's story of the "Good Man" from suffocating boredom.

Pamela; or, Virtue Rewarded, 1741 (for 1740).
Letters Written to and for Particular Friends . . ., 1741.
Clarissa, 1748.
Sir Charles Grandison, 1754.

Works, ed. L. Stephen, 12 vols., London: Sotheran, 1883.
Novels, Shakespeare Head edition, 18 vols., Oxford: Blackwell, 1929–31.
Correspondence, ed. A. L. Barbauld, 6 vols., London, 1804.   D.G.

RICHLER, Mordecai. See Canadian Literature.

RITSON, Joseph (1752–1803) was born at Stockton-on-Tees (co. Durham) and began life as a lawyer's clerk. This may have stimulated his antiquarian interests. In 1783 he published *A Select Collection of English Songs* (3 vols.) with an introductory essay on the origins of European folk songs. Other publications included *Pieces of Ancient Popular Poetry* (1791), *Ancient Songs from Henry III to the Revolution* (1792—title page, 1790) and a collection of *Scottish Song* (2 vols., 1794). In 1802 appeared *Bibliographica Poetica*, an amazingly full list which first called attention to various texts of *Piers Plowman*. Ritson is notable for his pioneering scholarly insistence on accuracy and for his controversial cantankerousness. (See also **Ballads**.) A.P.

ROBERT of Gloucester. See **Middle English Literature.**

ROBERTS, Sir Charles George Douglas. See **Canadian Literature.**

ROBERTSON, F. W. (Frederick William). See **Sermons.**

ROBINSON, Clement. See **Elizabethan Miscellanies.**

ROBINSON, Edwin Arlington (1869–1935) was brought up in Gardiner (Maine), the setting he used later as "Tilbury Town." His early literary interests were not encouraged, and a childhood ear infection troubled him all his life. In 1888 he fell in love with Emma Shepherd, but she married his brother Herman. (In 1909, when Herman died, Robinson asked Emma to marry him. She refused, both then and several times later.) In 1891 he went to Harvard, but was called home in 1893 because of family problems of ill health and failing finances. Already resolved to become a poet, he did some tutoring to earn money and published his first volume, *The Torrent and the Night Before*, at his own expense in 1896.

Life then began to fall into a pattern of restlessness, worry over money, loneliness and depression, relieved only by a few close companions and alcohol. In 1899 he obtained a secretarial job at Harvard and in 1902, with financial help from Mrs. Richards and Hays Gardiner, published the long narrative poem *Captain Craig*. From 1903 he worked on the New York subway and in advertising until in July 1905 President Roosevelt gave him a post in the New York Custom House. He published *The Town down the River*, his first independent commercial venture, in 1910 and in the following year first visited the MacDowell Colony in New Hampshire where he was to return every summer until his death. His friends there included Thornton Wilder and Constance Rourke.

The years 1911 to 1923 mark the main creative period of his life, and both the *Collected Poems* of 1921 and *The Man Who Died Twice* (1924) won Robinson a Pulitzer Prize. By the early 1920s he had fame and a certain amount of financial independence. In 1927 he published the third of his Arthurian romances, *Tristram*, which won a third Pulitzer Prize. A volume a year appeared from 1929 to 1935, including *Matthias at the Door* (1931) and *Amaranth* (1934). In January 1935 he entered a New York hospital with cancer, and died three months later, having completed his final work, *King Jasper*.

His best poems are the short, dramatic portraits—"Richard Cory," the quiet, rich, handsome man who one night puts a bullet through his head; "Aaron Stark," the hard, curlike miser; the mysterious "Fleming Helphenstine"; romantic old "John Evereldown"; bitter "Thomas Hood"; or the grief-stricken butcher, "Reuben Bright." The influence of Hardy and Browning is clear in these poems, but at a time when American poetry was at a low ebb, Robinson brought clarity of vision, a sympathetic understanding and, most important, a new directness and precision of language. The finest of these poems is "Mr. Flood's Party," in which old Eben Flood holds his solitary drinking session. Superficially comic, the poem brings out the man's loneliness and unhappiness. The best known is "Miniver Cheevy," in which Cheevy dreams of Thebes and Camelot and bemoans his being "born too late." The poem is at least partly an ironic dig by Robinson at himself, for a great deal of his own effort went into his Arthurian trilogy, *Merlin*, *Lancelot* and *Tristram*. Popular at the time, they contain a curious mixture of archaic and colloquial language and fail to hold the reader's attention. This is true of the many long, dramatic narratives—*Captain Craig*, "The Book of Annandale," *The Man Who Died Twice*, *Cavender's House*, *Matthias at the Door* and *King Jasper*; despite good passages, all are flawed. Robinson was not at his best when philosophizing; the short "Eros Turannos" is worth more than most of the longer poems.

The Torrent and the Night Before, 1896; reprinted, with additions and
    alterations, as *The Children of the Night*, 1897; 1905.
Captain Craig, 1902.
The Town down the River, 1910.
Van Zorn, 1914 (play).
The Porcupine, 1915 (play).
The Man against the Sky, 1916.
Merlin, 1917.
Lancelot, 1920.

The Three Taverns, 1920.
Avon's Harvest, 1921.
Collected Poems, 1921.
Roman Bartholow, 1923.
The Man Who Died Twice, 1924.
Dionysus in Doubt, 1925.
Tristram, 1927.
Cavender's House, 1929.
The Glory of the Nightingales, 1930.
Matthias at the Door, 1931.
Nicodemus, 1932.
Talifer, 1933.
Amaranth, 1934.
King Jasper, 1935.

Collected Poems, New York: Macmillan Co., 1937.
Selected Letters, ed. R. Torrence, New York: Macmillan Co., 1940.
Untriangulated Stars: Letters of Edwin Arlington Robinson to Harry de Forest Smith, ed. D. Sutcliffe, Cambridge, Mass.: Harvard Univ. Press, 1947.
Collected Letters, ed. W. L. Anderson, Cambridge, Mass.: Harvard Univ. Press, forthcoming.   D.N.C.

ROCHESTER, John Wilmot, 2nd Earl of (1647–80), educated at Burford Grammar School and Wadham College, Oxford, graduated M.A. after nine months' residence (1660). In 1661 he was granted a pension of £500 by Charles II, who also arranged for him to travel on the Continent. By 1665 he had returned to court. After a brief imprisonment for trying to abduct a Somerset heiress (whom he subsequently married in 1667), he entered the navy, distinguishing himself in the Dutch Wars. Rochester's subsequent life was a curiously double one. In the country he was a devoted husband, performing his private and many official duties conscientiously. In London he was a notoriously debauched rake (numbering among his many mistresses the actress Elizabeth Barry) and the leader of the irresponsible band of Court Wits, at once the kind patron and vicious satirist of the foremost writers. His libertine life undermined his health, and from 1671 he began to suffer the effects of venereal disease. Always a deep thinker, Rochester was led through discussions with Bishop Burnet to a dramatic death bed conversion.

Apart from *Valentinian* (1685), a tragedy adapted from Fletcher, Rochester's work consists of satires, love lyrics of a courtly pastoral type and burlesques of that form such as his "Love a woman! you're an ass." His philosophical and social satire constitutes his finest writing and reaches its bitterest intensity in *A Satire against Mankind*. A great deal of erotica was formerly ascribed to Rochester, but such attributions are largely spurious.

Collected Works, ed. J. Hayward, London: Nonesuch Press, 1926.
Complete Poems, ed. D. M. Vieth, New Haven: Yale Univ. Press, 1968.

H.N.D.

ROETHKE, Theodore (1908–63) was born and brought up in Michigan "in and around a beautiful green-house owned by my father and uncle." He was educated at Michigan State University and then at Harvard. He learned early, he said, how to get high grades and that rapidly seemed meaningless, so despite some good teachers, he professes to have hated both places. He did, however, write his first poems at Harvard and receive his first encouragement there. It then took ten years for him to write "one little book," *Open House*, which came out in 1941. Despite (or possibly because of) his own experience, Roethke was a teacher for most of his career, working from 1947 until his death at the University of Washington.

Roethke's early poems in *Open House* are characteristically short, intense, rhymed lyrics, several of which ("Death Piece," "Genesis," "On the Road to Woodlawn") are reminiscent of Emily Dickinson. His books from *The Lost Son* onwards contain many longer, more expansive poems, often using autobiographical material, though he has taken pains to point out that his protagonist's spiritual history is not that of himself personally, but of all "haunted and harried men." His work contains many moods and styles. *Words for the Wind* (1958), his collected earlier verse, includes a series of love poems together with his sequence "The Dying Man," in memory of Yeats. His next book, *I Am! Says the Lamb* (1961), is a volume of humorous nonsense poems and limericks, and *The Far Field*, published posthumously, contains another series of love poems and the important "North American Sequence."

Open House, 1941.
The Lost Son and Other Poems, 1948.
Praise to the End, 1951.
The Waking, 1953.
Words for the Wind: Collected Verse, 1958.
I Am! Says the Lamb, 1961.
The Far Field, 1964.

Collected Poems, New York: Doubleday, 1966; London: Faber & Faber, 1968.
On the Poet and His Craft, ed. R. J. Mills, Jr., Seattle: Univ. of Washington Press, 1965 (selected prose).

Selected Letters, ed. R. J. Mills, Jr., Seattle: Univ. of Washington Press, 1968; London: Faber & Faber, 1970.   J.P.W.

ROGERS, Samuel (1763–1855), born and educated in London, followed his father's profession as a banker until the latter's death in 1793 left him with independent means. For over half a century he was famous as entertainer, friend and helper of most contemporary artists and writers, and his wit was celebrated. His poetry is quiet and cultivated in the late eighteenth-century reflective-descriptive manner. *The Pleasures of Memory* (1792) was popular, but is less good than *Human Life* (1819). Rogers's great interest in the visual arts and travel can be seen in *Italy* (2 parts, 1822–28), the 1830 edition of which (illustrated by Turner and Stothard) is celebrated.

Poetical Works, ed. E. Bell (with memoir), London: Bell & Daldy (Aldine edition of the British Poets), 1875.   W.R.

ROLLE, Richard. See **Middle English Literature.**

RÖLVAAG, O. E. (Ole Edvart) (1876–1931) was born in Norway, emigrated to the United States in 1896 and was professor of Norwegian at St. Olaf's College, Minnesota (1907–31). His first novel, *Letters from America* (1912), was in the form of correspondence between an immigrant and relatives in Norway and, like all his books, was written in Norwegian. *Giants in the Earth* (1927), the first book of a trilogy, remains his greatest work. The sequels, *Peder Victorious* (1929) and *Their Fathers' God* (1931), complete an epic account of pioneer families and their adjustment to a tough existence in Dakota Territory, while coping with generational and religious conflicts.   R.W.

ROMANTIC MOVEMENT, The. The English Romantic movement in literature may be said to last from 1789 to 1824, from the publication of Blake's *Songs of Innocence* to the death of Byron. Of course, the influence of the movement was to be felt throughout the nineteenth century, not only in England, but in France and Germany as well, and many of its ideas and attitudes are still part of the assumptions on which contemporary Western culture is based. But by 1824 the period of great and fundamental innovation was over. Keats and Shelley were already dead; Wordsworth, Coleridge and Blake had produced their most characteristic and important work. As might be expected of any group of writers as heterogeneous as these clearly were, both their sources and their works were eclectic. Nevertheless, the characteristics of the movement can be defined, and the phrase retains its use as a vital term in literary history.

The central attitude of the Romantic movement may be described as an instinct to explode the rules and restrictions of eighteenth-century "culture"—particularly as these were characterized by Pope:

> God, in the nature of each being, founds
> Its proper bliss, and sets its proper bounds:
> But as he framed a whole, the whole to bless,
> On mutual wants built mutual happiness.
>
> (*An Essay on Man*, 3, 109–112)

The acceptance implied here, both of the divine and the social order, found its philosophical corollary in Locke's idea that the "mind is wholly passive." In such a world the function of the poet was to name and describe, for the purpose of producing a verbal mirror of the order and form which had been given to the universe by its Creator. The Romantics, on the other hand, overthrew the idea that the mind of man was passive, and with it the notion of a proper bliss, determined by a given position in a given hierarchy. In short, the Romantic movement reflected a change in psychological attitude which itself brought about an adjustment of the individual to the external world.

This world, for the Romantic poet, was no longer merely a place to describe; it aroused emotions in him, by no means all of which were pleasant. Pain, doubt, anxiety, fear and awe played as important a part in the Romantic response as a sense of order, tranquillity, joy and love; and these discordant emotions were equally a source of poetic pleasure. One part of this powerful emotional response derived from what T. E. Hulme attacked in *Speculations* (1924) as "spilt religion," an attribution to external nature of invisible powers at work within it; but the more important and interesting part lay in the recognition that the so-called given world was not given at all, but existed as a two-way traffic between what actually existed outside the observer and what his own individual mind brought to it. (The position of Coleridge needs qualification here because he regarded himself as a pure idealist.) Out of this dual relationship sprang the importance which the Romantic poet attached to nature, that inclusive concept which circumscribed the world of descriptive fact with the sublime, the elusive, the intangible—and, at times, the macabre as well as the decadent.

The recognition that the mind was a landscape to explore led also to a belief in individual aspiration, in freedom from the bondage of received ideas, and at the same time to an insistence on the value of the shaping spirit of imagination, making clear to the poet what were the "permanent realities" and the "eternal forms." Individualism of this sort intensified, too, a recognition of the deficiencies in prevailing social attitudes, and for the first generation of Romantics—Blake, Wordsworth and Coleridge—this found its focus in the enthusiasm aroused by the French Revolution in its earliest stages. The Reign of Terror from September 1793 to July 1794 shattered their hopes in France, but the Romantic movement continued to be characterized by an insistence on the value of liberty which, although rooted in individualism, was inseparable from political attitudes. In short, the force and direction of the movement may be defined as emotional and political rather than philosophical. Shelley, of course, was also deeply influenced by abstract ideas, but this was the temper of his mind, not the tenor of the movement.

Generalizations about the Romantic movement will not in fact be found to coincide precisely with the major Romantic poets considered together. Nevertheless, the Romantic attitude—and so the essential differences between the literature of the eighteenth and early nineteenth centuries—can be summed up, on the one hand, as the overthrow of a belief in a given world, and, on the other, in the ideas and feelings that grouped themselves around one or more of the following assumptions: (1) Nature was a complex and mysterious interassociation of mind and external world; (2) the imagination revealed to man, and particularly the poet, the discordant elements of which his mind was composed, and so made him aware of "truth" which he was able to embody in symbol and myth; (3) the individual genius of man was most nobly expressed when he was free from the slavery of received beliefs, religious, political and social. And out of this last was derived the Byronic spirit through which English Romanticism exercised its profoundest influence on the movement in Europe.

As the Romantic poets rebelled against eighteenth-century passiveness towards external nature, so they also reacted against the domination of poetry by the heroic couplet, in which elegance, neatness and wit were the main criteria (though Byron must be excepted here). Poetry now came to be defined as "memorable speech"—"memorable" because in meter as in verbal exactness it expressed a truth of the imagination, not merely a well-turned observation; and "speech" because it was not the product of a special poetic vocabulary, but the language of everyday usage. Both points may clearly be seen by comparing the following lines from Erasmus Darwin's *The Loves of the Plants* (1789):

> As yon gay clouds, which canopy the skies
> Change their thin forms, and lose their lucid dyes;
> So the soft bloom of Beauty's vernal charms
> Fades in our eyes, and withers in our arms.
>
> (canto 2, 195–98)

with a stanza from Coleridge's "The Rime of the Ancient Mariner" (1798):

> "I fear thee, ancient Mariner!
> I fear thy skinny hand!
> And thou art long, and lank, and brown,
> As is the ribb'd sea-sand."   (4, 1–4)

The ballad form which both Coleridge and Wordsworth used for their own poetic ends had not, of course, been revived by them. In 1765 Percy had published his *Reliques of Ancient English Poetry*, which had revealed the effectiveness of unsophisticated language in earlier ballads derived from popular oral tradition, as well as the opportunities provided by narrative poetry in which the narrator remained impersonal. Wordsworth, in particular, profited a great deal from the revival of interest in the ballad, as he did too from the poems of Cowper and Burns published in the mid-1780s. These moved away from the heroic couplet and showed indifference to urbanity, cultivated by an acceptance of the propriety and taste of classical ideals. Nevertheless, Wordsworth and Coleridge did modify the ballad tradition by the force of their own intellectual and ethical interests; and their penetration in this respect created a new form of memorable speech which brought to an end the supremacy of the heroic couplet and the aesthetic and moral assumptions which lay behind its success. In consequence, Romantic poetry is notable for the variety and frequent dexterity of its prosody in which eclecticism of feeling produces verse as dissimilar as Keats's Odes, Coleridge's "Kubla Khan" and Shelley's *Prometheus Unbound*. But the full significance of these changes in style is only made clear when considered beside the changes in attitude outlined above.

The English Romantic movement falls into two major generations of poets: (1) Blake, Wordsworth and Coleridge; (2) Keats, Shelley and Byron. It includes a number of less important poets, of whom the most notable is Southey, and one major novelist, Scott. The essential eclecticism of the movement naturally tended to proliferate as the influence of these first major Romantics diversified. The fruits of its first great flowering are plentiful in the literature of the middle and late nineteenth century. Keats's concern with the Middle Ages lives in much of the best work of Tennyson, as it does in the Pre-Raphaelite poets and painters. The Romantic spirit is to be found in Swinburne's search for the essence of poetry and in Morris's quest of *The Earthly Paradise* (1868–70). It lies behind the aesthetic theories of Pater's *Studies in the History of the Renaissance* (1873) and in the new religion which the young W. B. Yeats was determined to found from the "infallible church of poetic tradition." But by 1865, when Arnold published "The Function of Criticism at the Present Time," a new determination was setting in to see things as they "really" were. George Eliot had already published *Adam Bede* (1859) and was about to publish *Felix Holt* (1866) in which the social responsibility of the individual played a much larger part than his genius; and before long would emerge the open anti-Romanticism of Samuel Butler, George Gissing and George Bernard Shaw. The poets of the 1890s (Dowson, Lionel Johnson and Davidson) and the Georgians display the ultimate Romantic influence, as do Hardy and Housman. The latter's *The Name and Nature of Poetry* (1933) has been described as the last Romantic critical pronouncement in English literature.   P.G.M.

ROSENBERG, Isaac (1890–1918) was born of Jewish parents in Bristol. Seven years later his family moved to London, where he was educated. After winning a scholarship to the Slade School, he hoped to make his way as a painter, but was not able to support himself financially. In 1914 ill health forced him to emigrate to South Africa, but he returned to enlist in the following year and was killed in action in 1918. *Poems* (1922) and *Collected Works* (1937) reveal his developing art which culminates in the poems written directly from the trenches in the First World War. In the latter collection Siegfried Sassoon's foreword rightly draws attention to the original, vigorous fusion of English and Hebrew cultures, a rich tension between calm stoicism and prophetic fire in Rosenberg's poetry. As a poet he recognized both the pity and, especially, the horror of war, yet at times viewing the conflict with almost cool detachment. Despite the violence of his subject matter, he always brings to poetry the eye of the pictorial artist for shape and order. (See also **War Poets.**)

Collected Works, ed. G. Bottomley and D. Harding, London: Chatto and
    Windus, 1937.   O.K.

ROSS, Sinclair. See **Canadian Literature.**

ROSSETTI, Christina (1830–94), younger sister of Dante Gabriel Rossetti, appears in several of his paintings and had close connections with the Pre-Raphaelite Brotherhood. She began writing poetry in her teens and published first, under the pseudonym Ellen Alleyn, in their journal, *The Germ*. Her poems were later illustrated by her brother and by Arthur Hughes, and she was at one time engaged to James Collinson, a painter-member of the original Brotherhood. Her life, marred by persistent ill health, was spent quietly in London with her mother and she never married; the engagement was broken off because Collinson's conversion to Rome offended her devout Anglicanism.

    Much of her poetry is devotional and she was considerably influenced by the Oxford movement, but her Pre-Raphaelite affinities may be seen in narrative poems like "Goblin Market" with its rich pictorial sensuousness, in her ballads, her more frequently anthologized lyrics and her poems for children. Her lyrics characteristically deal with unrequited love, death and the separation of lovers, but are distinguished by their technical accomplishment and their music. Her religious poetry is the expression of deeply felt personal experience and conviction; more orthodox in its Christianity than the poetry of Emily Brontë or Emily Dickinson, it has a similarly vibrant spiritual intensity.

Goblin Market and Other Poems, 1862.
The Prince's Progress and Other Poems, 1866.
Sing-Song: A Nursery Rhyme Book, 1872.
Poems, 1890.

Poetical Works, ed. W. M. Rossetti (with memoir), London: Macmillan, 1904.   D.W.

ROSSETTI, D. G. (Dante Gabriel) (1828–82), the son of an Italian political refugee, studied art at the Royal Academy Schools and under Ford Madox Brown. In 1848 he founded the Pre-Raphaelite Brotherhood with Holman Hunt, John Everett Millais and four others. His marriage in 1860 to Elizabeth Siddal, a favorite Pre-Raphaelite model and herself an artist and poet, ended tragically in 1862 with her death from an overdose of laudanum. Rossetti had been writing poetry since about 1847 but had published only in periodicals, and he buried his manuscript poems in his wife's coffin. In 1869 he was persuaded to have it exhumed in order to publish a volume of poetry, a decision which attracted an understandable but unfortunate notoriety. In October 1871 *The Contemporary Review* carried an extravagantly abusive attack by "Thomas Maitland" (Robert Buchanan) under the title "The Fleshly School of Poetry." Rossetti replied responsibly and with dignity in "The Stealthy School of Criticism" (*Athenaeum*, 16 December 1871), but there is little doubt that the attack contributed to the melancholia and depression of his later years which replaced his earlier boisterous, good-humored energy, and which was aggravated by the chloral to which he became addicted as a pain-killer.

Excessive as it was, Buchanan's attack was not without foundation. Rossetti's poetry, like his painting, had a predominant sensuousness that many Victorians found exotic and distasteful. The sonnet "Nuptial Sleep" in "The House of Life" aroused such antagonism that he suppressed it. Yet this aspect of his work has, in many respects, proved more lasting in its appeal than the medievalism of some of his ballads, influential as these were on younger poets like Morris and Swinburne. He himself was much influenced by Keats, Tennyson (for the Moxon edition of whose poems in 1857 Rossetti was one of the illustrators), Poe (Rossetti thought of "The Blessed Damozel" as a counterpart to "The Raven") and, in dramatic monologues like "Jenny" and "The Last Confession," Browning. His main inspiration was Dante, and his first book was a volume of translations of *The Early Italian Poets* (1861), revised and reissued in 1874 as *Dante and His Circle*. Dante's relationship with Beatrice fascinated him: "The Blessed Damozel," published in 1850 in the short-lived Pre-Raphaelite journal, *The Germ*, attempts the expression of a mystical awareness of love transcending death. He saw his own relationship with Elizabeth Siddal increasingly in these terms, both in his painting and in his poetry.

The interrelationship between these two art forms is embodied in the colorful pictorialism of his poetry, its sharply visualized if sometimes lush imagery and its sensuous apprehension of physical experience. It shows, too, in the literary sources of many of his paintings and his treatment of the same subject in both media (at least six pictorial versions of "The Blessed Damozel" survive); but the relationship is more fundamental and less easily definable than this, as may be seen from the early prose tale "Hand and Soul" and the late sonnet sequence "The House of Life," which contains some of his most enduring work. A conscientious craftsman, he had a sensitive ear for poetic effect and the evocative use of language to express thought as well as emotion and visual experience.

The Early Italian Poets, 1861.
Poems, 1870.
Ballads and Sonnets, 1881.

Collected Works, ed. W. M. Rossetti, 2 vols., London: Ellis & Scrutton, 1886.
Poetical Works, ed. W. M. Rossetti, London: Ellis & Elvey, 1891.   D.W.

ROTH, Henry (1906–) was born in Tysmenica (Austria–Hungary). He is the author of a single novel, *Call It Sleep* (1934), which only in the 1960s came to be considered one of the masterpieces of the 1930s. It is a poetic work of intense compassion and great power. Similar in setting to many Jewish ghetto novels of the period, it creates from it a world of vision and nightmare. Roth, who, until recently, raised wildfowl in Maine, has refused all encouragement and enticement to write again.   D.V.W.

ROTH, Philip (1933–) was born in Newark (New Jersey) and graduated from Bucknell and Chicago Universities. His first novella, *Goodbye Columbus* (1959; f. 1969), was a critical and public success. The book's subject is the comedy of Jewish assimilation into Gentile culture, its pretensions and vulgarities. Roth showed himself an author of trenchant wit with an accurate ear for dialogue. The book won him a Guggenheim Fellowship and strong praise from authors such as Bellow and Kazin.

Roth's second book, *Letting Go* (1962), was subjected to considerable critical attack. A deliberate contrast to the first novel, it was an extremely long and serious work on the subject of detachment. Its hero, Gabe Wallach, is prone to indecision and is reluctant either to leave or to commit to permanent attachment. The book traces the dire effects of his vacillation but is full of overlong accounts of domestic conflict. In both this and his next novel, *When She Was Good* (1967), Roth seems to set out to extend the province of his writing. The later book is an attempt to create a Protestant Midwestern world, and its theme is the damage done by both moral laissez faire and extreme self-righteousness. Both books are largely without humor and the author is oddly detached.

Undoubtedly, Roth's most famous and probably most successful book is *Portnoy's Complaint* (1969). In it the novel of Jewish suffering has become a dirty joke. The book has a comedy that is both desperate and hilarious. The Jewish agony is Portnoy's father's constipation, his inherited guilt his penchant for masturbation. Guilt and insecurity are the basis of wildly comic in-fighting within the family. The book is a stylistic *tour de force* written in a prose that has the ease and spontaneity of the spoken language.

Goodbye Columbus and Other Stories, 1959.
Letting Go, 1962.
When She Was Good, 1967.
Portnoy's Complaint, 1969.
Our Gang, 1971.   D.V.W.

ROWCROFT, Charles. See **Australian Literature.**

ROWE, Nicholas (1674–1718) studied law at the Middle Temple, but gave it up to write tragedies of an affectingly sentimental kind. *The Fair Penitent* (1703) and *Jane Shore* (1714) are the best known. The latter professes to imitate Shakespeare's style and Rowe was, in fact, the first critical editor of Shakespeare's plays, which he brought out in 1709. A strong Whig, he held several government positions and in 1715 was made poet laureate. In 1718 he published his verse translation of Lucan's *Pharsalia*, much admired by Samuel Johnson in his life of Rowe.   J.C.

ROWLEY, William (?1585–?1642). Almost all that is known of Rowley is that he was a comic actor with Prince Charles's Men (1609–c. 12) and the King's Company (1623). Rowley seems to have been sole author of four plays, the best being the citizen comedy, *A New Wonder* (1632), but he was mainly known as a collaborator. He wrote at least five plays with Middleton, including the great tragedy *The Changeling* (p. 1622), for which he contributed the opening and closing scenes and the subplot. His work in general has vigor and humor but little grace. G.P.

ROYCE, Josiah (1855–1916), American philosopher, was born in California, graduated from the University of California (1875) and Johns Hopkins (Ph.D., 1878). Appointed by William James to teach philosophy at Harvard (1882), Royce remained there until his death. His greatest metaphysical work, *The World and the Individual* (1900–01), lectures delivered at the University of Aberdeen, expounded his beliefs in the necessary oneness of things and the ethical obligation of man to make his unique contribution to the moral order. He developed these concepts further in *The Philosophy of Loyalty* (1908), contending that the individual adjusts to life by pursuing a social aim which expresses loyalty to a cause. Royce's views stand in sharp contrast to the predominant materialism of his age. He also wrote books reflecting the influences of his California childhood, *California: A Study of American Character* (1886) and *The Feud of Oakfield Creek* (1887). J.W.

RUKEYSER, Muriel (1913–) was born in New York City and educated at Vassar College and Columbia. Best known as a poet, her writing covers an exceptionally wide field. *Theory of Flight* won the Yale Series of Younger Poets contest in 1935, and further volumes of poetry included *U.S. 1* (1938), *A Turning Wind* (1939), *Wake Island* (1942), *Beast in View* (1944), *The Green Wave* (1948), *Orpheus* (1949), *Elegies* (1949), *Selected Poems* (1951), *Body of Waking* (1958), *Waterlily Fire: Poems 1935–1962* (1962) and *The Speed of Darkness* (1968). Her early verse turned Depression experiences and observations into powerful documentary poetry. Later, in the 1940s, she celebrated universal love and the creative spirit. Among her other work is the biography *Willard Gibbs: American Genius* (1942), *One Life* (on Wendell Wilkie, 1957) and *The Traces of Thomas Hariot* (1970). J.P.W.

RUNYON, Damon (1884–1946), born in Manhattan (Kansas), enlisted in the army at fourteen and served in the Philippines. As a journalist he covered Mexican revolutions and the First World War, and ran syndicated columns. His last five years were spent as a Hollywood writer-producer. As a short-story writer he created an idiosyncratic universe and style. His Broadway "citizens" speak only in the present tense, as: "I am sitting in Mindy's restaurant . . . when in comes three parties from Brooklyn wearing caps as follows: Harry the Horse, Little Isadore, and Spanish John." Typical collections are *Guys and Dolls* (1932), the basis for the 1950 musical of that name (*f.* 1955), and *My Wife Ethel* (1939).   J.L.M.

RUSKIN, John (1819–1900), the only child of well-to-do middle-class parents, was educated at Oxford and traveled widely both in early life and later. His five volumes of *Modern Painters* (1843–60) contain a defense of the modern landscape artists in general, and of J. M. W. Turner in particular, against hostile critics. Making truth to nature his criterion of excellence, Ruskin undertakes to describe natural phenomena as they really are, so that the painters' representations of them can be judged. Much of his most eloquent writing occurs in these descriptions. Appealing to the same criterion, he defended the Pre-Raphaelites when they were attacked. This group had a medievalizing as well as a naturalistic strain; so some of its adherents responded enthusiastically to Ruskin's praise of Gothic and decrying of the Renaissance in *The Stones of Venice* (1851–53).

In this work and in *The Seven Lamps of Architecture* (1849) Ruskin advances the theory that the quality of art and craftsmanship is dependent upon the happiness of the workman producing them. Dissatisfaction with nineteenth-century art and craftsmanship naturally led him to ask what caused the unhappiness of the nineteenth-century workman. In *Unto This Last* and *Munera Pulveris* he blamed the prevalence of the orthodox doctrines of political economy which, by pretending that man is an acquisitive machine and therefore devoid of soul, social affections and moral sense, encourage him to act as if he were thus deprived—that is, selfishly. Ruskin later developed his social criticism in *Fors Clavigera*, a series of letters to the working men of the country.

Modern Painters, 5 vols., 1843–60.
The Seven Lamps of Architecture, 1849.
The Stones of Venice, 3 vols., 1851–53.
Unto This Last, 1862 (*s.* 1860).
Sesame and Lilies, 1865.
Fors Clavigera, 8 vols., 1871–84.
Munera Pulveris, 1872 (*s.* 1862–63).
Praeterita, 3 vols., 1886–89.

Works, ed. E. T. Cook and A. D. O. Wedderburn, 39 vols., London: G. Allen, 1902–12.
Diaries, ed. J. Evans and J. H. Whitehouse, 3 vols., Oxford: Clarendon Press, 1956–59.   J.D.J.

RUSSELL, Bertrand, 3rd Earl (1872–1970) was educated privately and at Trinity College, Cambridge, where he later became a fellow and one of a group of Cambridge philosophers, including G. E. Moore, A. N. Whitehead and Wittgenstein, who were to dominate philosophical thinking for many years. He wrote voluminously on philosophy, logic, ethics and politics and was awarded the Nobel Prize for literature in 1950. It was in the role of experimental investigator that he first made his important contribution to mathematical philosophy. Collaborating with Whitehead, he considered the relationship between logic and mathematics and questioned the assumptions of Aristotelian logic in *Principia Mathematica* (1910–13). In later writings, including *An Introduction to Mathematical Philosophy* (1919), *The Analysis of Mind* (1921) and *An Outline of Philosophy* (1927), he added to empirical philosophy a tenable theory of mathematical knowledge and reinforced it with new logical techniques.

The crisis of the First World War turned his attention from philosophy to ethics and politics, and much of his later writing deals exclusively, and often controversially, with social problems. His social criticism is always constructive, though it is often combined with a challenging wit and humor. From 1927 to 1932 he and his second wife, Dora Winifred Black, ran an experimental school for children, and Russell's views on education are put forward in *On Education* (1926) and *Education and the Social Order* (1932). He had extensive experience with politics and the effect of politics. His activities ranged from membership of the House of Lords to serving a term in prison for failing to agree with those in power on war policy. Latterly he played a leading part in the Campaign for Nuclear Disarmament. The inspired thinker and man are brilliantly revealed in his *Autobiography*, vols. 1–3 (1967–69) and *My Philosophical Development* (1959).

Collected Stories, ed B. Feinberg, London: Allen & Unwin, 1972.   O.K.

RUSSELL, George William ("Æ") (1867–1935), one of the main figures in the Irish intellectual movement, was born in county Armagh and became a poet, painter, economist and critic. He combined an interest in theosophy with an enthusiasm for Irish nationalism. The practical side of his work is represented by pamphlets on the Irish economy and by his interest in the Irish National Theatre, for which he wrote one play, *Deirdre* (1907; *p*. 1902). His interest in theosophy, which he shared with Yeats, inspired his own poetry, which he claimed was the product of mystical rapture. *Collected Poems* (1926) contains verse which expresses, with quiet grace, a mood of pantheism.   O.K.

"RUTHERFORD, Mark" was the pseudonym of William Hale White (1831–1913). Son of devout Dissenting parents, he studied for the ministry, but was expelled for heresy and spent most of his life in London as civil servant or journalist. Like George Eliot, who strongly influenced him, he never lost a sense of moral duty. *The Autobiography of Mark Rutherford* and *Mark Rutherford's Deliverance* are largely autobiographical, recounting a provincial Dissenter's loss of faith and subsequent behavior. *The Revolution in Tanner's Lane*, his finest work, portrays the lives of poor Dissenters through generations of religious and political change. Rutherford's novels are often digressive and poorly plotted, but his strong lucid style evoked admiration from such diverse observers as Gide and Lawrence.

The Autobiography of Mark Rutherford, 1881.
Mark Rutherford's Deliverance, 1885.
The Revolution in Tanner's Lane, 1887.
Miriam's Schooling, and Other Papers, 1890.
Catharine Furze, 1893.
Clara Hopgood, 1896.

Novels, 6 vols., London: Oxford Univ. Press, 1936.   C.P.

RYMER, Thomas (?1643–1713) lives now, somewhat unfairly, as the critic who thought "the tragical part" of *Othello* "a bloody farce, without salt or savour." He studied at Cambridge and at Gray's Inn, later doing useful work as historiographer royal from 1692. Misguided and polemical, he is nevertheless an early formal critic of English literature. *The Tragedies of the Last Age Considered* appeared in 1677, but he reserved the full vigor of his assault on Shakespeare until *A Short View of Tragedy: Its Original, Excellency, and Corruption* (1693). His own tragedy, *Edgar*, failed (1678).

Critical Works, ed. C. A. Zimansky, New Haven: Yale Univ. Press, 1956.
                                                                    J.C.

RYMOUR, Thomas, of Erceldoune. See **Middle English Literature.**

S

SACKVILLE, Thomas, 1st Earl of Dorset, Lord Buckhurst (1536–1608) studied at the Inner Temple and probably at Oxford and Cambridge also. He became a member of Parliament, privy councillor, chancellor of Oxford (1591), lord treasurer (1599) and lord steward (1601). Sackville was author of the two last acts of *Gorboduc* (written with Norton) and of the "Induction" and "The Complaint of Buckingham" pieces in *A Mirror for Magistrates* (1563). The "Induction" is perhaps the finest English poem between Chaucer and Spenser, with strong imaginative power and real stylistic grandeur.

G.P.

SALINGER, J. D. (Jerome David) (1919–) was born in New York City, attended Valley Forge Military Academy and saw military service in Europe. *The Catcher in the Rye* (1951), a brilliant, sensitive, vernacular novel about forty-eight hours in the life of Holden Caulfield as he crosses the line from puberty to adulthood, and the early stories (see *Nine Stories*, 1953; U.K. title: *For Esmé, with Love and Squalor*) established Salinger, especially with young readers, as a writer of remarkable moral, cultural and aesthetic sensitivity. His later work has been a sequence, running through several long stories, *Franny and Zooey* (1961); *Raise High the Roofbeam, Carpenters* and *Seymour: An Introduction* (1963), focused on a heroic family, the Glasses; it continues, though the ideals of aesthetic and verbal perfection embodied in the characters clearly makes for an artistic dilemma. He remains, nonetheless, one of postwar America's most important writers of fiction.

The Catcher in the Rye, 1951.
Nine Stories, 1953 (U.K. title: *For Esmé, with Love and Squalor*).
Franny and Zooey, 1961.
Raise High the Roofbeam, Carpenters and *Seymour: An Introduction*, 1963.

M.B.

SALKEY, Andrew. See **Caribbean Literature.**

SANDBURG, Carl (1878–1967) was born in Galesburg (Illinois) of Swedish immigrant parents. After an adolescence as hobo, farmworker, chore boy and dishwasher, he served in the Spanish-American War, worked his way through four years at Lombard College, Galesburg, wrote advertising copy, became an organizer for the Social Democratic Party and secretary to the mayor of Milwaukee, wrote for many Midwestern newspapers and became an editorial writer for the Chicago *Daily News*. His career as a lecturer began in 1908 with "Walt Whitman, an American Vagabond"; after 1920 he added the role of folk singer. Apart from some privately printed poems in 1904, his literary career dates from 1914 when *Poetry* printed "Chicago." The titles of his books of poetry— *Chicago Poems, Cornhuskers, Smoke and Steel, Slabs of the Sunburnt West, Good Morning, America* and *The People, Yes*—disarm criticism. Their relaxed omnivorousness invited comparison with Whitman, but Sandburg had nothing of Whitman's visionary eccentricity. His poems tend to achieve their impact through such banalities as the contrast between a child's questioning and the brute inscrutability of billboards or marching soldiers. The accuracy of his ear could transcend his vision, however; some of his best poems (in *The People, Yes*) are simply anthologies of American idioms, and he was a distinguished folk-song collector. His major prose work was his six-volume life of Lincoln, in which loaded atmospheric descriptiveness tends to triumph over the austerity of scholarship. *Remembrance Rock* is a 1000-page novel focusing four crucial epochs in American history. *Always the Young Strangers* is autobiographical.

Chicago Poems, 1916.
Cornhuskers, 1918.
Smoke and Steel, 1920.
Slabs of the Sunburnt West, 1922.
Abraham Lincoln: The Prairie Years, 2 vols., 1926.
Good Morning, America, 1928.
The People, Yes, 1936.
Abraham Lincoln: The War Years, 4 vols., 1939.
Bronze Wood, 1941.
Remembrance Rock, 1948 (novel).
Always the Young Strangers, 1953 (memoir).
Honey and Salt, 1963.

Complete Poems, New York: Harcourt, Brace, 1950.   M.T.

SANGSTER, Charles. See **Canadian Literature**.

SANTAYANA, George (1863–1952), philosopher, poet and novelist, was born in Spain, came to the United States in 1872, graduated from Harvard in 1886, where he was professor of philosophy (1889–1912), before returning to Europe. Santayana's philosophical concerns, the functions of reason and matter in human inquiry, are developed in *The Life of Reason* (5 vols., 1905–06) and *The Realms of Being* (4 vols., 1927–40). His philosophical theories are also reflected in his literary works, notably *The Last Puritan* (1935), a novel contrasting Puritanism and hedonism. Santayana's other writings include a play, *Lucifer: A Theological Tragedy* (1899; revised, 1924), a collection of *Poems* (1922), and *Character and Opinion in the United States* (1920), an analysis of materialism and idealism in America. *Persons and Places* (3 vols., 1944–53) is his autobiography. All of Santayana's writing is marked by a felicitous style and poetic sensitivity.

J.W.

SARGESON, Frank. See **New Zealand Literature.**

SAROYAN, William (1908–   ) was born in Fresno (California) of Armenian parents, spent his early years in an orphanage, then unsuccessfully occupied a wide variety of jobs. He is a prolific short-story writer of tremendous vitality and exuberance, breezy and tender, impetuous and somewhat undiscriminating in his love for his characters. From his first collection of short stories, *The Daring Young Man on the Flying Trapeze* (1934), his work had considerable popular success. *My Name Is Aram* (1940) is largely fictionalized autobiography but contains some of his finest short stories, and he has written several volumes of direct autobiographical reminiscence, such as *Here Comes, There Goes, You Know Who* (1961). Saroyan's plays, like *My Heart's in the Highlands* (1939), symbolic and sentimental by turns, have repeated his success in other areas. More recent fiction, such as *One Day in the Afternoon of the World* (1964), has concentrated on bitterness and loneliness.

D.V.W.

SASSOON, Siegfried (1886–1967), born in London, was educated at Marlborough and Cambridge. His early life was that of a moderately cultivated gentleman with a taste for writing verse. He was sent down from Cambridge and lived in London, where he published several volumes of minor verse. Commissioned in 1914, he served in France for most of the First World War, at first with enthusiasm and exceptional bravery. Later he introduced a new note of realism and satire into poetry about the war, reaching a high pitch of obsessive and contemptuous anger against civilians at home, the General Staff and the Church. He declared his opposition to the war and refused to take any further part. Thanks to the influence of friends, including Robert Graves, he was not court-martialed but declared temporarily insane and sent to Craiglockhart military hospital (where he met and greatly influenced Wilfred Owen). After the war he became an outspoken supporter of pacifism, and much of his work continued to be connected with his wartime experiences.

Sassoon's prose in his autobiographies and novels is always carefully written, rarely dull and often exuberant. His verse written outside the pressures engendered by his war experiences is unimpressive, but the poems of 1916–18 achieve a highly original style—terse, epigrammatic and colloquial, shaped by a fierce indignant energy.

(See also **War Poets.**)

The Old Huntsman, and Other Poems, 1917.
Counter-Attack, and Other Poems, 1918.
Memoirs of a Fox-Hunting Man, 1928.
Memoirs of an Infantry Officer, 1930.
Sherston's Progress, 1936.
The Weald of Youth, 1942.
Siegfried's Journey, 1916–1920, 1945.

Collected Poems, 1908–1956, London: Faber & Faber, 1961.   A.Y.

SATCHELL, William. See **New Zealand Literature.**

SAVAGE, Richard (?1697–1743) was probably of humble birth. He lived an irregular life and died in poverty. He was well regarded in his own day and was the subject of a lengthy but unreliable *Life* by his friend Dr. Johnson (1744). The circumstances of Savage's life probably find expression in some of the macabre episodes of his long didactic poem *The Wanderer* (1729), whilst *The Bastard* (1728) reflects on the countess of Macclesfield, whom he claimed as his mother. *The Progress of a Divine* (1735) is the best of his verse satires. He also wrote mediocre plays— *Love in a Veil* (1719; *p.* 1718); *Sir Thomas Overbury* (1724; *p.* 1723).

Poetical Works, ed. C. Tracy, Cambridge: Cambridge Univ. Press, 1962.
                                                                    A.P.

SCHREINER, Olive. See **African Literature.**

SCHULBERG, Budd (1914–) was born in New York. The son of a film producer, he satirized the Hollywood in which he grew up in *What Makes Sammy Run?* (1941), a novel, which he later translated into a musical, about a dynamic but vulgar movie mogul. *The Disenchanted* (1950) is a fictional rendering of F. Scott Fitzgerald's last Hollywood years. Schulberg's other writings include *The Harder They Fall* (1947; *f.* 1956), a novel about prize fighting, and *Sanctuary V* (1969), stories and distinguished scripts for such films as *On the Waterfront* (1954)—in novel form as *Waterfront* (1955)—and *A Face in the Crowd* (1957).   M.G.

SCHWARTZ, Delmore (1913–66) was born in Brooklyn and much of his poetry is involved with his life "amid six million souls." Educated at the University of Wisconsin, New York University and Harvard, he subsequently taught at several universities. His first volume of poetry, *In Dreams Begin Responsibilities*, appeared in 1938 and was well received for its combination of musicality and intellectual depth. *Genesis, Book I* (1943) and *Vaudeville for a Princess* (1950) followed, and he was awarded the Bollingen Prize for *Summer Knowledge: Selected Poems 1938–58* (1959). He was editor of *Partisan Review* (1943–47), and associate editor until 1955 when he became poetry editor of *The New Republic*. There is a memorable elegy to him in section 6 of John Berryman's *Dream Songs*.

Selected Essays, ed. D. A. Dike and D. H. Zucker, Chicago: Univ. of Chicago Press, 1970.   J.P.W.

SCIENCE FICTION is a branch of speculative literature whose modern origins may be traced to Jules Verne and H. G. Wells. Strictly defined, it deals in extrapolations of the future based on scientific or pseudoscientific hypotheses. Among its most popular themes are space flight, time travel, encounters with extraterrestrial beings, psychological or biological changes in human and alien life forms, and the effects of technology on social behavior.

The existence of science fiction as a distinct literary form is generally dated to 1928, when Hugo Gernsback founded the magazine *Amazing Stories*. Over the next two decades the American pulp magazines dominated the field. The "space operas" of this period often resembled, in plot and form, the traditional western transposed from the prairies to outer space. For the scientific content of their stories, writers drew heavily on the inspiration of H. G. Wells whom many regard as the true founder of science fiction. His early novels—*The Time Machine* (1895), *The War of the Worlds* (1898), *The First Men in the Moon* (1901)—and his short stories collected in *The Country of the Blind* (1911) set out the prototypes for nearly all the themes which characterize the genre.

The technological stimulus of the Second World War, particularly in the field of rocketry, created a boom in science fiction, reflected in the popularity of hard-core science fiction writers such as Isaac Asimov (e.g., *The Caves of Steel*, 1954), Arthur C. Clarke (e.g., *The Sands of Mars*, 1951), Robert Heinlein (e.g., *The Man Who Sold the Moon*, 1950; *The Green Hills of Earth*, 1951) and "John Wyndham" (J. B. Harris) (e.g., *The Day of the Triffids*, 1951; *f.* 1962), and in the editorial success of John W.

Campbell, Jr., editor of *Astounding Science Fiction*. In the 1950s scientific optimism began to give way to social and political concerns, taking their cue from Aldous Huxley's *Brave New World* (1932) and George Orwell's *Nineteen Eighty-Four* (1949). Among the most successful works of this type are *The Space Merchants*, by Frederik Pohl and C. M. Kornbluth, Kurt Vonnegut's *Player Piano*, Walter M. Miller's *Canticle for Leibowitz*, and the stories of Alfred Bester, Robert Sheckley, William Tenn, and Clifford Simak.

In the later 1960s the exhaustion of the traditional themes, and the decline of the pulp magazines, combined with increasing pessimism about the benefits of scientific progress, led to a fragmentation of the genre into subcategories, such as the nonscientific fantasies inspired by the writings of J. R. R. Tolkien, and gave rise to a new emphasis on form rather than content. These trends have been the source of much confusion about the precise definition of science fiction as a literary genre, and have raised the possibility that it may be reintegrated in the mainstream of literature under the more general label of speculative fiction.   A.J.C.

SCOTT, Duncan Campbell. See **Canadian Literature.**

SCOTT, F. R. (Francis Reginald). See **Canadian Literature.**

SCOTT, Sir Walter (1771–1832) was an Edinburgh lawyer's son. Infantile paralysis at an early age left him lame and resulted in his being sent to live on his grandfather's farm in the Border country, where he first revealed his lifelong passion for folk lore and ballad literature. In 1778 he was sent to Edinburgh High School. He read law at the university (1783), studied with his father, was called to the bar in 1792, became sheriff-deputy of Selkirkshire in 1799 and a clerk of session in Edinburgh in 1806. Scott's legal duties established the basic pattern of his life. After he married Charlotte Charpentier in 1797 they spent the law terms in Edinburgh, immersed in the intellectually modern, progressive society of that city in its golden age, and the rest of the year in the Border country, convenient for Scott's sheriff's duties, where they were surrounded by people and places that fed Scott's imaginative sympathy with his country's romantic past. In 1811 Scott bought Abbotsford, near Melrose, and the estate and house which he created in many ways expressed the same attempt as he made in the novels, to show a viable modern Scottish way of life, conscious of traditions but realistically awake to the demands of up-to-date commercial society.

The dual quality of Scott's mind can be felt in his first serious literary work, *The Minstrelsy of the Scottish Border* (1802–03). Apparent in it are his historicism, his appreciation of Scottish folk culture, his relish of heroic actions and strong emotion powerfully expressed, and his lifelong love of a good story. At the same period Scott was also editing Dryden's works (1808), an undertaking which emphasizes the breadth of his sympathies. His dual interest and equal competence in Augustan and Romantic writing suggests what is true of his best later work—that his romantic, picturesque imagination is allied with a strongly analytical, realistic interest in historical process as a means of explaining the character and qualities of modern life. As well as collecting ballads Scott had begun to imitate them. In addition to his natural love of the heroic spirit of balladry we may sense a masculine speed and directness of narration, not unlike Dryden's, in his first long narrative poem, *The Lay of the Last Minstrel* (1805), a work which made Scott the most popular British poet until Byron's *Childe Harold* was published.

From the beginning Scott's massive and various literary productivity was unfortunately involved with financial entanglements. He anticipated profits and spent far too much on the house and purchases of land at Abbotsford. In 1814 near-bankruptcy was averted by the immediate success of his first novel, *Waverley*. A spate of novels followed which made "The Great Unknown" (Scott published the novels anonymously till 1827) the most famous and influential author in Europe at that time. At first he dealt with episodes in recent Scottish history, but in *Ivanhoe* he turned to England in the Middle Ages. *Ivanhoe's* huge success encouraged him to write further medieval romances and the settings gradually extended to France (*Quentin Durward*) and even Palestine (*Tales of the Crusaders*). Though sometimes good stories, these medieval romances, deriving from his historical studies, are clearly inferior to Scott's best work, in which he could draw on his rich knowledge of his own country's culture and still-living traditions.

In 1821 George IV made Scott a baronet and in the early 1820s his friendship was sought by everyone in society. But in 1826 life changed dramatically. Scott's publisher failed and he found himself responsible for debts amounting to some £115,000. He determined to pay the money by writing and the strain to which he subjected himself is movingly revealed in his *Journal*, which he had started just before the disaster. Scott overworked till his health gave way, and after a winter in Italy he died at Abbotsford in September 1832, having paid off about half his debts in under six years. The creditors were paid in full after his death.

It has been said of Scott that "perhaps indeed he cared more for his stories than for his art." Any criticism of him must come to some such conclusion. He was a born storyteller, he absorbed a folk tradition in which heroic and tragic tales play a large part, and his own youthful experience of overcoming illness to achieve a firm constitution did much to increase his admiration for physical valor and adventure. Even the weakest of his narrative poems and novels show two basic qualities: a stirring plot and imaginative richness in re-creating past ways and appearances. His triumphs are of re-creation; the past lives in his work, for he saw that past societies conditioned men into forms of thinking which were often unlike our own, and that, though life in the past was different, it was not therefore inferior to the present and ought not to be patronized through superficial romanticism.

The unity of his best novels derives from his interest in the historic process through which Scotland had turned from a heroic-barbarous state into a modern commercial nation. In his major works character and setting alike contribute to the elucidation of a moment in which Scottish culture is at a crisis, two rival ideologies having reached a point of deadlock. Behind this lies Scott's knowledge of recent Scottish history, of a time full of dramatic religious, political and ideological conflicts. His early novels cover most of the great struggles in Scotland's recent past. Modern critics have agreed in singling out *Old Mortality* (1816), *The Heart of Midlothian* (1818) and *Redgauntlet* (1824) as being those in which Scott's view of the mixed blessing which modern civilization seemed to have proved for Scotland rises to a vision in which tragedy and the deepest vein of pathos play an essential part. But a high degree of interest also attaches to three of Scott's novels in which the story is set within his own lifetime. In these three books the eighteenth-century Scottish conflict between feudal-heroic values and modern common sense reveals itself, first through the survival into modern life of unruly social elements and a strain of folklore, magic and mystery (*Guy Mannering*, set in the 1770s), then in mere harmless quixotry in an individual's sentimental fondness for old ways and values (*The Antiquary*, set in the 1790s—its hero showing Scott's wry amusement at his own historical enthusiasms), and, finally, in a positive tragedy which derives from an inability and refusal to accept the absolute disappearance of the heroic element from the modern world (*St. Ronan's Well*, set in the opening years of the nineteenth century).

Scott's novels were innovatory in many respects. In his handling of setting, pathetic fallacy, atmosphere and picturesque elements generally to illuminate the basic purpose of his tale, he went far beyond his contemporaries. In his use of a wide range of socially representative characters, their speech patterns and jargon, and the linking of them in such a way that they create a sense of all layers of society being involved in the process of national evolution, he shows complete originality (bar a hint which he derived from Maria Edgeworth's *Castle Rackrent*, which he acknowledges in the preface to *Waverley*). The form of his novels is unadventurous; an uncommitted person from outside is brought into a scene of conflict and exposed to both sides in turn so that he can react as a free observer of ideologies and as recorder of the ultimate social-spiritual-cultural synthesis with its complex sense of gain balanced by inevitable losses and potential tragedy. The medieval and non-Scottish romances are simpler still, but as stories they are occasionally admirable (e.g., *Quentin Durward*); and Scott's historical imagination works under full pressure in his re-creation of Cromwellian England in *Woodstock* and the court scenes (and particularly the appearance of King James I) in *The Fortunes of Nigel*.

Scott's poetry is perhaps underestimated today, since the long narrative poem is firmly out of fashion. In *The Lay of the Last Minstrel* and *Marmion* (1808) the ballad feeling runs strongest and the narrative interest is commanding. The emotional directness and depth of ballad poetry can be felt in the battle scene of *Marmion* and also, where it is most movingly linked to personal autobiography, in the excellent introduction to each canto of the poem. The short lyrics in the novels sometimes touch greatness, and Scott had much of Moore's and Byron's flair for charming light poetry in the eighteenth-century artificial manner.

Scott's literary range was enormous, and in no field where he worked, except drama, was he less than competent. He had the most fertile imagination of his age and his influence on Victorian historicism, fiction, regional literature and architectural taste was so widely disseminated that no attempt can be made to define it here. For his contemporaries he was a romantic visionary, charming them with the picturesqueness of his Scottish scene painting and his dramatic revelation of the clash and excitement of history. The modern reader may feel much of the magic at times, but is likely to be most strongly impressed by the grasp and extent of Scott's historical vision, by his embodiment of the post-Union Scottish cultural crisis in terms which do not deny either its inevitability or its tragedy, and by the dry pawkiness of his comic imagination. His *Lives of the Novelists* can be strongly recommended for invaluable insights into his attitude to fiction and the whole field of the novel up to his time. He is one of the great diarists, and the standard biography by his son-in-law, J. G. Lockhart, brings Scott the man vividly before us.

(See also **Ballads; Essays; Romantic Movement, The.**)

Minstrelsy of the Scottish Border, 3 vols., 1802–03.
The Lay of the Last Minstrel, 1805.
Marmion, 1808.
The Lady of the Lake, 1810.
Rokeby: A Poem, 1813.
Waverley, 1814.
The Lord of the Isles: A Poem, 1815.
Guy Mannering, 1815.
"Old Mortality" in *Tales of My Landlord*, 1816.
The Antiquary, 1816.

"The Heart of Midlothian" in *Tales of My Landlord*, 2nd series, 1818.

Rob Roy, 1818.

"The Bride of Lammermoor" in *Tales of My Landlord*, 3rd series, 1819.

Ivanhoe, 1820 (for 1819; *f.* 1951).

The Monastery, 1820.

Kenilworth, 1821.

The Pirate, 1822 (for 1821).

The Fortunes of Nigel, 1822.

Peveril of the Peak, 1822.

Quentin Durward, 1823 (*f.* as *The Adventures of Quentin Durward*, 1955).

St. Ronan's Well, 1824.

Redgauntlet, 1824.

"The Talisman" in *Tales of the Crusaders* (*f.* as *King Richard and the Crusaders*, 1954).

Woodstock, 1826.

Lives of the Novelists, 1826 (as prefaces to Ballantyne's Novelist's Library, 1821–24).

Chronicles of the Canongate, 1827–28.

Tales of a Grandfather, 4 series, 1828 (for 1827); 1829 (for 1828); 1830 (for 1829); 1831 (for 1830).

Novels and Tales, Oxford Scott, 24 vols., London: Oxford Univ. Press, 1912.

Poetical Works, Oxford Complete edition, ed. J. L. Robertson, London: Oxford Univ. Press, 1904.

Letters, Centenary edition, ed. H. J. C. Grierson and others, 12 vols., London: Constable; New York: Columbia Univ. Press, 1932–37.

Journal, ed. J. G. Tait, 3 vols., Edinburgh: Oliver & Boyd, 1939–46; 1 vol., 1950.

W.R.

SEARS, E. H. (Edmund Hamilton). See Hymns.

SEDLEY, Sir Charles (?1639–1701) was a courtier, wit, poet and dramatist. With others he translated Corneille's *La Mort de Pompée* in 1664, wrote two comedies—*The Mulberry Garden* (1668) and *Bellamira* (1687)—and with his *Antony and Cleopatra* (1677) contributed to the Restoration vogue for rhymed heroic tragedy. His lyrical poems are easy and graceful; the duke of Buckingham's phrase, "Sedley's witchcraft," is apt, though Pope thought most of them insipid. Dryden dedicated *The Assignation* to Sedley, recalling their "genial nights" of literary discussion.

Poetical and Dramatic Works, ed. V. de S. Pinto, 2 vols., London: Constable, 1928.

J.C.

SELBY, Hubert, Jr. (1928–) was born in Brooklyn. From 1944 to 1946 he served in the U.S. Merchant Marine. *Last Exit to Brooklyn* (1964) has been the subject of several obscenity cases. Set in Brooklyn it depicts a fragmented, violent society where a typical character is the homosexual "Georgette": "Her life didn't revolve, but spun centrifugally, around stimulants, opiates, johns . . ." Attempts to communicate end in the murder of Harry and the communal rape of the prostitute "Tralala." The novel argues that "the disintegration of urban, industrial civilization is the current reenactment of our damned state." *The Room* (1971) describes the appalling revenge fantasies of a man picked up by the police.   J.L.M.

SELDEN, John. See **Ballads.**

SELVON, Samuel. See **Caribbean Literature.**

SERMONS. Poetry, dance and drama take their origin from religious ceremony, and for long the sermon itself was regarded as a matter of public performance and literary worth. It was seen as rhetoric in form, content and delivery, and until our own century it attracted crowds to hear it and publishers to print and sell it.

The sermon was especially important in times of widespread illiteracy. Thus in the medieval period the coming of mendicant friar or pardoner, accomplished as a preacher, was occasion for gathering together and enjoyment. People came with certain expectations about the way in which the preacher would perform and with ideas about his style derived from well-established rhetorical modes. There were conventions about the division of sermons and choice of illustrative examples.

With the coming of the Reformation, preaching became a means of propaganda against Roman Catholicism. It also gained in importance as a result of the Protestant belief that every man was responsible for his own eternal destiny and therefore must have the opportunity of hearing God's word in a form which he might understand. The result was vivid popular preaching, well illustrated in the work of Latimer. In the late sixteenth century a more academic style came into favor, certainly in court circles. This is variously exemplified in the noble and weighty periods of Hooker, the somber and imaginative manner of Donne and the quaint and learned discourse of Andrewes.

After a last full-bodied efflorescence in Jeremy Taylor this mode of preaching was succeeded by the plain method of Tillotson and his contemporaries. In an age of unadorned expression and severely methodical sermons the acid wit of Robert South (1634–1716) provides welcome diversion. Yet arid though it often appears, the manner of Tillotson dominated the English pulpit for over a century. The exceptions, and the figures who stand out in the eighteenth century, are the new generation of mendicants, the Methodists of the evangelical revival, John Wesley (1703–91) and George Whitefield (1714–70). To a people untouched by the Church of England, the new working classes of the Industrial Revolution, they brought new joy and hope into drab lives. They did so, Whitefield especially, by direct, vigorous, emotional preaching. Their Anglican counterpart, but a man much more restrained in manner and expression, was Charles Simeon (1759–1836).

The next phase of outstanding Anglican preaching comes with the reaction to the evangelical revival, the Oxford or Tractarian movement, which stressed the role of the Church over against man's need to find his own salvation. Its leader was Newman, endowed at once with a powerful intellect, refined emotions, poetic vision and a lucid style. Unmatched in all else, in one thing his contemporary F. W. Robertson (1816–53) outstrips him—as a psychological preacher, able to analyze situation and character with consummate brilliance. The nineteenth century was the great age of English preaching, and yet it does not seem to have left behind so rich a heritage as it might have done. There were others like Charles Kingsley with his vigor and firmness, H. P. Liddon (1829–90), learned, mannered and rich in style, William Connor Magee (1821–91), witty and polemical, and the Baptist C. H. Spurgeon (1834–92), simple, popular, colloquial; but for an age in which religion played so prominent a part both in the public beliefs and social habits of the nation the harvest might well have been fuller. With the decline of religion our own century does not look like producing any harvest at all.

A.P.

SERVICE, Robert W. (William) (1874–1958) was born in England and emigrated to Canada in the 1890s. He worked at a number of jobs, including banking and farming, and achieved literary success through his vigorous, rhythmic ballads of adventure, which have often lent themselves to parody. His most popular poems, *Songs of a Sourdough* (1907), later retitled *The Spell of the Yukon*, were inspired by his experiences at the time of the Klondike Gold Rush, and include the famous "The Shooting of Dan McGrew." He traveled widely, lived in France for much of his life, and continued to write verse, including *Bar-Room Ballads* (1940). *Harper of Heaven* (1948) recalls his life story. (See also **Canadian Literature.**)

R.W.

SEWALL, Samuel (1652–1730), essayist and diarist, was born in England, went to Boston in 1661 and graduated from Harvard in 1671. He served as a judge of the superior court of the colony and as a special commissioner (1692) for the Salem witchcraft trials. His public confession of error five years later illustrates his great integrity. He published essays on a variety of subjects, including the first antislavery tract in America, *The Selling of Joseph* (1700), and a plea for the humane treatment of Indians, *A Memorial Relating to the Kennebeck Indians* (1721). Sewall's literary reputation is based on his diary, covering the period 1674–1729, a detailed and engrossing account of the thoughts and life of a New England Puritan.

Diary in *Collections of Massachusetts Historical Society*, fifth series, 5–7, 1878–82.   J.W.

SEXTON, Anne (1928–), born in Newton (Massachusetts), began to write poetry only in 1957, following a nervous breakdown. The five volumes published subsequently trace the poet's autobiography from memories of the asylum and separation from her children, *To Bedlam and Part Way Back* (1960), the deaths of her parents, *All My Pretty Ones* (1962), mediations on death and suicide, *Live or Die* (1966), to a new assertion of life through love, *Love Poems* (1969). Anne Sexton admits to simplifying and dramatizing her experiences in order to shock, but insists that "To really get at the truth of something is the poem, not the poet." The expected flaws of confessional poetry are sometimes present, but Anne Sexton's blunt honesty is refreshing, her self-awareness more than mere narcissism, and her poetic skills considerable.   S.C.

SHADBOLT, Maurice. See New Zealand Literature.

SHADWELL, Thomas (?1642–92), son of an East Anglian landowner, was educated at Bury St. Edmunds and Caius College, Cambridge (1655–58). Like his father, he entered the Middle Temple. After travel abroad he lived in London, between 1668 and his death producing seventeen plays, mainly Jonsonian comedies of humors, like *The Virtuoso* (1676), ridiculing scientists. The best of his comedies are *Bury Fair* (1689) and *The Squire of Alsatia* (1688), whilst *Epsom Wells* (1673) also deserves a mention. Dryden satirized him devastatingly, but unjustly, as the poet of dullness in *MacFlecknoe*, mocking his flatulent writing and corpulent physique, but in 1688 Shadwell replaced Dryden as poet laureate.

Complete Works, ed. M. Summers, 5 vols., London: Fortune Press, 1927.
H.N.D.

SHAFTESBURY, Anthony Ashley Cooper, 3rd Earl of (1671–1713), grandson of Dryden's "Achitophel," who arranged for Locke to superintend the boy's education, was at school at Winchester and then traveled abroad. He was elected to Parliament in 1695 as an ardent Whig, but retired through ill health in 1698 and devoted his time increasingly to literature. He succeeded to the earldom in 1699, married in 1709 and left one son.

The essays making up the *Characteristics of Men, Manners, Opinions and Times* (1711; enlarged, 1713), though attacked by Christian apologists (Warburton and Berkeley) for their Deistic tendency, influenced ethical thought throughout the century, mainly through the concept of natural morality, that man is naturally endowed with a "moral sense." There are distinct traces of optimistic philosophy in Pope's *An Essay on Man*.

Characteristics, ed. J. M. Robertson, 2 vols., London: Grant Richards, 1900.   D.G.

SHAKESPEARE, William (1564–1616) was the son of John Shakespeare, a glover and leading citizen of Stratford-upon-Avon (Warwickshire). Although 23 April is traditionally celebrated as Shakespeare's birthday, the true date is unknown; he was baptized, according to the parish register, on 26 April 1564. Most of the facts about his life are derived from official records and legal documents; the absence of more intimate kinds of evidence, though not surprising, has doubtless permitted the growth of the popular legends and extravagant conjecture that have surrounded the figure of Shakespeare since the seventeenth century. Nevertheless, we know more about Shakespeare than about any other playwright of his time, except Jonson.

Shakespeare was almost certainly educated in the local grammar school. The school's records for the relevant years are not extant, but there is every reason to suppose that a man of John Shakespeare's standing would have sent his son to school from about the age of seven, and that he would have attended for at least six or seven years. The curriculum of a sixteenth-century grammar school, as the name implies, was based upon grammar and rhetoric, and the chief medium of instruction was Latin. Shakespeare's plays and poems show a familiarity with, and sometimes (as in the case of Ovid) a deep interest in, several of the Latin authors that were studied in the schools. He also clearly knew some of the standard textbooks and anthologies used by Elizabethan schoolboys, while his earliest works display rhetorical skill of a kind that presupposes the exercises of the schoolroom.

There is no reliable evidence to tell us when Shakespeare left school, but he may have left to help in the family business when his father ran into financial difficulties in 1577. In November 1582, when he was eighteen, Shakespeare married Anne Hathaway, and six months later, in

May 1583, their first child, Susanna, was baptized. Despite the romantic and less romantic fictions which have been woven around the circumstances of this marriage, it is quite possible that the couple had entered the married state legally and respectably some time before the ceremony in church, by making an exchange of vows, or "precontract," of the kind that was recognized by Elizabethan law. The notion that Anne was several years older than her husband rests upon the testimony of a seventeenth-century transcription from her gravestone, on which her age is now illegible. In February 1585 the twins Hamnet and Judith were baptized (Hamnet died in 1596).

Apart from the baptismal records of these children, nothing is known of Shakespeare's life during the ten years between his marriage and the first reference to him in a theatrical context in London. He may have been "a schoolmaster in the country," as the actor William Beeston told John Aubrey. Whenever it was that he went to London, it is clear that by September 1592 he was becoming known there as an actor-playwright, for he was then attacked in a pamphlet by Robert Greene as "an upstarr crow, beautified with our feathers . . . in his own conceit the only Shake-scene in a country." Greene was here warning his fellow playwrights, graduates of the universities, against a common player who was forgetting his place by setting himself up as a rival dramatist. The identification of this upstart as Shakespeare is made doubly sure by Greene's pun on his name and by the quotation of a line from *Henry VI*, part 3. The attack, of course, would not have been launched if Shakespeare had not already proved himself successful.

Although his theatrical career must have kept Shakespeare in London for most of the time during the ensuing years, it is not necessary to suppose that he forsook his family or that there was any estrangement between himself and his wife. While there is no direct evidence about Shakespeare's private life, the fact that he invested his growing prosperity in purchasing property in Stratford suggests that he maintained connections with his home town throughout the twenty years of his career. In a legal deposition of 1612 he described himself as a resident of Stratford, and it seems probable that he retired from the active life of the theater at about this time to spend the remainder of his life with his family. He died in Stratford on 23 April 1616, and was buried in the parish church where he had been baptized.

The emergence of professional acting companies with permanent theaters in London was quite a recent development when Shakespeare embarked on his career; the first building designed specifically for stage performances had been erected in 1576 by James Burbage, the father of Shakespeare's future colleague. Like its successors, this was sited on ground beyond the jurisdiction of the city authorities, whose attitude as keepers of the public morals was distinctly hostile to the growth of public theaters and other threats to good order and sober industry. Acting companies were required by law to seek the protection of a nobleman as members of his household, but, provided this condition was satisfied, the Privy Council resisted pressure from the city to suppress theatrical activities. Thus the actors were allowed to draw regular audiences of citizens to the public theaters, while maintaining themselves in readiness for the profitable summons to perform at court or on some special occasion in a noble household. The economic advantages of this situation were a necessary condition for the flourishing of the drama in Shakespeare's London, but the circumstances also called for plays that would please both popular and courtly tastes, and Shakespeare exploited the broad social spectrum of his audiences more successfully than any of his contemporaries. In this respect, too, he arrived on the scene at a propitious moment, for he followed hard on the heels of dramatists such as Marlowe, Kyd, Lyly, Greene and Peele, who brought to the popular stages some of the spirit of courtly humanism and provided new models for witty, lyrical and heroic dramatic speech.

Nevertheless, the livelihood of the professional actor in 1592 was still precarious and his social standing one of dubious respectability. Acting companies in London were often short-lived and there was continual disbanding and regrouping, not least as the result of the closing of the theaters in time of plague, a common hazard of life in the city at that time. Indeed, Shakespeare's first published works, *Venus and Adonis* (1593) and *Lucrece*, which was printed in the following year, were both written in the years between 1591 and 1594 when the London theaters were closed for much of the time and many of his fellow actors were touring the provinces. These poems were dedicated to the earl of Southampton, and they suggest that in those uncertain times Shakespeare was endeavoring to make himself known among sophisticated courtly circles as a poet as well as on the common stages as a workaday actor-playwright.

When the theaters reopened in 1594, Shakespeare joined the Lord Chamberlain's Men, as we learn from a record of payment made to three leading members of this newly formed company for court performances during the Christmas festivities of 1594. The other two actors named in this entry are Will Kemp, the famous clown, and Richard Burbage, the great tragic actor. Since Shakespeare never enjoyed a comparable reputation as a performer (though legend has it that he played the parts of old men), he presumably earned his place alongside Kemp and Burbage by the success he had already achieved as a playwright.

Provided with such abilities as these, and with the obvious advantages of a patron so well placed to help them, the Lord Chamberlain's Men emerged as the leading acting company of the 1590s, and in 1598 embarked on an unprecedented venture in building their own theater on Bankside, the Globe. Customarily, the acting companies only leased the theaters in which they played. The ambitious enterprise by which Shakespeare and his fellows came to possess a theater of their own made them unique among their rivals, confirming their supremacy and stability as a company and ensuring their increasing prosperity in the future. When James I succeeded to the throne in 1603, he gave official recognition to their preeminence by allowing them to change their title to that of the King's Men, a name which they continued to keep until the closing of the theaters in 1642. Further proof of the company's high standing and its shrewd business sense occurs in 1608, when the King's Men made arrangements to lease the Blackfriars Theatre. This was an indoors theater in a former Dominican monastery; it had been leased to the boys' companies, until the last of them was suppressed in 1608. Richard Burbage was landlord of the theater, like his father before him, and in leasing it to a syndicate of leading members of the King's Men (including Shakespeare) he provided the company with premises which it could use during the winter months when performances on the open-air stage of the Globe had to be suspended. Moreover, the Blackfriars Theatre was more exclusive, with smaller but more expensive accommodation, which attracted an audience of fashionably sophisticated and courtly tastes. Nevertheless, the Globe was still the home of the King's Men, and that they intended to retain their larger popular audiences is indicated by the fact that this theater was immediately rebuilt after a fire in 1613.

Shakespeare's professional fortunes were therefore bound to those of the company in which he spent all but the first few years of his career. Coming to the theater at a time when it was still a hazardous and socially disreputable calling to be a "common player," Shakespeare eventually retired to Stratford as a gentleman of substance. In this respect his career, like those of Burbage and the other great Elizabethan actor, Edward Alleyn, illustrates the social advancement that accompanied the increasing economic stability and artistic distinction of London's theatrical life. The grant of a coat of arms to his father in 1596 (to which John Shakespeare was entitled as a former bailiff of Stratford) no doubt also contributed to Shakespeare's rising status in the community, while his acquisitions of land and other property in Stratford prepared not only for his own comfortable retirement at about the age of forty-eight, but for the settlement he was able to make upon his heirs.

Shakespeare's plays themselves made only an indirect contribution to the material success of his career. They were doubtless essential to the preeminence achieved by the Lord Chamberlain's Men, but the fact remains that Shakespeare's prosperity was derived from his position in that company. From its formation in the summer of 1594 Shakespeare seems to have been one of the "sharers," the principal members who owned the company and divided its profits between them, as distinct from the "hired men" who were paid a fixed wage. Not surprisingly, therefore, he was also one of the seven "housekeepers," or landlords, both of the Globe Theatre and at Blackfriars. As a member of the company for which he wrote his plays, he would have had more influence than most dramatists of the time upon the performance and adaptation of his work. But there are no grounds for assuming that the plays would have been regarded as Shakespeare's personal property.

Elizabethan plays written for the public stages belonged to the companies that had bought and performed them. The author possessed no further rights in his work once he had sold it to the actors, although in general it was much more profitable to write for the stage than for publication. Since the text of a successful play was obviously a valuable asset of the company to which it belonged, printing rights were usually sold only when a play had outlived the first wave of popular demand, or when the fortunes of the company were low, or when a play could be pirated by a printer, perhaps by striking a bargain with "hired men" who reconstructed the text from memory. No play was kept in the repertoire for very long; when the supporters of the Essex conspiracy in 1601 hired Shakespeare's company for a special performance of *Richard II*, the actors were surprised at the request for a play "so old and so long out of use," though it was written barely six years before. Although all printed works needed the license of the censor, there was no copyright law to protect the interests of the author or the owner of a text. Printers tried to regulate affairs amongst themselves by requiring the registration with the Stationers' Company of all works intended for publication. The entry could then be challenged if a printer felt he had a prior claim to the book. Equally, a book could be entered by a printer who had no immediate intention of publishing it, but who wished to forestall his rivals in this way.

Shakespeare probably had no direct involvement with the printing of any of his plays. Eighteen of them were published individually in quarto form before 1623. Some seven or eight of these quartos give a notoriously inaccurate and corrupt text (they are now referred as as the "Bad Quartos"), and it is generally believed today that these derive from reconstructions by actors. Other quartos seem to have been printed directly from Shakespeare's manuscript (or "foul papers," as bibliographers call them), which were not used by the acting company once a fair copy had been made for use as a promptbook. An acting version of this kind would no doubt contain fuller stage directions, with whatever cuts were made in the text, and other practical details related to performance. The case of the late quarto of *Othello*, published in 1622, may be one of the rarer examples of a text deriving from a promptbook. Sometimes, after a play had been printed in an authoritative text, the company may have used an annotated copy of the quarto as their promptbook.

The decision to collect Shakespeare's plays and edit them for publication in a single volume may have been made while he was alive, and he may have begun to revise some of them for this purpose. In the year of Shakespeare's death (1616) a collected folio edition of Ben Johnon's *Works* was published, and this also doubtless encouraged the project that led to the First Folio of Shakespeare's plays in 1623. The chief editors, Heminge and Condell, were members of the King's Men with personal knowledge of Shakespeare and his work, and the evident care which was taken to establish a satisfactory text for each play lends authority to their attribution of the thirty-six plays in the volume to Shakespeare. The only plays excluded from the First Folio which are now thought to be at least partly the work of Shakespeare are *Pericles* and *The Two Noble Kinsmen*, and rejection by Heminge and Condell therefore reinforces the attribution of the remainder as wholly Shakespeare's. The claim of the First Folio title page, that its contents are "according to the True Originall Copies" is, on the whole, a just one, for whoever prepared the texts for the printer can often be shown to have collated the quarto texts of plays previously printed with independent sources, either "foul papers" or promptbooks. Nevertheless, the Folio version of a given play is certainly not a definitive text, nor is it in every case closer to Shakespeare's words than any of the quartos. Editorial revisions, theatrical adaptations and mere errors in the Folio make it necessary for the modern editor to refer to the good quarto texts where they exist, and sometimes to prefer their readings.

Ignorance or misunderstanding of the intellectual, social and dramatic traditions in which Shakespeare worked has produced some strange vicissitudes in the history of his critical reputation. The contrast between a supposedly unlettered Shakespeare and the learned Jonson, fostered partly by Jonson himself, rapidly became a commonplace during the seventeenth century. As neoclassical principles gradually supplanted the old-fashioned tastes of Shakespeare's generation, it was falsely assumed that because Shakespeare did not appear to follow the critical precepts of classical authority, he therefore wrote without any rules at all. Thus Milton referred to Shakespeare "warbling his native wood-notes wild," as though his plays were wholly the product of natural, untutored and unsophisticated genius. The customary pairing of Shakespeare and Jonson as convenient exemplars of the traditional antithesis between nature and art persisted into the eighteenth century, when more romantic spirits acclaimed Shakespeare precisely because they believed that he was, according to the well-established tradition, a poet by instinct and not by learning. In this way a misconception first bred by neoclassicism was eventually given a further lease of life by the very rejection of neo-classical canons. In fact, Shakespeare's knowledge and use of classical literature, like many other aspects of his work, reflect the partial survival of medieval attitudes and ideas in the sixteenth century. Although his plays (with two significant exceptions) pay little regard to the unities, they do derive from a rich and complex literary and dramatic heritage and were not the offspring of purely intuitive and original genius working in a creative vacuum.

The popular image of an uneducated, provincial genius developed more than one significance for the nineteenth century. On the one hand, Romantic presuppositions about the nature of genius led to interpretations of the plays as the spiritual autobiography of their author, the expressions of a personal philosophy reflecting the poet's own emotional crises. On the other hand, there were those who found in the plays evidence of an acquaintance with the worlds of learning, politics, law, courtly behavior and so on, which was incompatible with the image of a rustic and ignor-ant author. This realization prompted the numerous theories denying Shakespeare's authorship and attributing the plays to Francis Bacon, the earl of Oxford or other suitably eminent Elizabethans. Apart from the specious reasoning on which such theories depend, they show insufficient understanding of the period as a whole and of Shakespeare's plays in particular, for what is thought to signify learning or ignorance differs from age to age, and if Shakespeare's grammar school education was undervalued, the level of specialized knowledge reflected in the plays was grossly overestimated. Similarly, the philosophical thoughts and con-ceptions which many Victorians held to be Shakespeare's personal con-tribution to human wisdom were, in fact, part of the common property of his age, while they ignored the very nature of drama by ascribing to Shakespeare himself the views expressed by his characters.

Although there are few today who would read the plays as evidence for Shakespeare's convictions or his private life, the *Sonnets* are still often regarded as his most intimate self-revelations and the belief that they were inspired by a particular episode in his life is difficult to dislodge. This is due partly to a mistaken belief that an Elizabethan sonnet sequence, and Shakespeare's in particular, forms a continuous narrative or contains a story that can be pieced together, and partly to the mysterious circum-stances in which Shakespeare's sonnets were published. They appeared in print in 1609, long after the fashion for sonnets had declined, and pre-sumably more than a decade after most of them were composed. The dedication to "Mr. W.H.," described as "the only begetter" of the son-nets, has aroused extensive and ingenious conjecture about his identity.

Of those who understand "Mr. W.H." to be Shakespeare's patron and the inspiration of the sequence, some believe the initials to represent William Herbert, the earl of Pembroke, and others are equally convinced that they signify Henry Wriothesley, the earl of Southampton. Skeptics point out that since Shakespeare had nothing to do with the publication of the *Sonnets*, the dedication is not the poet's but the printer's, and that "Mr. W.H." may therefore be whoever it was that procured the copy for the printer, an "only begetter" possibly quite unknown to Shakespeare. The desire to interpret the *Sonnets* as the history of an actual situation in which Shakespeare was involved is really a tribute to the unusual degree of psychological realism and complexity of feeling they possess. Certainly Shakespeare treats the conventions of the form with unprecedented originality and power of expression. The sequence is very different from that of any of his contemporaries; the idealism and humility of the lover is directed towards a young man instead of a mistress, and the relationships between the poet, his friend and the treacherous mistress are treated with a dramatic intensity and conviction that greatly extend the range and scope of the sonnet form. One would expect no less from a poet of Shakespeare's stature; the main themes of the sequence, concerned with love's transcendence of time and mutability, show a conventional subject raised to a grandeur and eloquence of almost heroic proportions. It is, of course, possible to read the opening sonnets, addressed to the young man and urging him to marry, as written by Shakespeare for a particular patron, without supposing that an autobiographical significance extends to the sequence as a whole.

The image of Shakespeare which emerges from the main trends of twentieth-century criticism and scholarship is based upon more information about his historical context than previous generations possessed, even if that information is still subject to misinterpretation. In contrast with the earlier Romantic emphasis on a self-sufficient and self-revealing Shakespeare, the modern conception is that of an artist accepting and working within the conventions of his time, remarkable not for the originality of his thought nor for any revolution in taste or sensibility, but for his skill in manipulating the available resources. The Elizabethan drama was highly conventional, yet moulded as they were by medieval traditions and by the values of Renaissance humanism, the conventions were flexible and rapidly changing throughout the years of Shakespeare's career. The notion that Shakespeare was no more than a craftsman, bound by narrow theatrical conventions and the need to satisfy the demands of an illiterate and simple-minded audience, was an early twentieth-century reaction to the idolatry of Shakespeare and one that underestimated both the scope of the conventions and the interests of the Elizabethan theatergoing public as much as it slighted Shakespeare's artistic integrity. There is still a tendency to regard Shakespeare in his work as the spokesman for Elizabethan orthodoxy and as a slave to the changing theatrical fashions of the time. It is certainly true that Shakespeare drew upon the commonplaces of contemporary political, ethical and literary doctrines in composing his plays, but it does not follow that he wrote in order to propagate these or any other ideas. He used them to dramatize and give meaning to the issues of his plots; the very fact that they were orthodox, and therefore familiar, is sufficient warrant for their dramatic usefulness.

Shakespeare was receptive to new developments in dramatic methods and to the influence of his contemporaries throughout his career. A career of such unusual length and continued success as a playwright presupposes his versatility and his ability to sustain the constant development of his own powers. But to imagine that Shakespeare was motivated solely or even chiefly by the desire to keep up with the fads of popular taste is a travesty of his genius and a distortion of the facts, for he was not an imitator of other men's work in the sense that this implies. The ways in which Shakespeare adapted to his own use the dramatic trends and innovations at hand suggest a professional interest in techniques and style rather than a submission to box office appeal. Even in his earlier plays, where Shakespeare drew upon Lyly, Greene and Peele for comedy and Kyd and Marlowe for tragedy and tragical history, his work bears little resemblance to theirs, because he took only what he needed, and their influence is subordinate to his own more complex designs. The same is true of his treatment of the satirical spirit introduced at the turn of the century by Marston and Jonson, the influences of which have been traced in *As You Like It, Hamlet* and *Troilus and Cressida*. The radical differences between these plays and the intrinsic interests of each of them individually are far more striking than any elements they shared with the current vogue for tragical and comical satire. Similarly, the romantic plays at the end of his career show a new interest in the court masque, and it has been suggested that they were composed particularly to please the courtly audience at the Blackfriars; yet there is no reason to suppose they did not equally please at the Globe, where in fact the first recorded performances of two of these plays took place. It is easy to exaggerate Shakespeare's debt to contemporary influences, while underestimating the extent to which he constantly drew upon and developed the methods of his own earlier work throughout his career. There is a continuity in his work that implies an artist who learned much and wasted little. Moreover, the great series of history plays, unparalleled as a sequence in Elizabethan drama, shows that Shakespeare was quite capable of traveling in his own chosen direction, while he had little interest in certain other popular types of play —for instance, citizen comedy or domestic tragedy.

Like most Elizabethan dramatists, Shakespeare did not invent his own plots. A study of his treatment of his sources strengthens the impression of his receptive mind and of his ability to adapt and reshape material according to his own designs. It has been well said that if Shakespeare had read even half the number of books that scholars have claimed he used, he would have had no time to write the plays. Nevertheless, there is little doubt that in many cases he not only combined different stories in a single play, but also consulted two or more versions of the same story. Sometimes, by changing a few significant details in the events of a story, Shakespeare radically recast the whole spirit and conception of his action; the differences between *Othello* and the sordid tale by Cinthio on which it is based or the removal of the happy ending in the old play of *Leir* are cases in point. Sometimes Shakespeare dramatized an author whose interests were so close to his own that little alteration was needed; for instance, in Plutarch's *Lives* Shakespeare not only found the narrative basis for his Roman plays, but a model for the methods of intimate characterization which he was already developing as a dramatist. The study of his sources often brings one close to Shakespeare's particular interests and intentions.

Interpretative criticism in the twentieth century has turned away from the kind of approach to character and motivation that preoccupied nineteenth-century critics such as A. C. Bradley, although Bradley's study of the four "great" tragedies, concerned primarily with their heroes, is still a model of perceptive insight and close study of the text. Many modern critics, however, have felt that Bradley's speculations press the text too closely for evidence of a psychological realism that it will not bear, and his assumptions were challenged early in the present century by critics like E. E. Stoll, in *Art and Artifice in Shakespeare* (1933), who argued, from what was really a limited acquaintance with the dramatic conventions within which Shakespeare worked, that the theatrical effectiveness of the plays does not depend upon a naturalistic conception of character. In reaction to the Romantic adulation of Shakespeare, the school of criticism represented by Stoll conducted a skeptical campaign to clip the wings of speculative interpretation by appealing to the simplifying influences of Elizabethan theatrical conventions and the practical considerations of stagecraft. Other critics in the last thirty years, of whom G. Wilson Knight, with, for example, *The Wheel of Fire* (1930), *The Imperial Theme* (1931) and *The Crown of Life* (1947), has been perhaps the most influential and certainly the most prolific, have focused attention on the poetic unity of the plays, especially upon the coherence of verbal imagery and symbolic patterns. This concern with artistic unity in the plays is one of the chief features of modern Shakespeare criticism, and it has also manifested itself in the emphasis on the "themes" underlying the dramatic action. In this respect the endeavor to interpret Shakespeare in terms of his own age has stressed the continuity of medieval traditions and habits of thought, especially those of the allegorical morality plays, and the application to Shakespeare's plays of the belief in a divinely appointed hierarchical order of creation, or "chain of being," in which man has his fixed place. The history plays (e.g., in E. M. W. Tillyard's interpretation) and the so-called "problem plays" have lent themselves particularly to this kind of approach, and it is arguable that if modern criticism has been alert to the dangers of excessively psychological character analysis, it has not always avoided the tendency to impose a somewhat abstract doctrinal scheme upon the dramatic life of the plays. There is no simple "key" to the interpretation of Shakespeare, either in Elizabethan terms or in those of Freud and Marx. But with these tendencies it is not altogether surprising that the literary critics have had less influence upon modern productions of the plays than the contemporary dramatic styles of Brecht and Beckett. On the other hand, thanks not least to the example and criticism of Harley Granville-Barker in his *Prefaces to Shakespeare*, 5 series (1927–48), theatrical producers generally now recognize the advantages of the kind of large, open stage for which the plays were designed. It is commonly accepted that each age must interpret Shakespeare anew, but this is not necessarily to say that we understand him best when we impose on him our own preconceptions and obsessions.

The nature of Shakespeare's greatness is not easily defined. What little is known of his methods reveals a mind that readily assimilated a great diversity of material, that turned more naturally to the concrete and particular than to the abstract and theoretical, and that expressed itself with superlative fluency and facility. His imagination was of unparalleled breadth in its human sympathies, and, related to this, his creative temperament was mobile, acutely discerning and undogmatic. He has been described as the poet of human nature, as though his supreme achievement lay in his creation of convincing, complex and highly individualized characters. Yet, while this will probably remain the most universally satisfying description of his genius, it inadequately represents Shakespeare's incomparable command of the resources of language and of his theatrical medium. Although his work is for all time, as Jonson perceived, Shakespeare was first and foremost an Elizabethan artist; and that Elizabethan ideal of unity-in-variety which is fulfilled in his plays is also reflected in Dryden's famous tribute to him as "the man, who, of all modern and perhaps ancient poets, had the largest and most comprehensive soul."

(See also **Masques; Renaissance Humanism.**)

PLAYS

It is impossible to fix the chronology of the plays exactly. The list below is based on that given by E. K. Chambers, whose overall authority is still the most generally accepted, although recent evidence suggests an earlier dating is possible in certain cases. Dates of the first quarto publication are given in brackets, with an asterisk to denote those quartos now usually classified as "bad"; otherwise, the date of first publication is assumed to be 1623, in the First Folio.

Henry VI, part 2, 1590–91 (*The First Part of the Contention between York and Lancaster*, 1594).

Henry VI, part 3, 1590–91 (*The True Tragedie of Richard Duke of York*, 1595).

Henry VI, part 1, 1591–92.

Richard III, 1592–93 (Q.1597) (*f*.1955).

The Comedy of Errors, 1592–93.

Titus Andronicus, 1593–94 (Q.1594).

The Taming of the Shrew, 1593–94 (*The Taming of a Shrew*, 1594) (*f*. 1933; 1966).

Two Gentlemen of Verona, 1594–95.

Love's Labour's Lost, 1594–95 (Q.1598).

Romeo and Juliet, 1594–95 (*Q. 1597) (*f*. 1936; 1954; 1956; 1968).

Richard II, 1595–96 (Q. 1597).

A Midsummer Night's Dream, 1595–96 (Q. 1600) (*f*. 1935; 1969).

King John, 1596–97 (?*The Troublesome Raigne*, 1591).

The Merchant of Venice, 1596–97 (Q.1600).

Henry IV, part 1, 1597–98 (Q.1598).

Henry IV, part 2, 1597–98 (Q.1600).

Much Ado about Nothing, 1598–99 (Q.1600).

Henry V, 1598–99 (*Q. 1600) (*f*. 1945).

Julius Caesar, 1599–1600 (*f*. 1953; 1970).

As You Like It, 1599–1600 (*f*. 1936).

Twelfth Night, 1599–1600.

Hamlet, 1600–01 (*Q. 1603) (*f*. 1948; 1970).

Troilus and Cressida, 1601–02 (Q. 1609).

All's Well That Ends Well, 1602–03.

Measure for Measure, 1604–05.

Othello, 1604–05 (Q.1622) (*f*. 1956; 1966).

King Lear, 1605–06 (*f*. 1971).

Macbeth, 1605–06 (*f*. 1951; 1960; 1972).

Antony and Cleopatra, 1606–07 (*f*. 1972).

Coriolanus, 1607–08.

Pericles, 1608–09 (Q.1609).

Cymbeline, 1609–10.

The Winter's Tale, 1610–11 (*f*. 1968).

The Tempest, 1611–12.

Henry VIII, 1612–13.

POEMS

Venus and Adonis, 1593.

Lucrece, 1594.

The Passionate Pilgrim, 1599.

"The Phoenix and the Turtle," in *Love's Martyr; or Rosalin's Complaint*, 1601.

Shakespeare's Sonnets, 1609.

Complete Works, ed. P. Alexander, London: Collins, 1951; New York: Random House, 1952.

Complete Works, ed. C. J. Sisson, London: Odhams; New York: Harper, 1954.

The New Arden Shakespeare, general ed. U. Ellis-Fermor, H. F. Brooks, and H. Jenkins, London: Methuen; Cambridge, Mass.: Harvard Univ. Press, 1951– .

The New Cambridge Shakespeare, ed. J. Dover Wilson, A. Quiller-Couch, and others, 37 vols., Cambridge: Cambridge Univ. Press, 1921–62.

Complete Pelican Shakespeare, general ed. A. Harbage, London: A. Lane, Penguin Press; Baltimore: Penguin Books, 1969.   D.J.P.

SHAKESPEAREAN APOCRYPHA. The value of Shakespeare's name was such that even in his lifetime printers attributed to him a number of plays which the editors of the First Folio rejected—for example, *Locrine*, *Sir John Oldcastle*, *Thomas*, *Lord Cromwell*, *The London Prodigal*, *The Puritan*, and *A Yorkshire Tragedy*. In 1619 Pavier and Jaggard issued a number of quartos, including *Pericles*, among which were apocryphal plays; and a version of the Third Folio (1664) included the seven plays mentioned above.

In the mid-seventeenth century booksellers and publishers haphazardly ascribed plays to Shakespeare. Excluding those known to be by other writers, these were *The Taming of a Shrew*, *Edward III*, *Edward IV*, *The Merry Devil of Edmonton*, *King Stephen*, *Duke Humphrey*, and *Iphis and Iantha*. King Charles II had a volume of Shakespeare's plays containing *The Merry Devil*, *Fair Em* and *Mucedorus*. *Arden of Faversham* has been ascribed to Shakespeare and so has *Sir Thomas More*, which may contain genuine writing, though it is the work of a consortium later revised by others.

Few of the above plays deal with subjects that interested Shakespeare and the styles rarely suggest his hand. As Heminge and Condell knew him intimately, they were unlikely to make mistakes in selecting plays for the First Folio. When his share in a play had been slight, they preferred to reject the whole work; therefore they omitted *Pericles*, despite the existence of quartos giving Shakespeare's name. They also ignored *The Two Noble Kinsmen*, although it was eventually published as the work of Fletcher and Shakespeare and comes nearer than any of the above to deserving consideration as a play by Shakespeare.

The Shakespeare Apocrypha, ed. C. F. T. Brooke, Oxford: Oxford Univ. Press, 1908. G.G.U.

SHAPIRO, Karl (1913–) was born in Baltimore (Maryland). He attended the University of Virginia and Johns Hopkins University and, between 1942 and 1945, served in the South Pacific. His first collections of verse, *Poems* (1935) and *Person, Place and Thing* (1942), demonstrated his ironic wit and sense of form. *V-Letter and Other Poems* (1944), based on war experiences, won a Pulitzer Prize. The blank verse *Essay on Rime* (1945) was a lively critique of intellectualized modern poetry, an attack continued in his essays—*Beyond Criticism* (1953) and *In Defense of Ignorance* (1960). *The Bourgeois Poet* (1964) was written in rhythmic blocks of prose poetry. R.W.

SHAW, George Bernard (1856–1951), born in Dublin, acquired from his mother his early knowledge of music, especially opera, and painting. He was also well-read in Shakespeare, Bunyan, Shelley, Byron and Dickens. His Irish childhood, with its lessons of the evils of poverty and the unhealthy inhibitions encouraged by church religion, developed that moral passion and independence of viewpoint which characterized his later writing on matters of politics and belief. These factors outweighed the effects of his short-lived formal education. In 1871 he became junior clerk to a Dublin land agent, but five years later decided to move to London in the hope of satisfying "the enormity of his unconscious ambition." Within a year he had been commissioned to write musical reviews for *The Hornet* and, with the help of the editor, had killed the paper by his outspoken criticism. For the next nine years he did not earn a living and was dependent upon his mother who had established herself in London as a teacher of singing. But in this time Shaw wrote five novels, mastered the economics of Marx (who, he said, "made a man" of him), became the leading intellect among the Fabians and formulated his lifelong objections to meat eating, vaccination and blood sacrifice (which included both vivisection and the Crucifixion). On subjects which interested him Shaw also acquired the habit of factual exactitude which, together with his keenness of observation and his wit, was to provide a solid foundation for his success as original thinker, playwright and socialist.

In 1885 Shaw became a reviewer for *The Pall Mall Gazette*, and in the following year his novel *Cashel Byron's Profession*, which had already been serialized, was published in book form. Three years later, under the pen name of "Corno di Bassetto," he began to write musical criticism. He was also actively propagating his political beliefs, and in 1889 he published his *Fabian Essays in Socialism*, the basis some forty years later of *The Intelligent Woman's Guide to Socialism and Capitalism*. Shaw's work as a drama critic also led to *The Quintessence of Ibsenism* (1891) in which he championed the "depraved" Norwegian for the moral seriousness of his view, that conduct could only be justified by its effect on life, and not by reference to received ideals.

Shaw's early career as a dramatist aroused the interest of a small enthusiastic audience and the censor, who banned his third play, *Mrs. Warren's Profession* (1892). In 1898, unwilling to accept the general neglect of his work, Shaw published two volumes of his plays with prefaces, *Plays Pleasant and Unpleasant*, and these, together with the success of *The Devil's Disciple* in America and his marriage to an heiress, proved the turning point in his personal and economic fortunes. Shaw was then forty-two, and the remaining years of his long life may be described as the history of his dramatic successes and the persistent application of his ideas to practical affairs. From his demands for equality of income to his recognition of the dangers that would ensue from the victimization of Germany after the First World War and his support for Russia in the early 1930s, Shaw's ideas exercised widespread influence, but perhaps even more important was the Shavian spirit of tireless attachment to the "golden heresy of Truth."

During the sixty years of Shaw's life as a playwright neither his characterization nor his dramatic techniques moved a great deal in the direction of richness or complexity. The success of his dialogue depends to a large extent on witty surprise or deliberate outrage, as in the first scene of *Caesar and Cleopatra*. The majority of his characters live in unexceptional circumstances, but are inspired by Shaw's own exuberance for saying—and sometimes doing—the unexpected. Among his major creations in this respect are Bluntschli, Candida, John Tanner, Undershaft, Captain Shotover, the Inquisitor and King Magnus.

The central criticism directed against Shaw as a dramatist is a deficiency of feeling in his characters, whose existence depends on words and wit, not on emotion. Shaw's plays, it is true, do not attempt to draw the audience deeper into a world of conflicting desires and impulses in the manner of Ibsen and Strindberg. These desires and impulses fall under the collective heading of the Life Force, which Shaw shows at work not by probing its inner life, but by crossexamining the conscious assumptions and ideas which influence behavior, and so the fabric of social relationships. If Ibsen and Strindberg work from the surface of the ocean down to its bed, Shaw starts from the surface and works upwards; his plays are concerned with the means of achieving a "higher life" than his anti-romantic view of the individual and his social realism gave him any reason to suppose might yet be in existence. It is consequently not surprising that Bunyan's *The Pilgrim's Progress* was among his favorite books. The absence, too, of any Celestial City in his belief, except that in part 5 of *Back to Methuselah*, afforded problems that not even his unfailing wit could completely conceal.

Shaw's philosophy of creative evolution, derived from Samuel Butler, rationalized his will to abolish the poor and lay behind his desire to find some way of controlling the able. But he also recognized, particularly in *Saint Joan*, that the successive hierarchies created by the Life Force could only be good if the individual members of them were saintly.

Cashel Byron's Profession, 1886 (*s.* 1885–86).

(ed.) *Fabian Essays in Socialism*, 1889.

The Quintessence of Ibsenism, 1891; revised, 1913.

Widowers' Houses, 1893 (*p.* 1892).

The Perfect Wagnerite, 1898.

Plays Pleasant and Unpleasant, 2 vols., 1898.

Three Plays for Puritans, 1901.

Man and Superman, 1903.

Major Barbara, 1907 (*p.* 1905; *f.* 1941); with *John Bull's Other Island* (*p.* 1904) and *How He Lied to Her Husband*.

The Doctor's Dilemma, 1911 (*p.* 1906; *f.* 1958); with *Getting Married* (*p.* 1908) and *The Shewing-Up of Blanco Posnet* (*p.* 1909).

Misalliance, 1914 (*p.* 1910); with *The Dark Lady of the Sonnets* (*p.* 1910) and *Fanny's First Play* (*p.* 1911).

Androcles and the Lion, 1916 (*p.* 1913; *Everybody's*, September 1914; *f.* 1952); with *Pygmalion* (*p.* 1914; *f.* 1938; as *My Fair Lady*, 1964) and *Overruled* (*p.* 1912; *English Review*, May 1913).

Heartbreak House, 1919.

Back to Methuselah, 1921.

Saint Joan, 1924 (*p.* 1923; *f.* 1957).

Immaturity, 1930 (written 1879).

The Apple Cart, 1930 (*p.* 1929).

The Millionairess, 1936 (*f.* 1960).

The Intelligent Woman's Guide to Socialism and Capitalism, 1928.

The Bodley Head Bernard Shaw, collected plays with their prefaces, London: Bodley Head, 1970.

Correspondence between Shaw and Mrs Patrick Campbell, ed. A. Dent, London: Gollanz; New York: Knopf, 1952.

Correspondence between Shaw and Granville Barker, ed. C. B. Purdom, London: Phoenix House; New York: Theatre Arts, 1957.
Collected Letters, ed. D. H. Laurence, vol. 1 (*1874–1897*), London: M. Reinhardt; New York: Dodd, Mead, 1965; vol. 2 (*1898–1910*), London: Bodley Head, 1972.   P.G.M.

SHELLEY, Mary Wollstonecraft (1797–1851), daughter of William Godwin and Mary Wollstonecraft, was influenced from an early age by her father's religious and social radicalism. In 1814 she fell in love with Shelley and eloped with him; the couple were married in 1816. After Shelley's death she devoted herself to preserving his work, although her life with him had not been entirely happy. Important editions of his work were prepared by her in 1824, 1839 and 1840, and she also began his biography. As a novelist she is remembered for *Frankenstein; or, The Modern Prometheus* (1818; *f.* 1931; as *The Curse of Frankenstein*, 1957), a Gothic melodrama of considerable power.

Letters, ed. F. L. Jones, 2 vols., Norman: Univ. of Oklahoma Press, 1944.
Journal, ed. F. L. Jones, Norman: Univ. of Oklahoma Press, 1947.   I.W.

SHELLEY, P. B. (Percy Bysshe) (1792–1822) was born at Field Place, near Horsham (Sussex), the eldest son of Sir Timothy Shelley, a hard-headed country landowner. He was educated at Eton (which he detested and where he was known as "mad Shelley"), and in 1810 went up to University College, Oxford. His Oxford career was brief; in 1811 he and his close friend Thomas Jefferson Hogg were sent down for publishing a rather innocuous pamphlet entitled *The Necessity of Atheism*. In the same year he met and married Harriet Westbrook, the daughter of a London publican, and began corresponding with William Godwin, who was to have a profound influence on his life and thought. After ineffectual attempts to engage in revolutionary politics he found an outlet for his radical idealism in his first important poem, *Queen Mab* (1813). By 1814 he had tired of Harriet—his relationships with women were invariably febrile—and he discovered a new love in the person of Godwin's daughter, Mary. The couple eloped in 1814 and married in 1816 following Harriet's tragic death. The rest of Shelley's short life was marked by periods of acute restlessness and misfortune. In 1816 he and Mary visited Byron in Switzerland and, apart from a brief period at Marlow where he knew Peacock and Leigh Hunt, Shelley spent most of the remainder of his life on the Continent, especially in Italy which he loved. By the end of his life his marriage with Mary had frozen; after the early ecstasy their union was overshadowed by guilt and grief—their two children died and Shelley was refused custody of Harriet's children after her death. He died in 1822 in a boating accident off Lerici and his body was cremated on the shore, with his two friends, Byron and E. J. Trelawny, as witnesses.

In his essay "A Defence of Poetry," written in 1821, Shelley defined what he believed to be the true function of a poet: "For he not only beholds intensely the present as it is, and discovers those laws according to which present things ought to be ordered, but he beholds the future in the present, and his thoughts are the germs of the flower and the fruit of latest time." This concept of the poet as a philosopher who deals with elemental laws of human life and society is one to which Shelley adhered in much of his major poetry from *Queen Mab* to "The Triumph of Life," which he was working on when he died. It is often difficult to disengage Shelley's poetry from the political and social beliefs which inform it, beliefs which formed part of a radical European tradition and which Shelley supported in clear methodical essays such as "A Philosophical View of Reform" (1819). *Queen Mab* was written under the influence of Godwin's ideas and has been described as "a pamphlet in verse" and as "a poetical handbook to the philosophy of the Enlightenment." Although uninspired as poetry, *Queen Mab* contains the germs of what were to become Shelley's major poetic preoccupations—a radical vision of history, the Prometheus myth, and his faith in a Platonic idealism. *Alastor* (1816) is a far more personal poem, and its dominant theme of loneliness is recurrent in Shelley's work, especially in the lyric poems. In *Alastor* Shelley is engaged in the creation of a private mythology; significantly, the poem is filled with narcissistic water imagery, and the visionary woman whom the poet seeks is but a projection of his own soul. *The Revolt of Islam* (1818) is a more mature poem which combines the revolutionary idealism of *Queen Mab* with the search for personal fulfillment of *Alastor*. The poem uses the elemental imagery of crags, water, stars, caves etc., which recur throughout Shelley's poetry. This imagery does not derive from observed nature; it is the projection of an inner landscape. As Yeats observed, Shelley's imagery has about it an element of "rootless fantasy" that can become arid. Shelley's travels in Italy and Switzerland together with his reading of Greek tragedy gave him the subject of his next major poem, his lyric drama *Prometheus Unbound* (1820). The poem concerns the liberation of Prometheus, an embodiment of "the strength of suffering man," from the tyranny of Jupiter, an embodiment of social, religious and political oppression, and the consequent transfiguration of the world in truth and beauty. The impressive landscapes of the poem are still dreamlike, but they are more clearly imagined than they were in *Alastor*.

For many readers, however, Shelley's greatest achievement lies in his shorter lyric poetry. *Adonais* (1821) was inspired by the death of Keats and is a formal elegy in the tradition of "Lycidas." The poem displays no great sense of personal loss; rather it uses a traditional form to express the poet's beliefs. It is at once a passionate lament for the fate of the romantic poet in an uncaring age, and an assertion that the dead poet has become one with a higher Platonic reality. In two of his finest shorter lyric poems, "To a Skylark" and "Ode to the West Wind," Shelley succeeded in discovering a satisfactory reality in which to embody his own feelings and emotions. Unfortunately, in many of his brief lyric poems there is no such focus available and they seem rather vague disembodied emotions, lacking in form and substance. Shelley himself seems to have cared little for these lyric fragments, many of which are unfinished. Despite popular belief, Shelley's poetic range was not narrow. Some of his more personal poems, such as "To William Shelley" and "Letter to Maria Gisborne," have a warmth and generosity of feeling often lacking in his major poetry. He also wrote an effective political ballad, *The Masque of Anarchy* (1822); a political burlesque, *Oedipus Tyrannus; or, Swellfoot the Tyrant* (1820); a clever parody of Wordsworth, "Peter Bell the Third," written in 1819; and one actable melodrama, *The Cenci*. Current criticism tends to deprecate the sentimental and emotional in Shelley's poetry and to stress its philosophical and mythic qualities. Some scholars, however, feel that this emphasis is wrong and that Shelley's gifts were primarily lyrical, despite his own concept of himself as a philosopher-poet.

(See also **Political Pamphlets; Romantic Movement, The.**)

Queen Mab, 1813.
Alastor, and Other Poems, 1816.
Laon and Cythna, 1818; reissued as *The Revolt of Islam*, 1818.
The Cenci, 1819.
Prometheus Unbound: A Lyrical Drama, 1820.
Epipsychidion, 1821.
Adonais, 1821.
Hellas: A Lyrical Drama, 1822.

Posthumous Poems, ed. M. W. Shelley, 1824.
"A Defence of Poetry," 1840 (in *Essays, Letters from Abroad, Translations and Fragments*, ed. M. W. Shelley, 2 vols.).

Complete Works, ed. R. Ingpen and W. E. Peck, 10 vols., London: Benn; New York: C. Scribner's Sons, 1926–30.
Poetical Works, ed. T. Hutchinson, Oxford: Clarendon Press, 1904.

I.W.

SHENSTONE, William (1714–63) was a contemporary of Samuel Johnson at Pembroke College, Oxford, but his later life expresses the dilettante feeling for sensibility, naturalness, fancy and the Gothic, which characterizes the later eighteenth century. He cultivated his estate, The

Leasowes (Shropshire), in the new landscape manner and wrote experimental poetry in a variety of forms. *The Schoolmistress* (1742), an early Spenserian imitation, shows his characteristic mixture of lyrical charm and artifice. Shenstone suggested the idea of the *Reliques* to Percy and is partly responsible for the heavy editing of the ballads which it contains. He is at his best in his letters.

Poetical Works, ed. G. Gilfillan, Edinburgh: Nichol, 1854.
Letters, ed. M. Williams, Oxford: Blackwell, 1939.   w.r.

SHERIDAN, R. B. (Richard Brinsley) (1751–1816) was born in Dublin, his father being an actor and lecturer on rhetoric. After schooling at Harrow he lived in Bath, eloped in 1773 with Elizabeth Linley, the celebrated beauty and singer, and settled in London. Being short of money, he wrote *The Rivals* (1775), which was revised after an unsuccessful first night at Drury Lane, and then triumphed. The same year saw the first performance of Sheridan's short comedy *St. Patrick's Day*, and his comic opera *The Duenna*, which had a great success. In 1776 he purchased a half share of Drury Lane from Garrick and for this theater adapted (and rather watered down) Vanbrugh's *The Relapse* as *A Trip to Scarborough* (p. 1777). Also in 1777 he had his greatest success, with *The School for Scandal*. He bought the other share of Drury Lane, went into politics, and apart from his splendid burlesque tragedy, *The Critic*, wrote no further plays of any significance. In Parliament he was a brilliant orator and a friend of the chief Whig figures of his day, but he was never trusted with public office and died poor in 1816.

Technically, Sheridan's plays belong to the Restoration comic tradition. He refined existing stage techniques, and his forte lay in the perfect managing of situation and vivid characterizations drawn from the surface behavior of contemporary life. He had a fondness for dealing with contemporary fads, hypocrisies and fashionable vogues and topics of discussion. Much of his comedy can be directly related to popularized versions of new ideas as they could be found among Sheridan's contemporaries, and his verbal comedy, which is unfailingly brilliant, gains some of its finest effects from this fact.

The Rivals, 1775.
The Duenna; or, The Double Elopement, 1775.
The School for Scandal, 1780 (p. 1777).
A Trip to Scarborough, 1781 (p. 1777).
The Critic; or, A Tragedy Rehearsed, 1781 (p. 1779).
St. Patrick's Day; or, The Scheming Lieutenant, 1788 (p. 1775).

Speeches, 5 vols., London: Martin, 1816.

Plays and Poems, ed. R. C. Rhodes, 3 vols., Oxford: Blackwell, 1928.
Letters, ed. C. J. L. Price, 3 vols., Oxford: Clarendon Press, 1966.   w.r.

SHERWOOD, Robert E. (Emmet) (1896–1955) was born in New Rochelle (New York). A master of dramatic techniques, he sometimes allowed melodrama to mar an intelligent and compassionate insight. His best-known plays are *Idiot's Delight* (1936; *f.* 1939), on the absurdity of war, and *The Petrified Forest* (1935; *p.* 1934; *f.* 1936), about lost illusions. Pulitzer Prizes were also awarded for *Abe Lincoln in Illinois* (1939; *p.* 1938; *f.* 1939); *There Shall Be No Night* (1940), a reaction to the Russian invasion of Finland; and the historical work, *Roosevelt and Hopkins* (1948). During the Second World War he held a number of government offices. He wrote the film script for *The Best Years of Our Lives* (1946), which won nine Academy Awards.

r.w.

SHIRLEY, James (1596–1666) was born in London and educated at the Merchant Taylors' School and, probably, at both Oxford and Cambridge. After being ordained an Anglican priest, Shirley was converted to Roman Catholicism and was for some time a teacher at St. Albans Grammar School. About 1625 he moved to London and began writing for the stage, receiving encouragement from Queen Henrietta Maria. A Royalist during the Civil War, he taught again during the Commonwealth and died during the Fire of London.

Apart from masques (for which he was famous) and nondramatic verse, Shirley was the author of about forty plays. Of his tragedies perhaps the best are *The Traitor* (*p.* 1631) and *The Cardinal* (*p.* 1641). Most memorable of the comedies are *Hyde Park* (*p.* 1632), *The Gamester* (*p.* 1633) and *The Lady of Pleasure* (*p.* 1635). He also wrote tragicomedies in the manner of Fletcher and in imitation of Spanish drama. Historically, Shirley is particularly interesting as a link between Jacobean and Restoration theater; intrinsically, his work is unpretentious and unoriginal, often structurally effective and with a style which is fluent if finally rather shallow. Although Shirley lacks the strong involvement and moral alertness of the great Jacobean dramatists, he remains aware of a wider range of emotion and social stimuli than Restoration comedy was to be. (See also **Masques.**)

Works, ed. W. Gifford and A. Dyce, 6 vols., London: Murray, 1833.
Poems, ed. R. L. Armstrong, London: Oxford Univ. Press; New York: Columbia Univ. Press, 1941.

g.p.

SHORTHOUSE, J. H. (Joseph Henry) (1834–1903), a Birmingham businessman, was originally a Quaker, but later became an Anglican. He achieved fame with his first novel, *John Inglesant* (1881; published privately, 1880), which has a seventeenth-century setting, but his later novels of contemporary life were much less successful. The themes of his work are in the widest sense religious, being treated from the standpoint of an enlightened but vaguely mystical Anglicanism. They cover, for example, the relation between spiritual culture and personal development (*John Inglesant*) and the redeeming effect on others of self-sacrifice undertaken in response to conscientious scruple, as in *Sir Percival* (1886) and *Blanche, Lady Falaise* (1891). M.P.

SIDNEY, Sir Philip (1554–86) was educated at Shrewsbury School and Oxford, traveled widely in Europe, served at the court of Elizabeth I, and went on military service to the Netherlands. Wounded in a skirmish near Zutphen, he died a month later at Arnhem.

He was a courtier, a diplomat and a soldier; and as a writer he was equally versatile. In *An Apology for Poetry* (1595) he theorizes about literature. He argues that poetry is the best teacher because it embodies general truths in specific images and examples such as the memory can easily retain, and he acknowledges that this fact places a heavy responsibility on the poet. In *Astrophel and Stella* (written probably in 1582) he is himself a poet, composing the first sonnet sequence in the English language. Stella was perhaps Penelope Rich (née Devereux), and Astrophel Sidney. The sonnets are formal, lucid, graceful and ingenious; the accompanying songs show the poet at his most lyrical. In *Arcadia* (1590) Sidney turns again to prose for a long epic and pastoral romance which, like Spenser's *The Faerie Queene*, celebrates the ideal of chivalry as revived in the Elizabethan court. *Arcadia* has an intricate plot, with many episodic digressions; the characters unburden themselves in elaborate set speeches; and the prose style, though athletic enough, is certainly leisurely. Readers who expect a novel may find it tedious, but readers who accept it for what it is can be captivated by it as a product of the romantic imagination and moral seriousness of a great Englishman.

(See also **Renaissance Humanism.**)

Arcadia, 1590; enlarged, 1593.
Astrophel and Stella, 1591.
An Apology for Poetry, 1595.

Complete Works, ed. A. Feuillerat, 4 vols., Cambridge: Cambridge Univ. Press, 1912–26. J.D.J.

SILLITOE, Alan (1928–), born in Nottingham, is one of that group of novelists who established themselves in the 1950s with their portrayals of provincial life. His *Saturday Night and Sunday Morning* (1958; *f.* 1960) is, however, more definitely and more stridently working-class than many of the novels of this group. It is the story of a highly-paid factory worker, whose underlying attitude is one of revolt against what he regards as the prevailing social and ethical mores. The title story of his collection *The Loneliness of the Long-Distance Runner* (1959; *f.* 1962) has for its central character a juvenile delinquent, whilst *Key to the Door* (1961) takes a national service setting in the Malayan emergency. *The Death of William Posters* (1965) has been compared with Lawrence's *Aaron's Rod* as a study of a dissatisfied artist of working-class origins seeking fulfillment. Later works include *A Tree on Fire* (1967), *A Start in Life* (1970), a pastiche of the eighteenth-century picaresque novel put into a modern setting, and *Travels in Nihilon* (1971), a satire recalling another eighteenth-century mode, best illustrated by *Gulliver's Travels*. He also writes poetry, some of which was collected in *A Falling Out of Love, and Other Poems.* (1964).   A.P.

SIMEON, Charles. See **Sermons.**

SIMMS, William Gilmore (1806–70), a defender of slavery and secession, was born in South Carolina. He began his extensive literary career by writing romantic verse. His first novel, *Martin Faber* (1833), was a psychological study of a criminal, but his reputation was made with his so-named Border and Revolutionary romances, written in the tradition of Sir Walter Scott and James Fenimore Cooper, though at times deficient in realism. The former series includes *Guy Rivers* (1834), *The Yemassee* (1835) and *Beauchampe* (1842). *The Partisan* (1835), *Mellichampe* (1836) and *The Forayers* (1855) are among the latter.   R.W.

SIMPSON, Louis (1923–   ) was born in the West Indies. He served in the Airborne Division during the Second World War. Since then he has studied at Columbia, taught in American universities, and produced several collections of verse: *The Arrivistes* (1949), *Good News of Death and Other Poems* (1955), *A Dream of Governors* (1959), *At the End of the Open Road* (1963, Pulitzer Prize) and *Adventures of the Letter I* (1971).

His chosen forms are short lyrics, and long, topical, historical or dramatic poems. A subjective poet, he combines romantic lyricism and irony in the manner of Marvell. In "Walt Whitman at Bear Mountain" he relates his literary inheritance to the vastness of nature. This is finally a search for American and personal identity, which also occupies him in "Lines Written near San Francisco" and "Pacific Ideas—a Letter to Walt Whitman."   R.W.

SIMPSON, N. F. (Norman Frederick) (1919–), born in London, worked in a bank for two years before the Second World War, and afterwards wrote plays while following his profession as a teacher. His first popular success was *One Way Pendulum*, performed at London's Royal Court Theatre in 1959. This experimental comedy, described as "a farce in a new dimension," is characteristic of the author's work. Using fantasy, obsessed characters, seemingly nonsensical situations and replacing plot by a number of interconnected jokes, he strives to confuse the audience's view of the logical and the absurd, sense and nonsense.

A Resounding Tinkle, 1958 (*p.* 1957).
The Hole, 1958 (*p.* 1957).
One Way Pendulum, 1960 (*p.* 1959; *f.* 1964).
The Cresta Run, 1966 (*p.* 1965).   O.K.

SINCLAIR, Upton (1878–1968) was born in Baltimore, the son of an impoverished line of Southern aristocracy. Moving to New York he worked as a hack writer of jokes and stories. His first novels were romances, but their failure led him into muckraking with an article in *Collier's* in 1904 entitled "Our Bourgeois Literature." *The Jungle* (1906), dealing with corrupt business methods and unbearable exploitation of immigrant labor in the Chicago meat-packing factories, was an immediate success and led to the reform of the Food and Drug Laws. The money from this book went towards Helicon Hall, a settlement for radical writers and activists, where for a while Sinclair Lewis was the janitor. Together with Jack London, Sinclair founded the Inter-collegiate Socialist Society, and he was a New Jersey candidate for the House of Representatives on a Socialist platform in 1906. In 1934 he ran for Democratic governor of California, fighting for a system of old-age assistance. Meanwhile, he had produced a stream of novels directed against a variety of social ills and was to continue producing them at a steady rate until the late 1940s, in addition to his political activities and sociopolitical studies. The quality of his work remained on the level of journalism, vivid and striking but lacking in genuine personal or social perceptiveness. However, his persistence and energy in pointing out corruption and injustice cannot be denied, nor can his sincerity.

A Captain of Industry, 1906.
The Jungle, 1906.
The Metropolis, 1908.
King Coal, 1917.
They Call Me Carpenter, 1922.

Oil!, 1927.
The Lanny Budd series, 11 vols., 1940–53.
  World's End, 1940.
  Between Two Worlds, 1941.
  Dragon's Teeth, 1942.
  Wide is the Gate, 1943.
  The Presidential Agent, 1944.
  Dragon Harvest, 1945.
  A World to Win, 1946.
  Presidential Mission, 1947.
  One Clear Call, 1948.
  O Shepherd, Speak!, 1949.
  The Return of Lanny Budd, 1953.   D.C.

SINGER, Issac Bashevis (1904–   ) was born in Radzymin (Poland) and educated at Tachkemoni Rabbinical Seminary. The son and grandson of rabbis, Singer, like his brother Israel Joshua (author of *The Brothers Ashkenazi*), rejected a rabbinical career in favor of journalism and literature. He joined the staff of the *Jewish Daily Forward* when he went to he United States in 1935. His work is written in Yiddish and normally first published in the newspaper.

Singer's is a modern sensibility attempting to come to terms imaginatively with the previous 300 years of Polish Jewry. The principal tension in his work is between the demands of the old faith and of new science. A born storyteller, his writings employ fables, fantasy and saga to examine the rich Jewish heritage. His supreme creation is the vivid world of *shtetl* life, a world that gives equal time to the claims of passion, science and eternity.

A major branch of Singer's novel writing comprises multilayered novels containing many diverse characters and spreading over several generations. In both *The Family Moskat* (1950) and the double epic *The Manor* (1967) and *The Estate* (1969) the construction contrasts a believer in the old order and a man who embraces the new. Singer shows remarkable sympathy and understanding for the strengths and weaknesses of both viewpoints. Overall, his finest achievements are probably *The Magician of Lublin* (1960) and *The Slave* (1962). The former centers around the personality of Yasha Mazur, a strangely contemporary mixture of self-indulgent hedonism and all-pervading guilt. The latter is a simple and moving love story of two persecuted lovers united only in death.

Singer has written many short stories, the best of which are in *Gimpel the Fool* (1957), several books for children, and a set of autobiographical sketches.

The Family Moskat, 1950.

Satan in Goray, 1955.
Gimpel the Fool, 1957.
The Magician of Lublin, 1960.
The Slave, 1962.
In My Father's Court, 1966 (memoir).
The Manor, 1967.
The Estate, 1969.   D.V.W.

SINGH, Khushwant. See **Indian Literature.**

SITWELL, Dame Edith (1887–1964) was born at Scarborough (Yorkshire), the eldest child of Sir Reresby Sitwell and sister of two gifted brothers, Osbert and Sacheverell, and educated privately at the family seat at Renishaw near Sheffield. She never married, but occupied her adult life with writing and the company of a number of literary friends. Her early poetry was controversial, particularly *Façade*, poems written to be accompanied by dancing and music. Afterwards she published many volumes of verse, criticism and biography.

A writer whose poetry was to undergo continual development, she began by reacting strongly against conventional Georgian poetry. Her early volumes, *Clowns' Houses* and *Bucolic Comedies*, are notable for their spectacular technical experiments and affinities with music. During the 1930s economic pressures forced her to turn to prose and she wrote a number of biographies—on Pope, Queen Victoria and a semifictional life of Swift. It is likely that her poetry written during and after the Second World War will be considered her most significant achievement. In the poems included in *Street Songs*, *Green Song and Other Poems* and *Gardeners and Astronomers* she is still intensely aware of the importance of music and texture in her verse, but these are fused with more direct statements of feeling. A wide-ranging symbolism conveys the author's vision with dignity and gravity.

Façade, 1922.
Bucolic Comedies, 1923.
Rustic Elegies, 1927.
Alexander Pope, 1930.
Street Songs, 1942.
Green Song and Other Poems, 1944.
Gardeners and Astronomers, 1953.

Collected Poems, New York: Vanguard Press, 1954; London: Macmillan, 1957.
Selected Letters, 1919–1964, ed. J. Lehmann and D. Parker, New York: Vanguard Press, 1971.   O.K.

SKELTON, John (?1460–1529), mentioned by Caxton in 1490 as a scholar and translator, probably graduated from Oxford in 1484. At court, under the patronage of the countess of Richmond, he became tutor to Prince Henry in 1498 and probably entered the Church. After 1502 he was rector of Diss (Norfolk), but about 1512 returned to court under Henry VIII as *orator regius*, writing commissioned works, and lived at Westminster. Although for a time he was critical of Wolsey, Skelton's final poems suggest a reconciliation with him. Skelton died on 21 June 1529 and was buried at St. Margaret's, Westminster.

His first major poem, *The Bowge of Court* (?1498), was a vision allegory of the "ship-of-fools" type. At Diss he evolved a new, rough verse form, the Skeltonic, and moved into a new kind of poetry best seen in *Philip Sparrow*, a mock mass on Jane Scrope's pet sparrow with overtones reminiscent of Catullus, and in the low-life vitality of *The Tunning of Eleanor Rumming*. In 1515 he wrote his only extant play, *Magnificence*, a morality which is secular, giving advice to a ruler. Some critics have detected in it the beginnings of the attacks against Cardinal Wolsey which characterize the poems of 1521–22. *Speak, Parrot, Speak* veils the attack in learned allusions given by a parrot-persona. *Colin Clout* is a more direct attack in plainer style, and *Why Come Ye Not to Court?* a poem of outspoken and direct abuse that becomes uncontrolled. His works are listed in *The Garland of Laurel* (early 1523).

Skelton escapes from the stock themes and rhetorical devices of medieval tradition to produce poetry which suggests concern and involvement, conveyed particularly through his own plain style.

(See also **Morality Plays.**)

The Bowge of Court, ?1498.
The Garland of Laurel, 1523.
Magnificence, ?1530.
Colin Clout, ?1535.
Philip Sparrow, ?1545.
Why Come Ye Not to Court?, ?1545.
The Tunning of Eleanor Rumming, c. 1554.
Speak, Parrot, c. 1554.

Poetical Works, ed. A. Dyce, 2 vols., London: Rodd, 1843.
Complete Poems, ed. P. Henderson, 1931; revised, London: Dent; New York: Dutton, 1948.
                                                           A.D.M.

SLESSOR, Kenneth. See **Australian Literature.**

SMART, Christopher (1722–71) was born in Kent, but moved north as a boy with his family and was befriended by the duchess of Cleveland. He was educated at Durham Grammar School and Pembroke Hall, Cambridge, where his precocious scholarship and talent for verse attracted the attention of his contemporary, Thomas Gray. He very early contracted the habits of insobriety and extravagance which helped to ruin his life, but he was accepted as a friend and equal by many of the most distinguished men of his time. He won the Seatonian verse prize in 1750, the year of its inauguration and four more times in succession. Between 1749 and 1754 he mingled life in Cambridge with work as a hack writer in London, but after his marriage in 1752 his Cambridge fellowship was of necessity withdrawn. Like Collins, he seems to have undergone a religious crisis, but unlike that of Collins his religious enthusiasm was optimistic and took the form of unceasing prayer in public. He was in a madhouse at intervals from 1754 to 1763, and while there produced his greatest poem, *A Song to David* (1763), which to his contemporaries showed "melancholy proofs of the recent estrangement of his mind." It is a hymn on the psalmist, his character and his subjects, concluding in a great paean of adoration from all created things. In its associations, imagery and lyrical fervor it points the way to the intuitive manner of Blake. His other great poem, *Jubilate Agno*, was rescued from apparent meaninglessness by transposing the order of the leaves of the MS. His last work was a series of grave and demure *Hymns for the Amusement of Children* (1770), written in the King's Bench prison, where he had been taken for debt..

Collected Poems, ed. N. Callan, 2 vols., London: Routledge; Cambridge, Mass.: Harvard Univ. Press, 1949.   A.N.M.

SMITH, Adam (1723–90), most renowned of economists and author of the eminently readable and long influential *An Inquiry into the Nature and Causes of the Wealth of Nations* (1776), was born in Scotland at Kirkcaldy (Fifeshire). He was educated at Glasgow and Oxford Universities, and subsequently lectured at Edinburgh, mainly on English literature. In 1750 he was appointed to the chair of logic at Glasgow University and in 1751 moved over to the chair of moral philosophy. He now began to gestate the ideas which were later to give him such a *succès d'estime*, lecturing on topics in political economy. Being as much at home in town as in gown, he learned much about the practical facts of economic life from his friends the merchants of a prosperous Glasgow, and he was a lifelong friend of Hume. His shrewd and down-to-earth approach is everywhere apparent in *The Wealth of Nations*, but there is also a general philosophical basis to his political economy, set out in the earlier *Theory of*

Moral Sentiments (1759), which itself gave him a contemporary reputation at home and on the Continent. After 1764 first a private tutorship and then a pension and a sinecure enabled him to concentrate on *The Wealth of Nations*.

His economic thinking is suffused with the notion of natural law, "the hidden hand" operating through "the uniform, constant and uninterrupted effort of every man to better his condition" so as to achieve a harmony of interests and the greatest national product which resources allow. Any attempt to interfere with or improve upon this natural process was "a most unnecessary attention." He notably propounded the advantages of the division of labor, using the well-known example of a pin factory. His labor theory of value descended with mutations through Ricardo to Marx. His own main concern, however, was with economic progress, which has returned as an economic preoccupation at the present time.   R.H.B.

SMITH, Alexander. See **Spasmodics, The.**

SMITH, A. J. M. (Arthur James Marshall). See **Canadian Literature.**

SMITH, John (1580–1631), adventurer extraordinary, was born in Lincolnshire and died in London, after travels throughout Europe, the Balkans, Turkey and Russia and voyages to most parts of North America. His major works were concerned with his part in or the promotion of English colonization of Virginia and New England, and *A True Relation of Virginia* (1608) is one of the earliest accounts of the Virginia settlement. *A Description of New England* (1616) was one of the first English books to comment on this region. Smith tended to exaggerate but not, as was once thought, particularly of his *True Travels* (1630), to fabricate. His accounts of Indians are especially valuable.

Travels and Works, ed. E. Arber, 1884; revised A. G. Bradley, 2 vols., London: Grant, 1910.   R.S.

SMITH, Samuel F. (Francis). See **Hymns.**

SMITH, Sydney (1771–1845) was educated at Winchester and New College, Oxford, obtaining a fellowship in 1791. He took orders and became tutor to Michael Hicks Beach, whom he accompanied to Edinburgh. There he originated the idea of *The Edinburgh Review*, helped

Jeffrey to get it under way and became a regular contributor. In 1803 he moved to London, lectured on moral philosophy at the Royal Institution and became a member of the Whig circle connected with Holland House. In 1808 he settled at his living of Foston, near York, though he continued to be well known as a wit and much sought after on his annual visits to London. He later became a prebendary at Bristol and then a canon of St. Paul's Cathedral. He was known to most of the writers of his day.

As a clergyman Sydney Smith diverted some and horrified others with his strong-minded dislike of enthusiastic religion, love of openness and clarity, straightforward views and sturdy wit. His collected reviews show these qualities and are notably without trace of early nineteenth-century reviewing pomposity. He was equally able to give wit or seriousness to the service of worthy causes or an attack on anything which looked like a source of social injustice. His wit served his love of progress away from all kinds of outmoded prejudice. He was at his best in *The Letters of Peter Plymley* (1807–08) on the (supposed) terrors of Catholic emancipation. His letters, too, are unfailingly delightful.

(See also **Essays.**)

Works, 4 vols., London: Longman, 1839–40.
Selected Writings, ed. W. H. Auden, New York: Farrar, Straus, 1956;
    London: Faber & Faber, 1957.
Selected Letters, ed. N. C. Smith, London: Oxford Univ. Press, 1956.
                                  W.R.

SMITHYMAN, Kendrick. See **New Zealand Literature.**

SMOLLETT, Tobias (1721–71), born of good family in Dunbartonshire, studied medicine in Glasgow, but, fired by literary ambitions, set out for London in 1739 with his tragedy, *The Regicide*. His ambitions were deferred by service as a surgeon on the Cartagena expedition in 1741 and temporary residence in the West Indies, where he married an heiress who brought him enough money to set up a practice in London in 1744. The tragedy languished, creating animosities, but Smollett published two verse satires and then, in 1748, *The Adventures of Roderick Random*, which established him as a comic novelist also capable of vivid statement (witness the use made in this work of Smollett's naval and literary experience). Thus began a life of extensive literary activity which included novels, history, translation, laborious compilation, vicious political journalism and the provocative editorship (1756–63) of *The Critical Review*. The range of Smollett's activities at this time places him second only to Johnson as a man of letters.

Smollett was, however, less fortunate; and in 1763, "traduced by malice, persecuted by faction, abandoned by false patrons," he left England and spent two years on the Continent, of which his *Travels* (1766) forms a memorable record. Return and occasional residence in Bath brought no better fortune. In 1768 he departed to Northern Italy and lived near Leghorn till his death in 1771.

The bulk of Smollett's writing is now forgotten and, though the laborious publishers' ventures did serve their purpose well at the time, not unjustly forgotten. But despite a general critical inability to deal with the novels except as crude variants of Fielding's work, these continue to be read for their high style of articulate comedy (the quality Dickens so much admired in Smollett and which he incorporated in his own work) and for another level of style, vividly communicating a heightened moral and physical sense, which can only be matched by Swift in eighteenth-century prose.

If the early novels, *The Adventures of Roderick Random* and *The Adventures of Peregrine Pickle*, are predominantly comic, then *The Adventures of Ferdinand, Count Fathom* and *The Adventures of Sir Launcelot Greaves* show Smollett experimenting uneasily with a more flexible form. The neglected *Travels*, composed of forty long letters, miraculously apt and forceful in their description, perhaps suggested the epistolary structure of *The Expedition of Humphry Clinker*. In this, the fruit of Smollett's last years in Italy, the potentially disruptive "mixture of styles" is turned to good account as each correspondent is clearly identified in his own voice—notably Bramble (who speaks for the Smollett of the *Travels*), reviling the pretensions of Bath and the sophistication and degeneracy of London, and his nephew Jerry, seeing the same things but in a comic perspective as part of "the farce of life."

The Adventures of Roderick Random, 1748.
The Adventures of Peregrine Pickle, 1751.
The Adventures of Ferdinand, Count Fathom, 1753.
A Complete History of England Deduced from the Descent of Julius Caesar to the Treaty of Aix La Chapelle, 1748, 4 vols., 1757–58.
Continuation of the Complete History of England, 5 vols., 1760–65.
The Adventures of Sir Launcelot Greaves, 1762 (s. 1760–61).
The Expedition of Humphrey Clinker, 1771.

Works (prose fiction), ed. G. Saintsbury, 12 vols., London: Gibbings, 1895.
Letters, ed. L. M. Knapp, Oxford: Clarendon Press, 1970.   D.G.

SNODGRASS, W. D. (William De Witt) (1926–) was born in Wilkinsburg (Pennsylvania) and educated at the State University of Iowa. He has held various academic posts and was awarded the Pulitzer

Prize in 1960. Snodgrass became known almost overnight with the publication of his first volume of poetry, *Heart's Needle* (1959). Belonging to no particular school, he seems to have taken from both formalist and antiformalist poets. Some of the verse of the collection is colloquial, metaphysical and seriously witty. The best, however, is odd, local and personal. His portrait of man's suffering and action reformulates the theme of life as naked experience. His language is at all times individual, tense and idiomatic.

Heart's Needle, 1959.
After Experience: Poems and Translations, 1968.   D.V.W.

SNOW, C. P. (Charles Percy), Lord (1905–   ), born in Leicester, the son of a clerk, started his career as a scientist, though writing was his ultimate ambition. He enjoyed a distinguished career at Cambridge University, then after the Second World War became increasingly involved in public life—as a Civil Service commissioner, as a commentator on public affairs and as an adviser. In later years Snow has been better known as a social theorist than as a novelist, and his Rede Lecture, *The Two Cultures and the Scientific Revolution* (1959), was widely discussed. He married the writer Pamela Hansford Johnson in 1950.

Snow's novels are the direct outcome of his public and professional career. In 1940 he published the first of a sequence of novels, given the collective title of *Strangers and Brothers*, in which he set out to show the anatomy of society from 1920 to 1950 and to follow the career of Lewis Eliot, as he is involved in a struggle for power. Each novel may be read separately, but they are all linked by common themes, persons and places, Snow's chief strength lies in binding together the public and the private, social fact and character, in the consideration of a man's career from the lower middle class to Whitehall. At best, his vision is equable, objective and wide-ranging, and his modest artistry is in accord with his intention of giving a realistic account of the workings of power.

Strangers and Brothers, 1940.
The Masters, 1951.
The New Men, 1954.
The Conscience of the Rich, 1958.
The Affair, 1960.
Corridors of Power, 1964.   O.K.

SNYDER, Gary (1930–   ) was born in San Francisco and raised "on a feeble sort of farm just north of Seattle." He majored in anthropology at Reed College in 1951, and then spent time in logging and forestry, alternating with classical Chinese study at Berkeley. He spent 1956–57 undergoing formal Zen training in Japan, and after a spell working on a tanker, returned to Japan from 1959 until 1968. He has since lived in northern California. Eastern mysticism and his deep knowledge of the wilderness ("I hold the most archaic values on earth") are fundamental to his clean, precise poetry.

Riprap, 1959.
Myths and Texts, 1960.
Hop, Skip, and Jump, 1964.
Six Sections from Mountains and Rivers without End, 1965.
A Range of Poems, 1966.
The Back Country, 1967.
Earth House Hold, 1969 (essays).
Regarding Wave, 1970.   J.P.W.

SORLEY, Charles. See **War Poets.**

SOUSTER, Raymond. See **Canadian Literature.**

SOUTH, Robert. See **Sermons.**

SOUTH AFRICAN LITERATURE. See **African Literature.**

SOUTHEY, Robert (1774–1843) was the son of a Bristol draper. After expulsion from Westminster School for an antiflagellation article, Southey went to Balliol College, Oxford in 1793 and left the following year without taking a degree. He was in Bristol during 1794–95, full of ardor for revolutionary ideals, and at that time was Coleridge's closest friend. They formulated "pantisocracy" and married two sisters, but eventually quarreled and were temporarily estranged. Southey spent 1795–96 in Spain with his uncle, then studied law and wrote for the newspapers in London (1797–99). He was in Portugal during 1800–01 and in Dublin in 1801–02, then settled at Greta Hall, Keswick (Cumberland), with the Coleridge family, for whom he ultimately took on financial responsibility. In 1813 he became poet laureate. Southey's second wife was the poet Caroline Bowles. He wrote prolifically, and after years of vast scholarly undertakings his mind gave way about 1840.

Though a friend of Wordsworth and Coleridge, Southey can scarcely be grouped with them. His bent was scholarly (his library was famous) and he soon turned towards historical work. He wrote frequently for *The*

Quarterly Review on questions of church and state and was much reviled as an ultraconservative. His early ballad poems are at times rewarding, but the epics such as *Thalaba* and *Madoc*, which he wrote to illustrate various kinds of exotic mythology, are almost unreadable. His laureate odes have been granted a comic immortality by Byron's glorious answer to *A Vision of Judgement* (1821). But Southey's prose has always been admired. The biographies of Nelson (1813) and Wesley (1820) are impressive and, at the other extreme, his fantastic "Shandyan" work, *The Doctor* (1834–37), provides "The Three Bears."

(See also **Romantic Movement, The.**)

Poems, 2 vols., 1797–99.
Thalaba the Destroyer, 1801.
Madoc, 1805.
Letters from England, by Don Manuel Alvarez Espriella, 1807.
The Curse of Kehama, 1810.
The Life of Nelson, 2 vols., 1813.
A Vision of Judgement, 1821.

Poetical Works, collected by himself, 10 vols., London: Longman, 1837–38.   W.R.

SOUTHWELL, Robert (1561–95) came of well-to-do Norfolk stock, was educated abroad, entered the Jesuit order in 1578 and returned as a missionary to England in 1586. Arrested and tortured in 1592, he was imprisoned until his execution in 1595. His verse, entirely on Christian subjects, was written in the six years before his arrest, and was avowedly didactic in purpose. Its directness, force and sense of conviction are always effective, its style looking back to medieval lyrics in form and colloquial usages and forward to the baroque of Marvell and Crashaw in conceits and emblematic use of Christian truths and paradox.

Poems, ed. J. H. McDonald and N. P. Brown, Oxford: Clarendon Press, 1967.   A.E.

SOYINKA, Wole. See **African Literature.**

SPARK, Muriel (1918–   ) was born and educated in Edinburgh. After spending some years in Central Africa she worked in the Foreign Office during the Second World War. She then edited two poetry magazines and published biographies of Mary Shelley and John Masefield. She became a Roman Catholic in 1954. Her novels generally show religious patterns manifesting themselves in a godless society through the building up of seemingly inexplicable patterns of events and behavior. Apart from her novels she has also published poems, short stories and a play, *Doctor of Philosophy* (1962).

The Comforters, 1957.
Robinson, 1958.
Memento Mori, 1959.
The Ballad of Peckham Rye, 1960.
The Bachelors, 1960.
The Prime of Miss Jean Brodie, 1961 (*f.* 1969).
The Girls of Slender Means, 1963.
The Mandelbaum Gate, 1965.
The Driver's Seat, 1970.
Not to Disturb, 1971.   W.R.

SPASMODICS, The. The Spasmodic poets, chief of whom were P. J. Bailey, Sydney Dobell and Alexander Smith, enjoyed a remarkable popularity in England and in America during the 1840s and early 1850s. They were, throughout, championed by the influential critic George Gilfillan.

The first Spasmodic poem (not so called at the time) was Bailey's epic drama *Festus* (1839), a Byronic rendering of Goethe's *Faust*. After *Festus* came poems and verse dramas, such as Westland Marston's *Gerald* (1842), Sydney Dobell's *The Roman* (1850) and Alexander Smith's "A Life Drama" (1853), which, individually imitative of the style of such earlier poets as Byron, Shelley and Keats rather than of *Festus*, nevertheless had sufficient characteristics in common with Bailey's poem to warrant the labeling of their authors as a "school." Features common to these long verse dramas were the morbid introspection of Werther-type heroes, an extravagance of style, and, above all, a lack of formal discipline and structural organization which arose from an unconsciously shared belief, derived from Romantic poetic theory, of poetry writing as spontaneous and intuitively, or divinely, inspired creation. "Poetry," said Dobell, "should roll from the heart as tears from the eyes—unbidden."

The term "Spasmodic," which aptly describes the pulsations of frenzied emotionalism in their verse, was not applied to these poets until 1853, when Charles Kingsley, voicing an emerging sociological aesthetic which sought to disown the type of poetry the Spasmodics were writing, complained of "this spasmodic, vague, extravagant, effeminate school of poetry." It was William Aytoun, however, who gave the term notoriety in his attack on the Spasmodics in 1854 in *Blackwood's Magazine* and in his damaging parody, *Firmilian; or, The Student of Badajoz: A Spasmodic Tragedy*.

Tennyson's *Maud*, the poetry of Elizabeth Barrett Browning, and the sensation-novels of the period (including, perhaps, those of the Brontës) record the influence of the Spasmodics on their contemporaries.

Aytoun, William Edmondstoune (1813–65).
Firmilian; or, The Student of Badajoz: A Spasmodic Tragedy (pseud. "T. Percy Jones"), 1854.

Bailey, Philip James (1816–1902).
Festus, a Poem, 1839.
The Angel World, and Other Poems, 1850.

Bigg, John Stanyan (1828–65).
Night and the Soul, 1854.

Dobell, Sydney (1824–74).
The Roman (pseud. "Sydney Yendys"), 1850.
Balder, part 1, 1853; with preface, 1854. Part 2 never completed.

Jones, Ebenezer (1820–60).
Studies of Sensation and Event: Poems, 1843.

Marston, John Westland (1819–90).
Gerald: A Dramatic Poem, and Other Poems, 1842.

Massey, Gerald (1828–1907).
Voices of Freedom and Lyrics of Love, 1850.
The Ballad of Babe Christabel, and Other Lyrical Poems, 1854.

Smith, Alexander (1829–67).
Poems, 1853.
City Poems, 1857.   M.S.

SPENCE, Catherine. See **Australian Literature.**

SPENCER, Herbert (1820–1903) was born at Derby of a Dissenting family. After other abortive careers he turned to journalism in 1846. His work on *The Economist* led him to try to apply the principle of evolution in a sociological context. Thereafter he sought to extend it to ethics. He believed in an inevitable progress—towards the fullest individual freedom, for he was also an extreme adherent of laissez faire attitudes.

Social Statics, 1851.
Principles of Psychology, 1855; revised, 1870–72.
First Principles, 1860.
Principles of Sociology, 1876. } *A System of Synthetic Philosophy*, 10 vols,
Principles of Ethics, 1879.   1860–96.

The Man versus the State, 1884.
Autobiography, 2 vols., 1904.   A.P.

SPENDER, Stephen (1909–), son of a journalist with Jewish and
German antecedents, became known in the 1930s as one of the new Oxford
left-wing poets with Auden and Day Lewis. His experience of the
Depression and the Spanish Civil War produced poems remarkable for
their lyrical intensity and pity for human suffering. He has also published
fiction, verse drama (*Trial of a Judge*, 1938), autobiography (*World within
World*, 1951) and literary criticism (*The Destructive Element*, 1935; *The
Creative Element*, 1953). In 1933 he became a founder-editor of *Encounter*
and most of his subsequent work has been in literary journalism.

Collected Poems, 1928–1953, 1955.
Selected Poems, 1965.
The Generous Days, 1971.   D.W.

SPENSER, Edmund (?1552–99) was born in London of a family
which, in spite of its poor circumstances, was probably connected with the
noble Spencers of Althorp in Northamptonshire. He was educated at the
Merchant Taylors' School and at Pembroke Hall, Cambridge, where he
graduated B.A. in 1573 and M.A. in 1576. Cambridge was at that time a
scene of religious controversy, the Puritan Thomas Cartwright opposing
the more moderate John Whitgift. The Puritan sympathies which become
evident in *The Shepherd's Calendar* may therefore have developed in
these university days. From this period, too, dates the friendship with the
humanist scholar Gabriel Harvey, who figures as "Hobbinol" in the
Calendar. The unsuccessful courtship of the "Rosalind" referred to both
in the *Calendar* and the later *Colin Clout's Come Home Again* probably
belongs to the period after Spenser left Cambridge and before his appointment in 1578 as secretary to the bishop of Rochester. By 1579 he had
moved to London and found influential friends in the earl of Leicester,
Philip Sidney and Edward Dyer, all of whom encouraged aspiring poets.
Spenser's association with Sidney's circle, which at that time was deeply
concerned with plans for the reformation of English poetry, undoubtedly
influenced his development; and *The Shepherd's Calendar*, now regarded
as the opening manifesto of the new English Renaissance, is dedicated to
Sidney, chief among the architects of the change. Spenser's strong attachment to Leicester and Sidney is apparent both in "The Ruins of Time,"
in which he laments their deaths in high rhetoric and emblematic vision,
and in their partial, shifting allegorical reflections among Gloriana's
knights in *The Faerie Queene*. For Sidney he also composed a pastoral
elegy, *Astrophel*.

In 1580 the circle of friends was broken by Spenser's departure for Ireland as secretary to Lord Grey de Wilton, the new lord deputy. Ireland was then in a desperate condition, threatened by rebellion from the oppressed native population and intervention from powerful Catholic Spain, and Grey's efforts to control his uneasy charge were unsuccessful. He was recalled in 1582, disgraced by reports that, in Spenser's words, "he was a bloody man, and regarded not the life of her [the queen's] subjects, no more than dogs, but wasted and consumed all, so as now she had almost nothing left but to reign in their ashes." Spenser, however, was loyal to Grey and stoutly defended his policy, both in the prose *A View of the Present State of Ireland* and in the verse portrait of the conscientious Artegall, knight of justice in book 5 of *The Faerie Queene*. After Grey's recall Spenser stayed in Ireland, having obtained the lease of a country estate, where he lived for two years before taking up work in 1584 as clerk to the Munster council. He moved to Kilcolman Castle in county Cork, where he settled, a few years later. In 1589 Ralegh visited him, and together they sailed for England, where Spenser arranged the publication of the first three books of *The Faerie Queene*. Elizabeth expressed approval, and Spenser was granted a pension of £50 before his return to Kilcolman in 1591. His low opinion of court life, in spite of his reverence for Elizabeth, is displayed both in the satirical "Mother Hubberd's Tale" and in *Colin Clout's Come Home Again*, while his warm feeling for the countryside to which he returned is made evident in the delightful rural description of the final cantos of *The Faerie Queene*.

In 1594 he married Elizabeth Boyle (his first marriage, about which little is known, must have taken place about 1579), and celebrated the occasion with the ecstatic *Epithalamion*. His *Amoretti*, which describes the courtship, is unusual among Elizabethan sonnet sequences in that it, too, deals in happiness, presents a responsive lady, and looks forward to joyful fulfillment rather than endless frustration. In late 1595 Spenser revisited London to arrange publication of books 4–6 of *The Faerie Queene*, returning to Ireland probably in the following year. In 1598 an Irish rebellion under the earl of Tyrone caused him to flee from Kilcolman with his family, and in December he was sent to England with dispatches for the Privy Council. Shortly after his arrival at Whitehall he died and was buried in Westminster Abbey. The poets of England gathered round his tomb and threw into it elegies, together with the pens that wrote them.

The homage which Spenser has received from generations of English poets is a sufficient indication of his formative place in England's literary tradition. Milton told Dryden that Spenser was his original, Pope read his poems aloud and Keats was ecstatic when introduced to them. Wordsworth and Yeats also admired him greatly. In the sixteenth century his poems constituted the first glorious proof that England, too, could have a

Renaissance, however late, fit to stand beside those of Italy and France; and when he opened his career with a volume of pastorals, the Virgilian epic promise was implicit. *The Shepherd's Calendar* is the richest and fullest pastoral in English. It contains both vigorous satire and lyrical idealism, pagan despair and Christian comfort, homely humor and stern morality. All these elements are interwoven in a cyclical structure in which the revolution of the seasons and the duties of the shepherd are matched to man's life in its various aspects, as lover, priest and poet.

This intricate structural sense reappears, on a far larger scale, in *The Faerie Queene*, where the plot, complicated as it is (especially in books 3 and 4) by the influence of the diffuse epic manner, reminiscent of Ariosto, is held together by a pervasive use of parallel and analogy. Thus, though situations may seem to recur in an aimlessly repetitive way, closer examination will reveal each instance of their occurrence as deliberately reflecting back on what has gone before, and when the parallel is drawn, a further level of Spenser's meaning becomes plain. It is no accident, for instance, that both Guyon (book 2) and Artegall (book 5) begin their quests with the discovery of a dead lady, for justice and temperance, as their stories develop, are shown to have much in common. This process of parallel and analogy is peculiarly suited to the Ariostan method, whereby instead of following the fortunes of a single epic hero the poet takes several characters, or groups of characters, and deals with them individually, frequently switching from one to the other, until all are interwoven at the end. In book 3, for example, the adventures of Britomart are set off by those of Amoret, Florimell and Belphoebe, and the meaning unfolds as their stories develop. Until recently the subtlety of this method was not appreciated, and Spenser was accused of rambling, digressive construction.

A similar revolution of theory has taken place with respect to his characteristic imagery, with its beautiful lengthy similes, which were once thought of as diffuse and inorganic, a hindrance to narrative rather than, as they are, a deliberate commentary upon it. Most of the old-fashioned views on Spenser may be traced to influential Romantic critics, who saw in him a languid poet of idyllic escape—as Lamb said, "to read him is like dreaming awake"—instead of a highly intellectual poet of complex and subtle meaning, demanding close and intelligent reading.

The allegory, which Hazlitt recommended his readers to ignore, works on several levels. The purpose of the epic was, as Spenser put it in the prefatory letter to Ralegh, "to fashion a gentleman or noble person in virtuous and gentle discipline," and the Elizabethan gentleman was required to be an expert in many fields. The virtue which Gloriana's knights pursue and embody is at once Christian, Aristotelian and Neo-platonic, and their adventures have political, spiritual, moral, historical and personal analogies. Of these the contemporary topical level is perhaps the least interesting, but it is rarely intrusive (book 5 is the exception here), and when handled discreetly, as in the account of the Protestant church in book 1, it plays a comparatively minor part in the whole. The allegory cannot be flat and lifeless, as Coleridge thought it, because it is continually changing. Its quality varies; from the simple and prosaic, as when Guyon loses his horse at the start of his quest to indicate that temperance is a pedestrian virtue, it proceeds through the romantic and symbolic, as in the account of the mysterious, destructive and yet fertile sea in books 3 and 4, to the high philosophic, as in the Neoplatonic dance of the Graces in book 6. Spenser is never dull, because he is always changing. Yeats considered the main distinction between his work and modern poetry rested in his superior energy and more "active will," and Douglas Bush, more recently, sums up the extraordinary variety of his performance when he says that he is "among other things, the wistful panegyrist of an imagined chivalry, the bold satirist of ugly actuality, cosmic philosopher and pastoral dreamer, didactic moralist and voluptuous pagan, Puritan preacher and Catholic worshiper, eager lover and mystical Neoplatonist."

(See also **Renaissance Humanism.**)

The Shepherd's Calendar, 1579.
The Faerie Queene, books 1–3, 1590; 1–6, 1596.
Complaints, 1591.
Daphnaïda, 1591.
Amoretti and Epithalamion, 1595.
Four Hymns, 1596.
Prothalamion, 1596.

Works, a Variorum edition, ed. E. Greenlaw, C. G. Osgood, F. M. Padelford, and R. Heffner, 9 vols., London: Oxford Univ. Press; Baltimore: Johns Hopkins Press, 1932–49; index, 1957.
Poetical Works, ed. J. C. Smith and E. de Selincourt, Oxford: Clarendon Press, 1909–10.   R.E.

SPRIGG, Christopher St. John. See **"Caudwell, Christopher."**

SPURGEON, C. H. (Charles Haddon). See **Sermons.**

SQUIRE, J. C. (Sir John Collings) (1884–1958) was born at Plymouth and educated at Blundell's School, Tiverton and Cambridge. He edited both the *New Statesman* and *The London Mercury*, the latter of which he founded in 1919. With this journal Squire succeeded Sir Edward Marsh as the leader of the Georgian poets. Much of his own work is in the Georgian tradition, but his finest productions are in the realm of light verse and especially parody. He was knighted in 1933. His autobiographical sketches appeared in *The Honeysuckle and the Bee* in 1937. (See also **Georgians, The.**)

Collected Poems, London: Macmillan, 1959; New York: St. Martin's Press, 1960.   A.P.

STEELE, Sir Richard (1672–1729) was born in Dublin and educated, with Addison, at the Charterhouse and Merton College, Oxford, after which he became a captain in the Life Guards. He lived carelessly and drank too much, but wrote an edifying treatise, *The Christian Hero* (1701), and also four comedies. He started *The Tatler* (1709–11), a thrice-weekly paper dealing with matters of general social interest in short essays, and he soon enlisted Addison as a regular contributor. This was followed by their joint periodical, *The Spectator* (1711–12), which came out on weekdays, usually consisting of a single essay of the kind that had been featured in *The Tatler*, but more extended, covering the social scene, moral issues and intellectual themes. These were given a readily acceptable, elegant presentation and clearly rooted in the everyday social milieu which would be familiar to their readers. From 1712 to 1714 Steele edited *The Guardian*, and *The Spectator* had a short second run in 1714. He engaged in party journalism against Swift and the Tories, became a Whig member of Parliament in 1713 and was knighted in 1715. In 1719 he quarreled with Addison and shortly afterwards was driven from London by his debts. He spent his last years in Wales.

Steele's prose is lighter in tone and more prone to sentiment than Addison's, but it shows the same basic critical and social assumptions.

(See also **Essays; Political Pamphlets.**)

Dramatic Works, ed. G. A. Aitken, London: T. Fisher Unwin; New York: C. Scribner's Sons, 1894.
Plays, ed. S. S. Kenny, Oxford: Clarendon Press, 1971.
The Tatler, ed. G. A. Aitken, 4 vols., London: Duckworth, 1898–99.
The Spectator, ed. D. F. Bond, 5 vols., Oxford: Clarendon Press, 1964.
The Englishman, ed. R. Blanchard, Oxford: Clarendon Press, 1955.
Periodical Journalism 1714–16, ed. R. Blanchard, Oxford: Clarendon Press, 1959.
Correspondence, ed. R. Blanchard, London: Oxford Univ. Press; Baltimore: Johns Hopkins Press, 1941.
Occasional Verse, ed. R. Blanchard, Oxford: Clarendon Press, 1952. W.R.

STEFFENS, Lincoln (1886–1936), journalist and reformer, was born in San Francisco. After graduation from the University of California

(1889) and study abroad, he joined the staff of *McClure's Magazine* (1901), for which he wrote a series of pioneering "muckraking" articles. "Tweed Days in St. Louis," "The Shame of Minneapolis," and similar pieces exposed municipal corruption in the cities. His extended analysis of political corruption and of the alliance between business and government appears in such books as *The Shame of the Cities* (1904) and *The Struggle for Self-Government* (1906). After 1917 Steffens became a firm supporter of the Soviet Union and met Lenin (1919) on a visit to Russia ("I have seen the future, and it works"). Steffens's *Autobiography* (1931) contains an account of the reform movements of his day.

Letters, 2 vols., New York: Harcourt, Brace, 1938.   J.W.

STEIN, Gertrude (1874–1946) was born in Allegheny (Pennsylvania). She passed her early years in Vienna and Paris, and later in Oakland and San Francisco. She specialized in psychology at Radcliffe College (1893–97), where she was a pupil of William James. Bored by formal examinations, she did not take a degree there or at Johns Hopkins where she studied medicine for four years. In 1903 she went to Paris and lived the rest of her life, except for an American lecture tour in 1934, in France with her friend and secretary, Alice B. Toklas. They lived through the German occupation, and Gertrude Stein was planning another visit to America in 1946 when she died.

Picasso, Braque, Matisse and other avant-garde artists greatly impressed her as soon as she arrived in Paris, and she became strongly influenced by them, collecting their work and supporting them in her writings. She was a prominent and influential figure in Paris literary and artistic circles, especially among the young American writers, including Hemingway, who spent time in France in the years following the First World War. In her own writing she tried to cultivate a style akin to abstractionism as she admired it in the painters' work, developing an approach she had begun at Radcliffe of experimenting with spontaneous, automatic writing. She described her work as (writing in the third person)

> possessed by the intellectual passion for exactitude in the description of inner and outer reality. She had produced a simplification by this concentration, and as a result the destruction of associational emotion in poetry and prose.

Three Lives, 1909 (stories).
Tender Buttons, 1914 (experimental poetry).
Geography and Plays, 1922.
The Making of Americans, 1925 (novel, written 1906–08).
Composition As Explanation, 1926 (lectures at Oxford and Cambridge).

How to Write, 1931.
Operas and Plays, 1932.
The Autobiography of Alice B. Toklas, 1933.
Portraits and Prayers, 1934.
Lectures in America, 1935.
The Geographical History of America; or, The Relation of Human Nature to the Human Mind, 1936.
Everybody's Autobiography, 1937.
What Are Masterpieces, 1940.
Brewsie and Willie, 1946.
Four in America, 1947 (essays).
Last Operas and Plays, ed. C. Van Vechten, 1949.
Things As They Are, 1950 (novel).

Selected Writings . . . 1909–44, ed. C. Van Vechten, New York: Random House, 1946.
Unpublished Writings, ed. C. Van Vechten, 8 vols., New Haven: Yale Univ. Press, 1951–58; London: Oxford Univ. Press, 1952–59.
Writings and Lectures 1911–45, ed. P. Meyerowitz, London: P. Owen. 1967.   J.P.W

STEINBECK, John (1902–68) was born in Salinas (California), son of the treasurer of Monterey Country and a local schoolteacher. He read widely and was deeply influenced by his environment, the valleys and hills of Central California. Educated locally, then at Stanford University, which he attended sporadically without taking a degree, he acquired detailed knowledge of working-class life from many, mostly manual, jobs. Failing to become a writer in New York in 1926, he took work in California while he wrote a weak historical novel, *Cup of Gold* (1929), satirizing rugged individualism and exploiting mythical patterns. Undeterred by commercial failure, he married in 1930, lived in Pacific Grove on a paternal allowance and published *The Pastures of Heaven* (1932), realistic, ironic tales loosely linked, as in Sherwood Anderson's *Winesburg, Ohio*, by common setting and characters. *To a God Unknown* (1933), written earlier, ambitiously but unconvincingly portrays a farmer's struggle with the land as a myth of man's unity with nature. He established himself with *Tortilla Flat* (1935; f. 1942), a prizewinning best seller which was dramatized in 1938 by Jack Kirkland. The escapades of Danny and his rowdy band of illiterate paisanos living around Monterey are converted into farcical, mock-Arthurian romance. In this, his funniest book, Steinbeck slily castigates the property-minded middle class. He consolidated his reputation by his later books of the 1930s, nearly all rooted in reaction to the Great Depression, written from intimate knowledge of Californian locations and concern for the poor and dispossessed. *In Dubious Battle* (1936) is a cool, apparently disinterested account of a fruitpickers' strike, *Of Mice and Men* (1937) an allegorical play-novelette about the shattered dream of two oddly sorted migrant workers, and *The Grapes of Wrath* (1939), a protest novel which caused a tremendous stir and won Steinbeck the popularity that he feared.

Behind these various forms lies a consistent attitude considerably indebted to his friendship from 1930 with Edward F. Ricketts, owner of a small commercial laboratory in Monterey. Scientist, mystic, lecher, even saint, this engagingly paradoxical marine biologist makes numerous thinly disguised appearances in the fiction and is openly commemorated in a sketch affixed to *The Log from the Sea of Cortez* (1951), the separate publication of Steinbeck's share in their delightful collaboration, *Sea of Cortez* (1941). In this record of their expedition to the Gulf of California, Steinbeck enthusiastically interprets Ricketts's central concept, non-teleological (noncausal) thinking. Striving for detachment, regarding biological and sociological phenomena as subject to the same immutable laws, he could treat clinically the controversial strike materials of *In Dubious Battle* and publish *The Grapes of Wrath* only after shedding the angry polemics of his first draft and the newspaper articles collected as *Their Blood Is Strong* (1938). But Ricketts provoked a complex response: the novelist was energized by contradictory impulses, a conjugation of ecological and transcendental speculation, dispassionate observation and a compassionate alignment with the downtrodden and rebellious.

With fame came problems that Steinbeck could not resolve. Removed by traveling and residence in New York from his imaginative center, beset by marital difficulties (divorced twice, he remarried in 1950), robbed of Ricketts by a car accident in 1948, the prolific, versatile storyteller declined into dangerous facility. His interest shifted, too, from group action to individual ethics, and he alternated naturalistic and quasi-allegorical modes. The best of this minor work of the 1940s includes screenplays for *The Forgotten Village* (1941), Hitchcock's *Lifeboat* (1943) and Kazan's *Viva Zapata* (1952), the portrait of Ricketts as Doc in *Cannery Row* (1945) and the background of *The Pearl* (1947). Two considerable efforts stand out from the trifling of the 1950s. In *East of Eden* (1952) he unbalanced a promising family chronicle intended for his two sons by incorporating a modern Californian version of the Fall and the Cain-Abel conflict and a grossly mishandled point of view and exposition of theme. In *The Winter of Our Discontent* (1961), taking on the challenge of a New England setting and a sophisticated first-person narrator-hero, he buried authenticity and passion under whimsy and symbols. The rest was journalism, including towards the end articles from Vietnam supporting the U.S. government position on the war. He died in New York on 20 December 1968.

Steinbeck won the Nobel Prize in 1962; he earned it with his work from the 1930s. The excellent short story collection, *The Long Valley* (1938), boasts some of his finest near-Lawrentian descriptions, supremely in the contrasted initiation rites of "Flight," a grimly ironic tale of a hunted young paisano, and in "The Red Pony," a semiautobiographical four-part novella. In *In Dubious Battle* he concentrates forcefully on terse dialogue and taut dramatic construction and manipulates beneath the naturalistic surface a Miltonic parallel, subtly condemning the violence of his agitator-heroes. But politics and poetry are most arrestingly commingled in his social epic, *The Grapes of Wrath*. Here he dramatized on many levels the exodus of the work-hungry from the dust-bowl of Oklahoma into the inviting Californian fruitlands, latest of great westering movements across the continent. Realistic episodes deal with the journeying of the long-suffering Joads and their resourceful reactions to entrenched prejudice and brutal exploitation. Politically anatomized, in generalizing interchapters, they are victims of extreme laissez faire capitalism. Biologically considered, mainly through animal imagery, they are a family gradually being assimilated into the larger social unit of mass migration. Mystically, they belong to the community of love and partake of the natural order. The construction is solid, the biblical parallel identifying the Okies with the Chosen People is striking, there is abundant lyricism, vivid drama, earthy humor; yet flaws of journalistic overemphasis and obstrusive symbolism are prominent and Steinbeck's stress on the typical, on biological analogy and mythical precedent, often shrivels individual character into the idealized or the grotesque. Nevertheless, in spite of lapses into familiar vices of sentimentality and sensationalism, the novel is more than a social tract and achieves both panoramic sweep and individual moments of great intensity.

Cup of Gold: A Life of Henry Morgan, 1929.
The Pastures of Heaven, 1932 (stories).
To a God Unknown, 1933.
Tortilla Flat, 1935 (*f.* 1942).
In Dubious Battle, 1936.
Of Mice and Men, 1937 (*f.* 1939) (novel and play, published simultaneously).
The Long Valley, 1938 (stories).
Their Blood Is Strong, 1938.
The Grapes of Wrath, 1939 (*f.* 1940).
The Forgotten Village, 1941.
Sea of Cortez (with Edward Ricketts), 1941.
The Moon Is Down, 1942 (novel and play, published simultaneously).

Bombs Away, 1942.
Cannery Row, 1945.
The Wayward Bus, 1947.
The Pearl, 1947 (*f.* 1948; 1954).
A Russian Journal (with Robert Capa), 1948.
Burning Bright, 1950 (play in story form).
The Log from the Sea of Cortez, 1951.
East of Eden, 1952 (*f.* 1955).
Sweet Thursday, 1954.
The Short Reign of Pippin IV, 1957.
Once There Was a War, 1958.
The Winter of Our Discontent, 1961.
Travels with Charley: In Search of America, 1962.
America and Americans, 1966.
Journal of a Novel: The East of Eden Letters, 1969.

The Portable Steinbeck, revised edition, sel. P. Covici, New York: Viking Press, 1946; *The Steinbeck Omnibus*, sel. P. Covici, London: Heinemann, 1951.
Short Novels, ed. J. H. Jackson, New York: Viking Press, 1953; London: Heinemann, 1954.   A.S.

STEPHEN, J. K. (James Kenneth). See **Parody and Nonsense.**

STEPHEN, Sir Leslie (1832–1904), biographer and critic, came of a family associated with the Evangelical Clapham Sect and was the father of Virginia Woolf. He resigned his Cambridge fellowship on grounds of agnosticism. He edited *The Dictionary of National Biography* (1882–91), to which he contributed 378 articles. His other works include *Hours in a Library* (3 series, 1874–79; *The Cornhill Magazine* articles) and *The History of English Thought in the Eighteenth Century* (1876–81). His work is marked by a strong moral sense (which leads him to disapprove of some eighteenth-century novelists and Restoration drama) and by the sociological view that literature is a by-product of social conditions.   A.P.

STEPHENS, A. G. (Alfred George). See **Australian Literature.**

STERNE, Laurence (1713–68), born in Ireland, son of a subaltern, followed his father's postings and eventually settled to eight years' schooling in Halifax (Yorkshire). Left destitute, he was sent to Cambridge by an uncle, ordained in 1737 and was vicar of Sutton-in-the-Forest

(Yorkshire) from 1738 to 1759. He married in 1741, but his wife suffered from his "quiet attentions" to other women and went insane in 1758. The publication of *Tristram Shandy* in sporadic volumes in the 1760s brought Sterne fame; going to London to enjoy it, he lived in true Shandean manner. *A Sentimental Journey* was one result of the travels he made abroad for the benefit of his health. The innocent intrigue with Mrs. Draper of *Journal to Eliza* (1773, but kept in 1767) precipitated a separation from his wife and, more painfully, his daughter. Sterne died insolvent in London the next year.

   Tristram Shandy confused and outraged people on its first appearance and continues to do so. Horace Walpole described it as "a kind of novel . . . the great humour of which consists in the whole narration always going backwards." F. R. Leavis objects to Sterne's "irresponsible (and nasty) trifling." But it won readers then by its charm and eccentricity, and although modern taste reacts differently to Sterne's calculated sentimentality, obsession with the form of the novel has promoted interest in his extreme formal sophistication. It owes much to Locke's theories of sensation and association of ideas. It is as the self-conscious narrator of *Tristram Shandy* rather than as the Shandean exhibitionist of *A Sentimental Journey* that Sterne appeals today, though this ought not to blind us to the delicate inflexion and romantic flourish of his prose, evident in his correspondence as well as in his novels and journals.
   (See also **Parody and Nonsense.**)

Tristram Shandy, 1760–67.
The Sermons of Mr. Yorick, 1–2, 1760; 3–4, 1766; 5–7, 1769 (as *Sermons by the Late Rev. Mr. Sterne*).
A Sentimental Journey through France and Italy, 1768.

Writings, Shakespeare Head edition, 7 vols., Oxford: Blackwell, 1926–27.
Letters, ed. L. P. Curtis, Oxford: Clarendon Press, 1935; 1965.   D.G.

STEVENS, Wallace (1879–1955) was born in Reading (Pennsylvania); his ancestors on his mother's side were Dutch. He studied at Harvard (1897–1900) and the New York Law School (graduated 1903). He then practiced law in New York until he entered the legal department of the Hartford Accident and Indemnity Company in 1916, becoming its vice-president in 1934. He remained in Hartford until his death.
   Stevens began writing verses at Harvard. Later Harriet Monroe took some interest in his poetry and verse plays and the first version of "Sunday Morning" appeared in *Poetry* in 1915. His first volume of poetry, *Harmonium* (1923), received a lukewarm critical reception and it was not until 1935 that *Ideas of Order* was published. This included "The Idea of Order at Key West," a major poem in the Romantic tradition illustrating

Coleridge's assertion that "in our life alone does nature live." The title poem of *The Man with the Blue Guitar and Other Poems* was the first of several long pieces exploring the philosophical and aesthetic problems that constantly preoccupied Stevens. Two of these, *Notes towards a Supreme Fiction* (1942) and *Esthétique du Mal* (1944), were included in *Transport to Summer* in 1947. This was followed in 1950 by *The Auroras of Autumn* (1950), which included "A Primitive Like an Orb" (1948), a poem about perceiving the Supreme Fiction, "the huge high harmony." Stevens's *Collected Poems* (1954) contained the powerful, autobiographical "The Rock," a sequence of twenty-five poems celebrating the physical world and finally reconciling poetry and life, imagination and reality.

Stevens was certainly conscious of being an American poet. In "Like Decorations in a Nigger Cemetery" he describes "the sun of autumn" as being "like Walt Whitman walking along a ruddy shore" and continues:

> He is singing and chanting the things that are part of him,
> The worlds that were and will be, death and day.

Stevens is reminiscent of Whitman when he is writing about the sea, exalting the poet, or feeling melancholy, but his earliest work owes more to the French *symbolistes*, whose fluency and use of color appealed to him. Gaudy, elegant, foppish, exotic—these are the epithets usually applied to *Harmonium*, the collection which first set forth the contours and colors of Stevens's fictive world. But Stevens was forty-four in 1923—*Harmonium* is a middle-aged work, its gaiety suffused with weary resignation, its glittering displays of imagistic precision and radiance accompanied by interior dramas where the protagonists learn to adjust to perceptions of earthly things. Stevens's meditative manner is often in evidence, as in such poems as "The Man Whose Pharynx Was Bad" (about imaginative impotence) and the superb "Sunday Morning," a secular reflection on death. Acknowledging the disappearance of gods, Stevens sees that man is "dispossessed and alone in a solitude"; with gentle compassion and a brilliant command of image and rhythm, he argues for and projects a possible paradise on earth.

Harmonium remains notable for the originality of its imagery, its control of meter, the richness and density of its language. Its significance is gauged by Stevens's desire to call his collected poems *The Whole of Harmonium*. By the period of "The Man with the Blue Guitar," Stevens was writing in a more obviously philosophical manner, examining more directly and analytically the theme which was from the beginning the burden of his poetry—the tension between imagination and reality. His compositions sometimes look like versions of Santayana. Moving towards "the poem of the act of the mind" which "must take the place/

Of empty heaven and its hymns," Stevens reached a peak of achievement with *Notes towards a Supreme Fiction*, a sophisticated exposition of the redemptive role of the creative imagination: "It must be abstract [i.e. apprehend the pure essence], it must change, it must give pleasure," imperatives which satisfy and derive from "major man," the potentiality Emerson and Whitman perceived in the democratic individual.

Stevens's appeal has been limited, not only because of the difficulty of much of his verse, but because to many his persona was too dry, too lacking in warmth. In 1958 A. Alvarez could find no "continual deepening and broadening of experience" in Stevens's work, and some of the later poems particularly are open to the charge of being disembodied and remote from the "world of gutturals." Certainly, Stevens was unrepentantly patrician, even snobbish, and described money as "a kind of poetry." Such lapses are rare; it is Stevens's assurance and poise, his instinct for the right pace, the appropriate sounds and tones that impress the reader in the finest work. And although Stevens belongs in a Romantic tradition, he is very much a twentieth-century poet, recognizing empirically that the process of analyzing reality falsifies it (Uncertainty Principle) and that time is a sequence of unconnected moments (Quantum Theory). He places images—even whole sections—side by side, like flat blocks of color in modern painting. (Stevens's connection with modern art is as important as W. C. Williams's: his titles, such as "Sea Surface Full of Clouds," often sound like the titles of pictures, and in 1951 he wrote "The Relations between Poetry and Painting.") What matters is the relationship, the resonance between those images.

But

> Poetry is a finikin thing of air
> That lives uncertainly and not for long

and even the fixity of an image is dependent upon a single perspective. For Stevens there were (at least) thirteen ways of looking at a blackbird, just as for Melville the meaning of the doubloon in *Moby-Dick* varies according to the identity of the observer. So Stevens, wavering between the primacy of imagination and of reality, became skeptical of metaphor, describing it as "degeneration." Accepting and naming things unsymbolically, he placed at the end of *Collected Poems* the verses entitled "Not Ideas about the Thing but the Thing Itself." It was, however, the "intrepid and eager" imagination which made the abstraction of "the Thing Itself" possible.

Theodore Roethke, in celebration of Stevens, shouted: "Brother, he's our father!" but the continuity of Stevens's style is seen best perhaps in the poets of the New York School with their fanciful wordplay, dazzling images and close relationship with abstract expressionist painting.

Harmonium, 1923; revised, 1931.
Ideas of Order, 1935.
The Man with the Blue Guitar and Other Poems, 1937.
Parts of a World, 1942.
Transport to Summer, 1947.
The Auroras of Autumn, 1950.
The Necessary Angel: Essays on Reality and the Imagination, 1951.
Opus Posthumous, 1957.

Collected Poems, New York: Knopf, 1954; London: Faber & Faber, 1955.
Letters, ed. H. Stevens, New York: Knopf, 1966; London: Faber & Faber, 1967.
The Palm at the End of the Mind: Selected Poems and a Play, ed. H. Stevens, New York: Knopf, 1971.   R.W.

STEVENSON, Robert Louis (1850–94) was born in Edinburgh. He trained for a legal career, but at an early age his lungs were affected and he was forced to begin a lifetime of travel. The material which he soon collected resulted in several important books—*An Inland Voyage* (1878), *Travels with a Donkey in the Cévennes* (1879) and in 1883, as a result of a trip to California, *The Silverado Squatters*. Courageous and vigorous in the face of deteriorating health, Stevenson wrote novels, short stories (including *Dr. Jekyll and Mr. Hyde*), poetry, essays and a collection of letters, published in four volumes in 1912. *Treasure Island* (1883) was the first of a series of novels on which his popular reputation was built. In 1888 he settled in Samoa where his health recovered enough to permit him to write his last major work, *A Footnote to History: Eight Years of Trouble in Samoa* (1892).

Out of his affection for Scotland and its people, as well as a power to assimilate literature (which he said a writer should read "with his ear"), Stevenson developed a style that combines lucidity with a powerful narrative skill. Incapable of writing historical romances on the scale of Scott, Stevenson invested his tales with a verbal precision that was never pedantic, and a romantic grace that made his less sensitive critics dismiss him as a "faddling hedonist." In fact, Stevenson restricted his writing to the scale that would best exhibit his talents—craftsmanship in harmonious prose and an adventurous temperament that chose to control its resolute vivid affirmation of life through austerity in form. "A Puritan in fancy dress," he is best represented by his novels and essays, such as *Kidnapped* and *Virginibus Puerisque*, in which the influence of Scotland is most direct.

(See also **Essays**.)

Travels with a Donkey in the Cévennes, 1879.

Virginibus Puerisque and Other Papers, 1881.

New Arabian Nights, 2 vols., 1882 (vol. 1 *s.* 1878).

Treasure Island, 1883 (*s.* [in slightly different form] 1881–82; *f.* 1934; 1949).

[The] Strange Case of Dr. Jekyll and Mr. Hyde, 1886 (*f.* 1932; 1941; as *The Two Faces of Dr. Jekyll*, 1959).

Kidnapped, 1886 (*f.*1938; 1948; 1959).

The Black Arrow, 1888 (*s.* 1883; *f.* 1948).

The Master of Ballantrae, 1889 (*s.* 1888–89; *f.* 1953).

Catriona: A Sequel to Kidnapped, 1893 (*s.* 1892–93).

Weir of Hermiston, 1896 (unfinished).

Novels and Stories, selected V. S. Pritchett, London: Pilot Press, 1945; New York: Duell, Sloan & Pearce, 1946.

Complete Short Stories, with selection of best short novels, ed. C. Neider, New York: Doubleday, 1969.

Collected Poems, ed. J. Adam Smith, London: Hart-Davis, 1950.   P.G.M.

STEWART, Douglas. See Australian Literature.

STICKNEY, Trumbull (1874–1904)

was born in Geneva. Educated mostly by his father during the family's European travels, Stickney graduated from Harvard in 1895. He studied classics at the Sorbonne, where in 1903 he received the first doctorate ever awarded to an American. After a few months as instructor at Harvard he died of a brain tumor in 1904.

The publication of the posthumous *Poems* demonstrated his talent, but although R. P. Blackmur commented that his work occasionally rewards the persevering reader with sudden illuminating phrases, he has until recently received scant notice. His verse ranges from the Pre-Raphaelite to a firmer, more witty manner, which invites comparison with Hardy or Frost. Stickney's accomplishment lies in his accuracy of word and phrase and his neat control of rhythm.

Poems, ed. G. C. Lodge, W. V. Moody, and J. E. Lodge, Boston: Houghton, Mifflin, 1905.
                                                              M.L.

STOPPARD, Tom (1937–   )

was born in Czechoslovakia and came to England at the age of nine. He began to write plays after six years as a journalist in Bristol. *A Walk on the Water* was shown on British television in 1963; the stage version was seen in Hamburg and Vienna the following year and was presented with revisions at the St Martin's Theatre in 1968 under the title *Enter a Free Man*. By this time his reputation had been made by *Rosencrantz and Guildenstern Are Dead*, seen first at the Edinburgh

Festival, and then produced in 1967 by the National Theatre Company at the Old Vic, and by *The Real Inspector Hound*, presented at the Criterion Theatre in a double bill the following year.

Within a basically comic framework, the success of both these plays lies in their restoration of the value of language. The Rosencrantz and Guildenstern of the former are the Shakespearean characters outside their natural surroundings, aware of their own deficiencies, wary of the situation at the court of Elsinore, occasionally swept into the action of Hamlet against their will, and finally faded into the background as they outlive their usefulness. A similar dilemma concerns the two critics of *The Real Inspector Hound* drawn into the stage action of a play they have only come to review. The nature of identity, the absurdity of the nonhero and the realities of the theater itself are considered in dialogue that possesses a wit and intelligence rare in the contemporary theater, and certainly demonstrated again in *Jumpers* at the Old Vic in 1972.

Stoppard's other work includes radio plays (*The Dissolution of Dominic Boot*, *M Is for Moon among Other Things*, *If You're Glad I'll Be Frank* and *Albert's Bridge*), four plays for television (*A Separate Peace*, *Teeth*, *Another Moon Called Earth* and *Neutral Ground*), a novel (*Lord Malquist and Mr Moon*) and *After Magritte*, a one-act stage play.   J.M.W.

STOW, Randolph. See **Australian Literature.**

STOWE, Harriet Beecher (1811–96) was the second daughter of the Rev. Lyman Beecher, orthodox Calvinist and minister in Litchfield (Connecticut). The family also produced a worker for women's higher education and six clergymen. Harriet's education was along the conventional lines of her father's religion, at home and in her sister's school for girls in Hartford (Connecticut), where she herself also briefly taught. Her reading included the poems of Byron, as well as the novels of Walter Scott which influenced her towards realistic regionalism and perhaps a reliance upon improvisation in her plots. In 1832 her father went to Cincinnati to set up a theological seminary for frontier missionaries and took his family. Harriet joined her sister in running a girls' school there too, and began to write the religious sketches of New England life collected as *The Mayflower* (1843). In 1836 she married a colleague of her father's, the Rev. Calvin Ellis Stowe, a widower, and they had six children. A visit to Kentucky added a firsthand acquaintance of life in the South to the sympathetic interest in the Underground Railway for escaping slaves which she and her husband had developed in Cincinnati. In 1850 her husband became professor at Bowdoin College in Maine, and the family returned to New England from their long exile. While she was attending a communion service, all the emotion she had experienced about American slavery and the argument that raged over it in religious circles came to a head, and in answer to human and divine promptings she resolved to dedicate her pen, hitherto used mostly for small essays of piety and instruction, to writing *Uncle Tom's Cabin*. This was first serialized (1851–52) in the *National Era*, the Washington antislavery periodical, then published in 1852 as a book. It became a best seller; more than 300,000 copies were bought in less than a year after it appeared, and it quickly became the most popular work of fiction in the U.S. A pirated, dramatic version was made by George Aiken in 1852, which formed the staple offering of touring companies. In the second half of the nineteenth century, apart from the prose of the Bible and the hymns of evangelists like Moody and Sankey, *Uncle Tom's Cabin*, as a book or a play, was often the only form of the literary art familiar to hundreds of thousands of Americans.

The writing, publishing, popularity and effect of the book is less a matter for literary criticism than cultural history. Lincoln thought its effect on public opinion in the North precipitated the Civil War. It was widely translated, and formed the picture of the South and of the American racial situation held throughout the world. Harriet Beecher Stowe said that "God wrote it," and while we might decline to accept the precise meaning she gave this phrase, we would agree that there was an important impersonal side to the book. There are several layers of meaning embedded in it. A simplistic moral fable presents itself, of the noble Christian Tom, a black martyr, of the benevolent Shelbys, the saintly child Eva St. Clare, too good for this world, and of the degenerate planter Legree. In a neat propagandist turn Mrs. Stowe makes the latter a renegade Northerner corrupted by the situation. There is also to be seen from time to time her capabilities as a local colorist, though she developed these most successfully in her later New England sketches, *Oldtown Folks* (1869) and *Poganuc People* (1878). Her realism is strongly tinged with the genteel sentiment which has to a greater or lesser extent informed other American protest writing. The author shows flashes, however, of a much more interesting and, to our eyes, prophetic insight. She senses but cannot use, or allow herself to discuss, the connection between sexuality, slavery, violence and power. In Uncle Tom she has mythologized one of the roles forced on the blacks in America by white society. Her fumbled but suggestive contrast between the blonde, saintly Eva and the dark, unregenerate Topsy is another fragment of mythic feeling. Stowe's feeling for the blacks may be compared with the sympathy for the Indians shown by Cooper. Her accuracy was naturally attacked by the proslavery lobby once they grasped the effect of her book, and she rebutted the charges in a "factual" *Key to Uncle Tom's Cabin* (1853). In *Dred: A Tale of the Great Dismal Swamp* (1856) she returned to the problem of racial slavery, this time to show the degeneracy it engenders in the slaveholders. She twice traveled abroad, as the recognized spokeswoman of the American antislavery movement. *Sunny Memories of Foreign Lands* (1854; 1857) chronicles her impressions, and the defense in this volume of the duchess of Sutherland's clearance of the Celtic population from her vast Scottish estates shows her "progressivism." A third foreign tour brought her the acquaintance of Lady Byron, and in *Lady Byron Vindicated* (1870) she elaborated the charges of incest against the poet. The rest of Mrs. Stowe's *œuvre*, apart from the New England pieces, was copious, miscellaneous and undistinguished.

The Mayflower: or, Sketches of Scenes and Characters among the Descendants of the Pilgrims, 1843.
Uncle Tom's Cabin: or, Life among the Lowly, 1852 (*s.* 1851–52).
A Key to Uncle Tom's Cabin, 1853.
Sunny Memories of Foreign Lands, 1854.
Dred: A Tale of the Great Dismal Swamp, 1856.
The Minister's Wooing, 1859.
Agnes of Sorrento, 1862.
The Pearl of Orr's Island, 1862.
Oldtown Folks, 1869.
Lady Byron Vindicated, 1870.
Poganuc People, 1878.

Writings, 16 vols., Boston: Houghton, Mifflin, 1896.   A.M.R.

STRACHEY, Lytton (1880–1932), the eleventh child of distinguished parents, enjoyed a sheltered and prosperous childhood in London and went up to Trinity College, Cambridge in 1899, where he joined with J. M. Keynes, Clive Bell, E. M. Forster and others to form the exclusive intellectual coterie later styled the Bloomsbury Group. In 1918, after a long period of comparative obscurity as a literary critic, he suddenly became famous as the author of *Eminent Victorians* and soon confirmed his reputation as a stylish iconoclast by publishing a full-length study of Queen Victoria herself. Though he produced many other short critical pieces, he never equaled the achievement of these two biographical masterpieces, and his last major work, *Elizabeth and Essex,* proved to be disappointing.

Witty, felinely malicious and deliberately impressionistic, *Eminent Victorians* and *Queen Victoria* will ensure Strachey's survival as a stylist, whatever his failings as a historian; for, despite his judicious selection of only those facts that suited his preconceived view of his subjects, he knew how to make his characters come alive. Determined to undermine the pious solemnities of conventional biography, he introduced a new mode of interpretation, well-proportioned, urbane yet conversational, and above all entertaining.

Landmarks in French Literature, 1912.
Eminent Victorians, 1918.
Queen Victoria, 1921.
Elizabeth and Essex, 1928.
Portraits in Miniature, 1931.
Characters and Commentaries, 1933.

Collected Works, 6 vols., London: Chatto & Windus, 1948.   D.E.P.

STURT, George. See **"Bourne, George."**

STYRON, William (1925–   ), was born in Newport News (Virginia), served in the U.S. Marine Corps during the Second World War, and graduated from Duke University (1947). One of the founders and editors of *The Paris Review*, Styron traveled widely in Europe before settling in Connecticut. His first novel, *Lie Down in Darkness* (1951), the story (revealed in flashbacks) of the tragic life and eventual suicide of Peyton Loftis, daughter of a wealthy Virginia family, won wide critical praise. *The Long March* (1953), a short novel, recounts the forced thirty-six mile march of Marines in South Carolina that results in the death of eight men. Its protagonist, Captain Mannix, is an unwilling and awkward rebel who defies the bullying authority of his commander, Colonel Templeton. *Set This House on Fire* (1960), set in Italy, a complex story of crime and punishment, of murder and suicide, depicts the violent lives and relations of decadent American expatriates as recounted by Peter Leverett, "white, Protestant, Anglo-Saxon, Virginia-bred, just past thirty." Styron's controversial work *The Confessions of Nat Turner* (1967; Pulitzer Prize, 1968), a fictional account of the 1831 Virginia slave revolt, is, in his own phrase, "less a 'historical novel' in conventional terms than a meditation on history." Praised by white literary critics and historians as a consummate depiction of the antebellum South, Styron's fictional Nat Turner was regarded by black militants as a stereotyped portrait. Although Faulkner's influence is evident in Styron's early works, his writing, darkly poetic and broodingly imaginative, is distinctive and, at its best, stands outside of, while commenting on, the Southern tradition.

Lie Down in Darkness, 1951.
The Long March, 1953.

Set This House on Fire, 1960.
The Confessions of Nat Turner, 1967.   J.W.

SUCKLING, Sir John (1609–42) was born at Whitton (Middlesex)
and educated at Trinity College, Cambridge. He inherited large estates
in 1627, traveled abroad and on his return joined the court of Charles I.
He supported the king in the troubles that preceded the Civil War. He
died in Paris, probably by his own hand. His plays are now forgotten,
but he is remembered for some of the lyrics they contain ("Why so pale
and wan, fond lover?") and for others of his verses. He typifies the "mob
of [Cavalier] gentleman who writ with ease"; his poems are light, witty,
graceful and urbane. (See also **Metaphysical Poetry.**)

Plays, ed. L. A. Beaurline, Oxford: Clarendon Press, 1970.
Non-Dramatic Works, ed. T. Clayton, Oxford: Clarendon Press, 1970.
                                                                    A.P.

SURREY, Henry Howard, Earl of (?1517–47), courtier, soldier and
poet, a member of a powerful aristocratic family, was early distinguished
when chosen as companion to Henry VIII's natural son, the duke of
Richmond, whom he accompanied in 1532 to the French court, coming
into contact with its Italianate Renaissance culture. Surrey served against
the rebels of the Pilgrimage of Grace (1536), and in 1545–46 commanded
Henry's forces in France. He was finally executed on a questionable
charge of treason.

Surrey's verse is in the humanistic tradition of the Renaissance (see also
Renaissance Humanism). He followed his elder contemporary, Wyatt,
whom he admired, in writing sonnets, establishing the rhyme scheme
later favored by Shakespeare. Like Wyatt, Surrey was an innovator,
introducing blank verse in his translation of *Certain Books of Virgil's
Aeneid* in such a way as to foreshadow the flexibility with which later poets
and dramatists were to use the line. More truly neoclassical than Wyatt,
Surrey's best verse is imbued with restraint and dignity, as his fine elegy
on the elder poet demonstrates. His verse is characterized by a liquid,
smooth quality much prized by the Elizabethans, and his musical awareness lends a pleasing lyric grace even to poems in tedious "poulter's
measure." Surrey's dullest verse occurs in his biblical paraphrases, though
the psalms have a personal relevance which gives their versification
intensity. Many of his poems first appeared in Tottel's anthology, *Songs
and Sonnets* (1557) (see also **Elizabethan Miscellanies**).

Poems, ed. F. M. Padelford, Seattle: Univ. of Washington Press, 1920;
    revised, 1928.   J.M.P.

SURTEES, R. S. (Robert Smith) (1803–64), born of an ancient Durham family, qualified as a solicitor, but was a keen sportsman and contributed to *The Sporting Magazine*. In 1831 he helped found *The New Sporting Magazine* and edited it until 1836. He contributed to the magazine the adventures of his most famous character, John Jorrocks, the sporting grocer. (It was Jorrocks's success which the publisher Chapman and the artist Seymour intended to emulate when they asked Dickens to write the sketches which became *Pickwick Papers*.) The collected adventures appeared as *Jorrocks' Jaunts and Jollities*. Surtees was brilliantly served by the artist John Leech, who illustrated *Mr. Sponge's Sporting Tour* (1853), the expanded 1854 edition of *Handley Cross* (1843) and *Mr. Facey Romford's Hounds*, published posthumously in 1865.

Perhaps Surtees lacks the vision and powers of organization expected of a novelist, but he was a shrewd observer and he described an aspect of nineteenth-century life, the sporting world, which is neglected by most other novelists of his time. Only Charles Kingsley and Anthony Trollope can equal his description of a fox hunt. His comedy is broad, but he had a talent for vigorous farce, particularly that of the townsman trying his hand at country sport. It is also good-humored, and the pleasure with which he created characters such as Jorrocks and Pigg, the huntsman, has ensured him a small but appreciative audience.

Jorrocks' Jaunts and Jollities, 1838 (s. 1831–34).
Handley Cross, 1843.
Hillingdon Hall, 1845.
Hawbuck Grange, 1847 (s. 1846–47).
Mr. Sponge's Sporting Tour, 1853.
Ask Mamma, 1858.
Plain or Ringlets?, 1860.
Mr. Facey Romford's Hounds, 1865 (s. as *Mr. Romford's Hounds*, 1865).

Novels, 10 vols., London: Eyre & Spottiswoode; New York: C. Scribner's
    Sons, 1929–30.   S.M.S.

SWIFT, Jonathan (1667–1745) was probably born in Dublin, the posthumous son of Jonathan Swift, an English lawyer who had recently emigrated. He was educated through the generosity of an uncle, attending Kilkenny College (1673–82) and Trinity College, Dublin, where he took only a very poor degree (1686). He remained in residence for two more years, but when he was about to graduate M.A., violence broke out in Ireland and Swift, like many others, crossed to England in 1689. Here he joined his mother in her home county of Leicester before becoming secretary to Sir William Temple, a retired Whig diplomat and essayist.

Apart from two visits to Ireland, in 1690 in search of a better post and in 1694–96 when he was ordained and appointed to the prebend of Kilroot, Swift remained in Temple's household until the latter's death in 1699 and profited from his employer's fine library at Moor Park in Surrey. During this decade Swift obtained an Oxford M.A. by incorporation (1692) and wrote a number of odes in the style of Cowley, but he found his true genius in "The Battle of the Books" (1704, but written c. 1697) in which he entered the controversy between Temple, who had defended classical culture in his essay "Of Ancient and Modern Learning" (1690), and Bentley and Wotton, who had criticized the essay. It was during this decade also that Swift came to know the stepdaughter of Temple's steward, Esther Johnson, whom he called Stella.

After Temple's death Swift sought preferment in the Church and became domestic chaplain to the earl of Berkeley, with whom he traveled to Ireland. He received the living of Laracor (county Meath), and became prebendary of St. Patrick's Cathedral, Dublin in 1700, dividing his time during the following thirteen years between his parish, Dublin and England, where he acted on behalf of the Church of Ireland. During this period Swift became a figure of considerable political power in England, late in 1710 shifting his allegiance from Whig to Tory, editing *The Examiner*, a Tory periodical (1710–11), and writing pamphlets, of which the most notable is *The Conduct of the Allies* (1712), advocating the Tory policy of concluding the War of the Spanish Succession. Swift's circle of literary friends at this time was very wide, including Addison, Steele, Prior, Arbuthnot, Gay, latterly Pope, and Congreve, who had been Swift's junior at Kilkenny and Trinity College. Sometime before Swift returned to Ireland in 1714 the Scriblerus Club was formed, largely composed of literary men from this circle, and its members embarked on the collaborative project of writing the satirical *Memoirs of Martinus Scriblerus* to ridicule "false tastes in learning."

In 1710 Stella and her companion Rebecca Dingley moved to Ireland on Swift's advice, and the letters which Swift wrote to them between 1710 and 1713, collected later as *Journal to Stella*, vividly record many details about Swift's activities and display in their "little language" (a form of baby talk) Swift's linguistic playfulness. It was during these years, too, that Swift became friendly with Vanessa, as he called Esther Vanhomrigh, who also later lived in Ireland and corresponded with him. Their early friendship is celebrated in one of Swift's finest poems, *Cadenus and Vanessa* (1726, but probably written c. 1713). After causing Swift some embarrassment by what he regarded as her indiscretions and importunities Vanessa was to die of consumption in 1723, her health possibly undermined by an estrangement with Swift around 1722 about which there has been much speculation.

In 1713 Swift's political services were rewarded with the deanery of St. Patrick's, and in 1714 he returned to Ireland. The following five years were spent in comparative seclusion as Swift busied himself with cathedral reform and administration. His disappointment in not gaining preferment in the Church of England may have made this a period of bitterness. The twenty years following 1719 were responsible for his most enduring writings—*Gulliver's Travels*, worked on over a number of years and published in 1726, political pamphlets including *A Proposal for the Universal Use of Irish Manufacture* (1720), *The Drapier's Letters* (1724) and *A Modest Proposal* (1729), much of his best poetry including a number of poems to Stella, scatological and antifeminist or misogynist verses, and his *Verses on the Death of Dr. Swift* (written 1731), probably his finest poem. This is the second period when Swift was politically influential, this time inciting the Irish to resist English oppression. But he was not merely opposed to Irish economic and political subservience. In a much wider sense "fair liberty was all his cry."

In 1728 Stella died, after a long decline that greatly distressed Swift. *The Character of Stella*, which Swift wrote on her death, as he came to terms with his grief, movingly records his affection for "the truest, most virtuous, and valuable friend, that I or perhaps any other person ever was blessed with." He was too ill to attend the funeral, and over the succeeding years suffered frequently from Ménière's disease and became increasingly solitary. After 1738 periods of lucidity were only intermittent, and in 1742 he was declared "of unsound mind and memory." In 1745 Swift died in his deanery. He was buried next to Stella in St. Patrick's Cathedral beneath the Latin epitaph which he had composed and which records that he lies "where fierce indignation can lacerate his heart no more".

Of Swift's many writings in verse and prose, *A Tale of a Tub, Gulliver's Travels, The Drapier's Letters* and *A Modest Proposal* are especially noteworthy. *A Tale of a Tub* (1704), probably begun at Trinity College, "exhibits a vehemence and rapidity of mind, a copiousness of images, and vivacity of diction, such as [Swift] afterwards never possessed, or never exerted" (Johnson). The *Tale* satirizes the abuse of religion through the fable of three brothers representing the Catholic, Anglican and Puritan churches, and the coats (Christianity) bequeathed to them by their father. The fable is entertainingly interspersed with brilliant and wide-ranging satiric digressions.

Travels into Several Remote Nations of the World . . . by Lemuel Gulliver (1726), to give Swift's best-known book its fuller title, stems from the Scriblerus project, though it is in the third of Lemuel Gulliver's four extraordinary voyages, in which he visits a group of islands near Japan, that its origins are most clearly seen. Here the scientific learning of the virtuosi is ridiculed by its logical extension to patently absurd concepts; in particular, the Academy of Lagado parodies the Royal Society. There is also political satire when the Laputan treatment of the dependant island Balnibarbi is seen to relate to the English treatment of Ireland, and satire of false human ideals in the unhappy Struldbrugs, who, though immortal, are subject to senility.

The first voyage, to Lilliput, an island in the South Pacific where all things are a twelfth of normal size, has been widely enjoyed for its inventive fantasy and for the humor which comes from carefully manipulated incongruity. Gulliver extinguishes a dangerous palace fire by urinating on it and is suspected of adultery with the miniscule high treasurer's wife. But Gulliver's observations of the Lilliputians are also observations in an alien and ludicrous light of English manners and institutions, and although such satire is directed primarily at contemporary abuses, it has universal application. Political dexterity, translated into terms of acrobatics, and religious conflict, reduced to a quarrel about the right end at which to open an egg, both become ridiculous. The second voyage, to Brobdingnag on the west coast of North America where all things are ten times larger than normal, reverses the Lilliputian situation, though the satirical point remains the same. Here Gulliver, no longer a "man mountain" but a tiny plaything, trying to impress the king with an account of the achievements of his countrymen, succeeds only in persuading the royal giant that they are "the most pernicious race of little odious vermin that nature ever suffered to crawl upon the surface of the earth." But because certain physical features, such as pores in the skin, become unpleasant when grossly magnified, the Brobdingnagians themselves show a repulsive aspect of humanity.

The final voyage, to the country of the Houyhnhnms, has frequently been found distasteful. The Houyhnhnms, rational beings with an equine physiognomy who keep anthropoid Yahoos much as men keep horses, as beasts of burden, take Gulliver to be a form of Yahoo. Gulliver attempts to persuade them that his nature is essentially that of a Houyhnhnm, not that of the bestial, savage Yahoos. Although lack of emotion renders the Houyhnhnm master race coldly inhuman, when he returns home, Gulliver finds his own family disgusting and can find fellow feeling only with horses. But Swift seems to present both Yahoos and Houyhnhnms as aberrations, and Gulliver's misanthropy as a temporary derangement which may be cured by the human warmth of family life.

Infuriated both by English rapacity and Irish complaisance, Swift hated the mercantile system. In *The Drapier's Letters* (1724) he succeeded in arousing such bitter antagonism to an iniquitous scheme for introducing a new copper coinage into Ireland that a reward was offered for the disclosure of the identity of the anonymous Dublin draper whose practicality Swift had simulated so well, and the scheme was withdrawn. *A*

Modest Proposal with apparent benevolence and reasonableness outrageously recommends the regular butchering of most one-year-old children to solve the Irish food shortage by supplying meat and simultaneously reducing the population.

(See also **Augustans, The; Parody and Nonsense; Political Pamphlets.**)

A Discourse of the Contests and Dissensions between the Nobles and Commons in Athens and Rome, 1701.

A Tale of a Tub; to Which Is Added an Account of a Battle between the Ancient and Modern Books in St. James's Library; and the Mechanical Operation of the Spirit, 1704.

Predictions for the Year 1708 (pseud. "Isaac Bickerstaff"), 1708.

A Project for the Advancement of Religion and the Reformation of Manners, 1709.

A Meditation upon a Broomstick, 1710.

The Examiner, 32 weekly issues, 1710–11.

An Argument to Prove That the Abolishing of Christianity in England May . . . Be Attended with Some Inconveniences, 1711.

The Conduct of the Allies and of the Late Ministry, 1711.

A Proposal for Correcting, Improving and Ascertaining the English Tongue, 1712.

The Public Spirit of the Whigs, 1714.

A Proposal for the Universal Use of Irish Manufacture, 1720.

A Letter to a Gentleman Designing for Holy Orders, 1720.

A Letter of Advice to a Young Poet, 1721.

The Drapier's Letters, 1724.

Cadenus and Vanessa, 1726.

Travels into Several Remote Nations of the World . . . by Lemuel Gulliver, 1726 (*f.* as *Gulliver's Travels*, 1939; as *The Three Worlds of Gulliver*, 1959).

A Short View of the State of Ireland, 1727–28.

A Modest Proposal for Preventing the Children of Poor People from Being a Burthen to Their Parents or the Country, 1729.

The Lady's Dressing Room, 1732.

A Serious and Useful Scheme to Make an Hospital for Incurables, 1733.

A Beautiful Young Nymph Going to Bed, 1734.

A Complete Collection of Genteel and Ingenious Conversation, 1738.

Verses on the Death of Dr. Swift, 1739.

Directions to Servants, 1745.

The History of the Four Last Years of the Queen, 1758 (written 1713).

An Enquiry into the Behavior of the Queen's Last Ministry, 1765 (written c. 1721).

Journal to Stella (written 1710–13), ed. H. Williams, 2 vols., Oxford: Clarendon Press, 1948.

Prose Works, ed. H. Davis and others, 14 vols., Oxford: Blackwell, 1939–68.

Poems, ed. H. Williams, 3 vols., Oxford: Clarendon Press, 1937; revised, 1958.

Correspondence, ed. H. Williams, 5 vols., Oxford: Clarendon Press, 1963–65.   H.N.D.

SWINBURNE, A. C. (Algernon Charles) (1837–1909), born of a well-to-do Northumberland family, was educated at Eton and Oxford, where he became friendly with D. G. Rossetti, Morris and Burne-Jones. He subsequently shared a house in Cheyne Row, Chelsea with Rossetti and Meredith. His diminutive stature and fiery red hair were vividly caricatured by Max Beerbohm and, when linked with his high-pitched voice, suggested to Henry Adams "a tropical bird, high-crested, long-beaked, quick-moving." He never married, and from 1879 until his death lived with Theodore Watts-Dunton at Putney.

His first important work, *Atalanta in Calydon* (1865), was a brilliant re-creation in English verse of Greek tragedy. Its success was due to his knowledge and love of the classics and his unusual range and skill in metrical experiment, the virtuoso effect of the choruses being especially remarkable. In 1876 he returned with equal success to this form in *Erectheus*. The influence of the Pre-Raphaelites had stimulated an interest in medievalism which was reflected in *Poems and Ballads* (1866), where the sensuousness of Rossetti was reinforced by a sexuality and a hostility to Christianity that shocked many readers profoundly. Attacking the poetry of Rossetti, Buchanan thought Swinburne "wilder, more outrageous, more blasphemous . . . yet the hysterical tone slew the animalism." Swinburne retaliated vigorously in "Under the Microscope" (1872). Deeper-rooted than Buchanan recognized, Swinburne's antagonism to Christianity was connected with a passionate love of liberty derived in part from his enthusiasm for Shelley and in part from European revolutionary movements of the period. This found expression in *Songs before Sunrise* (1871). Two further volumes of *Poems and Ballads* followed in 1878 and 1889, much influenced by Baudelaire, while Swinburne's love of Elizabethan and Jacobean drama prompted several critical works and a number of verse dramas from the 1860s onwards.

In reaction against Tennyson's *Idylls of the King* he attempted an Arthurian theme in "Tristram of Lyonesse." He also wrote two novels, including the notorious *Lesbia Brandon*, which had lost some of its power to shock by the time of its eventual publication in 1952. Swinburne's poetry is his main claim to recognition, and that less for its sensationalism or its thought than for its rich sonorous music and its astonishing prosodic range and achievement. Long-winded, diffuse and repetitive in subject

matter, excessively addicted to tricks of style like alliteration and onoma-
topeia, facile and often predictable in the fondness for such rhymes as
lust/dust, rods/gods and tears/years, and so eminently open to parody
that Swinburne himself wrote some deliberate parodies of it, his poetry
still retains its aural appeal by its virtuosity and bravura. He is known to
have liked to compose while listening to music, especially Handel's; his
love of the sea produces some of his best work with its bold, surging
rhythms; and though scholars may debate the authenticity of their Greek
atmosphere, *Atalanta in Calydon* and *Erectheus* can still affect readers by the
tragic power of their imaginative rhetoric and poetry.
   (See also **Romantic Movement, The.**)

Atalanta in Calydon, 1865.
Poems and Ballads, 1866; second series, 1878; third series, 1889.
Songs before Sunrise, 1871.
Erechtheus, 1876.
Tristram of Lyonesse and Other Poems, 1882.
A Midsummer Holiday and Other Poems, 1884.

Lesbia Brandon, ed. R. Hughes, 1952.

Complete Works, Bonchurch edition, ed. E. Gosse and T. J. Wise, 20
   vols., London: Heinemann; New York: Wells, 1925–27.
Collected Poetical Works, 2 vols., London: Heinemann, 1924.
Letters, ed. C. Y. Lang, 6 vols., London: Oxford Univ. Press; New
   Haven: Yale Univ. Press, 1959–62.   D.W.

SYMONS, Arthur (1865–1945), son of a Methodist minister, made
writing his education and lived by his pen. A mental illness in 1908
significantly reduced his activities. He was a poet, translator and voluminous writer of essays which seek to establish a theory of all the arts. His
most influential work was done in the 1890s when his impressionist
Pateresque criticism, his symbolist-influenced poems in *Silhouettes* (1892)
and *London Nights* (1895) and his editing, with Beardsley, of *The Savoy*
(1896) gave him a reputation as "leader of the decadents." It was through
conversation with Symons that Yeats became acquainted with contemporary French writers, and it was Symons's book, *The Symbolist Movement in Literature* (1899), that revealed their importance to Eliot.

Collected Works, 9 vols., London: Secker; New York: Wells, 1924.   K.T.

SYNGE, J. M. (John Millington) (1871–1909), son of an Irish barrister,
was educated at Trinity College, Dublin, and then traveled in Europe,
earning a little money from journalism. In 1899 in Paris he met W. B.

Yeats, who urged him to return to Ireland, where a literary renaissance was beginning. Synge went to the Aran Islands, where he was fascinated by the primitive simplicity of the islanders' lives, by their folklore and by their "delicate exotic intonation that was full of charm." On these were based the poetry, prose and plays which he wrote in the last six years of his life. In 1904 he became a director of the Abbey Theatre, Dublin, and when he died he was engaged to its leading actress, Maire O'Neill.

Synge's subject was Irish peasant life and he treated it in the spirit that led him to remark, "It may almost be said that before verse can be human again it must learn to be brutal". His only completed full-length play, *The Playboy of the Western World*, occasioned riots at its opening because of its uncompromising exposure of bigotry, hypocrisy and raw cruelty in its characters, but its dominant mood is richly comic in its celebration of the folk imagination. Technically, the one-act play is better suited to Synge's genius, and *Riders to the Sea* is a rare example of a one-act play achieving tragic stature. Synge's plots are simple and his characterization is uncomplicated. His success depends always on his unfailing ear for Irish idiom and speech rhythms, which give these plays a poetic intensity even greater than that of the unfinished verse play, *Deirdre of the Sorrows*.

The Shadow of the Glen and Riders to the Sea, 1905.
The Aran Islands, 1907.
The Playboy of the Western World, 1907.

Collected Works, ed. R. Skelton and others, 4 vols., London: Oxford Univ. Press, 1962–68.   D.W.

T

TAGORE, Rabindranath. See **Indian Literature.**

TARKINGTON, Booth (1869–1946), was born in Indianapolis and educated at Purdue and Princeton. *The Gentleman from Indiana* (1899) is about a small-town editor who exposes political corruption but lives to see the community purified. *The Conquest of Canaan* (1905) is similarly hopeful: the sympathetic hero becomes a mayor of a bigoted community. *Penrod* (1914) and its sequels (*f.* as *Penrod and Sam*, 1937; as *By the Light of the Silvery Moon*, 1953) celebrate Midwestern boyhood, while *Seventeen* (1916; *f.* 1940) describes a boy's first love affair. More formidable is *The Magnificent Ambersons* (1918; *f.* 1942) where the hero ruins several lives, but finds forgiveness at the end. The picture of American small towns given by Sinclair Lewis and Sherwood Anderson is in reaction against Tarkington's.   J.M.

TATE, Allen (1899–), born in Kentucky, studied under John Crowe Ransom at Vanderbilt University and was a founder of the periodical *The Fugitive.* He wrote biographies of Stonewall Jackson (1928) and Jefferson Davis (1929), and contributed to the Agrarian symposium, *I'll Take My Stand* (1930). He remained a free-lance writer until 1934 when he began teaching, first at Southwestern University and later at Princeton, New York and Minnesota. From 1944 to 1946 he was editor of *The Sewanee Review.* An international man of letters, he retained his Southern affiliation.

Themes which run through his writings are the South, the fragmentation of personality in modern life, conditioned by science and industry, and the need and difficulties of belief. His one novel, *The Fathers* (1938), retrospectively narrates events in two families from 1858 to 1861 which counterpose the traditionalism of the father of a Virginian family and the new pragmatism of his son-in-law. Of the poems in his several collections, "Ode to the Confederate Dead," frequently revised since the first version (1926), is the best known. In his poetry since the first "Sonnets at Christmas," the sense of man suffering from unbelief is expressed in specifically religious terms.

He is one of the major writers of criticism. His essays contain fine studies of individual writers, notably of Emily Dickinson and Hart Crane,

662

and discussions of the function of literature. These discussions are imbued with a conviction of the importance of poetry in its own right and of the need in modern life for the restoration of the completeness which gives quality to experience.

Mr. Pope and Other Poems, 1928.
Poems: 1928–1931, 1932.
Reactionary Essays on Poetry and Ideas, 1936.
Selected Poems, 1937.
The Fathers, 1938 (novel).
Reason in Madness: Critical Essays, 1941.
The Winter Sea, 1944.
Poems: 1922–1947, 1948.
On the Limits of Poetry: Selected Essays, 1928–1948, 1948.
The Man of Letters in the Modern World, 1955.
Collected Essays, 1959.
Poems, 1960.
The Swimmers and Other Selected Poems, 1970.   R.V.O.

TAYLOR, Edward (?1645–1729) was born near Hinckley (Leicestershire), emigrated to Massachusetts in 1668 and entered Harvard as a student of advanced standing, which suggests that he may have had some higher education in England. On his graduation in 1671 he went to the recently incorporated town of Westfield, about 100 miles west of Boston and then on the frontier, as its first minister. As well as writing sermons and helping to organize the church, he had to serve as the town's physician and even encourage the settlers not to flee their homes during the threat of Indian raids posed by King Philip's War (1675–76). His sermons were full of learned references and intricately argued. A lifelong friend, the diarist and judge Samuel Sewall, records that on a visit to Boston Taylor gave a sermon at the Old South Church which "might have been preached at Paul's Cross." His grandson described him as "an excellent classic scholar, being Master of the three learned languages, . . . a vigorous Advocate for . . . civil and religious liberty . . . A man of small stature but firm; of quick passions, yet serious and grave."

It was not until 1937 that Taylor was discovered to have been a poet too, and the best of the American colonial period. A bound manuscript now referred to as the *Poetical Works* was found in the Yale University library, having been left there by his great-grandson (Taylor had asked his family not to publish his poetry). Manuscripts of his now available include a dispensatory, a commonplace book, *A Metrical History of Christianity* based on parts of *The Magdeburg Centuries* and Foxe's *Acts and Monuments*, and *Christographia* (1701–03), fourteen sermons on the nature of the Incarnation. The *Poetical Works* contain four groups of poems, three of which are arranged chronologically and span, roughly speaking, the period of Taylor's life in Westfield: (1) a collection of poems in honor of specific people (mainly elegies for prominent New Englanders, but including an elaborate acrostic love poem to his first fiancée, Elizabeth Fitch); (2) short topical lyrics moralizing specific events, such as "Upon a Spider Catching a Fly," "Huswifery," "Upon Wedlock and Death of Children"; (3) a long, didactic poem of many sections, called *God's Determinations Touching His Elect . . .*, Taylor's own dramatization of the Puritan way of doom. (cf. Wigglesworth's *Day of Doom*); (4) 217 *Preparatory Meditations . . .* written at intervals of roughly six weeks between 1682 and 1725 as part of Taylor's private spiritual preparation for the administration of the Lord's Supper.

The *Meditations* are in the tradition of Metaphysical divine poetry, suggesting Vaughan, Traherne or William Alabaster. Possible sources are Du Bartas, Quarles and especially Herbert, who finds several rhetorical echoes in Taylor's work. The typical *Meditation* starts from a short biblical excerpt, usually the text of the Lord's Supper sermon, then, after violently contrasting the status of Christ and that of the petitioner through vivid imagery of the exalted and the earthly, articulates a prayer for grace. Critical attention, which has centered mainly on these poems, began by questioning the orthodoxy, in the American Puritan context, of sensuous images of gold and silver, tuns of wine being broached, and trees of life, but gradually a better understanding both of traditional Christian metaphor and of the process of meditation has made Taylor seem less eccentric. In addition, Puritan commentaries on the Bible, twelve of which were in Taylor's library, did much to maintain the traditional typological and allegorical reading of the Bible which contributed to the wit of seventeenth-century divine poetry. A text-by-text comparison of a Taylor *Meditation* with passages in commentaries owned by him often reveals close parallels of argument and imagery.

Poems, ed. D. E. Stanford, New Haven: Yale Univ. Press, 1960.
Christographia, ed. N. S. Grabo, New Haven: Yale Univ. Press, 1962 (includes the meditation relevant to each sermon).
Treatise concerning the Lord's Supper, ed. N. S. Grabo, East Lansing: Michigan State Univ. Press, 1966 (sermons preached in 1694).

S.A.F.

TAYLOR, Jeremy (1613–67), onetime chaplain to Archbishop Laud, gave some support to the Royalists in the Civil War, but later withdrew to Golden Grove in Carmarthenshire. After the Restoration he became bishop of Down and Connor in Ireland. His best works were written at

Golden Grove, notably *Holy Living* (1650) and *Holy Dying* (1651). These, together with *The Worthy Communicant* (1660), were said by Heber to provide "a complete summary of the duties and specimen of the devotions of a Christian." In contrast with the Puritan divines of his time, Taylor laid stress upon works rather than upon faith. His prose style in his sermons is flowing and magniloquent, perhaps a little too rich and baroque.

(See also **Sermons.**)

Works, ed. R. Heber, 15 vols., London, 1822; revised, 10 vols., Oxford: Clarendon Press, 1847–52.   A.P.

TEMPLE, Sir William. See **Essays.**

TENNYSON, Alfred, Lord (1st Baron) (1809–92) was born at Somersby (Lincolnshire), where his father was rector, and educated by his father and at Trinity College, Cambridge. While an undergraduate he met A. H. Hallam, a young man of extraordinary promise, upon whom he grew intellectually and emotionally reliant. In 1830, the year which saw the publication of his first independent volume of poems, he traveled with Hallam in France as far as the Pyrenees. Two years later he issued his *Poems* dated 1833. J. W. Croker produced a brutally sarcastic review of this collection, writing with the declared intention of making another Keats of his victim. Within six months of Croker's onslaught, Tennyson received news of Hallam's sudden death.

Hurt and grieving, he lapsed into a ten years' silence. Only with difficulty was he persuaded to publish his *Poems* of 1842. Reviewers of this were not unfriendly. They recognized Tennyson's indebtedness to Keats, and they admired his art. But some of them felt that the art was too much in evidence and that his work was concerned too much with impressions passively received and too little with the satisfactions of successful activity. They wanted something more strenuous and more sustained than the short poems of 1830, 1833 and 1842. They asked him to compose a long poem, to handle an important contemporary subject, to display more human sympathy, and to inculcate sound doctrine. He responded with *The Princess* (1847), a fanciful contribution to the current discussion of women's education. Ironically, the poetic romance which forms the main part of this work has kept its appeal less well than have the exquisite and moving lyrics which are supposedly incidental to it.

In his next publication, *In Memoriam* (1850), Tennyson sought to construct a long prophetic poem, as demanded by his critics, from the short personal lyrics that came more naturally to him. Immediately on hearing of Hallam's death in 1833, he had begun to express his sense of desolation in lyrics written in what came to be called the "In Memoriam" stanza (four iambic tetrameters, rhyming *a b b a*). He went on adding to this collection and by 1842 had composed about one half of the items which he later shaped into the long poem of 1850. As we have it, this is both a sequence of intimate lyrics expressing his grief and his eventually successful effort not to be defeated by it, and, taken as a whole, a long philosophical work dealing with the problems of personal immortality and the purpose of human existence.

In Memoriam was immediately successful, but "Maud" (1855) met with considerable initial resistance. Again, Tennyson was trying to unite short lyrics into a complex whole. This time the protagonist is not the poet himself, but an unfortunate and neurotic young man whose conduct leads to disaster. "Maud" contains some of Tennyson's finest lyrics: "I have led her home," expressing the serenity of the accepted lover, for example, and "Come into the garden, Maud," expressing his feverish expectation of her approach. The monodrama's chief weakness is that its hero seems at times to become a mouthpiece for his creator. As a result, the reader is in doubt whether to interpret the hero's final enlistment to fight in the Crimean War as a natural outcome of his previous troubles or as Tennyson's remedy for the ills of a materialistic age.

In the eyes of many of his contemporaries, Tennyson's masterpiece was *Idylls of the King*. This, too, is a long work constructed from relatively short, separate items. He published four of these in 1859: "Enid," "Vivien," "Elaine" and "Guinevere." Readers understandably saw them simply as four cabinet pictures related to the Arthurian legends. But, as picture followed picture during the next quarter-century, it became clear that there was what Tennyson called "an allegorical or perhaps rather a parabolic drift" designed to unite them into a single whole. Thanks to this, the *Idylls* collectively offer an elaborate treatment of the struggle between soul and sense.

During his last two decades Tennyson wrote a number of plays. But his finest works of any length are those which he built up out of separable parts: *In Memoriam, Maud* and the *Idylls*. He had an extraordinary gift for creating poignant, highly subjective lyrics voicing fear, a sense of utter loneliness and despondency. He had an only less remarkable gift for composing short poems evoking a luxurious, Keatsian daydream. Both gifts have many representatives in his collections of 1830, 1833 and 1842. That of 1842, in particular, is one of the richest collections of short poems n the language. But his critics remained dissatisfied. They wanted something less negative, less enervating, less fragmentary. Tennyson, in any case, was devoting earnest and anxious thought to the problems confronting his generation and was not unwilling to give poetic form to his findings. The longer works in which he best succeeded in doing so are those in which he contrived to place his lyric impulses at the service of his prophetic purposes.

Tennyson's technical skill is famous. Not even Pope was his superior in fineness of ear and delicacy of touch. His craftsmanship served him well in the official utterances which he composed as poet laureate, an office to which he was appointed in the year of his marriage, 1850. But much more than is ordinarily understood by craftsmanship went to the creation of his most consummate pieces of verbal artistry—of "Tears, idle tears" and other songs from *The Princess*, for example, and of "Dark house" and others of the lyrics composing *In Memoriam*. It is natural that his contemporaries should have regarded him as "the Virgil of our time."

Poems by Two Brothers, 1827.
Poems Chiefly Lyrical, 1830.
Poems, 1833 (for 1832).
Poems, 2 vols., 1842.
The Princess, 1847.
In Memoriam, 1850.
Maud and Other Poems, 1855.
Idylls of the King, 1859; enlarged, 1869; enlarged, 1889.
Enoch Arden, 1864.
Tiresias and Other Poems, 1885.
Locksley Hall Sixty Years After, 1886.
Demeter and Other Poems, 1889.

Poems and Plays, London: Oxford Univ. Press, 1953.
Poems, ed. C. Ricks, London: Longmans; New York: Barnes & Noble, 1968.   J.D.J.

THACKERAY, William Makepeace (1811–63) was a civil servant's son, born in Calcutta and educated at the Charterhouse and Trinity College, Cambridge. He traveled, worked on two unsuccessful newspapers (one of which his stepfather bought so that Thackeray could be its Paris correspondent), studied art in Paris, married Isabella Shawe in 1836 and settled in London as a regular contributor to *Fraser's Magazine*. In 1840 his wife became permanently insane, leaving him to bring up their two daughters. He wrote for *Punch* from 1845, lectured in America (1852–53) and edited *The Cornhill Magazine* from 1859 to 1862.

Thackeray served a long literary apprenticeship before achieving fame with *Vanity Fair* (1848; *s.* 1847–48). In his early reviews, sketches and novels the basis of his later writings can easily be discerned. "Catherine" (*s.* 1839–40), "A Shabby Genteel Story" (1840, in *Fraser's Magazine*) and the very accomplished short pieces collected in *The Book of Snobs*, first published in *Punch* (1846–47) show Thackeray's comic roots to have lain in the Regency period (to which he returns in *Vanity Fair* and *Pendennis*) with its fondness for social satire, personalities and unsentimental astringency of tone. "The Great Hoggarty Diamond" (1841) first reveals the confessional element implicit in *Pendennis* and introduces a favorite Thackerayan figure—the young central character whose innocent amiability and unsuspecting nature leave him at the mercy of emotionally parasitic relatives, an unscrupulous world and the vagaries of his own conceit. "The Luck of Barry Lyndon" (1844), an excellent story set in the late eighteenth century, reveals Thackeray's complete familiarity with picaresque literature and its traditions, and his skill at re-creating the language and attitudes of an earlier age. It is still of interest as a successful historical novel, and it points forward to *Henry Esmond*. Also the story moves freely in Ireland, England and Europe, showing Thackeray's fondness for setting his stories in a large perspective (cf. Belgium and the German scenes in *Vanity Fair* and America in *The Virginians*).

Vanity Fair is Thackeray's masterpiece, for in it everything relates to his central intention, which is to satirize the hollowness of an acquisitive society and reveal the chaos of self-seeking, money, marriages and unscrupulous behavior at all levels, through which a declining aristocracy and a rising rich mercantile class jostle and push towards the top of English society. Thackeray's device of contrasted heroines, the quick-witted, gloriously unscrupulous Becky Sharp and the sentimental Amelia, whose related fates evolve together and show in varying lights the mostly hypocritical characters of the story, has often been criticized. In truth, Thackeray here reveals a weakness which besets his later books: the unscrupulous characters are so full of life and purposeful energy that they render the conventionally virtuous people more insipid and sentimental-seeming than they perhaps really are. Thackeray's difficulty in this respect is one he shares with most novelists of his generation. In *Pendennis* vital rascality or snobbishness of spirit generally steal the show. The opening country theatricals are brilliant, and Major Pendennis, crumbling pillar of majestic vanity, throws the good characters into the shade. The early part of *Pendennis* is cast as biography and is a lively account of the typical Thackerayan young man, progressing through adolescence and coming into contact with society for the first time. Thereafter the story slackens in interest, though the emotional voraciousness of its female characters is skillfully represented and there are scenes of brilliant social comedy. Thackeray's middle-class public wanted to read of the doings of its richer brethren, so *Pendennis*'s sequels, *The Newcomes* and *The Adventures of Philip* broaden into a great panorama of society's ways, its pretence of conventional morality and underlying self-seeking, its snobbery and mercenary values. The books are long and tend to be weakened by

Thackeray's increasing use of authorial interjections and rumination, but they throw interesting light on life in the early Victorian period.

Henry Esmond and *The Virginians* turn to an earlier society, that of the eighteenth century, which Thackeray re-creates with loving fidelity. Yet despite such things as the presence of Beatrix in *Henry Esmond* and the vast scale of Thackeray's picture of the American War of Independence in *The Virginians* the reader may feel that, like many historical novels, they have about them a certain atmosphere which is closer to brilliantly imagined theater than to complete reality.

Thackeray was a prolific journalist and produced a steady stream of stories, burlesques, comic verse and occasional writing of all kinds even during the years when he was writing the big novels. He was too busy and unmethodical to be an effective editor of *The Cornhill Magazine*, but he wrote the interesting "The Roundabout Papers" for it. His burlesque pantomime children's book, *The Rose and the Ring* (1855), preserves its freshness and it is one of the many books for which Thackeray designed his own vivid, exquisitely absurd and wholly appropriate illustrations.

(See also **Essays.**)

"A Shabby Genteel Story," in *Fraser's Magazine*, 1840.
"The Great Hoggarty Diamond," in *Fraser's Magazine*, 1841.
The Book of Snobs, 1848 (s. as "The Snobs of England," *Punch*, 1846–47).
Vanity Fair, 1848 (s.1847–48; f. 1932; as *Becky Sharp*, 1935).
The History of Pendennis, 1849–50 (s.1848–50).
The History of Henry Esmond, 1852.
The Memoirs of Barry Lyndon, 1852–53 (s. as "The Luck of Barry Lyndon," 1844).
The English Humourists of the Eighteenth Century, 1853 (lecture delivered in 1851).
The Newcomes, 1854–55 (s. 1853–55).
The Rose and the Ring, 1855 (for 1854).
The Virginians, 1858–59 (s. 1857–59).
The Four Georges, 1860.
Lovel the Widower, 1860.
The Adventures of Philip, 1862 (s. 1861–62).
Roundabout Papers, 1863 (s. 1860–63).
Dennis Duval, 1864.

Works, Centenary Biographical edition, ed. A. T. Ritchie (daughter), 26 vols., London: Smith, Elder, 1910–11.
Letters and Private Papers, ed. G. N. Ray, 4 vols., Cambridge, Mass.: Harvard Univ. Press, 1945–46.   W.R.

THOMAS, Dylan (1914–53) was born in Swansea where his father was senior English master at the grammar school. His remarkable poetic talent developed in his youth. After a short period as a journalist he moved to London in 1934. He married Caitlin Macnamara in 1937 and they lived for a short time in Laugharne (Pembrokeshire) where he made his home for the last four years of his life and where he is buried. During the Second World War he worked in London producing filmscripts, and he became well-known for his broadcast readings of verse. He made four visits to America where he gave many poetry recitals. He died in New York in November 1953.

Even before his death, when critical differences reached ridiculous extremes, there was strong disagreement about Thomas's stature as a poet. It had become almost impossible to separate the poet from the legendary bohemian figure which he himself had done much to create. His boyhood in South Wales is the subject of the semiautobiographical *Portrait of the Artist As a Young Dog* (1940), a collection of amusing and sometimes beautiful short stories which owe a clear debt to James Joyce. The early volumes, *18 Poems* (1934) and *Twenty-Five Poems* (1936), and even some of the poems in *The Map of Love* (1939) are developments of an intensely creative period between 1930 and 1934; the notebooks containing these embryo works were sold by Thomas before the outbreak of the Second World War when he entered a new stage of development. These early poems impressed with the power of their imagery, the incantatory rhythms, and the dazzling wordplay, but most readers found the multiplicity of meanings muddling rather than rich. Though some of the stories in *The Map of Love* are influenced by surrealist interest in dreams and madness, Thomas never adopted automatic techniques. In his later work he emerges as a painstaking and brilliant craftsman, still complex, still requiring considerable effort by his readers, but now absolutely clear in his ultimate meaning. The imagery of this late work is more unified and less private, because now he creates his metaphors from a more common experience of nature and art. The poems in *Deaths and Entrances* (1946) and his few last poems are among the finest in modern poetry.

Thomas thought in intensely visual images which are also strong metaphysical metaphors. His poetry is that of a man with powerful emotional and spiritual needs, while he wears his buffoon's mask to escape from an oversensitive and, at times, terrified personality. Throughout the poems his constant theme is the development of one man's experience, from feared and repulsive adolescent attitudes towards sex and the natural world, to a more mature and accepting, though always ambiguous, view of human and more-than-human love.

Under Milk Wood, a play for voices, shows Thomas as a superb entertainer, but the justifiable popularity of this last work has helped to deny a proper recognition of his more important achievements.

(See also **War Poets.**)

18 Poems, 1934.
Twenty-Five Poems, 1936.
The Map of Love, 1939.
Portrait of the Artist As a Young Dog, 1940.
New Poems, 1943.
Deaths and Entrances, 1946.
Twenty-Six Poems, 1950.
In Country Sleep, 1952.
Under Milk Wood, 1954 (*f.* 1972).
Quite Early One Morning, 1954.
Adventures in the Skin Trade and Other Stories, 1955.
A Prospect of the Sea and Other Stories and Prose Writings, ed. D. Jones, 1955.

Collected Poems 1934–1952, London: Dent; Norfolk, Conn.: New Directions, 1952.
Poems, ed. D. Jones, London: Dent; Norfolk, Conn.: New Directions, 1971.
Poet in the Making: The Notebooks, ed. R. Maud, Norfolk, Conn.: New Directions, 1967; London: Dent, 1968.   A.Y.

THOMAS, Edward (1878–1917), born in London of Welsh parents, was educated at St. Paul's School and Lincoln College, Oxford. He was killed in action at Arras. Much of his active life was spent in literary journalism, producing travel and topographical works and literary studies. His poetry, none of it written before 1912, is highly distinctive. Though far from experimental, it has great originality; its simple, direct vision of the English countryside is both moving and enlightening; it presents "the object as in itself it really is." Like Hardy, Thomas has the gift of making an apparently flat statement deeply suggestive in the context of the poem. It is significant that Thomas influenced the poetry of Robert Frost.

Poems, 1917.
Last Poems, 1918.

Collected Poems, with foreword by W. de la Mare, London: Selwyn & Blount, 1920.   C.H.

THOMAS, R. S. (Ronald Stuart) (1913–   ), an Anglican priest in a Welsh country parish, expresses in his poetry the experience of life in a

Welsh agricultural community. He often adopts an uncompromisingly critical attitude to his subject matter, revealing considerable austerity of vision, but he believes that a feeling for tradition is essential in a world threatened by materialism and anonymity. He finds this tradition embodied in the farmers of the hillsides rather than in the more obvious expressions of nationalism.

Song at the Year's Turning: Poems 1942–1954, 1955.
Poetry for Supper: New Poems, 1958.
Tares: Poems, 1961.
The Bread of Truth, 1963.
Pietà, 1966.
Not That He Brought Flowers, 1968.   A.J.S.

THOMPSON, Francis (1859–1907), son of a doctor and a Roman Catholic, was intended for the priesthood but proved unsuitable. From his unsuccessful studies to become a doctor he acquired a taste for opium, and from this and a life of squalor in London he was rescued by Wilfred and Alice Meynell, who gave him both physical and spiritual assistance. His finest poem, "The Hound of Heaven," is intense, visionary and religious. The same qualities appear elsewhere in *Poems* (1893), *Sister Songs* (1895) and *New Poems* (1897). In his last years he wrote mostly prose, largely reviews of a consistently high standard.

Works, ed. W. Meynell, 3 vols., London: Burns & Oates, 1913.
Poems, ed. T. L. Connolly, New York and London: Century, 1932; revised, 1941.
Literary Criticisms, ed. T. L. Connolly, New York: Dutton, 1948.
Letters, ed. J. E. Walsh, New York: Hawthorn Books, 1969.   K.T.

THOMSON, James (1700–48), born at Ednam (Roxburghshire), the son of a Scottish minister, went to Edinburgh University to study theology, then gave up the idea of ordination and went to London as a private tutor. With David Mallet's help and advice he published *Winter* (1726) and its success encouraged him to compose the other three poems which complete *The Seasons: Summer* (1727); *Spring* (1728); *Autumn* (1730). Thomson altered and added to the text several times, having some help from Pope, as well as from Arbuthnot and Gay. *The Castle of Indolence* (1748), a poem in Spenserian stanzas, was begun as a joke, but it developed into a delightful allegory on its author's way of life. Thomson also wrote five ponderous tragedies. His *Alfred: A Masque* (1740), written in collaboration with Mallet, contains "Rule Britannia."

The Seasons was popular all through the eighteenth century. Thomson's

Border childhood had made him sensitive to the aspects and moods of nature, as the poem, with its stress on "sublime" states of mind and the joys of solitary communion with nature, reveals. Thomson was a professed Deist. He interprets nature so that it becomes a philosophy and a religion, elevating the spectator to a purer state of mind through moods of rapture and sublimity. Yet his work has strong Augustan affinities: his worship of the picturesque goes along with delight in the orderliness and harmony of the universe and pleasure that observation and modern knowledge can demonstrate the attributes of God in it so plainly. Thomson's belief that nature is a moral influence on the human heart became one of the common assumptions of later nature poetry.

Britannia, 1729.
The Seasons, 1730; enlarged, 1744; 1746.
The Tragedy of Sophonisba, 1730.
Liberty, 5 parts, 1735–36; collectively, 1738.
The Castle of Indolence, 1748.

Poems, ed. J. L. Robertson, Oxford: Clarendon Press, 1908.
Letters and Documents, ed. A. D. McKillop, Lawrence: Univ. of Kansas Press, 1958. W.R.

THOMSON, James ("B.V.") (1834–82), son of a melancholic mother and a paralyzed alcoholic father, was born in Port Glasgow and educated in London. He became an Army schoolmaster, studied modern languages and was influenced by Leopardi and Heine, two poets whose temperament resembled Thomson's own. Dismissed from his teaching post for a trivial offence, he became a journalist in London and published under the initials "B.V." The remainder of his life was passed in poorly paid journalism and, although he gained some literary recognition in 1880 with the appearance of "The City of Dreadful Night," his tendency to melancholy and alcoholism asserted itself. The image of an isolated man, silent with incommunication in a city teeming with the muffled activity of its million inhabitants, is the paradoxical basis of his work. Although using conventional stanzaic forms, Thomson, especially in "The City of Dreadful Night," finds new rhythmic structures for his utterances and at times achieves an original powerful statement of ponderous despair.

Poems and Some Letters, ed. A. Ridler, London: Centaur Press; Carbondale: Southern Illinois Univ. Press, 1963.
The Speedy Extinction of Evil and Misery, ed. W. D. Schaefer, Berkeley and Los Angeles: Univ. of California Press; Cambridge: Cambridge Univ. Press, 1967 (selected prose). C.P.

THOREAU, Henry David (1817–62) was born in Concord (Massachusetts). The family originally came from Jersey, and his father was a manufacturer of pencils. Thoreau was educated at Concord Academy and Harvard. His life as a boy, with an early interest in natural history and religious discussion, together with a good grounding in the classics as well as in the best English, French and German writing, all helped to form both the expression of his maturity and his ideas as "a mystic, a transcendentalist, a natural philosopher." After graduating in 1837, Thoreau joined his brother John in pursuing a desultory career as a teacher. During this time, in 1839, he made the boating excursion with his brother which he recorded in his first book, *A Week on the Concord and Merrimack Rivers* (1849; revised, 1868). This miscellaneous and digressive work was badly received, like a good deal of the work Thoreau published in his own lifetime, but it contains nuggets of interesting travel material.

It was now that Thoreau made the acquaintance of Emerson, who in 1841 invited him to live in his house in return for help around the yard. This friendship, which ran into difficulties later, was of the greatest importance for Thoreau, since it gave him the run of Emerson's extensive library. He began to contribute to *The Dial*, the magazine of the transcendentalists, which was being taken over by Emerson from its founding editor, Margaret Fuller. Thoreau himself edited the issue of April 1843. He thus became a member, the only locally born one, of the group of Concord transcendentalists which, as well as Emerson, included Bronson Alcott, Orestes Brownson, who had taught Thoreau German, Hawthorne and W. E. Channing the younger. The group met as "the Symposium," which gives a flavor of the Platonic and Neoplatonic thought they admired. They developed a kind of eclectic, romantic, mystic feeling which, opposing the local Calvinist religion, stressed late-eighteenth-century individualistic humanitarianism, a recognition of the intuitive nature of knowledge and a respect for the immanent, indwelling divinity diffused throughout nature. Thoreau is an important expositor of such ideas, which were never formed into a system.

In 1843 he went briefly to Staten Island as a tutor, hoping to break into the New York literary world, but had to return to the Concord woods and the close companionship of his friend, Ellery Channing. Thoreau lived as simply as possible in Concord by working intermittently in his father's business, but in 1845 he began a solitary, uncluttered life, even closer to nature, in the cabin which he built in Emerson's woods at Walden Pond, half an hour's walk to the south of Concord. In July 1846 he spent a night in the Concord Jail for his six years' refusal to pay poll tax, a protest against the support given by the Commonwealth of Massachusetts to the institution of slavery. His spinster aunt Maria ruined his gesture by paying the arrears. The episode inspired his most famous essay, "On the Duty of Resistance to Civil Government," which he delivered as a lecture at the Concord Lyceum in January 1848 and published in 1849 in another transcendentalist periodical, the short-lived *Aesthetic Papers*, edited by Elizabeth Peabody. Lyceums were local societies for popular education and improvement, which often concentrated on natural history. The Concord Lyceum was an important part of Thoreau's life. He had given his first lecture there, on "Society" in 1838, and subsequently spoke regularly, as well as acting from time to time as its secretary and curator. His writing also has an oratorical form derived from this kind of communication, and the public speaking tone can be tedious to unwary readers. When in 1847 Emerson, one of the most popular speakers on the American lyceum circuit, went to England to lecture, Thoreau looked after his house and children, and on his return remained with the family until his own death.

Thoreau developed skill as a surveyor and practiced it locally to provide himself with the minimal income he needed. He also assisted his father's pencil business by improving the process of making the graphite filling. As well as frequenting the countryside around Concord, in 1845, 1853 and 1857 he made those excursions to the Maine woods which gave him the material for two lengthy magazine essays, "Ktaadn and the Maine Woods" in *The Union Magazine* (1848) and "Chesuncook" in the newly founded *Atlantic Monthly* (1858), both incorporated in the book posthumously published in 1864. Thoreau's response to his environment and his scientific interest in natural history were stimulated and formed by his experience of the disappearing American wilderness. As well as paying close attention to the harvesting of forest trees and to the wood-dwelling Indians who still lived in these areas, he also carried out fieldwork for the famous Harvard naturalist, Louis Agassiz.

The failure of his first book caused him to delay publishing his second, but finally in 1854, after five years' revision, he published *Walden; or, Life in the Woods*, his best-known single volume and the last book he published in his lifetime. This book, based on the years spent in his cabin, is framed as an account of the cycle of one year, beginning with summer. The revolving of the day, the season and the year sets out his own quiet spiritual revolution. Through his specific observation of natural life he deals with the life of quiet desperation most men lead, the erroneous economic thinking which leads them to accept their shackles, the liberating effects of nature on thought and living, and, lastly, the "higher laws" which can be glimpsed at least intermittently if a true life is united with true reflection. Thoreau became deeply involved, by speaking and writing, in the Abolitionist controversy, especially after the Fugitive Slave law of 1850. His attitude to that cause came to dominate his political thinking. His 1854 lecture on "Slavery in Massachusetts" was published in the

Abolitionist organ, *The Liberator*, and in 1860 he defended the unsuccessful raid on Harper's Ferry by John Brown, whom he knew, in "A Plea for Captain John Brown" in *Echoes of Harper's Ferry* and "The Last Days of John Brown" in *The Liberator*. But in the same year his health began to fail. He had been consumptive all his life, a condition aggravated by his work with graphite. In 1860 he contracted a chill while surveying tree stumps, and after a long decline, during which he unsuccessfully tried to find relief in travel to Niagara and the Midwest, he died on 6 May 1862.

Thoreau's work falls into three parts. His *Walden* and the essay on "Civil Disobedience" have had the widest circulation and most direct influence, the latter on Gandhi, for example, and on protest movements in America. The essay argues the old-fashioned individualistic position, "that government is best which governs least," but more important is the notion that each man must give his own personal assent to the actions of some external body called "government" and that, if he cannot, he is entitled to disobey any civil order. In much of this, as well as in his economic thinking which scorned accumulation, he gives early voice to several anarchic attitudes called forth by the intensive economic development of modern society and by the growth of highly organized and relatively efficient social structures such as national governments, communications or group pressures. His assertion of individual choice is expressed with humorous "Yankee cussedness" but touches a general romantic theme in modern life. Secondly, his *Journals*, not yet completely published, in their discursiveness, range and insights form his greatest work as an explorer of the self and stand as one of the greatest monuments to the sheer worth of the literary, humanistic yet natural culture of the early-nineteenth-century transcendentalists. Lastly, some of his other literary work is important in studying the development of American writing, thinking and consciousness. His eclectic reading, which included oriental literature, and his peculiar brand of egocentric humor make him a truly American writer.

A Week on the Concord and Merrimack Rivers, 1849.
Walden; or, Life in the Woods, 1854.
Excursions, 1863 (essays).
The Maine Woods, 1864.
Cape Cod, 1865.
Letters to Various Persons, 1865.
A Yankee in Canada, 1866.
Early Spring in Massachusetts, 1881 (from journal).
Summer, 1884 (from journal).
Winter, 1888 (from journal).
Autumn, 1892 (from journal).
Poems of Nature, 1895.

Writings, Walden edition, ed. B. Torrey, F. H. Allen, and F. B. Sanborn, 20 vols., Boston: Houghton, Mifflin, 1906.
Journals (reprinted from Walden edition above), 14 vols., Boston: Houghton Mifflin, 1949.
Writings, ed. J. L. Shanley and others, 12 vols., Princeton: Princeton Univ. Press, 1971– .
Collected Poems, ed. C. Bode, Baltimore: Johns Hopkins Press, 1943; enlarged, 1964.
Correspondence, ed. W. Harding and C. Bode, New York: New York Univ. Press, 1958.
Consciousness in Concord: The Text of Thoreau's Hitherto Lost Journal (1840–1841), ed. P. Miller, Boston: Houghton Mifflin, 1958.   A.M.R.

THORPE, Thomas Bangs (1815–78) was born at Westfield (Massachusetts) and is famous as a writer of "Tall Tales" and as a painter of portraits and frontier scenes. He owned and edited several newspapers in which appeared many of his most famous tales, notably "The Big Bear of Louisiana" and also coedited the New York magazine *Spirit of the Times*, in Arkansas (1841). Other collections of stories are *The Mysteries of Backwoods* (1846) and *The Hive of the Bee Hunter* (1854). The latter includes the tale of mighty Tom Owen who "on a clear day could see a bee a mile away." *Our Army in the Rio Grande* (1846) and *Our Army at Monterey* (1847) were based on Thorpe's experiences in Mexico. He was a colonel in the Civil War and, from 1869 to his death, held a Civil Service post in the New York Custom House.   D.V.W.

THRALE, Mrs. (Hester). See **Bluestockings.**

THURBER, James (1894–1961), born in Columbus (Ohio) and educated at Ohio State University, was a State Department code clerk before becoming a newspaper reporter in Columbus and then in Paris and New York City. After joining the staff of *The New Yorker* in 1927 he became a major contributor to the magazine and an outstanding humorist. The variety of his work is remarkable: *My Life and Hard Times* is a book of humorous autobiographical recollections; *The Years with Ross* is a biographical study prepared with care and unsentimental affection which evokes the complex personality of Harold Ross, editor of *The New Yorker* from 1925 to 1957; *Is Sex Necessary?*, written with E. B. White, provides an entertaining change from sex manuals, and *Let Your Mind Alone!* from books of self-improving popular psychology. In cooperation with Elliott Nugent he wrote *The Male Animal*, a successful comedy with a concern for academic freedom. *The Wonderful O* (1957) is seriously funny, well-written fantasy for children.

Thurber developed a form of drawing which achieved vivid expression with seemingly simple line, and he drew men, women, dogs, seals and other animals in an individual style. In essays, sketches, stories and drawings he maintained a high standard of sympathetic humor founded on good sense, and created a Thurber world in which resigned men, dominated by women and fate, find themselves in perplexing predicaments and seek compensation in secret lives of bravery and fame. The most representative collection is *The Thurber Carnival*.

Is Sex Necessary?, 1929.
The Owl in the Attic, 1931.
My Life and Hard Times, 1933 (*f.* as *Rise and Shine*, 1941).
The Middle-Aged Man on the Flying Trapeze, 1935.
Let Your Mind Alone! 1937.
The Male Animal, 1940 (*f.* 1942; as *She's Working Her Way through College*, 1952).
My World—and Welcome to It, 1942.
Men, Women, and Dogs, 1943 (collection of drawings).
The Thurber Carnival, 1945.
The Thurber Album, 1952.
The Years with Ross, 1959.   R.V.O.

TILLOTSON, John (1630–94) was influenced as a student by the Cambridge Platonists, Henry More and Cudworth. In his later career he progressed steadily to the deanery of Canterbury (1670), that of St. Paul's (1689) and finally to the archbishopric of Canterbury (1691). Firm without being extreme, Tillotson maintained the Protestant position against royal attempts to promote Roman Catholicism. He was a notable preacher of his time, and his prose style did much to form the modern manner. He sought clarity and lucidity and his sermons are models of clearly arranged, if not profound, argument. He appealed to the reason, and his strength was rather that of the moralist than the theologian. (See also **Sermons.**)

Works, ed. T. Birch, 3 vols., London, 1752.   A.P.

TOLKIEN, J. R. R. (John Ronald Reuel) (1892–   ) was professor of Anglo-Saxon at Oxford from 1925 to 1945, and then, until 1959, professor of English language and literature. His romantic fairy stories have since the late 1950s become the object of a cult. *The Hobbit*, professedly a children's book, was followed by the three-volume *The Lord of the Rings*, whose admirers included W. H. Auden and C. S. Lewis. The latter asserted that "if Ariosto rivalled it in invention (in fact he does not), he would still lack its heroic seriousness." Tolkien himself disclaims serious purpose and explains that it began as a philological game, with "no allegorical intentions, general, particular or topical, moral, religious or political." Edmund Wilson, chief opponent of the cult, attributed its growth to its admirers' "lifelong appetite for juvenile trash." (See also **Science Fiction.**)

The Hobbit, 1937.
The Lord of the Rings: vol. 1, *The Fellowship of the Ring*, 1954.
vol. 2, *The Two Towers*, 1954.
vol. 3, *The Return of the King*, 1955.   R.E.

TOLSON, M. B. (Melvin Beaunearus) (1898–   ) was born in Moberly (Missouri) and educated at Lincoln University and Columbia. He was for many years a professor at Wiley College, Texas, and Langston University, where he directed the campus Dust Bowl Theater. He wrote several plays himself, including *Southern Front* and *The Moses of Beale Street*, and won a prize at the Negro American Exposition in Chicago for his poem "Dark Symphony." He published his first volume of poetry, *Rendezvous with America*, in 1944 and followed this with *Libretto for the Republic of Liberia* (1953) and *Harlem Gallery* (1965). Although his work was widely admired by many of America's leading poets and Allen Tate even wrote a preface to the *Libretto*, their efforts to secure genuine recognition for his achievements were met for the most part with indifference.

C.B.

TOOMER, Jean (1894–   ) was born in Washington (D.C.) the grandson of a Reconstruction governor of Louisiana. Educated as a lawyer, he was drawn to the literary avant-garde of his day, being acquainted with Kenneth Burke, Hart Crane and Waldo Frank. *Cane* (1923) draws heavily on his own experiences as a teacher in Georgia. The book is impressive in its spirit of modernism, though this is in part vitiated by a sometimes cloying sentimentality. The book did not sell well, and subsequent works, such as "Essentials: Prose and Poems" (written 1930), "Portage Potential" (written 1931) and "Eight-Day World" (written 1932) remained unpublished, His later writings, therefore, failed to confer the literary reputation he earnetly sought and which has only recently shown signs of being secured.   C.B.

TOTTEL, Richard. See **Elizabethan Miscellanies.**

TOURGÉE, Albion (1838–1905) was born in Ohio, studied at the University of Rochester, served as a Union officer in the Civil War and moved to North Carolina (1865), where he practiced law and entered politics as a "carpetbagger." His romantic novels, depicting the South during Reconstruction, include the semiautobiographical *A Fool's Errand* (1879), which describes the sectional and racial problems of Reconstruction in North Carolina and is generally considered his best work. It gained him a prominent place in Republican and literary circles. *Figs and Thistles* (1879), a success story, was believed to be a thinly veiled biography of James A. Garfield, candidate for the Republican presidential nomination. Tourgée also published and edited *The Continent* (1882–84), a journal reflecting his staunch Republicanism, antipathy to the Ku Klux Klan and sympathy for the Negro.   J.W.

TOURNEUR, Cyril (c. 1575–1626). The date of Tourneur's birth is purely conjectural and nothing is known of his early life and education. His first literary work, the satire *The Transformed Metamorphosis*, was published in 1600. It was followed by a number of plays, written between 1606 and 1613, several occasional poems, published between 1609 and 1613, and by the prose work, *The Character of Robert Earl of Salisbury* (written 1612). This miscellaneous literary work would appear to have been incidental to Tourneur's somewhat obscure career in public affairs which included military service abroad.

Of the extant plays associated with Tourneur's name (*The Noble Man*, 1612, has not survived), only *The Atheist's Tragedy* (1611) seems reasonably certain to be his. *The Revenger's Tragedy* (1607), published anonymously, and *The Second Maiden's Tragedy* (1611) are of disputed authorship; yet it is primarily upon *The Revenger's Tragedy* that Tourneur's reputation rests. This play is one of the most powerful of the "tragedy of blood" genre and invites comparison with the work of Webster. It presents a world of all-pervasive evil, where death is omnipresent and corruption eats like poison into the mind. The less powerful *The Atheist's Tragedy* dramatizes the conflict between two opposing view of the nature of man: higher animal or God-created being. Both plays demonstrate Shakespearean influence.

Works, ed. A. Nicoll, London: Fanfrolico Press, 1930.   L.S.

TOWNS(H)END, Aurelian (?1583–1643) was born at West Dereham (Norfolk) and received the patronage of Sir Robert Cecil. His friends included Lord Herbert of Cherbury, Carew and Jonson. He replaced the last-named as composer of masques in the court of Charles I, for whom he wrote *Albion's Triumph* and *Tempe Restored* (1632), in both of which his collaborator was Inigo Jones. His other works consist of a few scattered poems, mostly either songs or commendatory verses that place him as a minor talent, whose work has a pleasing tinkle, within the school of Cavalier lyrists. (See also **Masques.**)

Poems and Masks, ed. E. K. Chambers, Oxford: Clarendon Press, 1912.

A.P.

TOYNBEE, A. J. (Arnold Joseph) (1889–   ), born in London, was educated at Winchester and Balliol College, Oxford, where he later became a fellow. After the First World War he pursued a distinguished academic career until he retired in 1955. An outstanding historian, particularly of Greek and Oriental civilizations, his work maintains high standards of scholarship and interpretation. His range and narrative powers are seen in *A Study of History* (1934–61; 10 vols. abridged to 2 vols. by D. C. Somervell, 1946–57), an ambitious twelve-volume survey of the decline and fall of all the great civilizations in terms of their response or lack of response to "the challenges from God."   O.K.

TRAHERNE, Thomas (?1637–74), son of a shoemaker, graduated from Brasenose College, Oxford in 1656, was ordained in 1660 and appointed to the benefice of Credenhill (Herefordshire). As spiritual adviser to Susanna Hopton he wrote the poems which were posthumously published as *Centuries*. In 1669 Traherne became chaplain to the lord keeper of the Great Seal, a post which he kept until his death.

During his lifetime only *Roman Forgeries* (1673) was published, although he had prepared *Christian Ethics* (1675) for publication shortly before his death. The majority of Traherne's works might well have remained lost but for a chance purchase of his manuscripts from a bookstall in 1896 and some excellent detective work by Bertram Dobell, who produced an edition of the *Poetical Works* (1903) and the prose *Centuries of Meditations* (1908). The manuscripts were at first ascribed to Vaughan, and there is a similarity between the two men especially in their idealization of the childhood state. Traherne believed that "It is of the nobility of man's soul that he is insatiable," and his poetry is a simple statement of inspiration and aspiration. The concern of all Traherne's writing is the pursuit of "felicity" in nature, the Bible, man and the Creator. He seems unaware of evil, finding only ignorance, and hence his work describes a quest for illumination rather than purgation. Only in *Roman Forgeries* and *Christian Ethics* is Traherne's philosophical learning at all complex. The simplicity of his mysticism and the directness with which he expresses it means that his devotional writings have none of the sense of struggle or the "toughness" which characterized much seventeenth-century writing, His chief importance is as a pleasing minor poet whose stress on the divinity of childhood makes him, like Vaughan, a precursor of Wordsworth.

Centuries, Poems and Thanksgivings, ed. H.M. Margoliouth, 2 vols., Oxford: Clarendon Press, 1958.   G.A.K.

"TRAVEN, B." (Berick Traven Torsvan) (1890–1969) was born in Chicago, and adventure stories by him, set in Mexico, first appeared in a German newspaper in 1925. *The Death Ship* appeared in German in 1926 and in English in 1934; capitalism is indicted when the stateless hero works aboard a ship liable to be scuttled for its insurance. *The Treasure of the Sierra Madre* (1935: *f.* 1948) concerns the greed of gold prospectors. *The Bridge in the Jungle* (1938) implies that a native child's accidental death may still be attributable, in the last analysis, to capitalist imperialism.

J.L.M.

TREGEAR, Edward. See **New Zealand Literature.**

TREVELYAN, G. M. (George Macaulay) (1876–1962), son of Sir Otto Trevelyan and a great-nephew of Lord Macaulay, came of a family of distinguished historians. He was regius professor of modern history at Cambridge and retired in 1951. He wrote both historical surveys and compressed histories and always adhered to the belief that history should be so written as to be enjoyed by general readers as well as students. Accordingly, his best work, including three books on Garibaldi (1907; 1909; 1911), *England under Queen Anne* (1930–34) and *English Social History* (1944), combines scholarship, biography and a masterly control of narrative.

O.K.

TROLLOPE, Anthony (1815–82) was the son of an unsuccessful barrister and a successful writer, his mother, Frances Trollope, turning out 114 volumes in thirty-one years in order to contribute to the family budget. Trollope was sent as a poor day boy to Harrow and Winchester where he suffered the scorn of wealthier companions. Influence enabled him to enter the Post Office at the age of nineteen where he first served as letter writer. Before resigning in 1867 he had risen to the higher ranks of the service, had been entrusted with missions abroad, some of which are recounted in his travel books, and had been responsible for the design of the English pillar-box. He began writing relatively late in life, his first book being published in 1847, but, having once started, he set himself a quota of completing forty pages a week—10,000 words. His enormous energy earned him, by his own figures, £68,939. 17. 5 for over sixty books. He remained in full-time employment with the Post Office, went hunting twice a week and frequented London clubs as an eager whist player.

Trollope's popular fame rested on his six Barsetshire novels—*The Warden, Barchester Towers, Doctor Thorne, Framley Parsonage, The Small House at Allington* and *The Last Chronicle of Barset*. These novels are set in the rural south of England and center on the activities of the clergy and squirearchy. Trollope was little concerned with intricate plot, and all his novels are variations on the delicate English opposition of love versus property. The heartrending problems of poor but well-bred girls seeking a suitable match, fathers in conflict with their sons over the family inheritance, and clerical ambition versus genuine piety provide a narrative base. Johnny Eames, a partially autobiographical portrait of a young, loyal but unheroic Civil Service clerk, was endearing to Victorian readers because of his faithful, but unrequited, love for Lily Dale. Mr. Harding, the old warden in the first novel of the series, is one of Trollope's finest creations: a gentle, unassuming cleric, he leads a much higher moral life than the other clergymen around him and is sharply, if unsubtly, contrasted with his son-in-law, the ambitious Archdeacon Grantly.

When Trollope later turned to more serious, and often satirical, fiction about English political life, he was criticized for not providing more of the adult fairy stories for which he had shown such capacity in the Barsetshire series. Although they are more questioning of current mores, the "political" novels again draw their narrative base from conflicts between property and love. This later group, comprising *Can You Forgive Her?, Phineas Finn, The Eustace Diamonds, Phineas Redux, The Prime Minister* and *The Duke's Children*, is more loosely knit as a series than the Barsetshire novels; all are concerned with political maneuverings in Parliament and in upper-middle-class society. It is likely that Trollope's own failure to gain a parliamentary seat in the election of 1868 made him both exaggerate and deflate the importance of serving one's country as a member of Parliament. Paradoxically, he exaggerates the sense of importance and self-esteem a young man may feel on his election, and also deflates the parliamentary role by showing how it operates as a gamelike ritual, although the game itself may be intensely serious.

Modern critics consider that Trollope's finest achievement is *The Way We Live Now*, a bitter satire on the new power of speculative finance in English life. Trollope himself states that certain tendencies in society were exaggerated by him, but that "I was instigated by what I conceived to be the commercial profligacy of the age." The solid rural virtues of the Tory squirearchy, represented by Roger Carbury, prove to be no match for the financial mesmerism of Augustus Melmotte. The spendthrift and dissolute behavior of the young members of the Beargarden

Club is intended to show a weakening in the moral fiber of the English aristocracy and Trollope anticipates the country's subsequent submission to American and foreign speculators.

In achieving his output of forty-seven novels he was more concerned with fulfilling his daily quota of words than with stylistic elegance. Apart from those already mentioned, the following are also important: *The Claverings, The Belton Estate, Orley Farm* and *Mr. Scarborough's Family*. His travel accounts of North America, the West Indies, Australia and New Zealand are difficult to obtain but are extraordinarily acute in their presentation of life and landscape in newly settled territories. In contrast to his mother, Trollope was most anxious to present a fair view of nineteenth-century America and his accounts of the various states are among the most knowledgeable of any English traveler. His *Autobiography*, published posthumously but written in 1875–76, created something of a furore, because veils of illusion, cherished by the Victorian reading public, were deliberately stripped away, and the romantic novelist revealed himself as one to whom novel writing was as methodical and clerical a task as letter writing had been during his early days with the Post Office.

Trollope has had his adverse critics. In 1863 *The Saturday Review* remarked that "there is a brisk market for descriptions of the inner life of young women, and Mr. Trollope is the chief agent for satisfying that market." The previous year Henry James had commented: "Mr. Trollope is a good observer; but he is literally nothing else. He is apparently as incapable of disengaging an idea as of drawing an inference." These are acute, if harsh, criticisms, although for the average reader Trollope provided, and still provides, a pleasant sojourn in a secure world, disturbed only by petty problems and minor disappointments.

The Macdermots of Ballycloran, 1847.
The Kellys and the O'Kellys, 1848.
La Vendee, 1850.
The Warden, 1855.
Barchester Towers, 1857.
Doctor Thorne, 1858.
The Three Clerks, 1858.
The Bertrams, 1859.
Framley Parsonage, 1861 (*s.* 1860).
Orley Farm, 1862 (*s.* 1861–62).
The Small House at Allington, 1864 (*s.* 1862–64).
Can You Forgive Her?, 1864 (*s.* 1864–65).
The Belton Estate, 1866 (*s.* 1865–66).
The Last Chronicle of Barset, 1867 (*s.* 1866–67).

The Claverings, 1867 (s. 1866–67).
Phineas Finn, 1869 (s. 1867–69).
He Knew He Was Right, 1869 (s. 1868–69).
The Vicar of Bullhampton, 1870 (s. 1869–70).
Ralph the Heir, 1871 (s. 1870–71).
The Eustace Diamonds, 1873 (s. 1871–73).
Phineas Redux, 1874 (s. 1873–74).
The Way We Live Now, 1875 (s. 1874–75).
The Prime Minister, 1876 (s. 1875–76).
The American Senator, 1877 (s. 1876–77).
Is He Popenjoy?, 1878 (s. 1877–78).
John Caldigate, 1879 (s. 1878–79).
The Duke's Children, 1880 (s. 1879–80).
Mr. Scarborough's Family, 1883 (s. 1882–83).
An Autobiography, 1883.

Letters, ed. B. A. Booth, London: Oxford Univ. Press, 1951.   C.P.

TRUMBULL, John (1750–1831) graduated from Yale (1767), where, remaining as a bachelor, then tutor, he tried to introduce modern literature into the curriculum and wrote his Hudibrastic satire on the shortcomings of contemporary education, *The Progress of Dulness* (1772–73). Practicing law in New Haven and Hartford (1774–1825), he became associated with the Connecticut Wits, took a cautious interest in the Revolutionary cause, and published *M'Fingal* (2 cantos, 1775–76; complete, in 4 cantos, 1782), his anonymous satire on the Tories. After the Revolution he became a strong Federalist and contributed to *The Anarchiad* (1786–87). He assisted in the publication of his *Works* (2 vols.) in 1820.   S.A.F.

TUCKER, James. See **Australian Literature.**

TUCKERMAN, F. G. (Frederick Goddard) (1821–73) was born in Boston and lived most of his adult life in Greenfield (Massachusetts). A retiring man, he preferred country seclusion to practicing the law and, apart from writing, his main interests were botany, astronomy and geology. These are reflected in his poetry, with its scientific precision and botanist's delight in obscure plants and flowers. The tragic death of his wife shortly after their third child's birth deepened a melancholy inherent in his nature, which infects all his poetry. Despite this self-imposed retirement Tuckerman had some slight acquaintance with contemporary literary figures. Hawthorne and Emerson wrote encouragingly of his single volume, *Poems* (1860); and once he was not only Tennyson's guest, but was presented with the manuscript of "Locksley Hall." Yet his poetry sank into obscurity before his death, remaining ignored until 1909.

Tuckerman is uncharacteristic of Romantic poets in his attitude to nature. As Yvor Winters remarks, he is neither mystic nor pantheist, but can make an obscure plant or flower so instinct with meaning that it becomes one with the poem's abstract theme. His sonnet sequences reveal this best, where he anatomizes the pains of bereavement as Sidney or Drayton treated love. Tuckerman's longer lyrics tend to diffuseness, irritating neologisms and obscure classical references, though a richly sensitive awareness of nature still prevails. Loneliness, grief, the unknown God, death, even violence are his poetic themes; yet there is neither Romantic optimism nor despair, but an accepting of "the beautiful and bitter miracle of life."

Complete Poems, ed. N. S. Momaday, New York and London: Oxford Univ. Press, 1965.   S.C.

TUPPER, Martin (1810–89) was born in London and educated at Charterhouse School and Oxford. He was called to the bar in 1835 but showed more interest in literature than in the law. His *Proverbial Philosophy* (1838) was an immediate and sustained success; in it he expressed, in verse that has neither rhyme nor meter, a commonplace and shallow moralizing view of life. His subsequent works included ballads on the Crimean war, church abuses, white slavery and emigration. (See also **Bible, The.**) A.P.

TURNER, Frederick Jackson (1861–1932), American historian, was born in Wisconsin, graduated from the University of Wisconsin and Johns Hopkins (Ph.D., 1890). He was professor of history at Wisconsin (1892–1910) and at Harvard (1910–24). In 1893 Turner delivered a paper before the American Historical Association on "The Significance of the Frontier in American History," an interpretation of the effect of the frontier on American democracy, institutions, individualism and national character. Turner's "frontier thesis," emphasizing environmentalism and evolutionary development, revolutionized American historiography and also influenced sociology, economics and literary criticism. His writings include *The Frontier in American History* (1920), *The Significance of Sections in American History* (1932, Pulitzer Prize) and *The United States, 1830–1850* (1935).   J.W.

TUTUOLA, Amos. See **African Literature.**

"TWAIN, Mark" was the pseudonym of Samuel Langhorne Clemens

(1835–1910), who was born in Florida (Missouri). In 1839 his family moved a few miles east to the little town of Hannibal on the banks of the Mississippi, and its recollected image dominates much of his best writing. His father's death cut short his schooling at twelve and forced him to earn a living (hence in part, perhaps, his frequent fictional idealizations of boyhood). He began as a printer, but in 1856 became a Mississippi steamboat pilot, a profession which, he was to say thirty years later, in *Life on the Mississippi*, he loved far better than any he had subsequently followed, for "a pilot, in those days, was the only unfettered and entirely independent human being that lived in the earth." It was from the river that he took his pseudonym.

The outbreak of the Civil War, however, put an end to the riverboats, and as a Confederate volunteer Clemens became one of the thousands he described in "The Private History of a Campaign That Failed" (1885) as having "entered the war, got just a taste of it, and then stepped out again permanently." He "stepped out" after a few weeks in order to accompany his brother Orion, who had been appointed secretary of the Nevada Territory. Prospecting disappointed his expectations and he turned to journalism, writing for the *Virginia City Territorial Enterprise* from 1862 to 1864 and thereafter for various California newspapers. For one of these he wrote up a visit to the Sandwich Islands (Hawaii) in 1866, and in 1867, with similar journalistic intentions, joined a party sailing from New York in the *Quaker City* for Europe and the Holy Land. This provided material for *The Innocents Abroad* (1869), which established him as a popular humorist and enabled him to marry, in 1870, Olivia Langdon, sister of one of his traveling companions on the boat. Tiring of journalism and of editing the Buffalo *Express*, he decided in 1871 to concentrate on creative writing and to move nearer to his publisher in Hartford (Connecticut), where he built an ostentatiously luxurious house at the cost of $131,000. One of his neighbors was Harriet Beecher Stowe; another was Charles Dudley Warner, with whom he collaborated to produce *The Gilded Age* (1873), an exposé of the politics, public life and extravagance of post-Civil War years. The book's main interest now lies in the ebullient Colonel Sellers, the comic creation who reappears in *The American Claimant* (1892).

Clemens had also achieved fame, in the United States and in England, as a lecturer and raconteur. Friendship with William Dean Howells and others strengthened still further his reputation in the cultural centers of Boston and New York, but his humble origins and his frontier spirit prevented his ever being wholly at ease there. Attempts to combine a literary career with publishing and other commercial ventures, however, ended in bankruptcy, his enthusiasm and confidence outrunning his capital and his business acumen. In 1895 he undertook a world tour, hoping to pay off his creditors with the proceeds of lectures on the way and the book that was to record his experiences (*Following the Equator*). In his absence his favorite daughter died in Hartford, and this, with the exhaustion induced by the trip, intensified a melancholic tendency, so that the work of his closing years was to become increasingly black in mood, despite the international success and honors he enjoyed. He died at Redding (Connecticut) in 1910, having outlived his wife, to whom he was devoted, and two of his three daughters.

Mark Twain's literary forebears were the midcentury American humorous writers whose popularity, on both sides of the Atlantic, is not easily understood today. Josh Billings, Petroleum V. Nasby, and Artemus Ward rendered mildly amusing anecdotes in a spelling which, in its grotesqueness, was intended to make funnier the unsophisticated artlessness of the teller. Mark Twain adopted a similar persona and colloquial idiom but, disdaining adventitious orthographic aids, exploited more imaginatively in print the cadences of the speaking voice. His first success, a tall tale of the California frontier called "The Celebrated Jumping Frog of Calaveras County" (1865; *f.* as *The Best Man Wins*, 1948), depends on exactly this technique, but there is also already apparent a dramatic instinct, a sense of character and a use of irony that outdistances his precursors. *The Innocents Abroad* extracts boisterous fun from the exposure to Europe of brash Americans with no pretensions to culture, while at the same time their fellow travelers who have such pretensions are castigated with sharper ridicule for their reverential servility. *Roughing It* (1872) gives a burlesque account of his own adventures in the Far West, but again there is sympathetic respect for the spontaneity of response possible only to the innocent. In these two books Mark Twain mastered a relaxed technique of comic anecdotes drawn from his own experience and learned to thread those anecdotes together on the tenuous story line of a journey. The inconsequential travel book became a standby for him. *A Tramp Abroad* is the most richly comic, *Life on the Mississippi* the most evocative in its nostalgia, *Following the Equator* the most socially conscious, though the least successful.

His best novels have a similarly picaresque and episodic structure; in *The Adventures of Huckleberry Finn* it is dictated by the river journey, in *A Connecticut Yankee in King Arthur's Court* by the travels of a nineteenth-century technologist in the Arthurian kingdom to which he has been mysteriously translated. The narrators characteristically think themselves knowledgeable but are constantly surprised and shocked by new experiences. This pattern was also congenial to Mark Twain in allowing him to show his characters at the mercy of chance and mischance rather than heroically commanding their own destinies. Even the Yankee's know-how is eventually defeated by circumstances, and the novel, which was begun as farce, ends in a despairing holocaust that prefigures the darker vision of human impotence and diminished responsibility that marks the later books.

Such an attitude precludes the stimulus to reform afforded by satire, and Mark Twain's characteristic stance is one of amused tolerance of human weakness and sympathy with human predicaments. He prefers instinct to dogma, and, like Huck Finn, is saddened by the awareness that "Human beings *can* be awful cruel to one another." In *The Prince and the Pauper* this awareness is sentimentalized; in *Following the Equator* he agonizes angrily and somewhat chauvinistically over race relations in Australia and South Africa. In *Pudd'nhead Wilson*, however, he handles slavery and human turpitude more imaginatively, blending comedy and tragedy into a moral equilibrium second only to the insight and humanity of *Huckleberry Finn*. The figure of Pudd'nhead, laughed at as a buffoon by the public but at last vindicated as a man of practical sagacity and a philosopher whose aphorisms are impregnated with worldly wisdom, is perhaps a projection of Clemens as Mark Twain would have liked him to be. Yet dreams of an idyllic boyhood and of the antebellum South were his strongest imaginative impulses, superbly fused in *The Adventures of Tom Sawyer*, and, in *Huckleberry Finn*, invigorated by the vernacular idiom and the dramatization of an adolescent coming to terms with the adult world. The warmth, humanity, humor, wisdom and originality of this book can excuse the exaggeration of Hemingway's claim that "All modern American literature comes from ... *Huckleberry Finn* ... it's the best book we've had."

The Innocents Abroad, 1869.
Roughing It, 1872.
The Gilded Age, 1873.
The Adventures of Tom Sawyer, 1876 (*f.* 1938).
A Tramp Abroad, 1880.
The Prince and the Pauper, 1882 (*f.* 1937; 1961).
Life on the Mississippi, 1883.
The Adventures of Huckleberry Finn, 1884 (*f.* 1939; as *Huckleberry Finn*, 1960).
A Connecticut Yankee in King Arthur's Court, 1889.
The American Claimant, 1892.
The Tragedy of Pudd'nhead Wilson, 1894.
Personal Recollections of Joan of Arc, 1896.
Following the Equator, 1897 (U.K. title: *More Tramps Abroad*).
The Man That Corrupted Hadleyburg and Other Stories and Essays, 1900.
The Mysterious Stranger, 1916.

Writings, Definitive edition, ed. A. B. Paine, 37 vols., New York: Wells, 1922–25. (A new edition in association with the Center for Editions of American Authors is currently in preparation.)

Papers, ed. H. Hill and others, Berkeley and Los Angeles: Univ. of Califor-
    nia Press; Cambridge: Cambridge Univ. Press, 1967–   .
Letters (Mark Twain—W. D. Howells), *1872–1910*, ed. H. N. Smith and
    W. M. Gibson, 2 vols., Cambridge, Mass.: Harvard Univ. Press;
    London: Oxford Univ. Press, 1960.   D.W.

TYLER, Royall (1757–1826), an eminent lawyer, was born in Boston.
After seeing *The School for Scandal* he wrote the first authentically Ameri-
can comedy, *The Contrast* (1787), in which plain, worthy Americans are
compared with the affected British. He is known to have written other
plays, satirical verse and essays, some of his work no longer being extant.
Of these he is now remembered chiefly for a long poem, *The Chestnut
Tree* (written 1824), which describes country life but foretells the Industrial
Revolution, a picaresque novel entitled *The Algerine Captive* (1797), and
Yankey in London (1809), a collection of fictitious letters.   R.W.

TYNDALE, William. See **Bible, The.**

U

UDALL, Nicholas (?1505–56), educated at Oxford, was headmaster of Eton (1534–41) and after various preferments to government and ecclesiastical posts became director of the court revels (1554). At Eton and at Westminster School (1555–56) Udall made acting part of the curriculum, and his pupils regularly performed at court. Of his masques and interludes, only *Ralph Roister Doister* (written before 1553) survives. This interlude (in *Five Pre-Shakespearean Comedies*, ed. F. S. Boas, 1934), which grafts the form, farce and character-types of Plautine comedy on to a native stock of song, proverbs and racy jest, is "school" comedy *par excellence*.

Dramatic Writings, ed. J. S. Farmer, London: Early English Drama Society, 1906.   L.E.P.

UPDIKE, John (1932–) was born in Pennsylvania, educated at Harvard and worked for *The New Yorker* between 1955 and 1957. A delicate and mannered writer, whose excellent short stories (see *Pigeon Feathers and Other Stories*, 1962) show his concern with the fleeting emotional and aesthetic responses that might redeem a bleakly secular age, he has also proved a robust, inventive novelist treating a remarkable range of themes—old age in *The Poorhouse Fair* (1959), the angst of a rather dull-witted basketball player in *Rabbit, Run* (1960; *f.* 1969), the mythological referents of modern life in *The Centaur* (1963), group sex in Massachusetts in *Couples* (1968), the peripatetic career of a novelist in *Bech: A Book* (1970), and the disastrous attempt, in *Rabbit Redux* (1971), of an earlier hero to bridge the 1960s' generation gap. Updike's technique is flamboyant, experimental and enormously impressive, his analytical sensitivity great. He has also written poems and children's books.   M.B.

V

VANBRUGH, Sir John (1664–1726) may well be unique in having combined the profession of comic dramatist with that of baroque architect. He was educated at the King's School, Chester, and then held a commission in the army for ten years in France. His first comedy, *The Relapse* (1697; *p.* 1696; *f.* as *Lock Up Your Daughters*, 1968) was written out of annoyance at the canting morality of a play by Cibber. In turn, he had his own morals attacked by Jeremy Collier and published a reply. Before this he had produced *The Provoked Wife* (1697). Another original play, *A Journey to London*, left unfinished at his death, was adapted by Cibber as *The Provoked Husband* (1728). Vanbrugh adapted several plays himself, of which *The Confederacy* (1705; from Dancourt) has quality. *The Pilgrim* (1700; from Fletcher) contained Dryden's *A Secular Masque*. After 1700 Vanburgh was chiefly concerned with architecture (Castle Howard, Blenheim, Seaton Delaval). He became controller of the royal works in 1702 and was knighted in 1714.

Vanbrugh's plays follow the usual conventions of Restoration drama. He had, however, to an unusual degree, the gift of creating solid, richly realized characters. His repartee, too, is characterized by bite and genuine humor, showing wit without frothiness. His last plays suggest that he had potential gifts as a domestic dramatist; his command of farcical stage situations is always admirable.

Works, ed. B. Dobrée (plays) and G. Webb (letters), 4 vols., London: Nonesuch Press, 1927.   W.R.

VAN VECHTEN, Carl (1880–1964) was born in Iowa. Selections of his critical articles on music, dance and drama appear in *Red* (1925) and *Excavations* (1926). *Peter Whiffle* (1922) marked the change from critic to novelist; purporting to be the autobiography of an aesthete and dilettante, it characterizes the sophisticated decadence of the 1920s. *The Blind Bow-Boy* (1923), about homosexuality, and *Parties* (1930), his last novel, also depict the New York smart set. Van Vechten worked hard to promote black writers and artists in the 1920s, though his notorious novel *Nigger Heaven* (1926) relied too much on primitivistic conceptions of "the Negro." He later edited some of the writings of his friend Gertrude Stein.

R.W.

VAUGHAN, Henry (1622–95), born of a Welsh family, lived most of his life in Newton-by-Usk (Brecknockshire). Both he and his twin brother Thomas were educated by a local clergyman (to whom each addressed a Latin poem) and at Jesus College, Oxford. Only Thomas graduated, Henry after two years going to London to study law in 1640. He was recalled to Wales at the outbreak of the Civil War and was to use his legal training in Brecon. By 1646 Vaughan had fought for the Royalists, and about then he married. By 1655 his wife had died and he had married her younger sister. An autobiographical letter (1673), solicited by his relative John Aubrey, says that he had practiced medicine "for many years with good success," but there is no record of his medical training.

Eight of his nine books appeared in the eleven years after 1646, a period of personal and political crisis for Vaughan. The 1646 volume includes a small collection of fashionable verse harking back to the Caroline past, and a translation of Juvenal's tenth satire on the vanity of human wishes, a choice which seems to indicate present discontent. Although another volume of poems and translations was ready by the end of 1647, Vaughan suppressed it, probably because of uneasiness about secular poetry or because some of the poems were politically dangerous. In 1651 "a Friend" published a version of this book as *Olor Iscanus* (the swan of Usk), on the title page giving Vaughan the appellation "Silurist," an allusion to Vaughan's association with the area anciently inhabited by the Silures. Meanwhile, in 1650, Vaughan had published *Silex Scintillans*, poems which show a greatly increased concern with religion and which, with the poems of the much enlarged edition of 1655, comprise his best work. In the intervening years of religious turmoil Vaughan published two devotional works in prose—*The Mount of Olives* (1652), an attempt to foster private devotions to replace the then banned services of the episcopal church, to which he appended a translation from Anselm, and *Flores Solitudinis* (1654)— three more translations and a life of Paulinus of Nola. Two other works belong to the Commonwealth period, *Hermetical Physic* (1655) and *The Chemist's Key* (1657), both translations of treatises by Heinrich Nolle and showing Vaughan's interest in medicine. Not till 1678 did *Thalia Rediviva*, the next and last work, appear. It is a miscellany of original poems and translations by the twin brothers, though Thomas had died in 1666.

Vaughan is one of the most imitative of poets. In his early secular poetry the debt is principally to Donne and Habington, whose Metaphysical imagery Vaughan used in an essentially decorative, inorganic manner, though his nature imagery displays a unique sensitivity. When Vaughan renounced secular poetry, he also renounced his pretentious mode of writing, condemning writers employed in "a deliberate search, or excogitation of idle words, and a most vain, insatiable desire to be reputed poets." The debt of the religious poetry is to "the blessed man, Mr.

George Herbert, whose holy life and verse gained many pious converts (of whom I am the least)." Although Vaughan frequently copied themes, titles, stanza forms and metrical effects, as well as phrases and images, from *The Temple*, the poems were now genuine and personal. Their intricate imagery is richly significant, and Vaughan's lack of Herbert's formal control is compensated for by a mystical perception of God in nature that is all his own.

(See also **Metaphysical Poetry.**)

Poems, 1646.
Silex Scintillans, 1650; 1655.
Olor Iscanus, 1651.
Thalia Rediviva, 1678.

Works, ed. L. C. Martin, 2 vols., Oxford: Clarendon Press, 1914; revised, 1958.　　　　　　　　　　　　　　　　　　　　　　　　　　H.N.D.

VAUX, Thomas, Lord (2nd Baron). See **Elizabethan Miscellanies.**

VEBLEN, Thorstein (1857–1929) was born in Cato township, Manitowoc County (Wisconsin), the son of Norwegian immigrants. Brought up in an isolated Norwegian community, it was not until he was seventeen that he left there to go to college, and this upbringing contributed to his detached, vitriolic view of American urban society. His research and career were, until after the First World War, continually disrupted by moves from one university to another due to his perpetual series of affairs or to his chagrin for not receiving proper acknowledgment of his brilliance. His first stable position was under J. Laurence Laughlin at Chicago University where he met Jacques Loeb, John Dewey, and Lester Ward, among others. His first and best-known book, *The Theory of the Leisure Class* (1899), was a cumbersome but bitingly perceptive analysis of "conspicuous consumption," the use of women as display cabinets of wealth and status, and the creation of life styles designed to distinguish the productive classes from those who made a goal of parasitism. Howells and the literary world accepted the book as an attack upon the aristocracy but failed to see its application to the middle classes. Veblen's next work, *The Theory of Business Enterprise* (1904), made the distinction between industry, the process of manufacture and creation, and business, the rapacious exploitation of credit and the labor of others. This book was based upon the *Reports of the Industrial Commission, 1900–1902*. His speculations thereafter moved into the field of instinct theory, and then to an application of his theories to the First World War, the institutions of higher learning in America and further aspects of economics, in all of which he saw business enterprise—"a marketable right to get something for nothing"—as the dominant obstacle to progress. He would have replaced such methods with a revolutionary soviet of technicians. He was one of America's greatest founders of sociology and economic theory, and his influence, through such people as Riesman, is still growing.

The Theory of the Leisure Class, 1899.
The Theory of Business Enterprise, 1904.
The Instinct of Workmanship, 1914.
Imperial Germany and the Industrial Revolution, 1915.
An Inquiry into the Nature of Peace, 1917.
The Higher Learning in America, 1918.
The Vested Interests and the State of the Industrial Arts, 1919.
The Engineers and the Price System, 1921.
Absentee Ownership and Business Enterprise in Recent Times, 1923.　　D.C.

VENKATARAMANI, K. S. See **Indian Literature.**

VERY, Jones (1813–80) was born at Salem (Massachusetts), the son of a sea captain. After graduating from Harvard in 1836 he studied at the Divinity School while a tutor in Greek. Although licensed, and often preaching, as a Unitarian minister, his visions and direct communications from the Holy Ghost led at one time to a voluntary stay in an asylum. Emerson, however, thought him "profoundly sane" and arranged the publication of *Essays and Poems* (1839), the only book to be published during Very's lifetime. He wrote little during the rest of his life, living in seclusion with his sister.

His interest in transcendentalism, though reflected in his poetry, is not its main concern. Very's poems use a language and style more like the English Metaphysical poets, particularly Herbert, to communicate the mystical experience of the surrender of personality and will to God. The figure of God here, and the whole religious experience, is more akin to Quaker and Puritan thought than to the optimism and faith in nature found in transcendentalism. Very does write about nature, but natural objects are seen as sacraments or material for spiritual allegory. The bareness of much of Very's poetry springs from his reliance on the voice of the Holy Ghost, which he claimed merely to reproduce. The resulting flat statements of dogma have lost in his transmission the visionary truth they once possessed. His faithfulness to his vision, however, when properly transmitted, reproduces the immediacy of the mystical experience lacking in his transcendentalist contemporaries.

Essays and Poems, 1839.
Poems, 1883.

Poems and Essays, ed. J. F. Clarke, Boston: Houghton, Mifflin, 1886.

D.M.

VESEY, Mrs. (Elizabeth). See **Bluestockings.**

VIDAL, Gore (1925–) was born in New York State and educated at Phillips Exeter Academy. Wartime army experience inspired *Williwaw* (1946) and since then Vidal's output has been prolific. Coming from a political family, Vidal has stood for Congress and has also shown his concern for American society in his plays—*Visit to a Small Planet* (1957; *f.* 1959); *The Best Man* (1960; *f.* 1964)—and essays, *Rocking the Boat* (1962) and *Reflections upon a Sinking Ship* (1969). His more recent works include *Myra Breckinridge* (1968; *f.* 1970), a satirical fantasy with a transsexual heroine created as much by the American film as by surgery; and *Two Sisters* (1970), described as "a memoir in the form of a novel." J.L.M.

VONNEGUT, Kurt (1922–) studied biochemistry at Cornell and anthropology at the University of Chicago. He served in the infantry during the Second World War, was taken prisoner and survived the fire-bombing of Dresden in a concrete abattoir. After the war he worked in journalism and was a public relations officer for General Electric. Vonnegut's war experiences feature in *Slaughterhouse-Five*, a novel which dissolves the boundaries between fact and fiction. The hero moves through the fictional microcosms of Vonnegut's previous novels, through all time, and also partakes in Vonnegut's factual war experiences. *Cat's Cradle* uses fantasy to explore the ambiguity of the human instinct to play, which is both creative and destructive. One character was "only playing" when he invented the atom bomb. His son builds miniature landscapes in plywood but later heads the small state of a Caribbean island. As game becomes reality, a philosophy emerges: man must live by harmless untruths rather than trust to outright lies with all their destructive potential. Vonnegut's other novels of futuristic satire are his earliest works, *Player Piano* and *The Sirens of Titan*. Behind the colloquial and avuncular tone, Vonnegut's pragmatism is often in danger of becoming pessimism. In tone and attitude and in his considerable popularity, especially with the young, Vonnegut resembles a modern Mark Twain. (See also **Science Fiction.**)

Player Piano, 1952.
The sirens of Titan, 1959.

Mother Night, 1961.
Cat's Cradle, 1963.
God Bless You, Mr Rosewater; or, Pearls before Swine, 1965.
Welcome to the Monkey House, 1968 (short stories).
Slaughterhouse-Five, 1969 (*f.* 1972).   J.L.M.

W

WALCOTT, Derek. See **Caribbean Literature.**

WALLACE-CRABBE, Chris. See **Australian Literature.**

WALLANT, Edward Lewis (1926–62) was born in New Haven (Connecticut) and worked as a graphic artist for various advertising agencies. He was only beginning to achieve recognition at the time of his tragically early death. He wrote four novels, two published in his lifetime, *The Human Season* (1960) and *The Pawnbroker* (1961; *f.* 1964), and two posthumously, *The Tenants of Moonbloom* (1963) and *The Children at the Gate* (1964). Each novel has a central character emotionally paralyzed and deals with his emergence into life and the recognition of his demands. In the case of the Pawnbroker and Angelo (*The Children at the Gate*) it involves the death of others. The heart of each book is the cross section of people, the suffering, the poor and the deprived, that the central character must face.   D.V.W.

WALLER, Edmund (1606–87) inherited at ten years of age valuable estates in Hertfordshire and Buckinghamshire. He was educated at Eton and King's College, Cambridge. He entered Parliament in 1621, and subsequently supported first the Puritan opposition and then the king. In 1631 he paid a large fine for abducting and marrying a young heiress, and after her death in 1634 unsuccessfully courted Lady Dorothea Sidney, whom he addressed as "Sacharissa" in many poems. In 1643 he instigated a scheme to secure London for the king ("Waller's Plot") and on its discovery narrowly escaped execution. Banished, he joined Charles in France, toured with Evelyn in 1646 and lived sumptuously in Paris. Returning to England in 1652, he published a panegyric on Cromwell in 1655, and then a celebratory poem for the Restoration in 1660. He again sat in Parliament, and enjoyed a high reputation, associating with the foremost literary figures and collaborating with some of them in a translation of Corneille's *Pompée* (1663). After the death of his second wife (1677) he lived in increasing seclusion.

Early in his career Waller professed an ambition to bring "smoothness" to English verse. His verse, small in quantity but highly polished, was extravagantly admired for about a century, and Waller was regarded as a refiner of the language. Now often associated with Cavalier poetry, Waller's lyrics lack the strength and vigor of Carew and Suckling, but the best-known pieces like "Go, Lovely Rose" and "On a Girdle" have undeniable charm.

Poems, 1645; enlarged, 1668.
Divine Poems, 1685.

Poems, ed. G. Thorn-Drury, 2 vols., London: Laurence & Bullen, 1893.

H.N.D.

WALPOLE, Horace (1717–97) was the youngest son of Sir Robert Walpole, prime minister from 1721 to 1742. He was educated at Eton and King's College, Cambridge, then sent on the Grand Tour with his schoolfellow, Thomas Gray, who quarreled with him in Italy. His father presented him with various sinecures and he was always a wealthy man. He ornamented his house at Strawberry Hill in the revived Gothic fashion, landscaped his grounds and lived what on the surface looked like a life of gentlemanly leisure but was, underneath, a dilettante but active existence of scholarship and writing. He became fourth earl of Orford on his nephew's death in 1791.

Walpole's greatest claim to attention is as a letter writer. Thousands of his letters survive and they record the events of the day with unmatched gusto and sense of comedy. He also wrote the important *Memoirs of the Last Ten Years of the Reign of George II* (1822) and *Memoirs of the Reign of King George III* (1845) and published a great deal of pioneering critical and historical work of all kinds. He established a press of his own at Strawberry Hill and wrote for it himself as well as printing works by other writers (e.g., Gray's *The Bard* and *The Progress of Poesy*). Most of his writing is of minor interest, but it all shows his characteristic flair for being in the van of emerging pre-Romantic taste. The new historicism is implicit in his *Historic Doubts on the Life and Reign of King Richard III* (1768), aesthetics in his *Anecdotes of Painting in England* (1762–71) and the shift towards imagination, the Gothic and medievalism in his romance *The Castle of Otranto* (1765), a work which seems rather comic now but which set the fashion for the whole school of Gothic fiction and ultimately for the medievalism of Victorian times.

Works, ed. M. Berry and others, 9 vols., London, 1798–1825.
Correspondence, ed. W. S. Lewis, c. 50 vols., London: Oxford Univ. Press; New Haven: Yale Univ. Press, 1937– .

W.R.

WALPOLE, Sir Hugh (1884–1941), born in New Zealand, the son of a clergyman, later worked in England as a schoolteacher and published his first novel, *The Wooden Horse*, in 1909. A talented and ambitious novelist, he never fulfilled the promise first shown in *Mr. Perrin and Mr. Traill* (1911; *f.* 1948), which portrays in a tragicomic manner the conflict between two teachers in a private school. Though his later work is competent in characterization and construction, it is marred by derivativeness. He wrote many different types of fiction—regional romance in *Rogue Herries* and its sequels, *The Herries Chronicle* (1939); novels with a Russian background, *The Dark Forest* (1916) and *The Secret City* (1919); and a series resembling Trollope's Barchester novels, including *The Cathedral* (1922) and *The Old Ladies* (1924)—but was master of none.   o.k.

WALTON, Izaak (1593–1683), born in Staffordshire, is best known for *The Compleat Angler*, which has been through hundreds of editions since it appeared anonymously in 1653. It is kept alive by its revelation of Walton's humorous and attractive personality rather than by its merits as a treatise. He was a friend of poets like Donne, Drayton, Bishop King and Cotton, and a strong Anglican and Royalist. He wrote with care and affection five *Lives* (of Donne, Wotton, Hooker, Herbert and Sanderson). The first four were collected in 1670; the *Life of Sanderson*, originally published in 1678, was included with the others for the first time in Zouch's edition of 1796.

Lives, ed. G. Saintsbury, London: Oxford Univ. Press, 1927.   j.c.

WARBURTON, William (1698–1779) was educated at Newark and Oakham Grammar Schools. He then trained as an attorney, but was ordained in 1727 and appointed bishop of Gloucester in 1760. After defending the orthodoxy of *An Essay on Man* Warburton became friendly with Pope and was later to be his literary executor and editor (1751). His principal work, the encyclopedic *The Divine Legation of Moses* (1737–41), argues a divine authority for a future state of rewards and punishments. Warburton's reputation for erudition in his own day was due to a pedantic display of massive reading, marked by a litigious quarrelsomeness and self-esteem, rather than sound scholarship. There is little to admire about his edition of Shakespeare (1747).

Works, ed. R. Hurd, 7 vols., London, 1788–94.   j.p.

"WARD, Artemus" was the pseudonym of Charles Farrar Browne (1834–67), a humorous writer born in Maine. While editor of the Cleveland *Plain Dealer* (1857–60), he wrote the first "Artemus Ward" letter, in dialect, deliberately misspelt and describing the adventures of a traveling showman. After a brief period with *Vanity Fair*, he published *Artemus*

Ward—His Book (1862) and the last few years of his short life were devoted to his famous and highly entertaining lecture tours delivered in the character he had created. He gave his "Artemus Ward among the Mormons" lecture in London in 1866 and was a contributor to *Punch*.

Complete Works, Boston: G. W. Dillingham Co., 1898. R.W.

WARD, Edward (Ned) (1667–1731) was a prolific pamphleteer and satirist in the heyday of Grub Street between 1695 and 1712. After *A Trip to Jamaica* (1698) he became the most sensitive barometer of public taste for subliterary genres. Yet despite ambitious ventures such as his three volume versification of Clarendon's *History* and a career of vituperative Tory pamphleteering which led him to the pillory for a serialized doggerel, *Hudibras Redivivus* (1705–07), he is now remembered only, as he proudly professed himself, as "the author of *The London Spy*." This narrative of low-life trivia, published serially (1698–1700), epitomizes Ward's undiscriminating vitality and crudely energetic style. (See also **Augustans, The; Essays.**) A.W.B.

WARD, Mrs. Humphry (1851–1920), granddaughter of Dr. Arnold of Rugby and niece of Matthew Arnold, grew up in Westmorland and Oxford amid the atmosphere of moral earnestness, combined with conflict and doubt in religious matters, which became characteristic of her best novels. The controversial subject of *Robert Elsmere* (1888)—concerning a clergyman who renounces his orders—initiated her immense popularity. Several ideological novels, drawing upon her own experience, portrayed with increasing literary skill the action of spiritual or political problems in human life. Acclaimed as the successor to George Eliot, Mrs. Ward received advice and encouragement from Henry James. However, after a series of novels based upon historical situations, most of her later works declined under financial pressure into romance or propaganda.

Writings, Westmoreland edition, 16 vols., London: Smith, Elder, 1911–12. E.M.J.

WARNER, Rex (1905–), born in Birmingham and educated at Oxford, subsequently became a teacher and lived in Greece and Egypt. In 1964 he took up a professorship at the University of Connecticut. His published works include poetry, translations, novels and criticism. Those of his novels set in the context of the politics of the late 1930s derive their power from the author's presentation of conflicting ideologies. He uses allegory to provide an appropriate vehicle for serious statement, though in his best work, *The Aerodrome* (1941), the allegory is rooted in an every-day world. Later novels, *The Young Caesar* (1958) and *The Converts* (1967), are given a historical setting.   O.K.

WAR POETS (1914-18 and 1939-45). The title "war poet" has been most meaningfully reserved for those writers who, directly involved in soldiering through battles of the First World War, set out to express their experience of modern mass warfare. In realistically conveying the hideous effects of the artillery bombardments, the gas attacks and, most terrible of all, the mass advances of infantry against well-defended trenches, machine-gun emplacements, mines and barbed wire entangle-ments, these poets learned to develop the expressive range of poetic language beyond a mere difference of degree. Their achievements, per-haps more than any other single factor, helped to bring about the gradual abandonment of more traditional and sentimentally romantic poetic modes and the acceptance of such experimental, even extremist, techniques as have characterized much English literature since the First World War.

During the early years of the war the dominant voices were those of older poets, such as Kipling and Hardy, naïvely exhorting patriotic re-sponses from the young, and of the young themselves naïvely dramatizing and romanticizing their roles. The vague sonnets of Rupert Brooke and the more vigorous but still idealized poems of Julian Grenfell (1888-1915) caught the general mood of excitement more surely than did the sober personal responses and questionings of Charles Sorley (1895-1915) and Graeme West (1891-1917), both of whom had seen more action and kept more open minds than those poets who uncritically shared the public's early enthusiasm.

After the bloody battles of 1915 and 1916 the need to convey the truth about the war to an obstinately ignorant civilian population in Britain became the obsession of Siegfried Sassoon and, partly through Sassoon's influence, of Wilfred Owen. Sassoon's poems are the most trenchant satires of the war, but Owen's, a controlled fusion of bitter anger at the stupidity of war and complete sympathy with the suffer-ings of the men he led, are the finer achievement. Isaac Rosenberg, a talented artist and writer, produced some of the most original and vivid poems of the war, though, as in the case of Owen's work, most of them were not published until after the armistice. Indeed, like many of the best prose accounts, one of the most impressive poetical works about the war, David Jones's *In Parenthesis* (1937), was not written until long afterwards, at a time when the probability of a new conflict was awaken-ing interest in the experiences of the First World War.

The techniques of Owen and Rosenberg, which their ways of looking and feeling had necessitated, were part of the consciousness of the poets who went to fight in 1939. This generation of young men was fully aware of what modern warfare meant; to them the journey from Versailles, through Manchuria, Abyssinia, Spain and Munich, to Poland in 1939 seemed inevitable. The crude if spirited politics of the verse of the 1930s were now abandoned (although that period's psychological and historical awareness was given a new personal direction), and many poets turned either to the restrained example of such a writer as Edward Thomas, whose few "war poems" had been essentially inward-looking, or, less frequently and less successfully, to the incantatory style in vogue during the early 1940s which set out both to console and to celebrate. There was certainly no need to "inform" a civilian population which itself was suffering bombing raids, and though there were many experiences which paralleled those of the First World War, a more mobile war fought on many more fronts produced a quite different poetry.

Sidney Keyes probed the meaning of the war and individual guilt for it in strong hard images, and his *War Poet* "who looked for peace and found/ My own eyes barbed" is representative of the firm rejection of any conventional patriotic role. Keith Douglas, generally estimated the greatest poetic loss of the war, wrote some of the most strongly visualized poems of the battles in the Western Desert, and Alun Lewis, a gifted lyrical poet, wrote sympathetically of the people of India and Burma where he served. Roy Fuller, Roy Campbell and Charles Causley all published interesting volumes of war poems, while a few rhetorical poems by Dylan Thomas presented a powerful emotional response to the deaths of civilians in air raids.

As after the First World War, the most terrible revelations about this war also came only after it had ended. What the dropping of the atomic bombs on Nagasaki and Hiroshima and the slaughter of millions in the Nazi concentration camps implied about human nature and man's future has been a continual concern of poets since 1945, and the problems of finding the appropriate form and language for, and the right critical attitudes towards, this extreme kind of poetry have been the subject of much heated controversy. Most volumes of poetry published since 1945, including, for example, those of such dissimilar poets as Philip Larkin, Ted Hughes and Thom Gunn, reflect to some extent, though in very different ways, attitudes towards the exploration of such painful areas of human experience.

First World War.

Anthologies: *Up the Line to Death*, ed. R. B. Gardner, London: Methuen, 1964.

Men Who March Away, ed. I. M. Parsons, London: Chatto & Windus; New York: Viking Press, 1965.

Second World War.
Anthologies: *The Poetry of War 1939–1945*, ed. I. Hamilton, London: A.
Ross, 1965.
Components of the Scene, ed. R. Blythe, Harmondsworth:
Penguin, 1966.
The Terrible Rain, ed. R. B. Gardner, London: Methuen,
1966.   A.Y.

WARREN, Robert Penn (1905–) was born and brought up in
Todd County (Kentucky), the setting for *Night Rider* (1939) and other
writings. In 1921 he entered Vanderbilt University where he came under
the influence of John Crowe Ransom, Allen Tate, Donald Davidson and
others connected with *The Fugitive*, a poetry magazine which championed
Southern regionalism and published Warren's first poems. He continued
his education at the University of California (1925–27), Yale (1928–29)
and as a Rhodes scholar at Oxford (1929–30). His subsequent career has
been equally devoted to writing and university teaching, including posts
at Vanderbilt (1931–34), Louisiana State (1934–42), Minnesota (1942–50)
and Yale (1950–). He also achieved distinction as a coeditor of *The
Southern Review* (1935–42) and of such anthologies as *A Southern Harvest*
(1937).

Although Warren has received many honors for writings in several
genres, it was his poetry which first attracted critical attention. *Thirty-Six
Poems* (1935) was heavily influenced by a wide range of figures, both
ancient and modern, but in *Eleven Poems on the Same Theme* (1942) he
began to find his own voice—highly rhetorical, allusive, sensuous, and
concerned with such themes as guilt, the emergence from childhood, and
corruption in time. *Selected Poems, 1923–1943* (1944) and *Promises* (1957)
contained new poems which are more nakedly emotional and, if sometimes marred by banalities of expression, nonetheless form an elegant peak
in his career, revealing his ability to wrest universal significance from
personal experience. Later collections include *You, Emperors* (1960), *Selected
Poems New and Old, 1923–1966* (1966) and *Incarnations* (1968). *Brother to
Dragons* (1953) is a "tale in verse and voices" based on the nineteenth-
century murder of a Negro by Jefferson's nephew.

Warren's novels, which all have a strong narrative combined with
firm intimations of a larger moral dimension, gained him a wider audience.
Night Rider (1939) explores the clash between tobacco and industrial
interests in Kentucky during the 1900s. *At Heaven's Gate* (1943), about a
corrupt Southern financier and politician, prepared the ground for his
most popular work, *All the King's Men* (1946). Apparently based on the
career of Huey Long, this novel concerns the charismatic power—for
both good and evil—exercised by a Southern demagogue, Willie Stark,

over Jack Burden, a newspaperman, and a range of other characters who come to do his bidding. Through a series of involved relationships and events reaching a violent climax, Burden ultimately begins to understand Stark's power and, also, his own responsibility as an individual human being. *Band of Angels* (1955) is a Civil War story treating miscegenation, and *The Cave* (1959) renders the profoundest motivations of a group of characters by exploring their varied reactions to a single event. His other fiction includes *World Enough and Time* (1950), *Wilderness* (1961) and *Flood* (1964).

Much of Warren's fiction has its basis in history in the largest sense, and his first book was a study of John Brown (1929). *Segregation: The Inner Conflict in the South* (1956), *The Legacy of the Civil War* (1961) and, for children, *Remember the Alamo!* (1958) reveal the persistence of this interest. Also, as a young man he believed in Southern Agrarianism as expressed in the symposium *I'll Take My Stand* (1930), to which he contributed; *Segregation* and *Who Speaks for the Negro?* (1965) constituted, in effect, a repudiation of his earlier views.

With the exception of occasional plays, including a dramatization of *All the King's Men* (1960), Warren's other important works are the products of a teacher–critic. His earlier essays and the textbooks written with Cleanth Brooks, including *Understanding Poetry* (1938) and *Modern Rhetoric* (1949), which stress close attention to the text, influenced a generation of teachers of literature towards the practices of the New Criticism, whereas his later criticism, such as the 1965 essay on Faulkner, has been more concerned to examine the total moral ambience of an author's works.

John Brown: The Making of a Martyr, 1929.
Thirty-Six Poems, 1935.
Night Rider, 1939.
Eleven Poems on the Same Theme, 1942.
At Heaven's Gate, 1943.
Selected Poems, 1923–1943, 1944.
All the King's Men, 1946 (*f.* 1949; dramatized, *p.* 1960).
The Circus in the Attic and Other Stories, 1948.
World Enough and Time, 1950.
Brother to Dragons: A Tale in Verse and Voices, 1953.
Band of Angels, 1955 (*f.* 1956).
Segregation: The Inner Conflict in the South, 1956.
Promises: Poems, 1954–1956, 1957.
Selected Essays, 1958.
The Cave, 1959.
You, Emperors, 1960.
Wilderness, 1961.

The Legacy of the Civil War, 1961.
Flood, 1964.
Who Speaks for the Negro?, 1965.
Selected Poems: New and Old, 1923–1966, 1966.
Incarnations: Poems, 1966–1968, 1968.
Meet Me in the Green Glen, 1971.   M.G.

WARTON, Joseph (1722–1800) and **Thomas** (1728–90) were the sons of Thomas Warton, vicar of Basingstoke (Hampshire) and onetime professor of poetry at Oxford. Joseph was educated at Winchester and Oxford, became a clergyman, and spent many years (1766–93) as ill-suited headmaster of his old school. A friend of William Collins, he published *Odes* in 1744 and 1746, in which he sought to "rise above the rhyming throng." *An Essay on the Genius and Writings of Mr. Pope* (1, 1756; 2, 1782) was informed by this same spirit, finding Pope "the great poet of Reason" and condemning his imitators. Joseph Warton produced an edition of Pope's works in 1797.

Thomas Warton, also educated at Oxford, like his father became professor of poetry (1757–67), Camden professor of history and eventually poet laureate (1785). The blank verse poem *The Pleasures of Melancholy* (1747), written in reaction against Augustan canons, celebrates individual experience, "religious horror," and "the solemn noon/ Of night" when "No being wakes but me." This was followed by *Observations on the Faerie Queene of Spenser* (1754) in the spirit of Richard Hurd, a pioneer *History of English Poetry* (1774–81), and an edition of Milton's early poems (1785).

Each a poet, critic, editor, man of letters and familiar of the Johnsonian circle, the Warton brothers were not, however, Augustans. They partook more of the pre-Romantic spirit, persistently urging the examples of Spenser, Shakespeare and Milton against the eighteenth-century ideals of correctness and invoking the "warm, enthusiastic" fancy that Shaftesbury and others mistrusted.

The Works of the English Poets, ed. A. Chalmers, London: Johnson, 1810, vol. 18.
The Three Wartons: A Choice of Their Verse, ed. E. Partridge, London: Scholartis Press, 1927.   D.G.

WASHINGTON, Booker T. (Taliaferro) (1856–1915), Negro spokesman and educational leader, was born a slave in Virginia and, after emancipation, attended Hampton Institute (Virginia), which stressed a program of industrial and agricultural training for Negroes. Washington taught at Hampton until chosen to organize Tuskegee Institute,

Alabama (1881), which he molded into a vocational college for blacks. Washington's Atlanta Exposition Address (1895), advocating Negro self-help and accommodation to white supremacy, gained him national prominence. He was to exercise an enormous influence over the distribution of white philanthropy and federal appointments for Negroes. His writings include the classic autobiography, *Up from Slavery* (1901), *Frederick Douglass* (1907) and *The Story of the Negro* (1909).   J.W.

WATTS, Isaac (1674–1748) was born at Southampton, the son of a persecuted Nonconformist, and studied in the Dissenting Academy at Stoke Newington (London). He became pastor at Mark Lane in 1698 and exercised his ministry till his death. His educational manual on *Logic* (1725) enjoyed some popularity and *The Improvement of the Mind* (1741) is at once instruction and unintentional autobiography. He is best known for his *Hymns and Spiritual Songs* (1707), which were followed by *Divine Songs in Easy Language for the Use of Children* (1715). These latter contain some bloodcurdling sentiments about punishment, but the best of the former collection, and especially such Christianized psalms as "O God, our help in ages past" and "Jesus shall reign," show Watts as among the greatest of hymn writers. In this direction his work was marked by its stress on God's power and strength. He usually contented himself with the common 8.6. measure. (See also **Hymns.**)   A.P.

WAUGH, Evelyn (1903–66), born in London, was the son of Arthur Waugh, publisher and critic, and brother to another novelist, Alec. He was educated at Lancing and Hertford College, Oxford. After leaving Oxford he was a schoolmaster for a time; something of what he thought of the profession can perhaps be seen in a somewhat decorated form in his first novel, *Decline and Fall* (1928). In 1930 he became a Roman Catholic. He spent most of the decade immediately preceding the Second World War in travel, visiting Abyssinia three times, once as a war correspondent, and putting the visits to good purpose in *Black Mischief* (1932) and *Scoop* (1938). During the war he served in the Royal Marines and the Commandos, an experience reflected in the trilogy of novels, *Men at Arms* (1952), *Officers and Gentlemen* (1955) and *Unconditional Surrender* (1961). After the war he lived quietly and uneventfully as an English country gentleman, cultivating an aggressive Tory-squirism which expressed part of his character but which at the same time concealed a shy, sensitive and, as one can guess from *The Ordeal of Gilbert Pinfold* (1957), tormented personality.

   Varied as it is, Waugh's work is very much of a piece. His early novels are brilliantly comic, showing that firm grasp of the ludicrous and the incongruous that is the essence of comedy. He depicts the life of upper-middle-class society with a mixture of affection and contempt and shows a toughness of mind that enables him to acknowledge injustice and folly as part of the human lot without being blinded to the strength of simple goodness. His characters are sometimes bizarre, but remain recognizable human beings; they and the situations into which he puts them have sometimes the legitimate exaggeration into fantasy that belongs to caricature. Even these early revels show the true satirist's concern for standards of conduct and decency. In *A Handful of Dust* (1934), beneath the ironic social survey is a terrifying vision of simple human goodness imprisoned in an amoral world: it starts as comedy and ends as nightmare. These novels have been mistakenly seen as eulogizing the "Bright Young Things" of Waugh's youth, but closer scrutiny shows their power of detached judgment and unmistakable condemnation. They depict a world of artificial hedonistic values which reality, in the shape of violence and death, constantly disrupts; underneath lie the fundamental moral values. In *Brideshead Revisited* (1945), for a long time his most popular novel, Waugh indulges to the full the sentimentality and snobbery that is elsewhere held in check. Sincere as the religious feeling is in intention, in effect it emerges as modish religiosity. His full power of *saeva indignatio* comes out clearly in what might be seen as a rather naughty *jeu d'esprit*, *The Loved One* (1948). Here his conservatism, his sense of the value of tradition and his hatred of the escapist unreality of modern civilization are expressed in terms of viciously comic satire.

The trilogy of novels dealing with the Second World War (which appeared together as *Sword of Honour*) is in some ways his most ambitious as well as his most difficult work. The first novel in particular is richly comic, but underneath the dispassionate and elegant prose is a sad indictment of the muddle and futility that accompany war. In the later volumes the effect of this futility is seen in the gradual disillusionment of the central character. For all the comedy and the richness of bizarre characterization, the general effect is undeniably somber, though the final emergence of the chastened hero as having come to terms with life is not without its consolatory effect.

Waugh also wrote *Helena* (1950), a novel based on the life of St. Helena, mother of Constantine the Great, a biography of the Elizabethan Jesuit, Edward Campion, and some travel sketches. All his work is meticulous in style and structure, and nowhere does he strive for meretricious effect. He saw himself as an honest craftsman, as indeed he was, but his satirical range, sheer comic force and essential seriousness make him much more than that.

Decline and Fall, 1928 (*f.* 1968).

Vile Bodies, 1930.
Black Mischief, 1932.
A Handful of Dust, 1934.
Mr Loveday's Little Outing and Other Stories, 1936.
Scoop, 1938.
Put Out More Flags, 1942.
Brideshead Revisited, 1945.
The Loved One, 1948 (*f.* 1965).
Helena, 1950.
Men at Arms, 1952.
Officers and Gentlemen, 1955.
The Ordeal of Gilbert Pinfold, 1957.
Unconditional Surrender, 1961.
Basil Seal Rides Again, 1963.

C.H.

WEBSTER, John (?1580–?1634) is, for the early part of his life, largely "in a mist," like most of his characters. No certain reference to him is found before 1602 when he collaborated with Middleton in the lost play, *Caesar's Fall*. Further collaborative works appeared in the next five years, including the popular *Northward Ho!* and *Westward Ho!*, written in conjunction with Dekker. A number of plays of sole authorship followed this dramatic apprenticeship of which three, *The Devil's Law Case* (*p.* ?1619), *The White Devil* (*p.* ?1609) and *The Duchess of Malfi* (*p.* ?1614), survive. Contemporary with these are the poem *A Monumental Column* and extensive additions to Overbury's *Characters*. In his later years he seems to have returned to collaborative work, apart from a single pageant, *Monuments of Honour*. He probably died in 1634, but 1625 has also been suggested.

Webster's reputation rests on two dramatic masterpieces, *The White Devil* and *The Duchess of Malfi*. These plays present a corrupt world dominated by intrigue and violence, in which moral values are confused and actions rarely produce their expected outcome. The darkness of his vision is reinforced by a macabre imagery frequently drawn from the hospital or the charnel house. The dramatist's prime debt is to Shakespeare, but the extent of his borrowing is vast. Nevertheless, his work remains entirely distinct and his major plays rank among the most important productions of a remarkably rich era.

The White Devil, 1612 (*p.* ?1609).
A Monumental Column, 1613.
The Duchess of Malfi, 1623 (*p.* ?1614).
The Devil's Law Case, 1623 (*p.* ?1619).
Monuments of Honour, 1624.

Works, ed. F. L. Lucas, 4 vols., London: Chatto & Windus, 1927; Boston: Houghton Mifflin, 1928.

L.S.

WEBSTER, Noah (1758–1843), born in Connecticut, graduated from Yale (1778) and, while teaching, began work on his "Blue-Backed Speller," published as *A Grammatical Institute of the English Language* (3 parts, 1783–85). It was instrumental in standardizing pronunciation and spelling in American, as distinct from British, forms and sold 15 million copies by 1837 and over 70 million by 1890. Webster edited *The American Magazine* (1787–88) and *American Minerva* and *Herald* (1793–1803). Webster's *Compendious Dictionary of the American Language* (1806), enlarged into *An American Dictionary of the English Language* (2 vols., 1828), established his international reputation as a lexicographer. In 1864 it was generally adopted in colleges and schools throughout the United States.   J.W.

WEEMS, Mason (1759–1825) was born in Maryland, studied theology in London, and on returning to America in 1794 combined the careers of Episcopal clergyman, subscription book agent and author. Writer of a variety of improving tracts, "Parson" Weems achieved fame with his didactic biography, *The Life and Memorable Acts of George Washington* (1800), which in its sixth edition (1808) was enlarged to include "Curious Anecdotes Equally Honourable to Himself and Exemplary to His Young Countrymen." The apocryphal story of "the little hatchet and the cherry tree," an enduring contribution to the Washington myth, had been introduced in the fifth edition (1806). Possessing a passionate belief in the value of good books, Weems also produced lives of Benjamin Franklin and William Penn.

J.W.

WELLS, H. G. (Herbert George) (1886–1946), born in Bromley (Kent), the son of a professional cricketer, was educated locally and, in order to relieve his father's financial troubles, apprenticed to a draper at the age of twelve. Later he became a teacher and subsequently graduated from the Royal College of Science. In 1891 he married one of his cousins, but divorced her after a short and unhappy marriage and married a former pupil, Amy Robbins. After taking many temporary teaching posts, he turned to writing in 1893 and combined his interests in literature, science and sociology by writing essays, reviews and textbooks. Ultimately Wells won greater fame as a novelist, for which he had no special training, than as a scientist or sociologist. In later life he retained a lively interest in public life and stood for Parliament as a Socialist candidate, though he was twice defeated.

Few writers have been more prolific or versatile than Wells—novelist, short story writer, historian and scientist. His first novels combine fantasy, fact and romance with a realistic prophecy of universal disorder and the degeneration of man. The first of these was *The Time Machine*, though *The War of the Worlds* is his best-known work of science fiction. Then followed a series of realistic social novels, of which *Love and Mr. Lewisham* is the first. These are "comic epics," to some extent autobiographical, in which, around the life story of a central character, there is a good deal of social comedy and satire at the expense of the upper classes, political and commercial interests. Others of this kind include *Kipps*, *Tono-Bungay* and *The History of Mr. Polly*. In Wells's later works, the novel is primarily a vehicle for his social, political and educational ideas. *The New Machiavelli* (1911) and *The World of William Clissold* (1926), for example, are novels in which a social thesis takes the place of realistic presentation. In other later works the emphasis falls upon the reconstruction of the world and upon Wells's semimystical idea of a corporate utopian universe. These are mainly nonfictional writings and include *The Elements of Reconstruction* (1916), an idealized picture of a future and better society.

Wells looked upon most of his work as social journalism and recognized that most of it would survive only so long as the ideas with which he dealt remained current. It is likely that his most lasting contribution to fiction will be his science fiction, which still remains compelling reading, and, more importantly, his works of social comedy and analysis. The strength of such works as *Kipps*, *Tono-Bungay* and *The History of Mr. Polly* derives from the author's semicomic, often Dickensian treatment of social and commercial life. Wells has a fertile comic imagination, a relish for describing and satirizing the feelings and habits of a number of social types and a sure grasp of middle-class life. At the same time his central characters, in their "passive endurance of dullness," show this society in depth. Like the unforgettable Mr. Polly, the hero is often divided against himself and in conflict with organized society. In all of Wells's "epic" novels, the realism and vitality of his social observation compensate for his diffuseness in style and construction.

(See also **Science Fiction.**)

The Time Machine, 1895 (f. 1960).
The Invisible Man, 1897 (f. 1933).
The War of the Worlds, 1898 (f. 1953).
Love and Mr. Lewisham, 1900.
Kipps, 1905 (f. 1941).
The War in the Air, 1908.
Ann Veronica, 1909.
Tono-Bungay, 1909.

The History of Mr. Polly, 1910 (*f.* 1949).
The New Machiavelli, 1911.
The Outline of History, 1919.
The World of William Clissold, 1926.

Complete Works, Atlantic edition, 28 vols., London: Fisher Unwin; New York: C. Scribner's Sons, 1924–27.
Complete Short Stories, London: Benn, 1927; Garden City, N.Y.: Doubleday, 1929.
Journalism and Prophecy, 1893–1946, ed. W. W. Wagar, Boston: Houghton Mifflin, 1964; London: Bodley Head, 1966.   O.K.

WELTY, Eudora (1909–   ) was born in Jackson (Mississippi) of non-Southern parentage. Educated in Mississippi and at the University of Wisconsin, she was briefly a journalist and copywriter. Since her moving short story "Death of a Travelling Salesman," appeared in 1936, she has published widely, collecting four volumes of stories. The high promise of *A Curtain of Green* (1941), compassionate studies of loneliness in grotesquely comic or disturbingly surreal terms, was amply confirmed by the brilliant *The Golden Apples* (1949). Her four novels have generally met with less success.

Selected Stories, ed. K. A. Porter, New York: Random House, 1954.

                                                          A.S.

WESKER, Arnold (1932–   ), an East End Jewish dramatist of Russo-Hungarian ancestry, has been a plumber's mate, a kitchen porter and a pastrycook. He has been mainly supported by the Royal Court Theatre in London which, after their initial run at the Belgrade Theatre, Coventry, put on three plays which later became known as the Wesker Trilogy—*Chicken Soup With Barley* (*p.* 1958), *Roots* (*p.* 1959) and *I'm Talking About Jerusalem* (*p.* 1960). The trilogy is less concerned with narrative progression than with the ideas it contains; its subject is the effort of two Jewish families to preserve their Socialist ideals against a background of political change. The middle play, *Roots*, set in Norfolk, is only tenuously attached to the rest.

Wesker followed the trilogy with an "angry" play, *Chips with Everything* (*p.* 1962), in which he attacks class distinctions and cultural values. In the same year he founded Centre 42, which aimed at providing the working classes with culture much as the Health Service provided them with doctors. *Chips* is a play about basic training for conscripts in the R.A.F., and if the detail is accurate, the central character, a rebellious youth who tries to betray his social class by not becoming an officer, is fairly unbelievable. Wesker's disillusionment with the lack of support the Trade

Unions gave his Centre (it takes its name from a declaration made at a Trades Union Congress) is reflected in his ambitious social play, *Their Very Own and Golden City* (p. 1965).

Chicken Soup with Barley, 1959 (p. 1958).
Roots, 1959.
I'm Talking about Jerusalem, 1960.
Chips with Everything, 1962.
The Four Seasons, 1966 (p. 1965).
Their Very Own and Golden City, 1966 (p. 1965).
Six Sundays in January, 1971.

The Wesker Trilogy, London: Cape, 1960.
Plays, ed. G. Leeming and S. Trussler, London: Gollancz, 1971. A.P.H.

WESLEY, John (1703–91) and **Charles** (1707–88), sons of Samuel Wesley, rector of Epworth (Lincolnshire), were much influenced both in Georgia and on their return to England by the Moravian Brethren. They both experienced evangelical conversions in 1738. This year marks the beginning of the Methodist movement, in the service of which John Wesley spent the rest of his life in itinerant outdoor preaching. Charles also carried on a similar ministry, though always on a lesser scale and much less strenuously in later years.

By contrast with their fellow preacher, the Calvinist Whitefield, the Wesleys preached a doctrine of full and free salvation to all men. On this question they separated from Whitefield, and there are many references in John's sermons and Charles's hymns and poems to this doctrinal difference. John Wesley also quarreled with the mystic, William Law, whose works had influenced him in earlier years. Here the difference lay in Wesley's emphasis on the operation of God's grace as opposed to the efficacy of man's works.

John was a prolific writer and especially a summarizer of other men's works for the benefit of his Methodist followers, but his chief publications are his *Journal*, in which he vividly describes his travels and experiences, and his *Sermons*, covering the whole range of his doctrines and expressed in confident reasoning terms.

Charles was the poet of Methodism and wrote over six thousand hymns. In these the notes of joy and praise are particularly characteristic, as is the exaltation of the love of God. His best-known pieces are "Jesu, Lover of My Soul," "Love Divine, All Loves Excelling," "O for a Thousand Tongues to Sing" and "Hark, the Herald Angels Sing."

(See also **Hymns; Sermons.**)

John Wesley.

Works, 32 vols., Bristol, 1771–74; 14 vols., London: Wesleyan Conference Office, 1872; reprinted, Grand Rapids, Mich.: Zondervan, 1958–59.

Journal, 21 parts, 1739–91; ed. N. Curnock, 8 vols., London: R. Culley, 1909–16.

Letters, ed. J. Telford, 8 vols., London: Epworth Press, 1931.

Standard Sermons, ed. E. H. Sugden, 2 vols., London: Epworth Press, 1921.

John Wesley, ed. A. C. Outler, New York: Oxford Univ. Press, 1964.

Charles Wesley.

Journal, ed. T. Jackson, 2 vols., London, 1849.

Representative Verse, ed. F. Baker, London: Epworth Press, 1962.   A.P.

WEST, Graeme. See **War Poets.**

"WEST, Nathanael" (1903–40) was born Nathan Wallenstein Weinstein in New York City, where he went to De Witt Clinton High School. He assumed his pen name, along with other affectations, as a dandyish student at Brown University. From there he went in 1924 to Paris; here he wrote and published, with an expatriate press, his first novel, *The Dream Life of Balso Snell*. Two more novels of greater polish and success, *Miss Lonelyhearts* and *A Cool Million*, followed in the early 1930s when he returned to the United States. In 1935, after working in a hotel, he went to Hollywood as a screenwriter, an experience that led directly into his fourth and last novel, *The Day of the Locust*. A year after its publication West and his new wife were killed in a car accident. His jokey, febrile novels held their coterie reputation until the 1960s, when West's intensely ironic view of American society and experience and his stylistic manner made him seem a precursor of the fashionable mode of black humor. He won high praise as a novelist in that line of bleak, ironic, detached fiction that runs from Melville's *The Confidence-Man* and Twain's *The Mysterious Stranger* to Heller's *Catch-22*.

West is undoubtedly a remarkable novelist, though a most uneven one; a writer one remembers for his vision, for his tone and the odd powerful images he distills, rather than for the particular texture of particular works. His novels all have the rough, slapdash quality of the pastiche. *Balso Snell* is obvious apprentice work, though a reminder that he knew a lot of fashionable experimental tactics; the three "mature" novels are insecure, yet virtuoso, performances. *Miss Lonelyhearts* is about a newspaper agony columnist suffering, incompetently, from the larger suffering of those who write to him. The theme lets West create a gallery of horrifying and pathetic grotesques. But, like "Miss Lonelyhearts," we have a problem in articulating our response to them; West's own is one of absurdist detachment. They are one-dimensional characters; their incompleteness may seem a satirical image of a dehumanizing society, but it may rather represent West's satirical view of serious, humanistic views of the human condition, or even his lack of creative resource. West's hard-edged comic method is intended to invoke the pathos of dehumanized people; it also takes pleasure in its own cool distance on them. His unconcern is evident in *A Cool Million*, a parody of that classic American success story, the rise of the virtuous innocent from rags to riches. In West's revised version the hero is gradually dismembered. The result is more the pastiche of a plot than a savage attack on America; and the central character's simple one-dimensionality makes for a gory, somewhat repetitious performance.

West's methods of simplified, grotesque characterization work much better in *The Day of the Locust*, perhaps the classic Hollywood novel. Because Hollywood is seen as a world of materialistic, tawdry, pastiche dreams, of images, traumas, delusions, false identities, accelerating neuroses and a hysteria culminating in the burning of the city of Los Angeles, West's technique becomes associated with a social and psychological world to which it is appropriate. His portrait of a denatured, urban, disturbed, dream- and identity-hungry world becomes successfully fleshed out; his way of writing so that all human actions and relationships are odd encounters with the physical and material world has an appropriate milieu. Here his comic grotesque manner does acquire the strength of a convincing modern style, a style rather like that sought by the significantly named artist-hero of the book, Tod Hackett, who paints while Los Angeles burns. West's fame as a modern absurdist novelist must rest especially on this book, where the very insufficiency of the rhetoric has an appropriateness to the world of decadent images and languages it contains, and where the strange, desperate dream world of modern mass urban life is caught in an appropriately fleeting, frightening and apocalyptic imagery.

The Dream Life of Balso Snell, 1931.
Miss Lonelyhearts, 1933 (*f*. as *Lonelyhearts*, 1959).
A Cool Million, 1934.
The Day of the Locust, 1939.

Complete Works, ed. A. Ross, London: Secker & Warburg; New York: Farrar, Straus, 1957.   M.B.

WHARTON, Edith (1862–1937) was born in New York into a family that she later described as one of the last of the "leisured class" in America.

She was educated privately at home, and taken on frequent trips to Europe. In 1885 she married Edward Wharton, and the next few years were divided between their homes first at Newport (Rhode Island) then Lenox (Massachusetts) and Europe. It was in Europe that she first met Henry James; and a friendship developed that was to last until James's death and have a considerable influence on her work. Her first volumes of stories were published around the turn of the century, at a time when her marriage was already a source of pain. She began to write partly as a kind of therapy, but none of this early work is of much interest. Her first significant work appeared in 1905, her novel *The House of Mirth*.

In 1907 she left America to make her home in Paris. Her husband was by this time too ill to travel, and they were finally divorced in 1912. These years before the outbreak of the First World War were some of the happiest and most creative of her life. The novels *Ethan Frome* (1911), *The Reef* (1912) and *The Custom of the Country* (1913) represent the core of her artistic achievement. The outbreak of the war had a tremendous impact on her, both physically and mentally. She remained in France organizing relief for Belgian refugees, work for which she was awarded the Legion of Honor, but she never forgave America for not rushing to help France. She eventually published two novels about the war, *The Marne* (1918) and *A Son at the Front* (1923), but neither is more than emotional melodrama. In contrast is *Xingu and Other Stories* (1916), published at the height of the war and containing the fine story "Bunner Sisters." Her other successful novel, *The Age of Innocence*, was published in 1920 and won her a Pulitzer Prize.

After the war she continued to live in France, but she never came to terms, either personally or artistically, with the changes the war had brought. She maintained a steady output of novels, stories and poems, but all are second-rate. In 1925 appeared a critical work, *The Writing of Fiction*, interesting both in relation to her own and to James's work. Her autobiography, *A Backward Glance*, was published in 1934. She died in France in 1937.

Edith Wharton is usually regarded as a novelist of manners. Her most typical setting is the old New York of her childhood, seen in *The House of Mirth* and *The Age of Innocence*, books that show very clearly the influence of James. She writes with the insight not only of having grown up in that world, but also of having seen it destroyed. This gives a fine edge of irony to her work; she reveals the thinness of the social veneer, and the destructive effect it can have on the individual. The most poignant example of this is Undine Spragg, heroine of *The Custom of the Country*. Thoroughly spoilt as a child, she wavers between the differing ways of life and their values that New York offers. Superficially she succeeds in getting all she wants, but emotionally she is destroyed and left empty and isolated. Edith Wharton's best novel is her least typical: *Ethan Frome* is a short, stark novel set in the bleak, barren landscape of New England. Ethan Frome is bound by the unceasing demands of labor to his farm, and to a wife who has an even more terrible and destructive hold over him. Ethan's one hope of happiness is with Mattie Silver, a young and attractive girl who comes to help on the farm, but he is unable to free himself to go away with her. The novel attains a very real sense of futility and waste, similar to the atmosphere of the story "Bunner Sisters," and marks Edith Wharton as an important novelist.

The Greater Inclination, 1899 (stories).
The Touchstone, 1900.
Crucial Instances, 1901 (stories).
The Valley of Decision, 1902.
Sanctuary, 1903 (long story).
The Descent of Man, and Other Stories, 1904.
The House of Mirth, 1905.
Madame de Treymes, 1907.
The Fruit of the Tree, 1907.
A Motor Flight through France, 1908.
The Hermit and the Wild Woman and Other Stories, 1908.
Tales of Men and Ghosts, 1910.
Ethan Frome, 1911.
The Reef, 1912.
The Custom of the Country, 1913.
Xingu and Other Stories, 1916.
Summer, 1917.
The Marne, 1918.
French Ways and Their Meaning, 1919.
The Age of Innocence, 1920 (*f.* 1934).
The Glimpses of the Moon, 1922.
A Son at the Front, 1923.
Old New York, 1924 (4 vols.: *False Dawn; The Old Maid; The Spark; New Year's Day*).
The Mother's Recompense, 1925.
The Writing of Fiction, 1925.
Here and Beyond, 1926.
Twilight Sleep, 1927.
The Children, 1928.
Hudson River Bracketed, 1929.
Certain People, 1930.
The Gods Arrive, 1932.
Human Nature, 1933.

A Backward Glance, 1934 (autobiography).
The World Over, 1936.
Ghosts, 1937.
The Buccaneers, 1938.

Best Short Stories, ed. W. Andrews, New York: C. Scribner's Sons, 1958.

D.N.C.

WHITE, Gilbert (1720–93), natural historian, scholar and country clergyman, was known as the "hussar parson" on account of his addiction to rambling the country on horseback. This sharpened White's natural talent for observation and his instinctive curiosity about nature, which had much in common with the natural theology of Ray and Derham in the previous century. He passed the major part of his life at Selborne (Hampshire) where in 1751 he began his *Garden Calendar* (later called *The Naturalist's Journal*), a record of plant and animal life. White produced one remarkable and scientifically important book, *The Natural History and Antiquities of Selborne* (1789), which is, in addition, a clear-grained and knowledgeable portrait of rural life in the eighteenth century.

Journals, ed. W. Johnson, London: Routledge, 1931.   P.G.M.

WHITE, Patrick. See **Australian Literature.**

WHITE, William Hale. See **"Rutherford Mark."**

WHITEFIELD, George. See **Sermons.**

WHITMAN, Walt (1819–92) was born on Long Island of farming stock of English and Dutch origin. He was brought up in Brooklyn and in 1830 he left school to work as office boy, printer's devil, printer and rural schoolteacher. From 1841 he was engaged in newspaper reporting and editing in Brooklyn and New York, and this continued until 1862, apart from a three-month trip in 1848 with his brother Jeff to New Orleans, Chicago and the Middle West. He was active politically in the press as a Democrat, and as well as some conventional verse he wrote some sentimental stories for *The Democratic Review* between 1841 and 1845. In 1842 he also wrote *Franklin Evans; or, The Inebriate: A Tale of the Times*, a temperance tract. He was made editor of the Brooklyn *Daily Eagle* but dismissed in 1848 for his sympathy with the Free Soil party, and in 1849 was editor of the Free Soil *Freeman*. His life at this time seems to have been spent in an easygoing enjoyment of the crowds and varying activities of city life, as well as wide-ranging reading, and his 1848 trip gave him experience of frontier life and the physical scale of America—all elements which are in evidence in the first *Leaves of Grass* volume in 1855. He began to dress as a working man rather than, as earlier, a dandy, and his fervently democratic attitudes are combined with his strong sense of his own individual self in the celebration in *Leaves of Grass* of the figure of Walt, both a unique individual and archetype; "an American, one of the roughs, a cosmos."

Nothing Whitman had previously written gives any hint of the possibility of the explosion of feeling in this first volume, and sexual experience (for instance, in New Orleans) or mystical experiences have been suggested as causes. Certainly the dominant note in the first edition is of a sexuality and sensuousness which leaks out of the poet's own body to inform the whole universe, and the expression of this sexuality in poetry seems to have acted as a sudden release. In spite of his claims, later in life, to have illegitimate children, there is no record of any heterosexual or homosexual relationships. What is displayed in the early editions of *Leaves of Grass* is more like Freud's view of infantile sexuality—innocent, anarchic and polymorphously perverse. The poetry has been called mystical in its sense of the poet's unity with the whole of creation, but it is a type of mysticism which presents a universe crowded with detail, rather than the nothingness of vastation. As *Leaves of Grass* grew in successive editions the original urgent expression of the highly personal sexual self diminishes and the generalized self—the persona of Walt as the democratic man—increases in importance. In successive editions Whitman added complete new sections, but he also expanded and rearranged the existing poems, so that the whole volume changes and grows organically. The third edition of 1860 added the "Calamus" and "Children of Adam" sections, "Calamus" dealing with homoerotic experiences and carrying more of the force and urgency of the original poems than "Children of Adam," which celebrated heterosexual love rather woodenly. A much more public note is present by the time of the 1867 edition, which includes "Drum Taps" and "Sequel to Drum Taps." In addition, the bolder sexual passages from earlier sections have been excised. The new additions here show the marked influence of the Civil War, Lincoln's death (e.g., "When lilacs last in the dooryard bloom'd") and, in particular, of Whitman's own experiences as hospital visitor in Washington from 1862 to 1865. He originally went to Virginia to search for his brother George among the wounded, then settled in Washington and became a familiar figure in the wards, bringing books and tobacco, dressing wounds and comforting the injured (see his prose accounts in *Specimen Days and Collect*). His reaction to the war was at first exhilaration and his poems are martial and patriotic for the North (e.g., "Beat! Beat! Drums!"), but these feelings are later balanced by the compassion for the casualties of both sides shown in, for instance, "The Wound-Dresser." Both the war fever in New York and the later experience in the hospitals in Washington seem to have given Whitman the sense of identity with the people of America which is such an important element in his poetry. He had known it before as an ideal; here it was actually experienced.

From 1865 until 1873 he worked as a government clerk in Washington (D.C.), although in 1865 he had to change departments when he was dismissed for the alleged immorality of *Leaves of Grass*. In 1873, after a paralytic stroke, he moved to Camden (New Jersey) where he remained, living in the style of the "good gray poet." The sixth or "Centennial edition" of *Leaves of Grass*, published in 1876, included the new section "Passage to India" which reflects Whitman's optimistic faith in scientific progress. (The title poem was prompted by the construction of canal, cable and railway links with the East.) The section also develops Whitman's belief in the regenerative possibilities for Western man of contact with the East. This easy combination of the material and the spiritual is typical of Whitman's method throughout his life, but in the later poetry the much-vaunted optimism and serenity becomes increasingly facile. In his later years he had acquired disciples who unfortunately bolstered up the public and representative side of his verse to the exclusion, in the later poetry, of the intense personal sensations of the earlier volumes.

It was only late in his life that he gained real public recognition, particularly in England by William Rossetti, Swinburne and Symonds. The notable exception to the early critical neglect of Whitman was Emerson's generous and whole-hearted appreciation of what he called Whitman's "free and brave thought" and "courage of treatment." Emerson rightly saw that Whitman had fulfilled his requirements for a new writing consonant with the new political and imaginative experience of being an American, and certainly Whitman's ideas owe much to Emerson and transcendentalist thought. In particular, Whitman found support for his feelings of unity with an ultimately beneficent nature. Given a faith in the natural rather than a suspicion of it, spontaneity rather than restraint or discipline, emotional expression rather than form and intellect will become the ideals to be achieved. But Whitman's achievement is to show in "Song of Myself" that these oppositions are not absolute; that spontaneity does not necessarily produce chaos but can produce a form organic to, and dependent on, the action or speech rather than superimposed on it. (Hence the importance of the leaves of grass which grow spontaneously, each separate and perfectly formed, and coexist in harmony.) Whitman's poetic forms reflect this faith in spontaneity, both locally and in large-scale structure. This is not to say that his poetry is without order, but that the order is based on the speaking or chanting voice rather than on the traditional English or classical meters, so that the phrase, regulated by the breath rather than the foot, becomes the basic unit, which is then developed on a larger scale in the poems in parallelism and repetition—rhetorical devices, but ones which give Whitman a chanting insistent rhythm rather than a studied, well-finished effect. The only earlier poetry that could have acted as model is that of the Old Testament, and Whitman often uses biblical phrases and vocabulary. Apart from the radical break with his predecessors in terms of form, Whitman also in much of his poetry completely drops extended metaphorical devices and similes, and only in the lyrics, which are untypical in their careful formal organization, does he use objects of the natural world as symbols.

His confidence in his own and every man's ability to be at one with the beneficent divine principle of the universe stems from his acceptance of Emerson's view of the universe as the "externalizaton of the soul," implying the unity of inner and outer through intuition. He also develops from Emerson the sense of everyman's life as a new beginning, and his poetry reflects this ecstatic realization of "a world primal again." This accounts not only for the *celebration* of the world, which Whitman can present, at his best, as if it had never been seen by anyone before, but for the insistent "enumerations" (Ginsberg) of objects and places, since Whitman, by acting as first man, as Adamic namer, is presenting the real world anew, in unison with the ideal, or Emersonian Oversoul.

The criticism leveled at Whitman, and Emerson too, is that this ecstatic vision leaves out of account the gap, painfully obvious to most people, between the real and the ideal, and that the tension which is generated by this gap is absent in Whitman. Certainly Whitman's poetry has no use for the irony or intellectual complexity which characterizes writers who acknowledge "the power of blackness," since for him the issues are very simple. His denial of a separate principle of evil does not, however, lead him to dwell only on the happier aspects of life. He visits, in "Song of Myself," scenes of pain and misery, and he had direct experience of the carnage in the Civil War and remained unshaken in his confidence in a divine principle; "Agonies are one of my changes of garments." Lawrence criticized him for his refusal to discriminate, his total acceptance and celebration of all aspects of life, comparing him to "a pipe open at both ends," and suggesting that far from being an extension and development of self, this "merging with everything" involved a breakdown of any real individual identity. In his later poetry this becomes true of Whitman, but in "Song of Myself" Whitman achieves a distinctive balance through the part-comic persona of Walt, whereby he is both empathetically merged with the sufferer and at the same time an observer who can still see the "form, union, plan" of life; "My hurts turn livid upon me as I lean on a cane and observe." In his celebrated lyrics ("When lilacs last in the dooryard bloom'd," "Out of the cradle endlessly rocking" and "As I ebb'd with the ocean of life") Whitman comes to terms with the existence of death, potentially an obstacle to his optimism, by seeing it as the ultimate union with the forces of nature and by stressing the cyclic qualities of life which guarantee regeneration. In these poems the careful, more formal organization of imagery and theme constitute a distinguished stratagem for dealing with the problems of death and dissolution, but it is in the earlier open-ended "Song of Myself" that Whitman's most distinctive and original work is found.

Leaves of Grass, 1855.
  (with 32 new poems), 1856.
  (with "Children of Adam" and "Calamus"), 1860.
  (with "Drum Taps" and "Sequel to Drum Taps"), 1867; 1871.
  (Centennial edition, with "Passage to India" and the prose "Democratic Vistas"), 1876; 1881.
  (with "November Boughs"), 1889.
  (with "Sands at Seventy" and "Goodbye My Fancy"), 1891.
Democratic Vistas, 1871.
Specimen Days and Collect, 1882.

Complete Prose Works, 1892.

Complete Writings, ed. R. M. Bucke, T. B. Harned, and H. L. Traubel, 10 vols., Putnam, New York, 1902.
Collected Writings, ed. G. W. Allen and E. S. Bradley, New York: New York Univ. Press, 1961– .   D.M.

WHITTIER, J. G. (John Greenleaf) (1807–92) was born of a Quaker farming family at Haverhill (Massachusetts). Mainly self-educated, he gave up farming because of delicate health and devoted himself to poetry and journalism. His early verse was influenced by Robert Burns and the Romantics. He edited a number of provincial newspapers and engaged in local politics; from the beginning his main cause was antislavery. He was at the forefront of the Abolition movement, and much of his poetry and prose is about the sufferings of slavery and similar themes such as Puritan religious persecution. Popular success and much of his lasting literary achievement came after the Civil War. An amiable and simple man, he never married and never traveled far from his native county, Essex.

Whittier is a poet of simplicity and serenity. Apart from slavery (where the note can be strident), his verse is concerned with New England history and legends (there are fine ballads, like "Skipper Ireson's Ride"), the New England rural scene, and religion, including his own Quaker belief. Parts of some of his poems became famous hymns (e.g., "Dear Lord and Father of Mankind" from "The Brewing of Soma"). His best work, like his masterpiece *Snow-Bound* (1866), one of the finest poems in English of this period, "Telling the Bees" and "The Last Walk in Autumn," is set in New England and permeated by a quiet sense of regret, acceptance and death.

Within a simplicity of rhyme and meter his verse can produce profound and startling imagery which is made an integral part of the serene surface. Though much of his work now appears flat and diffuse, a few of his poems have a unique and fine power. The best of his prose is *Margaret Smith's Journal* (1849), a fictional account of Puritan New England life in the late seventeenth century.

(See also **Hymns.**)

Legends of New England, 1831 (poems and tales).
Justice and Expediency, 1833.
Poems, 1838.
Lays of My Home, and Other Poems, 1843.
Voices of Freedom, 1846 (poems).
Songs of Labor, and Other Poems, 1850.
Home Ballads, Poems, and Lyrics, 1860.
In War Time, and Other Poems, 1863.
Snow-Bound, 1866.
The Tent on the Beach, and Other Poems, 1867.
The Pennsylvania Pilgrim, and Other Poems, 1872,

Writings, Riverside edition, 7 vols., Boston: Houghton, Mifflin, 1888–89.
Life and Letters, ed. S. T. Pickard, 2 vols., Boston: Houghton, Mifflin, 1894.

D.B.H.

WHYTE-MELVILLE, G. J. (George John) (1821–78) was born at Strathkinness (Fifeshire) and educated at Eton, held a captaincy in the Coldstream Guards and served in the Crimea. Returning in 1859, he devoted himself to field sports and to writing. His first work, *Digby Grand* (1853) portrayed the life of an officer on service abroad and at leisure in town, whilst *The Interpreter* (1858) drew on his experiences in the Crimea. *Holmby House* (1860) treats of the Civil War and *The Gladiators* (1863) is a study of Rome in decline. His best work, however, is about hunting, notably *Market Harborough* (1861) which is set in the Pytchley Hunt country. A.P.

WIGGLESWORTH, Michael (1631–1705) was born in England and graduated in 1651 from Harvard, where he taught for a while. From 1656 until his death he was minister and doctor at Malden (Massachusetts). A long illness kept him from preaching regularly, and he propagated the gospel through poetry. "God's Controversy with New England," written as a warning of God's displeasure after a serious drought (1662), in fact suggests great love for the place and for the people, if not for their sins. *The Day of Doom* (1662), a popular exposition of Augustinian and Calvinist soteriology, is written in rhyming fourteeners which sound, at worst, like Bottom playing Pyramus, and at best like plain, efficient morality-play dialogue. It was avidly read and went through twelve editions by the end of the eighteenth century.   S.A.F.

WILBUR, Richard (1921–) was born in New York City and is a graduate of Amherst and Harvard. He has held various academic posts and was awarded a Pulitzer Prize in 1957. He has translated Molière, edited Poe and written the lyrics for Leonard Bernstein's "Candide." Wilbur's poetry, as exemplified by *Things of the World* (1956), has all the civilized virtues—grace, precision and catholicity. He has deliberately limited the range of his writing, claiming that the genie gains his strength from the fact that he is confined within the bottle. Wilbur's verse has wider range than his detractors would allow and in work since *Advice to a Prophet* (1961) he has shown a new frankness and strength.   D.V.W.

WILDE, Oscar (1854–1900), son of an eminent surgeon, was educated at Trinity College, Dublin and Magdalen College, Oxford, emerging as the aesthete *par excellence* as a result of the unwitting influence of Mahaffy and Pater. The role of dandy and literary wit became his hallmark after a brief stay in Paris. His brilliant and frequently notorious career as an essayist, poet, novelist and dramatist was cut short in 1895. Accused of homosexuality, he was sentenced to two years' imprisonment. On his release, broken in health, he retired to France and died in Paris in November 1900.

Ultimately a series of confidences, Wilde's work is mainly concerned with the art-nature dialectic. In *Dorian Gray* (1891) he envisages life attempting to imitate art which exists in an ideal realm beyond space and time. In his critical work, *Intentions* (1891), he upholds the neutrality of art, denying society's claim on the artist. He seeks to resolve the aesthetic-moral conflict by means of Matthew Arnold's notion that art as "the most intense form of individualism" is a realized epitome of the life that social change will ultimately make generally possible. The comedies, Wilde's finest work, written in the tradition of such Restoration "comedy of manners" playwrights as Congreve, consolidate his literary theories with pungent wit and social criticism of philistines and puritans, whilst at the same time providing another vehicle for self-confession. When an outraged society condemned him, this element of ritual, so much a part of his poetic and dramatic technique, at length colored his life. The most representative figure of his age, he is also its scapegoat.

Poems, 1881.
Intentions, 1891.
The Picture of Dorian Gray, 1891.
Salomé (French edition), 1893; trans. Lord A. Douglas, 1894.
Lady Windermere's Fan, 1893 (*p.* 1892; *f.* 1949).
A Woman of No Importance, 1894 (*p.* 1893).
The Ballad of Reading Gaol, 1898.
An Ideal Husband, 1899 (*p.* 1895; *f.* 1948).
The Importance of Being Earnest, 1899 (*p.* 1895; *f.* 1952).
De Profundis, 1905; 1949.

Complete Works, introd. V. Holland, London: Collins, 1966.
Letters, ed. R. Hart-Davis, London: Hart-Davis; New York: Harcourt, Brace, 1962.
Literary Criticism, ed. S. Weintraub, Lincoln: Univ. of Nebraska Press, 1969.   J.O'M.

WILDER, Thornton (1897–   ) was born in Madison (Wisconsin). His father was a newspaper editor and strict Congregationalist, his mother the daughter of a Presbyterian minister. He was educated at Oberlin and Yale and, despite poor eyesight, served in the armed forces in both World Wars. His first novel, *The Cabala* (1926), passed unnoticed, but the success of his second, *The Bridge of San Luis Rey* (1927), enabled him to devote himself full time to writing. Both these works, set in Italy and eighteenth-century Peru respectively, showed the influence of his religious upbringing, for Wilder in a series of linked character sketches suggested the possibility of individual redemption even in a period of social and cultural decline. *Heaven's My Destination* (1935), his only American novel, showed Wilder at odds with the materialism of his age in his half-sympathetic, half-ironic portrait of George Brush, a naïve fundamentalist and holy innocent. *Our Town* (1938) sought to capture the rhythms of daily life in a small New England town, but it also exposed the limitations of Wilder's conception of theater as a "generalized experience." This is even more evident in the Joycean *The Skin of Our Teeth* (1942). Wilder, however, was influential in breaking down the conventions of naturalism in favor of a more flexible and self-conscious theatricality. He has also written *The Matchmaker* (1955), a comedy arguing the unfashionable Mandevillian thesis of private vices as public virtues, and two novels with classical settings, *The Woman of Andros* (1930), which depicted a pagan world struggling towards Christianity, and *The Ides of March* (1948), in which Wilder portrayed Caesar as an existential hero.

The Cabala, 1926.
The Bridge of San Luis Rey, 1927.
The Women of Andros, 1930.
Heaven's My Destination, 1935.
Our Town, 1938 (f. 1940).
The Skin of Our Teeth, 1942.
The Ides of March, 1948.
The Matchmaker, 1955 (f. 1958).   D.P.M.

WILKES, John (1727–97) found an exaggerated notoriety as a de-bauchee in the Hell-fire Club. His greatest achievements were those of an eminent radical politician, but his speeches, letters, libels and even his obscene poems show something of the intellectual agility and clever-ness which made him a success as member of Parliament and lord mayor of London. The same qualities inform his work for the successful, if limited, periodical, *The North Briton*, founded in 1762 to attack Lord Bute. There is still no complete edition.   A.W.B

WILLIAMS, Charles (1886–1945), born in London, even as a child showed a remarkable disposition towards religion. After two years at London University, poverty ended his academic career. He then worked for four years in the Methodist Bookroom in Holborn and in 1908 moved to the Oxford University Press. In spite of his lack of formal education, he was at the end of his life appointed lecturer at Oxford and awarded an honorary M.A. He died there suddenly in 1945.

Neglected by critics, particularly in the later Arthurian poems which he felt to be his most important work, Williams's achievement is difficult to assess. He began by writing poetry, publishing his first volume in 1912 privately under the auspices of Alice Meynell. His later work includes religious poetic dramas, seven novels or "metaphysical" thrillers, six biographies, a history of Christendom (*The Descent of the Dove*) and many essays on literature and religion. His work is characterized by a concern for mystical experience as part of ordinary life and consistently preaches what he terms the "affirmative way of life," illustrated in the "images" of poetry, love, nature and art. Although at home in Arthurian romance and contemporary London, there is a strong insistence in his writing on the importance of ritual in everyday life.

Poetry at Present, 1930.
War in Heaven, 1930.
Many Dimensions, 1931.
The Place of the Lion, 1931.
The Greater Trumps, 1932.

Descent into Hell, 1937.
Taliessin through Logres, 1938.
The Descent of the Dove, 1939.
The Figure of Beatrice: A Study in Dante, 1943.
The Region of the Summer Stars, 1944.
All Hallows' Eve, 1945.
Arthurian Torso (completed by C. S. Lewis), 1948.

Collected Plays, ed. J. Heath-Stubbs, London: Oxford Univ. Press, 1963.

A.P.H.

WILLIAMS, Denis. See **Caribbean Literature.**

WILLIAMS, Roger (c. 1604–83), born in London and educated at the Charterhouse and Cambridge, was ordained in 1628 or 1629, migrating shortly after to Massachusetts. A separatist, he fell foul of the authorities there, was expelled, and became a founder of Rhode Island. While he was in England in 1643 to 1644 and from 1651 to 1654 his polemical books, mainly against the practices of the Massachusetts churches, were printed. Williams is rightly remembered for advocacy of liberty of conscience and wrongly as an "early American democrat." His fame is higher in the United States, where he has been studied in isolation, than in England where he is seen as one of a number arguing for toleration. He is also remembered for his humane treatment of the Indians.

A Key into the Language of America, 1643.
The Bloudy Tenent of Persecution . . ., 1644.
The Bloody Tenent Yet More Bloody, 1652.
Letter to the Town of Providence, 1655.

Writings, 6 vols., Narraganset Club, 1866–1874.

R.S.

WILLIAMS, Tennessee (Thomas Lanier) (1911–) was born in Columbus (Mississippi), the son of a traveling salesman. Later his family moved to St. Louis. He graduated from high school in 1929 and attended the University of Missouri, but in 1932 he was forced to drop out and work in the International Shoe Company, in which his father was employed. After a breakdown three years later, he resumed his studies and eventually graduated from the University of Iowa in 1938. In 1939 he was awarded a Group Theatre prize for three one-act plays called *American Blues*. A Rockefeller Fellowship enabled him to write his first full-length play, *Battle of Angels* (1940) (reworked as *Orpheus Descending* in 1957), which closed without reaching New York. *The Glass Menagerie* (1945), by contrast, ran on Broadway for over a year. Both *A Streetcar Named Desire* (1947) and *Cat on a Hot Tin Roof* (1955) were awarded Pulitzer Prizes. Many of his plays have been made into films and he also wrote the original screenplay for *Baby Doll*. He has also written poetry, short stories and a novel, *The Roman Spring of Mrs. Stone* (1950).

Williams's favorite characters turn aside from a world in which they are ill at ease and out of place. After the pattern of Blanche Dubois in *A Streetcar Named Desire* they tend to be rootless wanderers, forever denied the security of a home and compelled by their sensitivity to take refuge in a world of their imagination. Williams's plays tend to focus on some traumatic, even horrifying, episode in which a brutal world abruptly shatters the fragile identity which they have built up—a moment which, as in *The Glass Menagerie* and *The Rose Tattoo*, is often treated in a spirit of grotesque comedy. Comedy, in fact, is crucial to Williams's vision, for it gives it greater reality and conviction, and when it disappears, his work. is always in danger of becoming unbalanced. After *Suddenly Last Summer* (1958), the Darwinian implications of his view of life as a brutal struggle for existence became explicit in imagery of turtles and iguanas, in a still greater concern with violence and destructiveness, in his own statement that "we are all savages at heart but observing a few amenities of civilized behavior." The fear of death and decay already present in *Cat on a Hot Tin Roof* became a central preoccupation in *Sweet Bird of Youth* and *The Milk Train Doesn't Stop Here Anymore*. In these plays, however, there was a straining after effect, a portentous solemnity, a reliance on vague and unconvincing symbolism that was a disappointment after the careful characterization, psychological insight, delicacy of feeling and sense of theater that marked his earlier work.

Battle of Angels, 1940.
The Glass Menagerie, 1945 (*p.* 1944; *f.* 1950).
You Touched Me! (with Donald Windham), 1947 (*p.* 1945).
27 Wagons Full of Cotton, 1946 (includes *This Property Is Condemned*, *f.* 1966).
A Streetcar Named Desire, 1947 (*f.* 1951).
American Blues: Five Short Plays, 1948 (collection enlarged from 3 of 1939).
Summer and Smoke, 1948 (*p.* 1947; *f.* 1961).
The Roman Spring of Mrs. Stone, 1950 (*f.* 1961).
The Rose Tattoo, 1951 (*p.* 1950; *f.* 1954).
Camino Real, 1953.
Cat on a Hot Tin Roof, 1955 (*f.* 1958).
Baby Doll, 1956 (*f.* 1956).
Orpheus Descending, 1958 (*p.* 1957; *f.* as *The Fugitive Kind*, 1960).
Suddenly Last Summer, 1958 (*f.* 1959).

Sweet Bird of Youth, 1959 (*f.* 1962).
Period of Adjustment, 1960 (*f.* 1962).
The Night of the Iguana, 1962 (*p.* 1961; *f.* 1964).
The Milk Train Doesn't Stop Here Anymore, 1964 (*p.* 1962; *f.* as *Boom*, 1968).
The Eccentricities of a Nightingale, 1965.
Kingdom of Earth: The 7 Descents of Myrtle, 1968.
Small Craft Warnings, 1972.   D.P.M.

WILLIAMS, William Carlos (1883–1963) was born in Rutherford (New Jersey) and, except for the years between 1897 and 1899 which he spent in Switzerland and Paris, went to school there. He then took a degree in medicine at the University of Pennsylvania where he began his lifelong friendship with Ezra Pound. He came to specialize in children's medicine and worked his internship in hospitals on the West Side of Manhattan. In 1909 he visited Europe again, staying in Leipzig, Paris, Italy, Spain, and for one week in London with Pound. There he found "an intense literary atmosphere," which, though he found it thrilling, "seemed completely foreign to anything I desired." Returning to America he began to practice medicine in Rutherford, where he was to work and live for the rest of his life. In 1912 he married Florence Herman.

Williams's first volume of poetry, *Poems*, "bad Keats, nothing else—oh well, bad Whitman, too," as he described it, was published privately in 1909. But several influences were combining to reduce this dependence on established poetic tradition, especially the English models. There were his friends and contacts who were developing contemporary poetry (Pound, Marianne Moore, Hilda Doolittle, Alfred Kreymborg), his excitement at what he saw happening in art, particularly as manifested at the Armory Show in New York in 1913, and most importantly there was his basic and growing sense of his own circumstances and *American* locality. "From the beginning I felt I was *not* English. If poetry had to be written I had to do it in my own way." His own way was a line determined not by metrical precedent but by the pace and rhythm of his own speech, and therefore in short lines, "because of my nervous nature." For subject matter he chose increasingly the sights and incidents that he encountered each ordinary working day. So throughout *The Collected Earlier Poems* (1951) are poems like "The Young Housewife," "Complaint," several poems called "Pastoral," "This Is Just to Say," which are brief rhythmic impressions of someone he might have passed in his car, or of ramshackle houses, a patient he is called to, his arrival home late at night after work. So simple in subject matter, these poems depend on the immediate clarity of Williams's language for their arrest in the reader's mind. It is this quality in Williams which led Kenneth Burke to call him "the master of the glimpse," and it is, even in more ambitious work, the vital thread of his poetry. This same long-standing fascination with portrayal of everyday scenes is the source of his obsession, right at the end of his career, with the painter Breughel.

But Williams's sense of American locality was not limited to these small pictures. He tried in his prose work *In the American Grain* (1925) to come to terms with the continent and nation as a whole—as he put it, "to possess it." The book is a series of essays, little influenced by conventional historical method, on various key figures and incidents in the history of America. Its heroes are those whom Williams recognized as able to live without fear or inhibition in the New World—Montezuma, Père Rasles, Daniel Boone—and his villains those like Cortez and the Puritan founders who had the Old World too much with them in their retreat into restriction and conservatism.

The five books of his long poem *Paterson* are similarly large in their scope. Making a start "out of particulars," Williams uses the geography of the Passaic river and its falls and the history and society of the New Jersey city, together with that of his own life, to write a poem "of a man identified with a city." It is at once a vision of modern America and of "the way I felt about life, like a river, following a course." Besides the familiar manner of Williams's colloquial verse, with occasional passages in more rhetorical vein, Williams makes use in *Paterson* of prose, documentary material and personal letters. Book 1 appeared in 1946 and book 5 in 1958, but Williams left fragments towards a sixth book which he was unable to finish before his death.

In his career Williams also wrote essays, plays, novels and short stories. His collected stories, *The Farmers' Daughters*, appeared in 1961, but together with *Pictures from Breughel* (1962), the most notable of his later work are the love poems in *The Desert Music* (1954) and *Journey to Love* (1955).

(See also **Imagism.**)

Poems, (privately) 1909.
Kora in Hell: Improvisations, 1920.
Spring and All, 1923.
The Great American Novel, 1923.
In the American Grain, 1925.
Collected Poems, 1921–31, 1934.
White Mule, 1937 (novel).
Complete Collected Poems, 1906–38, 1938.
In the Money, 1940 (novel).
Paterson, 5 books, 1946–58.
A Dream of Love, 1948 (play).

The Pink Church, 1949.
Make Light of It: Collected Stories, 1950.
Autobiography, 1951.
The Build-Up, 1952 (novel).
The Desert Music and Other Poems, 1954.
Journey to Love, 1955.
I Wanted to Write a Poem: The Autobiography of the Works of a Poet, ed. E. Heal, 1958.
The Farmers' Daughters, 1961 (collected stories).
Many Loves and Other Plays, 1961.
Pictures from Breughel and Other Poems, 1962.

Collected Later Poems, Norfolk, Conn.: New Directions, 1950; revised, 1963; London: MacGibbon & Kee, 1963.
Collected Earlier Poems, Norfolk Conn.: New Directions, 1951; London: MacGibbon & Kee, 1966.
Paterson, Books 1–5, Norfolk Conn.: New Directions, 1963; London: MacGibbon & Kee, 1964.
Selected Essays, New York: Random House, 1954.
Selected Letters, ed. J. C. Thirlwall, New York: McDowell, Obolensky, 1957.   J.P.W.

WILSON, Angus (1913–) spent his childhood in South Africa and then was educated at Westminster School and Oxford. He became a member of the staff of the British Museum, and after service with the Foreign Office during the Second World War, he returned there, becoming deputy superintendent of the Reading Room before his retirement in 1955 to devote himself fully to the pursuit of journalism and literature. His life during these years brought him into close touch with the scholars, academic administrators and dwellers on the literary fringe who play such a large part in his novels and stories.

He is most widely known as a novelist, but it is at least arguable that his short stories give his particular talent most scope. The main line of interest in these stories is best indicated by the titles of two of them, *The Wrong Set* (1949) and *A Bit off the Map* (1957). In the former, lively and at first sight simply comic stories present elegant and amusing accounts of various contemporary characters and situations; but, ultimately, the stories are seen to expose the pretentiousness and the pathetic futility of much of modern civilization by a fusion of contempt and compassion that is peculiarly Wilson's own. Here, as elsewhere in his work, the power of the stories lies chiefly in the absolute accuracy of the dialogue; the author has a remorselessly acute ear for the falsities and affections of semi-fashionable talk and he captures vulgarity of mind in a series of splendidly observed banalities. *A Bit off the Map* moves into a rather different kind of "wrong set." Here he explores not only the frontiers of society, but the frontiers of sanity; he catches with frightening force the half-world of the mind.

In the novels many of the characteristics and qualities of the stories remain, but they are diffused, and some of the astringency is lost. *Hemlock and After* (1952) and *Anglo-Saxon Attitudes* (1956) both deal in part with the academic and near-academic world. *Hemlock and After* has elements of grotesque and effective melodrama, ranging, like the stories, from the comic to the horrible. Though Wilson's style is very different, there are marked Dickensian elements. As a whole, however, the novel is seriously weakened in its handling of human relationships by more than a touch of sentimentality; what is actually offered to the reader does not seem to justify the degree of feeling that is demanded. *Anglo-Saxon Attitudes* is more secure in tone; the humor is more subtle, and the complex tangle of relationships is handled with clarity and dramatic control. Characterization is more mature and dispassionate, and the people of the novel take on individuality. The moral, emotional and intellectual problems are embodied in the interplay of personal relationships; people, as well as principles, are in conflict. The next novel, *The Middle Age of Mrs. Eliot* (1958), was something of a new departure, and something unusual in the serious novel of the postwar years in that it gains its strength from the direct detailed presentation and analysis of the central character. The many subsidiary characters and events are interesting in themselves, but they are all subordinated to Mrs. Eliot; their function is to display her. It is a *tour de force* of construction, all the more remarkable in that it produces the total effect of a very warm humanity; it is a generous and understanding novel. The later novels, particularly *Late Call* (1964) and *No Laughing Matter* (1967), are extremely intelligent but give the effect of being largely exploratory; they perhaps lack the individuality that distinguishes the works discussed here. Wilson is also author of a critical study of *Emile Zola* (1950), a play, *The Mulberry Bush* (1956; *p.* 1955), and a considerable body of good critical journalism.

The Wrong Set, and Other Stories, 1949.
Such Darling Dodos, and Other Stories, 1950.
Hemlock and After, 1952.
Anglo-Saxon Attitudes, 1956.
A Bit off the Map, and Other Stories, 1957.
The Middle Age of Mrs. Eliot, 1958.
The Old Men at the Zoo, 1961.
Late Call, 1964.
No Laughing Matter, 1967.   C.H.

WILSON, Edmund (1895–1972) was born in Red Bank (New Jersey). After a distinguished undergraduate career at Princeton he became a reporter on the New York *Evening Sun*. He returned to journalism after service in the First World War, first as managing editor of *Vanity Fair*, and later as the book review editor of *The New Republic*. He also had a long association with *The New Yorker*. In addition to his prolific output of criticism he wrote poetry, fiction and plays, and produced a number of books of social commentary based on his travels throughout the world. He also studied Hebrew and Biblical manuscripts and produced in 1955 a study of *The Dead Sea Scrolls*.

In the dedicatory letter to Christian Gauss at the beginning of his first major critical work, *Axel's Castle*, Wilson outlined his idea of what criticism ought to be—"a history of man's ideas and imaginings in the setting of the conditions which have shaped them." In fact, the context within which he studied literary works often tended to be much narrower than is suggested by that formulation—biographical and psychological rather than social, religious or political. For the most part, however, Wilson eschewed critical theory altogether and did not attempt to define critical terms or defend premises, but merely to judge particular works according to implicit standards derived pragmatically.

Wilson's passionate interest in social and moral problems is reflected in the subject matter of his novels, short stories and plays, the best of which, *Memoirs of Hecate County*, tales of social and moral disintegration in New York's suburbia, has been compared to Faulkner's *Go Down, Moses* and Sherwood Anderson's *Winesburg, Ohio*.

I Thought of Daisy, 1929 (novel).
Axel's Castle, 1931 (criticism).
The Triple Thinkers, 1938 (criticism).
The Wound and the Bow, 1941 (criticism).
Memoirs of Hecate County, 1946.
Classics and Commercials, 1950 (criticism).
The Shores of Light, 1952 (criticism).
Night Thoughts, 1961 (poetry and prose).
Five Plays, 1954.
Patriotic Gore, 1962 (criticism).   B.L.

WILSON, John ("Christopher North") (1785–1854) is best known as a prolific periodical journalist, but he was also professor of moral philosophy at Edinburgh University. With Lockhart he directed *Blackwood's Magazine* and was connected with it to the end of his life. As a critic he is to be numbered with the Romantics; he had an immense admiration for

Wordsworth. He contributed largely to the imaginary conversations, *Noctes Ambrosianae*, which appeared in *Blackwood's* from 1822 to 1835. This work covers a multiplicity of subjects and displays his characteristic energy, ingenuity and humor.

Collected Works, 12 vols., Edinburgh: Blackwood, 1855–58.   A.P.

WILSON, John Burgess. See **"Burgess, Anthony."**

WINCHILSEA, Anne Finch, Countess of (1661–1720) left the court, where before her marriage she had been maid of honor to the duchess of York, at the Revolution of 1688, and spent the rest of her life in retirement with her husband, writing in a variety of verse forms with a grace and delicacy that preclude neither ironic wit nor warm feeling. Wordsworth described her style as "chaste, tender and vigorous" and particularly admired poems such as "A Nocturnal Reverie"—in *Gildon's Miscellany* (1701)—in which she displays her sensitive feeling for nature. Her verse fables, which he disliked, rank second only to Gay's.

The Spleen: a Pindarique Ode, in C. Gildon's *New Miscellany*, 1701; 1709.
Miscellany Poems on Several Occasions, 1713; as *Poems on Several Occasions*, 1714.

Poems, ed. M. Reynolds, Chicago: Univ. of Chicago Press, 1903.
Minor Poets of the Eighteenth Century, ed. H. I'A. Fausset, London: Dent; New York: Dutton, 1930.   R.E.

WINSTANLEY, Gerrard. See **Political Pamphlets.**

WINTERS, Yvor (1900–68) was born and educated in Chicago. From 1928 until his death he lived and worked in California, where he taught at Stanford University. Winters's strongly individualistic criticism is characterized by a vehement rejection of all Romantic and *symboliste* theories of poetry. Poetry, he insists, must be based on the rational understanding and moral evaluation of experience. He has consistently attacked those poets who have abandoned logical, paraphrasable statement in favor of "pseudo-reference" and "qualitative progression," both of which reflect the "fallacy of imitative form." His thoroughgoing indictment of romantic vagueness and immorality has led him to attack the work of most modern major writers, including T. S. Eliot, Ezra Pound and James Joyce. Winters's most important books of criticism—*Primitivism and Decadence* (1937), *Maule's Curse* (1938) and *Anatomy of Nonsense* (1943)— were published collectively as *In Defense of Reason* (1947). His poetry—

awarded the Bollingen Prize in 1960—reflects the positive aspects of his preoccupation with classical technique.   B.L.

WINTHROP, John (1588–1649), descended from minor Suffolk gentry, spent time at Cambridge and was a member of Gray's Inn. Attorney at the Court of Wards in 1627, he joined the Massachusetts Bay Company and led the migration to the new colony where he was often governor. His main work was his "journal" or day to day account of life in Massachusetts, published first in 1790. An account of the trial of Ann Hutchinson is also attributed to him. His letters and papers are now printed. His writings are a major source for the history of Massachusetts and for their illumination of a seventeenth-century Puritan mind.

Journal (published as *The History of New England from 1630 to 1649*), ed. J. Savage, 2 vols., Boston: Little, Brown, 1825–26; 1853.
Papers, ed. A. B. Forbes, 5 vols., Boston: Massachusetts Historical Society, 1929–47.   R.S.

WISTER, Owen (1860–1938) was a Pennsylvanian who graduated from Harvard. He made trips to Wyoming, publishing *Lin McLean* (1898) and *The Jimmyjohn Boss* (1900), short stories concerning the cattle country of the West. *The Virginian* (1902; *f.* 1929), a very popular book which presented Wyoming cowboys of the late nineteenth century, made the cowboy an acceptable figure for serious fiction; in the figure of the hero Wister combined the values of the Wild West and the civilized East. He published *Philosophy 4* (1903), about Harvard, and *Lady Baltimore* (1906), a romantic novel set in Charleston. He also wrote biographies of Grant (1900), Washington (1907), and Roosevelt (1930).

Writings, 11 vols., New York: Macmillan Co., 1928.   E.A.

WITHER, George (1588–1667), born in Hampshire, was educated at Magdalen College, Oxford, and entered Lincoln's Inn. During the early part of his career he was twice imprisoned in the Marshalsea because poems by him had displeased the government. He was pro-Puritan (although he fought with Charles I against the Scots in 1639) and raised a troop of horse for Parliament in the Civil War, during which he emerged as the most prominent satirical propagandist in the Parliamentary camp. Wither became a man of substance as a result of the war, but his property was confiscated and he himself imprisoned at the Restoration. His chief literary friend was William Browne.

Although Wither is generally remembered as a satirist and although his first publication, *Abuses Stript and Whipt* (1613), was satirical, his best verse is probably in the pastoral lyricism to be found particularly in *The Shepherd's Hunting* (1615) and *Fidelia* (1615), the fluent prettiness and fresh delicacy of which are summed up in the famous lyric, "Shall I, Wasting in Despair." Wither was tremendously prolific, especially in his favorite seven-syllable couplets, and seldom wrote well for any extended period. His later career consisted mainly in writing religious poems like *Hallelujah* (1641) and satirical scribbling for the Parliamentary cause. This satirical work is often amazingly bad, but a few poems have some vividness and point.

Abuses Stript and Whipt, 1613.
Fidelia, (privately) 1615.
The Shepherd's Hunting, 1615.
A Collection of Emblems, 1635.
Hallelujah, 1641.

Poetry, ed. F. Sidgwick, 2 vols., London: A. H. Bullen, 1902.   G.P.

WODEHOUSE, P. G. (Pelham Grenville) (1881–   ), born at Guildford (Surrey) and educated at Dulwich, became a professional writer in 1903. Among his prolific output of novels have been *Enter Psmith* (in U.S.A., *Mike*) (1909), *Leave it to Psmith* (1923), *Ukridge* (1924), *Carry On, Jeeves!* (1925), *Right Ho, Jeeves* (1934), *The Code of the Woosters* (1938), *Ring for Jeeves* (1953) and *The Return of Jeeves* (1954). Wodehouse's world seems untouched by the pressures of twentieth-century life, but nonetheless he has converted artificiality into a skillful and individual comic art, and some of his characters have become household names. The lightness of his comedy does not disguise the fact that Wodehouse is a very professional and able technician. At his best he suggests an indulgent and affectionate view of the social world satirized in the early novels of Evelyn Waugh.   G.A.K.

WOLCOT, John ("Peter Pindar") (1738–1819), after an adventurous but unprofitable career as doctor and cleric in England and Jamaica, turned his talent for scurrilous jog-trot rhyming and his quick eye for the absurd to unashamedly economic use. He made his name with annual *Lyric Odes to the Royal Academicians* (1782–85), attacking the members of the Royal Society. Canto 1 of *The Lousiad*, the first and best of many satires on the royal family, appeared in 1785, followed by two blistering poems on the Johnson circle, *Bozzy and Piozzi* and *An Epistle to James Boswell* (1786). His great if inflated success was followed by blindness, death and equally disproportionate and rapid literary eclipse.

Works, 4 vols., London, 1816.   A.W.B.

WOLFE, Thomas (1900–38), the youngest of eight children, was born in Asheville (North Carolina) of affluent parents; his father was a stone-cutter and his mother ran a boardinghouse. At fifteen he went to the University of North Carolina, where he was active in the Debating Club and the Carolina Playmakers. In 1920 he went up to Harvard and to the 47 Workshop, George Pierce Baker's playwriting class, later treated satirically in *Of Time and the River*. Wolfe wrote several plays, took his M.A. and, between 1924 and 1930, taught intermittently at New York University. In 1925 he fell in love with Aline Bernstein (Esther Jack in *The Web and the Rock*); their affair lasted until 1930, just after the publication of *Look Homeward, Angel* (1929). Maxwell Perkins of Scribners had edited it from the original manuscript and later did the same for *Of Time and the River* (1935), quarried from the thousands of pages originally entitled "The October Fair." Wolfe's feelings during this period are recounted in *The Story of a Novel* (1936). For various reasons the Wolfe-Perkins partnership disintegrated soon afterwards and, in the spring of 1938, Wolfe gave to Harpers, his new publisher, a manuscript "breast high from the floor," which Edward C. Aswell later turned into *The Web and the Rock* (1939), *You Can't Go Home Again* (1940) and *The Hills Beyond* (short stories) (1941). Wolfe himself died later in 1938 after contracting pneumonia.

Wolfe's cultural roots lay in the nineteenth century; the Romantic tradition manifests itself in his doctrine of self-expression (and self-realization), in his feeling for the wonder and mystery of life, and in his Wordsworthian belief that existence moves us away from perfection. In his work, which is one continuous autobiographical narrative, there is an emphasis on the role of memory and on the need to rescue past moments from time and history. Undisciplined revelation often led to disjointedness, and not until *You Can't Go Home Again* did Wolfe achieve an awareness of the proper use of the personal past. But the epic strain in him was consistent. His deep interest in the vast American continent and its people is one of his redeeming qualities; along with the overflowing rhetoric, there are graphic descriptions of local sights, sounds and smells, conveyed, in Wolfe's phrase, with "concrete vividness."

Wolfe was a product of the social center, a recipient of Victorian humanistic idealism and thus, logically, an advocate of liberal democracy. His parents were upper bourgeois, and Wolfe made them the first of many remarkable portraits of dynamic, colorful, middle-class characters. In *Look Homeward, Angel* they are W. O. Gant, with his great appetite for life, and Eliza Gant, proud, egocentric, acquisitive. Wolfe's novel covers the first twenty years of Eugene Gant's life, describing the effects of money, death, art and sex on a single family whose daily activities open up small-town life. Some of the inhabitants of Asheville, people with "dusty, little pint-measure minds," resented Wolfe's honesty, but it is Wolfe's best novel, coherent, lyrical, humorous and evoking with great skill the atmosphere of a specific time and place. It is also "A Story of the Buried Life" (subtitle), a story of human loneliness, of youthful emotions and of Wolfe's desire, evident also in the later works, to "devour the whole body of human experience."

The two novels which followed have justly been criticized for their formlessness and verbosity. Diffuse, labored and overrhetorical, they are often lacking in narrative inventiveness, but they contain memorable passages. In *Of Time and the River*, which continues to chronicle Eugene Gant's career as a young man, at Harvard and in New York, the description of the death of W. O. Gant and the portrait of Bascom Pentland are evidence of Wolfe's talent. His accounts of trains, stations and railway journeys are notable, but the lonely hero's endless searching soon becomes wearisome. Most of the last part of *The Web and the Rock*, which traces, in a curiously nonphysical way, the affair between the shadowy hero (now named George Webber) and Esther Jack, is in the same fluid, lyrical style, but the episodic first part, which covers the same period as *Look Homeward, Angel*, is more objective and more controlled. Though *The Web and the Rock* is uneven and disconnected, it does contain some effective satire of New York's literary circle and of Southern Agrarians; Wolfe knew all about "the old stricken wounded 'Southness' of cruelty and lust."

You Can't Go Home Again is another matter. Although loosely constructed, it displays Wolfe in the role of social critic; in his exploration of business, politics, race and current affairs he observes his own times with acute penetration. For students of the American Depression the novel is essential reading. Wolfe brings to life the greed and madness of Libya Hill during the hysteria of a pre-1929 real estate boom and creates the figure of Judge Rumford Bland, who, in his blindness, lost potentiality and degeneration, symbolizes the town whose disastrous future he predicts. Then, in book 2, Wolfe exposes the moral hypocrisy and decadent aestheticism of the wealthy guests attending "The Party at Jack's" just before the stock market crash. Toughness, accuracy and control distinguish these assaults; later he focuses on homeless Depression victims, seeking warmth in public lavatories close to Wall Street, and on the fearful atavism of Hitler's Germany. Webber recognizes man's tragic destiny but also the need to "deny it all along the way." So the novel ends with his "Credo": "I believe that we are lost here in America but I believe we shall be found . . . I think the true fulfillment of our spirit, of our people, of our mighty and immortal land, is yet to come."

Wolfe was self-confessedly one of the "great putter-inners," so that his meandering prose and carelessness about structure have tended to conceal his virtues—his ability to depict character and scene, his verbal vitality, his moral awareness and his compassion. Like Cooper, he may be remembered as the creator of dazzling fragments, not only parts of the novels, but the poignant stories in *From Death to Morning*, including the Joycean short novel, "The Web of Earth," with its remarkable handling of spoken language.

Look Homeward, Angel, 1929.
Of Time and the River, 1935.
From Death to Morning, 1935.
The Story of a Novel, 1936.
The Web and the Rock, 1939.
You Can't Go Home Again, 1940.
The Hills Beyond, 1941.
Mannerhouse, 1948 (play).

Letters to His Mother, ed. J. S. Terry, New York: C. Scribner's Sons, 1943; ed. C. H. Holman and S. F. Ross, Chapel Hill: Univ. of North Carolina Press, 1968.
Letters, ed. E. Nowell, New York: C. Scribner's Sons, 1956.   R.W.

WOLFE, Tom (1931–) born in Richmond (Virginia), educated at Washington and Lee University and Yale, chronicles American pop culture, often in the language of advertisements and comic strips. He is fascinated by those status groups created as alternatives to conventional society—*Playboy's* Hugh Hefner and his special friends, surfer gangs, go-go girls, and Hell's Angels. His articles are collected in *The Kandy-Kolored Tangerine-Flake Streamline Baby* (1965), *The Pump House Gang* (1968) and *Radical Chic and Mau-Mauing the Flak Catchers* (1971). *The Electric Kool-Aid Acid Test* (1968) retails the adventures of Ken Kesey's peripatetic commune.   J.L.M.

WOOD, Anthony à. See **Ballads.**

WOODFORDE, James (1740–1803) was a fellow and for a time subwarden of New College, Oxford, where he began his diary in 1758. From 1774 till his death he was rector of Weston Longeville (Norfolk), and his diary is particularly valued for the exactness and truthfulness with which it describes English country life in the late eighteenth century. Woodforde was a man of no special gifts or intelligence. The very average, everyday quality of his record, revealingly preoccupied with food and drink, adds to its savor and authenticity.

The Diary of a Country Parson, 1758–1802, ed. J. Beresford, 5 vols., London: Oxford Univ. Press, 1924–31.   W.R.

WOOLF, Virginia (1882–1941), born in London at Hyde Park Gate, Kensington, was the daughter of Sir Leslie Stephen, the Victorian editor, scholar and critic. She drew on memories of her rationalist father for the character of Mr. Ramsay in *To the Lighthouse*. After his death in 1904 she moved to 46, Gordon Square with her two brothers and her sister Vanessa, who was to marry the art critic, Clive Bell, a few years later. The house became one of the meeting places of the "Bloomsbury group," including friends like J. M. Keynes, Lytton Strachey and E. M. Forster. Many of them had been influenced at Cambridge by G. E. Moore, author of *Principia Ethica*; they sought "love, beauty and truth" and felt their values threatened by a philistine world. In 1912 Virginia married Leonard Woolf, whose autobiography is most informative about members of the group.

It was not until her third novel, *Jacob's Room* (1922), that Virginia Woolf thought she had at last, at the age of forty, begun to find her own voice as a writer. She was not deterred by criticism of what some regarded as her idiosyncratic manner and her next novel, *Mrs. Dalloway*, shows how thoroughly she had come to reject traditional methods in order to capture the life of the mind by new techniques of writing. *To the Lighthouse* (1927) is often considered her masterpiece; fittingly, the book ends with an artist putting the final successful touch to her painting. Experiments in form followed. *Orlando: A Biography* is a fantastic work— Orlando, though born about 1570, does not die until 1928, aged thirty-six and mysteriously changed in sex. *The Waves*, too, is strikingly unusual, a poetic attempt "to give the moment whole," as she wrote in her diary. Her last novel, *Between the Acts*, is a brilliant combination of prose, poetry and dialogue, and its quality emphasizes the loss to literature when this most sensitive of writers committed suicide not long after its completion.

The sustained thought she gave to her art is as obvious in the variety of her novels as it is in the selections so far published from her diary and all the many critical reviews and essays she wrote. She abandoned the more conventional novel of Wells, Bennett and Galsworthy, always seeking what she thought they lacked—life itself:

> Let us record the atoms as they fall upon the mind in the order in which they fall, let us trace the pattern, however disconnected and incoherent in appearance, which each sight or incident scores upon the consciousness. Let us not take it for granted that life exists more fully in what is commonly thought big than in what is commonly thought small. (*Modern Fiction*, 1919.)

This abandonment of the solid properties of ordinary novels could have led to a sterile aestheticism, but her best work is wonderfully rich and suggestive, awakening the reader to those moments of intensity and significance she found in both life and art.

The Voyage Out, 1915.
Night and Day, 1919.
Jacob's Room, 1922.
The Common Reader, 1925; second series, 1932.
Mrs. Dalloway, 1925.
To the Lighthouse, 1927.
Orlando: A Biography, 1928.
The Waves, 1931.
The Years, 1937.
Roger Fry: A Biography, 1940.
Between the Acts, 1941.
A Writer's Diary, ed. L. Woolf, 1953.

Collected Works, 14 vols., London: Hogarth Press; New York: Harcourt, Brace, 1929–52.
Collected Essays, 4 vols., London: Hogarth Press, 1966–67; New York: Harcourt, Brace, 1967.   J.C.

WOOLMAN, John (1720–72), New Jersey Quaker minister and missionary, traveled extensively in North America and visited England in 1772 where he died of smallpox at York. He early advocated the abolition of slavery and was a pioneer in this field; his arguments were known and used by later writers. He was also interested in the humanitarian relief of poverty—*A Plea for the Poor* (1793). His *Journal*, first published posthumously in 1774, has been often reprinted and translated into other languages, as have some of his other writings. His plain and simple, even naïve style has attracted critical praise. His works have the appeal of Quaker honesty and openness.

Journal and Essays, ed. A. M. Gummere, New York: Macmillan Co., 1922.
                                                                        R.S.

WORDSWORTH, William (1770–1850) was born at Cockermouth (Cumberland), second son of an attorney. Left an orphan at the age of thirteen, he was educated at Hawkshead Grammar School and St. John's College, Cambridge. In 1790 he visited France and Switzerland, returning to France for a longer and more momentous stay in 1791–92. Animated by generous personal sympathy for the poor, by idealistic revolutionary fervor and the ideas and example of Michel Beaupuy, he was on the point of taking an active part in the Girondist movement when he was recalled to England. During his time in Blois he fell in love with

Annette Vallon, who after his return to England gave birth to his daughter, whom he acknowledged. The couple, in the face of poverty, different religious faiths and the embarrassments of the war, did not marry, and there was little communication between them for the rest of Wordsworth's life.

In 1793 were published *An Evening Walk* and *Descriptive Sketches Taken during a Pedestrian Tour in the Alps*, poems whose conventionality of manner and matter gives no hint of the future trend of Wordsworth's poetry. After a year or so of great perplexity and hesitancy, both intellectual (he was disillusioned by the excesses of the Revolution) and practical (he could not settle on a congenial career), the year 1795 brought two decisive events: first, a legacy of £900 from his friend Raisley Calvert gave him the financial independence to dedicate himself fully to the pursuit of poetry; and secondly, he met Samuel Taylor Coleridge. At Racedown (Dorset) and then at Alfoxden (Somerset) Wordsworth, his sister Dorothy and Coleridge were constant companions. Coleridge stimulated him, clarified and modified his poetic ideas, and confirmed him in his poetic ambitions. With Coleridge in 1796 he projected, and in 1798 published, *Lyrical Ballads*, a collection which was a deliberate challenge to contemporary taste and a manifesto of poetic revolution. At this time, too, he started on the great object of his life, the philosophical poem *The Recluse*, which was never completed, and *The Prelude*, an "antechapel to *The Recluse*." The first complete draft of *The Prelude* (addressed to Coleridge) was finished by 1805, but did not appear until, considerably revised, it was published in 1850. A second edition of *Lyrical Ballads* appeared in 1800, with the celebrated Preface formulating the principles underlying the poems and stating, somewhat aggressively, Wordsworth's poetical creed. Wordsworth's marriage to Mary Hutchinson in 1802 marked the beginning of a two-year period of intense creativity, during which many of the pieces in *Poems in Two Volumes* (1807), much of two books of *The Excursion* (1814) and parts of *The Prelude* were written. In 1810 a misunderstanding brought about a deep estrangement between Wordsworth and Coleridge and, though they were later reconciled (1812), the old close spiritual intimacy was never completely reestablished. Coleridge's tepid reception, justifiable enough, of *The Excursion* probably contributed to Wordsworth's failure to continue with *The Recluse*, of which it was a part.

In 1813 Wordsworth was appointed distributor of stamps for Westmorland and moved into Rydal Mount, which was his home for the rest of his life. By this time the great creative period was at an end; though he continued to write actively, and to publish works previously written, nothing new appeared that had the force and freshness of the earlier work. There is, however, much to charm or impress in *The River Duddon* . . .

(1820), in fugitive pieces, and even in *Ecclesiastical Sonnets* (1822). But, strangely, it is at this time that Wordsworth's ascendancy over English poetry of the nineteenth century began to make itself clear; his work grew steadily in reputation and influence, no longer merely with the avant-garde, but with the common reader. A succession of editions of *Collected Works* kept his earlier poetry current, and in 1843 he succeeded Robert Southey as poet laureate. These later years were saddened by the insanity of his beloved sister Dorothy, and the death of his daughter Dora in 1847 caused a grief that lasted till his death. He died on 23 April 1850 and is buried in the churchyard at Grasmere.

Wordsworth is so intensely a personal poet, so deeply concerned with the workings of his own inner life, that a study of the various forces influencing him as a man is relevant to his poetry. He is, in Keats's words, the poet of "the egotistical sublime"; he is, more deliberately and self-consciously than is usual, the raw material for the reworking into poetry of his own private consciousness.

In reading Wordsworth's poetry, one is constantly aware of a strong and sometimes assertive personality, a strength that was early channeled into a lifelong dedication to poetry. Speaking of the moment when he first felt absolute conviction of his appointed mission, as he saw it, he says:

> I made no vows, but vows
> Were then made for me; bond unknown to me
> Was given, that I should be, else sinning greatly,
> A dedicated spirit.
> (*The Prelude* (1805), 4, 341–44)

This sense of dedication was crystallized by Coleridge and fostered through Wordsworth's long life by the unselfish and completely convinced support of his sister Dorothy and his wife Mary. Dorothy, particularly, to a degree only to be guessed, was his eyes, his inspiration and his constant source of encouragement. These factors were external to him; his vision of life was essentially his own; he saw it and passed it through the re-creative processes of his imagination ("emotion recollected in tranquillity"). He turned repeatedly to his own childhood and the environment of that time for the material of his verse. One of the great discoveries of the Romantics was the recognition of childhood as a formative period, and not merely a state of regrettable, though pretty, nonage—"The child is father of the man." Wordsworth's best poetry is based on the impressions of his earlier years. Amongst these the scenery and society of what is now known as the Lake District were predominant. The austere and rugged beauty of the high fells impressed him; he saw daily the arduous, but free, lives of the farmers and the peasants; he saw nature in itself, and nature and man in combination. They imposed on him a sense of grandeur and doggedness wedded together, and a strong sense of man tied closely to a natural order that molded and supported him, but which, at the same time, had ways of being that were beyond his comprehension.

These largely instinctive feelings found rationalizing support in his early political beliefs, which were very much a product of the revolutionary element in eighteenth-century thought. He found justification for such feelings in theories of the greater purity of man in a state near to nature. He retained throughout his life, even when his ideological beliefs had faded in the light of experience, a feeling for the human dignity of hardship and poverty stoically endured; and he never lost a sense of the equality of men *as men*, and of their right to justice. These intuitions and convictions helped to create his doctrinaire and arbitrary theory of poetic diction: the nearer to nature, the purer the man; the purer the man, the purer the feelings; the purer the feelings, the purer the language. They also produced what is more important—a determination to perceive and state essentials rather than accidents, to reach what is common to all men; to give, in short, examples of "unaccommodated man." There is, unfortunately, a reverse and debit side to this admirable design. In his search for the simple and ordinary he sometimes ascribed too much importance to the unspectacular, the commonplace and the banal; he failed at times to re-create for the reader the significance that he saw in a trivial incident. The result is bathos and what his earliest contemporary critics regarded, perhaps with justice, as simple silliness. But he enlarged the range of what is permissible to poetry and took it out of the eighteenth-century drawing room into a wider world.

It is customary, and reasonable enough, to see Wordsworth's early poetry as a deliberate and self-conscious individual revolt against the modes and values of accepted eighteenth-century poetry and the society of which it was the expression. In doing so, it is advisable to apply a corrective by considering the depth of Wordsworth's indebtedness to that society, to the thought it produced and to minds other than his own. He was much more "bookish" than he cared to admit in print. He was thoroughly acquainted with the poetry of Chaucer, Shakespeare, Milton and Spenser, whom he saw as his direct masters. Both *The Prelude* and *The Excursion*, in particular, have many reminiscences and even echoes of these writers. He read Greek, Latin, Italian, French and Spanish, and though he probably could not be accounted a scholar in any of them, his reading was far-ranging and by no means confined to poetry.

Possibly an equally strong and direct influence on his thought, however, came from his study of the philosophies of John Locke and David Hartley. Locke, in *An Essay concerning Human Understanding*, argued that experience is the sole basis of all knowledge and that all that we can know is what is presented to our own minds; this theory made man indeed the proper study of mankind. Hartley, influenced by Locke's materialism, evolved a theory of perception and understanding that conditioned Wordsworth's poetic theories throughout his whole life. Roughly, Hartley's theory is based on sensation: phenomena, making an impact on the observer's senses, gradually "by association" build up the higher faculties of imagination, affection and morality. But Wordsworth's earlier acceptance of this theory was greatly modified by his association with Coleridge. Whereas Locke and Hartley had seen the mind as essentially passive, a blank sheet on which messages were written by outside agencies, Coleridge, either independently or under the influence of German metaphysical thought, saw the mind as essentially active and creative, building with the raw materials afforded to it by the senses. For him the imagination was the prime factor in *all* perception, and the secondary, or poetic, imagination was an extension of this basic faculty. He stresses the tendency of the imagination to see and create unity in all its manifestations: in simple perception of objects, scenes and situations, in the actual writing of a poem, and, at its highest, in the mystical apprehension of the metaphysical oneness of the diverse "goings-on" (Wordsworth's phrase) of the universe. These two philosophies, the Hartleian and the Coleridgean, fuse in a rather hazy and sometimes even contradictory way in Wordsworth's theory. Thus in *The Prelude* he can say, speaking of creative minds:

> They from their native selves can send abroad
> Like transformations, for themselves create
> A like existence.
> (*The Prelude* (1805), 13, 93–95)

(which is Coleridgean) and immediately afterwards say in completely Hartleian vein:

> . . . they build up greatest things
> From least suggestions.
> (98–99)

But Wordsworth, though highly intelligent, deeply thoughtful and profoundly concerned with the nature and meaning of life, was not really a philosopher in the restricted technical sense of the word. Dr. Leavis's comment is well worth noting:

> Even if Wordsworth has a philosophy, it is as a poet that he matters . . . even where he offers thought, the strength of what he gives is the poet's. ("Criticism and Poetry," *The Common Pursuit*.)

Wordsworth, for all his argumentation, is essentially a poet of the intuitions, and his philosophical concepts serve best as a means of fusing together the various instinctive sympathies and perceptions of his sensitive personality. In his highest poetry the various strands meet and interweave. An awareness of natural beauty, a sense of the dignity of man, a deep compassion, an austere moral concern and a reverent wonder before the mysteries of the universe all blend to produce moments of vision that re-create for the reader Wordsworth's own experience.

His methods of conveying this vision are surprisingly varied: surprisingly, because Wordsworth's poetic voice is always unmistakable. His diction ranges from extreme simplicity to highly formal magniloquence. "The language really used by men" from which he selects is not exclusively that of simple men, but that of Spenser, Milton and the philosophers, modified as it is by his own strong individuality. Equally, his approaches to his recurrent themes are diverse. Occasionally, much less often than the popular idea of Wordsworth as a "nature" poet suggests, he is directly, but never solely, inspired by the visual beauty of a scene, as in "I wandered lonely as a cloud," or moved to a contemplation of the combined simplicity and luxuriance of nature ("To a Daisy"). Even here, moral speculations follow. Wordsworth never describes purely for the sake of description as an end in itself; for him it is always a means to an end. More often, in the shorter lyrics, there is the poetry of utterly simple statement ("A slumber did my spirit seal") that by its very simplicity achieves an emotive force that defies analysis and is suggestive and profound. Then there is the narrative power which reaches its apex in "Michael." This poem is mainly an even-paced story of commonplace lives exposed to a common enough family disaster, told in terms of dispassionate flatness, but in its steady course it conveys the strength of human affection, the dignity of independent labor, the instinctive union of man with his natural environment, the power of sheer, unhoping endurance, and in its superb conclusion quietly states the fact of the transience of man and the permanence of nature.

Perhaps even more impressive are those poems and certain passages in *The Prelude* where some incident is described which, trivial in itself, acts as a catalyst for the whole range of Wordsworth's intuitions and becomes a moment of mystic revelation. In these passages, past and present, man and nature, the physical and the spiritual, the actual and the mysteriously possible are completely fused. So, too, are the poet and his readers; Wordsworth re-creates his experience for us. One such incident (*The Prelude* (1805), 11, 258–345) describes the young Wordsworth's seeing first a disused gibbet, then a beacon near a pool and a solitary

> Woman with her garments vexed and tossed
> By the strong wind.

This incident is the occasion for two of Wordsworth's most explicit statements of the significance of such incidents for him. He speaks of his sense of the revelation of a strange and new world, and his intimations of "unknown ways of being":

It was, in truth,
An ordinary sight; but I should need
Colours and words that are unknown to man
To paint the visionary dreariness. . . .

This "visionary dreariness" in later life became for him one of those

spots of time
Which with distinct pre-eminence retain
A vivifying virtue.

For him such experiences were a constant source of moral and spiritual strength, to be returned to time and again for consolation, support and exaltation. He successfully convinces his readers of the reality of such experiences, not by exhortation but by poetic re-creation. It is for this reason that the Victorians saw him as "the poet who taught us how to feel," and that John Stuart Mill could find that he was rescued from spiritual and emotional aridity by his discovery of Wordsworth's poetry.

Wordsworth's vision of the operative force of nature was extensive. He saw, at one extreme, nature working on man almost directly, giving him moral guidance and admonition, with

ample power
To chasten and subdue

and influencing his ethical behavior. At the other extreme, he envisaged what was for him nature's mightiest power—that of affording man apocalyptic visions of the unity of all created things and their essential connection with their Creator. These are exalted claims to make for nature. It is a measure of Wordsworth's stature as a poet that at his best he recaptures his awareness of these mighty forces, and in poetry that is "truth carried alive into the heart by passion" he reproduces the profoundest experiences of his own unique consciousness, enables his readers to see them and makes them feel that they share them. It is for this reason that Wordsworth has been for some, in successive generations, not only one of the greatest of poets, but also a guide, teacher and friend.

(See also **Romantic Movement, The.**)

An Evening Walk, 1793.
Descriptive Sketches, Taken during a Pedestrian Tour in the Alps, 1793.
Lyrical Ballads, 1798; with *Preface*, 1800; with additions, 1802.
Poems in Two Volumes, 1807.
The Excursion, 1814.
The White Doe of Rylstone, 1815.
Peter Bell, 1819.
The Waggoner, 1819.
The River Duddon, a Series of Sonnets; Vandracour and Julia; and Other Poems . . . A Topographical Description of the . . ., Lakes. . ., 1820.

The Prelude, 1850; ed., with 1805 version, E. de Selincourt, 1926; revised H. Darbishire, London: Oxford Univ. Press, 1959.

Poetical Works, ed. E. de Selincourt and H. Darbishire, 5 vols., Oxford: Clarendon Press, 1940–49.

Letters of William and Dorothy Wordsworth, ed. E. de Selincourt, 6 vols., Oxford: Clarendon Press, 1935–39; revised C. L. Shaver and others, 1967– .

Journals of Dorothy Wordsworth, ed. E. de Selincourt, 2 vols., London: Macmillan, 1941–52.   C.H.

WRIGHT, James (1927–) was born in Martin's Ferry (Ohio), and the world of the industrial Midwest—"the chemical riffles of the Ohio River"—figures large in his poetry. Educated at Kenyon College and the University of Washington, he spent time in Austria before returning to the United States to teach, first at the University of Minnesota and then at Hunter College, New York City. In 1957 he published traditional poems in *The Green Wall*, and in 1959 *Saint Judas*; in 1963 *The Branch Will Not Break* announced a movement to free form verse resembling Chinese poetry. With Robert Bly he translated *Twenty Poems of Georg Trakl* (1961), *Twenty Poems of Pablo Neruda* (1968), and with Bly and John Knoepfle *Twenty Poems of César Vallejo* (1963). He has also published a translation of Theodor Storm's short novels (1966). In 1968 *Shall We Gather at the River* appeared, and in 1971 *Collected Poems*.

Collected Poems, Middletown, Conn.: Wesleyan Univ. Press, 1971.

J.P.W.

WRIGHT, Judith. See **Australian Literature.**

WRIGHT, Richard (1908–60), was born near Natchez (Mississippi), the son of a sharecropper. His early life was scarred by poverty, rootlessness and racial and emotional repressions. Self-educated, he moved to Chicago in 1927 where he was attracted by the Communist party, and began writing for radical journals, including *Left Front* and *The New Masses*. As a member of the Federal Writers' Project he wrote *Uncle Tom's Children* (1938), a collection of tales that reveal the psychopathology of racial oppression in the South. His next book, *Native Son* (1940), was a best selling novel which brought him international fame. A compelling mixture of realism and Gothic nightmare, the novel tells the story of Bigger Thomas, a black boy driven by fear into the role of the "brute killer." In 1951 *Native Son* was made into a weak film starring Wright himself as Bigger Thomas. Wright's literary reputation was further strengthened by his moving autobiography, *Black Boy* (1945), a classic study of black suffering and fortitude. In 1945 he left America to live in France, but his novels written in exile are disappointing. *The Outsider* (1953) is a frenetic novel of existential violence, whilst *The Long Dream* (1958) covers old ground. More successful are the stories in *Eight Men* (1961), especially "The Man Who Lived Underground," which dates from 1942. In his later years Wright also produced several books on social and political topics.

Uncle Tom's Children, 1938.
Native Son, 1940 (*f.* 1951).
12 Million Voices: A Folk History of the Negro in the United States, 1941.
Black Boy, 1945.
The Outsider, 1953.
White Man Listen!, 1957.
The Long Dream, 1958.
Eight Men, 1961.
Lawd Today, 1963.   I.W.

WULFSTAN. See **Old English Poetry.**

WYATT, Sir Thomas (1503–42), born at Allington Castle (Kent), was a faithful servant to Henry VIII. His fortunes rose and fell, like those of other Tudor courtiers, but Wyatt was more fortunate than some in escaping execution. During a distinguished diplomatic career which provided the opportunity for firsthand knowledge of Continental literature, Wyatt survived periods of banishment from court, the stigma of a probable liaison, before her marriage, with Anne Boleyn (to which some poems possibly refer) and, more narrowly, the charge of treason in 1541, following the fall of his patron, Thomas Cromwell.

Wyatt's poetry marks the advent of the Renaissance in English verse, introducing the sonnet, terza rima and neoclassical satire. He also used native traditions, as his songs illustrate, and possibly the irregularities of some rhythms reflect the influence of the medieval "pausing line." Even when translating, Wyatt brings his own English tone to his original. Courtly love lyrics bulk largest in his verse and, though uneven in quality, are distinguished by an engaging plainness, a passionate desire for justice in an unjust world and a frequently bitter, cynical, resentful tone. His most accomplished works are the three satires, urbane and familiar, overlaying disillusion with court life with a cheerful resignation of worldly ambition. Some poems appeared without ascription in *The Court of Venus* (1539) and

in Tottel's *Songs and Sonnets* (1557). Authoritative modern texts are based on two major and several minor manuscripts.
(See also **Elizabethan Miscellanies; Renaissance Humanism.**)

Certain Psalms. . . ., 1549.

Collected Poems, ed. K. Muir and P. Thomson, Liverpool: Liverpool Univ. Press, 1969. J.M.P.

WYCHERLEY, William (1640–1716), born into a wealthy Royalist family, was sent at fifteen to complete his education in France, where he moved in aristocratic circles. In 1660 he returned to England, went to Queen's College, Oxford, and entered the Middle Temple. Four plays, performed between 1671 and 1676, earned him an entrée to the court but his secret marriage (1680) to the countess of Drogheda lost him royal favor. Lawsuits followed his wife's death in 1681 and in 1682 he was imprisoned for debt. In 1686 he was released and given a pension by James II, but this ceased with the Revolution. In 1704 the publication of his *Miscellany Poems* initiated a long friendship with Pope. He died soon after his second marriage.

The *Country Wife*, Wycherley's finest play, is one of the most outstanding examples of the "comedy of manners" genre. The play, which hinges on the feigned impotence of the rake, Horner, satirizes the sexual attitudes of jealous husbands, would-be wits, and "honorable" ladies who equate virtue with reputation. The comedy is essentially dark and the blend of laughter and savage satire recalls the work of Jonson. *The Plain Dealer* (based on Molière's *Le Misanthrope*) is a less successful though still considerable work. Lacking the structural unity of the earlier play, its satiric attack on an age when plain dealing was "quite out of fashion" degenerates into railing.

Love in a Wood; or, St. James's Park, 1672 (*p.* 1671).
The Gentleman Dancing-Master, 1673 (*p.* 1672).
The Country Wife, 1675.
The Plain Dealer, 1677 (*p.* 1676).
Miscellany Poems, 1704.

Complete Works, ed. M. Summers, 4 vols., London: Nonesuch Press, 1924.
L.S.

WYCLIF(FE), John (1320–84), a Yorkshireman, was the greatest and most controversial figure at Oxford in his century. Influenced by William of Ockham, Grosseteste and FitzRalph, he preached the doctrine that "dominion is founded in grace," and attacked every kind of abuse in the ecclesiastical system. He maintained transubstantiation to be a physical impossibility, and after his teachings were condemned in 1382 he retired to Lutterworth. Most of his enormous output is in Latin, but his sympathy with the masses led to the first complete English translation of the Bible. There are two versions of the Vulgate, but it is uncertain how far the translations are his own or inspired by him. (See also **Bible, The; Middle English Literature.**)

The Holy Bible . . . *in the Earliest English Versions*, ed. J. Forshall and F. Madden, Oxford: Oxford Univ. Press, 1850.

Select English Works, ed. T. Arnold, 3 vols., Oxford: Oxford Univ. Press, 1869–71.

English Works Hitherto Unprinted, ed. F. D. Matthew, London: Early English Text Society, 1880.   A.N.M.

WYNDHAM, John. See **Science Fiction.**

Y

YEATS, W. B. (William Butler) (1865–1939) was born in Dublin, the eldest child of John Butler Yeats, a lawyer who, soon after the birth of his son, gave up law for a career in art. The family moved to London in 1868, not to return to Dublin until 1880. The most memorable occasions of Yeats's childhood were the long holidays spent with his mother's family, the Pollexfens, in Sligo. Sligo was his ancestral home; Yeatses and Pollexfens, middle-class Protestant merchants and scholars, had lived and worked there for generations.

After seven years in Dublin John Butler Yeats again moved his family to London. During his young manhood in Dublin and London W. B. Yeats established important friendships and lifelong interests. As a boy he had developed a love of Irish legend and fairy story, and this now received stimulus and enlargement from his involvement in the Irish Nationalist movement and from his systematic inquiry into the occult as a member of the Theosophical Society and of the Order of the Golden Dawn, both of which he joined in 1890. His writings of this period—he had been publishing poems and stories since 1885—reflect these interests and also his association with late nineteenth-century writers and artists (William Morris, Lionel Johnson, Ernest Dowson, and others), with some of whom he founded the Irish Literary Society in 1891. In this year, too, he completed, with Edwin Ellis, an edition of the works of Blake, who was also an important literary influence on him.

Two years before this he had met Maud Gonne, an actress and Irish revolutionary, whom he was to love, vainly, for many years and whom he apotheosized in his poetry. For her he wrote his first play, *The Countess Kathleen* (1892), eventually performed by the Irish Literary Theatre which Yeats founded in 1899 with the help of Lady Gregory, whom he had met in 1896 and who was to remain until her death his friend and patron. The Irish Literary Theatre became the Irish National Theatre Company and in 1904 moved into the Abbey Theatre in Dublin. Yeats maintained his connection with the Abbey Theatre for the rest of his life, and was deeply implicated in all its crises. The most distressing to him was the violent rejection by an outraged audience of J. M. Synge's *The Playboy of the Western World*.

Yeats's own plays were almost as unpopular at the Abbey Theatre as Synge's. In theory and practice, his drama was a reaction against naturalism in the theater. What he aimed for was a drama of symbol and myth, "a ritual of passion ... remote, spiritual, and ideal." In 1913 Ezra Pound introduced him to Japanese No drama and Yeats eagerly adapted No conventions to his own use, to deepen and confirm earlier insights and practice.

In 1917 Yeats married Georgie Hyde-Lees and in the same year acquired Thoor Ballylee, a cottage in Galway with an adjacent Norman tower which was to become one of the most pregnant of his poetic symbols. He now discovered in his wife an ability for automatic writing. The messages from her Unknown Instructors seemed to verify and systematize his own previous thoughts on man, history and the nature of art. In a prose work, *A Vision* (privately, 1925; revised and enlarged, 1937), he set out the resulting philosophical system: it was recondite and idiosyncratic, but of structural and referential benefit to his poetry and plays.

Yeats's greatest work belongs to the last twenty years of his life. Living in Dublin and at Thoor Ballylee, with visits to the Continent for his health, he wrote more passionately and vigorously than ever before. He died at Roquebrune and was buried at Cap Martin on the French Riviera in 1939. In 1948 the Irish government, in honor of a man who, amongst so much else, had also been a senator of the Irish Free State (1922–28) and a Nobel Prize winner (1923), brought his remains home to Ireland to a permanent burial place in Sligo.

Yeats's talents as a dramatist and a prose writer are considerable, but his major achievement lies in his lyric poetry. The *Collected Poems*, drawing together individual volumes of poems published at intervals from 1888 to 1937, reveals his output as a developing body of verse unified throughout its progressive stages by a continual search for an ideal in life and art of "unity of being," a wholeness and harmony he found conspicuously lacking in his own age. Yeats embodied the search in images and symbols drawn from many sources—from magic and spiritualism, from neoplatonic and Indian philosophy, from Greek myth and Irish legend and history, and from his theories of the mask, or antiself, and the cyclic view of history which the Unknown Instructors of *A Vision* had set down as a philosophical system for him. Because of this range of reference, itself a search, Yeats's poetry is not simple; nor does it offer any final conclusion to this search for "unity of being." In place of assertion his poetry offers complex patterning of experience, dialectical parables in which truth is embodied rather than known and the only sure unity that of the poem itself which can confront and hold in equipoise the paradoxes of its vision.

Like his plays, Yeats's poetry is characterized throughout by a use of symbolism. Even his early poetry, which has some of the languor and escapism typical of late nineteenth-century verse, differs from that of his contemporaries in its insistent symbolism. What he sought for in symbolism was a passionate anonymity and universality: "poems where an always personal emotion was woven into a general pattern of myth and symbol." As he matured, his symbols became more substantial and localized; Ireland became his symbol of the world and through this microcosm the macrocosm was brought to hand.

His style developed also; the early "overcharged color inherited from the Romantic movement" gave place to the calculated austerity of the middle years, and this to the richly varied diction and rhythmic resonance—a style always oratorical, however colloquial, always the "singing voice" of the great public poet—of the volumes of 1919 and afterwards.

(See also **Romantic Movement, The.**)

The Wanderings of Oisin and Other Poems, 1889.
The Countess Kathleen, 1892.
The Celtic Twilight, 1893.
The Land of Heart's Desire, 1894.
The Secret Rose, 1897.
The Wind among the Reeds, 1899.
Cathleen Ni Hoolihan, 1902.
The Green Helmet and Other Poems, 1910; enlarged, 1912.
Responsibilities: Poems and A Play, 1914; 1916.
The Wild Swans at Coole, 1917; enlarged, 1919.
Michael Robartes and the Dancer, 1920 (for 1921).
The Tower, 1928.
The Winding Stair, 1929.
Words for Music and Other Poems, 1932.
Dramatis Personae, 1935.
A Vision, 1937.
New Poems, 1938.
Last Poems and Two Plays, 1939.

Autobiographies, London: Macmillan, 1955.

Poems, Definitive edition, 2 vols., London: Macmillan, 1949.
Variorum Edition of the Poems, ed. P. Allt and R. K. Alspach, London: Macmillan; New York: Macmillan Co., 1957.
Collected Plays, London: Macmillan, 1934; New York: Macmillan Co., 1935; with later plays added, London, 1952; New York, 1953.
Variorum Edition of the Plays, ed. R. K. and C. C. Alspach, London: Macmillan; New York: Macmillan Co., 1966.
Letters, ed. A. Wade, London: Hart-Davis; New York: Macmillan Co., 1954.
Senate Speeches, ed. D. R. Pearce, Bloomington: Indiana Univ. Press, 1960; London: Faber & Faber, 1961.   M.S.

YOUNG, Andrew (1885–   ), born at Elgin (Morayshire) and educated at Edinburgh University, moved south in 1920 and was made honorary canon of Chichester Cathedral in 1948. He is a contemplative nature poet who, while traditional in form, is original in sensibility and in the precision of his observation. With accuracy, freshness of vision and religious feeling he reveals an intimacy with the natural world and shows the familiar in a new light. His poems are recollections in tranquillity, characterized by simple language and unobtrusive rhythms.

Collected Poems, London: Cape, 1950.   O.K.

YOUNG, Edward (1683–1765), educated at Winchester and New College, Oxford, and later a law fellow of All Souls, did not enter the church until 1727 but, thanks to patronage, became a royal chaplain soon after ordination. Before that date he had written his tragedies *Busiris* (1719) and *The Revenge* (1721) and a series of six satires, *The Universal Passion* (1725–28). Following the death of his wife in 1741 he began *Night Thoughts* (1742–45). His later works include another tragedy, *The Brothers* (1753), the prose satire *The Centaur Not Fabulous* (1755), attacking the infidelity of his age, and *Conjectures on Original Composition* (1759)— addressed to the novelist Samuel Richardson. He died in 1765 at Welwyn (Hertfordshire), where he had been rector from 1730.

Young associated with the Addison coterie and his *Busiris* has much in common with the style of Addison's *Cato*. It is altogether too turgid to be dramatically successful. His satire is pungent and powerful, abounding in wit and epigram. His real fame, however, rests on *Night Thoughts*, prolix though this work is. In it Young provides the classic expression of the melancholy poetry of his time. He is occupied with the four last things—heaven, hell, death and judgment, and though he would claim that he stated the Christian hope, the overall impression is somber and overcast. There are inklings of a breakthrough to a freer expression of emotion than his age generally approved of, and if this is one indication of incipient Romanticism in his work, yet another is his praise of original genius in the critical *Conjectures on Original Composition*.

Busiris, King of Egypt, 1719.
The Revenge, 1721.
The Universal Passion, 1–7, 1725–28 (collected as *Love of Fame*).
The Complaint; or, Night Thoughts, 1742–45.
The Brothers, 1753.
The Centaur Not Fabulous, 1755.

Conjectures on Original Composition in a Letter to the Author of "Sir Charles Grandison," 1759.

Works, 4 vols., 1757; 5 vols., 1767; 2 vols., with life by J. Mitford, London: Pickering (Aldine edition of the British Poets), 1830.
Correspondence, ed. H. Pettit, Oxford: Clarendon Press, 1972.　A.P.

Z

ZUKOFSKY, Louis (1904–   ) was born in Manhattan and has lived there most of his life, teaching occasionally at colleges elsewhere in America and building a body of poetry and prose of the finest significance in twentieth-century letters. His poetic theory appears in *Le Style Apollinaire* (with R. Taupin, Paris, 1934), *A Test of Poetry* (1948) and *Prepositions* (1967), which includes major statements on poetics, including the "Five Statements for Poetry" (1951) and the bases of "Objectivism" (1932). His prose also includes *It Was* (1961), a fiction work which appears complete with *Ferdinand* (1968), and *Bottom: On Shakespeare* (1963), a magnificent large-scale work of aesthetics based on a lifetime's reading of Shakespeare and much else. *Autobiography* (1970) contains brief personal statements accompanying musical settings of his lyrics by Celia, his wife. She also contributed a musical score for *Pericles* as a second volume to *Bottom*, and collaborated with the poet in a large collection of translations from Catullus (1969). The great bulk and quality of Zukofsky's poetry between 1923 and the 1960s appears in two volumes of collected short verse, and in *"A" 1–12* (1959) and *"A" 13–21* (1969), a long poem celebrated for its lyrical intelligence and variety of inventive forms.

Le Style Apollinaire, 1934.
A Test of Poetry, 1948.
"A" 1–12, 1959.
Bottom: On Shakespeare, 1963.
Ferdinand, with *It Was*, 1968.
"A" 13–21, 1969.
Autobiography, 1970.

All the Collected Short Poems, 1923–1958, New York: Norton, 1965; London: Cape, 1966,
All the Collected Short Poems, 1956–1964, New York: Norton, 1966; London: Cape, 1967.
Prepositions: Collected Critical Essays, London: Rapp & Whiting, 1967; New York: Horizon Press, 1968.

E.M.

APPENDIX OF SECONDARY BIBLIOGRAPHY

Adams, Henry.

Samuels, E., *The Young Henry Adams*, Cambridge, Mass.: Harvard Univ. Press; London: Oxford Univ. Press, 1948.
Jordy, W. H., *Henry Adams, Scientific Historian*, New Haven: Yale Univ. Press, 1952.
Levenson, J. C., *The Mind and Art of Henry Adams*, Boston: Houghton Mifflin, 1957.
Samuels, E., *Henry Adams: The Middle Years*, Cambridge, Mass.: Harvard Univ. Press, 1958.
Hochfield, G., *Henry Adams: An Introduction and Interpretation*, New York: Barnes & Noble, 1962.
Samuels, E., *Henry Adams: The Major Phase*, Cambridge, Mass.: Harvard Univ. Press, 1964.

Addison, Joseph.

Johnson, S., *The Lives of the Poets*, London, 1779–81.
Macaulay, Lord, *Critical and Historical Essays*, vol. 2, London: Longman, 1843.
Graham, W., *English Literary Periodicals*, New York: Nelson, 1930.
Smithers, P., *The Life of Joseph Addison*, Oxford: Clarendon Press, 1954; revised, 1968.

African Literature (including South African).

Moore, G., *Seven African Writers*, London: Oxford Univ. Press, 1962.
Moore, G., *The Chosen Tongue: English Writing in the Tropical World*, London: Longmans, 1969.
Pieterse, C., and Munro, D. (edd.), *Protest and Conflict in African Literature*, London: Heinemann Educ., 1969.

Agee, James.

Ohlin, P. H., *Agee*, New York: Obolensky, 1965.
Seib, K., *James Agee: Promise and Fulfillment*, Pittsburgh: Univ. of Pittsburgh Press, 1969.

Aiken, Conrad.

Martin, J., *Conrad Aiken: A Life of His Art*, Princeton: Princeton Univ. Press, 1962.
Denney, R., *Conrad Aiken*, Minneapolis: Univ. of Minnesota Press, 1964; London: Oxford Univ. Press. Pamphlets on American Writers, no. 38.

Ainsworth, William Harrison.

Ellis, S. M., *William Harrison Ainsworth and His Friends*, 2 vols., London and New York: J. Lane, 1911.

759

Hollingsworth, K., *The Newgate Novel, 1830–1847*, Detroit: Wayne State Univ. Press, 1963.

Akenside, Mark.

Johnson, S., *The Lives of the Poets*, London, 1779–81.

Houpt, C. T., *Mark Akenside: A Biographical and Critical Study*, (privately) Philadelphia: Univ. of Pennsylvania Press, 1944.

Albee, Edward.

Amacher, R. E., *Edward Albee*, New York: Twayne, 1969.

Bigsby, C. W. E., *Albee*, Edinburgh: Oliver & Boyd, 1969.

Rutenberg, M. E., *Edward Albee: Playwright in Protest*, New York: D. B. S. Publications, 1969.

Alger, Horatio, Jr.

Gruber, F., *Horatio Alger, Jr.: A Biography and Bibliography*, Los Angeles: Grover Jones Press, 1961.

Gardner, R. D., *Horatio Alger; or, The American Hero Era*, Mendota, Ill.: Wayside Press, 1964.

Amis, Kingsley.

Rabinovitz, R., *The Reaction against Experiment in the English Novel, 1950–60*, New York: Columbia Univ. Press, 1968.

Anderson, Sherwood.

Burbank, R. J., *Sherwood Anderson*, New York: Twayne, 1964.

Weber, B., *Sherwood Anderson*, Minneapolis: Univ. of Minnesota Press, 1964; London: Oxford Univ. Press. Pamphlets on American Writers, no. 43.

Anderson, D., *Sherwood Anderson: An Introduction and Interpretation*, New York: Holt, Rinehart, 1967.

Andrewes, Lancelot.

Eliot, T. S., *For Lancelot Andrewes: Essays on Style and Order*, London: Faber & Gwyer, 1928; Garden City, N.Y.: Doubleday, Doran, 1929.

Welsby, P. A., *Lancelot Andrewes, 1555–1626*, London: S.P.C.K., 1958.

Anstey, Christopher.

Powell, W. C., *Christopher Anstey: Bath Laureate*, (privately) Philadelphia: Univ of Pennsylvania Press, 1944.

Arbuthnot, John.

Aitken, G. A., *The Life and Works of John Arbuthnot*, Oxford: Clarendon Press, 1892.

Beattie, L. M., *John Arbuthnot, Mathematician and Satirist*, Cambridge, Mass.: Harvard Univ. Press, 1935.

Arden, John.

Marowitz, C.; Milne, T.; and Hale, O. (edd.), *The Encore Reader: A Chronicle of the New Drama*, London: Methuen, 1965.

Hayman, R., *John Arden*, London: Heinemann, 1968.
Taylor, J. Russell, *Anger and After: A Guide to the New British Drama*, London: Methuen, 1962; revised, 1969; as *The Angry Theatre: New British Drama*, New York: Hill & Wang, 1962.

Arnold, Matthew.

Trilling, L., *Matthew Arnold*, London: Allen & Unwin; New York: Norton, 1939; 2nd edition, New York: Columbia Univ. Press, 1949.
Bonnerot, L., *Matthew Arnold, Poète*, Paris, 1947.
James, D. G., *Matthew Arnold and the Decline of English Romanticism*, Oxford: Clarendon Press, 1961.
Culler, A. D., *Imaginative Reason: The Poetry of Matthew Arnold*, New Haven: Yale Univ. Press, 1966.
Bush, D., *Matthew Arnold: A Survey of His Poetry and Prose*, London: Collier-Macmillan; New York: Macmillan Co., 1971.

Ascham, Roger.

Ryan, L. V., *Roger Ascham*, London: Oxford Univ. Press; Stanford: Stanford Univ. Press, 1963.

Aubrey, John.

Powell, A., *John Aubrey and His Friends*, London: Eyre & Spottiswoode, 1948; New York: C. Scribner's Sons, 1949.

Auden, W. H.

Hoggart, R., *Auden: An Introductory Essay*, London: Chatto & Windus; New Haven: Yale Univ. Press, 1951.
Beach, J. W., *The Making of the Auden Canon*, London: Oxford Univ. Press; Minneapolis: Univ. of Minnesota Press, 1957.
Spears, M. K., *The Poetry of W. H. Auden: The Disenchanted Island*, London: Oxford Univ. Press, 1963.
Spears, M. K. (ed.), *Auden: A Collection of Critical Essays*, Englewood Cliffs, N. J.: Prentice-Hall, 1964.
Blair, J. G., *The Poetic Art of W. H. Auden*, London: Oxford Univ. Press; Princeton: Princeton Univ. Press, 1965.
Fuller, J., *A Reader's Guide to W. H. Auden*, London: Thames & Hudson; New York: Farrar, Straus, 1970.

Augustans, The.

MacLean, K., *John Locke and English Literature of the Eighteenth Century*, London: Oxford Univ. Press; New Haven: Yale Univ. Press, 1936.
Willey, B., *The Eighteenth Century Background: Studies on the Idea of Nature in the Thought of the Period*, London: Chatto & Windus, 1940; New York: Columbia Univ. Press, 1941.
Lovejoy, A. O., *Essays in the History of Ideas*, Baltimore: Johns Hopkins Press, 1948; London: Oxford Univ. Press, 1949.
Sutherland, J. R., *A Preface to Eighteenth Century Poetry*, Oxford: Clarendon Press, 1948.

Davie, D., *Purity of Diction in English Verse*, London: Chatto & Windus, 1952; New York: Oxford Univ. Press, 1953.

Williams, K., *Jonathan Swift and the Age of Compromise*, Lawrence: Univ. of Kansas Press, 1958; London: Constable, 1959.

Fussell, P., *The Rhetorical World of Augustan Humanism: Ethics and Imagery from Swift to Burke*, London: Oxford Univ. Press, 1965.

Johnson, J. W., *The Formation of English Neo-Classical Thought*, Princeton: Princeton Univ. Press, 1967.

Trickett, R., *The Honest Muse: A Study in Augustan Verse*, Oxford: Clarendon Press, 1967.

Austen, Jane.

Lascelles, M. M., *Jane Austen and Her Art*, London: Oxford Univ. Press, 1939.

Chapman, R. W., *Jane Austen: Facts and Problems*, Oxford: Clarendon Press, 1948.

Mudrick, M., *Jane Austen: Irony as Defense and Discovery*, London: Oxford Univ. Press; Princeton: Princeton Univ. Press, 1952.

Wright, A. H., *Jane Austen's Novels*, London: Chatto & Windus; New York: Oxford Univ. Press, 1953.

Craik, W. A., *Jane Austen: The Six Novels*, London: Methuen; New York: Barnes & Noble, 1965.

Southam, B. C. (ed.), *Jane Austen: The Critical Heritage*, London: Routledge; New York: Barnes & Noble, 1968.

Australian Literature.

Green, H. M., *A History of Australian Literature*, 2 vols., Sydney and London: Angus & Robertson, 1961.

Dutton, G. (ed.), *The Literature of Australia*, Ringwood, Victoria: Penguin, 1964.

Moore, T. I., *Social Patterns in Australian Literature*, Sydney and London: Angus & Robertson, 1971.

Babbitt, Irving.

Manchester, F. A., and Shepard, O. (edd.), *Irving Babbitt: Man and Teacher*, New York: Putnam, 1941.

Bacon, Francis.

Broad, C. D., *The Philosophy of Francis Bacon*, Cambridge: Cambridge Univ. Press, 1926.

Craig, H., *The Enchanted Glass: The Elizabethan Mind in Literature*, London and New York: Oxford Univ. Press, 1936.

Knights, L. C., *Explorations: Essays in Criticism, Mainly on the Literature of the Seventeenth Century*, London: Chatto & Windus, 1946; New York: Stewart, 1947.

Anderson, F. H., *The Philosophy of Francis Bacon*, Chicago: Univ. of Chicago Press, 1948; Cambridge: Cambridge Univ. Press, 1949.

Crowther, J. G., *Francis Bacon: The First Statesman of Science*, London: Cresset Press, 1960.

Vickers, B., *Francis Bacon and Renaissance Prose*, Cambridge: Cambridge Univ. Press, 1968.
Vickers, B. (ed.), *Essential Articles for the Study of Francis Bacon*, Hamden, Conn.: Shoe String Press, 1969.

Bagehot, Walter.

St. John-Stevas, N., *Walter Bagehot: A Study of His Life and Thought*, London: Eyre & Spottiswoode; Bloomington: Indiana Univ. Press, 1959.
Buchan, A. F., *The Spare Chancellor: The Life of Walter Bagehot*, London: Chatto & Windus, 1959; East Lansing: Michigan State Univ. Press, 1960.

Baldwin, James.

Eckman, F. M., *The Furious Passage of James Baldwin*, New York: M. Evans, 1966; London: M. Joseph, 1968.

Ballads.

Sidgwick, F., *The Ballad*, London: Secker, 1915.
Gerould, G. H., *The Ballad of Tradition*, Oxford: Clarendon Press, 1932.
Hodgart, M. J. C., *The Ballads*, London: Hutchinson, 1950; revised, 1962.
Fowler, D. C., *A Literary History of the Popular Ballad*, Durham, N. C.: Duke Univ. Press, 1968.

Bancroft, George.

Nye, R. B., *George Bancroft: Brahmin Rebel*, New York: Knopf, 1944.

Barbour, John.

Neilson, G., *John Barbour: Poet and Translator*, London: Kegan Paul, 1900.

Barlow, Joel.

Woodress, J. L., *A Yankee's Odyssey: The Life of Joel Barlow*, Philadelphia: Lippincott, 1958.
Ford, A. L., *Joel Barlow*, New York: Twayne, 1972.

Barnes, William.

Baxter, L., *The Life of William Barnes*, London: Macmillan, 1887.
Dugdale, G., *William Barnes of Dorset*, London: Cassell, 1953.

Barrie, J. M.

Mackail, D. G., *The Story of J. M. B.*, London: P. Davies; New York: C. Scribner's Sons, 1941.

Baxter, Richard.

Nuttall, G. F., *Richard Baxter*, London: Nelson, 1966.

Beard, Charles Austin.

Beale, H. K. (ed.), *Charles A. Beard: An Appraisal*, Lexington: Univ. of Kentucky Press, 1954.

Beardsley, Aubrey.

Reade, B. E. (ed.), *Beardsley*, London: Studio Vista; as *Aubrey Beardsley*, New York: Studio, 1967.

Weintraub, S., *Beardsley: A Biography*, London: W. H. Allen; New York: Braziller, 1967.

Beattie, James,

Forbes, W., *An Account of the Life and Writings of James Beattie*, 2 vols., Edinburgh, 1806.

Beaumont, Francis.

See under **Fletcher, John.**

Beckett, Samuel.

Esslin, M., *The Theatre of the Absurd*, New York: Doubleday, 1961; London: Eyre & Spottiswoode, 1962.

Kenner, H., *Beckett: A Critical Study*, London: Calder; New York: Grove Press, 1962; new edition, Berkeley and Los Angeles: Univ. of California Press, 1968.

Fletcher, J., *The Novels of Samuel Beckett*, London: Chatto & Windus; New York: Barnes & Noble, 1964.

Esslin, M. (ed.), *Samuel Beckett: A Collection of Critical Essays*, Englewood Cliffs, N.J.: Prentice-Hall, 1965.

Fletcher, J., *Samuel Beckett's Art*, London: Chatto & Windus; New York: Barnes & Noble, 1967.

Barnard, G. C., *Samuel Beckett: A New Approac* London: Dent; New York: Dodd, Mead, 1970.

Beckford, William.

Chapman, G., *Beckford*, London: Cape; New York: C. Scribner's Sons, 1937; new edition, London: Hart-Davis, 1952.

Alexander, B., *England's Wealthiest Son: A Study of William Beckford*, London: Centaur Press, 1962.

Beddoes, Thomas Lovell.

Donner, H. W., *Thomas Lovell Beddoes: The Making of a Poet*, Oxford: Blackwell, 1935.

Beerbohm, Max.

Behrman, S. N., *Portrait of Max*, New York: Random House; as *Conversation with Max*, London: H. Hamilton, 1960.

Cecil, Lord D., *Max: A Biography*, London: Constable, 1964; Boston: Houghton Mifflin, 1965.

Behan, Brendan.

Taylor, J. Russell, *Anger and After: A Guide to the New British Drama*, London: Methuen, 1962; revised, 1969; as *The Angry Theatre: New British Drama*, New York: Hill & Wang, 1962.

Behn, Aphra.

Woodcock, G., *The Incomparable Aphra*, London and New York: Boardman, 1948.

Link, F. M., *Aphra Behn*, New York: Twayne, 1968.

Bellamy, Edward.

Bowman, S. E., *The Year 2000: A Critical Biography of Edward Bellamy*, New York: Bookman Associates, 1958.

Belloc, Hilaire.

Hamilton, R., *Hilaire Belloc*, London: Organ, 1945.

Speaight, R., *The Life of Hilaire Belloc*, London: Hollis & Carter; New York: Farrar, Straus, 1957.

Bellow, Saul.

Tanner, T., *Saul Bellow*, Edinburgh: Oliver & Boyd, 1965; New York: Barnes & Noble, 1967.

Malin, I. (ed.), *Saul Bellow and the Critics*, New York: New York Univ. Press; London: Univ. of London Press, 1967.

Opdahl, K. M., *The Novels of Saul Bellow: An Introduction*, University Park, Pa.: Pennsylvania State Univ. Press, 1967.

Benét, Stephen Vincent.

Fenton, C. A., *Stephen Vincent Benét: The Life and Times of an American Man of Letters, 1898–1943*, New Haven: Yale Univ. Press, 1958.

Benlowes, Edward.

Jenkins, H., *Edward Benlowes, 1602–1676: Biography of a Minor Poet*, London: Athlone Press; Cambridge, Mass.: Harvard Univ. Press, 1952.

Bennett, Arnold.

Allen, W., *Arnold Bennett*, London: Home & Van Thal, 1948; Denver: Swallow, 1949.

Wain, J., *Preliminary Essays*, London: Macmillan; New York: St. Martin's Press, 1957.

Hepburn, J. G., *The Art of Arnold Bennett*, Bloomington: Indiana Univ. Press, 1963.

Barker, D., *Writer by Trade: A View of Arnold Bennett*, London: Allen & Unwin; as . . . . : *A Portrait of Arnold Bennett*, New York: Atheneum, 1966.

Bentham, Jeremy.

Mack, M. P., *Jeremy Bentham: An Odyssey of Ideas*, London: Heinemann; New York: Columbia Univ. Press, 1962.

Letwin, S. R., *The Pursuit of Certainty: David Hume, Jeremy Bentham, John Stuart Mill, Beatrice Webb*, Cambridge: Cambridge Univ. Press, 1965.

Berkeley, George.

Warnock, G. J., *Berkeley*, Harmondsworth: Penguin, 1953.

Berryman, John.

Martz, W. J., *John Berryman*, Minneapolis: Univ. of Minnesota Press, 1969; London: Oxford Univ. Press. Pamphlets on American Writers, no. 85.

Besant, Sir Walter.

Keating, P. J., *The Working Classes in Victorian Fiction*, London: Routledge; New York: Barnes & Noble, 1971.

Betjeman, Sir John.

Stanford, D., *John Betjeman: A Study*, London: Spearman, 1961.

Bible, The.

Deanesly, M., *The Lollard Bible and Other Medieval Biblical Versions*, Cambridge: Cambridge Univ. Press, 1920.

Mozley, J. F., *William Tyndale*, London: S.P.C.K.; New York: Macmillan Co., 1937.

Robinson, H. W. (ed.), *The Bible in Its Ancient and English Versions*, Oxford: Clarendon Press, 1940.

Daiches, D., *The King James Version of the English Bible*, Cambridge: Cambridge Univ. Press; Chicago: Univ. of Chicago Press, 1941.

Lewis, C. S., *The Literary Impact of the Authorised Version*, London: Athlone Press, 1950.

Mozley, J. F., *Coverdale and His Bibles*, London: Lutterworth Press, 1953.

MacGregor, G., *The Bible in the Making*, Philadelphia: Lippincott, 1959.

Bruce, F. F., *The English Bible: A History of Translations*, London: Lutterworth Press; New York: Oxford Univ. Press, 1961.

Burrows, M., *Diligently Compared: The Revised Standard Version and the King James Version of the Old Testament*, Camden, N.J.: Nelson, 1964.

Nineham, D. E. (ed.), *The New English Bible Reviewed*, London: Epworth Press, 1965.

Bierce, Ambrose.

MacWilliams, C., *Ambrose Bierce*, New York: A. & C. Boni, 1929.

Fatout, P., *Ambrose Bierce: The Devil's Lexicographer*, Norman: Univ. of Oklahoma Press, 1951.

Bishop, Elizabeth.

Stevenson, A., *Elizabeth Bishop*, New York: Twayne, 1966.

Blackmore, R. D.

Burris, Q. G., *Richard Doddridge Blackmore*, Urbana: Univ. of Illinois Press, 1930.

Dunn, W. H., *R. D. Blackmore: The Author of "Lorna Doone,"* London: Hale; New York: Longmans, 1956.

Blair, Hugh.

Schmitz, R. M., *Hugh Blair*, London: Oxford Univ. Press; New York: Columbia Univ. Press (King's Crown), 1948.

Blake, William.

Gilchrist, A., *Life of W. Blake*, London, 1863.

Damon, S. F., *William Blake: His Philosophy and Symbols*, London: Constable; Boston: Houghton Mifflin, 1924.

Wilson, M., *The Life of William Blake*, London: Nonesuch Press, 1927; revised, London: Hart-Davis, 1948.

Schorer, M., *William Blake: The Politics of Vision*, New York: Holt, 1946.

Frye, N., *Fearful Symmetry: A Study of William Blake*, London: Oxford Univ. Press; Princeton: Princeton Univ. Press, 1947.

Davies, J. G., *The Theology of William Blake*, Oxford: Clarendon Press, 1948.

Blackstone, B., *English Blake*, Cambridge: Cambridge Univ. Press, 1949.

Erdman, D. V., *Blake: Prophet against Empire*, London: Oxford Univ. Press; Princeton: Princeton Univ. Press, 1954; revised, 1970.

Digby, G. F. W., *Symbol and Image in William Blake*, Oxford: Clarendon Press, 1957.

Beer, J. B., *Blake's Humanism*, Manchester: Manchester Univ. Press; New York: Barnes & Noble, 1968.

Raine, K., *Blake and Tradition*, 2 vols., London: Routledge; Princeton: Princeton Univ. Press, 1969.

Bluestockings.

Scott, W. S., *The Bluestocking Ladies*, London: Green, 1947.

Blunden, Edmund.

Hardie, A. M., *Edmund Blunden*, London: Longmans (for British Council), 1958. Writers and Their Work series.

Blunt, Wilfrid Scawen.

Reinehr, M. J., *The Writings of Wilfrid Scawen Blunt*, Milwaukee, Wis.: Marquette Univ. Press, 1940.

Bolingbroke, Viscount.

Trevelyan, G. M., introduction to *Bolingbroke's Defence of the Treaty of Utrecht*, Cambridge: Cambridge Univ. Press, 1932.

James, D. G., *The Life of Reason: Hobbes, Locke, Bolingbroke*, London: Longmans, 1949.

Merrill, W. M., *From Statesman to Philosopher: A Study in Bolingbroke's Deism*, New York: Philosophical Library, 1949.

Borrow, George.

Knapp, W. I., *The Life, Writings and Correspondence of George Borrow*, 2 vols., London: Murray, 1899.

Jenkins, H. G., *The Life of George Borrow*, London: Murray; New York: Putnam, 1912.

Shorter, C. K., *The Life of Borrow*, London: Dent; New York: Dutton, 1920.

768   *Boswell*

Boswell, James.

Pottle, F. A., *The Literary Career of James Boswell, Esq.*, Oxford: Clarendon Press, 1929.

Pottle, F. A., *James Boswell: The Earlier Years, 1740–1769*, London: Heinemann; New York: McGraw-Hill, 1966.

"Bourne, George."

Leavis, F. R., and Thompson, D., *Culture and Environment: The Training of Critical Awareness*, London: Chatto & Windus, 1933.

Bourne, Randolph.

Paul, S., *Randolph Bourne*, Minneapolis: Univ. of Minnesota Press, 1966; London: Oxford Univ. Press. Pamphlets on American Writers, no. 60.

Bowen, Elizabeth.

Brooke, J., *Elizabeth Bowen*, London: Longmans (for British Council), 1952. Writers and Their Work series.

Bowles, W. L.

Greever, G. (ed.), *A Wiltshire Parson and His Friends*, London: Constable; Boston: Houghton Mifflin, 1926.

Van Rennes, J. J., *Bowles, Byron, and the Pope-Controversy*, Amsterdam: H. J. Paris; New York: Stechert, 1927.

Brackenridge, Hugh Henry.

Newlin, C. M., *The Life and Writings of Hugh Henry Brackenridge*, Princeton: Princeton Univ. Press, 1932.

Marder, D., *Hugh Henry Brackenridge*, New York: Twayne, 1967.

Bradstreet, Anne.

Piercy, J. K., *Anne Bradstreet*, New York: Twayne, 1965.

White, E. W., *Anne Bradstreet: "The Tenth Muse,"* New York: Oxford Univ. Press, 1972.

Bridges, Robert.

Ritz, J. G., *Robert Bridges and Gerard Hopkins, 1863–1889: A Literary Friendship*, London: Oxford Univ. Press, 1960.

Brontë, Anne.

Gérin, W., *Anne Brontë*, London: Nelson, 1959.

Ewbank, I-S., *Their Proper Sphere: A Study of the Brontë Sisters as Early-Victorian Female Novelists*, London: Arnold; Cambridge, Mass.: Harvard Univ. Press, 1966.

Brontë, Charlotte.

Gaskell, E. C., *The Life of Charlotte Brontë*, London: Smith, Elder, 1857.

Ratchford, F. E., *The Brontës' Web of Childhood*, London: Oxford Univ. Press; New York: Columbia Univ. Press, 1941.

Ewbank, I-S., *Their Proper Sphere:* . . ., London: Arnold; Cambridge, Mass.: Harvard Univ. Press, 1966.

Martin, R. B., *The Accents of Persuasion: Charlotte Brontë's Novels*, London: Faber & Faber; New York: Norton, 1966.

Gérin, W., *Charlotte Brontë: The Evolution of Genius*, Oxford: Clarendon Press, 1967.

Craik, W. A., *The Brontë Novels*, London: Methuen; New York: Barnes & Noble, 1968.

Brontë, Emily.

Ratchford, F. E., *The Brontës' Web of Childhood*, London: Oxford Univ. Press; New York: Columbia Univ. Press, 1941.

Spark, M., and Stanford, D., *Emily Brontë: Her Life and Work*, London: P. Owen, 1953.

Visick, M., *The Genesis of "Wuthering Heights,"* Hong Kong: Hong Kong Univ. Press, 1958; revised, 1965.

Miller, J. H., *The Disappearance of God: Five Nineteenth-Century Writers*, London: Oxford Univ. Press; Cambridge, Mass.: Harvard Univ. Press, 1963.

Ewbank, I-S., *Their Proper Sphere:* . . ., London: Arnold; Cambridge, Mass.: Harvard Univ. Press, 1966.

Everitt, A. (ed.), *"Wuthering Heights": An Anthology of Criticism*, London: Cass; New York: Barnes & Noble, 1967.

Craik, W. A., *The Brontë Novels*, London: Methuen; New York: Barnes & Noble, 1968.

Gérin, W., *Emily Brontë: A Biography*, Oxford: Clarendon Press, 1971.

Brooke, Rupert.

Hassall, C., *Rupert Brooke: A Biography*, London: Faber & Faber; New York: Harcourt, Brace, 1964.

Rogers, T. (ed.), *Rupert Brooke: A Reappraisal and Selection*, London: Routledge; New York: Barnes & Noble, 1971.

Brooks, Van Wyck.

Vitelli, J. R., *Van Wyck Brooks*, New York: Twayne, 1969.

Brown, Charles Brockden.

Warfel, H. R., *Charles Brockden Brown: American Gothic Novelist*, Gainesville: Univ. of Florida Press, 1949.

Ringe, D. A., *Charles Brockden Brown*, New York: Twayne, 1966.

Browne, Sir Thomas.

Dunn, W. P., *Sir Thomas Browne: A Study in Religious Philosophy*, Minneapolis: Univ. of Minnesota Press, 1950; London: Oxford Univ. Press, 1951.

Bennett, J., *Sir Thomas Browne: A Man of Achievement in Literature*, Cambridge: Cambridge Univ. Press, 1962.

Huntley, F. L., *Sir Thomas Browne: A Biographical and Critical Study*, Ann Arbor: Univ. of Michigan Press, 1962.

Browning, Elizabeth Barrett.

Woolf, V., *The Common Reader*, London: Hogarth Press, 1925.

Hewlett, D., *Elizabeth Barrett Browning: A Life*, New York: Knopf, 1952; London: Cassell, 1953.

Hayter, A., *Mrs. Browning: A Poet's Work and Its Setting*, London: Faber & Faber, 1962; New York: Barnes & Noble, 1963.

Browning, Robert.

Chesterton, G. K., *Robert Browning*, London: Macmillan, 1903.

Griffin, W. H., and Minchin, H. C., *The Life of Robert Browning*, London: Methuen, 1910.

De Vane, W. C., *A Browning Handbook*, New York: Crofts, 1935; London: Murray, 1937; revised, New York: Appleton, 1955; London: Bell, 1956.

Raymond, W. O., *The Infinite Moment, and Other Essays in Robert Browning*, London: Oxford Univ. Press; Toronto: Univ. of Toronto Press, 1950; revised, 1965.

Miller, B., *Robert Browning: A Portrait*, London: Murray, 1952; New York: C. Scribner's Sons, 1953.

Langbaum, R. W., *The Poetry of Experience: The Dramatic Monologue in Modern Literary Tradition*, London: Chatto & Windus; New York: Random House, 1957.

Drew, P., *The Poetry of Browning: A Critical Introduction*, London: Methuen, 1970.

Litzinger, B. A., and Smalley, D. A. (edd.), *Browning: The Critical Heritage*, London: Routledge; New York: Barnes & Noble, 1970.

Brownson, Orestes.

Schlesinger, A. M., Jr., *Orestes A. Brownson: A Pilgrim's Progress*, Boston: Little, Brown, 1939.

Bryant, W. C.

Bigelow, J., *William Cullen Bryant*, Boston: Houghton, Mifflin, 1890.

Bradley, W. A., *William Cullen Bryant*, New York: Macmillan Co.; London: Macmillan, 1905.

Buchan, John.

Smith, J. A., *John Buchan*, London: Hart-Davis, 1965; Boston: Little, Brown, 1966.

Bunyan, John.

Tindall, W. Y., *John Bunyan, Mechanick Preacher*, New York: Columbia Univ. Press, 1934.

Talon, H., *John Bunyan: The Man and His Works*, London: Rockliff; Cambridge, Mass.: Harvard Univ. Press, 1951.

Sharrock, R., *John Bunyan*, London: Hutchinson, 1954.

Harding, M. E., *Journey into Self*, New York: Longmans, 1956.

Burke, Edmund.

Cobban, A., *Edmund Burke and the Revolt against the Eighteenth Century*, London: Allen & Unwin, 1929.

Magnus, P., *Edmund Burke*, London: Murray; New York: Transatlantic, 1939.

Copeland, T. W., *Our Eminent Friend Edmund Burke: Six Essays*, New Haven: Yale Univ. Press, 1949; as *Edmund Burke: Six Essays*, London: Cape, 1950.

Burke, Kenneth.

Rueckert, W. H. (ed.), *Critical Responses to Kenneth Burke, 1924–1966*, Minneapolis: Univ. of Minnesota Press, 1969.

Burnet, Gilbert.

Clarke, T. E. S., and Foxcroft, H. C., *A Life of Gilbert Burnet, Bishop of Salisbury*, Cambridge: Cambridge Univ. Press, 1907.

Burney, Frances ("Fanny").

Hemlow, J., *The History of Fanny Burney*, Oxford: Clarendon Press, 1958.

Bradbrook, F. W., *Jane Austen and Her Predecessors*, Cambridge: Cambridge Univ. Press, 1966.

Burns, Robert.

Snyder, F. B., *The Life of Robert Burns*, London: Macmillan; New York: Macmillan Co., 1932.

Daiches, D., *Robert Burns*, New York: Rinehart, 1950; London: Bell, 1952.

Crawford, T., *Burns: A Study of the Poems and Songs*, Edinburgh: Oliver & Boyd; Stanford: Stanford Univ. Press, 1960.

Craig, D., *Scottish Literature and the Scottish People, 1680–1830*, London: Chatto & Windus, 1961; New York: Hillary House, 1962.

Burroughs, William.

Mottram, E., *William Burroughs: The Algebra of Need*, Buffalo: Intrepid Press, 1971.

Burton, (Sir) Richard.

Brodie, F. M., *The Devil Drives: A Life of Sir Richard Burton*, London: Eyre & Spottiswoode, 1967.

Burton, Robert.

Babb, L., *Sanity in Bedlam: A Study of Robert Burton's "Anatomy of Melancholy,"* East Lansing: Michigan State Univ. Press, 1959.

Butler, Joseph.

Mossner, E. C., *Bishop Butler and the Age of Reason*, New York: Macmillan Co., 1936.

Jones, A. Duncan, *Butler's Moral Philosophy*, Harmondsworth: Penguin, 1952.

Butler, Samuel (1612–80).

Richards, E. A., *"Hudibras" in the Burlesque Tradition*, New York: Columbia Univ. Press, 1937.

Jack, I., *Augustan Satire*, Oxford: Clarendon Press, 1952.

Butler, Samuel (1835–1902).

Festing-Jones, H., *Samuel Butler . . .: A Memoir*, 2 vols., London: Macmillan, 1919.
Furbank, P. N., *Samuel Butler, 1835–1902*, Cambridge: Cambridge Univ. Press; New York: Macmillan Co., 1948.
Willey, B., *Darwin and Butler: Two Versions of Evolution*, London: Chatto & Windus; New York: Harcourt, Brace, 1960.

Byron, Lord.

Boyd, E. F., *Byron's "Don Juan,"* New Brunswick, N. J.: Rutgers Univ. Press, 1945.
Marchand, L. A., *Byron: A Biography*, 3 vols., New York: Knopf, 1957; London: Murray, 1958.
West, P., *Byron and the Spoiler's Art*, London: Chatto & Windus, 1960.
Rutherford, A., *Byron: A Critical Study*, Edinburgh: Oliver & Boyd; Stanford: Stanford Univ. Press, 1961.
Joseph, M. K., *Byron, the Poet*, London: Gollancz, 1964.
Marchand, L. A., *Byron's Poetry: A Critical Introduction*, Boston: Houghton Mifflin, 1965; London: Murray, 1966.

Cable, George Washington.

Turner, A., *George W. Cable: A Biography*, Durham, N. C.: Duke Univ. Press, 1956.
Butcher, P., *George W. Cable*, New York: Twayne, 1962.

Caldwell, Erskine.

Korges, J., *Erskine Caldwell*, Minneapolis: Univ. of Minnesota Press, 1969; London: Oxford Univ. Press. Pamphlets on American Writers, no. 78.

Campion, Thomas.

Kastendieck, M. M., *England's Musical Poet, Thomas Campion*, New York: Oxford Univ. Press, 1938.

Canadian Literature.

Pacey, D., *Creative Writing in Canada: A Short History of English-Canadian Literature*, revised and enlarged, Toronto: Ryerson Press, 1961.
Klinck, C. F. (ed.), *A Literary History of Canada*, Toronto: Univ. of Toronto Press, 1965.
Story, N., *The Oxford Companion to Canadian History and Literature*, London: Oxford Univ. Press, 1967.

Carew, Thomas.

Grierson, H. J. C., introduction to *Metaphysical Lyrics and Poems of the Seventeenth Century*, Oxford: Clarendon Press, 1921.
Williamson, G., *The Donne Tradition: A Study in English Poetry from Donne to the Death of Cowley*, London: Oxford Univ. Press; Cambridge, Mass.: Harvard Univ. Press, 1930.

Leavis, F. R., *Revaluation: Tradition and Development in English Poetry*, London: Chatto & Windus, 1936.

Caribbean Literature.

James, L. (ed.), *The Islands in Between: Essays on West Indian Literature*, London: Oxford Univ. Press, 1968.
Moore, G., *The Chosen Tongue: English Writing in the Tropical World*, London: Longmans, 1969.
Ramchand, K., *The West Indian Novel and Its Background*, London: Faber & Faber; New York: Barnes & Noble, 1970.

Carlyle, Thomas.

Froude, J. A., [*Biography of*] *Thomas Carlyle*, 4 vols., London: Longmans, 1882–84.
Neff, E., *Carlyle*, London: Allen & Unwin; New York: Norton, 1932.
Willey, B., *Nineteenth Century Studies: Coleridge to Mathew Arnold*, London: Chatto & Windus; New York: Columbia Univ. Press, 1949.
Williams, R., *Culture and Society, 1780–1950*, London: Chatto & Windus; New York: Columbia Univ. Press, 1958.
Seidel, J. P., *Thomas Carlyle: The Critical Heritage*, London: Routledge; New York: Barnes & Noble, 1971.

"Carroll, Lewis."

Williams, S. H., and Madan, F., *A Handbook of the Literature of C. L. Dodgson (Lewis Carroll)*, New York: Oxford Univ. Press, 1931; supplement, 1935; revised R. L. Green, 1962.
Empson, W., *Some Versions of Pastoral*, London: Chatto & Windus, 1935; as *English Pastoral Poetry*, New York; Norton, 1938.
Lennon, F. B., *Victoria through the Looking-Glass: The Life of Lewis Carroll*, New York: Simon & Schuster, 1945; as *Lewis Carroll*, London: Cassell, 1947.
Sewell, E., *The Field of Nonsense*, London: Chatto & Windus, 1952.

Cary, Joyce.

Wright, A. H., *Joyce Cary: A Preface to His Novels*, London: Chatto & Windus, 1958.
Mahood, M. M., *Joyce Cary's Africa*, London: Methuen, 1964; Boston: Houghton Mifflin, 1965.

Cather, Willa.

Brown, E. K., and Edel, L., *Willa Cather: A Critical Biography*, New York: Knopf, 1953.

Caxton, William.

Winship, G. P., *William Caxton*, London: Doves Press, 1909; Berkeley: Book Arts Club of California, 1937.
Bennett, H. S., *English Books and Readers, 1457–1557*, Cambridge: Cambridge Univ. Press, 1952.
Bühler, C. F., *William Caxton and His Critics*, Syracuse, N. Y.: Syracuse Univ. Press, 1960.

Centlivre, Mrs. Susanna.

Krutch, J. W., *Comedy and Conscience after the Restoration*, London: Oxford Univ. Press; New York: Columbia Univ. Press, 1924.

Bateson, F. N. W., *English Comic Drama, 1700–1750*, Oxford: Clarendon Press, 1929.

Bowyer, J. W., *The Celebrated Mrs. Centlivre*, Durham, N. C.: Duke Univ. Press, 1952; Cambridge: Cambridge Univ. Press, 1953.

Chandler, Raymond.

Durham, P., *Down These Mean Streets a Man Must Go: Raymond Chandler's Knight*, Chapel Hill: Univ. of North Carolina Press, 1963.

Chapman, George.

Ellis-Fermor, U. M., *The Jacobean Drama: An Interpretation*, London: Methuen, 1936.

MacLure, M., *George Chapman*, Toronto: Univ. of Toronto Press, 1966.

Spivack, C., *George Chapman*, New York: Twayne, 1967.

Chatterton, Thomas.

Meyerstein, E. H. W., *A Life of Thomas Chatterton*, London: Ingpen & Grant; New York: C. Scribner's Sons, 1930.

Chaucer, Geoffrey.

Root, R. K., *The Poetry of Chaucer*, London: Constable; Boston: Houghton Mifflin, 1906; revised, 1922.

Kittredge, G. L., *Chaucer and His Poetry*, Cambridge, Mass.: Harvard Univ. Press, 1915.

Curry, W. C., *Chaucer and the Mediaeval Sciences*, New York: Oxford Univ. Press, 1926; revised, London: Allen & Unwin; New York: Barnes & Noble, 1960.

French, R. D., *A Chaucer Handbook*, New York: Crofts, 1927.

Lewis, C. S., *The Allegory of Love*, Oxford: Clarendon Press, 1936.

Bennett, J. A. W., "*The Parlement of Foules*," Oxford: Clarendon Press, 1957.

Muscatine, C., *Chaucer and the French Tradition*, Cambridge: Cambridge Univ. Press; Berkeley and Los Angeles: Univ. of California Press, 1957.

Clemen, W. H., *Chaucer's Early Poetry*, London: Methuen; New York: Barnes & Noble, 1964.

Ruggiers, P. G., *The Art of "The Canterbury Tales*," Madison: Univ. of Wisconsin Press, 1965.

Gordon, I. L., *The Double Sorrow of "Troilus*," Oxford: Clarendon Press, 1970.

Chesterfield, Earl of.

Brewer, S. M., *Design for a Gentleman: The Education of Philip Stanhope*, London: Chapman & Hall, 1963.

Chesterton, G. K.

Belloc, H., *On the Place of Gilbert Chesterton in English Letters*, London and New York: Sheed & Ward, 1940.

Ward, M., *Gilbert Keith Chesterton*, New York: Sheed & Ward, 1943; London, 1944.

Churchill, Charles.

Blunden, E., *Votive Tablets: Studies Chiefly Appreciative of English Authors and Books*, London: Cobden-Sanderson, 1931; New York: Harper, 1932.

Brown, W. C., *The Triumph of Form: A Study of the Later Masters of the Heroic Couplet*, London: Oxford Univ. Press; Chapel Hill: Univ. of North Carolina Press, 1948.

Brown, W. C., *Charles Churchill: Poet, Rake, and Rebel*, Lawrence: Univ. of Kansas Press, 1953.

Hopkins, H. K., *Portraits in Satire*, London: Barrie Books; Chester Springs, Pa.: Dufour, 1958.

Churchill, Sir Winston.

Guedalla, P., *Mr. Churchill: A Portrait*, London: Hodder & Stoughton, 1941; New York: Reynal & Hitchcock, 1942.

Churchill, R. S., *Winston S. Churchill*, vol. 1, London: Heinemann; Boston: Houghton Mifflin, 1966; vol. 2, London, 1969; Boston, 1970.

Gilbert, M., *Winston S. Churchill*, vol. 3, London: Heinemann, 1971; Boston: Houghton Mifflin, 1972; and in progress.

Churchill, Winston.

Titus, W. I., *Winston Churchill*, New York: Twayne, 1963.

Cibber, Colley.

Krutch, J. W., *Comedy and Conscience after the Restoration*, London: Oxford Univ. Press; New York: Columbia Univ. Press, 1924.

Senior, F. D. P., *The Life and Times of Colley Cibber*, London: Constable; New York: Henkle, 1928.

Bateson, F. N. W., *English Comic Drama, 1700–1750*, Oxford: Clarendon Press, 1929.

Clare, John.

Martin, F., *The Life of John Clare*, London (printed), Cambridge, 1865; London: Cass; New York: Barnes & Noble, 1964.

Tibble, J. W., and Tibble, A., *John Clare: A Life*, London: Cobden-Sanderson, 1932; revised, London: M. Joseph, 1972.

Clarendon, Earl of.

Wormald, B. H. G., *Clarendon: Politics, History and Religion, 1640–1660*, Cambridge: Cambridge Univ. Press, 1951.

Knights, L. C., *Further Explorations: Essays in Criticism*, London: Chatto & Windus, 1965.

Cleveland, John.

Wedgwood, C. V., *Poetry and Politics under the Stuarts*, Cambridge: Cambridge Univ. Press, 1960.

Clough, Arthur Hugh.

Chorley, K. (Baroness), *Arthur Hugh Clough: The Uncommitted Mind*, Oxford: Clarendon Press, 1962.

Houghton, W. E., *The Poetry of Clough*, New Haven: Yale Univ. Press, 1963.

Harris, W. V., *Arthur Hugh Clough*, New York: Twayne, 1970.

Thorpe, M. (ed.), *Clough: The Critical Heritage*, London: Routledge; New York: Barnes & Noble, 1972.

Cobbett, William.

Cole, G. D. H., *The Life of William Cobbett*, London: Collins, 1924; revised, London: Home & Van Thal, 1947.

Chesterton, G. K., *William Cobbett*, London: Hodder & Stoughton; New York: Dodd, Mead, 1925.

Coleridge, Samuel Taylor.

Mill, J. S., *Coleridge*, 1840; *On Bentham and Coleridge*, ed. F. R. Leavis, London: Chatto & Windus, 1950; New York: Stewart, 1951.

Lowes, J. L., *The Road to Xanadu: A Study in the Ways of the Imagination*, London: Constable; Boston: Houghton Mifflin, 1927.

Richards, I. A., *Coleridge on Imagination*, London: Routledge, 1934; New York: Harcourt, Brace, 1935.

House, H., *Coleridge*, London: Hart-Davis, 1953.

Beer, J. B., *Coleridge the Visionary*, London: Chatto & Windus; New York: Macmillan Co., 1959.

Colmer, J. A., *Coleridge: Critic of Society*, Oxford: Clarendon Press, 1959.

Fogle, R. H., *The Idea of Coleridge's Criticism*, Cambridge: Cambridge Univ. Press; Berkeley and Los Angeles: Univ. of California Press, 1962.

Appleyard, J. A., *Coleridge's Philosophy of Literature: The Development of a Concept of Poetry*, Cambridge, Mass.: Harvard Univ. Press, 1965; London: Oxford Univ. Press, 1966.

Barfield, O., *What Coleridge Thought*, London: Oxford Univ. Press, 1972.

Collier, Jeremy.

Spingarn, J. E. (ed.), *Critical Essays of the Seventeenth Century*, vol. 3, Oxford: Clarendon Press, 1909.

Rose Anthony, Sister, *The Jeremy Collier Stage Controversy, 1698–1726*, Milwaukee, Wis.: Marquette Univ. Press, 1937.

Collins, Wilkie.

Phillips, W. C., *Dickens, Reade, and Collins: Sensation Novelists*, New York: Columbia Univ. Press, 1919.

Robinson, K., *Wilkie Collins*, London: J. Lane; New York: Macmillan Co., 1951.

Davis, N. P., *The Life of Wilkie Collins*, Urbana: Univ. of Illinois Press, 1956.

Marshall, W. H., *Wilkie Collins*, New York: Twayne, 1970.

Collins, William.

Garrod, H. W., *Collins*, Oxford: Clarendon Press, 1928.

Ainsworth, E. G., *Poor Collins: His Life, His Art, and His Influence*, London: Oxford Univ. Press; Ithaca, N. Y.: Cornell Univ. Press, 1937.

Carver, P. L., *The Life of a Poet: A Biography of William Collins*, London: Sidgwick & Jackson; New York: Horizon Press, 1967.

Colman, George (the elder).

Page, E. R., *George Colman the Elder*, London: Oxford Univ. Press; New York: Columbia Univ. Press, 1935.

Colman, George (the younger).

Peake, R. B., *Memoirs of the Colman Family*, 2 vols., London, 1841.

Colum, Padraic.

Bowen, Z. R., *Padraic Colum: A Biographical-Critical Introduction*, Carbondale: Southern Illinois Univ. Press, 1970.

Combe, William.

Hamilton, H. W., *Doctor Syntax: A Silhouette of William Combe, Esq.*, London: Chatto & Windus; Kent, O.: Kent State Univ. Press, 1969.

Compton-Burnett, Dame Ivy.

Burkhart, C., *Ivy Compton-Burnett*, London: Gollancz, 1965.

Congreve, William.

Taylor, D. C., *William Congreve*, London and New York: Oxford Univ. Press, 1931.

Hodges, J. C., *William Congreve: Letters and Documents*, London: Macmillan; New York: Harcourt, Brace, 1964.

Van Voris, W. H., *The Cultivated Stance: The Designs of Congreve's Plays*, London: Oxford Univ. Press, 1965; Chester Springs, Pa.: Dufour, 1967.

Conrad, Joseph.

Forster, E. M., *Abinger Harvest*, London: Arnold; New York: Harcourt, Brace, 1936.

Gordan, J. D., *Joseph Conrad: The Making of a Novelist*, London: Oxford Univ. Press; Cambridge, Mass.: Harvard Univ. Press, 1940.

Bradbrook, M. C., *Joseph Conrad: England's Polish Genius*, Cambridge: Cambridge Univ. Press, 1941.

Leavis, F. R., *The Great Tradition: George Eliot, Henry James, Joseph Conrad*, London: Chatto & Windus; New York: Stewart, 1948.

Guérard, A. J., *Conrad the Novelist*, Cambridge, Mass.: Harvard Univ. Press, 1958.

Baines, J., *Joseph Conrad: A Critical Biography*, London: Weidenfeld; New York: McGraw-Hill, 1960.

Hay, E. K., *The Political Novels of Joseph Conrad*, Chicago: Univ. of Chicago Press, 1963.

Stewart, J. I. M., *Joseph Conrad*, London: Longmans; New York: Dodd, Mead, 1968.

Conrad, B., *My Father: Joseph Conrad*, London: Calder & Boyars; New York: Coward-McCann, 1970.

Cooper, James Fenimore.

Spiller, R. E., *Fenimore Cooper, Critic of His Times*, New York: Minton, Balch, 1931.

Grossman, J., *James Fenimore Cooper*, New York: Sloane, 1949; London: Methuen, 1950.

Philbrick, T., *James Fenimore Cooper and the Development of American Sea Fiction*, Cambridge, Mass.: Harvard Univ. Press; London: Oxford Univ. Press, 1961.

Ringe, D. A., *James Fenimore Cooper*, New York: Twayne, 1962.

House, K. S., *Cooper's Americans*, Columbus: Ohio State Univ. Press, 1965.

Dekker, G., *James Fenimore Cooper: The American Scott*, New York: Barnes & Noble; as *James Fenimore Cooper: The Novelist*, London: Routledge, 1967.

Corbet(t), Richard.

Crofts, J. E. V., *A Life of Bishop Corbett*, in *Essays and Studies*, vol. 10, Oxford: Clarendon Press (for English Association), 1924.

Coverdale, Miles.

Mozley, J. F., *Coverdale and His Bibles*, London: Lutterworth Press, 1953.

Coward, Sir Noël.

Levin, M., *Noël Coward*, New York: Twayne, 1968.

Cowley, Abraham.

Nethercot, A. H., *Abraham Cowley: The Muse's Hannibal*, London: Oxford Univ. Press, 1931.

Walton, G., *Metaphysical to Augustan: Studies in Tone and Sensibility in the Seventeenth Century*, London: Bowes & Bowes; Philadelphia: Saifer, 1955.

Hinman, R. B., *Abraham Cowley's World of Order*, London: Oxford Univ. Press; Cambridge, Mass.: Harvard Univ. Press, 1960.

Cowper, William.

Cecil, Lord D., *The Stricken Deer; or, The Life of Cowper*, London: Constable, 1929; Indianapolis: Bobbs-Merrill, 1930.

Quinlan, M. J., *William Cowper: A Critical Life*, London: Oxford Univ. Press; Minneapolis: Univ. of Minnesota Press, 1953.

Ryskamp, C., *William Cowper of the Inner Temple, Esq.: A Study . . . to 1768*, Cambridge: Cambridge Univ. Press, 1959.

Hartley, L. C., *William Cowper: The Continuing Revaluation*, Chapel Hill: Univ. of North Carolina Press, 1960.

Cozzens, James Gould.

Bracher, F. G., *The Novels of James Gould Cozzens*, New York: Harcourt, Brace, 1959.

Maxwell, D. E. S., *Cozzens*, Edinburgh: Oliver & Boyd, 1964.

Hicks, G., *James Gould Cozzens*, Minneapolis: Univ. of Minnesota Press, 1966; London: Oxford Univ. Press. Pamphlets on American Writers, no. 58.

Crabbe, George.

Huchon, R., *George Crabbe and His Times, 1754–1832*, London: Murray, 1907.
Haddakin, L., *The Poetry of Crabbe*, London: Chatto & Windus, 1955.
Pollard, A. (ed.), *Crabbe: The Critical Heritage*, London and Boston: Routledge, 1972.

Crane, Hart.

Horton, P., *Hart Crane: The Life of an American Poet*, New York: Norton, 1937.
Dembo, L. S., *Hart Crane's Sanskrit Charge: A Study of "The Bridge,"* Ithaca, N.Y.: Cornell Univ. Press; London: Oxford Univ. Press, 1960.
Lewis, R. W. B., *The Poetry of Hart Crane: A Critical Study*, Princeton: Princeton Univ. Press, 1967; London: Oxford Univ. Press, 1968.
Leibowitz, H. A., *Hart Crane: An Introduction to the Poetry*, New York: Columbia Univ. Press, 1968.
Butterfield, R. W., *The Broken Arc: A Study of Hart Crane*, Edinburgh: Oliver & Boyd, 1969.

Crane, Stephen.

Berryman, J., *Stephen Crane*, New York: Sloane, 1950; London: Methuen, 1951.
Solomon, E., *Stephen Crane: From Parody to Realism*, Cambridge, Mass.: Harvard Univ. Press; London: Oxford Univ. Press, 1966.
LaFrance, M., *A Reading of Stephen Crane*, Oxford: Clarendon Press, 1971.

Cranmer, Thomas.

Hutchinson, F. E., *Cranmer and the English Reformation*, New York: Macmillan Co., 1951.
Bromiley, G. W., *Thomas Cranmer, Theologian*, London: Lutterworth Press; New York: Oxford Univ. Press, 1956.
Ridley, J. G., *Thomas Cranmer*, Oxford: Clarendon Press, 1962.

Crashaw, Richard.

White, H. C., *The Metaphysical Poets: A Study in Religious Experience*, New York: Macmillan Co., 1936; London: Macmillan, 1937.
Warren, A., *Richard Crashaw: A Study in Baroque Sensibility*, Baton Rouge: Louisiana State Univ. Press, 1939.
Willey, B., *Richard Crashaw: A Memorial Lecture*, Cambridge: Cambridge Univ. Press, 1949.

Crèvecoeur, M. (St. John de).

Philbrick, T., *St. John de Crèvecoeur*, New York: Twayne, 1970.

Croker, J. W.

Feiling, K. G., *Sketches in Nineteenth Century Biography*, London and New York: Longmans, 1930.
Brightfield, M. F., *John Wilson Croker*, Berkeley and Los Angeles: Univ. of California Press, 1940.

Crowne, John.

Boswell, E., *The Restoration Court Stage (1660–1702): With a Particular Account of the Production of "Calisto,"* London: Oxford Univ. Press; Cambridge, Mass.: Harvard Univ. Press, 1932; London: Allen & Unwin; New York: Barnes & Noble, 1966.

Cullen, Countee.

Ferguson, B. E., *Countee Cullen and the Harlem Renaissance,* New York: Dodd, Mead, 1966.

Cumberland, Richard.

Williams, S. T., *Richard Cumberland: His Life and Dramatic Works,* London: Oxford Univ. Press; New Haven: Yale Univ. Press, 1917.

Cummings, E. E.

Norman, C., *The Magic-Maker, E. E. Cummings,* New York: Macmillan Co., 1958.

Friedman, N., *E. E. Cummings: The Art of His Poetry,* Baltimore: Johns Hopkins Press, 1960.

Marks, B. A., *E. E. Cummings,* New York: Twayne, 1964.

Dallas, E. S.

Wellek, R., *A History of Modern Criticism: 1750–1950,* vol. 4, New Haven: Yale Univ. Press, 1965; London: Cape, 1966.

Dana, R. H., Jr.

Shapiro, S., *Richard Henry Dana, Jr., 1815–1882,* East Lansing: Michigan State Univ. Press, 1961.

Daniel, Samuel.

Lever, J. W., *The Elizabethan Love Sonnet,* London: Methuen, 1956; 2nd edition, and New York: Barnes & Noble, 1967.

Schaar, C., *An Elizabethan Sonnet Problem,* Lund, Sweden: Gleerup, 1960.

Rees, J., *Samuel Daniel: A Critical and Biographical Study,* Liverpool: Liverpool Univ. Press, 1964.

Darley, George.

Abbott, C. C., *The Life and Letters of George Darley, Poet and Critic,* London: Oxford Univ. Press, 1928.

Darwin, Charles.

West, G., *Charles Darwin: The Fragmentary Man,* London: Routledge, 1937.

Willey, B., *Darwin and Butler: Two Versions of Evolution,* London: Chatto & Windus; New York: Harcourt, Brace, 1960.

Darwin, Erasmus.

King-Hele, D. G., *Erasmus Darwin,* London: Macmillan, 1963; New York: C. Scribner's Sons, 1964.

Davenant, Sir William.

Harbage, A., *Sir William Davenant, Poet, Venturer*, Philadelphia: Univ. of Pennsylvania Press, 1935.

Nethercot, A. H., *Sir William D'Avenant, Poet Laureate and Playwright-Manager*, Chicago: Univ. of Chicago Press, 1938; with additional notes, New York: Russell & Russell, 1967.

Collins, H. S., *The Comedy of Sir William Davenant*, The Hague: Mouton, 1967.

Davidson, John.

Townsend, J. B., *John Davidson, Poet of Armageddon*, New Haven: Yale Univ. Press, 1961.

Davies, W. H.

Moult, T., *W. H. Davies*, London: Butterworth, 1934.

Defoe, Daniel.

Sutherland, J. R., *Defoe*, London: Methuen, 1937; revised, 1950.

Watt, I. P., *The Rise of the Novel: Studies in Defoe, Richardson and Fielding*, London: Chatto & Windus; Berkeley and Los Angeles: Univ. of California Press, 1957.

Starr, G. A., *Defoe and Spiritual Autobiography*, Princeton: Princeton Univ. Press, 1965.

Rogers, P. (ed.), *Defoe: The Critical Heritage*, London and Boston: Routledge, 1972.

Sutherland, J. R., *Daniel Defoe*, London: Oxford Univ. Press; Cambridge, Mass.: Harvard Univ. Press, 1972.

De Forest, John W.

Light, J. F., *John William De Forest*, New York: Twayne, 1965.

Dekker, Thomas.

Hunt, M. L., *Thomas Dekker: A Study*, New York: Columbia Univ. Press, 1911.

Gregg, K. L., *Thomas Dekker: A Study in Economic and Social Backgrounds*, Seattle: Univ. of Washington Press, 1924.

Judges, A. V., *The Elizabethan Underworld*, London: Routledge; New York: Dutton, 1930.

Knights, L. C., *Drama and Society in the Age of Jonson*, London: Chatto & Windus, 1937.

Bradbrook, M. C., *The Growth and Structure of Elizabethan Comedy*, London: Chatto & Windus, 1955; Berkeley and Los Angeles: Univ. of California Press, 1956.

Price, G. R., *Thomas Dekker*, New York: Twayne, 1969.

De la Mare, Walter.

Reid, F., *Walter de la Mare: A Critical Study*, London: Faber & Faber; New York: Holt, 1929.

Deloney, Thomas.

Lawlis, M. E., *Apology for the Middle Class: The Dramatic Novels of Thomas Deloney*, Bloomington: Indiana Univ. Press, 1960.

Denham, Sir John.

Johnson, S., *The Lives of the Poets*, London, 1779–81.

Dennis, John.

Paul, H. G., *John Dennis: His Life and Criticism*, New York: Columbia Univ. Press, 1911.

De Quincey, Thomas.

Eaton, H. A., *Thomas De Quincey: A Biography*, London: Oxford Univ. Press, 1936.
Sackville-West, E., *A Flame in Sunlight: The Life and Work of Thomas De Quincey*, London: Cassell; as *Thomas De Quincey*, New Haven: Yale Univ. Press, 1936.
Jordan, J. E., *Thomas De Quincey, Literary Critic: His Method and Achievement*, Berkeley and Los Angeles: Univ. of California Press, 1952; Cambridge: Cambridge Univ. Press, 1953.
Lyon, J. S., *Thomas De Quincey*, New York: Twayne, 1969.

Dewey, John.

Geiger, G. R., *John Dewey in Perspective*, New York: Oxford Univ. Press, 1958.

Dickens, Charles.

Gissing, G. R., *Charles Dickens*, London: Blackie, 1898.
Chesterton, G. K., *Charles Dickens*, London: Methuen; New York: Dodd, Mead, 1906.
Orwell, G., "Charles Dickens," *Inside the Whale*, London: Gollancz, 1940.
House, H., *The Dickens World*, London: Oxford Univ. Press, 1941.
Wilson, E., "Dickens: The Two Scrooges," *The Wound and the Bow*, Boston: Houghton Mifflin, 1941; London: Secker & Warburg, 1942.
Johnson, E., *Charles Dickens: His Tragedy and Triumph*, 2 vols., New York: Simon & Schuster, 1952; London: Gollancz, 1953.
Butt, J. E., and Tillotson, K. M. C., *Dickens at Work*, London: Methuen, 1957; Fair Lawn, N.J.: Essential Books (1955–), 1958.
Fielding, K. J., *Charles Dickens: A Critical Introduction*, London: Longmans, 1958; enlarged, Boston: Houghton Mifflin, 1965.
Miller, J. H., *Charles Dickens: The World of His Novels*, Cambridge, Mass.: Harvard Univ. Press, 1958.
Ford, G. H., and Lane, L. (edd.), *The Dickens Critics*, Ithaca, N. Y.: Cornell Univ. Press, 1961.
Gross, J., and Pearson, G. (edd.), *Dickens and the Twentieth Century*, London: Routledge, 1962.
Garis, R., *The Dickens Theatre: A Reassessment of the Novels*, London: Oxford Univ. Press, 1965.

Dickinson, Emily.

Whicher, G. F., *This Was a Poet: A Critical Biography of Emily Dickinson*, New York: C. Scribner's Sons, 1938.

Johnson, T. H., *Emily Dickinson: An Interpretative Biography*, Cambridge, Mass.: Harvard Univ. Press; London: Oxford Univ. Press, 1955.

Anderson, C. R., *Emily Dickinson's Poetry: Stairway of Surprise*, New York: Holt, 1960; London: Heinemann, 1963.

Ward, T. V., *The Capsule of the Mind: Chapters in the Life of Emily Dickinson*, Cambridge, Mass.: Harvard Univ. Press; London: Oxford Univ. Press, 1961.

Griffith, C., *The Long Shadow: Emily Dickinson's Tragic Poetry*, Princeton: Princeton Univ. Press, 1964.

Gelpi, A. J., *Emily Dickinson: The Mind of the Poet*, Cambridge, Mass.: Harvard Univ. Press; London: Oxford Univ. Press, 1965.

Disraeli, Benjamin.

Monypenny, W. F., and Buckle, G. E., *The Life of Benjamin Disraeli*, 6 vols., London: Murray; New York: Macmillan Co., 1910–20; 2 vols., 1929.

Pritchett, V. S., *The Living Novel*, London: Chatto & Windus, 1946; New York: Reynal, 1947.

Holloway, J., *The Victorian Sage: Studies in Argument*, London: Macmillan; New York: St. Martin's Press, 1953.

Smith, S. M. (ed.), *Mr. Disraeli's Readers*, Nottingham: Sisson & Parker, 1966.

Blake, R. N. W., *Disraeli*, London: Eyre & Spottiswoode, 1966; New York: St. Martin's Press, 1967.

Levine, R. A., *Benjamin Disraeli*, New York: Twayne, 1968.

Dixon, R. W.

Sambrook, J., *A Poet Hidden: The Life of Richard Watson Dixon, 1833–1900*, London: Athlone Press; New York: Oxford Univ. Press, 1962.

Dobson, Austin.

Evans, B. I., *English Poetry in the Later Nineteenth Century*, London: Methuen, 1933; revised, London: Methuen; New York: Barnes & Noble, 1966.

Donne, John.

Grierson, H. J. C., introduction to *Metaphysical Lyrics and Poems of the Seventeenth Century*, Oxford: Clarendon Press, 1921.

Simpson, E. M., *A Study of the Prose Works of John Donne*, Oxford: Clarendon Press, 1924.

Eliot, T. S., *Selected Essays, 1917–1932*, London: Faber & Faber; New York: Harcourt, Brace, 1932.

Leavis, F. R., *Revaluation: Tradition and Development in English Poetry*, London: Chatto & Windus, 1936.

White, H. C., *The Metaphysical Poets: A Study in Religious Experience*, New York: Macmillan Co., 1936; London: Macmillan, 1937.

Leishman, J. B., *The Monarch of Wit: An Analytical and Comparative Study of the Poetry of John Donne*, London: Hutchinson, 1951.

Alvarez, A., *The School of Donne*, London: Chatto & Windus, 1961; New York: Pantheon, 1962.

Mueller, W. R., *John Donne, Preacher*, Princeton: Princeton Univ. Press, 1962.

Smith, A. J. (ed.), *Donne and the Metaphysical Poets: The Critical Heritage*, London: Routledge; New York: Barnes & Noble, 1968.

Bald, R. C., *John Donne: A Life*, Oxford: Clarendon Press, 1970.

Doolittle, Hilda ("H.D.").

Quinn, V. G., *Hilda Doolittle (H.D.)*, New York: Twayne, 1968.

Dos Passos, John.

Wrenn, J. H., *John Dos Passos*, New York: Twayne, 1961.

Brantley, J. D., *The Fiction of John Dos Passos*, New York: Humanities Press; The Hague: Mouton, 1968.

Douglas, Gavin.

Lewis, C. S., *English Literature in the Sixteenth Century, Excluding Drama*, Oxford: Clarendon Press, 1954.

Douglas, Norman.

Tomlinson, H. M., *Norman Douglas*, London: Chatto & Windus; New York: Harper, 1931; enlarged and revised, London: Hutchinson, 1952.

Lindeman, R. D., *Norman Douglas*, New York: Twayne, 1965.

Dowson, Ernest.

Jackson, H., *The Eighteen Nineties*, London: Grant Richards, 1913.

Longaker, J. M., *Ernest Dowson*, Philadelphia: Univ. of Pennsylvania Press, 1944; London: Oxford Univ. Press, 1945.

Drayton, Michael.

Newdigate, B. H., *Michael Drayton and His Circle*, Oxford: Blackwell; New York: Salloch, 1941.

Berthelot, J. A., *Michael Drayton*, New York: Twayne, 1967.

Dreiser, Theodore.

Elias, R. H., *Theodore Dreiser: Apostle of Nature*, New York: Knopf, 1949; revised, Ithaca, N.Y.: Cornell Univ. Press, 1970.

Dreiser, H., *My Life with Dreiser*, Cleveland: World Publishing, 1951.

Matthiessen, F. O., *Theodore Dreiser*, New York: Sloane; London: Methuen, 1951.

Gerber, P. L., *Theodore Dreiser*, New York: Twayne, 1964.

Swanberg, W. A., *Dreiser*, New York: C. Scribner's Sons, 1965.

Moers, E., *Two Dreisers: The Man and the Novelist*, New York: Viking Press, 1969; London: Thames & Hudson, 1970.

Drummond, William.

Masson, D., *Drummond of Hawthornden*, London, 1873.

Fogle, F. R., *A Critical Study of William Drummond of Hawthornden*, London: Oxford Univ. Press; New York: Columbia Univ. Press, 1952.

Dryden, John.

Eliot, T. S., *John Dryden: The Poet, the Dramatist, the Critic: Three Essays*, New York: Holliday, 1932.

Bredvold, L. I., *The Intellectual Milieu of John Dryden*, Ann Arbor: Univ. of Michigan Press, 1934.

Van Doren, M., *John Dryden: A Study of His Poetry*, New York: Holt, 1946.

Nichol Smith, D., *Dryden*, Cambridge: Cambridge Univ. Press, 1950.

Ward, C. E., *The Life of John Dryden*, London: Oxford Univ. Press; Chapel Hill: Univ. of North Carolina Press, 1961.

Hoffman, A. W., *John Dryden's Imagery*, Gainesville: Univ. of Florida Press, 1962.

Moore, F. H., *The Nobler Pleasure: Dryden's Comedy in Theory and Practice*, Chapel Hill: Univ. of North Carolina Press, 1963.

Roper, A., *Dryden's Poetic Kingdoms*, London: Routledge; New York: Barnes & Noble, 1965.

King, B. A., *Dryden's Major Plays*, Edinburgh: Oliver & Boyd; New York: Barnes & Noble, 1966.

Swedenberg, H. T. (ed.), *Essential Articles for the Study of John Dryden*, London: Cass; Hamden, Conn.: Shoe String Press, 1966.

Hamilton, K. G., *John Dryden and the Poetry of Statement*, East Lansing: Michigan State Univ. Press, 1969.

Kinsley, J., and Kinsley, H., *Dryden: The Critical Heritage*, London: Routledge; New York: Barnes & Noble, 1971.

Du Bois, W. E. B.

Broderick, F. L., *W. E. B. Du Bois: Negro Leader in a Time of Crisis*, Stanford: Stanford Univ. Press; London: Oxford Univ. Press, 1959.

Rudwick, E. M., *W. E. B. Du Bois: A Study in Minority Group Leadership*, London: Oxford Univ. Press, 1960; Philadelphia: Univ. of Pennsylvania Press, 1961.

Dunbar, Paul Laurence.

Brawley, B. G., *Paul Laurence Dunbar: Poet of His People*, Chapel Hill: Univ. of North Carolina Press, 1936.

Cunningham, V., *Paul Laurence Dunbar and His Song*, New York: Dodd, Mead, 1947.

Dunbar, William.

Baxter, J. W., *William Dunbar*, Edinburgh: Oliver & Boyd, 1952.

Scott, T., *Dunbar: A Critical Exposition of the Poems*, Edinburgh: Oliver & Boyd; New York: Barnes & Noble, 1966.

Dunlap, William.

Coad, O. S., *William Dunlap: A Study of His Life and Works*, New York: The Dunlap Society, 1917.

Durrell, Lawrence.

Moore, H. T. (ed.), *The World of Lawrence Durrell*, Carbondale: Southern Illinois Univ. Press, 1962.

Weigel, J. A., *Lawrence Durrell*, New York: Twayne, 1966.

Fraser, G. S., *Lawrence Durrell: A Critical Study*, London: Faber & Faber; New York: Dutton, 1968.

Dwight, Timothy.

Cuningham, C. E., *Timothy Dwight, 1752–1817: A Biography*, New York: Macmillan Co., 1942.

Dyer, John.

Williams, R. M., *Poet, Painter and Parson: The Life of John Dyer*, New York: Bookman Associates, 1956.

Edgeworth, Maria.

Hare, A. J. C. (ed.), *The Life and Letters of Maria Edgeworth*, 2 vols., London: Arnold, 1894.

Newby, P. H., *Maria Edgeworth*, London: Barker; Denver: Swallow, 1950.

Butler, M., *Maria Edgeworth: A Literary Biography*, Oxford: Clarendon Press, 1972.

Edwards, Jonathan.

Miller, P. G. E., *Jonathan Edwards*, New York: Sloane, 1949.

Aldridge, A. O., *Jonathan Edwards*, New York: Washington Square Press, 1966.

Davidson, E. H., *Jonathan Edwards: The Narrative of a Puritan Mind*, Boston: Houghton Mifflin, 1966.

"Eliot, George."

Cross, J. W., *George Eliot's Life, As Related in Her Letters and Journals*, 3 vols., Edinburgh: Blackwood, 1885.

Bennett, J., *George Eliot: Her Mind and Her Art*, Cambridge: Cambridge Univ. Press: New York: Macmillan Co., 1948.

Leavis, F. R., *The Great Tradition: George Eliot, Henry James, Joseph Conrad*, London: Chatto & Windus; New York: Stewart, 1948.

Hardy, B., *The Novels of George Eliot: A Study in Form*, London: Athlone Press; New York: Oxford Univ. Press (Essential Books, 1955–   ), 1959.

Harvey, W. J., *The Art of George Eliot*, London: Chatto & Windus, 1961; New York: Oxford Univ. Press, 1962.

Haight, G. S., *George Eliot: A Biography*, Oxford: Clarendon Press, 1968.

Carroll, D. (ed.), *George Eliot: The Critical Heritage*, London: Routledge; New York: Barnes & Noble, 1971.

Eliot, T. S.

Matthiessen, F. O., *The Achievement of T. S. Eliot: An Essay on the Nature of Poetry*, 1935; 3rd edition, revised C. L. Barber, London and New York: Oxford Univ. Press, 1958.

Williamson, G., *A Reader's Guide to T. S. Eliot*, New York: Noonday Press, 1953; London: Thames & Hudson, 1955.

Smith, G. C., *T. S. Eliot's Poetry and Plays: A Study in Sources and Meaning*, Cambridge: Cambridge Univ. Press; Chicago: Univ. of Chicago Press, 1956.

Kenner, H., *The Invisible Poet: T. S. Eliot*, New York: McDowell, Obolensky, 1959; London: W. H. Allen, 1960.
Jones, D. E., *The Plays of T. S. Eliot*, London: Routledge, 1960.

Elyot, Sir Thomas.

Lehmberg, S. E., *Sir Thomas Elyot: Tudor Humanist*, Austin: Univ. of Texas Press, 1960.
Major, J. M., *Sir Thomas Elyot and Renaissance Humanism*, Lincoln: Univ. of Nebraska Press, 1964.

Emerson, Ralph Waldo.

Holmes, O. W., *Ralph Waldo Emerson*, Boston: Houghton, Mifflin, 1885.
Carpenter, F. I., *Emerson and Asia*, Cambridge, Mass.: Harvard Univ. Press, 1930.
Rusk, R. L., *The Life of Ralph Waldo Emerson*, New York: C. Scribner's Sons, 1949.
Whicher, S. E., *Freedom and Fate: An Inner Life of Ralph Waldo Emerson*, Philadelphia: Univ. of Pennsylvania Press; London: Oxford Univ. Press, 1953.
Nicoloff, P. L., *Emerson on Race and History*, New York: Columbia Univ. Press, 1961.

Empson, William.

Thwaite, A., *Contemporary English Poetry: An Introduction*, London: Heinemann; Chester Springs, Pa.: Dufour, 1961.
Fraser, G. S., *The Modern Writer and His World*, London: D. Verschoyle, 1953; revised, London: Deutsch, 1964; New York: Praeger, 1965.

Essays.

Walker, H., *The English Essay and Essayists*, London: Dent; New York: Dutton, 1915.
Marr, G. S., *The Periodical Essayists of the Eighteenth Century*, London: J. Clarke, 1923.
Graham, W., *English Literary Periodicals*, New York: Nelson, 1930.
Humphreys, A. R., *Steele, Addison and Their Periodical Essays*, London: Longmans (for British Council), 1959. Writers and Their Work series.

Etherege, Sir George.

Underwood, D., *Etherege and the Seventeenth-Century Comedy of Manners*, New Haven: Yale Univ. Press, 1957; London: Oxford Univ. Press, 1958.

Evans, Caradoc.

Williams, T. L., *Caradoc Evans*, Cardiff: Univ. of Wales Press, 1970.

Evelyn, John.

Hiscock, W. G., *John Evelyn and Mrs. Godolphin*, London: Macmillan, 1951; New York: St. Martin's Press, 1952.
Hiscock, W. G., *John Evelyn and His Family Circle*, London: Routledge, 1955.

Farquhar, George.

Connely, W., *Young George Farquhar: The Restoration Drama at Twilight*, London: Cassell, 1949.

Rothstein, E., *George Farquhar*, New York: Twayne, 1967.

Farrell, James T.

Branch, E. M., *James T. Farrell*, Minneapolis: Univ. of Minnesota Press, 1963; London: Oxford Univ. Press. Pamphlets on American Writers, no. 29.

Faulkner, William.

Vickery, O. W., *The Novels of William Faulkner: A Critical Interpretation*, Baton Rouge: Louisiana State Univ. Press, 1959; revised, 1964.

Beck, W., *Man in Motion: Faulkner's Trilogy*, Madison: Univ. of Wisconsin Press, 1961.

Meriwether, J. B., *The Literary Career of William Faulkner*, Princeton: Princeton Univ. Library, 1961.

Brooks, C., *William Faulkner: The Yoknapatawpha Country*, New Haven: Yale Univ. Press, 1963.

Volpe, E. L., *A Reader's Guide to William Faulkner*, New York: Farrar, Straus; London: Thames & Hudson, 1964.

Millgate, M., *The Achievement of William Faulkner*, New York: Random House; London: Constable, 1966.

Cowley, M., *The Faulkner-Cowley File: Letters and Memories, 1944–1962*, New York: Viking Press, 1966; London: Chatto & Windus, 1967.

Adams, R. P., *Faulkner: Myth and Motion*, Princeton: Princeton Univ. Press, 1968.

Fenollosa, Ernest.

Chisholm, L. W., *Fenollosa: The Far East and American Culture*, New Haven: Yale Univ. Press, 1963.

Ferrier, Susan.

Saintsbury, G., *Essays on English Literature, 1780–1860*, vol. 2, London: Percival, 1890.

Field, Nathaniel.

Brinkley, R., *Nathan Field, the Actor-Playwright*, London: Oxford Univ. Press; New Haven: Yale Univ. Press, 1928.

Fielding, Henry.

Dudden, F. H., *Henry Fielding: His Life, Works, and Times*, 2 vols., Oxford: Clarendon Press, 1952.

Watt, I. P., *The Rise of the Novel: Studies in Defoe, Richardson and Fielding*, London: Chatto & Windus; Berkeley and Los Angeles: Univ. of California Press, 1957.

Paulson, R. (ed.), *Fielding: A Collection of Critical Essays*, Englewood Cliffs, N. J.: Prentice-Hall, 1962.

Wright, A. H., *Henry Fielding: Mask and Feast*, London: Chatto & Windus; Berkeley and Los Angeles: Univ. of California Press, 1965.

Irwin, M., *Henry Fielding: The Tentative Realist*, Oxford: Clarendon Press, 1967.

Alter, R., *Fielding and the Nature of the Novel*, London: Oxford Univ. Press; Cambridge, Mass.: Harvard Univ. Press, 1968.

Firbank, Ronald.

Forster, E. M., *Abinger Harvest*, London: Arnold; New York: Harcourt, Brace, 1936.

Benkovitz, M. J., *Ronald Firbank*, New York: Knopf, 1969; London: Weidenfeld, 1970.

Merritt, J. D., *Ronald Firbank*, New York: Twayne, 1969.

FitzGerald, Edward.

Terhune, A. M., *The Life of Edward FitzGerald*, London: Oxford Univ. Press; New Haven: Yale Univ. Press, 1947.

Fitzgerald, F. Scott.

Mizener, A., *The Far Side of Paradise: A Biography of F. Scott Fitzgerald*, Boston: Houghton Mifflin; London: Eyre & Spottiswoode, 1951.

Turnbull, A. W., *Scott Fitzgerald*, New York: C. Scribner's Sons; London: Bodley Head, 1962.

Perosa, S., *The Art of F. Scott Fitzgerald*, Ann Arbor: Univ. of Michigan Press, 1965.

Piper, H. D., *F. Scott Fitzgerald: A Critical Portrait*, New York: Holt, Rinehart, 1965; London: Bodley Head, 1966.

Lehan, R. D., *F. Scott Fitzgerald and the Craft of Fiction*, Carbondale: Southern Illinois Univ. Press, 1966.

Sklar, R., *F. Scott Fitzgerald: The Last Laocoön*, New York: Oxford Univ. Press, 1967.

Flecker, James Elroy.

Hodgson, G. E., *The Life of James Elroy Flecker*, Oxford: Blackwell; Boston: Houghton Mifflin, 1925.

Fletcher, Giles (the younger).

Cory, H. E., *Spenser, the School of the Fletchers, and Milton*, Berkeley: Univ. of California Press, 1912.

Fletcher, John.

Lynch, K. M., *The Social Mode of Restoration Comedy*, London: Macmillan (Univ. of Michigan publications); New York: Macmillan Co., 1926.

Bradbrook, M. C., *Themes and Conventions of Elizabethan Tragedy*, Cambridge: Cambridge Univ. Press, 1935.

Wallis, L. B., *Fletcher, Beaumont and Company*, London: Oxford Univ. Press; New York: Columbia Univ. Press (King's Crown), 1947.

Danby, J. F., *Poets on Fortune's Hill: Studies in Sidney, Shakespeare, Beaumont and Fletcher*, London: Faber & Faber, 1952.

Waith, E. M., *The Pattern of Tragicomedy in Beaumont and Fletcher*, New Haven: Yale Univ. Press, 1952.

Appleton, W. W., *Beaumont and Fletcher*, London: Allen & Unwin; Fair Lawn, N. J.: Essential Books (1955–), 1956.

Leech, C., *The John Fletcher Plays*, London: Chatto & Windus; Cambridge, Mass.: Harvard Univ. Press, 1962.

Tomlinson, T. B., *A Study of Elizabethan and Jacobean Tragedy*, Cambridge: Cambridge Univ. Press, 1964.

Fletcher, Phineas.

Langdale, A. B., *Phineas Fletcher: Man of Letters, Science and Divinity*, London: Oxford Univ. Press; New York: Columbia Univ. Press, 1937.

Foote, Samuel.

Belden, M. M., *The Dramatic Work of Samuel Foote*, London: Oxford Univ. Press; New Haven: Yale Univ. Press, 1929.

Ford, Ford Madox.

Cassell, R. A., *Ford Madox Ford: A Study of His Novels*, Baltimore: Johns Hopkins Press, 1961.

Hoffmann, C. G., *Ford Madox Ford*, New York: Twayne, 1967.

MacShane, F. (ed.), *Ford Madox Ford: The Critical Heritage*, London and Boston: Routledge, 1972.

Ford, John.

Eliot, T. S., *Selected Essays, 1917–1932*, London: Faber & Faber; New York: Harcourt, Brace, 1932.

Sargeaunt, M. J., *John Ford*, Oxford: Blackwell; New York: P. Smith, 1935.

Ellis-Fermor, U. M., *The Jacobean Drama: An Interpretation*, London: Methuen, 1936.

Sensabaugh, G. F., *The Tragic Muse of John Ford*, Stanford: Stanford Univ. Press, 1944; London: Oxford Univ. Press, 1945.

Leech, C., *John Ford and the Drama of His Time*, London: Chatto & Windus; Fair Lawn, N. J.: Essential Books (1955–), 1957.

Forster, E. M.

Macaulay, R., *The Writings of E. M. Forster*, London: Hogarth Press; New York: Harcourt, Brace, 1938.

Trilling, L., *E. M. Forster*, Norfolk, Conn.: New Directions, 1943; London: Hogarth Press, 1944; revised, London, 1967.

Leavis, F. R., *The Common Pursuit*, London: Chatto & Windus; New York: Stewart, 1952.

Crews, F. C., *E. M. Forster: The Perils of Humanism*, London: Oxford Univ. Press; Princeton: Princeton Univ. Press, 1962.

Beer, J. B., *The Achievement of E. M. Forster*, London: Chatto & Windus, 1962; New York: Barnes & Noble, 1963.

Stone, W. H., *The Cave and the Mountain: A Study of E. M. Forster*, London: Oxford Univ. Press; Stanford: Stanford Univ. Press, 1966.

Foxe, John.

Mozley, J. F., *John Foxe and His Book*, London: S.P.C.K.; New York: Macmillan Co., 1940.

Haller, W., *Foxe's "Book of Martyrs" and the Elect Nation*, London: Cape, 1963; as *The Elect Nation: The Meaning and Relevance of Foxe's "Book of Martyrs,"* New York: Harper & Row, 1964.

Franklin, Benjamin.

Van Doren, C. C., *Benjamin Franklin*, New York: Viking Press, 1938; London: Putnam, 1939.

Granger, B. I., *Benjamin Franklin: An American Man of Letters*, Ithaca, N. Y.: Cornell Univ. Press, 1964.

Conner, P. W., *Poor Richard's Politicks: Benjamin Franklin and His New American Order*, New York: Oxford Univ. Press, 1965.

Frazer, Sir James George.

Downie, R. A., *James George Frazer: The Portrait of a Scholar*, London: C. A. Watts, 1940; New York: Macmillan Co., 1941.

Frederic, Harold.

O'Donnell, T. F., and Franchere, H. C., *Harold Frederic*, New York: Twayne, 1961.

Briggs, A. E., Jr., *The Novels of Harold Frederic*, Ithaca, N. Y.: Cornell Univ. Press, 1969.

Freneau, Philip.

Leary, L., *That Rascal Freneau: A Study in Literary Failure*, New Brunswick, N. J.: Rutgers Univ. Press, 1941.

Frost, Robert.

Thompson, L., *Fire and Ice: The Art and Thought of Robert Frost*, New York: Holt, 1942.

Cook, R. L., *The Dimensions of Robert Frost*, New York: Rinehart, 1958.

Lynen, J. F., *The Pastoral Art of Robert Frost*, New Haven: Yale Univ. Press, 1960.

Brower, R. A., *The Poetry of Robert Frost: Constellations of Intention*, London and New York: Oxford Univ. Press, 1963.

Thompson, L., *Robert Frost: The Early Years, 1874–1915*, New York: Holt, Rinehart, 1966; London: Cape, 1967.

Thompson, L., *Robert Frost: The Years of Triumph, 1915–1938*, New York: Holt, Rinehart, 1970; London: Cape, 1971.

Froude, J. A.

Paul, H. W., *The Life of Froude*, London: Pitman; New York: C. Scribner's Sons, 1905.

Willey, B., *More Nineteenth Century Studies: A Group of Honest Doubters*, London: Chatto & Windus; New York: Columbia Univ. Press, 1956.

Dunn, W. H., *James Anthony Froude*, 2 vols., Oxford: Clarendon Press, 1961–63.

Fry, Christopher.

Taylor, J. Russell, *Anger and After: A Guide to the New British Drama*, London: Methuen, 1962; revised, 1969; as *The Angry Theatre: New British Drama*, New York: Hill & Wang, 1962.

Roy, E., *Christopher Fry*, Carbondale: Southern Illinois Univ. Press, 1968.

Fuller, Thomas.

Addison, W., *Worthy Dr. Fuller*, London: Dent; New York: Macmillan Co., 1951.

Galsworthy, John.

Marrot, H. V., *The Life and Letters of John Galsworthy*, London: Heinemann, 1935; New York: C. Scribner's Sons, 1936.
Barker, D., *The Man of Principle: John Galsworthy*, London: Heinemann, 1963.

Galt, John.

Aberdein, J. W., *John Galt*, London: Oxford Univ. Press, 1936.
Frykman, E., *Galt's Scottish Stories, 1820–1823*, Upsala, Sweden: Lundequistska, 1959.

Garland, Hamlin.

Pizer, D., *Hamlin Garland's Early Work and Career*, Berkeley and Los Angeles: Univ. of California Press, 1960.

Gascoigne, George.

Prouty, C. T., *George Gascoigne: Elizabethan Courtier, Soldier and Poet*, London: Oxford Univ. Press; New York: Columbia Univ. Press, 1942.

Gaskell, Mrs. Elizabeth.

Cazamian, L., *Le Roman Social en Angleterre, 1830–1850*, Paris, 1904; 2 vols., 1935.
Cecil, Lord D., *Early Victorian Novelists: Essays in Revaluation*, London: Constable, 1934; Indianapolis: Bobbs-Merrill, 1935.
Hopkins, A. B., *Elizabeth Gaskell: Her Life and Work*, London: J. Lehmann, 1952.
Pollard, A., *Mrs. Gaskell, Novelist and Biographer*, Manchester: Manchester Univ. Press, 1965; Cambridge, Mass.: Harvard Univ. Press, 1966.
Wright, E., *Mrs. Gaskell: The Basis for Reassessment*, London: Oxford Univ. Press, 1965.

"Gawain Poet, The."

Borroff, M., *"Sir Gawain and the Green Knight": A Stylistic and Metrical Study*, New Haven: Yale Univ. Press, 1962.
Benson, L. D., *Art and Tradition in "Sir Gawain and the Green Knight,"* New Brunswick, N. J.: Rutgers Univ. Press, 1965.
Burrow, J. A., *A Reading of "Sir Gawain and the Green Knight,"* London: Routledge, 1965.
Blanch, R. J. (ed.), *"Sir Gawain" and "Pearl": Critical Essays*, Bloomington: Indiana Univ. Press, 1966.
Kean, P. M., *"The Pearl": An Interpretation*, London: Routledge; New York: Barnes & Noble, 1967.
Moorman, C., *The Pearl-Poet*, New York: Twayne, 1968.

Gay, John.

Irving, W. H., *John Gay, Favorite of the Wits*, Cambridge: Cambridge Univ. Press; Durham, N. C.: Duke Univ. Press, 1940.
Forsgren, A., *John Gay: Poet of a Lower Order*, Stockholm: Natur & Kulter, 1964.

George, Henry.

Geiger, G. R., *The Philosophy of Henry George*, New York: Macmillan Co., 1933.
Barker, C. A., *Henry George*, London: Oxford Univ. Press, 1955.

Georgians, The.

Ross, R. H., *The Georgian Revolt: The Rise and Fall of a Poetic Ideal*, London: Faber & Faber; Carbondale: Southern Illinois Univ. Press, 1967.

Gibbon, Edward.

Young, G. M., *Gibbon*, London: P. Davies, 1932; New York: Appleton-Century, 1933.
Bond, H. L., *The Literary Art of Edward Gibbon*, Oxford: Clarendon Press, 1960.
Trevor-Roper, H. R., *Gibbon*, London: New English Library, 1966.

"Gibbon, Lewis Grassic."

Munro, I. S., *Leslie Mitchell: Lewis Grassic Gibbon*, Edinburgh: Oliver & Boyd, 1966.

Gifford, William.

Longaker, J., *The Della Cruscans and William Gifford*, Philadelphia: Univ. of Pennsylvania Press, 1924.
Clark, R. B., *William Gifford: Tory Satirist, Critic and Editor*, London: Oxford Univ. Press; New York: Columbia Univ. Press, 1930.
Hopkins, H. K., *Portraits in Satire*, London: Barrie Books; Chester Springs, Pa.: Dufour, 1958.

Gilbert, W. S.

Darlington, W. A., *The World of Gilbert and Sullivan*, London: Nevill; New York: Crowell, 1950.

Gilpin, William.

Hussey, C., *The Picturesque: Studies in a Point of View*, London and New York: Putnam, 1927.
Barbier, C. P., *William Gilpin: His Drawings, Teaching, and Theory of the Picturesque*, Oxford: Clarendon Press, 1963.

Ginsberg, Allen.

Kramer, J., *Allen Ginsberg in America*, New York: Random House (Vintage), 1969; as *Paterfamilias: Allen Ginsberg in America*, London: Gollancz, 1970.

Gissing, George.

Donnelly, M. C., *George Gissing, Grave Comedian*, London: Oxford Univ. Press; Cambridge, Mass.: Harvard Univ. Press, 1954.

Korg, J., *George Gissing: A Critical Biography*, Seattle: Univ. of Washington Press, 1963; London: Methuen, 1965.

Glasgow, Ellen.

McDowell, F. P. W., *Ellen Glasgow and the Ironic Art of Fiction*, Madison: Univ. of Wisconsin Press, 1960.

Godwin, William.

Fleisher, D., *William Godwin: A Study in Liberalism*, London: Allen & Unwin, 1951.

Rodway, A. E. (ed.), *Godwin and the Age of Transition*, London: Harrap; New York: Barnes & Noble, 1952.

Monro, D. H., *Godwin's Moral Philosophy*, London and New York: Oxford Univ. Press, 1953.

Gogarty, Oliver St. John.

O'Connor, U., *The Times I've Seen*, New York: Obolensky, 1963; as *Oliver St. John Gogarty: A Poet and His Times*, London: Cape, 1964.

Golding Arthur.

Golding, L. T., *An Elizabethan Puritan: Arthur Golding, . . .*, New York: R. R. Smith, 1937.

Golding, William.

Kermode, F., *Puzzles and Epiphanies: Essays and Reviews, 1958–1961*, London: Routledge, 1962.

Hynes, S., *William Golding*, New York: Columbia Univ. Press, 1964.

Dick, B. F., *William Golding*, New York: Twayne, 1967.

Kinkead-Weekes, M., and Gregor, I., *William Golding: A Critical Study*, London: Faber & Faber, 1967; New York: Harcourt, Brace, 1968.

Babb, H. S., *The Novels of William Golding*, Columbus: Ohio State Univ. Press, 1970.

Goldsmith, Oliver.

Wardle, R. M., *Oliver Goldsmith*, Lawrence: Univ. of Kansas Press, 1957; London: Constable, 1958.

Hopkins, R. H., *The True Genius of Oliver Goldsmith*, Baltimore: Johns Hopkins Press, 1969.

Gosse, Sir Edmund.

Charteris, E. E., *The Life and Letters of Sir Edmund Gosse*, London: Heinemann; New York: Harper, 1931.

Gower, John.

Fisher, H., *John Gower: Moral Philosopher and Friend of Chaucer*, New York: New York Univ. Press, 1964; London: Methuen, 1965.

Granville-Barker, Harley.

Morgan, M. M., *A Drama of Political Man: A Study in the Plays of Harley Granville-Barker*, London: Sidgwick & Jackson, 1961.

Graves, Richard.

Hill, C. J., *The Literary Career of Richard Graves*, Northampton, Mass.: Smith College, 1935.

Graves, Robert.

Day, D., *Swifter than Reason: The Poetry and Criticism of Robert Graves*, London: Oxford Univ. Press; Chapel Hill: Univ. of North Carolina Press, 1963.

Cohen, J. M., *Robert Graves*, Edinburgh: Oliver & Boyd, 1960; New York: Barnes & Noble, 1965.

Kirkham, M., *The Poetry of Robert Graves*, London: Athlone Press; New York: Oxford Univ. Press, 1969.

Gray, Thomas.

Johnson, S., *The Lives of the Poets*, London, 1779–81.

Jones, W. P., *Thomas Gray, Scholar*, Cambridge, Mass.: Harvard Univ. Press, 1937; London: Oxford Univ. Press, 1938.

Hough, G. G., *The Romantic Poets*, London: Hutchinson; New York: Longmans, 1953.

Ketton-Cremer, R. W., *Thomas Gray*, Cambridge: Cambridge Univ. Press, 1955.

"Green, Henry."

Stokes, E., *The Novels of Henry Green*, London: Hogarth Press, 1959; New York: Macmillan Co., 1960.

Greene, Graham.

Allott, K., and Farris, M., *The Art of Graham Greene*, London: H. Hamilton, 1951.

Atkins, J. A., *Graham Greene*, London: Calder; New York: Roy, 1957; revised, London, 1966; New York: Humanities Press, 1967.

Lodge, D., *Graham Greene*, New York: Columbia Univ. Press, 1966.

Greene, Robert.

Jordan, J. C., *Robert Greene*, New York: Columbia Univ. Press, 1915.

Gregory, Lady.

Coxhead, E., *Lady Gregory: A Literary Portrait*, London: Macmillan; New York: Harcourt, Brace, 1961.

Greville, Fulke.

Rees, J., *Fulke Greville, Lord Brooke, 1554–1628: A Critical Biography*, London: Routledge; Berkeley and Los Angeles: Univ. of California Press, 1971.

Gunn, Thom.

Thwaite, A., *Contemporary English Poetry: An Introduction*, London: Heinemann, 1959; Chester Springs, Pa.: Dufour, 1961.

Rosenthal, M. L. (ed.), *The New Poets: American and British Poetry since World War II*, New York: Oxford Univ. Press, 1967.

Hakluyt, Richard.

Parks, G. B., *Richard Hakluyt and the English Voyages*, New York: American Geographical Society, 1928.

Halifax, George Savile, Marquess of.

Foxcroft, H. C., *A Character of the Trimmer: Being a Short Life of the First Marquis of Halifax*, Cambridge: Cambridge Univ. Press, 1946.

Hall, Joseph.

Kinloch, T. F., *The Life and Works of Joseph Hall, 1574-1656*, London and New York: Staples Press, 1951.

Hammett, Dashiell.

Nolan, W. F., *Dashiell Hammett: A Casebook*, St. Charlotte, N. C.: McNally & Loftin, 1969.

Hardy, Thomas.

Hardy, F. E., *The Early Life of Thomas Hardy*, London: Macmillan, 1928; *The Later Years of Thomas Hardy*, London: Macmillan, 1930; as single vol., London: Macmillan; New York: St. Martin's Press, 1962.

Cecil, Lord D., *Hardy the Novelist*, London: Constable, 1943; Indianapolis: Bobbs-Merrill, 1946.

Guérard, A. J., *Thomas Hardy: The Novels and Stories*, Cambridge, Mass.: Harvard Univ. Press, 1949; London: Oxford Univ. Press, 1950.

Brown, D., *Thomas Hardy*, London: Longmans, 1954; revised, 1961.

Hynes, S., *The Pattern of Hardy's Poetry*, London: Oxford Univ. Press; Chapel Hill: Univ. of North Carolina Press, 1961.

Bailey, J. O., *The Poetry of Thomas Hardy: A Handbook and Commentary*, Chapel Hill: Univ. of North Carolina Press, 1970.

Cox, R. G. (ed.), *Thomas Hardy: The Critical Heritage*, London: Routledge; New York: Barnes & Noble, 1970.

Stewart, J. I. M., *Thomas Hardy*, London: Longmans, 1971.

Harris, Joel Chandler.

Brookes, S. B., *Joel Chandler Harris, Folklorist*, Athens: Univ. of Georgia Press, 1950.

Hartley, David.

Bower, G. S., *Hartley and James Mill*, London: Sampson Low, 1881.

Hartley, L. P.

Bien, P., *L. P. Hartley*, London: Chatto & Windus; University Park, Pa.: Pennsylvania State Univ. Press, 1963.

Hawes, Stephen.

Lewis, C. S., *The Allegory of Love*, Oxford: Clarendon Press, 1936.

Hawker, R. S.

Burrows, M. F., *Robert Stephen Hawker: A Study of His Thought and Poetry*, Oxford: Blackwell, 1926.

Hawthorne, Nathaniel.

James, H., *Hawthorne*, London: Macmillan, 1879; New York: Harper, 1880.

Hawthorne, J., *Nathaniel Hawthorne and His Wife*, 2 vols., Cambridge, Mass.: Harvard Univ. Press, 1884; London: Chatto & Windus, 1885.

Stewart, R., *Nathaniel Hawthorne*, New Haven: Yale Univ. Press; London: Oxford Univ. Press, 1948.

Davidson, E. H., *Hawthorne's Last Phase*, New Haven: Yale Univ. Press; London: Oxford Univ. Press, 1949.

Fogle, R. H., *Hawthorne's Fiction: The Light and the Dark*, Norman: Univ. of Oklahoma Press, 1952.

Waggoner, H. H., *Hawthorne: A Critical Study*, Cambridge, Mass.: Harvard Univ. Press; London: Oxford Univ. Press, 1955.

Hoeltje, H. H., *Inward Sky: The Mind and Heart of Nathaniel Hawthorne*, Durham, N. C.: Duke Univ. Press; Cambridge: Cambridge Univ. Press, 1962.

Crews, F. C., *The Sins of the Fathers: Hawthorne's Psychological Themes*, New York: Oxford Univ. Press, 1966.

Crowley, J. D. (ed.), *Hawthorne: The Critical Heritage*, London: Routledge; New York: Barnes & Noble, 1970.

Hazlitt, William.

Howe, P. P., *The Life of William Hazlitt*, London: Secker, 1922; revised, 1947.

Schneider, E., *The Aesthetics of William Hazlitt*, London: Oxford Univ. Press; Philadelphia: Univ. of Pennsylvania Press, 1933.

Baker, H. C., *William Hazlitt*, London: Oxford Univ. Press; Cambridge, Mass.: Harvard Univ. Press, 1962.

Hemingway, Ernest.

McCaffery, J. K. M. (ed.), *Ernest Hemingway: The Man and His Work*, Cleveland: World Publishing, 1950.

Baker, C. H., *Hemingway: The Writer As Artist*, Princeton: Princeton Univ. Press, 1952; London: Oxford Univ. Press, 1953; revised, 1956.

Fenton, C. A., *The Apprenticeship of Ernest Hemingway: The Early Years*, New York: Farrar, Straus, 1954; London: P. Owen, 1955.

Baker, C. H., *Ernest Hemingway: A Life Story*, New York: C. Scribner's Sons: London: Collins, 1969.

Henley, W. E.

Buckley, J. H., *W. E. Henley: A Study in the Counter-Decadence of the 'Nineties*, London: Oxford Univ. Press; Princeton: Princeton Univ. Press, 1945.

Connell, J., *W. E. Henley*, London: Constable; New York: Macmillan Co., 1949.

"Henry, O."

Smith, C. A., *O. Henry*, Garden City, N. Y.: Doubleday; London: Hodder & Stoughton, 1916.

Henryson, Robert.

Muir, E., *Essays on Literature and Society*, London: Hogarth Press, 1949.

Stearns, M. W., *Robert Henryson*, London: Oxford Univ. Press; New York: Columbia Univ. Press, 1949.

MacQueen, J., *Robert Henryson: A Study of the Major Narrative Poems*, Oxford: Clarendon Press, 1967.

Herbert, George.

Leishman, J. B., *The Metaphysical Poets: Donne, Herbert, Vaughan, Traherne*, Oxford: Clarendon Press, 1934.

Knights, L. C., *Explorations: Essays in Criticism, Mainly on the Literature of the Seventeenth Century*, London: Chatto & Windus, 1946; New York: Stewart, 1947.

Tuve, R., *A Reading of George Herbert*, London: Faber & Faber; Chicago: Univ. of Chicago Press, 1952.

Summers, J. H., *George Herbert: His Religion and Art*, London: Chatto & Windus; Cambridge, Mass.: Harvard Univ. Press, 1954.

Alvarez, A., *The School of Donne*, London: Chatto & Windus, 1961; New York: Pantheon, 1962.

Eliot, T. S., *George Herbert*, London: Longmans (for British Council), 1962. Writers and Their Work series.

Stein, A. S., *George Herbert's Lyrics*, Baltimore: Johns Hopkins Press, 1968.

Herbert of Cherbury, Lord.

Williamson, G., *The Donne Tradition: A Study in English Poetry from Donne to the Death of Cowley*, London: Oxford Univ. Press; Cambridge, Mass.: Harvard Univ. Press, 1930.

Willey, B., *The Seventeenth Century Background: Studies in the Thought of the Age in Relation to Poetry and Religion*, London: Chatto & Windus, 1934.

Bottrall, M., *Every Man a Phoenix: Studies in Seventeenth Century Autobiography*, London: Murray, 1958.

Herrick, Robert.

Musgrove, S., *The Universe of Robert Herrick*, Auckland: Auckland Univ. College, 1950. Bulletin no. 38. English series no. 4.

Chute, M. G., *Two Gentle Men: The Lives of George Herbert and Robert Herrick*, New York: Dutton, 1959; London: Secker & Warburg, 1960.

Herrick, Robert (1868–1938).

Nevius, B. R., *Robert Herrick: The Development of a Novelist*, Berkeley and Los Angeles: Univ. of California Press; Cambridge: Cambridge Univ. Press, 1962.

Heywood, John.

Bolwell, R. W., *The Life and Works of John Heywood*, New York: Columbia Univ. Press, 1921.

Maxwell, I. R., *French Farce and John Heywood*, Melbourne: Melbourne Univ. Press, 1946.

Heywood, Thomas.

Clark, A. M., *Thomas Heywood, Playwright and Miscellanist*, Oxford: Blackwell; New York: P. Smith, 1931.

Eliot, T. S., *Selected Essays, 1917–1932*, London: Faber & Faber; New York: Harcourt, Brace, 1932.

Boas, F. S., *Thomas Heywood*, London: Williams & Norgate, 1950.

Bradbrook, M. C., *The Growth and Structure of Elizabethan Comedy*, London: Chatto & Windus, 1955; Berkeley and Los Angeles: Univ. of California Press, 1956.

Brown, A., "Citizen Comedy and Domestic Drama," *Stratford-upon-Avon Studies: no. 1, Jacobean Theatre*, London: Arnold; New York: St. Martin's Press, 1960.

Hobbes, Thomas.

James, D. G., *The Life of Reason: Hobbes, Locke, Bolingbroke*, London: Longmans, 1949.

Peters, R., *Hobbes*, Harmondsworth: Penguin, 1956.

Mintz, S. I., *The Hunting of Leviathan: Seventeenth-Century Reaction to the Materialism and Moral Philosophy of Thomas Hobbes*, Cambridge: Cambridge Univ. Press, 1962.

Hogg, James.

Batho, E. C., *The Ettrick Shepherd*, Cambridge: Cambridge Univ. Press, 1927.

Holcroft, Thomas.

Baine, R. M., *Thomas Holcroft and the Revolutionary Novel*, Athens: Univ. of Georgia Press, 1965.

Holmes, Oliver Wendell.

Small, M. R., *Oliver Wendell Holmes*, New York: Twayne 1963.

Hood, Thomas.

Jerrold, W., *Thomas Hood: His Life and Times*, London: Alston Rivers, 1907.

Reid, J. C., *Thomas Hood*, London: Routledge, 1963; New York: Hillary House, 1964.

Hooker, Richard.

Walton, I., *Lives*, 1670.

Paget, F., *An Introduction to the Fifth Book of Hooker's. . ."Ecclesiastical Polity,"* Oxford: Clarendon Press, 1899.

Sisson, C. J., *The Judicious Marriage of Mr. Hooker*, Cambridge: Cambridge Univ. Press; New York: Macmillan Co., 1940.

Marshall, J. S., *Hooker and the Anglican Tradition*, Sewanee, Tenn.: Univ. Press of Sewanee, 1963; London: A. & C. Black, 1964.

Hopkins, Gerard Manley.

Pick, J., *Gerard Manley Hopkins: Priest and Poet*, London: Oxford Univ. Press, 1942.

Peters, W. A. M., *Gerard Manley Hopkins: A Critical Essay towards the Understanding of His Poetry*, London: Oxford Univ. Press, 1948.

Gardner, W. H. (ed.), *Gerard Manley Hopkins, 1844–1889*, 2 vols., London: Secker & Warburg; New Haven: Yale Univ. Press, 1948–49.

Hartman, G. H. (ed.), *Hopkins: A Collection of Critical Essays*, Englewood Cliffs, N. J.: Prentice-Hall, 1966.

Housman, A. E.

Gow, A. S. F., *A. E. Housman: A Sketch*, Cambridge: Cambridge Univ. Press, 1936.

Marlow, N., *A. E. Housman: Scholar and Poet*, London: Routledge; Minneapolis: Univ. of Minnesota Press, 1958.

Haber, T. B., *A. E. Housman*, New York: Twayne, 1967.

Howells, William Dean.

Carter, E., *Howells and the Age of Realism*, Philadelphia: Lippincott, 1954.

Cady, E. H., *The Road to Realism: The Early Years, 1837–1885, of William Dean Howells*, Syracuse, N. Y.: Syracuse Univ. Press, 1956.

Cady, E. H., *The Realist at War: The Mature Years, 1885–1920, of William Dean Howells*, Syracuse, N. Y.: Syracuse Univ. Press, 1958.

Fryckstedt, O. W., *In Quest of America: A Study of Howells' Early Development As a Novelist*, Cambridge, Mass.: Harvard Univ. Press, 1958.

Kirk, C., and Kirk, R., *William Dean Howells*, New York: Twayne, 1962.

Hughes, Langston.

Emanuel, J. A., *Langston Hughes*, New York: Twayne, 1967.

Hughes, Ted.

Dyson, A. E., "Ted Hughes," *Critical Quarterly*, 1, pp. 219–26.

Hoffman, D., "Talking Beasts: The Single Adventure in the Poems of Ted Hughes," *Shenandoah*—Washington and Lee Univ. Review, Summer 1968, pp. 49–68.

Lodge, D., "'Crow' and the Cartoons," *Critical Quarterly*, 13, pp. 37–42 and 68.

May, D., "Ted Hughes" in *The Survival of Poetry*, ed. M. Dodsworth, London: Faber & Faber, 1970.

Hulme, T. E.

Lewis, W., *Blasting and Bombardiering*, London: Eyre & Spottiswoode, 1937.

Jones, A. R., *The Life and Opinions of Thomas Ernest Hulme*, London: Gollancz; Boston: Beacon Press, 1960.

Hume, David.

Mossner, E. C., *The Life of David Hume*, Austin: Univ. of Texas Press, 1954; London: Nelson, 1955.

Hunt, Leigh.

Blunden, E., *Leigh Hunt's "Examiner" Examined*, London: Cobden-Sanderson, 1928; New York: Harper, 1931.

Blunden, E., *Leigh Hunt: A Biography*, London: Cobden-Sanderson; as *Leigh Hunt and His Circle*, New York: Harper, 1930.

Hurd, Richard.

Trowbridge, H., "Bishop Hurd," *P.M.L.A.*, vol. 58, 1943.

Huxley, Aldous.

Henderson, A., *Aldous Huxley*, London: Chatto & Windus, 1935; New York: Harper, 1936.

Atkins, J. A., *Aldous Huxley: A Literary Study*, London: Calder, 1956; revised, 1967; New York: Roy, 1957; Orion, 1968.

Huxley, J. (ed.), *Aldous Huxley, 1894–1963*, London: Chatto & Windus, 1965; New York: Harper & Row, 1966.

Bowering, P., *Aldous Huxley: A Study of the Major Novels*, London: Athlone Press, 1968; New York: Oxford Univ. Press, 1969.

Huxley, T. H.

Irvine, W., *Apes, Angels, and Victorians*, London: Weidenfeld; New York: McGraw-Hill, 1955.

Bibby, C., *T. H. Huxley: Scientist, Humanist and Educator*, London: C. A. Watts, 1959; New York: Horizon Press, 1960.

Cockshut, A. O. J., *The Unbelievers: English Agnostic Thought, 1840–1890*, London: Collins, 1964.

Hymns.

Julian, J. (ed.), *A Dictionary of Hymnology*, London: Murray, 1892; 1907; 2nd edition reprinted, 2 vols., New York: Dover, 1957; London: Murray, 1958.

Benson, L. F., *The English Hymn*, London: Hodder & Stoughton; New York: Doran, 1915.

Reeves, J. B., *The Hymn As Literature*, New York: Century, 1924.

Manning, B. L., *The Hymns of Wesley and Watts*, London: Epworth Press, 1942.

Routley, E., *Hymns and the Faith*, London: Murray, 1955; Greenwich, Conn.: Seabury Press, 1956.

Pollard, A., *English Hymns*, London: Longmans (for British Council), 1960. Writers and Their Work series.

Imagism.

Coffman, S. K., Jr., *Imagism: A Chapter for the History of Modern Poetry*, Norman: Univ. of Oklahoma Press, 1951.

Read, H., *The True Voice of Feeling: Studies in English Romantic Poetry*, London: Faber & Faber; New York: Pantheon, 1953.

Indian Literature.

Iyengar, K. R. S., *Indian Writing in English*, Bombay: Asia Publishing House, 1962.

Irving, Washington.

Williams, S. T., *The Life of Washington Irving*, 2 vols., New York: Oxford Univ. Press, 1935.

Wagenknecht, E. C., *Washington Irving: Moderation Displayed*, New York: Oxford Univ. Press, 1962.

Hedges, W. L., *Washington Irving: An American Study, 1802–1832*, Baltimore: Johns Hopkins Press, 1965.

James, G. P. R.

Ellis, S. M., *The Solitary Horseman: or, The Life and Adventures of G. P. R. James*, London: Cayme Press, 1927.

James, Henry.

Dupee, F. W. (ed.), *The Question of Henry James*, New York: Holt, 1945; London: Wingate, 1947.

Leavis, F. R., *The Great Tradition: George Eliot, Henry James, Joseph Conrad*, London: Chatto & Windus; New York; Stewart, 1948.

Edel, L., *Henry James*, 5 vols., Philadelphia: Lippincott; London: Hart-Davis, 1953–72.

Krook, D., *The Ordeal of Consciousness in Henry James*, Cambridge: Cambridge Univ. Press, 1962.

Geismar, M. D., *Henry James and the Jacobites*, Boston: Houghton Mifflin, 1963; as *Henry James and His Cult*, London: Chatto & Windus, 1964.

Jefferson, D. W., *Henry James and the Modern Reader*, New York: St. Martin's Press; Edinburgh: Oliver & Boyd, 1964.

Putt, S. G., *Henry James: A Reader's Guide*, Ithaca, N. Y.: Cornell Univ. Press; London: Thames & Hudson, 1966.

James, William.

Perry, R. B., *The Thought and Character of William James*, 2 vols., Boston: Little, Brown, 1935; London: Oxford Univ. Press, 1936.

Allen, G. W., *William James*, New York: Viking Press; London: Hart-Davis, 1967.

Jarrell, Randall.

Lowell, R.; Taylor, P.; and Penn Warren, R. (edd.), *Randall Jarrell, 1914–1965*, New York: Farrar, Straus, 1967.

Jefferies, Richard.

Looker, S. J., and Porteous, C., *Richard Jefferies: Man of the Fields*, London: Baker; Mystic, Conn.: Verry, 1965.

Jeffers, Robinson.

Adamic, L., *Robinson Jeffers: A Portrait*, Seattle: Univ. of Washington Book Store, 1929. Univ. chapbooks, no. 27.

Powell, L. C., *Robinson Jeffers: The Man and His Work*, revised, Pasadena: San Pasquale Press, 1940.

Squires, R., *The Loyalties of Robinson Jeffers*, Ann Arbor: Univ. of Michigan Press, 1956.

Coffin, A. B., *Robinson Jeffers: Poet of Inhumanism*, Madison: Univ. of Wisconsin Press, 1970.

Jefferson, Thomas.

Chinard, G., *Thomas Jefferson: The Apostle of Americanism*, Boston: Little, Brown, 1929; revised, 1939.

Boorstin, D. J., *The Lost World of Thomas Jefferson*, New York: Holt, 1948.

Peterson, M. D., *The Jefferson Image in the American Mind*, New York: Oxford Univ. Press (Galaxy), 1962.

Jeffrey, Francis, Lord.

Clive, J. L., *Scotch Reviewers: "The Edinburgh Review," 1802–1815*, London: Faber & Faber; Cambridge, Mass.: Harvard Univ. Press, 1957.

Gross, J. J., *The Rise and Fall of the Man of Letters*, London: Weidenfeld; New York: Macmillan Co., 1969.

Jewett, Sarah Orne.

Cary, R., *Sarah Orne Jewett*, New York: Twayne, 1962.

Johnson, Lionel.

Pound, E., *Literary Essays*, London: Faber & Faber; Norfolk, Conn.: New Directions, 1954.

Johnson, Samuel.

Wimsatt, W. K., *The Prose Style of Samuel Johnson*, London: Oxford Univ. Press; New Haven: Yale Univ. Press, 1941.

Wimsatt, W. K., *Philosophic Words: A Study of Style and Meaning in the "Rambler" and "Dictionary" of Samuel Johnson*, New Haven: Yale Univ. Press, 1948; London: Oxford Univ. Press, 1949.

Leavis, F. R., *The Common Pursuit*, London: Chatto & Windus; New York: Stewart, 1952.

Bate, W. J., *The Achievement of Samuel Johnson*, New York: Oxford Univ. Press, 1955.

Clifford, J. L., *Young Samuel Johnson*, London: Heinemann; as *Young Sam Johnson*, New York: McGraw-Hill, 1955.

Boulton, J. T. (ed.), *Johnson: The Critical Heritage*, London: Routledge; New York: Barnes & Noble, 1971.

Jones, Henry Arthur.

Cordell, R. A., *Henry Arthur Jones and the Modern Drama*, New York: Long & Smith, 1932.

Jonson, Ben.

Knights, L. C., *Drama and Society in the Age of Jonson*, London: Chatto & Windus, 1937.

Partridge, E. B., *The Broken Compass: A Study of the Major Comedies of Ben Jonson*, London: Chatto & Windus; New York: Columbia Univ. Press, 1958.

Barish, J. A., *Ben Jonson and the Language of Prose Comedy*, Cambridge, Mass.: Harvard Univ. Press, 1960.

Trimpi, W., *Ben Jonson's Poems: A Study of the Plain Style*, Stanford: Stanford Univ. Press, 1962.

Orgel, S. K., *The Jonsonian Masque*, London: Oxford Univ. Press; Cambridge, Mass.: Harvard Univ. Press, 1965.

Joyce, James.

Budgen, F., *James Joyce and the Making of "Ulysses,"* London: Grayson & Grayson; New York: H. Smith, 1934.

Ellmann, R., *James Joyce*, London and New York: Oxford Univ. Press, 1959.

Tindall, W. Y., *A Reader's Guide to James Joyce*, New York: Noonday Press, 1959; London: Thames & Hudson, 1960.

Goldberg, S. L., *The Classical Temper: A Study of James Joyce's "Ulysses,"* London: Chatto & Windus; New York: Barnes & Noble, 1961.

Adams, R. M., *Surface and Symbol: The Consistency of James Joyce's "Ulysses,"* New York: Oxford Univ. Press, 1962.

Litz, A. W., *The Art of James Joyce*, New York: Oxford Univ. Press (Galaxy), 1964.

Keats, John.

Wasserman, E. R., *The Finer Tone: Keats' Major Poems*, London: Oxford Univ. Press; Baltimore: Johns Hopkins Press, 1953.

Muir, K. (ed.), *John Keats: A Reassessment*, Liverpool: Univ. Press of Liverpool, 1959.

Bate, W. J., *John Keats*, London: Oxford Univ. Press; Cambridge, Mass.: Harvard Univ. Press, 1963.

Ward, A., *John Keats: The Making of a Poet*, London: Secker & Warburg; New York: Viking Press, 1963.

Evert, W. H., *Aesthetic and Myth in the Poetry of Keats*, Princeton: Princeton Univ. Press, 1965.

Jack, I., *Keats and the Mirror of Art*, Oxford: Clarendon Press, 1967.

Mayhead, R., *John Keats*, Cambridge: Cambridge Univ. Press, 1967.

Gittings, R., *John Keats*, London: Heinemann; Boston: Little, Brown, 1968.

Matthews, G. M. (ed.), *Keats: The Critical Heritage*, London: Routledge; New York: Barnes & Noble, 1971.

Keble, John.

Abrams, M. H., *The Mirror and the Lamp: Romantic Theory and the Critical Tradition*, London and New York; Oxford Univ. Press, 1953.

Battiscombe, G., *John Keble: A Study in Limitations*, London: Constable, 1963; New York: Knopf, 1964.

Keynes, John Maynard, Lord.

Harrod, R. F., *The Life of John Maynard Keynes*, London: Macmillan; New York: Harcourt, Brace, 1951.

King, Henry.

Berman, R. S., *Henry King and the Seventeenth Century*, London: Chatto & Windus; New York: Oxford Univ. Press, 1964.

Kingis Quair, The.

Lewis, C. S., *The Allegory of Love*, Oxford: Clarendon Press, 1936.

Kinglake, A. W.

Tuckwell, W., *A. W. Kinglake: A Biographical and Literary Study*, London: Bell, 1902.

De Gaury, G., *Travelling Gent: Life of Alexander Kinglake, 1809–1891*, London: Routledge, 1972.

Kingsley, Charles.

Thorp, M. F., *Charles Kingsley, 1819–1875*, London: Oxford Univ. Press; Princeton: Princeton Univ. Press, 1937.

Pope-Hennessy, U., *Canon Charles Kingsley: A Biography*, London: Chatto & Windus, 1948; New York: Macmillan Co., 1949.

Martin, R. B., *The Dust of Combat: A Life of Charles Kingsley*, London: Faber & Faber, 1959 (for 1960); New York: Norton, 1960.

Kipling, Rudyard.

Carrington, C. E., *Rudyard Kipling: His Life and Work*, London: Macmillan; as *The Life of Rudyard Kipling*, Garden City, N. Y.: Doubleday, 1955.

Tompkins, J. M. S., *The Art of Rudyard Kipling*, London: Methuen, 1959; New York: Humanities Press, 1960.

Rutherford, A. (ed.), *Kipling's Mind and Art: Selected Critical Essays*, Edinburgh: Oliver & Boyd; Stanford: Stanford Univ. Press, 1964.

Gilbert, E. L. (ed.), *Kipling and the Critics*, New York: New York Univ. Press, 1965; London: P. Owen, 1966.

Dobrée, B., *Rudyard Kipling: Realist and Fabulist*, London and New York: Oxford Univ. Press, 1967.

Kyd, Thomas.

Freeman, A., *Thomas Kyd: Facts and Problems*, Oxford: Clarendon Press, 1967.

Murray, P. B., *Thomas Kyd*, New York: Twayne, 1969.

Lamb, Charles.

Lucas, E. V., *The Life of Charles Lamb*, 2 vols., London: Methuen; New York: Putnam, 1905; 5th edition, 2 vols., revised, 1921.

Blunden, E., *Charles Lamb and His Contemporaries*, Cambridge: Cambridge Univ. Press; New York: Macmillan Co., 1933.

Trilling, L., *The Liberal Imagination: Essays on Literature and Society*, New York: Viking Press, 1950; London: Secker & Warburg, 1951.

Barnett, G. L., *Charles Lamb: The Evolution of Elia*, Bloomington: Indiana Univ. Press, 1964.

Landor, Walter Savage.

Swinburne, A. C., *Miscellanies*, London: Chatto & Windus, 1886.

Super, R. H., *Walter Savage Landor: A Biography*, New York: New York Univ. Press, 1954.

Lang, Andrew.

Rait, R. S., *Andrew Lang As Historian*, London: Oxford Univ. Press, 1930.

Green, R. L., *Andrew Lang*, Leicester: E. Ward. 1946.

Murray, G., *Andrew Lang the Poet*, London: Oxford Univ. Press, 1948.

Langhorne, John.

Macdonald, H., "John Langhorne," in *Essays Presented to David Nichol Smith*, Oxford: Clarendon Press, 1945.

Langland, William.

Donaldson, E. T., *"Piers Plowman": The C-Text and Its Poet*, London: Oxford Univ. Press; New Haven: Yale Univ. Press, 1949.

Salter, E., *"Piers Plowman": An Introduction*, Oxford: Blackwell; Cambridge, Mass.: Harvard Univ. Press, 1962.

Lanier, Sidney.

Starke, A. H., *Sidney Lanier: A Biographical and Critical Study*, Chapel Hill: Univ. of North Carolina Press, 1933.

Parks, E. W., *Sidney Lanier: The Man, the Poet, the Critic*, Athens: Univ. of Georgia Press, 1969.

Lardner, Ring.

Elder, D., *Ring Lardner: A Biography*, New York: Doubleday, 1956.

Latimer, Hugh.

Chester, A. G., *Hugh Latimer, Apostle to the English*, London: Oxford Univ. Press; Philadelphia: Univ. of Pennsylvania Press, 1954.

Law, William.

Talon, H., *William Law: A Study in Literary Craftmanship*, London: Rockliff; New York: Harper, 1949.

Lawrence, D. H.

Murry, J. M., *Son of Woman*, London: Cape; New York: P. Smith, 1931; as *D. H. Lawrence: Son of Woman*, London: Cape, 1954.

Leavis, F. R., *D. H. Lawrence, Novelist*, London: Chatto & Windus, 1955; New York: Knopf, 1956.

Moore, H. T., *The Intelligent Heart: The Story of D. H. Lawrence*, London: Heinemann; New York; Farrar, Straus, 1955.

Hough, G. G., *The Dark Sun: A Study of D. H. Lawrence*, London: Duckworth, 1956; New York: Macmillan Co., 1957.

Sagar, K. M., *The Art of D. H. Lawrence*, Cambridge: Cambridge Univ. Press, 1966.

Draper, R. P. (ed.), *D. H. Lawrence: The Critical Heritage*, London: Routledge; New York: Barnes & Noble, 1970.

Lawrence, T. E.

Graves, R., *Lawrence and the Arabs*, London: Cape, 1927; as *Lawrence and the Arabian Adventure*, Garden City, N. Y.: Doubleday, Doran, 1928.

Lawrence, A. W. (ed.), *T. E. Lawrence, by His Friends*, London: Cape; Garden City, N. Y.: Doubleday, Doran, 1937.

Aldington, R., *Lawrence of Arabia: A Biographical Enquiry*, London: Collins; New York: Regnery, 1955.

Leavis, F. R.

Buckley, V., *Poetry and Morality: Studies on the Criticism of Matthew Arnold, T. S. Eliot and F. R. Leavis*, London: Chatto & Windus, 1959.

Lee, Nathaniel.

Ham, R. G., *Otway and Lee: Biography from a Baroque Age*, London: Oxford Univ. Press; New Haven: Yale Univ. Press, 1931.

"Lee, Vernon."

Gunn, P., *Vernon Lee: Violet Paget, 1856–1935*, London and New York: Oxford Univ. Press, 1964.

Le Fanu, Sheridan.

Browne, N., *Sheridan Le Fanu*, London: Barker; New York: Roy, 1951.

Le Gallienne, Richard.

Whittington-Egan, R., and Smerdon, G., *The Quest of the Golden Boy: The Life and Letters of Richard Le Gallienne*, London: Unicorn Press, 1960; Chester Springs, Pa.: Dufour, 1961.

Leland, John.

Rowse, A. L., *The England of Elizabeth: The Structure of Society*, London: Macmillan, 1950; New York: Macmillan Co., 1951.

L'Estrange, Sir Roger.

Kitchin, G., *Sir Roger L'Estrange: A Contribution to the History of the Press in the Seventeenth Century*, London: Kegan Paul, 1913.

Lever, Charles.

Stevenson, L., *Dr. Quicksilver: The Life of Charles Lever*, London: Chapman & Hall, 1939.

Lewis, C. S.

Gibb, J. (ed.), *Light on C. S. Lewis*, London: Bles, 1965; New York: Harcourt, Brace, 1966.

Robson, W. W., *Critical Essays*, London: Routledge, 1966; New York: Barnes & Noble, 1967.

Lewis, M. G. ("Monk.")

Peck, L. F., *A Life of Matthew G. Lewis*, London: Oxford Univ. Press; Cambridge, Mass.: Harvard Univ. Press, 1961.

Lewis, Sinclair.

Schorer, M., *Sinclair Lewis: An American Life*, New York: McGraw-Hill, 1961; London: Heinemann, 1963.

Dooley, D. J., *The Art of Sinclair Lewis*, Lincoln; Univ. of Nebraska Press, 1967.

Lewis, Wyndham.

Wagner, G. A., *Wyndham Lewis: A Portrait of the Artist As the Enemy*, London: Routledge; New Haven: Yale Univ. Press, 1957.

Pritchard, W. H., *Wyndham Lewis*, New York: Twayne, 1968.

Lillo, George.

Krutch, J. W., *Comedy and Conscience after the Restoration*, London: Oxford Univ. Press; New York: Columbia Univ. Press, 1924; revised, 1949.

Lincoln, Abraham.

Charnwood, Lord, *Abraham Lincoln*, New York: Holt; London: Constable, 1916.

Randall, J. G., *Lincoln the President*, 4 vols., New York: Dodd, Mead, 1945–55; London: Eyre & Spottiswoode, 1945–56.

Thomas, B. P., *Abraham Lincoln: A Biography*, New York: Knopf, 1952; London: Eyre & Spottiswoode, 1953.

Donald, D., *Lincoln Reconsidered: Essays on the Civil War Era*, New York: Knopf, 1956.

Lindsay, Vachel.

Masters, E. L., *Vachel Lindsay: A Poet in America*, New York: C. Scribner's Sons, 1935.

Harris, M., *City of Discontent: An Interpretive Biography of Vachel Lindsay*, Indianapolis: Bobbs-Merrill, 1952.

Ruggles, E., *The West-Going Heart: A Life of Vachel Lindsay*, New York: Norton, 1959.
Massa, A., *Vachel Lindsay: Fieldworker for the American Dream*, Bloomington: Indiana Univ. Press, 1970.

Locke, John.

MacLean, K., *John Locke and English Literature of the Eighteenth Century*, London: Oxford Univ. Press; New Haven: Yale Univ. Press, 1936.
Aaron, R. I., *John Locke*, London: Oxford Univ. Press, 1937.
James, D. G., *The Life of Reason: Hobbes, Locke, Bolingbroke*, London: Longmans, 1949.
Cranston, M., *John Locke: A Biography*, London: Longmans; New York: Macmillan Co., 1957.
Tuveson, E. L., *The Imagination As a Means of Grace: Locke and the Aesthetics of Romanticism*, Cambridge: Cambridge Univ. Press; Berkeley and Los Angeles: Univ. of California Press, 1960.

Lockhart, J. G.

Lang, A., *The Life and Letters of John Gibson Lockhart*, 2 vols., London: Nimmo, 1897.
Macbeth, G., *John Gibson Lockhart: A Critical Study*, Urbana: Univ. of Illinois Press, 1935.

Lodge, Thomas.

Paradise, N. B., *Thomas Lodge: The History of an Elizabethan*, London: Oxford Univ. Press; New Haven: Yale Univ. Press, 1931.

London, Jack.

Stone, I., *Sailor on Horseback: The Biography of Jack London*, Boston: Houghton Mifflin, 1938; London: Collins, 1940.
London, J., *Jack London and His Times: An Unconventional Biography*, Garden City, N.Y.: Doubleday, Doran, 1939.
O'Connor, R., *Jack London: A Biography*, Boston: Little, Brown; London: Gollancz, 1964.
Walker, F. D., *Jack London and the Klondike: The Genesis of an American Writer*, San Marino, Calif.: Huntington Library; London: Bodley Head, 1966.

Longfellow, H. W.

Arvin, N., *Longfellow: His Life and Work*, Boston: Little, Brown, 1963.
Wagenknecht, E. C., *Henry Wadsworth Longfellow: Portrait of an American Humanist*, New York: Oxford Univ. Press, 1966.

Longstreet, Augustus.

Wade, J. D., *Augustus Baldwin Longstreet: A Study in the Development of Culture in the South*, New York: Macmillan Co., 1924.

Lovelace, Richard.

Hartmann, C. H., *The Cavalier Spirit and Its Influence on the Literary Work of Richard Lovelace, 1618–1658,* London: Routledge; New York: Dutton, 1925.

Lowell, Amy.

Gregory, H., *Amy Lowell: Portrait of the Poet in Her Time,* New York: Nelson, 1958.
Flint, F. C., *Amy Lowell,* Minneapolis: Univ. of Minnesota Press, 1969; London: Oxford Univ. Press. Pamphlets on American Writers, no. 82.

Lowell, James Russell.

Howard, L., *Victorian Knight-Errant: A Study of the Early Literary Career of James Russell Lowell,* Berkeley and Los Angeles: Univ. of California Press, 1951; Cambridge: Cambridge Univ. Press, 1952.
Duberman, M., *James Russell Lowell,* Boston: Houghton Mifflin, 1966.
Wagenknecht, E. C., *James Russell Lowell: Portrait of a Many-Sided Man,* New York: Oxford Univ. Press, 1971.

Lowell, Robert.

Staples, H. B., *Robert Lowell: The First Twenty Years,* London: Faber & Faber; New York: Farrar, Straus, 1962.
Martz, W. J., *The Achievement of Robert Lowell,* Glenview, Ill.: Scott Foresman, 1966.
Cooper, P., *The Autobiographical Myth of Robert Lowell,* Chapel Hill: Univ. of North Carolina Press, 1970.
Cosgrave, P., *The Public Poetry of Robert Lowell,* London: Gollancz, 1970.

Lydgate, John.

Schirmer, W. F., *John Lydgate: A Study in the Culture of the Fifteenth Century,* trans. A. E. Keep, London: Methuen; Berkeley and Los Angeles: Univ. of California Press, 1961.
Pearsall, D. A., *John Lydgate,* London: Routledge; Charlottesville: Univ. Press of Virginia, 1970.

Lyly, John.

Wilson, J. Dover, *John Lyly,* Cambridge: Macmillan & Bowes, 1905.
Bradbrook, M. C., *The Growth and Structure of Elizabethan Comedy,* London: Chatto & Windus, 1955; Berkeley and Los Angeles: Univ. of California Press, 1956.
Hunter, G. K., *John Lyly: The Humanist As Courtier,* London: Routledge; Cambridge, Mass.: Harvard Univ. Press, 1962.
Saccio, P., *The Court Comedies of John Lyly,* Princeton: Princeton Univ. Press, 1969.

Lyndsay, Sir David.

Murison, W., *Sir David Lyndsay, Poet and Satirist of the Old Church in Scotland,* Cambridge: Cambridge Univ. Press; New York: Macmillan Co., 1938.

Lytton, Lord.

Sadleir, M., *Bulwer: A Panorama*, part 1, *Edward and Rosina, 1803–1836*, London: Constable; Boston: Little, Brown, 1931.

Hollingsworth, K., *The Newgate Novel, 1830–1847*, Detroit: Wayne State Univ. Press, 1963.

Macaulay, Rose.

Bensen, A. R., *Rose Macaulay*, New York: Twayne, 1969.

Macaulay, Thomas Babington, Lord.

Trevelyan, G. M., *The Life and Letters of Lord Macaulay*, 2 vols., London, 1876; enlarged, 1908.

Knowles, D., *Lord Macaulay, 1800–1859*, Cambridge: Cambridge Univ. Press, 1960.

McCarthy, Mary.

McKenzie, B., *Mary McCarthy*, New York: Twayne, 1967.

McCullers, Carson.

Evans, O. W., *Carson McCullers: Her Life and Work*, London: P. Owen, 1965; as *The Ballad of Carson McCullers: A Biography*, New York: Coward-McCann, 1966.

"MacDiarmid, Hugh."

Duval, K. D., and Smith, S. G. (edd.), *Hugh MacDiarmid: A Festschrift*, Edinburgh: Duval, 1962; Chester Springs, Pa.: Dufour, 1963.

Glen, D., *Hugh MacDiarmid (Christopher Murray Grieve) and the Scottish Renaissance*, Edinburgh: Chambers, 1964.

MacDonald, George.

Reis, R. H., *George MacDonald*, New York: Twayne, 1971.

Mackenzie, Henry.

Thompson, H. W., *A Scottish Man of Feeling: Some Account of Henry Mackenzie . . .*, London and New York: Oxford Univ. Press, 1931.

MacNeice, Louis.

Fraser, G. S., *Vision and Rhetoric: Studies in Modern Poetry*, London: Faber & Faber, 1959; New York: Barnes & Noble, 1960.

Macpherson, James.

Saunders, T. B., *The Life and Letters of James Macpherson*, London: Swan Sonnenschein, 1894.

Snyder, E. D., *The Celtic Revival in English Literature, 1760–1800*, Cambridge, Mass.: Harvard Univ. Press, 1923.

Mailer, Norman.

Kaufmann, D. L., *Norman Mailer: The Countdown*, Carbondale: Southern Illinois Univ. Press, 1969.

Leeds, B. H., *The Structured Vision of Norman Mailer*, New York: New York Univ. Press, 1970.

Malamud, Bernard.

Richman, S., *Bernard Malamud*, New York: Twayne, 1967.

Malory, Sir Thomas.

Vinaver, E., *Malory*, Oxford: Clarendon Press, 1929.

Bennett, J. A. W. (ed.), *Essays on Malory*, Oxford: Clarendon Press, 1963.

Lumiansky, R. M. (ed.), *Malory's Originality*, Baltimore: Johns Hopkins Press, 1964.

Moorman, C., *The Book of Kyng Arthur: The Unity of Malory's "Morte d'Arthur,"* Lexington: Univ. of Kentucky Press, 1965.

Malthus, T. R.

Keynes, J. M., *Essays in Biography*, London: Macmillan; New York: Harcourt, Brace, 1933.

Sraffa, P., and Dobb, M. H. (edd.), *Works and Correspondence of David Ricardo*, Cambridge: Cambridge Univ. Press, 1951-55, vols. 2; 6-10.

Mangan, J. C.

Sheridan, J. D., *James Clarence Mangan*, Dublin: Talbot Press, 1937; New York: Nelson, 1940.

"Mansfield, Katherine."

Alpers, A., *Katherine Mansfield*, New York: Knopf, 1953; London: Cape, 1954.

Marlowe, Christopher.

Bakeless, J., *Christopher Marlowe*, New York: Morrow, 1937; London: Cape, 1938.

Boas, F. S., *Christopher Marlowe: A Biographical and Critical Study*, Oxford: Clarendon Press, 1940.

Levin, H., *The Overreacher: A Study of Christopher Marlowe*, Cambridge, Mass.: Harvard Univ. Press, 1952; London: Faber & Faber, 1954.

Steane, J. B., *Marlowe: A Critical Study*, Cambridge: Cambridge Univ. Press, 1964.

"Marprelate, Martin."

Pierce, W., *An Historical Introduction to the Marprelate Tracts*, London: Constable, 1908.

Marquand, John P.

Gross, J. J., *John P. Marquand*, New York: Twayne, 1963.

Holman, C. H., *John P. Marquand*, Minneapolis: Univ. of Minnesota Press, 1965; London: Oxford Univ. Press. Pamphlets on American Writers, no. 46.

Marryat, Frederick (Captain).

Warner, O., *Captain Marryat: A Rediscovery*, London: Constable; New York: Macmillan Co., 1953.

Marston, John.

Campbell, O. J., *Comicall Satyre and Shakespeare's "Troilus and Cressida,"* London: Oxford Univ. Press; San Marino, Calif.: Huntington Library, 1938.

Bradbrook, M. C., *The Growth and Structure of Elizabethan Comedy*, London: Chatto & Windus, 1955; Berkeley and Los Angeles: Univ. of California Press, 1956.

Ornstein, R., *The Moral Vision of Jacobean Tragedy*, Madison: Univ. of Wisconsin Press, 1960.

Caputi, A., *John Marston, Satirist*, Ithaca, N. Y.: Cornell Univ. Press, 1961.

Martineau, Harriet.

Wheatley, V., *The Life and Work of Harriet Martineau*, London: Secker & Warburg; Fair Lawn, N. J.: Essential Books (1955–   ), 1957.

Webb, R. K., *Harriet Martineau: A Radical Victorian*, London: Heinemann; New York: Columbia Univ. Press, 1960.

Marvell, Andrew.

Eliot, T. S., *Selected Essays, 1917–1932*, London: Faber & Faber; New York: Harcourt, Brace, 1932.

Bradbrook, M. C., and Lloyd Thomas, M. G., *Andrew Marvell*, Cambridge: Cambridge Univ. Press, 1940; New York: Macmillan Co., 1941.

Legouis, P., *Andrew Marvell: Poet, Puritan, Patriot*, Oxford: Clarendon Press, 1965 (abridged).

Leishman, J. B., *The Art of Marvell's Poetry*, London: Hutchinson; New York: Funk & Wagnalls, 1966.

Wallace, J. M., *Destiny His Choice: The Loyalism of Marvell*, Cambridge: Cambridge Univ. Press, 1968.

Masefield, John.

Hamilton, W. H., *John Masefield: A Critical Study*, London: Allen & Unwin; New York: Macmillan Co., 1922.

Spark, M., *John Masefield*, London: Nevill, 1953.

Mason, William.

Draper, J. W., *William Mason: A Study in Eighteenth-Century Culture*, New York: New York Univ. Press, 1924.

Masques.

Chambers, E. K., *The Elizabethan Stage*, vol. 1, Oxford: Clarendon Press, 1923.

Welsford, E., *The Court Masque: A Study in the Relationship between Poetry and the Revels*, Cambridge: Cambridge Univ. Press, 1927.

Nicoll, A., *Stuart Masques and the Renaissance Stage*, London: Harrap, 1937; New York: Harcourt, Brace, 1938.

Furniss, W. T., "Ben Jonson's Masques," in *Three Studies in the Renaissance*, London: Oxford Univ. Press; New Haven: Yale Univ. Press, 1958.

Sabol, A. J., *Songs and Dances for the Stuart Masque*, Providence, R. I.: Brown Univ. Press, 1959.

Orgel, S. K., *The Jonsonian Masque*, London: Oxford Univ. Press; Cambridge, Mass.: Harvard Univ. Press, 1965.

Schoenbaum, S. (ed.), *Renaissance Drama*. New series, 1: *Essays Principally on Masques and Entertainments*, Evanston, Ill.: Northwestern Univ. Press, 1968.

Massinger, Philip.

Dunn, T. A., *Philip Massinger: The Man and the Playwright*, London: Nelson (for Univ. College of Ghana), 1957.

Mather, Cotton.

Wendell, B., *Cotton Mather, the Puritan Priest*, New York: Dodd, Mead, 1891.

Middlekauff, R., *The Mathers: Three Generations of Puritan Intellectuals, 1596–1728*, New York: Oxford Univ. Press, 1971.

Maturin, C. R.

Varma, D. P., *The Gothic Flame: Being a History of the Gothic Novel in England*, London: Barker, 1957.

Maugham, W. Somerset.

Cordell, R. A., *Somerset Maugham: A Biographical and Critical Study*, London: Heinemann; Bloomington: Indiana Univ. Press, 1961.

Brander, L., *Somerset Maugham*, Edinburgh: Oliver & Boyd; New York: Barnes & Noble, 1963.

Melville, Herman.

Olson, C., *Call Me Ishmael*, New York: Reynal & Hitchcock, 1947; London: Cape, 1967.

Howard, L., *Herman Melville: A Biography*, Berkeley and Los Angeles: Univ. of California Press, 1951; Cambridge: Cambridge Univ. Press, 1952.

Thompson, L., *Melville's Quarrel with God*, Princeton: Princeton Univ. Press; London: Oxford Univ. Press, 1952.

Bowen, M., *The Long Encounter: Self and Experience in the Writings of Herman Melville*, Chicago: Univ. of Chicago Press; Cambridge: Cambridge Univ. Press, 1960.

Mencken, H. L.

Stenerson, D. G., *H. L. Mencken: Iconoclast from Baltimore*, Chicago: Univ. of Chicago Press, 1971.

Meredith, George.

Trevelyan, G. M., *The Poetry and Philosophy of Meredith*, London: Constable, 1906.

Priestley, J. B., *George Meredith*, London: Macmillan; New York: Macmillan Co., 1926.

Stevenson, L., *The Ordeal of George Meredith*, New York: C. Scribner's Sons, 1953; London: P. Owen, 1954.

Kelvin, N., *A Troubled Eden: Nature and Society in the Works of George Meredith*, Edinburgh: Oliver & Boyd; Stanford: Stanford Univ. Press, 1961.

Beer, G., *Meredith: A Change of Masks*, London: Athlone Press; New York: Oxford Univ. Press, 1970.

Williams, I. (ed.), *Meredith: The Critical Heritage*, London: Routledge; New York: Barnes & Noble, 1971.

Metaphysical Poetry.

Williamson, G., *The Donne Tradition: A Study in English Poetry from Donne to the Death of Cowley*, London: Oxford Univ. Press; Cambridge, Mass.: Harvard Univ. Press, 1930.

Bald, R. C., *Donne's Influence in English Literature*, Morpeth: St. John's College Press, 1932.

Eliot, T. S., *Selected Essays, 1917–1932*, London: Faber & Faber; New York: Harcourt, Brace, 1932.

Tuve, R., *Elizabethan and Metaphysical Imagery: Renaissance Poetic and Twentieth Century Critics*, Cambridge: Cambridge Univ. Press; Chicago: Univ. of Chicago Press, 1947.

Walton, G., *Metaphysical to Augustan: Studies in Tone and Sensibility in the Seventeenth Century*, London: Bowes & Bowes; Philadelphia: Saifer, 1955.

Bennett, J., *Five Metaphysical Poets* (3rd edition of *Four Metaphysical Poets*), Cambridge: Cambridge Univ. Press, 1964.

Middle English Literature.

Wilson, R. M., *Early Middle English Literature*, London: Methuen, 1939; 3rd edition and New York: Barnes & Noble, 1968.

Kane, G., *Middle English Literature*, London: Methuen, 1951.

Loomis, R. S., *The Development of Arthurian Romance*, London: Hutchinson, 1963.

Woolf, R., *The English Religious Lyric in the Middle Ages*, Oxford: Clarendon Press, 1968.

Middleton, Thomas.

Eliot, T. S., *Selected Essays, 1917–1932*, London: Faber & Faber; New York: Harcourt, Brace, 1932.

Schoenbaum, S., *Middleton's Tragedies*, London: Oxford Univ. Press; New York: Columbia Univ. Press, 1955.

Mill, John Stuart.

Willey, B., *Nineteenth Century Studies: Coleridge to Matthew Arnold*, London: Chatto & Windus; New York: Columbia Univ. Press, 1949.

Packe, M. St. J., *The Life of John Stuart Mill*, London: Secker & Warburg; New York: Macmillan Co., 1954.

Letwin, S. R., *The Pursuit of Certainty: David Hume, Jeremy Bentham, John Stuart Mill, Beatrice Webb*, Cambridge: Cambridge Univ. Press, 1965.

Miller, Arthur.

Welland, D. S. R., *Arthur Miller*, New York: Grove Press; Edinburgh: Oliver & Boyd, 1961.

Hogan, R. G., *Arthur Miller*, Minneapolis: Univ. of Minnesota Press, 1964; London: Oxford Univ. Press. Pamphlets on American Writers, no. 40.

Huftel, S., *Arthur Miller: The Burning Glass*, New York: Citadel Press; London: W. H. Allen, 1965.
Hayman, R., *Arthur Miller*, London: Heinemann Educ., 1970.

Miller, Henry.

Widmer, K., *Henry Miller*, New York: Twayne, 1964.
Gordon, W. A., *The Mind and Art of Henry Miller*, Baton Rouge: Louisiana State Univ. Press, 1967; London: Cape, 1968.

Milton, John.

Masson, D., *The Life of Milton*, 7 vols., Cambridge, London: Macmillan, 1859–94.
Hanford, J. H., *A Milton Handbook*, New York: Crofts, 1926; London: Bell, 1927; 4th edition, revised, New York: Appleton-Century-Crofts, 1946.
Tillyard, E. M. W., *Milton*, London: Chatto & Windus; New York: Dial Press, 1930.
Lewis, C. S., *A Preface to "Paradise Lost,"* London: Oxford Univ. Press, 1942.
Rajan, B., *"Paradise Lost" and the Seventeenth Century Reader*, London: Chatto & Windus, 1947; New York: Oxford Univ. Press, 1948.
Waldock, A. J. A., *"Paradise Lost" and Its Critics*, Cambridge: Cambridge Univ. Press; New York: Macmillan Co., 1947.
Allen, D. C., *The Harmonious Vision: Studies in Milton's Poetry,* London: Oxford Univ. Press; Baltimore: Johns Hopkins Press, 1954.
Broadbent, J. B., *Some Graver Subject: An Essay on "Paradise Lost,"* London: Chatto & Windus, 1960; New York: Barnes & Noble, 1961.
Kermode, F. (ed.), *The Living Milton: Essays by Various Hands*, London: Routledge, 1960.
Ricks, C., *Milton's Grand Style*, Oxford: Clarendon Press, 1963.
Martz, L. L. (ed.), *Milton: A Collection of Critical Essays*, Englewood Cliffs, N. J.: Prentice-Hall, 1966.
Patrides, C. A. (ed.), *Milton's Epic Poetry*, Harmondsworth: Penguin, 1967.
Parker, W. R., *Milton: A Biography*, 2 vols., Oxford: Clarendon Press, 1968.
Shawcross, J. T. (ed.), *Milton: The Critical Heritage, 1628–1731*, London: Routledge; New York: Barnes & Noble, 1970; *1732–1801*, London and Boston: Routledge, 1972.

Miracle Plays.

Chambers, E. K., *The Mediaeval Stage*, 2 vols., Oxford: Clarendon Press, 1903.
Rossiter, A. P., *English Drama from Early Times to the Elizabethans*, London: Hutchinson, 1950.
Craig, H., *English Religious Drama of the Middle Ages*, Oxford: Clarendon Press, 1955.
Wickham, G., *Early English Stages, 1300–1600*, 2 vols. (vol. 2, 2 parts), London: Routledge; New York: Columbia Univ. Press, 1959–72.
Prosser, E. A., *Drama and Religion in the English Mystery Plays: A Re-Evaluation*, Stanford: Stanford Univ. Press, 1961.
Hardison, O. B., *Christian Rite and Christian Drama in the Middle Ages*, Baltimore: Johns Hopkins Press, 1965.

Kolve, V. A., *The Play Called "Corpus Christi,"* London: Arnold; Stanford: Stanford Univ. Press, 1966.

Mitford, Mary Russell.

Astin, M., *Mary Russell Mitford: Her Circle and Her Books*, London: N. Douglas, 1930.

Monro, Harold.

Grant, J., *Harold Monro and the Poetry Bookshop*, London: Routledge; Berkeley and Los Angeles: Univ. of California Press, 1967.

Moody, William Vaughn.

Henry, D. D., *William Vaughn Moody: A Study*, Boston: Humphries, 1934.

Moore, George.

Hone, J. H., *The Life of George Moore*, London: Gollancz; New York: Macmillan Co., 1936.
Cunard, N., *G. M.: Memories of George Moore*, London: Hart-Davis, 1956; New York: Macmillan Co., 1957.

Moore, Marianne.

Engel, B. F., *Marianne Moore*, New York: Twayne, 1964.
Nitchie, G. W., *Marianne Moore: An Introduction to the Poetry*, New York: Columbia Univ. Press, 1969.

Moore, Thomas.

Hazlitt, W., *The Spirit of the Age*, London, 1825.
Jones, H. M., *The Harp That Once—: A Chronicle of the Life of Thomas Moore*, New York: Holt, 1937.

Morality Plays.

Chambers, E. K., *The Mediaeval Stage*, 2 vols., Oxford: Clarendon Press, 1903.
Owst, G. R., *Literature and Pulpit in Medieval England*, Cambridge: Cambridge Univ. Press; New York: Macmillan Co., 1933.
Rossiter, A. P., *English Drama from Early Times to the Elizabethans*, London: Hutchinson, 1950.
Spivack, B., *Shakespeare and the Allegory of Evil*, London: Oxford Univ. Press; New York: Columbia Univ. Press, 1958.
Wilson, F. P., *The English Drama, 1485–1585*, ed. G. K. Hunter, Oxford: Clarendon Press, 1969.

More, Henry.

Powicke, F. J., *The Cambridge Platonists*, London: Dent, 1926; Cambridge, Mass.: Harvard Univ. Press, 1927.

More, Sir Thomas.

Chambers, R. W., *Thomas More*, London: Cape; New York: Harcourt, Brace, 1935.

Hexter, J. H., *More's Utopia: The Biography of an Idea*, London: Oxford Univ. Press; Princeton: Princeton Univ. Press, 1952.

Mason, H. A., *Humanism and Poetry in the Early Tudor Period*, London: Routledge, 1959; New York: Barnes & Noble, 1960.

Morgan, Charles.

Duffin, H. C., *The Novels and Plays of Charles Morgan*, London: Bowes & Bowes, 1959.

Morris, William.

Mackail, J. W., *The Life of William Morris*, 2 vols., London: Longmans, 1899.

Crow, G. H., *William Morris, Designer*, London: Studio Publications, 1934.

Thompson, E. P., *William Morris: Romantic to Revolutionary*, London: Lawrence & Wishart, 1955.

Morris, Wright.

Howard, L., *Wright Morris*, Minneapolis: Univ. of Minnesota Press, 1968; London: Oxford Univ. Press. Pamphlets on American Writers, no. 69.

Muir, Edwin.

Butter, P. H., *Edwin Muir: Man and Poet*, Edinburgh: Oliver & Boyd, 1966; New York: Barnes & Noble, 1967.

Munford, Robert.

Baine, R. M., *Robert Munford: America's First Comic Dramatist*, Athens: Univ. of Georgia Press, 1967.

Murdoch, Iris.

Byatt, A. S., *Degrees of Freedom: The Novels of Iris Murdoch*, London: Chatto & Windus; New York: Barnes & Noble, 1965.

Murry, John Middleton.

Griffin, E. G., *John Middleton Murry*, New York: Twayne, 1969.

Myers, L. H.

Bantock, G. H., *L. H. Myers: A Critical Study*, London: Cape, 1956.

Nabokov, Vladimir.

Field, A., *Nabokov: His Life in Art*, Boston: Little, Brown; London: Hodder & Stoughton, 1967.

Appel, A., Jr., and Newman, C. (edd.), *Nabokov: Criticism, Reminiscences, Translations and Tributes*, Evanston, Ill.: Northwestern Univ. Press, 1970; London: Weidenfeld, 1971.

Nashe, Thomas.

Hibbard, G. R., *Thomas Nashe: A Critical Introduction*, London: Routledge; Cambridge, Mass.: Harvard Univ. Press, 1962.

Newman, J. H.

Harrold, C. F., *John Henry Newman: An Expository and Critical Study of His Mind, Thought and Art*, New York: Longmans, 1945.

Holloway, J., *The Victorian Sage: Studies in Argument*, London: Macmillan; New York: St. Martin's Press, 1953.

Trevor, M., *Newman*, 2 vols., London: Macmillan, 1962; New York: Doubleday, 1962–63.

New Zealand Literature.

McCormick, E. H., *New Zealand Literature: A Survey*, London: Oxford Univ. Press, 1959.

Norris, Frank.

French, W., *Frank Norris*, New York: Twayne, 1962.

Pizer, D., *The Novels of Frank Norris*, Bloomington: Indiana Univ. Press, 1966.

O'Casey, Sean.

Koslow, J., *The Green and the Red: Sean O'Casey, the Man and His Plays*, New York: Arts, 1950.

Hogan, R. G., *The Experiments of Sean O'Casey*, New York: St. Martin's Press, 1960.

Krause, D., *Sean O'Casey: The Man and His Work*, London: MacGibbon & Kee; New York: Macmillan Co., 1960.

Cowasjee, S., *Sean O'Casey: The Man behind the Plays*, Edinburgh: Oliver & Boyd, 1963; New York: St. Martin's Press, 1964.

Malone, M., *The Plays of Sean O'Casey*, Carbondale: Southern Illinois Univ. Press, 1969.

Occleve, Thomas.

Bennett, H. S., *Chaucer and the Fifteenth Century*, Oxford: Clarendon Press, 1947.

O'Connor, Flannery.

Friedman, M. J., and Lawson, L. A. (edd.), *The Added Dimension: The Art and Mind of Flannery O'Connor*, New York: Fordham Univ. Press, 1966.

Hyman, S. E., *Flannery O'Connor*, Minneapolis: Univ. of Minnesota Press, 1966; London: Oxford Univ. Press. Pamphlets on American Writers, no. 54.

Hendin, J., *The World of Flannery O'Connor*, Bloomington: Indiana Univ. Press, 1970.

Odets, Clifford.

Clurman, H., *The Fervent Years: The Story of the Group Theatre and the Thirties*, New York: Knopf, 1945; London: Dobson, 1946.

Murray, E., *Clifford Odets: The Thirties and After*, New York: Ungar, 1968.

Weales, G., *Clifford Odets: Playwright*, New York: Pegasus, 1971.

Old English Poetry and Prose.

Whitelock, D., *The Audience of "Beowulf,"* Oxford: Clarendon Press, 1951.

Nicholson, L. E. (ed.), *An Anthology of "Beowulf" Criticism*, Notre Dame, Ind.: Univ. of Notre Dame Press, 1963.

Greenfield, S. B., *A Critical History of Old English Literature*, New York: New York Univ. Press, 1965; London: Univ. of London Press, 1966.

Stanley, E. G. (ed.), *Continuations and Beginnings: Studies in Old English Literature*, London: Nelson, 1966.

Wrenn, C. L., *A Study of Old English Literature*, London: Harrap, 1967; New York: Norton, 1968.

Irving, E. B., *A Reading of "Beowulf,"* New Haven: Yale Univ. Press, 1968.

Olson, Charles.

Charters, A., *Olson/Melville: A Study in Affinity*, Berkeley, Calif.: Oyez Press, 1968.

O'Neill, Eugene.

Clark, B. H., *Eugene O'Neill: The Man and His Plays*, New York: McBride, 1929; London: Cape, 1933; revised, New York: Dover, 1947.

Cargill, O., Fagin, N. B., and Fisher, W. J. (edd.), *O'Neill and His Plays: Four Decades of Criticism*, New York: New York Univ. Press, 1961; as . . . *Plays: A Survey of His Life and Works*, London: P. Owen, 1962.

Gelb, A., and Gelb, B., *O'Neill*, New York: Harper & Row; London: Cape, 1962.

Raleigh, J. H., *The Plays of Eugene O'Neill*, Carbondale: Southern Illinois Univ. Press, 1965.

"Orwell, George."

Atkins, J., *George Orwell: A Literary and Biographical Study*, London: Calder, 1954; New York: Ungar, 1955.

Rees, R., *George Orwell: Fugitive from the Camp of Victory*, London: Secker & Warburg, 1961; Carbondale: Southern Illinois Univ. Press, 1962.

Woodcock, G., *The Crystal Spirit: A Study of George Orwell*, Boston: Little, Brown, 1966; London: Cape, 1967.

Alldritt, K., *The Making of George Orwell: An Essay in Literary History*, London: Arnold, 1969; New York: St. Martin's Press, 1970.

Abrahams, W., and Stansky, P., *The Unknown Orwell* [to 1933], London: Constable; New York: Knopf, 1972.

Osborne, John.

Taylor, J. Russell, *Anger and After: A Guide to the New British Drama*, London: Methuen, 1962; revised, 1969; as *The Angry Theatre: New British Drama*, New York: Hill & Wang, 1962.

Hayman, R., *John Osborne*, London: Heinemann, 1968.

Trussler, S., *The Plays of John Osborne: An Assessment*, London: Gollancz, 1969.

Otway, Thomas.

Ham, R. G., *Otway and Lee: Biography from a Baroque Age*, London: Oxford Univ. Press; New Haven: Yale Univ. Press, 1931.

Taylor, A. M., *Next to Shakespeare: Otway's "Venice Preserved" and "The Orphan" and Their History on the London Stage*, Durham, N. C.: Duke Univ. Press, 1950; Cambridge: Cambridge Univ. Press, 1951.

Overbury, Sir Thomas.

Boyce, B., *The Theophrastan Character in England to 1642*, London: Oxford Univ. Press; Cambridge, Mass.: Harvard Univ. Press, 1947.

Owen, Wilfred.

Welland, D. S. R., *Wilfred Owen: A Critical Study*, London: Chatto & Windus, 1960.

Owen, H., *Journey from Obscurity: Wilfred Owen, 1893–1918*, 3 vols., London: Oxford Univ. Press, 1963–65.

Page, Thomas Nelson.

Gross, T. L., *Thomas Nelson Page*, New York: Twayne, 1967.

Paine, Thomas.

Aldridge, A. O., *Man of Reason: The Life of Thomas Paine*, Philadelphia: Lippincott, 1959; London: Cresset Press, 1961.

Thompson, E. P., *The Making of the English Working Class*, London: Gollancz, 1963; New York: Pantheon, 1964 (esp. chapter 7).

Palgrave, F. T.

Palgrave, G., *Francis Turner Palgrave: His Journals and Memories of His Life*, London: Longmans, 1899.

Parkman, Francis.

Doughty, H., *Francis Parkman*, New York: Macmillan Co., 1962.

Parody and Nonsense.

Stone, C. R., *Parody, 1915*, in *The Art and Craft of Letters*, 10 vols., London: Secker, 1914–16.

Kitchin, G., *A Survey of Burlesque and Parody in English*, Edinburgh: Oliver & Boyd, 1931.

Cammaerts, E., *The Poetry of Nonsense*, London: Routledge; New York: Dutton, 1925.

Read, H. (ed.), *Surrealism*, London: Faber & Faber, 1936; New York: Harcourt, Brace, 1937.

Sewell, E., *The Field of Nonsense*, London: Chatto & Windus, 1952.

Paston Letters, The.

Bennett, H. S., *The Pastons and Their England: Studies in an Age of Transition*, Cambridge: Cambridge Univ. Press, 1922; revised, 1931.

Pater, Walter.

Benson, A. C., *Walter Pater*, London: Macmillan, 1906.

Eliot, T. S., *Selected Essays, 1917–1932*, London: Faber & Faber; New York: Harcourt, Brace, 1932.

Cecil, Lord D., *The Fine Art of Reading, and Other Literary Studies*, London: Constable; Indianapolis: Bobbs-Merrill, 1957.

Patmore, Coventry.

Champneys, B., *Memoirs and Correspondence of Coventry Patmore*, 2 vols., London: Bell, 1900.

Patmore, D., *The Life and Times of Coventry Patmore*, London: Constable, 1949; New York: Oxford Univ. Press, 1950.

Reid, J. C., *The Mind and Art of Coventry Patmore*, London: Routledge; New York: Macmillan Co., 1957.

Peacock, Thomas Love.

Priestley, J. B., *Thomas Love Peacock*, London: Macmillan, 1927.

Campbell, O. W., *Thomas Love Peacock*, London: Barker; New York: Roy, 1953.

Dawson, C., *His Fine Wit: A Study of Thomas Love Peacock*, London: Routledge; Berkeley and Los Angeles: Univ. of California Press, 1970.

Pepys, Samuel.

Bryant, A., *Samuel Pepys*, 3 vols., Cambridge: Cambridge Univ. Press; New York: Macmillan Co., 1933–38.

Percy, Thomas.

Gaussen, A. C. C., *Percy: Prelate and Poet*, London: Smith, Elder, 1908.

Philips, Ambrose.

Johnson, S., *The Lives of the Poets*, London, 1779–81.

Phillips, David Graham.

Ravitz, A. C., *David Graham Phillips*, New York: Twayne, 1966.

Pinero, A. W.

Dunkel, W. D., *Sir Arthur Pinero: A Critical Biography with Letters*, Chicago: Univ. of Chicago Press, 1941.

Pinter, Harold.

Esslin, M., *The Theatre of the Absurd*, New York: Doubleday, 1961; London: Eyre & Spottiswoode, 1962.

Taylor, J. Russell, *Anger and After: A Guide to the New British Drama*, London: Methuen, 1962; revised, 1969; as *The Angry Theatre: New British Drama*, New York: Hill & Wang, 1962.

Esslin, M., *The Peopled Wound: The Work of Harold Pinter*, London: Methuen; New York: Doubleday, 1970.

Plath, Sylvia.

Newman, C. (ed.), *The Art of Sylvia Plath*, Bloomington: Indiana Univ. Press; London: Faber & Faber, 1970.

Poe, Edgar Allan.

Quinn, A. H., *Edgar Allan Poe: A Critical Biography*, New York: Appleton-Century, 1941.

Davidson, E. H., *Poe: A Critical Study*, Cambridge, Mass.: Harvard Univ. Press; London: Oxford Univ. Press, 1957.

Rans, G., *Edgar Allan Poe*, Edinburgh: Oliver & Boyd, 1965.

Allen, M., *Poe and the British Magazine Tradition*, New York: Oxford Univ. Press, 1969.

Jacobs, R. D., *Poe: Journalist and Critic*, Baton Rouge: Louisiana State Univ. Press, 1969.

Stovall, F., *Edgar Poe the Poet: Essays New and Old on the Man and His Work*, Charlottesville: Univ. Press of Virginia, 1969.

Political Pamphlets.

Kitchin, G., *Sir Roger L'Estrange: A Contribution to the History of the Press in the Seventeenth Century*, London: Kegan Paul, 1913.

Foot, M., *The Pen and the Sword*, London: MacGibbon & Kee, 1957 (on Swift).

Gregg, P., *Free-Born John: A Biography of Lilburne*, London: Harrap, 1961.

McGinn, D. J., *John Penry and the Marprelate Controversy*, New Brunswick, N. J.: Rutgers Univ. Press, 1966.

Novak, M. E., and Davis, H. J., *The Uses of Irony: Papers on Defoe and Swift*, Los Angeles: Univ. of California Press (William Andrews Clark Memorial Library seminar papers), 1966.

Woodcock, G., *The Crystal Spirit: A Study of George Orwell*, Boston: Little, Brown, 1966; London: Cape, 1967.

Béranger, J., *Les Hommes de Lettres et la Politique en Angleterre de la Révolution de 1688 à la Mort de George Ier*, Bordeaux: University of Bordeaux, 1968.

Pope, Alexander.

Warton, J., *An Essay on the Genius and Writings of Pope*, 2 vols., London, (with revisions) 1756–82.

Johnson, S., *The Lives of the Poets*, London, 1779–81.

Sherburn, G. W., *The Early Career of Alexander Pope*, Oxford: Clarendon Press, 1934.

Root, R. K., *The Poetical Career of Alexander Pope*, London: Oxford Univ. Press; Princeton: Princeton Univ. Press, 1938.

Tillotson, G., *On the Poetry of Pope*, Oxford: Clarendon Press, 1938; revised, 1950.

Williams, A. L., *Pope's "Dunciad": A Study of Its Meaning*, London: Methuen; Baton Rouge: Louisiana State Univ. Press, 1955.

Brower, R. A., *Alexander Pope: The Poetry of Allusion*, Oxford: Clarendon Press, 1959.

Mack, M. (ed.), *Essential Articles for the Study of Alexander Pope*, Hamden, Conn.: Shoe String Press, 1964; London: Cass, 1965; revised, 1968.

Porter, Katherine Anne.

Nance, W. L., *Katherine Anne Porter and the Art of Rejection*, Chapel Hill: Univ. of North Carolina Press, 1964.

Pound, Ezra.

Kenner, H., *The Poetry of Ezra Pound*, Norfolk, Conn.: New Directions; London: Faber & Faber, 1951.

Fraser, G. S., *Ezra Pound*, Edinburgh: Oliver & Boyd, 1960; New York: Grove Press, 1961.

Norman, C., *Ezra Pound : A Biography*, New York: Macmillan Co., 1960; revised and London: Macdonald, 1969.

Davie, D., *Ezra Pound: Poet As Sculptor*, New York: Oxford Univ. Press, 1964; London: Routledge, 1965.

Hesse, E., *New Approaches to Ezra Pound*, Berkeley and Los Angeles: Univ. of California Press; London: Faber & Faber, 1969.

Stock, N., *The Life of Ezra Pound*, New York: Pantheon; London: Routledge, 1970.

Homberger, E. (ed.), *Ezra Pound: The Critical Heritage*, London and Boston: Routledge, 1972.

Powell, Anthony.

Mizener, A., "A Dance to the Music of Time," *Kenyon Review*, Winter 1960.

Karl, F. R., *The Contemporary English Novel*, New York: Farrar, Straus, 1962; as *A Reader's Guide to . . .*, London: Thames & Hudson, 1963.

Russell, J. D., *Anthony Powell: A Quintet, Sextet, and War*, Bloomington: Indiana Univ. Press, 1970.

Powers, J. F.

Hagopian, J. V., *J. F. Powers*, New York: Twayne, 1968.

Powys Brothers.

Coombes, H., *T. F. Powys*, London: Barrie & Rockliff, 1960.

Knight, G. W., *The Saturnian Quest: A Chart of the Prose Works of John Cowper Powys*, London: Methuen; New York: Barnes & Noble, 1965.

Hopkins, H. K., *The Powys Brothers: A Biographical Appreciation*, London: Phoenix House; Rutherford, N. J.: Fairleigh Dickinson Univ. Press, 1967.

Praed, W. M.

Hudson, D., *A Poet in Parliament: The Life of Winthrop Mackworth Praed, 1802–1839*, London: Murray, 1939.

Priestley, J. B.

Cooper, S., *J. B. Priestley: Portrait of an Author*, London: Heinemann, 1970; New York: Harper & Row, 1971.

Prior, Matthew.

Legg, L. G. Wickham, *Matthew Prior: A Study of His Public Career and Correspondence*, Cambridge: Cambridge Univ. Press; New York: Macmillan Co., 1921.

Eves, C. K., *Matthew Prior, Poet and Diplomatist*, London: Oxford Univ. Press; New York: Columbia Univ. Press, 1939.

Quarles, Francis.

Freeman, R., *English Emblem Books*, London: Chatto & Windus, 1948.

Radcliffe, Ann.

Tompkins, J. M. S., *The Popular Novel in England, 1770–1800*, London: Constable, 1932.

Varma, D. P., *The Gothic Flame: Being A History of the Gothic Novel in England*, London: Barker, 1957.

Raine, Kathleen.

Grubb, F. S., *A Vision of Reality: A Study of Liberalism in Twentieth Century Verse*, London: Chatto & Windus; New York: Barnes & Noble, 1965.

Ralegh, Sir Walter.

Bradbrook, M. C., *The School of Night: A Study in the Literary Relationships of Sir Walter Raleigh*, Cambridge: Cambridge Univ. Press; New York: Macmillan Co., 1936.

Edwards, P., *Sir Walter Raleigh*, London: Longmans, 1953.

Ramsay, Allan.

Martin, B., *Allan Ramsay: A Study of His Life and Works*, London: Oxford Univ. Press; Cambridge, Mass.: Harvard Univ. Press, 1931.

Ransom, John Crowe.

Stewart, J. L., *John Crowe Ransom*, Minneapolis: Univ. of Minnesota Press, 1962; London: Oxford Univ. Press. Pamphlets on American Writers, no. 18.

Buffington, R., *The Equilibrist: A Study of John Crowe Ransom's Poems, 1916–1963*, Nashville, Tenn.: Vanderbilt Univ. Press, 1967.

Parsons, T. H., *John Crowe Ransom*, New York: Twayne, 1969.

Reade, Charles.

Reade, C. L., and Reade, C., *Charles Reade, Dramatist, Novelist, Journalist: A Memoir*, 2 vols., London: Chapman & Hall; New York: Harper, 1887.

Elwin, M., *Charles Reade: A Biography*, London: Cape, 1931.

Burns, W., *Charles Reade: A Study in Victorian Authorship*, New York: Bookman Associates, 1961.

Renaissance Humanism.

Thompson, J. W., and others, *The Civilization of the Renaissance*, Chicago: Univ. of Chicago Press, 1929; Cambridge: Cambridge Univ. Press, 1930.

Gilmore, M. P., *The World of Humanism, 1453–1517*, London: H. Hamilton; New York: Harper, 1952.

Bolgar, R. R., *The Classical Heritage and Its Beneficiaries*, Cambridge: Cambridge Univ. Press, 1954.

Hale, J. R., *England and the Italian Renaissance*, London: Faber & Faber, 1954.

Weiss, R., *Humanism in England during the Fifteenth Century*, Oxford: Blackwell, 2nd edition, 1957.

Mason, H. A., *Humanism and Poetry in the Early Tudor Period*, London: Routledge, 1959; New York: Barnes & Noble, 1960.
Bush, D., *Prefaces to Renaissance Literature*, London: Oxford Univ. Press; Cambridge, Mass.: Harvard Univ. Press, 1965.
Simon, J., *Education and Society in Tudor England*, Cambridge: Cambridge Univ. Press, 1966.
Seigel, J. E., *Rhetoric and Philosophy in Renaissance Humanism: The Union of Eloquence and Wisdom, Petrarch to Valla*, Princeton: Princeton Univ. Press, 1968.

Ricardo, David.

Hollander, J. H., *David Ricardo: A Centenary Estimate*, Baltimore: Johns Hopkins Press, 1910.

Richards, I. A.

Schiller, J. P., *I. A. Richards' Theory of Literature*, New Haven: Yale Univ. Press, 1969.

Richardson, Dorothy.

Blake, C. R., *Dorothy Richardson*, London: Mayflower; Ann Arbor: Univ. of Michigan Press, 1960.

Richardson, Samuel.

McKillop, A. D., *Samuel Richardson, Printer and Novelist*, London: Oxford Univ. Press; Chapel Hill: Univ. of North Carolina Press, 1936.
Sale, W. M., *Samuel Richardson, Master Printer*, Ithaca, N. Y.: Cornell Univ. Press, 1950; London: Oxford Univ. Press, 1951.
Watt, I. P., *The Rise of the Novel: Studies in Defoe, Richardson and Fielding*, London: Chatto & Windus; Berkeley and Los Angeles: Univ. of California Press, 1957.
Konigsberg, I., *Samuel Richardson and the Dramatic Novel*, Lexington: Univ. of Kentucky Press, 1968.
Eaves, T. C. D., and Kimpel, B. D., *Samuel Richardson*, Oxford: Clarendon Press, 1971.

Ritson, Joseph.

Bronson, B. H., *Joseph Ritson, Scholar-at-Arms*, 2 vols., Cambridge: Cambridge Univ. Press; Berkeley and Los Angeles: Univ. of California Press, 1938.

Robinson, Edwin Arlington.

Cestre, C., *An Introduction to Edwin Arlington Robinson*, New York: Macmillan Co., 1930.
Winters, Y., *Edwin Arlington Robinson*, Norfolk, Conn.: New Directions, 1946.
Neff, E. E., *Edwin Arlington Robinson*, New York: Sloane, 1948; London: Methuen, 1949.
Barnard, E., *Edwin Arlington Robinson: A Critical Study*, New York: Macmillan Co., 1952.

Fussell, E. S., *Edwin Arlington Robinson: The Literary Background of a Traditional Poet*, Berkeley and Los Angeles: Univ. of California Press, 1954; Cambridge: Cambridge Univ. Press, 1955.

Anderson, W. L., *Edwin Arlington Robinson: A Critical Introduction*, Boston: Houghton Mifflin, 1967.

Rochester, John Wilmot, Earl of.

Wilson, J. H., *The Court Wits of the Restoration*, London: Oxford Univ. Press; Princeton: Princeton Univ. Press, 1948.

Pinto, V. de S., *Enthusiast in Wit: A Portrait of John Wilmot, Earl of Rochester*, London: Routledge; Lincoln: Univ. of Nebraska Press, 1962.

Vieth, D. M., *Attribution in Restoration Poetry: A Study of Rochester's Poems of 1680*, New Haven: Yale Univ. Press, 1963.

Farley-Hills, D., *Rochester: The Critical Heritage*, London: Routledge; New York: Barnes & Noble, 1972.

Roethke, Theodore.

Stein, A. S. (ed.), *Theodore Roethke: Essays on the Poetry*, Seattle: Univ. of Washington Press, 1965.

Malkoff, K., *Theodore Roethke: An Introduction to the Poetry*, New York: Columbia Univ. Press, 1966.

Seager, A., *The Glass House: The Life of Theodore Roethke*, New York: McGraw-Hill, 1968.

Rogers, Samuel.

Roberts, R. E., *Samuel Rogers and His Circle*, London: Methuen, 1910.

Dyce, A., *Recollection of the Table Talk of Samuel Rogers*, ed. M. Bishop, London: Richards Press, 1952; Lawrence: Univ. of Kansas Press, 1953.

Romantic Movement, The.

Babbitt, I., *Rousseau and Romanticism*, Boston: Houghton Mifflin, 1919.

Praz, M., *The Romantic Agony*, trans. A. Davidson, London: Oxford Univ. Press, 1933.

Knight, G. W., *The Starlit Dome: Studies in the Poetry of Vision*, London: Oxford Univ. Press, 1941.

Lovejoy, A. O., *Essays in the History of Ideas*, Baltimore: Johns Hopkins Press, 1948; London: Oxford Univ. Press, 1949.

Bowra, C. M., *The Romantic Imagination*, Cambridge, Mass.: Harvard Univ. Press, 1949; London: Oxford Univ. Press, 1950.

Hough, G. G., *The Last Romantics*, London: Duckworth, 1949; New York: Macmillan Co., 1950.

Auden, W. H., *The Enchafèd Flood: The Romantic Iconography of the Sea*, New York: Random House, 1950; London: Faber & Faber, 1951.

Abrams, M. H., *The Mirror and the Lamp: Romantic Theory and the Critical Tradition*, New York: Oxford Univ. Press, 1953.

Hough, G. G., *The Romantic Poets*, London: Hutchinson; New York: Longmans, 1953.

Rodway, A., *The Romantic Conflict*, London: Chatto & Windus, 1963.

Fletcher, I. (ed.), *Romantic Mythologies*, London: Routledge; New York: Barnes & Noble, 1967.

Hayter, A., *Opium and the Romantic Imagination*, London: Faber & Faber; Berkeley and Los Angeles: Univ. of California Press, 1968.

Furst, L. R., *Romanticism in Perspective: A Comparative Study of Aspects of the Romantic Movements in England, France and Germany*, London: Macmillan, 1969; New York: Humanities Press, 1970.

Rosenberg, Isaac.

Bergonzi, B., *Heroes' Twilight: A Study of the Literature of the Great War*, London: Constable, 1965; New York: Coward-McCann, 1966.

Rossetti, Christina.

Sandars, M. F., *The Life of Christina Rossetti*, London: Hutchinson, 1930.

Stuart, D. M., *Christina Rossetti*, London: Macmillan; New York: Macmillan Co., 1930.

Packer, L. M., *Christina Rossetti*, Cambridge: Cambridge Univ. Press; Berkeley and Los Angeles: Univ. of California Press, 1963.

Rossetti, D. G.

Waller, R. D., *The Rossetti Family, 1824–1854*, Manchester: Manchester Univ. Press, 1932.

Doughty, O., *A Victorian Romantic: Dante Gabriel Rossetti*, London: Muller; as *Dante Gabriel Rossetti: A Victorian Romantic*, New Haven: Yale Univ. Press, 1949.

Welland, D. S. R., *The Pre-Raphaelites in Literature and Art*, London: Harrap; New York: Barnes & Noble, 1953.

Johnston, R. D., *Dante Gabriel Rossetti*, New York: Twayne, 1969.

Royce, Josiah.

Fuss, P. L., *The Moral Philosophy of Josiah Royce*, Cambridge, Mass.: Harvard Univ. Press, 1965.

Ruskin, John.

Ladd, H. A., *The Victorian Morality of Art*, New York: R. R. Smith, 1932.

Leon, D., *Ruskin, the Great Victorian*, London: Routledge, 1949.

Evans, J., *John Ruskin*, London: Cape; New York: Oxford Univ. Press, 1954.

Rosenberg, J. D., *The Darkening Glass: A Portrait of Ruskin's Genius*, New York: Columbia Univ. Press, 1961.

Russell, Bertrand, Earl.

Ayer, A. J., *Russell*, London: Fontana, 1972.

Russell, George William ("Æ").

Figgis, D., *Æ., George W. Russell: A Study of a Man and of a Nation*, Dublin: Maunsel, 1916.

"Rutherford, Mark."

Maclean, C. M., *Mark Rutherford: A Biography of William Hale White*, London: Macdonald, 1955.

Stock, I., *William Hale White (Mark Rutherford): A Critical Study*, London: Allen & Unwin; New York: Columbia Univ. Press, 1956.

Sackville, Thomas.

Davie, D., *Articulate Energy: An Inquiry into the Syntax of English Poetry*, London: Routledge, 1955.

Salinger, J. D.

Grunwald, H. A. (ed.), *Salinger: A Critical and Personal Portrait*, New York: Harper & Row, 1962.

Sandburg, Carl.

Detzer, K. W., *Carl Sandburg: A Study in Personality and Background*, New York: Harcourt, Brace, 1941.

Crowder, R., *Carl Sandburg*, New York: Twayne, 1964.

Sassoon, Siegfried.

Thorpe, M., *Siegfried Sassoon: A Critical Study*, London: Oxford Univ. Press; Leiden: Leiden Univ. Press, 1966.

Savage, Richard.

Tracy, C., *The Artificial Bastard: A Biography of Richard Savage*, Cambridge, Mass.: Harvard Univ. Press, 1953; London: Oxford Univ. Press, 1954.

Science Fiction.

Amis, K., *New Maps of Hell: A Survey of Science Fiction*, New York: Harcourt, Brace, 1960; London: Gollancz, 1961.

Philmus, R. M., *Into the Unknown: The Evolution of Science Fiction from Francis Godwin to H. G. Wells*, Berkeley and Los Angeles: Univ. of California Press, 1970.

Moskowitz, S., *Explorers of the Infinite: Shapes of Science Fiction*, Los Angeles: Nash, 1971.

Scott, Sir Walter.

Grierson, H. J. C. (ed.), *Sir Walter Scott To-Day*, London: Constable, 1932.

Hillhouse, J. T., *The Waverley Novels and Their Critics*, London: Oxford Univ. Press; Minneapolis: Univ. of Minnesota Press, 1936.

Grierson, H. J. C., *Sir Walter Scott, Bart.: A New Life*, London: Constable; New York: Columbia Univ. Press, 1938.

Daiches, D., *Literary Essays*, Edinburgh: Oliver & Boyd, 1956.

Welsh, A., *The Hero of the Waverley Novels*, New Haven: Yale Univ. Press, 1963.

Crawford, T., *Scott*, Edinburgh: Oliver & Boyd, 1965.

Hayden, J. O. (ed.), *Scott: The Critical Heritage*, London: Routledge; New York: Barnes & Noble, 1970.

Johnson, E., *Sir Walter Scott: The Great Unknown*, 2 vols., London: H. Hamilton; New York: Macmillan Co., 1970.

Sedley, Sir Charles.

Pinto, V. de S., *Sir Charles Sedley, 1639–1701: A Study in the Life and Literature of the Restoration*, London: Constable, 1927.

Sermons.

Owst, G. R., *Preaching in Medieval England*, Cambridge: Cambridge Univ. Press, 1926.

Mitchell, W. F., *English Pulpit Oratory from Andrewes to Tillotson*, London: S.P.C.K.; New York: Macmillan Co., 1932.

Mackerness, E. D., *The Heeded Voice: Studies in the Literary Status of the Anglican Sermon*, Cambridge: Heffer, 1959.

Pollard, A., *English Sermons*, London: Longmans (for British Council), 1963. Writers and Their Work series.

Blench, J. W., *Preaching in England in the Late Fifteenth and Sixteenth Centuries*, Oxford: Blackwell; New York: Barnes & Noble, 1964.

Sewall, Samuel.

Winslow, O. E., *Samuel Sewall of Boston*, New York: Macmillan Co.; London: Collier-Macmillan, 1964.

Shadwell, Thomas.

Borgman, A. S., *Thomas Shadwell: His Life and Comedies*, New York: New York Univ. Press, 1928.

Shaftesbury, Anthony Ashley Cooper, Earl of.

Willey, B., *The Eighteenth Century Background: Studies on the Idea of Nature in the Thought of the Period*, London: Chatto & Windus, 1940; New York: Columbia Univ. Press, 1941.

Brett, R. L., *The Third Earl of Shaftesbury: A Study in Eighteenth-Century Literary Theory*, London: Hutchinson, 1951.

Shakespeare, William.

Spencer, T. J. B., *Shakespeare and the Nature of Man*, London: Collier-Macmillan; New York: Macmillan Co., 1961.

Smith, G. R., *A Classified Shakespeare Bibliography, 1936–1958*, University Park, Pa.: Pennsylvania State Univ. Press, 1963.

Campbell, O. J., and Quinn, E. G. (edd.), *The Reader's Encyclopedia of Shakespeare*, New York: Crowell, 1966; as *A Shakespeare Encyclopaedia*, London: Methuen, 1967.

Gurr, A., *The Shakespeare Stage, 1574–1642*, Cambridge: Cambridge Univ. Press, 1970.

Muir, K., and Schoenbaum, S. (edd.), *A New Companion to Shakespeare Studies*, Cambridge: Cambridge Univ. Press, 1971.

The following monographs on Shakespeare and his plays, in the series Writers and

Their Work, London: Longmans (for British Council), are also useful. Each contains a select bibliography.

Sisson, C. J., *Shakespeare*, 1955.

Traversi, D. A., *The Early Comedies*, 1960.

Muir, K. A., *The Great Tragedies*, 1961.

Ure, P., *The Problem Plays*, 1961.

Hunter, G. K., *The Late Comedies*, 1962.

Knights, L. C., *The Histories*, 1962.

Leech, C., *The Chronicles*, 1962.

Kermode, F., *The Final Plays*, 1963.

Prince, F. T., *The Poems*, 1963.

Spencer, T. J. B., *The Roman Plays*, 1963.

Shaw, George Bernard.

Chesterton, G. K., *George Bernard Shaw*, London and New York: J. Lane, 1909; with additional chapter, London, 1935; New York: Devin-Adair, 1950.

Wilson, E., "Shaw at Eighty," in *The Triple Thinkers: Ten Essays on Literature*, London: Oxford Univ. Press; New York: Harcourt, Brace, 1938; as *Twelve Essays . . .*, revised, New York: Oxford Univ. Press, 1948.

Pearson, H., *Bernard Shaw: His Life and Personality*, London: Collins; as *G.B.S.: A Full Length Portrait*, New York: Harper, 1942.

Henderson, A., *George Bernard Shaw: Man of the Century*, New York: Appleton-Century-Crofts, 1956.

Purdom, C. B., *A Guide to the Plays of Bernard Shaw*, London: Methuen; New York: Crowell, 1963.

Stewart, J. I. M., *Eight Modern Writers*, Oxford: Clarendon Press, 1963.

Wilson, C., *Bernard Shaw: A Reassessment*, London: Hutchinson; New York: Atheneum, 1969.

Morgan, M. M., *The Shavian Playground*, London: Methuen, 1972.

Shelley, Mary Wollstonecraft.

Nitchie, E., *Mary Shelley, Author of "Frankenstein,"* New Brunswick, N. J.: Rutgers Univ. Press, 1953.

Shelley, P. B.

White, N. I., *Shelley*, 2 vols., New York: Knopf, 1940; revised, London: Secker & Warburg, 1947.

Hughes, A. M. D'U., *The Nascent Mind of Shelley*, Oxford: Clarendon Press, 1947.

Baker, C. H., *Shelley's Major Poetry: The Fabric of a Vision*, London: Oxford Univ. Press; Princeton: Princeton Univ. Press, 1948.

Cameron, K. N., *The Young Shelley: Genesis of a Radical*, New York: Macmillan Co., 1950; London: Gollancz, 1951.

Rogers, N., *Shelley at Work: A Critical Enquiry*, Oxford: Clarendon Press, 1956.

Bloom, H., *Shelley's Mythmaking*, New Haven: Yale Univ. Press, 1959.

Wasserman, E. R., *The Subtler Language: Critical Readings of Neoclassical and Romantic Poems*, London: Oxford Univ. Press; Baltimore: Johns Hopkins Press, 1959.

Wilson, M. T., *Shelley's Later Poetry: A Study of His Prophetic Imagination*, London: Oxford Univ. Press; New York: Columbia Univ. Press, 1959.

Cameron, K. N. (ed.), *Shelley and His Circle, 1773–1822*, 4 vols., London: Oxford Univ. Press; Cambridge, Mass.: Harvard Univ. Press, 1961–70.

Shenstone, William.

Humphreys, A. R., *William Shenstone: An Eighteenth Century Portrait*, Cambridge: Cambridge Univ. Press; New York: Macmillan Co., 1937.

Sheridan, R. B.

Darlington, W. A., *Sheridan*, London: Duckworth; New York: Macmillan Co., 1933.

Rhodes, R. C., *Harlequin Sheridan: The Man and the Legends*, Oxford: Blackwell; New York: P. Smith, 1933.

Cove, J. W. (pseud. Gibbs, L.), *Sheridan: His Life and His Theatre*, London: Dent, 1947; New York: Morrow, 1948.

Sherwood, Robert E.

Brown, J. M., *The Worlds of Robert E. Sherwood: Mirror to His Times*, New York: Harper & Row; London: H. Hamilton, 1965.

Shirley, James.

Nason, A. H., *James Shirley, Dramatist: A Biographical and Critical Study*, New York: Nason, 1915.

Harbage, A., *Cavalier Drama: An Historical and Critical Supplement to the Study of the Elizabethan and Restoration Stage*, London: Oxford Univ. Press; New York: Modern Language Association of America, 1936.

Shorthouse, J. H.

Shorthouse, S., *Life and Letters of J. H. Shorthouse*, 2 vols., London: Macmillan, 1905.

Sidney, Sir Philip.

Zandvoort, R. W., *Sidney's "Arcadia": A Comparison between the Two Versions*, Amsterdam: Swets & Zeitlinger, 1929.

Buxton, J., *Sir Philip Sidney and the English Renaissance*, London: Macmillan; New York: St. Martin's Press, 1954.

Boas, F. S., *Sir Philip Sidney, Representative Elizabethan: His Life and Writings*, London: Staples Press, 1955; New York: De Graff, 1956.

Rose, M., *Heroic Love: Studies in Sidney and Spenser*, Cambridge, Mass.: Harvard Univ. Press, 1968.

Simms, William Gilmore.

Ridgely, J. V., *William Gilmore Simms*, New York: Twayne, 1962.

Sinclair, Upton.

Dell, F., *Upton Sinclair: A Study in Social Protest*, New York: Doran, 1927; London: T. Werner Laurie, 1928.

Singer, Isaac.

Malin, I. (ed.), *Critical Views of Isaac Bashevis Singer*, New York: New York Univ. Press, 1969.

Siegel, B., *Isaac Bashevis Singer*, Minneapolis: Univ. of Minnesota Press, 1969; London: Oxford Univ. Press. Pamphlets on American Writers, no. 86.

Sitwell, Dame Edith.

Mégroz, R. L., *The Three Sitwells: A Biographical and Critical Study*, London: Richards Press, 1927.

Sitwell, O., *Left Hand, Right Hand!*, 4 vols., Boston: Little, Brown, 1944–48; London: Macmillan, 1945–49.

Lehmann, J., *Edith Sitwell*, London: Longmans (for British Council), 1952. Writers and Their Work series.

Skelton, John.

Gordon, I. A., *John Skelton, Poet Laureate*, London and Melbourne: Melbourne Univ. Press (in association with Oxford Univ. Press); New York: Stechert, 1943.

Heiserman, A. R., *Skelton and Satire*, Chicago: Univ. of Chicago Press, 1961.

Fish, S. E., *John Skelton's Poetry*, New Haven: Yale Univ. Press, 1965.

Harris, W. O., *Skelton's "Magnyfycence" and the Cardinal Virtue Tradition*, Chapel Hill: Univ. of North Carolina Press, 1965.

Smart, Christopher.

Devlin, C., *Poor Kit Smart*, London: Hart-Davis, 1961; Carbondale: Southern Illinois Univ. Press, 1962.

Dearnley, M., *The Poetry of Christopher Smart*, London: Routledge, 1968; New York: Barnes & Noble, 1969.

Smith, Adam.

Rae, J., *Life of Adam Smith*, New York: Macmillan Co., 1895.

Morrow, G. R., *The Ethical and Economic Theories of Adam Smith*, New York: Longmans, 1923.

Scott, W. R., *Adam Smith, As Student and Professor*, Glasgow: Jackson (Glasgow Univ. Publications), 1937.

Smith, John.

Barbour, P. L., *The Three Worlds of Captain John Smith*, Boston: Houghton Mifflin, 1964.

Smith, Sydney.

Pearson, H., *The Smith of Smiths: Being the Life, Wit and Humour of Sydney Smith*, New York: Harper, 1934; London: H. Hamilton, 1935.

Halpern, S., *Sydney Smith*, New York: Twayne, 1966.

Smollett, Tobias.

Introduction to *Travels through France and Italy*, ed. T. Seccombe, London: Oxford Univ. Press, 1907.

Boege, F. S., *Smollett's Reputation As a Novelist*, London: Oxford Univ. Press; Princeton: Princeton Univ. Press, 1947.

Knapp, L. M., *Tobias Smollett, Doctor of Men and Manners*, London: Oxford Univ. Press; Princeton: Princeton Univ. Press, 1949.

Spector, R. D., *Tobias George Smollett*, New York: Twayne, 1968.

Snow, C. P., Lord.

Greacen, R., *The World of C. P. Snow*, London: Scorpion, 1962.

Thale, J., *C. P. Snow*, Edinburgh: Oliver & Boyd, 1964; New York: C. Scribner's Sons, 1965.

Rabinovitz, R., *The Reaction against Experiment in the English Novel, 1950–1960*, New York: Columbia Univ. Press, 1968.

Southey, Robert.

Simmons, J., *Southey*, London: Collins, 1945; New Haven: Yale Univ. Press, 1948.

Carnall, G., *Robert Southey and His Age: The Development of a Conservative Mind*, Oxford: Clarendon Press, 1960.

Southwell, Robert.

Janelle, P., *Robert Southwell the Writer: A Study in Religious Inspiration*, London and New York: Sheed & Ward, 1935.

Devlin, C., *The Life of Robert Southwell, Poet and Martyr*, London: Longmans; New York: Farrar, Straus, 1956.

Spark, Muriel.

Stanford, D., *Muriel Spark: A Biography and Critical Study*, Fontwell, Sussex: Centaur Press, 1963.

Spasmodics, The.

Gilfillan, G., *Galleries of Literary Portraits*, 2 vols., Edinburgh and London, 1856–57.

Buckley, J. H., *The Victorian Temper: A Study in Literary Culture*, Cambridge, Mass.: Harvard Univ. Press, 1951; London: Allen & Unwin, 1952.

Weinstein, M. A., *William Edmonstoune Aytoun and the Spasmodic Controversy*, New Haven: Yale Univ. Press, 1968.

Spencer, Herbert.

Duncan, D., *The Life and Letters of Herbert Spencer*, London: Methuen, 1908.

Spenser, Edmund.

Jones, H. S. V., *A Spenser Handbook*, New York: Crofts, 1930.

Greenlaw, E. A., *Studies in Spenser's Historical Allegory*, London: Oxford Univ. Press; Baltimore: Johns Hopkins Press, 1932.

Lewis, C. S., *The Allegory of Love*, Oxford: Clarendon Press, 1936.

Ellrodt, R., *Neoplatonism in the Poetry of Spenser*, Geneva: Librairie E. Droz, 1960.

Parker, Mother P., *The Allegory of "The Faerie Queene,"* Oxford: Clarendon Press, 1960.

Hough, G. G., *A Preface to "The Faerie Queene,"* London: Duckworth, 1962; New York: Norton, 1963.

Nelson, W., *The Poetry of Edmund Spenser: A Study*, New York: Columbia Univ. Press, 1963.

Alpers, P. J., *The Poetry of "The Faerie Queene,"* Princeton: Princeton Univ. Press, 1967.

Rose, M., *Heroic Love: Studies in Sidney and Spenser*, Cambridge, Mass.: Harvard Univ. Press, 1968.

Cummings, R. M. (ed.), *Spenser: The Critical Heritage*, London: Routledge; New York: Barnes & Noble, 1971.

Steele, Sir Richard.

Graham, W., *English Literary Periodicals*, New York: Nelson, 1930.

Connely, W., *Sir Richard Steele*, London: Cape; New York: C. Scribner's Sons, 1934.

Stein, Gertrude.

Sutherland, D., *Gertrude Stein: A Biography of Her Work*, New Haven: Yale Univ. Press; London: Oxford Univ. Press, 1951.

Reid, B. L., *Art by Subtraction: A Dissenting Opinion of Gertrude Stein*, Norman: Univ. of Oklahoma Press, 1958.

Brinnin, J. M., *The Third Rose: Gertrude Stein and Her World*, Boston: Little, Brown, 1959; London: Weidenfeld, 1960.

Hoffman, M. J., *The Development of Abstractionism in the Writings of Gertrude Stein*, Philadelphia: Univ. of Pennsylvania Press, 1965.

Bridgman, R., *Gertrude Stein in Pieces*, New York: Oxford Univ. Press, 1970.

Steinbeck, John.

Moore, H. T., *The Novels of John Steinbeck: A First Critical Study*, Chicago: Black Cat Press (Normandie House), 1939.

Tedlock, E. W., and Wicker, C. V. (edd.), *Steinbeck and His Critics*, Albuquerque: Univ. of New Mexico Press, 1957.

Lisca, P., *The Wide World of John Steinbeck*, Brunswick, N. J.: Rutgers Univ. Press, 1958.

Watt, F. W., *John Steinbeck*, New York: Grove Press; as *Steinbeck*, Edinburgh: Oliver & Boyd, 1962.

Fontenrose, J. E., *John Steinbeck: An Introduction and Interpretation*, New York: Barnes & Noble, 1964.

Stephen, Sir Leslie.

Maitland, F. W., *The Life and Letters of Leslie Stephen*, London: Duckworth; New York: Putnam, 1906.

Annan, N., *Leslie Stephen: His Thought and Character in Relation to His Time*, London: MacGibbon & Kee, 1951; Cambridge, Mass.: Harvard Univ. Press, 1952.

Sterne, Laurence.

Cross, W. L., *Life and Times of Laurence Sterne*, New York: Macmillan Co., 1909; 3rd edition, 2 vols., revised, London: Oxford Univ. Press; New Haven: Yale Univ. Press, 1929.

Fluchère, H., *Laurence Sterne: From "Tristram" to "Yorick,"* trans. B. Bray (abridged), London: Oxford Univ. Press, 1965.

Thomson, D., *Wild Excursions: The Life and Fiction of Lawrence Sterne*, London: Weidenfeld, 1972.

Stevens, Wallace.

Kermode, F., *Wallace Stevens*, Edinburgh: Oliver & Boyd, 1960; New York: Grove Press, 1961.

Riddel, J. N., *The Clairvoyant Eye: The Poetry and Poetics of Wallace Stevens*, Baton Rouge: Louisiana State Univ. Press, 1965.

Doggett, F., *Stevens' Poetry of Thought*, Baltimore: Johns Hopkins Press, 1966.

Vendler, H. H., *On Extended Wings: Wallace Stevens' Longer Poems*, Cambridge, Mass.: Harvard Univ. Press, 1969.

Stevenson, Robert Louis.

Balfour, G., *The Life of Robert Louis Stevenson*, 2 vols., London: Methuen; New York: C. Scribner's Sons, 1901.

Swinnerton, F., *R. L. Stevenson: A Critical Study*, London: Secker, 1914; New York: M. Kennerley, 1915.

Daiches, D., *Robert Louis Stevenson*, Glasgow: W. Maclellan; Norfolk, Conn.: New Directions, 1947.

Furnas, J. C., *Voyage to Windward: The Life of Robert Louis Stevenson*, New York: Sloane, 1951; London: Faber & Faber, 1952.

Stickney, Trumbull.

Reeves, J., and Haldane, S. (edd.), *Homage to Trumbull Stickney: Poems*, London: Heinemann, 1968.

Stoppard, Tom.

Taylor, J. Russell, *The Second Wave: British Drama in the Seventies*, London: Methuen, 1971.

Stowe, Harriet Beecher.

Foster, C. H., *The Rungless Ladder: Harriet Beecher Stowe and New England Puritanism*, Durham, N. C.: Duke Univ. Press; Cambridge: Cambridge Univ. Press, 1954.

Adams, J. R., *Harriet Beecher Stowe*, New York: Twayne, 1963.

Wagenknecht, E. C., *Harriet Beecher Stowe: The Known and the Unknown*, New York: Oxford Univ. Press, 1965.

Strachey, Lytton.

Beerbohm, M., *Lytton Strachey [:Rede Lecture, 1943]*, Cambridge: Cambridge Univ. Press; New York: Knopf, 1943.

Johnstone, J. K., *The Bloomsbury Group: A Study of E. M. Forster, Lytton Strachey, Virginia Woolf, and Their Circle*, London: Secker & Warburg; New York: Noonday Press, 1954.

Sanders, C. R., *Lytton Strachey: His Mind and Art*, London: Oxford Univ. Press; New Haven: Yale Univ. Press, 1957.

Holroyd, M., *Lytton Strachey: A Critical Biography*, 2 vols., London: Heinemann, 1967–68; New York: Holt, Rinehart, 1968.

Surrey, Henry Howard, Earl of.

Berdan, J. M., *Early Tudor Poetry, 1485–1547*, New York: Macmillan Co., 1920.

Lever, J. W., *The Elizabethan Love Sonnet*, London: Methuen, 1956; 2nd edition and New York: Barnes & Noble, 1966.

Mason, H. A., *Humanism and Poetry in the Early Tudor Period*, London: Routledge, 1959; New York: Barnes & Noble, 1960.

Surtees, R. S.

Watson, F., *Robert Smith Surtees: A Critical Study*, London: Harrap, 1933.

Swift, Jonathan.

Jones, R. F., *Ancients and Moderns: A Study of the Background of the "Battle of the Books,"* Seattle: Univ. of Washington Press, 1936.

Quintana, R., *The Mind and Art of Jonathan Swift*, London: Methuen, 1936; revised and New York: Oxford Univ. Press, 1953.

Price, M., *Swift's Rhetorical Art: A Study in Structure and Meaning*, London: Oxford Univ. Press; New Haven: Yale Univ. Press, 1953.

Ewald, W. B., *The Masks of Jonathan Swift*, Oxford: Blackwell; Cambridge, Mass.: Harvard Univ. Press, 1954.

Williams, K., *Jonathan Swift and the Age of Compromise*, Lawrence: Univ. of Kansas Press, 1958; London: Constable, 1959.

Paulson, R., *Theme and Structure in Swift's "Tale of a Tub,"* New Haven: Yale Univ. Press, 1960.

Crane, R. S., "The Houyhnhnms, the Yahoos and the History of Ideas," in *Reason and the Imagination: Studies in the History of Ideas, 1600–1800*, ed. J. A. Mazzeo, London: Routledge; New York: Columbia Univ. Press, 1962.

Ehrenpreis, I., *Swift: The Man, His Works, and the Age*, 3 vols., London: Methuen; Cambridge, Mass.: Harvard Univ. Press, 1962– .

Ferguson, O. W., *Jonathan Swift and Ireland*, Urbana: Univ. of Illinois Press, 1962.

Davis, H., *Jonathan Swift: Essays on His Satire and Other Studies*, New York: Oxford Univ. Press, 1964.

Tuveson, E. (ed.), *Swift: A Collection of Critical Essays*, Englewood Cliffs, N. J.: Prentice-Hall, 1964.

Jeffares, A. N. (ed.), *Fair Liberty Was All His Cry: A Tercentenary Tribute to Jonathan Swift, 1667–1745*, London: Macmillan; New York: St. Martin's Press, 1967.

Swinburne, A. C.

Nicolson, H., *Swinburne*, London: Macmillan; New York: Macmillan Co., 1926.

Chew, S. C., *Swinburne*, Boston: Little, Brown, 1929; London: Murray, 1931.

Lafourcade, G., *Swinburne: A Literary Biography*, London: Bell; New York: Morrow, 1932.

Hyder, C. K. (ed.), *Swinburne: The Critical Heritage*, London: Routledge; New York: Barnes & Noble, 1971.

Symons, Arthur.

Temple, R. Z., *The Critic's Alchemy: A Study of the Introduction of French Symbolism into England*, New York: Twayne, 1953.

Kermode, F., *Romantic Image*, London: Routledge, 1957; New York: Macmillan Co., 1958.

Lhombreaud, R., *Arthur Symons: A Critical Biography*, London: J. Baker, 1963.

Synge, J. M.

Strong, L. A. G., *John Millington Synge*, London: Allen & Unwin, 1941.

Greene, D. H., and Stephens, E. M., *J. M. Synge, 1871–1909*, New York: Macmillan Co., 1959 (authorized biography).

Price, A., *Synge and Anglo-Irish Drama*, London: Methuen, 1961.

Tate, Allen.

Bradbury, J. M., *The Fugitives: A Critical Account*, Chapel Hill: Univ. of North Carolina Press, 1958.

Taylor, Edward.

Grabo, N. S., *Edward Taylor*, New York: Twayne, 1962.

Stanford, D. E., *Edward Taylor*, Minneapolis: Univ. of Minnesota Press, 1965; London: Oxford Univ. Press. Pamphlets on American Writers, no. 52.

Taylor, Jeremy.

Stranks, C. J., *The Life and Writings of Jeremy Taylor*, London: S.P.C.K., 1952.

Tennyson, Alfred, Lord.

Bradley, A. C., *A Commentary on Tennyson's "In Memoriam,"* London: Macmillan; New York: Macmillan Co., 1901.; revised, 1902; 1930.

Nicolson, H., *Tennyson: Aspects of His Life, Character, and Poetry*, London: Constable, 1923; Boston: Houghton Mifflin, 1925.

Baum, P. F., *Tennyson Sixty Years After*, London: Oxford Univ. Press; Chapel Hill: Univ. of North Carolina Press, 1948.

Tennyson, C. B. L., *Alfred Tennyson*, London: Macmillan; New York: Macmillan Co., 1949.

Buckley, J. H., *Tennyson: The Growth of a Poet*, Cambridge, Mass.: Harvard Univ. Press, 1960.

Killham, J. (ed.), *Critical Essays on the Poetry of Tennyson*, London: Routledge; New York: Barnes & Noble, 1960.

Jump, J. D. (ed.), *Tennyson: The Critical Heritage*, London: Routledge; New York: Barnes & Noble, 1967.

Ricks, C., *Tennyson*, London: Macmillan, 1972.

Thackeray, William Makepeace.

Saintsbury, G., *A Consideration of Thackeray*, London: Oxford Univ. Press, 1931.

Ray, G. N., *The Buried Life: A Study of the Relation between Thackeray's Fiction and His Personal History*, London: Oxford Univ. Press (for Royal Soc. of Lit.); Cambridge, Mass.: Harvard Univ. Press, 1952.

Tillotson, G., *Thackeray the Novelist*, Cambridge: Cambridge Univ. Press, 1954.

Tillotson, K., "Vanity Fair," in *Novels of the Eighteen-Forties*, Oxford: Clarendon Press, 1954.

Ray, G. N., *Thackeray*, 2 vols., London: Oxford Univ. Press; New York: Mc-Graw-Hill, 1955–58.

Tillotson, G., and Hawes, D. (edd.), *Thackeray: The Critical Heritage*, London: Routledge; New York: Barnes & Noble, 1968.

Thomas, Dylan.

Tindall, W. Y., *A Reader's Guide to Dylan Thomas*, London: Thames & Hudson; New York: Farrar, Straus, 1962.

FitzGibbon, C., *The Life of Dylan Thomas*, London: Dent; Boston: Little, Brown, 1965.

Cox, C. B. (ed.), *Dylan Thomas: A Collection of Critical Essays*, Englewood Cliffs, N. J.: Prentice-Hall, 1966.

Moynihan, W. T., *The Craft and Art of Dylan Thomas*, London: Oxford Univ. Press; Ithaca, N. Y.: Cornell Univ. Press, 1966.

Jones, D. (ed.), *Dylan Thomas: The Poems*, London: Dent; Norfolk, Conn.: New Directions, 1971.

Thomas, Edward.

Moore, J. C., *The Life and Letters of Edward Thomas*, London: Heinemann, 1939.

Coombes, H., *Edward Thomas*, London: Chatto & Windus, 1956.

Cooke, W., *Edward Thomas: A Critical Biography, 1878–1917*, London: Faber & Faber, 1970.

Thomas, R. S.

Clark, L., *Andrew Young*; with Thomas, R. G., *R. S. Thomas*, London: Longmans (for British Council), 1964. Writers and Their Work series.

Thompson, Francis.

Meynell, E., *The Life of Francis Thompson*, London: Burns & Oates, 1913; New York: C. Scribner's Sons, 1916.

Reid, J. C., *Francis Thompson, Man and Poet*, London: Routledge, 1959; Westminster, Md.: Newman Press, 1960.

Walsh, J. E., *Strange Harp, Strange Symphony: The Life of Francis Thompson*, New York: Hawthorn Books, 1967; London: Allen & Unwin, 1968.

Thomson, James.

Grant, D., *James Thomson, Poet of "The Seasons,"* London: Cresset Press, 1951.

Cohen, R., *The Art of Discrimination: Thomson's "The Seasons" and the Language of Criticism*, London: Routledge; Berkeley and Los Angeles: Univ. of California Press, 1964.

Cohen, R., *The Unfolding of "The Seasons": A Study of James Thomson's Poem*, London: Routledge; Baltimore: Johns Hopkins Press, 1970.

Thomson, James ("B.V.").

Schaefer, W. D., *James Thomson ("B.V."): Beyond "The City,"* Berkeley and Los Angeles: Univ. of California Press, 1965.

Thoreau, Henry David.

Canby, H. S., *Thoreau*, Boston: Houghton Mifflin, 1939.

Stoller, L., *After Walden: Thoreau's Changing Views on Economic Man*, Stanford: Stanford Univ. Press, 1957; London: Oxford Univ. Press, 1958.

Paul, S., *The Shores of America: Thoreau's Inward Exploration*, Urbana: Univ. of Illinois Press, 1958.

Harding, W., *A Thoreau Handbook*, New York: New York Univ. Press, 1959.

Edel, L., *Henry D. Thoreau*, Minneapolis: Univ. of Minnesota Press, 1970; London: Oxford Univ. Press. Pamphlets on American Writers, no. 90.

Thurber, James.

Black, S. A., *James Thurber: His Masquerades: A Critical Study*, The Hague: Mouton, 1970 (distributed New York: Humanities Press).

Tillotson, John.

Locke, L. G., *Tillotson: A Study in Seventeenth-Century Literature*, Copenhagen: Rosenkilde & Bagger, 1954.

Tourneur, Cyril.

Eliot, T. S., *Selected Essays, 1917–1932*, London: Faber & Faber; New York: Harcourt, Brace, 1932.

Bowers, F. T., *Elizabethan Revenge Tragedy, 1587–1642*, London: Oxford Univ. Press; Princeton: Princeton Univ. Press, 1940.

Murray, P. B., *A Study of Cyril Tourneur*, Philadelphia: Univ. of Pennsylvania Press, 1964; London: Oxford Univ. Press, 1965.

Traherne, Thomas.

Wade, G. I., *Thomas Traherne: A Critical Biography*, London: Oxford Univ. Press; Princeton: Princeton Univ. Press, 1944.

Martz, L. L., *The Paradise Within: Studies in Vaughan, Traherne and Milton*, New Haven: Yale Univ. Press, 1964.

Salter, K. W., *Thomas Traherne: Mystic and Poet*, London: Arnold, 1964; New York: Barnes & Noble, 1965.

Clements, A. L., *The Mystical Poetry of Thomas Traherne*, London: Oxford Univ. Press; Cambridge, Mass.: Harvard Univ. Press, 1969.

Trevelyan, G. M.

Plumb, J. A., *G. M. Trevelyan*, London: Longmans (for British Council), 1951. Writers and Their Work series.

Trollope, Anthony.

Sadleir M., *Trollope: A Commentary*, London: Constable, 1927; revised, 1945; New York: Farrar, Straus, 1947.

Gerould, W. G. (formerly Gregory, W.), and Gerould, J. T., *A Guide to Trollope*, London: Oxford Univ. Press, 1948.

Cockshut, A. O. J., *Anthony Trollope: A Critical Study*, London: Collins, 1955; Fair Lawn, N. J.: Essential Books (1955–   ), 1956.

Praz, M., *The Hero in Eclipse in Victorian Fiction*, trans. A. Davidson, London: Oxford Univ. Press, 1956.

Booth, B. A., *Anthony Trollope: Aspects of His Life and Art*, Bloomington: Indiana Univ. Press, 1958; London: Hulton, 1959.

Trumbull, John.

Bowden, E. T. (ed.), *The Satiric Poems of John Trumbull*, Austin: Univ. of Texas Press, 1962.

Tuckerman, F. G.

Golden, S. A., *Frederick Goddard Tuckerman: An American Sonneteer*, Orono: Univ. of Maine Press, 1952.

Tupper, Martin.

Hudson, D., *Martin Tupper: His Rise and Fall*, London: Constable, 1949; as *Unrepentant Victorian: The Rise and Fall of Martin Tupper*, New York: Macmillan Co., 1950.

Turner, Frederick Jackson.

Hofstadter, R., and Lipset, S. M. (edd.), *Turner and the Sociology of the Frontier*, New York: Basic Books, 1968.

"Twain, Mark."

Brooks, V. W., *The Ordeal of Mark Twain*, New York: Dutton, 1920; London: Heinemann, 1922; revised, New York: Dutton, 1933; London: Dent, 1934.

De Voto, B., *Mark Twain's America*, Boston: Little, Brown, 1932.

De Voto, B., *Mark Twain at Work*, Cambridge, Mass.: Harvard Univ. Press, 1942.

Bellamy, G. C., *Mark Twain As a Literary Artist*, Norman: Univ. of Oklahoma Press, 1950.

Wecter, D., *Sam Clemens of Hannibal*, Boston: Houghton Mifflin, 1952.

Blair, W., *Mark Twain and Huck Finn*, Berkeley and Los Angeles: Univ. of California Press; Cambridge: Cambridge Univ. Press, 1960.

Lynn, K. S., *Mark Twain and Southwestern Humor*, Boston: Little, Brown; London: Constable, 1960.

Smith, H. Nash, *Mark Twain: The Development of a Writer*, Cambridge, Mass.: Harvard Univ. Press, 1962.

Cox, J. M., *Mark Twain: The Fate of Humor*, Princeton: Princeton Univ. Press, 1966.

Kaplan, J., *Mr. Clemens and Mark Twain: A Biography*, New York: Simon & Schuster, 1966; London: Cape, 1967.

Vanbrugh, Sir John.

Dobrée, B., *Restoration Comedy, 1660–1720*, Oxford: Clarendon Press, 1924.

Dobrée, B., *Essays in Biography*, London: Oxford Univ. Press, 1925.

Whistler, L., *Sir John Vanbrugh, Architect and Dramatist, 1664–1726*, London: Cobden-Sanderson, 1938; New York: Macmillan Co., 1939.

Van Vechten, Carl.

Lueders, E., *Carl Van Vechten*, New York: Twayne, 1965.

Vaughan, Henry.

Hutchinson, F. E., *Henry Vaughan: A Life and Interpretation*, Oxford: Clarendon Press, 1947.

Garner, R., *Henry Vaughan: Experience and the Tradition*, Cambridge: Cambridge Univ. Press; Chicago: Univ. of Chicago Press, 1959.

Pettet, E. C., *Of Paradise and Light: A Study of Vaughan's "Silex Scintillans,"* Cambridge: Cambridge Univ. Press, 1960.

Durr, R. A., *On the Mystical Poetry of Henry Vaughan*, London: Oxford Univ. Press; Cambridge, Mass.: Harvard Univ. Press, 1962.

Martz, L. L., *The Paradise Within: Studies in Vaughan, Traherne and Milton*, New Haven: Yale Univ. Press, 1964.

Veblen, Thorstein.

Riesman, D., *Thorstein Veblen: A Critical Interpretation*, New York: C. Scribner's Sons, 1953.

Very, Jones.

Bartlett, W. I., *Jones Very: Emerson's "Brave Saint,"* Durham, N. C.: Duke Univ. Press; Cambridge: Cambridge Univ. Press, 1942.

Gittleman, E, *Jones Very: The Effective Years, 1833–1840*, New York: Columbia Univ. Press, 1967.

Vidal, Gore.

White, R. L., *Gore Vidal*, New York: Twayne, 1968.

Waller, Edmund.

Johnson, S., *The Lives of the Poets*, London, 1779–81.

Allison, A. W., *Towards an Augustan Poetic: Edmund Waller's Reform of English Poetry*, Lexington: Univ. of Kentucky Press, 1962.

Chernaik, W. L., *The Poetry of Limitation: A Study of Edmund Waller*, New Haven and London: Yale Univ. Press, 1968.

Walpole, Horace.

Ketton-Cremer, R. W., *Horace Walpole: A Biography*, London: Duckworth; New York: Longmans, 1940; revised, London: Faber & Faber, 1946.

Lewis, W. S., *Horace Walpole*, London: Hart-Davis; New York: Pantheon, 1961.

Clark, K., *The Gothic Revival: An Essay in the History of Taste*, London: Constable, 1928; New York: C. Scribner's Sons, 1929; 3rd edition, revised and enlarged, London: Murray, 1962.

Walpole, Sir Hugh.

Hart-Davis, R., *Hugh Walpole: A Biography*, London: Macmillan; New York: Macmillan Co., 1952.

Walton, Izaac.

Novarr, D., *The Making of Walton's "Lives,"* London: Oxford Univ. Press; Ithaca, N. Y.: Cornell Univ. Press, 1958.

Warburton, William.

Evans, A. W., *Warburton and the Warburtonians: A Study in Some Eighteenth-Century Controversies*, London: Oxford Univ. Press, 1932.

"Ward, Artemus."

Austin, J. C., *Artemus Ward*, New York: Twayne, 1964.

Ward, Edward (Ned).

Troyer, H., *Ned Ward of Grubstreet: A Study of Sub-Literary London in the Eighteenth Century*, London: Oxford Univ. Press; Cambridge, Mass.: Harvard Univ. Press, 1946.

Pinkus, P., *Grub Street Stripped Bare. . .*, London: Constable; Hamden, Conn.: Shoe String Press, 1968.

Ward, Mrs. Humphry.

Trevelyan, J. P. (formerly Ward), *The Life of Mrs. Humphry Ward*, London: Constable; New York: Dodd, Mead, 1923.

War Poets.

First World War.

Pinto, V. de S., *Crisis in English Poetry, 1880–1940*, London: Hutchinson; New York: Longmans, 1951.

Blunden, E., *War Poets, 1914–1918*, London: Longmans (for British Council), 1958. Writers and Their Work series.

Bergonzi, B., *Heroes' Twilight: A Study of the Literature of the Great War*, London: Constable, 1965; New York: Coward-McCann, 1966.

Second World War.

Currey, R. N., *Poets of the 1939–1945 War*, London: Longmans (for British Council), 1960. Writers and Their Work series.

Warren, Robert Penn.

Casper, L., *Robert Penn Warren: The Dark and Bloody Ground*, Seattle: Univ. of Washington Press, 1960.

Bohner, C. H., *Robert Penn Warren*, New York: Twayne, 1965.

Warton, Joseph and Thomas.

Wooll, J., *Biographical Memoirs of . . . Joseph Warton*, London, 1806.

Rinaker, C., *Thomas Warton: A Biographical and Critical Study*, Urbana: Univ. of Illinois Press, 1916.

Washington, Booker T.

Matthews, B. J., *Booker T. Washington: Educator and Interracial Interpreter*, Cambridge, Mass.: Harvard Univ. Press, 1948; London: S.C.M., 1949.

Spencer, S. R., Jr., *Booker T. Washington and the Hero's Place in American Life*, Boston: Little, Brown, 1955.

Watts, Isaac.

Manning, B. L., *The Hymns of Wesley and Watts*, London: Epworth Press, 1942.

Davis, A. P., *Isaac Watts: His Life and Works*, New York: Dryden Press, 1943; London: Independent Press, 1948.

Waugh, Evelyn.

Stopp, F. J., *Evelyn Waugh: Portrait of an Artist*, London: Chapman & Hall; Boston: Little, Brown, 1958.

Bradbury, M., *Evelyn Waugh*, Edinburgh: Oliver & Boyd, 1964.

Webster, John.

Brooke, R., *John Webster and the Elizabethan Drama*, London: Sidgwick & Jackson; New York: J. Lane, 1916.

Ellis-Fermor, U. M., *The Jacobean Drama: An Interpretation*, London: Methuen, 1936.

Leech, C., *John Webster: A Critical Study*, London: Hogarth Press, 1951.

Bogard, T., *The Tragic Satire of John Webster*, Cambridge: Cambridge Univ. Press; Berkeley and Los Angeles: Univ. of California Press, 1955.

Webster, Noah.

Lindblad, K. E., *Noah Webster's Pronunciation and Modern New England Speech: A Comparison*, Cambridge, Mass.: Harvard Univ. Press, 1954.

Wells, H. G.

Brooks, V. W., *The World of H. G. Wells*, London: Fisher Unwin; New York: M. Kennerley, 1915.

Nicholson, N., *H. G. Wells*, London: Barker, 1950; Denver: Swallow, 1951.

Brome, V., *H. G. Wells: A Biography*, London and New York: Longmans, 1951.

Bergonzi, B., *The Early H. G. Wells: A Study of the Scientific Romances*, Manchester: Manchester Univ. Press, 1961.

Dickson, L., *H. G. Wells: His Turbulent Life and Times*, London: Macmillan; New York: Atheneum, 1969.

Welty, Eudora.

Appel, A., Jr., *A Season of Dreams: The Fiction of Eudora Welty*, Baton Rouge: Louisiana State Univ. Press, 1965.

Wesker, Arnold.

Taylor, J. Russell, *Anger and After: A Guide to the New British Drama*, London: Methuen, 1962; revised, 1969; as *The Angry Theatre: New British Drama*, New York: Hill & Wang, 1962.

Hayman, R., *Arnold Wesker*, London: Heinemann Educ., 1970.

Wesley, Charles and John.

Jackson, T., *The Life of the Rev. Charles Wesley*, 2 vols., London: Mason, 1841; abridged, 1 vol., 1848.

Tyerman, L., *The Life and Times of the Rev. John Wesley*, 3 vols., London: Hodder & Stoughton, 1870–71.

Rattenbury, J. E., *The Evangelical Doctrines of Charles Wesley's Hymns*, London: Epworth Press, 1941.

Manning, B. L., *The Hymns of Wesley and Watts*, London: Epworth Press, 1942.

Rattenbury, J. E., *The Eucharistic Hymns of John and Charles Wesley*, London: Epworth Press, 1948.

Edwards, M. L., *John Wesley and the Eighteenth Century*, 1933; revised, London: Epworth Press, 1955.

Gill, F. C., *Charles Wesley: The First Methodist*, London: Lutterworth Press, 1964; Nashville, Tenn.: Abingdon, 1965.

"West, Nathanael."

Light, J. F., *Nathanael West: An Interpretative Study*, Evanston, Ill.: Northwestern Univ. Press, 1961.

Wharton, Edith.

Lubbock, P., *Portrait of Edith Wharton*, New York: Appleton-Century; London: Cape, 1947.

Nevius, B. R., *Edith Wharton: A Study of Her Fiction*, Berkeley and Los Angeles: Univ. of California Press; Cambridge: Cambridge Univ. Press, 1953.

Lyde, M. J., *Edith Wharton: Convention and Morality in the Work of a Novelist*, Norman: Univ. of Oklahoma Press, 1959.

Bell, M., *Edith Wharton and Henry James: The Story of Their Friendship*, New York: Braziller, 1965; London: P. Owen, 1966.

Walton, G., *Edith Wharton: A Critical Interpretation*, Rutherford, N. J.: Fairleigh Dickinson Univ. Press, 1971.

White, Gilbert.

Johnson, W., *Gilbert White: Pioneer, Poet and Stylist*, London: Murray, 1928.

Rye, A., *Gilbert White and His Selborne*, London: Kimber, 1970.

Whitman, Walt.

Arvin, N., *Whitman*, New York: Macmillan Co., 1938.

Allen, G. W., *The Solitary Singer: A Critical Biography of Walt Whitman*, New York: Macmillan Co., 1955.

Chase, R. V., *Walt Whitman Reconsidered*, New York: Sloane; London: Gollancz, 1955.

Miller, J. E., Jr., *A Critical Guide to "Leaves of Grass,"* Chicago: Univ. of Chicago Press; Cambridge: Cambridge Univ. Press, 1957.

Asselineau, R., *The Evolution of Walt Whitman*, 2 vols., Cambridge, Mass.: Harvard Univ. Press; London: Oxford Univ. Press, 1960–62. Translated from Paris: Didier edition, 1954.

Hindus, M. (ed.), *Walt Whitman: The Critical Heritage*, New York: Barnes & Noble; London: Routledge, 1971.

Whittier, J. G.

Pollard, J. A., *John Greenleaf Whittier, Friend of Man*, Boston: Houghton Mifflin, 1949.

Pickard, J. B., *John Greenleaf Whittier: An Introduction and Interpretation*, New York: Barnes & Noble, 1961.

Wagenknecht, E. C., *John Greenleaf Whittier: A Portrait in Paradox*, New York: Oxford Univ. Press, 1967.

Warren, R. P., *John Greenleaf Whittier's Poetry: An Appraisal and a Selection*, Minneapolis: Univ. of Minnesota Press, 1971; London: Oxford Univ. Press, 1972.

Wilde, Oscar.

Ervine, St. J., *Oscar Wilde: A Present Time Appraisal*, London: Allen & Unwin, 1951; New York: Morrow, 1952.

Ellmann, R., "The Critic As Artist As Wilde," *Encounter*, July 1967.

San Juan, E., *The Art of Oscar Wilde*, Princeton: Princeton Univ. Press, 1967.

Wilder, Thornton.

Burbank, R., *Thornton Wilder*, New York: Twayne, 1961.

Grebanier, B., *Thornton Wilder*, Minneapolis: Univ. of Minnesota Press, 1964; London: Oxford Univ. Press. Pamphlets on American Writers, no 34.

Wilkes, John.

Postgate, R., "*That Devil Wilkes*," New York: Vanguard Press, 1929; London: Constable, 1930.

Sherrard, O. A., *A Life of John Wilkes*, London: Allen & Unwin; New York: Dodd, Mead, 1930.

Nobbe, G., "*The North Briton*": *A Study in Political Propaganda*, London: Oxford Univ. Press; New York: Columbia Univ. Press, 1939.

Williams, Charles.

Hadfield, A. M., *An Introduction to Charles Williams*, London: Hale, 1959.

Williams, Roger.

Miller, P., *Roger Williams: His Contribution to the American Tradition*, Indianapolis: Bobbs-Merrill, 1953.

Morgan, E. S., *Roger Williams: The Church and the State*, New York: Harcourt, Brace, 1967.

Williams, Tennessee.

Falk, S. L., *Tennessee Williams*, New York: Twayne, 1962.

Jackson, E. M., *The Broken World of Tennessee Williams*, Madison: Univ. of Wisconsin Press, 1965.

Maxwell, G., *Tennessee Williams and Friends*, Cleveland: World Publishing, 1965.

Weales, G., *Tennessee Williams*, Minneapolis: Univ. of Minnesota Press, 1965; London: Oxford Univ. Press. Pamphlets on American Writers, no. 53.

Williams, William Carlos.

Koch, V., *William Carlos Williams*, Norfolk, Conn.: New Directions, 1950.

Wagner, L. W., *The Poems of William Carlos Williams: A Critical Study*, Middletown, Conn.: Wesleyan Univ. Press, 1964.

Guimond, J., *The Art of William Carlos Williams: A Discovery and Possession of America*, Urbana: Univ. of Illinois Press, 1968.

Paul, S., *The Music of Survival: The Biography of a Poem by William Carlos Williams*, Urbana: Univ. of Illinois Press, 1968.

Dijkstra, B., *The Hieroglyphics of a New Speech: Cubism, Steiglitz, and the Early Poetry of William Carlos Williams*, Princeton: Princeton Univ. Press, London: Oxford Univ. Press, 1969.

Breslin, J. E., *William Carlos Williams: An American Artist*, New York: Oxford Univ. Press, 1970.

Wilson, Angus.

Rabinovitz, R., *The Reaction against Experiment in the English Novel, 1950–1960*, New York: Columbia Univ. Press, 1968.

Wilson, Edmund.

Paul, S., *Edmund Wilson: A Study of Literary Vocation in Our Time*, Urbana: Univ. of Illinois Press, 1965.

Frank, C. P., *Edmund Wilson*, New York: Twayne, 1970.

Wilson, John ("Christopher North").

Swann, E., *Christopher North (John Wilson)*, Edinburgh: Oliver & Boyd, 1934.

Winthrop, John.

Morgan, E. S., *Puritan Dilemma: The Story of John Winthrop*, Boston: Little, Brown, 1958.

Wither, George.

Wedgwood, C. V., *Poetry and Politics under the Stuarts*, Cambridge: Cambridge Univ. Press, 1960.

Wodehouse, P. G.

Orwell, G., *Critical Essays*, London: Secker & Warburg; as *Dickens, Dali and Others: Studies in Popular Culture*, New York: Reynal & Hitchcock, 1946.

Usborne, R., *Wodehouse at Work: A Study of the Books and Characters of P. G. Wodehouse*, London: H. Jenkins, 1961.

French, R. B. D., *P. G. Wodehouse*, Edinburgh: Oliver & Boyd, 1966; New York: Barnes & Noble, 1967.

Wolcot, John.

Girtin, T., *Doctor with Two Aunts: A Biography of Peter Pindar*, London: Hutchinson, 1959.

Wolfe, Thomas.

Johnson, P. H., *Thomas Wolfe: A Critical Study*, London: Heinemann, 1947; as *Hungry Gulliver: An English Critical Appraisal of Thomas Wolfe*, New York: C. Scribner's Sons, 1948.

Nowell, E., *Thomas Wolfe: A Biography*, New York: Doubleday, 1960; London: Heinemann, 1961.

Kennedy, R. S., *The Window of Memory: The Literary Career of Thomas Wolfe*, Chapel Hill: Univ. of North Carolina Press, 1962.

Turnbull, A. W., *Thomas Wolfe*, New York: C. Scribner's Sons; London: Bodley Head, 1968.

Reeves, P., *Thomas Wolfe's Albatross: Race and Nationality in America*, Athens: Univ. of Georgia Press, 1969.

Woodforde, Rev. James.

Woolf, V., *The Common Reader*, second series, London: Hogarth Press, 1932.

Woolf, Virginia.

Bennett, J., *Virginia Woolf: Her Art As a Novelist*, Cambridge: Cambridge Univ. Press; New York: Harcourt, Brace, 1945; 2nd edition, Cambridge, 1964.

Hafley, J., *The Glass Roof: Virginia Woolf As Novelist*, Berkeley and Los Angeles: California Univ. Press, 1954.

Brewster, D., *Virginia Woolf*, New York: New York Univ. Press, 1962; London: Allen & Unwin, 1963.

Guiguet, J., *Virginia Woolf and Her Works*, London: Hogarth Press, 1965; New York: Harcourt, Brace, 1966. Translated from Paris: Didier edition, 1962.

Thakur, N. C., *The Symbolism of Virginia Woolf*, London: Oxford Univ. Press, 1965.

Bell, Q., *Virginia Woolf*, 2 vols., London: Hogarth Press; New York: Harcourt, Brace, 1972.

Woolman, John.

Cady, E. H., *John Woolman: The Mind of the Quaker Saint*, New York: Washington Square Press, 1966.

Wordsworth, William.

Havens, R. D., *The Mind of a Poet: A Study of Wordsworth's Thought with Particular Reference to "The Prelude,"* London: Oxford Univ. Press; Baltimore: Johns Hopkins Press, 1941.

Stallknecht, N. P., *Strange Seas of Thought: Studies in William Wordsworth's Philosophy of Man and Nature*, Durham, N. C.: Duke Univ. Press, 1945.

Darbishire, H., *The Poet Wordsworth*, Oxford: Clarendon Press, 1950.

Jones, H. J. F., *The Egotistical Sublime: A History of Wordsworth's Imagination*, London: Chatto & Windus, 1954.

Moorman, M., *William Wordsworth: A Biography*, 2 vols., Oxford: Clarendon Press, 1957–65.

Danby, J. F., *The Simple Wordsworth: Studies in the Poems, 1797–1807*, London: Routledge, 1960; New York: Barnes & Noble, 1961.

Salvesen, C., *The Landscape of Memory: A Study of Wordsworth's Poetry*, London: Arnold, 1965; Lincoln: Univ. of Nebraska Press, 1966.

Owen, W. J. B., *Wordsworth As Critic*, London: Oxford Univ. Press, 1969.

Wright, Richard.

Webb, C., *Richard Wright: A Biography*, New York: Putnam, 1968.

McCall, D., *The Example of Richard Wright*, New York: Harcourt, Brace, 1969.

Brignano, R. C., *Richard Wright: An Introduction to the Man and His Works*, Pittsburgh: Univ. of Pittsburgh Press, 1970.

Wyatt, Sir Thomas.

Berdan, J. M., *Early Tudor Poetry, 1485–1547*, New York: Macmillan Co., 1920.

Lever, J. W., *The Elizabethan Love Sonnet*, London: Methuen, 1956; 2nd edition, and New York: Barnes & Noble, 1966.

Mason, H. A., *Humanism and Poetry in the Early Tudor Period*, London: Routledge, 1959; New York: Barnes & Noble, 1960.

Stevens, J. E., *Music and Poetry in the Early Tudor Court*, London: Methuen, 1961.

Thomson, P., *Sir Thomas Wyatt and His Background*, London: Routledge, 1964; Stanford: Stanford Univ. Press, 1965.

Wycherley, William.

Dobrée, B., *Restoration Comedy, 1660–1720*, Oxford: Clarendon Press, 1924.

Fujimura, T. H., *The Restoration Comedy of Wit*, Princeton: Princeton Univ. Press, 1952.

Zimbardo, R. A., *Wycherley's Drama: A Link in the Development of English Satire*, New Haven: Yale Univ. Press, 1965.

Wyclif(fe), John.

Workman, H. B., *John Wyclif: A Study of the English Medieval Church*, 2 vols., Oxford: Clarendon Press, 1926.

Yeats, W. B.

Hone, J. M., *W. B. Yeats, 1865–1939*, London: Macmillan, 1942; New York: Macmillan Co., 1943.

Ellmann, R., *Yeats: The Man and the Masks*, New York: Macmillan Co., 1948; London: Macmillan, 1949.

Jeffares, A. N., *W. B. Yeats: Man and Poet*, London: Routledge; New Haven: Yale Univ. Press, 1949.

Hall, J., and Steinmann, M. (edd.), *The Permanence of Yeats: Selected Criticism*, New York: Macmillan Co., 1950.

Henn, T. R., *The Lonely Tower: Studies in the Poetry of W. B. Yeats*, London: Methuen, 1950; New York: Pellegrini & Cudahy, 1952.

Ellmann, R., *The Identity of Yeats*, London: Macmillan; New York: Oxford Univ. Press, 1954.

Unterecker, J., *A Reader's Guide to William Butler Yeats*, London: Thames & Hudson; New York: Noonday Press, 1959.

Ure, P., *Yeats the Playwright: A Commentary on Character and Design in the Major Plays*, London: Routledge; New York: Barnes & Noble, 1963.

Young, Edward.

Johnson, S., *The Lives of the Poets*, London, 1779–81.

Eliot, G., "Worldliness and Otherworldliness," in *Essays and Leaves from a Notebook*, Edinburgh: Blackwood, 1884.

Shelley, H. C., *The Life and Letters of Edward Young*, London: Pitman, 1914.

Wicker, C. V., *Edward Young and the Fear of Death: A Study in Romantic Melancholy*, Albuquerque: Univ. of New Mexico Press, 1952.